Notes and Queries

A Medium of Intercommunication for Literary Men,
General Readers
(Ninth Series) (Volume IX)
January – June 1902

Unknown

Alpha Editions

This edition published in 2020

ISBN : 9789354173820 (Hardback)
ISBN : 9789354174216 (Paperback)

Design and Setting By
Alpha Editions
www.alphaedis.com
email - alphaedis@gmail.com

LONDON, SATURDAY, JANUARY 4, 1902.

Notes.

MERCIAN ORIGINS.

THE following notes, gathered from Bede and the 'Anglo-Saxon Chronicle,' have been put together in the hope of contributing something to elucidate the early history of Mercia. The Mercian supremacy over the greater part of England lasted about 200 years (640–820), and although it may have been a loose Home-Rule arrangement, leaving great liberty to the subordinate or associated states, yet it must have had its effect on the gradual unification of the English peoples. For example, it may turn out that the "large hide" is Mercian, and the "small hide" Kentish, the squire and the yeoman, to use later terms, being the respective ideals of the landowning freeman. One of the earliest Mercian charters is a grant of a five-hide estate by Wulfhere (Birch, 'Cartularium,' i. 53). One important document has come down to us to show how Mercia was composed, the 'Tribal Hidage.' It will be assumed here that the solution proposed in 9th S. vii. 441 is in the main correct, but it may be pointed out that Mr. Corbett's solution in the *Transactions* of the Royal Historical Society for 1900, which makes the total to be 144,000 hides, assigns 100,000 to England south of the Humber, for he supposes the first 44,000 to belong to Northumbria, viz., Bernicia, 30,000, and Deira, 14,000.

The first question is, What was the territory originally occupied by the Angle tribes known as the Mercians? We have Bede's answer that the North Mercians had 7,000 hides and the South Mercians 5,000, and that the Trent divided them (iii. 24). The 'Tribal Hidage' gives us the Lindes farona with Hæth feld land, 7,000 hides, and Nox gaga, 5,000 ; and it has been already suggested that the latter district is a portion of the 7,000 hides of the Wocen sætna, occupying (roughly speaking) the present counties of Leicester and Northampton. The Lindes farona have their country defined by the "parts of Lindsey," and Hæth feld land seems to be used for the whole district on the west side of the Trent from Hatfield and Hatfield Chase to the south of Nottinghamshire. The part of Bassetlaw Hundred adjacent to Yorkshire was known as the Hatfield division, either because it was originally part of Hatfield, or at least bordered upon it ; and in the latter alternative the old "Heath field" must have stretched down to the borders of Derbyshire. On marking on a map the North Mercians over the northern half of Lincolnshire, the south-east corner of Yorkshire, and Nottinghamshire, and the South Mercians over Leicestershire and Northamptonshire, it will be seen how well the allocations fit in with Bede's description. It will also become evident that the Mercians entered England by the Humber and settled on its shores and along its tributaries the Don and Trent, the latter giving easy access into the centre of the country.

Another means of fixing the area is afforded by considering the districts occupied by the surrounding states. The Mercians occupied the "mark," or district separating the provinces of the Northumbrians, East Angles, and West (or South) Saxons, and we have clues as to the extent of these provinces. The Humber, it appears from Asser (a. 867) and Geoffrey of Monmouth (ii. 7), was the name, not only of the estuary now so called, but of the Ouse at least as far as York. Thus the limit of Northumbria is fixed not at the southern border of Yorkshire, but at the Ouse ; yet it probably always embraced what is called the Ainsty of York, between the Ouse, Wharfe, and Nidd, for it was to this district that the Northumbrian saint Hieu retired (Bede, iv. 23). Westward of this, to the south of the Wharfe or the Nidd, was the kingdom of Elmet, which Bede (*l.c.*) calls British, and which Nennius (app.) says became Northumbrian on its seizure by King Edwin. Elmet therefore was not Northumbrian, and the 'Tribal Hidage' shows it as having fallen to Mercia. It was in this district that Penda was killed at the battle of the Winwæd. The site is said to be Winmoor, to the north-east of Leeds, which place was reached by Oswy a little after the battle. Close by one of the great Roman roads passes northward through Aberford. The Northumbrians, being comparatively weak in numbers, seem to have waited for the attack on their own ground. The Wharfe gives the most probable boundary line. It is the boundary of the hundreds, one of which is named Skyrack (division oak?). For the Nidd, it may be said that it forms the boundary of the archdeaconry of York or the West Riding, the civil boundary of this district being still further to the north. Possibly the district between the Wharfe and the Nidd was a "mark" or No-man's-land. Nennius calls the district where the battle took place the Field of Gai; Guiseley and Kayley, places lying between Cawood and Keighley, may preserve this ancient name. Elmet is attached usually to Barwick-in-Elmet, and sometimes also to Sherburn.

The Northumbrians, however, made conquests further west, and Ethelfrith's descent on Chester in 607 or later, perhaps by way of Sedbergh or of Colne, secured for them most of the present counties of Lancaster and Chester, which probably remained Northumbrian till the overthrow of Oswald in 641. Oswestry seems a peculiar site for a battle between the kings of Mercia and Northumbria, but if we suppose that Oswald was trying to join the Wessex forces by way of the Severn Valley, it will be seen that Penda attacked him just after he had crossed the Northumbrian limit, at the southern boundary of Cheshire (now a detached portion of Flintshire)—as soon, in fact, as he became a trespasser on what Penda considered his own domains.

The East Angles occupied Norfolk and Suffolk, and their allies or subjects the Gyrwas spread themselves over the Fen country and its margin. It appears from Bede that the South Gyrwas were the dominant people among the Fenmen — he mentions them by name, and their chief was of rank to marry a daughter of the East Anglian king—and the 'Tribal Hidage' agrees with this by giving them the first place in its list, thus: South Gyrwa, North Gyrwa, East Wixna, West Wixna, (Herstina), and Spalda. The last named were certainly Fenmen by race,

as the position of Spalding and Spaldwick shows, and so we may conclude that the intermediate tribes belonged to the same group. The country occupied by the Gyrwas, to give them their general name, includes South Lincolnshire (Kesteven and Holland), Cambridgeshire, Huntingdonshire, and the northern end of Northamptonshire. Bede (iv. 6) tells us that Peterborough was in the country of the Gyrwas, and the historians of Ely call the people of their district by the same name. Further, Bede speaks of the "province" of Oundle, just as he speaks of the "province" of the East Angles or of the East Saxons; hence it may be inferred that Oundle was the chief city of the South Gyrwas, and so the seat of government for the whole group. This "province" of Oundle maintained a sort of distinction till a later period, being known as "The Eight Hundreds" in the time of Edgar ('A.-S. Chron.,' 963). The 'Tribal Hidage' assigns only 600 hides to the South Gyrwas, so that there had been some enlargement, either by addition or by natural growth, in the 300 years intervening. That the Gyrwas were East Anglian in sympathy and doubtless by race is proved by the story of their conversion. This was probably effected by St. Felix, who is said by tradition to have had a church at Soham, on the border of their country; and his successor in the East Anglian bishopric was "his deacon Thomas, of the province of the Gyrwas" (Bede, iii. 20). Then we have the story of St. Botolph. It can scarcely be doubted that Siwara, Queen of the "Southern English," was the ruler of the South Gyrwas in succession to Tonbert. Botolph obtained from her an islet in the Fens as the site for his hermitage, and the gift was ratified by the kings of the East Angles. If Boston be the site of Ikanho, the land granted him must have been near a Spalda district; and so his story shows that in 654, when Penda was in the zenith of his power, the Fenland tribes held together under the suzerainty of the East Angles. A little later St. Etheldreda settled at Ely, "in the province of the East Angles, a country of about 600 families"—probably the Herstina of the 'Tribal Hidage'—which had been assigned to her as dowry by her first husband Tonbert, and the people of which, as already stated, were Gyrwas (Bede, iv. 19; 'Liber Eliensis'). It is sometimes supposed that they were *the* South Gyrwas; but it is so unlikely that a chief would give the central district of his province as dowry that nothing further need be said as to this. Another piece of evidence is given incidentally by Bede (ii. 12), who, in mentioning the great battle between Redwald of East Anglia and Ethelfrith of Northumbria in 617, says it took place "on the borders of the kingdom of Mercia, on the east side of the river that is called Idle," showing that Redwald's domains extended at least as far as the Trent—*i.e.*, they included Kesteven and the Fen country of South Lincolnshire.

As on the north and east the Mercians were originally shut in by the Northumbrians and Elmet and by the East Anglians and Gyrwas, so on the south and west they met the West Saxons. It is singular that though the 'Chronicle' is a West Saxon compilation it gives but scanty details of their settlements. It would appear that Cerdic in 495 landed on the Hampshire coast near Christchurch and pushed his way inland; then (*c.* 519), leaving this district, with the Isle of Wight, conquered later, to his nephews or cousins Stuf and Wihtgar (514, 534), sailed away to make further conquests. If the names Chard and Chardstoke may be relied upon as indications, these new settlements were in the western part of Dorset. This may have given rise to the tradition that to rule the western part of the West Saxon country was more dignified than to rule the eastern (Asser, a. 855). About the same time as Cerdic, the mysterious Port, with his sons Bieda and Mægla, landed near Porchester (501), and, having conquered the Britons there, dwelt in the district. Nothing is told us of their tribe or ancestry or their subsequent history. Port himself has a name apparently derived from the place he conquered; but the situation indicates that they were the Meonwaras, or dwellers by the Meon, afterwards conquered by Wulfhere of Mercia (661) and given to the king of the South Saxons. Stuf and Wihtgar and their comrades were Jutes, but the Meonwaras may have been Saxons, as nothing is said to show that they differed from the great body of the settlers on the south coast. Bede, relating the story of Wilfrid's missionary work among the South Saxons (iv. 13), states that Ebba, the queen of Ethelwalch, "had been christened in her own island, the province of the Wiccii." If these Wiccii were the same as the inhabitants of the Severn Valley, the "island" is a difficulty, unless they had a settlement in Hampshire, say on Hayling Island, in which case Port and his sons may have been of this tribe.

From their settlements on the south coast the West Saxons pushed their conquests inland in two lines: across the Thames towards Bedfordshire (571) and to Cirencester and the Severn Valley (552, 577). In the former direction they would meet the Angle invaders from the north and east, and we may conjecture that in this manner were formed the districts of mixed race called the country of the Middle English or Middle Saxons (Bede, iii. 21; 'Chron.,' 653). They became part of the Mercian confederation, and seem to be those called in the 'Tribal Hidage' Færpinga, Wigesta, and perhaps Herefinna. In the former essay it was suggested that the latter occupied Worcestershire, on the ground that places called Harvington occur here, and that the traditional hidage of the county seems to have been 1,200; but there are some objections to this, and the Herefinna, with their "twice 600 hides," may have been settled in Buckinghamshire. In this case Middle England probably means the greater part of the present counties of Bedford, Hertford, and Buckingham, with some portion of Oxfordshire. Along the Severn the more permanent West Saxon conquests are indicated by the limits of the old dioceses of Hereford and Worcester, the tribes dwelling here being called Hecana, Megasæta, and Hwicca. How much further they may have been extended is unknown, but if the battle of Fethanleah (584) really took place at Faddiley, in Cheshire, it seems likely that the north of Shropshire and most of Cheshire and Staffordshire were, for a time at least, West Saxon, for we are told that as a consequence of this victory "Ceawlin took many towns and spoils innumerable." Another token of this advance may be afforded by Cuttlestone, the name of a hundred in Staffordshire. The Domesday form, Cudulvestone, points to Cuthwulf's Stone as the meaning, and Cuthwulf was the great West Saxon warrior who penetrated to Bedford in 571, and was slain in the same year at some place not mentioned. If this account of West Saxon advance be correct, the Westerna of the 'Tribal Hidage' must have been theirs originally, and even Staffordshire and Cheshire, afterwards so distinctively Mercian.　　　　J. B.

(*To be continued.*)

THE JUBILEE OF THE 'LEISURE HOUR.'
(*Continued from* 9th S. viii. 519.)

LIKE *Chambers's Journal*, which was started on the 4th of February, 1832, the *Leisure Hour* used to be published in weekly numbers as well as in monthly parts, but the sale of the weekly issue gradually fell off, while that of the monthly part increased, and in 1881 the weekly issue was abandoned. In the fresh series music was introduced, Sullivan contributing a duet, 'The Sisters,' based on newly published words, for the use of which Tennyson gave special permission. In 1900 great changes were again made, both in the size and appearance of the magazine, bringing it well up to modern requirements. My father frequently advised that advertisements should be taken for the monthly parts, and represented what an additional source of revenue they would prove; but for many years no advertisements except a few from its own publisher were inserted, "the commercial advantage being held to be subordinate to the general aim."

The *Leisure Hour* has always been noted for its excellent illustrations. Mr. (afterwards Sir) John Gilbert was for long its principal artist, and as a contrast to later times, it is interesting to note that at the height of his fame he never charged more than five guineas a drawing.

Through the kindness of Mr. James Bowden and the Rev. Richard Lovett, I am in a position to give the number of publications of all kinds issued by the Religious Tract Society during the year ending March 31st, 1901, and the total issues from the formation of the Society. During that year 682 new publications were issued, of which 268 were tracts. The Society has already published, or helped others to publish, books and tracts in 250 languages, dialects, and characters. The total circulation in the year from the home depôt, including books, tracts, booklets, handbills, periodicals (reckoned in numbers), cards, and miscellaneous issues, reached 31,646,560, including 15,227,990 tracts. The issues from foreign depôts, so far as can be ascertained, amounted to 20,000,000, making a total circulation of 51,646,560, and of 3,438,565,420 since the formation of the Society.

The Jubilee number records the important services rendered to the literature of the people by the Messrs. Chambers and John Cassell. And in addition to these mention should also be made of the father of our periodical literature, John Limbird, as well as Charles Knight. In January, 1822, Limbird started the *Mirror*, and it was published weekly at the then low price of twopence. It consisted of a sheet of sixteen demy octavo pages, with one or two woodcuts. In the *Athenæum* for the 22nd of January, 1831, the bound volume for the half year received high praise: "It is just the humanizing volume that ought to delight the fireside of every cottage in the kingdom." The notice was evidently written by Mr. Dilke. John Limbird died on the 30th of October, 1883,

aged eighty-eight. The *Penny Magazine* was started ten years after the *Mirror*, being commenced in March, 1832, Charles Knight undertaking the risk and becoming its editor, Alexander Ramsay acting as sub-editor. The title was originated by Mr. M. D. Hill, then member for Hull. Mr. Bulwer (afterwards Lord Lytton) in the House of Commons described it as "affording a trumpery education to the people," and Dr. Arnold described it as "all ramble-scramble." De Morgan was amongst its first contributors, writing for it a series of mathematical papers. Such was its success that at the end of its first year it had reached a sale of 200,000. The magazine terminated unexpectedly in 1845.

Of the progress made by *Chambers's Edinburgh Journal* when entering on its fourteenth year, the number for January 4th, 1845, contains an interesting account. The sale of the monthly part is given as forty thousand, while that of 'Chambers's Information for the People' had been about a hundred and thirty thousand; and the same article states that upwards of a quarter of a million of printed sheets left the house every week, "being as many as the whole newspaper press of Scotland issued in a month about the year 1833." It is curious that in the same article a suggestion should be made that books should be sold by general dealers.

Although *Chambers's Journal* is still issued in weekly numbers, the monthly-part sale is far the larger. In 1882 its Jubilee was celebrated, and in the number for the 28th of January Mr. William Chambers contributes 'Reminiscences of a Long and Busy Life,' and includes a history of the founding of the *Journal* and much interesting information concerning himself and his brother Robert. Seven months after the starting of the *Journal* literature had to mourn the death of Sir Walter Scott, which occurred on the 21st of September, 1832. At the funeral, which took place on Wednesday, the 26th, the brothers were present, and William writes of it: "The spectacle presented at the final solemnity—the large concourse of mourners clustered under the trees near the ruins of the Abbey of Dryburgh, the sonorous reading of the funeral service amidst the silent crowd, and the gloomy atmosphere overhead—is one never to be obliterated from remembrance."

JOHN C. FRANCIS.

(*To be continued.*)

KIPLING IN AMERICA.

Before giving a complete list of the books, poems, &c., written by Mr. Kipling and published in the United States, it may not be out of place to append a full list—for all of which, excepting a few items, I am indebted to Mr. W. M. Clemens's 'A Ken of Kipling' (New York, New Amsterdam Book Company, 1899)—of every original publication that has come from his pen up to the publication of 'Kim':—

1. Quartette. Christmas Annual. Lahore, 1885. 8vo, pp. 125.
2. On Her Majesty's Service Only. Departmental Ditties. Lahore, 1886. Oblong 8vo.
3. Plain Tales from the Hills. Calcutta and London, 1888. Cr. 8vo, pp. 283.
4. Soldiers Three. Allahabad, 1888. Cr. 8vo, pp. 97.
5. The Story of the Gadsbys. Allahabad, 1888. Cr. 8vo, pp. 100.
6. In Black and White. Allahabad. Cr. 8vo, pp. 106.
7. Under the Deodars. Allahabad, 1888. Cr. 8vo, pp. 106.
8. The Phantom 'Rickshaw, and other Tales. Allahabad, 1888. Cr. 8vo, pp. 104.
9. Wee Willie Winkie, and other Stories. Allahabad, 1888. Cr. 8vo, pp. 96.
10. The Courting of Dinah Shadd, and other Stories. New York, 1890. Cr. 8vo, pp. 182.
11. Departmental Ditties, and other Verses. Calcutta, London, and Bombay, 1891. Cr. 8vo, pp. 121.
12. The City of Dreadful Night. Allahabad. No date, probably 1891. Cr. 8vo, pp. 96.
13. Life's Handicap: Stories of Mine Own People. London and New York, 1891. Cr. 8vo, pp. 351.
14. Letters of Marque. Allahabad, 1891. 8vo, pp. 154.
15. Barrack-Room Ballads, and other Verses. London, 1892. Cr. 8vo, pp. 208.
16. The Naulahka: a Story of West and East. London, 1892. Cr. 8vo, pp. 276.
17. Ballads and Barrack-Room Ballads. New York and London, 1892. Cr. 8vo, pp. 207.
18. Many Inventions. London and New York, 1893. Cr. 8vo, pp. 365.
19. The Jungle Book. London and New York, 1894. Cr. 8vo, pp. 212.
20. The Second Jungle Book. London and New York, 1895. Cr. 8vo, pp. 238.
21. Soldier Tales. Macmillan, 1896. (Knowles.)
22. The Seven Seas. London and New York, 1896. Cr. 8vo, pp. 246.
23. Slaves of the Lamp. London and New York, 1897.
24. Captains Courageous. New York and London, 1897. Cr. 8vo, pp. 387.
25. The Day's Work. New York and London, 1898. Cr. 8vo, pp. 388.
26. A Fleet in Being. London, 1899. Cr. 8vo, pp. 88.
27. Stalky & Co. London and New York, 1899. Cr. 8vo, pp. 282.
28. From Sea to Sea. New York, 1899; London, 1900. 2 vols. 8vo, pp. 431.
29. Kim. London and New York, 1901. Cr. 8vo, pp. 420.

I have searched the catalogues of American publications from 1890, the year in which Kipling was first represented in the States, right up to 31 October, 1901, for the issues of Mr. Kipling's works, &c., which have appeared in America. This has not been done without some little trouble; so I trust any omissions (I have endeavoured to be absolutely accurate) will be pardoned. I add also the year of publication and the publisher. The list does not include volumes of selections.

1890.
Plain Tales from the Hills. F. F. Lovell.
Story of the Gadsbys. J. W. Lovell.
Ditto. Munro.
Courting of Dinah Shadd, and other Stories. With Biographical and Critical Sketch by A. Lang. Harper.
Departmental Ditties, Barrack-Room Ballads, and other Verses. United States Book Company.
Indian Tales. United States Book Company.
Phantom 'Rickshaw, and other Tales. Munro.
Ditto. Rand, McNally & Co.
Plain Tales from the Hills. Macmillan.
Ditto. Munro.
Soldiers Three, and other Stories. Munro.

1891.
Life's Handicap. Macmillan.
Light that Failed. Rand, McNally & Co.
Ditto. Munro.
Ditto. United States Book Company.
Mine Own People. With Introduction by H. James. Munro.
Ditto. Ditto. United States Book Company.
Story of the Gadsbys, and Under the Deodars. United States Book Company.
Under the Deodars. United States Book Company.
Wee Willie Winkie, and other Stories. Rand, McNally & Co.

1892.
Ballads and Barrack-Room Ballads. Macmillan.
Barrack-Room Ballads, and other Verses. United States Book Company.
Naulahka: a Story of West and East. Rand, McNally & Co.

1893.
Ballads and Barrack-Room Ballads, with Additional Poems. Macmillan.
Many Inventions. Appleton.

1894.
Jungle Book. Century Co.

1895.
Prose Tales. 6 vols. Macmillan.
The Naulahka: Story of West and East. Macmillan.
Out of India: Things I saw and failed to see in Certain Days and Nights at Jeypore and Elsewhere. Dillingham.
The Second Jungle Book. Century Co.

1896.
The Seven Seas. Appleton.
Soldier Stories. Macmillan.

1897.
The Writings in Prose and Verse of Rudyard Kipling. 18 vols. Outward Bound Edition. Vols. i.-xi. Scribner.

Barrack-Room Ballads. Mansfield.
Captains Courageous: a Story of the Grand Banks. Century Co.
Departmental Ditties. Mansfield.

1898.

Collectanea: Reprinted Verses. Mansfield.
Barrack-Room Ballads and Verses. Mansfield.
Barrack-Room Ballads and Departmental Ditties, and other Verses. Mansfield.
Barrack-Room Ballads, Recessional, &c. Doxey's.
The Courting of Dinah Shadd. Brentano's.
Ditto. Marion Press.
The Day's Work. Doubleday.
Departmental Ditties, and other Verses. Mansfield.
Departmental Ditties: Typographical Facsimile of the First Edition. Mansfield.
The Drums of the Fore and Aft. Brentano's.
Ditto. Estes.
The Man who would be King. Brentano's.
Mandalay. Mansfield.
Recessional. Critic Company.
The Vampire. Critic Company.
Ditto. Mansfield.
Ditto. Woodward & Lothrop.
Plain Tales from the Hills. Caldwell.
Soldiers Three. Caldwell.

1899.

Barrack-Room Ballads, and other Verses. Mansfield.
Betrothed. Grosset.
Ditto. Mansfield.
Departmental Ditties. Mansfield.
Gunga Din. Grosset.
Recessional. Grosset.
The Vampire. Grosset.
American Notes. Brown.
City of Dreadful Night; and other Stories. Ogilvie.
Ditto. Grosset.
Danny Deever. Grosset.
Mandalay. Grosset.
From Sea to Sea. Doubleday.
Works. Swastika Edition. 15 vols., 5 vols., and 6 vols. Claflin.
Writings in Prose and Verse. 18 vols. Outward Bound Edition. Vols. xii.-xv. Scribner.
Soldier Stories. Claflin.
Barrack-Room Ballads, and other Poems. Crowell.
Indian Tales. Caldwell.
His Majesty the King, also Wee Willie Winkie. Estes.
Plain Tales from the Hills. Burt.
Stalky & Co. Doubleday.
Mine Own People: The Courting of Dinah Shadd. Burt.
The Brushwood Boy. Doubleday.
Barrack-Room Ballads and The Story of the Gadsbys. Burt.
The Courting of Dinah Shadd. Street.
Mandalay. Doxey's.
The Light that Failed. Caldwell.
Letters of Marque. Caldwell.
Mine Own People. Caldwell.
Phantom 'Rickshaw. Caldwell.
Poems. Caldwell.
Story of the Gadsbys. Caldwell.
Under the Deodars. Caldwell.

1900.

Writings in Prose and Verse. 18 vols. Outward Bound Edition. Vols. xvi.-xviii. Scribner.

The Absent-Minded Beggar. Brentano's.
The Absent-Minded Beggar, Recessional, and Bobs. Elder & Morgan Shepherd.
Ditto. Madigan.
Indian Tales. 2 vols. Burt.
Recessional. Buckles.
Recessional and Bobs. Wieners.
The Vampire, and other Poems. Street.

1901.

Barrack-Room Ballads, Recessional, and other Poems. Doxey's.
Departmental Ditties, The Vampire, and other Poems. Doxey's.
Kim. Doubleday, Page.

In each case the above titles represent the publisher's first issue only for that year. In some instances several editions appeared from the same publisher in the same year.

It will be seen by the following figures how the popularity of the writer has increased or decreased year by year. The small number of editions issued in 1900 and 1901 suggests a falling off of the Kipling mania, and is extremely remarkable when compared with the previous years' figures :—

1890. Books and editions published		11
1891.	,, ,,	9
1892.	,, ,,	3
1893.	,, ,,	2
1894.	,, ,,	1
1895.	,, ,,	9
1896.	,, ,,	2
1897.	,, ,,	14
1898.	,, ,,	19
1899.	,, ,,	61
1900.	,, ,,	10
1901 (to October 31)	,,	3

Thus in twelve years the number of Kipling's books published amounts to 144. These figures are, of course, influenced considerably by the paragraph immediately following the issues above in 1901.

The editions are issued by thirty-one publishers, and are distributed among them as follows :—

Claflin	27	Estes		2
Scribner	18	Critic Co.		2
Mansfield	12	Lovell, F. F.		1
Macmillan	12	Lovell, J. W.		1
Caldwell	10	Harper		1
U.S. Book Co.	7	Dillingham		1
Grosset	7	Marion Press		1
Munro	6	Woodward & Lothrop	1
Doubleday	5	Brown		1
Brentano's	4	Ogilvie		1
Burt	4	Crowell		1
Rand, McNally & Co.	4	Elder & M. Shepherd	1
Doxey's	4	Buckles		1
Century Co.	3	Wieners		1
Appleton	2	Madigan		1
Street	2			

I may add that several of the above publishers are regarded as "pirates."

MATTHEW CRIPPS.

13, Marmion Road, Clapham Common, S.W.

"Rather."—A correspondent of the *Academy* discussing "rather," on 9 November last says the word is unique, implying that it stands alone in having a defective comparison. In this respect, however, it is hardly more remarkable than "good," "bad," "much," "erst," and "less." The same writer goes on to say that "long ago" the positive of the word was "rath," and he cites Bishop Hall and May's translation of Virgil in support of his statement. This is to overlook "hraðe" altogether, which in the form "rathe" recurs in Chaucer and later poets. The word, says the writer in the *Academy*, has no superlative, but, as he professes to treat the subject historically, he should have discovered that "rathest" ("radost"), though obsolete, had once a real and active existence. Finally, he says the positive degree has been out of use for many a day. But Tennyson is not a remote writer, and he has "men of rathe and riper years" in 'In Memoriam,' while he uses the word adverbially in the line

Till rathe she rose, half cheated in the thought.

THOMAS BAYNE.

ROMNEY AND THE ROYAL ACADEMY.—It is curious to note, in auctioneers' catalogues and elsewhere, how frequently George Romney is described as R.A. He never exhibited at the Royal Academy, and did not require the adventitious aid of the Academy to give him "bold advertisement." In looking over some old newspapers the other day I came across an amusing blunder in the *London Evening Post* of 29 April-2 May, 1780, in which is the following sentence, *à propos* of the opening of the Royal Academy of that year: "The portraits of Sir Joshua Reynolds, Dance, West, Gainsborough, and Romney gave great satisfaction." The writer clearly had not been to the Royal Academy.   W. ROBERTS.

JEWS AND PATRIOTISM.—Probably the following extract from the *Manchester Courier* of 9 December, 1901, is worthy of a place in 'N. & Q.,' especially in view of the last column (9th S. viii. 201) of the interesting notes entitled 'Bevis Marks Synagogue Bicentenary,' signed N. S. S.:—

"A grand synagogue parade of Jewish troops was held in the Central Synagogue, Great Portland Street, W., this evening [*i.e.*, 8 December]. The pulpit and other portions of the synagogue were draped with Union Jacks, and among others there were present the Lord Mayor and Lady Mayoress, the Sheriffs, and the Duke of Bedford. Fully 300 troops attended, the mingled uniforms of the Hebrew Lifeguardsmen, Scots Guards, Dragoons, Yeomen, Volunteers, &c., forming a brilliant and picturesque scene. The officiating clergy were the Chief Rabbi (who, with the Scroll of the Law in his hand, read a solemn prayer for the King and Queen), the Rev. E. Spero, and the Rev. F. L. Cohen, Chaplain to the Jewish members of the Forces. Mr. Cohen mentioned that fully 2,000 Jews (including 80 officers) had fought in the war. Of these 40 had been mentioned in dispatches, while two Jewish nursing sisters (one of whom had gone through the siege of Ladysmith and the other through the siege of Kimberley) had also received similar mention; 325 Jews had figured in the casualty list, nearly 100 of whom had been killed in action or had died of disease. The rev. gentleman solemnly read out the names of the fallen, all the congregation rising in their places. The service was brought to a conclusion by the singing of the National Anthem."

"Patria est, ubicumque est bene" — Cic., 'Tusc. Disp.,' v. 37 (108).

ROBERT PIERPOINT.

St. Austin's, Warrington.

BLACK BOTTLES FOR WINE.—The *Times* of 14 December, 1901 (p. 14, col. 2), says:—

"The familiar black bottle mainly used for wine was introduced into this country one hundred and fifty years ago by Lord Delaval, who brought over from Germany a number of Hanoverian bottle-blowers, and started some works adjacent to his mansion at Seaton Sluice, Northumberland, for the manufacture of black glass bottles, his main idea being to utilize some inferior qualities of coal which he had mined on his estate. At that time, it may be remarked in passing, the black colour of the bottles was the natural result of the materials used. Since then other materials have been adopted, and these by themselves would produce a glass which is transparent; but wine drinkers are so accustomed to having their wine in dark bottles that the black colour has been kept to, and is now produced by artificial means."

R. B.

"FADGE."—An extended application of the meaning of this word, as furnished in the 'E.D.D.,' is worth recording. There one finds, sb. 1, that the meanings "a bundle, a burden; a part of a horse's load," are given, among others; and a S. Lan. illustration runs "a fadge of potatoes, a fadge of beef."

In the last fortnight of autumn, when the days were approaching their shortest, and the weather was tempestuous, I met, struggling through the darkness, which was unrelieved in consequence of a temporary extinction of the street lights, a postman, who said, "I could get on better if I weren't hampered with this fadge o' parcels." He explained that fifty years ago a *fadge* was, for example, two hundredweight of coals carried in a sack on a donkey's back, and so arranged that the load as borne sideways was equally distributed on each side of the animal. He intimated parenthetically that short weight was supplied by the coal dealers as a rule. The 'H.E.D.' gives the word also.   ARTHUR MAYALL.

Queries.

WE must request correspondents desiring information on family matters of only private interest to affix their names and addresses to their queries, in order that the answers may be addressed to them direct.

EPITAPH AT CLIFFE, CO. KENT.—Close to the footpath leading through the churchyard, and within a few feet of the entrance porch on the south side of the grand old parish church of Cliffe, near Rochester (otherwise of late years incorrectly called Cliffe-at-Hoo), co. Kent, is a somewhat plain table monument or altar tomb in stone of three female members of the family of Somner, which formerly ranked as farmers, residing in the parish. On the north, south, and west sides of this monument, which was apparently erected in 1672 (about which date the burial register is unfortunately defective for some years), are inscriptions, evidently composed by an illiterate person, and displayed and cut in a rude and unworkmanlike manner, which, owing to time and weather causing decay and a scaling off of the stone, have hitherto been deemed illegible, many unsuccessful attempts being made to read them. Having, however, long been collecting materials, chiefly from original sources, for (*inter multa alia*) a history of that and the adjoining, and also very interesting, parish of Cooling, in both of which the county family whose head and representative I had then recently become have for upwards of 200 years past been lords and extensive landowners; and as the inscription on that side of the tomb which faces the church was believed to be curious, I, in the summer of 1900, took much pains and spent considerable time in endeavouring to make out the same, and with the following result—although it must be understood that several of the words are doubtful :—

" Passengers . weepe . heere . lies . a . wife . who . saved [=save or except ?]. none . | Jone . Somner . her . life . one . that . was . all . the . good . God. | sende . in . the . whole . peice . of . woman . kind . | withall . she . shvned . the . light . and . died . | the . light . that . mother . to . | one . too . dear . in . whose . worlds . death . before . Heaven . | to . her . Lord . God . and . Master . one [gone ?]. did . same . thing . hase [=as ?]. her . | went . to . the . one . now . powr . grate . have [gave ?]. to . walke . heere . | and . her . tombe . remains."

The whole is apparently in capitals of one size. The two other inscriptions, which are shorter and of no particular interest, I read with more ease and certainty. My chief object in inserting the principal one in 'N. & Q.' is to ascertain whether any reader,

having met with the same in MS., as copied long since and when fairly legible, can supply a correct transcript. That such inscription has appeared anywhere in print I do not suppose, although something similar might be met with elsewhere.   W. I. R. V.

TONTINE. — My grandfather invested in a tontine for his five children (100*l*. each) as they were born. My mother was the last of the children, and that money should be mine. The tontine started about 1817, and would be worth something now, as she has been dead twenty-four years. The family lived in Westmorland. Who would be likely to know of this tontine, and where would it be registered ?   J. C. C.

WEEKS'S MUSEUM.—I find on a clock of some merit in design and workmanship the following inscription : "Weeks' Museum, Tichborne Street." Can any reader tell me if this was a museum or merely a shop, and who Weeks was ? I should like to know the period when he flourished.
                        W. H. QUARRELL.
[Three clockmakers named Weeks or Weekes were admitted members of the Clockmakers' Company between 1654 and 1713. See Britten's 'Old Clocks and Watches,' 1899.]

HENRY CRISPE, Common Serjeant of London, 1678, till his death in October, 1700. What is known of his parentage and family ? He was a barrister of the Inner Temple, and, I believe, M.P. for Lancaster 1685-7.
                        W. D. PINK.

BEAU BRUMMEL AND BARBEY D'AUREVILLY. —I should be very glad if any reader of 'N. & Q.' could tell me whether there exists any English translation of Barbey d'Aurevilly's 'Du Dandysme et de G. Brummel.' I find that this book was originally published in 1845 at Caen, in an edition of only thirty copies. The third edition, published in 1879 by Lemerre at Paris, contains two portraits, one of Brummel and one of Barbey, both at the age of twenty. Is there any account in English of the reason why the French writer produced his extraordinary account of the English Beau ? I am acquainted with most of the English literature dealing with Brummel, but I should be glad to know anything of the history of Barbey's work.
                        CHARLES HIATT.

KNOCKER FAMILY.—I should be glad to learn anything about Arthur Knocker, gent., whose daughter was wife of Francis Thynne, of Kempsford, co. Gloucester, second son of Sir John Thynne, of Longleat, *temp*. Elizabeth. A monument or gravestone in Kempsford Church, no longer existing, bore his arms, 3 text K's impaled with Thynne. He is described in the 'Visitation of Gloucester, 1623,' as of "......in com. Suffolk," but elsewhere as of "......co. Stafford." There is no further information in Mr. Botfield's work. This very rare surname exists only in Kent, I believe.   A. S. ELLIS.

BRANDON, EXECUTIONER.—Can any reader of 'N. & Q.' inform me if there is in existence an authentic portrait of Richard Brandon, public executioner, who is supposed to have cut off the head of Charles I.? Richard was the son of Gregory Brandon, and died in 1649.   P. SIDNEY.

THE MUSICIANS' COMPANY OF THE CITY OF LONDON.—I am collecting information concerning this ancient guild, and I should be glad if any reader of 'N. & Q.' could tell me of any trials to restrain musicians who were not free of the Company from practising their art within the City precincts. I possess an account of the trial of a Mr. Green, organist of St. Giles's, Cripplegate, in 1724. I should be glad to know of anything else of interest relating to the Company, and also if any proof exists connecting the present guild, whose charter was granted by James I. in 1604, and the older guild whose charter was granted by Edward IV. *circa* 1461. In the records of the Company there is practically no information.   ARTHUR F. HILL.
140, New Bond Street, W.

ARMS OF DUTCH EAST INDIA COMPANY.—I should be glad to have a description heraldically correct of the arms of the old Dutch East India Company.   L. L. K.

GEORGE HENRY FITZROY, FOURTH DUKE OF GRAFTON, 1760–1844.—Is it known whether the above was ever at Harrow School? The 'Harrow Register, 1800–1901,' begins too late to be of use in this connexion, and the 'D.N.B.' mentions no place of education before Trinity, Cambridge. The fifth, sixth, and seventh dukes were all at Harrow.
A. R. BAYLEY.
St. Margaret's, Malvern.

ST. BRIAVEL.—I should be glad to be favoured with any particulars regarding this saint or name.   MILES.

PAINTED TILES are set all over the guardchamber floor in the remains of a castle of the Dukes of Normandy at Caen, and said to have been laid down during the time of William the Conqueror, having represented on them the arms of some of those who attended William in his conquest. In 1786 these were taken up and presented by the Benedictine monks of St. Stephen at Caen to Charles Chadwick, Esq., of Healey Hall, Lancashire. Some of the tiles bore the arms of the Malets, viz., three buckles. I should be glad to know where these are now.
HAROLD MALET, Colonel.
Radnor House, Sandgate.

WARLOW FAMILY.—I should be glad if any of your readers could give me any information regarding the pedigree of the Warlow family, and tell me whether it is of Welsh or English origin.   G. H. WARLOW.

OLDEST BOROUGH IN ENGLAND.—Can you or any of your readers tell me which is the oldest borough in England?   J. C.

SIR THOMAS MORGAN, OF ARKSTONE.—I am anxious to discover the parentage and arms of Sir Thomas Morgan, of Arkstone, who died 1595. He married a daughter of Jean, Sieur de Mérode, and his own daughter Anne was the wife of Henry Carey, created Baron Hunsdon in 1559.   KATHLEEN WARD.
Castle Ward, Downpatrick.

REV. JOHN TAUNTON, of Axbridge, Somerset, who died in 1592. Any information regarding this clergyman will be gratefully received.   C. J. T.

J. IMPEY was admitted to Westminster School on 16 October, 1809. I should be glad to obtain any information concerning him.
G. F. R. B.

BISHOPS' SIGNATURES.—I have derived from a visit to Hartlebury the impression that Stillingfleet, when Bishop of Worcester, signed himself Edw. Vigorn. Am I right? I wish I had followed your excellent advice and "made a note." There is now an opportunity of abandoning the very ugly and modern-looking use of "Worcester" tacked on to the initials; and, if I am right in supposing that the ancient style lasted till the eighteenth century, there can be no reason why a return should not be made to it in the twentieth. I wrote to the *Guardian* and *Church Times* to the same effect; but they either regard it as without their sphere or think it a matter of little general interest. Your readers will, I trust, be otherwise minded.   W. E. B.
[See 7th S. ix. 189; xi. 118; 8th S. iii. 449; xii. 84.]

"KNEVEL."—Charles Mackay, in his 'Lost Beauties of the English Language,' a work which has of course been corrected and superseded by later publications, says "knevel" means moustache. He indicates that we got

the word "moustache" from the Spanish, and
that we must have had an English word for
the hair on the upper lip long before the
Spanish name was introduced. The French,
Italian, and Greek forms of "moustache" are
ignored. But Mackay asserts that "knevel"
is pure English. One cannot suppose that
he would make this statement without some
ground for so doing. The questions are:
Where is this alleged English word to be
found; and, if found, what is its precise
meaning? See 9ᵗʰ S. v. 88, 196; but these
references under 'Whiskers,' while throwing
light on the case generally, do not answer the
questions.   ARTHUR MAYALL.

'L'ART DE PRECHER,' 1683.—Who is the
author of this didactic poem? One Jacques
Canier makes the requisition for a licence to
print, which is granted as follows: "Je
n'empêche pour le Roy la Permission requise.
A Lyon ce 15 Juillet, 1682. Vaginey." The
introductory lines are these:—

Enfin tu vas prêcher, la Liste le publie,
Et fait voir imprimé ton nom et ta folie;
Mais de tous les métiers, où l'on peut s'attacher,
Sçais tu que le plus rude, Abbé, c'est de prêcher.
            RICHARD H. THORNTON.
Portland, Oregon.

THE LOWNDES MOTTO.—The singular motto
"Ways and Means" (with these inverted
commas) is used to this day by the family of
Selby-Lowndes, of Whaddon Hall, co. Bucks.
Can this be the augmentation of the coat of
arms mentioned by Burke in his 'Landed
Gentry,' vol. ii., s.v. 'Lowndes,' as granted
by Queen Anne to William Lowndes, Secretary to the Treasury and Chairman of Ways
and Means? He is noticed by Macaulay in
his 'History of England' (chap. xxi.), and it
is added in a note that in 1695 he published
a pamphlet, an 'Essay for the Amendment
of the Silver Coins,' which was refuted by
John Locke.   JOHN PICKFORD, M.A.
Newbourne Rectory, Woodbridge.

GEE FAMILY.—I should be glad if any one
could inform me when members of this family
first settled in England, or when the name,
or any of its variants, is first met with as an
English surname.   JAMES H. GEE.
58, Park Street, Walsall.

PEARLS A CURE FOR CORNS.—The harvest
of folk-lore is by no means reaped. Dissolve
two pearl buttons in lemon juice until they
become a paste. Rub on corns three days
and three nights running, and the corns
disappear. An old man's recipe. Is it known
elsewhere?   THOS. RATCLIFFE.
Worksop.

Replies.

PINS IN DRINKING VESSELS.
(9ᵗʰ S. iv. 287, 358, 484.)

ANSELM'S decree of 1102 appears — not
literally—translated in 'The Acts and Monuments' of John Foxe. "That priests should
not resort to taverns or banquets, nor sit
drinking by the fire-side," stands for "Ut
presbyteri non eant ad potationes, nec ad
pinnas bibant" ("Church Historians of England, Reformation Period," 'The Acts and
Monuments of John Foxe, 1854,' vol. ii. p. 168,
i.e., book iv. of the 'Acts,' &c.).

In the Appendix to vol. ii. p. 835, is a note in
which "nec ad pinnas bibant" is rendered
"nor drink to pins." Reference is made to p. 59,
where Foxe says that, to check the excessive
drinking, which was owing to the "multitude
of Danes dwelling in divers places in England," Edgar

"ordained certain cups, with pins or nails set in
them, adding thereto a law, that what person drank
past the mark at one draught should forfeit a certain penny, whereof one half should fall to the
accuser, and the other half to the ruler of the
borough or town where the offence was done."

A note (Appendix, p. 818), saying that the
actual law has not been found, gives a passage from Malmesbury ('Script. post Bedam,'
p. 56, line 26). The following is the translation of it in Sharpe's translation of William
of Malmesbury's 'History,' London, 1815,
chap. viii., 'Of King Edgar, son of King
Edmund' (p. 171):—

"Indeed, so extremely anxious was he to preserve
peace even in trivial matters, that, as his countrymen used to assemble in taverns, and when a little
elevated, quarrel as to the proportions of their
liquor, he ordered gold or silver pegs to be fastened
in the pots, that, whilst every man knew his just
measure, shame should compel each, neither to take
more himself, nor oblige others to drink beyond
their proportional share."

The pegs are in the original "clavi." The
phrase "a little elevated" underrates, I think,
the meaning of "temulenti."

The note on p. 835 says:—

"The peg-tankards had in the inside a row of
eight pins, one above another, from top to bottom.
The tankards hold two quarts, so that there is a
gill of ale, i.e., half a pint of Winchester measure,
between each pin."

After describing how each person had to
drink to the next pin, it says the drinkers
were very liable to get drunk, "especially
when, if they drank short of a pin, or beyond
it, they were obliged to drink again." The
reference given is "Anonymiana, 125, Gent.
Mag. xxxviii. 426."

Further:—

"A very fine specimen of these peg-tankards, of undoubted Anglo-Saxon work, formerly belonging to the abbey of Glastonbury, is now in the possession of Lord Arundel of Wardour. It holds two quarts, and formerly had eight pegs inside, dividing the liquor into half-pints. On the lid is the Crucifixion, with the Virgin and John, one on each side of the cross. Round the cup are carved the twelve Apostles." — Fosbrooke's 'Encyclopædia of Antiquities,' vol. i. p. 258, London, 1835. See also Hone's 'Year-Book.'

Ducange in his Glossary, v. 'Potus,' mentions a canon being passed at a council in France which forbade "æquales potus," a canon of the same import as that of Anselm's.

On referring to Hone's 'Year-Book' I find a woodcut of the Glastonbury tankard. The letterpress says that the four uppermost pegs remain, and that the holes from which the other four have fallen out are discernible. It is made of oak and has been lackered with strong varnish, especially inside. It was saved from Wardour Castle by Blanch, Lady Arundel, who, on surrendering the castle to Sir Edward Hungerford and Col. Strode, withdrew this cup with certain articles of her property, and, retiring to Winchester, retained it as long as she lived. In one of the old inventories of the effects belonging to Wardour Castle this cup is mentioned as having been brought from the ancient abbey of Glastonbury. The above is only a little of Hone's account. A woodcut of the tankard appears (No. 794) on p. 189 of vol. i. of 'The Pictorial Gallery of Arts' (London, Charles Knight & Co.). It is mentioned, but there is no description of it in the letterpress. See also Brand's 'Popular Antiquities,' s.v. 'Drinking Customs: Pledging,' p. 491 of the 1877 edition of Chatto & Windus.

ROBERT PIERPOINT.
St. Austin's, Warrington.

STAUNTON, WORCESTERSHIRE (9th S. viii. 383, 510).—I can clear up this confusion, as the parish named by MR. MATTHEWS is in my division, and the other is on its edge and contains many of my constituents. The postal address of "Staunton, Worcestershire," is "Staunton, Gloucester." MR. MATTHEWS's parish, "Staunton, Gloucestershire," is a long way off, and lies between Coleford and Monmouth, with a view over the Wye.

CHARLES W. DILKE.

CASTOR-OIL PLANT (9th S. viii. 224, 511).— As M. M. L. writes from Costa Rica to suggest that eucalyptus trees drive away mosquitos and "might drive away flies," may I say that no one has ever suggested that the eucalyptus will affect flies, and that the opinion that it annoys mosquitos is a popular delusion? I may add that flies are put to sleep by the pungent smoke of a eucalyptus-leaf fire, but that mosquitos ply their trade unharmed in it as in tobacco smoke.

C. O. P.

HORN DANCERS (9th S. viii. 444). — I have just found an earlier reference to the Abbot's Bromley dancers, viz., 'Hobby-horse Dance,' 6th S. ii. 368 (6 November, 1880), where Dugdale's 'England and Wales,' vol. i. p. 7, is quoted. The querist was the late MR. EDW. WALFORD. On p. 397 various references are given, but not to Bromley. On p. 418 'N. & Q.'s' old contributor ST. SWITHIN quotes from Halliwell an extract from the *Mirror*, xix. 228, 'Bromley Pagets.' It is to be found on p. 452 of vol. i. col. 2, of first edition of Halliwell. There is also a reference to Strutt. I cannot lay my hands on my copy, and it is possible only hobby-horses are meant, not horn dancers.

S. L. PETTY.
Ulverston.

MANX GAELIC (9th S. viii. 460).—In the first place, I should like to thank your correspondent for the interest he shows in the preservation of Manx as a living language; and, in the next place, I should like, as president of the Manx Language Society, to explain what has been done, and what is being done, to keep the language alive.

We have all felt the need of a satisfactory grammar, and now that want is met for beginners by 'First Lessons in Manx,' by Edmund Goodwin, published by the Celtic Association, Dublin, price 6d. A convenient reading-book, 'Æsop's Fables,' in Manx and English, written by an old Manxman of Creigneish, and edited by Mr. Roeder, of Manchester, is also published at the same price at the *Examiner* office, Douglas. For more advanced students the appendices to vol. xxxiii. of the Manx Society's Publications (pp. 1-183) on Manx phonology, by Prof. Rhys, of Oxford, will be found to go into the matter very thoroughly.

During the winter months classes are held in the island for teaching Manx, but these have to be abandoned while "the season" lasts. The Manx Language Society is now trying to get Manx placed on the same footing as Welsh in the education code, and so to be officially recognized as an extra subject, which may be taught in elementary schools. This would be a great step forward, but we do not yet know what view those in authority will take.

There is much enthusiasm among real lovers of Manx in the island, as distinct from those mercenary folk who will learn and teach only what will pay; but such are in

the minority. If those who take an interest
in the preservation of Manx will communicate
with me (Canon Savage, St. Thomas's Vicarage,
Douglas), I shall be pleased to give all the
information I can, and to forward a report
of the annual meeting of the Society held
last month. In such a case as this outside
interest would greatly help to strengthen our
hands ; for we are looked upon by many here
as unpractical enthusiasts who are simply
hunting a shadow. It ought to stir up half-
hearted Manxmen to see the efforts that
intelligent people elsewhere are making to
prevent the language from dying out.

Manx is spoken far more than people know ;
but not before strangers. When going "after
the herrings" in some of the Peel luggers not
a word of English is spoken by the crew from
the time they leave the harbour to the time
of their return next morning, every order
being given in Manx. Dr. Clague, of Castle-
town, an excellent Manx scholar, has told me
that in many houses that he visits in the
south of the island all the directions as to
the treatment of his patients are given in
Manx, and frequently no word of English is
spoken during his visit ; so that it is a *living*
language, and more young people are able
to speak it than is commonly known. We
have asked to have the ages of those who
can speak Manx specified in the census
returns, which will give us accurate figures,
if they are published.

ERNEST B. SAVAGE, M.A., F.S.A.
St. Thomas's Vicarage, Douglas.

"GOD SPEED YOU AND THE BEADLE" (9ᵗʰ
S. viii. 422).—Considering the frequency with
which the word "beetle" occurs in proverbial phrases, like "Deaf as a beetle,"
"Blind as a beetle," "Between the beetle
and the block," and the employment of the
"beetle" or mallet as an implement of industry, not only in washing, but in many
other occupations, it is highly probable that
the saying implies merely a wish for prosperity, in the same way that "God speed the
plough" applied to the pursuit of agriculture. A large sledge-like implement for
driving wedges was known as a "beetle," and
there is a curious tavern-sign survival of the
"Beetle and Wedge." "To cleave a tree with
a beetle without a wedge" (Fuller, 'Holy
War,' iii. xxiv., 1840, 162). The phrase "As
deaf as a beadle" is sometimes used instead
of "As deaf as a beetle," meaning, of course,
the implement so called, since nothing could
well be more inanimate ; whereas deafness is
an affliction that would at once disqualify a
beadle for a post where the constant use of a

healthy sense of hearing is a *sine qua non*.
'There is no more conceit in him than there
is in a mallet" ('Hen. IV.,' Part II., Act II.
sc. iv.) ; and Halliwell has "beetle-headed,"
i.e., wooden-headed, thick-headed. We meet
again with the tendency to mispronounce
"beetle" in "black-beadle."
J. H. MACMICHAEL.

"SHIMMOZZEL" (9ᵗʰ S. vi. 266, 371 ; vii. 10 ;
viii. 471).—I am glad to see this interesting
topic is still to the fore. The opening letter
of the correspondence stated that *shimmozzel*
never occurred in print. In reply I quoted a
modern novel, and I have just met with it in
another, viz., 'The Golden Tooth,' by J.
Maclaren Cobban ("If Will comes out of this
shemozzle," p. 170). This may reach the eye
of Mr. Farmer, whose address I do not
know. Of the terms cited by MR. BRESLAR,
noff was explained in a letter to the *Academy*,
16 February, 1901. A synonym is *shickster*,
which will be found in Hotten, and must not
be confounded with *shicker*, which means
intoxicated. *Moskinner*, pledger, is better
known in English under the forms *moskeneer*
and *mosker*. The latter was once the subject
of an article in the *Daily Telegraph*, 9 July,
1883 ("The Mosker......is, in slang vernacular,
one who makes a living by taking advantage
of the business incapacity of persons engaged
in the pawnbroking trade"). Readers desirous
of enlarging their acquaintance with Anglo-
Yiddish should get A. M. Binstead's collection
of short stories, 'Houndsditch Day by Day'
(Sands & Co., 1899). JAS. PLATT, Jun.

DICKENSIANA : PHRASE OF MRS. GAMP (9ᵗʰ
S. viii. 324, 426).—Readers are too apt to base
their comments upon the manners and customs of the time in which they themselves live,
and fail to associate themselves with the
fashions of the period of which their authors
are attempting delineation.

In Mrs. Gamp's time the majority of the
retail liquor shops in London openly and
without interference carried on business as
gambling resorts, nearly every licensed
victualler announcing at the advent of
every important sporting contest that a
sweepstake might be joined on application
at his bar ; and in the thoroughfares nearly
every purveyor of penny pies (such as the
itinerant tradesman cited by Mr. Samuel
Weller, a decade before Mrs. Gamp's first
appearance, whose announcement was paraphrased by Sam as, "Fruits is in and cats is
out," and who was credited by his critic with
ingenuity, by judicious "accommodation"
of seasoning, in passing off a mutton for a
kidney, or *vice versâ*, confection) and brandy

balls and other sweets and such small deer paraded a circular tray furnished as described by the REV. W. D. SWEETING, or with an upright pillar rising from the centre, spirally hollowed out within, with a capital representing a Turk's head roughly carved, in the hollow turban of which the gambler, on payment of a penny, had the privilege of depositing a marble which, rolling down the spiral, came to its rest in one of the hollows, and on the inscription in this depended the investor's chance of receiving a supply of the displayed delicacies or of going empty and copperless away. Those peripatetic vendors who were not provided with such gambling machinery were equally ready to sell their wares without risk or to gratify the sporting instincts of those who preferred tossing to buying, and the humble penny or halfpenny would then suffice for the chance-deciding convenience.

Experto crede. I well remember the wandering mutton pieman. At this hour his familiar chant comes to my ears—"like an odour of brine from the ocean" might appeal to another sense—more especially as twilight deepened into gas-qualified night darkness: "Pies all hot! smoking hot! hot mutton pies!" But then in the early fifties a good, grandmotherly Government came in to take care of us and prevent our burying our own dead at our own street doors, and interfered with our British rights to poison our neighbours— sure they had the right to poison us in their turn—with our disdain of elementary sanitary mode of living, and swept away the temptation to us to "make ducks and drakes" of what means we possessed by sending Inspector Forester and his merry men to raid the recognized gambling hells, and to swoop down upon the Bonifaces and their alluring sweepstake combinations; and the men in blue at the same time harried the "dollies" and deluding pointing arrows out of the thoroughfares and shops, and the "coppers" sternly "ran in" the pieman and the sweet-seller who "skied" the current copper, not invariably without suspicion that the principle of "Heads I win, tails you lose," might be adroitly applied. And yet the British constitution has survived!   GNOMON.

Temple.

MR. F. G. KITTON would be right in assuming that it was formerly customary for boys to toss the hot-pie man for his wares. But those itinerant traders, with their steaming tin "cans," have, through the so-called march of civilization and improvement, apparently long since disappeared—at least in London—and even the pie-shops once so

popular are now few and far between. This kind of gambling was, as I have always understood, done with coin on the palm of the hand and guessing whether "heads or tails" (otherwise "man or woman") appeared uppermost, and not with any instrument of chance, although I have frequently seen in use at pleasure fairs a somewhat similar contrivance to that mentioned at the last reference by the REV. W. D. SWEETING—the "prizes" being of various kinds, and sometimes pieces of cake, but never, to my knowledge, pies, hot or cold. I well remember that about 1856-9, when, as a boy, I was home from boarding-school for the holidays, an old pieman used to go round the streets of Pimlico with small apple and other pies, in a basket on his arm, for disposal on the toss-or-buy system, the particular terms being that the intending purchaser, if winning the "toss," should have two for the price of one. This pieman was, of course, unable to cry "toss or buy," as he might have done with impunity in days of yore; but the same was unnecessary, as his method of doing business was so well known locally. I may mention that another noted itinerant trader (but on cash terms) in the same neighbourhood at the time, and I believe until a much later date either there or elsewhere, was the brandy-ball man — a somewhat younger individual, and more important, at least in his own estimation—who wore a sort of smoking cap with tassel and a white apron, and carried his commodities in front of him on a wooden tray suspended from his shoulders. Every now and again he announced his approach in a sort of chant, ending with "Bran—dy ball! They're all brandy!" But those were not, as at present, the days of cheap sweets and small profits, and no doubt he did well. *Tempora mutantur, et nos mutamur in illis.*   W. I. R. V.

When I was a boy I was a prodigious consumer of pies, which were perambulated round the purlieus of Petticoat Lane by one Sam the Pieman, whose "Pie hot! Pie nice, nice pie!" resounded far and wide, and was a clarion call to the hundreds of boys in the great public seminary where I received my primary education. About twelve o'clock Sam would reach the great iron gates, towards which we all bounded pell-mell, shouting and raving, and looking like so many prisoners behind the grill to any outside onlooker, and as fast as he could hand them through the bars his mince and mutton pies found ready customers. Sam was too honourable or shrewd ever to tempt any one of us to toss him for a pie. He was a merchant, and quite above such low practices. He must be dead years now.

M. L. R. BRESLAR.

J. Camden Hotten's 'A Dictionary of Modern Slang and Cant Words' has under 'Spin-em-Rounds':—

"A street game consisting of a piece of brass, wood, or iron, balanced on a pin, and turned quickly around on a board, when the point, arrow shaped, stops at a number and decides the bet one way or the other. The contrivance very much resembles a sea compass, and was formerly the gambling accompaniment of London piemen. The apparatus then was erected on the tin lids of their pie cans, and the bets were ostensibly for pies, but more frequently for 'coppers,' when no policeman frowned upon the scene, and when two or three apprentices or porters happened to meet."

This supplies the information required.

ARTHUR MAYALL.

BARBARA JOHNSTON (9ᵗʰ S. viii. 484).—Some pen-and-ink notes from an old copy of Burke's 'Extinct, Dormant, and Suspended Peerages' in my library may interest your correspondent MR. JOHNSTON. The copy is of the 1831 edition, and has the signature of "Jas. Gilbert Johnston, 39, Hyde Park Square," on a fly-leaf. The notes are on the page giving an account of the Montague family, Barons Halifax, Earls of Halifax, &c. George Montague, second Baron Halifax, created Earl of Halifax in 1715, married secondly Lady Mary Lumley, daughter of Richard, Earl of Scarborough, and had issue George, his successor, and six daughters: Frances, Anne, Mary, Elizabeth, Barbara (died unmarried), and Charlotte, married to Col. Johnston. A footnote in the same handwriting as on the fly-leaf says, "Col. J. was my gᵗ grandfather. After the death of Lady Charlotte he married the widow of the Rt. Revd. — Twisden, Bishop of Raphoe, and son of Sir Wm. Twisden, Bart." There are also other notes on the same page and elsewhere in the same handwriting.

The Barbara Johnston of your query may have been a daughter of this Col. Johnston. Assuming she was, she may have been named after her maternal aunt Barbara, who died a spinster. Another note states that Lady Mary Lumley has a sister Lady Barbara, who married the Hon. Chas. Leigh. The name Barbara "ran" in the Lumley family. The Rev. Robert Lloyd, who claimed the barony of Lumley in 1725, claimed as lineal descendant of Barbara Lumley, sister (daughter?) of George Lumley, who was attainted.

It will be odd if this stray marginal note, from an old book picked up years ago at a second-hand stall in a neighbouring city, and recalled by your correspondent's query from memory, where it had been unconsciously stacked, supplies the information sought for. If it does it will be a remarkable instance of the utility of 'N. & Q.,' and an instance also of "genealogical luck."

LIONEL CRESSWELL.

ORCHESTRA OR ORCHESTRE (9ᵗʰ S. viii. 424).—Our attention has been drawn to an editorial note in your issue of 23 Nov., 1901, referring to the word "orchestra," which reads, "'Orchestre' is said in the 'Century' to be obsolete, and is unmentioned by Funk & Wagnalls." Permit us to point out that in our 'Standard Dictionary,' on p. 1237, column 3, twelfth line from the foot of the page, the two obsolete forms of the word "orchestra," "orchester" and "orchestre," are given. We shall feel greatly obliged if you will do us the kindness of correcting this statement.

FUNK & WAGNALLS COMPANY.

POMEROY FAMILY OF DEVON (9ᵗʰ S. viii. 424).—See 'Visitations of the County of Devon,' by the late J. L. Vivian, pp. 605–9.

W. D. PINK.

DEVONIAN will find a pedigree of the above family in Vivian's 'Visitations of co. Devon,' which gives full particulars; also a short account in Archdall's edition of 'Lodge's Peerage of Ireland' under 'Harberton.'

JOHN RADCLIFFE.

Various articles respecting this family will be found in 6ᵗʰ S. ii. 328, 493; iii. 58; 8ᵗʰ S. xii. 388, 456.   EVERARD HOME COLEMAN.
71, Brecknock Road.

CROSSING KNIVES AND FORKS (9ᵗʰ S. viii. 325, 433).—ROBIN GOODFELLOW is not positive as to the religious significance of the Russian mode of placing table cutlery. I remember only too well the sharp rebukes my father was wont to administer to us youngsters if we happened to cross our knives and forks by way of artistic finish to a well-polished plate. My father was of Polish extraction and came largely into contact with all classes of the best Russian and Polish society of his day, and must frequently have observed this cruciforming habit at their tables.

M. L. R. BRESLAR.

The sight of accidentally crossed knives upon our luncheon table to-day (28 November) caused a distinct shudder to run through my wife and grown-up daughters, all of whom first saw the light within a few hundred yards of my present residence. The nearest one made a grab at the offending cutlery and at once carefully placed the knives parallel. Further, they almost simultaneously exclaimed, with evident concern, "Crossed knives! dear me, how *very* unlucky!" This belief is general throughout Devonshire.

HARRY HEMS.

Fair Park, Exeter.

BARRAS (9th S. viii. 202, 228, 267, 473).—The definition of this word by MR. NEILSON agrees very well with the position of Barras Lane, Barras Heath, and Barr's Hill in this town. They are all without the ancient walls of the city, and were used as outposts against attacks upon the gates and walls. It certainly seems to be a mutation of the word Barre.

J. ASTLEY.

Coventry.

BIRTHPLACE OF LORD BEACONSFIELD (9th S. viii. 317, 426, 512).—I thank MR. RALPH THOMAS for courteous mention of my article, but nevertheless cannot without another word let him throw cold water on my advocacy of a memorial to Isaac D'Israeli and Lord Beaconsfield on the house 22, Theobalds Road. I fancy MR. THOMAS visited it lately during a dreary day in November, and viewed it in its present uninhabited condition. All houses in such circumstances look miserable, and, indeed, the favour of the sun's brightening rays is always needed to render prepossessing the aspect of a London house, be it of dingy brick or grimy stucco. I have paid it another visit, even in the bleak December, and standing opposite, under the wall of Gray's Inn Gardens, have impartially viewed the block, which now consists of five houses, occupied chiefly as the offices of solicitors. Of these No. 22 only is vacant, and as the letting board is gone, I hope it is not to remain so. The four occupied houses look as cheerful and well cared for as a block of offices ever does, and even more cheerful than others, on account of the street being free of houses on the opposite side, and the aspect that of the verdant gardens. No. 22, with its pretty old doorway, only wants paint, varnish, clean window glass, and a bright new knocker and name-plate, to render its appearance as imposing as that of many houses which have received the decoration of the tablet, and even more so than some. I hope MR. THOMAS will go again, six months hence, and give it another chance.

It must have been but a few years old in 1802 when Isaac D'Israeli went to live in it, and the busy, noisy thoroughfare of to-day was at that time perhaps scarcely a thoroughfare. But changed as it is, it is not in the degraded condition of the purlieus of the now partially reformed Seven Dials and Drury Lane, and, if I remember rightly,

tablets are found in that neighbourhood where famous people once lived. For even when a street has suffered degradation, it is a relief to be reminded that it was not always as now, that it was not always mean and ugly; and certainly by the erection of a tablet the memory of the famous one is not besmirched. Also the transformation of London, the transmigration of the upper class of its habitants from one area to another, is a part of its history interesting to observe.

I hardly think the object of the tablet is so much to impress the passing public as to give welcome information to those interested in the past, to preserve for these a fact in the life of the commemorated, and possibly to preserve the house itself. Were these memorials only to be erected in fashionable or respectable quarters the series would be indeed incomplete; so I will hope that the London County Council—who, as announced, are to continue the work happily until now conducted by the Society of Arts—will soon place the tablet on 22, Theobalds Road, which will thereby be enhanced in value to its future tenant, a worthy Conservative lawyer cherishing the memory of Lord Beaconsfield in his birthplace.

W. L. RUTTON.

HARVEST BELL (9th S. viii. 201, 308, 427).—It is part of the sexton's duty here to ring the curfew bell in the church tower every night at eight o'clock. He also rings the same bell at twelve o'clock every day. This latter is known as the dinner bell. These bells have been so rung from time immemorial.

JOHN T. PAGE.

West Haddon, Northamptonshire.

MR. BRESLAR is surely mistaken in his version of the words painted on the Ripon post office (formerly, I believe, the town hall). If my memory serves they run thus: "If ye Lord keep not ye city, ye Wakeman waketh in vain."

A curfew bell is rung nightly during the winter at nine o'clock at Mytton, in Yorkshire, and I fancy also at Whalley, the neighbouring Lancashire village.

FRED. G. ACKERLEY.

Seemannsheim, Libau, Russia.

The church of St. George-in-the-East has, since its consecration in 1729, regularly used a bell to call to labour at six o'clock each morning, and (presumably to discontinue work) at eight o'clock each evening. From childhood I have been familiar with the "eight o'clock bell," as it is familiarly spoken of in the parish, although very early in my education I learnt to associate it with the curfew, a connexion still retained in my mind.   GNOMON.

Temple.

SURNAMES DERIVED FROM FRENCH TOWNS (9ᵗʰ S. viii. 464).—MR. HILL has started an interesting subject. Some of our old Norman families, deriving their names from places in Normandy, are still represented amongst the nobility of that province, in which the Duc de Harcourt holds the foremost position. Amongst the lesser nobility, of which branches attained to a far higher rank on this side the Manche, we still find the families of Reviers, Rivers, or Redvers (which derived its name from a seigneury in the neighbourhood of Caen*) and of Bailleul, which gave a king to Scotland, and of which the original ancestor hailed from a village near Hazebrouck, in French Flanders, which is passed by every tourist travelling between Calais and Brussels. The great family of St. John—which, if the descent of Sir Oliver St. John of Bletsho, who died in 1437, from the feudal barons of that name can be established, can claim descent in the male line from a great Domesday tenant-in-chief (Hugh de Port), a very rare, if not unique distinction, according to Mr. Round—derived its origin from St. Jean-le-Thomas, overlooking the bay of Mont St. Michel, in the extreme west of Normandy.† The family of Mohun (De Monteminori) was from Moyon, in Normandy, a commune of the canton of Tessy, arrondissement of St. Lo and department of La Manche (Stapleton, introduction to 'Liber de Antiquis Legibus,' p. xx). Bethune, from which the Bethunes and Beatouns of Scotland were descended, is a railway station, canton, and arrondissement in the Pas de Calais. The great family of De Courcy is from Courcy-sur-Dive, a commune of the canton of Coulibœuf, arrondissement of Falaise, department of Calvados (ib., p. xl). Ferrières, from which the illustrious family of Ferrers (De Ferrariis) derived its origin, is in Normandy, while Forz or Fors, whence the equally historic family of De Fortibus descended, is a commune of the canton of Prahecq, arrondissement of Niort, department of Deux Sèvres, in Poitou (ib., p. xxxiv). The distinguished family of Gurney derives its name from Gournay-en-Bray, chef-lieu of the canton of that name, arrondissement of Neufchâtel-en-Bray, department of the Seine Inférieure (ib., p. cxvi).

---

* Huet, in his work 'Origines de la Ville de Caen,' derives the name of this seignory (Ripuariæ) from its situation on the banks of several rivers.

† The *Genealogist*, xvi. 1.

The baronial family of Tregoz was not Cornish by origin, as might be inferred from the name, but derived from the commune of Troisgots, in the canton of Tessy, arrondissement of St. Lo, department of La Manche (it., p. xcviii). Numerous other instances might be given, and I may further state that a book published several years ago, called 'The Norman People,' though not to be relied on as absolutely accurate, will afford your correspondent some valuable information regarding the origin of many of our old Norman families.

W. F. PRIDEAUX.

The Editor is of course quite right. Camden says ('Remains,' p. 118, J. R. Smith's edition) there is no village in Normandy "that gave not denomination to some family in England," and the names which represent towns elsewhere in France, and those reminiscent of the provinces of that delightsome land, are probably too numerous to be repeated with profit in the pages of 'N. & Q.'

ST. SWITHIN.

"SPATCHCOCK" (9ᵗʰ S. viii. 403).—Halliwell adopts this explanation: "A hen just killed and quickly broiled for any sudden occasion." The Rev. A. Smythe Palmer in his 'Folk Etymology' illustrates the same meaning by quotations from Kettner's 'Book of the Table,' 'Memoirs of Thos. Moore,' King on the 'Art of Cookery,' Webster's 'Northward Ho,' Cartwright's 'The Ordinary,' T. Brown's 'Works,' and Cotton's 'Burlesque upon Burlesque Poems.'   EVERARD HOME COLEMAN.

71, Brecknock Road.

Grose's 'Classical Dictionary,' 1796, gives "*Spatchcock* [abbreviation of dispatch cock], a hen just killed from the roost or yard, and immediately skinned, split, and broiled. An Irish dish upon any sudden occasion."

JOHN RADCLIFFE.

Mr. A. G. Bradley, in his 'Highways and Byways in the Lake District,' p. 62, speaks of a man's "being made a *spatchcock* of," that is (as he explains), "of his head being stuck in a rabbit hole, and his legs staked to the ground." This, I gather, is a Cumberland custom.   C. C. B.

FIRE ON THE HEARTH KEPT BURNING (9ᵗʰ S. viii. 204, 412).—Sixty years ago, in the rural districts of Aberdeenshire, where almost the only fuel burnt was peat or turf, the kitchen fires were never intentionally allowed to go out. The cinders were carefully covered with ashes over-night, and when raked out in the morning were almost invariably alive. When it was the reverse, which did not occur more than once in half a dozen years or so, the task of producing a light was often a formidable one. We had no matches, the tinder-box was not known in our parts, and the servantmaid had to enlist the services of one of the ploughmen with his pocket flint and steel. The touch paper was speedily ignited, but to produce a flame sufficient to light a candle was by no means easy, and often took up a considerable amount of time. The first time I ever saw lucifer matches was, if I remember rightly, in 1843 or 1844.

ALEXANDER PATERSON.
Barnsley.

COMIC DIALOGUE SERMON (9th S. vii. 248, 339; viii. 309, 433).—In a review of 'Memorials of William Charles Lake, Dean of Durham, 1869-1894,' is given a passage from (as I suppose) his own pen, which cannot fail to be of interest to those involved in the present quest :—

"One course at the Church of the Gesù used to amuse us much. It was in the form of a dialogue conducted on a stage between a good man and a sinner, and the repartees of the sinner in answer to the remonstrances of the good man were often rather telling. On the whole, it certainly struck me that the Roman Catholic clergy had all the power of dealing with the lower classes which our Methodists have, and in which our own clergy (at that time, at least) were very deficient. Another point I thought remarkable was the character of the tracts which I was fond of collecting in the bookshops of the lower parts of Rome, and which almost always referred entirely or were addressed to our Lord, and seldom either to the Virgin or to the saints."

ST. SWITHIN.

ARMS OF SCOTLAND (9th S. vii. 368, 452).—MR. EASTON (p. 368), in speaking of the royal tressure of Scotland, states that it was "the emblem of the ancient league with France, from whose kings it was a gift to the kings of Scotland." The high authority of the late Dr. Woodward was not in favour of this origin. His observations upon this point ('Heraldry, British and Foreign,' ed. 1896, vol. i. p. 187) are, I think, worthy of reproduction here :—

"Popular belief long associated this bearing in the arms of Scotland with a supposed alliance between one Achaius, King of the Dalriadic Scots, and Charlemagne; and declared that it commemorated the agreement that the French lilies should be for all time coming a defence to the lion of Scotland.

"It is easier to laugh at the transparent absurdity of this fable than to account for the first introduction of the fleur-de-lis into the royal coat of Scotland. Historically no alliance between Scotland and France can be found earlier than the reign of Robert Bruce.

"On the seal of Alexander II. the lion is the sole charge. On the great seal of Alexander III. (1249-1286) the lion rampant appears alone upon the

shield borne by the monarch, but the caparisons of this [? his] charger have the lion surrounded by a bordure; this is charged with small crosslets, but the inner edge has a border of demi-fleurs-de-lis. (Vrée, 'Généalogie des Comtes de Flandre,' plate xv.) A portion of this seal is engraved in Laing's 'Scottish Seals,' vol. ii. plate ii. fig. 1, and, I am inclined to think, not so accurately given as in Vrée's example, where the whole seal is given, and the crosslets distinctly shown on the bordure. To this bordure I believe we must trace the origin of the tressure flory-counter-flory, which had no direct connection with any French alliance, connubial or political."

From this extract MR. EASTON will see that the lion of Scotland was borne alone upon the seals of the second and third Alexanders, and this certainly at a period long anterior to the time given by him (1471), when King James III. decided to eliminate the double tressure from the royal arms, though long subsequent to that pre-heraldic period when the supposed alliance with Charlemagne led to the popular belief, as Dr. Woodward states, that it was the origin of the tressure in the Scottish arms.

Dr. Woodward would seem to have been aware of the Act of Parliament in 1471, mentioned by MR. EASTON, by which James III. affected to do away with the tressure. He gives the enacting words (p. 189): "In tyme to cum thar suld be na double tresor about his armys, but that he suld ber hale armys of the lyoun without ony mar," and says that it is not easy to explain the motive for the Act, which, however, was never carried into effect.

J. S. UDAL, F.S.A.
Antigua, W.I.

BEAULIEU AS A PLACE-NAME (9th S. vi. 87, 216; viii. 397).—The abbot of a monastery de Bello Loco is recorded in various documents of Honorius III., which SIR E. BEWLEY will easily find from the index to Pressuti's magnificent edition of that Pope's 'Regesta' (Typ. Vat., 1888-95). My diplomatic and geographical knowledge does not go far enough to say whether the place is in the diocese of Châlons-sur-Marne, Troyes, or Toul, or identical with any of those already mentioned.

O. O. H.

"OUTRIDER" (9th S. viii. 462).—This word, formerly applied to sheriffs' officers and postillions, and still used in the latter capacity, may have been utilized locally as an expansion or variant of "rider"; for in the north of England, before steam was applied to locomotion, commercial travellers, riding on horseback from place to place soliciting orders, were very widely designated "riders." Hence that fine old farce in one act (was it not George Colman's?) entitled

'Ducks and Green Peas; or, the Newcastle Rider,' in which the bagman, waiting for his dinner at a Harrogate inn, sings

> 'Tis Riders only life enjoy,
>   They travel through the land;
> Variety can never cloy,
>   All pleasures they command.
>   Tol lol de rol.

> Then who would not a Rider be,
>   To lead a life like this;
> From every care and trouble free,
>   Enjoying earthly bliss.
>   Tol lol de rol.

And then soliloquizes in the following fashion:—

"There's for you, ye parchment-bound 'prentices, ye hen-peck'd husbands, ye gouty-footed drones! Get a horse like me, and travel from place to place, live like kings, and sup upon ducks and green peas, as I am going to do!"

           RICHARD WELFORD.

Upwards of a quarter of a century ago the representatives of brewers, grocers, drapers, &c., who drove into this village from the neighbouring towns of Northampton and Rugby, soliciting orders from the local shop-keepers, were always spoken of as "out-rides." This designation has now fallen largely into disuse, the gentlemen in question being invariably alluded to as "travellers."

           JOHN T. PAGE.
West Haddon, Northamptonshire.

DISSINGTON FAMILY (9ᵗʰ S. viii. 365).—In answer to MR. HERBERT SOUTHAM's inquiry I may say that I find it stated by Jan Brouwer in his pocket encyclopædia that Elden is a village in Gelderland, three-quarters of an hour's distance N.N.E. from Elst (another Dutch village in the same province)—for that is the quaint way in which Brouwer indicates position—meaning, I take it, that if a man, walking at an ordinary pace, were to start from Elst in a N.N.E. direction, he would arrive at Elden in three-quarters of an hour.

           H. G. K.

Gentleman's Magazine, vol. l., for the year 1780, p. 494, amongst deaths has "Sept. 27, Andr. Dishington, esq., aged 66. He was one of the oldest lieutenants in the royal navy."

           H. J. B.

There is a place named Elden in Gelderland, Netherlands, latitude 51° 57′ N., longitude 5° 52′ E.; also a village in Suffolk (England), about four miles from Thetford, which has also been known under the names of Elvedon and Elveden.

           EVERARD HOME COLEMAN.

BOTTLED ALE: ITS INVENTION (9ᵗʰ S. vii. 287, 412, 514).—The following extract from 'Cavalier and Puritan,' on p. 327, is interesting, in that it shows that English bottled ale could be purchased in Paris in 1699. The diary of Sir Richard Newdigate: "Bought English bottled Ale at sixteen pence a quart."

           HERBERT SOUTHAM.

Miscellaneous.

NOTES ON BOOKS, &c.

Caroline the Illustrious. By W. H. Wilkins, M.A. 2 vols. (Longmans & Co.)

"ILLUSTRIOUS" is a strong term to apply to the queen consort of George II. and the four times queen regent of England. In that Hanoverian invasion to which England was subjected after the death of Queen Anne she is, however, the most pleasing and attractive—it might almost be said the only pleasing and attractive—figure. Mr. Wilkins, who holds a brief for her, has written, from sources many of them now first employed, a life which is to some extent a continuation of his 'Love of an Uncrowned Queen,' in which he told, practically for the first time, the story of Sophia Dorothea, the ill-starred consort of George I. The book thus constituted is interesting and stimulating, though the picture it presents of life in Hanover and subsequently in England is necessarily saddening. At no period in English history was the Court more coarse, immoral, corrupt, and depraved than during the reigns of the early Georges. No whit more refined were the Courts of Saxony and Hanover, and the examples set before the young princess were the least edifying that could easily be conceived. No breath of scandal attaches to her life; and though she had in England periods of extreme unpopularity, and was even burnt in effigy by a London mob, she enjoyed general respect and admiration, and she certainly was, as Mr. Wilkins says, "by far the greatest of our Queens Consort, and wielded more authority over political affairs than any of our Queens-Regnant, with the exception of Elizabeth and, in quite another sense, Victoria." As woman and as wife she is no less remarkable than as monarch, and it is singular that she has had to wait so long for her historian. Much information concerning her and her environment is obtainable from books with which most are now familiar. Some of this, however, has but recently become accessible, and Mr. Wilkins's book brings her almost, if not quite, for the first time before the public as a recognizable being. It is a good book in the main, hurried in parts, in need of some *labor limæ*, and marred by some slovenlinesses or inaccuracies of diction. These are of no great significance, and history is seldom more picturesque, attractive, and pleasurable than herein it appears. In depicting her early life both in Germany and England Mr. Wilkins has had access to documents previously unused. The Hanoverian archives have for the first time been consulted with regard to the betrothal and marriage of the princess, and dispatches not hitherto published of Poley, Howe, and D'Alais, English envoys at Hanover 1705-14, have been employed. Less interesting and less important than the proceedings when, in concert with Walpole, Queen Caroline led her brutal husband by a silken thread are those of her early days in Saxony, Prussia, and elsewhere in Germany. Without a study of these it is, however, impossible to understand her life as queen in England. Her early association with Leibniz and the delight she conceived in metaphysical and theological discussion are responsible for the unpopularity with the High Church party begotten of her ecclesiastical appointments and for the charge of Erastianism brought against her in common with her husband and Walpole. On these matters Mr. Wilkins dwells at some length, and what he says concerning them is neither the least interesting nor the least important portion of his book. Caroline was "an unorthodox Protestant." Her theological inquiries "carried her into the shadowy regions of universalism and the refined Arianism of her favourite chaplain Dr. Samuel Clarke." In an infallible Bible she had, we are told, no more faith than in an infallible Pope, and her views, had they been known, would have been regarded with horror by the Protestant Dissenters whom she patronized. Ecclesiastical patronage was bestowed for purely political reasons. The High Church clergy were Jacobites, the Low Church were Whigs, and Walpole took care that none other than Whigs should obtain advancement.

A study of her wooing by George II. and of the conditions attending the marriage is indispensable to a comprehension of her bearing to the king. It is difficult to acquit her of a measure of duplicity and cunning, but her affection for George must have been genuine; and the manner in which she studied his requirements, ministered to his prejudices and jealousies, and protected his amours is in its way unique. Her diplomacy was wonderful. Rarely, indeed, did the monarch—the suspiciousness and meanness of whose nature were remarkable—perceive with how light a hand he was guided; and when once and again the satirists pointed out to him the truth, Caroline so effaced herself that his mistrust disappeared. In spite of his atrocious behaviour to her, George felt for her something as near affection as he was capable of experiencing, and left directions that on his burial the sides of both coffins should be opened so that their joint bones should mingle. Caroline's consistent support of Walpole is no less remarkable than the other features in her character. At heart as much a German as her husband, her diplomacy succeeded in concealing the fact. There is something pathetic in her struggles to retain her empire over the king, and her silence concerning the rupture she so carefully concealed was probably due to her fear of producing physical disgust and so losing her influence over him. Mr. Wilkins's book deserves to be generally read and studied. We should like to have chapter and verse for a few of the stories, which are doubtless accurate, but have been narrated concerning others. It is difficult to understand her dislike to her son Frederick, which was of course shared by her husband. One of the best-known incidents in the relations between Caroline and George occurred on her deathbed. She advised him to marry again when she was dead. At this George burst into sobs and tears, and assured her he would not, saying, with a strange mixture of *naïveté* and brutality, "Non, non ! j'aurai des maîtresses." To this the queen could only reply, pathetically and wearily, "Mon Dieu ! cela n'empêche pas." A great attraction in the book consists of the portraits, which are numerous and admirable. We could have done with an ampler index.

A Genealogical Dictionary of the Peerage and Baronetage, the Privy Council, Knightage, and Companionage. By Sir Bernard Burke, C.B. Edited by Ashworth P. Burke. (Harrison & Sons.)

A NEW edition of 'Burke'—the best, the most authoritative, the most widely recognized, and the longest established of the guides to British titles, rank, and precedency—leads off the new year's list of peerages. Always welcome and indispensable, it is this year more welcome and indispensable than ever, since it chronicles a change of monarch and the re-establishment of some of the oldest and most exalted of honours. The accession to the throne of His Majesty Edward VII. is, of course, the matter of primary importance in its pages, but the creation of the Queen the Lady of the Most Noble Order of the Garter, the augmentation of the royal title, and the creation of the Duke of Cornwall, York, and Rothesay, Prince of Wales and Earl of Chester, are conspicuous events in royal annals. Large accessions to titles of honour have come as a natural result of the war. It will strike some readers with amazement to learn that close upon two thousand distinctions have been awarded in the course of the year. In order to supply a chronicle of all these this bulkiest of volumes has had to be further enlarged, and the 1976 pages of last year's peerage have in the present, or sixty-fourth edition, expanded into 2058. Mr. Ashworth Burke, to whom the preparation and accomplishment of this huge labour are due, owns his indebtedness to his brother, Mr. H. Farnham Burke, Somerset Herald, to the three Kings of Arms, Garter, Lyon, and Ulster, and to other heraldic authorities. The information supplied is naturally up to date, and its value to all engaged in genealogical pursuits needs no fresh testimony. So comfortable are we in the possession of a work of so much authority and value that we forget to condole with other countries less happily situated. If any country possesses a work supplying like information in a shape equally serviceable and attractive we are unaware of the fact. The conditions attending the transmission of title in the chief European countries render it little probable that another such book can be found. Among the familiar features to the student are the essays on 'The Royal Lineage' and the 'Tables of Precedency,' which supply full information not elsewhere given. Almost the only suggestion we can make is that the time is approaching when the work should be issued in two volumes. It is easy to see the difficulties in the way of such a division, but the task of lifting this peerage from a shelf on to a table involves some labour, and every possessor and lover of books of reference does not possess space enough to enable him to keep them on tables or anywhere but on shelves.

AN article in the *Fortnightly* by Mr. Arthur Symons on Wordsworth is wholly commendable. It is, indeed, a specimen of a kind of paper far too uncommon in our leading monthlies. We cannot sum up Mr. Symons's argument. Wordsworth's limitations and his powers are justly appraised. Wordsworth had, it is declared, "a quality of mind which was akin to the child's fresh and wondering apprehension of things. But he was not content with using the faculty like a man ; it dragged him into the depths of a second childhood, hardly to be distinguished from literal imbecility." And again :

"While other men search among the images of the mind for that poetry which they would impute to Nature, Wordsworth finds it there, really in things, and awaiting only a quiet, loving glance." It is impossible, however, by quotation to convey an idea of the value of the essay. M. Georges Bourdon, late manager of the Odéon, has been commanded by the French Minister of Fine Arts to inquire into the organization of foreign theatres. Beginning with England, he has sent to the *Fortnightly* a summary of his observations on 'Staging in French and English Theatres.' He awards a hearty preference to the English stage, and has much to say about the triumphs, mechanical and poetical, obtained at Drury Lane, Her Majesty's, the Haymarket, Lyceum, Wyndham's, &c. Mr. Tree's mounting of 'Le Chemineau' ('Ragged Robin') and Sir Henry Irving's mounting of 'The Bells' are specially eulogized. M. René Doumic writes on 'The French Drama in 1901,' which he depicts as in a very flourishing condition. It is satisfactory to find that he regards M. Hervieu and M. Brieux as the leading dramatists, and that the bubble of M. Edmond Rostand, whose popularity is one of the most whimsical features of the day, seems to have been pricked. M. Doumic deals briefly with the present condition of the Comédie Française. Mr. Stobart writes on 'The "Either—Or" of Soren Kirkegaard.' —Sir Herbert Maxwell sends to the *Pall Mall* 'Mary, Queen of Scots, and the Mystery of the Casket Letters.' His article, giving a good insight into a matter concerning which the general public has little information, is principally derived from Mr. Lang's 'Mystery of Mary Stuart,' reviewed in our last volume. It is accompanied by a portrait of Mary by Clouet at present in St. Petersburg, and by a reproduction of 'La Reine Blanche' of the same artist. Not wholly satisfactory is Lady Stanley's account of her treatment of her own pets given under the title of 'Tragic Blunders.' A personage quite so thoughtless should not keep pets. 'Tunnelling the Alps' describes the attempts being made to lessen the journey on the Simplon from Brigue to Domo d'Ossola. 'The Trap-door Spider' tells a remarkable story of the attempts of spiders to guard themselves against implacable enemies. The story of the Portland Vase is told afresh. 'As Others see Us' gives American cartoons of English statesmen. Mr. Max Beerbohm writes on 'The Naming of Streets' very whimsically, but also very sensibly.—In the *Cornhill* 'Thackeray in the United States,' by General James Grant Wilson, is continued. It supplies much interesting correspondence with celebrities, English and American, and has many portraits and other designs. New serial novels begin by Anthony Hope and Mr. A. E. W. Mason. So far as can be judged, Mr. Hawkins will deal with irresistible tendencies to parsimony and Mr. Mason with congenital cowardice. 'At the Justice's Window,' by Mrs. Woods, depicts negro life. Under the title 'The Eighteenth-Century Place-Hunter' Mr. Innes Shand presents Richard Rigby, the parasite of the Duke of Bedford. 'The Great Duchess,' by Mr. Street, is, of course, the Duchess of Marlborough. 'A Londoner's Log-Book' is excellent at the outset; we care less about its closing pages. In 'A Forgotten Poet' Dr. Hutton writes about Shenstone, concerning whom we are disposed to ask, Is he quite forgotten; and is he as a poet worthy of being resuscitated?—In the *Gentleman's* 'Pot-Pourri from a Theatrical Library' is not very good nor very instructive. Mr. J. B. Firth writes on 'Public Readings in Ancient Rome'; Dr. Strauss depicts and defends what is called 'Zionism'; Dr. Japp gives an interesting account of 'The Dabchick, or Little Grebe'; and Mr. James Sykes writes on Tom Duncombe.—'A Smuggler's Diary,' by W. H. Hunt, in *Longman's* gives some account of the price of things at the close of the penultimate century, but is not very stirring. 'What we Breathe' deals naturally with microbes. 'Catching Mullet at the Land's End' is readable. Mr. Lang's 'At the Sign of the Ship' remains the most interesting portion of the magazine. In the present instalment he answers Mr. Edward Garnett, who had volunteered some criticism, deals with an antiquarian controversy on some marked and perforated stones found at Dunbuie and Dumbuck, and has something to say concerning advertisements for books wanted.

OUR old correspondent the REV. JOHN PICKFORD, M.A., notes that the time-honoured custom of bringing in the boar's head on Christmas Day at Queen's College, Oxford, was omitted last year, the cause being the lamented death of the senior Fellow of the college, Mr. Henry George Madan, M.A., which took place at his residence near Gloucester. He was the eldest son of the Rev. George Madan, for many years rector of St. Mary Redcliffe, Bristol, and the brother of Mr. Falconer Madan, sub-librarian of the Bodleian, Fellow of Brasenose College, an old contributor to our columns.

Notices to Correspondents.

We must call special attention to the following notices:—

ON all communications must be written the name and address of the sender, not necessarily for publication, but as a guarantee of good faith.

WE cannot undertake to answer queries privately.

To secure insertion of communications correspondents must observe the following rules. Let each note, query, or reply be written on a separate slip of paper, with the signature of the writer and such address as he wishes to appear. When answering queries, or making notes with regard to previous entries in the paper, contributors are requested to put in parentheses, immediately after the exact heading, the series, volume, and page or pages to which they refer. Correspondents who repeat queries are requested to head the second communication "Duplicate."

N. NEVILLE.—"Upwards of a hundred pounds" is a purposely vague way of saying "More than a hundred pounds."

REPLIES on 'The Mitre' and 'The West Bourne' have been received without signature to identify the writer.

NOTICE.

Editorial communications should be addressed to "The Editor of 'Notes and Queries'"—Advertisements and Business Letters to "The Publisher"—at the Office, Bream's Buildings, Chancery Lane, E.C.

We beg leave to state that we decline to return communications which, for any reason, we do not print; and to this rule we can make no exception.

LONDON, SATURDAY, JANUARY 11, 1902.

CONTENTS. — No. 211.

Notes.

EDMUND BOLTON'S 'NERO CÆSAR,' 1627.

THE literary value of this very interesting book has long been recognized both by Warton in his 'History of English Poetry' and by Hearne in his 'Reliquiæ Hearnianæ' The latter, for example, thus expresses himself regarding it (ed. 1869, vol. i. pp. 292, 298) :—

"He [Bagford] likewise says, that one Mr. Bolton was author of 'Nero Cæsar,' which is an excellent thing."
"The book called 'Nero Cæsar,' printed in a pretty big character, in a small folio, was written by Mr. Bolton......The said Life of Nero is very well written. There is great variety of learning in it, managed with very much judgment."

Hearne does not exaggerate. 'Nero Cæsar' throughout is "an excellent thing"; and notwithstanding a certain inflation of style, I think I could cite from it not a few passages at once picturesque, epigrammatic, and suggestive. My object in this note, however, is to draw attention to what interested me in the perusal of the volume. On p. 11 Trajano Bocalini's 'I Raggvagli Di Parnasso : or Advertisements from Parnassus,' is referred to in these words :—

"Of this poinct the Italian author of the famous Ragvalias of Parnassus makes vnfriendly vse, in the imagery inauguration of Cornelivs Tacitvs, to the fained kingdome of Lesbos, smally to the honor of Tacitvs, whom hee makes throwne out againe for affectation of tyranie."

As Bocalini's curious and entertaining work has been translated into English by Henry, Earl of Monmouth, Bolton's allusion will be found on p. 38 of the second edition of 1669.

George Sandys's 'Travels' are thus commendably mentioned (p. 50) :—

"That very sepulcher, at this day extant, and called Agrippina's, is figured on the roofe, and sides with sphinxes, and griphons, but greatly sullied with the smoake of torches, and lights borne in by such as enter. George Sandys, as an eye-witnesse testifies it, in his generous trauails."

The following extract may be taken for what it is worth ; but it is sufficiently interesting in itself (p. 66) :—

"The riotous youths of these our times vniuersally more studious of wittie then discreete, of odde conceipts then solid......Wittie flashes doe condimentally well ; but, if that were their best vse, the gnift of poësie were with little reason styled diuine. There are who lay other studies in the bottome to balasse the fiërie lenities of conceipt, and only they doe honor the Muses with their manners. Those other while they vnlearnedly, and miserably mistake licence for freedome, are oftentimes pleasant companie, but neuer good."

Bolton tells us he wrote a life of Tiberius—it was never printed (p. 82) : "In the life which I haue diligently written of Tiberivs there is more."

Our author's references to some of his distinguished contemporaries are very interesting. William Camden is "that most modest, and antient good friend of mine"; "worthie Camden"; "the king of our antiquaries and not one of arms onely." Sir Henry Saville "was another Tacitvs for grauitie and iudgement." Selden, like Camden, appears to have been personally known to Bolton (p. 156) :—

"They who would see more of this, may satisfie themselues out of Clavdivs Salmasivs, the Selden of Gallia, if without creating enuy to my learned friend, Iohn Selden, I may compare them so."

The illustrious author of 'The Faërie Queene' comes in for honourable mention in what follows (p. 161) :—

"Edmund Spencer, who was in his time, the most learned poet of England, layes it [the scene of the battle between the Romans and Britons] to haue beene further off [than Salisbury Plain]; for he names besides Severn. But without praying in aide of his poëms, I seeme to my selfe to haue made it vehementlie probable, that the field was hereabout, by hauing shewed that Pavllinvs was marcht hitherwards."

On p. 87 Bolton acknowledges an obligation. Who was the "great and generous Earle"?

"What the left hand of the image held, vn-
luckely appeares not, in that faire printed copie,
with which it pleased a great, and generous Earle
to befriend me."

In the next extract we have an early use
of the word "boss" (p. 100) :—

"In Dio she [Boadicia] doth not appeare old, or
decayd, but a strong and perfect woman. Her
picture hangs vp there in such words as showe the
person of some martial Bosse, or Amazonian Gian-
tesse."

Himself a translator, Bolton appears to
have the confident assurance of one who feels
he does not live in a glass house. The
following passage does not lack vigour
(p. 109) :—

"The wrongs, and dishonors, which the most
noble authors sustain oftentimes by many translatours, are infinite and intollerable. Scarce one
booke among one hundred honestlie done, and not
one of one hundred exactlie."

Following up this general accusation, he has
a word of disparagement, evidently against
Richard Grenewey—although he does not
mention him by name—whose translation of
the 'Annals' of Tacitus was first published in
1598, and between that date and 1612 three
editions appeared (p. 112) :—

"The Ocean betweene Britain, and Gall, at the
full tide did ouerflowe, of a bloudie colour, and at a
low water the prints of mens bodies were seene
vpon the bare, and not the dead bodies themselues,
which the englished 'Annals of Tacitvs' mistak-
ingly say."

As the edition of 1612 of Grenewey's
translation of 'The Annales of Cornelivs
Tacitvs' is now before me, I shall quote, for
the sake of comparison, the passage (p. 210)
referred to by Bolton :—

"Further the Ocean bloudy in shew and dead mens
bodies left after an ebbe as they brought hope to
the Britans, so they droue the old souldiers into a
feare."

Nor does the venerable Philemon Holland
escape a mild censure from our persistent
critic (p. 252) :—

"The translatour of Plinies 'Naturall Historics,'
hath rendred the originall in such words, as if the
place were not to be meant of treasure conueighed
away for trade, but onely laid out to furnish a
voiage. For what reason I know not. Cleare it is,
that Plinie speakes of money not expended, but
exhausted."

And as if this were not enough, William
Warner, in another way, is put upon the
"pikes"—to use one of Nash's words—for his
'Albions England' (p. 160) :—

"But amongst her [Boadicia] strengths at this
time, wee must not reckon the flockes of British
wiues and women, who were brought to sit spectators of the expected vtter ruine of Pavllinvs (the
cause and hope of their iourney) though the versifier
in his 'Albions England,' pleasantly encroaching

vpon the poet, doth furnish this Queene-Mother,
and her martiall daughters, with sixe thousand
armed Ladies, out of his Homericall hearsayes. A
licence of wit not vnbeseeming the musicke of
rimes, but incompetent for the grauity of storie,
which admits no fables."

The reference in the following extract to
the Isthmus of Panama is singularly interesting (p. 270) :—

"Reasons which preserued those two huge peniles
of America (naturally combined at the creation of
the world, by a farre broader necke of earth then
that which annexed Peloponnesvs to Greece) from
being sundred by the pickaxe, and spade ; though
that necke alone is the cause of fetching a circuit
from Nombre de Dios to Panama, many thousands
of miles about."

Appended to the edition of 1627 of 'Nero
Cæsar' is a short essay, entitled 'An Historical Parallel,' which Bolton previously privately
communicated to his friend Endymion Porter,
extending to only sixteen pages. The concluding part is so interesting that I cannot
forbear reproducing it here :—

"That renowned Savile, who gaue vnto vs; 'The
end of Nero, and beginning of Galba.' A maister-
peece, and a great one. His praises, as the praises
also of that short essay, are at their high-water
marke in the Epigrams of my antient friend,
Beniamin Ionson, not without the equall praises of
Ionsons selfe, though in a diuers kinde. I for my
part make no vse of the Savilian compositions,
though they handle a finall part of the Neronian
argument. His example in ciuill, and noble letters,
I would gladly commend, vpon this occasion, to all
the free students of our nation ; many of them
growne delicate, and fine of wit, and not of life
alone. Whereas his contrary courses in studie, and
eloquence, nearest to the common nature of things,
void of phantasticke notions, fluent, manly, graue,
vnaffected, smooth, yet full of vigour, and sinewes,
made it easily appeare, that hee had the best of the
antients in his maine imitations. The generall
Latin Historie of our countrey a subiect for a Savile,
and a cherishment for a King, nor of any rather
then of our owne most peacefull Prince, King
Iames."

A. S.

[*Complimentally*, quoted above from p. 66 of 'Nero
Cæsar,' does not appear in the 'H.E.D.,' which,
however, cites Lyly's 'Euphues,' 1579, for *boss* in
the sense of a big fat woman. The example of
penile, from p. 270 of 'Nero Cæsar,' may be useful
presently to Dr. Murray.]

THE AUTHOR AND AVENGER OF EVIL.

On reflecting upon religious or poetical
conceptions, Christian or pagan, ancient,
mediæval, or modern, one is struck by the
confused ideas with regard to the *rôle* acted
by that awful being, the generally accepted
irreconcilable foe of God and man. If man
knows not how anthropomorphic he is, as
little does he foresee where sincere emotion
will lead him, and what extraordinary con-

ceptions—not all illogical—his mind will evolve when applied to the lifelong problems of good and evil, this world and the next, the natural and the supernatural. A *Spectator* essayist remarked not long since that the human imagination recoils before the effort to depict a four-legged angel. Our fixed type is no doubt the traditional angel of art, the fair, winged, female figure with flowing robe and hair and benignant smile. "Great Pan is dead," leaving his horns, hoof, and tail for the adornment of Satan, the result being the bogey whose objective existence is still unquestioned by numbers of pious souls, although Luther treated him with supreme disdain, and brave Tom Ingoldsby and others did their best to reduce the monstrosity to the level of a November Guy Fawkes. This is but a minor instance of the effects of heathenism upon Christianity, strange *Aberglauben* tenaciously held—though happily without serious detriment to genuine religious knowledge and faith—often vividly present to the minds of vigorous denouncers of "paganism" and "idolatry." Carlyle says that Dante had no more doubt of the existence of the *città dolente* and the *Malebolge* pool than we have that we should see Constantinople if we went there, but it is probable that the Sage of Chelsea goes beyond the Florentine bard.

The Hebrew and Christian rebel archangel and his compeers, whose fall has not deprived them of dignity, are paralleled by the shadowy Typhon of the Egyptians, and to a certain extent by the Titans of Greek mythology, though these are mostly tremendous ogres, with forms and passions of men and brutes combined. Milton makes Satan naturally grand, nay beautiful, even if for his vile ends he assumes for a short time the shape of the despised toad or serpent. Ahriman is a powerful force wrestling with Ormuzd on something like equal terms, though the issue of the conflict is predestined. A clergyman once told me in the Sunday school that the devil should be respected, no doubt on account of his superior powers and intelligence. The quaint ideas of children with regard to the evil principle were the subject of an article and correspondence in the *Spectator* a few years ago. To them he is a vague black spectre, perhaps hiding round the corner or in the cupboard playing spy; but if they feel that a temptation to petty theft or falsehood has been resisted, they are sometimes known to crow over Satan's discomfiture. I remember mentally chuckling at his supposed chagrin, because I decided not to touch a tempting dish within reach.

When at a later date I was discussing with a schoolfellow the futility, as it seemed to me, of an intelligent being waging obstinate war against Omnipotence, with full knowledge of ultimate defeat—Robbie Burns in a kindly mood advises the deil to take a thought and mend—my companion bluntly assented in these words, "Depend upon it, the fellow is a fool!" The character loses something of its strength and impressiveness when "some paltry, juggling fiend" is described in legend or fable as *the* devil, reducing the arch-enemy to the size and influence of a malicious conjuror, as Mephistopheles, devoted to the pursuit of one man's soul, or to the dimensions of a Puck or a "Gabriel hound," in which form he once disturbed a service at Bungay Church. Robinson Crusoe, a man of signal courage in an age when superstition was rampant, thought it most likely that the gleaming eyes of the poor old goat in the cave belonged to the devil, who had surely more pressing employment than scaring the solitary inhabitant of a desert isle. The inexplicable footprint in the sand was ascribed to the same source.

Thus much for conflicting conceptions of one definite being. The problem which I think needs to be faced is the tacitly assumed destiny of the prince of darkness to act as an infernal *bourreau.* By what mandate is he who causes the ruin of souls to execute judgment upon them through the ages, in which hateful task he takes characteristic delight? Is he not rather their companion in misery? As Goethe puts it:—

Auch hier sind jene grossen Scharen,
Die mit ihm gleiches Lasters waren,
Doch lange nicht so bös als er.
Hier liegt die ungezählte Menge,
In schwarzem, schrecklichem Gedränge,
Im Feuerorkan um ihn her;
Er sieht, wie sie den Richter scheuen,
Er sieht, wie sie der Sturm zerfrisst,
Er sieht's und kann sich doch nicht freuen,
Weil seine Pein noch grösser ist.

Pluto, the grisly god lately discussed in the columns of 'N. & Q.,' with his train of furies, Cerberus, and other monsters, cannot be called a fallen angel, nor can they. He is the brother and equal of Jupiter and Neptune, and does not appear to share the woe which he contemplates in iron majesty. Hela, the fearsome Norse goddess of Niflheim, was, I understand, a daughter of the Allfather Odin, and no rebel. The Hindoo Yamen, if I mistake not, is a parallel to Pluto. Are Azrael, the Mohammedan angel of death, and those grim inquisitors Munkar and Nakir, evil beings or ministers of Allah's stern justice? In Dante's 'Inferno' the arch-rebel is embedded in ice, suffering terribly, and incidentally inflicting hideous torture on others. Judas Iscariot, Brutus, and Cassius are crushed in his triple jaws, while the incessant flapping of his wings raises the blast which congeals Cocytus, where lie the traitors :—

Con sei occhi piangeva, e per tre menti
Gocciava 'l pianto e sanguinosa bava.
'Inferno,' xxxiv.

Lucifer's mental agony is too profound to admit of his rejoicing over those whom he has led to their doom (and note that Dante punishes the Titans as enemies of Jehovah). Singing of the Egyptian plagues, Asaph says (Psalm lxxviii. 49) that Jehovah "sent evil angels among them" (*immissiones per angelos malos*). It is not clear to my mind whether these are ministers of Divine wrath, as St. Michael, or malignant spirits allowed to work their pleasure on Pharaoh and his subjects. In the Apocalypse commissions of dire severity are assigned to celestial beings.

I do not know whether this point has been satisfactorily dealt with, but it seems repulsive that a being whose set purpose is "evil, be thou my good," and who seeks to pervert and wreck the lives of men, should be regarded as their remorseless tormentor hereafter. The assumption is clearly implied in the *juron* of the French king, which has its expression in most languages. The question of bargaining with Satan for temporary advantage, as in the case of Marlowe's and Goethe's hero, I do not discuss.

FRANCIS P. MARCHANT.
Brixton Hill.

THE JUBILEE OF THE 'LEISURE HOUR.'
(*Concluded from p. 4.*)

MR. WILLIAM CHAMBERS had formed high expectations as to the success of the *Journal*, but these were far exceeded. In a few days there was, for Scotland, the unprecedented sale of thirty thousand copies. An agency was established in London, and the circulation rose to fifty thousand, which in after years increased to eighty thousand. It has been the custom of the *Journal* from time to time to take its readers into its confidence and to give articles on its progress. Mr. Robert Cochrane has called my attention to these. On January 19th, 1895, 'Some Notable Beginners in *Chambers's Journal*' mentions that on July 7th, 1849, George Meredith's first contribution, 'Chillianwallah,' appeared. This memorializes the bloody fight which took place at the village of that name in the Punjab during the second Sikh war, on the 13th of January, 1849. Mr. Payn also contri-

buted his first novel, 'The Family Scapegrace.' He was editor from 1858 to 1871.

On November 6th, 1897, another contribution to the history of the *Journal* was made, and again on the 17th of November, 1900.

Its contributors have included, among many other well-known names, Robert William Jamieson, the father of "Dr. Jim," who contributed 'Who Wrote Shakespeare?' August 7th, 1852; Mr. Stanley J. Weyman on Oxford life; Thomas Hardy, 'How I built myself a House,' March 18th, 1865; Dr. A. Conan Doyle, whose first short story appeared in 1879, 'The Mystery of Sasassa Valley,' a South African story; Mr. D. Christie Murray; Sir Wemyss Reid; and Mr. Leslie Stephen.

Dr. A. K. H. Boyd was wont to say that "the *Journal* was read in Scotland by everybody who read anything at all." There can be no doubt that its early success was largely due to the fact that at that time the price of newspapers was usually sevenpence, owing to the heavy stamp and advertisement duties; *Chambers's Journal*, being free from these exactions, sold at threehalfpence, and in point of size was nearly as large as a newspaper. But while the publications of the Chamberses were free from the stamp and advertisement taxes, they had to bear a heavy burden in the shape of the paper duty; and when my father founded the Press Association for its abolition the three brothers William, Robert, and David took an active part in the movement until repeal was secured. On the occasion of the presentation made to my father on the 19th of January, 1863, to commemorate his services in promoting the repeal of the taxes upon literature and the Press, Mr. David Chambers stated that during the twenty years previous to the tax being abolished it had cost the firm 160,000*l.*, while on their "Tracts for the People" alone they paid 10,000*l.* These had to be abandoned on account of the heavy duty.

It is pleasing to know that all the useful publications issued by the firm are prospering. The new edition of 'Chambers's Encyclopædia' is selling well; the first large impression of 'Chambers's Twentieth Century Dictionary,' edited by the Rev. T. Davidson, is almost exhausted; and the new edition of the 'Cyclopædia of Literature,' edited by D. Patrick, LL.D., the first volume of which has just been published, has met with a good reception. The present editor of the *Journal* is Mr. Charles E. S. Chambers, grandson to its distinguished founder.

John Cassell came into the field of cheap literature much later than the Chamberses, the *Working Man's Friend and Family In-*

structor not appearing until January, 1850. It consisted of thirty-two pages, crown 8vo, price one penny, and was published at 335, Strand. Mr. Pike, in his life of John Cassell, gives an extract from the *Working Man's Friend* of November 1st, 1851, as to the sale of the ten daily papers then published in London, the total being 64,408. Of these the *Times* absorbed 38,382, the *Morning Chronicle* 2,915, and the *Daily News* 3,630, the united circulation of the seven other papers being under 20,000. On the 3rd of April, 1852, 'The Popular Educator' was started, its first editor being Prof. Wallace, of Glasgow, and in July of the same year Cassell removed from the Strand to La Belle Sauvage Yard, the home of the present firm. Mr. F. J. Cross amusingly relates that when John Cassell came there was a public-house at the end of the yard, but that gave way to the publishing house, and "little by little we have monopolized the square, and also stretch to Fleet Lane." Mr. Cross tells me that there are now eight monthly magazines and nearly fifty serials published by the firm. John Cassell was the first editor of the *Quiver*, started in 1861. He was succeeded by the Rev. Henry Wright, followed by John W. Clark, then by Canon Teignmouth Shaw, who was followed by the present editor, the Rev. Dr. H. G. Bonavia Hunt, who has been editor for the last twenty-five years. Its Christmas number contains three beautiful photogravures—'The Good Samaritan,' from the painting by William Small; 'The Love-Letter,' by George A. Storey; and 'Home,' by T. B. Kennington.

Cassell's Magazine started on the 9th of March, 1867. Its first editor was W. Moy Thomas. He was among the early contributors to *Chambers's Journal*, a poem of his entitled 'Autumn' appearing on the 27th of November, 1847, when he was only nineteen. It is a sweet picture of the country in autumn, when

> Sometimes, day by day, the hazel tint
> Grows deeper on the mass of forest trees,
> And not a single breath from heaven is sent
> To cool the ruddy fruits, that by degrees
> Wax ripe and riper in a dreamy ease.

. . . . . .

> Till the sharp north wind cometh unaware,
> And half relieves the laden orchard-bough;
> And like hoar death, that kills the good and fair,
> Lays autumn's loveliest bells and blossoms low,
> And sudden winter falls wherever it doth blow.

Mr. Moy Thomas was followed in the editorship by the Rev. H. R. Haweis, John Lovell, G. M. Fenn, and Dr. Hunt. The present editor is Mr. Max Pemberton. With the Christmas number is given a photogravure, beautifully executed, of 'The Pirate's Prize,' from the painting by B. F. Gribble. The *Saturday Journal* was established on the 6th of October, 1883. Its first editor was Dr. Hunt, followed by Mr. Laird Clowes. Mr. Ernest Foster has edited the *Journal* for the past fifteen years. It should not be forgotten that Messrs. Cassell also founded the *Echo* (see 9th S. ii. 504)

Of the original partners of the firm in 1859 Mr. Thomas Dixon Galpin alone survives. The number of hands at present employed is about twelve hundred. It is curious that John Cassell, the originator of this large business, had no knowledge of publishing. He died at the early age of forty-eight, on the 2nd of April, 1865, the same day as Richard Cobden, who had shown him much friendship. Cassell took an active part in the repeal of the Paper Duty, and with my father visited Edinburgh and Dublin, where they formed branch associations in connexion with the one in London to forward repeal. One cannot close this rapid glance at some of the men who have rendered such service to our cheap literature without an expression of gratitude to them for having served their generation so faithfully and so well.   John C. Francis.

"Macaw" and "Macaco."—In his 'Notes on English Etymology,' 1901, p. 349, Prof. Skeat appears to confuse these two distinct terms. He says: "The 'Century Dictionary' derives *macaw* from Brazilian *macao*, which I fail to find. The 'Hist. Nat. Brasiliæ' has nothing like it. The modern Spanish form is *macaco*." *Macaco*, however, means a monkey, not a parrot, and according to the 'Hist. Nat. Brasiliæ,' 1648, is a Congo word, like *chimpanzee* and *pongo*. The only dissentient from this is Von Martius, 'Beiträge zur Ethnographie,' 1867, ii. 461, who describes it as "vox a Brasiliensibus recepta, in insulis Antillis a primis Europæis audita, Caraibice *mecou*"; but here, again, there seems to be confusion between two distinct terms, as this should surely rather apply to *mico* than to *macaco*. As to the origin of *macaw*, the Brazilian, or rather Portuguese, *macao*, according to a statement quoted by Buffon from Albin, was applied to these birds because they were supposed to come from Macao in the East Indies. It is some confirmation of this that the older English explorers used it to designate Oriental parrots. Thus Dampier, 'Voyages,' 1697, ii. 128, ascribes "maccaws" and "parakites" to Acheen.   Jas. Platt, Jun.

'Budget of Paradoxes': Diderot.—De Morgan, in the 'Budget,' twice relates the story of the algebraical proof of the existence of God which was presented to Diderot at the Court of Catherine II. The statement at p. 474 is the more detailed :—

"The scorner was informed that an eminent mathematician had an algebraical proof of the existence of God, which he would communicate before the whole Court, if agreeable. Diderot gladly consented. The mathematician, who is not named, was Euler. He came to Diderot with the gravest air, and in a tone of perfect conviction said, 'Monsieur ! $\frac{a+b^n}{z} = x$, donc Dieu existe ; répondez !' Diderot, to whom algebra was Hebrew, though this is expressed in a very roundabout way by Thiébault, and whom we may suppose to have expected some verbal argument of alleged algebraical closeness, was disconcerted ; while peals of laughter sounded on all sides. Next day he asked permission to return to France, which was granted."

Now Thiébault ('Mes Souvenirs de Vingt Ans de Séjour à Berlin,' Paris, 1804, tome iii. pp. 141-2) says

"que Diderot, voulant prouver la nullité et l'ineptie de cette prétendue preuve, mais ressentant malgré lui l'embarras où l'on est d'abord lorsque on découvre chez les autres le dessein de nous jouer, n'avait pu échapper aux plaisanteries dont on étoit prêt à l'assaillir ; que cette aventure lui en faisant craindre d'autres encore, il avoit témoigné peu de temps après le désir de retourner en France."

Here, instead of anything approaching to a hint that algebra was Hebrew to Diderot, which De Morgan says Thiébault "expressed in a very roundabout way," there is a very reasonable explanation of Diderot's defeat. Besides, it is not true that Diderot was ignorant of algebra. His 'Mémoires sur Différents Sujets de Mathématiques' (Paris, 1748) are sufficient proof of the contrary.

I think it must be admitted that, for once, De Morgan's "odium theologicum" got the better of his accuracy.   J. R—N.

HARVEY AND THE CIRCULATION OF THE BLOOD: AN INEDITED POEM, c. 1673.—On the back of the title of a copy of Dr. William Harvey's 'Anatomical Exercises concerning the Motion of the Heart and Blood,' with preface by Zachary Wood, physician of Rotterdam, 1673, 12mo, which was included in lot 827 of a book sale at Sotheby's Rooms on the 5th ult., is the following curious MS. poem, without title or name of author, but probably contemporary with the date of the book (i.e., some sixteen years after Harvey's death), or, if we may judge by the last two lines thereof, in reference to the rebuilding of St. Paul's Cathedral after the Great Fire of 1666, not later than the year 1675. Although I have (inter alia) unquestionably given more attention to the subject of the great anato-

mist than any other person during a long series of years—at an enormous expenditure of time and money, and with many remarkable results—I do not remember to have met with this poem elsewhere, either in MS. or print ; and I should think that its author was himself a physician and a former owner of the volume in question. As the latter contains on its pages some autographs and MS. notes, I hoped by such means either to ascertain the authorship of the poem or to obtain a clue thereto, but in vain, as the same are evidently in other and later hands ; and the initial fly-leaf, which may have borne the writer's name, or afforded some other interesting information, is wanting, owing possibly to the looseness of the covers. The last half of the poem no doubt refers to the loss during the great Civil War of Harvey's papers, which our poet appears to imagine would otherwise have been given to the world in print, either by the doctor himself in his lifetime, or by others after his decease.

Considering the great and world-wide interest which is attached to everything of early date relating to the "immortal" discoverer of the circulation of the blood, I venture to think that no apology is needed for seeking to enshrine in the columns of 'N. & Q.' this curious and apparently hitherto unknown *morceau*.

Methinks in Arts great Circle others stand
　　Lock't vp together hand in hand,
　　Ev'ry one leads as he is led,
　　The same bare path they tread,
A dance like Fairies a Fantastick round,
But neither change their motion, nor their ground :
Had Harvey to this Road confin'd his Wit,
His noble Circle of ye Blood had been vntrodden
　　　　yet.
Great Doctor, ye [altered from "in"] Art of
　　Curing's cur'd by thee,
　　We now thy Patient Physick see
From all inveterate diseases free,
　　Purg'd of old errors by thy care,
New dieted, put forth to clearer air,
　　It now will strong & healthfull proue,
It selfe before Lethargick lay, & could not moue.

These Usefull Secrets to his Pen we owe,
And thousands more 'twas ready to bestow ;
Of wch a Barbarous War's vnlearned Rage
　　Has robb'd the ruin'd Age ;
O cruell Loss ! as if ye Golden fleece
　　With so much cost and labour bought
　　　　　　　[altered from "brought"],
And from afar by a great Heroe brought,
　　Had sunk ev'n in ye Ports of Greece.
O cursed War ! who can forgiue thee this ?
　　Houses & Townes may rise again
　　　　And ten times easier 'tis
To rebuild Pauls, than any work of his.
　　　　　　　　　　　W. I. R. V.

JOHN KANE, A FORGOTTEN ACTOR.—As I always look upon 'N. & Q.' as a medium for preserving from oblivion ("not for an age only") the names of bygone heroes and heroines who "fought till they fell and died," may I quote a few lines from the *Era* of 9 Nov., 1901? In 'A Chat with Mr. Arthur Willoughby, Acting-Manager of the Buxton Pavilion,' that gentlemen said, speaking of old times :—

"A very respectable family, the Thornhills, performed at the old theatre in Spring Gardens ; then a more modern theatre was opened at the bottom of Hall Bank. The Thornhills are buried in the little secluded church of St. Anne's, in Higher Buxton, the mother church of Buxton, where also lies all that is mortal of John Kane."—"Kean ?" "No, Kane. You were speaking of dear old Toole a moment ago. When he opened our present theatre, he and his company visited, in the pouring rain, the grave of this 'poor Yorick.' Mr. Toole paid a handsome sum for it to be reverently restored."—"We should like to see this grave." "You will find it at the east end of the churchyard. Close to the fence wall is a headstone placed at the foot of the grave, the inscription facing *westwards*, while every other inscription faces, of course, the east. The inscription reads as follows:—

This stone is placed here
In Memory of
John Kane, Comedian,
Who departed this Life Dec. 10th, 1799,
Aged 58 years.

A pathetic story is associated with this strolling player's grave. John Kane was about to dine off roast beef. He went out in the fields for some horseradish, to serve as a condiment, but instead of horseradish he pulled up the roots of hemlock, or monkshood (aconite), and died in dreadful agony two hours after he had dined. Mr. Toole, with tears in his eyes, bareheaded, before the mouldering tombstone, said, pointing to the hundreds of graves in front of Kane's, 'What an audience he will have when the curtain is rung up at the last great performance !'"

HERBERT B. CLAYTON.

39, Renfrew Road, Kennington, S.E.

TENNIS : ORIGIN OF THE NAME. (See 9ᵗʰ S. viii. 236.)—M. Jusserand, as noted at the above reference, confirms Prof. Skeat's derivation of the name of the game. "I suppose," says Prof. Skeat, "it meant 'take heed' or 'mark' as an exclamation ; if so, it is precisely the equivalent of the modern 'play.'" M. Jusserand quotes from 'Lusus Puerilis,' Paris, 1555, and deduces that the *excipe* of Cordier and the *accipe* of Erasmus were the Latin version of the French *tenez*, an exclamation used on commencing play. It is curious to find that at a late period the server on beginning a set said, "Y êtes-vous?" just as we now say, "Are you there?" at the telephone.   JOHN HEBB.

[*Tenez* = "take it," which may still be heard. A player at fives is still said to "take" a serve which is offered to him.]

Queries.

WE must request correspondents desiring information on family matters of only private interest to affix their names and addresses to their queries, in order that the answers may be addressed to them direct.

CARLYLE ON SYMBOLS.—The *Daily Telegraph* of 11 December last, in its first leading article, refers to "Carlyle's belief in the value of traditional symbols." I would ask some kind student of the Chelsea Sage to inform me in which of his works this is found. For to those who confess an affection for symbols it cannot but be gratifying to know that they had the appreciation of the hard-headed philosopher, who certainly did not wear his heart upon his sleeve—an indiscretion, indeed, to which his countrymen are not prone.

It will be interesting to notice the symbols to which the Sage refers, and his testimony will add assurance to the conviction that as the world grows old, *et nos in illo*, the use of emblems, whether political, religious, or social, prevails to-day as through precedent ages it ever did. And how, indeed, can it be otherwise so long as in living beings the material and the immaterial are welded and inseparable? The one must express the other. "An outward and visible sign" must represent the inward and invisible mind, and so subtle, necessary, and universal is the representation that it is often made unconsciously.

Theological symbols have perhaps chief observance and notoriety ; they have been overturned and smashed when the represented doctrines have also suffered subversion, but others have replaced them. The Puritan and the Covenanter destroyed objects of beauty which to them seemed to represent falsehoods ; but they gave expression to their own conceived ideas of truth by the simplicity of whitewash, and the self-abasement of cropped hair and straight-cut sombre garments. The Irish Orangeman also effaced the sacred Christian emblem, and, more cheerful-minded than the Protestant of England or of Scotland, adopting colours as his symbol, flaunted his flag of orange and blue in the face of his Roman Catholic brother, who, under his banner of green, eagerly accepted the gauge of battle, their differences being referred to the arbitrament of the shillelagh !

The resuscitation and cultivation of art in our own time, joined to our more recent seizure of the Imperial idea, have refreshed our affection for symbols. Then we have been blessed in the prolonged reign of a great and good Queen, for so many years the head and symbol of the nation whose best qualities she represented. So our pride in the monarchy, proved to be the best form of government under which we can live, is renewed, and we hail the coming coronation of the King with all its aforetime stateliness and significant symbolism. The pageantry may, perhaps, to some appear childish, but happier they who have not lost their zest in the pleasures of childhood, and can yet enjoy the stately show of a great symbolic ceremony. And whatever may be the difference in sentiments, it is certain that in the display of dignity and patriotism each member of the united monarchy will claim its due position. "Caledonia stern and wild" will be careful that her "ruddy lion ramps in gold" in all rightful and accustomed places; and "gallant little Wales," democratic and severely religious though she be, will not be slack to exhibit "the Dragon of the great Pendragonship," happily of late restored to the national heraldry by the gracious sovereign.

So let symbols flourish; and after a long digression (which is committed to the forbearance of the Editor) I would again ask for Carlyle's reference to them.
                                W. L. RUTTON.

ARMS OF A MARRIED WOMAN.—Is a married woman, who is not herself entitled to arms, allowed to bear the arms of her husband (who is an armigerous person) on a lozenge?
                                W. G. D. F.

'FAERIE QUEENE': SUPPLEMENT TO.—I have a memorandum among my papers that there is in the Public Library at Cambridge a manuscript supplement to the 'Faërie Queene,' in three books (Ee. iii. 53). Will some one tell me its date, authorship, and whether it has ever been printed?   ASTARTE.

PICTURE OF NEW CROSS GATE.—A friend has an old painting most execrably executed, but valuable to the local historian if the date could be ascertained. It represents a large coach outside the public-house called "The Five Bells," at New Cross Gate; on the signpost the landlord's name appears as Dyke, while the customers are supplied with Calvert & Co.'s "Intire." The coach has "John Court, Greenwich to London," and "I.A.C." in a circle on the panel. Under the seat behind is what appears to be a spread eagle; on the panel is a representation of St. George and the dragon, and on the dickey five bells. There are three passengers abreast shown inside; two seats behind, holding five persons, three and two; and three on top besides the driver, one a lady, wearing a hat like that worn by Queen Caroline at her trial. Has any reader access to records which would enable me to arrive at a proximate date?
                                AYEAHR.
New Cross, S.E.

"FOUNTAIN-PREGNANT."—At the age of fourteen Alfred Tennyson wrote:—

> The fountain-pregnant mountains riven
>   To shapes of wildest anarchy,
> By sacred fire and midnight storms
>   That wander round their windy cones.

I suppose the epithet "fountain-pregnant" was of his own imagination, but Dante many centuries earlier made Guido del Duca say:

> Ben è che il nome di tal valle pera;
> Chè dal principio suo (dov' è si *pregno*
> L' alpestro monte, ond' è tronco Peloro,
> Chè in pochi luoghi passa oltra quel segno)
> Infin là, 've si rende per ristoro
> Di quel che il ciel della marina asciuga.
>   'Purg.,' xiv. 30-35.

Dean Plumptre has a note in which he remarks ('Purgatory,' p. 103):—

"The word *pregno*......may be a rendering of Lucan (ii. 397). Speaking of a district in the Apennines, he says:—

> Nulloque a vertice tellus
> Altius intumuit propriusque accessit Olympo.

And in this case it would point simply to height. Another rendering refers the word to the character of that part of the Apennines as a watershed, the sources of the Arno and Tiber, the Lamone, the Savio, and two other rivers lying within the compass of eighteen miles."

Did our great English poet owe anything at fourteen to Dante, or was the idea born of his own genius?   ST. SWITHIN.

DONNE'S BURIAL. — Walton in his life of Dr. Donne states that "the next day after his burial some unknown friend, some one of the many lovers and admirers of his virtue and learning, writ this epitaph with a coal on the wall over his grave:—

> Reader! I am to let thee know,
> Donne's Body only lies below;
> For, could the grave his Soul comprise,
> Earth would be richer than the Skies!"

Has this friend ever been surmised? It would appear unlikely he was Dr. Fox. Was he Walton himself? He was present at Donne's death, and presumably at his funeral and in London the day after.
                        STAPLETON MARTIN.
The Firs, Norton, Worcester.

"PEN-NAME."—I have not read Mrs. Elizabeth Wells Gallup's 'Bi-literal Cypher of Sir Francis Bacon,' but in a sympathetic article in the *Publishers' Circular* of 14 December last a statement is quoted which is said by Mrs. Gallup to have been found in the

1595 edition of 'Colin Clout,' and in which Bacon claims to be the son of Queen Elizabeth. In this statement Bacon is made to say that "Marlow is also a pen-name emploi'd ere taking Wm. Shakespeare's as our masque or vizard." I have always been under the impression that "pen-name" was an Americanism of somewhat recent date for pseudonym or *nom de guerre*, but I may be wrong. I should therefore be glad if some authority could be shown for the use of the term in the acknowledged writings of Bacon or any of his contemporaries. Into the general merits of the question raised by Mrs. Gallup I do not, of course, propose to enter.   W. F. Prideaux.

Moat's 'Stenography.'— I am in possession of a copy of Moat's 'Stenography,' bearing date 1833, though, according to a quaintly worded preface, completed for publication twenty years earlier. It is an octavo with some twenty pages of steel-engraved "characters." The work seems to me to be of unique interest, as very patently most systems of a later date are based upon it. Could any of your readers inform me of the history of the work or its author?
                              George Jesson.
525, George Street, Sydney, N.S.W.

[Thomas Moat's 'Shorthand Standard Attempted' was published in 8vo by Thomas Tegg, price 8s., between 1816 and 1851.]

Gordon, a Place-name. — What is the meaning of the name Gordon? I believe it is to be found in many countries, and I have heard it described as a hill fort.
                              J. M. Bulloch.

Sir Thomas Smith, of Parson's Green.— I am in search of the ancestry of Sir Thomas Smith, of Parson's Green, who married the Hon. Frances Bruges (or Brydges) *temp.* Elizabeth. Was he identical with the Sir Thomas Smith who was Secretary of State to that queen?   Kathleen Ward.
Castle Ward, Downpatrick.

Archange de Pembroke.—A writer in a recent number of the *Dublin Review*, in a paper on Angélique Arnauld, incidentally refers to "a Franciscan friar, well known in the religious circles of the day as Father Archange de Pembroke." He was, we are told, "an English nobleman" by birth, and therefore was probably a member of the race of the Earls of Pembroke. Can he be identified?   Astarte.

'The Little Picture Bible.'—What is the date of this excellent little book? My copy is written by Isabella Child, and the publisher is "London: Charles Tilt, Fleet Street." The book is 3 in. by 2½ in., and the paging runs to 191. It contains "48 pretty plates."   Thos. Ratcliffe.

Feeding Birds. — In the *Sheffield Daily Telegraph*, 28 December, 1901, is the following interesting notice with reference to the feeding of birds :—

"In old times a sheaf of wheat was sometimes hung outside the porch of village churches, and renewed at intervals during winter, as food for the birds—a sermon surely in itself—a charming reminder that Christian kindness should not end with suffering humanity, but should embrace all God's creatures."

I should like to know if this custom is still practised.   Charles Green.
18, Shrewsbury Road, Sheffield.

Epitaph at Llanrhidian Lower. — On the outside of the south wall of the nave of the church of Llanrhidian Lower, in the "rural district of Gower," Glamorganshire, they have suspended a tombstone bearing the following epitaph :—

"Here lieth the body of Robert Harry who deceased the xxi day of September : aged. 65 : anno Domini 1646 : who maried two wives and had issve by them x children.
Here lyeth my lifeles corps bereved of liveing breath :
Not slaine by sinne which is the cavse of death.
But by decree which God hath said all men shall dy :
And come to jvdgement to know how they shall try.
And now o heavenly God that liveing breath thov gavest to mee :
That mortall life and sovle I yeeld and give againe to thee.
My corps to earth for short time I doe give :
My sovle vnto my saviovr Christ eternally to live."

The passive or middle use of "try" is noteworthy. Has this inscription been published in any book?   E. S. Dodgson.

'Cornhill Magazine' Illustrations.— Who was the artist of the initial letter T designs, illustrating chaps. iii. and iv. of 'Lovel the Widower,' in the March and April numbers, 1860? The former is initialled S., and the latter E. S., reversed in a circle. Also, Who was the artist of the outline 'Ariadne' in the December number, 1860?
                              R. D. C. N.

'Rotuli Scotiæ,' 1814-9, Glossary.—A slip was inserted in vol. i. as follows :—

"With volume second, containing the Reigns of King Richard II.......Edward IV., will be printed an Index of Matters and Names of Persons and Places, a Glossary, Table of the Contractions, and General Preface."

Were the index of matters, the glossary, and the general preface ever published? They are not in the Bodleian copy.   Q. V.

𝕽𝖊𝖕𝖑𝖎𝖊𝖘.

KINBOROUGH AS A FEMALE CHRISTIAN NAME.
(9ᵗʰ S. viii. 504.)

KINBOROUGH is not a place-name, but the modern form of the Old English (=Anglo-Saxon) female name Cyneburgh or Kyneburh, latinized Cyniburga, well known as that of the sainted daughter of King Penda of Mercia, the sister of Kings Peada and Wulfhere, who was married in 653 to Alchfrid, son of Oswiu, King of Northumbria, as recorded by Bæda, 'Hist. Eccles.,' III. xxi., where she appears as "Cyniburgam filiam Pendan regis." (One may assume that every reader of 'N. & Q.' knows that Latin and Old English C was = K.) The Old English Chronicle (Laud MS.) contains in the annal of 656 the account of the consecration of the Minster of Medeshamstede (later Peterborough), built by the Kings Peada and Wulfhere, at which the latter was present with his two sisters Kyneburg and Kyneswith, written in the later annal of 675 Kineburh and Kineswith. And the annal of 963 tells how, three centuries later, Abbot Ælfsi took up the bodies of St. Kyneburh and St. Kyneswith that lay at Castor, and brought them to Peterborough, and presented them there to St. Peter. For the traditional accounts of the sister saints, see Rev. C. Plummer's edition of Bæda (III. xxi. note). *Cyne*, "kingly, royal," is the first element of a long list of Old English personal names, male and female ; the feminine *burh*, "fort, fortress," is an equally frequent second element of names of women, of which Æthelburh, Eadburh, and Seaxburh—latinized Ethelburga, Edburga, and Sexburga—are perhaps the best known ; but more than twenty others occur in the Durham 'Liber Vitæ' and Bæda's 'History.' The Old English proper names in Cyne- mostly take Ken- in their modern form, as in Cynehelm = Kenelm, Cyneric = Kenrick or Kendrick, Cynewulf = Kennulph ; but Kin- or Kyn- is the regular phonetic representative of Cyne-, Kyne-, already, even in Old English times, shortened to Cyn-, Kyn-: Cyneburh itself appears as Cynnburg, Kynnburug (see Sweet, 'Oldest English Texts,' 553). It would be of interest to know whether the group of related Kinboroughs in the sixteenth and seventeenth centuries had had their name handed down from Old English times, or whether it was introduced at a later date as a baptismal name, perhaps for a female child born or baptized on 6 March, St. Cyneburh's or Kinborough's day. J. A. H. MURRAY.

G. D. B. says that this name occurs at times spelt Kynburgh, though Kinborough is the more usual form. I therefore do not think there can be much room for doubt that the ladies he mentions were called after the Anglo-Saxon saint Kyneburga, whose festival was observed on 6 March, under which date an account of her may be seen in the 'Acta Sanctorum,' Alban Butler's 'Lives of the Saints,' and the late Rev. Richard Stanton's 'Menology of England and Wales.'
EDWARD PEACOCK.

DESBOROUGH PORTRAITS AND RELICS (9ᵗʰ S. viii. 497).—SIR E. F. DU CANE writes of engravings of portraits of General and Mrs. Desborough, and wishes for some information about them. There is a reproduction of a photograph of a family portrait of Major-General Disbrowe (Desborough), in possession of Miss Desborough, facing p. 172 of my 'Oliver Cromwell' (Goupil, 1899), which may assist him in determining whether his engraving represents the general or not.
SAMUEL R. GARDINER.

ST. BRIAVEL (9ᵗʰ S. ix. 9).—The accounts of his hundred and parish in various Gloucestershire and Dean Forest books seem to prove that he was a Norman St. Brulé. D.

ADULATION EXTRAORDINARY (8ᵗʰ S. x. 152, 322 ; 9ᵗʰ S. viii. 473).—The following is bad to beat. It occurs in a speech addressed to Charles I. by Thos. Widdrington, Recorder of Berwick, when his Majesty was passing through the town in June, 1633, on his way to be crowned at Edinburgh (Rushworth, ii. 179) :—

"It were unseasonable for us to represent to Your Majesties view the Gloomy Cloud of our Pressures and Wants : No I need not do it......for that Cloud is suddenly vanished by the Radiant Beams of Your Sun-like Appearance. By whose approach these Rusty Ordnances, these Solitary Walls, these Souldiers, this now despicable *Town*, have all instantly received their former Life, Luster, and Vigour; and hence we are induced to think, that this Year (being the Year of Your Majesties most Royal Progress) is likewise the Year dreamed on by *Plato*, wherein all things were to return to their former Life, Splendor and Excellency......We well know (as indeed who knoweth not) that Royal Blood running in Your Majesties Veins, to be Extracted from the most Renowned Kings of both these Kingdoms, and by those Kings (Most Dread Sovereign) especially by Your Royal Father of ever Blessed and Happy Memory, hath this Town, though in the Skirts of either Kingdom, been richly Imbroidered, with many Priviledges, Franchises, and Immunities : And therefore we doubt not but Your Majesty, in whom each Man may behold the Worth of all Your Ancestors, You being no less Rightful Inheritor of their Vertues, than of their Crowns, will gratiously maintain what they have

most benignly granted......Your Majesty is now
going to place a *Diadem* upon Your most Sacred
Head, which God and Your own Right have long
since given into Your Hands......And we most
affectionately wish, That the Throne of King
Charles, the Great and wise Son of our Brittish
Solomon, may be like that of King *David*, the
Father of *Solomon*, established before the Lord for
ever."

On 30 March, 1639, Widdrington, who had
been appointed Recorder of York, made
another speech to the king, in which, among
other extravagant phrases, he said (Rushworth, ii. 887) :—

"The beams and lightnings of those Eminent
Vertues, Sublime Gifts and Illuminations wherewith you are endowed, do cast so forcible Reflections upon the Eyes of all Men, that you fill, not
only this City, this Kingdom, but the whole
Universe with splendor."

A few years later this royal adulator had
become "Speaker of the Parliament of the
Commonwealth of England, Scotland, and
Ireland," and as such installed Cromwell as
Lord Protector! His address on that memorable occasion was pitched in a milder key,
but is extolled by Carlyle as "Eloquent mellifluous speech," "Speech still worth reading,"
&c.   RICHARD WELFORD.

The following ascription may be worth a
note :—

Mal. iii. 3.   Numb. xxxi. 22.
Jehovah Chimista Supremus.
Carolus D.G. Secundus.

It occurs on the title-page of a work entitled
"The Laws of Art and Nature in Knowing,
Judging, Assaying, Fining, Refining, and
Inlarging the Bodies of confin'd Metals.—
By Sir John Pettus, of Suffolk, Kt. Of the
Society for the Mines Royal.—London: 1683."
And, that the "merry monarch" may be sure
to see the point of the reference, the author
is careful to remark in a dedication that
"tis hinted in the Title Page Your Majesty
is (in the Science of Chimistry, as in all
Sciences of Humanity) *Nulli Secundus*."
                          R. OLIVER HESLOP.
Newcastle-upon-Tyne.

ANCIENT BOATS (9th S. viii. 366, 407, 507).—
In 1860 a canoe was found in the turbary of
Mercurago, near Arona; there is an account
of it, with a woodcut of a section, in Prof.
Gastaldi's 'Lake Habitations of Italy,' 1865,
p. 102. A canoe found at Giggleswick is now
in the museum of the Leeds Philosophical
Society; for a description and picture see
'Old Yorkshire,' ed. Smith, N.S., 1890,
pp. 2, 3.   W. C. B.

PECHÉ FAMILY (9th S. viii. 232, 392).—This
family were also early settled in Suffolk,
where the name still abounds. D'Ewes in the
autobiography printed by Halliwell (i. 326)
mentions a William Peccatum, or Peché, as
holding land in Wickhambrook, Suffolk,
20 William I. See also Harl. MS. 537, fo. 105,
as to lands in Stowlangtoft held by Reginald and Galfridus Peché.
                          L. B. CLARENCE.

ACLAND OF CHITTLEHAMPTON (9th S. viii.
464).—Lieut.-Col. J. L. Vivian's 'Visitations
of the County of Devon' contains the above
from before 14 Edward II. to 1879. It includes the Aclands of Acland, Columbjohn,
Killerton and Hawkridge, &c.
                          JOHN RADCLIFFE.

See under 'Acland' in the 'Dictionary of
English and Welsh Surnames.'
                          ARTHUR MAYALL.

References to families bearing this name
from the time of Henry VII. will be found in
3rd S. iv. 452; v. 320; 8th S. i. 106, 159; and
the *Western Antiquary*, vols. i., iv., v., viii.,
ix.   EVERARD HOME COLEMAN.
71, Brecknock Road.

PEWS ANNEXED TO HOUSES (9th S. vii. 388,
517; viii. 89, 191, 288, 428).—Such a pew as
those to which your correspondents refer was
until some nine years ago in existence in
St. Mary's Church, Willesden. It was known
as the "Faculty" pew, and contained a brass
plate announcing (I quote from memory) that,
by a faculty granted by the Consistory Court
of the diocese, the pew was the private property of the family at Neasden House. The
huge pew was a very ugly structure, and
being situated on the south side of the nave,
against the chancel, quite obstructed the
view of the chancel from all worshippers
seated in the south side of the nave and the
south aisle. The former vicar made several
attempts to get the structure removed, but
without success. Shortly after the present
vicar was inducted, however, the abomination
was taken down, to the improved appearance
of that fine old church.   F. A. RUSSELL.
Catford, S.E.

An interesting addition to this subject will
be found at vol. ii. pp. 67-119 of 'Reminiscences, chiefly of Towns, Villages, and
Schools,' by the Rev. T. Mozley (Longmans,
1885), where is the narrative of the claim by
the author's father to a pew appurtenant in
St. Werburgh's Church, Derby. It begins :—

"Early in 1828 my father bought the Friary, and
with it a gallery pew of five sittings. The pew was
distinctly described in the deed of conveyance as
part of the consideration for which the price was
paid, the market price of such a pew being at that
time one hundred guineas."

The final phase of the matter was the appointment by the Bishop of Lichfield (Ryder) of a lay commission, which, after looking into opinions which had been given by Sir Herbert Jenner and Dr. Lushington, reported, in 1831, "that pews cannot be held to be appurtenant to houses."

The soundness of this view must, however, now be judged by the light of the Warminster pew case, decided by the House of Lords in 1891, and the Sharnbrook pew case, heard in 1896 before Sir Arthur Charles, the present Dean of Arches, then a judge of the Queen's Bench Division. W. B. H.

From time immemorial it has been the custom in South Tawton, Devonshire, to apportion a pew to an owner of property of any significance in the parish. During the restoration of the church, some twenty years or so ago, I remember that Mr. Arnold, the then owner of North Wyke, threatened to go to law because he considered his rights in this matter had been infringed.

The following is an extract from a catalogue of deeds, &c., offered for sale by Mr. Coleman, of Tottenham :—

"Gloucestershire.—The original faculty granted to Robert Brown, who in 1733 kept the White Hart publichouse in Stroud, in the county of Gloucester, claimed his right to a seat in the Parish Church there for the use of himself and family, he then being the owener of the tennement called the White Hart, in the said town, signed by Edward Stephens, registrar, 27 March, 1733."

W. CURZON YEO.
Richmond, Surrey.

"ALL FOURS," A KENTISH GAME (9ᵗʰ S. viii. 462).—Why not quote from the original book, Cotton's 'Compleat Gamester' of 1674 (chap. x. p. 111)? The passage there is as follows :—

"*All Fours* is a Game very much play'd in *Kent*, and well it may, since from thence it drew its first original ; and although the Game may be lookt upon as trivial and inconsiderable, yet I have known *Kentish* Gentlemen and others of very considerable note, who have play'd great sums of money at it, yet that adds not much to the worth of the Game, for a man may play away an estate at *One and Thirty* ; as I knew one lose a considerable sum *at most at three throws*."

I.e., three throws of dice. J. S. MᶜTEAR.

REGIMENTAL NICKNAMES (9ᵗʰ S. v. 161, 224, 263, 377, 438 ; vi. 235).—There is a monument in the cemetery at Trimulgherry (Deccan, India), raised by the officers, non-commissioned officers, and men of the 76th Regiment to the memory of those of their corps who died during its time of service in India. On this monument the regiment is called the "76th Hindoostan Regiment." The 76th—at present

the 2nd Battalion of the West Riding Regiment—was raised for service in India at the time of the war with Hyder Ali. It remained in India until peace was proclaimed in the Deccan, having been at Seringapatam and Assaye. I regret that I have forgotten the date of the monument. FRANK PENNY.

KIRJATH-JEARIM (5ᵗʰ S. vi. 346 ; vii. 250).—The question here was, why Sir Walter Scott took this place-name for the name of a Jew. I would suggest that he borrowed from Marlowe's 'The Jew of Malta.' See Dyce's edition of Marlowe's plays, 1865, p. 147 :—

There 's Kirriah Jairim, the great Jew of Greece,
Obed in Bairseth, Nones in Portugal,
Myself in Malta, some in Italy,
Many in France, and wealthy every one.
RICHARD H. THORNTON.
Portland, Oregon.

A SURVIVAL OF PAGANISM (9ᵗʰ S. viii. 463).—There are still a few people left in this village who profess to believe that it is unlucky to kill a pig during the waning moon. I cannot, however, say that any one acts up to the superstition. I have heard the belief stated at a pig-killing, prefixed by the usual "They say," but it seems to me that people here always kill their pigs at the time most convenient to themselves, regardless of consequences. JOHN T. PAGE.
West Haddon, Northamptonshire.

"RACING" (9ᵗʰ S. viii. 104, 150, 291, 347).—When the grinder races a grindstone he uses a piece of pointed cast steel, called a racing-iron, to make the working surface of the stone flat, as grindstones have often soft places in them, and when the grinder has worked upon them it causes the stone to become uneven on the surface. Old grindstones when discarded by the grinder are often utilized for various purposes. I have seen several well-built sheds for cattle in the neighbourhood of Sheffield with excellent pillars formed of grindstones. To support the roof of the shed a post has been driven in the ground, and the grindstones have been placed one upon another, forming in some cases picturesque pillars, reminding one of the primitive age of the construction of early classic columns. Grindstones too were very frequently used to form stepping-stones over the millstreams. Numbers of these stones are still to be seen in the river-bottoms near Sheffield, where bridges are now constructed. I have seen some excellent vases turned out from grindstones. When the grindstone is of no further use to the grinder it becomes a useful commodity to the housewife for cleansing floors, &c. It is a very common occurrence in Sheffield to-day to see men going about with these grindstones on their heads, disposing of them for the above purpose. In my early days I remember these stones were broken up and crushed to a fine powder for sanding floors, which reminds one of the words in Longfellow's poem 'Nuremberg,' in which he refers to it in speaking of the house of Hans Sachs, the cobbler poet,

> But his house is now an alehouse,
> With a nicely sanded floor.

We have in Sheffield parish churchyard a grindstone used as a monumental stone, dated 1818. There is also in the same churchyard, to the memory of William Hobson, grinder, a flat stone with these lines inscribed on it, dated 1815 :—

> Beneath this stone a grinder lies
> A sudden death ath closed his eyes
> He lost his life by the breaking of a stone
> We hope his soul to Heaven 's gone.

In Attercliffe churchyard are two grinder's stones used for monumental purposes, the earlier dated 1776. Grindstones were used as seats in gardens, also for a covering over wells, the hole in the centre being enlarged to let the bucket pass through. I remember in my boyhood frequently seeing them on the hearths of cottagers' homes in Yorkshire. It was a common saying, "Sit thee down on t' grindlestone, i' t' ingle nook." There are several old songs on the grindstone, which would take too much of your valuable space to quote. The following is a verse from one of the songs, entitled 'The Grinder's Hardships,' which was probably written during the formation of the Grinders' Misfortune Society, established at Crookes, Sheffield, 1804 :—

> There seldom comes a day but our dairymaid* goes
>   wrong,
> And if that does not happen, perhaps we break a
>   stone,
> Which may wound us for life, or give us our final
>   blow,
> For there 's few that brave such hardships as we
>   poor grinders do.
>   CHARLES GREEN.
18, Shrewsbury Road, Sheffield.

COPPERPLATE CUTS (9th S. viii. 444). — During the eighteenth and early nineteenth centuries (probably earlier) copperplate engravings used as illustrations to books were known, professionally, as "cuts." In the British Museum Library are two histories of England (which I have already mentioned in the pages of 'N. & Q.'): Temple Sydney's, 1775, and Russel's, 1777, which contain many (full-page) copperplate prints,

* Water-wheel.

excellently engraved. Although on the title-page the books are described (respectively) as "Illustrated with plates engraved from the drawings of Mr. Wale," and "Illustrated with upwards of one hundred Copper plates," yet in the directions to the binder special instructions are given as to the proper placing of the "cuts." According to most dictionaries a "cut" is described as (apart from its other meanings) "a picture cut or carved upon a stamp of wood or copper, and impressed from it" (I quote from Walker, edition 1809). Originally, I believe, "cut" was the trade name for the block, stamp, or die upon which the picture had been engraved, and not, as subsequently, used to denote the impression taken therefrom. With the revival of wood-engraving came a composite (sometimes hyphen) word, "woodcut"; but when, in the early years of the last century, "wood-chopping" superseded metal engraving, "cut" was applied by the profession almost exclusively to drawings engraved on wood. I do not think "cut" was ever much favoured by the "man in the street," but I recollect when a child, during the fifties, hearing artists, engravers, journalists, printers, &c., usually speak of the "large cut in Punch"—which we should now style the cartoon. Since the introduction of "process" the word "cut" as applied to illustrative art has, I fancy, become almost obsolete. Process blocks could hardly be termed "cuts," although the better class of "half-tone" pictures are frequently finished up by hand with the graver.
                               HERBERT B. CLAYTON.
39, Renfrew Road, Lower Kennington Lane, S.E.

See 'N.E.D.' under 'Cut,' sb. 2, iv. 21. Among the uneducated any picture, even a painted glass window, is called a "cut." See Peacock's 'Manley and Corringham Glossary.' Much in the same way, every figure, whether in sculpture, brass, or glass, is called a "picture" in 'Rites of Durham.'   J. T. F.
Durham.

ENTRIES IN PARISH REGISTER (9th S. viii. 464).—The "septum," not "septem," was the name given to the low marble wall or balustrade which divided the nave of the ancient basilican church into three, inside the middle one of which were the clergy.

By 8 & 9 William III., c. 30, it was enacted that every person who, after the first day of September, 1697, shall be in receipt of relief of any parish, and the wife and children of any such person, "shall upon the shoulder of the Right Sleeve of the uppermost garment in an open and visible manner wear such

Mark or Badge as is herein mentioned, that is to say, a large Roman P together with the first letter of the name of the Parish, cut either in red or blue cloth."   H. S. V.-W.

The "septêm" is probably a transept, if the church has one. "Septum," a walled enclosure, unfurnished building, points that way.   T. B. WILMSHURST.
Tunbridge Wells.

The Rev. Frederick George Lee, D.C.L, in his 'Glossary of Liturgical and Ecclesiastical Terms,' London, 1877, explains that "septum" was a term used by certain seventeenth-century Anglican writers for the fixed or movable rail, placed on each side of the entrance of the sanctuary, to support the communicants when they knelt to receive the Lord's Body and Blood.
      EVERARD HOME COLEMAN.
71, Brecknock Road.

LEIGH HUNT (9ᵗʰ S. viii. 64, 130).—A newspaper cutting in my possession, unfortunately without date or recorded origin, states that the question of identity had been agitated in Chicago, and that the *Dial* of that city published, as evidence in support of Mr. Froude's denial of the reference being to Mrs. Carlyle, a little poem which its editor found in the *Monthly Chronicle* for November, 1838. The "little poem" is the same in every respect as the well-known lines, except that for Jenny one reads "Nelly": an important difference. This may be evidence *per se*, or it may be evidence of piracy only.
      ARTHUR MAYALL.

VANCOUVER (9ᵗʰ S. viii. 504).—On my way back from Australia a few months ago, I spent a week in the remarkably progressive British Columbian city of Vancouver. At the entrance to the Public Library I noticed an oil painting of the circumnavigator from whom the city derives its name. To the best of my recollection the inscription underneath this picture contains the information desired. No doubt a letter to the librarian would elicit a copy.   J. F. HOGAN.

CURE BY THE HAND OF A CORPSE (9ᵗʰ S. viii. 483).—The severed human hand was frequently used in magic. The "hand of glory," as it is commonly called, is often mentioned in folk-lore books and elsewhere. The late Bishop Forbes, quoting the Aberdeen Breviary, tells how St. Fillan used one of his hands as a source of light :—

"He secretly constructed a cell not far from the cloister, in which, on a certain night, while the brethren of the monastery announced by a little servant that the supper was ready, the servant,

kneeling and peeping through a chink in that cell to see what was taking place, saw the blessed Faelanus writing in the dark, with his left hand affording a clear light to his right hand. The servant, wondering at this occurrence, straightway returned to the brethren and told it."—'Kalendar of Scottish Saints,' p. 342.

Candles made of the fat of the dead were also often used in incantations.
      EDWARD PEACOCK.
Wickentree House, Kirton-in-Lindsey.

The Rev. R. H. Barham had been reading 'Secrets Merveilleux de la Magie Naturelle et Cabalistique du Petit Albert' (Lyons, 1776) when he wrote 'The Nurse's Story.' He says himself in that poem :—

For another receipt the same charm to prepare
Consult Mr. Ainsworth and *Petit Albert*.

The complete "specification" of this charm, with an illustration, is to be found on p. 104 of the 'Secrets Merveilleux.'
      EDWARD HERON ALLEN.

"PROSPICIMUS MODO" (9ᵗʰ S. viii. 445).—This ingenious specimen of literary trifling in the shape of "retrograde verses," something like the palindrome (for which see Brewer), is quoted in the Appendix to Dr. Morley's edition of 'Gulliver's Travels' (Routledge, 1890), p. 417, with the reading "nobis" for "patriæ" in the second line, which, however, does not affect the characteristic form of the thing. The author is not mentioned, but the elegiac couplet is given as a specimen of the kind of knowledge that Cyrano de Bergerac (born 1620) got from his schoolmaster in Perigord, and of the literary taste in France about that time.
      C. LAWRENCE FORD, B.A.
Bath.

WEARING THE HAT IN THE ROYAL PRESENCE (9ᵗʰ S. viii. 368, 452).—The licence to Sir John Pakington is referred to in the 'Letters and Papers, *temp.* Henry VIII.,' iv. 3, No. 5510, 5. The reference there given is "S. B." [? Signet Bills], and "Patent Roll 20 Henry VIII., pars 2, m. 24." The date of the licence is 5 April, 20 Henry VIII., 1529. In Nash's 'Worcestershire,' i. 352, the reference to the Patent Roll is (probably wrongly) given as "Patent 28 Henry VIII., pars 2."

As this licence apparently differs from the others hitherto printed, I venture to ask whether some London correspondent would kindly search the Patent Rolls and see whether it is in reality different from the ordinary form of licence. Was the licence given to Sir John Pakington because of some disease or infirmity in his head? And did it really extend beyond the reign of Henry VIII.?

The 'D.N.B.' mentions the presence of Henry's successors, whilst Nash omits these words.

W. G. D. FLETCHER.

"PILLAGE, STALLAGE, AND TOLL" (9th S. viii. 420).—The first word is doubtless a misreading of *piccage*, which will be found in most English dictionaries. In 1376 the Corporation of Calais was reconstituted on the English model, and it was enacted ('Rolls of Parliament,' vol. ii. p. 359) that the mayor, aldermen, and commons should have the assize of wine, bread, and ale, and "la stallage des Bouchers, et la stallage des Drapers et Mercers, et auxint le picage en la Marche."

The distinction between *piccage* and *stallage* will be noticed.　Q. V.

Bailey's English dictionary (1731) is useful for reference when old law terms are in question. "Pillage" is therein explained as in use among architects, and as meaning a square pillar that usually stands behind columns to bear up arches—manifestly a support with a foundation. "Stallage" is the right to erect stalls, which need have no foundation in the ground ; it also includes the money paid for the right. The right is that of occupying the ground without breaking it. Is not "pillage" the right of occupying and breaking for the necessary support of the pillar? Some market-places have permanent fixed holes for this purpose, as at Cambridge. In many others the stalls are merely erected on the surface of the ground. By inference "pillage" would mean also the money paid for the right of setting up the pillar.

FRANK PENNY.

MERCHANTS OF LUKES : MERCHANTS OF LUK (9th S. viii. 481).—With regard to the above, I am of opinion that the extracts from the Hundred Rolls and the Patent Rolls set forth below are evidence that the merchants of Lukes and the merchants of Luk were merchants of Lucca, in Italy.

From the Hundred Rolls.

Permission for Lucas de Luk, Thomas of Basing, and other Lombards to export wool. —*Temp.* Edward I.

Permission for Luc de Lukes and Deodatus and their fellows to export wool to Flandr'.— Edward I.

From the Patent Rolls.

Luke of Lucca and colleagues, merchants of Lucca, appointed to collect the new custom at Boston.—3 Edward I.

Receipt to Bauruncinus and Reyner de Luk, merchants of Lucca, for 3,000 marks paid into the Wardrobe at Chester.—10 Edward I.

Luke de Luk and his fellows are requested to lend the king 500 marks for the expenses of his household.—3 Edward I.

Letters for Baruncinus de Lucca and Burnettus his son nominating Andrew de Florentia their attorney.　EDWARD J. LUCK.

LONDRES (9th S. viii. 443). — William de Londre (Loundre, Lounder, as the name is variously spelt) evidently did not come in with the Conqueror, as the first clear evidence we have concerning him is contained in the Bull of Honorius II., 1128, anathematizing him and several others, whose notions of *meum* and *tuum* were equally hazy, for "spoiling the Church." He appears to have been the founder of the family, and erected Ogmore Castle, in the county of Glamorgan. He evidently spelt his name Londre, if he could spell, and was, I think, an illegitimate son of the Conqueror. He was in high favour with Henry I., by whom this lordship marcher appears to have been bestowed upon him. He was the founder of Ewenny Priory in intention, although he did not live to complete it, and a fragment of his tombstone is extant there with grand Lombardic lettering. As evidence of spelling of the name see the seal attached to deed No. 176, Duchy of Lancaster records : "Vesica shaped, horse and rider, cour. to left, round exergue Sigillum Will [.........]ndoniis" ; and again, MS. 177. same series, grant by William de Londinis to his daughter Sibilla, on the seal of which the name is spelt "Lundonis." The penultimate heiress, Haweisia, joined with Patric de Carducis in payment of a fine on obtaining seisin of the estates of his wife 19 Henry III. (1235) ; and the penultimate heiress of this branch, Blanche, on her marriage to John of Gaunt, carried these wide domains into the royal house, where a small part yet remain as Duchy of Lancaster lands.

From various sources I have collected the pedigree and descent of the lords and ladies of Ogmore. They are not of sufficient public interest to give in 'N. & Q.,' as mainly derived from contemporary MSS., lengthy, and opening too many side issues of interest only to the genealogist and historian, but much at the service of those who care for such curious information.　G. E. R.

The Anglo-Norman family inquired about must have been so called from some early connexion with London. The only place in Northern France with a name resembling London is Londinières, a canton in the department of Seine Inférieure. I suspect the ancestor of this family was a certain "Willelmus nepos Episcopi" of Domesday Book, a nepos possibly of Maurice, Bishop of London, whose rather uncommon Christian name we find used by William's descendants. William was called "de Londoniâ," and gave the tithes of Eastgarston to Herley Priory ('Form. Angl.,' p. 252). Madox had the original before him, which was endorsed in an old hand "Carta Willelmi de Londoniis." Maurice, his son, was a witness. It is not improbable it was a sister of William who married Harding fil. Eadnoth (see 6ᵗʰ S. ii. 11), and was mother of Robert fitz Harding, the founder of Bristol Abbey, Maurice, and other sons. Robert, in conjunction with a William de London, gave Blacksworth, in Kingswood, to the abbey. It should be further noted that Robert called his eldest son Maurice, which has continued to be the favourite name of the Berkeley family ever since.

William de London was one of the knights who went with Robert fitz Hamon into Glamorganshire, founded Ewenny Priory, and was a donor to Neath and Kidwelly, &c.

Thomas de London, a contemporary who may have been another son, went into Scotland with King David, and had a grant of Lessedwyn. He left a son Maurice, and it is this circumstance that makes me think he was one of this family. Of course much more about the Londons of Ogmore and Kidwelly is known, but these notes and suggestions may be enough for MR. A. HALL's purpose.

A. S. ELLIS.

Westminster.

BIBLIOGRAPHY OF THE BICYCLE (9ᵗʰ S. viii. 304, 490, 530).—The following *obiter dicta* might appropriately fall under the head of 'Wrong Forecasts by Eminent Men,' but as they may not have come under the notice of some of your readers who are interested in the subject the reference may be worth advancing. They are thus related by Bransby B. Cooper in the 'Life of Sir Astley Cooper' (vol. ii. p. 309):—

"One morning our visitor was Prof. Vince, of Cambridge, and my uncle almost immediately began to talk to him upon the subject of these velocipedes. The doctor said he had heard of them and admitted the ingenuity of the contrivance. This induced Sir Astley at once to declare all his fears resulting from their universal employment. 'Sir,' said he, 'it will alter the face of the country: no grass will be grown, but all farms will become arable; for who will keep horses, when a machine can be substituted which does not cost more than two or three pounds, and the first outlay is the whole expense?' 'Sir,' said Mr. Vince, 'I misunderstood you; the expediency of its application I merely admitted to the extent of a toy, for it can never facilitate or expedite a lengthened journey. It would be contrary to every axiom in mathematics to suppose it could, for it is impossible by any mechanism to increase your velocity without diminishing your power; and as, in this instance, the power emanates from the employer, he would soon become too happy to be satisfied with the speed of his natural progression, and glad to cease exhausting himself by sustaining an additional weight to his own body. In two months you will hear no more of them.'"

These opinions were expressed in or about 1823.　　RICHARD LAWSON.

Urmston.

WILLIAM THE CONQUEROR'S HALF BROTHERS AND SISTERS (9ᵗʰ S. viii. 199, 293, 525).—Robert, Earl of Mortain, did not found the abbey of St. Evroult, where Orderic Vital was, also called Ouche. He founded, with the Countess Matilda, his wife, in 1082, the collegiate church of St. Evroult at Mortain. I did not make this clear in my previous communication.　　F. S. VADE-WALPOLE.

Stagbury, Banstead.

THE SIGNATURE OF THE DUKE OF CAMBRIDGE (9ᵗʰ S. viii. 525). — MR. CHARLES HIATT says he has the duke's signature "Cambridge." This was probably written by his equerry, as I have it; certainly not by the duke himself.

The Prince of Wales, if he follows his father's precedent, will sign "George, P."

A. F. T.

'HYMNS ANCIENT AND MODERN' (9ᵗʰ S. viii. 101, 230, 388).—It is quite true that W. C. B.'s criticism "hardly meets the point" of my note, but much of MR. PHINN's is equally irrelevant. I do not see why, as regards grammar, original hymns and translations should not be "measured by the same tests." A translator ought no more to retain foreign constructions than foreign words. It is unfortunately true, as the late Mr. Palgrave lamented in a note on this subject which I had from him many years ago, that translated hymns, like all translated verse, are "rarely effective as poetry." Sometimes, indeed, they are, for Mr. Palgrave himself, in an essay on hymns in *Good Words*, once named one of Miss Winkworth's translations—'Christ will gather in His own'—as worthy to stand beside Newman's 'Lead, kindly Light,' but then he had forgotten the fact that it *is* a translation. All this, however, is again away from the point, as is also MR. PHINN's remark that in original compositions—why not in translations too?—many phrases such as those of which he cites examples may be tolerated, although they are usually disallowed in public worship. My point is simply that on which John Wesley laid such stress—that hymns for general use ought to have not only "the purity, the strength, and the elegance of the English language," but also, and above all, "the utmost simplicity and plainness, suited to every capacity." That this last desideratum is so often lacking in 'Hymns Ancient and Modern' is no doubt partly owing to the fact that so many of the hymns in this collection are translations, but this is no excuse. If a translator cannot turn a Latin hymn into English, he can at any rate let it alone. John Wesley's own translations from the German are models in this respect; they are amongst the most cherished hymns in his collection, and comparatively few of his followers suspect that they are translations.

I do not think the reading of Mrs. Adams's hymn which O. O. H. quotes is much better than the generally accepted one, and the subject of alterations in hymns is too wide for these columns. I may say, however, that a compiler has surely as much right to correct an author's grammar as to tamper with his theology.   C. C. B.

The history of that most beautiful hymn 'Nearer, my God, to Thee,' is given in M. D. Conway's 'Centenary History of the South Place Society' (London, 1894), where a facsimile of the draft in Sarah Flower Adams's handwriting is given. The verse under discussion reads :—

> Tho like the wanderer
> The sun gone down
> Darkness be over me
> My rest a }
>   pillow } stone
> Yet in my }
>   night } dreams I'd be
> Nearer my God to thee
>   Nearer to thee

Of the alternative readings here given, the *first* in each case was adopted—an instance that second thoughts are not always best. Dr. Garnett regards her hymn beginning "He sendeth sun, He sendeth shower," as superior to the more famous 'Nearer, my God, to Thee,' but the latter has found its way to acceptance by the most diverse of creeds and temperaments. Mrs. E. Bridell-Fox issued from the *Christian Life* office in 1894 a pamphlet of forty-six pages, containing a memoir of Sarah Flower Adams, her hymns, and 'The Flock at the Fountain,' a catechism for children. This is a modest and inspiring memorial of a woman who has given voice to the spiritual aspirations of millions.
WILLIAM E. A. AXON.
Manchester.

ROWE OF CORNWALL (9th S. viii. 305, 349, 470).—I am inclined to think that the tradition of an ancestor of the West-Country Rowes joining one of the Crusades arose in the following manner. An ancient family of "a-Rowe," or Rowe, was long seated in Kent. A very fine seventeenth-century illuminated pedigree of this family in the British Museum (Add. 29,797) shows that "Richard Rowe of Kent married the da' and heire of Phillipp Rurd," and was the father of William Rowe, who "married yᵉ Daughter of Viueon" (*i.e.*, Vivian, a West-Country name), whose son "John Rowe, Sergeant at Lawe in the tyme of H. 8," married "Agneta, daug. and heir of Will Barnhouse of Kingston in Deuonshiʳ."

Turning to the Visitation of Devon, 1620 (Harl. Soc., p. 247), the above-mentioned three generations of Rowes are given as the ancestors of "John Rowe de Kingston in parochia de Staverton in com. Devon, æt. 76 superstes 1620," who duly enters and signs the pedigree.

This, I think, is strong evidence that the Devonshire family of Rowe was a branch of the old Kentish stock.

From what I can gather, the Crusade story appears to be based on the fact that the West-Country Rowes bear as their arms Gules, three holy lambs argent, which are said to have had their origin in one of the Crusades. Now these were not the ancient arms of Rowe, which were Gules, a quatrefoil or, and later, Argent, a chevron azure between three trefoils slipped per pale gules and vert. The arms of the Rurd family, however, whose heiress married the Richard Rowe mentioned above, were Gules, three holy lambs couchant argent, and this coat was at the time of the Visitation of 1620 merely quartered by the Devonshire Rowes (see pedigree of Rowe of Lamerton, Harl. Soc. 248) ; subsequently, however, they were borne alone, unsupported by the paternal coat, as they are at the present day (the lambs becoming passant instead of couchant). The ancient paternal Rowe coats, having thus been discarded, were soon forgotten, while the Crusade tradition, which was not improbably imported into the West-Country branch of the Rowe family along with the holy lambs at the time of the Rurd alliance (Edward III.), continued to live, being kept in remembrance by the exclusive use of the more favoured Rurd quartering with which it is associated.
ARTHUR F. ROWE.
Walton-on-Thames.

"MACHINE"=PUBLIC COACH (9th S. viii. 462).—Beckmann, in his article on 'Coaches' ('History of Inventions,' 1846), omits any mention of the "machine" carriage, or "New

Post Machine," as it was called, although it played an important part in the history of long-distance travelling. The vehicle appears to have been adopted about the year 1756, at least it does not seem to have been advertised before that time, which is seven years before the date given at the above reference. On 25 December, 1756, "Two New Post Machines" were advertised to

"set out every Monday, Wednesday and Friday for Bath and London in two days, one from the Rose Inn, and the other from the White Swan, Holborn Bridge, at 6 A.M. precisely. One pound three shillings for each passenger, allowing each 14 lb. weight of luggage, and all above to pay Three Half-pence per pound."—*Whitehall Evening Post*, 25 December, 1756.

The Bristol machine, which left the "Saracen's Head" in Friday Street, also took two days for the journey, setting out "at five in the morning every Monday, Wednesday, and Friday, and putting up at the White Lion, Bristol. Fare, 1*l.* 5*s.*; each fare allowed 14 lb. weight, all above to pay Three Half pence per Pound, by the way of Chippenham, and not to go to Bath" (*Whitehall Evening Post*, 6 April, 1756). In the year 1757 a "flying machine" on steel springs was established by the merchants of Liverpool after the manner of the Manchester "flying coach" (Capt. Malet, 'Annals of the Road,' 1876, p. 14).   J. HOLDEN MACMICHAEL.
Wimbledon Park Road.

In a book just published by Chapman & Hall, viz., 'The Norwich Road,' by C. G. Harper, at pp. 34-5, is a description of the "Norwich Machine," that ran three times a week to London in March, 1762. I think this may be interesting to your correspondent.   ROBERT BURNINGHAM.

The Rev. Lewis Davies, in his 'Supplementary English Glossary,' quotes to the above effect from Goldsmith, 'Citizen of the World,' letter xlviii.; Anstey, 'New Bath Guide,' letter xiii.; Walpole, 'Letters,' iv. 12 (1775); and 'Sketches by Boz' (Mr. Minns). He adds that the only vehicle now so called is a bathing-machine. In horse-dealing parlance a "machiner" is a van horse at the present day.   H. P. L.

[Cycles are commonly so called.]

PAYING RENT AT A TOMB IN CHURCH (9ᵗʰ S. viii. 302, 355, 411).—In Scotland the usual place for paying a redemption or mortgage was at or on an altar in the parish or other church. After the Reformation the style of the deed frequently ran as where "Sanct James Altar the Apostell sumtym was situat" or where "the hie altar usit to stand." One reversion dated 1567 has the unusual locus "in the place quhair the hie poulpet is situat" (Home Writs, Hist. MSS. Comm.). A favourite place was on the tomb of the Regent Murray in St. Giles's Church, Edinburgh, this altar-tomb being probably the most convenient counter or table on which to count the coin, after the removal of the altars.
           J. G. WALLACE-JAMES, M.B.
Haddington.

Miscellaneous.

NOTES ON BOOKS, &c.

The Tower of London. By Lord Ronald Sutherland Gower, F.S.A.   Vol. I. (Bell & Sons.)

NUMEROUS and important as are existing works on the Tower, there is always room for one more, and a welcome for it is certain also when, as in this case, it comes with such numerous and valuable illustrations. Lord Ronald Sutherland Gower's opening volume deals with the Tower during Norman, Plantagenet, and Tudor times; that is, during the most interesting and picturesque, and also the most bloodthirsty period of its annals. He is safe in affirming that it would be vain to search any other city—Rome itself not excepted—for another such group of buildings, or to endeavour to match the historic interest or splendid record of the ancient Norman structure. With most that is vital in our national life and all that is superb in historical pageantry this building is associated, and there are no stories "of the death of kings" so sad as those which its walls could tell. The early records are, as Lord Ronald avows, meagre and scanty. With a purpose such as that by which he is animated of being accurate rather than picturesque, he finds the task impossible to infuse into them much life, movement, or interest. From the period of Edward III. the case is different. Through the Wars of the Roses, and during the short reign of Richard III., the action is spirited enough, and during almost the entire period of Tudor rule the place is a shambles. Englishmen are wont to congratulate themselves upon the fact that their streets have witnessed few such scenes of ferocity and carnage as have polluted the fairest cities of France. In order to rival the bloodshed in the Tower of London under the five rulers of Tudor race—for, child though he were, Edward VI. need not be exempted—we should turn to the Courts of Dahomey or other savage countries of Africa. Interesting and absorbing enough is the story of the Tower at this point, and its cruel record—which, so far as the present instalment is concerned, closes here—will be kept up during the reign of James I., will be revived with the accession of James II., and will not lose all its brutality until after the massacres of 1746 and 1747. A history of the Tower, so far as it is now carried out, is necessarily a condensed history of the English monarchy. Lord Ronald begins, however, with a picturesque and topographical account of the various buildings and their environment from the first mention by Tacitus of London as a place of importance. This description, which occupies some four score pages, is accompanied by a series of admirable illustrations, taken by Messrs. Colls, most of them photogravure plates. The frontispiece consists of a coloured plate, from a MS. in the British Museum, depicting the Duke of Orleans a prisoner in the Tower, a striking, vivid, and characteristic presentation of mediæval life as it showed itself to the illuminating scribe. Following this comes a vivid picture of the Tower and the river as both are seen under the conditions, atmospheric and other, of to-day. Forty photogravures, sixteen blocks, and a couple of plans are given in the present volume. Most of them are views of the Tower and its appurtenances. The portraits include Anne Boleyn, Fisher (Bishop of Rochester), Sir Thomas More, his daughter Margaret Roper (as is supposed)—the last three from drawings by Holbein—Bloody Mary, Lady Jane Grey and Lord Guildford Dudley (by Lucas van Heere), Lady Jane Grey (from Holbein), Henry Grey, Duke of Suffolk (by Joannes Corvus), and Robert, Earl of Essex. In addition there are many presentations of ancient armour and an accurate representation of the block and axe. In their fidelity and beauty these designs render the work unique in its class, a fine historical monument, and a book which all lovers of English annals will be bound to possess. Lord Ronald has done his work well, his chapters vii. to xi. inclusive, dealing with the Tudor monarchs, being especially well written and effective. We are not greatly impressed by the parallel he institutes between Sir Thomas More and Mr. Gladstone, and still less by some further comparisons in which he indulges. Should not the Sir Henry Ellice whom at p. 144 he couples with Froude the historian as an authority on Tudor MSS. be Sir Henry Ellis? It seems implied (p. 170) that the title of Lord Sudley (Thomas, Lord Seymour of Sudley, Lord High Admiral of England) and that of Lord Sudeley were, in the days of Edward VI., the same. Lord Ronald should be an authority on the subject, but we knew not the fact he advances. To the charge brought against the Duke of Norfolk and the Earl of Surrey of quartering upon their family shield the arms of Edward the Confessor we may advance the assertion (9th S. viii. 495) that Edward the Confessor belongs to a time when arms were not borne in England. We have more to say concerning Lord Ronald's interesting and valuable volume, but must wait till his second volume, for which we look with anxiety, brings the indispensable index.

Modern English Biography. By Frederick Boase. —Vol. III. *R—Z.* (Truro, Netherton & Worth.)
As we anticipated, Mr. Frederick Boase was not able to complete within the nineteenth century what is practically a supplement to the biographical records of its latter half. One additional year has had to be accorded him for the discharge of his onerous and responsible task, and the close of 1901 saw the completed work in the hands of the subscribers. The appearance of each separate part has been chronicled (see 8th S. i. 345; xi. 440). MR. RALPH THOMAS (8th S. i. 487) bore also a tribute to the importance of the work then begun (and now achieved), and gave a half promise, still unredeemed, to supply further comment upon it. We are glad to see within the period we ourselves judged indispensable the completion of a work the utility of which to all concerned in historical, political, and genealogical pursuits cannot easily be overestimated. Two hundred and fifty copies in all have been printed. As there are more than five hundred public libraries, the absence from which of a book of this kind should count as

a reproach, we shall be justified in the assumption that the book, except to those who have secured a copy or are in the neighbourhood of a library on the shelves of which it rests, is now inaccessible. It is at least to be presumed that it will shortly become so, and those who cannot already boast its possession are counselled at once to obtain it.
Turning over incidentally pages naturally intended for consultation rather than perusal, we come on the names of many dear and distinguished friends. One of the first is W. R. S. Ralston, the famous Russian scholar, found dead in his bed in 1889. Then follow William Brighty Rands (the Matthew Browne of 'Chaucer's England,' an exquisite and but half-recognized writer), Charles Reade, his nephew William Winwood Reade, John Edmund Reade, Robert Reece, Alfred German Reed (the entertainer), Sir Charles Reed, Henry Reeve (editor of the *Edinburgh Review*), Henry Robert Reynolds (of Cheshunt) and his brother Sir John Russell Reynolds, James Rice (collaborator with Sir Walter Besant), Col. Alfred Bate Richards (of Volunteer fame), Sir Benjamin Ward Richardson, F.R.S., Sir Matthew White Ridley, David Roberts, R.A., with his constant friend and associate in life and art Clarkson Stanfield, R.A., Thomas William Robertson, Thomas Frederick Robson (actor), Lord Romilly (Master of the Rolls) and Hugh Hastings Romilly (explorer and writer), James Anderson Rose (collector), Gabriel Charles Dante Rossetti, and Clara Marion Jessie Rousby, known as the beautiful Mrs. Rousby. These names, taken with a solitary exception from the first letter in the volume, and consisting, also with a solitary exception, of those with whom we had more or less association or intimacy, convey an idea of the class with whom the three volumes are principally concerned. Some others—such, for instance, as Peter Robinson, draper—are well known to the public, though without claim to literary, artistic, or social recognition. It is, however, in connexion with people obscure enough to escape inclusion in general biographical dictionaries that a work of this class is specially useful. The lives run from about a fifth of a column to a column; in one or two cases, as that of George Augustus Sala, they are slightly over a column. All accessible facts of birth, paternity, descent, occupation, works, death, and sepulture are supplied, and for immediate reference the work is, in its line, the best we possess. Being so nearly up to date, it all but serves, so far as England is concerned, the purposes of a dictionary such as that of Vapereau. It at any rate leaves far behind works such as 'Men of the Time' and 'Men of the Day.' We are happy in commending the completed work to our readers. Whatever their occupation or pursuit, it can scarcely fail to be useful to them. An ample index facilitates reference, and indicates uses, not always obvious, to which the work may be put.

Art Sales of the Year 1901. Edited by J. Herbert Slater. (Virtue & Co.)
EMBOLDENED by the conspicuous success which has attended his 'Book-Prices Current,' a work which, in the course of little over a dozen years, has developed into one of the most prized of bibliographical possessions, Mr. Slater has, not unnaturally, essayed to do for pictures and prints what he has previously done for books. The result of his efforts is the work before us, the sub-title of which

is "Being a record of the prices obtained at auctions for pictures and prints sold from January, 1901, to the end of the season." Holding to the view that all collecting is good, even if some collecting is better than others, we greet the new volume, and wish it a career as distinguished as its predecessor. This we dare not, however, presage. A collector for over half a century of books, we have found that luxury sufficiently costly to dispense with the pursuit of all others; and while we can meet Mr. Slater as editor of 'Book-Prices Current' on his own ground, we are mum when he comes before us as editor of 'Art Sales,' having, indeed, everything to learn. This much we may say: his goodly volume contains some 550 pages, considerably over 100 of which are occupied with an admirably full index with cross-references galore. The sale is chronicled of 3,118 items, the prices of which range from a couple of pounds or less to a good many hundreds and thousands. A glance through the volume, which we do not profess to have closely studied, shows us that the topmost price paid for a Hobbema was 9,870l., a second work from whose brush brought 2,362l. 10s. It is to be hoped that the soul of the artist received in the shades some hint of his modern reputation, since he and his wife died in want. The biggest prices we detect for English pictures are 14,752l. for a Hoppner and 5,800l. for a Romney; Millais's 'No' brought 1,471l.; Turner's 'Buckfastleigh Abbey,' 840l.; a Reynolds went for 1,701l.; portraits by Gainsborough were sold for 1,869l. and 2,257l. A Mabuse brought 2,520l.; a Rubens, 3,360l.; a Velasquez, 997l.; a Van der Helst, 1,995l.; a Murillo, 2,730l., and so forth. We are attempting to draw no inferences from these prices, but are simply extracting a few plums from Mr. Slater's book. Not less remarkable are the prices paid for engravings, especially those of J. R. Smith after Reynolds. Of great value are the notes supplied by Mr. Slater with regard to the sales and the individual pictures. Some useful information is interpolated as to the prices realized by a few French sales. The book is handsomely and even luxuriously got up, and is a credit to the publishers. It is to be hoped that it will establish itself in public favour and become a "hardy annual." That it will rank with 'Book-Prices Current' we hesitate, as has been said, to believe. We shall be glad, however, to see our vaticinations falsified, and the book is, at least, likely to take its place on shelves of reference and to prove equally useful to the amateur and the dealer.

In the *Nineteenth Century*, through the medium of which it first reached a general public, the cypher "fad" of Mrs. Gallup receives what will probably prove to be its quietus. Two articles on the subject approach it from different sides. Mr. H. Candler shows how unsatisfactory are the historic assumptions and how far astray Mrs. Gallup goes in her philology. Mr. R. B. Marston, expanding his letter to the *Times*, proves that if the bi-literal cypher is trustworthy and acceptable Pope's 'Homer' is to be added to the works written by Bacon. Will no American investigator add to the list of Bacon's productions the letters of Junius and the quatrains of Omar Khayyam? Mr. Herbert Cook inquires 'Did Titian live to be Ninety-nine Years Old?' and answers his own question in the negative. Mr. Cook leans to the view that Titian was born about 1489 and died about 1576-7 at the age of eighty-seven. The Hon. Rollo Russell holds cheery views as to the ultimate extinction of London fogs. We can but hope that he is not too sanguine. Col. Pedder asks 'Where are the Village Gentry?' and shows some of the evils that attend the process of centralization ever proceeding. Mr. Fuller Maitland has an interesting and valuable paper on 'Music *versus* the Opera.' Lady Priestley writes on 'Sir James Paget and Louis Pasteur,' and Lady Hely-Hutchinson on 'Female Emigration to South Africa.' It is saddening to hear that three out of the four classes of women available consist of "Lady Helps.—Pretentious, delicate, incapable; Girls.—Flighty, self-assertive, purposeless, ignorant, lazy, and inefficient; Kaffirs.—With the understanding and demeanour of children and the vices of men."—In *Scribner's* appears the first of three papers by Mr. Frank A. Vanderlip on 'The American "Commercial Invasion" of Europe.' In this M. de Witte, the Russian Minister of Finance, is made to speak with compromising frankness. No preacher of pleasant things is he. "France hates England, and England hates France; Germany detests France, and France detests Germany; Russia hates Germany, and Germany hates Russia." There are illustrations showing American "binders" in the Steppes and the Highlands, electric lines by the Pyramids, cars in Cairo, coalhauling machines in Germany, bridges in Russia, pumps in Bombay, and so forth. 'Sub Umbra Liliorum' is the title of some impressions concerning Parma. Mr. H. Cabot Lodge writes on 'The Treaty-making Powers of the Senate,' and Mr. Macgowan on 'Military Parades and Parade Training.'

Notices to Correspondents.

We must call special attention to the following notices:—

On all communications must be written the name and address of the sender, not necessarily for publication, but as a guarantee of good faith.

We cannot undertake to answer queries privately.

To secure insertion of communications correspondents must observe the following rules. Let each note, query, or reply be written on a separate slip of paper, with the signature of the writer and such address as he wishes to appear. When answering queries, or making notes with regard to previous entries in the paper, contributors are requested to put in parentheses, immediately after the exact heading, the series, volume, and page or pages to which they refer. Correspondents who repeat queries are requested to head the second communication "Duplicate."

F. M. ("Bogus Degrees"). — A few universities still supply these.

H. J. MEIGS ("Taxation in Glasgow"). — Your friends are wags.

CORRIGENDUM.—9ᵗʰ S. viii. 509, col. 2, l. 20 from foot, for "1845" read *1825*.

NOTICE.

Editorial communications should be addressed to "The Editor of 'Notes and Queries'"—Advertisements and Business Letters to "The Publisher"—at the Office, Bream's Buildings, Chancery Lane, E.C.

We beg leave to state that we decline to return communications which, for any reason, we do not print; and to this rule we can make no exception.

LONDON, SATURDAY, JANUARY 18, 1902.

CONTENTS. — No. 212.

Notes.

HEYFORD FREE SCHOOL: EARLY RULES.

BELOW are the "School Orders" of the Heyford Free School, as they appear in an old folio which was written by Mr. William Taylor, *circ.* 1724. He was (see Baker's 'Northamptonshire,' p. 192)

"son of the rev. George Taylor, rector of Keston in Kent, many years master of the free school here [Heyford], was employed by Mr. Bridges; and subsequently, during the editorship of Dr. Samuel Jebb, entered into a similar engagement with Gibbons the bookseller, to copy monumental inscriptions and collect local information for the intended history of the county. His correspondence on the subject from the year 1718 to 1739, in which he bears the warmest testimony to the liberal and honorable conduct of Mr. Bridges towards him, and bitterly complains, apparently with too much reason, of the inadequate compensation he received from the London bookseller, has lately come into my possession; and a selection of the most interesting letters will probably be introduced into a retrospective view of the labors of my predecessors, in the introductory portion of the present work. He lived to an advanced age in a state of abject poverty, and was buried here [Heyford, co. Northampton] 1 July, 1771."

His baptism is recorded in the Keston register on 11 June, 1695.

I may add that Mr. William Taylor was a most industrious man with the pen. I have in my possession three of his MSS. in folio, bound in vellum. They are written most beautifully, and look more like engrossing than ordinary writing. In these volumes (and they are the only three extant, although he wrote about a dozen or more of them) he has copied many notes, deeds, &c., of local interest. I have also two volumes of his father's sermons copied by him. The two volumes embrace about 1,000 pages and contain about 100 or more sermons.

The 'Leges Scholasticæ' may interest some who have studied the advance of education in this country. As master of the Free School at Heyford Taylor apparently, from letters which are copied into one of these folios, fell out with the powers that be, and among these letters are some to the then Lord Bishop of Peterborough asking his intervention. These orders are dated 1724.

HEYFORD FREE SCHOOL.
School Orders.

The Laws or Orders of the said Free School were engrossed on Parchment & putt into a Frame & hung up for the Perusall of Every Boy belonging to the sᵈ School.

Leges Scholasticæ
sive,
Monita Pædagogica.

Articles.

1. Imprimis, Whatsoever Boy comes to School past 7 o' th' Clock In the Morning In Summer time, and past 8 o' th' Clock In yᵉ Winter time [without Shewing good reason] Shall receive 3 Lashes.

2. Item, Whosoever absents himself from School, Either by Truantry, by trying to stay at home, or otherwise; Shall incurr his Master's highest displeasure, Suffer the hissing and Scoffing of yᵉ whole School, Tarry behind the Rest one hour at Night for a week, and besides [as a suitable Reward for his   ] shall suffer 12 Lashes.

3. Item, Whatsoever Boy shall at any time Curse, Swear, or take the Lord's Name in vain, Shall assuredly suffer for such offence 15 Lashes.

4. Item, What Boy soever addicts himself to Obscene Talking or foolish Jesting, shall Suffer for each such Transgression.

5. Item, What Boy soever absents himself from the Service of Almighty God on the Sabbath day, and spends that Day in a wicked man'er In playing & running about, Shall receive 20 Lashes.

6. Item, Whosoever steals from or defrauds his School-fellow of Ink, Pens, Paper, Quills, or any Other Thing Whatsoever, Shall certainly, when found out and detected, receive 9 Lashes.

7. Item, Whosoever tells tales, Or divulves [*sic*] What is transacted in School, On any accoᵗ whatever, shall receive 8 Lashes.

8. Item, What Boy soever Loiters in the Way, Either in Coming to Or Going from School, Shall suffer for each Offence 4 Lashes.

9. Item, What Boy soever is catch'd in telling a Lye, Upon any Account whatever, shall receive 7 Lashes.

10. Item, Whosoever is found Deficient in point of Manners (viz) In not putting off his hatt, and

demeaning himself Orderly and Schollar-like On all Occasions, Shall suffer 5 Lashes.

11. Item, Whosoever strikes, challenges, or quarrells with Any of his Schoolfellows at any time or in any place, Shall [after due Examinacon thereof had] surely receive 8 Lashes.

12. Item, Whosoever is found Guilty of a small Fault Three Times together, and instead of amending Behaves himself stubbornly and contumaciously, Shall receive 9 Lashes.

13. Item, Whatsoever Boy is found Five times successively In the Monitor's Bill (tho' but for petty faults) Shall suffer 3 Lashes.

14. Item, Whatsoever Monitor is found Negligent and Remiss In the discharge of his Duty and Office, Shall receive 10 Lashes.

15. Item, What Boy soever omitts the doing of his Exercise at Night, without Good reason can be given, shall suffer 5 Lashes.

16. Item, What Boy soever performs not his Exercise appointed in the holy-days, Shall on his return to School receive 10 Lashes.

17. Item, What Boy soever in Buying or Selling In or out of School shall fraudulently cheat or impose On his schoolfellows or Any Other, shall on due conviccon receive 9 Lashes.

18. Lastly and to conclude, Whatsoever Boy finds or knows his Schoolfellows To be guilty of the Breach of any One of These Articles [or any other Misdemenour, which is contrary to good discipline & the known orders of yᵉ School] and does not give the Weekly Observator timely Information Who is presently to acquaint the Master therewith; But connives at the sᵈ Delinquent, Shall (if found out) assuredly suffer for the Other, whom he foolishly spar'd, and receive Without yᵉ benefitt of Clergy 15 Lashes.

Nisi exequantur, pereunt Leges.

H. H. CRAWLEY.

Stowe-Nine-Churches, Weedon.

MERCIAN ORIGINS.
(Concluded from p. 3.)

ONE district remains—that of the Pec-sætna dwelling in our Derbyshire. The 'Tribal Hidage' shows that these people were distinct from the Mercians proper, just as the Gyrwas were. They may have come from the north-east through Doncaster and Sheffield, or along the Trent Valley; or it is just possible that they were an offshoot of the West Saxon settlements along the Severn. The hills provided them with a boundary on the north and west, while on the east the great forest of Sherwood (does this mean Division Wood?) would cut them off from the people of Nottingham.

Thus the limits of the states bordering Mercia have been roughly traced; they confirm the conclusions derived from Bede's statement about the Northern and Southern Mercians, and show how small was the area these occupied before the rise of Penda. The doubtful districts are Derbyshire and Staffordshire, with parts of Cheshire and Shropshire; and in the south Surrey. The latter seems to have been originally Kentish, but early conquered by the West Saxons ('Chron.,' 568), and then practically annexed by the Mercians; while, ecclesiastically, it was at first by turns attached to the South Saxon or Winchester diocese, finally adhering to the latter, from which it may be concluded that, whatever their political fate, the people were in the main West Saxon.

In course of time many of these difficulties may be cleared away by the patient efforts of students. each pursuing the portion of the inquiry he finds congenial. Dialect and folklore, with such customs as borough English, the physical peculiarities of the people, place-names and the names in the old pedigrees of the kings, and church dedications may all contribute. In the last-named branch of the inquiry we have St. Chad in Lichfield diocese, St. Edmund in East Anglia, and St. Botolph in the Fen country. The Fenmen also seem to have had a devotion to St. Andrew; and St. Helen is popular within the York sphere of influence. Place-names have yet to be properly investigated and classified. It may be found that such names as Stoke and Stow have a bearing on the settlement of England; for instance, the Stokes appear most numerous in the south, and spread north on the lines of the West Saxon advance; yet there do not seem to be any in the Isle of Wight or in the Jutish district of Hampshire, and there is but one in Kent, by the mouth of the Medway, where it may represent an East Saxon colony. In place-names there is a distinction to be made between personal or family names and tribal names: the former are naturally attached to the homestead or group of homesteads where the person or family dwelt, but the latter belong to a whole district, and when found attached to a single township it is reasonable to assume that this township was either just on the boundary of the tribal district or quite outside it. For example, a Kentish Town in the middle of Kent would be an anomaly, there would be no distinctiveness about it; but in London it would be appropriate for a settlement of Kentish men, though it appears that the London district so called has no connexion with Kent. Similarly a family name like English must have been first given to Englishmen living outside their country, and the Scotts are border families.

II. The expansion of Mercia begins with Penda, who "first separated the kingdom of Mercia from that of the Northmen" (Nennius, Appendix). The 'Chronicle' gives the outline of his career thus:—

626. Penda succeeded to the kingdom and reigned thirty years ; and he was fifty years old when he succeeded. (This was the year in which Edwin chastised the West Saxons for their attempted assassination of him.)

628. This year Cynegils and Cuichelm fought against Penda at Cirencester, and then made a treaty.

633. This year King Edwin was slain by Cadwalla and Penda at Heathfield, 12 October. ......After that went Cadwalla and Penda and laid waste the whole country of the Northumbrians. (Bede, iii. 1, attributes this wasting of the North to Cadwallon only, and he it was who was defeated and slain by Oswald in 635 at Denisesburn or Catscaul. Oswald re-established the suzerainty over all England which had been acquired by Edwin.)

(635. Penda conquered East Anglia. Bede, iii. 18.)

642. This year Oswald, King of the Northumbrians, was slain by Penda and the Southumbrians at Maserfield on 5 August. (From this time till his death in 655 Penda had no one south of the Humber who could resist him.)

645. This year Kenwalk was driven out of his (West Saxon) kingdom by King Penda. (He took refuge in East Anglia, where he was baptized, and in 648 was restored to his place, apparently without war. Bede, iii. 7.)

654. This year King Anna was slain (by Penda, who then ravaged East Anglia for the second time. Bede, iii. 18).

655. This year King Oswy slew King Penda at Winwidfield......and Peada, the son of Penda, succeeded to the kingdom of the Mercians.

This last statement proves that Penda was by origin King of the Southern Mercians, for it was over this part of Mercia that Peada was by Oswy allowed to rule (Bede, iii. 24). The pedigrees of the kings may be cited in confirmation : the men of Lindsey had had a line of kings of their own, which ceases at the tenth descent from Woden ; the Mercian line is quite distinct, and, singularly enough, the first who is known to have had any kingly rank in England is Creoda, the eleventh from Woden, whose remote ancestor Offa ruled the Angles before they came over to this island. The kingdom therefore to which Penda "succeeded" was that of the South Mercians, perhaps with the Pec sætna added ; and with these the North Mercians (men of Lindsey and Nottingham) associated themselves. The "treaty" of Cirencester and the peace with Kenwalk, the great victories over Edwin and Oswald, and the two invasions of East Anglia would have

results in the expansion of the boundaries of Mercia to include districts formerly held by the West Saxons, Northumbrians, and East Anglians ; and the first part of the 'Tribal Hidage' (excepting the 1,500 hides belonging to Hampshire and the Isle of Wight) probably shows the extent of the kingdom at Penda's death, while the second part shows that his overlordship extended over all England south of the Humber. In the latter part of his reign he allowed his son Peada to rule over the Middle English (Bede, iii. 21), and to these were probably added the Gyrwas, detached from the East Angles, for the foundation of Peterborough is attributed to Peada. There is no record that Penda conquered the East or South Saxons or Kent ; these kingdoms probably submitted without resistance after the overthrow of Oswald. It seems clear that England south of the Humber had had some sort of unity for a long period, for Bede in his list of Bretwaldas (ii. 5) says that the earlier of them—Ella, Ceawlin, Ethelbert, and Redwald—governed this district, Edwin being the first to govern north as well as south of the Humber ; so that Penda's rule was really a continuation of the old state of affairs — the most powerful of the princes having the overlordship.

After Oswy's brief revival—for two or three years—of the wider lordship of Edwin and Oswald, the youthful Wulfhere (658-675) regained the domains which his father Penda had governed, and in 661 added the Jutish districts of Wight and Hampshire. He seems to have pushed the Mercian boundary southwards to the Thames, and to have designed further annexations of the West Saxon lands, for in the last year of his reign he was fighting with Escwin at Beadenhead (Bedwin ?). His brother and successor Ethelred (675-704) managed to maintain the Mercian limits as extended, and though greater kings, in Ethelbald and Offa, exercised probably a more direct and coercive authority, the boundaries remained unaltered. One point about Wulfhere's reign may be noticed : he seems to have moved his chief residence westward as time went on (Beresford's 'Lichfield Diocese,' p. 28); and a similar movement is noticeable in the life of his daughter St. Werburgh, for while her early associations are with Ely and Weedon, she afterwards founded Hanbury and Trentham. Lichfield also became the principal see of Mercia, and Leicester and Lindsey occupied subordinate positions.

III. With the growth of Mercia in area changes took place in its administration. The king associated with himself some ealdormen. These were normally five in number

('Chron.,' a. 825), and the arrangement may be traced back as far as Wulfhere's time, if the abstract of his charter of 664 given in the 'Chronicle' is trustworthy. There is nothing obviously suspicious either in contents or signatures, but it does not profess to be an exact copy. Here there are five ealdormen named as witnessing the endowment of Peterborough—Immine, Edbert, Herefrid, Wilbert, and Abon. The first two of these are named by Bede (iii. 24) as having, in conjunction with a third named Eafa, broken the Northumbrian yoke and set Wulfhere on the throne. There is an Imingham in Lindsey, so that Immine may have been the ealdorman of this district, the people of which were so jealous of their freedom that they would certainly take their share in the overthrow of Oswy's rule (see Bede, iii. 11). At that time, then, the Mercians had probably the three ealdormen named for the districts of the North Mercians, the South Mercians (King Peada being dead and leaving no successor), and the Middle Angles, the Gyrwas being, perhaps, joined with these last. The two other ealdormen would govern the annexed districts in the west, the Hwiccas and Hecanas.

1. With respect to the North Mercians, it has been stated above that the men of Lindsey had traditions of a royal line going back to Woden. When Paulinus visited the district (c. 628 ; Bede, ii. 16) Blecca was the principal man there. In 702 "Kenred succeeded to the kingdom of the Southumbrians," becoming King of Mercia in 704. 2. The South Mercians provided the king for the whole, and therefore would have no special ealdorman, except in such an interregnum as that between Peada's death and Wulfhere's successful insurrection. But on the east they had the Gyrwas, who, under the old East Anglian rule, had an ealdorman (of the South Gyrwas), and this ruler may have continued for a time until the Gyrwas were thoroughly merged in the general body of Mercians. Tonbert, the husband of St. Etheldreda, died in 653, and was succeeded by the young son (Ethelwald) of some unnamed chieftain, whose widow Siwara was actually governing in 654, when St. Botolph's story mentions her. When the King of Mercia became more absorbed in the western portion of his dominions, an ealdorman would be found necessary for the eastern half. 3. The Middle Angles were assigned to Peada by his father Penda, and Beortwald, son of Wulfhere, may have had a similar position under his uncle Ethelred. Later Dudda, father of St. Frideswide, occurs as under-king in the Oxford

district. 4. The Hwiccas had a line of under-kings, whose names are preserved in the Worcester charters. Often there seem to have been two rulers at once, a chief and an assistant. Among the names are Osric (676), Oshere (680), the brothers Osric and Oswald (681), Ethelweard, son of Oshere (706), Eanbert (757), Uhtred and Aldred, his brothers (767), Ethelmund (800). 5. The Hecanas had Merewald, brother of Wulfhere, as their under-king for a time.

This distribution of authority in the secular sphere may be compared with the ecclesiastical arrangements sanctioned by archbishop and king in 679 (Florence of Worcester, Appendix) :—

The king	Bp. of Lichfield.
Ealdorman of N. Mercians	,, Lindsey (or Sidnaceaster).
,, S. Mercians (Gyrwas)	,, Leicester.
,, Middle Angles	,, Dorchester.
,, Hwiccas	,, Worcester.
,, Hecanas	,, Hereford.

The bishopric of Dorchester did not continue, being merged in Leicester, the three originally distinct countries of the South Mercians, Gyrwas, and Middle Angles becoming a united whole, though they appear to have retained the double ealdormanship.

IV. The Lindsey bishopric.—It is well known that not only Yorkshire, but Nottinghamshire also belonged to the diocese of York, and that when it was, after the Conquest, proposed to transfer the Midland see of Dorchester (representing the older Leicester) to Lincoln, the Archbishop of York objected, on the ground that Lindsey was in his diocese. Thus it might be argued that originally Lindsey and Hæthfeld land, identified above as the country of Bede's Northern Mercians, originally belonged to Northumbria, York being certainly within the bounds of the latter country. Yet it is quite clear not only that the men of Lindsey were not Northumbrians politically, but that Nottinghamshire was Mercian. Was, then, the diocese of York from the beginning a composite one, partly Mercian and partly Northumbrian? This seems unlikely in itself ; for it would be extremely difficult for a bishop to administer a district lying in the territories of two independent kings who from time to time made war on each other. It is better, therefore, to take the only alternative, and define the old diocese of Lindsey as comprising the Lindsey, Hatfield (this extending over all Nottinghamshire), and Elmet of the 'Tribal Hidage.' Thus it would be entirely Mercian, and York entirely Northumbrian. This theory seems confirmed by the story of St. Wilfrid.

When exiled from his own sees of York and Hexham he found a refuge in Mercia, and for a time (692-705) administered the diocese of Leicester. Had York been a composite diocese he might have continued to govern the Mercian portion after being expelled from Northumbria, but there is no hint of anything of the sort. It may be objected that, "in the opinion of Bishop Stubbs," the small archdeaconry of Stow, lying between the Ancholme and the Trent, represents the original diocese of Lindsey (Venables and Perry, 'Lincoln Diocese,' p. 7). This, however, must have been a mere *obiter dictum* of that great scholar, for it is a singular fact that the places Bede mentions as lying in Lindsey are outside the limits of this archdeaconry — Bardney, Partney, Barrow-on-Humber, and Lincoln itself ('H. E.,' ii. 16; iii. 11; iv. 3). Then, as Lindsey had its first separate bishop from Northumbria, during a brief period of conquest (Bede, iv. 12), so it is not difficult to imagine that on the destruction of the bishopric about 860, as a result of the Danish invasions, the administration of Church affairs, so far as anything of the kind was possible, would fall to the archbishops of York as being close at hand. From 950 to 1000 the title was revived by the bishops of Leicester or Dorchester, but "all real episcopal power had ceased long before, and the very name was soon to pass away" (Venables and Perry, p. 33). From a remark in the work cited (p. 51), it may be conjectured that the archdeaconry of Stow is really a fragment of the archdeaconry of the West Riding, which would in turn indicate that its small district had formed part of the Hæth feld land of the 'Tribal Hidage,' the eastern limit being not the Trent, but the Ancholme.

The see was at Sidnaceaster. If this be Stow, it would be a convenient centre for the diocese, as would Retford also. It is curious that old Roman stations or chesters should have been so commonly adopted as episcopal sees—Canterbury, Rochester, London, Winchester, Dorchester, Leicester, York, Worcester, Exeter; and Lichfield has a Chesterfield close at hand. Some of these also were border cities, as London and York, so that a central situation was not a primary requisite.

J. B.

St. Heliers.—In Black's 'Guide to the Channel Islands,' eighth edition, 1896, pp. 6-7, we find these words: "*Royal Square*, originally the market-place. The market-cross used to stand where we see now that odd, gilt statue of George II., erected in July, 1751." I remember that some few years ago, when the statue referred to was so begrimed with the dirt of generations that doubts were felt as to whom it was intended to represent, some discussion was raised on the point, but—not being in a position to refer to your General Indexes—I cannot call to mind whether the discussion was carried on in your columns or in the local newspapers published in St. Heliers. At all events, the statue about that date was thoroughly cleaned, and it was then made out to be a statue of George II., but I am not able to say what the favour was which that king had conferred on the islanders in return for which this statue was erected.

In an account of St. Heliers by M. de la Croix, published in Jersey by Richard Gosset in 1845, on pp. 11-12 of No. 1, we may read (I condense the French) that between the west gable of the Royal Court-house and the house known under the name of "L'Hôtel de l'Union" there existed in old times a narrow passage (*ruelle*), which afforded a communication from what is now called Hill Street to the market-place. The soil of this passage —subject to the above public right of way —belonged to a certain Mr. Gosset. We further learn that about the year 1750 the Royal Court-house was being rebuilt. I will now carry on this story in somewhat fuller detail than as here set out by recalling what I read of it a few years ago in another work, by the same author, I think, and of about the same date (1845). Mr. Gosset was some sort of a builder or contractor, and when he happened to be in Plymouth a few years before—say in 1745 or thereabouts—a privateer brought in a Spanish ship captured in the Mediterranean. Among the miscellaneous goods which made up the cargo of this prize was an old statue, supposed to date from Roman times, and possibly representing an emperor. At the auction of the cargo which followed Mr. Gosset, probably for a mere trifle, bought this statue, and, carrying it to Jersey, stored it in his builder's yard. The States of Jersey, having in 1750 nearly finished their court-house, seem to have thought that some embellishment of the ground in front would be desirable, and no embellishment could be more appropriate than that of their reigning sovereign. By good luck also at about this date Mr. Gosset, wishing much to enlarge his own premises, which could only be done by stopping up the narrow passage, applied to the States for their assent, and as a result—I condense again now from M. de la Croix's pages—the States gave the required permission in exchange for that statue. The statue was then gilt, and on 9 July, 1751, having been baptized with the title of George II., was unveiled and inaugurated with all possible ceremonial. A representative company of each division of the island militia and of the garrison, and all the civil authorities in due form, were present, and Mr. Charles Marett, Deputy Viscount, having mounted the pedestal whence public notifications are usually made, and which for that occasion was dressed with carpets, declared that the aforesaid statue had been set up in honour of his Majesty King George II. Three rounds of cheering followed this declaration, and at the signal given by the hoisting of a flag on the steeple of the town church the garrison of Elizabeth Castle three times saluted with seven guns, each round of seven guns being followed by a small-arms volley on the part of the troops in the Royal Square. Then wine was brought to the vicinity of the statue, and his Majesty's health was drunk by the civil and military officials. After these ceremonies the mace, the emblem of the authority wielded by the States, was taken back in charge of the proper officials, and with a very solemn and dignified escort, to the place where it was usual to keep it ; and refreshments were supplied to the soldiers, some being detained to serve as guard of honour to General Hurst, the Governor-in-Chief, who was expected to arrive that day. However, when the tide turned, and it was thereby evident that the Governor could not make the port till the morrow, all the rest of the soldiers were allowed to go ; and in the evening there were public fireworks. From the foregoing history we may conclude that all parties concerned were satisfied : the king with the honour, Mr. Gosset by having got his wish on easy terms, the States and the Jersey public because they felt that they had done the right thing at the smallest possible outlay, and the soldiers and others who took part in the ceremony with the extra refreshments and drink. One thing only was lacking to fill up the cup of joy—the Governor-in-Chief, General Hurst, had not been present. Whether he reached the island on the next day I do not know, but it seems to me highly probable that he also may have been satisfied, for to miss his tide on 9 July was a way, without offending any one, of getting out of a ceremony in which he was reluctant to take part.

Having concluded the account of this incident, I should like to draw the attention of those who infer, from the existence of so many Vine Streets in this country, that wine was formerly made in England from grapes grown out of doors, to the following passage on p. 38 of M. de la Croix's book. The houses in St. Heliers,

"for the most part covered with thatch, were tapestried externally with trellis-work, over which a vine spread itself. People were so fond of the vine, and the habit of cultivating it was so general, that the street which starts from 'Royal Square' and terminates at the 'little Douet' is called Vine Street to this day" (1845).

H. G. K.

THE SOURCE OF THE "SEVEN AGES."—The Variorum editor of 'As You Like It' cites numerous allusions to the idea that "All the world's a stage," &c. ; but, apparently, Dr. Furness has overlooked Shakespeare's indebtedness to Lodge, from whom the dramatist appears to have borrowed. Lodge attributes the allusion to Plutarch, an authority not mentioned heretofore by commentators. In 'A Margarite of America,' 1596 (p. 91), there is this passage :—

"True it is that Plutarch saith (quoth he) that life is a stage-play, which even unto the last act hath no decorum : life is replenished with al vices, and empoverished of all vertue."

Here is a description of the lodging of Protomachus in the fortress of Arsinous :—

"About the walles of the chamber in curious imagerie were the seven sages of Greece, set forth with their seuerall vertues, eloquently discovered in Arabiccke verses: The bed appointed for the prince to rest himselfe, was of black Ebonie enchased with Rubies, Diamons and Carbuncls, made in form of an arch on which by degrees mans state from infancie to his olde age was plainly depictured, and on the testerne of the bed the whole contents of the same most sagelie deciphered in these verses :—

HUMANÆ MISERIÆ DISCURSUS.

O wherof boasteth man, or by what reason
Is filthy clay so much ambitious ?
Whose thoughts are vaine, and alter euery season.
Whose deeds are damned, base, and vitious,
Who in his cradle by his childish crying,
Presageth his mishaps and sorrowes nying.

An infant first from nurces teat he sucketh
With nutriment corruption of his nature :
And from the roote of endless errour plucketh
That taste of sinne that waits on every creature,
And as his sinewes firme his sunne increaseth
And but till his death his sorrow never ceaseth.

In riper years when youthly courage raineth,
A winters blast of fortunes lowring changes,
A flattering hope wherein no trust remaineth,
A fleeting love his forward ioy estranges :
Atchive he wealth, with wasteful wo he bought it,
Let substance faile, he grieues, and yet he sought it.

In staied yeares whenas he seekes the gleaning :
Of those his times in studious Artes bestowed,
In summe, he oft misconstrueth wise-mens meanings,

Soiling the spring from whence his science flowed,
In all he gaines by perfect iudgement gained,
A hate of life that hath so long remained.

From height of throne to abiect wretchednesse,
From woonderous skil to seruile ignorance ;
From court to cart, from rich to recklessnesse
The ioyes of his life have no continuance :
The king, the caitife wretch, the lay, the learned,
Their crowns, woes, wants and wits with griefe
        have erned.

The Iudgement seate hath brawles, honour is hated,
The soldiers life is a dayly thrall to danger,
The merchants bag by tempest is abated
His purse still serves for prey to every stranger,
The scholler with his knowledge learns repent,
Thus each estate in life hath discontent.

And in these trades and choice estates of living,
Youth steales on manly state, and it on age,
And age with weakned limmes, and mind misgiving,
With trembling tongue repenteth youthly rage,
And ere he full hath learnd his life to governe,
He dies, and dying doth to dust returne.

There are four more verses in similar
vein, but enough have been quoted to show
the striking similarity of treatment.
                    CHAS. A. HERPICH.
New York.

"TWO BLADES OF GRASS." (See 7th S. iv. 24.)
—The Week-End of 11 January ascribes to
either Adam Smith or Bentham the well-
known observation of the king in 'Gulliver's
Travels' that he who makes two blades of
grass grow where only one grew before is a
benefactor of his race. This was, in fact,
"chaff" of the platitudes of our king's
speeches.   T. W. E

AMBERLEY, SUSSEX.—I do not know whether
the following has ever been communicated to
'N. & Q.' In the chancel of Amberley
Church are two memorial tablets : on the
left, that of John Hanley, vicar of Amberley-
cum-Houghton for forty-five years, who died
20 February, 1840, aged eighty-two years ;
on the right, that of George Arthur Clarkson,
who was vicar for fifty-seven years, and died
18 July, 1897, aged eighty-two years. So
from 1795 until 1897 this parish had only two
incumbents.   DE V. PAYEN-PAYNE.

"LA BELLE IMPÉRIA." (See 9th S. viii. 455.)
—At this reference your reviewer suggests a
source from which Balzac may have taken
"La Belle Impéria." It has always seemed
to me that he may have been indebted to
'Le Moyen de Parvenir,' section vii.—couplet.
                            F. R. R.

THE SMALLEST CHURCH IN ENGLAND.—I
see in the daily papers that the Bishop of
Carlisle said recently that he believed the
church at Wasthead to be the smallest in
England. More than twenty years ago, when
I was there, the incumbent said to me, " Here
you have the deepest lake—Wastwater ; the
highest hill—Scafell ; and the smallest church
—Wasthead—in England."
                            GEORGE ANGUS.
St. Andrews, N.B.

[See 6th S. vi. 514 ; vii. 392, 434, 472 ; viii. 74.]

COWPER AND THE 'TIMES.' — In turning
over recently some old numbers of the Times
I came across, in the issue of 15 June, 1789,
an apparently original contribution by William Cowper, 'The Queen's Visit to London
on the 17th March, 1789,' consisting of nineteen four-line verses.   W. ROBERTS.
47, Lansdowne Gardens, S.W.

Queries.

WE must request correspondents desiring information on family matters of only private interest
to affix their names and addresses to their queries,
in order that the answers may be addressed to them
direct.

REV. ANTHONY WARTON, 1657.—In 1856 a
query was inserted concerning the above.
About three years ago you repeated it for
me. I have found his will in the P.C.C., 1661.
He died at Breamore, Hants, where he went
in 1626. How can I prove or disprove his
identity with Anthony Wharton, at Lincoln
College, Oxford, 1596, aged thirteen, from
Lancashire ? The Breamore Warton was
ordained by the Bishop of London in 1607/8,
and I am trying to trace him between that
date and 1626. Any clue to the burial-
place of his descendant Joseph Warton, R.N.,
born 1780, at Tunworth, Hants (in the 'Navy
List' up to 1863), will oblige.   A. C. H.

A LINE OF BROWNING.—In the second verse
of the 'Epilogue' to 'Asolando' there is a
passage which seems to run entirely out of
connexion with the general train of thought
this poem conveys. Will some experienced
traveller in Browning kindly enlighten me
as to the relation of this line with the preceding ones, and tell me how it fails to
contradict those which follow ?—
Like the aimless, helpless, hopeless, did I drivel—
                Being—who ?
                            L. K.

WILLIAM EDWARDS, OF EGLWYSILAN.—Can
any one give me a complete list of the bridges
built by this Welsh farmer-builder and his sons?
The 'Dict. Nat. Biog.' ascribes to William
Edwards a bridge over the Taff, three over
the Towy, the Usk bridge, Bettws and Llan-

dovery bridges in Carmarthenshire, Aberavon bridge in Glamorganshire, and Glasbury bridge in Brecknockshire ; and to his son David Llandilo bridge over the Towy and Newport bridge over the Usk. Two other sons were also builders. Did any of them build or design any bridges not in Wales ?
                S. W. R.

THOMAS MAURICE, 1754–1824.—Will some one who has access to Maurice's 'Memoirs' very kindly tell me whether the author of 'Indian Antiquities' was ever at Harrow School ? He refers apparently to the democratic spirit which prevailed thereat under Dr. Sumner, and the 'D.N.B.' says he devoted himself to classics under the tuition of Dr. Samuel Parr at Stanmore.
                A. R. BAYLEY.

St. Margaret's, Malvern.

CONFESSIONALS.—In the Roman Catholic Church in Libau I notice that the confessionals are quite open, there being a seat for the priest with a wooden grating on either side, but the front is open, and the penitent must be in full view of any one in the church. A lady informs me that she has seen penitents kneeling at the chancel step while the priest sat within the rails. Is this at all usual, or is it a Polish custom ? I understand that the sermon is preached in Polish one Sunday, Russian the next, and Lettish the next, but that the majority of the congregation are Poles.   FRED. G. ACKERLEY.

Seemansheim, Libau, Russia.

"MISCHIEF-NIGHT."—What is the origin of this term for the eve of Gunpowder Plot ? After dark on 4 November of last year a maid from my house (near Bramley, Leeds) was in Kirkstall, when she was set upon by a number of small boys armed with sticks. She alleges that they struck her pretty sharply, and that to her remonstrances they merely said : "Oh, it 's ahl reight, missis, it 's 'mischief-neight,' doan't you knoa ?" Are such forms of assault and battery on the night before "the Fifth" purely local ?
                DOWNHAULER.

Leeds.

THE EARTH MOTHER.—Under St. Walburga (25 February), Baring-Gould says :—

"There can be no doubt that S. Walburga has inherited the symbols and much of the cultus anciently devoted to Walborg, or Walburg, the Earth Mother."

Where shall I find particulars of this Walborg cultus ?   PRESBYTER.

[We find nothing directly bearing on this point in either Grimm's 'Teutonic Mythology' or Frazer's 'Golden Bough.']

'ROBINSON CRUSOE.'—I should be much pleased to correspond with any one interested in the early editions of this work, in which I have observed several curious discrepancies— e.g., in the preface to the first edition it reads "because all such things are dispatch'd," instead of "disputed," as in later editions Also in the fifth edition, 1720 (which I have), the frontispiece, though similar, is not exactly the same. Will any one having an early edition kindly communicate with
              WM. A. CLARKE.

1, Warnborough Road, Oxford.

MINIATURE OF COL. GEO. FLEETWOOD.—In looking through some Fleetwood wills, I came across that of John Fleetwood, citizen and glass seller, of London (Ludgate Hill?), proved 17 January, 1760, by John Fleetwood, son of his late brother Robert, sole executor. There is a bequest to his niece Jane Fenton, widow, of 50l.,

"in case she gives my executor hereinafter named within one month after my decease the picture for a watch of my late grandfather Colonel George Fleetwood deceased, otherwise the said legacy of 50l."

to sink into the residuary estate.

Can any of your readers inform me who the Col. Geo. Fleetwood alluded to was ? I have seen the engraving at the British Museum of a miniature of the regicide, and also the original thereof, painted by Samuel Cooper, now in the possession of Mr. Gery Milner-Gibson-Cullum, F.S.A., and have had indisputable proof that the miniature named in the will is not the one engraved. This one was left by the regicide to his daughter Anne, in his will, 1651 (this must be the date of the will), as follows :—

"I do hereby give and bequeath to my daughter Anne......and also my Picture set in a gold Box enamelled, in lieu whereof I give unto my wife the sum of one hundred pounds."

By her it was left to her aunt, Mrs. Honoria Cradock, by her will proved 1676 (made 1674), in the following words : "Item to my dear aunt Mrs. Honoria Cradock I give my Father's little Picture." It remained in the Cradock family till, at the death on 22 November, 1772, of Thomas Priest, of Gesyngs, Suffolk, who married Elizabeth Cradock (she died without issue), it was sold and purchased by Mrs. Ashley Palmer, great-grandaunt of the present possessor.

The miniature named in the will may be a replica, or it may be the portrait of another George Fleetwood. If it be still in existence, perhaps the present owner would give information as to how it came into his possession, and a pedigree of the branch of the family. Was the Ludgate Hill family related to Robert Fleetwood of Abchurch Lane, will proved 6 February, 1790; and was either connected with a family of the same name settled in Clerkenwell?

Is there any record of the regicide's death, which is supposed to have occurred in America, and is his will printed in any publication? He must not be confused with George (brother of Charles, Cromwell's son-in-law), who was made a Swedish baron, and was present at the battle of Lutzen.   R. W. B.

AN OLD CHARM.—The editor of the *Chemist and Druggist* sends me some slips of parchment (seven in number), evidently of great age, being much worn and disfigured, which were found recently in an old hall near Bradford, and had been sent to him by a firm of chemists in that town as old medical prescriptions. Each of the slips bears the same inscription, but on none of them is it legible throughout, and it is only by comparison of one with another that I have been able to read the whole. Possibly, as it is, I have misread a letter here and there, but my reading is certainly substantially correct. The dots represent crosses :—

```
Aon . hora . Cammall . . .
Naadgrass . Dyradgrass . . .
Arassund . yo . Sigrged . . .
dayniss . Tetragrammaton E
Inurmed E Soleysicke . . .
domend . Ame . dias . hora . . M
            Fiat.
```

That this formula is magical in character there can, I suppose, be no doubt. The word Tetragrammaton probably gives the key to the whole, but it does not enable me to unlock the mystery. The writer of the article on 'Witchcraft' in 'Chambers's Encyclopædia' states that when the Earl of Gowrie was slain (at Perth in 1600) he was wearing an amulet inscribed with this word, which kept his body from bleeding "even when dead." This is probably as true as the kindred superstition that the word Abracadabra—which is, according to a quotation in the 'H.E.D.,' of somewhat similar import—when written in the form of a triangle and worn round the neck, is a preventive of ague. The Bradford charm, if it is one, is the most elaborate that I have seen, and is worthy of a place in 'N. & Q.'   C. C. B.

P.S.—A friend versed in such matters tells me the handwriting on these slips is apparently the legal hand of George III.'s time, and adds : "It is interesting that a whole batch of charms should have been made at so late a date." The person who found them says they are three hundred years old. I should say the *formula* is a good deal older than that.

KITTENS USED AS CHARMS.—The following is an extract from a letter which I lately received. Can any reader of 'N. & Q.' throw light on the matter?

"A friend of some friends of mine was an army surgeon during the Crimean war. Once, when he with others was picking up the wounded after an engagement, he stooped over a Cossack who was dying, in order to help him, and the wounded man put his hand into his coat and brought out a white kitten. The doctor brought it to England, and my friends used to go to see it and its children. Now for the point—the Cossacks took kittens into the battlefield as charms. Can you explain this?"

The story of a dying Cossack giving to an Englishman the kitten he had taken into battle is familiar to me, but I never before heard that the animal was carried as a charm.   M. P.

PICTORIAL GRAMMAR.—Can any one tell me the name of the artist who drew the quaint woodcut illustrations to B. Steill's 'Pictorial Grammar for Children,' published at 20, Paternoster Row, in 1844? They are much in the style of Cruikshank.   OWEN.

"FLITTINGS."—This term, I am informed, is applied to gatherings in Ireland at Easter for the purpose of hiring farm servants, of a similar character to our old "mops." Can any one tell me where I can find an account of them?   AYEAHR.

HERRICK : SILVER-PENCE.—The following lines occur in 'Oberon's Palace' of Herrick's 'Hesperides,' and I shall be glad to have them explained :—

> And these among
> Those silver-pence, that cut the tongue
> Of the red infant, neatly hung.

The decorations, or curiosities, on the walls of a room are referred to.   H. P. L.

EDWARD LEE, APOTHECARY, OF STEPNEY, in 1710, entered into a bond (Add. MS. 22,230, fo. 63, Brit. Mus.) bearing a seal engraved with a fesse between three crescents. Can any reader give particulars as to descent, dates of birth and marriage, or information as to his right to use the above arms? He is conjectured to have been born c. 1670-80 near Doncaster, and married a Rebecca Woodfine. Another Edward Lee, a nephew, carried on the practice after his uncle's death in 1756. A history of the Lee-Jortin family was published. Can any reader tell me where a copy can be seen?   HENRY J. LEE.

168, Finborough Road, S.W.

Replies.

ROBERT SHIRLEY.
(9ᵗʰ S. viii. 244, 433.)

It should be noted that the Wiston branch of the Shirley family always spelt the name Sherley. The founder of the Wiston family was Ralph, the only son of Ralph Shirley, of Ettington and Shirley, by Elizabeth his second wife, daughter of Sir John Blount and sister of Walter, Lord Montjoy. He succeeded to the family property in Sussex and Buckinghamshire on the death of his father in 1466. These estates had been inherited by the Shirleys by their descent from the noble house of Braose of Bramber, by the marriage of Sir Hugh Shirley, great-grandfather of Ralph, with Beatrix, sister and sole heir of Sir John de Braose, Knt., of the younger branch of the baronial house of that name, Lords of Bramber and Knep Castles in Sussex, and of Brecknock and Gower in Wales.

This Ralph Sherley, of Wiston, &c., was the great-grandfather of Sir Thomas, the father of the three celebrated "Sherley brothers," of whom Sir Robert was the youngest. The late Mr. Evelyn Philip Shirley, of Ettington (which was bequeathed by the first Earl Ferrers to his eldest son by his second wife and his heirs in 1717), wrote a memoir, 'The Sherley Brothers,' which was published for the Roxburghe Club in 1848. On p. 59 he writes :—

"The period of R. S.'s marriage is not exactly known : it must have taken place previous to 1607, as it is recorded in Nixon's pamphlet of that year, tho' not without considerable exaggerations and inventions. The lady was Teresia, the daughter of Ismael Khan, a Circassian of noble birth and Christian faith. She was, on the authority of her husband, related to one of the Circassian wives of King Abbas......; according to Nixon two children were the issue of this marriage, born in Persia, to one of whom the king stood godfather ; the same veracious author informs us that Shah Abbas was half inclined by Sherley's arguments to embrace the Christian faith, 'To strengthen which hope,' he adds, 'Robert Sherley hath also erected there a church called after his own name, in which he hath divine service as duely read, as here it is on this side the seas.'"

These assertions, Mr. E. P. Shirley adds, "are entirely without foundation, and 'more fit,' as Cartwright writes in 1611, 'for a stage for the common people to wonder at than for any man's private studies.' Malcolm, vol. i. p. 559, misunderstands this passage and quotes it as an authority for the fact of Abbas having stood godfather to Sherley's firstborn."

In the same memoir (pp. 78-9) Mr. E. P. Shirley states that the firstborn and only son was born in the autumn of 1611, and was named Henry, after the Prince of Wales, who, with the queen, stood sponsor.

Sir Robert's letter to the prince, asking him to be godfather, is preserved in the Harleian Collection (MS. 7008, 73). Nothing is known as to what became of the son, except that he was alive in 1614.

Sir Robert himself died at Casbin, in Persia, 13 July, 1628, and after his death his widow retired to Rome, whither she transported his bones in the year 1658, as appears from a Latin inscription on a large slab of marble in the church of Santa Maria della Scala in that city. From certain papers preserved in the convent of that church it appears that Lady (Teresia) Sherley survived till the year 1668, when she died, and was buried in the same tomb as her husband ; it is decorated with the coat of Shirley, and round it are eleven others connected with the family.

Facsimile copies of the engraving which Lady Russell describes are not uncommon ; at any rate, I have purchased some for 1s. 6d. or 2s. each. Under the Latin inscription are the words : "A Facsimile from the Original : Penes Th. Brand Hollis Armig. March J. F. Sculp 1789."

For further particulars I would refer Lobuc to 'Stemmata Sherleiana' and 'The Sherley Brothers,' both by Mr. E. P. Shirley ; also vol. xi., *Journal Royal Asiatic Society* (May, 1840), and 'The Three Brothers,' by an anonymous author, published by Hurst, Robinson & Co., London, 1825 ; also to the various State Calendars, Domestic, Venetian, East Indian, &c., and Records of the East India Company.

If there is any special point on which Lobuc desires information, I should be glad to communicate with him privately if he will address a letter through the Editor, as I have copies of various contemporary accounts by Parry, Cartwright, and others.

C. S. Harris.

"Kathmath," a Precious Stone (9ᵗʰ S. viii. 464).—Perhaps a form of *cadimirus*, "a species of precious stone" (Ducange). This, however, takes us no further with the meaning of the word. Might I suggest that it is from *katimia* for *kadimia*, the mineral we know as cadmium, which the ancients confused with that which we know as cobalt? Cobalt was used to make a blue glass or smalt which was used by the ancients for enamel. The fine permanent blue pigment of the Egyptians is smalt, and doubtless the Romans, who were famed enamellers, used the same material, and from them the mediæval workers derived it. "Kathmath," therefore, may mean an enamel of preferably a blue colour.

"Hardillone" is from the French *ardillon*, the tongue of a buckle. The firmaculum was probably in two parts, one sewn to each edge of the garment.

J. G. WALLACE-JAMES, M.B.
Haddington.

I cannot at once send Q. V. the meaning of "kathmath," but "hardillo" is *ardillon*, *i.e.*, the iron point which goes through the leather strap and holds it in passing through the buckle :—

> Femme par homme est enceynte,
> Et de une ceynture est ceynte,
> De la ceynture le pendaunt
> Passe par my le mordaunt
> Queinsy doyt le hardiloun
> Passer par tru de subiloun.
> Gautier de Bibelsworth.

I quote from M. de Laborde's 'Notice des Emaux, &c., Musée du Louvre.'

E. F. S. D.

L'ardillon is the tongue of a buckle.
G. KRUEGER.
Berlin.

PETOSIRIS AND PTOLEMY (9th S. viii. 520).— MR. LYNN, mentioning the connexion between the two Egyptian astronomers Petosiris and Necepso, writes, following a note in Thomas Taylor's translation of 'Firmici Thema Mundi,' that "Necepso, to whom Petosiris wrote as being coeval with him, is believed to have flourished about the year 800 of the Attic era, *i.e.*, about the beginning of the Olympiads." Taylor has the authority of old Fabricius for this thesis. Allow me to call the attention of MR. LYNN and of the readers of 'N. & Q.' to W. Kroll's 'Aus der Geschichte der Astrologie,' in the *Neue Jahrbücher für das klassische Alterthum*, &c., 8 Oct., 1901 (Leipzig, Teubner). Prof. Kroll, of the University of Greifswald, in Prussia, is the greatest authority on the history of old astronomy, astrology, and magic. He asserts that Petosiris and Necepso must have lived between 170 and 100 B.C., and advances the thesis that Necepso and Petosiris were one and the same person. He asks, "Have, indeed, in the year 150 B.C. two good friends, one under the mask of Petosiris, the other under the mask of Necepso, written astronomical or astrological works, controlling one another so strictly and constantly that no contradiction steals in ? I think the presumption is allowed that Petosiris and Necepso are identical, and that the man who is at the bottom of the two pseudonyms expected to recommend his astrological knowledge better by distributing it between two illustrious names." Indeed, the astrologer of the second century before Christ may quite well have borrowed the names of old Egyptian kings. (Manetho has a king Necepso in the twenty-sixth dynasty.) As to the details, I refer to the very clever note of Prof. Kroll in the *Neue Jahrbücher*. DR. MAX MAAS.
Munich, Bav.

It is difficult to understand why Dryden should have made a change so perversely ; but he did not do so because the name could not be brought readily into his verse. The couplet would sound better with the right name in it :—

> No nourishment receives in her disease
> But what the stars and Petosiris please.

Dryden takes the same liberty in another place. In the third pastoral of Virgil he says :—

> My Phyllis me with pelted apples plies.

The name is Galatea in the original.
E. YARDLEY.

THE WEST BOURNE (9th S. viii. 517).—In my article on this subject I wrote, by a slip of the pen, that in 1258 the manors of West-bourne and Knightsbridge were held by the "Dean" and Chapter of Westminster. This, of course, should have been the *Abbot* and Chapter.

I avail myself of this opportunity to add to the list of valuable London articles in the *Builder* one which appeared in the issue of 4 January, entitled 'Knightsbridge, Kensington, South Kensington, and Earl's Court, 1801–1900.' W. F. PRIDEAUX.

DEMON REPENTANT (9th S. viii. 242, 494).— Carlyle remarked upon the last stanza of this most weird apostrophe (quoted by DOLLAR at the latter reference) :—

"Burns even pities the very de'il, without knowing, I am sure, that my Uncle Toby had been beforehand there with him. 'He is the father of curses and lies,' said Dr. Slop, 'and is cursed and damned already.' 'I am sorry for it,' said my Uncle Toby."

Carlyle adds, while he makes this apt quotation from Sterne, "A poet without love were a physical and a metaphysical impossibility" ('Poetical Works of Burns,' London, Routledge & Sons, 1885).

B. D. MOSELEY.

CHARLES WESLEY, GEORGE LILLO, AND JOHN HOME (9th S. viii. 402, 492).—In a reply under the above heading MR. C. LAWRENCE FORD cites—no doubt appropriately—the line touching the death of Camilla, 'Æneid,' xi. 831 :—

Vitaque cum gemitu fugit indignata sub umbras,

It may be not out of place to recall the fact that the same idea is expressed, and in precisely the same words, regarding the death of Turnus, in the last line of the 'Æneid'; and that the same curious conception is presented in the description of the death of Lausus, although in somewhat different terms, in 'Æneid,' x. 820 :—

Tum vita per auras
Concessit mæsta ad Manes, corpusque reliquit.

Furthermore, it is, perhaps, worth while to remember that the idea in question was taken by Virgil from Homer, since in 'Iliad,' xvi. 856, in the account of the death of Patroclus, the following lines occur :—

ψυχὴ δ' ἐκ ῥεθέων πταμένη "Ἀϊδόσδε βεβήκει,
ὃν πότμον γοόωσα, λιποῦσ' ἁδροτῆτα καὶ ἥβην.

and the same lines are applied to the death of Hector, 'Iliad,' xxii. 362.

Finally, in the description of the apparition of the shade of Patroclus to Achilles, a nearly similar sentiment is introduced, although in slightly varied terms, 'Iliad,' xxiii. 100 :—

ψυχὴ δὲ κατὰ χθονὸς, ἠΰτε καπνός,
ᾤχετο τετριγυῖα.

PATRICK MAXWELL.
Bath.

A RIME ON EDWARD VII. (9ᵗʰ S. viii. 445, 532).—From thirty to thirty-five years ago I distinctly remember some of the ecclesiastical newspapers alluding to an old rime to the effect that

When Edward the Seventh shall come to reign,
Edward the Sixth's Prayer Book shall be used again.

On several occasions I remember hearing these or similar words quoted.

W. G. D. F.

ST. CLEMENT DANES (9ᵗʰ S. vii. 64, 173, 274, 375 ; viii. 17, 86, 186, 326, 465).—MR. HENRY HARRISON unreservedly condemns the derivation of the A.-S. wīc from the Latin vīcus. I do not profess to have a very deep knowledge of Anglo-Saxon etymologies, and in expressing this "old-fashioned idea" I was merely following the lead of Prof. Skeat, who is generally supposed to know something about these matters, and has more than once laid down the proposition to which MR. HARRISON objects.* Perhaps, however, like Kluge, he "has not devoted enough attention to the archæology of the matter and to the lessons taught by place-names." At any rate, the younger school of German philologists have developed new ideas, and it would be interesting to learn how they connect wīc with

* See, for instance, 'The Place-names of Cambridgeshire,' 1901, p. 27.

wāc or wæc, weak, from which primâ facie it would seem, both in meaning and in etymology, to be pretty far removed. Perhaps the Pan-Germanic idea may be as powerful in effecting a revolution in vowel-mutation as it is in depriving the countries of Europe of all ownership in their national anthems.

MR. HARRISON points out that "vicus has left a meagre legacy behind it in France and South Germany, where Roman influence was strongest." But where do we find traces of stratum and castrum in France, Germany, and Italy ? The places compounded with château and castel in France, and castel or castello in Italy, are all of comparatively recent date, and do not equal in antiquity the casters and chesters of England. Other Latin words were adopted by the Saxons in their local nomenclature, such as port, a town, from portus, and camp, a field, from campus. We know that vicus was the usual word in Latin documents to express a village or street, and I gave some examples in a previous paper (9ᵗʰ S. vii. 65). MR. HARRISON can understand the Germanic races borrowing a Latin word for "a paved road," but to borrow a word for "village" is, he thinks, a different matter. But there are villages and villages. The hām was the first settlement of the family or tribe, when huts were "dumped down" with no regard to symmetry or order ; the tūn was a collection of cottages within an enclosure ; while the wīc in all probability consisted of the rows of houses which lined a road on either side, such as we see to be the case with many villages situated on high roads at the present day, or, in the case of seaside places, those which ran parallel to the shore.

W. F. PRIDEAUX.

"NANG NAILS" : "NUBBOCKS" (9ᵗʰ S. viii. 306, 431).—The former of these words appears in a form I have not met with elsewhere in Prof. Henslowe's 'Medical Works of the Fourteenth Century,' p. 16 : "Pro wrangnoylis in pedibus. Take gandres dryt [? dyrt] and eysil and het it to-gedre and ley it ther-to."

C. C. B.

NEWCASTLE (STAFFS) FAMILIES (9ᵗʰ S. viii. 225, 431).—The family of Colclough or Coleclough seems to have been of considerable importance before migrating from Staffordshire to Ireland. As is well known, John Colclough was one of the rebel chiefs in Ireland in 1798, and, after being apprehended with his wife and B. B. Harvey in one of the Saltee Islands, was executed with Harvey at Wexford. In the south-east angle of the south aisle of the old parish church of Brereton, co. Chester, not very far from Newcastle-under-Lyme, Staffordshire, is the monument of William Smethwicke of Smethwicke, Esq., and Frances Coleclough, his wife, who died 1 May, 1632, surmounted by their half-figures. On a tablet underneath her effigy is the following epitaph :—

> Here also lieth the body of
> Frances Smethwicke, daughter
> of Sir Anthony Coleclough,
> Knight, married to William
> Smethwicke aforesaid, and lived
> in wedlocke with him 58 yeares,
> a devout and hospitall matron,
> borne anno Dom. 1557, in the castle
> of Kildare, in Ireland, Novemb. 6,
> and died 1° of May 1632.
> Mors absorpta est in victoria.

The arms of Smethwicke (a family long extinct) were : Or, three crosses patée fitché sable ; those of Colclough : Argent, five eaglets displayed in cross sable. Smethwick is a township in the parish of Brereton, but the old hall has long since been pulled down. There is a pedigree of the family in Ormerod's 'History of Cheshire,' showing them to have intermarried with good county families.   JOHN PICKFORD, M.A.
Newbourne Rectory, Woodbridge.

CHOCOLATE (9th S. viii. 160, 201, 488).—An early English book on this subject is that by Dr. John Stubbe, scholar, and physician to King Charles II., called "The Indian Nectar, or a Discourse concerning Chocolata...... Lond., 1662." Its use was widely spread even at that time, as the following from p. 2 shows :

"The Northerly tract thereof [of America] principally seems to use the drink called Chocolata, in New Spain, Mexico and the neighbouring Provinces......And indeed it hath prodigiously spread itself not only over the West·Indies ; but over Spain, Portugal, Italy, France, high and low Germany, and England, yea Turkey, and Persia : and hath been recommended by sundry learned Physicians to the world."

The author quotes several times from Thomas Gage's 'Survey of the West Indies,' the first edition of which appeared in 1648.
                              W. R. B. PRIDEAUX.

In Addit. MS. (British Museum) 10,116, being vol. i. of Thomas Rugge's 'Mercurius Politicus Redivivus, 1659-72,' p. 14, is the following interesting note :—

"Nov. 1659. Theere ware also att this time a Turkish drink to bee sould, almost in eury street, called Coffee and another kind of· drink called Tee [sic], and also a drink called Chacolate [sic], which was a very harty drink."

This, I presume, refers to the sale in London only. The date of the first introduction of chocolate into England (probably from Spain) could not, I think, have been long prior to 1659—which is, indeed, earlier than that

generally ascribed to it, viz., temp. Charles II., as dating from the Restoration of 1660.
                              W. I. R. V.

DOROTHY CECIL (9th S. viii. 362, 386, 490, 529). —When I made my inquiry as to the church in which the curious epitaph appears I assumed that it was in Wimbledon Church, but I wished for confirmation. I must refer H. to Dalton's 'Life of Sir Edward Cecil, Viscount Wimbledon,' vol. ii. p. 363, as authority for stating that Dorothy Cecil died unmarried in France, and the quotation there from her will induced me to ask where she was buried. I do not gather from the pedigree of the Earl of Ranfurly in Burke's 'Peerage' that any member of the family could have a right to quarter the arms of Cecil.   JOS. PHILLIPS.

ANTHONY FORTESCUE (9th S. vii. 327, 435 ; viii. 73, 449). — Further search enables me to answer both the questions asked by MR. EVERITT at the last reference, at the end of his valuable notes upon the relations between the families of Pole and Fortescue.

1. Proof that Anthony Fortescue, the rector of Symondsbury, held that living after October, 1562, when Anthony Fortescue, the conspirator, was sent to the Tower, is furnished by the following entry, dated 3 May, 5 Eliz. (1563), in the 'Composition Books' at the Record Office :—

"Dorset, Symondisborough.—Antonius Fortescue, juris civilis bacchalarius, composuit pro primitiis rectoriæ prædictæ. Extenditur ad xxxvili. 3s. 4d. Decimæ inde lxxiis. 4d. Et remanet clare xxxiili. 11s. (1° Novem. 1563, 1° Maij 1564, 1° Novem. 1564, 1° Maij 1565.)

"Obligantur Johannes Fortescue, magister magnæ garderobæ dominæ reginæ, armiger, Nicolaus Payne de Wallingforde in com. Buck. [sic], generosus, et Adam Wormall de parochiæ Sti Christopheri apud le Stocks, London."

According to the index to these 'Composition Books,' the next entry therein concerning the rectory of Symondsbury is that which is dated 5 Nov., 14 Eliz. (1572), when William Hemmerford, "clericus," became rector. Hemmerford is not in the list of the rectors of Symondsbury given in Hutchins's 'Dorset.' Some particulars about him appear in Foster's 'Alumni Oxon., 1500-1714,' p. 692, No. 7. His successor, Edmund Hund, who compounded 16 Feb., 26 Eliz. (1583/4), is mentioned by Hutchins.

The style of B.C.L. seems sufficient proof that Anthony Fortescue, the rector, was the Wykehamist, younger brother of (Sir) John Fortescue, Keeper of the Great Wardrobe and afterwards Chancellor of the Exchequer ('D.N.B.,' xx. 45). The records of New College, Oxford, show that this Anthony

Fortescue was admitted there as a scholar on 9 Nov., 1552, and as a full Fellow two years later, and that on 11 May, 1564, Edward Capell was admitted scholar in Fortescue's place, on account of his absenting himself "ultra tempus in statutis limitatum." It seems reasonable to infer that his absence was caused by his attention to his duties as parish priest. The theory that he was identical with Anthony Fortescue (the husband of Katherine Pole) who was convicted of treason in February, 1562/3, must be rejected as untenable. By the statutes of the college (rubric 38) no married man could hold a fellowship ; and this is only one out of several fatal objections to the theory. It has been already pointed out (at the first reference) that the conspirator's marriage with Katherine Pole probably took place in 1544.

2. The style "*Sir* Anthony Fortescue," when applied to the conspirator, indicates neither a knight nor a cleric, but a blunder. In the special commissions, dated 18 and 22 Feb., 5 Eliz. (1562/3), for the trial of this conspirator and his companions, he is described as "Anthonius Fortescue, nuper de Lambehethe, in com. Surr., generosus," and it is incredible that he received the honour of knighthood after his conviction. The proceedings relating to his trial are epitomized in the 'Fourth Report of the Deputy Keeper of Public Records,' App. II., p. 263, and the original documents are at the Record Office, in Baga de Secretis, pouch xl.

In making the conspirator a knight, as also in making him brother of Sir John Fortescue, Chancellor of the Exchequer, Lord Clermont merely followed 'Biographia Britannica,' vol. iii. (1750) p. 2002, where it is stated that "the second great misfortune" of Sir John's family was "the conviction of his brother Sir Anthony Fortescue, Knt., for high treason." For this statement 'Biographia' cites Camden's 'Annals,' p. 89 ; but Camden neither styles the conspirator a knight nor suggests that he was related to Sir John Fortescue. 'Biographia' makes a further blunder (p. 2003, *in notis*). which Lord Clermont detected (p. 12), by identifying Sir John's younger brother also with the Anthony Fortescue who, on the death of Sir Osburn Ichingham, was appointed to the "officium marescalli armatus exercitus soldarium et aliorum belligerorum nostrorum in regno Hiberniæ." This appointment, under which the new marshal was to have 4s. a day for his own pay and 9d. sterling for each of his thirty-two "equites," was made by letters patent dated 23 Dec., 38 Henry VIII. (1546). In the patent the marshal is described simply as "armiger"; but in the 'Visitations of Worcestershire, 1569,' and the 'Visitations of Surrey, 1530, 1572, and 1623' (Harl. Soc. Publ., xxvii. 56, xliii. 14), he is called "*Sir* Anthony." It is possible, therefore, that he became a knight, and that his knighthood has sometimes been transferred by mistake to the conspirator.

In searching for the marshal's patent I found another, dated 21 Oct., 38 Henry VIII. (1546), whereby "our welbeloved servant Anthony Fortescue, one of the gentylmen ushers of our chamber," was licensed to sell and export 200 dickers of tanned leather hides or their value in calf-skin. For his "offences and demeryts" this gentlemanly leather-seller was a prisoner in the Tower on 29 March, 1547, when, notwithstanding his imprisonment, his licence was continued for the benefit of his assignees and of the "poore jentylwoman" his wife. See 'Acts of Privy Council,' N.S., ii. 462. On the question whether or not he was the future conspirator it would be unwise to hazard any guess.

H. C.

"ODOUR OF SANCTITY" (9th S. viii. 483).—This phrase refers to a belief which has prevailed that the dead bodies of persons who were remarkable for the holiness of their lives and saintly deaths have emitted a miraculous odour of surpassing sweetness—whether immediately after death or on long-subsequent uncovering of their remains. The phrase, in English as in other languages, must be traceable to a remote period.

JOHN HOBSON MATTHEWS.
Town Hall, Cardiff.

In an announcement in *Faulkner's Dublin Journal* of the death on 1 March. 1744/5, of the Hon. Rose Mapas, widow of Christopher Mapas, of Rochestown, and second daughter of William, third Viscount Fitzwilliam, of Merrion, it is stated that

"she was endowed with amiable qualities, being an extraordinary wife, mother and family woman, most pious, truly charitable, and departed this life in the Odour of Sanctity."

F. ELRINGTON BALL.

ST. KILDA (9th S. viii. 324, 487).—Here is another theory as to the origin of this name. There is, or was, in the island a spring of water called Kilder. Now as the name Kilda is said to be given to some springs of cold water in Iceland, it is not impossible, according to a writer in the 'Edinburgh Encyclopædia' (1830), that the appellation St. Kilda may have originated from the abundance of springs in the island. The same writer mentions that the religious woman named Kilda, who may perhaps have reached this lonely rock and left her name attached to it, is mentioned by Bede in his 'Ecclesiastical History' and also by Camden; but he does not say what editions he used, and so I have not been able to verify his references.　　　　T. P. ARMSTRONG.

A SIMILE IN 'SAMSON AGONISTES' (5th S. vii. 186, 296, 437).—The comparison of a woman in movement with a full-rigged vessel—

But who is this? what thing of sea or land?
Female of sex it seems, &c.,

may be traced back to Aristophanes. In 'The Birds,' l. 1192, when Peisthetairos sees Iris coming through the air, he asks whether this is a vessel or a petasus.

Ὄνομα δέ σοι τί ἐστι; πλοῖον, ἢ κυνὴ;

I am indebted for this note to the edition put forth by Prof. Felton of Harvard (the friend of Charles Dickens) in 1849. He illustrates the Greek line by the passage from Milton.　　　RICHARD H. THORNTON.
Portland, Oregon.

ENGLISH CONTINGENT IN THE LAST CRUSADE (9th S. viii. 343).—'The English Crusaders,' by James C. Dansey, gives an account of all the English knights who engaged in Crusades—also their arms. In the seventh (?) Crusade, under Prince Edward, Dansey states that the under-mentioned persons were his followers: Walter de Molesworth, Hugh Kynnardsleye, Herbitus Chaworth, Pain Chaworth, Patric Chaworth, John St. Lo, Ralph Gorges, Otho de Grandeson, William de Latimer, Roger Leiburne(?), Sir John Hautville, William de Rythie, Brian Fitzalan, Lord of Bedale, John de Gayton (chamber valet to Prince Edward), William de Fienes (?).　Mr. ROWE might find some information in Bentley's 'Excerpta,' Lond., 1831.　　　JOHN RADCLIFFE.

EARLIEST EUROPEAN MENTION OF VEDAS (9th S. viii. 464).—The passage in the book 'De Tribus Impostoribus' for which Mr. CROOKE inquires is, no doubt, the following:

"Et Sectarii istorum, ut et Vedæ et Brachmanorum ante MCCC retro secula obstant collectanea, ut de Sinensibus nil dicam. Tu, qui in angulo Europæ hic delitescis, ista negligis, negas; quam bene videas ipse. Eadem facilitate enim isti tua negant. Et quid non miraculorum superesset ad convincendos orbis incolas, si mundum ex Scorpionis ovo conditum et progenitum terramque Tauri capiti impositam, et rerum prima fundamentis ex prioribus III Vedæ libris constarent, nisi invidus aliquis Deorum filius hæc III prima volumina furatus esset !"

I think this is the only specific reference to the Vedas, though the Brahmins are named elsewhere. The authorship of the tract 'De Tribus Impostoribus' has excited much

curiosity and controversy, and its bibliography is intricate. Of the original edition, dated MDIIC, only some three copies are known, but there are modern reprints : that of Philomneste Junior (i.e., Gustave Brunet), printed at Brussels in 1867, is based on the copy in the French Bibliothèque Nationale, whilst that of Emil Weller, printed at Heilbronn in 1876 (and earlier in 1846), is from the exemplar in the Königlichen Bibliothek at Dresden. There are also others.
　　　　　　WILLIAM E. A. AXON.
Manchester.

MR. CROOKE will find a full bibliographical account of the book, or supposed book, 'De Tribus Impostoribus' in the work 'Le Traité des Trois Imposteurs, et précédé d'une notice philologique et bibliographique par Philomneste Junior' (i.e., Brunet), Paris and Brussels, 1867.　　　A. COLLINGWOOD LEE.
Waltham Abbey.

"YCLEPING" THE CHURCH (9th S. viii. 420, 486).—The spelling of this word by the newspaper writer quoted in the first reference is mere priggishness; he deviates into right when he says "or, as it is now put, 'clipping' the parish church." "Clippan," to clasp or embrace, is, of course, a real old English word, and is still the word most in use here in the West Country. (See 'West Somerset Word-Book,' E.D.S.)

The custom of "clipping the tower" was practised within living memory in the parishes of Wellington and Langford Budville, but there is much uncertainty as to the dates on which it was observed. This is to be accounted for by the confusion of tradition when the purpose of a custom became forgotten, and when, from some cause or other, the original dedication of the church became changed : a change that has happened at both the above parishes — Wellington, originally and down to 1500 St. Mary the Virgin, is now St. John Baptist; while at Langford St. James has become St. Peter.

Functions of forgotten origin in connexion with churches usually came to be associated with the patron saint, and it should be noted that the traditional name of this one is not "clipping the church," but "clipping the tower"; and thus I submit the true meaning is preserved.

So far as I can ascertain, Hone's account is correct. Whether at Easter or at Lady Day (as we say), it was a spring performance, and both sexes took part in it, the essential point being the clipping, or surrounding the tower with joined hands. Thence the tower represented the same idea as the maypole, whatever that may have been—a question into which we need not now inquire. The whole custom seems to be a survival of the ancient worship of the spirit of vegetation, whose cult was practised at various seasons of the year, but chiefly in the spring, when she had to be awakened and propitiated to put forth renewed vigour.

"Clipping the tower" is, then, a vestige of old nature worship, and had nothing whatever to do originally with either churches or saints.   F. T. ELWORTHY.

Here we undoubtedly have the old English word to "clip," meaning to embrace, to encircle with the arms. "Clipping and kissing" was a phrase often employed to express the mutual embracing of a pair of lovers.
      JOHN HOBSON MATTHEWS.
Town Hall, Cardiff.

["Clip" in this sense is Shakespearian.]

MOTTO FOR DOOR OF A HOUSE (9ᵗʰ S. viii. 443, 469).—A very suitable Scottish motto for the door of any house is "Better rue sit than rue flit"; and if the arms of a country may be said to stand for the experiences of the royal bearers thereof, then the motto loses none of its aptness in that relation.
      ARTHUR MAYALL.

There is a very interesting list of house mottoes, with their origins and significations, by William Norman Brown, F.R.H.S., in *Country Life*, 8 April, 1899. Among them are several Scotch.
      J. HOLDEN MacMICHAEL.

In reply I suggest the words "Enter; you have been long expected" (Beaconsfield's 'Coningsby').   LL. LLOYD.

DENHAM, LAIRD OF WISHIELS (9ᵗʰ S. viii. 484).—The first of this family evidently was Symon Dennum, who on 16 June, 1506, was retoured heir to his grandfather, John Liddaill, in the lands of Westschull, in the barony of Carnwith (in shire of Lanark).
      J. G. WALLACE-JAMES.
Haddington.

FIRST CHRISTMAS CARD (9ᵗʰ S. viii. 504).—In the absence of a dated Christmas card prior to 1845, I believe the evidence is conclusive that "Cuthbert Bede"—the Rev. Edward Bradley—was the designer of the first printed Christmas card. Mr. Bradley entered Durham University in 1845, and at the end of his first year sent designs of a picture card to Mr. Lambert, belonging to the well-known firm of printers and publishers of Newcastle-upon-Tyne, to be printed for private circulation at Christmas and

New Year among his friends. During the following year Messrs. Lambert printed several of his designs for him; and for three or four years the private Christmas design was printed. The printers conceived the idea of putting such picture cards into the market, and in 1847-8 the first Christmas cards were offered for sale by Messrs. Lambert to the trade of Newcastle and district. These facts were given me by Mr. Thomas Smith, who in 1845 was foreman printer for Lambert, and afterwards began business for himself in 1847, when he did several engravings for Mr. Bradley. The date of the first sale of Christmas cards by stationers was confirmed on the authority of Messrs. Thomas & George Allan, the well-known stationers of Newcastle-upon-Tyne, who began business about that time, and at the death of the Rev. Mr. Bradley—"Cuthbert Bede"—informed me in the presence of Mr. Smith, then the oldest printer in the north of England, that there was no doubt about Messrs. Lambert's Christmas cards being the first on sale in England, and "Cuthbert Bede" being the first to design a picture card for Christmas greetings.   JOHN ROBINSON.
Delaval House, Sunderland.

STONE PULPIT (9ᵗʰ S. viii. 325, 394, 489).—There is an excellent example of a stone pulpit, partly sunk in the wall, in the old refectory of the abbey at Beaulieu, Hants, a structure now used as the parish church. Here Margaret of Anjou took sanctuary after the battle of Barnet, and Perkin Warbeck in the reign of Henry VII. In the ruined abbey of Rievaulx, Yorkshire, may be seen the marks of the spot where the stone pulpit stood from which the monk read during meals.   JOHN PICKFORD, M.A.
Newbourne Rectory, Woodbridge.

MERCHANTS OF LUKES: MERCHANTS OF LUK (9ᵗʰ S. viii. 338, 481; ix. 35).—I am engaged in an investigation which closely involves the history of Lucchese merchants in England, and shall be very glad to receive references to any books, other than Rymer and Record Office Calendars, which your readers may kindly send. Those in unofficial documents, such as the work cited by MR. WEARE, will be especially valuable.
      ROBT. J. WHITWELL.
C.C.C., Oxford.

"ULLIG" = CHRISTMAS IN MANX (9ᵗʰ S. viii. 504).—The real Manx for Christmas is "Nolick." See Bishop Phillips's Prayer-Book (1610) in Manx Society's Publications, vol. xxxii. pp. 17, 51, 55. But it is now often

written *Laa yn Ullick*, the day of Christmas, the *n* of *yn* having attracted and absorbed the *N* of "Nolick," very much in the same way as "a nadder" has become "an adder" (see 'H.E.D.'). It will thus be seen that the word can certainly be identified with the Gaelic, Irish, and Welsh forms, and with the Latin origin, that are suggested at the above reference (see Manx Society's vol. xxxiii. p. 139). ERNEST B. SAVAGE, M.A., F.S.A.
St. Thomas's, Douglas.

There can, I think, be little doubt that *Ullig* is the phonetic representation of the Gaelic *Nollaig*. The question is, how came the *N* to be lost? I would suggest the following explanation. When the article *y* (*yn*) is prefixed (Gaelic *an*), we get *y Nullig* = the Nativity, and in process of time the initial *N* got transferred, making *yn Ullig;* just as in English the terms *a nadder, a napron*, with some others, became *an adder, an apron*, &c., by transference of the *n* to the article.   C. S. JERRAM.
Oxford.

THACKERAY'S EARLY WRITINGS (9th S. viii. 383).—The sale of 'The Exquisites' mentioned at the above reference was lot 922 in Messrs. Sotheby's sale of December 17–20, 1898. See 'Book-Prices Current,' 1899, No. 2,209.
W. ROBERTS.

THE LOWNDES MOTTO (9th S. ix. 10).—The coat of arms exemplified and confirmed in the grant of augmentation of arms made to William Lowndes, Esq., in 1704, is at the present time used by several of the families representing the three original lines of descent, viz., of Winslow, of Astwood, and of Chesham, together with the motto "Ways and Means," which was probably adopted by Mr. Lowndes in relation to his office of Chairman of the Court of Ways and Means I possess a copy of the grant and also a copy of the essay referred to.
CHARLES LOWNDES.
Stratford-on-Avon.

THE YOUTHFUL YEAR (9th S. viii. 484).—I think the third line should begin "E già le notti." When I was travelling in Italy, in 1883, I bought in Milan a copy of a very small edition of 'La Divina Commedia,' published by Sonzogno in that year, at the very small price of "una lira." The notes, collected by Camerini, are copious and valuable, and I have found the handy little volume a pleasant and instructive companion during many journeys. The note to the passage quoted at the above reference is, "*Giovinetto*, di fresco incominciato—comin-

ciando l' anno dal primo di gennaio, secondo lo stile romano." And this note is based on Brunone Bianchi's work on Dante, Florence, 1863.   W. S.

Can this be the explanation of Dante's speaking of the sun being in Aquarius when the year was young? The year of Julius Cæsar's calendar, 45 B.C., began with January. This would be the civilian's reckoning. The Church year began with Advent, a little before the winter solstice. Dante was a son of the Church and a disciple of Virgil. Was he not likely to think of the year as these authorities thought of it?   T. WILSON.
Harpenden.

Dante was perhaps referring to the natural new year as perceptible in the sprouting of the new vegetation, just commencing by the end of January or the beginning of February. Or he may have had in mind the ecclesiastical year, which commences at vespers of Saturday before the first Sunday in Advent, *i.e.*, about the beginning of December.
JOHN HOBSON MATTHEWS.
Town Hall, Cardiff.

"THERE IS A DAY IN SPRING" (9th S. viii. 423, 511).—From Miss Smedley's 'Story of Queen Isabel.' In 1887 the editor of the *Fortnightly Review* (Mr. Frank Harris) invited various writers to "name the one passage in all poetry which seems the finest" to them. The Dean of St. Paul's (Dr. Church) gave the ten lines beginning as above as one of the quotations "recurring oftenest to his mind at the present time."
H. S. MUIR, Surgeon-General.

THE COMING CORONATION (9th S. viii. 485). —Fortunately it does not require a great deal of erudition to be able to answer the query of the REV. FATHER ANGUS, but only access to a library and some knowledge as to where to look the subject up. Lingard says in his 'History of England':—

"On the feast of St. George, the king [James II.] and queen were crowned by the hands of Archbishop Sancroft in Westminster Abbey, after the usual form, but with the omission of the Communion service and a few minor ceremonies, which were confessedly of modern origin and had been introduced since the Reformation."
T. P. ARMSTRONG.

PRESIDENT ADAMS (9th S. viii. 485).—John Quincy Adams, sixth President of the United States of America, was probably of English "extraction," but was born 11 July, 1767, in that part of Braintree, Mass., which was subsequently incorporated into a town by the name of Quincy. He was son of John Adams, and died in the Capitol at Washington

23 February, 1848. I do not deem it necessary to burden the columns of 'N. & Q.' with further particulars, but would refer A. L. W. P. to a pamphlet entitled 'Token of a Nation's Sorrow. Addresses in the Congress of the United States, and Funeral Solemnities on the Death of John Quincy Adams,' second edition, Washington, 1848, 8vo, which contains much information respecting this worthy, as well as an engraved portrait of him.   W. I. R. V.

There is a pretty full notice of him in 'The Penny Cyclopædia,' which says that he was "of a family which had come from England at the first settlement of the colony." There are lives of him by G. Gibbs, 1848, and C. F. Adams, 1851.   C. S. WARD.

"IN PETTO" (9ᵗʰ S. viii. 413).—The error to which attention is drawn by H. in constructing Italian phrases from corresponding French ones had once an amusing illustration in my experience. When in Italy my sister and I were invited to dine at her "pensione" with a friend who constantly boasted that, knowing French well, she could get on anywhere in Italy by converting literally the French phrases into Italian. On the day appointed my sister was unwell and unable to go with me ; and when the "padrone," who had been told to expect two extra, saw only one sit down, he asked my friend why the other lady had not come. "Sua sorella *non se porta bene*," replied my friend, which she thought the equivalent of *ne se porte bien*. "Oh, never mind !" said the kindly padrone, looking compassionately at me, "let her come, let her come," when I, laughing, had to explain to my friend that she had told the padrone that my sister did not behave herself well enough at table to be invited out.   K. M. ROBERTS.
Condover.

Miscellaneous.

NOTES ON BOOKS, &c.

A New English Dictionary on Historical Principles. Edited by Dr. James A. H. Murray.—Vol. VI. *Lap—Leisurely.* By Henry Bradley. (Oxford, Clarendon Press.)

SOME points of extreme interest are illustrated in the last instalment—a double section—of the great Dictionary. Modern editors of Shakespeare, so far as we know without exception—it is certainly the case in all the editions we have consulted, including the 'Cambridge Shakespeare'—have in 'King Henry VIII.' altered into *legatine* the "legative" of the First Folio. Dr. Schmidt even, in his admirable 'Shakespeare Lexicon,' falls into the same error. The Dictionary shows, however, that *legative* was in use from 1537 to 1886. This furnishes a further proof how dangerous it is to tamper with

Shakespeare, and how frequently increasing knowledge vindicates his true text from the conjectures of the commentator and the phrase-mender. *Lastery*, which, on the strength of Spenser, appears in most dictionaries, is shown to be a ghost-word. The passage in which it appears—

> Polisht ivory
> Which cunning Craftesmans hand hath overlaid
> With faire Vermilion or pure lastery—

occurs in 'The Faërie Queene,' book ii. canto ix. stanza 41. We quote from the edition of 1609. The word should, however, be *castory*, a colour extracted from *castoreum*. It is a misprint which was duly corrected in the *errata* to the first edition. Under *lavender*, the current hypothesis that *lavendula*, in mediæval Latin, is a corrupt form of *lavandula*, and is connected with *lavanda*, washing, is not favoured, the sense development from washing to a non-essential adjunct thereto not seeming plausible. The resemblance of *lavendula* to *calendula*, marigold, is obvious. M. Paul Meyer, the eminent French scholar, suggests *livindula* for "lividula," "livid." Prof. Skeat derives *lawn*, fine linen, from Laon, in France, where there was a manufactory of linen. *Lawn*=a glade in its original form is *laund*. *Larder* is defined as "a room or closet in which meat (? originally bacon) and other provisions are stored." Should Corporal Gregory Brewster's constant interjection in Dr. Conan Doyle's 'A Story of Waterloo,' "Lardy ! Lardy !" find a place beside *lardy dardy ? Larrikin*, which is chiefly Australian, is said to be of uncertain origin, being first known in Melbourne shortly before 1870. Popular suggestions concerning its use are not accepted. *Lasher*=the body of water that lashes or rushes over a barrier or weir, is said to be chiefly local (on the Thames). A well-known name for such a spot on the Aire at Bingley, Yorks, is "the lasher." A lateen sail—which is, of course, a Latin sail—is not heard of until early in the eighteenth century. Under *lather* we find a quaint quotation from Bailey's 'Erasmus's Colloquies': "Such as by the Lather of Tears, and Soap of Repentance have washed away their Pollutions." The use of *lather* as a verb=to thrash, is, we suppose, dialectal. It used to be familiar. That pretty word *lattice*—pretty, at least, in its suggestion—is derived from "lath." *Lay* occupies the most space of any word in the section. To our surprise, since we thought it a modern word, *to laze*=to enjoy oneself lazily, dates back to the sixteenth century, being used by Robert Greene. That abominable word *leaderette* first intrudes into the language in 1880. "When Little's leadless pistol met his eye," from 'English Bards and Scotch Reviewers,' is naturally the first quotation under *leadless*. In this, as in other parts of the 'Dictionary,' the supremacy over all rivals is maintained, and the work remains a source of undying information and delight.

The Last Words (Real and Traditional) of Distinguished Men and Women. Collected from Various Sources by Frederic Rowland Marvin. (New York, Fleming H. Revell Company.)

WITH the limitations conveyed in its title, this work is not quite what it professes to be. This is of little consequence, since it is an edifying and an entertaining work of a kind of which the Anglo-Saxon race does not soon tire, and may be read with the certainty of interest and the possibility of advantage. 'Deathbed Utterances,' though inaccurate so far as those are concerned who died in action or on the scaffold, would more clearly indicate the character of the work. It would be interesting to trace, were such a thing possible, how many so-called last words are exact. That the last word of Charles I. was "Remember!" may probably be accepted. The "Don't let poor Nelly starve," though it was possibly said by Charles II., appears apocryphal. "I beg pardon, I have been an unconscionable time dying," is just as defensible; and "Give Monsieur Dairolles a chair" have been advanced as the very last words of all. The first utterance given is that of Dr. Adams, the author of 'Roman Antiquities': "It is growing dark, boys. You may go." This is a quite natural sentence of a dying schoolmaster, and the words have been put in the mouth of Dr. Arnold. "Animula, vagula, blandula," &c., will ever be associated with the Emperor Adrian, but cannot easily have been his last words. Two utterances are said to be assigned to Rabelais: "Let down the curtain, the farce is over," and "I am going to the great perhaps" ("Je vais chercher un grand peut-être"). He is also said to have wrapped himself in a domino and said, "Beati sunt qui moriuntur in Domino." A vast majority of the sayings are naturally pious. Some of the most striking rest on the authority of Foxe of the 'Acts and Monuments.' If Leigh Hunt's last words were "Deep dream of peace," the self-quotation is at least pardonable. Gainsborough's "We are all going to heaven, and Vandyke is of the company," is one of the most satisfactory. What is the authority for Gambetta's gloomy foreboding, "I am lost, and there is no use to deny it"? and that of George IV.'s almost cheery utterance, "Wally [Sir Walthen Waller, his page], what is this? It is death, my boy; they have deceived me"? Many utterances of American soldiers are new to us. Those who supply columns of edifying anecdotes to the newspapers will find the book a treasure-house. An admirably apt passage from Montaigne constitutes a capital preface.

The History of the Family of Sherborn. By Charles Davies Sherborn. (Mitchell & Hughes.)

THOUGH it contributes but two names to the 'Dictionary of National Biography,' the family of Sherborne or Sherburne of Stonyhurst and elsewhere stands fairly conspicuous in English annals. Strong Roman Catholics and devoted Loyalists, its members swell the lists of recusants and are in constant hot water during the period of Commonwealth rule and under the early Hanoverian kings. Their family history has been traced by Mr. Charles Davies Sherborn, the son of the eminent painter-etcher C. W. Sherborn, himself a descendant, in a book which is in many respects a model of the class of work. Records concerning the family have appeared in Whitaker's 'Whalley' and his 'Craven,' in Gerard's 'History of Stonyhurst College,' in various local histories, the *Gentleman's Magazine*, and other books and periodicals. The earliest member of the Lancashire - Yorkshire family is Robert de Sherborn, according to the Stow MS. grandson of Geoffrey l'Arbalastier, whose name appears in the Feet of Fines in a fine made at Westminster 25 June, 1200. With Sir Nicholas Sherborn, died 16 December, 1717, the direct line of the Sherborns came to an end. Branches of the family settled in various places, Wolfhouse, Heysham, Ribbleton, Little Mitton, Dighton, Dutton, Odiham, and elsewhere, and some of the members are naturally located in the United States. The name has been spelt two score different ways, including such forms as Schyrebourne, Churborne, and Cherbron. There is also a family of Shernborn of Shernborn, near Hunstanton, in Norfolk, which is said to be traceable to the Conquest. Such researches as Mr. Sherborn has made fail to trace any connexion between the two. As to the origin of the name Sherborn, the author quotes two letters from Prof. Skeat, for the conclusions in which the reader must turn to the book. Concerning Robert de Sherborne or Sherburn, Bishop of Chichester, who died in 1536 at the reputed age of ninety-six, no successful attempt to trace the descent has been made. The 'D.N.B.' gives no particulars of birth, and all that Mr. Sherborn has discovered about him is that he used the Sherborn-Bailey arms. Sir Edward Sherburne or Sherborn, 1618-1702, the other man mentioned in the 'D.N.B.,' is, from the literary standpoint, the most eminent of his race. He descended from the Stonyhurst stock, but is classed under Sherborn of London, Essex, and Southants. He succeeded his father as Clerk of the Ordnance, joined the king's standard at Nottingham, was at Edgehill and Oxford, and was deprived of his place by the House of Lords. His library—one of the best of the day—was seized, and he was for a time dependent upon the charity of Thomas Stanley, the poet, his kinsman, to whom he dedicated his 'Salmacis, Lyrian, and Sylvia, Lydia, The Rape of Helen,' &c. Shirley, the dramatist, was also among his friends. In the case of the Sherborns of Stonyhurst a connected history is supplied. Sir Richard Sherborn, 1526-1594, who held the Stonyhurst and adjacent properties for fifty-seven years, was conspicuous in Lancashire history, and seems to have been a high-handed and turbulent gentleman with a keen eye to the main chance. Retaining the goodwill of four successive monarchs, Henry VIII., Edward VI., Mary, and Elizabeth, he must have been a time-server, but stuck to his allegiance to the Church of Rome. In the 'Calendar of State Papers: Domestic Series, 1591,' we are told that he and his family are recusants, and do not go to church, or, if they do, stop their ears with wool lest they should hear. Other enormities are charged against him, and he is believed to be a Jesuit. His Roman Catholicism was, however, winked at, and he was allowed to have a chapel with priest. Among the charges against him were that he laid too high taxes for soldiers on the inhabitants of Lancashire, that he threatened to hang constables by martial law if they did not collect taxes, that he was guilty of incest and adultery, and that, though worth more than 1,000l. a year, he never lent money to Queen Elizabeth. Concerning a Charles Sherborn, of Bedfont, an engraver of the middle of the eighteenth century, information will be found in 8th S. iv. 358. All one can do is to dip into the book and furnish matter which is of family and not seldom of historic interest. Mary Winifreda Sherborn, born 22 November, 1692, married Thomas, eighth Duke of Norfolk. Other distinguished marriages are reported. A special feature in an excellent book is an index to all the Sherborns who have been traced. A frontispiece by Mr. Charles W. Sherborn gives from a roll of arms, *circa* 1514, the armorial bearings of Thomas Sherborn and those of four other members of the family, including the Bishop of Chichester.

King Horn: a Middle-English Romance. Edited from the Manuscripts by Joseph Hall, M.A. (Oxford, Clarendon Press.)

Though presumably the earliest of the English romances, 'King Horn' is an excellent specimen of the purely narrative kind. The work has been familiar to scholars from the edition of the MS. Gg. 4, 27, 2, in the Cambridge University Library, edited, 1866, by Mr. J. Rawson Lumley, with fragments of other poems, for the Early English Text Society. Under the care of Mr. Joseph Hall, head master of the Hulme Grammar School, Manchester, the three MSS. known to exist have been printed opposite each other, two on one page and the other facing. With them are given an introduction, essays on grammar and metre, an account of the story, notes, glossary, and index of names, together with, in an appendix, the romance of 'Horn Child.' Not easy is it to exaggerate the care or the labour involved in the production of the book, the chief interest of which is naturally philological. It speaks well for our improvement in scholarship that works of this class, long left to the Germans, are now undertaken by Englishmen, and executed at our great university presses.

The Cathedral Church of Manchester. By the Rev. Thomas Perkins, M.A. (Bell & Sons.)

If the latest addition to Bell's admirable "Cathedral Series" is less interesting than some of the previous volumes, it is because the edifice with which it deals is also less interesting. In spite of the additions that have been made to it in recent days, it is small in comparison with the great cathedrals, and even with some abbey churches. Neither the style of the architecture nor the historical associations can be regarded as particularly impressive. It has neither transept nor central tower, no cloister walls with surrounding walks, and its environment is poor and unpleasing. So dark, moreover, is the interior that in the height of summer it cannot be seen without the aid of artificial light, and in winter the gas is practically always burning. Much work (some of it beautiful) is there that will repay a visit, especially in the screens. The ancient rood screen is, indeed, a fine piece of work. It is long since we saw the church; our recollections of it, even when freshened up by the well-executed photographs, are but dim, and we have no immediate purpose of revisiting it. In the same volume Mr. Perkins includes a short history and description of the collegiate building known as Chetham's Hospital.

An old and valued contributor, Mr. A. G. Reid, of Auchterarder, died on 12 December last, after a short illness. He was seventy-seven years of age, and one of the oldest and best-known members of the legal profession in Perthshire. He was educated at Edinburgh University, where he took some of the highest honours. He attained his jubilee as a procurator in June, 1897, when he was presented with an address expressing appreciation of his honourable career and of his eminence in literary and antiquarian pursuits. He recently published 'The Annals of Auchterarder' and 'Memorials of Strathearn.' He also edited 'The Diary of Andrew Hay of Craignethan, 1659-60,' with introduction and notes. This has just been issued by the Scottish History Society. For some years past scarcely a volume of 'N. & Q.' has appeared without some contribution from his pen. Among many of general interest was one on 'Cervantes and Burns' (9th S. iv. 144), in which he called attention to one of the tales in the 'Exemplary Novels' of Cervantes, 'The Dialogue between Two Dogs,' and its resemblance to 'The Twa Dogs' of Burns.

A correspondent reminds us that we passed without comment the number for 2001 of the *Scarborough Post*, a supplement to the first number of the new century, and declares that the paper was not only a *jeu d'esprit*, but a carefully thought-out forecast, which in a century (a long time to wait) will be profoundly interesting. The paper was suggested by Sir George Sitwell, who is believed to be responsible for many of the articles. It was sprung without notice upon the public, and arrested much attention. We admit our neglect; but the space we can devote to reviews is so small, and the claims upon it are so considerable, we are driven to selection, and much matter of interest is crowded out. We have not kept the *brochure*, and can only give publicity to what is said about it.

'Notes and Queries' for Sale (9th S. vii. 387, 520; viii. 76). — At the present date the thirty-one half-yearly volumes issued between July, 1853, and December, 1868, viz., 1st S. viii. to 4th S. ii., are offered for 2*l*. 2*s*. at Bright's Stores, 22 and 23, Town Hall Avenue, Bournemouth.

EVERARD HOME COLEMAN.

Notices to Correspondents.

We must call special attention to the following notices:—

On all communications must be written the name and address of the sender, not necessarily for publication, but as a guarantee of good faith.

We cannot undertake to answer queries privately.

To secure insertion of communications correspondents must observe the following rules. Let each note, query, or reply be written on a separate slip of paper, with the signature of the writer and such address as he wishes to appear. When answering queries, or making notes with regard to previous entries in the paper, contributors are requested to put in parentheses, immediately after the exact heading, the series, volume, and page or pages to which they refer. Correspondents who repeat queries are requested to head the second communication "Duplicate."

M. S. T. ("Of love which never knew its earthly close").—This is the opening line of Tennyson's 'Love and Duty,' p. 92 of Macmillan's complete edition in one volume.

R. M., Brussels ("Collection of Posters").—This application is only suited to our advertisement columns.

CORRIGENDUM.—P. 25, col. 1, l. 29, for "Canon Teignmouth Shaw" read *Shore*.

NOTICE.

Editorial communications should be addressed to "The Editor of 'Notes and Queries'"—Advertisements and Business Letters to "The Publisher"—at the Office, Bream's Buildings, Chancery Lane, E.C.

We beg leave to state that we decline to return communications which, for any reason, we do not print; and to this rule we can make no exception.

LONDON, SATURDAY, JANUARY 25, 1902.

CONTENTS. — No. 213.

Notices to Correspondents.

Notes.

CITIZEN BARONETS.

THE number of citizens who have attained to the dignity of bearing the " red hand of Ulster " is far from insignificant. Yet when we remember that this dignity was at its institution, or soon afterwards, conferred upon any one who was willing to pay down the comparatively trifling sum of 1,095l.—the cost of supporting thirty foot soldiers in Ireland for three years—it is remarkable that we do not find a single citizen availing himself of the opportunity. So far as the citizens of London are concerned the coveted title has always been conferred spontaneously by the sovereign.

It is not pretended that the following list is exhaustive of those who attained to this dignity through their connexion—official or otherwise—with the City. It will, however, probably be accepted as a liberal instalment towards the compilation of such a list. The names are arranged chronologically, and so far as possible the civic connexion, or the occasion for the bestowal of the honour, is indicated.

1621, 19 July. Sir John Rivers, of Chafford, Kent. He was grandson of Sir John Rivers, Knight, who was Lord Mayor in 1573-4. This baronetcy became extinct 31 Oct., 1870.

1621/2, 2 Feb. Sir Paul Gore, of Magherabegg, co. Donegal, Baronet of Ireland. He was eighth son of Gerard Gore, Alderman of Bridge Out (1594-1607), and brother to William Gore, who was Sheriff in 1615-16 and Alderman of Bridge Out 1615-24; also brother to Sir John Gore, Lord Mayor in 1624-5; Sheriff in 1615-16; and Alderman successively of Aldersgate (1615-18), Castle Baynard (1618-21), and Walbrook (1621-36). This baronetcy still continues.

1621/2, 16 Feb. Sir John Garrard, of Lamer, Herts, who had been knighted 26 Feb., 1615/16. He was eldest son and heir apparent of Sir John Garrard, Knight (died 7 May, 1625), who had been Lord Mayor in 1601-2; Sheriff 1592-3; and Alderman successively of Aldgate (1592-1606) and Candlewick (1606-1625). Baronetcy extinct in 1767.

1623, 26 June. Sir Edward Barkham, of Southacre, Norfolk. Eldest son and heir apparent of Sir Edward Barkham, Knight (died 15 Jan., 1633/4), who had been Lord Mayor in 1621-2; Sheriff in 1611-12; and Alderman successively of Farringdon In (1611-21) and Cheap (1621-34). Baronetcy extinct in 1695.

1629, 31 May. Sir William Acton, of London. He was Alderman of Aldersgate 1628-1643; Sheriff 1628-9, and was created a baronet whilst serving that office, being the first person to receive the honour in that position ; elected Lord Mayor in Sept., 1640, but discharged by the House of Commons in the following month for his adherence to Charles I. Baronetcy extinct at his death in 1651.

1629, 28 Nov. Sir Robert Ducie, of London. Alderman successively of Farringdon Out (1620-5), Billingsgate (1625-7), and Bassishaw (1627-34); Sheriff 1620-1; Lord Mayor 1630-1. Was banker to Charles I., in whose cause he is said to have lost 80,000l. Baronetcy extinct in 1703.

1641, 28 June. Sir Thomas Whitmore, of Apley, Salop. His father and grandfather were merchants of London, and his uncle, Sir George Whitmore, Knight, of Hackney, was Alderman successively of Farringdon In (1621-6) and Langbourn (1626-43); Sheriff in 1621-2; and Lord Mayor 1631-2; being one of the Royalist Aldermen discharged and imprisoned in 1643. Baronetcy extinct in 1699.

1641, 14 Dec. Sir Richard Gurney, of London. Alderman successively of Bishopsgate

(1634-7) and Dowgate (1637-42); Sheriff in 1633-4; Lord Mayor in 1641, until discharged by the House of Commons 11 Aug., 1642. He was the first Lord Mayor to receive a baronetcy during his mayoralty, and was one of the Royalist Aldermen who were deprived, impeached, and imprisoned for loyalty to Charles I. His baronetcy failed with him in 1647.

1660, 7 June. Sir John Langham, of Cottesbrooke, co. Northampton. Alderman successively of Portsoken (1642-8) and Bishopsgate (1648), until discharged by the House of Commons in 1649 for refusing to proclaim the abolition of monarchy; Sheriff 1642-3; restored Alderman Sept., 1660, but discharged a few days afterwards at his own request; knighted 26 May, Baronet 7 June, 1660. Baronetcy continues.

1660, 13 June. Sir Thomas Adams, of London. Alderman successively of Portsoken (1639-41), Billingsgate (1641-6), Cornhill (1646), till discharged in 1649 for refusing to proclaim the abolition of monarchy; Sheriff 1639-40; Lord Mayor 1645-6; restored Alderman of Cornhill 1660, till death in 1668; knighted at Breda, May, 1660. Baronetcy extinct in 1770.

1660, 14 June. Sir Thomas Allen (or Alleyne), of London. Alderman successively of Cheap (1653-60), Aldgate (1660-79), Bridge Out (1679), till superseded in 1683; restored 1688, till decease in 1690; Sheriff 1654-5; Lord Mayor 1659-60, being in office at the Restoration; knighted 29 May, 1660, upon delivering the keys of the City to the king at St. George's-in-the-Fields; Baronet a few days after. Title extinct in 1730.

1660, 18 June. Sir Thomas Cullum, of Hawsted, Suffolk. Alderman of Cordwainer 1643, till discharged in 1652; Sheriff 1646-7; imprisoned in the Tower in 1647 by order of the House of Commons; created Baronet for forwarding the Restoration. Baronetcy extinct in 1855.

1660, 22 June. Sir John Robinson, of London. Alderman successively of Dowgate (1655-8), Cripplegate (1658-63), Tower (1663) till decease in 1680; Sheriff 1657-8; Lord Mayor 1662-3; knighted 26 May, 1660; Baronet shortly afterwards for zeal in promoting the Restoration. Nephew of Archbishop Laud, and sometime Lieutenant of the Tower. His baronetcy continues.

1660, 22 July. Sir Richard Browne, of Dibden, Essex. Alderman of Langbourn 1648, till discharged by Parliament in 1649; restored 1662-3; Bridge Out 1663-4; Sheriff 1648-9; Lord Mayor 1660-1; knighted 19 May, 1660; Baronet shortly afterwards, just before his elevation to the civic chair. Had been a distinguished Parliamentary officer and well known in the Civil War as Major-General Browne, but had retired from that party at the king's death; imprisoned for several years by Cromwell; created Baronet as a reward for his zeal in the cause of the Restoration. Title extinct or dormant about 1727.

1661, 18 June. Sir Thomas Viner, of London. Alderman successively of Billingsgate (1646-1651) and Langbourn (1651), till discharged in 1660; Sheriff 1648-9; Lord Mayor 1653-4; knighted by Cromwell when Mayor 8 Feb., 1653/4; reknighted by Charles II. 1 Aug., 1660. Baronetcy extinct about 1680.

1661/2, 7 March. Sir Thomas Proby, of Elton, co. Hunts. He was grandson of Sir Peter Proby, who was Lord Mayor in 1622-3; Sheriff 1614-5; and Alderman successively of Queenhithe (1614-23) and Broad Street (1623), till his death in 1625. Sir Thomas Proby was M.P. for Amersham 1660-79 and for co. Hunts 1679-81. Baronetcy extinct at his death in 1689.

1664, 31 Aug. Sir Thomas Bateman, of How Hall, Norfolk. Son of Robert Bateman, who was Chamberlain of London 1631-40 and M.P. for the City 1621-6. His baronetcy became extinct at his death.

1666, 10 May. Sir Robert Viner, of London. Alderman of Broad Street 1666-79 and Langbourn 1669, till discharged in 1686; Sheriff 1666-7; Lord Mayor 1674-5; knighted 24 June, 1665, and created a Baronet shortly before his election as Sheriff. His dignity expired with him in 1688.

1678, 18 July. Sir Josiah Child, of London and of Wanstead, Essex. A London merchant and Governor of the E.I. Co. Baronetcy merged in earldom of Tylney 1731; extinct 1784.

1684, 16 Sept. Sir Robert Dashwood, of Northbrooke, Oxon. Son of George Dashwood, of Hackney (who had a warrant for a baronetcy, but never took out the patent), and nephew of Sir Samuel Dashwood, Knight, who was Alderman successively of Cheap (1683-7) and Aldgate (1688-1705); Sheriff 1683-4; and Lord Mayor in 1702-3. Baronetcy continues.

1688, 21 July. Sir Henry Ashhurst, of Waterstock, Oxon. Alderman of Vintry 1688-1689; son of Henry Ashhurst, merchant of London, and brother to Sir William Ashhurst, who was Alderman successively of Bread Street (1687-8) and Billingsgate (1688-1720); Sheriff 1691-2; and Lord Mayor in 1693-4. Baronetcy extinct 1732.

W. D. PINK.

(*To be continued.*)

JUNIUS.—Two portraits of an Under-Secretary of State in the reign of George III. being likely to be sold shortly at Christie's, it may be well the public should know somewhat more about their original than is generally the case. He was Mr. Jackson, Secretary of the Admiralty during the whole of the great American war, and subsequently Judge-Advocate of the Fleet. To him was imputed, and not without good reason, the authorship of the 'Letters of Junius,' but there are facts that must have been quite unknown when he was taken for Junius which bring the probability of the ascription within reasonable belief. Having entered the Civil Service about 1743, he afterwards married, when twenty-one, the only daughter of his uncle, William Ward, by one of the Vincent family of Stoke d'Abernon. This connected him with the Clanricardes and Osborns of Chicksands, and soon brought him into good society. But his intercourse with the Pitts of Dorsetshire is the main consideration. When he first became acquainted with that family is not very certain, but there are two electioneering badges, on blue silk, bearing in gold and silver letters the words "Pitt and Jackson." It does not appear by reference to the Parliamentary returns for what constituency these badges were used. It would seem as though it were for the county of Dorset; nevertheless, although the name of Pitt occurs frequently in boroughs in that county, no name of Jackson appears conjointly with Pitt to satisfy his election on that occasion. But Mr. Jackson was returned M.P. for Weymouth at an early date, and subsequently stood twice for the borough of Colchester, the first occasion being a contested election, of great notoriety at the time, which cost him a fabulous sum of money. There are several letters between himself and the Chatham family extant at Hayes, where he was a constant visitor, Lady Chatham writing to ask intelligence of her son Henry, who was in the navy—as to the whereabouts of his ship, and so forth. This Henry, by-the-by, was brother of the great statesman William Pitt, and I have often failed to find his name in any peerage. Whether the supposed Junius set up by different persons as the veritable Junius had all these advantages of familiar intercourse with the Pitt family I do not know, but Mr. Jackson had that advantage.

The handwriting of the 'Letters of Junius' is certainly not that of Mr. Jackson, who wrote a large, good hand; but it is not at all likely that a man who had been in office all his life would have allowed his identity to be known by his handwriting. There is every reason to believe that a gentleman named Aust, who still lived in 1822, might have been employed by Mr. Jackson for this purpose. Mr. Jackson, who was created a baronet in 1791, left three daughters by his first wife and one son by his second wife, the late Sir George Duckett, who was an original member of the Pitt Club. Why the secrecy of the authorship of the 'Letters of Junius' should have been so strictly observed, or even thought requisite, is now not easy to understand. But as for controversies and those who set up as authorities to solve them, I know from experience that the wildest and most absurd solutions are put forth to serve a purpose, more especially in the present day; but the object of this communication is simply to put the saddle on a probable horse. The secrecy in the matter is quite unexplainable, but "Omnia mutantur, nos et mutamur in illis." G. F. D.

"BARRACKED"=HOOTED.—The *Daily News* of 18 December, 1901, contains the following note on the use of the word "barracked":—

"According to the telegrams, the disappointed spectators at Sydney 'barracked' at the Australian cricketers for the feeble stand they were making against MacLaren's eleven. This is a comparatively new specimen of colonial slang. In the same way 'barracking' is only an elongated form of 'barking.' It originated with the rowdy supporters of rival football teams, and has now spread to cricket and various other forms of sport. It has even forced its way into the political arena. People who vociferously cheer a particular public man are not infrequently referred to in Australian papers as his 'barrackers.' A colonial reporter would probably have remarked that Lord Rosebery had a regiment of 'barrackers' at Chesterfield."

While I am quite willing to admit that all hooting or shouting may be described as "barking," I am somewhat sceptical as to the elongation into "barracking." I think this word is far more likely to have been formed from *barreter* or *barrator*, which Bailey (edition 1733) defines as "a wrangler, a stirrer-up, a maintainer of quarrels," and gives as a law term derived from the old French *barratter*.

G. YARROW BALDOCK.
South Hackney.

'THE LAST OF THE DANDIES.'—As, thanks to the brilliant talents of Mr. Tree, there has of late been a revival of interest in the career of D'Orsay, I should like, trusting once again to the kindness of the Editor and the patience of the readers of 'N. & Q.,' to recall (may I say rescue?) from oblivion the name of Thomas Henry Nicholson, who was (if I am not mistaken) "foreman artist" at Gore House.

Although "by trade" a wood-draughtsman and engraver, he was at his best as a modeller for sculpture. He was also, however, a capable black-and-white artist; and although his figure drawing was imperfect, he had an almost thorough knowledge of the anatomy of the horse. After the "break up" at Gore House he went back to wood-drawing. In 1848 he contributed sketches to the *Illustrated London News* in the (almost) record "French Revolution" number. In the same year, I think, he sketched a two-page block for the *Pictorial Times* (a speculation of the Spottiswoodes and Henry Vizetelly) —'Going to the Derby'—beginning with the "swell" in his drag, and finishing with the coster whipping up his "moke"—"Kim up! D'ye think I stole yer?" For a few months in 1850 he supplied the place of John Gilbert on the *London Journal*. About 1856 he was "leading artist" on *Cassell's Illustrated Family Paper*, but after 1860 he was superseded by F. J. Skill, Morten, dear old Charles Green, and other "more up-to-date" artists, whose names are legion. I have always been given to understand that Nicholson, as manager of the studio at Gore House, was, after D'Orsay removed to France, made responsible for the hundred or so of debts owing to artist-colourmen. But for this I cannot vouch. I conclude with a few words from "Redgrave": "Of a shy and retiring disposition, he did not enjoy the credit which his works deserved. He died at Portland, Hants, 1870."

If T. H. Nicholson had drawn in a more "attractive" style, as he undoubtedly possessed "genius," he might have been another Sir John Gilbert.

HERBERT B. CLAYTON.
39, Renfrew Road, Kennington, S.E.

THE DONIBRISTLE MINERS. — Sir George Douglas, Bart., of Springwood Park, Kelso, alluding, in a letter to the *Scotsman* of 25 December, 1901, to the touching extracts printed in that journal from the time-book of the Donibristle miners, calls attention to a curious literary reminiscence. "'Oh, wonderful is Death, Death and her brother Sleep,' writes one of the doomed men. These are practically," Sir George remarks, "the first two lines of Shelley's 'Queen Mab.' But the idea is far older, being, in fact, the ὕπνος κασίγνητος θανάτοιο of Homer's 'Iliad.'"

JOHN GRIGOR.

"ENDORSEMENT": "DORSO-VENTRALITY."— The dividend warrants of a commercial undertaking having its registered office in the north of England bear on their *face*, below the space for the receipt stamp and the indication for the place of the signature, the singular statement "This cheque requires endorsement." In other words, the shareholders are asked to back the instrument on the front, which is clearly wrong. The point would be scarcely worth mentioning if there were not a word in the language, "dorso-ventrality," which seems to justify the peculiar usage, in that it would appear to mean "back-frontness." But this scientific term is not really self-contradictory. The two parts of the compound are not mutually self-destructive. The idea is that both back and front have to be considered. See 'H.E.D.,' *s.v.* 'Dorso-.'

ARTHUR MAYALL.

"BAR SINISTER." — This heraldic impossibility still flourishes, and that, too, among those for whom there is no excuse. Speaking of King James II., the *Daily Chronicle* of 18 September, 1901, said :—

"Macaulay's History may be unduly severe on James's character, but Hallam's is little more favourable, and one of the mildest of his critics has written 'through the greater part of his life he was the slave of the immorality then universal in his rank, in which he contrived to caricature the excesses of his brother.' At any rate, he contributed a good many bars sinister to the arms of the Members of the House of Lords."

Not long ago the same journal had a headline to a speech by John Morley, "A Bar Sinister on the Empire."

AYEAHR.

MADAME DE SÉVIGNÉ. — In a review of 'The Marquis d'Argenson and Richard II.,' by Mr. R. Rankin, which recently appeared in 'N. & Q.' (9th S. viii. 534), it said of D'Argenson, "One of the most humane of men, he wrote to Voltaire after the battle of Fontenoy, the close of which he witnessed, a letter such as, said Voltaire, Madame de Sévigné might have written had she found herself similarly situated." This is questionable, for, whatever Voltaire may have said, a certain want of humanity was a flaw in the character of that admirable woman, and it is doubtful if she was ever really touched by the sufferings of any one outside the immediate circle of her family and friends. Sainte-Beuve, who is cited in the review, notices this failing in the essay on Madame de Sévigné, which was originally published in the *Revue de Paris* in 1829, and was afterwards prefixed to the 'Lettres Choisies.' He says :—

"Il est une seule circonstance où l'on ne peut s'empêcher de regretter que madame de Sévigné se soit abandonnée à ses habitudes moqueuses et légères; où l'on se refuse absolument à entrer dans son badinage, et où, après en avoir recherché toutes les raisons atténuantes, on a peine encore à le lui pardonner: c'est lorsqu'elle raconte si gaiement à sa fille la révolte des paysans bas-bretons et les horribles sévérités qui la réprimèrent......Quand, pour châtier Rennes......qu'on prend *à l'aventure* vingt-cinq *ou* trente hommes pour les pendre, qu'on chasse et qu'on bannit toute une grande rue, femmes accouchées, vieillards, enfants, avec défense de les recueillir, sous peine de mort; quand on roue, qu'on écartelle, et qu'à force d'avoir écartelé et roué l'on se relâche, et qu'on pend: au milieu de ces horreurs exercées contre des innocents ou de pauvres égarés, on souffre de voir madame de Sévigné se jouer presque comme à l'ordinaire; on lui voudroit une indignation brûlante, amère, généreuse; surtout on voudroit effacer de ses lettres des lignes comme celles-ci: 'Les mutins de Rennes se sont sauvés il y a longtemps; ainsi les bons pâtiront pour les méchants; mais je trouve tout fort bon, pourvu que les quatre mille hommes de guerre qui sont à Rennes, sous MM. de Forbin et de Vins, ne m'empêchent point de me promener dans mes bois, qui sont d'une hauteur et d'une beauté merveilleuses'; et ailleurs: 'On a pris soixante bourgeois: on commence demain à pendre. Cette province est un bel exemple pour les autres, et surtout de respecter les gouverneurs et les gouvernantes, de ne leur point dire d'injures et de ne point jeter des pierres dans leur jardin'; et enfin: 'Vous me parlez bien plaisamment de nos misères: nous ne sommes plus si roués; un en huit jours seulement pour entretenir la justice: la *penderie* me paroît maintenant un rafraîchissement.'"

These extracts render it probable that a lady who could make a jest of the atrocities that were being perpetrated within a few miles of her château would have borne with equanimity any losses that might have occurred in a distant battle, and one cannot but echo the regret expressed by Sainte-Beuve that her heart, which among her contemporaries was famed for its "bonté," "ne se soit pas élevé au-dessus des préjugés de son temps." W. F. Prideaux.

"Rout."—The late Francis Pulszky in his autobiography, writing of the doings of Society (with a capital S) in London in 1848-9, mentions the crowded state of drawing-rooms "at the so-called 'routs' (which word means about the same as *soirées*)." The word is not to be found in my copy of Skeat's 'Etymological Dictionary,' but it survives in the vocabulary of some West-End confectioners and other caterers, who lend out on hire "rout-chairs," and advertise the fact on their carts and in their shop windows. L. L. K.

[Annandale's four-volume edition of Ogilvie gives a quotation from Thackeray, and the 'Encyclopædic' one from Wharton's 'Ranelagh House,' to illustrate this use of *rout*.]

'Chronicles of Carlingford.' — Dr. Richard Garnett, in his life of Margaret Oliphant ('Dictionary of National Biography,' Supplement, vol. iii. p. 231), makes very misleading and, indeed, quite incorrect statements relative to the publication of the 'Chronicles of Carlingford.' He says three of them "were published anonymously in *Blackwood's Magazine* between 1862 and 1865. The earliest was 'Salem Chapel,' 1863, 2 vols.; and it was followed by 'The Rector and the Doctor's Family' (1863), 'The Perpetual Curate' (1864, new ed. 1865), and 'Miss Marjoribanks' (1866)." The dates for the appearance in *Blackwood's Magazine* are not precisely correct, and from the passage taken as a whole a reader naturally infers that the series opened with 'Salem Chapel.' The order of publication in *Blackwood's Magazine* is 'The Rector,' without the general title of 'Chronicles of Carlingford' (Sept., 1861), 'The Doctor's Family' (Oct., 1861–Jan., 1862), 'Salem Chapel' (Feb., 1862–Jan., 1863), 'The Perpetual Curate' (June, 1863–Sept., 1864), and 'Miss Marjoribanks' (Feb., 1865–May, 1866). It is thus interesting to note that Mrs. Oliphant reached 'Salem Chapel' through two slight experiments with Carlingford themes. In a similar manner Anthony Trollope explored Barsetshire after its discovery in 'The Warden.'

Wilbur L. Cross.

Yale University.

Farthing on Shorthand.—I do not know whether anything has been recorded of the professional worth of "Mr. Farthing," a teacher of the stenographic art in the middle of the seventeenth century. The following extract from the address "To the Christian Reader" in 'The Saints' Treasury,' 1654, by Jeremiah Burroughes, may prove interesting to some readers of 'N. & Q.' I may mention that one of the signatories to that address—there are six—is the well-known Ralph Venning.

"We shall adde this also for thy encouragement, that these Sermons have been very happily taken by the pen of a ready writer, Mr. Farthing, now a Teacher of Short writing; one who hath given ample testimonie of his great skill and dexteritie in writing Short-hand. We think we may say, there are not many words delivered by the Author, that are left out. However, confident we are that there is nothing materiall which was by him preached, but is here by the care and faithfulnesse of the Scribe presented to thy view."

A. S.

Nathaniel Booth.—Nathaniel Booth, the second son of Nathaniel Booth, of Mottram St. Andrew, co. Chester, arm., was born about 1660. He seems to have entered at Brasenose College, Oxford, but not to have graduated. He was admitted at Gray's Inn 21 May, 1683, and was called to the Bar 10 June, 1689. He collected a good library of books and manuscripts, which were used by William Oldys, the herald and antiquary, and afterwards bought and catalogued by Thomas Osborne. In 1702 he became Supervisor-General of the Green-Wax-Monies in the Court of Exchequer, and held this office until his death. In 1707 he was appointed, by patent, Steward of the Honour and Castle of Windsor and of the Courts of Record there, and Clerk of the Constable of the said Castle, and Clerk of the same, and Keeper of the Seal of the said Courts. These places he surrendered in 1721. Gray's Inn made him an Ancient 8 July, 1709; Bencher, 6 July, 1715; and Treasurer, 27 June, 1729. He died, without issue, 9 October, 1745, aged eighty-five.

Mr. Booth published the following:—

1. The Rights of His Majesty's Forest Asserted, in a Charge given at a Swanimote-Court, held in the Castle Court belonging to the Honor and Castle of Windsor, before the Verderers of the Forest of Windsor, the 27th of Septem. 1717. 8vo, 1719.

2. The Right of Succession to the Crown of England, in the Family of the Stuarts, exclusive of Mary, Queen of Scots, asserted against Sir Anthony Brown, by Sir Nicholas Bacon. Published from the Original Manuscript by Nathaniel Boothe. 8vo, 1723.

3. An edition of 'God and the King' in defence of the Hanoverian succession. 1727.

4. A Military Discourse whether it be better for England to give an invader battle, or to temporize and defer the same. By Sir Walter Ralegh. Published by Nath. Booth, of Gray's Inn, Esq. 8vo, London, 1734.

Some surnames seem to attract certain Christian names. Our Nathaniel was the son of a Nathaniel. Contemporary with him was a Nathaniel Booth, clothier, of Batley, in Yorkshire, Constable of Batley in 1659. He lived at Staincliffe Hall, became a trustee of the Grammar School at Batley in 1664, and was buried at that place 27 September, 1675. In 1694 his son, also Nathaniel, became a trustee of the Batley Grammar School; and his son in turn, a third Nathaniel, was master of the same school (for which he built a house), and died without issue in 1723 ('Records of Batley,' by Michael Sheard, 1894). Another Nathaniel Booth was of Merton College, Oxford, M.A. 1764, B.D. 1776.

The authorities for the preceding account are 2nd S. iv. 141; xi. 102, 202; 3rd S. i. 23; vii. 324; xi. 133; Foster's 'Collectanea' (Gray's Inn); Jones, 'Originalia,' 1793, i.; Chamberlayne's 'Present State,' ed. 36, 1745; Sixth Rep. Dep.-Keeper, 1845, App. ii. 116; Lowndes, 'Bibl. Man.,' ed. Bohn, 1861, part vii. p. 2040b.

W. C. B.

THE MARKING OF MEMORABLE LONDON HOUSES. — The advocates of this worthy enterprise will with pleasure hail the an-nouncement that at the London County Council meeting of 17 December last the Historical Records and Buildings Committee reported that they had been in communication with the Society of Arts, which society had proposed that the Council should continue the good work of affixing commemorative tablets on houses of the metropolis once inhabited by distinguished men and women, and that, the Committee having reported favourably on the proposition, the Council accepted their recommendation. Therefore we will hope that, with all proper discretion, the erection of tablets will systematically proceed.

It was, of course, not to be expected that any individual society should undertake to carry out this work to its completion; and, indeed, there can be no completion of it, for we anticipate a continued progression of worthy men and women whom London will delight to honour. The Society of Arts have well earned our gratitude for what they have already accomplished, and also for their present offer to furnish the Council with whatever information they have gathered towards the object in view, and generally to give the assistance of their advice and experience. And as the interests of archæology, art, and literature are very much concerned in the project, careful verification being necessary both of the houses and the claims of those proposed to be commemorated, it seems advisable that the Society of Arts, if not a body composed of members of the various societies fostering the above studies, should from time to time be consulted by the Historical Records Committee of the London County Council.

We learn that up to the present thirty-four tablets have been affixed. May I venture to suggest that a record of them would find a fitting place in the pages of 'N. & Q.'?

W. L. RUTTON.

ANCIENT SHIPS STILL AFLOAT.—The following extract from the *Daily Chronicle* of 28 November last seems worthy of permanent record in 'N. & Q.':—

"It is stated that a ship dating from the time of Columbus is still trading between Spain and America. One wonders how much of the original timber remains. The condition of the Anita—such is said to be her name—must resemble that of the ancient sloop Lively, wrecked at Bacton, near Cromer, described as follows in the *Whitby Gazette*, July, 1888: 'The Lively was built by Mr. Spence in 1786, and is therefore more than 100 years old, and was the oldest Whitby-built ship afloat......We believe she had but one of her original planks in her, having been partially rebuilt once or twice.' Another ancient ship was the Liberty, wrecked in 1856. It was built in Whitby in 1750, and was employed in the coal and Baltic trades. The Russian admiral at

Cronstadt inspected her in 1850, and expressed surprise at her age and build, remarking that he had commanded a ship of 100 guns, but never a ship 100 years old."

It may lead to further information on an interesting subject.   CHARLES HIATT.

[For other old ships see 'Whittington and his Cat,' 9ᵗʰ S. viii. 485.]

HOUR OF SUNDAY MORNING SERVICE IN 1688.—This would seem to have been not later than 9 o'clock. The writer of 'A Complete History of the Late Revolution,' London, 1691, an eighty-page pamphlet, examines in curious detail the birth of "James the Third," adducing circumstances in support of the warming-pan story. He says, *inter alia*, that the lying-in of the queen "was contrived to be at Church-time on the Sunday, between the hours of nine and ten in the morning, that the Business might be over before the Protestant Ladies were come from Church." I presume that the change of hour to 11 o'clock came about gradually.

RICHARD H. THORNTON.

Queries.

WE must request correspondents desiring information on family matters of only private interest to affix their names and addresses to their queries, in order that the answers may be addressed to them direct.

GREEK TRIMETER IAMBICS.—I shall be glad if any of your correspondents can tell me who was the author of an anonymous book published (in the year 1820 or thereabouts) at Oxford under the title 'An Introduction to the Metres of the Greek Tragedians.' I had never heard of it until a few years ago, when I accidentally met with a little pamphlet containing some "Observations" on this work, in which it is said that some of Porson's well-known metrical canons, as laid down in his preface to the 'Hecuba,' are impugned, and even condemned, as useless and not deserving of attention; nor should I have been disposed to trouble myself much further about it had not the author of these "Observations" alluded to "the high character of the author of the 'Introduction' and the generally favourable opinion of it that deservedly prevails." As for the "Observations" themselves, I can only say that they seem to have been rather hastily put together, and are not very easy to follow; but I should like to know a little more about the author of the 'Introduction' who ventured to attack Porson in one of many strongholds of Greek criticism.   F. N.

[It is attributed to Dr. J. Burton.]

EAST INDIA BADGE.—What is the origin of the badge used by the East India Company on some of its copper coinage—a circle surmounted by the figure 4 reversed standing on the diameter? I noticed a similar badge on a tablet in the cloisters of Basle Cathedral some years ago.   J. P. LEWIS.

'LIFE,' BY MRS. BARBAULD.—In what collection of poems may I find that short and beautiful poem on 'Life' by Mrs. Barbauld? Who was Mrs. Barbauld? The last two lines of this poem run :—

Say not "Good night," but in some brighter clime
    Bid me "Good morning."

GEORGE SHELDON.

[You will presumably find the poem in question in 'Works of A. L. Barbauld,' 1825. We fail to trace it in any collection to which we have access. As to who Mrs. Barbauld was you must consult the 'Dict. Nat. Biog.' Our own General Indexes contain several references to her.]

'THE GAMBLER DETECTED.'—I have a small print, about 6½ in. by 4 in., called 'The Gambler Detected.' It represents two men in the dress of the early part of the eighteenth century, one of whom has risen from his chair, which he has upset, and is pinning the left hand of the other to the table with a fork; cards are scattered about, and the other end of the table is laid out for a meal. The print has evidently been a frontispiece or illustration to some book. Can any one tell me what book?

I venture to add to the many appeals which have been made to MR. JULIAN MARSHALL to continue his very interesting bibliography of books on gaming, which ended so abruptly at the thirteenth edition of Hoyle. In January, 1899 (9ᵗʰ S. iii. 35), he promised some further articles on the subject.

F. J.

HENRY VIII.—This crowned Moloch is spoken of by one of the late Restoration writers, I think Thomas Brown, as "this great king who never spared woman in his lust or man in his anger." Was this writer the first so to class him? The expression seems above his level.   H. T.

SUNFLOWER ORNAMENT ON CRUCIFIX.—In a list of second-hand books and other things is a description of a crucifix : "This is apparently of Dutch make, and after the Spanish occupation, as is shown by the sunflower ornament behind the figure of Christ." Why is this? Did the Dutch specially cultivate sunflowers? I suppose it would be the Spaniards who might regard the sunflower as sacred, from the belief that it always turns towards heaven, and their habit of looking for a religious meaning in everything. Are many instances known of sunflowers or other flowers being placed on a cross behind the head of Christ?   C. F. Y.

"A MAD WORLD, MY MASTERS."—Does this expression occur anywhere in Shakespeare's works? It is quoted in a letter to the *Times* of 10 January as being his, and the editor gives it special prominence by using it as a headline. I had always understood it was Middleton's, as it certainly forms the title of one of his plays. I should be glad to know whether he borrowed it from Shakespeare or not.   E. F. BATES.
  Kew Gardens.

  [The phrase is not in Shakespeare. It appears to have been proverbial. Nicholas Breton so named a pamphlet issued in 1603. Middleton's play was acted and printed in 1608.]

DATE OF OLD CLOCK.—I have an old grandfather's clock made by "Wm. Lasseter, Jun.," of Arundel. Can any one enable me to trace its date, and was the maker well known?
                              URLLAD.

  [William Lasseter was a maker of long-case clocks at Arundel about 1770.]

LORD MAYORS' "PAGEANTS."—Can any of your readers possibly furnish the title and name of author of the printed "Pageant" of each of the following Lord Mayors of London? Mr. G. E. Cokayne, in his interesting book 'The Lord Mayors and Sheriffs of London, 1601-1625,' issued in 1897, appears to have omitted these five as being unknown to him. I presume they are "very rare." Sir Thos. Cambell, 1609; Sir Wm. Craven, 1610; Sir Edw. Barkham, 1621; Sir Peter Proby, 1622; Sir Martin Lumley, 1623.
                              E. C.

KELLY.—Four boys of this name were admitted to Westminster School in 1786. Their Christian names were (1) Hinton, (2) James Francis, (3) John Francis, and (4) Montague Henry. If any correspondent of 'N. & Q.' can help me to identify them I shall be greatly obliged.   G. F. R. B.

CLAYTON FAMILY.—Can any Irish contributor, or any one having access to suitable records, give information respecting a certain John Clayton who was an M.D. in Dublin (see Chetham Soc., 'Norris Papers,' p. 51) and brother of Wm. Clayton, M.P. for Liverpool, who died 1715? I have reason to believe that the individual for whom I inquire was father of John Clayton, Dean of Kildare, and grandfather of Bishop Robert Clayton, of

Clogher. The 'Nat. Dict. of Biog.' is incorrect as to the parentage of the bishop.
                              W. STUART WHITE.

OXFORD DIOCESAN ARMS.—Who are the three royal ladies whose heads are charged on the shield borne by the diocese of Oxford? The arms of the see are thus blazoned: Sa., a fesse arg.; in chief, three ladies, couped at the waist, heads affronté, arrayed and veiled of the second, crowned or; in base, an ox of the second, passant over a ford, barry wavy arg. and az. In regard to these persons Dr. Woodward, in his invaluable work on 'Ecclesiastical Heraldry' (London, 1894), writes thus:—

  "Probably the heads in chief should be rather of kings than of queens, and they, like the crowns in the University arms, may refer to the Royal Founders of the University."

  Possibly some one may be able to enlighten me on this point.   H. BASKERVILLE.

GOWER.—Wanted the connexion between the Gowers of South Wales and Lord Trentham of Trentham.   (Mrs.) J. COPE.
  13c, Hyde Park Mansions, W.

PORTRAITS OF FEMALE FIGHTERS.—I should be very grateful if any one could tell me if they know of any portraits extant of the following women, as I am anxious to find some to illustrate an article on 'Women who Fought': Phœbe Hassel (or Hessel), Mary Ralphson, Jenny Cameron (Jacobite), Anne Oetzliffin, Chevalier d'Éon (1761), Catherine II. of Russia (wife of Peter III.), any of "The Furies" during the Reign of Terror, "William Roberts," the Manchester heroine, Peggy Monro, Susan Frost, Mrs. Dalbiac, Rose Lacombe, Marie Adrian, Mary Schlienck (or Shellenck), Martha Glar, the Maid of Saragossa, and Miss Wheeler (of Cawnpore).
                              EMILY KERR.
  The Eves, Chapel-en-le-Frith.

GORDON RIOTS.—Can any one inform me where I can obtain any precise information about the houses which were destroyed in the Gordon riots? Some sort of inquiry must have been held on the subject. If so, is the evidence now at the Public Record Office? One of the houses was that of Marmaduke Langdale, a distiller in Holborn. Was he related to the Lord Langdale of the period?
                              ST. CLEMENT.

"STREAM OF TENDENCY."—Matthew Arnold has the expression "the stream of tendency, in which all things seek to fulfil the law of their being." Emerson has also the phrase "a" or "the stream of tendency," probably

before Arnold, though I am unable at this moment to say in what essay. Hazlitt has the expression "a mighty stream of tendency" in his essay on 'Why Distant Objects Please,' and even there he puts it in quotation marks. May I ask if the phrase can be traced to its origin, or, if not, how far back can it be traced?   JAS. B. LAURENCE.
Lerwick.

ROYAL TENNIS COURT AND NELL GWYN. —I shall be very much obliged for any information about the royal tennis court which, I believe, stood near the Haymarket, and is supposed to have been connected with St. James's Palace by an underground passage. I think there is some record of Nell Gwyn visiting the court, but I cannot trace the reference, and shall be very glad for help.
K.

EARLIEST PRINTED INSTRUCTIONS TO SUNDAY-SCHOOL TEACHERS.—In my possession is, and previously for many years in that of Mr. Thomas Pell Platt, M.A., J.P., was, a carefully preserved printed broadside (in foolscap folio), which is said to be unique, containing the earliest "[Instructions] To the Masters and Mistresses of Sunday-Schools." It is undated, but, judging by the paper and other circumstances, was probably printed between 1780 and 1790. These instructions are in ten numbered paragraphs, the first being :—

"I. ENDEAVOUR to know and practise the best Method of Instruction."

And the last, longest, and most interesting :

"X. Above all, keep the Religious Ends of the Institution always in Sight; and be constantly reminding all under your Care, that SUNDAY-SCHOOLS are designed
"......To check and reform vicious Habits, and all Tendencies towards them in the rising Generation.
"......To inculcate upon them a becoming Regard for the Word and Worship of Almighty GOD.
"......To require their keeping holy the Sabbath-Day.
"......To warn them of the Evil of Sin in general, and of youthful Sins in particular, such as Pride, Pilfering, Idleness, Swearing, Lying, Disobedience to Parents, &c.
"......To set before them the Excellency and Importance of Justice, Diligence, Humility, and a conscientious Regard to Truth in all they say, and a respectful Subjection to those whom the Providence of GOD has set over them.
"......Finally, to explain, in a Manner suited to their Understandings, all the Truths and Duties recommended in the Holy Scriptures; and promote a believing and obedient Regard to them for their Happiness both here and hereafter."

It would be well if this rare broadside were reprinted in bold type on cardboard, and a copy hung in every Sunday-school in the kingdom. My chief object, however, is to ascertain whether any of your readers have met with a copy of these instructions in any printed book, or any reference thereto; and, if so, where.   W. I. R. V.

"FOOT-CLOTH NAG," &c.—What was this? The expression occurs in a curious book entitled "Observations, Rules, and Orders Collected out of Divers Journals of the House of Commons, entred in the Reigns of Edward VI., Q. Mary, Q. Elizabeth, K. James I., K. Charles I., and K. Charles II. London: Printed for Bernard Lintot between the Temple-Gates; and Sold by Ch. King in Westminster-Hall. MDCCXVII."

"27 Jan. 23 Eliz. Upon Motion to the House in regard of the Infirmity and pains in the Serjeant's Feet, he is licensed by the House to ride upon a Foot-Cloth-Nag."
"8th Feb. 18 Jac.   Leave given to the Serjeant to ride before the Speaker."

Two other extracts are :—

"1 May, 1584......The Speaker's Excuse for his Absence, which was occasioned by his taking Physick this day."
"4th Junij, 19 Jac.   Moore and Lock who arrested Sir James Whitlock's Servant, for which they were Adjudged to ride on a Horse bare-backed, Back to Back, from Westminster to the Exchange, with this Inscription on their Breasts: 'For Arresting a Servant to a Member of the Common-House of Parliament.'"

HAROLD MALET, Colonel.
[See quotations in 'H.E.D.' s.v. 'Foot-cloth.']

ST. ANTHONY.—Where may I find a coloured print of 'St. Anthony preaching to the Fishes'?   OWEN.

SIR NICHOLAS BACON.—In Lodge's 'Portraits' (Bohn's edition, 1849) is an account of Sir Nicholas Bacon (vol. ii. pp. 107-14), illustrative of a portrait of a man facing to the right, "from the collection of His Grace the Duke of Bedford at Woburn Abbey." On 21 June, 1888, the present Viscount Dillon told the Society of Antiquaries that the late Sir George Scharf had told him that the portrait engraved was *not* that of the Keeper of the Great Seal. Can any reader say whose portrait it is?
T. CANN HUGHES, M.A., F.S.A.

"SACRAL."—In the new illustrated edition of 'Social England' Prof. Maitland, referring to trial by battle, speaks of it as "sacral." Is there any warrant for the use of the word in this connexion? The only meaning given by the ordinary dictionaries ('Century,' &c.) to the word "sacral" will assuredly not express the professor's intention.   YGREC.

Replies.

'THE TEMPEST' ANAGRAM.

(9ᵗʰ S. viii. 442, 512.)

ONE need not slay the slain, and Q. V., MR. MOUNT, and MR. YARDLEY have sufficiently demolished MR. SIBREE'S anagrammatical argument; but it may be amusing to follow on his lines by way of illustration.

A true anagram must run letter by letter with its original. It is then entertaining, but absolutely useless, reminding me of Dr. Johnson's recipe for dressing a cucumber: "Open your window towards the west. Peel your cucumber, slice it as thin as you can, add salt, oil, and vinegar, *quant. suff.*, and then—throw it out of window." That is what one may safely do with the best of anagrams.

A second and less legitimate kind, and if possible more worthless, is when you "add an *a*," as MR. SIBREE does, *i.e.*, when you make a letter or letters do double or triple duty. The anagrams below take this liberty.

A third kind—more illegitimate still, but giving scope for more entertainment — is when you settle what dogma you wish to inculcate or what is the particular lie on which you desire to throw a somewhat favourable light, pick out the letters you want from any sentence, and discard those which you may find unmanageable.

MR. SIBREE does not do full justice to his hero. It is evident, on the lines of his argument (if it is an argument, and not a mere *jeu d'esprit*), that Bacon wrote the 'Canterbury Tales,' commonly attributed to a mythical personage of the name of Chaucer. Take the 'Prologue,' ll. 623-4 :—

> A Somnour was ther with us in that place,
> That had a fyr reed Cherubynnes face,

words which artfully conceal the fact that

> Francis of Verulam, Bacon hett that Peer,
> Thys verse dyde write whan Chanse*ler*.

I have italicized the letters lent by those which do double duty; and there are, besides, an *a* and an *h* left out—unimportant chips on the floor of the workshop. That the 'Prologue' saw the light about two hundred years before Bacon was born will be, I am persuaded, no obstacle to any earnest Baconian. A man who in the sixteenth century could write bad nineteenth-century English, and who gives England "colonies in all regions of the earth" when she had none but in America, would be capable of anything.

To come to my next illustration, he would, of course, have had no difficulty in making the Prayer-Book translation of the Psalms commonly attributed to Coverdale; for that saw the light only twenty-two years before he was born.

See Psalm vii. 15, "Behold he travaileth with mischief: he hath conceived sorrow, and brought forth ungodliness"; in which we find :—

> Sir Francis Bacon made this translation;
> With godlie sorowe he brought it fourthe.

There are a few unconsidered trifles left out : five *h*'s, a *d*, and an *e*, &c.; but the passage is there—not very good sense, indeed, but that can disagree with nobody who has been able to digest MR. SIBREE's second line.

MR. SIBREE has not, I think, gone deep enough to discover the hidden meaning of the last two lines of the Epilogue to 'The Tempest.' A more careful study will disclose the following passage contained in it :—

> Bacon yᵉ Tempest! A mere dreame! Go to!
> I! I! none else! Sir Ffrauncis couldn't do it! W.S.

An *l*, an *r*, a *u*, and a *y* have been left out; but each letter has one or more representatives; and *a, e, i, c, d, o, m, n, s, t,* are repeated more often than in the original lines.

Enough of anagrams. As to the main question, it has not, I think, been sufficiently observed that the whole Baconian craze sprang from the letter of Sir Tobie Matthews *from abroad* to Sir Francis Bacon, with whom he was in close intimacy. A passage in it runs thus : "The most prodigious wit that ever I knew of any nation, and *of this side of the sea*, is of your lordship's name, though he be known by another." This has been interpreted as if "of your lordship's name" meant "your lordship's self." But there is little doubt that the person referred to was Thomas Bacon, a Jesuit, one of the most learned controversialists of his day on the Roman side under the name of Southwell. Sir Tobie had become a Roman Catholic during his stay in Italy, where Father Southwell was living, and it is highly probable that it was to him that Matthews referred. See the 'D.N.B.' under Southwell (Nathanael and Thomas).   ALDENHAM.

In conjunction with this, it should be noted that the names of Francisco and Antonio occur in the list of persons represented in 'The Tempest.' They seem to suggest those of Francis and Anthony Bacon.

     E. SIBREE.

BRANDON, EXECUTIONER (9ᵗʰ S. ix. 9).—If MR. P. SIDNEY turns to the pamphlet, a member of the Thomason Tracts in the Library of the British Museum, which is entitled 'A Dialogue; or, a Dispute betweene the late

Hangman and Death' (press-mark 669 f. 14/51), he will find a woodcut which represents Richard Brandon, the executioner, immediately after cutting off the head of Charles I., with the body of the king kneeling before the block, &c. If he turns further to the tracts named 'The Confession of Richard Brandon' (press-mark E. 561/14) and 'A Great and Bloody Plot' (press-mark E. 1021/8), which are both in the same library as 'A Dialogue,' &c., he will see that the identical cut was used a second and a third time. It was probably, according to the practice in such cases, used still more frequently, and to illustrate very different themes. The cuts in question here are, in the above order, B.M. Satirical Prints Nos. 762, 761, and 949. As portraits, Mr. Sidney must take them for what they are worth, and he will bear in mind that, whereas King Charles was put to death 30 January, 1649, Thomason, who was a bookseller in St. Paul's Churchyard, and to whom 'The Confession,' &c., belonged, wrote with a pen and ink upon the copy of the tract here in view the date "June 25, 1649," while the publication line of the work is "Printed in the Year of the Hang-mans downfall, 1649." On the title of 'A Dialogue,' &c. (which has no publication line), he wrote "July 3ᵈ." It is understood that these holograph dates refer to the days upon which Thomason bought these tracts, which are comprised in a prodigious gathering of similar publications, numbering nearly 30,000.

There might have been earlier issues of the cut than that which the old bookseller of blessed memory dated "June 25" as above—that is, prints of Richard Brandon in the performance of that function to which Mr. Sidney refers; but if such is the case, they did not come to my notice while I was examining the whole stupendous collection of tracts (including Thomason's) and broadsides in the British Museum which Carlyle (more suo) actually ventured to call "rubbish heaps." At any rate, 25 June, 1649, should be taken into account while we are studying the history of 30 January in the same year. According to the text of 'The Confession,' Richard Brandon "departed this life," with a conscience much troubled, 20 June, 1649, i.e., five days before Thomason bought the tract in question. Richard Brandon was sometimes called "Gregory," as if, with the office of his father Gregory Brandon, he had accepted his name. More frequently Richard was described as "Young Gregory," who "claimed the gallows as an inheritance." In reading about these worthies one has to hold tight to one's chronology.

In 'The Last Will and Testament of Richard Brandon, Esquire' (B.M., press-mark E. 501/12 ; see Satirical Print No. 760), the testator expresses his wish to benefit various distinguished members of the Parliamentary party by bequests from his estate, e g., his "Manor of Tyburn to the Iuncto and all Rebels in General," and "a parcel of land lying by Mary bone Park, to build a Chapell on, and one piece of ground lying by the Kings high-way for a burying-place for them, and their heirs for ever." This may interest those correspondents of 'N. & Q.' who have recently been illustrating the descent of the "Manor of Tyburn." The beneficiaries were to bind themselves to "build a Colledge on the same parcell of ground known by the name of Doctor Stories Cap." I understand that the "Colledge" was to be a gallows, i.e., the "triple tree" so often mentioned in the literature of London crime, which was a triangle of stout timbers mounted high upon tall wooden legs, a record of which is preserved in Hogarth's delineation of the last scene in the career of Mr. Thomas Idle, who came to grief by its means at Tyburn. This structure was called after Dr. Story, who, temp. Elizabeth, 1571, preceded Idle from that spot into the other world. The doctor's offences were alleged to be cursing the queen at meals, employing magical devices, and invoking foreign enemies against her. He was one of those who, vide 'The Purchasers Pound' (B.M., E. 1040/13), were

English Traytors, that have had their scope,
To act a part, upon their Sovereign King ;
for which on Dr. Story's Cap theyl swing.

Some of 'N. & Q.'s' correspondents who, not long since, were exercised anent the attitude assumed by King Charles at the final moment of his life—that is to say, whether he lay prone with his neck upon a very low block, or whether he knelt before a block such as that in the Tower—may find comfort in the woodcut of 'A Dialogue,' which distinctly illustrates the latter mode, and was actually published in London within a few weeks of the event it professes to represent.

'The Last Will and Testament of Richard Brandon' tells us that, after having flatly refused to perform his office upon the "White King," he was fetched out of his bed by a troop of horse ; paid thirty pounds, all in half-crowns, for the deed ; went into Rosemary Lane, where he lived, to his wife, gave her the money, and then had a drinking bout, with effects which look very like those which often attend delirium tremens ; finally, the minister of death died in "a most sad condition," "apparitions and visions," called up by his troubled conscience, terrifying him to the last. This event happened 20 June, 1649; the next day his remains were carried to Whitechapel Churchyard and there interred amid strange and portentous "actions."

F. G. STEPHENS.

If your correspondent will refer to 5th S. v. 177, he will find the titles of three tracts in the British Museum Library, published soon after the execution of Charles I.; also references to many works bearing on that event, in some of which he may find the required information; but in no case is a portrait mentioned.

EVERARD HOME COLEMAN.
71, Brecknock Road.

LONDON COFFEE - HOUSES AND TAVERNS (9th S viii. 224, 345, 509).—A full and very interesting account of Pontack's will be found in the 'Dictionary of National Biography,' vol. xlvi. pp. 94-5. R. B.
Upton.

"PARVER ALLEY" (9th S. viii. 325, 451, 514).—To speak of the "middle aisle" of a church is a thing so general, and to speak of the "middle alley" an expression so comparatively rare, that I am tempted to ask whether a word which has been accepted as current by the majority of writers on church architecture and ecclesiology may not be used to mean what we know is meant, without perpetual references being made to its original signification. Scores of other good nouns have been dissociated from their etymologies, and are being blamelessly employed in novel senses. It would be well if *aisle* were permitted to be the name of the main passage through the nave of a church as well as of the lateral gangs—I might say gangways, had not *way* been "unnecessarily added"—which are means of access to the wings. In common speech *alley* calls up associations which are not connected with the inside of a church, though it gets there in Lincolnshire and in some other delightsome parts of the kingdom. MR. ARTHUR HUSSEY'S philological knowledge is probably not far inferior to that of MR. HARRY HEMS. ST. SWITHIN.

Neither MR. CHARLES HIATT nor J. T. F. appears at all clear as to the word "aisle." Parker, in his 'Glossary of Terms used in Grecian, Roman, Italian, and Gothic Architecture' (Oxford, 1869), defines it tersely enough (p. 5):—

"Aisle or Aile (French, from Latin *ala* = wing), the lateral division of a church. They may also be

considered as an inward portico. In England there are seldom more than two, one on each side of the nave or choir, and frequently only one; but examples may be found of two aisles on one side and one on the other. In foreign churches there are many examples of five parallel aisles, or two on each side of the nave."

The same author adds in a foot-note, "Alley, allye, used for aisle."

No one who has the slightest knowledge of accepted architectural phraseology could possibly speak of the nave of a church, or its central approach to the altar, as a "middle aisle." HARRY HEMS.
Fair Park, Exeter.

"OH, LIFE SO SHORT!" (9th S. viii. 525.)—The lines "O world! so few the years we live," &c., will be found in the notes to Longfellow's Spanish translation 'Coplas de Manrique.' They form the opening portion of some stanzas "found in the author's pocket after his death on the field of battle."

ALEX. P. STEVENSON.

MODEST EPITAPHS (9th S. viii. 421).—See 1st S. viii. 491 for an American anonymous epitaph. A tombstone at Agra has simply the words "Happy Seaton" upon it. Is not "Miserrimus" to be seen at Winchester?

H. S. MUIR, Surg.-General.

["Miserrimus" is in Worcester Cathedral.]

"PEN-NAME" (9th S. ix. 28).—I notice that COL. PRIDEAUX, in asking a question as to when "pen-name" was first used, says it was referred to in a "sympathetic article" in the *Publishers' Circular* of 14 December last on Mrs. Gallup's 'Bi-literal Cypher.' Kindly allow me to say that soon after writing that article I found that Mrs. Gallup's "Bacon" was really Pope's 'Homer,' and that the less said about her claim for "absolute veracity" the better. R. B. MARSTON,
Ed. *Publishers' Circular.*

"ALRIGHT"=ALL RIGHT (9th S. viii. 240, 312, 413, 493).—In the present unsettled state of English spelling the poor child has to remember a great many things. There being no fixed rule, he has to learn by heart all words in which the second *l* is dropped before a consonant, as in *welcome, welfare, fulfil, fulfilment, almighty, almost, already,* &c. Why should not the rule be carried logically through, and why do not we write either *welbehaved, illtreatment, alright, fulgrown, fulmoon,* &c., or *well-come, full-fill, all-mighty,* &c.? L. L. K.

LADY MARY TUDOR (9th S. viii. 484).—I have a pamphlet, 'The Last of the Derwentwaters,' by the late J. Fisher Crosthwaite, Esq., of Keswick, in which it is stated that "Edward" (son of Sir Francis Radcliffe) "was married to the Lady Mary Tudor, the youngest natural daughter of Charles the Second, who was at the time of her marriage in the fourteenth year of her age. In the month following this event (1688) Sir Francis was created Earl of Derwentwater, Baron Tynedale and Viscount Radcliffe and Langley." If this be correct, it thus appears Lady Mary was born in 1674.   MISTLETOE.

According to Fisher's 'Companion and Key to the History of England,' p. 312, this lady was born 16 October, 1673.   E. A. FRY.

According to Anderson ('Royal Genealogies,' second edit., 1736), she was born 16 October, 1673, and received the name of Tudor, 10 December, 1680.   C. S. WARD.

PETER LYLY (9th S. viii. 504). — Though Peter Lily, or Lilly, Archdeacon of Taunton, is described in the 'Dictionary of National Biography' (vol. xxxiii. p. 263) as the son of Peter Lily, Prebendary of Canterbury, the only Lily who held a stall in that cathedral was George Lily, who was collated to a canonry in the first prebend of the church of Canterbury 13 March, 1557/8 (Le Neve's 'Fasti Ecc. Anglic.,' vol. i. p. 47).
                                        G. F. R. B.

CASTOR-OIL PLANT (9th S. viii. 224, 511; ix. 11). — When in Oporto I found, *pace* C. O. P., that the tincture of eucalyptus gently dabbed on face, hands, &c., before going to bed, afforded a considerable protection from the attacks of mosquitos. I am bound to say, however, that the long, vicious, and shrill swear-words with which the angry insects wheeled away from the (to them) obnoxious odour of their prey were somewhat a deterrent from peaceful slumbers.
                                        E. E. STREET.

ZOAR CHAPEL, SOUTHWARK (9th S. viii. 521). —During the reign of James II. (1685-9) one Poulter, a zealous Papist, opened a school in Southwark to teach the children of the poor gratis. This excited considerable attention, and three gentlemen of St. Saviour's parish, Messrs. Mallet, Warburton, and Holland, all members of the church in St. Thomas's Street, used their utmost endeavours to frustrate Poulter's designs. They obtained the lease of a piece of ground in what was called The Park, Southwark, on which they erected a building at an expense of 300*l*., for the purpose of a school and a meeting-house. When the place was no longer used as a place of worship, the service was removed to the meeting-house in St. Thomas's Street. Thus originated the Gravel Lane Charity School. In 1740 the meeting-house was removed to Deadman's Place, the building was let for various purposes, and the profits were devoted to the support of the school. Shortly after 1783 a new meeting-house was erected in Union Street, whither the congregation of the Protestant Dissenters was removed.

The place was for some time called John Bunyan's Meeting-house. The lease of the ground was dated January, 1687, and the building must have taken some months to erect. Now as John Bunyan died on 31 May, 1688, at Bedford, and only visited London once in a year, he could not have preached in it on more than one occasion. For further particulars see Wilkinson's 'Londina Illustrata,' London, 1825, with two illustrations.   EVERARD HOME COLEMAN.
71, Brecknock Road.

The building to which MR. HIBGAME refers can hardly be the original Zoar Chapel in which Bunyan preached, for John Timbs, in his 'Curiosities of London' (1855), says, "The chapel was used as a wheelwright's shop prior to its being pulled down, when the pulpit in which Bunyan had preached was removed to the Methodist Chapel, Palace Yard, Lambeth." Where is this pulpit now? There is an engraving of it in 'Interesting and Remarkable Places,' by C. Mackenzie (n.d.), and the accompanying letterpress is as follows :—

"This treasured relic is in the Methodist Chapel, Palace Yard, Lambeth. It appears that the pulpit came from the Meeting-house in Zoar Street, where Bunyan was allowed to deliver his discourses, by favour of his friend Dr. Thomas Barlow, Bishop of Lincoln, to whom it belonged. Here Bunyan preached whenever he visited London; and if only one day's notice were given, the place would not contain half the people who assembled. Three thousand had been sometimes gathered together in that remote part of the town; and even on a dark winter's morning, at seven o'clock, not less than twelve hundred."

In my copy of 'Old and New London,' vi. 40 (n.d.), I observe that the writer was apparently uncertain as to whether Zoar Chapel did or did not then exist. He, however, mentions the existence of two engravings, one dated 1812 and the other 1864. Probably a comparison of these with the present building before it finally disappears might throw some valuable light upon the point.

While on the subject of Bunyan, I should like to ask if it is known where "Mr. Gammin's meeting-house, near Whitechapel,"

NOTES AND QUERIES.

stood. Here it was that Bunyan preached his last sermon, on Sunday, 19 August, 1688. This sermon was, I believe, eventually printed, but I am at present unaware of its title. JOHN T. PAGE.
West Haddon, Northamptonshire.

GUINEA (9th S. viii. 461).—The following epigram from 'Elegant Extracts,' 1790, vol. i. p. 838, if not taking up too much room in your columns, may prove amusing and interesting. The name of the author is not given :—

As Quin and Foote, one day walk'd out
  To view the country round,
In merry mood, they chatting stood,
  Hard by the village-pound.

Foote from his poke, a shilling took,
  And said. "I'll bet a penny,
In a short space, within this place,
  I'll make this piece a guinea."

Upon the ground, within the pound
  The shilling soon was thrown :
"Behold," says Foote, "the thing's made out,
  For there is one pound one."

"I wonder not," says Quin, "that thought,
  Should in your head be found,
Since that's the way, your debts you pay—
  One shilling in the pound."

What are called spade-ace guineas are frequently hung on watch-chains.
JOHN PICKFORD, M.A.
Newbourne Rectory, Woodbridge.

SHELLEY'S COTTAGE AT LYNMOUTH, DEVON (9th S. viii. 523).—Prof. Edward Dowden, in his life of the poet (1886), vol. i. p. 278, says in a foot-note :—

"The house occupied by Shelley has been pulled down and another is built on the site. The precise spot was pointed out by Mary Blackmore, adopted daughter of Shelley's landlady, to Miss Blind. 'It is,' Miss Blind writes, 'at Lynmouth, not Lynton, not touching the river, but some way back on the other side of the road.' Mrs. Blackmore had a vivid recollection of Shelley."
A. R. BAYLEY.

"HALSH" (9th S. viii. 81, 255, 327, 411, 509, 529).—Courtesy seems to require that I should acknowledge the communication at the last reference of the writer who signs Q. V. (If I knew that those letters were his initials it would save a seeming circumlocution.) Firstly, then, does not his instance show that the 'Dictionary' is incorrect in indicating that "halch" is obsolete, seeing that he cites it as in use ? I cannot at the moment decide this question definitely, because I have not seen the paper mentioned. And, secondly, "halch" being conceded, "halsh" also should be recorded as a main word. Moreover, "halsh" and "halsh-band" should be given as substantives, ARTHUR MAYALL.

"KNEVEL" (9th S. ix. 9).—This is certainly not "pure English." It is Low German and Dutch. The corresponding form in High German is Knebel, of which Dr. Kluge, in his 'Etymological German Dictionary,' 1891, remarks that it is still doubtful whether in this sense, first recorded in modern High German, it is developed out of the O.H.G. knebil, "cross-beam, girder, cross-bar, cord, fetter, knuckle," or whether it is another word, connected with Anglo-Saxon cenep, Old Frisian kenep, Old Norse kampr, "moustache." Be this as it may, the lost English word for the hair on the upper lip is not knevel, but rather kemp, which is defined by Dr. Murray as now meaning "coarse or stout hair......occurring in wool," but must once have had the force of the Anglo-Saxon cenep, from which it appears to be derived. JAS. PLATT, Jun.

Mackay's assertion that knevel is pure English is utterly erroneous. It is Dutch, and is more explicitly written knevelbaard, defined as "barba vestiens superius labrum, cornua superioris barbæ" ('Kilianus Auctus,' 1642) ; "the Muschadoes on the upper-lipp" (Hexham, 1658). Knevel has other meanings, especially, e.g., those of a packer's-stick (pakstok) and a "korte dikke knuppel, dien men sommige dieren dwars door den bek doet" (i.e., a short thick stick put transversely through the muzzle of certain animals), whence probably the application of the word to the moustache.

The moustache, which we know from Julius Cæsar was cultivated by the ancient Britons ("capilloque sunt promisso atque omni parte corporis rasa præter caput et labrum superius," 'De Bello Gall.,' v. 14), was also retained by the Anglo-Saxons ("The Englysshemen, at those dayes," says Fabyan, "vsed the heer of theyr ouer lyppes shadde [i.e., parted] and nat shauen"), in whose tongue it was called cenep.* Whether there was another word for it, my acquaintance with Old English is not sufficient to enable me to say. Cenep, however, appears to have no affinity with knevel.

Our word moustache was taken, not from the Spaniards, but from the French, who had borrowed it from the Italians, the earliest known use of the French word dating from the fifteenth century ("Grec portant la barbette moustache," Jean Le Maire, quoted in Hatzfeld's dictionary). The Old French

* I find this word in the plural in the 'A.-S. Chronicles,' an. 1056, ed. Thorpe, who hazards a wrong rendering; and it is given with the meaning of bridle or bridle-bit (lupatum) in Wright-Wülcker's 'Vocabularies' (31, 4; 486, 16; cf. 430, 14),

word (see 9th S. ii. 389) was *grenon, gernon,* or *guernon,* which presumably fell into disuse when shaving became general in France in the fifteenth century ; and the 'Dictionnaire de Trévoux' tells us that *moustache* was sometimes employed to denote the side whiskers. Mackay is equally at fault in asserting that we must have had an English word for the hair on the upper lip long before "moustache" was introduced. I have never met with such a word in Middle English, and after our adoption of the French word writers made a sad hash of the spelling, as may be seen by the examples quoted by Fairholt in his 'Costume,' a book not at my hand, or by those given in Nares's 'Glossary' under the words 'Monchato,' 'Mouchato,' 'Mutchato,' as well as by Hexham's *muschado* (mentioned above), *muchato,* and *mouchato* ("een Snot-baerdt, ofte Knevel-baerdt, A Snottie-beard, or Snottie Muchatoes," and " Mouchatoes. Siet Mustaches"—a cross-reference not carried out). The quotation from Le Maire is curious for its allusion to the Greeks. For whereas there is no word in classical Latin for "moustache," the ancient Greeks denoted it by μύσταξ (see the fourteenth idyl of Theocritus), which, passing into mediæval Latin in the form *mystax,* gave origin to the Romance words.

The Dutch *knevel,* it may be observed in conclusion, is identical with the German *Knebel.*   F. ADAMS.
115, Albany Road, Camberwell.

BEAULIEU AS A PLACE-NAME (9th S. vi. 87, 216 ; viii. 397 ; ix. 17).—Beaulieu-en-Argonne is a beautiful village of 237 inhabitants in the diocese of Verdun (Meuse). The Abbey of Beaulieu, which was founded in the year 642 by St. Rouin, a native of Scotland, received in 1610 the reform from the Benedictine Abbey of St. Vannes, and is now a ruin. Please to read 'Recherches Historiques sur l'Abbaye de Beaulieu,' by Aug. Lemaire, in-8 (Bar-le-Duc, 1873).   ABBÉ BENOIT.

TENNIS : ORIGIN OF THE NAME (9th S. ix. 27).—The difficulty about accepting the origin proposed here is twofold : (1) the word *tenez,* in French, does not, and never did, mean "take it," as suggested ; and (2) there is no iota of evidence that the exclamation was ever habitual in French tennis-courts with anything like that meaning. Prof. Skeat, of course, suggests nothing of the sort. He knows well enough that the exclamations "tiens!" and "tenez!" are mere expressions of surprise. I suppose, I may have played in French tennis-courts more frequently, per-

haps, than any other contributor to 'N. & Q.,' and I have certainly heard those exclamations many hundreds of times, but never from a server who was delivering or had just delivered a service, and only from a player surprised by the unlooked-for bound of a ball in one direction when he had expected it to bound in another. As to the first difficulty, *tenir* means, in its primary sense, *to hold,* not *to take.* A very rudimentary knowledge of French should be sufficient to settle that. As to the Latin words *excipe* and *accipe,* I do not think they are enough to establish the peculiar use of a French exclamation, which rests on no other foundation whatever.   JULIAN MARSHALL.

LONDON M.P.s (9th S. viii. 524).—I have much pleasure in affording the following information, extracted by me from the parish register of St. Andrew Undershaft, London, relating to William Love (citizen and draper), Alderman and Sheriff of London, and M.P. for same 1661-81, and in 1689 until his death, which must, I think, have taken place in April (rather than "in May," as stated by MR. W. D. PINK) of the latter year, considering the date of his burial. He appears also to have resided at Clapham, in Surrey, where he died, and where probably some of his children were born and baptized. In any history of that parish further particulars respecting the family will no doubt be met with, but I have not had time to make the reference.

Baptisms.
1651, Dec. 20. William, s. of Wm. and Ellisabeth [*sic*] Loue.
1660, April 17. Sammuell [*sic*], s. of Mr. Wm. Loue, Alderman.
Burials.
1654, Sep. 30. A d. of Mr. Wm. Loue.
1664, March 25. Edwd., s. of Wm. Loue, Esqr.
1664, April 3. Joseph, s. of Wm. Loue, Esqr.
1677-8, Feb. 23. Sarah Ward, died in Ald. Loues ho.—bur. at Bethlehem.
1689, May 1. Wm. Loue, Essq. [*sic*], died at Clapham in Surry.
1694, Aug. 3. Mrs. Elizabeth, relict Wm. Love, Esq., from Clapham.

The same parish register contains other (and later) burial entries relating to the family.
       W. I. R. V.

"SAWE" (9th S. viii. 424, 448). — May I trouble F. P. to construe the rest of the phrase in which this word occurs ? "William ......carpenter and top-sawyer who is to be made in Calais," strikes one as an odd expression. Did *saw-pits* and the relative *top-sawyers* exist at all in 1369 ?   Q. V.

Your correspondent gets the meaning of top-sawyer (which sounds smart) out of "maistre de la sawe" by disregarding the adjected phrase "qu'est a ffaire"—an easy, but far from commendable mode of interpretation. One may wonder why an English word should be used when a French one was handy, *sie* or *sigue* (see Scheler, *s.v.* 'Scier'). But fancy the post of *maître* of a *saw in course of manufacture!*　　　F. ADAMS.

VERSES WANTED (9ᵗʰ S. viii. 144).—The verses referred to are probably those beginning

　　Comes, at times, a stillness as of even,

and forming hymn No. 641 in the 'Office Hymnbook' (Pickering & Chatto, 1890). They are there said to be the property of the Rev. I. Gregory Smith.

　　　　JOHN B. WAINEWRIGHT.

ANNE BILSON (9ᵗʰ S. viii. 464).—Anne, the wife of Thomas Bilson, Bishop of Winchester, was one of the five daughters of Thomas Mill, Esq., of Grove Place, Nursling, co. Hants, by his wife Jane, daughter of Richard Sutton, of Sarum (see addenda to 'Vis. Dorset, 1623,' Colby and Rylands, p. 17).

Thomas Mill (younger son of John Mill, a wealthy merchant of Southampton, d. 1551) was Recorder of Southampton, and represented that borough in Parliament in 1553; he died in 1560. His only son, Sir Richard Mill, Knt. (born 1556-7), was Sheriff of Hants in 1593-4; M.P. for Hants 1597; died, *s.p.*, 20 Oct., 1613. The remains of a handsome monument erected to his memory may still be seen in Nursling Church.

The bishop had two children by his wife Anne: a daughter Amy, the wife of Sir Richard Norton, Bart., of Rotherfield, co. Hants, and a son, Sir Thomas Bilson, Knt. (born 1591; married Susanna, daughter of Sir William Uvedale, Knt., of Wickham, co. Hants, on 6 August, 1612; knighted at Royston 25 Oct., 1613; M.P. for Winchester 1614; died 1649), of Mapledurham, near Petersfield, co. Hants, where his descendants resided until the death, without issue, of his great-grandson Leonard Bilson, M.P. for Petersfield, on 6 Oct., 1715.

There is a record in the Petersfield parish registers of the burial of "Anne Bilson, widow," on 6 Nov., 1643, which doubtless refers to the bishop's widow.

　　　　ALF. T. EVERITT.

High Street, Portsmouth.

BURIAL SERVICE READ OVER A RAIL (9ᵗʰ S. viii. 524).—I find this paragraph unsatisfactory. It is not yet possible for a man to fall into "a furnace of molten metal," nor is iron now "run into rails"; while the article usually described as "a rail" would be some yards in length. If your correspondent had addressed the two unanswerable inquiries direct to the "brother of his friend," he would probably have been informed that no such occurrences took place. If the statement can have had its origin from reports of an occurrence at one of the blast furnaces at Middlesbrough some years ago, the actual circumstances were widely different.

　　　　WILLIAM G. NORRIS.

Coalbrookdale.

OLD SONGS (9ᵗʰ S. viii. 104, 212, 351, 472).—The author of the 'Beggar's Petition,' beginning "Pity the sorrows of a poor old man," was the Rev. Thomas Moss, B.A., who died in 1808. There is a notice of him in the 'Dictionary of National Biography' (vol. xxxix. p. 184).

　　　　WILLIAM E. A. AXON.

Manchester.

'CORNHILL MAGAZINE' ILLUSTRATIONS (9ᵗʰ S. ix. 29).—Mrs. Richmond Ritchie says:—

"My father drew the designs [of the initial letter T], and an employé at Smith & Elder's copied them on to the wood. But it wasn't satisfactory altogether. Then came Mr. Walker's drawings."

　　　　HENRIETTA COLE.

96, Philbeach Gardens, S.W.

COMMISSION OF SEWERS (9ᵗʰ S. viii. 485).—The Commissioners of Sewers were in early reigns appointed at the pleasure of the Crown, in all parts of the realm wherever needful, by commission under the Great Seal, granted *pro re nata*, such commissions to endure for five and sometimes for ten or fifteen years.

By statute 23 Henry VIII. it was enacted that the commissions were to be at the discretion and nomination of the Lord Chancellor, Lord Treasurer, and Chief Justices, and to continue ten years unless repealed by a new commission. The duties of the Commissioners of Sewers were to overlook the repairs of sea-banks and sea-walls, the cleansing of rivers, public streams, and ditches, &c., for the carrying off of water, and were limited to the county for which they were specially appointed. They were empowered to make laws and ordinances for the carrying out of such repairs, and to assess and levy such rates as they deemed necessary for that purpose. They might decree the sale of lands in default of payment of such rate, but their decrees were to be certified into Chancery and to have the royal assent; and the Commissioners were subject to the jurisdiction of the Court of King's Bench.

The Commissions of Sewers are enrolled on the dorse of the Patent Rolls.

Proceedings before the Commissioners of Sewers range from Edward II. to Henry VI.

Laws and ordinances of the Commissioners range from 42 Elizabeth to 1831, and include decrees relating to the Bedford Level made in Charles II.'s reign.

The above information is taken from Mr. Scargill-Bird's 'Guide to the Public Records,' and the documents themselves are to be found in the Public Record Office.   E. A. Fry.
Birmingham.

G. A. M. will find some information as to the existing law on this subject (from stat. 23 Henry VIII. c. 5 onward) in the current edition of the 'Index to the Statutes in Force,' under 'Drainage and Improvement of Land,' heading 1. He will also find a Commission of Sewers ordered as early as 1314-5 for the Yorkshire Dove ('Rolls of Parliament,' vol. i. p. 319, col. 1).   O. O. H.

Your correspondent G. A. M. will find much information on this subject in Robert Callis's 'Reading upon the Statutes of Sewers,' the first edition of which was issued in 1647. The late Serjeant Woolrych wrote a useful book on the law of sewers, but I cannot give the title. Dugdale's 'History of Embanking and Draining' may also be consulted with advantage.   Edward Peacock,
A Commissioner of Sewers.

For a brief history of the formation and doings of the above see article on 'Drainage of the Great Level' in *Fenland Notes and Queries* for April, July, and October, 1901.
J. H. S.

Irish in Pembrokeshire (8th S. i. 434).— A query at this reference still, I believe, remains unanswered. Mr. R. Linn, of Christchurch, New Zealand, quoting a review in the *Edinburgh Review* of April, 1886, of Bagwell's 'Ireland under the Tudors,' wants to know whether the settlement of Irish in Pembrokeshire was made in the time of Henry VIII., and whether their descendants can be recognized at the present time in any way. The following is an extract from 'The Welsh People,' by Principal J. Rhys and D. Brynmor Jones, a work published in 1900, referring to this settlement :—

"We read in the history of Pembrokeshire by George Owen, who lived in the time of Elizabeth, that the Anglo-Flemish portion of his native county was so overrun by Irishmen, that in some parishes the clergyman was found to be the only inhabitant who was not Irish. This it is true was an exceptional time, as it was at the end of the war known as Tyrone's Rebellion, but many of the exiles must have settled in Pembrokeshire. In fact Mr. Henry Owen, the learned editor of George Owen's works, remarks that the descendants of these Irishmen can still be traced."

I am informed that this colony is still in evidence. The east end of the town of Pembroke is largely composed of Irish folk, whose ancestors probably settled there at the time of the colonization above referred to.
J. P. Lewis.

Song Wanted (9th S. viii. 364, 510). — I cannot give Gnomon any information as to the 'National Song-Book' about which he inquires, but I can give him the song which he wants. It is in 'The Banquet of Thalia ; or, the Fashionable Songster's Pocket Memorial,' p. 94 :—

THE GODS OF THE GREEKS.
Words by G. A. Stevens.

I.

Once the gods of the Greeks, at ambrosial feast,
  Large bowls of rich nectar were quaffing ;
Merry Momus amongst them was sat as a guest :
  (Homer says the celestials love laughing.)
On each in the synod the humourist droll'd,
  So none could his jokes disapprove ;
He sung, reparteed, and some smart stories told,
  And at length he began upon Jove :

II.

"Sire ! Atlas, who long has the universe bore,
  Grows grievously tired of late ;
He says that mankind are much worse than before,
  So he begs to be eas'd of his weight."
Jove knowing the earth on poor Atlas was hurl'd,
  From his shoulders commanded the ball ;
Gave his daughter Attraction the charge of the world,
  And she hung it high up in his hall.

III.

Miss, pleas'd with the present, review'd the globe round
  To see what each climate was worth ;
Like a diamond the whole with an atmosphere bound,
  And she variously planted the earth :
With silver, gold, jewels, she India endow'd—
  France and Spain she taught vineyards to rear ;
What suited each clime, on each clime she bestow'd,
  And Freedom she found flourish'd here.

IV.

Four Cardinal Virtues she left in this isle,
  As guardians to cherish the root ;
The blossoms of Liberty then 'gan to smile,
  And Englishmen fed on the fruit.
Thus fed and thus bred, from a bounty so rare,
  O preserve it as free as 'twas given !
We will whilst we've breath ! nay, we'll grasp it in death !
  Then return it untainted to heav'n.

The prefatory address "to the public" in 'The Banquet of Thalia' is signed "F. Atkinson," and is dated "York, Nov. 19, 1792." At the end of the book is "From the Herald-Office, York, by Wilson, Spence, and Mawman, anno M,DCC,XC."

These dates disagree, but they take the song back to the eighteenth century.

According to Allibone's dictionary, George Alexander Stevens, a strolling player, dramatic author, vocalist, and lecturer, died 6 Sept., 1784.   ROBERT PIERPOINT.
St. Austin's, Warrington.

Miscellaneous.

NOTES ON BOOKS, &c.

Traces of the Elder Faiths of Ireland. By W. G. Wood-Martin, M.R.I.A. 2 vols. (Longmans & Co.)

A ZEALOUS worker in the fields of archæological research, Col. Wood-Martin is known as the historian of Sligo and the author of 'Pagan Ireland : a Handbook of Irish Pre-Christian Antiquities,' and, other works. His present book is to some extent an expansion of the Handbook previously mentioned. It is almost too comprehensive in scheme, and, though primarily intended for the folk-lorist, aims also at being, among other things, a summary of geological conditions. While maintaining generally that investigations into and speculations concerning the great glacial epoch have an important bearing upon the development of the human race, the author holds that, as almost all parts of the world except "these Islands" have been regarded as the cradle of the human race, "man must necessarily have been some time in existence, and must have acquired some faint religious ideas before he found a home on these, at that time, icebound shores." He begins, accordingly, with an account of the period when Ireland, as well as Britain, was united to the Continent, and furnishes maps showing the area of volcanic action in Great Britain and Ireland during part of the Tertiary period. The illustrations, it may be said, which are very numerous, constitute a striking and important feature in the volumes. The first of these, the frontispiece to the first volume, shows an ideal landscape of the north of Ireland in the Tertiary period, with two huge volcanoes, each throwing forth a pall of smoke. Similar designs and maps follow, presenting the aspects of the land and its occupants, concerning which our knowledge is of the scantiest. Quitting this domain, where all is practically conjecture, Col. Wood-Martin comes to first proofs of human action in the shape of flint weapons, quoting from the 1881 edition of Sir John Evans's 'Ancient Stone Implements' (the latest edition is 1897). We are here on more familiar ground, though even here the imagination is afforded some play, and we have a characteristic, if fanciful, picture of two fair-skinned warriors combating the grizzly bear with a rude lance and a hatchet of stone. Representations of the mammoth, the gigantic Irish deer, and other extinct animals follow, and there is a design, by which the collector may well profit, of the manufacture of sham Irish antiquities, which seems now to be a fairly prosperous occupation. At this early stage, even, we come upon an illustration of the paganism which, as students know, still exists beneath the veneer of Christianity. To use a happy phrase of Col. Wood-Martin, Christianity has smoothed over and swallowed paganism, and "the contour of its prey, as is the case of the boa constrictor, can be distinctly traced under the glistening colours of its beautiful skin." The pagan illustration of which we speak is that of kindling the "need fire," which was practised in the last century. When cattle were affected with a disease called "big-head" every fire in the townland in which it had broken out was extinguished, and the inhabitants, assembling at the infected farm, produced fresh fire by the well-known and primitive process of friction. When the sticks were ignited a great smoke was produced from "scraws" (sods covered with soot), and the animals were compelled to inhale this till water ran plentifully from mouth and nostrils. This curious survival is more pleasant to contemplate than the barbarous persecutions for witchcraft which have been practised at a period still later in date. Flint arrow and spear heads are supposed to possess the power of healing cattle, and instances are known of farmers finding it more profitable to keep them for such purpose than to sell them to collectors. Cave remains are familiar in Ireland, though no very startling discovery of such has been made. Fairy doctors, as they are called, still regard flint instruments as elf bolts, and sometimes use them as a cure for human ailments as well as those of cattle. So late as 1480 we hear of an Ulster chief O'Kane, whose house, when he received a visit from a Bohemian nobleman, lodged sixteen women, all naked except for a loose mantle. The chief himself had only the same scanty garb and shoes, and took off both on entering the house, inviting the guest to follow his example. Some interesting particulars are given concerning bonefires. The views of the Colonel on Irish literature and Irish MSS. will be far from acceptable to the younger school of Irish students. The former is said to be mere protoplasm, and with certain reservations it is alleged to be difficult to discover an Irish MS. which to the ordinary nineteenth-century reader does not appear "extremely childish." "We possess," says the Colonel, "in Irish no work of genius comparable to the 'Nibelungen Lied' or the 'Song of Roland.' To speak of the 'Táin-Bó-Cuailnge' as a Gaelic 'Iliad' seems, to say the least, an imprudent comparison." Again he says : "There is nothing, either in material or literary remains, to support the assertion of the monastic chroniclers as to the glories of the Green Isle of the West at the time when the first missionaries began their attempt to convert the people to Christianity."

In the second volume we are more strictly in the land of folk-lore. The opening chapter of this, concerning fairies, is the most interesting in the work. Those which follow on marriage lore, well worship, tree worship, stone worship, and similar subjects are of signal value. Some of the information given is from our own columns, and much of it is familiar to the general student. Enough that is characteristically Irish remains to render the book indispensable to the scholar. So well has Col. Wood-Martin done his work, and so valuable is the information he has collected, that we feel disposed to be lenient to some proofs of carelessness, such, for instance, as talking of the 'Urn Burial' of Sir John (*sic*) Browne, and to a rather aggravating habit of calling antiquaries "antiquarians." He displays much zeal and much erudition, and his work, from which, did space permit, we should like largely to quote, is a fine contribution to a study of unending interest.

Besides being pleasant reading, it fulfils his aim, and is "the romance of religion in Ireland."

Isopel Berners. By George Borrow. Edited by Thomas Seccombe. (Hodder & Stoughton.)

IN printing as a consecutive and integral story the chapters in 'Lavengro' and 'Romany Rye' which deal with Borrow's life in "the dingle" and his association with Isopel Berners, Mr. Seccombe renders a genuine and an almost ideal service to the lovers of romantic fiction. It would be easy to assert that the words employed are inappropriate. Let them stand, however. To us the story of Isopel Berners belongs to romantic fiction of the most enchanting class. Isopel is in some respects to be numbered with the heroines who will never leave us, with much, as the author would say, of Brynhild and something of Tess of the Durbervilles. She is best, however, taken as herself, and as such she is far too good for her lover, who lets her go, and pules unavailingly over her loss. We thank Mr. Seccombe for reintroducing us to her. We were young when we made her acquaintance, and failed to estimate her aright. Now we serve her and are of her train. We thank Mr. Seccombe, too, for a delightful introduction, worthy of the story, though we disagree with every word of it. With regard to Borrow, we dissent from received opinion. As was said by a Frenchman of a woman, "She is not pretty, she is worse," we say of Borrow's descriptions they are not true, they are more alluring than truth. We have no more idea as to what "the dingle" is like than if it were in fairyland, and we are not sure that it is not. It has no more reality than that scene in an Irish schoolroom where the master is shown us poring over a "huge Elzevir Flaccus"! or than Borrow's linguistic acquirements, whether obtained from the "émigré of the ancien[ne] cour" or from whispered conferences with Ursula behind the hedge. Borrow has, however, a truth beyond truth, and is always to be prized and loved, though for reasons precisely different from those often advanced in his favour. As for Isopel Berners, she dwells with Di Vernon, with whom she has this in common that her creator got afraid of her, as Shakespeare is said to have done of Mercutio. Her leavetaking is not her own, however. That is all Borrow. It is a wonderful composition, but from Borrow we expect no less.

Frederick the Great on Kingcraft. From the Original MS. By Sir J. William Whittall. (Longmans & Co.)

THE story of the MS. "Les Matinées du Roi de Prusse, écrites par Lui-même, A.D. 1764," which is here printed in its integrity for the first time, reads like a page out of one of Haggard's or Stevenson's romances. Marshal Savary, Duke of Rovigo, the Buonapartist general, arrives at Smyrna as a destitute *réfugié* in the year 1816. He and his companion General Lallimand had been picked up at sea in an open boat, with "only the clothes they were in." Happily these clothes had a pocket, and the pocket contained as his inseparable *vade-mecum* this remarkable MS. Having been hospitably sheltered and entertained by Mr. Charles Whittall, who was a resident factor at Smyrna, Savary, on his departure, presented his host with a copy of the 'Matinées' as a small souvenir of his gratitude. The original MS., he said, he had surreptitiously

appropriated when visiting the palace of Sans Souci in company with the Emperor Napoleon. This autograph exemplar has disappeared, so that we have to accept the copy on the authority of Sir J. Whittall's grandfather, which, he assures us, is unimpeachable. Carlyle, however, utterly discredited the authenticity of the document.

These instructions of Frederick the Great, written for the benefit of his nephew and heir, in their cynical revelation of his private thoughts and the *naïveté* of their non-morality, often remind us of the similarly ingenuous counsels of Chesterfield to his son. His ideas on religion, politics, and military affairs are set down with startling sincerity, naked and unashamed. "When I arrive at a place I always have a fatigued air, and I show myself to my people with a bad overcoat and a badly combed wig. These are but trifles, but they often make a singular impression." One poor fellow pitied him on seeing his bad overcoat: "He did not know that I had a good coat underneath." When about to review his troops he gets up beforehand the names of three or four of the lieutenants and sergeants, which he produces as he passes along the ranks: "This gives me a singular reputation for memory and reflection." He eats and drinks sparingly in public at a dinner prepared by a German cook, but "when I am in my private apartments my French cook does all he can to satisfy me, and I confess that I am somewhat fastidious. I am near my bed, and that is what removes any anxiety as to how much I drink." Religion is a very good thing for one's subjects, "but a king is not wise to have any himself." "I understand by the word 'politics' that we must always seek to make dupes of others." If the picture here revealed of a libertine in morals, a sceptic in religion, a posture-monger in matters of state and government, was really drawn by his own hand, this Machiavellian monarch had little claim to be entitled "Great."

The remaining and larger portion of Sir J. Whittall's book has nothing to do with Frederick. It consists partly of family reminiscences of a gossiping anecdotal character and partly of a collection of Turkish folk-tales and parables picked up in Asia Minor. The best of these are attributed to Nasreddin Hoja, the Eulenspiegel or Joe Miller of the Turks in the fifteenth century. The likeness of the author and his family referred to on p. 140 as forming the frontispiece of the volume *non est* in the copy before us.

Selections from the English Poets. — The Dunbar Anthology, 1401-1508. — The Surrey and Wyatt Anthology, 1509-1547. Edited by Prof. Edward Arber, F.S.A. (Frowde.)

PROF. ARBER'S admirable 'Anthology,' the best and most comprehensive we possess, has already received full recognition at our hands. It is now being reissued in a form even more attractive than that it formerly assumed, and with the agreeable addition of portraits of the most eminent poets. As the series is now complete, it is appearing in consecutive volumes, each of which may be obtained separately. In the first volume the portraits consist of Geoffrey Chaucer, John Lydgate presenting a work to the Earl of Salisbury, and Earl Rivers doing the like to King Edward IV.; in the second the frontispiece is a medallion portrait of Wyatt, other likenesses being the Earl of Surrey, Sir Thomas More, Lord Vaux, and Andrew

Boorde. Prof. Arber's services to literature merit, and, indeed, obtain the highest recognition. No previous or contemporary compiler has done so much to spread a knowledge of the best poetry. In his short introductory notes he might with advantage supply beside the praise of poetry of Coleridge that even more inspired of George Wither. Prof. Arber justly claims that the collection is the most diversified and representative in the language. It is that and more.

The Era Annual for 1902. (*Era* Office.)

During more than thirty years the 'Era Almanack' has constituted a trustworthy and useful theatrical record, supplying in its later numbers the dates of first performances of plays in London and the country, in Paris, and in Berlin, a stage obituary, and similar matters. At the outset, when E. L. Blanchard, with his unrivalled stage knowledge, furnished an account of the principal London theatres, it had even stronger claims. The latest volume gives portraits of the theatrical celebrities who have died during the past year.

The Upper Norwood Athenæum again sends us its *Record of Winter Meetings and Summer Excursions, 1900-1901.* This little society, established a quarter of a century ago, still flourishes, and is doing good work. During the year many places were visited for the first time, and the papers read are full of interest. Considerable pains have evidently been taken in collecting the various facts. It is pleasant to find the help so cordially given by clergymen and owners of property in the different districts. Among the papers read was one by Mr. Truslove on Crowhurst Place and church, in which mention is made of the slab in the church to the memory of John Angell, who died in 1670, in his seventy-eighth year, and who "bequeathed his soul to God, his body to the earth, his faith to the Carlists, and his example to his children." There is also a tablet to Justinian Angell, who married Elizabeth, eldest daughter of John Scaldwell, of Brixton, and it would seem that the present Angell Road, Brixton, is named after her; also that Crowhurst Road derives its title from the fact of the lady's residence at Crowhurst. Mr. Potter read a paper, 'Bexley and Crayford,' when the tomb in Bexley Churchyard of Francis Moore the elder, the founder of 'Old Moore's Almanac,' who died March 31st, 1684, was visited. In this district the custom used to prevail of selling beer by the yard, some of the measures being still in existence. Mr. Thomas Stock also read a paper on Hertford, and mentions the kind way in which the ramblers were received at the church of St. Andrew by the Rev. Evan Killan Roberts, who produced the old registers, and showed the Pre-Reformation altar, which is one of the few remaining that contain the slot for the Holy Relics. The 'Record' is well illustrated, some of the illustrations being original, while many are due to the kindness of the proprietors of the *Illustrated London News* and *Sketch* and the *Lady's Pictorial*, and the *Sporting and Dramatic* Publishing Company. Nothing but praise can be said of the careful editing of Mr. J. Stanley and Mr. W. F. Harradence.

The excellent *Astronomy for the Young* of Mr. William Thynne Lynn, B.A., F.R.A.S., the best existing work of its class, has reached a second edition. Prefixed to this is a view of the Royal Observatory, Greenwich. Mr. G. Stoneman is the publisher.

The *Playgoer*, edited by Fred Dangerfield (Dawbarn & Ward), has reached its fourth number. It is not enough of a chronicle. Its value would be increased were a *résumé*, with casts, supplied of the month's theatrical novelties.

The 'English Dialect Dictionary' is now sufficiently advanced to enable the editor to state definitely the date of its completion. The whole of the Dictionary, consisting of about 4,700 pages, contained in six volumes, will be completed before the end of 1905. Four of these six volumes are already printed, viz., Vol. I. (A to C, 855 pages), Vol. II. (D to G, 772 pages), Vol. III. (H to L, 698 pages), Vol. IV. (M to Q, 688 pages). Vol. V. (R, S, about 850 pages) is now being printed, and will be finished in November. Vol. VI. will consist of the letters T to Z, the supplement, the bibliography of the many thousands of books specially excerpted for the Dictionary, and a comprehensive comparative grammar of all the dialects treated historically. Great advantages are offered to subscribers willing to compound for the remaining portion of the work. Such should communicate with Mr. Henry Frowde at the Clarendon Press.

Mr. Fred Hitchin-Kemp's 'History of the Kemp and Kempe Families' is now all but ready for delivery to subscribers by the Leadenhall Press, and the author is already contemplating further genealogical labour.

Notices to Correspondents.

We must call special attention to the following notices:—

On all communications must be written the name and address of the sender, not necessarily for publication, but as a guarantee of good faith.

We cannot undertake to answer queries privately.

To secure insertion of communications correspondents must observe the following rules. Let each note, query, or reply be written on a separate slip of paper, with the signature of the writer and such address as he wishes to appear. When answering queries, or making notes with regard to previous entries in the paper, contributors are requested to put in parentheses, immediately after the exact heading, the series, volume, and page or pages to which they refer. Correspondents who repeat queries are requested to head the second communication "Duplicate."

Brandon Hill.—1. 'Jacqueline: a Tale' (1814) is by Samuel Rogers, the banker-poet. It originally appeared in the same volume with Lord Byron's 'Lara.' 2 'The Garden of Florence,' by John Hamilton (1821), is by John Hamilton Reynolds, the friend of Keats.

NOTICE.

Editorial communications should be addressed to "The Editor of 'Notes and Queries'"—Advertisements and Business Letters to "The Publisher"—at the Office, Bream's Buildings, Chancery Lane, E.C.

We beg leave to state that we decline to return communications which, for any reason, we do not print; and to this rule we can make no exception.

LONDON, SATURDAY, FEBRUARY 1, 1902.

CONTENTS. — No. 214.

Notes.

FATHER PAUL SARPI'S 'LETTERS,' 1693.

I CAN learn nothing of "Edward Brown, Rector of Sundridge in Kent," the translator of these 'Letters,' except what he tells us in his dedication to the Earl of Nottingham. The late Mr. Henry Huth issued in 1874 for private circulation a volume entitled 'Prefaces, Dedications, and Epistles.' I never had the pleasure of seeing that book, but I am free to say that if Edward Brown's preface to Father Paul's 'Letters' has not been included, the volume is infinitely the poorer for it. But probably it might be found to be too long and too polemical for such a collection. A more truly unconventional preface could scarcely be. Brown writes as if he had his readers seated round his parlour table, and in the intervals, so to speak, of dispensing the social amenities, pours forth all he knows about these 'Letters,' not in the formal language of the schools, but in the free-and-easy colloquialism of the market and the street. The very opening at once arrests attention :—

"Courteous Reader ; It may be, upon the great Credit and Repute that Father Paul has most deservedly with religious, wise and learned Men, that know how to value his Worth and Excellence, you will be so eager to know what there is in these Letters of his, which I have made ready for your Perusal, that you will skip over Prefaces, and every thing else that stands in your way, between this and them. And truly upon that Account, I could have been as well contented to say what I have to say about these things, at the further End of the Book, and to wait upon you there, but that a Preface must be what it is called, and cannot change its Place without changing its Name ; though a very excellent Person [Dr. Donne], and a very good Friend of Father Paul's, was once of the Mind, that a Man could not well be called a Reader, till he had read a Book over ; and did therefore design, he says, to have met his Reader at the End of his Book, and there tell him what he had to say about it. And if you should really do thus, you are welcome to begin where you please ; only be so kind, as to call in here as you come back, and let me tell you a few things about this excellent Person and these Letters, and others, which you ought to know, sooner or later, for your better Acquaintance with them. But if this Conceit of mine should chance to stop you a little here, and tempt you to stay till you come fairly to the Letters ; I hope that besides the Conquest of your Impatience, you will find somewhat that may help you to read them with better Judgment, and a more settled and pois'd Expectation."

The "Courteous Reader," it is to be presumed, is paying due heed to all that is being said, but on the eighteenth page the author breaks the even flow of his discourse in this somewhat unceremonious fashion :—

"Whilst I have been thus tediously talking of Letters in general, for ought I know, you have given me the slip, and are got somewhere else ; but 'tis all one if you have, you will read this some time or other. But to come a little nearer to our Business ; let me only tell you that this part of the Age has been happy (how miserable soever in other Respects) in the Publick Knowledg of many great Mens Letters."

Then he goes on again in his usual breezy way.

I may here say Father Paul's 'Letters' are, in themselves, singularly interesting ; and I am sure it is a matter for regret that Brown did not carry out his intention (as stated in the advertisement on p. cxviii) of issuing a second volume, which was meant to include a translation of Fulgentio's 'Life' of Father Paul (that of 1651, "by a Person of Quality," is a very disappointing production, and justly comes under our author's censure) as well as other interesting pieces. The purpose of this note, however, is not with the 'Letters,' but simply to register a number of familiar phrases scattered throughout the volume :—

Riff-raff stuff ; no better than it should be : which has been a Bone for them to pick ever since ; they call it a Nose of Wax, and the old Canary-bird Melchior Canus has a pretty Note to the same Tune ; Fardel of Lies ; addle-headed Greeks ; for ought I know, you have given me the slip ; the same Game they were playing ; 'tis not a farthing matter who sees it : finely japann'd and varnish'd over ; 'tis a thousand to one ; piddling Work ; 'tis as good looking for a Needle in a Bottle of Hay; here's a whole Knot of good Books; shewed his Teeth; like a Cock upon his own Dunghil; what is Sawce for a Goose, we say, is Sawce for a Gander; the more's the Pity; the Words and the Sense jump together; knowing Men to have an Eye to; to see the World turn'd topsy-turvy; his Disciple in all his Whimseys; a slippery sort of Man; was hugely put to it; rants and hectors; one Eye in their Heads; Bug-bear sort; betwixt sixes and sevens; another bout there; the Searchers are as sly as can be; as it is possible for such Sharks to be; sleep in a whole skin; let the future shift for itself; wheedled by them; we shall take a good nap; catch us napping; made use of for a stalking Horse; though they do not yet play above-board; buy a Cat in a Sack or a Pig in a Poke; dance Attendance; down in the Mouth; I do not value it a farthing; in spight of my own Teeth; shall be defended Tooth and Nail; meer hotch-potch; by hook or by crook; this rare Gim-crack; pinning Mens Faith upon other Mens Sleeves; from the Teeth outward; laugh on the wrong side of their Mouths; his Friend may go whistle to understand it; away they slip through his Fingers; in spight of his Teeth; no body would give a farthing for all the Wit and Craft they have; scared out of their seven Senses; set them together by the Ears; slink behind the Curtain; end in Smoak and nothing; have got the whipping Hand of us; but ten to one; no Army will budg a foot; they never boggle at any Promise; lay all their Heads together; not yet been as good as their word; Matter fit to hammer it out of; they have cock'd their Caps; it must needs be the Ace of Trumps; like a Turn-coat as he was; fit to leap out of their Skins; at the fag-end of all; still in his Swadling Clouts; There is something here upon the Anvil; trip up a Man's Heels that stands; go point-blank against it; They are buzzing their Pates about it; accept the Will for the Deed; the same hurly-burly; dive over Head and Ears; to stand in a Quondary; have been fain to let go the Fish; a sudden Occasion that call'd me out of Town; bestir his Stumps; his Empire handsell'd with more Work; ill will cannot forbear to shew its Teeth; takes into his Army Tag Rag and Bobtail; so they can but feather their own Nest; there are some that can swallow it as glibly as they do here; he trusts him no further than he can fling him; they do it bare-fac'd.

On the first fly-leaf of my copy of these 'Letters,' 1693, there is to be found the name of "Stuart Bickerstaffe," written in a round, bold, and legible hand. Immediately under this name there is written, apparently in a different hand and in a less decided colour of ink, "Donum Authoris." Then on the second fly-leaf there is written, "Mr. Brown Rector Sundridge and Editor of this book gave it me." But as this was not exactly what the writer meant to express, the whole is obliterated by the pen, and these words are substituted underneath: "The Authour gave me this book." The writing of these last two I take to be in character the same as that of "Stuart Bickerstaffe."

I should be much obliged if some kind reader of 'N. & Q.' could tell me anything regarding both "Stuart Bickerstaffe" and "Edward Brown, Rector of Sundridge in Kent."   A. S.

THE BIRTHPLACE OF MARGARET, COUNTESS OF RICHMOND.

SOME seven miles from Bedford, on the road between that town and Higham Ferrers, the birthplace of Archbishop Chicheley, and on the banks of the slow-flowing Ouse, is situated the quiet village of Bletsoe, with its church grey with antiquity, not far from the Midland Railway. Bletsoe was once the residence of one of the greatest families in England, the Beauforts, and now has for some four hundred years been the property of the noble family of St. John, styled Barons St. John of Bletsoe. Here was born that most benevolent of ladies Margaret Beaufort, the foundress of St. John's and Christ Colleges at Cambridge and the Lady Margaret Professorship of Divinity at Oxford. She is known by the names of Lady Margaret Beaufort, Margaret of Lancaster, and the Countess of Richmond, but usually by the simple title of Lady Margaret.

The old castle where this benevolent lady first saw the light in 1441 has been razed to the ground, but a considerable portion of the great mansion where the St. Johns lived is still in existence, a venerable structure covered with ivy, and the church continues to this day to be their burial-place. The vault is in the northern arm of the transept, and on the wall is a curious monument of Sir John St. John, who was brought up by Lady Margaret with her grandson Henry VIII., who made him guardian of his daughters the Princesses Mary and Elizabeth. There are one or two monuments of modern date to members of this ancient family, but of no great interest. From a common ancestor descended Henry St. John, Viscount Bolingbroke, in the days of Queen Anne, the great statesman, the friend of Harley and Atterbury, to whom Pope dedicated his fine poem 'An Essay on Man,' which has this [altered] address:—

> Awake, my St. John! leave all meaner things
> To low ambition, and the pride of kings.
> Let us (since life can little more supply
> Than just to look about us and to die)
> Expatiate free o'er all this scene of Man;
> A mighty maze! but not without a plan.

Bolingbroke died childless in 1751, and was buried in Battersea Church. It is probable that on the death of Queen Anne in 1714, had prompt measures been taken, her brother would have ascended the throne of England, and the story goes that Atterbury offered to put on his lawn sleeves and proclaim King James III. Thackeray, in 'Esmond,' has given a remarkable and graphic description of the state of parties at that era, when certainly at least one-half of the people of England were on the side of the exiled family of Stuart.

There are many portraits in existence of Lady Margaret. One at Knowsley, the seat of the Earl of Derby, is engraved in Lodge's 'Portraits.' The artist does not seem to be known, but was probably Holbein, as he painted the portrait of her third husband, Thomas Stanley, Earl of Derby, who predeceased her in 1504 Another very fine portrait, probably a replica of this, is in the hall of St. John's College, Cambridge; and there is a third at Melchbourne Park, the seat of Lord St. John. There are many smaller portraits in oils in existence of her, all depicting a nunlike figure with the hands clasped in prayer, bearing out the idea of her devotional character; and her effigy in Henry VII.'s Chapel in Westminster Abbey exactly corresponds. Her munificence was directed towards abodes of learning, and not to monastic foundations, though the object of both was much the same.

The first husband of this noble lady is buried in the presbytery of St. David's Cathedral, under a sumptuous tomb, on which it is said that Edmund Tudor was "father and brother of kings." He died in 1456, leaving an infant son only fifteen weeks old, afterwards Henry VII. This tomb was beautifully restored at the expense of the late Rev. John Lucy, of the ancient line of the Lucys of Charlecote, and rector of Hampton Lucy, co. Warwick. He also inserted at his own expense the beautiful mosaics and stained glass in the east window of the cathedral, which now needs a similar kindly and liberal hand for the restoration of the Lady Chapel at the eastern end. The well-known arms of Lucy, the three pikes or luces hauriant, may be seen on the encaustic tiles on the pavement of the presbytery. Her second husband was Sir Henry Stafford, second son of the great Duke of Buckingham, who probably fell in battle, and by him she had no issue. Her third husband was Thomas Stanley, the first Earl of Derby, who turned the scale in favour of her son at Bosworth Field in 1485, and proclaimed him king by the title of Henry VII. after the victory. He died in 1504, and was buried in the priory church of Burscough, in Lancashire, and by him she had no issue.

Lady Margaret just witnessed the accession of her grandson Henry VIII. in 1509, then a youth of great promise. She had seen many changes in her long life—the fierce struggles in the Wars of the Roses, the fatal battles of Towton, Mortimer's Cross, and Barnet, the accession of Richard III. and his final overthrow; but she seems to have held aloof from strife as much as one in her prominent position possibly could. Her great and wise counsellor was John Fisher, Bishop of Rochester, "a man," as Macaulay says, "worthy of a better age and a better cause." In her funeral sermon, preached by that prelate, it is said :—

"She was bounteous and lyberal to every person of her knowledge or acquaintance. Avarice and covetyse she most especially hated, and sorrowed it full moche in all persons, but specially in ony that belonged unto her."

The Ouse still flows by Bletsoe, and, although sluggish, it is rather picturesque, and the water-lilies are very beautiful. Cowper, who dwelt at Olney, some few miles higher up the river than Bletsoe, thus wrote of it and the lilies in some of his best-known lines :—

> The moon was shady, and soft airs
> Swept Ouse's silent tide,
> When, 'scaped from literary cares,
> I wandered on his side.
> It was the time when Ouse displayed
> His lilies newly blown:
> Their beauties I, intent, surveyed,
> And one I wished my own.

JOHN PICKFORD, M.A.
Newbourne Rectory, Woodbridge.

'BURIAL OF SIR JOHN MOORE.'—Although several articles have appeared in early volumes of ' N. & Q.' on the authorship of Wolfe's ode on the burial of Sir John Moore, I do not think there is any reference therein to the famous mistake that it was done

By the struggling moonbeams' misty light.

My attention was again directed to the subject recently by reading a "leader" in the *Daily News* in which the writer, commenting on mistakes made by popular writers on astronomical matters, shows a not very profound acquaintance with them himself, for he tells us that Sir Robert Ball (now Plumian Professor of Astronomy at Cambridge) took the trouble to make the calculation, and found that the moon was not visible at the date of the battle of Corunna. Now whether Sir Robert was the first person to point out the mistake in question I do not remember, but it is quite certain that he did *not* take the trouble to calculate what he could find at once in the 'Nautical Almanac' or any similar ephemeris. The moon was new at about 1 o'clock,

Greenwich time, on the afternoon of 16 Jan., 1809, the very day of the battle, so that "moonbeams" were quite out of the question. In the First Series of 'N. & Q.' (vol. vi. p. 274) is a letter from the clergyman, H. J. Symons (then at Hereford), who officiated at the interment, which did not take place until the morning after the general's death, when the principal part of the troops had embarked. Perhaps it may be permissible to mention that I feel a special interest, in addition to that which all my countrymen feel, in the circumstances connected with Moore's retreat, victory, and death, arising from the fact that the first service in which my father was employed as an army surgeon was as one of those who attended to the wounded brought back from Corunna.

W. T. LYNN.

Blackheath.

[For summary of early references see 9th S. vii. 463.]

"SITTING ON THE FENCE."—We are familiar with this phrase in politics. MR. DELEVINGNE in 7th S. i. 6 notes a classical illustration of what he describes as the Transatlantic phrase "Sitting on both sides of the fence." As regards the simpler phrase, we may note a passage written to Newman by

"a gifted and deeply earnest lady, who in a parabolical account of that time [1843] has described both my conduct as she felt it and her own feelings upon it. In a singularly graphic, amusing vision of pilgrims, who were making their way across a bleak common in great discomfort, and who were ever warned against, yet continually nearing, 'the King's highway' on the right, she says, 'All my fears and disquiets were speedily renewed by seeing the most daring of our leaders......suddenly stop short, and declare that he would go no further. He did not, however, take the leap at once, but quietly sat down on the top of the fence with his feet hanging towards the road, as if he meant to take his time about it, and let himself down easily.'"— 'Apologia pro Vita Sua,' 1882 ed., pp. 218–9.

When one remembers the very wide circulation of Newman's 'Apologia,' and the close attention with which it has been read, it is not difficult to think that the memory of this passage has unconsciously made the "Transatlantic phrase" more familiar to our lips than it might otherwise have become.

WILLIAM GEORGE BLACK.

Ramoyle, Dowanhill Gardens, Glasgow.

"GROAT."—An "Order in Council approving Proclamation declaring certain silver Groats or Fourpences current in the Colony of Trinidad and Tobago" ('Statutory Rules and Orders of 1901,' No. 985) is mentioned in the current 'Monthly List of Official Publications.' Miss G. B. Rawlings ('Story of the British Coinage,' 1898, p. 209) states that "in

1888 the coinage of the silver groat or fourpenny piece was resumed for" British Guiana.

It would be interesting to know whether the name *groat* is now used in either of the colonies named, or whether the proclamation archaizes merely fancifully. The 'H.E.D.' mentions the reissue of 1888, with the note, "The name was neither officially recognized nor commonly used."

May I invite MR. UDAL, as nearest to the spot, to investigate this point? Q. V.

AERONAUTICS.—In view of the recent successful experiments in Paris of M. Santos Dumont with regard to aërial navigation, the following extract is interesting. It is taken from Thomas Wright's introduction to his 'Biographia Britannica Literaria' (Anglo-Saxon Period), p. 68, in which he refers to

"a learned and ingenious monk of Malmesbury, named Ailmer, who not many years afterwards made wings to fly, an extraordinary advance in the march of mechanical invention, if we reflect that little more than a century before Asser the historian thought the invention of lanterns a thing sufficiently wonderful to confer an honour upon his patron King Alfred. But Ailmer, in the present instance, allowed his zeal to get the better of his judgment. Instead of cautiously making his first experiment from a low wall, he took flight from the top of the church steeple, and, after fluttering for a short time helplessly in the air, he fell to the ground and broke his legs. Undismayed by this accident, the crippled monk found comfort and encouragement in the reflection that his invention would certainly have succeeded had he not forgotten to put a tail behind."

RICHARD LAWSON.

"YARD OF ALE."—The following extract from the *Tatler* of 8 January (No. 28, p. 52) seems worth preservation in 'N. & Q.':—

"The extraordinary-looking glass which is illustrated on this page belongs to Dr. Ernest Fincham, who bought it four years ago at Shrewsbury. It is believed to be the only genuine specimen of a 'yard of ale' glass to be found in the United Kingdom. A hundred years ago these glasses were comparatively common, and were to be found in most inns suspended from the wall by a coloured ribbon."

Underneath the illustration it is stated that the glass is 38 in. high and contains two pints of ale. It would be interesting to know if the specimen referred to is entitled to the unique honour claimed for it. URLLAD.

[See *ante*, p. 80, *Record* of the Upper Norwood Athenæum; also 6th S. v., vi., vii., x., *passim*.]

THE COURT OF ST. JAMES'S. — Under the word 'Court,' 8, the 'H.E.D.' prints the phrase "accredited as ambassador to the Court of St. James's," but I look in vain for any syllable to show what is meant by "the Court of St. James's." Nothing appears under the words 'Accredited' or 'Court' or

'James.' What I had long ago found wanting in the treatment of 'Accredited' and 'Court' I was confident I should find supplied in the article 'James.' There was reason for my expectation, for both the Apostles of that name are mentioned, and the sacred day of one of them. The name James is brought forward in connexion with a crowbar, a coin, and a sheep's head. We are told what St. James's wort and St. James's powder signify, but regarding St. James's Palace there is utter silence.

It is to be hoped that this omission did not escape the eye of the lamented Fitzedward Hall, and that it will be made up in the supplementary volume which will crown the lifelong labours of a lexicographical legion.

Readers who despair of seeing this far-off consummation will not refuse to read a note concerning the most noteworthy phrase, in the eyes of English speakers, in which the Apostolic names have entered. At some point in the present London park of St. James a hospital bearing his name had been built before the Conquest as a home for fourteen leprous maidens by the Londoners— a tradition which Maitland says cannot be questioned, for he saw in the Cotton Library a MS. stating that Gisbert, Abbot of Westminster, visited it *anno* 1100, &c.

In 1532 Henry VIII. bought the hospital and eighty acres of marsh ground around it to form a deer park, and therein erected a goodly palace, but never made it his own home, though it still exists in part, and bears the name of St. James.

Soon after William came over, at the Revolution, Whitehall was burnt, and he made St. James's the royal residence. During the Stuart dynasty it had been a Stuart nursery, and was the site of the royal Court during the whole era of George III., and perhaps long before.

The phrase "Court of St. James," in the sense of the British Royal Government, may be as old as the Revolution, or may not be older than the accession of George III.; or may it not have been coeval with the second or first King James? It is used in the latest 'Encyclopædia Britannica.'

How early a use of the words in the sense desiderated can be found, who first used them, and in what connexion, are facts which some among the multitudinous readers ought to have early ascertained for Dr. Murray. In America the locution "Ambassador to the Court of St. James" has been long common in the mouths of people too ignorant to supply the ellipsis of "palace," and at a loss for a reason why James was preferred as a patron saint to George. English antipathy to Spaniards would have forbidden, one would think, the bestowal of such a high honour on one who, as Dr. Murray tells us, was chosen as the patron saint of Spain

JAMES D. BUTLER.

Madison, Wis., U.S.

[Our correspondent in his last paragraph settles his own difficulty. The ellipsis in "Court of St. James's" is merely of the word "Palace."]

SIR THOMAS BROWNE'S SKULL.—The *Norfolk Chronicle* of 18 January has an account of the casket for Sir Thomas Browne's skull presented to the Norfolk and Norwich Hospital.

In July last Dr. Osler expressed to Mr. Chas. Williams, surgeon, of Norwich, a wish to present a silver casket for the skull. The Museum Committee of the hospital were pleased to accept so generous an offer, but suggested that the casket should be formed not of silver, but of plate-glass.

Early in December it was presented by Mr. Williams in the name of Prof. Osler to the Committee, who directed that an appropriate pedestal should be made for it.

The casket is of oblong shape, about 13 in. in length by 11 in. in width, and 11 in. in height. The four sides and top consist of crystal glass with silver-gilt mountings, and set on a stand of ebony. On the stand are placed four gilt plates, on one of which is engraved the name of the donor, &c., and on the other three quotations selected by Prof. Osler from the 'Religio Medici.' The inscription runs :—

"This casket was presented to the Norfolk and Norwich Hospital by William Osler, M.D., F.R.S., Professor of Medicine, Johns Hopkins University, Baltimore, 1901."

JOHN PICKFORD, M.A.

Newbourne Rectory, Woodbridge.

THE FEAST AND THE RECKONING.—On turning over the pages of a reprint of the debates on the Education Bill of 1870, I have come across a speech delivered by Col. Barttelot on 7 July of the year mentioned, in which the then gallant member for West Sussex quotes with excellent effect "the old saying," as he terms it,

We laugh and revel till the feast is o'er ;
Then comes the reckoning, and we laugh no more.

I take it that the feeling expressed in the two verses is as old as civilization, for we should scarcely expect to find it existing at the time

When wild in woods the noble savage ran.

But it may be otherwise ; if so, I trust that the distinguished artist E. T. Reed, who is

so steeped in " prehistoric " lore, will give us
in black and white a " peep " of how it was
done in those dim and distant days. I cannot
ask the speaker who was the author of the
couplet, for he and Gladstone, Disraeli,
Forster, Lowe, Northcote, Fawcett, Hors-
man, with others that might be named,

> All, all are gone, the old familiar faces.

I should like to know if the lines can be
traced to any particular writer. Perhaps
they are only a translation of the old proverb
expressed in the macaronic distich, quoted
in his 'Compitum' (book i. chap. xi. p. 403)
by K. H. Digby, who excels even Robert
Burton in power of quotation :—

> A boire et manger exultamus,
> Mais au débourser suspiramus.

John T. Curry.

[Mr. Granger Hutt stated in 5ᵗʰ S. xii. 39 that
"So comes a reck'ning" is from Gay's ' What d'ye
Call It,' Act II. sc. ix.]

"Late."—I notice that Mr. Bradley writes
in the 'H.E.D.': " *Late*, a.¹...5. Of a person :
That was alive not long ago, but is not now :
recently deceased." The charter of the Royal
Historical Society (dated 30 July, 1889)
recites that

"the said Society......did also in the year 1886
appoint a committee for the due celebration of the
eight hundredth anniversary of the completion of
the Domesday Book of His late Majesty William
the First."

I carefully sent a quotation from this to Mr.
Bradley ; but I presume he judged that
though a ninth-century royal charter, if not
in Latin, was in English, the same reasoning
did not apply to a nineteenth-century royal
charter. I have no doubt that he was right ;
but the painful super-accuracy of the drafts-
man should be recorded in ' N. & Q.,' even if
it be not worthy of note in the 'H.E.D.'

Q. V.

Earl of Cardigan.—The 'Dictionary of
National Biography' states that James
Thomas Brudenell, seventh Earl of Cardigan, was born at Hambledon, in Hampshire, 16 October, 1797. He was, in fact, born
at Hambleden, Bucks, where his baptism is
entered in the parish register as follows :
"1797. Nov. 5. James Thomas, son of Robert
Brudenell, Esq., and Penelope Ann."

J. C. F.

Christmas Decorations and Shrove
Tuesday.—It is proper to take down Christmas decorations at Candlemas, but they
ought to be kept till Shrove Tuesday, and
then burnt in the fire over which the
pancakes are fried. I have this from a Welsh
cousin.   C. C. B.

Death of an Aged Chartist. — It has
hitherto been assumed that George Julian
Harney, who died at Richmond, in Surrey, on
9 December, 1897, was the oldest survivor of
those connected with this famous movement.
But it would now appear that Samuel
Bartlett, who has recently passed away at
the great age of ninety-three, was considerably his senior. Apart from the
notoriety gained in the ranks of Chartism,
Mr. Bartlett was noteworthy as affording
another instance of the long life so often
granted those who practise total abstinence,
of which creed he was always a staunch
advocate and disciple.   Cecil Clarke.
Authors' Club, S.W.

Distraint on Wearing Apparel, 1790-4.—
In a case tried before Lord Kenyon the
plaintiff had rented furnished rooms from
the defendant. When eight weeks' rent was
in arrear, the latter distrained on clothing, a
part of which was in the wash. His lordship
sustained the proceeding. A note says that
a few years previously a landlord distrained
the clothes of his tenant's wife and children
while they were in bed ; and this was held
good, on the ground that the things were not
in actual use ! See Baynes *v.* Smith, Isaac
Espinasse's Reports, p. 206 (Dublin ed.,
1799).   Richard H. Thornton.
Portland, Oregon.

"Ludi magister." (See 9ᵗʰ S. viii. 516.)—
In your review of the *Northern Genealogist*,
edited by A. Gibbons, F.S.A., the writer
asks, " What is the exact significance of *ludi
magister* used at this period [1588]? Qy.
schoolmaster ?" To which I reply, Yes, certainly schoolmaster.   W. I. R. V.

Queries.

We must request correspondents desiring information on family matters of only private interest
to affix their names and addresses to their queries,
in order that the answers may be addressed to them
direct.

Drawing-knife.—In a journal written in
1781 I have an account of a schooner that
had come to great grief in a squall, and was
lying nearly water - logged. Her crew of
fifteen men were on deck, where " with the
utmost difficulty they prevented themselves
from being washed overboard." After some
eighteen or twenty hours of this " the mate
accidentally got hold of an old *drawing-knife*
with his foot, which was in the cabin ; with
this they cut away the mainmast of 16 or 17
inches, and the vessel came upon her legs."

Can any one tell me what is meant by a "drawing-knife"? The passage, in its literal sense, means that with it they cut through a mast some sixteen inches in diameter; but it may probably be merely a careless way of saying that they cut the shrouds, and the mast broke off by its own weight. But at any rate what was a "drawing-knife"?

J. K. Laughton.

[There is a full explanation in the 'H.E.D.']

"Say not that he did well."—Can you tell me the author of the following quotation?

Say not that he did well or ill,
But say he did his best.

F. M. Camilleri Major, F.S.I.

Method of testing cloth.—Can you tell me of any means by which one can ascertain if flannel—or cloth of any kind—is really made of wool or not? A. J. E.

[If a small fragment of cloth is cut off the piece, you may by a simple process of unravelling distinguish if the warp is of cotton. Supposing the material to be made of what is called wool, the presence of what is technically known as "shoddy" is revealed when the fragment on being stretched by the thumbs with the leverage of the forefingers is inelastic, soft, and spongy, yields easily, and having yielded does not return to its original firmness.]

Moore's 'History of Dunstable.'—Information as to date, author, price, &c., earnestly requested. F. C. Beazley.
Fern Hill, Oxton, Birkenhead.

[We fail to trace any such work.]

Window Glass.—Was any kind of "window glass" (apart from coloured mosaic) used by the Romans. or any other ancient people? My impression is that such was not employed at all until the eleventh or twelfth century, and that any statements to the contrary are mistakes of historians or translators.

G. C. Warden.

Psalmorum Codex Latinus. —I have a beautiful copy of a Latin edition of the Psalms, with a commentary by Bishop Bruno. The book is a folio of 276 printed leaves, measuring 11¾ in. by 8¼ in., and is in three sizes of type. There are two columns to a page, the large type of the Psalms having twenty-five lines to a full column, and the commentary fifty lines. The book is without colophon, or numerals, or signatures, or catchwords, and has no printer's name, place, or date, and therefore was, in all probability, issued while printing was in its infancy, and the art was a secret, and printed copies were sold as MSS. It is one of the earliest books printed in two colours, red and black. My object in giving these par-

ticulars is that the edition may be identified. It has an introduction of fourteen pages, which cannot have been written by Bishop Bruno, seeing that it records his death in 1045. Can any of the readers of 'N. & Q.' tell me who is supposed to have written it? Internal evidence points to its having been written about two hundred years after the commentator's death, for the introduction speaks of the testimony of Origen as dating back one thousand years; and as Origen died in 253 or 254, that brings the date of the introduction to about 1253. The Psalms are from the Vulgate.

Geo. Washington Moon, Hon.F.R.S.L.
21, Hove Park Villas, Hove, Sussex.

Dalrymple on the Fur Trade.—I am anxious to learn the correct title and date of Dalrymple's "admirable pamphlet on the Fur Trade," thus described in the preface to Meares's 'Voyages,' London, 1791. Lowndes states that several of this writer's minor works are in the British Museum. An answer direct will oblige. C. King.
101, Union Street, Torquay.

"With affection beaming."—Can you identify this description: "With affection beaming in one eye and calculation in the other"? R. Lucas.

Mummers.—I shall be greatly obliged if you or some of your correspondents will kindly state where full and trustworthy information may be found with reference to mummers and their quaint dialogues or plays and their origin. H. W.

[Consult 2nd S. x. 466; xi. 271. See also Brand's 'Popular Antiquities,' ed. Hazlitt, 1870, vol. i. pp. 245 et seq., and Gomme's 'Dictionary of British Folk-lore,' part i. vol. ii.]

Markoe or Marcou Family: Records of Nevis, St. Eustatius, and Santa Cruz.—The Markoe or Marcou family, from Salins and Montbeliard in the Franche-Comté of France, were, with a Count Crequi, early settlers in the above islands, and some systematic search is now being made to discover genealogical data as to the family and the existence of any records of the islands in England, as a consequence of naval operations or military successes in the West Indies. Careful inquiry in the islands discloses the not unexpected fact that not a single public record antedating 1780 is in the custody of the local authorities. The church records and gravestones which I am about to examine personally are reported as few and fragmentary. Recitals in legal documents as to St. Eustatius show that one

Pieter Markoe was the commandant of that island towards the close of the eighteenth century, and presumably under English rule. Family tradition as to Nevis says that a Markoe was a member of the island council. In Santa Cruz the family were among the leading planters, and thence a branch came to Philadelphia and founded a noted American family. Were any records removed from the above islands by the naval or military authorities, and are any such to be found in any repositories of records in England? Any information will be gratefully acknowledged.
STUART C. WADE.

121, West 90th Street, New York.

CORBYN FAMILY.—Can any correspondent give information about the family of William Charles Corbyn (? of Manchester), who by Elizabeth his wife had a son Frederick, born in Manchester 11 May, 1791, and baptized at St. Giles's-in-the-Fields 24 April, 1807? He had other sons distinguished in the navy and elsewhere. SIGMA.

AUTHOR OF POEMS WANTED.—I should be pleased if any reader could give me the author of two poems entitled 'Lord Byron's Pilgrimage to the Holy Land,' to which is added 'The Tempest,' Lond., 1817; and 'Childe Harold's Pilgrimage to the Dead Sea,' Lond., 1818. S. J. KIRK.

CLIII.—I should be glad to obtain additional instances of the ecclesiastical number 153, at which Dean Colet fixed the free scholars of St. Paul's School. The traditional (and no doubt correct) reference is to the number of fishes in the miraculous draught, as typical of all the various kinds of fishes, and therefore of "all nations and countries," to which Dean Colet expressly threw his school open. But I also find that St. Augustine tells us that the martyrs of Utica numbered 153—those martyrs who were thrown into a lime-kiln, and whose remains are consequently styled the "white mass." Are there any other instances of this particular number that might have more particularly appealed to Dean Colet? R. J. WALKER.

FIREPLACES IN CATHEDRAL CHURCHES.—At Lincoln, Hereford, and Durham fireplaces have been inserted in the west walls of the south transepts. They have been supposed to be for heating obley-irons, and for supplying the thuribles with burning charcoal. But is anything really known about their former use, and are there other examples of fireplaces in the same situation? That at Lincoln is not in the great transept, but in the eastern south transept, in the place with a lavatory known as "Ancient Choristers' Vestry." See Murray's 'Cathedrals: Lincoln,' p. 311, and No. 26 on the plan, p. 263.
J. T. F.

Durham.

BÉRANGER : 'LE ROI D'YVETOT.'—In 'Chambers's Concise Gazetteer,' 1895, it is stated, s.v. 'Yvetot,' that Béranger's well-known song was a satire on Napoleon. Was this really the case? A satire, however chargé, must have some sort of resemblance to the person satirized, or it would be unrecognizable; but what resemblance is there between the King of Yvetot, "dormant fort bien sans gloire," who

> Sur un âne, pas à pas,
> Parcourait son royaume,

and him who, like a thunderbolt,

> Scoppiò da Scilla al Tanai,
> Dall' uno all' altro mar?

It is true that Béranger's song, in my edition, is dated "Mai, 1813," shortly after the Russian débâcle, which might, by a very far-fetched "gloss," account for the "sans gloire" and "peu connu dans l'histoire." But had Béranger any thought at all of Napoleon when writing his song? Besides, was not Béranger a great admirer of Napoleon? One would naturally think so, judging from his touching song 'Les Souvenirs du Peuple.' If 'Le Roi d'Yvetot' is really a satire on the great captain, what is the evidence on the point?
JONATHAN BOUCHIER.

Ropley, Hampshire.

WIMPOLE STREET EIGHTY-FIVE YEARS AGO.—Can any one say what was the maximum rent of a house in Wimpole Street about the year 1816, when Miss Austen wrote 'Mansfield Park'? We know that it was then a fashionable quarter, but it is difficult to suppose the rents so high in those days as the novel suggests in a passage in a letter from Miss Crawford to Fanny Price :—

"Mrs. Rushworth......will open one of the best houses in Wimpole Street......Henry [Crawford] could not have afforded her such a house. I hope she will recollect it, and be satisfied, as well she may, with moving the queen of a palace, though the king may appear best in the background."

Yet Henry Crawford, we are told, had 4,000l. a year. My recollections of Wimpole Street go back more than fifty years. In 1849 my father became tenant of a comfortable house in it at 120l. a year, and some seven years later of another (I should think nearly as spacious as any in the street) at 160l., taking over an old lease. When did the value of houses in Wimpole Street decline

so greatly as they must have done if Mr. Rushworth's house was beyond Crawford's means when 'Mansfield Park' was written?
C. C. M.

CHALICES OF WOOD.—At what date were chalices of wood forbidden? Durandus says by Pope Urban and the Council of Rheims in 874, but De Caumont writes: "Le pape Léon IV. (IXᵉ siècle) défendit de se servir de calices de bois ou de verre. Cette défense fut renouvelée par le Concile de Tibur, tenu en 895" ('Abécédaire d'Archéologie,' 1886, p. 116). The Rev. John O'Brien, in his 'History of the Mass,' fifteenth edition, n.d., but *circa* 1879, says, "Sometimes, too, in diffi- cult circumstances chalices of wood were used......The canons of King Edgar of Eng- land (tenth century) wholly interdicted chalices of wood" (p. 71). His authority is Bona, 'Rev. Liturg.,' to which I have not access. Mr. Walter Lowrie, whose 'Christian Art and Archæology,' 1901, is the most recent handbook and one of the best, puts it thus: "Vessels of glass, of the baser metals, or even of wood were, in fact, used by poor churches till late in the Middle Ages" (p. 343). A chalice (more properly a mazer) bearing date 1567, with a wood cup and silver stem, belonging to St. Mary's College, St. Andrews, was exhibited at the Glasgow Exhibition last year; it is figured in the *Proceedings* of the Society of Antiquaries of Scotland, 1882-3, p. 141, but it is not quite in point, and I only mention it in case some reader should kindly refer me to it. I have read the communica- tions in 8ᵗʰ S. ii.
WILLIAM GEORGE BLACK.
Ramoyle, Dowanhill Gardens, Glasgow.

ROYAL PERSONAGES. (See 9ᵗʰ S. viii. 184, 252, 349.)—Some of my former queries remain unanswered, and I shall be much obliged for replies.
I have found it necessary to affix dates in order to avoid confusion.
I desire to know the places of birth and death of the brothers and sisters of George III., and the dates of funerals of the first two princesses *only* :—
Louisa Anne, b. 8 March, 1749; d. 13 May, 1768.
Elizabeth Caroline, b. 10 Jan., 1740; d. 4 Sept., 1759.
Frederic William, b. 24 May, 1750.
Wm. Henry, Duke of Gloucester and Edin- burgh.
Henry Frederic, Duke of Cumberland.
Augusta, Duchess of Brunswick-Wolfen- büttel.
Where were the Dukes of Gloucester

and Cumberland married, respectively on 6 September, 1766, and 2 October, 1771, to Maria, Countess Dowager Waldegrave, and the Hon. Mrs. Anne Horton?
With regard to the children of George II., can any reader supply the precise dates and places of birth and death of the following, also places and dates of funerals ?—
Anne, Princess Royal, b. 1709; died (where?) 12 Jan., 1759.
Mary, Princess of Hesse Cassel, b. 1723 (married at Cassel 8 May, 1740?).
Louisa, Queen of Denmark, b. 1724 (married where?).
I wish to know the place of death of the following :—
Amelia Sophia, d. 31 Oct., 1786.
Caroline Elizabeth, d. 28 Dec., 1757.
George William, d. 6 Feb., 1718.
I shall be glad to obtain also the following information :—
Dates of burial of George III.'s youngest sons, Octavius and Alfred; place of death of latter (on 26 Aug., 1782), and date of removal to Windsor.
Elizabeth, his daughter, date of burial and place of death (d. 10 Jan., 1840).
Augustus Frederic, son of the Duke of Sussex; places of birth and death, and date of funeral.
Ellen or Emma Augusta, his sister; place of death and burial, and date of latter. Married to Lord Truro: where?
Birthplace of H.R.H. the present Duke of Cumberland and his sisters, and his two eldest children, Marie Louise and George William. Did his father, George Frederick Alexander Charles Ernest, die in Paris, 12 June, 1878? Where was he married, 18 Feb., 1843?
A. W. B.

Replies.

KIPLING IN AMERICA.
(9ᵗʰ S. ix. 5.)

MR. CRIPPS deserves credit for his industry in compiling the list of American issues of Mr. Kipling's works; but if he had travelled further through the thorny jungle of biblio- graphy he would have hesitated before apply- ing the epithet "complete" or even "full" to any essay in that science. The "full list" of original publications, for which MR. CRIPPS is indebted to Mr. W. M. Clemens's 'A Ken of Kipling,' has many *lacunæ*, which I will endeavour to supply; but before doing so I may observe that instead of relying on Mr. Clemens, MR. CRIPPS would have acted more wisely in consulting the bibliography of Mr.

Kipling's books which forms a supplement to Mr. Le Gallienne's 'Rudyard Kipling,' 1900. Further information he would also have found in G. F. Monkshood's book on 'Rudyard Kipling,' 1899; in Mr. F. L. Knowles's 'A Kipling Primer,' 1900; and in 'The Kipling Guide-Book,' by W. Roberton, 1899. But the finest book hitherto published on Kipling bibliography has just reached me from America. It is entitled :—

The Works | of | Rudyard Kipling | The Description of a Set | of the First Editions of | his Books, in the Library | of a New York Collector | with Facsimiles | [Monogram] New York | Dodd, Mead & Company | 1901. Royal 8vo, pp. viii-92.

This beautiful volume, of which only seventy-seven copies have been printed, including twelve on Japan paper, contains a large number of facsimiles of title-pages and wrappers, the latter being printed in the colours of the originals, and as far as possible on the same paper, and, in the slang of the day, is the *dernier cri* of scientific American bibliography.

I will now enumerate some of the original works omitted by Mr. Cripps in his first list :—

Schoolboy Lyrics. Lahore, 1881. Fcap. 8vo, pp. iv-46.

All these poems have been reprinted, with one exception, in the volume entitled 'Early Verse' in Scribner's "Outward Bound" edition of Kipling's 'Works.'

Echoes. By Two Writers [Rudyard and Beatrice Kipling]. Lahore, n.d. [1884]. 16mo, pp. iv-72.

The thirty-two poems by Mr. Kipling in this volume have also been reprinted in 'Early Verse.'

The Seven Nights of Creation. 8vo, pp. vi.

This is a privately printed issue of a poem in 'Schoolboy Lyrics,' and is probably the rarest (with the exception of the two that follow) of all Mr. Kipling's works. It bears neither date nor imprint.

The City of Dreadful Night, and other Sketches. Allahabad, 1890. 12mo.

Of this edition only three copies were preserved. The volume contained 'The City of Dreadful Night,' as reprinted in 1891, with the addition of eleven stories not reprinted.

The Smith Administration. Allahabad, 1891. Extra crown 8vo, pp. ii-92.

Of this book also only three copies were preserved. It was reprinted in 'From Sea to Sea.'

The Light that Failed. London and New York, 1891. Crown 8vo, pp. viii-339.

This story, with a different ending, first appeared in *Lippincott's Magazine* (see below).

Cleared. Edinburgh, n.d. [1891].

A private reprint by the *Scots Observer* of a poem that first appeared in that journal, and was afterwards published in 'Barrack-Room Ballads.'

Good Hunting. London, 1895. 8vo, pp. 16.

A reprint by the *Pall Mall Gazette*.

An Almanac of Twelve Sports for 1898. Illustrated by William Nicholson. London, 1897. 4to, pp. 32.

White Horses. London, 1897. 12mo, pp. 10.

A private reprint of a poem that appeared in *Literature* for 23 October, 1897.

The Absent-Minded Beggar. A folio leaflet.

Reprinted from the *Daily Mail* of 31 October, 1899.

The Science of Rebellion. London, n.d. [1901]. 8vo, pp. 10.

The Sin of Witchcraft. London, 1901. 8vo, pp. ii-8.

Reprinted from the *Times* of 15 March, 1900.

Mr. Cripps mentions only the first and sixth editions of 'Departmental Ditties.' It may, therefore, be useful to give a list of the various editions of these poems until they assumed their final form :—

First edition, Lahore, 1886, contains twenty-six poems.

Second edition, Calcutta, 1886, contains thirty-two poems.

Third edition, Calcutta and London, 1888, contains forty-two poems, one of which, 'Diana of Ephesus,' has never been republished.

Fourth edition, Calcutta, London, and Bombay, 1890, contains fifty poems. This was the first edition printed in England.

Fifth edition, Calcutta, London, and Bombay, 1890. A reprint of the fourth edition with a new title-page.

Sixth edition, Calcutta, London, and Bombay, 1891. Contains the glossary for the first time.

Alterations were made in many of the poems in the various editions.

Mr. Cripps includes in his first list two items which should not properly find a place there. One of these is the collection called 'Ballads and Barrack-Room Ballads,' which is not an original work and was only published in America, and the other is 'Slaves of the Lamp,' which was originally published in *Cosmopolis*, and made its first appearance in England in book form in 'Stalky and Co.'

Turning now to the American list of Mr. Kipling's books, I notice that Mr. Cripps omits the first original work of that writer which was issued in the United States. This is 'The Record of Badalia Herodsfoot,' which made its first appearance in *Harper's Weekly* for 15 and 22 November, 1890, and was reprinted in the Christmas number of the *Detroit Free Press* for that year. Next came 'The Light that Failed'—also omitted by Mr. Cripps—which was published in *Lippincott's Magazine* for January, 1891, and had such a large sale that separate title-pages were printed for it by Messrs. Lippincott and by the English publishers as under :—

The | Light that Failed. | By | Rudyard Kipling, | Author of 'Plain Tales from the Hills,' 'Soldiers Three,' 'The Story | of the Gadsbys,' 'Departmental Ditties,' etc. | Ward, Lock, Bowden, & Co., | London, New York and Melbourne.

Another American book which is unnoticed by Mr. Cripps is of some importance, as it contains the first issues in this form of productions by R. L. Stevenson and Rudyard Kipling. This is :—

American Series. | American Notes, | by Rudyard Kipling, | Author of 'Soldiers Three,' 'Plain Tales from the Hills,' | 'The Story of the Gadsbys,' 'The Phantom 'Rickshaw,' | 'The Courting of Dinah Shadd,' etc., etc. | and | The Bottle Imp, | by | Robert Louis Stevenson. | New York : | M. J. Ivers & Co., Publishers, | 86 Nassau Street. 16mo, pp. 160.

Shortly after printing the first edition Messrs. Ivers removed to 379, Pearl Street, New York, and this address appears on the title-page of most copies. An immense number were printed, and the later issues are extremely common. The first impression was issued on 14 February, 1891.

Under the year 1898 Mr. Cripps has

The Courting of Dinah Shadd. Brentano's. Ditto. Marion Press.

It may be noted that the second item is not a reprint of the story, but 'A Contribution to a Bibliography of the Writings of Rudyard Kipling,' of which one hundred and twenty copies were privately printed for subscribers in March, 1898. It is really "a reprint, with notes by Mr. Paul Lemperly, of the correspondence between Messrs. Harper & Brothers and Mr. Kipling, relative to copyright on the stories included in 'The Courting of Dinah Shadd'" (see Mr. Cripps's list under 1890), as printed in the *Athenæum*, with Kipling's poem 'The Rhyme of the Three Captains' ('The Works of Rudyard Kipling,' p. 81).

I may add, in conclusion, that the American work from which I have just quoted gives lists of Kipling's contributions to the *United Services College Chronicle*, to the *Week's News* of Allahabad, and to 'Turnovers from the Civil and Military Gazette,' Lahore. In addition to the facsimiles it is adorned with a beautiful etching on Japan paper, by Mr. T. Johnson, of the well-known portrait by the Hon. John Collier.

W. F. Prideaux.

1, West Cliff Terrace, Ramsgate.

Baron de Grivegnée and Power (9ᵗʰ S. vii. 409, 476 ; viii. 170).—The following pedigree of the Kirkpatricks, from whom the Empress Eugénie is descended, though meagre, I believe to be accurate :—

Thomas Kirkpatrick had issue James and Robert ; the latter had two sons. Thomas, and William of Conheath, co. Dumfries. William had (1) John, (2) William.

(1) John of Conheath had issue :—

a. William Escott. Descendants living.

b. Thomas James, who married Carlota Catalina, daughter of his uncle William. Descendants living.

c. Robert.

d. Maria Isabella, who married Joseph Kirkpatrick. See below.

(2) William had issue :—

a. Maria Manuela, who married the Count de Teba and Montijo (died 1823), and became mother of the Empress Eugénie.

b. Carlota Catalina, who married Thomas James Kirkpatrick.

c. Henraquita, who married Count Cabarrus. Descendants living.

The pedigree of the family from which Thomas James Kirkpatrick, who married Carlota Catalina, sprang is as follows :—

James Kirkpatrick, born in 1668, left Scotland in 1686, and married Anne Hoar, of Romney. Had a son James, who was the father of

(1) James, living in 1815.

(2) John, living in 1815.

(3) Joseph, sometime of the parish of Carisbrooke, in the county of Southampton, who married secondly, at St. Mary's, Woolwich, 21 April, 1796, Henrietta, daughter of Lieut.-General Geo. Fead (see 'D.N.B.').

Joseph had a son Joseph, who married Maria Isabella, daughter of John Kirkpatrick of Conheath, and they had issue :—

(1) Isabella, who married Roger, son of Roger, and grandson of Sir James Kirkpatrick, fourth baronet. Descendants of Isabella living.

(2) John Everett, now living in Canada.

Traditionally connected with the Kirkpatricks of Conheath was Wm. Kirkpatrick, Bailie of Dumfries in the eighteenth century, who had issue :—

(1) Henrietta, who married Capt. John Johnstone, of the Royal Marines, and was served heir to her father and her brother Roger 29 March, 1794.

(2) Roger.

(3) Agnes, who married Thomas Gordon of Dumfries, and was served heir to her father and her brother Roger 29 March, 1794.

(4) Elizabeth, who married Lieut.-General Geo. Fead, of the Royal Artillery. Mrs. Fead died on 17 January, 1836, in her eighty-sixth year, and was buried in St. Mary's Church-yard, Woolwich.   J. Scott.

STAUNTON, WORCESTERSHIRE (9th S. viii 383, 510; ix. 11).—MR. MATTHEWS may find some information in a book published in 1883 at Bristol, by the late Sir John Maclean, entitled 'History of the Manor and Advow-son of Staunton in the Forest of Dean.' I cannot trace the paper to which MR. JOHN HOBSON MATTHEWS refers in the volumes of the Bristol and Gloucestershire Archæological Society during the last ten years.
T. CANN HUGHES, M.A., F.S.A.
Lancaster.

Permit me to amplify my reply. Sir William Whittington, of Pauntley, Gloucester-shire, married the heiress of Staunton in the same county. Sir Richard Whittington, Mayor of London, is believed to have been their fifth son. The society to whose *Trans-actions* I referred MR. HAWKINS is the Glou-cester Field Club.
JOHN HOBSON MATTHEWS.
Town Hall, Cardiff.

THE WEST BOURNE (9th S. viii. 517; ix. 51). —I cannot follow COL. PRIDEAUX to his con-clusion about this name. He doubts whether "in early times the stream had any specific name." Very possibly it had not, but the absence of any such name from early maps seems to me insufficient proof thereof. Here is a case which seems to be in point. Some years ago I was fishing in the river running through Cassiobury Park. After a good morning's sport I asked the keeper what was the name of the river. "Well, sir," said he, "it's got a name right enough, but dang me if I can remember un. We just calls it 'the River.'" Presently, a respectably dressed man coming by, the keeper stopped him and asked whether he could remember the name. He, too, was sure the stream had a name, but he could not call it to mind. An hour or two later the same person returned and said to me, "I found what you wanted to know, sir. There is an old fellow in the village tells me that this is the river Gade; and I remember now hearing that name when I was a boy." Thinks I to myself, Here is a case of Avon and Esk over again; the specific is for-gotten, the generic remains. When English

speech shall have passed away this stream will perhaps retain its name as "the River."

Well, on reading COL. PRIDEAUX's interest-ing note I turned up the only map of Hert-fordshire which happened to be at hand—that in vol. xi. of the 'Encyclopædia Bri-tannica.' I find the river in Cassiobury Park without any name given, although Gaddesden and Gadesbridge are marked on its course, and although the nearest stream on the east is duly marked the Ver and the nearest on the west is marked the Chess, neither of them of greater volume than the Gade.

Assuming, then, that the suffix of West-bourne is "bourn, burn," a stream, A.-S. *burne*, and not "bourn," a boundary, French *borne*, is it not the case that this term for a stream has entirely dropped out of the Southern English vernacular, although it is retained in common use in Northern English and Scots? Before it so dropped out of use, the West Bourn may have given its name to the manor of Westbourne, where it remained fixed, although the stream — the eponymus of the manor — lost its title through the meaning thereof having become hidden from the people on its banks.

I will offer another illustration from my own name. In the twelfth century Maccus, the son of Undewyn, obtained a grant of land near Kelso, now called Springwood, from David I. of Scotland. Included in this grant was a salmon pool in the Tweed, which thence-forward was known as Maccus' Wiel, the pool of Maccus. From this pool the neighbouring land got the name of Maccuswel or Maxwell (Maxwellheugh is just above Springwood Park); then the family became known feudally as De Maxwell, and conferred their name on other and distant places—Maxwell-ton, &c. To this day the salmon pool is known as Maxwheel (it is the first below Kelso Bridge). Its etymology very likely has been forgotten, but the important industry of salmon fishing has preserved the name in constant use for eight hundred years; whereas the Westbourne, it seems, has been diverted to the purpose, and received the inglorious name, of the Ranelagh Sewer.

Instances of the disappearance of a river name, coupled with its retention in the ad-jacent topography, might be given in num-bers far exceeding the dimensions of a "note"; but I may be permitted to adduce one from the remote end of the kingdom, in a district very well known to me. The river running parallel with the north-eastern boundary of the county of Sutherland was known of old in Gaelic speech as Amhuinn Ullidh, the river Ullie, and its valley as Strath Ullie;

but when the Norsemen occupied that land in the eighth or ninth century they renamed many of the local features in their own speech, and Strath Ullie became Helmsdale. At the present day no native of that strath would understand an inquiry about the river Ullie; it has become the Helmsdale River. Yet still the brae along which the high road runs from Helmsdale to Kildonan, about a mile north of the town of Helmsdale, is called, and appears on the Ordnance maps as, Creagbun-Ullidh—that is, the crag at the foot (or estuary) of the Ullie.

Again, Col. PRIDEAUX is probably familiar with the pier and hotel of Inversnaid, on Loch Lomond, where a fine burn falls in a cascade into the lake. Now Inversnaid means "the mouth of the Snaid," but the burn no longer bears that name. It is called on the Ordnance map the Arklet Water, from the lake out of which it flows. And note, the smaller the stream, the more likely it is to change its name. Great rivers—Thames, Tay, Tweed, &c.—make their names in history and become fixed; but I have a couple of trout streams running through my property, the longer of which has but a course of ten miles, yet the names of each vary between source and mouth according to the farms through which they flow.   HERBERT MAXWELL.

I am surprised at one sentence in Col. PRIDEAUX's interesting note: "It seems reasonable to suppose that Westbourne received its name from its situation on the west bank of the rivulet." Is there any analogy for this? Does it explain the name Eastbourne in Sussex, a little inland from South Bourne on the coast? Or of Norborn, near Deal, in Kent? All analogy from the numerous Nortons and Suttons, Westminster, &c., seems the other way, and to show that West Bourne should mean the burn or brook west of some other brook.   T. WILSON.
Harpenden.

In regarding the word *bourne* (*burn, burne,* &c.) only in the sense of stream (rivulet), is there not the danger of forgetting another meaning of the word—viz., limit, boundary (Fr. *borne,* Webster)? It is true that very often the limit or boundary would be found to consist of a stream or rivulet, but not necessarily so. When the poet wrote of "that *bourne* from whence no traveller returns," one does not imagine he was thinking of a rivulet.   W. H. B.

HENRY CRISPE (9th S. ix. 8).—Apparently only one Henry Crispe whom it would be reasonable to identify with Henry Crispe,

the Common Serjeant 1678–1700, was admitted member of the Inner Temple—viz., "Henricus Crispe de Universitate de Cambrige generosus," who was admitted on 21 Nov., 1666 (Register of Admissions). He seems to have been called to the Bar on 26 Nov., 1676, and to the bench of his Inn on 9 Feb., 1696/7 ('Calendar of Inner Temple Records,' vol. iii.). In the 'Masters of the Bench of the Inner Temple, 1450–1883' (privately printed, 1883), the parentage, &c., of the Common Serjeant is noted thus, but, I would suggest, erroneously:—

"Henry Crispe, of the Custom House, London. Eldest son of Henry Crispe, rector of Catton, Yorkshire, and grandson of Henry Crispe, of Monkton, in the Isle of Thanet, Kent, a member of the Inn...... Died 1700."

The source of this note is probably the pedigree in Berry's 'Kent Genealogies,' p. 491. But there is nothing in that pedigree to suggest that the Common Serjeant was identical with the Henry Crispe there mentioned as being of the Custom House, London, and a son of Henry Crispe, rector of Catton; and the identification seems erroneous, because:—

1. The 'Liber Institutionum' at the Record Office records the following institutions to Catton Rectory: Henry Carvile, 1630; Thomas Cary, 1677/8; Henry Crispe, 1685; Richard Sowray, 1737. Apparently the only Henry Crispe instituted to Catton Rectory was instituted on 1 Dec., 1685.

2. Musgrave's 'Obituary' (Harl. Soc.) states, with a reference to "Carter's Camb., 152," that "Henry Crisp, rector of Catton, Yorks, Fell. King's Coll.," died on 23 Feb., 1736 (? 1736/7), æt. 80. This rector was probably the Henry Crispe who is mentioned in 'Graduati Cantab., 1659–1823,' as Fellow of King's, B.A. 1680, M.A. 1684.

3. A man who was aged *circa* eighty in 1736 must have been born *circa* 1656, and could not have had a son who became Common Serjeant in 1678.

This note does not supply the particulars sought for by MR. PINK, but seems to dispose of the parentage assigned to Henry Crispe, the Common Serjeant, in a book liable to be consulted and cited.   H. C.

CHAPLAINS (9th S. viii. 463).—Among the earliest records and writs of Scotland occur the names of ecclesiastics who evidently held offices corresponding to what we know nowadays as domestic and institution chaplains. Many deeds and charters have among the names of the witnesses men designated chaplain in contradistinction to others who are designated rectors or vicars.

The priors or masters of the nuns that appear in writs of various nunneries of the twelfth and thirteenth centuries are evidently the chaplains of these institutions.

We have various licences to landowners from bishops permitting founding of chapels at their castles, with provisions that the mother or parish church shall not be injured from withholding the usual offerings of the parishioners. Thus at Congilton, in parish of Gullane, in this county, the following was arranged in 1224: No services were to take place at the chapel there on St. Andrew's Day, Christmas Day, nor at Easter; and there were to be no baptisms at the chapel, but only at the parish church at Gullane.

Froissart in his 'Chronicles' narrates the "valyaunt" deeds of "a chapelayne of his" (the Earl of Douglas) at Otterburne, 19 August, 1388, which prove him in verity a member of the church militant in a double sense. Towards the end of the fifteenth century (1471) we have mention of Isabella, relict of Sinclair of Hirdmanston, and "her chaplain," Sir Wm. Stevenson.

The Papal letters give many instances of licence granted to people to choose a confessor and to have a portable altar.
J. G. Wallace-James.
Haddington.

The record, register, or statutes under which the appointments have been made have often been asked for in the pages of 'N. & Q.'

From the replies given, it appears that the statute in which chaplains to noblemen are first named is 21 Henry VIII., c. 13 (1529), in which by section ii. every archbishop and duke may have six chaplains; every marquis and earl, five chaplains; viscount and bishop, four chaplains; the Chancellor of England for the time being, and every baron or Knight of the Garter, three chaplains; the Master of the Rolls, two; and the Chief Justice of the King's Bench, one.

By 25 Henry VIII., c. 16 (1533-4), every Judge of the King's Bench and Common Pleas, the Chancellor and Chief Baron of the Exchequer, the Attorney and Solicitor General may have one chaplain each.

The appointments are registered in the Faculty Office in Doctors' Commons.
Everard Home Coleman.
71, Brecknock Road.

Sarten (9ᵗʰ S. viii. 345, 410, 533).—Mr. Ackerley's mention of the Leipzig catalogue gave me a clue which enabled me to trace out and examine both the Russian books to which he refers. They are in the British Museum. The grammar is by Z. A. Aleksyeev

(Tashkend, 1884), and is very short. It contains no exercises, readings, or vocabularies. The other book, however, by V. P. Nalivkin (Samarcand, 1898), which Mr. Ackerley calls a "reading book," is a grammar of a much superior class, with exercises, readings, and two vocabularies, Russian-Sart and Sart-Russian. Unfortunately, neither of these works gives any information on the subject of what the difference is between Sart and ordinary Eastern Turkish. That Sart is closely allied to Turkish is clear from every page.
Jas. Platt, Jun.

The Sarts are fully described in 'Samarkand la Bien Gardée,' by A. Durrieux and R. Fauvelle (Paris, Librairie Plon, 1901). They are a caste rather than a race; they are the working class of Samarkand, as opposed to the nomads of the Steppes. The nomads despise the Sarts; but the Sarts seem to be continually finding recruits among those nomads who prefer the delights of settled life to a life of roaming. The authors quoted consider the Sarts to have been originally Iranians.
Herbert A. Strong.
University College, Liverpool.

Duels (9ᵗʰ S. viii. 364, 491).—There is a long and an interesting history of 'Duels and Ordeals' in 'Memoirs of Extraordinary Popular Delusions, and the Madness of Crowds,' by Chas. Mackay, LL.D. (London, Routledge & Sons, 1869); but as there is no mention therein of the duels between English and French officers in Paris immediately after Waterloo, perhaps I may be permitted to relate that when the Allies were in the occupation of the capital of France the French officers, boiling with rage and indignation at their recent defeat, sought out, by every means in their power, opportunities of insult, but always so artfully contrived as to render the opposite party the challenger, thus reserving to themselves the choice of weapons. When, therefore, it is borne in mind that the French are the most expert swordsmen in Europe, little doubt can exist as to the issue of the combats; and, in fact, scarcely a morning passed without three or four English or Prussian officers being carried through the Barrière de l'Etoile, if not dead, at least seriously wounded and condemned to carry with them through life the inflictions of a sanguinary and savage spirit of revenge.

My authority for this statement will be found in Charles Lever's 'Confessions of Harry Lorrequer,' in which work is also recorded how an English officer, Capt. Trevanion, punished an insulting remark uttered by Capitaine Augustin Gendémar, the president of a duelling club associated for the express and avowed object of provoking to insult, and certainly dooming to death, every English officer upon whom they could fasten a quarrel.

HENRY GERALD HOPE.
Elms Road, Clapham, S.W.

'The Origin and History of Ordeals, &c., with a Chronological Register of the Principal Duels,' by James P. Gilchrist (London, 1821), contains information respecting duels which were fought during the period 1762 to 1821, the number mentioned being 172. In some cases the correspondence and the results of the trials are given.   JOHN RADCLIFFE.

WATERPROOF CLOTHING (7th S. xii. 67 ; 9th S. v. 229, 294. See also 'Mackintoshes,' 7th S. iii. 227 ; 8th S. i. 127, 215 ; ii. 58, 92).—On 13 Dec., 1634, John Eyres, Charles Mowat, and John Walles had granted to them by Privy Seal the

"Privilege for fourteen years to put in practice in England and Ireland ways by them newly invented, for making woollen cloth impenetrable of wet and serviceable for coaches and wagons."—Forty-eighth Report of Deputy-Keeper of P.R., App. iii. 521.

O. O. H.

THE JUBILEE OF THE 'LEISURE HOUR' (9th S. viii. 518 ; ix. 3, 24).—To the deeply interesting papers contributed by MR. JOHN C. FRANCIS at the above references may I be allowed to append a small postscript?

The great pioneer of cheap literature, John Cassell, is buried in Kensal Green Cemetery. His grave, No. 19,094, in Square 16, nearly opposite the main entrance, is covered by a coped recumbent slab of granite, and bears the following inscriptions :—

In loving Memory.
John Cassell,
Publisher,
Born January 23rd, 1817.   Died April 2nd, 1865.
Mary Hannah Cassell,
Daughter of the above,
Born June 29th, 1844.   Died June 13th, 1848.
Mary Cassell,
Born April 9th, 1811.   Died July 6th, 1885.
Interred at Hove Cemetery, Brighton.

JOHN T. PAGE.
West Haddon, Northamptonshire.

MICHAEL BRUCE AND BURNS (9th S. vii. 466 ; viii. 70, 148, 312, 388, 527).—This controversy, as I have already pointed out, has made no progress in thirty years, and it is surely futile to continue it unless something new can be offered. I am now asked to study the defunct *Scots Magazine* on the subject, but the specimen of evidence quoted from that periodical does not encourage further investigation of its contents. MS. copies of the 'Ode to the Cuckoo,' according to this authority, are

"said to have been circulating in East Lothian in or about 1767, before the Bruce MSS. came into Logan's possession, which was not till the succeeding summer, or probably as late as 1769."

The writer of this ought to have shown reason for disbelieving the statements of Bruce's biographers that Logan got the MSS. in 1767. The story of the "circulating" copies, however, is more than a century old, and is thus disposed of by Dr. Grosart :—

"Here is the cautious language of his eulogist, Dr. Robertson, in his 'Life' of Logan prefixed to his 'Sermons': 'The only pieces which Logan himself ever acknowledged, in his conversations with the compiler of this biographical sketch, were the story of "Levina," the "Ode to Paoli," and "The Cuckoo." The *last* was handed about and extolled among his literary acquaintances in East Lothian long before its publication, probably (though not certainly) in 1767, as he did not reside there at all in 1768, and very little in 1769. This fact, and his inserting it as his own in a small volume eleven years afterwards, seem pretty decisive of his claim.' *Credat Judæus!* Only first seen in 1767, and yet 1767 was the year of his reception of Bruce's MSS. ; not to say that, as a correspondent of the Poet, he might even have received and 'shown' it earlier, though it is nowhere attempted to be proved that he did this. The claim on such a miserable chance probability—'not certainly'—is monstrous ; and, as the strength of a chain is measured, not by its strongest but by its weakest part, this link failing, the after publication shares its worthlessness."—' Works of Michael Bruce,' p. 64, ed. 1865.

Dr. Grosart further deals in a note (p. 65) with the letter from Robertson of which Dr. Rae appears to be enamoured. This is how he disposes of its claim to consideration :—

"David Laing, Esq., LL.D., of the Signet Library, Edinburgh, has kindly favoured me with a copy of the first edition of Bruce's 'Poems' (1770), in which some anonymous former possessor of the volume has marked the pieces usually claimed for Logan as his ; and, of course, the 'Ode to the Cuckoo' is one of them. But this is of no value whatever, seeing it only shows that the writer, whoever he may have been, accepted Logan's own statement. Dr. Laing has also sent me a copy of a letter by Dr. Robertson, of Dalmeny, containing nearly the same list ; but we have seen all that *he* had to adduce (*supra*). In short, wherever I have come upon any attempt at evidence in favour of Logan, an examination has invariably resolved it into his own publication and self-assertion."

It seems almost necessary to apologize for using the columns of 'N. & Q.' in the reproduction of this ancient controversial matter. I crave indulgence, however, in defence of my statement that nothing new on the problem has come to light since Dr. Grosart advanced his damaging indictment of Logan in his edition of Michael Bruce's poems. He may have been wrong, but his error is still to be proved. The method of the late *Scots Magazine* (if we may judge from the illustrative extract presented for consideration) does not seem likely to affect his position. Nor is it of any avail to advance against him the opinion of Robertson of Dalmeny, whom he himself disposed of as a very insignificant factor in the discussion. There will always be room for regret that Dr. Grosart did not live to issue, as he thought of doing, a new edition of his 'Works of Michael Bruce.' Possibly he might not have been able to add much to his original memoir, but I have the best reasons for saying that he would have emphasized his contention that Bruce was the author of the 'Ode to the Cuckoo.'

THOMAS BAYNE.

ST. TEILO (7ᵗʰ S. viii. 9, 194; 9ᵗʰ S. viii. 511). —Any of your readers who are interested in this subject may be glad to be referred to a booklet published at Preston, Lancashire, in 1893, entitled 'The Life and Memorials of Saint Teilo, Patron of Llandaf and Cardiff,' by J. H. M.; printed for Saint Teilo's Catholic Historical Society of South Wales.

JOHN HOBSON MATTHEWS.
Town Hall, Cardiff.

"FRAIL" (9ᵗʰ S. iv. 436, 507; v. 51, 158; vi. 378; vii. 33, 177; viii. 531).—At the present time this name for a rush basket is seldom used in Shropshire. I do not remember hearing it for many years, except about two months ago when in Bridgnorth I was asked if I would like a parcel put in a "frail," as I could then carry it easily. HERBERT SOUTHAM.
Shrewsbury.

GEORGE HENRY FITZROY, FOURTH DUKE OF GRAFTON, 1760–1844 (9ᵗʰ S. ix. 9).—According to G. E. C.'s 'Complete Peerage' (vol. x. p. 68) the fourth duke was educated at Harrow School and Trinity College, Cambridge. His father, who filled the offices of Secretary of State and First Lord of the Treasury in the first decade of George III.'s reign, was educated at Westminster School and Peterhouse.

G. F. R. B.

BIRTHDAY CAKE WITH CANDLES : A GERMAN CUSTOM (9ᵗʰ S. viii. 344, 486).—DR. KRUEGER says: "The Norns sit at Nornagest's cradle and proclaim that his life will last only as long as the candle burning there lasts." This reminds me of one of the folk-tales collected by Bechstein. Death introduces a man into a cavern, and shows him a number of candles burning, some nearly burnt to the end and others not so. These candles represent the lives of men; and, when they are burnt or blown out, the lives come to an end.

Macbeth, speaking of life, says: "Out, out, brief candle!" It may be that Shakspeare had heard the tale. In one folk-story, at least, Death is represented as hewing down trees, which signify the lives of men. An idea somewhat similar to that of these folk-stories is expressed in Washington Irving's tale of 'The Devil and Tom Walker.' Althæa's brand, which finished the life of Meleager, has some connexion with the foregoing.

E. YARDLEY.

Two years ago I was staying at a hotel in the Highlands, and amongst the guests was an American family. When the birthday of one of the party came round—a young lady some seventeen or eighteen years old—at dinner there was a sugared birthday cake placed in the centre of the table, with seventeen or eighteen lighted candles round it, one for each year of the young lady's life. They told us it was a common American custom to do this on a birthday.

W. G. D. F.

The phrase mentioned by DR. G. KRUEGER occurs in the Walpurgisnacht scene in Goethe's 'Faust.' Mephistopheles threatens the apologetic will-o'-the-wisp, who cannot keep a straight course to guide Faust and himself up to the Brocken—

Ei, ei! Er denkt's den Menschen nachzuahmen,
Geh er nur grad', ins Teufels Namen!
Sonst blas' ich ihm sein Flackerleben aus.

FRANCIS P. MARCHANT.

BEAU BRUMMEL AND BARBEY D'AUREVILLY (9ᵗʰ S. ix. 8).—Has MR. HIATT seen Mr. Charles Whibley's book 'The Pageantry of Life'? If my memory serves me, the article on Brummel contained in it will give him the information he asks for. C. C. B.

BURIAL OF A SUICIDE (9ᵗʰ S. viii. 502).— Mention has been made, under this heading, that the body of a certain unfortunate wretch in Lincolnshire who had committed suicide was buried in a standing position. A Frenchman was interred near the top of a hill in the immediate neighbourhood of Reigate, early last century, perpendicularly and head downwards. This was at his own request. He declared that, when at the last day everything was turned topsy-turvy, he was anxious to rise right side up. HARRY HEMS.
Fair Park, Exeter.

"HEP! HEP!" THE CRY AGAINST THE JEWS (7ᵗʰ S. xi. 420; 9ᵗʰ S. viii. 471).—K. G. Andresen, in his 'Ueber Deutsche Volksetymologie' (pp. 19, 20), says:—

"The cry 'Hep! Hep!' directed against the Jews is said to owe its origin to the three letters H. E. P.

written on the colours of the gangs pursuing them at the time of the first Crusade, signifying, it is pretended, Hierosolyma est perdita. This, interesting as it may be, is deserving of no credit. It can be proved that the cry in question was applied at first to animals, especially goats—the goat has the dialectal names of Hippe, also Heppe—and as a long Jew's beard was also dubbed goat's beard, the extension of the sense can be easily conceived. That 'hep' is the imperative of 'heben'—heb den Fuss—is possible, as far as form goes, but improbable."

"The common people," he adds, "tried to account for their war-cry by the explanation that the Jews, when the Saviour was drawn up on the Cross, called out, Heb! Heb! (Lift! Lift!)."

Of course, this cannot be taken seriously; the Jews of those times spoke as little German as the German mob used Latin. The derivation from the goat's beard sounds more plausible; but is it not more natural to assume that "Hep" is only the shortened "Hebräer," Hebrew? In my boyhood, when catching sight of a Jew we saluted and pursued him—naughty boys as we were—with "Jude, Jude!" or "Jude, hep!"

G. Krueger.
Berlin.

DISSINGTON FAMILY (9th S. viii. 365; ix. 18).—Is it too fanciful to connect this family with the place-name Tissington, in Derbyshire, where the far-famed well-dressing still survives?

T. Cann Hughes, M.A., F.S.A.

"MINE HOST OF THE TABARD" (9th S. viii. 505).—It is more than probable that Harry Bailly, of the Cook's Prologue in Chaucer's 'Canterbury Tales,' was identified more than forty-four years ago. See 2nd S. iii. 228.

Everard Home Coleman.
71, Brecknock Road.

WEEKS'S MUSEUM (9th S. ix. 8).—The sale of the automatic figures and other pieces of mechanism from Weeks's Museum took place at Messrs. Christie's rooms on 26 May, 1864. Many of the articles offered for sale are described in 3rd S. vi. 46. The museum was established about 1810 at 3, Tichborne Street, Haymarket. The grand room was 117 ft. long and 30 ft. high. It was covered entirely with blue satin, and contained a variety of mechanical curiosities. The architecture was by Wyatt, and the ceiling was painted by Rebecca and Singleton. There were two temples nearly 7 ft. high, supported by sixteen elephants, and embellished with 1,700 pieces of jewellery. Among the automata were the tarantula spider and the bird of paradise, the surprising efforts in a minute compass of the proprietor's ingenuity. The price of admission to the temple was 2s. 6d.,

one shilling extra being charged for the tarantula or the bird.

Everard Home Coleman.
71, Brecknock Road.

The following description appears in Leigh's 'New Picture of London,' 1824-5, under 'Exhibitions of Works of Art,' &c., p. 384:—

"Weeks's Museum, Tichborne Street, is an exhibition of some curious and surprising mechanism. A tarantula spider, made of steel, comes independently out of a box, and runs backward and forward on the table, stretches out and draws in its paws, as if at will; moves its horns and claws, and opens them with ease. This singular automaton, that has no other power of action than that contained in its body, is composed of 115 pieces! Here also are shown two magnificent clocks in the form of temples, supported by sixteen elephants, and embellished with upwards of seventeen hundred pieces of jewellery, in the first style of elegance.—Admission, 2s. 6d."

G. Yarrow Baldock.
South Hackney.

John Timbs, in his 'Curiosities of London,' first edition, 1855, says that this museum was established at 3, Tichborne Street about 1810, and was famed for its mechanical curiosities. The grand room, by Wyatt, had a ceiling painted by Rebecca and Singleton. In it were two temples, 7 ft. high, supported by sixteen elephants, and embellished with 1,700 pieces of jewellery. Among the automata were the tarantula spider and bird of paradise. He adds:—

"Weeks's Museum has long been dispersed; the premises were subsequently the show-rooms of the Rockingham Works, where, in 1837, was exhibited a splendid porcelain dessert-service made for William IV.; 200 pieces, painted with 760 subjects, occupied five years and cost 3,000l. In 1851 the place was refitted by Robin (?Houdin), the conjuror."

'The Picture of London for 1820,' a contemporary account, says:—

"WEEKS'S MUSEUM; TOP OF THE HAYMARKET, ST. JAMES'S.

This Museum, on the plan of the celebrated Mr. Cox, forms an interesting object to the curious. The grand room, which is 107 ft. long, and 30 ft. high, is covered entirely with blue satin, and contains a variety of figures, which exhibit the powers of mechanism. Admittance 1s. 6d. from one till four; and 2s. from seven till ten. The price of admission to the temple is 2s. 6d. from twelve till four, and from six till nine. A curious tarantula and bird are shewn at 1s. each."

I believe I have seen at least one engraving of this museum.

E. E. Newton.
7, Achilles Road, West Hampstead, N.W.

CARLYLE ON SYMBOLS (9th S. ix. 27).—In 'Sartor Resartus,' book iii. chap. iii., my friend MR. W. L. Rutton will find the reference he asks for under the above heading.

The paragraph relating to the coming Coronation in MR. RUTTON's interesting note is probably due to an unconscious reminiscence of the time when he read 'Symbols' himself, the last paragraph of which will to-day bear amendment. It reads as follows :—

"When, as the last English Coronation [that of George IV.—Ed.] was preparing, concludes this wonderful Professor, I read in their Newspapers that the 'Champion of England,' he who must offer battle to the Universe for his new King, had brought it so far that he could now mount his horse with little assistance, I said to myself: Here also we have a Symbol well nigh superannuated. Alas, move whithersoever you may, are not the tatters and rags of superannuated worn out Symbols (in this Ragfair of a World) dropping off everywhere, to hoodwink, to halter, to tether you; nay, if you shake them not aside, threatening to accumulate, and perhaps produce suffocation."

Fortunately, to-day circumstances are different, as are the principal personages in the ceremony referred to.   W. S. S.

SEVEN (9ᵗʰ S. viii. 525).—The "Seven Sisters" was the name of an old inn at Tottenham, in front of which was a cluster of seven elms in a circle, with a walnut tree in the middle. An engraving showing the trees as they appeared in 1830 will be found in 'Old and New London,' v. 373. The Seven Sisters Road leads from Holloway to Tottenham. Elms and other trees seem to have been often planted in clumps of seven.

I do not think the origin of Seven Kings at Ilford has ever been satisfactorily determined.

There is a farm called Seven Score near Ramsgate. The local etymologist derives the name from "Sea-vent-score, to which the sea scored, or marked up, close up, on the south, in the olden time." The word *score*, however, is merely equivalent to *share*.

     W. F. PRIDEAUX.

The number seven is more favoured than any other digit, for which various reasons have been assigned. Bedwell, who wrote a history of Tottenham about 270 years ago, describes Page Green, near that village, as having a group of seven elms in a circle, each planted by a sister, and a walnut tree in the centre by the eighth. He says :—

"This tree hath this many years stod there, and it is observed yearely to live and beare leavs, and yet to stand at a stay, that is, to grow neither greater nor higher. This people do commonly tell the reason to bee, for that there was one burnt upon that place for the profession of the Gospel."

The tree planted by the most diminutive of the sisters was always low in its growth, and when the eighth sister died the walnut tree died also.

In Ireland there is the legend of the seven sisters at Ballybunion, situated a few miles from Kerry Head, co. Cork, fully given in 1ˢᵗ S. ix. 465 ; x. 112.

The favouritism of this number is remarkable. Nine places in England have this prefix, six in our colonies, and seven in other parts of the world.

     EVERARD HOME COLEMAN.
71, Brecknock Road.

I have always understood that Seven Sisters Road was named after seven elm trees which stood outside an old public-house in the locality bearing the sign of the "Seven Sisters." In 'Old and New London,' v. 373, is an engraving showing the seven trees as they appeared in 1830, and the letterpress, p. 380, states : "They were upwards of five hundred years old, and the tradition ran that a martyr had been burnt on the spot where they stood."

As to Seven Kings, near Ilford, the name appears to have originally belonged to a large farm in the locality. The legend is that the Seven Kings of the Saxon Heptarchy once watered their horses at the neighbouring stream, which here crosses the main road. It was anciently known as Seven Kings Watering.   JOHN T. PAGE.
West Haddon, Northamptonshire.

STOWE MISSAL (9ᵗʰ S. viii. 484).—The Stowe Missal has not occurred in any of the Ashburnham sales by public auction. But surely it would have been included among the Stowe MSS. which the late Earl of Ashburnham purchased *en bloc*, and which his successor, the present earl, sold to the British Government. This collection is divided between the British Museum and the Dublin Library. I have no means at hand for making a more definite reply, but this may put H. A. W. on the right track.   W. ROBERTS.

"AS MAD AS A TUP" (9ᵗʰ S. viii. 501).—In Scotland it is said of a young woman who incontinently seeks the society of men that she "rins like a blind tup-in-the-wind." "As mad as the baiting bull of Stamford" is a similar phrase which had its origin in a custom that took place annually in that town, derived from a traditional incident recorded in histories of Lincolnshire. In the proverb "As mad as a March hare," which occurs in Heywood's 'Epigrams,' 1567, the allusion is said to be to the fact that hares are unusually shy and wild in that month, their rutting time ; but Erasmus in his 'Aphorisms' (p. 266, 1542) says that "hares are wilder in marshes from the absence of hedge and cover." The question, therefore, is, Do hares exhibit any exceptional symptoms of wildness at their rutting time? And, if so, is it of such a remarkable character as to be likely to have given rise to the proverb?

J. Holden MacMichael.

Miscellaneous.

NOTES ON BOOKS, &c.

Twelfth Night; or, What You Will. Edited by Horace Howard Furness. (Philadelphia, Lippincott Co.)

One more volume—the thirteenth—has been added by Dr. Horace Howard Furness to that Variorum edition of Shakespeare which is the crowning achievement, as regards Shakespearian literature, of American scholarship, and puts to the blush all rival English effort. The thirteen volumes already issued include twelve plays, 'Hamlet,' as our readers presumably know, with the immense amount of criticism and exegesis to which it has given rise, occupying two volumes. Of the works now published, seven are comedies and five tragedies. With the historical plays Dr. Furness, it is understood, does not propose to concern himself, leaving that portion of his task to other and younger hands.

It is with delight that we watch on the shelves the augmenting row of volumes, and express a hope that the full series contemplated by the editor will appear under his supervision. Enough for fame, and enough also to constitute a proud lifetime's accomplishment, will be such productiveness.

In its present shape 'Twelfth Night' makes direct and strong appeal to the public. Facts of extreme value conspire to make the initial matter of keen interest. So far as regards the text, which is wholly based upon the First Folio, and of which no copy published in Shakespeare's lifetime exists, little difficulty is experienced. The principal errors are held to be typographical; and though there are some diverting cruces that seem now all but incapable of explanation, the text, by comparison with those of other works, is of exemplary purity. From the outset, however, what commentators persist in regarding as obscure faces the student. Whence comes the name, it is asked, and what is the significance of the second portion of the title? So well known are the revels attendant on Twelfth Night salutations, and so well remembered are the Saturnalia, that it requires more than the average denseness of the commentator to boggle over the words "what you will," while the orgies of the two knights, Feste, and Maria, and the sour-faced disapproval of Malvolio, who, according to the assertion of Maria, is sometimes "a kinde of a Puritane," are enough to satisfy us from what observations of current proceedings Shakespeare drew his notions. It is, of course, true that Sir Thomas Herbert, the Master of the Revels, in a copy of the Second Folio presented to him by King Charles I. altered the title to 'Malvolio,' this being one of five plays he treated after a similar fashion. To the man who gave us 'As You Like It,' 'Much Ado about Nothing,' 'The Winter's Tale,' and 'A Midsummer Night's Dream,' what title so likely to commend itself as 'Twelfth Night; or, What You Will'? the "what you will"

corresponding as closely as it well can to 'As You Like It.' Before the play is begun Dr. Furness has to deal with the reference in Manningham's 'Diary' to the performance of the piece at the Middle Temple on 2 February, 1601, the conjectures concerning the date of production on the strength of internal evidence being shown by this to be amusingly inaccurate. On this subject Dr. Furness makes merry, and in this the reader will probably follow him. We have only glanced over, not studied, the diary in question, but are curious to know whether the date should not be 1601/2, which would, of course, make it 1602, according to modern computation. Another question to be carefully settled is whether the original MS., which Collier was the first to use, has undergone any of the customary processes of that prince of falsifiers. With a view to settling this it should be closely inspected with the aid of a powerful lens. In this diary the Italian origin of the story is first indicated. A full history of this constitutes an attractive portion of the work. The well-known difficulties of the play, the "Lady of the Strachy," the "Equinoctial of Queubus," and other delightful puzzles, which we, as well as Dr. Furness, are glad to leave as mysteries, are treated at length. A full account of the music sung by the topers or by the clown is given, and the book is in all respects equal to the best of its predecessors. Dr. Furness is, indeed, the best of editors, and has learnt better than any other the all-important lesson that he edits best who meddles least. The reasonableness and sanity of his comments are in striking contrast with the rage for misunderstanding and meddling with which most men who approach Shakespeare seem afflicted. We sincerely hope that the whole of the comedies will be issued under his conscientious and intelligent supervision. Once more we note with profound sympathy the pious dedication, which, to those who know all, conveys so much which has passed into the region of sanctities.

What Great Men have said of Great Men: a Dictionary of Quotations. By William Wale. (Sonnenschein & Co.)

This volume is the latest addition to the useful "Dictionaries of Quotations" series, but scarcely rises to the high level of its predecessors. Familiarity with its contents is likely to make a man glib rather than well informed. The second name in the book, the arrangement of which is alphabetical, is Addison, the first being Abelard. Of the twenty-three passages given concerning the English writer many are quite superfluous. Tickell is not "a great man," and so does not come within the scope of the book. No one is the better for reading his assertion that "every Muse was fond of Addison." Lytton's eulogy is extravagant and James Ferguson's fantastic. By going through the volume, and striking out those—such as Richard Glover, Christopher Smart, Walter Harte, Elijah Fenton, William Hayley, and others—with no claim to greatness, and who are, indeed, already forgotten, the congested volume might be greatly relieved. If with them went some modern writers, altogether incapable of giving critical opinions of the slightest value, none would have a right or a disposition to complain. We are, however, no wise disposed to censure the manner in which Mr. Wale's task has been accomplished. His volume is not complete; it is undesirable, and almost impossible, that it should be so. It shows, none the less, omnivorous reading and wide research, and may be taken up at any time, ransacked with satisfaction, and laid aside. For this class of book we have, however, a dislike. Your purveyor of matter for magazine and periodical may turn to it and obtain a cheap and spurious reputation for knowledge. No genuine scholar will often employ in his work information he has not himself quarried, and the experienced critic mistrusts the assertion that A calls B such and such a thing, with no hint where this is done. Such assertions are, as a rule, misleading when not inexact. No great harm is perhaps done, since work constructed on facile principles is like jerry-built houses that collapse of themselves. We could suggest to Mr. Wale one or two extracts that might with advantage have appeared, but refrain, since his book is large enough. *Apropos* of the Georges I., II., III., IV., he might with advantage supply in his next edition the well-known lines beginning

> George the First was always reckoned
> Vile, and viler George the Second.

The Babylonian and the Hebrew Genesis. By H. Zimmern, Ph.D. (Nutt.)

The value of a book like this—the third issue of "The Ancient East" series—is not to be estimated by its size, which is small, or by its price, which is only one shilling. It gives us the mature and reasoned judgment of a great scholar on a problem of the most far-reaching interest—no less than the origin and development of those early beliefs which are recorded in the opening pages of the Hebrew Scriptures. No sincere and earnest student of the Old Testament should fail to possess himself of this concise but authoritative statement of the most recent results of Babylonian discovery in their bearing on the Book of Genesis. If the large number of people who profess to be readers of the Bible, and also lovers of truth, ignore this valuable series of manuals which Mr. Nutt is placing within their reach, we can only say that it is one more instance of the cant and obscurantism which are often characteristic of the popular religionism of the day. Our fathers, such people argue, did not, because they could not, know of these discoveries, and therefore we will not. "This they willingly are ignorant of."

Among the many subjects of historical interest in the later numbers of the *Intermédiaire* may be mentioned the faith-cures of Prince Alexander Leopold of Hohenlohe-Waldenburg-Schillingfürst, uncle of the late German Chancellor. The notes on the conduct of Rossel, immediately before his execution after the fall of the Commune, are also worthy of attention. Antiquaries who make a study of Christian relics will find, in a communication relating to the so-called nails of the Passion, that there used to be "une dent de Jésus-Christ" at Noyon. Unfortunately, however, the authority for this curious fact is not quoted.

Mélusine still continues to add to the hoard of ancient customs, rites, and beliefs which M. Gaidoz and his fellow-workers are indefatigable in bringing together.

The *Library Journal* gives all kinds of information on the methods used in developing the public libraries of America. If the average man of the Transatlantic communities does not speedily become a model of erudition it will be because inherent tendency still leads him to expend whatever energies he may possess in personal action on his own environment rather than to the acquirement of book-learning.

Dr. F. G. Lee, F.S.A., who has just died at the age of seventy, after the announcement of his conversion to the Church of Rome, was a well-known antiquary, and was long recognized as an authority on all matters pertaining to ecclesiological lore. As an author he will be best remembered for his large and learned volume on the 'History and Antiquities of the Prebendal Church of the Blessed Virgin Mary of Thame,' published in 1883. This was a work of singular interest and value, and one of which the late Bishop of Oxford (Dr. Stubbs) had the highest opinion as a learned historical work. He edited three editions of that well-known volume the 'Directorium Anglicanum,' which was originally brought out by his friend Mr. Purchas in 1858. He likewise compiled a 'Glossary of Liturgical and Ecclesiastical Terms,' containing many illustrations from his own pen and that of Mr. Pugin, and a 'Manuale Clericorum,' both dealing with many interesting liturgical questions. He contributed numerous papers on antiquarian subjects to the pages of *Archæologia*, the *Herald and Genealogist*, the *Ecclesiologist*, the *Ecclesiastic*, the *Records of Buckinghamshire*, and many similar serials. He was a contributor also to 'N. & Q.' He was a Fellow of the Society of Antiquaries of London, as well as of Scotland, and an honorary member of the Archæological Societies of Normandy and Rome, and of many bodies of a like nature. Dr. Lee, who was educated at Oxford, where he won the Newdigate in 1854, received the honorary degree of D.C.L. from the University of Salamanca in 1864, and that of D.D. from the Washington and Lee University, in Virginia, in 1879.   H. B.

Notices to Correspondents.

We must call special attention to the following notices:—

On all communications must be written the name and address of the sender, not necessarily for publication, but as a guarantee of good faith.

We cannot undertake to answer queries privately.

To secure insertion of communications correspondents must observe the following rules. Let each note, query, or reply be written on a separate slip of paper, with the signature of the writer and such address as he wishes to appear. When answering queries, or making notes with regard to previous entries in the paper, contributors are requested to put in parentheses, immediately after the exact heading, the series, volume, and page or pages to which they refer. Correspondents who repeat queries are requested to head the second communication "Duplicate."

M. L. R. B. ("The Essenes").—Shall appear next week.

NOTICE.

Editorial communications should be addressed to "The Editor of 'Notes and Queries'"—Advertisements and Business Letters to "The Publisher"—at the Office, Bream's Buildings, Chancery Lane, E.C.

We beg leave to state that we decline to return communications which, for any reason, we do not print; and to this rule we can make no exception.

LONDON, SATURDAY, FEBRUARY 8, 1902.

CONTENTS. — No. 215.

Notes.

EDWARD DE VERE, EARL OF OXFORD, AND THOMAS WATSON.

WHILST looking through the 'Shakespeare Anthology,' edited by Prof. Arber, I recently came across a sonnet which, on the strength of a manuscript in the Bodleian Library, is attributed to the above noble poet. But the words seemed so familiar that I felt certain I had read them elsewhere and that they were by a different writer. The same indefatigable editor furnished me with the means of showing that I was not mistaken, for, on turning to his reprint of Thomas Watson's poems, I found that the lines form the sixtieth and last sonnet of 'The Tears of Fancie; or, Love Disdained,' published in 1593. The discovery is so curious and interesting that I hope to be excused for quoting both pieces. De Vere's, printed for the first time in 1899, is as follows :—

Who taught thee first to sigh, 'Alas!' my heart?
                Love.
Who taught thy tongue the woeful words of plaint?
                Love.
Who filled your eyes with tears of bitter smart?
                Love.
Who gave thee grief, and made thy joys so faint?
                Love.
Who first did paint with colours pale thy face?
                Love.
Who first did break thy sleeps of quiet rest? Love.
Above the rest in Court, who gave thee grace? Love.
Who made thee strive in honour to be best? Love.
In constant troth, to bide so firm and pure? Love.
To scorn the World, regarding but thy friends?
                Love.
With patient mind, each Passion to endure? Love.
In one desire to settle to the end? Love.
    Love then thy choice! wherein such choice thou bind;
    As nought but death may ever change thy mind.*

I will now give the sonnet as it was printed more than three hundred years ago, when the last of the Tudors sat on the throne of England :—

Who taught thee first to sigh Alasse sweet heart?
                love.
Who taught thy tongue to marshall words of plaint?
                love.
Who fild thine eies with teares of bitter smart? *love.*
Who gave thee griefe and made thy ioyes so faint?
                love.
Who first did paint with coullers pale thy face? *love.*
Who first did breake thy sleepes of quiet rest? *love.*
Who forst thee unto wanton love give place? *love.*
Who thrald thy thoughts in fancie so distrest? *love.*
Who made thee bide both constant firme and sure?
                love.
Who made thee scorne the world and love thy friend?
                love.
Who made thy mind with patience paines indure?
                love.
Who made thee settle stedfast to the end? *love.*
    Then love thy choice though love be never gained,
    Still live in love, dispaire not though disdained.†

Now, as they stand, it is manifestly impossible that these poems could have been written by two separate persons, for the one is almost a copy of the other, as the reader may see for himself. It is, however, very strange that the imitator should have ascribed the verses to De Vere, Earl of Oxford, as I shall show. Thomas Watson's life was short; he was about forty-five years old, or thereabouts, when he died in 1592. De Vere, born in 1545, ended his career, about which there was no "odour of sanctity," in 1604, so there could not have been much difference between the ages of the poets. But now comes in the curious fact that Watson's poem 'The Ἑκατομπαθία, or Passionate Centurie of Love,' published in 1582, is dedicated "To the Right Honorable my very good Lord Edward de Vere, Earle of Oxenford, Vicount Bulbecke, Lord of Escales, and Badlesmere, and Lord High Chamberlaine of England,"

---

* 'The Shakespeare Anthology,' p. 48. The words *your* in the third line, and *friends* at the end of the tenth, are enough of themselves to prove that the MS. is valueless. See the corresponding lines in the next poem.

† Thomas Watson's 'Poems,' p. 208. Arber's reprint, 1870.

who had, we are told, "at convenient leisures favourablie perused it, being as yet in written hand." It has been suggested that the earl may have written the introductory notices which precede the poems in this work. But that supposition is altogether untenable, for, although they are mostly put in the third person, they are of such a character and so fully describe the sources whence the poet drew his inspiration, that we are forced to the conclusion that no other hand than his could have composed them.

However, that is a matter which needs no further argument on this occasion. We are now only concerned with the above-quoted sonnet and its authorship, which must be unhesitatingly ascribed to Thomas Watson. That it was printed in 1593 is indisputable. Furthermore, one might call it an echo of another poem in the 'Passionate Centurie of Love' (lxxxix.), the first twelve lines of which begin with the word "love," just as the corresponding number end with it in the one under discussion. And what is still more remarkable is the fact that the "annotation" prefixed to this piece is written in the first person, so that all doubt is removed.* I do not claim any great merit for the lines, but they are peculiar in their way, and should be assigned to their rightful author, who was Thomas Watson, despite their attribution to the Earl of Oxford on the authority of "MS. Rawl. Poet. 85, in Bodleian Library," by Prof. Arber in his excellent volume.

De Vere's fame as a poet is for the most part legendary. We have scarcely anything left that we may regard as the genuine offspring of his muse. There can be no doubt that he once enjoyed a considerable reputation. Puttenham, in his 'Arte of English Poesie,' published in 1589, writes as follows:

"And in her Maiesties time that now is are sprong up an other crew of Courtly makers Noble men and Gentlemen of her Maiesties owne servauntes, who have written excellently well as it would appeare if their doings could be found out and made publicke with the rest, of which number is first that noble Gentleman Edward Earle of Oxford."—Arber's reprint, p. 75.†

This testimony is emphatic, but indefinite, and savours of adulation, in which the writer was an adept. We get something more specific on p. 77, where he bestows praise on "Th' Earle of Oxford and Maister Edwardes of her Maiesties Chappell for Comedy and Enterlude." In this, the last chapter of

* This is not the only one; there are two more: see poems xli. and lxii.
† Puttenham here seems to borrow from Webbe's 'Discourse of English Poetrie,' 1586. See pp. 33, 35, Arber's reprint, 1870.

book i., we have a very interesting criticism of English poets, dead and living, from Chaucer and Gower to "Sir Philip Sydney and Maister Challenner, and that other Gentleman who wrate the late shepheardes Callender," which proves he did not know Spenser's name; but no mention is made of Thomas Watson, though his chief poem had been in print for seven years. But the greatest genius of all, according to Puttenham, was Elizabeth herself! Here are his own words :—

"But last in recitall and first in degree is the Queene our soveraigne Lady, whose learned, delicate, noble Muse, easily surmounteth all the rest that have written before her time or since, for sence, sweetnesse and subtillitie, be it in Ode, Elegie, Epigram, or any other kinde of poeme Heroick or Lyricke, wherein it shall please her Maiestie to employ her penne, even by as much oddes as her owne excellent estate and degree exceedeth all the rest of her most humble vassals."

I have quoted this amazing piece of flattery to show that the praise was as ill bestowed in the case of the queen as of the earl. What has the latter left to justify Puttenham's eulogium? A few pieces, among which the best is the one entitled 'The Judgment of Desire,' that has held a place in almost every anthology since the publication of Percy's 'Reliques.' Percy tells us that he found it entire in the 'Garland of Good-will,' printed about the close of the sixteenth century. Of this poem Ellis says it is the "only one of his productions which can be said to rise a little above mediocrity," which opinion confirms Percy's, where we read (vol. ii. book ii.): "Perhaps it is no injury to his reputation that few of his compositions are preserved for the inspection of impartial posterity." This well-known piece is not given in the 'Golden Treasury,' nor in Prof. Arber's 'Shakespeare Anthology,' but it is quoted in full by Prof. Saintsbury in his 'History of Elizabethan Literature,' pp. 127-8, to prove that Lord Oxford was "a charming writer of verse." But are the lines really his, though, so to speak, guaranteed by Puttenham himself, who quotes a portion of them? At the third reference to the 'Arte of English Poesie' we find the following passage, which I beg to transcribe in its entirety, as so much depends on it :—

"Edward Earle of Oxford a most noble and learned Gentleman made in this figure of responce an emble of desire otherwise called Cupide which from his excellencie and wit, I set downe some part of the verses, for example.

When wert thou borne desire?
In pompe and pryme of May,
By whom sweete boy wert thou begot?
By good conceit men say,

Tell me who was thy nurse?
Fresh youth in sugred ioy.
What was thy meate and dayly foode?
Sad sighes with great annoy.
What hadst thou then to drinke?
Unfayned lovers teares.
What cradle wert thou roeked [*sic*] in?
In hope devoyde of feares.   Pp. 215-6.

Puttenham's volume, as I have said, was published in 1589; Watson's 'Passionate Centurie of Love' in 1582, with a dedication to De Vere; and it is beyond doubt that the latter was indebted to the twenty-second poem in that book for his subject and much of his language. Watson's inspiration was derived from the Italian, as he himself informs us. I cannot quote the whole piece, but the following lines will show that the earl's verses are only an adaptation and can claim no originality:—

When werte thou borne sweet Love? who was thy sire?
When Flora first adorn'd Dame Tellus lap,
Then sprung I forth from Wanton hote desire:
Who was thy nurse to feede thee first with pap?
Youth first with tender hand bound up my heade,
Then saide, with Lookes alone I should be fed;
What maides had she attendant on her side,
To playe, to singe, to rock thee fast a sleepe?

Though this is not such a glaring case as the other, it may perhaps be assumed that De Vere could never have written the lines attributed to him had he been unacquainted with those of Thomas Watson. There I leave the matter.   John T. Curry.

THE ESSENES.

Few problems have vexed the souls of historians more intensely than the product called Essenism, which apparently sprang into being during the tempestuous reigns of the Hasmonean princes in the second century B.C. At any rate, nothing seems to be definitely known of their existence prior to this date, unless the Beisussim mentioned in the Talmud, who were in open contest with the Sopherim or Scribes, may be the party subsequently designated the Essenes. Their political influence on their brethren was practically nil, and it is even questionable whether their impress on literature and morals was much more. One or two famous dicta in the Gemara seem directly traceable to them, such as "Heaven can control all things except reverence," "Work is preferable to worship," "Work not for personal gain, but for its own sake," "Communism or death." In these relics there may lurk much indirect material by which we can reconstruct the popular attitude towards these Jewish Socialists, and also gauge the ethical value of their services to posterity.

It might prove interesting to sketch what seem to be the "converging lines" of the ethnic developments that made the Maccabean era a fitting *nidus* for the reception of Essenic germs in the Hebraic organism. Essenism is briefly a compound of Judaism, Parseeism, and Hellenism. Now Judaism, much as it is a sensuous religion, partakes also of the nature of asceticism, which it derives in the first instance from the Egyptian hierarchy. The question of "clean and unclean," the Sabbath dogmas, the Expiation regulations, and so forth, all indicate a considerable degree of self-repression and monastic reserve which came to Jewry *viâ* Egypt. The Nazarite and Rechabite groups, also the Cohanim (priestly caste), show strong tendencies towards groupings or classifications even in pre-exile times. So that a disposition towards a principle which apparently wars with the major forces of Mosaism lay latent in its bosom, needing merely the confluence of generating stimuli to excite it into a living entity in any given era of the Jewish state. Unfavourable conditions alone must be alleged for its non-arrival or birth sooner than later, among which the most favourable was the spread of Hellenism in Judæa through the domination of the Seleucidæ on the one side, and of the Lagidæ in Alexandria on the other. Parseeism, to which a short reference is necessary, made its appearance in the literature and dogmas of the Jews in the fourth century B.C., during which period it is surmised that the 'Jobeid' and many of the Psalms were composed. Angelology, which is a striking feature of Essenism and of the Zohar, chisels its features deeply into the tenets of this strange sect. The Hebrews themselves derived many practices from their Persian rulers, one of which (introduced by Ezra—*i.e.*, of reading portions of the Scriptures on Sabbaths) has survived to this day. Moreover, there are not wanting thinkers who hold, from the similarity of many of the rites of the ancient Parsees and the Jews, that they both sprang from some common ancestor. In any case, Persian dualism is unmistakably imbedded in many of the later writings of the Jews. How far this Parsee element was powerful to colour the ceremonies of the Greek world before and after Persia was conquered by Alexander, 331 B.C., has always remained an unsettled point; but that the early settlers in Greece (who came from Asia Minor, and brought with them the Lydians, whose Semitic origin has been clearly ascertained) imported many Persian rites seems quite feasible, and may help to explain the existence of Orphism in Homer and elsewhere, albeit some contend that these passages are spurious. Many of these early settlers in the plains of Attica worshipped the Pelasgian Zeus, whose temple is the sky, the unseen father dwelling alone, whose resemblance to the Hebraic Jahveh is, to say the least, noteworthy. These immigrants built a temple in which they hung "a perpetual lamp," and from certain remains it is conjectured they lived on rocks, resembling the "rock-dwellers" of the Scriptures. There are many other citable facts, all pointing more or less directly to Semitic strands in the rites and ceremonies of the Greeks. Nor can the relation of the Pythagoreans to the question be overlooked. Herodotus records that Pythagoras brought back from Egypt a complete insight into the arcana of Egyptian priestcraft, among which was the theory of metempsychosis, of the immortality of the soul, and of "clean and unclean." The Pythagoreans possessed many traits in common with the Essenes.

All this heterogeneous evidence shows that the barriers between Hellenism and Judaism were never so wide but a day would come when the two systems could merge and flourish in one camp. That camp was to be Essenism. In fact, the Rabbis, whose tolerance is constantly receiving signal demonstration, favoured Hellenism, and even discovered in Gen. ix. 27 a prophetic sanction to harmonious intercourse between Aryan and Semite. Reference to Alexander has already been made *supra*. Now when that emperor founded Alexandria, 332 B.C., he little dreamt that the decaying forces of Hellenism were to spring into renewed activity in less than a century from his death. About 260 B.C. the Alexandrian Jews translated the Scriptures into Greek, and so enabled the Therapeutæ—a similar sect to the Essenes — to obtain an insight into Mosaism. Regarding the existence of this band of Socialists there raged a battle royal between Graetz and Zeller. But if Zeller is correct, it follows that the Alexandrian Jews must have had an object-lesson in communistic living ready made. Now intercourse between Judæa and Alexandria was continuous, despite the fact of the building of the Onian temple near Heliopolis. Regular pilgrimages were made to Jerusalem, and tribute and offerings were religiously dispatched. Moreover, when Philo wrote his 'De Vitâ Contemplativa' it may reasonably be assumed that there were communistic ideas afloat in the philosophic and doctrinal controversies of the learned Alexandrine Jews, some of whom, bolder than the rest, may have returned to Judæa to put into a practical form what they had learnt from the Therapeutæ in Egypt. Hence, in all likelihood, arose the Essenes.

A sect that discouraged marriage was not destined to grow into a multitudinous race; and, apart from this destructive factor, the religious tenets of the Essenes were lacking in the warmth and colour of the parent faith, and thus could hardly compete with Judaism, even if the "selective" conditions of membership did not oppose an impassable barrier to successful development.

M. L. R. Breslar.
Percy House, South Hackney.

Rollo on North Wyke alias Moreton Wyke.—I should be glad if through your columns I could communicate with one Rollo, who, in 1899, wrote to the owner of North Wyke, in South Tawton, Devon, suggesting the identity of that estate with the Wica that in Edward the Confessor's day was held by Ordulf, and at the time of the Domesday survey by Robert, Earl of Moretain. Premising that in the opinion of the Rev. O. G. Reichel (based, he believes, principally on the sequence in the Exeter Book) this Wica is represented by Wick in Shobrook, and certainly not by Teignweek *als.* Highweek, as sometimes conjectured, Rollo maintains that there are many grounds for passing over these claims in favour of North Wyke, in South Tawton. Accepting Worthy's statement that this North Wyke* was, in or about the reign of Henry II., held by William de Wigornia, "a grandson of Waleran de Bellomonte, Earl of Mellant, created in 1144 first Earl of Worcester" (Comes Wigorniæ), and noting that in the Visitation of 1564 the name of the house appears as Moreton Wyke, Rollo advances the theory that it must have been included in those Devonshire estates of the Earl of Moretain which were bestowed by Henry I. on Reginald FitzHenry, Earl of Cornwall, and which upon Reginald's death were resumed by the king, with the exception of such estates as Reginald had given to his daughters.† One of these daughters being Maude, wife of Robert Bellomonte, Earl of Mellant and Worcester, there would be no difficulty in supposing her to

* The topographers seem to have fallen into some confusion between North Wyke in South Tawton, North Wyke in North Tawton, and Chawleigh Wyke *als.* Flambert's Wyke, near Chulmleigh.
† What historic evidence is there for the gift of *Devonshire* estates to Reginald's daughters?

have handed down a part of her share to William de Wigornia (whom Rollo, probably following Worthy, describes as "one of her own younger sons"); while that the Earls of Moretain did hold land in the parish of South Tawton is testified by the grant (recorded in Oliver's 'Monasticon,' p. 228) by King John, when Earl of Moretain ("dum essemus Comes Moritonensis"), of certain rents in Allingeston (now Allison), within the manor of South Tawton, to the priory of Canonsleigh. I may add that, from comparison of ancient records, I should judge Allingeston to have been the lordship-house of the manor later known as Ytton, and comprising Collibeare, Serslande, &c., in which case part of it was contiguous to the lands of North Wyke proper (which, as Rollo points out, very nearly correspond in acreage with the Wica of Domesday). The Rev. Wm. Wykes-Finch informs me that Itton, Powlesland, Youldens, Collibeare, Sessland, &c., were long held by the North Wyke family. As to Worthy's assertion that William de Wigornia was possessed of North Wyke and of divers other lands in the parish (in particular the manor of East Ash), besides Wray in Moreton Hampstead and Cheverston in Kenton (the last three "by royal grant"), I have yet to learn—and should be very pleased to know—his authority. Certain it is that Bellomontes were at that time lords of the manor of South Tawton.

My own paper in the *Transactions* of the Devon Association for 1901 contains some early local matter that in an expert's hands might throw further light upon the case.

ETHEL LEGA-WEEKES.

EARLY HOTELS OF ROME.—In 1469, close to St. Peter's, was an inn bearing the sign of "The Ass" (Asino), managed by Giorgio Britanno.[*] This reminds one that here was that ancient Anglo-Saxon quarter, dating from the days of Ina and Ceadwalla, the quarter of S. Spirito, where doubtless Raher, of St. Bartholomew the Great, and certainly Thomas A'Beckett, a little later, lodged when in Rome. In the commencement of the sixteenth century we find a Pietro de Leone keeping a hotel there "in casa dell' Ospedale de l' inglesi." The Piazza di Spagna already had "l' osteria del Cavalletto" in 1701, as Valesio records in his diary, where he like-

[*] "Georgio de Brectania hospiti hospitii Asini apud S. Petrum Fl(or) ij b(on) liiij pro expensis factis iiij equis cursorum Imperatoris."—'Arch. di Stato di Roma,' Mandati Camerali, vol. 1468-9, fol. 180. Cf. 'Ricerche Storiche intorno Agli Alberghi di Roma,' F. Cerasoli. The emperor here referred to was Frederick III.

wise refers to a robbery at another "locanda" there, called Monte d' Oro, at the mouth of the street leading to Trinità di Monti, called S. Sebastianello. ST. CLAIR BADDELEY.

"PATTLE." (See 'Brattle,' 9th S. viii. 500.)—In the 'Durham Account Rolls' (Surtees Soc.), the third volume of which, containing the Glossary, &c., is just about to be issued, we find the terms *patele, patil,* and *plogh pattyl,* used of "a ploughpaddle or spud, to clear off adherent soil or weeds, or for breaking large clods." The Glossary gives a reference to Deut. xxiii. 13, A.V. J. T. F.

CAPT. S. FORSTER TO N. TILSON, 1673: A CURIOUS HISTORICAL LETTER.—Among my collections is the following original autograph letter, dated 18 August, 1673, from a Capt. S. Forster, at Fleet (near Holbeach), in Lincolnshire, to Mr. Nathan Tilson, who appears to have resided opposite to the "Red Hart" Inn, in Fetter Lane, London. The writer, who was evidently a wag—or, as some would say, "a jolly fellow"—humorously refers to matters and things of historical interest, and his letter is therefore, I think, worthy of publication in 'N. & Q.' Moreover, many of your readers would, like myself, no doubt be glad to know more of these correspondents, as well as of the Mr. Lawrence (Tilson's neighbour) and Mr. Peter referred to therein. The explanatory foot-notes, it must be understood, are mine.

fleet. 18. Aug. 1673.

Deare Sr,—I am here safe, (God be thanked,) I left my bagg and baggage att Lyn,[*] drinkeing helter Skelter in King John's cupp,[†] but I hope the washes wilbe more kinde to my neice,[‡] I 'le venture it howeuer. I intreat you doe me the kindnesse to deliuer the inclosed wh the french Edict, Decree, I know not what you call it to my Lord priuy Seale, if it be knowne I shalbe hangd, but the right I thinke ought to take place, especially belonging to the late Kings sonne and our Kings-brother,[§] wee say here that the french wud not fight the last Engagement, marry hang them for cowardly traytorly whorelily rogues.[‖] My most humble service to Amorous

[*] Lynn Regis (or King's Lynn), co. Norfolk.

[†] The Corporation of Lynn boasts of having been presented by King John with a very rich double-gilt cup and cover, weighing 73 oz., which is still preserved and used on public occasions; and at the same time a large sword with a silver mounting from his own side, as is engraven on the inscription on the hilt.

[‡] Referring to King John crossing the washes of Lincolnshire.

[§] James, Duke of York, brother to Charles II., and afterwards King James II. He resigned his place of Admiral of the Fleet 9 April previously (1673), and was succeeded by Prince Rupert.

[‖] Alluding to Prince Rupert's engagement with the Dutch fleet, 11th of same month (August, 1673), in which, owing to the French squadron (our allies)

Mary, and incomparable Ann, if their husband and gallant Mr Peter be amongst the lineing, tell him I am not dead and so forth. I am

yors euer
S. Forster.

pray seale this. pray faile not the speedy deliuery. pray tell my Lord* That you must call for it whin a week's tyme.

yors whout date I receaued yesterday, and am heartily sorry for mrs Tilson's sicknesse, I wish wh my heart that Peter had hers and his owne too, I returne my vnfeigned thanks for yor care of my Tally, methinkes the king and I should not differ for the interest of 35l. for 2 or 3 yeares,† present my humble Seruice to yor good neighbour mr Lawrence, and tell him what I say.

Addressed :—
To Mr Nathan Tilson
over agt the red-hart Inn‡
in ffetter lane
London
dd.

Endorsed :—
18 August 1673
Captn fforster.
W. I. R. V.

Discovery in the Churchyard of Malvern Priory.—Some excavations made for drainage purposes in the churchyard of Malvern Priory early this year have led to a discovery which is, I think, of sufficient interest to deserve record here. Although lately on a brief visit to Great Malvern, I was unfortunately away on the day on which the kiln described below was brought to light. I therefore quote the remarks of a writer in the *Malvern Gazette* of Friday, 10 January. All antiquaries are aware that the monks of "Moche Malverne" carried on the manufacture of so-called "encaustic" tiles on a large scale. The fine old priory church still retains many examples of them. According to the writer in the *Gazette*:—

"The discovery of the old kiln in which the encaustic tiles were baked was a very interesting one, and it was a wonder local archæologists did not more carefully investigate it when the opportunity was afforded, which may never occur again, as it is now covered in with several feet of earth. The kiln was apparently a facsimile of those discovered in the Hendon grounds, and which are pictured and described at page 71 of Mr. Nott's book, 'Malvern Priory Church.' The kiln was semicircular in plan, with an upper and lower chamber, the former being for the tiles and the latter for the heat source, which was probably derived from charcoal, supplies of which would be abundant and suitable.

standing neuter the latter part of the day, his victory was not so complete as it might have been.
* The Lord Privy Seal.
† Perhaps referring to money lent the king for the Dutch war.
‡ This and the "Crose Keys" are the only two taverns in Fetter Lane named in a MS. 'List of Taverns in London and Westminster and Ten Miles round London, 1690-8' (*penes me*).

The tiles found this week were in almost every case imperfect, and were apparently the failures which had been utilised in the building or repair of the kiln. Doubtless all the perfect ones would be removed from the kiln before it was abandoned by the monks. Those unearthed were either over-burnt or imperfect in design or shape, and very few of them were of ecclesiastical character, the religious symbols being practically absent. But in the interests of archæology, it seems a pity that, as they were found in the churchyard itself, they were not retained for inspection and report by some one qualified to do so. As it was, they became the possession of any one who cared to carry them off, and are now dispersed beyond recovery."

One cannot help sharing the regret expressed in the above paragraph. Malvern teems with clergy and retired professional men. It is, therefore, the more remarkable that the ancient kiln, while exposed, was not accurately measured and delineated. The tiles, which are described as apparently failures, might have shed light on the process by which the monks achieved interesting artistic results. Charles Hiatt.

The First Gentleman of Colour to receive Knighthood.—The *Daily Telegraph* of February 1st records the death of Sir William Conrad Reeves, who was the first gentleman of colour to receive the distinction of knighthood and to occupy the position of a British Chief Justice. He was, according to 'Whitaker's Peerage,' born in 1841, and married, in 1868, Margaret, *née* Rudder. In early life he came from the Barbados to England, entered the Middle Temple, was called in 1863, and after returning to the West Indies practised for some time at the Bar. He became Attorney-General in St. Vincent in 1867, was appointed Q.C. in 1883, in 1886 was made Chief Justice of Barbados, and in 1889 received the honour of knighthood.
N. S. S.

"Gun."—
Caistor was a city when Norwich was none,
And Norwich was built with Caistor stone.

This is still the vulgar pronunciation of "stone" and "bone." We know the pronunciation "bun," witness Bunhill Fields; *done* is still called "dun," and *none* "nun." Now I have a new etymology for the word "gun." Any ordinary dictionary will tell you it is probably derived from "engine." This is absurd. It is evidently "gone," gone off, old pronunciation, neither "gawn" nor "gone."
Brutus.

[The origin suggested in the 'H.E.D.' seems much more probable. Your conjecture is not likely to find favour with philologists.]

The Gourou Nut.—This is a synonym for the *kola* nut, highly prized by cyclists for its stimulating and sustaining properties, which are analogous to those of the South American *coca*. The term is included, of course, in the 'N.E.D.,' but without etymology, unless we count as such the vague remark, "Presumed to belong to some African language." In view of its importance, it may be worth while to place on record here the actual forms which I have found in some African tongues. In the Wolof of Senegambia it is called *gourou*, in the wide-spread Hausa it is *goro*, in the Songay of Timbuctoo it is *gouro*, in the Fulah it is *garru*. This last may account for a third orthography sometimes met with in English—namely, *karoo* nut. In the Mandingo, spoken in the French Soudan, it changes its initial, and becomes *wourou* or *woro*, according to J. B. Rambaud's 'Dictionnaire,' 1896.

JAS. PLATT, Jun.

Queries.

WE must request correspondents desiring information on family matters of only private interest to affix their names and addresses to their queries, in order that the answers may be addressed to them direct.

"TO POUR OIL UPON THE WAVES," &c.—We want for the Dictionary examples of this, in the figurative sense, before 1847. As the practice itself was discussed before the Royal Society and in the press in 1774, the figurative use might arise at any time after that date, and ought to be found long before 1847.

J. A. H. MURRAY.

Oxford.

[Perhaps first from some translation of Plutarch, who discussed the question before the Royal Society did.]

THACKERAY QUOTATION.—Where in Thackeray's works shall I find the following on Washington Irving: "The first ambassador of the New World to the Old"?

RUDOLF GROSSKUNZ.

Leipzig.

MILTON: A TRACT ON LOGIC.—In 1672 was published 'Artis Logicæ Plenior Institutio ad Petri Rami Methodum Concinnata,' by John Milton. Has this ever been reprinted, either separately or as part of a collected edition of Milton's works?

CHARLES R. DAWES.

EARL OF CROMARTIE. — In ' Links with the Past,' by Mrs. Charles Bagot, is the following extract from the diary of Miss Mary Bagot :—

" 1823, Aug. 4. Miss Hay and Mrs. Bowdler, who are both with us, mentioned the following circumstance, which both had *seen* [*sic*]. Lady Augusta Murray, who was born three months *after the execution of her father*, the Earl of Cromarty, came into the world with the mark of an axe and three drops of blood upon her throat, which she bore to her dying day."

How is this to be reconciled with the following entry in the ' Annual Register ' ?—

"Sept. 29, 1766, died the Earl of Cromartie, in Poland Street. He received his late Majesty's pardon for being concerned in the rebellion in 1745."

H. S. V.-W.

ROYAL DESCENDANTS.—Will any of your correspondents kindly inform me when replies appeared concerning descendants (?) of Princess Cicely, Viscountess Wells, daughter of Edward IV.? Also a reply relative to the family of Wellesbourne, said to descend from Princess Eleanor, daughter of King John?

C. H.

SIR GEOFFREY FENTON.—Is anything known of the parentage of Sir Geoffrey Fenton, Secretary of State for Ireland, *temp.* Elizabeth? He married Alice Weston, and his daughter Catherine was the wife of "the great Earl" of Cork.

KATHLEEN WARD.

Castle Ward, Downpatrick.

WATERLOO ENGRAVINGS.—A friend of mine has a set of coloured prints representing the scenes of Waterloo. Some of these are both drawn and engraved by Rouse, others by Rouse and Hamilton ; while portraits of the leading characters at the famous battle are by G. Cruikshank. Evidently they were originally bound up with letterpress. Perhaps one of your readers could tell me what value they possess at the present time. Their artistic merit does not appear to be great, but otherwise they seem to possess a considerable interest.

HOLCOMBE INGLEBY.

Heacham Hall, Norfolk.

FRANCES B. IRVING. — Can any reader kindly furnish me with any particulars of a lady named Frances B. Irving, who was living about 1850?

CORONATION.

[Fannie B. Irving published in 1888, through Fisher Unwin, ' Six Girls: a Home Story,' illustrated.]

DAKIN FAMILY.—I am collecting material for a history of the Dakin family in America, and should greatly appreciate any information of or clue to the birthplace and parentage of Thomas Dakin, who was born, according to his will, in 1624, and who was at Concord, Massachusetts, about 1654.

A. H. DAKIN, Jun.

Tenafly, New Jersey, U.S.

"Roof-tree."—What is the origin of this?
LEIGH MORRIS.

["Two pairs of bent trees, in form resembling the lancet-shaped arches of a Gothic church, were set up on the ground, and united at their apexes by a ridge-tree" (Addy's 'Evolution of the English House,' p. 27). We recommend the purchase of this book, which appeared in 1898, as a volume of the "Social England Series" of Messrs. Swan Sonnenschein & Co., price 4s. 6d. It is full of information on such subjects.]

FUNERAL FOLK-LORE.—What is the origin of the notion that a path or road along which a corpse is carried on its way to burial becomes thereby a public highway, if it was not one before? This doctrine seems to be widely held.   D. C. I.

[See 4ᵗʰ S. xi. 213, 285, 374, 433; xii. 96, 158; 5ᵗʰ S. x. 49, 197.]

STONING THE WREN.—I should be glad if any of your readers could tell me in what parts of England the custom of stoning wrens to death is carried on on 26 December, also if any one would give me a full account of this ceremony.   N. W. OSBORNE.

[See 6ᵗʰ S. x. 492; xi. 58, 177, 297. Consult also Croker's 'Researches in the South of Ireland' and Dyer's 'British Popular Customs,' and you will find what you seek.]

"SKIRRET."—Is this word associated with the craft of Freemasonry? I am informed that in gardening it is applied to a reel with cord for aligning paths, beds, &c.   V.

BURKE'S VISITS TO MONMOUTHSHIRE.—Mr. John Morley, on p. 10 of his 'Burke' ("English Men of Letters," 1882 edit.), says of Burke's early years, "At the date of which we are speaking, he used to seek a milder air at Bristol, or in Monmouthshire or Wiltshire." Can any of your readers give me any information as to Burke's visits to Monmouthshire? The local histories I have consulted do not mention any visits made by him to the neighbourhood, nor have I been able to glean any details from the works of Burke to which I have access.   A. G.

"SAULIES."—What is the derivation of this old Scottish word, which was in use at the beginning of the seventeenth century, and meant hired mourners at funerals? The only suggested derivations which I have seen are the Anglo-Saxon *sal*, black; the Gaelic *sall*, mockery; and the Latin *salve reginam*. It has occurred to me that the appearance of these men, dressed in black cloaks with hoods, and carrying drooping black flags or banners ("deule weedes"), may have suggested a resemblance to weeping willows, and that the name was derived from the French word *saule*—"un saule pleureur, un saule qui pleure" (Littré). Many Scottish words in use at the beginning of the seventeenth century had French parentage. Sir Walter Scott, in his 'Antiquary,' describes common "saulies" as miserable-looking old men clad with threadbare black coats, and tottering as if on the edge of that grave to which they were marshalling another; but at funerals of the great there were sometimes as many as fifty "saulies," and these were of a better class. The Rev. Robert Blair, of Athelstaneford, in his poem 'The Grave,' thus alludes to the hired mourners (I quote from my copy of the first edition, 1743):—

But see! the well-plum'd *Herse* comes nodding on
Stately and slow; and properly attended
By the whole Sable Tribe, that painful watch
The sick Man's Door, and live upon the Dead,
By letting out their Persons by the Hour
To mimick Sorrow, when the Heart's not sad.
     W. S.

KINGSMAN.—George William Kingsman and Thomas Kingsman were admitted respectively to Westminster School in 1771 and 1775. Any information which would lead to their identification is desired.   G. F. R. B.

ANTINOMIAN SECT.—Mr. Havelock Ellis, in his useful work on 'The Criminal,' pp 125, 126 (Walter Scott, 1895), says :—

"On the whole, we may conclude that the practice of the instinctive and habitual criminal corresponds very closely with the faith of that religious sect who in Commonwealth days held 'that heaven and all happiness consists in the acting of those things which are sin and wickedness,' and 'that such men and women are most perfect and like to God or eternity, which do commit the greatest sins with least remorse.'"

Can this peculiar sect be identified?
RICHARD H. THORNTON.
Portland, Oregon.

GAZLAY FAMILY.—Search is now being made for the birthplace of John Gazlay, an Englishman, who emigrated to America in 1717, and settled at Goshen, Orange County, New York. Family tradition, possibly erroneous, attributes to him a Welsh origin. Major-General Sir Alfred Gaselee is of opinion that there is no possibility of relationship with his family, which deduces a descent from a Gaselee, possibly a continental emigrant, who is found at Portsmouth in 1650. There is, of course, the village of Gasely, in Suffolk, to supply a place-name, and Sir Alfred Gaselee is so kind as to inform me of a family of Gazeley in England. I shall be very grateful for names and addresses of members of this family, or for extracts from church registers, or instances of the occurrence of the name, for an account of the family which I am now printing.

ARIBERT GAZLAY.
Chamber of Commerce Building, Cincinnati.

TIB'S EVE.—The other day I was conversing with a man about a prospective event. "Yes," said he, "it will be on Tib's Eve, neither before nor after Christmas," expressing thus his incredulity as to the function ever coming off. I see that Miss Baker records the saying, but makes no comment as to its origin. Is it known in other counties?

JOHN T. PAGE.
West Haddon, Northamptonshire.
[See 8th S. iv. 507; v. 58, 132, 193, 298, 438; vi. 213.]

MRS. JAMES DENN OR DENNE.—Can any reader of 'N. & Q.' supply the maiden name and parentage of Mrs. James Denn or Denne (mother of the first Countess Beauchamp), whose portrait by Reynolds is at Madresfield? It is said that her name was Hippisley, but it is not known upon what evidence. Information concerning her husband, James Denne, is also desired. ST. GEORGE.

UNCOVERING AT THE NATIONAL ANTHEM.—It would be interesting to know when this practice first became a recognized custom. Can any of your correspondents decide this question? I have an impression that it was unknown before the accession of the late Queen, and that it became a common observance especially to denote public sympathy after the death of the Prince Consort. In country places it has not yet taken root, for many of the most enthusiastically loyal people will neither stand nor uncover at the well-known sounds. F. T. ELWORTHY.

GWYNETH.—This is an old Welsh Christian name. What is the proper form—Gwyneth or Gweneth? On a tombstone in Monkton Priory Church, Pembroke, it is spelt Geneth. Gwynedd, pronounced Gwyneth, was the old name for a portion of North Wales, but I presume this is a different word.

J. P. LEWIS.

WILLIAM GERARD HAMILTON, 1729-96.—In M. E. Cumming Bruce's 'Family Records of the Bruces and the Cumyns' (1870), p. 366, it is stated that James Bruce of Kinnaird (the African traveller) entered Harrow School on 21 January, 1742, together with the above and other kinsmen. The 'D.N.B.' says that "Single-Speech Hamilton" was educated at Winchester and Oriel, where he matriculated, in 1745, at the age of sixteen. Was he also at Harrow under Dr. Cox? A. R. BAYLEY.
St. Margaret's, Malvern.

SILVER ORNAMENTS.—I have an old silver necklet (in two parts as bracelets) in ten small plates, with representations of the Annunciation, &c., on them, some worn so that the subject is difficult to distinguish. The plates are three, four, and five sided, and slightly open-worked at the top of each. No hall-mark. Can any one tell me of a work on silver ornaments, or any way in which I could find the probable date and history? C. F. Y.

"WYRALL."—In Harl. MS. 1419a (a list of the effects of Henry VIII. in 1547) the following is said (on folio 169) to be "at Westminster":—

"Item three staves, every of theym having a picke with two graynes at the nether end and a *wyrall* of Iron tynned."

There are several references to "a *virall* of golde" in other parts of the same MS. What is the meaning of this word? There is no trace of it in my edition of Halliwell's 'Archaic and Provincial Words' (1855).

T. CANN HUGHES, M.A., F.S.A.
Lancaster.

Replies.

OBELISK AT ST. PETER'S.
(9th S. viii. 405, 505.)

MR. PIERPOINT has copied his inscriptions well, albeit I note the absence of DE before TRIBV IVDA in his first one. The inscription which he cites from Gorringe is not so illegible as he imagines; nor is its comparative illegibility due so much to three centuries of rain and dust (called in to account for it by Gorringe) as to its great altitude above the spectator. It is also on the west side, and just at the summit. I was able to make out nearly half of it without the aid of glasses. It may be of interest to remind him that Poggio Bracciolini, who visited and noted well what he saw of the ancient monuments in the Eternal City at the close of the Pontificate of Martin V. (1445), refers to the obelisk "qui est in Vaticano a C. Cæsare Caligula positus Divo Augusto et Divo Tiberio sacer." It is also mentioned by the Pilgrim of Einsiedeln *circa* A.D. 800. It was probably the first imported to Rome of the non-Egyptian obelisks, that is to say, of the imitation ones. As Pliny says, "factus in imitatione eius quem fecerat Sesostridis filius Nuncoreus" ('H.N.,' lib. xxxvi. c. xi.). The lunacy of Caius, as we know from other evidences, was conspicuously megalomaniac. It has been attempted by Middleton, Lanciani, and others to make out that his bridge (*pons*) from the Palatine to the Capitoline Temple of Jove must have been of wood. Closer study of Caligula's works and life should convince the intelligent that such a man was not to be put off by a piece of merely dexterous carpentry. As, however, the present excavations at that site have revealed conclusively that the Augusteum, over the roof of which the said bridge passed to that of the Basilica Julia, was reconstructed *e fundamentis* by Hadrian, it is unlikely that any traces of that earlier, and maniacal, experiment will be found, such, for instance, as bases of its piers, &c. The bringing over of the gigantic obelisk, however, was grandly on the side of sanity, as well as the construction of the magnificent ship that brought it. Later on, however, Caius must needs construct a mole and two colossal barges on the tiny lake of Nemi, beneath whose placid waters they must lie probably for ever.

ST. CLAIR BADDELEY.

Absence from England has prevented my correcting in due time an error which appears in one of the inscriptions in my reply at the last reference. TRIBV IVDA should read DE TRIBV IVDA.   ROBERT PIERPOINT.

STAUNTON, WORCESTERSHIRE (9th S. viii. 383, 510 ; ix. 11, 92).—The heading is again inappropriate to the contribution of MR. CANN HUGHES regarding the history of "Staunton in the Forest of Dean," inasmuch as that Staunton is Staunton, Gloucestershire, not "Staunton, Worcestershire."

With regard to the other contribution which appears with it from MR. JOHN HOBSON MATTHEWS, I should be inclined to doubt if the gentleman of "Pauntley, Gloucestershire," who "married the heiress of Staunton," found his bride "in the same county." Pauntley, Gloucestershire, adjoins Staunton, Worcestershire, but is a long way from Staunton, Gloucestershire.

CHARLES W. DILKE.

BEAU BRUMMEL AND BARBEY D'AUREVILLY (9th S. ix. 8, 96).—With regard to this query, I have pleasure in replying that a translation by my friend Mr. Douglas Ainslie was published by Dent & Co. in 1897. I was especially interested in this, for ten or twelve years earlier I had myself translated the booklet, for the publication of which I had obtained M. Calmann Lévy's or M. Lemerre's written permission. But it was too soon for the renascent interest in dandyism, and no publisher could be found for my MS. Consequently, when M. Lévy wrote to Mr. Ainslie to ask his authority for publishing his translation, I had the pleasure of transferring to him the rights granted to me.

If MR. HIATT will refer to a short paper on 'Dandyism' in *Temple Bar* (January, 1891 or 1892, I think), it may partly answer his question as to how and why D'Aurevilly and other French writers interested themselves in the "Dux dandiorum." Barbey d'Aurevilly was a native of Caen, and when a youth had seen Brummell in his decadence and consulship there, before Palmerston, on the dandy's own representation of its uselessness, had abolished the office. At Caen Brummell lies under a modest stone in the Protestant cemetery. But D'Aurevilly (as is patent in all his writings) had dandyism in the blood and marrow, and he was "suckled" upon its not then "outworn creed." He was the first to show its inner meaning and philosophy (before Baudelaire) as the quintessence of character, and, moreover, he perused Jesse's proof-sheets before the "Magpie's" book on Brummell was published. The ordinarily accepted cock-nosed portrait of Brummell is most unsatisfactory, and I possess what I believe to be a far more authentic likeness of him after his fall from the hand of Wilkie. This was exhibited at the Eton Exhibition, when Sir George Scharf (the editor of the catalogue) declined to give the attribution his sanction on the ground that it differed too greatly from the accepted portrait ; but it far more closely resembles that by Dighton (exhibited in the Victorian Exhibition) and the little figure published in Gronow's book.   A. FORBES SIEVEKING.

[D'Aurevilly's tract is one of a few opuscules he printed in Caen in very limited editions, some dozen or so copies. Before the production of Mr. Tree's 'Last of the Dandies' we purchased a copy of the book in question for twenty-five francs.]

GATES OF CAROLINE PARK, EDINBURGH (9th S. vii. 288).—With reference to a question about the disappearance of the fine old wrought-iron gates from the lodge at Gogar House, Midlothian, I have to say that they have been removed for the purpose of their being repaired. When so repaired they are to be erected at Sauchieburn, in Stirlingshire, the property of Mrs. Steel-Maitland, who also owns Gogar House. The gates were designed to guard the north or seaward entrance of Caroline Park House (near Granton, Edinburgh), built by George, first Earl of Cromartie. At the time he built the house (1685) he was Viscount Tarbat, by which title he was long known in Scottish affairs. He was all for the Union, and along with his peers received English gold for his services towards that end. He thus sat in the last Scots Parliament, that which dissolved itself in 1707 on the consummation of the Union. Throughout the filigree ironwork in Caroline Park—in the balustrades for the staircases and in the railing of a balcony over the south entrance, as well as in the above-mentioned gates—the rose and thistle are conspicuously worked, symbols of the union of England with Scotland, which the builder of Caroline Park had so much at heart. Tarbat's character is excellently drawn in 'The Union of England and Scotland,' by my colleague Dr. Mackinnon, Lecturer on History in this university.

DAVID FRASER HARRIS.
University, St. Andrews, N.B.

AN HEUSKARIAN RARITY IN THE BODLEIAN LIBRARY (9ᵗʰ S. viii. 378).—MR. E. S. DODGSON states that "the late Mr. Llewelyn Thomas, Vice-Principal of Jesus College......marked (illegally) in pencil upon the margin of the Bodleian copy of M. Vinson's 'Bibliography' some useful corrections," &c. The corrections were not written by Mr. Thomas, but by a member of the staff of the library, and I do not understand why MR. DODGSON, who knew Mr. Thomas's handwriting, should charge him after his death with an "illegal" act.

REGINALD L. POOLE.
Magdalen College, Oxford.

WILLIAM THE CONQUEROR'S HALF BROTHERS AND SISTERS (9ᵗʰ S. viii. 199, 293, 525; ix. 36).—Following up MRS. VADE-WALPOLE'S interesting investigations as to the relations of the Conqueror, perhaps some reader could inform me if there be any truth in a statement which I have heard that a sister (perhaps own sister) was married to a certain nobleman named Le Nez, who was killed at the battle of Hastings, and whose name appears on the roll of Battle Abbey. I should be glad to know if the story has any foundation.

P. L. N. F.

"ALRIGHT"=ALL RIGHT (9ᵗʰ S. viii. 240, 312, 413, 493; ix. 72).—None of the compounds cited by L. L. K. is quite on all fours with *alright*. To speak only of those of which *all* forms a part. In these the first element (*al-*) either entirely alters the meaning, as in *already*, *almost*, or gives it force and extension, as in *almighty*. These words, in short, are needed, and it is merely a question of convenience whether we write *all-mighty* or *almighty*. We cannot, however, say "all most hysterical" when we mean "almost hysterical." Look, now, at *all right*. This phrase, in nine cases out of ten in which it is used, is pleonastic; the *all* is not needed, and adds nothing to the force of the phrase. In

such cases, then, nothing can be said in favour of *alright*; it does but tend to perpetuate a vicious form of expression. But when *all right* is needed—as when we predicate rightness of a number of things or of one thing in its totality—*alright* would still be objectionable, being ambiguous. It is true that *all right* may be used ambiguously too, but that is beside the mark.   C. C. B.

Is it quite certain that the phrase "all right" has had "such a long lease of colloquial importance" as MR. BAYNE supposes? In a letter bearing date 28 April, 1824, from Mr. Robert Hamond, a well-known sporting character, to Selby, the naturalist, and printed in the *Transactions* of the Norfolk and Norwich Naturalists' Society (vol. ii. p. 400), it is used apparently as a neologism: "I am happy in being able to say I am now in the fashionable term 'all right.'" It would be well to know what earlier instances could be cited. I have not succeeded in finding one in Dr. Murray's 'Dictionary,' and I cannot help thinking that the expression originated in coaching days, when it was certainly the common exclamation of guard or ostler as a signal for the coachman to drive off.

A. N.

BREADCRUMBS AND THE DEVIL (9ᵗʰ S. viii. 383).—When we children were careless with our bread our mother used to admonish us very seriously to be more careful of it, and never to throw away "das liebe Gut" (the precious thing), always adding, "Perhaps you will one day eat sharp stones." That was in Anhalt. In Berlin it is regarded as a sin to throw the remnants of bread into the dust-bin; they should be put on the fire.

G. KRUEGER.
Berlin.

COSSEN OR COSEN (9ᵗʰ S. viii. 523).—A family named Cossens resided at St. Ives, Cornwall, in the seventeenth century. Many references to them will be found in my 'History of St. Ives,' &c. (Elliot Stock, 1892). One or two families of the same name were resident in Gloucestershire from the fourteenth to the eighteenth century. As to these I have many notes.   JOHN HOBSON MATTHEWS.
Town Hall, Cardiff.

"GOD SPEED YOU AND THE BEADLE" (9ᵗʰ S. viii. 422; ix. 12).—MR. MACMICHAEL has made an attempt to explain this saying which demands no criticism beyond a reminder that a different meaning is possible if we construe the phrase with both substantives in the same grammatical case; the interpretation then is "God and the beadle save you." There is no need to dwell on the characteristics of the human representative of authority, which are sufficiently embodied in the word "beadledom."

Your correspondent's assertion that "beetle" in the phrase "as deaf as a beetle" means the implement so named does not accord with the popular interpretation, which connects the word with the insect. It may be supported by citing the phrase "as deaf as a post"; but "as deaf as a beetle" may with equal likelihood be an offshoot of "as blind as a beetle," where identity with the coleopter need hardly be questioned. Popular ideas of animal life, as expressed in similar phrases, are not always correct. Compare "as deaf as an adder," "as blind as a bat," &c.   F. Adams.

Mortara: Arro (9th S. viii. 443).—The following work, which may be of assistance to your correspondent, will be found in the library of the South Kensington Museum :—

"Parmigiano (Francesco Mazzola, called): Della Vita e del Lavori di Francesco Mazzola detto Il Parmigianino; Memoria di Anton Enrico Mortara. 8vo, Casalmaggiore, 1846."

Everard Home Coleman.
71, Brecknock Road.

Snow-feathers (9th S. viii. 403, 494).—The idea that snowflakes are the feathers of geese seems general in Europe. In Thorpe's 'Northern Mythology,' vol. iii. p. 98, we read :

"The German traditions relating to Holda are current chiefly in Hesse and Thuringia. She is believed to influence the atmospheric phenomena. When the sun shines Holda is said to be combing her hair; when it snows, she is making her bed."

See also Grimm's 'Teutonic Mythology,' vol. iii. p. 1088. A common German nursery rime begins :—

The angels have made their beds on high,
And down to the earth the feathers fly.

And according to Köhler the children in Voigtland have a game in which they sing :

Ring, a ring of roses,
Who sits within?
The old emperor.
What does he do?
He strips feathers,
And bites quills :

which seems to imply that the Barbarossa of legend spends his enchanted hours in manufacturing snowstorms. It is in Voigtland, too, that snow is personified as a goose in the saying :—

The white goose in February
Broods blessing for the whole year.

And the same conception is to be met with elsewhere, for, according to an article on Russian children in the Ural mountains, pub-lished in *St. Nicholas*, November, 1891, the little ones have a song beginning :—

Daddy, daddy Winter,
Let your white geese fly;
Send the wind to drive them
All across the sky.

In Poitou when snow falls it is said that the Holy Virgin is plucking her geese and shaking the down (Léon Pineau, 'Le Folklore du Poitou,' p. 520, ed. 1892).   G. W.

The following old rime is still popular in Sheffield, and sung by the children when snow begins to fall. There are various versions of it, but this is the one I remember in my early days :—

Snow, snow faster,
Old Sally Baster,
She's killing geese in Scotland
And sending feathers here.

Charles Green.
18, Shrewsbury Road, Sheffield.

Ranulph, Earl of Chester (9th S. viii. 404).—Ormerod's 'History of Cheshire,' 1882, vol. i. p. 53, gives a charter of Randle the third, surnamed Blundevill, to his barons of Cheshire (in Latin, also an English translation), made about the year 1218, granting them many privileges. The above liberties were confirmed by Prince Edward, son of Henry III., in 1265, which confirmation is given in Latin. The prince when king (1300) again confirmed it. It contains other deeds of grants by the Earls of Chester.

John Radcliffe.

"Two blades of grass" (9th S. ix. 47).—T. W. E. says that "the well-known observation of the king in 'Gulliver's Travels'......was, in fact, 'chaff' of the platitudes of our king's speeches." Surely the whole passage might be more accurately described as a biting criticism of politicians who placed personal and party interests above those of their country.   W. H. Helm.

A Seventeenth-century Plagiary: 'Vindex Anglicus' (9th S. viii. 457). — It seems doubtful whether many of the words vilipended by Vindex had, when he wrote, got into circulation. John Cockeram's 'English Dictionarie' of 1623 seems to be responsible for the bulk of them. The Oxford University Press have cut down Cockeram's *bubulcitate* ("to cry like a cowboy") to *bulbitate*. I notice that the 'Dictionary of National Biography' states (vol. ix. 62) that Carew's 'Epistle' "appeared in the second edition of Camden's 'Remains,' 1605."

Were there really two editions of 1605; and, if so, in what points do they differ?

There is, as Mr. Curry says, an edition of 1614 in which the 'Epistle' appears ; and the edition of 1623 is called "the third impression reviewed, corrected and encreased." A fourth edition appeared in 1629 ; and the 1636 edition is described on the title as "The fift impression, by the industry and care of John Philipot."

Are we to assume an error in both the title-pages quoted ?   O. O. H.

ADJECTIVAL CHANGE (9th S. viii. 462).—The form "a large-size bowl" is, I think, a revival of that which poets of the sixteenth and seventeenth centuries not seldom employed. I instance Spenser's "light-foote Faeries" ('Teares of Muses,' 31) ; Chapman's "the curl'd-head Greeks" ('Iliad,' ii. 380) ; Herrick's "sweet-breath nimphs" ('Hesper.,' 355, ed. Ald.), "every......smooth-skin tree" (522, l. 41), and—in a prose title 599—"a sowre-breath Lady."   CHAS. P. PHINN.
Watford.

TONTINE (9th S. ix. 8).—Your correspondent will find much interesting information on this subject in the *Gentleman's Magazine* for January, 1791, and several long communications in 3rd S. ii. ; 4th S. ix , x.
EVERARD HOME COLEMAN.
71, Brecknock Road.

"GENTLE SHEPHERD, TELL ME WHERE" (9th S. viii. 423, 530).—The glee entitled 'The Wreath,' to which Dickens refers in 'Edwin Drood,' and of which MR. EBSWORTH supplies the words, was composed by J. Mazzinghi and forms No. 2634 of the 'Musical Bouquet.' I am not aware exactly when this piece of music was published, but it has certainly been in my possession for thirty-five years.
JOHN T. PAGE.
West Haddon, Northamptonshire.

ARMS OF MARRIED WOMEN (9th S. ix. 28).— Nisbet gives the following :—

"By the custom of nations wives may use the arms of their husbands : for being in their families they have a right to the honour and privileges of the same : as Hoppingius de Iure Insignium, par. 8, 'Ratio qui transit in alterius familiam is ejus origine, nomine et privelegiis gaudet, nobilitatisque et dignitatis sit particeps, adeo ut insignia deferendi jus transeunti denegari non possit, atque omnis uxor transit in familiam mariti ; ergo uxori jus deferendi insignia mariti recte denegari non poterit.' Though the wife be ignoble and a bastard, she has the right to make use of the arms of her husband ; as our author, 'Non impedit quod uxor ignobilis et plebeia, maritus vero nobilis extat, similiter non refert, quod mulier spuria ; nam nulla major unio quam conjugalis, nec negamus quin oleum non consecratum consecrato possit oleo commisceri.' But it is not so with the ignoble husband

who has a noble wife ; by her he is not nobilitate, nor can properly carry her arms, because wives receive honour from their husbands, but do not give it ; as our author, 'Vir ignobilis ducendo uxorem nobilem, non nobilitetur per eam cum accipiant non adferunt nubentes mulieres dignitatem.' After the husband's decease the widow may continue to have the arms of her husband upon all her utensils, but if she proves vicious or unchaste she loses the honours of her husband, says our author ; and if she marry again, she must follow the condition of her second husband, and cannot use the arms of her first husband, whose honour she loses, which holds with us and in England," &c.

Guillim does not agree with the above. After giving various examples of the arms of widows impaled with the arms of their husbands in a lozenge, he says :—

"Thus much for the bearing of widows, who may on no pretence whatsoever bear either their Paternal Coat or their Husbands single ; for if in an Escutcheon or Shield then it will be taken for the bearing of a man, and—if in a Lozenge, then the proper bearing for a Maiden Gentlewoman."

JOHN RADCLIFFE.

BORROW'S 'ZINCALI' (9th S. viii. 523).—The original MS. of Borrow's collection of Transylvanian gipsy words is in the British Museum. It consists of about 25 pages, not overcrowded with writing, and, to the best of my belief, it has not yet appeared in print. The late Mr. Groome once stated that the compiler had not collected the vocabulary in Transylvania, but had simply extracted the words from Bright's 'Travels in Hungary' (1818), and Borrow never refuted the accusation (cf. *Academy*, 13 June, 1874). The collection is poor compared with that published by the Archduke Joseph, who has written also a grammar of the tongue spoken by the Hungarian gipsies (under the title of 'Románo Csibákero Sziklariben,' 1889). The Lord's Prayer printed by Borrow in his 'Románo Lávo-lil' differs considerably from the text given by the archduke, though both versions are professedly derived from the same source.   L. L. K.

O, I am not of gentle clan,
   I am sprung from Gypsy tree ;
And I will be no gentleman,
   But an Egyptian free.

I may perhaps mention that I have in my copy of 'The Zincali,' published by John Murray, London, 1872, not only a charming portrait of the author of that delightful book, containing pictures of life, high, middle, and low, in the byways of the land of Gil Blas, entitled 'The Bible in Spain,' but also a long chapter on 'The Language of the Gitanos,' and one on 'Specimens of Gypsy Dialects,' from which the following is quoted : "Llundun baro foro, bishwar mai baro sar Cosvaro"

("London [is] a big city, twenty times more big than Colosvar").

HENRY GERALD HOPE.
119, Elms Road, Clapham, S.W.

THE OLDEST BOROUGH IN ENGLAND (9th S. ix. 9).—I believe Ripon claims this privilege, and alleges that it began in 886, and in this belief held a most gorgeous "Millenary Celebration" in August, 1886, which is beautifully and fully rendered in a volume published by Mr. William Harrison, of Ripon, in 1892. The earliest wakeman was James Percival in 1400, and the first charter is dated 26 June, 1604, under which Hugh Ripley, the last wakeman, was made first mayor.

Lancaster claims, and with justice, I think, to be the oldest town in the North, and possibly in England. There is in my custody as Town Clerk the earliest existing charter, that granted by the Earl of Moreton (afterwards King John) in 1193. A detailed account of this and our other charters, written by my predecessor and friend Mr. W. O. Roper, F.S.A., will be found in *Archæological Journal*, lv. 359-66, and in the *Transactions* of the Historic Society of Lancashire and Cheshire (vol. xxxv., O.S., 1-14). There are seventeen charters of Lancaster, many in beautiful condition and with rare seals. The town also possesses a fine seal, believed to be of the time of Henry III.

Your correspondent will, I hope, draw much information as to the charters of towns which may be older than Lancaster—*e.g.*, Winchester, York, Southampton—but as its Town Clerk I shall require very strong proof before I admit any evidence more conclusive than the grand old Moreton charter of the Burgh of the Camp on the Loyne—Loynecaster.

T. CANN HUGHES, M.A., F.S.A.
Lancaster.

Lostwithiel in Cornwall may or may not be the oldest borough in England, but it certainly ranks as one of the oldest.

There is in possession of the Corporation a charter by Robert de Cardinan, Ric. I., 1190-1200,

"Quod ego Rob(ertus) de Cardinan dedi et concessi et hac presenti carta confirmavi omnibus Burgensibus meis et hominibus de Lostuuidiel," &c.

The report made by the Hist. MSS. Com. on the muniments of the borough (but not yet published) states that

"the wording and provisions of this deed are alike extremely interesting; they illustrate the first growth of a borough out of a village and manor by the grant of liberties by the private owner and lord, which afterwards are confirmed and enlarged by the authority of the king."

There is also an *Inspeximus* by Edw. II. of a charter granted by Richard, Earl of Cornwall and King of the Romans, to the burgesses of Lostwythiel and Penkneke, dated at Watlington, 13 July, 12th of his reign (1268).

R. BARCLAY-ALLARDICE, F.S.A.(Scot.).
Lostwithiel.

"EVE STOOD AT THE GARDEN GATE" (9th S. viii. 463).—I believe that the author is Rudyard Kipling and that the lines are not to be found in any "collection of poems." They occur as a pseudo-quotation in one of his short stories, called 'Mrs. Hauksbee Sits Out,' originally published, I think, as the Christmas number of one of the illustrated papers, and republished in 'Under the Deodars.'

The verses as they appear in the story are not consecutive, as conversation breaks in at intervals, but the poem as it stands is as follows :—

Fair Eve knelt close to the guarded gate in the hush of an Eastern spring,
She saw the flash of the Angel's sword, the gleam of the Angel's wing.

. . . .

And because she was so beautiful, and because she could not see
How fair were the pure white cyclamens crushed dying at her knee

. . . .

He plucked a Rose from the Eden Tree where the four great rivers met.

. . . .

And though for many a Cycle past that Rose in the dust hath lain
With her who bore it upon her breast when she passed from grief and pain,
There was never a daughter of Eve but once, ere the tale of her years be done,
Shall know the scent of the Eden Rose but once beneath the sun !
Though the years may bring her joy or pain, fame, sorrow or sacrifice,
The hour that brought her the scent of the Rose, she lived it in Paradise.

I should add that all editions of 'Under the Deodars' do not contain this story. I quote from the *édition de luxe*, vi. 68, 69.

E. R.

"MISCHIEF-NIGHT" (9th S. ix. 48).—The date for the mischievous practices is Hallowe'en, 31 October, but at Leeds the celebrations of 5 November have evidently attracted without absorbing the mischief and the bonfires of the earlier date. The following tricks have been perpetrated to my knowledge on "mischief-night." One custom is to ask at a cottage for a drink of water, and while the water is being fetched to stuff the hinge side of the door with mussel shells. Then when the water has been drunk, and an attempt is made by the cottager to shut the door, there is a considerable crunching of the shells and some annoyance. A worse trick is to select two houses with doors exactly opposite to one another, in a quiet street, and tie the handles together with a strong rope, allowing just so much slackness on the rope that one of the doors may be opened a short distance. It is the custom then to arrange that both doors shall be knocked at simultaneously. The fun begins with seeing the different occupiers pulling against one another in the attempts to open their doors. The usual result is that the door with the stronger individual behind it is opened a little, and the other not at all. The cabbage stump, which also plays a part in Hallowe'en divination, is sometimes flung at a door and left there. There are many other mischievous practices for the occasion, but it is remarkable that 4 November, as stated by the querist, has been selected as the date at Leeds.   ARTHUR MAYALL.

J. O. Halliwell, in his 'Dictionary of Archaic and Provincial Words,' 1878, says that in Yorkshire it is held on May eve ; and the Rev. Thomas Wright, M.A., in his 'Dictionary of Obsolete and Provincial English,' adds that the evening of 30 April in Yorkshire was so called because many pranks are played by youths of both sexes.
EVERARD HOME COLEMAN.
71, Brecknock Road.

HOGNEL OR HOGNAYLE MONEY (4th S. ii. 275 ; 9th S. v. 287, 459 ; vi. 56*).—To the information already collected I add a reference to the facts given in the *Sussex Archæological Collections*, vol. xli. pp. 37, 47, and note, and to *Archæologia*, vol. xxxv. p. 413, where *hogling money* is stated not to have been paid in Minchinhampton after the year 1595. I hope that some one interested in the matter will investigate all these instances and the others noted in 'H.E.D.' (where *hogler* also should be looked up) and 'E.D.D.,' and ascertain, if possible, the time of payment† and the geographical distribution of the words. Thereafter will arise the question of the origin of the name and its relation, if any, to the French *aguillauneuf* (see the many

---

* See also 'Hoglinge Money' (3rd S. iii. 423) and 'Hogenstore,' 'Hognor Bread,' 'Hoggenor's Money' (9th S. iii. 265).
† I believe I am correct in stating that the churchwardens' accounts presented at Easter do not contain payments and receipts of the Easter festival, but only those since the preceding Michaelmas. The Easter offerings would fall into the Michaelmas account.

variants of this word in Godefroy) and the Scottish *hogmanay*.   Q. V.

"OUTRIDER" (9th S. viii. 462 ; ix. 17).—My mother (who was born in 1821) well remembers in her young days, near Drewsteignton in Devon, hearing what we now call "travellers" spoken of as "outriders" when they came to visit the country districts.
T. CANN HUGHES, M.A., F.S.A.
Lancaster.

This word, as applied to travellers from the neighbouring towns who drive round the villages for orders, principally beer and grocery, is still used daily by the cottagers of the Down country.   GEORGE C. PEACHEY.

FREAKS OF NATURE (9th S. viii. 482).—The issue for December, 1901, of the *Stone Trades Journal* contains a paragraph headed 'Curious Markings on Marble.' It has evidently been culled from a U.S. contemporary, and (somewhat shortened) runs :—

"Many persons look for pictures in the graining and markings of stone, and frequently some very beautiful effects are traced in marble slabs. Perhaps some of the most curious of these *lusi* [*sic*] *naturæ* are to be found in the Illinois State House, where presentments ranging from a portrait of Commodore Vanderbilt to a donkey are to be found. On one panel is to be seen a convalescent boy reclining in a chair, a white covering drawn diagonally across his body. The sad smile, wan face, lines made by recent suffering, are all clearly shown. Another panel presents a mountain crag and a bird's nest. The mother bird sits on a scraggy tree, and her open mouth shows her screaming a protest against the intrusion of a boy bent on despoiling her home. Across the corridor is a mountain scene. A huge leopard and a human giant are face to face, with a narrow chasm dividing the ledges on which they stand. The leopard is in a crouching attitude, indicative of a determination to leap the barrier of space and have it out with his adversary. The most striking representations are likenesses of Napoleon and Josephine. Oddly enough, the panels on which they appear are close together, and so placed that Josephine is looking across at the man who made her love a football. Each picture is full length. There is something regal in the bearing of Josephine as she holds her fan in one hand and with the other draws about her the ermine robe she wears. The once mighty conqueror is gazing sorrowfully over the waters from the shore of the Island of St. Helena. The Napoleonic hat and features are finely depicted, and there is something in the pose that suggests the memory of great power, while on the face of Josephine may be traced something of pity and forgiveness."
HARRY HEMS.
Fair Park, Exeter.

A remarkable instance of this *lusus naturæ* occurred a few days after the death of the late Dean Vaughan, of Llandaff. There suddenly appeared on the wall of Llandaff

Cathedral a large blotch of dampness or some minute fungus, forming a lifelike outline of the dean's head and face. It was photographically reproduced in one or both of the Cardiff daily papers at the time.

JOHN HOBSON MATTHEWS.
Town Hall, Cardiff.

MAJOLICAN BACINI ON OLD CHURCHES AT PISA AND ELSEWHERE (9th S. viii. 503).—See an article by Mr. C. D. Fortnum in *Archæologia*, vol. xlii. (1869), at pp. 379-86. The bacini at S. Pietro in Grado, S. Andrea, S. Sisto, and S. Francesco, at Pisa, seem to be considered by Fortnum to be in general Italian. At S. Cecilia, among many Italian bacini, he found one which he describes as ancient Persian or Damascus faïence. After describing the bacini in churches at Rome and elsewhere, he sums up thus:—

"From the foregoing facts it may be inferred that very few of the bacini now found in the churches of Italy are other than of Italian manufacture. The adoption of such a method of decoration may or may not have had its origin at Pisa, and was manifestly in great favour there; but I am inclined to think that the story of the Majorcan dishes, captured and built in as trophies in the church walls, is apocryphal."

ALIQUIS.

"MACHINE" = PUBLIC COACH (9th S. viii. 462; ix. 37).—The "machine" was known in Bristol in 1754, two years earlier than the date quoted by MR. HOLDEN MACMICHAEL at the last reference. In an advertisement in *Felix Farley's Journal*, issued at Bristol, the "Bristol Flying Machine" was announced to start for London on 24 February, 1754, at 2 A.M. The journey was performed in two days. My collection of broadsheets, newspaper cuttings, &c., relating to Bristol contains woodcuts of two of the "machines" that went from Bristol to London in 1756, viz., "The Bristol Machine," which started from the "White Lion," Broad Street, Bristol, and arrived at the "Saracen's Head," Friday Street, London; and "The Old London Machine," which started from the "White Hart," Broad Street, Bristol, and on the return journey took up passengers at the "One Bell," in the Strand, the "Bell Savage," on Ludgate Hill, and the "Three Cups," in Bread Street. These two machines were built on steel springs: one has the appearance of a miniature state carriage, the other looking unmistakably like a sedan chair on a large scale elevated on a frame. They were drawn by six horses, a man riding on one of the leaders, the coachman or "whip" being seated on the front of the machine, on a platform detached from the body or coach.

In the year 1763—and probably before—the journey was performed in one day by the machines which started from the "Rummer Tavern," High Street, Bristol, and arrived at the "Three Cups," Bread Street, London. Incidentally, I may mention that an original board, with particulars of the fares of the coaches to London, is still preserved at the "Rummer Hotel." It is somewhat curious that some of my newspaper cuttings relating to the light post coaches and machines which performed the journey from Bristol to London, *viâ* Bath, in the year 1784, contain—among the names of the persons by whom the journeys were performed—the name of Pickwick, who probably resided in or near Bath. The earlier advertisements contain the words "performed if God permit," or "God permitting," in much the same form as the old bills of lading relating to the cargo of a ship. Long before 1754 there were coaches running between Bristol and London which were called "Flyers," and advertisements of other coaches announced that they would "fly"—hence, probably, the term "fly," which even now is frequently used as a description of the ordinary cab. It is, I think, not very difficult to imagine how the "machine" came to be described as a "flying machine."

G. E. WEARE.
Weston-super-Mare.

When I lived in Scotland the name "machine" was almost the only one used for a carriage in country places, especially, if I remember rightly, one with a single horse. No doubt the name is so used there still.

H. J. MOULE.
Dorchester.

"FADGE" (9th S. ix. 7).—*Apropos* of "a fadge of potatoes" in this note, I remember that fifty years ago—and it probably is so still—in the north of Ireland the ordinary potato bannock was spoken of as *fadge*. It was a circular unleavened cake, made of potatoes and flour and done on a griddle, like a very thick Indian chapatti. It was thick enough to be split and buttered, to be eaten hot.

MICHAEL FERRAR.
Little Gidding, in Ealing.

FLOWER GAMES (9th S. vii. 329, 397, 474, 511; viii. 70, 232, 466).—Devonshire children call the dandelion piss-a-bed (and sometimes something worse), and have the keenest apprehension of consequences from gathering it. I have seen youngsters throw away handfuls when warned by another youthful wiseacre. This belief was prevalent at a big Watford school some twenty years ago among children from all parts of the empire. At the same school it was believed the "milky juice" was capable of removing warts. Emmet=ant in Devon; indeed, some people would not recognize the word "ant."

W. CURZON YEO.

Richmond, Surrey.

FIRE ON THE HEARTH KEPT BURNING (9th S. viii. 204, 412; ix. 16).—It was the custom —as I have heard my mother say—to keep the house-place fires in all the year round in farmhouses and cottages in Derbyshire. And in the early fifties fires were regularly "raked" each night when the household retired. To "rake" the fire meant to pull the cinders from the fire-back on to a raking coal, then place on top a shovelful of slack. This ensured a slow fire during the night, and all the first riser had to do was to rake out the ashes at bottom, and break up the lump of partly burnt raking coal, with the result that a good fire and a boiling kettle were ready for those who had to turn out for early farmwork. I may add that "it isn't every one that can rake a fire"—that is, do it so that it will neither go out nor burn out. There is "an art" in the doing of common every-day things.   THOS. RATCLIFFE.

Worksop.

HORN DANCERS (9th S. viii. 444; ix. 11).— MR. ELWORTHY will find a very interesting illustrated paper by Miss C. S. Burne on this subject, entitled 'The Folk-lore of Staffordshire,' in vol. ii. of the new series of the *Journal* of the British Archæological Association (pp. 24–35). It was contributed to the Stoke-on-Trent Congress on 13 August, 1895.

T. CANN HUGHES, M.A., F.S.A.

Lancaster.

"JOHNIAN PIGS" (6th S. xi. 328, 414; xii. 36). —James Johnson's "Book of Epigrams in Latine. Printed at London by John Beale, 1615," is described in the British Museum Catalogue as 'Epigrammatum Libellus, sive, Schediasmata Poetica,' &c., and bears the press-mark 1213, g. 15 (1). Perhaps one of your readers will find out whether the epigram in question happens, as suggested at the last reference, to be in English, spite of the Latin title.   O. O. H.

BIBLIOGRAPHY OF THE BICYCLE (9th S. viii. 304, 490, 530; ix. 36).—My impression is that whether there be an angel with a wheel or not in a window at Stoke Poges, there is a representation of some toy with a wheel for a child to ride on, and also one of a toy to be spun round by means of a long string. The window was made up of fragments when

I saw it some years ago, and I hope it has not been destroyed in order to make room for modern glass. When the "hobby-horse" was mentioned I wrote to the vicar to ask if my memory served me rightly, but a day or two after I saw a notice of his death in the papers, and I have had no reply. I should be very glad to learn something about it.   J. T. F.

Durham.

ADULATION EXTRAORDINARY (8th S. x. 152, 322; 9th S. viii. 473; ix. 30).—The address of Recorder Widdrington, of Berwick, to Charles I. is well supplemented by the following address of Recorder Thorpe, of Hull, to the same monarch on his visit to that town in April or May, 1639 (Symonds, 'Hullinia,' p. 69):—

"Most Gracious Sovereign! If the approaches to the thrones of heaven and earth had been by the same way of access, we had done [?]. Since learning by our daily prayers unto the 'King of Kings,' to speak as might become us, unto your sacred Majesty, whom God has now blessed and honoured us with the presence of. But since these are different, and we not so much conversant in the latter as in the former, we most heartily crave your sacred pardon and grace for our rudeness, which is or may be committed, opining, your Majesty, that they proceeded from nothing but want of knowledge and skill how to receive and to express ourselves upon the happy reception of so much glory.

"Our full hearts make us almost unable to undergo what we most thankfully undertake, and would stop all passages of speech and make us dumb with the awful majesty that happy we behold and adore.

"This town was always faithful and true, in respect of the zealous and loyal affections of the people of the same, to your Majesty's honour and service. It may be said, as it is of the city of Saville in Spain, 'not only to be walled, but also to be garrisoned by fire,' not dead nor asleep, nor absconded in senseless flints, but continually vivacious, waking, ardent, apparent, and sensible in their courageous and boiling heat for your Majesty's long life, welfare and happiness. So that the town is not only yours by name, but also by nature—so shall it ever remain to be.

"Your Majesty hath not only here a magazine of all military provisions of your own loyal collecting, ordering and appointment, but also a richer store, a more noble and safe prize, even a magazine of faithful and true hearts all the town over, which renders it stronger for your Majesty's service, than if it had walls of brass or iron.

"Your Majesty's most noble predecessors built, encouraged, and honoured it. The pious and good King Edward VI. committed the castle and blockhouses of it to the perpetual keeping of the corporation. May your Majesty live for ever and ever, and may all the thorns in your travels grow up into crowns; may your battles be always crowned with laurels, and may good success always attend your actions and desires; may your years be added unto your days, and length of time, till time shall be no more."

But alas for consistency! three years afterwards, in April, 1642, when Charles I.—accompanied by Prince Rupert, the Duke of Kingston, the Marquis of Winchester, the Marquis of Northampton (killed at Hopton Heath), the Earls of Lindsey (killed at Edgehill), Derby (executed at Bolton), Montrose (executed in 1650), Worcester, Chesterfield, and Lichfield, Viscount Fauconberg, Thomas, Lord Arundell of Wardour (killed at the battle of Lansdown, 5 July, 1643), Lord Wentworth, and others—appeared before the gates of Hull, the governor, Sir John Hotham, declined to admit them, on the ground that he had orders from Parliament to that effect. It was this action of the governor of Hull that began the civil war between the king and the Parliament. Recorder Thorpe, of Hull, seems to have acted on all fours with Recorder Widdrington, of Berwick, for he afterwards became a judge and a great enemy of the king.

RONALD DIXON.
46, Marlborough Avenue, Hull.

ARMS OF DUTCH EAST INDIA COMPANY (9th S. ix. 9).—I do not think that this company had any arms, but it used a monogram V. O. C., standing for "Vereenigde Oost-Indische Compagnie" (United East India Company). By resolution of 28 February, 1603, it was decided that the monogram should take the form of a large V transfixing an O and a C of less than half its size, and that the letters should be azure on a silver field. Accordingly we find this monogram everywhere that the Company went, in India, Ceylon, Malacca, the Cape of Good Hope, &c., cut on stone or wood, cast in metal on cannon, swords, bayonets, and coins, graven on the glass, and painted on the Delft ware used by the officials of the Company.

J. P. LEWIS.

THE LOCOMOTIVE AND GAS (9th S. vi. 227, 358).—William Murdock's name was originally spelt Murdoch, but he is said to have changed the spelling to Murdock because of the inability of Englishmen to pronounce the final *ch* of his name (see the 'Dict. of Nat. Biog.,' vol. xxxix. pp. 324-8). When I was a boy I used sometimes to stay with William Murdock's son (Mr. John Murdock) at his residence in Handsworth called The Sycamores or Sycamore Hill. This was in the early sixties. I remember Mr. John Murdock showing me a gold snuff-box with an inscription, and his telling me that that snuff-box was the only reward his father ever received for his invention of gas. He also had some models of steam locomotives which his father designed, I believe before Watt's discoveries.

Probably these models and the snuff-box may be still in the possession of his relatives, the Waltons.

W. G. D. F.

BISHOPS' SIGNATURES (9th S. ix. 9).—My father informs me that in a vicarage library in Worcestershire there is a volume of Stillingfleet's charges, with preface by himself, dated Hartlebury Castle, 23 April, 1698, and signed "Edw. Wigorn." So my recollection was not unfounded. I am much obliged to you for allowing me to call attention to the subject. Before this appears in print the point will have been decided one way or the other—let us hope in the right way—by the person most nearly concerned.

W. E. B.

I find on reference to a volume of Stillingfleet's 'Discourses' that the preface, which is dated 24 April, 1696, is initialled "E. W." This would almost point to the fact that Stillingfleet's signature would be "Edward Worcester." A very handy addition to 'Mowbray's Churchman's Kalendar' for this year is a list of the signatures of the present archbishops and bishops.

JOHN T. PAGE.
West Haddon, Northamptonshire.

KEYS TO NOVELS (9th S. viii. 505).—See *L'Intermédiaire* (xxxviii.; xxxix.; xliv. 480, 819, 956), under the heading of 'Les Romans à Clef de Balzac'; also (xliv. 945) under that of 'La Clef des Maritimes.'

I have somewhere seen that in Lord Lytton's 'Paul Clifford' the highwaymen "Old Bags," "Fighting Attie," and "Gentleman George" represent respectively Lord Eldon, the Duke of Wellington, and George III.

F. E. R. POLLARD-URQUHART.
Castle Pollard, Westmeath.

Miscellaneous.

NOTES ON BOOKS, &c.

Pleadings and Depositions in the Duchy Court of Lancaster, Time of Edward VI. and Philip and Mary. Edited by Lieut.-Col. Henry Fishwick. (Lancashire and Cheshire Record Society.)

THIS volume relates to one of the most unsettled times in our history. The violent changes which had recently occurred and were still in progress had so disturbed the minds of men that no one could calculate what would happen next, so there was a widespread feeling that it behoved every one to look out for himself. The greater part of the book relates to disputes, often attended with violence, as to real and personal property, in which Stanleys, Gerrards, Townleys, Leighs, and Traffords figure conspicuously. Such documents are of unquestionable value to the local historian and the genealogist, but do not throw much light on the manners and feelings of the people, and still less on general history. There is, however, another class of papers which are very important, as illustrating social life. We gather from some of them that, although there was no organized uprising against authority on the suppression of the chantries, the change was viewed with great disfavour, and that means, of course very ineffectual, were frequently adopted for evading it. The pillage of the churches of their cherished ornaments was also resented by a large portion of the inhabitants. Of this we find here several instances. For example, the churchwardens of Farnworth were rash people. Whether they were merely covetous persons, inflamed with the desire of making all they could for themselves out of the things in their charge, or whether they were moved to what they did by strong sympathy with the reformed faith, we cannot tell. They were informed against in the reign of Mary for having destroyed a "rancke" of iron, curiously wrought and decorated with floral ornaments, "whereupon divers and many lights used to stand before the Holy Sacrament." This "rancke"—or "hersse," as it is also called—was, we conclude, a sumptuous piece of ironwork. It is spoken of as thirty feet long. There were also three other "ranckes," of a smaller size, which we think, though there is no evidence in proof thereof, were placed around tombs. These churchwardens had received an order from Sir William Norres, a man in authority, to restore the damage they had done; but as they refused to do as they were bidden, they were commanded to appear in the Duchy Chamber to answer for their evil deeds. Hearses, as they were commonly called, of this kind are now of extreme rarity. There is one in the Warwick Chapel; another at Tanfield, near Ripon; and a third, probably one side only, in the South Kensington Museum. They were not uncommon before the Reformation.

Another curious example of the lawlessness of the time occurred in the same reign at Billinge, in the parish of Wigan, where the people of all ranks and conditions had built for themselves a chapel. For permission to have service therein they had obtained authority from the rector of the parish. They furthermore paid out of their own pockets the stipend of a priest, who said mass and administered the sacraments, "to the great ease of all the said people, and to the increase of godliness and virtuous living in those parts." This, however, displeased James Winstanley, of Winstanley, Gent., for on 6 August—the year is unfortunately not given—he assembled twenty unknown persons, and with their help pillaged the chapel of all its ornaments, including even the bell, which was worth three pounds. We wonder whether anything further is known of Winstanley. That he was a turbulent person is evident; but it by no means follows that this audacious act was inspired by motives of greed.

We meet here with more than one instance of child marriage and divorce, which throw unfavourable light on the manners of the time.

Who's Who, 1902: an Annual Biographical Dictionary. (A. & C. Black.)

'WHO'S WHO' has now reached its fifty-fourth annual issue. It goes on improving in interest and value, the present volume including two hundred pages more than its predecessor. Three or four years ago it made a great spurt, and it is now the most frequently consulted book of reference on our shelves. Its arrangement and the information it supplies are such that it enables us to dispense with all rival publications—'Men of the Time,' 'Men of the Reign,' and other works of the class. It is in part a peerage and in part a Red or Blue Book, since it supplies the addresses of most of the people with whom a man of letters is likely to have to associate or correspond. The biographical portion is of supreme excellence, and the facts concerning men of eminence are quite trustworthy, being as a rule supplied by the subjects themselves. As proof of the utility of the work our readers may refer to the Right Hon. Joseph Chamberlain, Lord Milner, William Marconi, Lord Charles Beresford, the Rev. Sabine Baring-Gould, the Rev. Prof. Skeat, and innumerable others. This excellent work is the nearest approach to an English Vapereau we possess, and has an advantage over that book, seeing that, being an annual, it is always up to date.

Whitaker's Peerage for the Year 1902. (Whitaker & Sons.)

'WHITAKER'S PEERAGE,' now in the sixth year of its appearance, has vindicated its utility, and has obviously come to stay. It is a cheap and trustworthy guide to titled persons, and contains this year nearly a hundred pages more than last year. Its very title-page is serviceable. In the prefatory matter there is a rather mordant article on claimant-baronets and others. In the case of recent changes in the peerage, such as the Earldom of Arran, the information is up to date. The work is a useful companion to the indispensable 'Whitaker's Almanack.'

No doubt was ever felt that the inaccuracy and absurdity of the alleged bi-literal cipher of Bacon would be shown before long by some duly qualified historian. Mr. Andrew Lang was the first to point out the discrepancy in date between the allegations of Mrs. Gallup and the known facts of history. The subject is treated at greater length by Mr. R. S. Rait in the *Fortnightly.* Mr. Rait shows that if the marriage of Elizabeth and Leicester took place, as is alleged in the cipher, while both were imprisoned in the Tower, Bacon's birth was illegitimate. It is once more shown that Bacon had not acquired rudimentary knowledge concerning his own times, and is made to use forms of speech which were not in employment at that date, nor for long after. A strange error assigned Bacon by Mrs. Gallup is that of employing "curricula" in a sense it only acquired in quite modern times. A proportion much smaller than usual of the number is occupied by politics, home and foreign, and there are many valuable essays on literary subjects. Mr. Havelock Ellis writes on Victor Hugo, à propos of the coming centenary, and holds rightly that Hugo's permanent position cannot as yet be definitely fixed. Mr. Arthur Symons gives an interesting foretaste of his shortly to be expected translation of the 'Francesca da Rimini' of Signor Gabriele d'Annunzio. Dr. Todhunter has some valuable comments on 'Blank Verse on the Stage.' Mr. Gosse writes on 'Aubrey de Vere,' Miss Hannah Lynch on 'A. Mary F. Robinson,' and Mr. T. H. S. Escott on 'The Analysis of Jingo.'—The most important paper in the *Nineteenth Century* consists of Mr.

Sidney Lee's ' Shakespeare in Oral Tradition,' which constitutes a valuable addition to his monumental life of Shakespeare. In their anxiety to preserve a balance between Shakespeare's moral rectitude and his literary and dramatic supremacy, Shakespearean biographers have regarded as things not to be mentioned the rumours which among the unregenerate find readiest acceptance—the report that he killed the king's deer, or the record of the practical jokes he played upon his contemporaries. Almost for the first time Mr. Lee mentions without a shudder Shakespeare's reputed paternity towards D'Avenant, and shows the things that tell to some extent in its favour. If we study closely the epoch, we shall wonder, Mr. Lee holds, "not why we know so little, but why we know so much." Lady Paget supplies some deeply interesting information concerning ' The Empress Frederick in Youth.' A curious article is that of Miss Hannah Lynch on ' The Young French Girl Interviewed.' Unfortunately, the utterances of these *ingénues* cannot be implicitly trusted. ' Art and Eccentricity,' by Mr. Herbert Paul, deals with modern Tyrtæuses, which is not precisely what we expected from its title. 'Metternich and Princess Lieven' is a long paper derived from Metternich's autobiographical memoirs. — To the *Pall Mall* Mr. Frederick Wedmore sends an interesting contribution on ' The Great Queen's Monument,' with illustrations no less pleasantly suggestive by Mr. Hedley Fitton. Following this comes a capital reproduction of the pleasing portrait of Marie Antoinette by Madame Vigée Lebrun, a coloured reproduction of which serves for the cover. Sir Harry Johnston writes on ' The Pygmies and Ape-like Men of the Uganda Borderland,' and Mr. Archer on ' Paolo and Francesca.' Both letterpress and illustrations are of high interest. ' A Great Cavalry Leader' gives a record of the career of Major-General Sir John French, on whom all eyes are now fixed. It is accompanied by a portrait. ' Brighton Revisited and a Contrast' has a certain amount of interest. It is, some may be glad to know, a eulogy of a place with few defenders. What is the place chosen as a contrast we know not. Mr. George Stronach defends the Baconian origin of Shakespeare's plays, gives a history of the growth of the delusion, and marshals together what facts seem to him to support it. Major Hoenig deals with the question ' Is an Invasion of England Possible?' Mr. Max Beerbohm supplies some further reproductions of his wonderful caricatures. — Very interesting in the *Cornhill* is a lady's account of ' Browning in Venice,' which is ushered in by a prefatory note by Mr. Henry James. Mr. J. B. Atlay tells afresh the story of Governor Eyre and Jamaica. Mr. Godley is amusing in describing ' The Consolation of Mediocrity,' and Mr. Stephen Gwynn thoughtful in dealing with ' The Luxury of Doing Good.' Prof. Beeching has an interesting and valuable article on ' The Sonnets of Shakespeare.' ' A Londoner's Log-Book' is capitally continued. ' La Doctoresse malgré Elle' gives a graphic account of the conditions of peasant life in the district of the Cevennes. —Mrs. Creighton's ' Reminiscences of J. R. Green' in *Longman's* are both readable and valuable. ' Parson and Parishioner in the Eighteenth Century,' by Mr. W. H. Legge, has archæological interest. ' A Friend of Nelson' is continued. Mr. Lang deals with customary outspokenness with the Bacon ciphers, and is, after his wont, both

witty and wise.—In the *Gentleman's* are articles on ' Shakespeare as History,' ' Scent in Dogs,' ' The Scot Abroad,' and ' On Senlac Hill.' Mr. Percy Fitzgerald sends what he calls some ' Bozzyana.'— ' Washington, a City of Pictures,' by Francis E. Leupp, with illustrations by Jules Guérin, in *Scribner's*, is interesting and instructive. Its title would perhaps be more explanatory if it were ' A City of Sites and Vistas,' since it consists of designs of edifices and avenues, and not, as we expected, of paintings. Some of the views are very effective: not less so are those of the proposed Isthmian Ship-Canal. ' Paul Troubetzkoy, Sculptor,' introduces to us an artist concerning whom little is known in this country, except to the esoteric. Among the illustrations is one of the sculptor at work on a bust of Count Tolstoy. Other contents which may be read with pleasure or advantage are ' The American "Commercial Invasion" of Europe' and ' In Oklahoma.'

Mr. Bertram Dobell's catalogues, issued from Charing Cross Road, are well known to book-lovers. That now issued is the hundredth, and is inferior in interest to none of its predecessors. With it Mr. Dobell issues a literary supplement, dealing with the gallant fight he is making against the Westminster City Council in the matter of bookstalls. We have not space to deal with the subject, but we shall bitterly deplore the removal of the bookstalls from a road in which they are the least possible of an obstruction. It needs a Charles Lamb to express in proper terms the resentment the book-lover feels against the Council's highhanded and superfluous action.

Notices to Correspondents.

We must call special attention to the following notices:—

On all communications must be written the name and address of the sender, not necessarily for publication, but as a guarantee of good faith.

We cannot undertake to answer queries privately.

To secure insertion of communications correspondents must observe the following rules. Let each note, query, or reply be written on a separate slip of paper, with the signature of the writer and such address as he wishes to appear. When answering queries, or making notes with regard to previous entries in the paper, contributors are requested to put in parentheses, immediately after the exact heading, the series, volume, and page or pages to which they refer. Correspondents who repeat queries are requested to head the second communication " Duplicate."

E. B. Matthew.—Your query shall very shortly appear.

Corrigenda.—P. 59, col. I, l. 13, for " Adams" read *Adam*; p. 60, col. I, l. 9, for " Lumley" read *Lumby*.

NOTICE.

Editorial communications should be addressed to " The Editor of ' Notes and Queries'"—Advertisements and Business Letters to " The Publisher"— at the Office, Bream's Buildings, Chancery Lane, E.C.

We beg leave to state that we decline to return communications which, for any reason, we do not print; and to this rule we can make no exception.

LONDON, SATURDAY, FEBRUARY 15, 1902.

CONTENTS. — No. 216.

Notes.

PONTEFRACT-ON-THAMES.

(See 1st S. ii. 56, 205 ; 2nd S. ix. 343, 395 ; 7th S. v. 69, 136, 293, 512.)

A POINT which has puzzled the correspondents of ' N. & Q.' for the last fifty years has been the exact situation of Pontefract-on-Thames. The question was first raised in the second volume of the First Series in connexion with certain writs which were issued from that place in the reign of King Edward II. I quote below some of the attestations to these writs which will be found in Rymer's ' Fœdera,' vol. ii. pt. i. p. 461 :—

"Teste Rege, apud Pountefreit super Thamis' xxviii die Nov^{bris} 1321.

"*Ditto*, apud Pountfreyt super Thamis' xxx die Nov^{bris} 1321.

"*Ditto*, apud Pontem Fractum super Thamis' xxx die Nov^{bris} 1321.

"*Ditto*, apud Pontem Fractum, xxx die Nov^{bris} 1321 (15 Edw. II.)."

The context rendered it clear that when these writs were issued the king was staying at some place on the Thames between Windsor and the mouth of the river, and various guesses were accordingly hazarded. One correspondent thought the probabilities pointed to Kingston Bridge, another to Staines, and a third to Shepperton Ashford. In more recent times a much-lamented correspondent, who wrote under the pseudonym of HERMENTRUDE, suggested that the locality might be Woolwich or Erith, basing her view on the Wardrobe Accounts (31/17) showing the "expenses of John of Eltham, son of the King (Edward II.), in wardship of Lady Alianora Le Despenser, from 30 April to 13 June, 1326." From these accounts it appeared that on 30 May this lady and her royal charge dined at Shene and supped at Pontfreit, where they spent the following day. On 1 June they travelled on to Rochester, where they arrived in time for dinner. As Woolwich or Erith was further from Shene than Kingston or the other places which were previously equated with Pontfreit, HERMENTRUDE concluded that this unknown locality might be identical with one of those she had mentioned, although she furnished further evidence tending to show that Broken Wharf, near Queenhithe, might be an alternative place.

It seems odd that none of the correspondents who dealt with this question should have referred to any standard work on London topography, as such a course would have at once removed their difficulties. Mention is made of Pontefract-on-Thames in Strype's ' Stow,' in Maitland's ' History of London,' in Lysons's ' Environs of London, and in Cowper's ' History of Millwall.' From these authorities it is clear that it was situated in Stepney Marsh, otherwise known as Poplar Marsh, and for some hundreds of years as the Isle of Dogs. The manor seems to have been a sub-infeudation of the great manor of Stepney, under which heading it is dealt with by Lysons. The following quotation from Maitland's ' History of London,' ed. 1739, p. 753, embodies Strype's views on the subject :—

"The *Chapel House* in the *Isle of Dogs*, or *Poplar* Marsh ; is the Ruins of a Stone Chapel, but when, or by whom built, is unknown. However, I am of opinion, that it either belong'd to the Manor of *Pountfret* (or to his Majesty's Servants who attended the Royal Kennels, whilst the King's Hounds were kept here), which anciently lay in this Marsh ; the capital Mansion whereof, by the Discovery of large Foundations and Gatehooks, may not only be presumed to have stood here, but likewise divers other Houses, which probably were inhabited till the great Inundation toward the Close of the Fifteenth Century, occasion'd by a Breach in the Bank of the River *Thames* near the Great Shipyard at *Lime house.*"

There is no historical reason for believing that the king's hounds were ever kept in the

Isle of Dogs, and the story was probably invented in order to account for the name of the locality. This name does not occur earlier than the time of Elizabeth. The Chapel House was converted into a farmhouse some time in the sixteenth century, and it figures in Norden's map of Middlesex, 1593, as the "Isle of Doges Ferme." When Lysons wrote, the old chapel was the only dwelling-place upon the marsh. It exhibited no remains of antiquity, except in the lower parts of the walls, which were full of small stones and flints. A Gothic window was removed about 1792. When Mr. Cowper wrote in 1853 the condition of the Chapel House was much the same as when Lysons's description was written. Two or three additional tenements had been erected on the west side of the farmhouse, but they were mean and inconvenient. The trees had been nearly all removed. The ground in the vicinity showed traces in every direction of having, at some remote period, been occupied with buildings, &c., but more especially to the south-west, from the Chapel House to the river. On the formation of the Millwall Dock, in 1867–8, all traces of the Chapel House were swept away, its site being absorbed in the new docks (Walford's 'Greater London,' i. 537).

This chapel, which was dedicated to St. Mary, was thought by Mr. Cowper to have been connected with, or dependent on, the Abbey of St. Mary of Graces, near the Tower of London. I venture to think that it was originally attached to the manor house of Pontefract, of which the foundations are mentioned by Strype and Maitland, and of which traces were visible up to fifty years ago. The Abbey of St. Mary does not seem to have been possessed of any property in Stepney Marsh till the end of the fifteenth century, when the manor of Pontefract apparently lapsed to the Crown. On this point, however, the evidence is not satisfactory.

The first owner of the manor of whom we have any knowledge was a certain John de Castello, otherwise known as John Attecastle. In the year 1302, 31 Edward I., the manor was purchased from John de Castello and Joan his wife by John Abel and Margery his wife.* John Abel, although he has not obtained the honour of a niche in Messrs. Stephen and Lee's Valhalla, was a personage of considerable importance in his time. He was a trusted official of King Edward I., and during the reign of that monarch and of his successor his name repeatedly occurs in the Patent Rolls as a Commissioner of Oyer and

* 'Calendar of Feet of Fines for London and Middlesex,' ed. Hardy and Page, i. 72.

Terminer. He was also an escheator south of Trent, and steward to Queen Margaret. On 8 March, 1311/12, 5 Edward II., on the promotion of Walter de Norwych to be Chief Baron of the Exchequer, John Abel was appointed a Baron of that Court in his place. In 1317 he was appointed envoy to the King of France ('Cal. Close Rolls, Edward II., 1313–18,' pp. 553, 622). He had a son named Walter (ib., p. 98), who seems to have died in the lifetime of his father, as on John Abel's death in 1323 it appears from his Inquisition post mortem that he left only three daughters, coheirs. The manor of "Ponfrayt super Thamis'," of which he died seised, consisted of eighty acres of arable, a windmill, &c. (Escheat. 16 Edward II., No. 41). He was also in possession of other manors, including West Tilbury, in Essex. The manor of Pontefract was divided into three portions, one of which was inherited by each daughter. Of these daughters, Joan married Sir William Vaughan, Margaret married Walter Heryng, and of the third I have no record, unless it were Katherine, the wife of John Chicche, who in 1333, 7 Edward III., levied a fine with William Vaughan and his wife for a third part of this manor.* Sir William Vaughan seems to have been succeeded by his son Sir Thomas Vaughan, who died seised of "Pomfreyth maner' ut de maner' de Storteford" in 1362 (Escheat. 36 Edward III., part 2, No. 64). Sir Thomas Vaughan left a son Hamon, who died without issue, and after his death and that of Margaret Heryng, who died in 1369, seised of a third part of the manor (Escheat. 43 Edward III., part 1, No. 53), the property seems to have split up into severalties, which were divided among the families of Strange, Molyneux, Mitton, Bokilton, and Falk. We find from the inquisitions that "Ricardus Mutton, chivaler," and Margaret his wife were seised of "sexta pars duarum partium manerii Pountfreit" (Escheat. 8 Henry V., No. 8), and that "Philip' Bokilton, ar'," was seised of exactly the same amount (Escheat. 8 Henry V., No. 48). Katherine, the daughter and heir of Philip Bokilton, married John Falk. Margery, the widow of Sir Baldwin Strange, held at her death, in 1432, a third part of the manor of "Pountfreit in Stepheneth Marsh," and was succeeded by her daughter and heir Elizabeth, who at the age of fourteen was already the wife of Robert Molyneux (Escheat. 10 Henry VI., No. 10). From the Feet of Fines it seems that half the manor came into the possession of John Harpur, as in 1422, 1 Henry VI., John Falk

* Ibid., p. 111.

and Katherine his wife levied a fine with him and others for a moiety of the third part; while in 1435 William Mitton, son and heir of Sir Richard and Margaret Mitton, levied another fine with John Harpur and others for another moiety of the third part. Having thus acquired a moiety of the manor, "John Harpur of Ruysshale, esquire, and Alianora his wife," parted with it in 1458, 36 Henry VI., to Thomas Hethe.* Of the further fortunes of the manor I have no information.

To end with the point from which we started, I think we have in the descent of the manor a clear explanation of the reason why the king's writs were attested at Pontefract-on-Thames. King Edward II., in travelling from Surrey or Essex into Kent, stayed a day or two with his trusty counsellor John Abel, in the manor house of which the last vestiges have been absorbed in Millwall Dock, and there transacted his official business. Although John Abel was dead in 1326, when the king's little son passed the night at Pontefract with his *gouvernante*, the hospitable traditions of the house survived, and Joan Abel, with her husband Sir William Vaughan, doubtless did their best to entertain the party. In conclusion, I may say that while I am gratified at being able to throw some light on one of the obscurer points connected with the history of mediæval London, I should be glad to receive some further information on the later history of the manor, which seems to have been closely connected with the Essex manor of West Tilbury.†

W. F. PRIDEAUX.

TOBACCO: NEW ITEMS.

1. IN 'Travels of Evliya Effendi' (2nd S. v. 453) it is stated that, in converting a building about one thousand years old at Constantinople into a monument of Sultan Mustafa, a tobacco pipe was found among the stones which smelt of smoke.

Here is a coincidence taken from the *Evening News*, 20 Sept., 1901 :—

"Whilst digging up the soil in the garden connected with the Egerton (Manor) House at Wine-wall, near Colne, the gardener came upon a clay smoking-pipe in fairly good condition, having a short stem. The date is 1450, the initials are 'P. W.' With the exception of being of a smaller concentration, the style is somewhat similar to the current make. A strong tobacco odour is emitted from the pipe.—*St. James's Gazette*."

2. In the *Athenæum* for 1 August, 1857, is a long article on tobacco. There it is stated

* 'Calendar of Feet of Fines,' ed. Hardy and Page, i. 236-8.
† Cf. the *Genealogist*, xviii. 183.

that the Chinese say that they had a knowledge of tobacco long, long ago. In Hone's 'Every-Day Book' is a short article, in which it is stated that

"Mr. Crocker describes a pipe which was found at Bannockstown, County Kildare, sticking between the teeth of a human skull, and it is accompanied by a paper, which on the authority of Herodotus: Strabo: Pomponius Mela: and Solinus: goes to prove that the Northern Nations of Europe were acquainted with tobacco, or an herb of similar properties, and that they smoked it through small tubes—of course, long before the existence of America was known."

3. Although 'N. & Q.' records James I.'s hatred of tobacco and Charles I.'s and Charles II.'s dislike for it, yet it does not mention, I think, that

"*the Tobacco pipe Makers' Company* were Incorporated by Charter, their privileges existing through the City of London and Westminster, the Kingdom of England and Dominion of Wales; they have a Master, four Wardens, and about twenty Assistants. They were first Incorporated by King James I. in his seventeenth year. Confirmed again by Charles I.; and lastly, the 29th April in the fifteenth year of King Charles II. in all the privileges of their aforesaid Charter. Their Coat of Arms is a tobacco plant in full blossom, and the device is said to be given by this Company on all their Publick Occasions."—Stow.

4. No contributor has yet referred to 'Particulars concerning Tobacco, digested in a Chronological Order from Prof. Beckmann's "Introduction to Technology."' It is much too lengthy to send you. I extract the last paragraph only :—

"He remarks that even before the discovery of the fourth Quarter of the Globe, a sort of tobacco was smoked in Asia. This conjecture being made to the celebrated traveller, M. Pallas, he gave the following answer: 'That in Asia, and especially in China, the use of tobacco for smoking is more ancient than the discovery of the New World.' I, too, scarcely entertain a doubt. Among the Chinese, and among the Mogul tribes who had the most intercourse with them, the custom of smoking is so general, so frequent, and become so indispensable a luxury; the tobacco purse affixed to their belt so necessary an article of dress; the form of the pipes, from which the Dutch seem to have taken the model of theirs, so original; and lastly the preparation of the yellow leaves, which are merely rubbed to pieces and then put into a pipe, so peculiar; that we cannot possibly derive all this from America by way of Europe; especially as India, where the habit of smoking tobacco is not so general, intervenes between Persia and China. May we not expect to find traces of this custom in the first account of the Voyages of the Portuguese and Dutch to China?......Ulloa says it is *not* probable that the Europeans learned the use of Tobacco from America, for, as it is very ancient in the Eastern Countries, it is natural to suppose that the knowledge of it came to Europe from those regions, by means of the intercourse carried on with them by the commercial States on the Mediterranean Sea. No where, not even in those parts of America where the tobacco plant grows wild, is the use of it, and that only for smoking, either general, or frequent."

It seems that there is yet something more to be learnt about tobacco. Perhaps the knowledge is coming, as witness my final extract from the *Daily Mail* of 11 Oct., 1901 :—

"AN ETYMOLOGICAL DISCOVERY.

"Ottawa, Sept. 27.

" Intelligence was received here to-day from the Yukon of a strange discovery that the language of the Nulato Indians who live within the Arctic Circle and that of the Apaches of New Mexico and Arizona are the same.

"The facts have come to light through the return to Dawson City of Father John René, Prefect Apostolic of the Roman Catholic Church in Alaska, from a journey to the fathers working among the aboriginal tribes of the Lower Yukon.

"The reverend father says: 'It is one of the most peculiar facts ascertained in connexion with the inhabitants and their origin that has ever been discovered, and one for deep study and research. It indicates, if anything, that the theory that the people of New Mexico and Arizona must have travelled southward from the Arctic regions is correct, and lends colour to the belief that the inhabitants of America came from Asia by the way of Behring Straits."

G. J. S.

HERALDRY BEFORE THE CONQUEST.

WHEN referring to early Saxon and other coats of arms I have more than once been pulled up by friends who are heraldic enthusiasts by being told that heraldry did not exist prior to 1066. Let me premise all that follows by stating I do not profess any knowledge of the subject, being led to make these few observations from unskilled reading. If gentlemen versed in matters heraldic, when making the assertion named, qualified it by some such remark as that the present system of heraldry was not in existence before William's time, a novice might be better able to understand what is meant ; but the bald statement that heraldry did not exist before 1066 has so worried me that I am obliged to unburden myself in these columns, feeling sure that I shall, by their aid, find solid ground upon which I can in future stand when heraldic authorities may perchance fling at me a similar retort.

I do not feel competent, nor is there any reason, to enter upon the subject " What is or was heraldry ? " except in the sense these observations clearly convey. I suppose it is called a science (which personally I demur to) of recording genealogies and blazoning coats of arms. Well, then, did heraldry exist prior to 1066 ? I venture to think it did, in

that genealogies are recorded and coats of arms were in use, for argument' sake, say, seven hundred years before William I.'s time. We have genealogies recorded in the Bible, and for coats of arms I will not go further back than 3928 A.M.

Was there any system observed ? Suppose we have not any trace of a system which existed in the early days, so far as written rules and regulations go, with respect to heraldry. If it can be demonstrated that the arms of any one family or person were promiscuously used by another and totally distinct family or person, it would clearly prove to a certain extent that there was not any recognized system. If, on the other hand, we can show that the arms of one particular family were handed down or carried by succeeding generations, this would surely prove the existence of " system."

That there were in the early days unwritten laws of habit and custom, use and wont, as now, which were quite as binding as any by law established, may be accepted without any great pleading. Did arms pass through families ? From Cæsar I., 3928, to A.D. 304, the coat of arms of each emperor was the same, and from Claudius, 43, to Constantinus III., 401 (with one slight difference in Constantinus Mag. in 308).

Take Egbert, first King of England, 800 ; his arms were Quarterly azure and or, a cross patonce counterchanged of the same. Ethelwolph and Ethelbald had Azure, a cross potent fitched or, as their arms. Ethelbert succeeded in 858, and we find his coat of arms was the same as his grandfather's, while the former's brother Ethelred carried the same.

If we turn to Edward the Elder, in the year 900, and trace the kings' arms to the year 1016, we find very certain evidence of a continuity which cannot be mistaken for chance, or put down to a lack of " system." This Edward's arms were Azure, a cross patonce between four martlets or. Edgar's in 959 were the same ; Edward the Martyr, son of Edgar, had the arms of his father, but four crowns take the place of the martlets. Ethelred succeeded to the throne, and his coat of arms in 978 was the same as Edward's in 900. That of Edmund Ironside in 1016 was Egbert's in 800.

Glancing at the Danish monarchs' arms, we find Eric III. in 950 had the same as Eric in 905 ; that Anlaff III. in 980 carried the same arms as his namesake in 946 ; that Hardicanute in 1041 had, I think, the same coat of arms as Knute in 1017. Edward the Confessor, 1042, had the same coat of arms as

Edward the Elder in 900, with the addition of one martlet.

What shall we say as to the "science" so called? Edmund's coat of arms in 940 was Azure, three crowns, each transfixed with two arrows saltirewise, or. Keeping in mind that a doubt exists as to there being any such thing as invention, I ask, in all humility, Is there no "science" in this coat of arms; was it by chance that such a coat of arms was chosen; does it exhibit the art of a herald; and does it not point to the "science" of conventional distinctions?

Again, Uther Pendragon's arms: Vert, a cross argent, on the first quarter our Lady, with her Son in her arms. Will any one say this has no more meaning or significance than a simple coat of arms chosen or fixed upon for self, being evolved simply from the consciousness of Pendragon? Does it speak anything for even the superior heraldic order of things from 1066 to 1442 when we find that the coat of arms of John Talbot, Earl of Shrewsbury, was Teudar Mawr's in 1073? Was this an appropriation; or does it mean "continuity"?

In connexion with this subject I may be allowed to refer to Shakspere. Horatio, speaking of Fortinbras of Norway, uses the words "who, by a seal'd compact, well ratified by law and heraldry." More to the point, perhaps, is the first player's speech, which begins, "The rugged Pyrrhus, he whose sable arms, black as his purpose, did the night resemble......With *heraldry* more dismal; head to foot now is he total *gules*: horridly *trick'd*" (the italics are my own). There are other references to heraldry in Shakspere, to which I need not now call attention.

May I hazard the opinion that heraldry existed long before William's time; that it was a "science" as much then as now; that it was equally an art; that there was a system which regulated it; that heraldry pointed then, as now, to conventional distinctions of caste; and that any difference existing between the heraldry prior to William and the present day is simply a development or extension of what existed on the Continent, if not in our own country, long before heraldry was introduced by William, if its introduction is due to him? I may mention that I have before me 'Divi Britannici,' 1660, Dr. Heylyn's 'Help to English History,' 1773, and 'A Synopsis of Heraldry,' 1682.

ALFRED CHAS. JONAS.

FILBERT.—Prof. Skeat expresses a decided opinion that this word is clearly taken from a proper name, but adds, "We have no sufficient evidence to show from whom the nut was named. A common story is that it was so named after *Philibert*, King of France, but there was no such king." In Syme's 'English Botany' the derivation from a supposed King Philibert is mentioned, but preference is given to that proposed by Wedgwood, "quasi *fill-beard*," because the nut "just fills the cup made by the beards of the calyx." This is rejected by Prof. Skeat, because "the spelling *fylberde* is a mere corruption of the earlier trisyllabic form in Gower." (That poet's suggestion of a derivation from Phillis is not worth notice, as it takes no account of the last syllable.) There is no historical record of any *King* Philibert; but it was the name of two dukes of Savoy, the earlier of whom (called "the hunter") died of excess at Lyons in 1482, when only eighteen years of age, while on a visit to the King of France (Louis XI.). Prof. Skeat contends strongly for a derivation from St. Philibert of Jumièges, similar to the German word for the nut, *Lambertsnuss*, from St. Lambert of Maestricht. The day of the former is 20 August, that of the latter 17 September. But is it not rather remarkable that the English name of the nut should be derived from that of a French saint not recognized in any Anglican calendar? The two saints, it may be mentioned, were nearly contemporary, the date usually assigned for the death of St. Philibert being A.D. 684, and that of the martyrdom of St. Lambert A.D. 708. The days given for the deaths would correspond in the Gregorian style of the calendar to 23 August and 20 September, and it is supposed that the connexion with the filberts is that they become ripe about that season.

W. T. LYNN.

[The 'H.E.D.' says probably from the nut ripening near St. Philibert's day.]

"VERIFY YOUR QUOTATIONS."—This counsel is always needful, for one is constantly coming across a citation that either is not in verbal agreement with the original or is attributed to a wrong source. An instance illustrating both points has just come under my notice. Canon Hicks, of Manchester, in addressing the Manchester and Salford Equitable Co-operative Society at Ardwick on Saturday, 25 January, concluded his remarks by begging his hearers to "take as their motto the words of a great poet and reformer, William Morris":—

I will not cease from mental strife [fight],
Nor shall my sword sleep in my hand,
Till I [we] have built Jerusalem
In England's green and pleasant land.

The poet of the 'Earthly Paradise' was certainly a reformer, and was in sympathy with the co-operative movement, but Canon Hicks should have known that William Blake was the author of the lines he attributed to Morris, and at the same time misquoted.

JOHN GRIGOR.

LAST WORDS OF GAMBETTA. (See *ante*, p. 58.)—In your review of Marvin's 'Last Words' you ask what is the authority for Gambetta's foreboding, "I am lost, and there is no use to deny it." I have a cutting from the *Pall Mall Gazette* of 1 January, 1883, the words of which are given as taken from the *Times* of the same day, the day after Gambetta's death. They are as follows:—

"M. Gambetta died without recovering his senses, but in the afternoon he exclaimed, 'Je suis perdu, il est inutile de dissimuler. Mais j'ai tant souffert que ce sera une délivrance.'"

NOSA.

THE SOBIESKI STUARTS: "AN UNSOLVED MYSTERY."—The following is from the *Times*, 11 January:—

"Hay-Allen.—On the 1st Jan., 1902, at East Finchley, Gilbert Hay-Allen, aged 72, son of Lieut. Thos. Allen by Ann Salmon (his second wife), grandson of Admiral Carter Allen, and half-brother of John Sobieski and Charles Edward Stuart, Count d'Albanie. Buried in Old Finchley Churchyard. 'Per Enses ad Astra.'"

This inspired paragraph leaves the mystery no nearer solution. ROBERT RAYNER.

Herne Hill, S.E.

ARCHÆOLOGICAL DISCOVERIES. — In the *Graphic* of 8 June, 1901, and in *Black and White* of 29 June, 1901, appeared notices and illustrations of discoveries at Jerusalem and Rome. At the former place a mosaic of Orpheus was found. Compare with the Orpheus at the back of the Delhi Peacock throne, now at the India Museum, South Kensington. Also at Rome was discovered a Christian church with a carving of figures and garlands, which compares with a carving of figures and garlands found on the Afghan border, for information concerning which consult the authorities at the Kensington Museum, as this latter is in a plate published by the Government of India, Simla Branch Press, before 1884, in an official report on the monuments. H. H. COLE.

Virginia Water.

BIBLIOMANIA.—The following extract from the *Daily Telegraph* of 14 November last seems worthy of a note in 'N. & Q.':—

"At the meeting of the Yarmouth Board of Guardians, on Tuesday, it was reported that a pauper named Stokes, who lived alone, had recently died, and that on searching his cottage the relieving officer found hundreds of books, some of great rarity, the collection being valued by a bookseller at some hundreds of pounds. Over 150 prints, framed and unframed, were also discovered, and receipts were found for considerable sums sent to Paris for books. Some of the works—in French—were ordered to be sent to the retort house at the gas works to be destroyed, while the remainder are to be valued and disposed of. The deceased pauper, who had received out-relief for years, had paid considerable sums for bookbinding, as was shown by receipts; and one guardian said he had purchased over 50*l.* worth of books from him, not knowing that he was a pauper. The only money found in the house was 1½*d.* on a key-ring."

W. H. QUARRELL.

"MOST REVEREND," "RIGHT REVEREND," AND "VERY REVEREND."—When a bishop retires he still retains the title of "Right Reverend," and is spoken of as "The Right Rev. Bishop X." But when, as in the case of Bishops Johnson and Welldon, the see is metropolitan, does he in his retirement retain his title of "Most Reverend," or does he go down a step and become "Right Reverend"? What are the corresponding Latin honorifics of which these are translations, and within what period have they become stereotyped in English use? That they were not fixed for some time after the Reformation is shown by the inscription on a monument in Monkton Priory Church, Pembroke, which runs:—

"Here Lyeth intombed the body of Sr Francis Meyricke, Knight, who departed this life upon Friday the xxix Day of July Ano Dni 1603, Beinge the son of the Reverend Father Rowland Meyricke, late Bishop of Bangor and Katherine Meyricke His Wife Hee Married Anne Laugharne the Daughter of Francis Laugharne of S^t. Bride Esquire and Geneth Phillips His Wife and had issue Gelly Meyricke Francis Meyricke, Henry Meyricke and John Meyricke, Frances Meyricke and Jane Meyricke."

It is curious that in Ireland within the last thirty years or so the Roman Catholic Church has advanced its dignitaries a step as it were —apparently in order to "go one better" than the disestablished Church in this respect—so it seems at least to the uninitiated. All its bishops are now "Most Reverend" and its canons "Very Reverend" (its deans and archdeacons seem to be almost extinct). This course, however, has not been taken in England or the colonies, with regard to the bishops at least, who still remain "Right Reverend," though canons, I think, are "Very Reverend."

While on this subject I may note that in the *Daily Mail* of Christmas Day last I saw the Moderator-Elect of the "Presbyterian Church of England" described as the "Very Rev. So-and-So." It is, I think, a new departure on the part of that body to give its Moderator an honorific of this kind; and if it has been taken, why was the Scottish practice not followed—viz., of making him a Right Reverend for a year, instead of assimilating him to the principals of the Scotch universities for that period?

These questions, I should add, are not asked in any spirit of controversy. The first has, in fact, become unnecessary, for I have since recollected that Bishop Barry, who was a metropolitan, is always styled "The Right Reverend." A retired archbishop, however, would remain the "Most Reverend." The only instance in the Anglican Church that I can recall is that of the late Archbishop Lewis, of Canada. But if so, why should not a metropolitan, though he did not bear the title of archbishop? The difference is one of name only.

An archdeacon who, like Archdeacon Diggle, resigns his office and removes to another diocese, would not, I presume, retain the title of the "Venerable Archdeacon" or the honorific of "The Venerable," as the office is entirely a local one. It is not usually done in the case of colonial archdeacons returning to England. But the same argument might be applied to the case of a retired archbishop, as it is, in fact, to the case of a retired metropolitan who had not borne the title of archbishop. J. P. L.

Queries.

WE must request correspondents desiring information on family matters of only private interest to affix their names and addresses to their queries, in order that the answers may be addressed to them direct.

"OLIVER."—This is the name of a small lift-hammer (of from four or five to fifty or sixty pounds weight) worked by the foot by means of a treadle and spring-pole. It is used by nailmakers, chainmakers, and others. Why is it so called? The name looks like a surname—perhaps of the inventor. The earliest reference to it we have found is only of 1858, but it was then in ordinary use, and apparently had been for some time. I shall be glad of any information as to its origin. Readers who have friends in the nailmaking districts might help by making inquiries there.
J. A. H. MURRAY.

"OMNEITY": "OMNIETY."—This word was used by Archbishop Usher and by Sir Thomas Browne, in the sense of "allness," "allhood," and has been used by later metaphysicians. I should like to know whether it is an English formation, or whether it occurs in any mediæval or modern Latin writer, as *omneitas*, or *omnietas*, or (correctly) *omnitas*.
J. A. H. MURRAY.

CHRONOGRAMS.—Who was the originator of this form of wit? I lately saw a golden key, with an ecclesiastical device, which bore the following inscription :—

En fIDeI nostræ testIs plaCet aVrea CLaVIs PrInCeps nVnC serVos faC frIDerICe tVos.

This would give the date of the key as 1732. Perhaps some of your readers could throw more light on its history. Addison remarks that this form of wit was very popular in Germany, and quotes a medal struck in honour of Gustavus Adolphus. As the primary object was to include the numeral letters which gave the key to the date, we have not much to look for in the form of the Latin. CECIL H. S. WILLSON.
Weybridge.

[The word "chronogram" is said to have been first used in verses addressed, in 1575, to the King of Poland. See 'Chronograms: Five Thousand and more in Number,' &c., by James Hilton, F.S.A. (Stock, 1882). Many references to chronograms occur in our General Indexes.]

ITALIAN SUNDIAL INSCRIPTION.—On the front wall of the Albergo Rossazza, the solitary old inn upon the top of Mont Cenis, is a sundial, whereupon is a half-obliterated inscription. It reads

OMBRAONDEL
MEFEGEM.

I carefully copied the characters during a leisurable tramp across the mountain last summer, and the (apparently) two words are displayed precisely as now given. *Ombra*, of course, is "a shadow," but what of the rest. Is it patois? The tumbledown posada in question is in Italy, but within a mile or two of the French frontier. HARRY HEMS.
Fair Park, Exeter.

"ALL COOPER'S DUCKS WITH ME."—A short time ago I heard a respectable young master-butcher in London use the following curious saying, viz., "It would soon have been all Cooper's ducks with me," meaning that death would have resulted had he not quickly recovered from a recent attack of influenza. This person was born and bred in Kent; but, although myself a Kentish man, I have not previously heard the same either there or elsewhere; nor is any reference to it to be met with in Hotten's 'Slang Dictionary'—unless it have anything to do with a "duck" (otherwise better known as a "faggot"), which that book describes, somewhat incorrectly, as "a bundle of bits of the 'stickings' of beef sold for food to the London poor." Can any

of your readers throw light on the origin of
the saying?   W. I. R. V.

DE LA POLE OR POLE FAMILY.—Edmund of
this surname fought at Agincourt (Walsingham, 'Hist. Angl.,' ii. 169; Nicolas, 'Agincourt,' pp. 128, 354; *Archæologia*, iii. 18). He
is supposed to have been the grandson of Sir
William de la Pole (died 1366), the father of
Michael, first Earl of Suffolk. Is anything
known of the father of this Edmund and of
his marriage and descendants (if any)?

Sir William de la Pole (died 1366) had four
sons and two daughters—Michael (first Earl
of Suffolk), Sir Walter, Sir Thomas, Sir Edmund (Captain of Calais), Blanche (who
married Richard, first Lord Scrope of Bolton),
and Margaret (who married Richard Neville,
of Hornby, Lancashire). Is anything known
of the marriages and descendants of Sir
Walter, Sir Thomas, Sir Edmund, and the
descendants of the two daughters? Sir
Thomas, I believe, had an only daughter and
heiress, named Catherine, who died in 1362.
Who was Richard Neville, of Hornby?

Michael de la Pole, first Earl of Suffolk
(died 1389), had three sons and one daughter
—Michael (second earl), Thomas, Richard
(Foss, ii. 76), and Anne, who married Gerald
de l'Isle. Is anything known of the descendants of Thomas, Richard, and Anne?

Michael de la Pole (died 1415), second Earl
of Suffolk, had eight children — Michael
(third earl), William (fourth earl and first
duke), Sir John (died in captivity), Alexander (slain at Jargeau, 1429). Thomas (died
1433 in captivity), and three daughters.
Is anything known of the marriages and
descendants of Sir John, Alexander, Thomas,
and the three daughters?

John de la Pole, second Duke of Suffolk
(died 1491), who married Elizabeth, sister of
Edward IV. and Richard III., had ten children—John, Earl of Lincoln (killed at Stoke,
1487), Edmund, Earl of Suffolk (executed
1513), Humphrey, Edward, Richard (killed
at Pavia, 1525), Sir William, and four
daughters. Is anything known of the marriages and descendants of Humphrey, Edward, Richard, William, and the four
daughters?

The 'Dict. Nat. Biog.,' under the heading
of Margaret Pole, Countess of Salisbury (wife
of Sir Richard Pole), refers to an article in
1ˢᵗ S. v. 163 as dealing with the relationship between the St. Johns, the Beauforts,
and the Poles. I am anxious to see this
article, but Mr. Francis tells me that the
First Series has long been out of print. If
any reader of this has the issue I shall be

very much obliged if he will let me have a
copy of the article in question.
                              RONALD DIXON.
46, Marlborough Avenue, Hull.

ISLE OF ROSENEATH.—The error of Sir
Walter Scott in describing the peninsula of
Roseneath as an island in his 'Heart of Mid-
lothian' has often been commented on. But
I see that the Marquess of Argyll speaks of
"his isle and county" of Roseneath (State
Trials, 13 Charles II., 1661). Probably Scott
had this designation in his mind. But how
came it that Roseneath was called an island?
                              J. WILLCOCK.
Lerwick.

"IN EARTHLY RACES."—Who wrote the following? It was a favourite quotation with
the late Sir William Gull:—

> In earthly races
> To victors only do the heralds call;
> But oh! in yonder high and heavenly places
> Success is nothing and the work is all.
                                    J. F. P.

LADY NOTTINGHAM.—In the life of 'Caroline the Illustrious' is a reference to Lady
Nottingham, who is said to have had thirty
children. Is this a substantial fact? One
would like to know how many came at a
time and at what intervals. If true, is not
this a record in maternity?   E. F. D. C.

ALEXANDER KEITH was admitted to Westminster School on 27 January, 1812. Can any
reader of 'N. & Q.' give me any particulars
of his parentage and career?   G. F. R. B.

KEATING.—James and Alfred Keating were
admitted to Westminster School in 1825 and
1828. I should be glad to obtain any information concerning them.   G. F. R. B.

GREGORY LEWIS WAY.—Is anything known
of the writer of this name who in the
eighteenth century translated a selection
from the twelfth and thirteenth century
'Fabliaux' of Legrand d'Aussy? I find no
mention of him in the 'D.N.B.,' although the
names suggest a connexion with the Way
family which counted Albert the antiquary
and Sir Gregory the soldier among its members. Both of these men were sons of Lewis
Way, of Stanstead Park, Sussex. It seems
just possible that Gregory Lewis Way may
be the full names of Lewis Way, but scarcely
probable, as the latter was born in 1772, and
in 1796 George Ellis edited G. L. Way's translations. In an old bookstall find (Homer's
'Battle of the Frogs and Mice,' 1717) I have a
steel book-plate, showing a knight in full
armour seated on the shore of a moonlit sea;

the name on the plate is "Gregorius Ludovicus Way." WALTER JERROLD.
Hampton-on-Thames.

BATTLE OF NAVARINO. — Did Codrington allege in his defence a remark of George IV., "Il me faut une bataille à tout prix"?
W. MILLER.

NUMIDIAN COINS. (See the 'Hawson Oak,' 9th S. viii. 522.)—MR. THORPE refers to "the finding of Numidian coins of B.C. 200 on Carnbrea." Where are these coins, and where were they found? I was unaware of any such find, except of one coin of Micipsa of Numidia, described in vol. xiii. of the *Journal* of the Royal Inst. of Cornwall, p. 103. YGREC.

REBECCA CROMWELL. — Are any portraits known of this lady? (Mrs.) J. COPE.
13c, Hyde Park Mansions, W.

W. E. PHILLIPS. — This gentleman was Governor of Penang from 1820 to 1826. Can any of your readers supply me with data relating to parentage, place of birth, and descendants? Was he related to that "builder of Greater Britain," Admiral Arthur Phillips, the founder of the settlement of New South Wales? V.

[The founder of New South Wales was named Phillip.]

LE NEVE FAMILY. — I should be glad to have some information respecting the Le Neve family, who appear to have settled in Norfolk before the fifteenth century. The first of whom I have any record is Robert Le Neve, of Tivetshall, who lived in the reign of Henry IV. Sir William Le Neve, of Aslacton, Clarenceux King of Arms, was herald at Edgehill. Francis Le Neve, born 1573, died 1652, was Master of the Merchant Taylors' Company in 1629. A very fine portrait of him by Cornelius Jansen can be seen in the hall of that company. Peter Le Neve, of Great Witchingham, Norfolk, born 1662, died 1729, was Norroy King of Arms. I believe that there are monumental tablets to several members of the family in Great Witchingham Church, and I should be glad to know if others can be found in any other part of the country. As many of the family appear to have settled in London, probably some traces exist in London churches. Can any reader furnish particulars? P. L N. F.

LOUIS PHILIPPE AND FAMILY AT THE "STAR AND GARTER," RICHMOND.—I am wishful to know how long they stayed at the "Star and Garter" before going to Claremont in 1848; more especially whether they were there till the Christmas Day of that year. They came over from France in February. One day during the year, being inquisitive about celebrities, I went to Richmond and saw the king and queen and three sons going out, I think to Cardinal Wiseman's cathedral. The old people bowed politely to the spectators, as they drove in a closed carriage. The sons walked, and seemed very cheerful. E. M. JONES.

SIR MARTIN STUTEVILE.—I shall be glad to be referred to sources of information touching Sir Martin Stutevile, of Dalham Tower, Herts, the correspondent of Joseph Mede. He married one of the Ishams of Lamport, Northants. LOBUC.

PORTRAITS OF JOANNA BAILLIE.—I should be obliged if any reader of 'N. & Q.' could inform me of the present location of original portraits of Joanna Baillie (1762-1851).
J. L. C.

HOLME OF WEARMOUTH.—It appears from Harleian MS. 1540 (45) that Robert Holme, of Wearmouth, son of John Holme, of Holme Hall, in Lancashire, married Anne, one of the Middletons of Silksworth, and that Raffe Holme, the grandson of Robert Holme, married Margaret, one of the Greys of Horton Grange. Can any reader enable me to find out the precise parentage of these ladies?
FRANCIS P. MARCHANT.

"TWOPENCE FOR MANNERS."—The Rev. E. J. Hardy, in an article 'Talk to Young People,' gives the origin of this saying :—

"Formerly in Ireland twopence, or a penny, or a few pieces of turf were brought to the schoolmaster each week by every scholar in payment for tuition in manners. Accordingly it would be said of an uncourteous boy, 'Oh! he never paid his twopence.' I am afraid in some Board schools twopennyworth of manners is not imparted in the year. You will hear them [children], as they rush out of school, calling passers-by nicknames, and making remarks about their personal appearance as rude as were those of the young people who said to Elisha, 'Go up, thou bald head!'"

I am reminded by this remark that in the year 1699 more attention must have been paid to manners than in the present day. In that year there was published an octavo volume entitled 'An Account of the Societies for the Reformation of Manners in London and Westminster.' Are those societies still in operation; if not, when and why did they cease to exist?
EVERARD HOME COLEMAN.

[For much information see 6th S. xii. 454 and the references to 'N. & Q.' there quoted.]

Replies.

THE DUCHY OF BERWICK.
(9th S. viii. 439, 534.)

Is Mr. Curwen correct in saying that St. Dominic was not the founder of the Inquisition? He certainly instigated the "inquisitorial missions" sent out by Pope Innocent III. in 1210-15 against the Albigenses in the south of France, and every Spanish account of the institution which I have ever seen claims St. Dominic as its founder. It was in consequence of St. Dominic's connexion with these Inquisitorial Commissions that the Inquisition, when regularly organized by Gregory IX. in 1233, was placed in the hands of the Dominicans.

As regards the Duchy of Berwick, which, of course, was created as a peerage of England in 1687, what I meant to say was that the first holder—who, in consequence of the Revolution of 1688, never took his seat in the House of Lords previous to his attainder in 1695—had his English duchy bestowed on him as a Spanish grandeeship by Philip V. of Spain, and hence the present holder very legitimately describes himself as "Duke of Berwick," and *not* "Duque de Berwick," in the 'Almanach de Gotha,' and is so addressed by all English officials. Curiously enough, William III. did much the same thing when he created Marshal Schomberg an English duke by the title of Duke of Schomberg. I confess I quite forgot that Lord Bridport holds the Duchy of Bronte. Admiral the Earl of Dundonald held the Brazilian title of Maranhaõ for life. Lords Rothschild and Pirbright hold Austrian baronies, just as Sir William Walrond, M.P., holds the old Spanish Marquisate of Vallado. I find I also omitted from my list the Austrian honours held by Viscount Taaffe, and the Papal principality held by the Earl of Newburgh (Prince Giustiniani Bandini). Lord Perth, as Duc de Melfort in France, is another instance in which a title originally bestowed by James II. was reconferred on the holder during his exile by a foreign sovereign; and, as I have already said, it is a very open question whether or not the English Duchy of Wharton and James III.'s Duchy *in partibus* of Northumberland were not recognized as Spanish grandeeships by Philip V.

Fitz-James as a royal surname may, of course, be paralleled by Fitz-Charles, which was bestowed by Charles II. upon his son by the Viscountess Shannon, whom he created Earl of Plymouth; but I should be surprised to learn that *Fitz* is necessarily or always a sign of illegitimacy. How about Fitz-Gerald and Fitz-William? The present Earls of Pembroke are Herberts, not Fitzherberts, although they are undoubtedly illegitimate descendants of the old Earls of Pembroke, whilst the Fitzherberts of Tissington have no bend sinister. Is Mr. Easton certain that there is no documentary proof older than Scott for the assumption that James V., when on frolic bent, used to call himself Fitz-James? Moreover, if Fitz is a proof of illegitimacy, why is Henry II. so constantly described as Henry Fitz Empress? Was there any earlier instance of its use in England to denote illegitimate descent from royalty than that of Henry Fitzroy, Duke of Richmond, illegitimate son of Henry VIII. by Elizabeth Blount? The illegitimate descendants of John of Gaunt took the name of Somerset, not Fitzjohn. Fitzroy, Duke of Grafton, was not the eldest child of Charles II., who went back to history for the surnames of his children in the instance of Lady Mary Tudor, his daughter by Moll Davies.

Your readers may be interested in one title which, according to G. E. C. in his 'Complete Peerage,' vol. i. p. 60, is possessed by the Duke of Berwick. The Marquisate of Jamaica in the English peerage was conferred upon his ancestor the Duke of Liria by James III. in 1720, and, according to G. E. C., is still borne by the family. It is curious that James III. should have chosen for his cousin—a grandee of Spain—a title derived from a former possession of the Spanish Crown. Readers of Beckford's 'Letters from Spain and Portugal' may recollect his frequent mention of a Marquis of Jamaica, presumably the then heir of the Berwick family. He evidently had not a notion that the title was English, but a Jacobite creation. I recollect some years ago taking part in a controversy in the *Globe* as to whether or not the Marquisate of Jamaica was one of the titles borne by the descendants of Columbus. Other titles *in partibus* conferred by James III. upon foreigners seem to have included an English Duchy of Castelbranco, granted by him to the Spanish Count of Castelbranco, and a Scotch Earldom of Almond given to Sig. Davia, senator of Bologna. With the exception of two or three baronetcies given by Charles II. to friends in Holland these are, probably, the only instances since the time of the Plantagenets in which English honours have been conferred upon non-naturalized foreigners. Are any instances known in which the Garter has been granted to foreign subjects?   H.

"Wyrall" (9ᵗʰ S. ix. 109).—Cotgrave has French *virole*, "an iron ring put about the end of a staffe, &c., to strengthen it, and keep it from riving." Just because it was often made of iron, the corresponding E. word was "derived" from Latin *ferrum*, and is now spelt *ferrule*. See 'Ferrule' in 'H.E.D.,' or in any dictionary that is at hand.

CELER.

GEE FAMILY (9ᵗʰ S. ix. 10).—William Gee was Mayor of Hull in 1573. He left money to build almshouses in that city, and in 1575 at his own expense he replaced the great east window of Holy Trinity Church, which had been damaged by a mob. A half life-size portrait of him on wood is or was in the Hull Grammar School, and on this appears his coat of arms. His will is reprinted in 'Hullinia,' a work written by Alderman John Symonds, and published in 1872. It begins:

"Whereas, in the Scriptures, the great God has willed, by the Prophet, to say to Hezekiah, to make his will and put things in order, for that he must die, so I do now pray, and humbly beseech the great God, to confound and destroy all those men, lawyers, and others whosoever, to the Devil, in the Pit of Hell, which do, or shall do, or take upon them to alter this my will. Amen. Good Lord, Amen!" &c.

This will gives "to my son William Gee, 2,000*l.*; my son Walter, 200*l.*," &c.

William Gee the younger seems to have lived at Bishop Burton in the East Riding of Yorkshire, and to have had a wife named Mary, but possibly this was his mother's name. By deed these two agreed to fulfil the wishes of the elder William Gee.

The Gees appear to have been connected with Hull for generations, and one of the nine divisions of the west window of Holy Trinity Church is a memorial to Joseph Gee, "of Hull, merchant, who died in 1860."

RONALD DIXON.

46, Marlborough Avenue, Hull.

An early instance of this family name occurs in the charter of the Company of Stationers, dated 4 May, 1556, Thomas Gee being one of the ninety-four members whose signatures were attached thereto. The name appears frequently in the City of London. The registers of St. Botolph, Bishopsgate, commenced in 1558. During the next century there were eleven baptisms, fifteen marriages, and nine deaths, of which I will furnish MR. GEE with details should he require them. See also 6ᵗʰ S. ii. 71.

EVERARD HOME COLEMAN.

71, Brecknock Road.

BOWYER WILLS (9ᵗʰ S. viii. 444).—William Bowyer, senior, died in 1737, and William, his son, in 1777, both at Low Leyton, Essex, where a monument was erected to their memory. Would not their wills be probably proved at the District Registry, Ipswich? A copy of the will of the latter is given in 'Nichols's Literary Anecdotes' with a biographical memoir, vol. viii. p. 270. This work may be consulted in the Corporation Library, Guildhall. Extracts therefrom may be found in Timperley's 'Dictionary of Printers and Printing,' and 2ⁿᵈ S. iv. 209.

EVERARD HOME COLEMAN.

71, Brecknock Road.

QUOTATIONS (9ᵗʰ S. vi. 489; vii. 74, 170, 497; viii. 113).—"Cum rerum natura nusquam magis, quam in minimis, tota sit" (Plin., 'Nat. Hist.,' xi. i. (2).

"Veuve d'un peuple-roi, mais reine encore du monde." According to Ramage's 'Beautiful Thoughts from French and Italian Authors,' second edition, this saying is by Gabriel Gilbert, who flourished about 1650. The heading is 'Papal Rome.' No more particular reference is given.

ROBERT PIERPOINT.

GREEK PRONUNCIATION (9ᵗʰ S. vii. 146, 351, 449; viii. 74, 192, 372, 513).—While noting M. HAULTMONT's interesting comments upon certain remarks of mine in the above connexion, I cannot own to being as much convinced by the arguments brought forward as that writer will probably expect me to be, for I conceive that the Italian would not be more likely than the French to have retained the old Latin sound of *sal*, but less so. Words received by the French language from the Latin would more naturally remain unaltered and unaltering in sound in the land of their adoption than they would in the land of their origin, where they would be part of a living and always moving tongue, and open to all the changes of such a tongue, and it is in the vowel-sounds more particularly that changes in such a tongue would be found to occur.

In modern times, English, as talked in rural America, is more likely to retain the vowel-sounds of English speech two hundred years ago than to-day's island English, and especially to-day's London English, is. Many words of old French origin, embedded in our own tongue, are surely more likely to retain the old French vowel-sounds than the same or similar words in their modern form in the French of to-day. It was an ancient dictionary that gave the derivation of *salt* as from the Latin *sal*. I need not defend it. If *salt* is rather from the A.-S. *sealt* (cf. N.H.Ger. *Salz*), we only see more clearly

still how strangely a word in our own living tongue can alter, when in a few hundred years the letters *sealt* can now by many be represented by the sound *sorlt*. Evidently, then, the Italians may just as easily have altered the sound *vas* (or *vazz*) into *varze*; though possibly few of them will have as yet Romanced the word into *vorze*, as some of us have done. The modern Italian sound, then, for the commodity *salt* does not attract my attention nearly so much as the uncommon French sound, and that sound seems to the present writer to require some explanation. As to the A.-S. word *sealt*, if that is indeed our root-word, it and the French *sel* seem apparently very similar in the vowel-sounds, which is noteworthy. We are told that all living languages are ever moving; thus we might expect that the word *sel*, if it were not a Latin fossil, preserved, as fossils are apt to be, in a foreign tongue, would have drifted to *sal* in sound, and possibly into *sol*, just as our *sealt* has drifted into *sorlt*. I submit, then, that the *sel* sound is one not to be expected, and requires accounting for. That the word *vas* has also the form *vasum* does not seem to me altogether conclusive against what I had submitted. The lack of absolute knowledge of what the sounds were was the point I was more particularly endeavouring to urge, and I note that M. HAULTMONT only contends for what, to that writer, seem the probabilities.
                     W. H. B.

VANCOUVER (9th S. viii. 504; ix. 34).— George Vancouver was born about 1750. He was a midshipman in the Royal Navy, and served under Capt. James Cook. He was appointed to the command of an expedition to ascertain whether there was any communication between the North Pacific and North Atlantic oceans. The island which now bears his name was originally called Nootka, discovered in 1774, but was first circumnavigated by Capt. George Vancouver in 1792. He compiled an account of this voyage under the title of 'Voyage of Discovery to the North Pacific Ocean and round the World, in which the Coast of North-West America has been carefully examined and accurately surveyed, principally with a view to ascertain the existence of any navigable Communication between the North Pacific and North Atlantic Oceans, 1790-95,' 3 vols., 1798. This work was ready for publication when the author died on 10 May, 1798.
               EVERARD HOME COLEMAN.

George Vancouver was born at King's Lynn, 22 June, 1757. "Which after the place

of my nativity, the town of Lynn in Norfolk, obtained the name of Lynn Canal": so writes Vancouver in vol. iii. p. 249 of his book 'A Voyage of Discovery to the North Pacific Ocean and round the World.' St. Margaret's register contains the following: "Mar., 1761, George s. of Mr. John Gaspar Vancouver, and Bridget his wife (born 22 June, 1757)."
               ALFRED SMITH.
Stonegate House, King's Lynn.

SIR THOMAS SMITH, OF PARSON'S GREEN (9th S. ix. 29).—He was son of Thomas Smith, Mayor of Abingdon in 1584, by Joan, daughter of Thomas Jennings. He was born 1556; matric. at Christ Church, Oxon, in 1573 (see Foster's 'Alumni Oxon.'); M.P. for Cricklade, 1588-9; Tamworth, 1593; Aylesbury, 1597-8; secretary to the Earl of Essex; Clerk of the Privy Council, 1587; Clerk of the Parliament, 1597; Latin Secretary to James I., 1603; knighted at Greenwich, 20 May, 1603; and appointed one of the Masters of Requests in 1608. He died at Fulham, 27 Nov., 1609, and was buried there 7 December following. Will dated 12 Sept., 1609; proved in P.C.C., 21 Dec., 1609. He married Frances, eldest daughter of William Brydges, fourth Lord Chandos, and she afterwards, about 1610, became the second wife of Thomas Cecil, first Earl of Exeter, whom she survived forty years, dying in 1663 at the age of eighty-three, and was buried in Winchester Cathedral. Her will, dated 20 Jan., 1662, was proved 17 July, 1663. By Sir Thomas Smith she had an only son, Robert Smith, who died *s.p.* in 1626, and a daughter Margaret, who became the wife successively of Sir Edward Herbert, Attorney-General to Charles I., and of Thomas Carey, second son of Robert, Earl of Monmouth. Sir Thomas Smith, the Secretary of State to Queen Elizabeth, died in 1577, so before Frances Brydges was born. Sir Thomas of Parson's Green must also be distinguished from Sir Thomas Smith, the well-known Treasurer of the Virginia Company and ambassador to Muscovy. He was knighted in the same month as his namesake, but died in 1625.
               W. D. PINK.
Lowton, Newton-le-Willows.

Sir Thomas Smith was son of Thomas Smith, of Abingdon, by Jone, daughter of Thomas Jenings (Harl. MS. 1551, Visitation of Middlesex). Born at Abingdon about the year 1556. In 1573 a student of Christ Church, Oxford; B.A. 1574, M.A. 1578. He became Public Orator and Proctor in 1584; 1587, Clerk of Privy Council; M.P. for Cricklade, 1588-9; Tamworth, 1593; 1597, Clerk of the Parliament; knighted at Greenwich, by James I., 1603; 1608, Master of the Court of Requests. In 1606 he purchased Parson's Green of Sir William Billesbie, and died at Brightwells 28 November, 1609. His Inq. p.m., the inscription on his tomb in Fulham Church, and extracts from his will are given in Feret's 'Fulham Old and New.' He left, by the Hon. Frances Brydges, a son Robert, who was educated at Christ Church, and d. *s.p.*, in his mother's lifetime, 1626 (Harl. MS. 1551). His daughter Margaret married first Hon. Thomas Carey, and secondly Sir Edward Herbert.

H. S. V.-W.

Frances, eldest daughter of William Brydges, fourth Baron Chandos of Sudeley, was married first to Sir Thomas Smith, of Parson's Green, co. Middlesex (died 1609), Master of Requests and Latin Secretary to King James I.; secondly to Thomas Cecil, Earl of Exeter, who died 1623. She was thirty-eight years younger than her husband, and survived him more than forty years, dying in 1663, aged eighty-three years. She was buried under a flat stone in the cathedral of Winchester. A painting of her by Vandyke was at Strawberry Hill, and a print from it was engraved by Faithorne. The above Sir Thomas is not identical with the Secretary of State *temp.* Elizabeth.

JOHN RADCLIFFE.

GORDON, A PLACE-NAME (9th S. ix. 29).— The following, taken from the 'Minute Book kept by the War Committee of the Covenanters in the Stewartry of Kirkcudbright (1640-1),' may be of interest. Speaking of the Gordons of Kenmure and Lochinvar, the writer says (p. 183):—

"Whence the origin of the Gordons, who were one of the most ancient and powerful families in Scotland, there are now no means of accurately ascertaining. Some historians, reasoning from the similarity of names, have alleged that the first of the name came from Gordonia, a city in Macedon, whilst others trace them to Normandy, where there was once a manor called Gordon, and conclude them to be sprung from the same family as Bertrand de Gordoun, the archer who shot Richard I. at the siege of Chalos in Aquitaine. The traditionary account of the origin of the name is that in the reign of Malcolm III. there was in the south of Scotland a wild boar of tremendous strength and ferocity, which had killed many knights and gentlemen who had attempted to destroy it, and had at length become such a terror to the whole country that none durst encounter it, whereupon the king offered a great reward to whoever should kill it and bring its head to the Court. This being done by a brave yeoman called Adam, the king inquired of him how he slew the monster. He replied that having wrapped his plaid about his arm, he thrust

it into the mouth of the boar and *gored him down* with his dagger. Malcolm, pleased with the intrepidity of the action, conferred upon him the honour of knighthood, and commanded him to assume the surname of Goredoun in commemoration of the circumstance. By some the boar is said to have been killed in the forest of the Glenkens (Kirkcudbrightshire), whilst others lay the scene of the exploit in the parish of Gordon, in Berwickshire."

L. CAMPBELL-JOHNSTON.

ARCHITECT'S NAME WANTED (9th S. viii. 384, 487).—*Apropos* of churches at Colombo, may I recall my impression of an old native Catholic church I saw there in 1876? It was built by the labour of Singhalese or Tamils, and the interior adornments were most curious and interesting. The "sanctuary" was carved in the Indian manner, resplendent with gold and colours, but somewhat tarnished with age. I should much like to have some information as to this church, which stands, or stood, near the large Portuguese church, between the lake and the sea.

JOHN HOBSON MATTHEWS.
Town Hall, Cardiff.

BARRAS (9th S. viii. 202, 228, 267, 473; ix. 15).—I note that in vol. vii. of the *Transactions* of the Cumberland and Westmorland Antiquarian and Archæological Society there is a paper by the late Chancellor Ferguson, F.S.A., on 'Barras Gate, Dalston.' There is a locality in Chester, now known as "The Bars," some distance along Foregate Street, in front of the east gate of the city, and along the Roman road, where the Bars gate formerly was believed to have stood. This may quite easily have been "Barras Gate" on the derivation given by MR. NEILSON.

T. CANN HUGHES, M.A., F.S.A.
Lancaster.

IRISH BADGES (9th S. viii. 484).—I think D. B. is under a false impression, for neither Cicely Nevil nor her husband, the Duke of York, used the greyhound for a badge. Thomas de Lancaster, Duke of Clarence, son of King Henry IV., who was lieutenant in Ireland 1401–13, had a greyhound gorged with a plain collar for that purpose. Robert de Vere, Earl of Oxford, did not take the three crowns to Ireland; just the reverse. King Richard II. created him Duke of Ireland 13 October, 1386, and granted him the ancient arms of that country, Azure, three crowns or, with a bordure argent, as an augmentation to his arms. The tower triple-towered or, from the portal a hart springing argent, attired and unguled, also or, has been the crest since 1801; and, as Willement says, "it is rather curious that the badge given for Ireland assimilates very closely to that of King Richard (II.), being a white hart issuing from the portal of a golden castle." King Richard made two visits to Ireland during his short reign ; whether he left the above badge as a legacy to the Irish to gain their favour I am unable to find out. According to MS. Harleian No. 304 the following are the arms of Ireland : Gules, a castell argent, a hart issuing out of the gat in his prop. colour, horned gold. The oval seal of Queen Eleanor, wife of King Edward I., has upon it a figure representing herself, with a castle (with the hart) and lion on each side, which refer to the arms of the kingdom of Castile. The war-cry of "Farrah ! Farrah !" was probably a general one amongst the Irish chiefs in battle, as I cannot find that it appertained to any special family or sept.

JOHN RADCLIFFE.

'LIFE,' BY MRS. BARBAULD (9th S. ix. 67).— MR. G. SHELDON will find this poem in Palgrave's 'Golden Treasury,' Crawford's 'Lyrical Verse' (1896), Mowbray Morris's 'Poet's Walk,' and 'The Oxford Book of English Verse.'　　　　　　G. A. M.

Respecting the query concerning Mrs. Barbauld's poem on 'Life,' it may not be without interest to some readers of 'N. & Q.' to know that in the 'Golden Treasury' F. T. Palgrave gives the first four and the last eight lines of the poem, without any title or headline ; that Dr. Charles Mackay, in 'A Thousand and One Gems,' gives under the heading 'Life' only the last eight; and that Mr. Quiller-Couch, in 'The Oxford Book of English Verse,' published in the beginning of last year, gives the entire poem, headed 'Life,' which contains altogether thirty lines.

JOHN GRIGOR.

Your correspondent will find these lines by Mrs. Barbauld at p. 215 of 'Lyra Elegantiarum' (Moxon, 1867) [p. 211 of the modern edition in Ward & Lock's " Minerva Library "].

J. R. FITZGERALD.

A POSSIBLE GLOUCESTERSHIRE ORIGIN FOR GEOFFREY CHAUCER (8th S. xii. 341, 449).—Sir Patricius de Chaurse, or Chaworth, is the subject of three Wiltshire Inquisitiones post mortem of 42 Henry III. (1258), as owning land, &c., in the vill of Stepillavinthon, the manor of Berewik, and half a knight's fee both in Standene and Hokhull. The great-grandfather of Chaucer's two patronesses— Blanche, Duchess of Lancaster, and Elizabeth, Duchess of Clarence—is styled indifferently throughout the above Patricius de Cadurcis, Patricius de Chawrtes, and Patricius de

Chawrces. In the manor of Berewik one Agnes de Chawrces holds half a virgate of land freely for term of her life, and pays therefor per annum 4s.　　A. R. BAYLEY.

"WAGE"=WAGES (9th S. viii. 404, 508).— It is safe to say that this word was never used in the singular number by operatives ; and the old dramatists, if my memory does not deceive me, always adopted the plural form. In the comic opera of 'The Maid of the Mill,' Ralph, in throwing up his service, sings to the miller :—

Henceforward take care of your matters who will ;
They are welcome to slave for your wages who
　　need 'em.
Fol lol de rol lol, I have purchas'd my freedom,
And never hereafter shall work at the mill.

The chorus of the 'Servants' Medley' in 'Love in a Village' is :—

My masters and mistresses, hither repair ;
What servants you want you 'll find in our fair ;
Men and maids fit for all sorts of stations there be ;
And as for the wages we shan't disagree.

I cannot locate the following couplet :—

　　Ten pounds a year my standing wages,
　　With beans and bacon and cabbages.

It occurs in one of the old classical dramas.

B. D. MOSELEY.

Burslem.

RANULPH, EARL OF CHESTER (9th S. viii. 404 ; ix. 112).—The date of the document referred to by O. O. H. is c. A.D. 1218. It was confirmed by Prince Edward 27 August (1265), 49 Hen. III., and was again confirmed by him (Edward I.) 30 March, 1300, in the twenty-eighth year of his reign. The charter is set forth at large by Leycester, 'Antiq. Ches.,' p. 107, from which it has been reproduced in a 'Pedigree of Lord Massy from 876 to 1782,' printed in Dublin in 1890 "for private circulation only." Peter Leycester's 'Historical Antiquities' was published in London in 1673.　　　　GEO. S. CARY.

Laurel Lodge, Terenure, co. Dublin.

ROYAL ANTEDILUVIAN ORDER OF BUFFALOES (9th S. viii. 524).—Many books have been recently published descriptive of the rules, rites, and ceremonies of this good old society. In the Catalogue of the British Museum Library may be found the names of seven works upon this subject. As the earliest of these publications is dated 1893, there would hardly, I should say, be much difficulty in procuring a copy of a text-book relative to "initiation," &c. However, I would like, if the Editor of 'N. & Q.' could spare enough "elbow-room," to draw attention to what is probably the earliest printed record of the "Buffs." It occurs in the 'Finish of Tom and Jerry,' by Pierce Egan. Joe Lisle, the founder of the society—though now, alas! forgotten by all save print collectors—was in his day regarded as almost the equal of Seymour. His clever caricature sketches (printed from stone, coloured by hand, published, I believe, at one shilling each, by, I think, Tregear of Cheapside) are now very scarce. As they were mostly purchased for screens or scrap-books, the few surviving prints would probably be "cut down," and therefore, according to trade usage, of little value at the present day. The complete extract from Pierce Egan would, I fear, be far too long for insertion in the pages of 'N. & Q.'; but I will venture upon the chance offer of a few lines from the 'Finish.' I might add, before concluding, that when "Buffalo Bill" visited London in 1887 Mr. J. W. Rowley utilized the chorus, hereafter mentioned, in a topical-burlesque sort of way, as applied to the show at Earl's Court :—

Now we mash the ladies, a shilling for the show ;
In the Wild West of Kensington we chase the
    Buffalo.

"The initiated Buffaloes are waiting outside the door; the orator being decorated with a wig for the occasion. On a given signal they all enter the room with what they term the kangaroo leap, and jump round the chair of the 'degraded wretch' (as the victim is termed).

Come, all you young fellows who's a mind for to
    range
Unto some foreign country, your station for to
    change,
Your station for to change, away from here to go,
Through the wide woods we'll wander to chase the
    buffalo.
            Chorus.
We'll lay down on the banks of the pleasant shady
    Wo,
Through the wide woods we'll wander to chase the
    buffalo.

"This is succeeded by a solemn march and the following chant, the Buffaloes carrying brooms, shovels, mops, and a large kettle by way of a kettle-drum—

        Bloody head and raw bones !
        Bloody head and raw bones !
            Be not perplexed,
            This is the text,
        Bloody head and raw bones !

"The charge is then given to the 'victim' by the Primo Buffo, accompanied by the most extravagant and ridiculous gestures.

"At the 'Harp,' in Great Russell Street, opposite Drury Lane Theatre, the Buffalo Society was first established, in August, 1822, by an eccentric young man of the name of Joseph Lisle, an artist, in conjunction with Mr. W. Sinnett, a comedian, to perpetuate, according to their ideas upon the subject, 'that hitherto neglected ballad of "We'll chase the Buffalo." '"

                HERBERT B. CLAYTON.
39, Renfrew Road, Lower Kennington Lane.

If your correspondent will refer to 4th S. iii. 106, 267 ; iv. 124, 372, he will find all the information respecting this society which he can require.   EVERARD HOME COLEMAN.
71, Brecknock Road.

LECTERN IN DURHAM CATHEDRAL (9th S. viii. 483). — If the inquiry is not strictly limited to lecterns, it may be useful to draw attention to this extract from Parker's 'Concise Glossary' (1869, p. 185) :—

"The representation of this bird [pelican] vulning herself occurs not unfrequently as a sacred emblem among the ornaments of churches. A beautiful specimen is preserved at Ufford, Suffolk, at the summit of the elaborately carved spire of wood which forms the cover of the font ; and another occurs over the font at North Walsham, Norfolk."

Tyack's 'Lore and Legend,' &c. (p. 152), states that at Wimborne, and formerly at Waterford, were lecterns such as the Durham example.   RICHARD LAWSON.
Urmston.

The late Frederick George Lee, D.C.L., in his 'Glossary of Liturgical and Ecclesiastical Terms,' London, 1877, describes the pelican in her piety as a mediæval symbol or Christian emblem, representing a pelican feeding her young from the blood of her own breast —a symbol of our Blessed Saviour giving Himself for the ransom and redemption of the whole world. This symbol is frequently found represented both in sculpture and painting in ancient churches, and is now very commonly used in chapels dedicated in honour of the Blessed Sacrament in the Roman Catholic Church.

The subject has been discussed in 'N. & Q.' on more than one occasion. See 1st S. v., vi.; 4th S. iv. ; 7th S. vii., viii.
                EVERARD HOME COLEMAN.
71, Brecknock Road.

The pelican in her piety, with "wings addorsed and feeding her young with her own blood," forms the lectern from which the lessons are read in St. Mary's Cathedral, in Edinburgh. So far as I remember, it was made of latten. In St. Peter's Church, Congleton, above the reredos, is a representation of the pelican in her piety, excellently carved in oak, the probable date of which may be 1740. The coat of Richard Fox, Bishop of Winchester (1501–1529), founder of Corpus Christi College, Oxford, is a pelican in her piety. Bishops usually impale the arms of the see with their own paternal coat.
                JOHN PICKFORD, M.A.
Newbourne Rectory, Woodbridge.

ANAGRAMS (9th S. viii. 521). — C. E. D. says of the anagram given, "It is difficult to imagine one much worse than this." It has been said that the next best thing to a very good pun is a very bad one ; and, conversely, the next best thing to a very bad anagram may perhaps be admitted to be a very good one. I hope, therefore, that I may be allowed in this connexion to revive the memory of what seems to me to be a first-rate anagram, if not at once so striking as the briefer ones, such as "Horatio Nelson—honor est a Nilo," yet remarkable for its very length as well as for its appositeness. I transcribed it from some public print in the early time of the Crimean War, and, if I remember rightly, *before* the death of the Czar Nicholas.

I may say beforehand (1) that the form "Tsar" is recognized in French dictionaries ; (2) that the two O's have been inserted by myself to make the anagram complete ; but it is just possible that there may have been a slight inaccuracy in my transcription.

"A sa Majesté impériale, le Tsar Nicolas, souverain et autocrate de toutes les Russies." This, transposed, will be found exactly to make the following :—"O, ta vanité sera ta perte ; O, elle isole la Russie ; tes successeurs te maudiront à jamais."

Another example of a very good anagram is the following :—'Confessions of an Opium Eater' : "If so, man, refuse poison at once." This, like the other, is perfect. The source of it I have quite forgotten.

C. Lawrence Ford, B.A.

Bath.

Pins in Drinking Vessels (9ᵗʰ S. iv. 287, 358, 484 ; ix. 10).—Lord Arundell of Wardour kindly informs me that the earliest and fullest account of the Glastonbury Cup was written by the Right Rev. Dr. Milman, and appeared in the eleventh volume of *Archæologia*. Strangely enough, Mr. Pierpoint, while writing so fully about this tankard, *ante*, p. 10, omits reference to this account by the author of the 'History of Winchester.'

Ronald Dixon.

46, Marlborough Avenue, Hull.

Royal Tennis Court and Nell Gwyn (9ᵗʰ S. ix. 69).—There never was a *Royal* tennis court in the Haymarket, or near it. There was a tennis court in James Street, Haymarket, which was called "Royal" by its lessee in the last century, but without any authority for so doing. There was a tennis court in St. James's Palace, just north of the stable-yard and south of Cleveland Row ; and of this there is a ground-plan in the Office of Woods and Forests, a copy of which I possess, by the kindness of an old friend. K. will find what is known about those two

old courts in my 'Annals of Tennis,' of which a copy is in the British Museum ; or I should be happy to show it to him. The book is out of print. There is no trace of an underground passage in either of these courts ; and I should think that the "record" of Nell Gwyn visiting the court, if it exist, must be only to be found in some work of fiction. At Windsor, indeed, there was a court near her house, St. Alban's Lodge, close under the walls of the Castle ; but no subterranean approach was needed there, for the court stood in her garden, or at its boundary.

Julian Marshall.

The Royal Tennis Court was situated on the south side of James Street, Haymarket, and originally formed part of the celebrated gaming-house which was known as Shavers' Hall, from its proprietor, Simon Austbiston, having been barber to the Lord Chamberlain, Philip, Earl of Pembroke and Montgomery. The building was converted in 1866 into a storehouse for military clothing ; but an old tablet, inscribed "James Street, 1673," was preserved in the wall, and is, I believe, still in existence. The Tennis Court was a favourite resort of Charles II., and may very probably have been visited by Nell Gwyn, though I can find no record of the fact.

W. F. Prideaux.

Movable Stocks (9ᵗʰ S. vi. 405 ; vii. 14, 118, 214).—The *Western Daily Mercury* for 22 January is responsible for the following :

"Earl Brownlow, speaking at the Lincolnshire Police Court Mission at Lincoln, remarked that although the punishment of the stocks was done away with legally so many years ago, he had himself seen a man in the stocks. He was staying once in a small town in Shropshire, and in the middle of the market-place saw a man in the stocks. The stocks were on wheels, and were kept in one of the archways of the market, and when any of the market people were caught using light weights or selling bad meat or fish, or in any way cheating, the stocks were run out into the middle of the market and the person was placed in them and kept there until the market was over. Lord Brownlow added that he did not know but that, with proper organization and proper arrangements, it would be a good thing if the stocks could be used again."

Harry Hems.

Fair Park, Exeter.

St. Clement Danes (9ᵗʰ S. vii. 64, 173, 274, 375 ; viii. 17, 86, 186, 326, 465 ; ix. 52).—In a genealogy of the family of Clapham, of Clapham and elsewhere, co. York, deduced from Pharamund, King of the Franks, as contained in one of the original note-books (1720) of the Rev. John Lambe, M.A., rector of Ridley, co. Kent, now in my possession, it is stated that William (who was apparently son of Arthur) Clapham, Lord of Dente (or Denton, "called so from yᵉ River Dent") and Sudbrough (Sedbroughe or Sedbrough, a barony given him by William the Conqueror), in the West Riding of Yorkshire, had by gift of the same king "certain hydes of Land juxta Camberwell besides Lambithe where he builded the Clappsham or Clapsam near London in the year of our Lord 1066." The MS. contains also extracts in Latin from 'Floriacensis Wigorn : his Chronicle,' with other references to Osgod Clapa (or "Clapham") and the death of Hardicanute in June, 1042, of drunkenness at the marriage feast of Osgod's daughter and a noble Dane at "Lambeth, near Clapham."

As the above bears upon the subject of some of your correspondent's statements herein, but is not in accord with the same, I give it for what it is worth, without expressing any opinion in the matter.

W. I. R. V.

COL. PRIDEAUX, in his most interesting defence of the traditional derivation of *wick* from *vicus*, has pointed out the comparative absence of compounds of "street" and "castle" in the nomenclature of Southern Europe. Is not the explanation simple? In Southern Europe the great roads were very numerous and were built to connect pre-existing centres of habitation. In Northern Europe the Roman roads, like the railways in North America, created centres of population along their course, to which names like "Ad Decimum," "Stone-street," &c., might be applied, just as "Railhead" figures on colonial maps to-day.

As for "castle," few centres of population in Italy (although some did in Spain and Portugal) sprang up on the site of Roman camps. When *castro* is used in an Italian name it usually marks the site of a post-Roman military settlement, whether Lombard, Saracenic, or German, intended to overawe the native population. Of course, *turris* is found in Southern Europe, as fortified towers became numerous in the periods of disturbance after the fall of the Roman empire. May I ask COL. PRIDEAUX, in view of his last remark as to *vicus* being used for villages built along the seashore, whether he would derive names like Harwich, Ipswich, Dunwich, Wick (Caithness), from *vicus*, or *vik*= bay ?

H.

If homonyms of different origins can dwell together in unity by the score in the pages of our dictionaries, why cannot the *-wichs* and *-wicks* in *England* of Norse and Saxon and Latin origin be allowed to run their course? Attempts to assign one origin to them appear to be irrational. I italicize England, because the amount or intensity of Roman influence at a certain time per unit of area was probably greater there than in Germany. The littoral and estuaries of England and North-West Europe lent themselves to the Norse influence ; inland of that sphere may very well have predominated the Saxon and Latin influence, in England especially.

H. P. L.

"RATHER" (9th S. ix. 7).—The use of this word by Tennyson proves that it is not obsolete in literature, while in the dialects—the great repository of old English—it is not even obsolescent. Here in Somerset *rathe* or *rave* is the common form by which early maturity or forwardness in growth is expressed, when speaking of either young persons, cattle, or fruits. "A *rave* spring" (early) is the usual phrase. "Your children be *rave*, sure 'nough," "A *rave* piece of wheat," may be heard constantly (see also 'West Som. W. Book,' E.D.S., p. 616). As an adverb, such as Tennyson's use, I have never heard it spoken. The pronunciation is invariably with long *a*, as in *pave*, and the old *th* has mostly become *v*, though we preserve the former in the name of a well-known early apple, "the rathe-ripe."

In the comparative the word is equally common, though confined to the same limitations of use respecting time or season. This shows the true conservatism of the dialect, for in Mid. Eng. *rathe* and *soon* were alternative terms (see 'Promp. Parv.'). The country folk never by any chance use *rather*, as in modern English, to express preference. We should always say "I'd so soon," or "I'd sooner have one o' they" ; never "I should prefer." So the broad *a* in the modern *rather* is as unknown as the common slang affirmative "Rather!" in reply to any ordinary question ; *e.g.*, "Were you there last night?" "Rather!" As a superlative, *ravest* would be well understood, and, if needed, constantly used. "They be the *ravest* sort ever I'd a-got," "Mr. ——'s young stock be always the *ravest* in the market." It is unsafe to pronounce any old English word obsolete.

F. T. ELWORTHY.

The "positive degree" of this adjective still lingers in the west of England. You may hear of a "*rathe* piece of oats." There is also an early apple, the "rathe-ripe," now grown somewhat scarce. This adjective supplies a noteworthy instance of the steadfastness with which poorer folk adhere to ancient pronunciation, while the more educated classes make changes. Poor folk still say *rayther*, as their forefathers did, but the higher ranks are accustomed to pronounce this *rarther*. Similarly in such words as *ask, wasp, hasp*, the educated folk agree to transpose the two consonants, while humbler people adhere steadfastly to the A.-S. *akse, wops, apse*. Nor is this conservatism confined to Anglo-Saxon words. Witness, for instance, *theatre*, which the humbler of the lieges steadfastly continue to pronounce *theāter*.

Lobuc.

Mr. Bayne should follow up his comparison of this interesting word. Here are some instances of its use. 1. As adjective : "The rathe primrose" ('Lycidas'), "Rathe and riper years" ('In Memoriam,' which he quotes), "The rather lambs" ('Shepherd's Calendar,' ii. 83). *Rathest* as an adjective I cannot find. 2. Adverb : "All too rathe" ('Shepherd's Calendar,' xii. 98), "Why rise ye so rathe?" (Chaucer, 'Cant. Tales,' l. 3768) "Beginning ever rathest" (King James I., 'Basilicon Doron,' p. 162, fol., 1616). Morris, p. 93, gives "rathest-riping" from Palladius, which I cannot verify.

W. T.

[Lydgate, in his 'Chronicle of Troy'—not the full title—has *rathest* (book i. c. 5). We find this in a note taken very many years ago, but have not the book for reference.]

John Byrom's Epigram (9th S. viii. 445, 533).—The true reading is asked for. I transcribe from Byrom's 'Poems' (1814, Leeds), vol. i. p. 241. It is there headed "To the same [*i.e.*, to an officer in the army] extempore, intended to allay the Violence of Party-Spirit."

God bless the king, I mean the faith's defender ;
God bless—(no harm in blessing)—the pretender ;
But who pretender is, or who is king,
God bless us all—that 's quite another thing.

In that very interesting pamphlet by the Rev. Dr. Hoole entitled 'Byrom and the Wesleys' (Lond., Nichols, 1864), where on p. 5 the epigram forms a foot-note, the first line reads :—

God bless the King, *and bless* the Faith's Defender.

C. Lawrence Ford, B.A.

St. Heliers (9th S. ix. 45). — This statue seems to have exercised the minds of writers on Jersey a good deal. 'The Picturesque and Historical Guide to the Island of Jersey,' by Rev. Edward Durell, A.M., published by Philip John Ouless, artist, 50, Paradise Row, Jersey, 1852, says (chap. vi.) :—

"There is a statue at the upper end of the [Royal] Square which passes for one of George II., though doubts are entertained on the matter. It was given in exchange for permission to build against one of the ends of the Court House, by one

Gosset, a Frenchman, in 1749. It was inaugurated with a good deal of ceremony by all the local authorities, civil and military. The statue is gilt, and in a Roman dress, but is said to be of lead, with a new head which was fitted to its bust, when it was allowed to assume the name of George II. That head is not unlike those on the coins of that sovereign."

The statue is thus referred to in 'The Complete Guide to Jersey' (London, Elliot Stock, 1896) :—

"The gilt statue in the middle of the Square represents, as will be seen by the monogram on the pedestal, George II. Critics say that the casting was meant for some Roman emperor, taken from a Spanish vessel, and pressed, *nolens volens*, into the honour of the king."

W. B. H.

Pronunciation of Nietzsche (9th S. viii. 362).—It sounds like *neeche*, the last vowel being short and unaccented, as in "finger." Very likely the name is derived from the element *Nid*=envy ; compare the compounds Nid-hart, Nied-mar, Nit-perht ; Nîd+el= Niedel, Neidel ; Nîd+k=Niedke ; Nîd+z= Nizs, Nietze, Nizze, Nitz, Nitzsch(e), with lengthened *i*, Nietzsche.

G. Krueger.

Berlin.

Miscellaneous.

NOTES ON BOOKS, &c.

Nova Legenda Anglie. Edited by Carl Horstman, Ph.D. 2 vols. (Oxford, Clarendon Press.)

Dr. Horstman is already well known as an indefatigable student of English hagiology. His accurate editions in German of the 'Alt-englischen Legenden,' and in English of the works of Richard Rolle of Hampole, are held in high esteem by all who are interested in the religious life and literature of England. Few of our native writers have such a grasp of the subject as he. In the two handsome volumes here noticed he devotes himself to re-editing, with fresh material from MS. and printed sources, the Latin lives of the saints which long passed current under the name of John Capgrave. This text, which was printed under that ascription, with sundry additions, by Wynkyn de Worde in 1516, Dr. Horstman has carefully collated with the fourteenth-century original among the Cottonian MSS. of the British Museum, and has further supplemented with some additional lives from the Bodleian and Dublin libraries which have not hitherto been printed. He demonstrates that the honour of compiling this ample collection of legends is really due to John of Tynemouth, who in his 'Sanctilogium Angliæ' brought together from the most varied sources all the material he could glean concerning the pious worthies whom his country had produced. He intended it to be essentially and exclusively a national work, not admitting any saint except those belonging to England, Wales, Scotland, and Ireland. He relaxed this rule, however, in favour of a few, like Joseph of Arimathea and Augustine, who were intimately identified with the history of the English Church. Accordingly, we look in vain for such popular, but foreign, saints as St. Nicholas,

St. Catherine, or St. George. For these we must have recourse to a kindred work—the famous 'Legenda Aurea' of Jacobus de Voragine. John of Tynemouth was a monk of St. Albans in the early part of the fourteenth century, and it is one of Dr. Horstman's discoveries that the mediæval chronicle which was published by Hearne under the name of Walter Hemingford is only a part of the 'Historia Aurea,' written by him when annalist of that renowned foundation. The good monk was, indeed, nothing more than a compiler, but a very faithful and conscientious one, of what he found ready to his hand in the archives of the abbeys and monasteries which he visited for the purpose, making excerpts as he went, with all the bibliographical zeal of a Dibdin. To the lives proper he appends what he calls a "narratio," *i.e.*, a brief story or amusing anecdote, with often but little bearing on the foregoing life, but useful to enliven the flagging attention of the brotherhood or gain the ear of the ignorant folk. What makes this collection particularly valuable, as the editor notes, is the fact that the original MSS. upon which John of Tynemouth drew for his material have in many instances perished, with the result that this remains the only authority for certain Anglo-Saxon and Celtic saints. Like most mediæval chroniclers, he has an unbounded appetite for prodigies and visions. He delights in retailing those curious stories of the apparitions of demons and visits to the Inferno which were so rife in the Middle Ages. Among the more remarkable of these are the descent of the Roman knight Owen into St. Patrick's Purgatory and the strange experiences of Tundal (vol. ii. p. 303). In his introduction, which displays a really marvellous knowledge of the contemporary sources of information, Dr. Horstman deals with the personality and *milieu* of his author. We wish that he could have found time to supply out of his treasures a commentary or illustrative notes on the subject-matter of his text. The latter is very accurately printed, but we notice "Cloufert" (vol. i. p. 153, note), a misprint for Clonfert.

The Use of Sarum. Edited by the Rev. W. H. Frere, M.A. (Cambridge, University Press.)

OSMUND, Bishop of Salisbury, one of the Conqueror's prelates, arranged and systematized the services and ritual of his cathedral with such judgment and learning that his service-book became the recognized standard of liturgical propriety, so that in ecclesiastical matters "according to the use of Sarum" was a phrase almost tantamount to "according to Cocker" in business affairs at a later day. How predominating was its influence may be inferred from the fact that it was adopted so far north as Elgin in 1242, when it was decreed that "in the divine offices, in psalm-singing, reading, chanting, and other things pertaining to divine service, the order be observed which is known to have been adopted in the church of Salisbury." In 1542 the Convocation of Canterbury ordered all the clergy of the province to follow this use in their churches. Mr. Frere has sedulously devoted himself to the editing of this important document of the Anglican Church, which he evidently finds a congenial task. In a previous volume he gave us the 'Consuetudinary' and 'Customary,' which dealt with the Sarum ceremonies and *ceremoniarii*. In the present issue he edits the 'Ordinal' and 'Tonal,' the former of which regulated the order and conduct of the various offices, and was held to be so essential an adjunct for the correct rendering of divine service that every parish church was required to possess a copy of it. The 'Tonal' was a directory for the musical part of the services, to ensure a systematic classification of the antiphons and of the tones and endings to which they were to be sung. A number of these latter are printed in score in an appendix extending to eighty pages. Mr. Frere is inclined to believe that this part of the 'Use' may be ascribed to Bishop Richard Poore, and thus date from the beginning of the thirteenth century. The actual text, however, seems hardly earlier than about 1270. Just a century later we find Wiclif raising a loud protest against the amount of time and attention that was given—and, as he maintained, misspent—by the clergy in conning the elaborate rules of this mediæval manual when they might be better occupied. "A Lord," he cries, "gif alle the studie & traueile that men han now abowte salisbury uss......weren turned in-to makynge of biblis & in studiynge & techynge ther-of, hou moche schulde goddis lawe be forthered & knowen & kept" ('Unprinted Eng. Works,' E.E.T.S., 194). We are reminded of the later outcry against the crabbed and complex "Rules called the Pie," which were felt to be a sore burden from their "number and hardness." The volume, as might be anticipated, abounds in minute technicalities which appeal only to the liturgical antiquary, but to him it will be invaluable.

Renderings of Church Hymns. By the Rev. R. M. Moorsom. (Clay & Sons.)

IN a preface, in which emphasis is weakened by reiteration, Mr. Moorsom strongly urges the Church's need of a book of common praise, which is to embrace the best hymns of every branch of the Church Catholic, and in especial those of the Greek, Syrian, and other Oriental Churches. As a contribution to this desirable object he offers this little volume—the solace of his hours of blindness—of translations or free renderings of hymns from foreign sources—Italian, Celtic, German, as well as Eastern. We cannot say that we are much impressed with the freshness or originality of these specimen versions. The fact is, that the language and ideas of praise, thanksgiving, and petition are common to all Churches and everywhere very similar; when reduced to English they do not differ greatly from our native efforts in this kind. We are surprised to find that Mr. Moorsom includes in his selection one hymn which he admits is unorthodox from an Anglican standpoint, and two at least which are sacred poems, and in no sense hymns. He also labours under the erroneous impression that there was a time when "Ye Englishe Chyrche" was good vernacular. Tunes to twenty of the hymns have been composed by the Rev. G. W. Griffith, and one by Mr. W. S. de Winton, which are here given.

Time Table of Modern History, A.D. 400-1870. Compiled and arranged by M. Morison. (Constable & Co.)

THIS is a work which serious students of modern history ought to have at hand. The labour of compiling it must have been great, for, so far as we have been able to test it, the ordeal has been gone through very fairly. Of course it would have been possible to make corrections, and it must be borne in mind that there are some dates which cannot be fixed with precision. Contemporary authorities, even, not infrequently contradict each other, for not only were the mediæval chroniclers sometimes almost as regardless of chronological accuracy as we moderns, but there were various ways of recording time in common use, so that without that minute knowledge which so very few of us possess it is often impossible to tell what system the writer had taken for his guide. We are pleased to find that as to names of persons Mr. Morison has been content to use those which are commonly accepted, though he must have been aware that it would lay him open to adverse criticism. We need not say that this is, strictly speaking, an error which on certain occasions ought to be sternly condemned; but the great point in a work of reference such as this is that it should be handy, so that we can find our way about in it, and be spared the pains of racking our brains to remember how the name of some obscure potentate was spelt by his contemporaries. The pedigrees near the end of the volume will be found useful, but they might have been made fuller than they are with advantage. That of the house of Bonaparte is miserably thin. Surely all the descendants of Charles, the father of Napoleon I., should have been given. It is true that to-day no member of the race is among the sovereigns of Europe; but it is mere pedantry not to regard them as scions of a royal house with chances in the future. We think, too, that it might have been well to give a list of the illegitimate children of Charles II. and James II., with their marriages. Readers of the history of the Stuart time do not, we have observed, always carry the needful information in their minds. The compiler has given more than he promised. The title-page leads us to anticipate that the end would be reached in 1870, but the entries are carried on for ten further years.

Patent Rolls of the Reign of Henry III., 1216-1225. (Stationery Office.)

This, the earliest volume of the Patent Rolls of King Henry III., has not the name of the editor on its title-page, but the preface is signed by Sir H. C. Maxwell Lyte, and we learn that the text has been prepared by Mr. J. G. Black. We believe that there are no omissions or condensations. The text is given as it stands in its original Latin. From the second to the ninth year of the reign the rolls are in duplicate, or one is a transcript of the other. The latter is the more probable, as words or passages cancelled in the original are almost always left out in the duplicate.

The volume must be of great interest not only to historical students, but to all persons engaged in topographical inquiries or on the history and growth of surnames. Members of the great families are mentioned over and over again, and we encounter a very fair share of the common folk. Surnames, though coming into use, were not by any means stable as yet. Men changed them at will, or had them altered for them when they moved from one place to another. In a list of certain persons, all of whom, we may presume, lived in the neighbourhood of Tavistock, we find a Robertum Cocum, an Adam Fabrum, and an Adam Longum. These people were no doubt called by their friends Cook, Smith, and Long. Did the last one, we wonder, acquire his name because he was abnormally tall? or was it given him on account of his occupying a long strip of ploughland or meadow? The latter is, we think, the more probable suggestion. A man called Humphrey de la Slowe lived in Buckinghamshire in 1225. There is a possibility that he may have acquired his name from some town or village, but we strongly incline to the belief that it originated from some boggy place or large puddle near to which he lived. The number of safe-conducts on returning to the king's peace is very large. Any one might be able to make a most interesting list of those who had been adherents of Louis of France and the barons from the documents here registered. We trust if this be ever done the names will be, so far as is possible, arranged under counties. We shall then in some degree be able to estimate to what extent the manifold injustices of the previous reign had moved men to fight for their liberties. We believe the tyranny had been far more crushing in some parts of the country than in others.

There is not so much regarding the action of the Pope in this country as we should have expected. We have, however, in 1217 a notice of the Papal absolution of the lords who had been in rebellion, conveyed through the hands of the Bishop of Chichester, and we also find a letter from Henry, dated 16 October, 1220, thanking the Pope for good offices in his behalf.

In the index, under 'Castles,' there is a long list of fortresses in the king's hands or fortified by him, which will be of frequent use to those studying the disturbed time to which this volume relates.

Notices to Correspondents.

We must call special attention to the following notices:—

On all communications must be written the name and address of the sender, not necessarily for publication, but as a guarantee of good faith.

We cannot undertake to answer queries privately.

To secure insertion of communications correspondents must observe the following rules. Let each note, query, or reply be written on a separate slip of paper, with the signature of the writer and such address as he wishes to appear. When answering queries, or making notes with regard to previous entries in the paper, contributors are requested to put in parentheses, immediately after the exact heading, the series, volume, and page or pages to which they refer. Correspondents who repeat queries are requested to head the second communication "Duplicate."

E. H. Y.—The lines you send—

A cottage he saw, with a double coach-house,
Full of *ton*, full of taste, and gentility:
And the Devil he smiled,—for his favourite vice
Is the pride that apes humility—

are a sad hash of a quatrain in 'The Devil's Drive,' by Coleridge and Southey, to be found in most editions of the works of these poets.

S. H. ("Mit Dummheit," &c.).—From Schiller, 'Jungfrau von Orleans,' III. vi., though not quite correctly quoted.

NOTICE.

Editorial communications should be addressed to "The Editor of 'Notes and Queries'"—Advertisements and Business Letters to "The Publisher"—at the Office, Bream's Buildings, Chancery Lane, E.C.

We beg leave to state that we decline to return communications which, for any reason, we do not print; and to this rule we can make no exception.

LONDON, SATURDAY, FEBRUARY 22, 1902.

CONTENTS. — No. 217.

Notes.

THE BACON—SHAKSPEARE QUESTION.

As considerable attention has been paid of late to the question as to whether or not Francis Bacon wrote the Shakespeare plays and poems, and as no scholar of repute deems it worth his while fully to refute the theory of the Baconians, it has occurred to me that readers of 'N. & Q.' may not be indisposed to listen to what I can say concerning the matter. I gave five or six years' close attention to the subject, and carefully examined the statements of those who deny the claims of Shakespeare. I will not waste many words, as—to use a Baconian phrase—I wish to "come to the matter"; but this I will say, that it seems to me that scholars are making a big mistake in allowing this question to assume such serious proportions. The lie ought to have been caught up years ago, and nailed to the counter ; and it is such an easy thing to show that it is a lie, that I often wonder somebody has not proved it to be such long ere this. I am going to demonstrate that it is easy not only to refute the Baconians, but to show that they are lamentably wrong in many of their strongest assertions, which, moreover, prove them to be very badly versed in Elizabethan literature. Indeed, I shall have to prove that they are not only ill acquainted with contemporary writings, but that they do not even know the work of their own master—Bacon. In the course of my argument I shall show that if Bacon wrote anything for the stage at all, in addition to masques, inquirers who are eager to add to his honours are making a great mistake in troubling themselves about the work of Shakespeare—they ought to try Ben Jonson. There is a really wonderful field open for Baconian speculation in the work—or, for the sake of the argument, the supposed work—of Ben Jonson, and if what I have to say concerning it has the effect of absorbing some of the superabundant energy of Bacon's eager followers, I shall consider that the time I have devoted to this matter has not been spent quite in vain.

Ciphers, anagrams, and cryptograms are, I regret to say, things with which I am not competent to deal—

Quæ supra nos nihil ad nos.

Things above us are not for us ; such lofty matter I shall leave severely alone ; but if after what I allege it can be clearly proved that Bacon used his ciphers in Shakespeare's work, then nothing will be proved except that Bacon was a greater rogue than his contemporaries took him to be. I hope that warning will be taken to heart, for I do not say Bacon was a rogue—far from it ; but it would be a pitiful thing if the followers proved the master to be such.

Now to the matter. Bacon, needless to say, was an omnivorous reader who was perpetually taking notes. Like all other men, he took notes for the purpose of lightening his labour and of refreshing his thoughts. He not only did so, but he was extremely methodical in arranging them. We are able to say so much of him, because a portion—perhaps a very small portion—of these notes has escaped the ravages of time, and is now safely deposited in the British Museum. These notes play a very considerable part in the discussion of the Bacon-Shakespeare question ; they are, in point of fact, the sheet-anchor of the advocates of the Bacon authorship of the Shakespeare plays. He used them, say they, in the plays and poems ascribed to Shakespeare, but he did not, they further say, use them in his acknowledged works. Moreover, it is alleged that allusions to these notes cannot be found in any work prior to the appearance of the Shakespeare plays, or but very sparingly ; and in order to prove that this is the case, it is said that contemporary literature has been carefully examined, but with negative results. Not only so, it is asserted that the notes are of such an exclusive character, so uncommon in phrase and suggestion, that all English literature will be vainly searched to find them as we find them in the pages of Shakespeare.

It is a very pretty theory; but pity 'tis, 'tis not true. Bacon *does* use his notes in his acknowledged works; they are *not* used in the same way in Shakespeare; they are, contrary to the Baconian assertion, mostly common-places in all English literature up to the end of the seventeenth century; and they are more frequently alluded to in Ben Jonson than in Shakespeare.

Before I enter into a minute examination of the Bacon notes, I wish to draw special attention to the assertion that Bacon used the notes in the plays, but not in his acknow-ledged works. Does any reasonable being think that a man could so order his thoughts as to divide himself, as it were, in that way— to scatter through the plays, as one writer has it, allusions to his notes "as thick as grains of wheat through the surface of a fresh-sown field," and to ignore them so completely in his acknowledged work as to defy discovery of allusions to them? It will be my business to show that the Baconians have tried to prove too much, and that a further course of their master is a matter of urgent necessity.　CHARLES CRAWFORD.

53, Hampden Road, Hornsey, N.

(*To be continued.*)

WHERE DWELLS TRUTH?

A DOZEN years ago my friend Prof. J. E. B. Mayor introduced me to the writings of August Schwarzkopff, in whose book 'Aus Natur und Welt' (Leipzig, 1888, S. 5), among other striking verses, the following is to be found :—

SPRECHT, IHR VIER, WO WOHNET IHR?
(Nach einer alten Sage.)

Feuer, du wildes, wo finden wir dich?
"Sucht euch einen Stein im Thal,
Schlagt daran mit hartem Stahl,
Augenblicks spring ich heraus;
Denn das ist mein Bett und Haus
Und da schlaf und wohne ich!"

Luft, du leichte, wo finden wir dich?
"Wo ein Blättlein bebt am Baum,
Oder fliegt ein zarter Flaum,
Oder ringelt grauer Rauch,
Weht von meinem Mund ein Hauch;
Allda leb und atme ich!"

Wasser, du feuchtes, wo finden wir dich?
"Wo die schwanke Binse steht,
Grabt, bis ihr die Wurzel seht,

Da blitzt euch mein Auge an,
Weil kein Berg mich bergen kann;
Horcht, da ries'le, da hause ich!"

Wahrheit, du heil'ge, wo finden wir dich?
"Ach, ich hab kein Haus, noch Zelt,
Niemand will mich auf der Welt;
Klopf ich,—auf geht keine Thür,
Ruf ich,—keiner folget mir,
Lug und Hass verjagen mich:
Drum—zum Himmel flücht ich mich!"

Of this little poem an English version ap-peared in the *Academy*, and was reprinted in my 'Ancoats Skylark,' but is now, in Lamb's phrase, "as good as manuscript" :—

Fire, so wild, where shall we find thee?
"In the valley seek a rock:
Strike with steel, and at the shock
In a moment outspring I:
There the bed wherein I lie,
There seek and ye shall find me."

Air, light air, where shall we find thee?
"Where leaflets tremble on the tree,
Where the curling smoke you see,
Where the down floats north or south,
'Tis the breathing of my mouth,
There seek and ye shall find me."

Water bright, where shall we find thee?
"Mighty mountains cannot hide
Flow of spring and force of tide;
Where the roots of rushes grow
You will find me, dig below,
There seek and ye shall find me."

Holy Truth, where shall we find thee?
"Through the weary world I roam,
No house have I, no place, no home.
I knock, I call, but no reply,
Therefore heavenward I must fly,
There seek and ye shall find me."

The story is to be found in 'A Hundred Mery Talys,' where it takes this shape :—

"In the old world when all thyng could speke the iiii elementys mette to geder for many thynges whych they had to do, because they must meddell always one wyth a nother: and had communication to gyder of dyvers maters, and by cause they could not conclude all theyr maters at that season they appoynted to breke comunicacion for that tyme, therefore ech one of them shewed to other where theyr most abydyng was and where their felows shoulde fynde them yf nede shuld requyre and fyrste the erthe sayde bretherne ye know well as for me I am permanent alway and not remouable: there-fore ye may be sure to haue me alway whan ye lyste. The wather sayde yf ye lyst to seke me ye shal be sure to haue me under a toft of grene rushes or under a woman's eye. The wynde sayde yf ye lyst to speke wyth me ye shal be sure to haue me among aspyn leuys or els in a womans tong. Then quod the fyre yf any of you lyst to seke me ye shal euer be sure to fynd me in a flynt stone or els in a womans harte.

"By thys tale ye may lerne as well the properte of the iiii elementys as the properteis of a woman."

This forms number nineteen of Dr. Herman Oesterley's edition, and he mentions that Hans Sachs wrote 'Ein Gesprech der vier Element mit Fraw Warheit,' and that the story appears in a Danish translation of Pauli's 'Schimpf und Ernst.' In that curious and interesting book is the earliest example of the story which I have so far found :—

"Es kamen einmal vier Jungfrauen zusammen und scherzten mit einander und waren guter Dinge. Die eine sprach zu den anderen dreien: Ach, nun ist uns doch wohl bei einander! Aber wenn wir einander gern wiederum hätten, wo finden wir einander? Und die eine hiess Ignis (Feuer), die andere Aqua (Wasser), die dritte Aër (Luft), und die vierte Veritas (Wahrheit). Ach sprach die eine, Feuer, wo finden wir dich? Sie sprach: In einem harten Stein; da schlaget mit einem Stahl daran, so findet Ihr mich!—Da sprach sie: Luft, wo finden wir dich? Wo bist du daheim? Sie sprach: Ihr müsset lugen, wo ein Blättlein an einem Baum zittert und sich bewegt, da findet Ihr mich, da bin ich daheim!—Da sprach sie: Wasser, wo finden wir dich, wo bist du daheim? Sie sprach: Wo Ihr Binsen findet da grabet zu den Wurzeln; da findet Ihr mich, da bin ich daheim!—Da sprach sie: O edle Wahrheit, wo finden wir dich? Die Wahrheit antwortete ihnen allen dreien: O ihr lieben Schwestern, ihr habt alle eure Orte genannt, da man euch weiss zu finden; aber ich habe leider kein eigen Haus; Niemand will mich beherbergen; ich bin von Jedermann gehasst!"—'Schimpf und Ernst,' von Bruder Johannes Pauli. Ausgewahlt und sprachlich erneuert von H. A. Junghaus, Leipzig o. J. S. 9.

The preface to Brother Johannes Pauli's book is dated 1519. The manner in which the names are given suggests that the good Franciscan had before him a Latin version of the story. Some reader of 'N. & Q.' may perhaps be able to point out the source which I have failed to identify. WILLIAM E. A. AXON.
Manchester.

ADDITIONS TO THE 'N.E.D.'

Abdomenistic (not in).—1891, Roy Tellet, 'Draught of Lethe,' iii. 5, "I am everything the other way, realistic, materialistic, abdomenistic."

Aberrometer (not in).—1895, G. E. Davis, 'Practical Microscopy' (third ed.), p. 183, "Like the aberrometer of Dr. Piggott."

Achromat (not in).—1901, *Brit. Journ. Photog.*, 1 November, p. 694, col. 2, "The apochromatic microscope objectives first introduced by Abbe proved to be much more efficient in their correction for the secondary spectrum than the usual achromats."

Acrometer (not in).—1844, M. Hennell, 'Social Systems and Communities,' p. 212.

Adopter (cf. def. in Dict.).—1758, tr. Macquer, 'Elem. of Chym.,' i. 177, "These ballons with two necks are called Adopters."

Aerotonometer (not in).—1894, *Times*, 15 Aug., p. 11, col. 5, "Prof. Frédericq read a paper on the Aerotonometer and Gas-pipette."

Afghan (not in).—1887, F. R. Stockton, 'Hundredth Man,' xxii., "Miss Burns was crocheting an afghan. ......She got the wools at cost price from the store in which she was employed, and could therefore afford to make a fine large afghan."

Afternoony (not in).—1900, Huxley, 'Life,' ii. 96, "There is something idle and afternoony about the air which whittles away one's resolution."

Agronomic.—1891, *Times*, 28 Sept., p. 13, col. 5, "Agronomic stations have been created for the purpose of enlightening agriculturists."

Agrostical (not in).—1800, *Gent. Mag.*, i. 151 (rev. of Sonnini, 'Trav. Upper and Lower Egypt'), "Agrostical, p. 63, must be sought for in a botanical dictionary."

Agrypnotic.—1849, Pereira, 'Mat. Medica,' third ed., i. 214.

Aidur=Eider.—1747, *Gent. Mag.*, 172.

Algometer (not in).—1897, E. W. Scripture, 'New Psychology,' p. 303, "Experiments have been made on pains produced by pressure. The pressure algometer consists essentially of a strong spring, by means of which a rubber disc or point is pressed against the surface to be tested."

Alkalizate, v. (prob. only as pa.pl.).—1758, Reid, tr. Macquer, 'Chym.,' i. 320, "The Phlogiston contained in this quantity of Tartar is more than sufficient to alkalizate the Nitre."

Allemand (verb, not in).—1890, Baring-Gould, 'Arminell,' xlviii.

Alliole (chem., not in).—1865, Gesner, 'Pract. Treat. on Coal, Petroleum, &c.,' second ed., p. 94.

Alternativeness (no quot.).—1844, M. Hennell, 'Social Systems and Communities,' p. 194.

Ambergris=amber (not in).—1575-91, Horsey, 'Trav.' (Hakluyt Soc.), p. 248, "A paire of perfumed gloves and a chaine of ambergrece, which the chauncelor receaved thanckfully."

Amberous (not in).—1890, *Century Mag.*, Aug., p. 500, "Its chambers paved with amberous lights."

Amidol (not in).—1894, *Brit. Journ. Photog. Alm.*, p. 830, "Diamidophenol or amidol, both as the chlorhydrate and the sulphate, was originally prepared by T. Gauche in 1869." Also, 1894, *Amer. Ann. Photog.*, p. 182, "Solutions of amidol must be made with neutral sulphites." *Ibid.*, p. 132, "The density of an amidol developed plate."

Amorphism.—P. M. Roget claims the coinage of this word, 'Thesaurus,' 1852 (ed. 1875, introd., xxii).

Ampaline (not in).—Gesner, *ut supra*, p. 94.

Amphimixis (not in).—1901, *Nature*, p. 482, col. 2, "The origin of a variation is equally independent of selection and amphimixis (Weismann, 'The Germ-plasm,' p. 431)."

Anabolic (not in).—1889, Geddes and Thomson, 'Evolution of Sex,' p. 88, "The ascending, synthetic, constructive series of changes are termed 'anabolic.'"

Anabolism (not in).—Geddes, *ut supra*, p. 122, "The upbuilding, constructive, synthetic processes are summed up in the phrase anabolism."

Anastate (not in).—Geddes, *ut supra*, p. 88, "The various special lines of anabolism and katabolism respectively, and the definite component substances ('anastates' and 'katastates') which it is the task of the chemical physiologist to isolate."

Anastigmat (not in).—1894, *Amer. Ann. Photog.*, p. 100, "The Anastigmat......is the most rapid lens I have tried." Also, 1901, *Brit. Journ. Photog.*, 1 November, p. 694, col. 2, "The new glasses, called barium silicate glasses, without which the modern anastigmat could not be constructed."

Anastigmatic (not in).—1901, *Brit. Journ. Photog.*, 22 November, p. 744, col. 1, "The anastigmatic flatness of field."

Androdiœcism (not in).—1888, Henslow, 'Orig. Flor. Struct.,' p. 227, "Androdiœcism signifies the same species has both male and hermaphrodite plants."

Andromonœcism (not in).—Henslow, *ut supra*, p. 227, "Andromonœcism signifies that the same plant bears both male and hermaphrodite flowers."

Anemophily (not in).—1883, Müller, 'Fert. Flowers' (tr. Thompson), p. 591, "In a few cases reversion to anemophily has taken place."

Anthophilous (not in).—1883, Müller, *ut supra*, p. 25, "Anthophilous insects"; *ibid.*, p. 33, "Beetles which are anthophilous."

Aplanat (not in).—1901, *Brit. Journ. Photog.*, 1 November, p. 695, col. 1, "The selection of the glasses for his aplanats. These aplanats consist of strong refracting flint glasses, whose quotient and colour dispersion do not much differ."

Apochromat (not in).—1901, *Brit. Journ. Photog.*, 1 November, p. 693, col. 2, "Remarkably perfect objectives—the Abbe apochromats—are available."

Apochromatic (not in).—1895, G. E. Davis, 'Practical Microscopy,' third ed., p. 201, "These lenses have been called by Prof. Abbe apochromatic."

Apolausticism (not in).—1894, X. L., 'Aut Diabolus aut Nihil,' p. 6, "He was indeed only fervent in his apolausticism."

Apospory (not in).—1889, Geddes and Thomson, 'Evolution of Sex,' p. 206, "The production of spores may be suppressed......This exceptional occurrence is technically called apospory."

Apotheme (chem., no quot.).—1853, C. Morfit, 'Art of Tanning,' p. 55, "Apotheme is also an accompanying product of the slow conversion of tannin and tanning solutions by exposure to air. It is a dark brown substance, soluble in water, and is the source of the objectionable colour of several kinds of leather."

Apprenticeage (obs.).—1797, *Monthly Mag.*, iii. 303, "An apprentissage of three months is sufficient to learn the nature of this trade."

Apriorist (not in).—G. B. Shaw, 'Fabian Essays in Socialism,' 1890, p. 177, "The apriorist notion that among free competitors wealth must go to the industrious."

Apron (shipbuilding, earlier).—1711, Sutherland, 'Shipbuilder's Assistant,' p. 25, "Raising the stem and false stem (or apron) together."

Archæsthetism (not in).—1901, *Nature*, p. 482, col. 2, "By a mixture of 'use-inheritance' (Kinetogenesis) and Lamarck's neck-stretching theory (Archæsthetism)."

Archoplasm (not in).—Geddes, *ut supra*, p. 98, "Within the last year Boveri has drawn attention to a special element in the protoplasm, which he calls archoplasm."

Argon (not in).—1895, *Times*, 1 February, p. 6, col. 4, "Argon, a new constituent of the atmosphere."

Arse (not in?).—1848, G. Biddlecombe, 'Art of Rigging,' p. 73, "A heart, or dead-eye, is seized in the bight, with a splice at the arse of the heart." *Ibid.*, p. 89, "The standing-part of the fall makes fast to the becket in the arse of the single-block."

Artisticism (not in).—1891, H. Herman, 'His Angel,' p. 40, "Our present-day, lackadaisical, sham artisticism."

Aryanisation (not in).—1890, I. Taylor, 'Origin of Aryans,' p. 212, "The Aryanisation of Europe doubtless resembled that of India."

Astay (cf. Astays).—1607, Topsell, 'Hist. Four-footed Beasts' (ed. Rowland, 1673), p. 125, "The inhabitants of Caramair and Carib do drive astay the dogs."

Auntship (earlier).—1813, 'Sketches of Character,' i. 109, "Won't your auntship take cold without your usual number of petticoats?"

Automobile, Automobilist (not in).—1902, *Munsey's Mag.*, February, p. 699, "They purchase their automobile without an idea as to its manner of construction. This is alike unfair to the manufacturer and to the aspiring automobilist."

Avalanchy (not in).—1894, G. M. Fenn, 'In Alpine Valley,' i. 117, "Rather an avalanchy place."

Axes (obs.).—1893, Crommelin, 'Bay Ronald,' i. 283, "Amos......wagged his head slowly, grumbling that his boy had got the axey."

Azoxy (not in).—1894, *Times*, 15 August, p. 12, col. 1, "Very interesting in point of fastness to light were the azoxy colours."

J. DORMER.

Redmorion, Woodside Green, S.E.

(*To be continued.*)

DISAPPEARING CHARTISTS.—Samuel Bartlett, whom MR. CECIL CLARKE mentions in an interesting note (*ante*, p. 86), was not much known as a Chartist outside Chelsea. I do not remember his name in early Chartist days. The Charter was drawn up by Place in 1838. I was a few months older than Harney, and we were both young men in the Chartist movement at the time it took the field. We first met at Birmingham at the Bull Ring Riot in 1839. I was living in the town then. It does not seem long ago. There must be some yet living who, if not prominent, may have been in the ranks; but in a few years more all the pioneer Chartists will disappear, as the Waterloo veterans have. W. H. Chadwick is counted the oldest living Chartist in Manchester. He is seventy-five or seventy-six and still appears on the platform. I had not only knowledge but friendship with Julian Harney, Feargus O'Connor, Thomas Cooper, Rev. Joseph Rayner Stephens, Bronterre O'Brien, Joshua Hobson, James Watson, Henry Hetherington, John Cleve, Henry Vincent, Linton, Gammage, George White, William Lovett, John Collins, and many others. Collins and I were Sunday-school teachers. He was much older than I. In 1848 I was appointed to address the delegates at the Convention, who the next day were going to Kennington Common with a great petition. I was a member of the last Chartist Executive with Feargus O'Connor, who would ask me to walk round Covent Garden with him and talk things over on nights when he was earlier than other members. In Brighton we lately buried William Woodward, who was in his ninetieth year. He was a real old Chartist, who came from prison to Brighton seventy years ago. Like Harney, he was one of the unstamped-newspaper prisoners. I delivered the oration at his grave, as I did at the grave of Hetherington fifty-one years before; but though I was in the Chartist agitation from beginning to end, I am not generally counted as one of the survivors, being better known to this generation in other agitations than that.

              G. J. HOLYOAKE.

Eastern Lodge, Brighton.

JACK = KNAVE —The interesting review (9th S. viii. 474) of the fifth volume of the 'New English Dictionary' led me to refer to the work to see what it said on the above subject in its relation to playing-cards. I found therein the following definition and quotation (*s.v.* 'Jack') :—

     "5. *Cards.* Name for the knave of trumps in the game of all-fours; hence *gen.* any one of the knaves.
     "1674-80. Cotton, 'Compl. Gamester,' ix., This game......is called *All Fours*, from highest, lowest, jack, and game, which is the set as some play it. *Ibid.*, He turns up a Card, which is Trump: if Jack (and that is any knave) it is one to the dealer."

The conclusion come to that the term Jack was applied to a knave generally, through its use in the old game of all-fours, is the natural one, and without doubt correct; but that Cotton employed it in the general sense, which is the inference meant to be taken from the form and position of the quotation, is quite a misapprehension. The record, therefore, from the historical or chronological point of view is misleading. The mistake is a natural and easy one to any one not thoroughly acquainted with the subject; and, unfortunately, if there is any ordinary matter that savants show want of knowledge of in their writings, it is of games. Cotton's diction in the 'Gamester' is generally loose, and it is often unsafe to take him literally, without going below the surface to find out his meaning. When he applies the term Jack to knave in the above quotation, he means that any knave turned up will be Jack (as the turned-up card is trump, and Jack is the knave of trumps), and not that Jack is any or every knave—two very different things. To Cotton, Jack is simply the term for the trump-knave in the game of all-fours, as Tom is the term for the trump-knave in the game of gleek. If his description of all-fours is carefully read with this knowledge, it will be found that in none of the several instances in which the word Jack is used does Cotton apply it to anything else than the knave of trumps. When he speaks of another knave, he calls it a knave. To term every knave Jack, where there is only the one Jack, would make the description a jumble of nonsense. Nowhere, outside of all-fours, does Cotgrave, Cotton, or Seymour (our early describers of card-games) write Jack for knave. Nor have I met with it in any of the early writers. Accordingly, by the 'Dictionary' corrected, Benjamin Martin (1749) is the first recorder of the use of the term in the general sense. Do any of your readers know of an earlier?

              J. S. McTEAR.

"HAKATIST."—This word deserves to be added to the list of those which, like *cabal*, are of political coinage. We have heard lately of weighty Prussian measures against the Poles in Posen, among the supporters of severity being three gentlemen named Hannemann, Kinnemann, and Tidemann. From their initials this adjective is derived, and it is a curious accident that the terminations are identical.

            FRANCIS P. MARCHANT.

Brixton Hill.

CORONATION INCIDENT. — The following extract from the 'Memoir of Richard Redgrave, R.A.' (Cassell & Co., 1891), p. 299, may be of interest. The writer refers to a visit to the late Marquis of Salisbury at Hatfield in January, 1868 :—

     "In the course of an after-dinner conversation on the rather curious subject of the advantages of perspiration, Lord Salisbury remarked that he was one of the train-bearers at the coronation of George IV., and that the weight of the robes gave each of the bearers a Turkish bath of some hours' duration. I added that the king seemed equally to suffer on that occasion (I was in the Abbey and close to him). 'Ah,' said my lord, 'the king had an hour's rest and freedom from his robes; for after the coronation he retired for a time before he left the Abbey, and Lord ——, going into the room which had been fitted up as a dressing-room, found the king walking up and down in a state of nudity, but with the crown on his head.'"

             W. B. H.

SIDE-WHISKERS.—May I object to the word "side-whiskers" for whiskers? I last met with it in the 'Dictionary of National Biography,' article 'Ruskin.'   R. S.

BEN JONSON'S REPETITIONS. — The advocates of the Baconian theory of the origin of Shakespeare's plays seem to be particularly struck with the fact that Ben Jonson employed the same phrase in writing of both Shakespeare and Bacon. In both cases he compares their works to anything produced by "insolent Greece or haughty Rome," and every one who has read the arguments of the Baconians knows the inference they draw from this fact. I should like to point out that this is not the only instance in which Jonson repeats himself. He uses the same phrase both of Bacon and of no less august personages than their majesties King Charles I. and his queen. Readers of Jonson's works will remember his poem addressed to Bacon on his birthday, which appeared in the collected edition of Jonson's miscellaneous poems, entitled 'Underwoods.' In it occur the lines :—

Whose even thread the Fates spin round and full
Out of their choicest and their whitest wool.

This phrase is repeated—this time in prose, but without any considerable alteration—in his 'Love's Welcome : the King and Queen's Entertainment at Bolsover, at the Earl of Newcastle's, the 30th of July, 1634.' One of the characters in this entertainment, named Philalethes, speaking of the king and queen, who were present, is made to say of them, amongst other things : "The Fates spinning them round and even threads, and of their whitest wool, without brack or purl." This statement may not give the Baconian theorists their quietus, but it is, at least, an interesting instance of Jonson's employment of the same expression with respect to different individuals on different occasions.

E. F. Bates.

Kew Gardens.

Compound Words.—It is not always easy to say when a term should be expressed in two words, when the words should be linked with a hyphen, and when they should be arranged in a single undivided form. This difficulty gives variety of usage according to the divergent tastes and inclinations of different writers. It would be well, however, if the same writer were uniform in his practice, and consistent with himself. In one especially who affects authoritative deliverance a want of precision is readily noticeable, and looseness of method inevitably challenges comment. What might have been easily overlooked in another provokes wonder and inquiry when presented by the uncompromising critic. Thus the attention is arrested in the first essay of Mr. Churton Collins's 'Ephemera Critica' by three phrases in which the same expression is given in three different forms. On p 34 the writer protests against "the puffers of bookmakers"; on p. 35 he exposes "the creed of the modern book-maker"; and on p. 40 he decries "the study of such Epitomes, Manuals, and Histories as are the work of mere irresponsible book makers." Mr. Collins might surely have selected one arrangement of the term and given it authoritative value by his *imprimatur.* Thomas Bayne.

Residential State of Broad Street and Bishopsgate Street in 1677.—In the Introduction (written, I believe, by John Camden Hotten, the bookseller, of Piccadilly) to the reprint of the first 'London Directory of Merchants,' 1677, it is stated that "comparatively few merchants then [1677] resided in Broad Street, or in Bishopsgate Street. Rents were therefore low in that quarter." May we infer from this that these neighbourhoods were then also "low"? I believe the statements to be quite unfounded, and should like to know what evidence (if any) there is to support the same. I have also grave doubts whether the writer had any information as to the annual value of house property either in those or any other parts of the City at the period in question — information which he should have possessed before making the last of such statements except as a quotation. After giving him the credit of certain knowledge, which he was not at all likely to have had, one can only imagine that he based his conclusions on a comparison of the modern rentals of the houses in such streets with those of some two hundred years previously, without regard to the altered value of money, &c. I have always looked upon Broad Street and Bishopsgate Street as fashionable residential neighbourhoods in former times; but as they escaped the great fire of 1666, while most, if not all, of the destroyed portion of the City had in 1677 been recently rebuilt, it is probable that rents were lower for the old than the new buildings, to which latter the majority of the merchants and others may have flocked in preference, on account of the better accommodation and access.

E. C.

Queries.

We must request correspondents desiring information on family matters of only private interest to affix their names and addresses to their queries, in order that the answers may be addressed to them direct.

Tower : St. Peter in the Chains. — What was the ceremony that was alluded to in the papers recently in connexion with the erection of tablets and the transfer of bones at the chapel of the Tower? I ask as representing a lady who was buried there in the time of Elizabeth. D.

Portuguese Naval Supremacy.—I should be grateful for information as to the chief works in English which tell one briefly how, why, and when the Portuguese lost their former military and mercantile supremacy over the world's seas. I am anxious to supplement the scattered information about the Portuguese former power, as too briefly described in Capt. Mahan's magnificent monograph upon 'The Influence of Sea Power upon History, 1660-1783.'

J. LAWRENCE-HAMILTON, M.R.C.S.
30, Sussex Square, Brighton.

LADY CARRINGTON'S PORTRAIT BY LAWRENCE. — Some of your readers probably noticed in Messrs. Goupil's Gallery the beautiful engraving published by them in the early part of last year of Sir Thomas Lawrence's portrait of Lady Carrington, *née* Paulina Belli. The original portrait was bequeathed by Miss Laura Carrington to the South Kensington Museum. The object of the present communication is to inquire if any of your readers can tell me in what year the Belli family went to England, and from what part of Italy the family sprang.

Lady Carrington's father, John Belli, secretary to Warren Hastings, was, I believe, born in England ; but I am not sure of this. His wife was a Miss Cockerell. His three daughters married Dr. Howley, Archbishop of Canterbury, Mr. Horsley Palmer, and Sir C. E. Carrington, Chief Justice of Ceylon (whose sister was the mother of Lord Napier of Magdala). John Belli's youngest son, the Rev. Charles Almeric Belli, vicar of South Weald, died only a few years ago at a great age. Lady Carrington's extraordinary beauty was not quite equalled by her sisters, but they also were handsome.

E. MARTINENGO-CESARESCO.
Palazzo Martinengo, Salò, Lago di Garda.

ARMS.—Can any reader identify this bearing ? Vair, on a canton......a buck's head cabossed......impaling Argent, two bendlets wavy gules. The plate with these arms bears the date-mark of the reign of Charles II. and the initials A. B.   H.

BIBLE : AUTHORIZED VERSION.—Which of the previous versions differs least from the Authorized Version of the Bible? In other words, which version did the translators of 1611 revise or take as the basis of their version ?   FRANCIS J. PAYNE.

[It is founded on the work of Tyndale and Coverdale.]

GREEK EPIGRAM.—Can you give me the full text of a Greek epigram— or perhaps, more precisely, an epigram in Greek, as I fancy it may have been the composition of a modern scholar — beginning Τέσσαρες αἱ Χάριτες......καὶ δέκα Μοῦσαι, and of its ren-

dering in English, "Four are the Graces and the Muses ten"?   CHARLES F. T. FURRAN.
Sydney, N.S.W.

GALLEY HALL ESTATE.—This is situated in the parish of Great Baddow, in the county of Essex. In the year 1831 William Polley, the occupier, died, and letters of administration were granted to his son, William Polley. He died in 1848. The history of this Galley Hall—viz., the occupiers or owners from time to time, from the beginning of its existence down to the present—is wanted.

HENRY OLIVER.

"WEALD," NAME OF PART OF ESSEX.— In old maps of Essex this is printed North and South Weald, also in old records. I find several Essex names now being spelt as Weal and Wheal. How has this change come about ? On searching an old church register at North Benfleet recently I found the name written in a baptismal register of 1830 *Weald*.

T. A.

"O SAW YE MY FATHER."—I shall be glad if some one will tell me the title of, and in what collection I can see, a song beginning :

O saw ye my father, O saw ye my mither,
Or saw ye my true love John?
I saw na your father, I saw na your mither,
But I saw your true love John.
He 's met with some delay
That has caused him to stay,
And he will be here ere long.

BENEDICK.

WEEK.—The week is distinctly a Jewish and Christian institution. How is it that the names of the days are — Latin and Teutonic—invariably pagan ; and to what period may these names be traced back ?

M.

[Christianity adapted to its use existing mythology and pagan elements and customs which survive in various names. The word "week," German *Woche*, is probably true Teutonic, like the names of the days. References for their English forms will be found in Prof. Skeat's 'Etymological Dictionary.']

JEREMIAH CLIFTON.—When did this London clockmaker flourish ?   PRESTER.

[The only Cliftons traceable in Britten's 'Old Clocks and Watches and their Makers' are Thomas Clifton, a Brother of the Clockmakers' Company in 1651, and another Thomas admitted in 1687.]

PRICE OF EGGS. — In the eighth volume of the 'Calendar of the Cecil Papers' (Hist. MSS. Com., 1899) is a letter dated 23 July, 1598, from Paul Delahay, who (under the impression that he was "marrying money") had become the son-in-law of William Cecil of Alt-yr-ynys, and had undertaken certain

financial responsibilities in connexion with
the estate of his father-in-law, then deceased.
"Being subject," he complains, "to my
father-in-law's debts, the widow's dowries,
Winston's copyhold, the present heriots, and
the continued clog of service issuing out of
the lands, and harbouring and relieving of
many of my father-in-law's children and
kindred, I shall have as good a bargain as
an egg for a penny" (*op. cit.*, 272). How
many eggs could then be purchased for a
penny in the ordinary course?   O. O. H.

WIDOW OF PROTECTOR DUKE OF SOMERSET,
HANWORTH, MIDDLESEX.—I find mention in a
seventeenth-century MS. of the Protector's
widow as having lived at Hanworth, Middlesex. Can any reader of 'N. & Q.' identify
this place or house?   LOBUC.
  [Hanworth is two miles south-west of Twicken-
ham. The 'D.N.B.' states that the Duchess subsequently married Francis Newdigate, the Duke's
steward, and died 16 April, 1587, being buried in
Westminster Abbey.]

"THE MOSS-COVERED BUCKET."—Some years
ago I read a poem in which the writer stated
his conviction that the world could not offer a
more acceptable draught than that which he
used to obtain at home "from the moss-
covered bucket that hangs in the well."
Can any reader furnish me with a copy of
the words of this poem? I believe it comes
from an American source.   JOHN T. PAGE.
  West Haddon, Northamptonshire.

IRISH NAMES IN MANUSCRIPT BOOK.—This
appears to be copied from another list, and
made about a century ago. It contains over
2,000 entries, giving the name, abode, and
date of admission; there is also a column
headed "Number," but not filled in. The
dates of admission appear at irregular intervals and range from 1736 to 1791, whilst some
one has marked as "dead" nearly 400 entries.
Most of the names are those of people of
standing, but various trades are represented,
as well as several clergy and military men.
In one case nine Shearmans, the sons of
Robert Shearman, Esq., were admitted on
the same day, and the same applies to other
families in a lesser degree. Several different
counties are included; but the list was probably kept in Dublin, "Dawson" and
"George's" Streets being the only places of
abode in two cases. The names include Wm.
Beresford, Bishop of Ossory; Lords Sudley,
Mountgarret, and Mountmorris; several
baronets or knights; Peter Metge, a Baron of
the Exchequer; and John, Duke of Rutland,
admitted at the age of ten. I have been told
the names are those of Protestants, probably

willing to render assistance in case of any
rising among the Irish against the Government. Can any readers kindly enlighten me
on this point?   T. D. DUTTON.
  17, Keyes Road, Cricklewood, N.W.

FRENCH NOVEL.—Can any one tell me the
title (possibly 'Les Inconsolables'), the author,
and the publisher of a French novel (read
by me not later than 1891) in which, at a
woman's grave, her two husbands meet, and
express a warm appreciation of her, and,
striking up a close friendship, resolve to live
together, mourning her constantly? They vie
with each other as to the outward signs of
bereavement, one of them using a pocket-
handkerchief with a black border so deep
that the white centre is "no larger than a
postage stamp." Gradually a reaction sets
in, and each one tries to hide from the
other that he is growing cheerful and im-
patient of the restrictions of "le deuil."
                              UNE ANGLAISE.

GORDON AS A RUSSIAN SURNAME —Many
Russian Jews bear the surname of Gordon.
Is there anything in the theory that it is a
transposition of "Grodno," which is said to
be an impossible combination of letters in
Hebrew?   J. M. BULLOCH.
  118, Pall Mall.

MOLYNEUX.—I should be glad of information about a preacher named Molyneux, who
was living in the middle of the last century.
Can any one tell me if his memoirs have been
published?   M. G. SELLON.

"BRISTOL LOOK."—In the 'Life of Lord
Houghton' (Reid, vol. i. p. 57) the following
passage from a letter is given: "It is really
very hard that Boulogne should have so bad
a name, I hardly dare mention it. Harvey
gave me such a Bristol look when I said
where I had been." Can some reader kindly
describe a Bristol look?
                              RICHARD LAWSON.
  Urmston.

WIND FOLK-LORE. — Can any reader of
'N. & Q.' furnish further examples of the
following superstition? "To-morrow is
Equinox Day, when if the wind should
return to north-east, north-east will it blow
till June 21, as we all believe down here"
('Letters of Edward FitzGerald to Fanny
Kemble,' 1871-83, No. xc.). I also find in *Bye-
Gones*, vol. iii. p. 479, that if the wind is
in the east on the eve of All Saints', *i.e.*,
31 October, it will be the prevailing wind for
the next three months, and the weather will
be fair and open; but the locality in
which this superstition is held is not men-

tioned. In the Vosges, according to Laisnel de la Salle's 'Croyances et Légendes du Centre de la France,' vol. ii. p. 280, it is believed that the wind which blows during the midnight mass on Christmas Eve will be the predominant wind during the approaching year. G. W.

JACKSON FAMILY, CO. DURHAM.—I should be much obliged if any of your readers would tell me the descent of Philip Jackson, of West Rainton Hall, co. Durham. West Rainton Hall was conveyed to him in or soon after 1760, and he married Penelope, daughter of John Goodchild, Esq., of Pallion, in the same county. G. B.

SMALLNESS OF THE INFANT JESUS. — In a translation of 'A Prayer of the Blessed Francis to obtain Holy Poverty,' appended to Mr. Montgomery Carmichael's rendering of 'Sacrum Commercium Beati Francisci cum Domina Paupertate,' occurs the following passage :—

"She [Poverty] clung to Thee with such Fidelity, that even within Thy Mother's womb she paid Thee homage, for Thy Infant Body was, it is thought, the smallest of all."—P. 186.

This tradition is new to me. Where does the first notice of it appear? ST. SWITHIN.

ULISSE BARBIERI.—Edmondo de Amicis, in his very interesting 'Memorie,' has the following in his article on the above :—

"Così egli gira il mondo da quindici anni......e sarà tale e quale fra trent' anni, salvo qualche pelo bianco di più sulla testa e qualche centinaio di drammi di più sulla coscienza."

The article is dated Torino, 1878. Is this prolific and erratic author still *inter vivos*? J. B. McGOVERN.
St. Stephen's Rectory, C.-on-M., Manchester.

FOUNTAIN FAMILY.—After the Revocation of the Edict of Nantes a branch of my family settled in England, Scotland, or Ireland. They formerly resided at Royan, near Bordeaux, and in the sixteenth century in Touraine. I should much like to hear from any member of this family.
HUBERT DE FONTAINES.
Château de Serigny, Foussais, Vendée.

SOURCE OF QUOTATION WANTED. — An American correspondent wants to know where the following line occurs :—

The raucous clamouring of crows and choughs.
J. A. H. MURRAY.

REDEMPTION OF CAPTIVES, 1659. — In a curious tract published in 1660, entitled 'The Mystery of the Good Old Cause Briefly Unfolded, &c.,' giving details of "such Aldermen and Common-Councilmen as made profit by the Continuance of the War, Excise, Taxes, and oppressive proceedings of the Long Parliament," mention is made of Alderman Richard Hill, who died in 1659, as "a receiver of one per cent. of merchants' goods for redemption of captives."

I should be glad to know what this refers to. It could not have been anything to do with briefs for collections for redemption of captives, as apparently none was issued between 1624 and 1668. Was the receivership a permanent post created by the Parliament, or only a temporary one by the City? I may mention that I have found frequent references to Hill in the State Papers as commissioner for sale of goods taken in the Dutch war, but nothing to throw light on this one.
R. H. ERNEST HILL.

Replies.

'THE GAMBLER DETECTED.'
(9th S. ix. 67.)

THE engraving with this inscription about which F. J. inquires is British Museum Satirical Print No. 4836, and it came from the *Covent Garden Magazine*, March, 1773, where impressions face p. 82. The impression in the Print Room, British Museum, is accompanied (*vide* the entry under No. 4836 in the Trustees' 'Catalogue of Satirical Prints') by a cutting from that periodical to the following effect: "This design represents a circumstance in the career of 'Baron Neuman,' who is called Crooked-finger Jack." He is stated to have been a German of doubtful origin, educated by charity, apprenticed to a grocer, and of vicious habits. He became a gambler, assumed the character of a gentleman, but was detected or suspected of unfair play, and driven in succession from various resorts. He then came to England, assumed the title of baron (Neuman), was very successful, and set up a handsome establishment. His usual game was piquet :—

"An unlucky discovery, however, occurred at Scarborough, where our hero repaired to improve his finances. Being at play with a gentleman one day at all fours, whilst dinner was getting ready, and the cloth laid, with knives and forks at one end of the table, the gentleman was astonished how Jack always became possessed of the knave of trumps, and having watched him with great accuracy and attention, at length perceived a corner of a card in his hand while he was dealing; upon which the gentleman, immediately seizing a fork that lay by him [forks were twi-prongs in those days], pinned his hand down to the table, saying, 'By G—d, I've got you now.' There was the knave sure enough, and so the party ended."

It is said that the gentleman "gave him a cant" from the first floor into the street, and that Foote, passing by, reminded him of the advice he had often given

"not to play so high as the danger was imminent. 'Jack' still continued to play, but wears his *card curtains*, which are the largest ruffles ever seen, that hang over his fingers' ends and conceal the long shuffle and the slip."

They concealed his manœuvres, and hid the lameness of his fingers, from which he derived his nickname :—

"The print is likewise accompanied by a cutting from a book, or newspaper, containing 'The Little Baron Newman : a Sketch,' being an obituary notice of the man in question,"

the little baron, of crook-fingered memory, which states that some had said that it was Lord Chesterfield who detected the cheat, and avers that it was not he, but a brother sharper, who achieved this act. Lord Chesterfield often played at piquet at Bath with the "Baron." The paper gives a miserable account of the sharper's killing his last and only friend, a little spaniel, and final hanging of himself at his lodgings in Duke Street, Bath. No. 4651 in the national collection above named is "Baron Forchetta, after a Bett of Fifty (Baron Neuman) (Bath). By an Officer in the Guards." This is a coloured etching, published by Mathew Darly, "Jan. 24, 1774, Strand," and represents a dwarfish old man holding a pinch of snuff and a snuff box. The text of the Catalogue in view here states this is a portrait of Neuman, who, having been suspected of foul play, was watched, and a gentleman, seizing a fork, dashed it through the baron's hand, with the apology, "Sir, if such a card is not under your hand, I must beg your pardon."   F. G. STEPHENS.

This print, I venture to suggest, depicts an incident in the career of that well-known eighteenth-century gambler "Savage" Roche or Rock, who actually "pinned" to the table with a steel fork or knife the hand of a fellow-gambler who, he had occasion to think, was playing unfairly. The subject would have been easier of solution had F. J. given name of engraver, &c.
    JOHN ROBERT ROBINSON.

This print occurs as the frontispiece to a book on games called "Annals of Gaming...... By a Connoisseur. London : Printed for G. Allen, No. 59, Paternoster-Row, 1775." The operator with the fork is "Capt. Roche, *alias* Tyger, *alias Savage* Roche, who stuck his gaming companion's hand to the table with a fork for concealing a card under his hand" ('The Gaming Calendar,' 1820, 8vo, p. 63).

The name of the "gaming companion" has not come down to us, so far as I know.

In reply to F. J.'s flattering appeal, I must offer a sincere apology to those who have done me the honour to ask me to continue my bibliography of books on gaming, together with a promise that I will do so as soon as possible. The well-known result of undertaking too many things is that one never finishes anything, or but rarely. At least, that has been rather constantly my fate.
    JULIAN MARSHALL.

WINDOW GLASS (9ᵗʰ S. ix. 87).—The use of glass in windows was practised by the Romans certainly in the first century A.D., if not before. Three years ago I had what I considered unusual luck in drawing a small pane from the remains of a great villa near Porto d'Anzio (Antium), a considerable portion of which is in my possession now. The edges are thickened and rounded, probably for the grip of the metal or wooden frame. It lay about three feet below the present grassy level, among a quantity of broken pottery, &c. Similar panes, and also portions of bronze framing, were found in another first-century villa, known to me, near Marino, on the Alban Hill. At Pompeii, in the tepidarium of the bath in the villa of Diomedes, four panes of glass ten and a half inches square and portions of their frame (wooden) were taken. Others were found in the baths near the Forum.
    ST. CLAIR BADDELEY.

I believe that MR. G. C. WARDEN is right in his impression that window glass was not used until the eleventh century. The windows of Saxon and Anglo-Norman buildings were frequently filled in with oiled canvas, which kept out the wind and rain and admitted a certain quantity of light. According to Sir Gilbert Scott, canvas was bought so late as 1253 to close the windows of the Chapter-house of Westminster Abbey. In books dealing with ancient churches one reads of stained glass of the eleventh century, but though I have examined many churches with supposed eleventh-century glass, I am persuaded that the glass is much more recent than the writers profess. CHARLES HIATT.

Window glass is found in all the Roman camps in the north of England. There can be no doubt that it was in use in the time of the Romans. If I knew MR. WARDEN's address I would send him a fragment.   R. B—R.
    [Further replies to come.]

STOWE MISSAL (9ᵗʰ S. viii. 484 ; ix. 98).— MR. ROBERTS is correct in stating that the

Stowe Missal was among the Stowe MSS. bought by Government in 1883 from Lord Ashburnham. One hundred and forty-eight volumes connected with Ireland from this purchase were deposited in the library of the Royal Irish Academy in Dublin, the Stowe Missal being among them. The remaining and larger portion of the MSS. was similarly deposited in the British Museum. The Stowe Missal is thus at present preserved in the Academy's care in Dublin.   GRENVILLE A. J. COLE, R.I.A.

GOWER (9th S. ix. 68).—There is no connexion. Gower is a land barony in Glamorganshire. It is the name of a man in Yorkshire.   H. R. GRENFELL.

"SAULIES" (9th S. ix. 108).—It is Jamieson who gives an "A.-S. *sal.*" There is no such word. He means *salu*, which is Mod. E. *sallow*. *Saule*, a willow tree, would have given a monosyllabic word *saule*, without *-ie*. In order to obtain a dissyllabic *saul-ie*, we must go back to a dissyllabic French form; and if we are to guess (which is still yearned after), we might as well go back to the O. Fr. *saoulé*, glutted, which was frequently used to mean simply drunk, or a drunken fellow. But let us hope that the hired mourners knew better.   CELER.

"IN PETTO" (9th S. viii. 443; ix. 58).—I notice that Mr. Kipling, in 'Kim,' p. 341, makes his Russian say, with reference to Hurree Babu, "He represents *in petto* India in transition—the monstrous hybridism of East and West." The meaning of *in petto* in this passage seems to be "in miniature"—not "in the recesses of his breast." The first reference is misprinted "413" in the heading to MISS ROBERTS's reply.   W. F. PRIDEAUX.

"PEN-NAME" (9th S. ix. 28, 151).—Dr. Annandale's 'Imperial Dictionary' (1882) attributes this expression to Bayard Taylor. Now if this statement be correct, Bacon could not have used the word, for his Excellency the United States Minister at Berlin was born on 11 January, 1825, and died on 19 December, 1878. I fail to find the word in any dictionary of an earlier date than the above named, though I have searched in many.
EVERARD HOME COLEMAN.
71, Brecknock Road.

REV. JOHN TAUNTON (9th S. ix. 9).—The Composition Books for First Fruits show no trace of him as vicar of Axbridge. A John Taunton, clerk (index gives Tainton), compounded for first fruits of Castle Carey, 7 February, 1592, and had for bondsmen

George Yonge, of Compton Dando, co. Somerset, and James Kyrton, of Almisforde, co. Somerset, gent. Bondsmen, being very often relatives of the compounder, help in identification.   GERALD MARSHALL.
Wandsworth.

LONDRES (9th S. viii. 443; ix. 35).—I venture to think that G. E. R. is in error when he states that the first mention of William de Londres is found in 1128. William de Londres, or London, was one of the twelve knights who accompanied Robert Fitzhamon, who was persuaded by Eineon to come to Wales to help Jestyn. This was about the year 1090. I think it will be found that William de Londres, or Londinensis, was born in London, and that Fitzhamon gave him the castle and manor of Ogmore, and William thus became Lord Ogmore. This William de Londres had a son Maurice; the former soon after the conquest of Glamorgan founded a priory at Ewenny for the Benedictines, the latter in 1141 made a cell there to St. Peter's Abbey of Gloucester.

Maurice left a son named, after his grandfather, William de Londres. The ruins of Ewenny Abbey are among the most interesting architectural studies in this country. There is, or was, a sepulchral stone to the memory of Maurice de Londres, an ornamental cross in relief, extending the whole length, with the inscription—

Ici gist Morice de Londres le fondeur,
Dieu lui rend son labeur.

The flat, coffin-shape stone, with its Norman-French inscription, is of considerable value, assisting as it does the tracing of the history of other monuments of the class.
ALFRED CHAS. JONAS.

BRANDON, EXECUTIONER (9th S. ix. 9, 70).—I am deeply indebted to MR. STEPHENS for his able account of the various original papers relating to Richard Brandon. I had, however, previously read all these papers, but MR. STEPHENS's review of them will, I am sure, prove of much aid to others interested in the subject. The print, which represents the headsman cutting off the head of the "kneeling" king, must, as MR. STEPHENS points out, be admitted as some evidence in favour of the theory of the "high" block, but I consider, nevertheless, that the evidence adduced in support of the "low" block, or slab, is far stronger. Nearly all the best contemporary records describing the execution state that Charles "lay down," that he asked why the block was not higher, and that he was told it was high enough. Moreover, a Spanish contemporary manuscript mentions its size, which was only one foot high and one foot and a half long. I think it may now be taken for granted that no portrait of Brandon exists beyond those on the headings to the papers referred to by MR. STEPHENS.

PHILIP SIDNEY.

"BAR SINISTER" (9ᵗʰ S. ix. 64).—The *Daily Chronicle* errs in good company. Lord Rosebery, speaking of the "unreliability of Las Cases" in his 'Napoleon,' pp. 20, 21, says :—

"We think we have said enough to show that these various fabrications lie like a bar sinister athwart the veracity of his massive volumes, and make it impossible to accept any of his statements, when he has any object in making them."

His lordship may have thought that the literary poise of this passage would suffer if, with pedantic accuracy, he had used the correct term, "bâton sinister."

A more important error in the *Daily Chronicle* article is the statement that James II. "contributed a good many bars sinister to the arms of the members of the House of Lords." James II. created his mistress Catherine Sedley Countess of Dorchester in January, 1685/6, but she died childless in 1692, and the honour died with her. He also created his illegitimate son James Fitz-James Duke of Berwick in 1687, but the duke was attainted in 1695, and his English honours became forfeited. No descendant of James II. sits, or has sat for over two hundred years, in the House of Lords.   W. F. PRIDEAUX.

"BORE" OR "BOAR," AND OTHER FASHIONABLE SLANG (9ᵗʰ S. viii. 481).—The word is said to have originated in the eighteenth century with the Macaroni Club, whose members used the word *boar*, not *bore*, of any one opposed to dandyism or macaroni manners (see *Cassell's Magazine*, 'London Legends ').   J. H. MACMICHAEL.

R. B.'s interesting quotation would have been doubly valuable if he had given the date at which it was written, and the page of the 'Life' on which it occurs.   Q. V.

CROLLY FAMILY (9ᵗʰ S. viii. 484).—Stanislaus I., Leszczynski, King of Poland and Duke of Lorrain, was the son of Frederick Augustus I., Elector of Saxony and King of Poland, and Christina Eberhardine, daughter of Christian Ernest, Margrave of Bayreuth, and Erdmuth Sophia, daughter of John George II., Elector of Saxony, his wife. Born November, 1677, and married Catherine of Alinskaia, daughter of Henry Opalinski, Castellan of Posen. Succeeded to the throne 12 July, 1704; deposed 2 Oct., 1709; re-

turned 12 Sept., 1725; redeposed June, 1736, and 21 March, 1737. Died 23 Feb., 1736 [?]. Lady Anne, the eldest daughter of Lewis, the third Marquis of Huntly, married the Comte de Crolly, of whom I can find no information; probably he was connected with one of the Irish families of Crolly. A Captaine Aide Major Croly [*sic*] was in the Regiment de Rothe in 1746-52, that being one of the Irish brigades in the service of France. There is a pedigree of the Crolly family in O'Hart's 'Irish Pedigrees,' but it will not help MR. BULLOCH.   JOHN RADCLIFFE.

CHARLES V. ON THE DIFFERENT EUROPEAN TONGUES (9ᵗʰ S. viii. 523).—In Ravizzotti's 'Italian Grammar,' fifth edition, Lond., n.d. (dedicated to Lord Palmerston), on p. 402, and towards the close of a section headed 'Costumi delle Nazioni,' I find the following :

Diceva Carlo-Quinto che parlerebbe
In lingua Francese ad un amico,
  „   Tedesco al suo cavallo,
  „   Italiano alla sua signora,
  „   Spagnuolo a Dio,
  „   Inglese agli uccelli.

Here the first four parts correspond very nearly to MR. NORTH'S quotations, but the last is different. He says, "I fancy he described English as the language of birds," but the Italian given above evidently means that birds should be spoken to in English.

Brewer's 'Dictionary of Phrase and Fable,' ed. 1895, p. 728, has : "L'Italien se parle aux dames ; le Français aux hommes ; l'Anglais aux oiseaux ; l'Allemand aux chevaux ; l'Espagnol à Dieu" (misprinted "Dieux," see his 'Reader's Handbook,' 1898, p. 591). This is followed by a note : "Charles Quint used to say, ' I speak German to my horses, Spanish to my God, French to my friends, and Italian to my mistresses.'"

Preceding this is another note which may serve to explain "English to birds": "English, according to the French notion, is...... sing-song."

Apropos of this one naturally recalls another well-known saying of this emperor, or at least generally attributed to him : "For every new language one acquires, one becomes a new man." But, if really uttered by him, was it original? Vámbéry, in his 'Travels in Central Asia,' 1864, p. 219, quotes, as a Latin proverb, "Quot linguas cales, tot homines vales," where "cales" seems to be either a misprint for "calles," or to be so spelt for the sake of the rhyme.

In Donaldson's 'New Cratylus,' 1839, p. 10, we read :—

"It was a great mistake of Ennius to say that he had three hearts because he understood three languages (Aulus Gellius, 'Noctes Atticæ,' xvii. 17); the heart of a people is its mother tongue only (Jean Paul, xlvii. p. 179). The Emperor Charles V. was nearer the truth when he said, 'Autant de langues que l'homme sçait parler, autant de fois est-il homme'—for every language that a man learns he multiplies his individual nature, and brings himself one step nearer to the general collective mind of Man."

C. LAWRENCE FORD, B.A.
Bath.

"FITZ" (8th S. vi. 443 ; vii. 31, 77, 136).— At 9th S. viii. 534 MR. GRAHAM EASTON makes the astounding statement: "'Fitz' denotes illegitimacy." The phrase he uses can only mean that this is a general rule, not confined to the FitzJameses. Has he any evidence in support, or even positive proof in this particular instance ?

O. O. H.

WARBURTON=WERBURH'S TOWN (9th S. viii. 460).—In this connexion it may be worth mentioning that in a will, undated, but of about 1525, the testator, residing at Hoo St. Werburgh, in Kent, describes himself as "of Saint Wartown."

GEORGE C. PEACHEY.

TENNIS : ORIGIN OF THE NAME (9th S. ix. 27, 75).—Surely the most likely derivation of "tennis" is from O.G. tenni, modern German Tenne, threshing-floor. The word "area" in the Reichenau glosses is explained by danea. See Diez, 'Recueil de Travaux Originaux ou Traduits,' &c., s.v. 'Area.' H. A. STRONG.

CONFESSIONALS (9th S. ix. 48).—It does not appear that what MR. ACKERLEY saw at Libau was anything very remarkable. No doubt it would strike an Englishman or a person who has been brought up in Protestant surroundings, but on the Continent such sights, if not familiar, are, at any rate, not unusual.

In a church frequented almost entirely by Poles I have seen one of the boxes mentioned. It may best be described as a cross between a chair and a confessional. The precautions for secrecy were of a minimum description. Nor was it very wonderful. In the same church, very undermanned with priests in proportion to the numbers of the congregation, at any time on a Sunday, when low Mass is being said, or when the church is open, the people may be seen tailing off, three deep at first, then two, then one, on either side of a confessional, while in front of it some half-dozen individuals are standing in the hope that their turn may come some time. In the same church the sermon is preached in Polish, but is submitted, I am told, before-

hand to the Government censor. If ecclesiastical doings and regulations in Poland are somewhat defective—and I do not wish to imply that they are so to any considerable extent—it must be remembered that the Church in Russia labours under many disadvantages. T. P. ARMSTRONG.

The form of confessional described by MR. ACKERLEY, in which both priest and penitent are visible to any one who is in front of the "box," is the only form to be found in the very numerous churches of Malta. This kind of confessional, moreover, if I am not mistaken, is general throughout Italy. The confessions of men are in no country restricted to the "confessional-box" (to use an English term), being heard frequently in any part of the church, in the sacristy, or even in the priest's private apartment. I believe that ecclesiastical regulations require that the confession of a female (except, of course, in case of sickness or other emergency) shall be heard in a confessional.

JOHN HOBSON MATTHEWS.
Town Hall, Cardiff.

The Rev. Frederick George Lee, in his 'Glossary of Liturgical and Ecclesiastical Terms,' London, 1877, states that in England anciently the priest sat in the chancel to receive confessions. Very few of the old constructional confessionals exist. At Tanfield, near Ripon, Yorkshire, there is an ancient confessional or shriving-pew supposed to be unique, the front of which is open, and the penitent must have been in full view of any one in the church.

EVERARD HOME COLEMAN.
71, Brecknock Road.

STRAWBERRY LEAVES (9th S. viii. 463, 513). —The reason and the meaning of the ornamental leaves, commonly known as strawberry leaves, which are placed upon the coronet of a duke, &c., is a question which has puzzled the writers on honour and heraldry. Selden, a learned man on the subject, mentions "the rose (or as some would have oak leaves or some other leaves)," but gives no definite explanation. Nisbet says, "they [coronets] are brightened with leaves like those of the oak, smallage or great parsley." Randle Holme, in his usual loquacious style, gives the following :—

"An Earl's crown, Crownett or Coronet.—The circle of this is raised into spires like sun-beams, with buttons between ; each spire having a pearl fixed on the point thereof ; some describe the Crown to have small Roses between the spires, but that is only the fancy of the workman as a further flourish or garnish to the Crown when the largeness of it will admit of such curiosities, but the old way was

Pearls, for the Earl, being a degree higher than a Viscount and lower than a Marquess, hath the Crown composed of both theirs."

In former times the commander of the army was called a Duke, the word meaning leader, as long as he held the office, and when he kept the districts he conquered he often retained the title. The oak leaf was considered a symbol of victory, and the probability is that this leaf was originally intended to be represented by the leaves on the coronets.

As A. N. wishes to know why this leaf is used, I will give the only reason I can find, which is in the article on heraldry in the 'Encyclopædia Londinensis,' the name of the writer being unknown. He says:—

"The decoration by the strawberry-leaves is very ancient, and we do not doubt but the honour of adorning the brows of majesty was reserved to this humble plant in order to remind sovereigns that though elevated to so high a station in society, they never ought to forget that they are but men, and but a single leaf in the great scale of nature and in the dispensation of Divine Providence."

JOHN RADCLIFFE.

KNOCKER FAMILY (9ᵗʰ S. ix. 8).—This name exists in other counties than Kent, for the two sons of the late Mr. Dibb, of Hull, are Col. Arthur Knocker Dibb and Mr. Oscar Knocker Dibb. No doubt their use of the name is derived from a near relative who bore it as a surname.   RONALD DIXON.

46, Marlborough Avenue, Hull.

SURNAMES DERIVED FROM FRENCH TOWNS (9ᵗʰ S. viii. 464; ix. 16).—As your querist seems to be interested in these, when next he is in Normandy he should take an opportunity of examining the list of "Compagnons de Guillaume à la conquête de l'Angleterre en MLXVI.," which he will find graven over the main doorway (inside) of the old church at Dives. He can there feast his eyes on famous Anglo-Norman names galore—Durand, Giffard, Talbot, Malet. de Venables, Tirel, de Colleville, Archer, Gibard, Gilbert, de Malleville, Basset, Lovvet, de Perci, de Manneville, de Vernon, de Laci, de Maci, de Chandos, Corbet, de Harcourt, de Mortemer, de Glanville, Maltravers, de Tilly, Bertran, &c.— that is to say, unless he choose the more comfortable and fashionable occupation of lounging in the gateway of the old "Hostellerie de Guillaume le Conquérant" in the Rue d'Hastings.

The monument in the church was erected by the Société Française d'Archéologie in August, 1862, just about a year after Arcisse de Caumont set up his celebrated "Colonne Commémorative" on the hill overlooking the mouth of the D···es, whence the Bastard

started on his eventful voyage. This column, by the way, is now getting as hard to reach as the Bayeux Tapestry is on cattle-market day.

But, after all, your querist will probably prefer to consult the various printed lists of the names he wants.   HY. HARRISON.

In 1874 Henry S. King & Co., of London, published an anonymous volume entitled 'The Norman People,' the larger portion of which is devoted to an "Alphabetical Series of Norman Names and Families from the 'London Post Office Directory.'" I think this book will amply answer the above query, as its author states that one-third or more of the English population is of Norman origin, and substantiates his statements by testimony from the 'Rotuli Hundredorum,' 'Testa de Neville,' 'Proceedings of the Curia Regis,' 'Pipe Rolls, temp. Henry I. and II.,' 'Rotuli de Libertate of King John,' and other works of authority.

It seems to me a pity that such a work should be anonymous, for the learning and labour requisite to its production would lend dignity to a name already honoured.

N. W. J. HAYDON.

Boston, U.S.

MINIATURE OF COL. GEO. FLEETWOOD (9ᵗʰ S. ix. 48).—Has not R. W. B. confused the two George Fleetwoods? As I make it out, the regicide George, who died in America, was the brother of the well-known Charles Fleetwood, Cromwell's son-in-law. Sir George Fleetwood, his cousin, knighted in 1632, was the Swedish baron, and died in Sweden in 1667 (see Noble's 'Lives of the Regicides'). So much interest, and at the same time obscurity, attaches to the later generations of the Fleetwood descent that any little item of addition is most welcome. Possibly R. W. B. may be able to note something further from the wills he has examined.

W. D. PINK.

EARLIEST PRINTED INSTRUCTIONS TO SUNDAY-SCHOOL TEACHERS (9ᵗʰ S. ix. 69).—I have a great collection of Sunday-school material. It has been freely consulted by Mr. Leslie Stephen and other biographers of Raikes. It is my impression that the broadsheet in the possession of W. I. R. V. was compiled or written by the brother of Robert Raikes, who really took a more active part in the management of Sunday schools than his brother, the reputed founder of the institution. The Rev. Richard Raikes was a most exemplary, pious, and energetic clergyman, and he wrote things for the guidance and promotion of

Sunday schools. His brother Robert was the proprietor, printer, and editor of the venerable *Gloucester Journal;* and if I could see the broadsheet I could no doubt readily recognize the type of Robert's printing office. The Archbishop of Canterbury and other influential men and representatives of influential bodies have memorialized the Gloucester municipal authorities to repair and restore the Raikes and other Sunday-school monuments. The Rev. Richard Raikes was buried in the churchyard of St. Mary de Lode. His tomb is rapidly decaying, and if it be not speedily repaired it will disappear. This is to be deplored, especially when so many persons visit Gloucester as the shrine of Sunday schools.　　H. Y. J. TAYLOR.
3, Falkner Street, Gloucester.

HOUR OF SUNDAY MORNING SERVICE (9ᵗʰ S. ix. 67).—Much collateral evidence may be seen at 8ᵗʰ S. xii. 269. Thomas Scott, the commentator, had a sermon and a celebration on alternate Sundays at 6 A.M. at St. Margaret's, Lothbury, 1785-8 ('Life,' ninth edition, 1836, pp. 149-51). See Hatton's 'New View of London,' 1708, vol. i. p. xxxvii.　　W. C. B.

In North Lincolnshire sixty years ago the Sunday morning services in the churches usually began at ten o'clock, but I have heard that in some few places an older custom was followed and nine continued to be the hour.　　COM. LINC.

CLAYTON FAMILY (9ᵗʰ S. ix. 68).—In Cameron's 'History of the Royal College of Surgeons in Ireland' John Clayton is named, at p. 72, as one of the original brothers of the Gild of Barber-Chirurgeons under the charter of James II. of 10 February, 1687. In the lists of the members of the Gild in the original records now in the library of Trinity College, Dublin, the name of John Clayton does not appear, but in the first list after the charter of James II., dated 22 July, 1688, one of the brothers is given as "John Creighton," with "gone away" written after his name. No will of any medical man named John Clayton, nor grant of letters of administration of his effects, is to be found in the Public Record Office, Dublin, amongst the records of the Prerogative Court, or the Consistorial Court of the Diocese of Dublin.

The 'D.N.B.' is in error in describing the father of Robert Clayton, Bishop of Clogher, as "Dr. Robert Clayton, minister of St. Michael's, Dublin." He was the Rev. John Clayton, M.A., rector of St. Michan's, a totally different parish from St. Michael's, and is mentioned in the Act 9 Will. III. c. 16

(Ir.), by which the old parish of St. Michan's was divided into three distinct parishes. As the Rev. John Clayton does not appear to have been a graduate of the University of Dublin, he is possibly the John Clayton, son of Richard Clayton, of Preston, co. Lancaster, who obtained the degree of M.A. at Oxford in 1682 (see Foster's 'Alumni Oxonienses').
　　E. T. B.

CUCKLAND (9ᵗʰ S. viii. 384, 510).—Because Cuckhamsley Hill, in Berkshire, seems to be the A.-S. *Cwichelmes-hlǽw,* it certainly does not follow that all our *cuck* names are from Cwichelm. *Cuck* is normally a variant of *cock:* cf. Chaucer's *cokkow* = cuckoo, and *cokewold* = cuckold.　　HY. HARRISON.

WARLOW FAMILY (9ᵗʰ S. ix. 9).—The name of Warlow is an old Pembrokeshire name, yet it is not of Welsh origin. Neither is it Flemish nor Norman, but most probably of Danish or Norse origin. It is found as a surname in Pembrokeshire about the time of Henry III., and occurs several times in the Bronwydd MS. in connexion with the district of Kemeys, a district which was conquered by a Norman knight, Martin of Tours.

There was a Thomas Warlaugh who died in 1274, and there is extant an agreement between him and Robert de Valle respecting lands at Morvill and Redwalles ('Arch. Cambren.,' 1862, p. 27, supp). Then there were David and Philip Warlagh or Warla, whose names occur on several Latin documents in connexion with Newport, Pem. (Fenton, p. 72, appen.; 'Arch. Cambren.,' 1862, p. 60; Owen's 'Pem.,' p. 189, part ii.). There does not appear to be a pedigree of the family published, but the name appears several times in 'Dwynn's Visitations' (vol. i. pp. 74, 116, 168, 175, 244). It is also found in Law's 'Little England beyond Wales,' p. 432. There is a river and town of the name of Warnow in Mecklenburg, indicating a Norse origin.　　H. A. R.

A similar question appeared in 'N. & Q.' upwards of forty-four years ago (2ⁿᵈ S. iv. 69), to which no reply has been given. The querist then suggested that the name was Flemish, and that it might be connected with Warlock, through the softening of the final letters of that word.
　　EVERARD HOME COLEMAN.
71, Brecknock Road.

EAST INDIA BADGE (9ᵗʰ S. ix. 67).—The Indexes of 'N. & Q.,' under 'Merchants' Marks,' will reveal many references which furnish several ingenious explanations of this figure 4.　　W. C. B.

PORTRAITS OF FEMALE FIGHTERS (9ᵗʰ S. ix. 68).—A portrait of the well-known warrior Hannah Snell, who fought and was wounded twelve times at Pondicherry, and was pensioned by the Duke of Cumberland, will be found in the Victoria Gallery of the Chelsea Public Library. It may be added that Mrs. Spragg, "who, long declining wedlock and aspiring above her sex and age, fought under her brother, with arms and manly attire, in a fire-ship against the French for six hours on the 30th June, 1690," is buried in Old Chelsea Church. The sentence quoted above is part of the inscription on her monument there.	CHARLES HIATT.

Your correspondent includes, under the above heading the Chevalier d'Éon, who at his death was proved to have been a male. His portrait will be found in Kirby's 'Wonderful and Eccentric Museum,' 1820, vol. iv., and Wilson's 'Wonderful Characters,' 1821, vol. iii. There is a biographical sketch in Granger's 'Wonderful Museum,' 1807, vol. v., but no portrait.
EVERARD HOME COLEMAN.
71, Brecknock Road.

There is a portrait of "Phebe Hassel, aged 106," in Hone's 'Year-Book,' p. 105. In the account of this redoubtable woman which accompanies it is the following note :—

"In looking over the drawings of Mr. Chatfield, the artist (No. 66, Judd Street, Brunswick Square), I found a fine full-sized portrait of Phebe Hassel, which that gentleman sketched at Brighton in her lifetime, and has obligingly copied for the engraving before the reader."

Several notes concerning Phebe or Phœbe Hessel, or Hassel, have appeared during the last year or so in the Antiquities column of the *East London Advertiser*. A drawing of her gravestone in Brighton Churchyard is to be found in 'Curious Epitaphs,' by William Andrews, F.R.H.S. (1899).

Some twenty years ago I remember seeing a biography of the Chevalier d'Eon which contained a number of portraits taken at various periods of his life.
JOHN T. PAGE.
West Haddon, Northamptonshire.

DENHAM, LAIRD OF WISHIELS (9ᵗʰ S. viii. 484 ; ix. 56).—A pedigree of the Denholms or Denhams of Westshield, deduced from Andrew Denham of Braidstain, who married Marion Liddell, heiress of Westshield, will be found prefixed to the memoir of Sir James Steuart Denham, Bart., of Coltness and Westshield, which forms part iii. of the 'Coltness Collections,' printed for the Maitland Club, 1842.

In the churchyard of the parish of Dunlop, co. Ayr, stands a monument which includes effigies of the Janet Denham mentioned at the first reference, and the Rev. John, *alias* Hans Hamilton, her spouse, with an inscription. It was erected in 1642 by the first Lord Clanboyes. An outline engraving of it faces p. 24, part i. vol. i. of 'Selections from the Family Papers preserved at Caldwell,' printed at Glasgow, also for the Maitland Club, in 1854.	R. E. B.

KINBOROUGH AS A FEMALE CHRISTIAN NAME (9ᵗʰ S. viii. 504 ; ix. 30).—Kinborough is not unlike Cyneburgh, but Kimmerjum seems far removed from "Cyneburgh's home." And still a place so pronounced (but spelt Kimmerghame) has perhaps from this beginning derived its very curious name. It lies (mansion-house, mains, and mill all called alike) in the centre of the Merse in Berwickshire. On the north it is bounded for two miles by the river Blackadder. On the south it runs to within a mile of the old Saxon village of Swinton. In the later centuries the name has altered little. In Bleau's 'Atlas,' c. 1648, it is spelt Kymmerjemm ; but when we get back to the early Coldingham charters in Raine's 'North Durham,' it assumes quite a different character. In charter dxliii., date c. 1240, we find it as Kymbringeham and Kinebriggeham ; in charter cxvii., date c. 1200, it is Kyneb'gham ; in charters ccccxxxv. and ccccxxxvi., date c. 1100, it is Cynebrihthā and Cynebrithā ; and in charter vii., also c. 1100, it is Chynbrygh'm. Now DR. MURRAY quotes Bæda to the effect that in 653 Cyneburgh, daughter of King Penda of Mercia, was married to Alchfrid, son of Oswiu, King of Northumbria. Perhaps he will tell me if he agrees with my idea that Kimmerghame was this lady's Northumbrian home.

I ought to add that Kimmerghame is under fifty miles from Bewcastle. There stands the celebrated cross erected in memory of Alchfrid's victory, and on it, according to the newly published history of Cumberland, the name of Cyneburgh is clearly decipherable.
GEORGE S. C. SWINTON.

The Wedmore parish registers record the baptism of Kimboroe, daughter of James Montague, on 11 September, 1584. In February, 1609, she (Kinbora) is married to Richard Renion. In December, 1661, she (Kinborough) is buried.	S. H. A. H.

BALL'S POND ROAD, NORTH LONDON (9ᵗʰ S. viii. 461).—The paragraph preserved by MR. HIBGAME, giving the origin of this name, does not contain any mention of the fact that the "pond" was a famous ducking-pond attached to Ball's tavern. Cunningham had seen a token of this tavern, with that name upon it, of the reign of Charles II., and quotes the following from D'Avenant, 'The Long Vacation in London' ('Works,' 1673, p. 289) :—

But Husband gray now comes so stall,
For Prentice notch'd he strait does call:
Where 's Dame, quoth he,—quoth son of shop,
She 's gone her cake in milk to sop :
Ho, ho ! to Islington ; enough !
Fetch Job my son and our dog Ruffe !
For there in Pond, through mire and muck,
We 'll cry hay Duck, there Ruffe, hay Duck.

Thomas Cromwell, in his 'Walks through Islington,' 1835, p. 198, says that the tavern was the "Salutation," and that the token alluded to represented two male figures in the costume of the day, each bowing, hat in hand, while an inscription surrounds them and covers the reverse, containing the words "John . Ball . at . the . Boarded . House . neere . Newington . Greene . his . penny."

J. HOLDEN MACMICHAEL.

'LES LAURIERS DE NASSAU,' SMALL FOLIO, 1612 (9th S. viii. 464).—'Les Lauriers de Nassau ; ou, Description des Victoires gagnees par les Etats du Pays-bas sous la Conduite du Prince Maurice de Nassau,' fol., Leyden, 1615. It is considered only a translation of the last piece of the Dutch work 'Nassaure Laurekrans,' by Jo. Jans Orlers ende Henrich van Haustens, fol., Leyden, 1616.

JOHN RADCLIFFE.

LADY LOUISA STUART (9th S. viii. 505).—Although I am unable to answer MR. LEVI'S inquiry, it may interest him to know that some long and interesting communications relating to this lady appeared in 5th S. iv. 484, 524 ; v. 110, 177, 193, 256, 313.

EVERARD HOME COLEMAN.
71, Brecknock Road.

COMPULSORY COSTUME FOR JEWS AND CHRISTIANS (9th S. viii. 521). — It is stated that the Jews so late as 1736 were at Avignon and other parts of the Pope's dominions compelled to wear hats of a yellow colour (*Athenæum*, 16 April, 1898, p. 493).

Southey, quoting from Kennett's 'Parochial Antiquities,' says that Henry III. ordered that the Jews, when they went abroad, should bear on their upper garments a badge of two white tablets on the breast, made of linen, cloth, or parchment, so as to distinguish them from Christians ('Common-Place Book,' First Series, p. 460).

N. M. & A.

"OWL IN IVY BUSH" (9th S. vi. 328, 396 ; vii. 16, 116).—The last reference gives 1678 as an early instance of the above proverb. The following quotation from Miss Cruwys-Sharland's recently printed (from MSS. in the British Museum) 'Story Books of Little Gidding, 1631-2,' p. 221, goes still further back. The Guardian is relating to his little community in the great hall of the manor house a story of Sir Thomas More's about the disagreement of a jury in the Pypouder Court at Sturbridge Fair :—

"Nay, stay, I pray, Mr. Dickinson (that was his name), sayde the Southerne [the other jurors were North-Country men] Jurer ; meethinks both reason and law are on the defendants part. With that they all fell upon him, as an Oule in an ivie bush. With what doe your two eies see more than our two and twenty ?"

The "Pypouder Court" was a temporary court held at the principal fairs to dispose of petty cases on the spot :—

"From Fr. *pied* and *poudre* because the litigants are commonly country people with dusty feet : or from the Dispatch in determining the Causes even before the Dust goes off from their Feet."—Bailey, 1727.

MICHAEL FERRAR.
Little Gidding.

STONE PULPIT (9th S. viii. 325, 394, 489 ; ix. 56).—Another famous stone pulpit is that in the ancient refectory of the Abbey of St. Werburgh (now Chester Cathedral) ; the room was used for many years for the grammar school. I was at school there from August, 1875, to the spring of 1877, when the school was transferred to the new building between the cathedral and the Town Hall Square. A fine plate (by J. H. Le Keux) of the pulpit and its details will be found in Mr. J. H. Parker's 'Mediæval Architecture of Chester' (1858). Mr. Parker says :—

"The eastern part of the refectory, now the King's Grammar School, is a very fine Early English vaulted chamber, with a beautiful stone pulpit and staircase to it, one of the finest examples we have remaining. The windows at the back of this beautiful pulpit and of the passage leading to it have unfortunately been walled up ; it would be a great and easy improvement to have them reopened and glazed."

This has never been done. The room is now used only as a practice-room for the cathedral choir. The good Churchmen of the Chester diocese could not more fitly celebrate the coronation of King Edward VII. than by opening out this fine room to the original length, and filling its windows with really good stained glass.

T. CANN HUGHES, M.A., F.S.A.
Lancaster.

A choice little engraving of the stone pulpit standing south-east of the Abbey

Church at Shrewsbury appeared in the *Mirror* of 30 March, 1833.   JOHN T. PAGE.
West Haddon, Northamptonshire.

PEARLS A CURE FOR CORNS (9ᵗʰ S. ix. 10).—
Two or three years ago I was told by the shampooer at the Doncaster Turkish Baths that pearl buttons dissolved in lemon juice would cure corns. It never occurred to me that this was "folk-lore" based on the doctrine of "signatures," but I dare say it is. I thought it quite possible that the citrate of lime might penetrate and bring about painless extinction and exfoliation of the corn, tried it, and persevered for perhaps three weeks running, but could not tell that it did the slightest good. I should now have more faith in the solution with excess of lemon juice, which may have answered in some cases, or still more in lemon juice alone.   J. T. F.

In response to a query from MR. RATCLIFFE, I write to say that the recipe for corn-curing which he gives is not new. I have seen it elsewhere, but believe vinegar was to be used in it, not lemon juice. There seems to be some misunderstanding about the material of which "pearl buttons" are made—this is "mother-of-pearl," not the marine gem itself.   B. B.

I should like to say that, to my personal knowledge, this quaint remedy has been used for many years in Yorkshire. In Driffield, in the East Riding, also in Whitby thirty years ago, I knew several people who used it. As to its efficacy I can speak favourably, having tried it with advantage to myself.
   W. D. RIDLEY.

REV. ANTHONY WARTON, 1657 (9ᵗʰ S. ix. 47).
—This is the second occasion on which A. C. H. has made inquiries respecting this divine, the author of 'Refinement of Zion,' London, 1657. I now refer him to 1ˢᵗ S. ii. 56, an interesting communication of MAGDALENSIS, to which no reply ever appeared.
   EVERARD HOME COLEMAN.
71, Brecknock Road.

THE YOUTHFUL YEAR (9ᵗʰ S. viii. 484; ix. 57).—I am obliged to W. S. for amending my citation. I have now come to the conclusion that Dante did not count the age of the year in the Tuscan mode, but that he followed the prescription of Boniface VIII., who, according to Sir Harris Nicolas's 'Chronology of History,' p. 191, began "the year at Christmas, which custom was followed by nearly all his successors in the fourteenth century." I do not quite follow MR. T. WILSON's argument. The sun enters Aquarius on 20 January, and if the poet's year began on the 1st of that month, he had more right to call it "youthful" than if it had been born with Advent, though in either case the epithet would be appropriate.
   ST. SWITHIN.

AN OLD CHARM (9ᵗʰ S. ix. 49).—"Naadgrass Dyradgrass" seems to be Welsh. If I am correct in this surmise, the proper spelling would be "Na ad gras, Dyro dy ras," and the meaning "Prevent not grace, Give Thy grace." Unless C. C. B. is quite sure of his reading, I would suggest as more probable, "Na ad dy rass, Dyw dy rass," for "Na ad dy ras, Duw dy ras" (Prevent not Thy grace; God, Thy grace). Both these supplications, but especially the latter, are well known as bardic mottoes. Mediæval charms of this kind, made up of phrases from Latin and Greek liturgies, interspersed with Welsh words, were common in the Principality right down to the early part of the nineteenth century. The most usual form had its origin in an ancient prayer attributed to St. Augustine of Hippo, which appears in a MS. French Book of Hours of the early fifteenth century, in my possession.
   JOHN HOBSON MATTHEWS.
Town Hall, Cardiff.

BURIAL OF A SUICIDE (9ᵗʰ S. viii. 502; ix. 96).—It is possible that the story mentioned by MR. HARRY HEMS, of a Frenchman being buried near Reigate head downwards, may have had its origin in the following facts. Mr. Richard Hull built a tower on Leith Hill, in the parish of Wotton, in the year 1766, and, dying in 1772, was buried in the basement. Old folks in the neighbourhood told me, some twenty years since, the same story; but there is no foundation for it. He was, no doubt, buried in the tower, but my inquiries resulted in my being assured that he was buried in the usual way; all the rest of the story is fiction. Leith Hill tower was repaired by Mr. J. P. Perrin, who purchased the property after Mr. Hull's death. It is now in the possession of Mr. J. Evelyn, of Wotton, who repaired and heightened the tower. The hill is 993 feet above the level of the sea, and on a fine day parts of some ten counties can be seen from it.
   F. CLAYTON.
Morden.

SIR THOMAS MORGAN, OF ARKSTONE (9ᵗʰ S. ix. 9).—The Morgans of Arkstone, in the county of Hereford, were a junior branch of the widely distributed Herbert clan, whose chief is Col. Ivor John Caradoc Herbert,

of Llanarth, C B., C.M.G., D.S.O. Col.
Herbert is alone entitled to bear the un-
differenced arms of Herbert, to wit, Per
pale azure and gules, three lioncels rampant
argent. Like some other offshoots of this
male stock, Morgan of Arkstone bore
different arms, viz., Argent, a lion rampant
sable, ducally crowned or.

　　　　　　　JOHN HOBSON MATTHEWS.
Town Hall, Cardiff.

Miscellaneous.

NOTES ON BOOKS, &c.

The Life of Napoleon I. By John Holland Rose,
M.A. 2 vols. (Bell & Sons.)

NUMEROUS and important as are the books concerning Napoleon, no historical collection can afford
to dispense with this latest addition. Mr. Rose
has scarcely had canvas enough for the picture he
has sought to paint. Many details have had to be
hurried over, and the design in places is blurred.
The necessity for compression renders the language,
and sometimes the idea, obscure, and the passages
in which occur explanations of the impossibility of
carrying further a portion of the argument are
numerous. These things are inherent in the scheme,
and we are compelled to accept the book as it is
planned and executed by the author. The work might
have been better had double the amount of time been
spent on its composition and double the amount of
space been awarded to the exposition. It is excellent, however, as it is, and we are only justified
in going behind the author's purpose and aim so far
as to say that there are times when we should be
thankful for more. Mr. Rose's book is a specimen
of the rewritten histories which must in time
replace in almost all cases the half-informed and
often prejudiced compilations of earlier days. The
influence of the opening of the archives of Simancas
to English research, and the careful investigation
of those of Venice, have, for instance, rendered
necessary a recasting of the history of Tudor times.
In history, as in other things, there is no finality,
and further research — opportunities for which
multiply as international jealousies, so far as access
to literary documents is concerned, diminish—
leads to a constant reshaping of facts and recasting
of judgments. It is curious that close investigation
into those portions of our archives embracing the
period covered by the Napoleonic wars should have
been long deferred. This has, however, been the
case, and Mr. Rose is practically the first to bring
to bear upon the career of the great French emperor
the information contained in our national archives.
This constitutes the chief value of his important
and profoundly interesting volumes. Not wholly
consoling is it to read of the ineptitude of the
British Government after the death of Pitt, of the
disastrous consequences of aristocratic jobbery, of
widespread corruption, and of disloyalty on the
part of a political opposition which the author
denounces as lack of patriotism. To the study of
these things the merest tiro in history is accustomed, and he is a sanguine man who expects to
find more gratifying reading in the records of
present or future campaigns.

Little in the present work is more striking than
the contempt Napoleon displayed for English diplomacy—a contempt so justified that the student
accepts it as inevitable, and shrugs his shoulders
over it as part of the appanage—shall we say
as the curse?—of our race. It is natural that,
though the work deals with the entire career
of Napoleon, the most interesting portion should
be to English readers the descriptions of the
sustained struggle against England, the most
resolute and, thanks to her insular position, the
most triumphant of Napoleon's opponents. Of the
men arrayed against Napoleon three only can come
into any sort of comparison with him, and these
were all Englishmen—Pitt, Nelson, and Wellington. Anything approaching to an adequate review
of Mr. Rose's work is not to be expected. Every
episode in the career of Napoleon is of highest
interest, and we turn as reluctantly from the man
of Toulon and of Vendémiaire as from the conqueror of Marengo, of Austerlitz, and of Jena, the
fugitive from Moscow, the defeated of Waterloo,
and the prisoner of St. Helena. We can but take
a few distinct and distinguishing assertions or
opinions of the author. Of the French Revolution
he says that discontent and faith were the ultimate
motive power: "Faith prepared the Revolution,
and discontent accomplished it." The three writers
whose influence on revolutionary politics was to be
definite and practical were Montesquieu, Voltaire,
and Rousseau. With purely speculative writers
he concerns himself no more than with such half-
unconscious agents as Beaumarchais. As his is a
history of Napoleon, and not of the Revolution,
such omissions are excusable. In his short and
valuable preface Mr. Rose quotes the words employed by Napoleon to Gallois: "Je n'aime pas
beaucoup les femmes, ni le jeu, enfin rien : *je suis
tout à fait un être politique.*" This shows the point
of view from which the book is written. Mr. Rose
avowedly treats with special brevity the years
1809-11, which he considers to represent the *con-
stans atas* of the emperor's career, and has dedicated proportionately more space to showing how
Napoleon's "continental system was setting at
work mighty economic forces that made for his
overthrow, so that after the *débâcle* of 1812 it came
to be a struggle of Napoleon and France *contra
mundum.*" It is pleasant to find from the same
preface that British policy comes out the better
the more fully it is known. Beginning in feeble-
ness and ineptitude, it attained to firmness and
dignity, and "Ministers closed the cycle of war
with acts of magnanimity towards the French
people which are studiously ignored by those who
bid us shed tears over the martyrdom of St. Helena."
Of Napoleon's passion for Josephine in the days
of the Italian campaign an interesting account is
given, Marlborough's letters to his peevish duchess
during the Blenheim campaign being "not more
crowded with maudlin curiosities than those of the
fierce scourge of Austria to his heartless fair." The
"facile fondnesses" of Josephine welled forth far
too widely "to carve out a single channel of love
and mingle with the deep torrent of Bonaparte's
early passion." With these passages will naturally
be compared those when the position was changed,
it may almost be said reversed. Nelson's career
in Naples—"the worst Court in Europe"—is un-
sympathetically treated, and that hero is said to have
tarnished his fame on the Syren (*sic*) coast. Napoleon's behaviour at Jaffa is held to compare favour-

ably with that of Cromwell at Drogheda. Special attention is merited by the passages descriptive of the events of Brumaire, when Napoleon, Sieyès, and others ran imminent risk of the guillotine. To the disaster of Marengo British dilatoriness is shown to have contributed. At vol. i. p. 335 is quoted a valuable document showing the contempt felt, at the period of the Peace of Amiens, in the Parisian *salons* for the conduct of the British Government. After this it is pleasant to read of the behaviour of Wellesley, "our great proconsul at Calcutta, by whose foresight our Indian Empire was preserved and strengthened." Not half way are we through the passages we marked for comment in the first volume, and those in the second have not yet been approached, yet we must stop. So limited is the space that we can, under the most favourable conditions, award to reviews that in the case of a work of this kind, which we have diligently perused, we can deal with no more than an occasional point. The book is pleasantly written, though the epithets used in describing battles are, perhaps necessarily, sometimes conventional. Perusal is, however, a pleasure rather than a task, and once begun is quitted with difficulty. Many an hour has in our case been stolen from sleep in order to continue the study. The illustrations are numerous and well selected, and the maps are useful. Nothing is wanting to the book so far as regards enjoyment, and as a work of reference it is invaluable.

The Vowel-Sounds of the East Yorkshire Folk-Speech. By the Rev. M. C. F. Morris, B.C.L. (Frowde.)
Mr. Morris has in a previous volume proved his intimate acquaintance with the folk-speech of East Yorkshire, and in the present *brochure* he endeavours to make plain to outsiders how its vowel-sounds are pronounced. He essays to do this, not by any scientific method of phonetics, such as the glossic of Mr. Alexander Ellis, but in a popular and untechnical way, by the rule of thumb, which is in this case the rule of rime. On the whole, he succeeds better than might be expected in giving us a fair idea of the pronunciation. Many of its peculiarities may be traced to Scandinavian influences, and in particular to the dialect of West Jutland. It is rather amusing to find Mr. Morris in the very sentence in which he reprobates "new-fangled Americanisms" himself expressing a preference for words which have "a lengthy past history."

King Henry VI., Part I., Part II., and Part III. 3 vols. With an Introduction and Notes by John Dennis and Illustrations by Byam Shaw. (Bell & Sons.)
The latest additions to the lovely "Chiswick Shakespeare" comprise the three parts of 'King Henry VI.,' edited and illustrated in the same admirable fashion as the previous volumes. On the question of the authorship of the three plays Mr. Dennis has little to add to the current opinion that, though Shakspeare took them and stamped portions of them with the seal of his genius, they are not wholly his. The subject, which has given rise to endless controversy, and will continue so to do, is not to be opened out afresh. Each volume has its separate glossary and notes. In none of the plays yet given to the world are Mr. Byam Shaw's talents and knowledge of mediæval life seen to greater advantage.

Crowns and Coronations: a History of Regalia. By William Jones, F.S.A. (Chatto & Windus.)
A reissue of the excellent account of 'Crowns and Coronations' by the erudite author of 'Finger-Ring Lore' is a natural outcome of the approaching ceremonial. In the volume, which extends to six hundred pages, and swarms with illustrations, a summary — the first, so far as we remember — of coronations in all ages of the world's history is given. Nearly nineteen years have passed since the first edition saw the light, and so thoroughly was the work done that neither change nor addition has been found necessary. During this period it has been in constant use on our shelves as a work of reference. Under present conditions it deserves to be restudied, and is sure to be frequently consulted.

Mr. Herbert Chitty has reprinted from the *Wykehamist* of December a few copies, for private circulation, of *An Index of Names of Winchester Scholars in the 'Dictionary of National Biography.'* The list, which is large and brilliant, extends from 1401 to 1854. Mr. Chitty was himself a commoner of the college, and is a contributor to our columns. Corrections which he has made therein reappear in his pages.

Mr. E. H. W. Dunkin, of The Heath, Fairlight, Hastings, writes: "May I draw the attention of your readers to a society lately formed for printing records relating to the county of Sussex? If those interested in such matters would become members of the society, and forward their subscription (one guinea) to Mr. Turner, The Castle, Lewes, the important work promoted by the society would be greatly encouraged. The first volume, now in the press, will be 'Sussex Marriage Licences (1586-1642) for the Archdeaconry of Lewes.'." This volume is sure to interest American genealogists.

Notices to Correspondents.

We must call special attention to the following notices:—

On all communications must be written the name and address of the sender, not necessarily for publication, but as a guarantee of good faith.

We cannot undertake to answer queries privately.

To secure insertion of communications correspondents must observe the following rules. Let each note, query, or reply be written on a separate slip of paper, with the signature of the writer and such address as he wishes to appear. When answering queries, or making notes with regard to previous entries in the paper, contributors are requested to put in parentheses, immediately after the exact heading, the series, volume, and page or pages to which they refer. Correspondents who repeat queries are requested to head the second communication "Duplicate."

Clifton.—Shall appear next week.

NOTICE.

Editorial communications should be addressed to "The Editor of 'Notes and Queries'"—Advertisements and Business Letters to "The Publisher"—at the Office, Bream's Buildings, Chancery Lane, E.C.

We beg leave to state that we decline to return communications which, for any reason, we do not print; and to this rule we can make no exception.

LONDON, SATURDAY, MARCH 1, 1902.

CONTENTS. — No. 218.

Notes.

"FAMOUS SCOTS."

IN the December number of the *Pall Mall Magazine* Mr. W. E. Henley somewhat rudely dispels cherished illusions regarding the late Mr. R. L. Stevenson. Apparently there are two main points in Mr. Henley's contention : (1) Stevenson was in large measure the creation of Mr. Henley ; and (2) the designer is dissatisfied with the admiration now lavished on what he calls "this faultless, or very nearly faultless, monster." In the fashioning process there was no aiming at monstrous results at all, but now, apparently, we have a vivid illustration of the tendency in ill-considered transactions to come home to roost. Mr. Henley will not recognize the Stevenson that never returned from America, because that is not the finished product which, in his own words, " I knew, and loved, and laboured with and for, with all my heart and strength and understanding." One recalls the supreme agony of Frankenstein, similarly wrestling with the tortures supervening on the untoward development of his strange creation. He, too, was cruelly exercised by the unexpected wonders that sprang up in the wake of his "very nearly faultless monster" after that agent had fairly struck out on his own account. He fled afar, and made every effort to avoid him, but his sin was prone to find him out even in the uttermost parts of the earth. He exhausted his ingenuity in discovering every possible contiguity of shade that would hide him, and every vast wilderness in which he might roam in lonely misery ; but the creature of his heart and strength and understanding was ubiquitous, hopelessly present, even as mocking Care that sits behind the horseman. Mr. Henley, too, struggles to get free from Stevenson, but finds him in constantly recurring biographies, monographs, estimates, and what not. He avoids his books—those painful products of the hard toil by which he nourished their author into strength—and he seeks the pleasant shades of Lamb and Hazlitt, the romantic retreats of Scott and Thackeray and Dickens, nay even the universe of Shakespeare itself, only to find that his efforts are all in vain. R. L. S. is with him, and will not be denied, and the world is now asked to sympathize with his mourning.

Meanwhile trustful souls have accepted Mr. Henley and certain journalistic henchmen as impeccable prophets on their own showing, and have duly completed the solemn apotheosis of Mr. R. L. Stevenson. Mr. Henley's abortion has been formally and triumphantly exalted into high places. Not only have cousins and others written his biography, as one of those whose burial-place Pericles declared to be the world, but his schoolfellows have been allowed to blossom into purring authorship on the strength of intimate acquaintance, and writers of literary text-books have solemnly recognized him as one of the potent forces of letters in these decadent days. If he is not a shepherd of the seals he is at least a triton of the minnows, and there is infinite pother over his inherent greatness. The publishers of a series of books under the general title of "Famous Scots" distribute a prospectus of their monographs with ornamental covering, prominent on which are prints representing the most distinguished Scotsmen of all time. To simplify identification they considerately print the names under the respective portraits, which (taken chronologically) are found to be John Knox, Robert Burns, Walter Scott, and R. L. Stevenson. Thus do we find what Mr. Henley has to answer for ! It is not as a man of letters only that this "nearly faultless monster " wins distinction here, but it is as a representative Scotsman. The series, of which he and his compeers are taken to be outstanding ornaments, includes books on patriots like Wallace and Bruce, on physicians, statesmen, poets, historians, and yet Stevenson is the only one among them whose genius the publishers and their advisers have deemed worthy of being associated with the three about whom there is no possibility of doubt. This concrete presentment is a striking illustration of the work accomplished by Mr. Henley and his coadjutors. They persisted in comparing Stevenson with Scott; he was not, they admitted, his equal in invention and breadth of work, but he had that charm of style which Mr. Henley now says palls upon his taste; and, at any rate, it was safe to assert that he was the foremost of Scott's successors. The general result is that, apparently, no one of the Scottish "makers" is so great as Stevenson in the present estimate of his influential fellow-countrymen; that Knox is the only man between them and Burns that can be considered on the same page with him; and that he and Sir Walter Scott represent the nineteenth century together and alone. Allan Ramsay, Hume, Smollett, Robertson, Christopher North, Sir William Hamilton, Thomas Carlyle—to mention only a few men of letters, and to exclude statesmen and warriors altogether—are of a lower order of greatness, according to the prevalent method of estimate. If due effect is to follow the pathetic expression of Mr. Henley's sorrows there will need to be a revision of view. But perhaps the mischief has already reached too far, and time alone may be expected to adjust the perspective.   THOMAS BAYNE.

"BROD."

AMONG the Scottish proverbs given by Ray in the second edition of his 'Collection of Proverbs,' 1678, is this one, "It is hard to fling at the brod (a stick that children use when they play at penny-prick) or kick at the prick." In the sense in which it is there used, brod meant a goad, such as was used for driving oxen, a straight and pointed weapon. Hence another Scottish saying, or a variation of the same one, "He was never a good aver that flung at the brod," meaning a draught ox that resented the use of the goad, kicked at the prick.

Another meaning of the word was a flat piece of wood, such as the top of a table, from which it came to signify the small table or stool placed at church doors in Scotland to receive the contributions of the congregation for the poor. In some churches these collection stools had no plate or basin, but

merely the top scooped or hollowed out for the reception of coin. On all occasions an elder stood by to watch and guard and be responsible for the safe custody of the amount contributed.

Robert Burns makes no mention of lifting the collection by ladles, nor does he use the word brod, but he writes:—

> When by the plate we set our nose,
>   Weel heaped up wi' ha'pence,
> A greedy glow'r Black Bonnet throws,
>   An' we maun draw our tippence.

In Mr. Colville's admirable little book, 'Byways of History,' the following mention is made of one of the items in a Glasgow merchant's ledger about the year 1621:—

"Here occurs the interesting item of half a dozen kirk stools. For long after this period pews were unknown, the worshippers carrying their folding creepies to church with them......Often the stools remained in the charge of the beadle, from whom a stranger might obtain the use of one for a consideration."

I think these six stools must have been for church-door collections. Half a dozen would have been a very small number to supply as seats for worshippers at even one church on ordinary occasions, and there were often overflow congregations in a tent in the churchyard at Communion times. Folding or clasp stools, and chairs too, were used in great numbers. In the records of the kirk session of Kilmarnock, under date 1676, mention is made of

"the great oppression that is in the church floore through a multitude of chaires......whereby many old deserving women cannot win neir to heir sermon......The session doe unanimouslie conclude that ther be only five score chaires in the kirk floore."

And in the records of the kirk session of the West Church (St. Cuthbert's), Edinburgh, there is an entry as to a "Visitation of Presbytery" in 1711, when among other "uttencills" found in possession were "six pouther basons" and "six wanscot stools for the collections." I remember that in some of the larger churches in Edinburgh in the early fifties of last century it was customary to have two plates at each of the entrances—in St. Stephen's Church, for instance, which had three entrances.

Galt, in his 'Ayrshire Legatees' (Blackwood's Magazine, July, 1820), makes more than one allusion to church-door collections; but his spelling of brod is peculiar:—

"We had taken a gold guinea in our hand, but there was no broad at the door......I asked at him for the plate......No wonder that there is no broad at the door to receive the collection for the poor."

In the story of the eccentric elder at

Muthill, as told by Dean Ramsay, *brod* is used in the double sense of a goad and an instrument for taking a collection :—

"As he went round with the ladle, he reminded such members of the congregation as seemed backward in their duty, by giving them a poke with the brod, and making in an audible whisper such remarks as these, ' Wife at the braid mailin, mind the puir'; ' Lass wi' the braw plaid, mind the puir.'"

By about the year 1715 it had become customary in many Scottish churches to have a large black board on which were inscribed the names of benefactors, and this was known as the legacy *brod*.

A board for the game of draughts used to be known in Scotland as a *dambrod*—hence the common name, still in use, of the dambrod pattern in articles of napery.

The boards of a book were often called *brods*, as, for example, in the following quotation from a kirk session's records in 1703: "For a calf's skinn to be a cover to ye Kirke bible. For dressing ye skinn bought to cover ye Kirke bible, and alm'd leither to fasten ye cover to ye brods."

We read, too, of painted *brods*—paintings on wood. W. S.

'DICTIONARY OF NATIONAL BIOGRAPHY':
NOTES AND CORRECTIONS.
(*Continued from* 9th S. vi. 325.)

Supplement, Vol. I.

P. 83 a, l. 2. For "afterwards" read *now*.

P. 160 b, "Tangiers"; 161 a, "Tangier."

Pp. 169-71. W. J. E. Bennett also published a pamphlet on the Mackonochie case—'Obedience to the Lesser ; Disobedience to the Greater.'

P. 194. Edward Bickersteth, Dean of Lichfield, took a Licence in Theology at Durham ; see more in the *Durham University Journal*, x. 80-1.

P. 204 a, l. 14. For "John Edward" read *Edward John*.

P. 212. Blagdon's ed. of Dr. Johnson's 'Poems' was published by Suttaby & Crosby in 1806.

P. 228 b, l. 17. For "afterwards" read *now*.

P. 229 a. "Wathington"? probably *Whatlington*.

P. 230. Boehm's Jubilee coins were not successful.

P. 251 b, l. 38. For "and February" read *February and March*.

P. 256 a, "Wilshere"; 257 b, "Wilshire."

P. 260 b. "Brantingham, near Barnard Castle, Durham." Brantingham is near Brough, on the Humber, in the East Riding of Yorkshire.

P. 284 b, l. 5. "Parental legislation." Perhaps *paternal* may be intended.

P. 321 b, l. 27 from foot. Correct press.

P. 344. George Burnett. The controversies between him and Joseph Foster should be mentioned. See also the *Genealogist*, N.S., vi. 213-5.

P. 358 b. George Butler, "admitted *ad eundem*" what ?

Pp. 359-60. Dean Butler printed his Westminster School Commemoration Sermon, and also one in memory of Canon Liddon, in Lincoln Cathedral, 1890.

P. 381 b. Sir Alex. Campbell. For "village of Heydon" read *town of Hedon*. His father, James Campbell, described as of Hedon, surgeon, a bachelor, married at Hedon, 31 July, 1811, Lavinia Scatcherd Roberts, of that place, spinster. For Thomas Sandwith, father of Sir Alexander's wife, see 'D.N.B.,' vol. l. 281 b.

P. 396 b. W. L. R. Cates. "Articled clerk" must be an error ; he could not attempt "to establish a practice" before he had been articled.

P. 418. Mrs. Charles's first publication was 'Light in the Dark Places ; or, Memorials of Christian Life in the Middle Ages,' translated from Neander, 1850, without her name.

P. 421 b, l. 29. Correct press.

Vol. II.

P. 7, l. 11 from foot. Correct press.

P. 9 b, l. 7. For "Paschal" read *Pascal*.

P. 58 b. "Returned to Gainsborough." Nothing has been mentioned of her having been there before.

P. 59 a, l. 4 from foot. For "Bason's" read *Baron's*.

P. 123 b. For "afterwards" read *now*.

P. 124 a, l. 8 from foot. "Pseudepigraphia"?

P. 128. Archd. Denison also printed 'The Present Persecution. A Letter to the Lord Bishop of Rochester' (on the Tooth case), 1876, and 'Some Outlines of the History of Philosophy. A Paper read at Hull,' 1879.

Pp. 130-1. William Denton. See more of him in *Church Times*, 6 January, 1888 ; *Church Quarterly Review*, ii. 260 ; Spurgeon, ' Commentaries' ; he also printed a sermon, ' Christianity, True Manliness,' preached at Forest School, Walthamstow, 1875. He was a contributor to 'N. & Q.' He married Jane, youngest daughter of William Hurst Ashpitel ; she died at St. Leonards-on-Sea, 9 September, 1901.

P. 175 b. Edersheim was not Grinfield Lecturer in 1890, for he died in March, 1889.

P. 232 a. For "Sedburgh" read *Sedbergh*.

P. 255 b, l. 3. For "Mary's" read *Mary*.

P. 268 b. The Durham degree was D.C.L., not LL.D.

Pp. 330-2. Sir Henry Goodyer. There are three epigrams in John Owen's collections, one being on the death of his wife.

P. 445. "Present." In other places "afterwards" has been used.

Vol. III.

P. 1. Bishop W. How. See *Durham University Journal*. xii. 414, 428.

Pp. 62-3. Samuel Kettlewell. See *Durham University Journal*, x. 197-8.

P. 78, Dean Lake. See more of him in *Durham University Journal*, xii. 464 ; xiii. 48, and elsewhere.

P. 78 a, l. 2 from foot. For "court's" read *courts*.

P. 78 b, l. 17. For "Katherine" read *Katharine*.

P. 91. Mr. Lenihan was a contributor to 'N. & Q.' See 8ᵗʰ S. ix. 40.

P. 215 b, Vergil ; 216 b, Virgil.

P. 216 b, l. 10 from foot. Correct press.

Pp. 221-3. F. W. Newman. See *Athenæum*, 9 October, 1897 ; 'N. & Q.,' 9ᵗʰ S. i. 251.

P. 293. Sims Reeves. The *Illustrated London News*, 11 December, 1847, p. 388, has a portrait of him as Edgardo.

P. 374. Sir Arthur Sullivan. See *Illustrated London News*, 12 April, 1862, p. 365.

P. 397 a, last line. For "Bishopsthorpe" read *Bishopthorpe*.

P. 507 b. Mary Ward's inscription at Osoaldwick is as follows : "To loue the poore perseuer in the same liue dy and Rise with them was all the ayme of Mary Ward who Hauing Lived 60 years and 8 days dyed the 20 of Jan. 1645."

Throughout the 'Dictionary' the exact dates and places of the consecration of bishops, and the names of the consecrators, might well have been added. In many of the biographies it is not stated where the person spent the bulk of his life. "University College" is often mentioned without the needful addition of "London," a tiresome and pretentious way of writing, not a little ridiculous in the eyes of Oxford men. The stupid phrase "ill-health" occurs times out of count.   W. C. B.

HOLTS AT WINCHESTER.—In the life in the 'D.N.B.,' vol. xxvii. p. 202, of Sir John Holt (1642-1710), the famous Chief Justice of the King's Bench, it is stated that he was "educated at Abingdon Grammar School, Winchester College, and Oriel College, Oxford"; but, so far as Winchester is concerned, this statement is not supported by the authority cited for it, Wood's 'Athenæ Oxon.,' iv. 505. I cannot find any record that Sir John Holt was a Wykehamist, and suspect that the statement in the 'Dictionary' is erroneous. Can any reader throw light upon this matter ?

The statement is possibly due to confusion between Sir John Holt and the Mr. Holt, M.P., who on 18 June, 1689, upon the question whether Sir Edward Herbert should be excepted from the Bill of Indemnity, informed the House that he had his education at Winchester College with Herbert, and pleaded in vain for his old schoolfellow (Cobbett's 'Parl. Hist.,' v. 336). Mr. Cotton Minchin, in 'Our Public Schools.' identifies this member with Henry Holt, Winchester scholar 1660 (Kirby). But according to the 'Return of Members,' the only Holt then in the House was Richard Holt, M.P. for Lymington, Hants. I should be grateful for particulars of this Richard Holt. He is not mentioned in Mr. Kirby's 'Scholars,' and I therefore suppose that he was a commoner at Winchester.

The above Henry Holt was a soldier who, after acting as adjutant of the Holland Regiment, became colonel of the Duke of Bolton's Regiment on service in the West Indies. He was afterwards colonel of a regiment of marines, and rose to be lieutenant-general (see Dalton's 'English Army Lists'). He died in Cecil Street, Strand, on 19 December, 1714 (Le Neve's 'Monuments,' 293). In 1699 he married Lucy Hare, of Docking, Norfolk (Harl. Soc. Publ., xxiv. 234), who proved his will (P.C.C, 25 Fagg). The probate shows that Mr. Kirby's statement that Henry Holt was knighted is incorrect. Who were his parents ?   H. C.

GEORGES I.-IV. (See *ante*, p. 100.)—There is a version of the lines which opens more crisply than the one here cited :—

> Vile as George the First was reckoned,
> Viler still was George the Second.

           ST. SWITHIN.

"DOUBLE JOES."—It has been stated in some of the daily papers that an enterprising American, immediately on the issue of King Edward VII.'s stamp, addressed 10,000 letters to himself with Queen Victoria's stamp and Edward VII.'s stamp, under one post-mark, dated 1 January, 1902. These treasures he is retailing at a dollar each, and the trade name is "Double Joes," a name that was formerly given to gold coins of Ferdinand and Isabella with the heads of both sovereigns on the face. "Double Joes" can still be manufactured, but they can no longer be given the historic post-mark of 1 January, 1902. As the name is likely to survive, it may be as well to note its origin.

B. D. MOSELEY.

"SHINNANICKIN'": "HANNICROCHEMENS." —Most words among the major parts of speech carry with them their own pictures, so to speak ; and it would appear that these two words have companion pictures that may be described as of the bizarre order. The first is frequently used as a Lancs dialect word, and perhaps most often in the Liverpool district, but it is not to be found in the three glossaries of the vernacular that I have consulted. In a mild sense it means "shammocking," "shaffling," or, as polite speech has it, "shuffling." But there is a spirit of contention, and a putting forth of methodical effort, suggested by *shinnanickin'* that these meanings do not naturally convey. It may be an Irish slang word. If due allowance is made for the plurals, Cotgrave's meanings for the word *hannicrochemens* provide the best synonyms. He gives for the O.F. word "subtilties, entanglements, cavils, troublesome vexations." M.F. uses and spells the word differently ; and indeed in the sixteenth century it took the form "anicrochements," as when a certain M. le connétable was instructed to make "quelques petits anicrochements" (see Littré, Supplement, *s.v.* 'Anicroche'). This, too, was shinnanickin'.

ARTHUR MAYALL.

PORTRAIT OF ERASMUS. — In a book entitled 'Plantz, Povrtraitz et Descriptions de Plvsievrs Villes et Forteresses,' by Antoine du Pinet (fol., Lyon, 1564), occurs on p. 78 a woodcut portrait of Erasmus, said to be taken from the life. It is three-quarter face, and looks to the right. On his head he wears a cap, and round his neck a fur collar. The size of the woodcut is 4 in. by 3¼ in. The author speaks thus of it :—

"Apres la description de Germanie, ie ne veux oublyer de mettre le pourtraict du Grand Erasme, lequel i'ay recouuré d'vn mien amy Alleman, qui l'auoit fait au vif. Car encores fait-il bon voir la physionomie de ces grans personnages, qui ont eu vn esprit diuin & celeste : veu que ceste representation induyt encores les hōmes à les admirer......Et par-ainsi veu que nostre Erasme (ie le diz nostre, car il nous a bien seruy) a tant illustré nostre Siecle par ses œuures diuines, ie ne me suis contenté vous faire entendre qu'il estoit de Roterdam, ville maritime de Hollande : ains ay bien voulu monstrer par son pourtrait, fait au vif, que ce petit corps (car il estoit bas de stature) a seruy d'organe à vn esprit autant diuin, & autant excellent qui ayt esté depuis Cicero."

It is not mentioned in Larousse, 'Grand Dic. Univ. du XIX. Siècle,' where there is a fairly full account of the portraits of Erasmus, but doubtless some reader of 'N. & Q.' will be able to name the artist.

W. R. B. PRIDEAUX.

"CE N'EST QUE LE PREMIER PAS QUI COUTE." —I should be glad to learn what is the authentic story of the origin of this saying. I dimly remember its being attributed to Voltaire (or some other wit), who was asked by a lady, "Can it be really true that St. Denis walked *all the way* from Montmartre to Paris with his head in his hand ?" to which query came the answer, "Ah, madame, ce n'est que," &c. In a review in the *Times* Literary Supplement of 14 February I find the following sentence :—

"It was this Cardinal [the 'gifted but indolent' Cardinal Polignac] who, when remonstrating with a sceptical lady, related that St. Denis carried his head in his hand for a distance of seven leagues, and received for a reply, 'C'est le premier pas qui coûte.'"

R. B. LITCHFIELD.

31, Kensington Square, W.

["Il n'y a que le premier pas qui coûte."— Madame Deffand, Lettre à d'Alembert, 7 Juillet, 1763.

"Il n'y a que le premier obstacle qui coûte à vaincre, la pudeur."—Bossuet, 'Pensées Chrétiennes et Morales,' ix.

Le premier pas, mon fils, que l'on fait dans le monde, Est celui dont dépend le reste de nos jours.

Voltaire, 'L'Indiscret,' I. i.]

ISLE OF DOGS.—The meaning of this name now given to Poplar Marsh has often been discussed, or rather guessed at, with the aid of fiction, instead of looking to its origin, which—it seems to me—at once explains it. Elizabethan maps—notably the one reproduced in Bruce's report on the defences of 1588—show that the name belonged then to a small islet—a mud bank—off the southwest corner of the marsh, which, from its situation, must have been a trap for every dead dog or cat that came down the river. The channel between the islet and the main has long ago been silted up ; perhaps the islet itself has been washed away ; and dead bodies of all kinds, no longer trapped there, are now stranded on the opposite shore, where the burying of those of one class is a regular charge on the rates. But the name Isle of Dogs has been extended to the whole marsh, and a mythical kennel invented to account for it.

J. K. LAUGHTON.

AMAZON.—The ordinary derivation of this word (ἀ- and μαζός, from a supposed mutilation, probably invented to account for it) is said by Prof. Skeat, in his 'Etymological Dictionary,' to be "perhaps fabulous," which

expression is repeated in the errata and addenda to his third edition, with the addition, "and the story an invention intended to satisfy a popular craving for an etymology." But Prof. Ridgeway, in 'The Early Age of Greece,' vol. i. p. 651, puts before us the much more probable theory that the word means that that people were very far from being vegetarians, the true etymology being from ἀ- and μάζα. This is suggested by a passage in Æschylus ('Suppl.,' 283), τὰς ἀνάνδρους κρεοβόρους Ἀμαζόνας, the husbandless, flesh-eating Amazons. This may be new to some of your readers, and worth a corner in 'N. & Q.'   W. T. Lynn.
Blackheath.

[The 'H.E.D.' in its first part, issued in 1884, stated that the Greeks explained the word as from ἀ and μαζός, but Dr. Murray added that this was probably a popular etymology to explain a foreign word.]

"Opodeldoc." (See 7th S. vi. 167, 316.)— Dr. Murray will soon arrive at this word, and he may be glad to know that a discussion has recently taken place in one of the organs of the drug trade as to what opodeldoc really is. In one or two cases that I have noticed the definitions of popular names of drugs given in the 'H.E.D.' have not been quite correct. In the Lap—Leisurely section, for instance, *lapis infernalis* is said to signify lunar caustic. It is true that under 'Infernal' quotations are given which seem to justify this definition, and it is also true that lunar caustic has this name assigned to it in some continental pharmacopœias; but I believe I am correct in saying that in England it is almost invariably given to caustic potash. I rely partly on my own experience, which is fairly wide, and partly on what I find in our dispensatories. These, without exception, so far as my own collection goes, give the name to caustic potash if they mention it at all. My collection of these books is not a large one, but it begins with Culpeper (1654) and ends with Phillips (1851).

The opodeldoc of Paracelsus was undoubtedly a plaster, but he gives several different formulas for it. The first occurrence of the word in English (so far as I know) is in a version of the 'Chirurg. Min.' of Paracelsus, published in 1656 under the title 'Paracelsus his Dispensatory and Chirurgery,' in which the translator invariably uses the form *oppodeltoch*, and applies it to a plaster. How it afterwards came to be transferred to a liniment composed mainly of soap I do not know; but from the notes of different correspondents of the *Chemist and Druggist*, and an article in that journal, under date 1 Feb.,

I gather that the first saponaceous preparation to which it was given was the *Unguentum opodeldoch* of the Edinburgh Pharmacopœia, 1722. The name, however, continued in use for a time in the old sense, for an *Emplastrum opodeldoc*, founded on that of Paracelsus, appears in Alleyne's 'Dispensatory,' 1733. In 1744 the Edinburgh *Unguentum* took the name *Balsamum saponaceum, vulgo oppodeldoch*; and in 1745 it appeared, in a simplified form, in the London Pharmacopœia, under the name *Linimentum saponaceum*. Of this preparation the *Linimentum saponis* of the present British Pharmacopœia is the lineal descendant, and to this, in England at any rate, the name opodeldoc is generally applied. In the Merchant Shipping Acts (1867), however, for some unknown reason, opodeldoc is described as liniment of opium, which is really composed of equal parts of soap liniment and tincture of opium; and on the Continent the name is given to a preparation based on Steers's Opodeldoc, a famous nostrum of the eighteenth century, which was, I believe, an imitation of the old Edinburgh *Unguentum opodeldoch*, with the addition of ammonia. In Scotland, I understand, liniment of opium is frequently sold as opodeldoc, in accordance with the Acts of Parliament just mentioned. It is to be hoped that in the 'H.E.D.' the word will be properly defined.   C. C. B.

"Penile" in 'Nero Cæsar.' (See *ante*, p. 22.)—The Rev. L. Davies, in his 'Supplementary English Glossary,' gives an earlier quotation for *penile*, from Speed's 'Hist. Great Britain' (1611), bk. ix. chap. xii.
     H. P. L.

Sir Henry Cromwell.—I am not aware whether the following reference has been noticed by writers on the Cromwell family:

"Also I give and bequeathe to either of Sir Henry Cromwell Knighte and to the ladye his wife and to every one of theire children a black gowne apiece."

I have extracted it from a copy (which lately came into my possession by the death of a near relative) of the will of Sir Thomas White, Knt., citizen and alderman of London and merchant tailor, the will being in the Prerogative Court of Canterbury. It is dated 8 Elizabeth, being the 8 November, 1566, and the year of his death. This Sir Thomas is the well-known founder of St. John's College, Oxford.

The grandfather of the great Oliver was Sir Henry Cromwell, Knt., and as Oliver was born in 1599 the dates and name would agree with the conclusion that the friend of the founder of St. John's was the grand-

father of the Protector, whose father, therefore, would have received one of Sir Thomas's
black gowns.   D. J.

Queries.

We must request correspondents desiring information on family matters of only private interest
to affix their names and addresses to their queries,
in order that the answers may be addressed to them
direct.

The London Library Catalogue.—The
following is the final list of queries
which have arisen during the preparation
of the new catalogue now in the press. All
ordinary books of reference and catalogues
have been consulted, and if there is a query
about an apparently well-known person it is
because there is disagreement between two
or more authorities. Will persons who are
kind enough to answer these queries give the
exact source of their information, without
which no statement can be accepted?

(1) Wanted full Christian names and particulars of :—

Lévy (le Président de). Journal Histor. ou Fastes de
    Louis XV. 2 vols. 1766.
St. Marie (Count). Algeria in 1845. 1846.
Scott (Col.   ). K.S.F., K.C. Journal in the
    Esmailla of Abd-el-Kader, &c. 1842.
Smith (Edgar). Letter to the Chancellor of the
    Exchequer proposing that Public Stocks should
    be rendered Transferable, &c. 1852.
Stewarton (   ). Revolutionary Plutarch. Fourth
    edition, 1805. The Female Revolutionary
    Plutarch. 1806. Memoirs of Talleyrand. 1805.
    Secret History of the Court and Cabinet of St.
    Cloud. 1806.
Walker (Mrs.). Eastern Life and Scenery, with
    Excursions in Asia Minor, &c. 2 vols. 1886.
Warren (le Comte Edouard de). L'Inde Anglaise en
    1843. 3 tomes. 1844.
Wickham (J. A.). Synopsis of Doctrine of Baptism.
    1850.
Williams (D. E.). Life and Correspondence of Sir
    T. Lawrence. 2 vols. 1831.
Williamson (A.). British Industries and Foreign
    Competition. 1894.
Wilson (Mrs. R. F.). The Christian Brothers. 1883.
Wood (C. F.). Yachting Cruise in the South Seas.
    1875.
Wylde (A. B.). '83 to '87 in the Soudan. 1888.

(2) Who are the authors of the following?—

Commonplace Arguments against Administration,
    with Answers. 1780. (? Richard Tickell.)
Scenes and Adventures in Spain. 1835–40. By
    Poco Mas. 2 vols. 1845.
State of the Nation. 1765. (? D. Hartley, M.P.)
Viking, The. By M. R. 1879.
Volunteer. The True History of the Origin of our
    Volunteer Army. 1867.
Vonved the Dane. 1861.
Warm Corners in Egypt. By "One who was in
    Them." 1886.
White Witch, The. 1884.

Whitecross and the Bench. By author of 'Five
    Years' Penal Servitude.' 1879.
Wild Flowers from the Glens. By E. L. L. 1840.
    (? Eliza Lynn Linton.)

(3) Are these the same person?—

Douglas (J. W.). World of Insects. 1856.
Douglas (John William). British Hemiptera. Vol. I.
    1865.
Rutherford (John). Fenian Conspiracy. 1877.
Rutherford (John). The Troubadours. 1873.
Stead (Alfred). How to grow Peaches. 1886.
Stead (Alfred) and Mackenzie (W. D.). South
    Africa. 1900.
Stuart (J. M.). Ancient Goldfields of Africa. 1891.
Stuart (J. Maitland). How No. 1 became 1½ in
    Norway. 1890.
Taylor (Augustus). Poems. 1874.
Taylor (John William Augustus). Translator of
    Vinet (A. R.), 'Solitude Recommended.' 1841.
Westoby (W. A. S.) Adhesive Postage Stamps of
    Europe. 1898–1900.
Westoby (W. A. S). Legal Guide for Residents in
    France. 1858.

(4) Is the following a pen-name?—

Search (Simon). Spirit of the Times. 1790.
            C. T. Hagberg Wright,
                    Secretary and Librarian.

[Perhaps R. B. may be willing to supplement the
information with regard to " Poco Mas" which he
gave 9th S. i. 413.]

Brook and Brookes Families.—I shall be
glad if any persons interested in genealogical
and historical facts concerning these families
will kindly communicate with me, in view of
publishing a general history of the Brook,
Brooke, and Brookes families of Great Britain
and her empire.   Fred. Hitchin-Kemp.
    6, Beechfield Road, Catford, S.E.

Household of George III.—Can any of
your correspondents inform me where it
would be possible to find the names of the
tutors of Prince Adolphus, son of George III.?
I should be greatly obliged for help, as this
is the only clue possessed of a relative whom
it is desired to trace.   Clifton.

Shakespeare's Vocabulary.—I am told
that some ingenious person once took the
trouble to produce a list of the words that
he believed to occur in Shakespeare's plays
for the first time in English literature, and
that such list contains some 2,000 words. As
an instance of misdirected ignorance this
must be interesting; and I shall be very
grateful to any of your readers who will send
me a post-card to say where that list may be
consulted.   Robt. J. Whitwell..
    70, Banbury Road, Oxford.

Gurbs or De Gurbs Barony. — Stephen
Gurbs, Surrey, matriculated at King's College, Aberdeen, in 1823, and took the degree
of M.A. there in 1829 as Hutton Prizeman—

i.e., the most distinguished graduate of the year. He appears to have been known in later life as the Baron de Gurbs. Information is desired as to this barony.   Q. K. B.

HUXLEY AS REVIEWER.—In Darwin's 'Life and Letters,' vol. ii. p. 189, Huxley wrote:— "The only review I ever had qualms of conscience about, on the ground of needless savagery, is one I wrote on the 'Vestiges.'" I believe Mr. Huxley's review of the 'Vestiges of Creation' was written about 1853. Can any of your readers tell me where it was published?   FRANCIS DARWIN.
Botanical Laboratory, Cambridge.

HYMN OF ST. PETER DAMIANI.—Will you or any of your correspondents inform me in what work (easily procurable) I can find the Latin version of St. Peter Damiani's hymn "Ad perennis vitæ fontem meus sitivit arida"?   ALEXANDER PATRICK.
1, Higher Brimley Terrace, Teignmouth.

[This hymn of Cardinal Damiani is given in Loftie's 'Latin Year,' p. 124, 'Dominica Quarta a Trinitate,' Pickering, 1873. This is not a common book, but some one may possibly be able to copy the poem for you at the British Museum or elsewhere. But for its length we would ourselves have quoted it. The 'Latin Year' is a book to be secured when it is found. Daniel's 'Thesaurus Hymnologicus,' Mone's 'Hymni Latini Medii Ævi,' and Trench's 'Sacred Latin Poetry' will probably contain it; but these we do not possess.]

"CISSURA ROBARUM WALLENSIUM."—In the account of Robert de Wodehouse, Cofferer of the Wardrobe, 1330-32, in MS. Tanner 197, fo. 54 b, are two entries, marked in the margin "Cissura robarum Wallensium":—

"Audoeno ap yeuan & viij. sociis suis sagittariis Wallensibus de dono Regis pro cissura robarum suarum, cuilibet xij*d.* per manus dicti Audoeni ibidem [sc. apud Bere Wicum super Twedam] xxiij die Aprilis, ix*s.*"
"Johanni le Waleys & Ade Gough sagittariis Wallensibus de dono Regis pro cissura robarum suarum vtrique xij*d.* per manus dicti Johannis ibidem secundo die Maij, ij*s.*"

Are there any contemporary pictures showing in what way the Welsh dress had to be modified to suit that of English archers?
O. O. H.

ARMS OF LE NEVE FOSTER.—The arms of this family, I believe, are Argent, on cross sable five fleurs-de-lys. The crest is a lily springing from ducal coronet. I should like to know the family motto.   P. L. N. F.

TITIAN'S 'SACRED AND PROFANE LOVE.'—One or two years ago appeared in an English review or weekly paper a very interesting note on the so-called 'Amore Profano e Sacro,' the famous picture of Titian in the Galeria Borghese. It was said that in a Paris edition of the 'Argonautica' of Valerius Flaccus, printed in the middle of the sixteenth century, a copy of the 'Amore Divino e Profano' figured as a frontispiece, and that the tenor of the masterwork would be Venus persuading Medea to fly with Jason. I shall feel obliged for the name of the publisher.
DR. MAX MAAS.
Munich.

'SWEET RICHARD.'—In Miss Strickland's 'Lives of the Queens of England,' vol. i., in the account of the life of Isabella of France, second wife of Richard II., occurs a reference to a ballad composed by Owen Glendower entitled 'Sweet Richard.' Can any one furnish information as to where the words of this ballad may be found?   E. A. M.
[See 8ᵗʰ S. ix. 388.]

'LA BLANCHE FÉE.'—Can any of your readers tell me the name of the author and publisher of a French song called 'La Blanche Fée,' which I used to hear some forty years ago in Paris and Versailles?
F. E. R. POLLARD-URQUHART.
Castle Pollard, Westmeath.

PARISH REGISTERS: THEIR CARE AND PROTECTION.—I should like an expression of opinion from some of your readers more experienced than I am in such matters on the following state of affairs, which—through a search made recently in the marriage registers of a certain parish (the parish shall be nameless in order to wound no susceptibilities)—was disclosed to me by the correspondent who had undertaken the search on my behalf.

I was not seeking the date of the marriage —that I knew already—but I wanted to prove the existence at that date of a certain person, who was, I believe, one of the witnesses signing the record of that marriage, and accordingly I asked for a complete copy of that certificate of marriage. The reply comes back that the original registers, up to a certain date late in the eighteenth century, have been recopied and then destroyed. The copies omit the names of the witnesses and other matter not judged material, the object seemingly having been to reduce the number of volumes to be stored. The destroyed registers have therefore been replaced by a record taken from them, or purporting so to have been, which contains at the head of each page a note of the year, and then, in two columns, the precise date of the particular marriage in one column, and the names of the couple who were married on the corresponding line in the adjoining column. Each page of this list is signed by the curate and the two churchwardens at foot, as having been examined and found correct.

I confess that the whole proceeding seems to me monstrous, and possibly, if a title or inheritance were at stake, the courts might hold that this copy of a portion only of a missing register could not be accepted as evidence. As to the suppression of the witnesses' names, apart from other objections, the whole picturesqueness of an entry is gone when the materials for reconstructing that family party have been taken away.

H. G. K.

JOHN DYKE ACLAND, DIED 1778.—Is it known whether this soldier and politician was ever at Harrow School? "J. D. Acland" is apparently cut upon one of the panels in the fourth-form room; but the first letter may be only a clerical error for "T.," and the tenth and eleventh baronets (Sir Thomas D. Acland) were undoubtedly at the school.

A. R. BAYLEY.

St. Margaret's, Malvern.

DESCENT OF THE TSAR.—At the time of the Crimean war it was stated in various newspapers that the Tsar of Russia was a lineal descendant of Jingis Khan. Can this be proved, or was it a mere guess or fable?

N. M. & A.

SIR WILLIAM DAMSELL OR DANSELL was one of the knights made at the coronation of Queen Mary in 1553. M.P. for Arundel in 1555, and for Hastings 1563-7. His will proved in 1582 in P.C.C., wherein he is described as "of London." Any information as to his parentage, &c., will oblige. I believe that at one period he was on the Council of the Welsh Marches.

W. D. PINK.

APPLE-TREE FOLK-LORE.—Why is the apple-tree specially connected with Christmas? That it is so the ancient rites of our cider counties bear witness. Moreover, continental customs show that the same belief is held abroad.

To begin with, in Courland apple-trees are struck with a stick on the first day of Christmas, so that there may be a good crop of fruit (W. Mannhardt, 'Der Baumkultus der Germanen,' p. 276). And in Swabia a violent wind at Christmas foreshows a fruitful year (Birlinger, 'Volksthümliches aus Schwaben,' vol. i. p. 466), while in Voigtland they say: "If the wind shakes the trees well at Christmas there will be much fruit." Also: "If

much 'Rauchfrost' is on the trees there will be much fruit" (Köhler, 'Volksbrauch im Voigtlande,' pp. 341, 342). The wind is also imagined to be potent in Berry, where it is said :—

> Plus les avents sont venteux
> Plus les vergers sont plantureux.

For the peasant asserts that high winds blowing during "les avents de Noël" render the trees fruitful (Laisnel de la Salle, 'Croyances et Légendes du Centre de la France,' vol. ii. p. 279).

The Montenegrins place the remains of the Christmas log between the boughs of young fruit-trees to promote their growth ('Der Baumkultus,' p. 225).

According to Baader ('Volkssagen aus dem Lande Baden,' p. 47), apple-trees bloom, cast their flower, and bear fruit during the Christmas matins; and from Gerard's 'Land beyond the Forest' (vol. ii. p. 44) we learn that on Sylvester Night—that is, New Year's Eve—bright moonlight means full granaries among the Transylvanian Saxons, which seems an allied belief, as does the German notion which teaches "so many stars to be seen in the heavens on Christmas night, so many 'Mandeln' of corn at harvest" ('Der Baumkultus,' p. 234. See also 'Volksthümliches aus Schwaben,' i. 465). The Normans, it may be remarked, will tell you, "If the sun shines on St. Eulalia's day there will be more than enough apples and cider" (F. Pluquet, 'Contes Populaires de l'Arrondissement de Bayeux,' deuxième édition, p. 130), the Voigtlanders being of opinion, according to Köhler (p. 341), that when Michaelmas falls in a waxing moon much fodder will grow in the following year.

M. P.

Replies.

HENRY VIII.
(9th S. ix. 67.)

IN the first canto of 'England's Reformation,' a Hudibrastic poem, generally known by the title of 'Ward's Cantos,' the following lines occur :—

> A blessed race !
> Race like its parent, whom we find
> A man to every vice inclined,
> Revengeful, cruel, bloody, proud,
> Unjust, unmerciful, and lewd;
> For in his wrath he spared no man,
> Nor in his lust spared any woman.

The writer (Thomas Ward, 1652-1708) in a note refers us to Dr. P. Heylin as his authority for the saying. But on consulting the latter's principal work, the 'Ecclesia Restaurata; or, the History of the Reformation of the Church of England,' this is all that I find : "Which brings into my mind a sharp, but shrewd character of the king, occurring in the writings of some, but more common in the mouths of many, that is to say, that he 'never spared woman in his lust, nor man in his anger'" (vol. i. p. 30, Cambridge, 1849). It is, therefore, a quotation, but Heylin supplies no reference, and, from his indefinite language, was apparently ignorant of the author's name. The book just quoted was published in 1661, but the phrase is to be found in a volume printed exactly twenty years before that date. In Sir Robert Naunton's 'Fragmenta Regalia' we find it given thus : "The atrocity of the father's nature was rebated in her [Elizabeth], by the mother's sweeter inclinations ; for (to take, and that no more than the character out of his own mouth) 'he never spared man in his anger, nor woman in his lust.'" I quote from the reprint in the fifth volume of the 'Harleian Miscellany,' p. 122. But it will take much stronger evidence than this to make one believe that Henry himself was the originator of so cynical a phrase. Until such be forthcoming, we may well believe that the "character" is, so to speak, a crystallization of the sayings of several writers, among whom the first is the one cited by Robert Burton in his 'Anatomy' (part iii. sec. ii. mem. ii. subs. i.) : "Nicholas Sanders relates of Henry VIII. (I know not how truly), Quod paucas vidit pulchriores quas non concupîerit, et paucissimas concupîerit quas non violârit. He saw very few maids that he did not desire, and desired fewer whom he did not enjoy." Burton's reference is simply "Vita ejus," but this must mean the celebrated work 'De Schismate Anglicano' (to give the short title used by Fuller and Heylin), which was published long before the close of the sixteenth century. This is surely authority enough for the first part of the saying ; if any be wanted for the second, we find it in the words of Sir Walter Raleigh in the preface to his 'History of the World,' p. 8, London, 1614 : "If all the pictures and patterns of a merciless prince were lost in the world, they might all again be painted to the life, out of the story of this king." And yet Peter Heylin (who quotes these words), Thomas Fuller, and Gilbert Burnet would have us believe that this "Moloch's" vices were redeemed by his virtues, and that he was a chosen instrument of the Almighty to do great things.

JOHN T. CURRY.

In Thomas Ward's 'England's Reformation, from the Time of King Henry VIII. to the End of Oates's Plot, a Poem in Four Cantos,' 1716, Henry is described as one who

In his hate spared no man,
Nor in his lust spared any woman ;
Who ne'er was rul'd by any law,
Nor gospel valued he a straw.

I quote from memory, so may not be verbally accurate.   K. P. D. E.

This terrible epigram has been long familiar to me as occurring in Naunton's 'Fragmenta Regalia.' I quote from the first edition (1641), p. 3. Naunton is writing of Queen Elizabeth :—

"The atrocitie of the Fathers nature was rebated in her, by the Mothers sweeter inclinations for to take, and that no more then the Character out of his owne mouth, *he never spared man in his Anger, nor woman in his Lust.*"

Is it possible that this attribution of the words to King Henry VIII. rests on any earlier authority than Naunton's ?

C. E. D.

'THE PALATINE'S DAUGHTER' (9ᵗʰ S. viii. 505).—The bilingual verses quoted may be compared with those (A.-S. and Lat.) in the 'Oratio Poetica,' published in 'Be Domes Dæge' (E.E.T.S.), the reading of which is, as will be seen, continuous. I append four lines :—

& se soðfæsta . summi filius .
fo on fultum . factor cosmi .
Se of aeðelre wæs . virginis partu .
Clæne acenned . Christus in orbem .

The alliteration of *wæs* and *virginis* may be noted, though well known.   H. P. L.

FATHER PAUL SARPI'S 'LETTERS,' 1693 (9ᵗʰ S. ix. 81).—Edward Browne, who was collated to the rectory of Sundridge, Kent, on 29 January, 1688/9, was described in the certificate of his collation as "clericus, artium magister." His degree may possibly provide a clue to further particulars of him. Edward Tenison, his successor in the rectory, was collated on 12 October, 1698.   H. C.

STAUNTON, WORCESTERSHIRE (9ᵗʰ S. viii. 383, 510 ; ix. 11, 92, 110).—If SIR CHARLES DILKE is able to say that there was a family of Staunton which derived its surname from Staunton in Worcestershire, *cadet quæstio.* The Staunton near Coleford, in Gloucestershire, certainly gave its name to a baronial house. Johannes de Staunton and Alicia relicta Philippi de Staunton are rated to the Subsidy of 1327, under the heading "Libertas de S'c'o Briauell', Villa de Staunton," *i.e.,* Staunton juxta Coleford. The county histories seem to imply that it was a Staunton of this house who was married to Sir William de Whittington of Pauntley. I should like to see the point cleared up.

JOHN HOBSON MATTHEWS.
Town Hall, Cardiff.

SIR GEOFFREY FENTON (9th S. ix. 107).— The 'Dictionary of National Biography,' vol. xviii., gives a life both of Sir Geoffrey (1539?–1608) and of his elder brother Edward, who commanded the Mary Rose in the fleet for opposing the Invincible Armada. They were sons of Henry Fenton, of Fenton, in the parish of Sturton (formerly Stretton-le-Steeple), Nottinghamshire, and of Cecily, daughter of John Beaumont, of Coleorton, in Leicestershire. A. R. BAYLEY.

Sir Geoffrey Fenton was a son of Henry Fenton, of Fenton, in Nottinghamshire, and of Cecily, daughter of John Beaumont, of Coleorton, in Leicestershire ('Dict. Nat. Biography,' vol. xviii. p. 323). A pedigree of the Fenton family, comprising sixteen generations, from Sir Richard Fenton, Knt., Lord of Fenton, to the children of Sir Geoffrey Fenton, will be found in 'The Visitations of the County of Nottingham in the Years 1569 and 1614,' edited by George W. Marshall, Harl. Soc., vol. iv. p. 33. E. T. B.

Sir Geoffrey Fenton was the son of Henry Fenton by Cecily, daughter of John Beaumont, of Coleorton. Henry Fenton was son of Thomas Fenton by a daughter of Thomas Burgh, of Burgh, in Yorkshire. His father was Ralph Fenton, who married Dorothy, daughter of Robert Staunton; and his father Thomas Fenton married Eleanor, daughter of Ralph Nevill, of Liversedge. Alice Weston was daughter of Robert Weston by Alice Jenyns. H. S. V.-W.

BLACK ARMLET AS A SIGN OF MOURNING (9th S. viii. 520).—The 'H. E. D.,' s.v. 'Knot,' sb. 2, and under the date 1708, gives the quotation, "The Officers to wear......a mourning Knot on their left Arm." This badge differs from the armlet, but may well be its immediate forerunner. ARTHUR MAYALL.

BRISTOW FAMILY (9th S. viii. 404).—John Bristow, of Quidenham Hall, co. Norfolk, M.P., Sub-Governor of the South Sea Company, was the son of Robert, of London, and Catherine, daughter of Robert Woolley, of London. He married Anne Judith, daughter of Paul Foisin, an East India merchant in Paris. He had issue three sons and eight daughters: 1. Henry, of Dover Street, Piccadilly, captain in the Coldstream Guards, whose four grandsons were in the H.E.I.Co.'s military service; 2. John, President of the

Board of Trade at Calcutta. represented by Bristows of Ensemere Hill, Ulleswater; 3. William, who had two sons; 1. Ann Margaret, married the Hon. H. Hobart; 2. Catherine, married Lieut.-Gen. Hon. Simon Frazer; 3. Louisa, married Tillieux Girardot, of Putney; 4. Frances, married Sir Richard Neave, Bart.; 5. Caroline, married William Henry, Lord Lyttelton; 6. Mary, d. umd.; 7. Harriet, married General Slessor, Governor of Oporto; 8. Sophia, d. umd.

JOHN RADCLIFFE.

BIBLIOGRAPHY OF THE BICYCLE (9th S. viii. 304, 490, 530; ix. 36, 117).—I have received an obliging letter from the new vicar of Stoke Poges, the Rev. J. F. Hoyle, confirming my recollections in every particular. He writes as follows :—

"The two figures you ask about have no relation to each other. The child with the 'whirligig' is an infant (? our Lord) on his mother's lap, the latter figure some three or four feet in height. The debated 'bicycle' is ridden by a very much smaller figure, and the treatment of design and colour of glass is altogether different from the former. The design is something like the enclosed (I draw from memory), and the action (in the glass) is not unlike that of one pushing or 'paddling' a hobbyhorse. He holds a trumpet as shown (? a primitive bicycle bell), and has nothing to indicate an angel."

Mr. Hoyle's sketch indicates a wooden hobbyhorse with a front and back wheel, not much more rude in construction than the hobbyhorse that immediately preceded the "bone-shaker" bicycle, but there is no indication of any steering apparatus. If there was none the machine must have been steered as well as driven by the feet, which are on the ground. The rider holds a long trumpet to his mouth with his left hand, while his right appears to be at liberty. Perhaps the trumpet was not blown so much to give a warning note as to express simple joyousness of heart, as the modern "Harry" sometimes blows a long paper trumpet now.

Mr. Hoyle describes the window as made up of fragments, thought to be chiefly brought from the old Elizabethan manor house, which was half pulled down in 1760.

I think that the Stoke Poges hobbyhorse and its rider ought certainly to be reproduced in any work on the evolution of the bicycle. J. T. F.
Durham.

EARL OF CROMARTIE (9th S. ix. 107).—With reference to this inquiry, the Earl of Cromartie was not executed, being reprieved by the king. It is believed that he owed his life mainly to his wife's intercession. At all events, the circumstances of his forfeiture and condemnation made so great an impression on the mind of his wife that on the birth of her daughter Augusta (who afterwards married Sir William Murray, Bart., of Ochtertyre) she was found to have on one side of her neck the mark of an axe with three drops of blood.   J. B P.

Miss Mary Bagot made a slight slip, as George Mackenzie, Earl of Cromartie, was not executed, but, at the earnest intercession of his wife, received a respite, and in 1749 was pardoned and allowed five hundred pounds a year out of his forfeited estates. His attainder was not removed. The story of his daughter, Lady Augusta Mackenzie, who subsequently became the wife of Sir William Murray, of Ochtertyre, is well known. Lady Cromartie was *enceinte* when sentence was pronounced upon her husband, and in the words of Jesse in his 'Memoirs of the Pretenders and their Adherents,' the little girl, who was born shortly afterwards, was "said to have borne on her neck the evident mark of an axe, which had been impressed there by the imagination of her mother, while labouring under the terrors of suspense on account of her unhappy lord."

Lord Cromartie was captured by a body of Lord Sutherland's militia in the dining-room of Dunrobin Castle on the eve of the battle of Culloden. In 1849 the title of Countess of Cromartie was revived in favour of Anne Mackenzie, wife of the third Duke of Sutherland, and is now borne by her granddaughter. In consequence of the Act of Union it was necessary to make it a peerage of the United Kingdom.   W. F. Pʀɪᴅᴇᴀᴜx.

Tʜᴇ Sᴘʟɪᴛ Iɴғɪɴɪᴛɪᴠᴇ (8ᵗʰ S. xii. 205, 375, 491).—In the bedrooms of the Charing Cross Hotel may be found one of the most striking " splits " in the following :—

"Notice.—This Room is protected by Pearson's Automatic Fire Alarm Indicator, which upon an undue rise of temperature causes the fire bells situated throughout the Hotel to instantaneously and continuously ring until attended to by the fireman on duty."

The splitting has in this case a distinct rhetorical effect, as it seems to me.   O. O. H.

"Sᴛʀᴇᴀᴍ ᴏғ ᴛᴇɴᴅᴇɴᴄʏ" (9ᵗʰ S. ix. 68).— This now common phrase may be traced further back than Matthew Arnold, Emerson, or Hazlitt. In Wordsworth's 'Excursion,' ix. 87-90, we find what is, perhaps, its true source :—

> And hear the mighty *stream of tendency*
> Uttering, for elevation of our thought,
> A clear sonorous voice, inaudible
> To the vast multitude.

Here Dr. W. Knight has this note : "A phrase familiarized to English ears by Mr. Arnold's use of it." Does the word "English" suggest in any way a possible foreign origin? It is for others to say whether the phrase was original with Wordsworth. An instance of its use without marks of quotation—one, no doubt, among very many—may be found in Dr. W. B. Pope's 'Higher Catechism of Theology' (1883), p. 269. 'The Excursion' was published in 1814. Hazlitt is obviously quoting Wordsworth.

    C. Lᴀᴡʀᴇɴᴄᴇ Fᴏʀᴅ, B.A.
Bath.

Dɪᴄᴋᴇɴsɪᴀɴᴀ : Pʜʀᴀsᴇ ᴏғ Mʀs. Gᴀᴍᴘ (9ᵗʰ S. viii. 324, 426 ; ix. 12).—I am not nearly so old as Mrs. Gamp would be were she alive now, but I remember very well a sort of "gambling machine" that was one of the chief attractions of the "stalls" that used to visit our village on the occasion of the annual feast. It consisted of a round board divided into compartments, with a revolving pillar and index finger in the centre. Each of the compartments held an article of greater or less value—as a packet of sweets, a small toy, a bootlace, or what-not—some of them being very fair pennyworths and others very bad ones. We used to pay a penny for a spin, and I dare say the excitement round the tables at Monte Carlo is not greater than ours was while the finger was revolving. I do not know whether those machines are still allowed.   C. C. B.

In 'London Labour and the London Poor,' by Henry Mayhew, vol. i. p. 204, is a whole-page engraving called 'The Coster Boy and Girl tossing the Pieman,' from a daguerreotype by Beard. At p. 196 is a description of the process, indulged in chiefly, it is said, by boys, though the pieman observes, "Gentlemen out on the spree at the late public-houses will frequently toss when they don't want the pies ; and when they win they will amuse themselves by throwing the pies at one another, or at me." There is a description given of the not very appetizing materials of which the pies were made. The date of my copy is 1861 ; but I fancy there is a much earlier edition of the work. Times have indeed altered since its issue.

    Jᴏʜɴ Pɪᴄᴋғᴏʀᴅ, M.A.
Newbourne Rectory, Woodbridge.

I remember, as a small boy in the early sixties, seeing an apparatus on a dial with a pointer, where you paid your penny and took your chance of getting any article (not a pie, I think) opposite which the pointer rested, in the booths which came in those days to the racecourse on the Roodee at Chester, for the four days of the Chester May meeting. The races were then in the afternoons, and the shows were sought after by the children in the mornings.

T. CANN HUGHES, M.A., F.S.A.
Lancaster.

PORTRAITS OF EARLY LORD MAYORS (9th S. viii. 485).—On 26 April, 1840, Mr. William Smith sold at his great rooms, 73, New Bond Street, the following lot No. 650, to Mr. Molton, Printseller, Pall Mall. It was described as

"Lord Mayors—A View of all the Right Honourable the Lord Mayors of this Honourable City of London, &c., beginning at the first year (1558) of Her Majesty's Happy Raigne and continued unto this present Yeare 1601. Printed at London for William Jaggard and Thomas Pauyer, and are to be sold at his House in Cornhill, at the Signe of the Cat and two Parots, 1601. Portraits in Wood, of all the Lord Mayors during the Reign of Elizabeth, with Historical Accounts under each. A highly interesting series of prints, in fine Condition and presumed to be Unique. From the Gulston Collection."

It would be very fortunate if the name of the present possessor could be ascertained.
EVERARD HOME COLEMAN.
71, Brecknock Road.

There are numerous portraits of Lord Mayors belonging to the City companies and other owners. Many of them have been engraved, and I have about sixty in my collection, starting from Fitz-Alwine, first Lord Mayor, 1199, down to recent times.   J. D. FRY.
Hadley Hurst, Barnet.

A LINE OF BROWNING (9th S. ix. 47).—In reply to the query as to the meaning of the words

Like the aimless, helpless, hopeless, did I drivel—
Being—who?

I would suggest, to begin with, that the punctuation is bad. The comma after "hopeless" is unnecessary, as is also the dash after "Being." Even the dash before "Being" is not grammatically necessary, but is doubtless inserted to show that there is a pause for deliberation before asking the two final words of the question. It seems to me that the passage would be best printed thus:—

Like the aimless, helpless, hopeless did I drivel?
—Being who?

Thus punctuated it may be freely paraphrased: "Did I drivel like the aimless, helpless, and hopeless? And this, too, when I was such a man as—what shall I say?" The passage is very concise, and is only one of many instances of how the lack of mental discipline in early life induced in Browning a

habit of putting into words that cannot be clearly understood by his readers thoughts that were quite clear to himself. So far as my experience of him goes, I find the difficulty of interpretation is frequently enhanced by bad punctuation. If from such passages one eliminates the stops and proceeds to translate into Latin or Greek, one finds the connexion between the words becomes much clearer. In the above passage "who" is used as equivalent to the Latin "qualis," not "quis"; and the present participle "being" agrees with "I." The third stanza is an answer to the query contained in the last two words of the second. In effect, he asks of himself: "What sort of man am I really?" and then replies:—

One who never turned his back but marched breast forward.
J. B. EAMES.

The poet confesses that he drivelled like the aimless, helpless, and hopeless, and was, all the while, he cannot, or will not, at once say who. He leaves the answer to the reader. After a little pause, we learn from verse 3 that he is

One who never turned his back but marched breast forward,

und so weiter, as the Germans say.
ST. SWITHIN.

JAMES THE DEACON AND AYSGARTH (9th S. viii. 359, 488).—I was, of course, aware of the supposed connexion of James the Deacon with Aikbar, but it is not clear that Ayksbarghe of the 'Monasticon' is Aikbar. Aikbar is now in the parish of Fingal, in which parish, as in Patrick Brompton, Hawkswell, and most of the neighbouring parishes, Jervaulx Abbey owned property; but there is an entry in the 'Valor Ecclesiasticus' of the payment by the abbey, "Rector' de Patrik Brompton p' pens' sua exeunt' de decim' de Ayksbarghe 1l. 13s. 4d" This would seem to connect Ayksbarghe rather with Patrick Brompton. But even supposing Ayksbarghe to be Aikbar, and not Aysgarth, there remain the Domesday form Echescard, the Patent Roll of 1397 Ayksgarth, the 'Valor Ecclesiasticus,' 1536, Ayksearth and Ayscarth, and Spelman's 'Villare Anglicum,' 1655, Ayskarth, all of which refer without a doubt to Aysgarth; and if Ayksbarghe is to be Jakesbargh, then very well also may Ayksgarth be Jakesgarth, as I believe it is. I was aware also that Canon Isaac Taylor derived Aysgarth from Asgard: "Asgardby and Aysgarth, however, probably refer to Asgard, the home of the gods" ('Words and Places,' 222, ed. 1896). And on p. 111 he refers to the district between Tattershall, New Boling-broke, Horncastle, and Spilsby as being the most exclusively Danish district in the king-dom. Here under Bolingbroke we find Asgardby in Domesday (f. 351); but it appears as Asgerebi, a very different form from the Echescard which represents Aysgarth. It certainly seems that Canon Taylor cannot have compared the Domesday forms of the two place-names, for they are entirely different. So in the 'Monasticon' (vi. 1275) it appears as Asgherbie in a confirmation of the prebend to Lincoln Cathedral by Henry I. The resemblance between the two names is clearly only superficial. It is likely enough that Hauxwell, Aikbar, Aysgarth, and even Aikton, near Carlisle, bear the deacon's name, but it would have been at Aysgarth by the Cataract that he most of all baptized. C. S. TAYLOR.

THE MITRE (9th S. viii. 324, 493, 531).—I venture to think that practically all the queries of your correspondents on this subject could easily be answered by themselves, if they would refer to the following, for the most part, easily attainable books. I have verified each quotation, and found these references after about fifteen minutes' search. I fancy many other references might be found in books of the same kind if a little time was given to the quest. I have made the references as short as is consistent with their usefulness.

Pugin's 'Glossary,' p. 157 (Bohn, 1844).
'Church of our Fathers,' Rock, pp. 91 to 122 (Dolman, 1849).
'Dict. des Antiquités Chrétiennes,' Martigny, p. 258 (1865).
'Early Drawings and Illuminations,' Birch and Jenner, pp. 113, 116 (Bagster, 1869).
'Glossary,' F. G. Lee, p. 217 (Quaritch, 1877).
'Polity of the Christian Church,' Pelliccia, Bellett's trans., p. 83 (Masters, 1883).
'A Catholic Dictionary,' Addis and Arnold, fifth edition, pp. 644, 645 (Kegan Paul, &c., 1897).
'Ecclesiastical Heraldry,' Woodward, pp. 53, 67, 122, &c. (Johnston, 1894).

May I add a mild protest against the use of the term "ecclesiastical millinery" to describe what many of your readers regard as the sacred vestments of the Church of God? This term is so used 9th S. viii. 532.
H. W. M.

There is in the 'Assize Roll of Northumberland, 7 Edw. I.' (printed by the Surtees Society):—

"Et dicunt [juratores] quod Wapentak de Sadberg fuit in manibus Regum, prædecessorum domini Regis nunc, de corpore comitatus Northumbriæ, quousque dominus Rex Ricardus vendidit illud Hugoni de Pusat, Episcopo Dunelmense."

From this it appears that the Wapentake of Sadberge was formerly parcel of the county of Northumberland, and that is probably the reason why Bishop Pudsey acquired it with the earldom of Northumberland. The latter was only held for life, but Sadberge was annexed in perpetuity to the County Palatine. The Wapentake of Sadberge appears to have comprised a large strip of land, bounded on the south by the river Tees. I believe that until recently writs were addressed to the sheriff of the "County Palatine of Durham and Sadberge," and it is possible they are still so addressed.
JAMES PEACOCK.
Sunderland.

In the DEAN OF YORK's paper at the last reference, col. 2, near the middle, I suspect a misprint after the words "Westminster Abbey"; in the phrase, "But the coronet never appears round the mitre or the episcopal seal," qy. for "or" read on? I am not sure whether the Dean intends a distinction between "the mitre, surrounded by a coronet," and "the coronet never appears round the mitre." T. WILSON.
Harpenden.

Your correspondent F. DE H. L. will find all about the pagan origin of the mitre, as well as of "various articles of ecclesiastical millinery," in Hyslop's 'Two Babylons,' price 5s., from any bookseller.
F. CLAYTON.
Morden.

In my possession is a case of silver-handled knives and forks which belonged to my ancestor Thos. Lamplugh, Archbishop of York (1688-91). The knives bear the arms of the see—saltire keys, and in chief what Boutell calls an imperial crown, but the DEAN OF YORK a coroneted cap—it looks most like a crown here—impaling his own arms (Or, a cross fleury sa.). This shield the mitre surmounts, coming from a plain circlet only.

Is the Harsnett brass really "the latest representation of an Anglican bishop clad in the ancient vestments"?

My recollection—I may be mistaken, it is some years since I saw it—is that the above-named Archbishop Lamplugh is represented in a mitre with pastoral staff in his hand—a standing coloured statue in the south-choir aisle of York Minster.

I have before me the Earl Marshal's summons to the archbishop to attend at the coronation of William and Mary, "furnished and appointed as to yor Degree and

order appertaineth." Unluckily, no particulars are given as to the dress required.
                                                                    Ibagué.

MINIATURE OF COL. GEO. FLEETWOOD (9th S. ix. 48, 154).—Peter Wentworth, M.P., the Puritan leader, had a son-in-law called by him "my sonne Fleetwoode at Wygan." Can MR. PINK find him in the family of the regicide or of Cromwell's son-in-law?   D.

HENRY CRISPE (9th S. ix. 8, 93).— I am obliged to H. C. for his note. Henry Crispe, the Common Serjeant, who died in office in 1700, was clearly not the son of the rector of Catton.

The will of Henry Crispe, of the Custom, London, dated 27 July, 1745, with codicil 17 June, 1746, was proved 4 November, 1747. Names his wife Mary, mother Ann Crispe, sister Ann, brother Thomas and his daughter, niece Susan, cousin Ann Smith, cousin Richard Wiatt of Boxley. To be buried in the ancient burying-place in Birchington. Had property in Kent and London, and land at Cambridge. His father, Henry Crispe, rector of Catton, is stated in Carter's 'Cambridge' to have been allied to the family of the Duke of Somerset by marriage with Anne, daughter of Francis Percey, of Haverill, in Suffolk.

There was a Henry Crispe, citizen and blacksmith of London, of St. Mary's, Whitechapel, whose will, dated 9 July, 1701, was proved 27 October, 1701, leaving his son Henry residuary legatee.   W. D. PINK.

DESBOROUGH PORTRAITS AND RELICS (9th S. viii. 497 ; ix. 30).—Referring to my notes and queries on the Desborough portraits, which I believe to represent Cornelius van den Anker and his wife Sarah Norden, widow of Andrew Sane, of Dort, I should be glad of any information about C. van den Anker, who was a merchant in London in the seventeenth and eighteenth centuries.
                                                  E. F. DU CANE.

DUELS (9th S. viii. 364, 491 ; ix. 94).—Information about duels is to be found in Douglas's 'Duelling Days in the Army.' Some duels which took place between French and English officers in France soon after Waterloo are mentioned in Gronow's 'Recollections.'   W. S.

HEYFORD FREE SCHOOL : EARLY RULES (9th S. ix. 41).—The rules at this ancient school, and the usual penalty of so many "lashes" for non-attention to any one of them, recall the fact that my late father went to a boarding-school at Cheshunt (Essex), in

the early years of last century. Whipping there was so much in evidence that I have heard him frequently say scarcely an hour passed without the dominie, or his ushers, administering severe corporal punishment. On such occasions they would cry sternly to the offender the all-too-often heard and dreaded command :—

Down with your breeches, and up with your shirt ;
Twenty-four lashes will do you no hurt !

With ultimate disastrous consequences to the poor little victim better imagined than described.   HARRY HEMS.
Fair Park, Exeter.

"WITH AFFECTION BEAMING" (9th S. ix. 87).— The description occurs in the eighth chapter of 'Martin Chuzzlewit' :—

"Mrs. Todgers stood for some moments gazing at the sisters [the Miss Pecksniffs] with affection beaming in one eye and calculation shining out of the other."
                                   WALTER B. KINGSFORD.
[Replies also from W. T. and others.]

BLACK BOTTLES FOR WINE (9th S. ix. 7).— I have a black bottle eight inches in height, half of which appertains to the neck, and eleven inches in circumference. When filled to the top it holds fifteen fluid ounces. It is very strongly but rudely made, and has a curious warped appearance. Upon a raised circle on the side are stamped the letters and date G : C 1744, the date being beneath the letters.

This bottle was dug up, some years ago near the shore of a large lake in this neighbourhood ; along with it was found a cannon-ball of cast-iron, which now weighs almost eleven and a half pounds, but has, no doubt, lost weight by rust.

Can any of your readers enable me to trace the source of this bottle ?
                                           S. A. D'ARCY.
Rosslea, Clones, co. Fermanagh.

THE MUSICIANS' COMPANY OF THE CITY OF LONDON (9th S. ix. 9).—Is MR. HILL acquainted with what has already appeared in ' N. & Q.' respecting this company ? See 8th S. xii. 407, 510.   EVERARD HOME COLEMAN.

THE FEAST AND THE RECKONING (9th S. ix. 85).— I think this runs :—
Men laugh and riot till the feast is o'er,
Then comes the reckoning, and they laugh no more.

I have seen these words so printed on an engraving called 'A Day's Pleasure' (painted by E. Prentis, engraved by James Scott, published 18 April, 1843, by Tilt & Bogue, Fleet Street, London). The engraving represents a room at the "Star and Garter Hotel,"

Richmond, and depicts the presentation of the bill to a party of gentlemen after they have dined. I believe the waiter is " from life," and I have heard that he afterwards became the proprietor of the hotel.

JAS. CURTIS, F.S.A.

"HIGH-FALUTING" (9th S. viii. 505).—If, as D. K. T. says, this is by J. R. Lowell deemed an "odious word," Lowell himself nevertheless employs it in his 'Rebellion' ('Political Essays'), when he says, speaking of 'The Southern History of the War,' by E. A. Pollard, that "in point of style it is a curious jumble of American sense and Southern *high-faluting.*" The word, meaning " tall talk," is thought by Dr. Brewer, in his 'Dictionary of Phrase and Fable,' to be from the Dutch *verlooten,* high-flown, stilted.

J. HOLDEN MACMICHAEL.

THE PARENTAGE OF CÆSAR BORGIA (9th S. viii. 524).—Your correspondent MR. DAWES mispresents my treatment of this subject in 'Chronicles of the House of Borgia,' which obvious *satura* he, deluded by its pretentious form, has mistaken for an attempt at serious history. The narration of Varillas is cited there as "an extraordinary story," "an extremely probable tale," "in the absence of anything more authoritative ......the most probable solution," a narration which "deserves consideration as a contribution to the solving of the mysteries of the unquenchable hatred of Dellarovere for Borgia, and of Duke Cesare's relations with the Lord Alexander P.P. VI." If MR. DAWES had studied my gallimaufry he would have failed to find terms more absolute than these. Varillas is offered for what he is worth. He may be a slipshod historian, "proverbially discredited" (Hallam); but he is not esteemed a deliberately malignant liar, like Infessura or Guicciardini, for example. At all events, I myself am not solicitous to compurge him, if MR. DAWES can give me cause for incredulity in the present instance: otherwise Varillas's tale will remain for me "humanly probable." I wrote the 'Chronicles' "vnder correction of benyuolence" certainly; but I deem it inconvenient that a member of my tribe (*corvus monedula*), imperfectly informed of my writings, should intend himself as cavillator. *Nihil cum fidibus gracculo.* FREDERICK BARON CORVO.

MOAT'S 'STENOGRAPHY' (9th S. ix. 29).— Moat's system of stenography, as developed in his 'Shorthand Standard' of 1833, has long been virtually obsolete, though copies of the work are by no means rare. Any collector may procure one without much effort for a few shillings. It is an able and scholarly work, but as a shorthand treatise is much too elaborate ever to have been widely popular. MR. JESSON is mistaken in his assumption that most modern systems are based upon it. It is constructed upon what is known as the stave or bar principle, introduced by Samuel Richardson in 1800, specially ruled books having to be provided for the reporter who desires to turn it to the best possible account. Without the lines it can only be used at an immense disadvantage in the matter of speed. Of the nearly two hundred systems and modifications of systems that had been published prior to 1833, not more than five were then used to any extent, the authors of these being Gurney (in reality Mason), Byrom, Mavor, Taylor, and Lewis. Since then three hundred odd additional systems have been given to the world, and only some two or three of these have borne any resemblance to Moat's. One Eneas Mackenzie, who published a cheap treatise on the stenographic art about 1838, adopted Moat's alphabet without the staves, but probably only few ever succeeded in mastering the art as he presented it. The basis of Pitman's, with most of the other modern systems, is phonetic, and that most certainly Moat's was not. Of his career nothing seems to be known. His name finds no place in the 'Dictionary of National Biography,' and the shorthand historians know nothing of him beyond what may be gleaned from his work. It is dated from 59, Fleet Street, London, 8 August, 1833. There were two writers of the Moat system in the Parliamentary "Gallery" in 1882, to nearly a hundred of the Pitman, and nearly half that number of the Taylor system, with Gurney men and others. ALEXANDER PATERSON.

Barnsley.

THE EARTH MOTHER (9th S. ix. 48).—Inquiries were made for St. Walburge in 1st S. x. 186, to which the Editor gave a long reply. He stated that she was daughter of St. Richard, and cousin to St. Boniface, was abbess of a nunnery at Heidenhaim, and died there on 24 February, 779. Reference is also made to 'Britannia Sancta; or, Lives of the Celebrated British Saints,' 1745, and Butler's 'Lives of the Saints' (25 February), 1812. A copy of the latter in 12 vols. may be seen in the Corporation Library, Guildhall, E.C.

EVERARD HOME COLEMAN.

71, Brecknock Road.

PRESBYTER will find some interesting information bearing on the subject of his query in Mr. Conway's 'Demonology and Devil-Lore,' vol. ii. chap. xxvi. Mr. Conway, relying apparently on Dr. Wuttke (with whose work I am not acquainted), takes it for granted that St. Walpurga, the original May Queen, is really one with the Bertha or Mother Rose of Teutonic mythology. C. C. B.

It is probable that the information PRESBYTER is seeking may be found in E. L. Rochholz's 'Drei Gaugöttinnen, Walburg, Verena, und Gertrud, als deutsche Kirchenheiligen.' M. P.

WILLIAM GERARD HAMILTON (9th S. ix. 109).—"Single-Speech" Hamilton was undoubtedly a Wykehamist. He was a pupil at Winchester of Dr. Burton, and his name appears as a Commoner on the annual school lists (or "Long Rolls," as they are called) of the college for September, 1740-4, as will be seen some day, I hope, in a second series of these documents from 1723 onwards, which I have in preparation for the press. He matriculated at Oriel College, Oxford, 4 March, 1744/5, then aged sixteen; consequently, if he was also at Harrow it must have been before September, 1740. In after years Hamilton identified himself with Winchester by attending the gatherings of the "Wykehamist Society," founded in 1758, whose meetings were held at the "Crown and Anchor Tavern" in the Strand. A letter of his to Dr. Joseph Warton, then head master of Winchester, dated 16 April, 1765, printed in Wooll's 'Memoirs of Warton,' 1806, p. 306, gives further proof of his association with some distinguished members of his old school. C. W. H.

FILBERT (9th S. ix. 125).—May I be allowed to make a personal observation with respect to this matter, as my name is cited in the article at the above reference?

I wish to say, in particular, that philology, especially as regards English, is a progressive science, and that the rate of progress is very fast. New facts turn up literally every week, even within my own knowledge. And this is why the last edition of my 'Concise English Etymological Dictionary' had to be almost rewritten.

As to this very word *filbert*, I found two new facts myself. Of these, the former was printed in 1891, eleven years ago, and is obviously material. It is, that the word is not English at all, but Anglo-French; so that the remark upon the strangeness of deriving "the *English* name of the nut from a French saint" has, obviously, no point at all. I gave the reference in 1891 (as said above),

and it is now reprinted in my 'Notes on English Etymology' at p. 97. Perhaps it is worth while to quote the passage in full.

In Britton, ed. Nichols, vol. i. p. 371, we have the following sentence: "Et ausi est pasture un noun commun a herbage, et a glan, et a pesson, et as noiz"; and a foot-note tells us that another MS. adds at the end "e a philbers." The translation is: "Pasture likewise is a general name for herbage, acorns, mast, and nuts, and philberts." Of course, the A.-F. *philbert* loses its *t* (as usual) before the plural suffix -*s*, in accordance with grammar, though the earlier form would have been *philberz*, with *z* for *ts*.

The allusion is unmistakable, and this shows that the A.-F. name for "filbert" was certainly *philbert* in the thirteenth century.

My second find was that the word is still known in France. In Moisy's dictionary of the Normandy *patois* we are told that the actual name of the nut is still *noix de filbert*. This note was printed in 1888, and is given in the *last* (rewritten) edition of my 'Concise Dictionary,' and in no previous one.

I need not point out to an expert in chronology the improbability that a name already current before 1300 should be derived from that of a duke who was alive in 1482.

The statement that the "nut of Philbert" is connected with St. Philibert's Day is only a guess; but I shall be much obliged to any one who will make an obviously better one. WALTER W. SKEAT.

ENGLISH CONTINGENT IN THE LAST CRUSADE (9th S. viii. 343; ix. 55). — The Patrick Chaworth mentioned by MR. JOHN RADCLIFFE seems to have done as did the younger De Montforts after the Crusade, and taken office under Charles I. of Anjou-Naples. His name appears as Chevalier de l'Hôtel in the 'Reg. Angev.,' 25, fo. 211; 26, fo. 292 b; 44, fo. 89. He became Justice de la Terre d'Otranto in 1280, and so remained until 1282, when, I think, his death took place. His heiress, if I mistake not, was Maud de Cadurcis, Chaurs, otherwise Chaworth, who became ward to the king, and eventually ancestress to the Dukes of Lancaster, which royal duchy still owns some of her Gloucestershire estates. ST. CLAIR BADDELEY.

AERONAUTICS (9th S. ix. 84).—Bishop Lesley, in his 'History of Scotland,' gives the following account of the attempt of Damian, the abbot of Tungland, to fly. The story forms the subject of Dunbar's satirical poem of 'The Fenyeit Frier of Tungland.' The ingenious explanation of the failure was not the want of a tail, which seems to have crippled Ailmer, the monk of Malmesbury, in his earlier attempt, but the grovelling propensities of the domestic fowl, whose feathers he had thoughtlessly used to fashion his wings.

An ambassador was sent to France by King James in September, 1507, when the abbot of Tungland

"tuik in hand to flie with wingis, and to be in Fraunce befoir the saidis ambassadouris. And to that effect he causet mak ane pair of wingis with fedderis, quhilkis beand fessinit apoun him, he flew of the Castell wall of Strivelling [Stirling], bot shortlie he fell to the ground, and brak his thee [thigh] bane; bot the wyt [blame] thairof he ascryvit to that thair was sum hen fedderis in the wingis quhilk yarnit and covet the mydding [dung-heap] and not the skyis."

J. G. WALLACE-JAMES.

MILTON: A TRACT ON LOGIC (9th S. ix. 107). —Milton's 'Artis Logicæ,' &c., is reprinted in the sixth volume of the edition of Milton's prose works by Symmons, London, 1806.

MEMA.

HERRICK: SILVER-PENCE (9th S. ix. 49).—I think this may refer to the custom of cutting a membrane under the tongue of an infant to ensure the freedom of its "little member." If so, a silver penny must have been a popular instrument for the operation. In France matrons and *sages-femmes* make use of the nail of the little finger when they do not venture to employ scissors. ST. SWITHIN.

The reference is to tongue-tied children. The "tie" is cut by the sharp edge of a much-worn silver coin. The note to the line in Grosart's 'Herrick' confirms this. By the same means the tongues of starlings are loosened. ARTHUR MAYALL.

The allusion seems to be to the practice of using a silver coin for cutting the superfluous ligament in the mouth of a tongue-tied infant. This practice was probably due to a primitive prejudice against the employment of a metal instrument, and so allied to the survival among the Jews of the use of a sharp flint for performing the rite of circumcision.

JOHN HOBSON MATTHEWS.

Miscellaneous.

NOTES ON BOOKS, &c.

The Works of Lord Byron.—Poetry. Vol. V. Edited by Ernest Hartley Coleridge, M.A. (Murray.)

THE penultimate volume of Mr. Ernest Hartley Coleridge's authoritative edition of Byron's poetry now sees the light, and will, according to the rate of progress hitherto maintained, be succeeded during the present year by the concluding volume. It com-

prises works belonging to the last two years of Byron's life as a poet, and constitutes in itself a remarkable accomplishment. When it is considered that cantos vi. to xv. of 'Don Juan,' 'The Vision of Judgment,' 'The Blues,' 'The Irish Avatár,' and other poems were written during the same period one marvels at such industry and productiveness. The principal portion of the volume is occupied by the dramas, six of which appear—'Sardanapalus,' 'The Two Foscari,' 'Cain,' 'Heaven and Earth,' 'Werner,' and 'The Deformed Transformed.' It is to be feared that, as Mr. Coleridge says, the greater part of the contents of this volume has been "passed over and left unread by at least two generations of readers." None the less, he holds, "these forgotten works of the imagination are full of hidden treasures." We ourselves read them all duly something less than two generations ago. Feeling the justice of his observations, and moved, mayhap, by some implication of rebuke, we have reread a considerable portion of the volume, a task facilitated by the type in which the whole is printed and the companionship of Mr. Coleridge's introductions and notes. Not wholly pleasurable was the exertion. In 'The Island,' the weakest of Byron's tales and the last sustained flight his muse was to make, positive resolution was requisite to get through it. On the other hand, by 'The Deformed Transformed,' all of which except the opening lines, full of Byron's moody introspection, had faded from memory, we were stimulated, feeling a distinct regret that the work was left incomplete. Unlike 'Manfred,' it trenches on nothing uncomfortable in domestic relations, and the obligation to 'Faust,' though real, is far from being so great as has been assumed. It does not seem likely that any of these plays will be seen again on the stage. 'Werner' has been given under the Irving management at the Lyceum, and 'Manfred,' which belongs to an earlier epoch, was more than once revived in the latter half of the century. 'Sardanapalus' was produced by Charles Kean at the Princess's in 1853, the temptation to mount it being found in the then recent discoveries in Nineveh. The performance of either 'Cain' or 'Heaven and Earth' is not conceivable under existing conditions; and the Venetian play has, so far as we recall, slept since its performance in the year of its production. That Byron was careful in his investigation of authorities is to his credit, but scarcely atones for lack of interest in his dramas. The frontispiece consists of a portrait of Byron by W. E. West. Other portraits are of Goethe, from a drawing by Maclise; of Georgiana, Duchess of Devonshire, after Sir Joshua Reynolds; and Mary Wollstonecraft, by R. Bothwell. Assur-Bani-Pal, from a slab in the British Museum, illustrates 'Sardanapalus,' and the Lion of St. Mark's 'The Two Foscari.' Mr. Coleridge's labours remain interesting and illuminative.

The Tower of London. By Lord Ronald Sutherland Gower, F.S.A. Vol. II. (Bell & Sons.)

NOT long have the readers of Lord Ronald Sutherland Gower's history of the Tower had to wait for the second and concluding volume. The first volume (see *ante*, p. 38) carried the story through Norman, Plantagenet, and Tudor times; the second prolongs the tale from the accession of the Stuarts until the present day. Though less pathetic than the early record, since we have now no innocent female victims of a king's unbridled licentiousness or a father's vaulting ambition, no execution upon an Anne Boleyn or a Jane Grey, the later is wanting in no tragic or heroic respect. Pathetic cases there are—witness the service of

That sweet saint who sate by Russell's side—

and not all end unhappily, as is seen by the escape of Lord Nithsdale on the eve of his execution, through the heroism and resourcefulness of his wife. Full particulars of an incident that angered greatly George I. are supplied by Lord Ronald. The most illustrious victim of royal malignity, cowardice, and spite with whom the second volume deals is, of course, Sir Walter Raleigh, though the fate in the following reign of Lord Strafford caused greater consternation. Raleigh had been so long in prison, and experienced so many unkind visitations of fortune, that his death when brought about created less sensation than might have been anticipated. Says Lord Ronald, "Sir Walter Raleigh died a martyr to the cause of a Greater Britain; his life thrown as a sop to the Spanish Cerberus by the most debased and ignoble of our kings." This is true, though hardly well said. Who is the "Spanish Cerberus"? He adds: "The onus of the guilt of his death — a judicial murder, if ever there was one—must be borne by the base councillors who truckled to the king, and by the king himself, who, Judas-like, sold Raleigh to Spain." The use of "truckle" is quite defensible. To the reign of James belong the death of Lady Arabella Seymour, which took place in the Tower, and, without being sanguinary, was due to her long and hopeless confinement, and that of Sir Thomas Overbury, which James might have been powerless to prevent, but which, at least, he basely condoned. Among those subject to detention in the Tower were Bacon and Coke.

The victims in the days of Charles I. and the Commonwealth were numerous and renowned. The deaths of Strafford and Laud are perhaps the most picturesque and touching. Concerning Laud's additions to St. John's College, Lord Ronald says that in the library of that college his spectre is said to be seen "occasionally gliding on moonlight nights between the old bookshelves." Is not the tradition rather that he and his royal master indulge with their heads in a nocturnal game of bowls? Many noble heads were lopped during the following reigns before we come to the death of Monmouth, perhaps the handsomest victim of all. In the reigns of the Georges the executions were fewer, being chiefly confined to participants in the revolts of 1715 and 1745. During the late reigns we hear only of the fire of 1841 and the attempt to blow up the White Tower in 1885, the executant of which crime issued from imprisonment a year or two ago. Most of the stories which Lord Ronald tells are necessarily familiar. Some are, however, less known than others. The tale of Blood's attempt to carry off the regalia is told afresh, and the supposition that Charles II. connived at it is not very strongly reproved. An idea that Charles II. and his brother had a private cognizance of, or participation in, the death of Arthur Cecil, Earl of Essex, is not favoured. It may safely be consigned to the same limbo in which now rests the once famous story in the following reign of the child and the warming-pan. The illustrations are, as in the previous volume, numerous and excellent. In addition to portraits of the principal victims they include views of the Tower from all aspects and in various

times. The work is indeed one of the best illustrated of modern days, and will be warmly prized by all students of history and antiquity and collectors of what are now called Londoniana.

Selected Essays and Papers of Richard Copley Christie. Edited, with a Memoir, by William A. Shaw, Litt.D. (Longmans & Co.)

FEW works of the same class deserve a warmer welcome than this. Richard Copley Christie, a firm friend and supporter of 'N. & Q.,' was primarily a man of action, discharging many important and responsible functions. What these were, and how they were discharged, was told in various periodicals on his lamented demise little more than a year ago (see, *inter alia*, 9th S. vii. 60). In the intervals of his various avocations he became a scholar all but, if not quite, unequalled in his line. A man of fine tastes and wide sympathies, he wrote one work, his life of Etienne Dolet, which is accepted as a masterpiece, and remains the principal—and, in a sense, unique—tribute to one of the most interesting and tragic figures of the French Renaissance. To that life in its English dress, and in the subsequent French translation, we have more than once drawn attention, and other writings of his have been noticed in our columns. Of few men can it be said that their work was equally varied, trustworthy, erudite, and scholarly, or animated by so fine a taste; of still fewer that they were so complete masters of their subject. Possessor of a fine library, ever at the disposition of his friends, and of what most scholars would regard as affluence, he pursued his studies in a fashion that recalls Gibbon. The articles, accordingly, he contributed to the quarterlies and other periodicals are so careful and elaborate as to be of permanent value, and a collection of them is a boon alike to the student and the bibliophile. So fresh is his memory with us, and so many were the services he rendered, we can scarcely even now persuade ourselves to think of him as dead. His brief memoir is adequate and sympathetic; the portraits present faithfully his refined, clear-cut face; and the illustrations of his haunts, and especially his library, add greatly to the value of the volume. The chief attraction of this will, however, be found in the collected essays and sketches, which will always be the delight of the scholar, and abound in information on out-of-the-way subjects. Had Christie been less occupied he might well have given us a history of the literary renaissance, and what he leaves behind constitutes no unimportant contribution to the subject. Knowing well both the man and his work, we have nothing but praise for this tribute to his memory and his fame.

The King and Queen of Hearts. Written by Charles Lamb, illustrated by William Mulready. Reissued in facsimile by E. V. Lucas. (Methuen & Co.)

IN the course of his Lamb studies Mr. E. V. Lucas came upon a letter from Lamb to Wordsworth, dated 1 February, 1806, claiming the authorship of 'The King and Queen of Hearts,' issued in 1805. He was also fortunate enough to find a copy of a little work of extreme rarity, and to obtain permission from the proprietor to issue it in facsimile. The task has been executed with so much skill that any owner of the book without its modern environment, which is separated, would believe himself possessed of a genuine curiosity. From the date 1805, this is the earliest of Lamb's books written for children. Such details must be sought in the introduction, in which Mr. Lucas justly says that the fact that it is by Lamb is vindication enough for its reappearance. Mulready's illustrations, executed when he was a youth, are very quaint and characteristic. Concerning these the reader may consult, if he can, the facsimile of 'The Looking-Glass' issued by Mr. F. G. Stephens in 1885. Lovers of Lamb and collectors of curiosities will at once secure this delightful little volume.

The Gold of Ophir. By A. H. Keane, F.R.G.S. (Stanford.)

WHERE the auriferous Ophir, the Eldorado of the ancients, was situated is a problem that has been waiting its solution for many a century. At last the hour and the man have come—the man of insight capacitated by the arrival of the hour of increased knowledge and discovery. If it were not, indeed, for the latter the best scholar might theorize in vain. But in Prof. Keane we find one standing on the firm foundation of modern research, and able, consequently, to draw a conclusion which, strange and unexpected as it is, as bringing the most ancient and most modern of interests into close connexion, yet demands our assent. It makes Mr. Rhodes shake hands across the ages with King Solomon, and finds the earliest outpost of prehistoric colonization in a country so *actual* as the Transvaal. Working on the discoveries by Mr. Theodore Bent of the Zimbabwe monuments in the present Rhodesia, and bringing these into connexion with the researches of Dr. Glaser and others in Southern Arabia, Prof. Keane makes out a strong case for identifying the Biblical Ophir with Ptolemy's Sapphar, Arrian's Portus Nobilis, *i.e.,* Moscha, the harbour *par excellence* on the south coast of Arabia, to the east of Hadhramout. Ophir itself seems to be the same word as Aphar, which is only a variant of Saphar or Sapphar, the metropolis, of which the port was Moscha. But his chief point is that Ophir itself was not a gold-bearing district, but merely the emporium or mart where gold was imported and distributed to other countries, and that the actual seat of the gold mines which yielded the supply must be sought in Rhodesia; and, further, that Rhodesia was really the Havilah of Genesis ii. 11, the gold of which land is good. Thence it was conveyed to Moscha in the trading vessels of the Himyarites, Sabæans, and Phœnicians. All this is very cleverly worked out in Prof. Keane's ingenious and learned essay, which also identifies Sheba with Yemen, and Tarshish with Sofala, in Rhodesia. Another interesting surprise is provided for us in his proof that the Himyarites, on their way to South Africa, to some extent colonized and occupied Madagascar, and that undoubted remains of this prehistoric occupation may still be traced in the language and calendar of the Malagasy. "It is certainly a revelation," as the author remarks, "to find the Sabæo-Babylonian astronomic nomenclature still surviving amongst the unlettered and semi-barbarous Oceanic populations of Madagascar."

THE current number of *Folk-Lore* begins with an excellent paper on the difficult subject of totemism, which is followed by a minute description of the festival known as Garland Day at Castleton, in Debyshire, while a third article relates to the silver bough in Irish legends. The collectanea and correspondence of this useful journal embody many notes which must in the future prove of great value to students of ancient custom and belief.

THE *Antiquary* for February contains a brief account of the old hall at Mickleover, Derbyshire, and a notice of some Essex brasses which illustrate Elizabethan costume. It also gives a description of mediæval library fittings.

THE *Intermédiaire* for 10 February is quite as good as any of the numbers preceding it. Among the subjects with which it deals are the nails of the Passion, Louis XVI. and the Swiss Guard, and churches used by both Catholics and Protestants.

GREATLY to our regret, we find that with the conclusion of the tenth volume our lively and erudite friend and rival *Mélusine* comes to a temporary stop. Whether M. Gaidoz will be able in any shape or at any time to reissue it we know not. We are at least sure that many readers, French and English, will regret the interruption, temporary even though it be, to its appearance.

WE hear with much regret of the death of Dr. Samuel Rawson Gardiner, one of the most capable and distinguished of English historians. On the subject of England under the first two Stuart kings, the Civil War, and the Protectorate he was our greatest authority. Born on 4 March, 1829, at Alresford, he was on the point of reaching his seventy-fourth year. Dr. Gardiner was educated at Winchester and Christ Church, Oxford. In 1884 he was made Fellow of All Soul's, in 1892 Fellow of Merton. He held the Professorship of Modern History at King's College, London, and was Examiner in History at Oxford. A frequent contributor to our columns, his name appears from the Fourth Series up to p. 30 of our present volume.

Notices to Correspondents.

We must call special attention to the following notices:—

ON all communications must be written the name and address of the sender, not necessarily for publication, but as a guarantee of good faith.

WE cannot undertake to answer queries privately.

To secure insertion of communications correspondents must observe the following rules. Let each note, query, or reply be written on a separate slip of paper, with the signature of the writer and such address as he wishes to appear. When answering queries, or making notes with regard to previous entries in the paper, contributors are requested to put in parentheses, immediately after the exact heading, the series, volume, and page or pages to which they refer. Correspondents who repeat queries are requested to head the second communication "Duplicate."

O. E.—Not suitable for our columns.

NOTICE.

Editorial communications should be addressed to "The Editor of 'Notes and Queries'"—Advertisements and Business Letters to "The Publisher"—at the Office, Bream's Buildings, Chancery Lane, E.C.

We beg leave to state that we decline to return communications which, for any reason, we do not print; and to this rule we can make no exception.

LONDON, SATURDAY, MARCH 8, 1902.

CONTENTS. — No. 219.

Notes.

ST. MARGARET'S CHURCH AND WESTMINSTER BENEFACTORS.

St. Margaret's Church is one of many memories, and among them all there are none that cling closer than those relating to the benefactors of the poor of this city. Until about one short year ago the city of Westminster was virtually comprised in the two parishes of St. Margaret and St. John the Evangelist, for then the "Greater Westminster" had not been called into existence. St. Margaret's Church, again, is rich in monuments, and among them are at least half a dozen commemorating local worthies who, with hearts to feel for the woes of the poorer parish folk, devoted a portion of their substance to aid in the alleviation of the troubles of those who fell upon evil times in old age, and in attempting to make the paths of the young brighter and better than they would have been without their aid. In those days almshouses were often the admirable manner in which charitable impulses found an outlet, and their foundation has given comfort to the poor of these parishes for some centuries, and bids fair to do so for many more to come,

and many are the cheerful and pious souls who hourly bless the names of their ancient benefactors. The monuments of the worthies in the church are, as they should be, among the handsomest and most interesting and elaborate specimens of the mason's work, and were formerly—before Father Time had dimmed their lustre—rich in colour and gilding ; but, if somewhat dull and dingy, they still retain enough to make them pleasant to look upon and stir the emotions of the true citizen of what is certainly no mean city.

It is but reasonable to suppose that some charitable bequests may get diverted in the course of time, and even be lost altogether, which is the case of the first benefactress whose monument adorns the walls of our old parish church. At the west end of the church, over the churchwardens' pew, is the monument of this lady, which for our edification records :—

"Hereunder is intombed Blanche Parrye, daughter | of Henry Parry, of New Courte in the County of Heref[d], | Esq[ier] Gentlewoman of Queene Elizabethes most honor | able bedchamber and Keper of her Maties iuells | whome she faithfullie served from her Highnes | birth. Beneficiall to her Kinsfolke and Countrye | men charitable to the poore insomuch that | she gave to the poore of Bacton and Newton | in Herefordshire scaven score bushells of | wheate and rye yearlie for ever w[h] divers somes | of money to Westminster and other places for good uses she died a maide | in the eighte two yeers of her age the twelfe of Febrvarye 1589."

A report published by the late vestry in 1890 states that this inscription " is the only record traceable of the gifts above referred to." There is at Bacton a most interesting monument to her memory, as, although buried here, her heart was deposited there. The monument there has a quaint inscription of twenty-eight lines, setting forth her long life and good work. My old friend the late Mr. Henry Poole has put it on record that she seems to have served as a "go-between with the queen and her ministers, her courtiers and her suppliants." Altogether we may, I think, take it for granted that she was really a person of considerable importance in her day, and at various times subsequently we meet with members of the family, some of whom were not in quite such saintly odour as this lady ; but our chief concern is that her benefaction has been lost to us. Not so the others, for which Westminster is profoundly thankful.

On the north wall of the church is another monument, exceedingly quaint, and much the worse for its over 300 years of existence, that to the memory of Cornelius Vandon, who also thought of the poor who are always with us. The inscription records that

"Cornelius Vandon lieth here borne at Breda | in Brabant a soldiour with K. Henry at Turney | yeoman of the gard and usher to K. Henry. K. | Edward. Q. Mary. and Q. Elizabeth of honest and vertuous lyfe a careful man to poor folke | who at the end of this toune did buyld for | poor widowes 20 howses of his owne cost."

The monument has a half-length figure of Vandon in the dress of a Yeoman of the Guard, curiously but effectively carved. Round the effigy are inscribed the words, "Obiit Anno Domini 1577. Buried yᵉ 4ᵗʰ Sepʳ Aetatis suae 94." Upon reference to the 'Will Book of St. Margaret's, Westminster,' for the year 1577 we find this entry :—

"Cornelius Vandon, born at Breda, in Brabant, yeoman of the guard, and usher to their Maᵗⁱᵉˢ K. Hen. K. Edwᵈ the 6ᵗʰ Queen Marie, and Q. Elizabeth, he did give eight almshouses in Pettie France, next to the end of St. James-street, for the use of Eight poor women of the parish and did also give eight other almshouses near Sᵗ Ermin's-hill, by Tuttle side, for the use of eight poor widows of this parish."

Again quoting from the vestry report of 1890, we are told that the

"'Charity Book of St. Margaret's' refers to the Petty France houses as having been founded 'for relief, succouring, and harbouring eight poor women, who in time of sickness, as need should require, might help to keep and attend such as should be diseased within the parish of Sᵗ Margaret, Westminster,' the intention being, according to some, to provide nurses in the time of 'plague' or other visitations, when few would undertake the office of nurse, to the increased distress and suffering of poor people."

The ground and almshouses at Petty France were bought by the vestry, under the powers given by the Westminster Improvement Act, in 1850, for 2,992l., and in 1852 land was bought in Carlisle Street, Lambeth, for 450l., and the following year two new almshouses, each containing eight rooms, were built, at a cost of 950l., for four poor women, and the balance invested. There was a continual buying, selling, and reinvesting of the funds in order to increase the usefulness of the charity. The almshouses were at last let "at a fair occupation rent," for the support of visiting nurses among the poor. In 1879–83 80l. was the average rent derived, but three years later it had dwindled down to 37l., and next year the London and South-Western Railway paid 2,000l. to the trustees for the purchase of the site and the almshouses, and they ultimately demolished them for the widening of the line, the funds being now administered by the Westminster Nursing Committee. W. E. Harland-Oxley.

71, Turner Buildings, Millbank, S.W.

(To be continued.)

LEATHER FOR BOOKBINDING.

Having perused with much pleasure the report of the committee on this subject, I feel that the moral to be drawn therefrom is still an open one, as it was in 1859, when I read a paper upon the subject of the 'Library : Books and Bindings,' with regard to their preservation and restoration, in our great room at the Adelphi, the discussion on which was adjourned and gave rise to much correspondence.

Things have not greatly changed since that period, for the adage that there is "nothing like leather" still exists, and for highly ornate bindings, decorated by the use of hot metal tools, no other material is so beautiful, though its endurance can be measured by time.

All leathers seem to be equally good if used in their primitive state and not tampered with by the dyer or by the bookbinder ; but then we should lose the glorious hues of the dyes and the beautiful forms of the marbles, and this particularly applies to calf, which is the most used and the most tampered with, though it takes time to develope the cause of this. Calf is often washed with oxalic acid, or polished by hot irons, when shellac varnish might have been used ; but even then the joints at the back of the books may become brittle, and they alone rely upon the hempen cords on which the book is sewn, and which are drawn into the boards.

With regard to hogskin, that is a material which is to be commended in its undyed state, and though it cannot be worked upon in gold, it seems to be less affected by worms, and, if undyed, to continue to be fairly sound at the joints.

To illustrate this, I would note that I have two saddles that have been most enduring, one of which is at least fifty years old. Noting its great durability, and hearing that it took dye well, I ordered a set of dining-room chairs to be covered therewith, with, alas ! the result that in five years these covers perished, and became as tinder. I send you a sample of this material that has been kept free from light, air, and gas fumes. If you will put this in an ordinary room, and under the same conditions, doubtless it will become the same.

As a further evidence of the effect of time upon russia, I send you a writing-case that is seventy years old, from which may be seen how light, air, and heat have affected the same externally, whilst internally it is perfect. I forward also a thin green russia pocket-book that has been in use since 1861, and is still serviceable.

This now brings us to the subject of a substitute for leather ; and that is not difficult to find in the very great improvement in bookbinders' cloth, much of which has endured since its introduction in 1836, and has outlived the library bindings affected since then. I have now before me a copy of 'Sketches by Boz' which is as perfect, as regards durability, as if done yesterday, though the back is faded, the decoration on the sides, marking the transition period, being embossed in imitation of a "blind" pattern suggested by single-line gouges.

I send you also a specimen of durable binding in buckram, a binding that is devoid of animal or mineral aid, being a vegetable product, save and except the size that may have been used in binding.

As a test of durability the great thing is the hinge, and to test materials stuffs should be subject to a perpetual hinge motion to see which endures the test for the longer period.

Of course, if a high class of decoration with exquisite finish be desired, leather must be used ; and if the tooling is to be very fine, then the leather must be as thin as paper, that the heated metal may reveal the sharpest form.

As a destroyer the bookbinder is quite as great a culprit as the currier, his beautiful tree marbles and inlays being greatly detrimental—indeed, many of the books bound within the last thirty years are only held together by their vegetable sewing and the bands that are "drawn in" at the hinge.

This brings us to the lasting quality of flax, and the importance of binding in buckram, which is most enduring, samples having been found in the Egyptian tombs, where all leather has perished.

I would note that the samples of hogskin have had imparted to them a morocco grain, and I am told that all leathers suffer soon in warm and hot climates, ants being very destructive to leather and paper, though colocynth or bitter aloes, if used in the paste employed, deters them.

Finally, as to sewing, I say 'ware wire, as damp rusts it. Vellum is an excellent material, and, indeed, books sewn upon vellum bands, with flaxen thread in lieu of sunken saw cuts, have proved most excellent. Nearly every kind of material has been used as a covering for books, including even the *peau humaine*, which somewhat, in colour, resembles vellum, probably the most durable of all. JOHN LEIGHTON, F.S.A.
Ormonde, Regent's Park.

THE MARLBOROUGH FAMILY. — In cataloguing the library of the Catholic Cathedral, Northampton, I came upon a Book of Common Prayer, London, 1678, which, from the internal evidence, had plainly been the property of the Marlborough family. It bore the autograph of the haughty duchess, "S. Marlborough," dashed off in a bold imperious hand very characteristic of the writer. Above it, at the top of the page, was a note in another hand : "This Bible [*sic*] was my dear mother's, and was......the 27 day of July, 1693." The binder has cut away two or three words, which we may, however, assume were "given me." To judge from the context, the recipient must have been the Lady Anne Churchill, second daughter of the Duke and Duchess of Marborough, who was married in January, 1700, to Charles Spencer, third Earl of Sunderland, and by whom she had three sons. One of these now became possessor of the book, for just below his grandmother's autograph he records the untimely deaths of both his parents as follows : "My dear Mama Sunderland Died April the 15, 1716"; "My dear papa Died April the 18, 1722." It was popularly supposed at the time that his death was attributable to poison, but the doctors failed to detect any evidence to support it. At the end of the book, still in the same handwriting, is the following interesting note recording the death and burial of the greatest of our military leaders, the only one of whom it can be said that he never fought a battle without winning it, or sat down before a fortress without taking it : "June the 16, 1722, about four a clock in the morning, The Duke of Marlborough Died, my dear Grandpapa, and he was interred the 9 of August at Westminster Abby."

It is most probable that the writer and possessor of the book was the Hon. John Spencer, the third son of the Earl of Sunderland, and the ancestor of the present Earl Spencer, as there is a book-plate with the Spencer crest with "Wimbledon" written on the scrollwork. The great duchess bought Wimbledon Manor, after the South Sea collapse, from Sir Theodore Jansen, and built a house which became her favourite residence. The manor afterwards descended to the Spencer family, but the mansion was burnt down in 1785. J. S. S.

BURNS AND JAMES CRIRIE.—In one of his letters to Peter Hill, the bookseller, Robert Burns criticizes and somewhat extravagantly praises James Cririe's 'Address to Loch

Lomond.' As a copy of the original edition of the 'Address' (1788) has been searched for in vain by Mr. Wallace, the new editor of Robert Chambers's 'Burns' (vol. ii. p. 382, note), I venture to draw attention to the fact that I found a copy in the British Museum Library (press-mark 11602. h. 14 ; not in the Catalogue *s.v.* 'Cririe'). I may add that the first three lines quoted by Mr. Wallace from the version given in Cririe's 'Scottish Scenery' (1803) are not contained in the original edition. The "compliment" referred to by Burns—"one of the most elegant compliments I have ever seen"— reads thus :—

Along thy banks,
In playful youth, unconscious of their powers,
They sportive rov'd ; where, sacred to each name,
A tribute due, the monumental stone,
With sculpture deck'd, with praise well-earn'd
    inscrib'd,
The grateful pride of kindred souls proclaims.

OTTO RITTER.

Berlin.

EGMONT AND THE 'ENCYCLOPÆDIA BRITANNICA.'—One of the most atrocious judicial murders recorded in history is that of Count Egmont by the Duke of Alva, who had got the former into his hands by treachery. That in ordering his execution and that of Hoorn he was carrying out the intentions of the marble-hearted Philip there is no doubt ; but it may be worth while to point out an odd mistake of that generally accurate authority the 'Encyclopædia Britannica,' in its life of Egmont (ninth edition, vol. vii. p. 699), where we read :—

"It was in vain that the most earnest intercessions had been made in his behalf by the emperor Charles V., the order of the Golden Fleece, the states of Brabant, the electors of the empire, and the regent herself."

The date of Egmont's execution was 5 June, 1568 ; that of the death of Charles V. (some time after his abdication) was 21 September, 1558, nearly ten years before. Prescott discredits the report of a brutal jest sent to the countess by Alva the day before her husband's execution, but says there is more reason to believe that the emperor (then Maximilian II., son of Ferdinand I. and nephew of Charles V.) sent her a letter during the trial assuring her that she had nothing to fear. The cruelties of Philip through the agency of Alva had, as is well known, far-reaching consequences which they little anticipated. W. T. LYNN.

Blackheath.

" KEEP YOUR HAIR ON."—The 'N.E.D.' does not take this phrase further back than 1883 ; but it must be much older. In 1799 Thomas Holcroft sailed from the Thames to the Elbe. During the voyage he was told by the sailors that "the waves in the western ocean are sometimes so oily, from dead whales, that they are not much disturbed by a brisk gale." Another described to him " a stiff breeze"; he " swore that it shaved him, that he could not keep his hair safe on his head, and that it made the ship sneeze" ('Memoirs of Thomas Holcroft,' 1816, iii. 228-9).

W. C. B.

[Is not the slang sense illustrated in the 'N.E.D.' distinct from the literal meaning in the above quotation from Holcroft ?]

"AND YOUR PETITIONER SHALL EVER PRAY, &c."—An inquiry was recently made as to the meaning of " &c." in this common ending to a petition. West's 'Symboleography,' published in the reign of Elizabeth, gives many forms, some of which I have copied below :—

"And your said almoner shall pray unto almighty god for the prosperous estate of your Majestie according to his most bounden dutie in most high honour and felicitie long to reign over us."

"And your said suppliant shall daily pray unto God for your highnes prosperous estate in royaltie long to reign."

"And your said subject shall daily pray to God for the prosperous estate of your majesties Raigne."

"And your said humble subject shall daily pray to God for the preservation of your highnesse in all felicitie most happily long to reigne."

"And your said supplyant shall daily pray for your honor."

"And your supplyant as nevertheless by duetie bounden shall daily pray to God for the increase of your Honour."

It is evident that the " &c." may be filled up according to individual fancy.

W. P. W. PHILLIMORE.

[Numerous endings of petitions are supplied in 8th S. ix. 377, with references to 1st S. i. 43, 75; vii. 596; 3rd S. ii. 113, 148, 178.]

PICTURE RESTORING IN FRANCE UNDER NAPOLEON I.—'A Visit to Paris in 1814,' by John Scott (editor of the *Champion*), second edition, 1815, at pp. 162-3, contains the following :—

" M. Hacquin could not be content only to clean Titian's picture of Pietro Martire, but he must lay it on its face, and plane away the board till he came to the actual colour. He then put down pasted and glued canvas, that stuck to the colour, and thus transferred the picture from wood to canvas. The members of the Institute were in an agitation of delight as this curious trick was in progress: 'Sacre Dieu ! What an undertaking !' An eye or a toe, a white cloud, a speck of colour, on which much of the effect of this inestimable performance of the Venetian depended, was as nothing to the dexterity of the French remover. M. Hacquin was made member of the Legion of Honour, and the whole body of artists and literati ran with wonder —not to study the picture of Titian......but to chatter, to shrug, to take snuff, and to express admiration of the talents of M. Hacquin. The whole system of this cleansing and restoring is hateful...... An English artist told me that he was within the Louvre, studying the cartoon of the 'School of Athens,' when from a private door came forth an old Frenchman, who regularly set his palette and began to work on a large picture, the back of which was towards the Englishman. The latter thought it must be the performance of the person who was so busily employed on it, and from curiosity went over to examine it. To his horror he found the Frenchman engaged in regularly painting over an early and curious specimen of Italian art, touch by touch. He had painted the drapery of the Virgin entirely over, a fine staring blue. 'Good God!' said the startled Englishman, 'who is this picture by?' 'Je ne sais pas, Monsieur,' was the reply. 'Je ne suis pas peintre—Je suis Restorateur!' It afterwards turned out that this painting, so honoured by the attention of Monsieur le Restorateur, was by Cimabue, and a most rare and singular relic."

WILLIAM GEORGE BLACK.
Ramoyle, Dowanhill Gardens, Glasgow.

"LURDEN."—The following account of the origin of this word, as it is too lengthy for Dr. Murray, may yet be worth putting within ready reference by 'N. & Q.':—

"And besydes this, the common people were so of them oppressed, that for feare and dreade, they called them in every such house as they had rule of, Lord Dane: But in processe of tyme, after the Danes were voyded the lande, this worde Lord Dane, was in dirision and despite of the Danes turned by Englishe men into a name of opprobry called Lurdane,......for if one Englishe man will rebuke another, he will for the most part say, thou art but a Lurdane."—Grafton, 1568, 'Chron.,' i. 163.

This is given in connexion with the massacre of the Danes, about 1002, or as a result after it.

Halliwell gives also "lordeyn fever"= idleness, and "lurdy"=lazy, with references, but suggests no origin, and this may not be a sound derivation, and yet be worth noting.
X.

CHILDREN'S AFFIRMATIONS.—Children soon learn to distinguish nicely between various degrees of affirmation. The bare word they rarely consider binding. One of the most curious forms of oath (for such it really is) that I have met with among them is the wet finger. The child holds up a wet finger, and asks, "Is this finger wet?" then dries it, and holds it up again, with the question, "Is this finger dry?" and adds, "Cut my throat before I'd lie." Only the most depraved will tell an untruth with this formula. An approved way of getting at the truth is to ask, "Are you sure?" "Yes." "Are you certain?" "Yes." "Are you shot down dead?" "Yes."

"Are you sure and certain, shot down dead?" "Yes." This, I believe, is, or was in my own young days, the most binding form of all.
C. C. B.

IN PRAISE OF BURNS.—Mrs. Annie Vincent Burns Scott (great-granddaughter of Robert Burns), of Ortunga, Largs, South Australia, made application recently to the secretary of the Burns Federation for assistance to discover the author of some verses on Burns, "deciphered in manuscript on a very old hand-painted memorial card." The "poem," consisting of six stanzas, the first two of six and the remainder of four lines, appeared in the *Glasgow Evening News*, and evoked a reply, in which the writer ascribed most of the verses to John Nicholson, of Airdrie, who penned them in 1826. Nicholson's poem, I think, will interest some readers of 'N. & Q.':—

Learning hath many a rhymer made
To flatter near the throne,
But Scotia's genius hath displayed
A poet of her own.

His lyre he took to hill and glen,
To mountain and to shade ;
Centuries may pass away, but when
Will such a harp be played?

His native strain each bird may try,
But who has got his fire?
Why, none! For Nature saw him die,
And took away his lyre.

And for that lyre the aspiring youth
The world may search in vain ;
She vowed she ne'er would lend it more
To sound on earth again.

Then call'd on Fame to hang it by ;
Fame took it, with a tear,
And broke the strings to bind the wreath
Which Burns shall ever wear.
J. GRIGOR.
105, Choumert Road, Peckham.

MOSES MENDELSSOHN.—The witty distich quoted in your 'Notes on Books' (*ante*, p. 100),—

George the First was always reckoned
Vile, and viler George the Second,—

recalls an anecdote told of Moses Mendelssohn. With more refinement of wit than Heliogabalus, Frederick II. was wont to play practical jokes on his intimates. These invariably took the form of sportive sallies when men like Voltaire, Lessing, and Mendelssohn were his guests. One night Frederick had the tables turned upon himself most adroitly by the little humpbacked scholar. As soon as Mendelssohn took his customary seat at the festive board there was a universal titter. Frederick, pretending innocence, inquired why he was making such a wry face. Holding the paper close to his nose (for the philosopher was, in addition, very near-sighted), Mendelssohn blurted out, "Some fellow has been very rude to your Highness. He has written 'Mendelssohn is one ass—Frederick the Second.'" The original was: "Mendelssohn is an ass—Frederick II."   M. L. R. Breslar.

"Vicuña."—This has been badly treated by our lexicographers. Firstly, the 'Century Dictionary' derives it from "Peruvian *vicuña*, Mexican *vicugne*," which is half right and half wrong, since it has about as much to do with Mexican as with the fabled "Lingua Angelorum." Secondly, Prof. Skeat, in his 'Notes on English Etymology,' 1901, p. 345, says: "I do not find this word in the Peruvian dictionary, and suspect it to be a corruption." It may not be in all Peruvian dictionaries, but it is to be found in several of them. Thus Domingo de S. Thomas, the earliest writer who applied the now familiar name Quichua to the Peruvian, has in his 'Lexicon de la Lengua General del Peru,' 1560, "*Oveja*, llama, ó paco, ó guaca, ó guanaco, ó vicuña." Similarly Juan Martinez, in his 'Vocabulario en la Lengua General del Peru,' 1604, has "*Oveja silvestre*, vicuña, huanacu." These references may be of use to the editors of the 'N.E.D.' The term occurs in English in Acosta's 'Naturall Historie,' 1604, iv. xl.: "There is another kinde of beasts, which they call Tarugne, which likewise are wilde and more nimble than the Vicugne." I mention this because it contains a curious misprint. By the change of a letter two terminations are levelled under one. *Tarugne* should be *taruque*, representing Spanish *taruga*, which in Martinez is spelt *taruca* and glossed "ciervo ó venado."
    J. Platt, Jun.

Pope Leo.—Pope Leo, who completed his ninety-second year on Sunday last, March 2nd, is, the *Daily News* reminds us, the only Pope who has strolled along Piccadilly and occupied a seat in the Distinguished Strangers' Gallery at the House of Commons, where he had the pleasure of hearing a speech by Daniel O'Connell, the Irish leader of the period. The Pope, then Archbishop Pecci, spent the whole of February, 1846, in London. Queen Victoria, whom he had previously met when Papal Nuncio at Brussels, invited him to a State reception at Court, and he was also present at "a great ceremonial in which the Queen took part."   N. S. S.

Political Nicknames : Chamberlain and Bülow.—Political nicknames are often amus-ing, but it is sometimes difficult to trace their history. Let 'N. & Q.' register two. 'A Bismarck en Pantoufles' is the title of a searching article in the February number of the *Fortnightly Review* on the political career of Chancellor of the Empire Bülow. The other nickname I take from another article in the same number, 'The Man of Emergency': "The *Vorwärts*, the Socialist organ in Berlin, had the good fortune to coin the wittiest thing yet said of the Chesterfield speech, 'Lord Rosebery is Mr. Chamberlain —*édition de luxe*'" (p. 193).
    William George Black.
Ramoyle, Dowanhill Gardens, Glasgow.

Swift's Visits to England : the "Four Crosses" Inn. — In collecting material for a work on the Holyhead Road I have come upon traces of Dean Swift here and there, and particularly at Willoughby, a wayside village four and a half miles from Daventry, where the old "Four Crosses" Inn stood until 1898, when it was demolished, owing, perhaps, to the alterations in the neighbourhood incident upon the completion of the Great Central Railway, crossing over the road near by, and with the station for Willoughby within sight. Many years ago the late Mr. Cropper, an auctioneer of Rugby, who was born at Willoughby, purchased from an old woman in the village a pane of glass credibly said to have once been in a window of the "Four Crosses," and bearing the inscription, apparently scratched with the diamond of his ring :—

There are three
Crosses at your door :
Hang up your Wife
and you 'l count Four.
        Swift D.   1730.

This pane—an old diamond-shaped piece of green glass, that bears its antiquity plain to see — is now in the possession of Mrs. Cropper at Rugby. I have seen it on two occasions, and carefully copied the inscription as above. The story told is that the dean, staying at the inn, then called the "Three Crosses" (presumably from roads that even now run in three directions from the spot), was annoyed by the landlady, who would not put herself to any extra trouble for him, and that, on leaving, he scratched this uncomplimentary suggestion. It seems that, if the landlord did not suspend his wife, he at least altered his sign. When the pane was removed does not appear, but evidently a great many years ago. Perhaps the landlady herself saw to it !

But, strange to say, another inn called the "Four Crosses" claims this distinction, and has often been accorded it in print. This house is the much older and greatly superior "Four Crosses" at Hatherton, on the old Chester road, near Cannock—a road Swift certainly would also have travelled on his journeys between London, Chester, and Holyhead, on his way to or from Dublin. He also probably stayed there. (There are, by the way, four cross-roads at that point.) The inn at Willoughby was always a very humble one, and were it not that Swift is known to have enjoyed visiting the pothouses on the way to listen to the talk of the waggoners and others, we might think it too mean a place for that dignitary of the Church to have honoured.

The lines have almost always been egregiously misquoted, probably by writers following the incorrect version given in the *Gentleman's Magazine* in 1819. It would be of the greatest interest if any light could be thrown upon the circumstances that led to Swift writing this; and, moreover, if it can be reconciled with the apparently irreconcilable, *i.e.*, the invariable statements of all Swift's biographers that his last visit to England was in 1727. And while we are about it, what has become of the epigram he similarly scratched on a window-pane at Chester: something to the effect that the churches and the clergy of that city were alike unfurnished within?   CHARLES G. HARPER.
Petersham, Surrey.

Queries.

WE must request correspondents desiring information on family matters of only private interest to affix their names and addresses to their queries, in order that the answers may be addressed to them direct.

METEMPSYCHOSIS AMONG THE SWEDES.— The Illuminati, who were influential in Swedish society during the reign of Gustavus III. and subsequently, held, I have been informed, among other tenets, that the souls of certain great men passed into the bodies of other persons endowed with similar great qualities of genius or courage. I shall be glad to know where references to this belief of theirs can be found.   SEARCHER.

KING CHARLES I. AT THE NEW GALLERY.— One of the most interesting pictures in the Winter Exhibition at the New Gallery is that marked No. 104, although, by a curious oversight, the compilers of the catalogue have omitted to record the point that makes it famous. It is a seated figure of King Charles I., and portrays him as he sat at his trial in the High Court of Justice— the latter fact unnoticed in the catalogue. His beard is worn full and quite grey; in his right hand he holds the historic ebony cane, whose silver top fell off during one of the sittings; and his head is covered by a high-crowned black hat, a royal prerogative which the king resolutely maintained during the memorable scene. The picture must have been painted from memory after the trial, but it makes Charles I. look considerably older than in his usual and better-known portraits, while the grizzled beard, less carefully trimmed than of yore, imparts a touching and lifelike aspect to the whole.

The chair, with its covering of red velvet, is still extant, preserved in a cottage hospital at Moreton-in-the-Marsh, Gloucestershire. It was on view in the Stuart Exhibition some years ago. What a pity it cannot be acquired for the nation, and placed either in Westminster or Whitehall! Similar pictures, of various sizes, may yet be found in the possession of old Jacobite families, and some rough copies on glass, with an inscription below, can occasionally be purchased in curiosity shops; but all Stuart relics are now becoming rare, and fetch high prices. Can any one throw some light on the artist of the picture? It is signed "Edward Bower, att Temple Bar, 1648."   PERCY CLARK.
[For Bower see Bryan's 'Dict.,' 1885, under his name.]

CHAPMAN FAMILY.—Information is desired as to the parentage and descendants of John Chapman, who lived at Checkley Hall in the first half of the nineteenth century. Where is Checkley Hall? In Yorkshire? The person in question was of the Chapmans of Whitby.
B. P. SCATTERGOOD.
Moorside, Far Headingley, Leeds.

"I DOE LOVE THESE AUNCYENT ABBAYES."— Who is the author of the following lines?—

I doe love these auncyent abbayes;
We never tread within them but we set
Our foote upon some reverend historie.

JOHN A. RANDOLPH.
128, Alexandra Road, Wimbledon, S.W.

["Abbayes" is a mistake. The lines run:—

I do love these ancient ruins;
We never tread upon them but we set
Our foot upon some reverend history.

They occur in 'The Duchess of Malfi,' V. iii. (Webster's 'Works,' ed. Hazlitt, 1857, vol. ii. p. 270).]

WARREN AND CLEGG.—Can you tell me if Esther Clegg, who was born 15 September, 1693, and who married Jonathan Warren, of Limehurst, at Ashton-under-Lyne, on 2 April,

1716, was a descendant of Bernulf de Clegg, the founder of Clegg Hall, near Rochdale, in the reign of Stephen; also the Christian name of Esther Clegg's father, and where she was baptized; also the Christian name of Jonathan Warren's father? Jonathan Warren was born 8 December, 1694. Where?—and where baptized?   G. J. WATTS.

STEEVENS's 'SHAKESPEARE.' — Will you kindly inform me the value of a set of Steevens's 'Shakespeare,' Boydell, 1802? My copy is in 9 vols., and belonged to Mr. Martin, who inserted many illustrations.
    H. W. B. GLOVER.
Norfolk, Va.
[No man except an expert can give you the value of an exceptional copy. The only plan is to sell it by auction, and buy it in if you want to keep it. Consult the successive volumes of 'Book-Prices Current.']

AUTHOR OF BOOKS WANTED.—Who is the author of 'Experiences of a Gaol Chaplain,' 'Notes from the Diary of a Coroner's Clerk' (published in *Bentley's Miscellany*, but, I believe, never published separately), 'Stray Leaves from a Freemason's Note-book'; and what are the names of any other works of his?   WILLIAM ELAM.

WILLIAM AND ROBERT BENT. — Can any one give me biographic data of William Bent, the compiler and publisher of English catalogues, and the founder of *Bent's Literary Advertiser*, established in 1802; also of Robert Bent, his successor?   A. G.
New York.

ASHTEAD, SURREY.—The parishioners are anxious to trace, and if possible recover, the registers of baptisms, marriages, and burials prior to 1660; also the accounts of the churchwardens and overseers from the end of the eighteenth century as far backwards as possible. Suggestions or information will be welcomed.   (Rev.) F. G. L. LUCAS.
The Rectory, Ashtead.

MINAS AND EMPECINADOS. — Macaulay, in his essay on 'Lord Mahon's War of the Succession in Spain,' writes, "The Earl [of Peterborough] therefore made war after the fashion of the Minas and Empecinados of our own times." Ignorance, sheer ignorance, induces me to ask some reader to enlighten me as to Minas and Empecinados, and in what fashion they made war.   JAMES WATSON.
[The Minas, uncle and nephew, and Empecinado were celebrated leaders in the Spanish guerilla war against the Napoleonic invaders.]

"CADAVER."—In Coke's 'Institutes,' vol. iii. p. 203, appears the following: "The burial of the *cadaver* (that is *caro data vermibus*) is," &c.; and the passage is quoted verbatim, without comment, by Mr. Justice Holroyd in Rex *v.* Coleridge, 2 Barnewall and Alderson's Reports, p. 809. Did the learned author intend his readers to consider that he believed *cadaver* to be derived from the union of the first three syllables of the other three following Latin words; or is it a little ghastly pleasantry? Is the joke his own? Lexicographers are unanimous in tracing the derivation *a cadendo*—cadaver being that which no longer stands, but has fallen. Cf. πτῶμα and πίπτειν.   G. B. F.

RICHARD EDWARDS was admitted to Westminster School in 1770. Can any correspondent of 'N. & Q.' tell me whether this was Richard Edwards of Nanhoron, Carnarvonshire?   G. F. R. B.

"LIMERICK."—Why is a certain form of nonsense verse known by this name; and by whom was the name first given? The question has already been asked (9ᵗʰ S. ii. 470), but has not, I believe, been satisfactorily answered.   HENRY BRADLEY.
Clarendon Press, Oxford.

BULL-BAITING.—I have seen reference to a statute ordering bulls to be baited as a condition precedent to their flesh being exposed in the shambles for sale. In 'Records of the Borough of Leicester,' vol. ii. p. 289, there is notice of a borough enactment that "no bocher kylle no bull to selle within this town but yf hit be bayted before in payne of forfeture thereoff." The order has its counterpart in a Cambridge ordinance of 1376 (Cooper's 'Annals,' i. 114), where "baiting" is explained as being fed with grass in a stall. Was there a statute such as that mentioned above, and did it enjoin baiting by bulldogs or baiting as contemplated by the Cambridge ordinance?   G. T.

COMIC ANNUAL. — Wanted the title and names of author, artist, and publisher of a comic annual (?) which appeared about sixty years ago. On p. 53, under the heading 'Rhetoric and Elocution for the Million,' are two illustrations, a large face on a small body, and a sulking boy leaning against a wall. On p. 54 (dealing with teeth) is represented an old nurse offering pap to an infant in its chair. On p. 55 is a clown shooting a gigantic tooth out of the mouth of a pantaloon. On p. 56 is a carpenter seated over a signboard ("The Queen's Head"), and sawing it away from its post. These are all the pages that I possess, but on one there was, I recollect, an illustrated description of a boy teasing his mother for an apple. He says, "All apples are not put into puddings and pies, are they, mamma? I should so like an apple." I think he threatens to go and catch some illness if he does not get the apple, and it ends with "Pretty dear! he has got the apple!" POMANDER.

'THE SPIRIT OF THE WYE.'—I can remember to have read many years ago, when a boy, in a book entitled 'The Romance of History,' by Henry Neale, a story called 'The Spirit of the Wye.' It narrated how a shadowy form was occasionally seen sailing in a boat on the river Wye, near Hereford. Is this tradition lost or forgotten?—for I have mentioned it to several people resident at Hereford, and they have never heard of the legend.

JOHN PICKFORD, M.A.

CLEBURNE: BOWES: WARD.—Who were the descendants of Elizabeth Bowes, daughter of Sir George Bowes, of Streathlam, co. York, and goddaughter of Queen Elizabeth? Her daughter Elizabeth Hutton married Edward or Edmund Cleburne, of Killerby, co. York (the eldest son of Thomas Cleburne, of Cleburne Hall, co. Westmoreland), whose eldest son William, of St. John's Manor, co. Wexford, married Bridgetta, sister or niece of Michael Ward, Bishop of Ossory, *ob.* 1643. Any information or printed pedigrees of these families will oblige and be of assistance.

WALTER J. BURKE.

HAMBLEY ARMS. — The arms of Hambley of Cornwall are Sa, on a pale or three torteaux; the crest, a dolphin haurient azure (9th S. v. 92). Harl. MSS. 5871, 2129, 1538, 1091, give for the Hambly or Hamley arms Arg., three talbots passant az. Harl. MS. 3288 says Hamley has for coat of arms (quartered by Trevylyan) Arg., a chevron between three talbots passant sa. Harl. MS. 1080 describes this family's coat of arms as Arg., three talbots sa. What reasons might there be for these differences in the arms? Will some one learned in heraldic lore explain the remarkable connexion between these coats of arms and that of Sir Wm. Hollys (presumably of Devon), which is Sa., on a bend, between a talbot courant in chief and a dolphin naiant embowed in base arg., three torteaux?

CORNUBIAN.

BIDDULPH FAMILY OF BIDDULPH.—Has the early pedigree of this old Staffordshire family ever been worked out in a scientific manner? There are, of course, various pedigrees in Burke's 'Commoners' and 'Landed Gentry,' in Sleigh's 'Leek,' in the 'Visitations of Staffordshire,' published by the Wm. Salt Arch. Soc., and elsewhere, but none of these are complete or convincing, and various discrepancies occur. I am especially desirous of discovering the connexion with the main line (which I naturally assume) of Thomas Bedulf, of Horton, co. Staffs, who by his will dated 9 June, 1535, and proved at Lichfield 1 December, 1535, nominates as one of his overseers "Richard Bedulf of Bedulf gent.," the then head of the family. Horton and Biddulph are adjoining parishes.   ALEYN LYELL READE.

Park Corner, Blundellsands.

QUEEN CUNEGUNDA. — Wippo, 'De Vita Chunradi Salici' (p. 442 of the Frankfort edition, 1654), tells us that the body of Queen Cunegunda (who died in 1038) "in præpositura Lutburg sepultum est." I should be glad to know where this burial-place was.

WILFRID C. ROBINSON, F.R.Hist.S.

FITZGERALD QUOTATION. — In which of Edward FitzGerald's works shall I find the following lines?—

> For like a child, sent with a fluttering light
> To feel his way along a gusty night,
> Man walks the world. Again, and yet again,
> The lamp shall be by fits of passion slain;
> But shall not He who sent him from the door
> Relight the lamp once more, and yet once more?

They were quoted by Mr. Asquith in an article in last December's *Contemporary Review.*   C. L. S.

DAVID POLE, SECOND BISHOP OF PETERBOROUGH, DIED 1568.—This Churchman is said to have been a relation of Reginald Pole, the cardinal. Is it known whether any relationship did really exist between these two?   RONALD DIXON.

46, Marlborough Avenue, Hull.

"HOP THE TWIG."—I have it in my mind that this expression has at some period been in vogue to indicate decease in persons or animals. Can any reader put me in the way of tracing the origin of the term, and say if it is still used in metropolitan or county areas? I have searched many likely shelves in vain.   CECIL CLARKE.

SEASALTER.—What is the origin of the name of this parish, west of Whitstable in Kent, and on the Swayle, which separates the Isle of Sheppey from the mainland in Kent? At the Domesday Survey it is mentioned as "a small burgh called Seseltre." A popular idea is that the place received its name from the open salt-pans, for the production of salt by evaporation of the sea-water.

ARTHUR HUSSEY.

Tankerton-on-Sea, Kent.

Replies.

THE WEST BOURNE.
(9ᵗʰ S. viii. 517 ; ix. 51, 92.)

In my former note I produced evidence to show that the stream which we conventionally call the Westbourne passed under several other names, and I asked for evidence to prove that it was ever called the " West Bourne" previous to the nineteenth century. The weapons of deduction, inference, and analogy have been employed to assail my position, but the irrefragable arm of evidence has not yet been produced.

My note has, however, been fortunate in eliciting the valuable and suggestive article of Sir Herbert Maxwell. I quite agree with Sir Herbert that the absence of the name of West Bourne as the designation of a stream in early maps is no proof that the stream had no specific name. To my mind it affords a probability, but certainly no proof. On the other hand, the illustrations given by Sir H. Maxwell seem to show that, to his mind, the absence of a name at the present time affords a probability that in early times the stream had a specific name. Where there is room for such varying opinions the safest course to pursue is to accept nothing except on the clearest evidence.*

Sir H. Maxwell alludes to the case of Avon and Esk, and adds, "The specific is forgotten, the generic remains." In the case of the Gade in Hertfordshire, he is doubtless right ;† and if the Thames were not so big its name might be forgotten too, for no one talks of rowing on the "Thames"; one has an afternoon on "the river." But the numerous Avons and Usks, Ouses and Axes, certainly

* By a curious coincidence, I had written thus far (1 February) when the *Morning Post* was brought into my room, and on opening it I found a most admirable article by Mr. Andrew Lang, entitled 'Belief and Disbelief,' which should be read and inwardly digested — like all Mr. Lang's writings it contains its own pepsin — by every correspondent of 'N. & Q.'

† Norden has some quaint remarks on this river. He says: " *Caishoo* should import a water, called *Cais* or *Caegs*, the name, it may bee, of the riuer that passeth through this hundred, called *Caishoo* or *Caegshoo* hundred, called of *Hollenshed Gades* and giues name to the *Gadesdens*, where the riuer riseth : And so by corruption of pronunciation they call it *Caishoo* for *Gadeshoo*, *Gades* river, or else is *Gades* mistaken for *Cais* or *Caegs*, and so for *Caisden* or *Caegsden* pronounced *Gadesden*, for doubtless, the riuer giueth name to *Caishoo* or *Caegshoo*, or *Gadeshoo-berye*" ('Speculum Britanniæ,' Herts, ed. 1723, p. 15). Not very conclusive, perhaps.

afford a probability that in early times specific names were not so commonly used as generic ones. People did not travel much out of their own districts, and it was not until communications were developed that any necessity was felt for a specific name. No one made any mistake as to what was meant by the "stream" or the "river."

As I have just shown in the case of the Thames, this habit is not entirely lost at the present day. I may perhaps be allowed to give a further illustration from my own personal experience. On my occasional visits to London—or "town," as it is called by an analogous process—I usually occupy rooms in a house on the east side of Welbeck Street. One morning, in the course of a talk with the landlord—a very intelligent man, who has lived many years in the district—on the geology of that part of London, he said that from excavations made when old houses were pulled down, as was just then happening in Bentinck Street, he observed that the gravel practically ended in the middle of Welbeck Street, and that onwards to the "river" the soil consisted of gravel mixed largely with mud. I said, "The 'river'? What river?" "Oh!" he replied, "the bourne." "Ah," I rejoined, "I suppose you mean the Tyburn." "Well, sir," he said, "I suppose you would call it the Tyburn." Now, I may observe *en passant*, I never would call it the Tyburn, except in a conventional way, for, with the exception of a doubtful passage in a charter of uncertain date, there is as little evidence to show that the King's Scholars' Pond Sewer was ever known as the Tyburn as there is that the Ranelagh Sewer was ever known as the Westbourne. But this, of course, is another question.

The term "bourne" applied by my landlord to this stream shows that this word has not entirely dropped out of the Southern English vernacular, and if Sir H. Maxwell will turn to Dr. Murray's dictionary, *s.v.* 'Bourne,' he will find stronger evidence on this point in the shape of a quotation from Richard Jefferies's 'Wild Life in a Southern County,' 1879, p. 22 :—

"The villages on the downs are generally on a bourne, or winter water-course......In summer it is a broad winding trench......along whose bed you may stroll dryshod......In winter the bourne often has the appearance of a broad brook."

The same invaluable dictionary will also show Sir H. Maxwell and W. H. B. that the second constituent of Westbourne cannot be "bourn," a boundary, French *borne*, as the word in that sense was first employed in English by Lord Berners in his translation of Froissart, 1523; then seven times by Shakespeare, including the world-wide quotation from 'Hamlet' cited by W. H. B.; and then apparently not till the eighteenth century, the modern use, according to Dr. Murray, being probably due to Shakespeare.*

Mr. T. Wilson questions my supposition, which I made on the authority of Bosworth, that Westbourne received its name from its situation on the west bank of the rivulet. "Bourne" is a common termination in East Kent, especially round Canterbury, where we have Littlebourne, Bekesbourne, Patrixbourne, and Bishopsbourne. There is also Northbourne (not Norburn), near Deal, which gives its name to a peerage. This is a small hamlet, not a stream, though it is seated near one. Unfortunately I do not know Eastbourne or South Bourne, and cannot say whether they are situated on streams bearing those names, or whether they owe their names to streams called respectively the East Bourne and the South Bourne. Further inquiry into the origin of all these names might throw light on the subject.

The earliest mention of the so-called West Bourne occurs in a charter of King Æthelred, A.D. 986, on which Prof. Hales has partly founded an interesting paper in the *Transactions* of the London and Middlesex Archæological Society, vi. 560. In this charter the stream is called "mær-burne," or boundary-brook, and rightly so, as it marked the boundary of the parish of Hampstead. Thence it meandered down to Kilburn, a very ancient name which is evidently derived from the stream, though I have never met with any indication that the stream itself was so called. And thence to Westbourne, where we will leave it, while awaiting the evidence for which I asked.   W. F. Prideaux.

With regard to the word *bourne*, otherwise *burn, brun*, in the sense of limit, boundary, may one suggest some further considerations? *Bourne* has come to mean in our time pretty generally in England, and (as *burn*) even still more in Scotland, simply a stream or rivulet. How has this particular and simple meaning come to attach itself so generally to this word? May it not possibly be because the idea limit, boundary, originally always underlay the thought stream, rivulet? and this perhaps through the fact that the first natural limits and boundaries regarded by men would most frequently be streams and rivulets, which are helpfully common, which run through territories in a clear-cut and continuous dividing line, and which are readily seen from every little eminence. In ancient deeds it is often very noticeable how greatly limits and boundaries are defined even by the smaller water-courses. Webster, under 'Bound, Boundary, *n.*,' gives O. Fr. *borne* as a root of that word; and, as said already, he gives *borne* also as a root of "burn," when that word stands for river, rivulet—so that limit, boundary, may clearly be called the original underlying idea in both cases. It might be remarked that where streams and rivers give names to our dales and valleys, what we call their "watersheds" are in effect their limits and boundaries—so that we speak of the district within such a watershed as the dale or valley of such and such a river. The fiat of nature which decreed that water falling upon this side of the top of this moorland shall flow, say, to the course of the river Aire, while the water falling upon that other side shall flow to the course of the Wharfe, decreed that the stream name should thus likewise form a boundary name, so that we still say "Airedale" and "Wharfedale" (that is, "Aire's" -dale and "Wharfe's"-dale)—the districts so by name apportioned being in effect the boundaries and limits of the basins which they drain, and thus the districts distinctly assigned—dealt out—to those rivers. In the case of smaller streams that have not been deemed important enough to give names to their watersheds, may they not still have served as limits and boundaries in themselves—inward boundaries only in this case, and not both outward and inward; and, where *bourne* or *burn* is the name received from old time for a stream or river, may not that name point back to that old function of boundary marking? Such a name as *Burnley*, in Lancashire, on the river *Burn* or *Brun*, occurs to one as an example.   W. H. B.

THE FIRST GENTLEMAN OF COLOUR TO RECEIVE KNIGHTHOOD (9th S. ix. 106).—It may be useful to add to the paragraph quoted by N. S. S. the following letter, dated 31 January, which appeared in the *Times* over the signature of Sir J. W. Carrington :—

"The late Sir Conrad Reeves, Chief Justice of Barbados, was so distinguished and striking a personality, and his career was in many respects so remarkable, and, indeed, it may be said, unique, that I cannot help thinking the readers of the *Times* would like to know something more of him than appears in the brief obituary notice which is printed in your columns this morning. Perhaps, therefore, you will allow one who for some years

---

* The fact that Shakespeare uses this word seven times in a sense unemployed by any of his contemporaries is worthy of notice.

enjoyed his friendship—a friendship not unmixed with rivalry at the Bar and in the local legislature—to bear somewhat fuller testimony to his signal worth and achievement.

"It is not correct to describe him as a 'negro' in the sense in which that word is used in the West Indies. He was a dark man of colour—that is to say, of mixed European and African blood. He was born in Barbados some eighty years ago in very humble circumstances. He began life, with little or no advantages of education, as a printer's devil. By-and-by he rose to be a reporter. His ability and industry in that capacity were so marked that his friends made shift to send him to England to read for the Bar. After he had been 'called' by the Middle Temple, he returned to his native island, and soon acquired a considerable practice as an able and eloquent advocate. For some years he abstained from politics, but in 1873 he was elected to the House of Assembly, where he rapidly came to the front. In 1876, at the instance of Mr. Pope Hennessy, then Governor of the island, he was appointed Solicitor-General. This office, however, he held but for a few months, resigning it in order to take the leading part in the bitter contest between Mr. Hennessy and the local legislature. His conduct in that crisis secured for him in a high degree the respect and regard of his countrymen. Nor, in the result, did it permanently alienate him from her Majesty's Government, for in 1881 he was appointed to the higher office of Attorney-General of the island. After good service in this post, he was advanced in 1886 to the dignity of the Chief Justiceship, and not long afterwards received the honour of knighthood. In that office he administered the law so fairly, so firmly, so courteously, and so efficiently as to win in an extraordinary measure the esteem, the confidence, and the affection of all classes of the community. When he died on the 8th inst., the Governor, with the consent of the members of the local legislature, accorded him the honour of a public funeral, and the sorrow of the people of the island was testified by the immense number of persons who attended at and witnessed the ceremony. In the history of Barbados his will always be *clarum et venerabile nomen.*

"But there is even a wider point of view from which his character and career are interesting. So far as my knowledge goes, he is the most distinguished man of colour ever born in the British dominions, and it is not too much to describe him as the fine flower of that liberal and enlightened policy which the mother country practises towards the weaker races under her sway."

This is a generous and valuable testimony.
WILLIAM E. A. AXON.
Manchester.

TOWER: ST. PETER IN THE CHAINS (9ᵗʰ S. ix. 146).—For the ceremony on placing a brass tablet in the crypt, having reference to human remains there deposited several years ago, see *Illustrated London News,* 22 February.
R.U.S.I.

BEN JONSON'S REPETITIONS (9ᵗʰ S. ix. 145).—It was pointed out at this reference that Ben Jonson uses the same phrase of different persons on different occa-

sions in other instances besides that on which stress is laid by believers in Bacon's authorship of the Shakespearian plays as showing that, after becoming one of Bacon's secretaries, he transferred to Bacon the striking expression employed of Shakespeare in the lines prefixed to the First Folio. It has not to my knowledge been observed that this particular expression is not original in Jonson. John of Salisbury, in his 'Policraticus' (ii. 22), a book familiar to scholars of Jonson's time, thus speaks of Cicero: "Ille in quo Latinitas nostra solo invenit quicquid insolenti Græciæ eleganter opponit aut præfert." I should not be surprised to find that John himself had taken this from some older author; but I have not discovered it elsewhere. It is scarcely possible to suppose that Jonson's passages are independent of that in John of Salisbury: speaking of an English writer, he had to couple Rome with Greece, and to find an appropriate epithet for Rome to balance "insolent" applied to Greece; and there is nothing wonderful in the same epithet, which had satisfied his ear once in this connexion, recurring to him in the same connexion on a like occasion. It is worth pointing out also that there is nothing remarkable in the omission of Shakespeare from the 'Catalogus Scriptorum' in the 'Discoveries,' since that is a list of orators only, and does not include poets at all.
C. C. J. W.

OXFORD DIOCESAN ARMS (9ᵗʰ S. ix. 68).—The arms of the diocese are the ancient arms of the priory of St. Frideswide, the church of which is now the cathedral of Oxford, as well as the college chapel of the house. Antony Wood ('City of Oxford,' ed. Clark, ii. 159) testifies that these arms were "not long since extant in several places of this monastery," and are over the monument of Dr. King, the first bishop of Oxford. He also shows that the three "virgins' heads" were probably originally King Didanus, Queen Safrida, and their daughter St. Frideswide, the last of whom founded the nunnery (as it then was) in the eighth century.
LOCRINIDES.

"GUN" (9ᵗʰ S. ix. 106).—Surely philologists should welcome with rapture BRUTUS's exceedingly ingenious etymology of the word *gun,* which is so beautifully convincing, even to the simplest beginner. They might save themselves much trouble and useless searching if they applied this method to other words. I venture to offer one or two similar self-evident elucidations. The word *dun* is evidently "done," done brown, old pronunciation, neither "dawn" nor "done"; "tun"= *tone*, a vessel which gives a hollow tone; "bun"=*bone*, a cake made of crushed bone. As *come* and *some* are pronounced "cum" and "sum," so "hum"=*home*, a home-sound. The new etymology of *gun* is surely proved up to the hilt by the interesting light it throws on the abusive expression "son of a gun"=son of a gone person, gone off his head, of course, son of a lunatic.

Possibly the professional jealousy which endeavours to make etymology a select science, protected from the competition of the *vulgus* by an elaborate hocus-pocus system of absurd rules, will not permit such simple explanations to "find favour with philologists." Have they not haughtily condemned many equally ingenious etymologies offered in olden times by worthy monks and others, and covered with ridicule their praiseworthy attempts to explain the language in an intelligible way? It is time to protest against this pedantic trades-unionism. There may yet be many things concealed from the philologists and revealed to babes and Brutuses.

SIMPLICISSIMUS.

'LES LAURIERS DE NASSAU' (9th S. viii. 464; ix. 157).—The copy that I have of this book bears the date 1612, so it can hardly be a translation of the Dutch book published in 1616. Is there an earlier edition of the Dutch text, or is the French edition the original one which was afterwards translated into Dutch? Can your correspondent MR. JOHN RADCLIFFE tell me whether the book (either in Dutch or French) is one of any authority as an historical record?   B. D.

SIR NICHOLAS SMITH (9th S. viii. 283, 373). —Perhaps these references to Chancery Proceedings, Car. I., may be useful to your correspondents on this subject.

P. 38, 34. The Lady Smith, wife of George Parry, Chancellor of Exeter, having bought the marriage of her eldest son Nicholas Smith for 1,500*l.* from the Court of Wards, and borrowed 500*l.* to do so and further on his marriage with Rosse, daughter of Hester, Lady Lambert, her sons Lord Lambert and Sir Carew Lambert having taken over the bond as part of her marriage portion—the said Lamberts did not pay, and Lady Smith is now threatened with proceedings, which she prays the Court to avert. Her brother, Sir George Horsey, of Clifton, Dorset, is mentioned. 1628.

P. 39, 35. The same on behalf of her infant children, Ralph and Lettice Smith, claims alimony for them under the will of her husband, Sir N. Smith, of Larkbeere, pr. 1622,

of which James Walker and Ralph Symes were trustees, and also under an indenture of 17 Jac. I. In the answer it is stated that her eldest daughter Edith had married William Bruton.

P. 39, 36. The same, with her son James Smith, complains that Lady Smith (once Grace Bevil, of Cornwall), widow of Sir George Smith, of Maddeford, had a right of dower on an estate at Ottery St. Mary under an indenture of 40 Eliz. made with said Sir George and his sons Thomas and Nicholas, and had agreed with Nicholas, after the death of Sir George and Thomas Smith, to give up this right, but had never done so, whereby the complainants were injured. 1628.

R. 15, 7. John Richards claims moneys from Sir George Parry as executor of his stepson George Smith, who with his brother owned the manor of Ivedon Penne, Devon. 1648.

P. 34, 14. Dorothy, Lady Parry, and her son John Smith make certain claims on Grace, Lady Smith. Also see S. 15, 22.
　　　　　　　　　　　　J. H. PARRY.

I wish to thank the gentlemen who have replied to my inquiry about this knight for the information they have sent. They tell me a great deal about his ancestors, but I want also to connect him with the Smith family of Great Torrington, Canonsleigh, parish of Burlescombe, and St. Audries, Somerset, from whom I claim descent. If Sir Nicholas Smith is really my ancestor, as I have been assured, I would only ask for about two generations of Smiths to connect him with a James Smith, of Great Torrington, who married about 1680 Thomasine, daughter of a Henry Rowland and Elizabeth Bickford. I will ask any one who is kind enough to take an interest in this pedigree to look at my former letter.   DOMINICK BROWNE.

Christchurch, New Zealand.

ST. BRIAVEL (9th S. ix. 9, 30).—The earliest occurrence I have met with of St. Briavel's as a place-name is in the Gloucestershire Subsidy Roll of 1313, where it is called "S'c'us Browel'." It is supposed to be the name of a Cambro-British saint; and, indeed, there can be little doubt as to this, though a very full calendar of the Welsh Church which I have compiled from various sources contains no mention of such a person. "Briauail filius Luuarch" (Briafael ap Llywarch, in modern spelling) occurs several times in the 'Book of Llandaff' as the name of a layman witnessing various grants of land to that see in the tenth century ('Liber Landavensis,' Oxford, 1893, pp. 143, 145, 148, 149, 151, 217).

The name is undoubtedly Welsh, and must at an earlier period have been "Briamail." It should be remarked that Western Gloucestershire, historically considered, is more Welsh than English.

JOHN HOBSON MATTHEWS.
Town Hall, Cardiff.

He was not a Norman, but a Welshman. His father was Lumarch and his grandfather Tydwr. As son of Lumarch he tests several charters (as the grant of Llowes to Bishop Oudoceus) about the beginning of the seventh century, some four hundred years before the Normans came. Briavail's daughter Cenedlon married Arthfaiel ap Ithel, King of Gwent. The whole history of the family to which he belonged is one of singular interest, because it is almost the only family of country squires or petty chieftains of those early days of which we have notices of some six generations, and what adds to the interest is that they were earnest agents in founding the Christian Church in Monmouthshire, for there they seem chiefly to have lived, though Briavail's activity was extended to Gloucestershire and Radnorshire. One of Briavail's nephews gave Usk to St. Cadoc, and another, who seems to have lived in Llansoy, gave a large gift to the Bishop of Llandaff down in Glamorganshire, apparently, anyhow, not of his own property, but bought to give. This man Brychan had a son Dingad, who is called St. Dingad and founded Dingestow near Monmouth, and his son again, St. Gwytherine, founded Llanvetherine in North Monmouthshire.

THOS. WILLIAMS.
Aston Clinton.

ANCIENT BOATS (9ᵗʰ S. viii. 366, 407, 507; ix. 31).—The following appeared in the *Morning Leader* of 31 December, 1901 :—

"An ancient Irish corrack, or canoe boat, has been discovered by workmen employed turf-cutting in a bog near Tuam, and the find is to be dispatched to-morrow *via* Limerick to be placed in a royal museum at Dublin. The corrack, which is in a good state of preservation, was found several feet below the surface. It measures 52 ft. long, and the Great Southern and Western Railway Company have provided a special double compartment for its conveyance to Dublin, where it will be placed among the other Celtic relics in the museum."

W. CURZON YEO.
Richmond, Surrey.

TINTAGEL (8ᵗʰ S. i. 434).—A correspondent at this reference asks whether this word and Tintageux in Sark have the same meaning, whether that meaning is "the Devil's Castle," and whether the word is in both cases of Celtic origin. These queries have not, I believe, been answered. Borrow, in 'Wild Wales,' says that Tintagel means "'the house in the gill of the hill,' a term admirably descriptive of the situation of the building," and scouts the idea that it means "the castle of guile, as the learned have said it does." According to his derivation, the first part of the word, therefore, is the Welsh *ty*=a house (old Welsh *tig*, Greek τέγος) combined with the preposition *yn*=in. But according to Mr. Ward ('Thorough Guide to North Devon and North Cornwall') Tintagel is a corruption of Dundagel, and means "the impregnable hill fort." Which is, or is either, correct?

J. P. LEWIS.

LADY MARY TUDOR (9ᵗʰ S. viii. 484; ix. 72).—"The Peerage of England. Second edition. London, 1710. Printed by G. F. for Abel Roper and Arthur Collins, at the Black-Boy in Fleetstreet," has the following on p. 27:—

"A daughter of K. Charles II. by Mrs. Mary Davis. Mary, surnam'd Tudor, born 1673 (was brought up under the Government and Tuition of Anne Countess Marshal, Wife of the Earl-Marshal of Scotland); to whom the King gave the Surname of Tudor; married Francis Lord Ratcliff, at that time, Son and Heir to Francis, Earl of Derwentwater, whom he succeeded in the Earldom."

A reference in the margin is made to Derwentwater, under which heading on p. 332 we find :—

"To him succeeded Francis, his Son and Heir, anno 1696, who, in his Father's Life, married the Lady Mary Tudor, Natural Daughter of King Charles II. (begotten on the Body of Mrs. Mary Davis) by whom he had Issue, James Lord Ratcliffe, son and Heir, now Earl of Derwentwater, born 1695."

HERBERT SOUTHAM.
Shrewsbury.

"OMNEITY": "OMNIETY" (9ᵗʰ S. ix. 127).— I find "Omneity, the allness, or all being of a thing," in the 'English Dictionary,' by "E. Coles, School Master and Teacher of Tongue of Foreigners," London, 1692. Dr. John Ash, in his 'Dictionary of the English Language,' 1776, says it is derived from the Latin *omnis*, all, the state of containing all things.

EVERARD HOME COLEMAN.
71, Brecknock Road.

"OLIVER" (9ᵗʰ S. ix. 127).—There is a serial story now running through the *Quiver*, entitled 'Nebo the Nailer,' by the Rev. S. Baring-Gould, in which reference is continually being made to what the writer calls the "ollifer." The mechanism of the instrument is fully described, but whether the details given of the invention are fiction or fact I am unable to say.   JOHN T. PAGE.
West Haddon, Northamptonshire.

Peter Pett (3rd S. x. 127).—Though it be a long call from 1866 to 1902, some readers may be interested in the following lines concerning Charles II.'s shipwright. They occur in the Third Part of the 'Collection of Poems on Affairs of State,' London, 1689, no printer's name. I see that the 'D.N.B.' ascribes the verses to Marvel, the accuracy of which I am inclined to doubt :—

> After this loss, to rellish discontent,
> Some one must be accus'd by Punishment.
> All our miscarriages on *Pett* must fall ;
> His Name alone seems fit to answer all.
> Whose Counsel first did this mad War beget ?
> Who all Commands sold thro' the Navy ? *Pett.*
> Who would not follow when the *Dutch* were bet ?
> Who treated out the time at *Bergen ?* *Pett.*
> Who the *Dutch* Fleet with Storms disabled met,
> And rifling Prizes, them neglected ? *Pett.*
> Who with false News prevented the *Gazette ?*
> The Fleet divided ? Writ for *Rupert ?* *Pett.*
> Who all our Seamen cheated of their Debt ?
> And all our Prizes who did swallow ? *Pett.*
> Who did advise no Navy out to set ?
> And who the Forts left unrepair'd ? *Pett.*
> Who to supply with Powder, did forget
> *Languard, Sheerness, Gravesend,* and *Upnor ?* *Pett.*
> Who all our Ships expos'd in *Chathams* Net ?
> Who should it be but the *Phanatick Pett ?*
> *Pett,* the Sea Architect, in making Ships,
> Was the first cause of all these Naval slips :
> Had he not built, none of these faults had bin ;
> If no Creation, there had been no Sin.

Some of this resembles the Fitzgerald poem in 'Rejected Addresses' :—

> Who makes the quartern loaf and Luddites rise ?
> Who fills the butchers' shops with large blue flies ?

Richard H. Thornton.
Portland, Oregon.

Louis Philippe and Family at the "Star and Garter," Richmond (9th S. ix. 129).—Louis Philippe and his queen arrived at Newhaven on 3 March, 1848 ; on the following day they travelled by rail to Croydon, and drove thence direct to Claremont. The children had arrived in England earlier, and stayed at East Sheen, but they joined the royal party at Croydon on 4 March, and went with them to Claremont. Many interesting particulars and pictures are given in the *Illustrated London News,* March, 1848, pp. 166, 176, 179, 206.
W. C. B.

Gregory Lewis Way (9th S. ix. 128).—This gentleman was the second son of Lewis Way, Esq., of Old Court House, Richmond, Surrey, and Denham Place, Bucks, a director of the South Sea Company and President of Guy's Hospital, by his fourth wife Sarah, daughter of the Rev. Thomas Payne, vicar of Holme Lacy, Herefordshire, and sister of Frances, Countess of Northampton. He was born in 1756, and married 9 December, 1779, Ann Frances, daughter of the Rev. William Paxton, rector of Taplow, Bucks, by whom he had four sons and two daughters. He died 26 April, 1799, aged forty-three. Major-General Sir Gregory Holman Bromley Way, K.C.B., was a son of Mr. G. L. Way's elder half-brother, Benjamin Way, M.P. for Bridport and President of Guy's Hospital (1740–1808), and not of Mr. Lewis Way, as stated by Mr. Walter Jerrold. I think Mr. G. L. Way should have found a place in the 'Dict. Nat. Biog.,' as he was one of the most cultivated men of his time. In his translation of Le Grand's 'Fabliaux' he was associated with George Ellis, who saw the work through the press. The book-plate described by Mr. Jerrold is, of course, a creation of the fancy, illustrative of Mr. Way's chivalric tastes.
W. F. Prideaux.

Much information respecting the Rev. Lewis Way will be found in 5th S. xi. 349, 453, under the head of 'Palingenesia, the World to Come,' being the title of a work written by him, published in 1824. Consult also 7th S. i. 87, 137, under the name of Lewis Way.   Everard Home Coleman.
71, Brecknock Road.

Early Hotels of Rome (9th S. ix. 105).—Ælfred the Great may probably be added to the list of illustrious Englishmen who, like Rahere and St. Thomas of Canterbury, have at one time or another lodged in the quarter of S. Spirito. Ælfred, when only four years old, was sent to Rome in 853 by his father, where the Pope, Leo IV. (although he was Æthelwulf's youngest son), hallowed him king. His father Æthelwulf, King of the West Saxons, made his own pilgrimage thither in 855, and, returning the next year, brought Ælfred back to England with him. They would, doubtless, inhabit the quarter already well known to them through the residence therein of their ancestors, Kings Ine and Cædwalla. Ælfred ever remained a devoted son of Holy Church, Prof. Earle, indeed, considering the double-sceptred figure of *cloisonné* enamel, which forms the interior of the Ælfred Jewel, to be the conventional effigy of Christ's Vicar and Vicegerent upon earth.   A. R. Bayley.

Arms of Married Women (9th S. ix. 28 113).—I think there can be no doubt as to the correctness of Guillim's dictum that a widow cannot bear her husband's arms unimpaled, nor yet her own paternal coat. Neither can she bear them impaled, except on a lozenge with a black background to the dexter side, and that for the obvious reasons mentioned by Guillim, and cited by Mr. Radcliffe.

John Hobson Matthews.

Royal Personages (9ᵗʰ S. ix. 89).—Louisa Anne, born at Leicester House, died at Carlton House, buried 21 May, 1768, in Westminster Abbey.

Elizabeth Caroline, born at Norfolk House, St. James's Square, died at Kew, buried 14 September, 1759, in Westminster Abbey.

Frederic William, born at Leicester House, died there, or at Savile House, which adjoined it.

The Dukes of Cumberland and Gloucester, both born at Leicester House; the former died at Cumberland House, Pall Mall.

Augusta, Duchess of Brunswick, born at St. James's Palace, died at Spring Gardens.

Reference is made in Mrs. Delany's 'Life and Correspondence' to the Duke of Gloucester's marriage. She writes, 28 May, 1773, as follows:—

"When evidences were ask'd for, none were to be had; no register! no certificate, and no witness; the person that married them dead, and nothing remain'd but the oath of the D. and Dss. of G. that they were married."—Vol. iv. p. 507.

Anne, Princess Royal, born 22 October, 1709, in Hanover.

Mary, Princess of Hesse Cassel, born 22 February, 1723, at Leicester House; married at Cassel; died 14 June, 1771.

Louisa, Queen of Denmark, born 7 December, 1724, at Leicester House; married at Copenhagen; died 8 December, 1751.

Amelia Sophia died at her house in Harley Street, corner of Cavendish Square.

Caroline Elizabeth died at St. James's Palace.

George William died at Kensington Palace.

Prince Octavius was buried 10 May, 1782

Prince Alfred died at Windsor, buried 27 August, 1783.

These two princes were removed from Westminster to Windsor 10 February, 1820.

These dates are gleaned from Chester's 'Registers of Westminster Abbey,' Hare's 'Walks in London,' Miss Tytler's 'Six Royal Ladies of the House of Hanover,' Mrs. Delany's 'Life,' 'D.N.B.,' &c.

T. Colyer-Fergusson.

CLIII. (9ᵗʰ S. ix. 88).—I beg to refer Mr. R. J. Walker to pp. 164-6 of the Rev. J. H. Lupton's 'Life of Dean Colet' (1887). It would seem that a memorandum in Colet's handwriting is in existence, which apparently throws some light on his selection of the number 153. It is to be found on the fly-leaf

of a MS. copy of Colet's 'Statutes' now in the British Museum Library (Add. and Egerton MSS., S. 6274), and is quoted by Mr. Lupton as follows: "Of halidayes and halfe halydayes all noumbred togyder in whiche ys no teachinge ther be yn the hole yere viiˣˣ and xiij." Presumably this is the only evidence extant directly referring to the number 153. It seems as though the draught of fishes theory has been seized upon and made to do duty simply because of its coincidence.   John T. Page.

West Haddon, Northamptonshire.

"Barracked" (9ᵗʰ S. ix. 63).—Mr. Yarrow Baldock questions whether "barracking" (i.e, a word so spelt) can be "an elongated form of 'barking'"; yet is not the word "larrikin" or "larrakin" usually allowed to be only an elongated form of "larking"? The latter word, by-the-by, in the sense in which it is often used by us now, does not seem to figure in the older dictionaries I have at hand. In them the only meaning given is catching larks. May we not therefore conclude that "larking" in the later sense is only a corrupted form of the N.C. "laking" (or, to be exact, and to give to the word its full N.C. sound, "lā-āking")? If so, the first vowel in that word has evidently undergone that lowering of tone which has altered the character of the sound in so many of our words that they become almost unrecognizable. "La-aking" is the N.C. word for "not working." A mill-hand may not be "playing" in the S.C. sense; but he is "lā-āking" (and that amounts to "playing" in the N.C. sense) when not steadily at work—in that position, in fact, which is rather apt to produce (in young men) a "larky" frame of mind, and eventually, perhaps, a "larrikin" or "larrakin" person in the colonial sense.   Boscombrosa.

Bricks (9ᵗʰ S. viii. 404, 449, 528).—In a valuable article by the late Mr. G. E. Street on 'Brickwork in the Middle Ages' (Church Builder, 1863, pp. 53-64) the north porch of Lübeck Cathedral is described as

"a thirteenth-century addition of two bays in depth, with groining piers of clustered shafts with sculptured capitals, and a many-shafted doorway of the best character. Its interior is probably mainly of stone, but the exterior is all of brick. The archway is boldly moulded, and above it is a horizontal arcaded corbel table, stepped up in the centre to admit the arch. The gable is boldly arcaded upon shafts, and has a stepped corbel table, with a double line of moulded bricks above it next to the tiles. A couple of simple open arches are pierced in each side wall, and there are flat pilasters at the angles. In the gable enclosed within the arcading are some circular openings, one of which is cusped with small foliations formed of brick. The moulded bricks in the main arch are of two kinds only, one a large boltel, the other a large hollow, and these, arranged alternately with plain square-edged bricks, produce as much variety as is needful. The jamb of the doorway is of plain bricks, built with square recesses, in which detached stone shafts are placed. The capitals throughout are of stone with simple foliage."

J. HOLDEN MACMICHAEL.

WHIPS IN THE HOUSE OF COMMONS (8th S. iv., v., vi., vii., viii.).—A recently published pamphlet by Mr. George Walpole, entitled 'House of Commons Procedure ; with Notes on American Practice,' is responsible for the following :—

"Origin of the term 'Whip.'—This has been traced to a sally of Burke's in 1768, during the trouble over the election of Wilkes. Ministers sent messengers to bring back their supporters from the North of England, and even from France. Burke compared an official thus sent to the 'whipper in' of a pack of foxhounds."

EVERARD HOME COLEMAN.
71, Brecknock Road.

"UTILITARIAN" (9th S. vii. 425).—As supplementary to what is said at this reference, it may be mentioned that Mahony uses "Utilitarian" freely in his quaint and scholarly 'Reliques of Father Prout.' At the opening of the chapter on the 'Songs of France,' contributed to *Fraser's Magazine* in 1834, he applies the epithet to Sir John Bowring, who was then engaged on his commercial inquiry on the Continent. He scouts the proceedings of such an emissary as futile, and roundly asserts that they forcibly illustrate "that sad mixture of imbecility and ostentation too perceptible in all the doings of Utilitarianism." Here, then, is the abstract term itself, used, of course, with a purpose different from that which it was made to serve twenty years afterwards by John Stuart Mill, but still fully developed and ready to be turned to account. Mill's note, in chap. ii. of 'Utilitarianism,' remains defensible from his point of view, but such a statement as that made in the 'Encyclopædic Dictionary.' viz., that "Utilitarianism is a word coined by John Stuart Mill," will henceforth need to be modified.

THOMAS BAYNE.

CHESELDEN, RADCLIFFE, AND PRIDMORE (9th S. viii. 65).—I am indebted to the vicars of Somerby, Leicestershire, and of Braunston, Rutlandshire, to MR. JOSEPH PHILLIPS, MR. EDWIN HOLTHOUSE, and MR. VERE L. OLIVER for information. William Cheselden, son of George Chisseldine, gent., and Deborah his wife, was baptized "October ye 26th, 1688,"

at Burrough, Leicestershire, and was one of at least eight children. Is anything known of Peter Cheselden, born 24 September, 1696, and afterwards of Leicester, surgeon? He was a brother of William Cheselden. Peter Cheselden married and had issue. Was the Rev. Edward Cheselden, M.A., J.P., rector of West Charlton, Somersetshire, and of Somerby, Leicestershire, who married Jane, daughter of the Rev. William Dodd, one of the children of Peter Cheselden? The Rev. Edward Cheselden died 9 June, 1780, aged fifty-eight, and had a son Edward Cheselden, who died 10 November, 1804, aged fifty-five, and a daughter Wilhelmina Jane, who married John Suffield Brown, of Leesthorpe, in the parish of Pickwell, and died 31 January, 1832, aged eighty-three. I fail to trace any descendant in the male line of the family of Cheselden, formerly of Uppingham, Braunston, Ridlington, Burrough, Somerby, Manton, Melton Mowbray, or of any other place. James Weltden Roberts, of Thurnby, and lord of the manor of Thorpe Langton, is given as having married Mary, only daughter of Richard Cheselden, of Melton Mowbray, and Elizabeth (Nedham, of Gaddesby), his wife, and as having had issue.

REGINALD STEWART BODDINGTON.
15, Markham Square, Chelsea.

THE SOURCE OF THE SEVEN AGES (9th S. ix. 46).—

Who in his cradle by his childish crying
Presageth his mishaps.

Lodge in the above seems to have the words of Sidney in his mind :—

The childe...............................
Which cries first borne, the presage of his life.
'Arcadia.'

At a later time Shakspeare wrote :—

When we are born we cry that we are come
To this great stage of fools.　　'King Lear.'

Shakspeare's description of the seven ages appears to me something like the lines in Horace's 'Ars Poetica' beginning :—

Reddere qui voces jam scit puer.

Horace is not comparing the world to a stage, but he passes the ages of man in review. E. YARDLEY.

GAZETTEER (3rd S. iv. 25).—Many years have elapsed since a query appeared at the above reference asking for the origin of the word "gazetteer" as applied to a geographical dictionary. The explanation is given in the 'New English Dictionary.' The word was first used by L. Echard in 1704 in the preface to the edition published in that year of his 'Gazetteer's or Newsman's Interpreter, being a Geographical Index.' Echard says in the preface, "The kind Reception the Gazetteer has met with......induced us to go on with a second Part." In 1751 there appeared a work entitled 'England's Gazetteer.'

R. B. P.

"Rout" (9ᵗʰ S. ix. 65).—To the citations of "rout" I beg to add the following earlier examples :—

1782. "And, as I have a frank and a subject, I will leave my bothers, and write you and my dear brother Molesworth a little account of a *rout* I have just been at, at the house of Mr. Paradise."— 'Diary and Letters of Madame D'Arblay,' ii. 89 (London, Henry Colburn, 1854, 7 vols.).

1775. "He told us that the Prince was to dine with Lord Buckingham and a multitude of others, and begged the concert might not wait for him, as he was obliged to go in for a few minutes to Lady Harrington's before he came, it being her *Rout* Day."—'The Early Diary of Frances Burney,' iii. 94 (London, George Bell & Sons, 1889, 2 vols.).

You've heard of my Lady Bunbutter, no doubt,
How she loves an Assembly, Fandango, or *Rout* ;
No Lady in London is half so expert
At a snug private Party, her Friends to divert.

'The New Bath Guide,' p. 97 (London, J. Dodsley, 1766).

E. P. Merritt.

Boston, U.S.

See 'The Faithful Bird,' by Wm. Cowper, "Fandango, ball, and rout"; and 'Our Ball,' by Praed, "Miss Hyacinth threatens a rout."

J. R. FitzGerald.

L. L. K. in his note talks of "rout-chairs" being advertised by West-End caterers. In the East-End we talk of "rout-seats," and you will find the word listed among the many articles hirable for parties, &c., from catering firms. These "rout-seats" are long forms, the seatings of which are made of cane. They usually afford accommodation for six persons. I presume the reason these are used at public dinners is that they can be more expeditiously handled and stacked up than chairs, and also because they form excellent sittings for those who are tired of waltzing, &c., at the balls that generally follow on at these functions.

M. L. R. Breslar.

Percy House, South Hackney.

The word comes into the old epigram :—

Marriage, as some men say and old men note,
Is like some public feast or common rout,
Where those that are without would fain get in,
And those that are within would fain get out.

H. A. St. J. M.

In 1857, when I resided in Derbyshire, 'Rout Polka' was the title of a pianoforte piece which I heard strummed in every house.

Charles A. Federer.

Bradford.

"Frail" (9ᵗʰ S. iv. 436, 507 ; v. 51, 158 ; vi. 378 ; vii. 33, 177 ; viii. 531 ; ix. 96).—The term "frail," or more commonly "flail," is applied to a bag made of brown cord, such as is used by women for shopping. The word is so employed, at least, by people who belong to East Monmouthshire. I have not heard it in London.   John Hobson Matthews.

Town Hall, Cardiff.

Markoe or Marcou Family : Records of Nevis, St. Eustatius, and Santa Cruz (9ᵗʰ S. ix. 87).—Possibly the following extract from Capt. J. H. Lawrence-Archer's 'Monumental Inscriptions of the British West Indies,' p. 188, may be of use to Mr. Wade, viz., "New West Ground (Kingston)," Jamaica, "Francis Marcaud, who obit [*sic*] April 29th, 1826, aged 77 years."   Geo. S. Cary.

Laurel Lodge, Terenure, co. Dublin.

Miscellaneous.

NOTES ON BOOKS, &c.

History of the Church of England. By R. W. Dixon, D.D. Vols. V. and VI. (Oxford, Clarendon Press.)

It is the too common fate of any literary work projected on a scale of unusual magnitude that it is left a fragment. If the compasses be extended too widely at the start the proposed circle never gets described, and only a partial arc suggests what the completed orb might have been, time and material favouring. But the life of the artist is all too brief for the exacting longitude of art. So it has proved with Canon Dixon's copious 'History of the Church of England.' Taking the abolition of the Roman jurisdiction as his starting-point, in his first three volumes he gave us (1881-84) the history of Church affairs under Henry VIII. and Edward VI ; in 1890 appeared the fourth volume, devoted to the short reign of Mary (see 5ᵗʰ S. x. 119 ; 6ᵗʰ S. iii. 399) ; and now we have the fifth and sixth volumes—which are also, alas ! to be the last —published two years after his death, and covering only the first twelve years of Elizabeth's reign. The "spacious days" of the great queen no doubt demanded a spacious canvas, and Canon Dixon had no lack of interesting matter wherewith to give it life and colour. He loved an ample stage to set out his stirring drama with due effect, and here he has to deal with a critical period, when the National Church assumed its present form, and gained new life by being severed from the Roman Curia, which, with hasty improvidence, itself did the severing.

Canon Dixon is well known to have been a diligent explorer of ancient muniments, and he supplies abundance of "justificative pieces" to establish all his conclusions, which are eminently fair and judicial. Whole pages from contemporary sermons or forgotten pamphlets are made to give actuality and local colour, as well as authentication, to the events chronicled. Indeed, if a trustworthy and impartial account of the Reformation in England is desired, we know not where it can be found sooner than here. Elizabeth's and Cecil's astute policy of holding the balance between the conflicting extremes of Church parties is skilfully depicted, and we commiserate the hard lot of good Archbishop Parker, who was employed as the necessary cat to draw the chestnut of Uniformity out of the fire, so that his royal patron might not burn her fingers. Among the points incidentally cleared up is the disuse of the title "Supreme Head of the Church," which died out with Henry VIII., it having been repealed in the first year of Mary and Philip and never afterwards revived. The "Nag's Head" fable is shown to be not even *ben trovato*, and is traced up to its first concoction in 1604 in Holywood's 'De Investiganda Vera ac Visib. Christi Ecclesia.' The same conclusion is arrived at as in Dr. Gee's 'Elizabethan Clergy and the Settlement of Religion,' that the Reformation movement was so thoroughly national that not more than 200 out of 9,400 parish priests were deprived for not accepting it.

Regarding Canon Dixon's work from a literary point of view, we cannot say we are admirers of his style, although we are aware that we here dissent from the judgment of many competent critics. He uses words in a slovenly manner sometimes, with a want of precision and choice which we should not have expected from one who was also a considerable poet. We may give two instances. He speaks of a declaration which "bears the *images* of the hammers wherewith it was forged." He tells of a poor comedy "which descended to midnight, but not to posterity," meaning, we suppose, that it lasted till midnight, but has not survived to our own times. Occasionally, indeed, the sentences are so peculiar as to remind one of a foreigner writing in an unaccustomed language. Thus, Elizabeth's "charm lay in the feminine quality which met all men with that which seemed the partner of their several tastes, resembling that which they preferred, and yet not the double, but the counterpart and completion of it." Again: "Ireland will be difficultly stayed in obedience......For France, try for peace ; kindle religious controversy. Scotland the same : augment the hope of them who incline them to good religion : and fortify Berwick and get demilances. Ireland wants some money spent on it. How is the alteration to be done?" "Awaking spicery of conscience," "an incident in midst exemplifying" something, are crabbed phrases; and such archaisms as "regiment" for *régime* or rule, and "they perused the rest of the diocese," are at least unusual. A sentence like the following stands self-condemned : "This cleansing of temples, taking place the most part about Bartholomew tide ; on the eve, the day, the day after the day of St. Bartholomew, may be said to make a Bartholomean era in our annals, an era to which the epithet that denotes the colour of darkness may be considered inappropriate." Among verbal eccentricities we mark an "abscondite" clerk (something new for Dr. Murray), "inter-religion," "to nonconform," "martyric" boldness, a "manifest" (for *manifesto*). "Romanensian" does not seem to us a happy substitute for *Romanizer*, nor "Calvinian" for *Calvinist*, nor "parochs" for *parochial clergy*, nor "executor" at Holy Communion for *celebrant*. After these we hardly staggered at reading that "the queen *besigned*, as some say, to exhibit her reformation in a fair aspect to the foreign world"; but, as Dr. Murray again fails us here, we are charitable enough to believe that this is only a misprint.

These volumes have been seen through the press by the author's friend Dr. Henry Gee, who undertook the laborious task of verifying all the citations taken from documents in the Record Office and public libraries. Quotation marks to define the beginning of an important passage which ends on vol. v. p. 22 are missing, leaving its extent quite ambiguous. The index is excellent.

Arundel Hymns, and other Spiritual Praises. Chosen and edited by Henry, Duke of Norfolk, and Charles T. Gatty, F.S.A.

These hymns, intended for the use of Catholics, are published with Papal permission and with an introductory letter from Pope Leo XIII. They are wholly from Roman Catholic writers. The Latin in many cases accompanies the English text. As a rule the compositions are more notable for devoutness than for poetical facility. The volume is published by the editors, 3, Queen Street, Mayfair.

A close study of the political articles in the leading reviews can scarcely be recommended to those of a nervous temperament. Time was when it was part of the scheme that those who frightened us with prospects of invasions, coalitions against us, and every form of European complication, used to sign their own names, so that we might judge as to the value of their opinions. Those days are long past, and those who now set before us the inevitable results of our modern actions employ pseudonyms implying the possession of oracular wisdom and unequalled sources of information, but so far as regards their identity veil their heads in the obscurity of the clouds whence they fulminate. The temptation to deal with these prophets of evil has never been strong, and is now weaker than ever. For different reasons we cannot discuss Sir Henry Thompson's thoughtful contribution to the *Fortnightly*, 'The Unknown God.' Mr. G. H. Powell's 'The Care of Books' appeals very directly to our readers, and may, indeed, be warmly commended to them. Concerning the wisdom of what he says there is no doubt. His are, however, counsels of perfection. It is well to have the advice given by the Marquis of Macciucca to frequenters of the library, though some of the counsels, such as "Do not steal the books," belong to elementary forms of morality. M. Maeterlinck, now a frequent writer in the *Fortnightly*, has an article on 'Our Past,' and is as fantastically ingenious and paradoxical as needs be wished. A line or two from this will suffice: "'The past is past,' we say, and it is false ; the past is always present : 'We have to bear the burden of our past,' we sigh, and it is false ; the past bears our burden." This is the right butterwoman's rate to market, and a continuance of it will almost console us for the loss of 'Proverbial Philosophy.' Miss Elizabeth Robins writes on 'Pleasure Mining.' The nature of her communication seems scarcely indicated in her title. Miss Janet Hogarth discusses 'Lucas Malet's Novels.'—In the *Nineteenth Century* Mr. Walter Frewen Lord berates Thackeray as 'The Apostle of Mediocrity.' We will leave others to answer this railer, and wait with some curiosity to see how large a nest of hornets he will bring about his ears. The article is not written in banter, but is as serious as it can be. Mr. Claude Phillips speaks strongly, as is but due, on the 'Increasing Export of England's Art Treasures.' This is a difficult subject, and will become more so as times go on. The great English portraits should, of course, be kept in England, but who is to keep them in presence of American competition? Mr. Stephen Gwynn eulogizes eloquently 'The Masque of "Ulysses."' Mr. W. S. Lilly writes 'Concerning Ghost Stories,' and the Countess of Jersey deals with 'The Young English Girl Self-portrayed.' The whole constitutes an admirable number, which unfortunately we get too late to be able to do full justice to its contents.— A curious and not altogether agreeable effect is obtained in the *Pall Mall* in the reproduction of the 'Portrait of a Lady,' by Velasquez, which serves as frontispiece. A character-study of President Loubet, by Ada Cone, declares him to be the first President of the French Republic who has realized completely the democratic ideal of a chief magistrate. No very intimate knowledge of President Loubet seems to be possessed by the writer. 'The Real Siberia,' by Mr. John Foster Fraser, is an account by an American of a Siberia in which in September he was frizzled with heat and munched by mosquitoes. In the coldest winter, even, the place is described as not destitute of attraction. The views seem to us the chief feature of the contribution. Mr. Walter Maunder has a valuable and scientific article on the moon, which also is well illustrated. Mrs. Gallup contributes her account of Bacon's bi-literal cipher. This leaves matters where they were, so far as Bacon's claim to be every one is concerned, and requires closer investigation than we are at present able to bestow. An account of Chancellor von Bülow may be read with interest. — 'The Heart of England,' in *Scribner's*, gives some striking pictures of the life of labour in London, near London Bridge, and in the port of London. The views are taken from all sorts of places, including a balloon, and are very impressive to those most familiar with the spots depicted. The third instalment appears of 'The American "Commercial Invasion" of Europe.' Very interesting, both as regards designs and letterpress, is Miss Wharton's 'Sanctuaries of the Pennine Alps.' To the charms of the waters of the Lago d' Orla we have long been sensible. In defiance of authority, Mr. Richard Harding Davis calls a story of his 'The Bar [*sic*] Sinister.' The fiction, with which we are unable to deal, is excellent.—Mr. J. W. Mackail, an elegant scholar, sends to the *Cornhill* a rendering of the scenes between Calypso and Odysseus, or Ulysses, as, after the example of Mr. Stephen Phillips, the wanderer is called. The passages translated are from the fifth book, lines 148-224, and the metre resembles that of the quatrain of Omar Khayyam. "An Old Fogey" contrasts the Bohemia of yesterday with that of to-day. Part xiv. of 'A Londoner's Log-Book' holds out the promise of a contested election in Stuccodom. Lady Grove deals with 'Social Solecisms,' without, however, quite understanding her subject. General Maunsell, C.B., gives his reminiscences of the Punjaub campaign. Mrs. Moffat, in 'On Safari,' describes life in Central Africa. 'What is "Popular Poetry"?' by Mr. W. B. Yeats, leaves us still a little in the dark.—Mr. Hudson's articles on natural history in *Longman's* are always good, and 'Selborne Revisited' is one of the best. It inspires a strong desire to follow in the writer's track. 'Canvassing in 1832' is brightly written. Mrs. Clement Shorter tells pleasantly in verse the opening of the story of King Cophetua. Mr. Lang is once more admirable in 'At the Sign of the Ship,'

the most entertaining, although the most personal, of the miscellanea contributed to magazines.—Canon Wood, in the *Gentleman's*, writes on 'Arthur, "King of England,"' by which, we are told, is not to be understood the famous husband of Guinevere, but the Prince Arthur who married Katherine of Arragon and never came into his kingdom. Mr. Charles Wilkins writes on 'The King of the Dandies' without ever apparently having read the 'Dandyism and G. Brummel' of Barbey d'Aurevilly, the best thing ever written on the subject.

CHARLES KENT, an old contributor to our columns, who died on the 23rd of February, was born in London on the 3rd of November, 1823, and was the son of William Kent, R.N., who was born at the old Government House, Sydney, on December 23rd, 1799. At the early age of twenty-two Charles Kent became editor of the *Sun* evening newspaper, and from 1874 to 1881 he edited the *Weekly Register*. He was a contributor to the 'Dictionary of National Biography' and the 'Encyclopædia Britannica,' and was an authority on the works of Leigh Hunt, Lytton, and Charles Dickens. In 'N. & Q.' for September 4th, 1875, he wrote an interesting reply to MR. TOWNSHEND MAYER in reference to Lord Lytton's introduction of several of his contemporaries in his 'King Arthur.' Kent's long life was devoted to literature, and in recognition of his services a Civil List pension of 100*l*. a year was conferred upon him. He was one of the most lovable of men, and the inscription he caused to be placed on Leigh Hunt's tomb might well find a place on his—"Write me as one who loves his fellow-men." We who knew him say of him, as Leigh Hunt said, "Right Friend and Gentleman."

Notices to Correspondents.

We must call special attention to the following notices:—

ON all communications must be written the name and address of the sender, not necessarily for publication, but as a guarantee of good faith.

WE cannot undertake to answer queries privately.

To secure insertion of communications correspondents must observe the following rules. Let each note, query, or reply be written on a separate slip of paper, with the signature of the writer and such address as he wishes to appear. When answering queries, or making notes with regard to previous entries in the paper, contributors are requested to put in parentheses, immediately after the exact heading, the series, volume, and page or pages to which they refer. Correspondents who repeat queries are requested to head the second communication "Duplicate."

H. P. L. ("Lifting").—See 6th S. vii. 308; viii. 37, 94, 234, 436; 8th S. vi. 29, 192.

NOTICE.

Editorial communications should be addressed to "The Editor of 'Notes and Queries'"—Advertisements and Business Letters to "The Publisher"—at the Office, Bream's Buildings, Chancery Lane, E.C.

We beg leave to state that we decline to return communications which, for any reason, we do not print; and to this rule we can make no exception.

LONDON, SATURDAY, MARCH 15, 1902.

CONTENTS. — No. 220.

Notes.

'A DREAM OF A QUEEN'S REIGN': 'GOD SAVE THE QUEEN.'

IN my possession is a fine uncut copy, in the original buff-coloured paper covers, of an extremely rare small 8vo book, entitled 'A Dream of a Queen's Reign,' containing fifty-five pages with six preliminary leaves, and published by John Templeman, of 248, Regent Street (near Oxford Street), London, in 1843. It includes, at the end, a sixteen-page catalogue of books issued by the same publisher. The title-page bears the quotation from Shakspeare, "I have had a most rare vision." There is no copy in the British Museum, nor can the existence of any but my own, or even any mention of the book, be traced. This singular production is stated in the somewhat lengthy preface to be edited from a MS. belonging to the "Rev. Theophilus C——, the octogenarian curate of G—— [apparently in one of the Midland counties of England]. lately deceased," who, in consequence of its evident interpolations and alterations by different hands, at different periods, and for different purposes, had little or no faith in its general authenticity, nor

could he read it in so connected a manner as to understand its drift or moral, or to determine the locality to which it refers, or the period or periods when the chief portions of the context were written. The editor, who obtained the MS. direct from his friend the owner as above, upon due examination and reflection, concludes, however, that the main portion of this report of the dream was probably written a little after the accession of King James I. It appears from the editor's statement that the names of all persons and places had been erased in the MS., except the initial letters, and from certain crowded interpolations and marginal addenda it would seem that somebody wanted to publish the dream in the reign of Queen Elizabeth, and that amongst the various illuminated title-pages which were rolled up with the MS., one bears a date coeval with the reign of Queen Mary, her sister and predecessor ; and that there are plain directions to the printer, with dates to them, showing that in the time of Queen Anne the necessary steps were actually taken to put this dream forth in a connected form to the world ; but, owing, probably, to the constitutional timidity or unexpected demise of that princess, it was considered to be totally inapplicable, and the manuscript was reconsigned to oblivion, or passed from hand to hand only amongst the curious.

This MS. was purchased, with other literary curiosities, by the said reverend gentleman's grandfather, at the public sale of the effects of a learned antiquary at Huntingdon, whose ancestors had been for ages forming the collection. And it is added, with some expression of doubt as to the truth of the statement, that the MS. was greatly desired by Sir Robert Cotton, sometime of Connington, Bart., at any price ; but that all his offers were rejected.

The dream deals with the events of the reign and the conduct of an imaginary or ideal Queen of England, and the dreamer—whose Utopian ideas were possibly stimulated by Sir Thomas More's famous philosophical romance, and who had probably studied such works as 'The Trauayled Pylgrime,' printed in 1569—was one Master Bernard M——, of S——, who, as the editor infers, was a bachelor and a gentleman of what is called a good family, a scholar, and had travelled, of a religious and kindly disposition, and of a cultivated taste for the period in which he lived. We are further informed by the editor that the book produces the dream for the first time printed in one uniform contexture. Among the more noteworthy contents is (on p. 54) mention of the playing and singing of the "hymn" of 'God save the Queen' (alluding, of course, to the imaginary queen of the dream), as follows :—

1.

God save our righteous Queen,
Bless our most faithful Queen,
   God save the Queen.
Send her victorious,
In goodness glorious,
Long to reign over us,
   God save the Queen.

2.

O Lord our God, arise,
Turn the Queen's enemies,
   And let none fall.
Confound base politicks,
Flatt'rers and factions' tricks,
In thee our hopes we fix,
   God save us all.

3.

Thy choicest favours pour,
Now and for evermore,
   On our fair Queen :
Bless her dominions all,
Home and colonial,
Round the revolving ball :
   God save the Queen !

The editor appears to have previously compiled a little work dealing with the history and antiquities of a small rural district in one of our Midland counties, in which he was greatly assisted by his reverend friend, but, through lack of subscribers, the same did not go to press.

It has occurred to my mind whether the book 'A Dream of a Queen's Reign' was really from a MS. of the period stated (in the style of which it is certainly written), or a "modern antique"; and if the latter, who was its author? If the former, who was the Master Bernard M—— referred to, and where is now the original MS., and who was its editor in 1843? Can the rarity of the book be accounted for, and is any reader able to refer to an earlier publication of the dream in any form? Any further information on the subject will be appreciated.

W. I. R. V.

THE BACON—SHAKESPEARE QUESTION.
(*Continued from p. 142.*)

Bacon's MS. consists of about forty quarto pages; it is mostly in Bacon's own handwriting, and the title of one of the sheets, 'Promus of Formularies and Elegancies,' was given to the whole collection by the late Mr. Spedding. "It consists," to quote from Mr. Spedding's description, "of single sentences set down one after the other without marks between, or any notes of reference and explanation." The collection is of the most miscellaneous character, and it includes proverbs in English, French, Italian, Spanish, Latin, and Greek; verses from the Bible, and sentences from Latin authors; single words, small turns of expression, certain forms of salutation, and jottings concerning the sayings of Bacon's own friends. It remains to add that there is very little in it that is original or Bacon's own, and that the collection is mostly from books which were then in every scholar's hands.

Those who favour the Bacon authorship of the Shakespeare plays not only wish us to believe that these notes, which were put down with such care, are not used in Bacon's own work, but that they are not commonplaces. They know their master's work so well that you may take their word for it that there is little or no trace of the 'Promus' entries in Bacon's acknowledged work. And, they argue, Bacon would never have collected about 1,700 sayings, words, &c., if they had been commonplaces, or if he had not intended using them in his work. What, then, did Bacon do with his notes? He used them, say the Baconians, in the work of Shakespeare.

A quotation from Bacon's "acknowledged work" will assist us in this part of our inquiry :—

"Therefore to speak plainly of the gathering of heads or commonplaces, I think first in general that one man's notes will little profit another, because one man's conceit doth so much differ from another's; and also because the bare note itself is nothing so much as the suggestion it gives the reader. Next I think no profit is gotten of his notes that is not judicious in that whereof he makes his notes."—'Advice to Sir F. Greville,' about 1596.

The gathering of commonplaces is advocated by Bacon not only in the advice to Greville, but in several places in his work, notably in the 'De Augmentis,' book vi. The notes may be commonplaces, but they must be selected with care and with particular reference to the suggestions they offer; for not only will one man's notes little profit another, but the same sayings or sentences will conjure up in another man's mind quite different trains of thought, which would be controlled by a differing experience and environment. In other words, so many heads, so many wits. Now let us compare Bacon's wit with Shakespeare's.

I will first deal with one or two single words that are noted in the 'Promus,' and will quote Bacon and Shakespeare as they are quoted in Mrs. Pott's work, which seeks to show that the notes are used in the great dramatist's work.

Entry No. 1422 is as follows: "Removing (Remuant)."

Mrs. Pott could not find Bacon using the note in his acknowledged work; but, nevertheless, he did so:—

"A hasty fortune maketh an enterpriser and remover (the French hath it better, *entreprenant*, or *remuant*); but the exercised fortune maketh the able man."—'Essay of Fortune.'

The following passages from Shakespeare are supposed to illustrate Bacon's note:—

She moves me not, or not removes, at least,
Affection's edge in me.
　　　　　　'Taming of the Shrew,' Act I. sc. ii.

Any soul removed.
　　　　　　'1 Henry IV.,' Act IV. sc. i. l. 35.

All thy safety were remotion.
　　　　　　'Timon of Athens,' Act IV. sc. iii.

This act persuades me that this remotion is practice only.
　　　　　　'Lear,' Act II. sc. iv.

Under No. 1432 occurs the note "The avenues."

In illustrating the note from Shakespeare Mrs. Pott quotes many passages which use the words "gates," "pathways," "road," "way," &c., just as if these words, like "remove" and "remotion" in the preceding instance, were peculiar to Shakespeare and Bacon; and she goes further than this, for in her preface, p. 50, she asserts that the word "avenues" is not only not in Shakespeare, but it is absent also from Bacon's prose work. I will quote from Bacon, and it will be seen that he not only has a fixed way of employing the word, but that he always associates it with the words "approaches" or "entrances."

1. "Since the last parliament, it is also notorious in every man's knowledge and remembrance that the Spaniards have possessed themselves of that avenue and place of approach for England," &c.—'Speech on the Subsidy Bill,' 1597.

2. "How great the honour is, to keep the approaches or avenues of this kingdom, I hear many discourse."—'Advice to Essex,' March, 1599.

3. "If physicians will learn and use the true approaches and avenues of nature," &c.—'Advancement of Learning,' book ii.

4. "But their approaches and avenues are taken away." — 'General Naturalization,' February, 1606/7.

5. "Causeways in the avenues and entrances of the towns abroad beyond the seas."—'Charge on Opening the Court of the Verge,' 1611.

Other cases could be cited to show that Bacon employs the word in the same very peculiar way.

Then there is the word "real," which is put under No. 461, and which Mrs. Pott thinks Bacon may have introduced into the English language. "Real," in the sense of "royal," was a common word in English several hundred years before Bacon was born, and it occurs many times in Chaucer. "Real," as opposed to "nominal," was also in use in England long before Bacon was born, as witness the opposing sects of the Nominalists and the Realists. The Spanish coin, a *reale*, was also well known to Englishmen before Bacon's time. Yet Mrs. Pott, mistaking the object of Bacon's note, which is revealed by the entry that he places under it, "Forma dat esse," makes a parade of the fact that Shakespeare uses "royal" for "real," that he puns upon the coins "noble" and "real," and that he employs "real" in the sense of being opposed to "unreal." Shakespeare is quoted thus:—

Host. My lord, there is a nobleman would speak to you.
P. Hen. Give him as much as will make him a royal man, and send him back.
　　　　　　'1 Henry IV.,' Act II. sc. iv.

Mrs. Pott does not attempt to show that Bacon anywhere associated the Spanish coin with the English word "real," and she overlooks the fact that the dramatists of the time were often guilty of making most wretched puns on the names of coins. It was a common device to play on "angel," "ducats," &c. Thus in 'The First Part of Jeronimo' Kyd has several nonsensical puns on "ducats," which become "ducks, dainty ducks"; and in 'Sir John Oldcastle' and in many other plays money is given the cant name of "golden ruddocks" or "robin-redbreasts." Hence Shakespeare was but following a general lead, and there is nothing unusual or strange in his pun, supposing him to be connecting "royal" with the Spanish "reale"—a point which is open to serious question. He may have merely meant "royal" to stand for "kingly," or something greater in rank than a "nobleman." "Royal" in this sense is used in a somewhat similar passage by Massinger, and in relation to money:—

Wellborn.　　　　　I will pay you in private.
Order. A royal gentleman!
Furnace. Royal as an emperor!
He'll prove a brave master; my good lady knew
To choose a man.
　　　　'A New Way to Pay Old Debts,' Act IV. sc. ii.

'The Fable of Cupid,' as told by Bacon, and his interpretation of it, explain the precise use to which he meant to put his note, for there and elsewhere he associates the scholastic "real" with the Platonic dictum "Forma dat esse," as well as with his other 'Promus' note, No. 765, "He came of an egge." Now if there were no other evidence to disprove Bacon's title to the Shakespeare plays and poems it could be found in this word "real," for, strange to say, it seems to have almost completely dropped out of common speech for at least fifty years before it became the subject of Bacon's note. I have been unable to find it in any part of the writings of Peele, Greene, Marlowe, or other poets and dramatists of the same or an earlier period. Bacon and men of his acquaintance and scholars like Gabriel Harvey use it frequently. Shakespeare, on the other hand, uses "real" and its variants only five times, whereas Beaumont and Fletcher in twenty plays employ it eight times, and Ben Jonson twenty-three. I can quote sixty-nine passages from Bacon's work in which the word occurs, and have no doubt if I were to go over all his work I could find it many times more. Now if Bacon wrote the Shakespeare plays why is it that we find "real" so seldom in them? See how much closer Ben Jonson is to Bacon in his vocabulary than Shakespeare. The word does not occur in Shakespeare in any work that is known to have been written earlier that 1598, whereas it is a common word in Bacon before that time.   C. CRAWFORD.

53, Hampden Road, Hornsey, N.

(To be continued.)

RICHARD ARGENTINE, ALIAS SEXTEN.—In the account of this "physician and divine" in the 'D.N.B.,' vol. ii. p. 80, it is stated that "in January, 1563/4, he appears to have been living at Exeter, but the statement that he was a prebendary of Exeter and Wells is without foundation."

This statement can scarcely be regarded as strictly accurate, for, according to the Composition Books at the Record Office, Richard Argentine, clericus, compounded for the first-fruits of one of twenty-four prebends in Exeter Cathedral on 20 March, 4 Eliz. (1561/2). A cleric of the same name compounded in respect of Stokeleigh Pomeroy rectory, Devon, on 16 February, 4 Eliz. (1561/2), and of Stoke Fleming rectory, Devon, on 1 August, 5 Eliz. (1563).

Argentine's career starts in the 'Dictionary' with his going to Ipswich "in a serving-man's coat," and becoming "successively usher and master of the grammar school" there. He perhaps was the native of Milton, Dorset, who, under the name of Richard Sexten, or Sexton, became scholar at Winchester in 1524 (Kirby), and was Fellow of New College, Oxford, 1528–38; M.A. 1536 (Foster, 'Alumni Oxon.'). According to an old marginal note against his name in the Winchester College register, this Sexten became doctor of medicine and under-master (*hypodidascalus*) at Ipswich. I am ignorant, however, of the

reasons why writers have stated that Richard Argentine was "*alias* Sexten" (see Tanner, 'Bibliotheca Britannico - Hibernica,' 48; Cooper, 'Athenæ Cantab.,' i. 275), and should be glad of information upon the point.

According to the 'Dictionary' Argentine was rector of St. Helen's, Ipswich, 1556–68. The index to the Composition Books mentions no composition in respect of this rectory intermediate between that by William Baker on 29 September, 1554, and that by William Burges on 15 June, 1570. Perhaps some Ipswich correspondent may be able to throw further light on Argentine's connexion with this rectory.   H. C.

'THE CAMBRIDGE CONFESSOR.'—In 1836 there appeared at Cambridge (printed for I. Stevenson, Trinity Street, and J. Fraser, Regent Street, London) the first and only number of the *Cambridge Confessor; or, the Guide to the Church*, which was apparently intended to rival the 'Tracts for the Times,' then in course of publication at Oxford. It is stated in the introduction, which is dated 6 May, 1836, that the publication would appear monthly during term, and that the contents would be "partly original and partly selected." The sub-title of the first number is 'The Claims of the Catholic Church on the Love and Reverence of the Faithful,' 12 pp. 8vo, and it bears a close resemblance to its Oxford prototype. I believe that the publication stopped at the first number on account of the small support which the venture received, though in point of quality the number is at least equal to some of the 'Tracts for the Times.' The title was somewhat unfortunate, as it suggested auricular confession, and so cast suspicion on the whole thing. Amongst those who were connected with the publication was the late Rev. Henry Goldsmith Vignes, vicar of Sunbury from 1842 to 1895, or thereabouts. I am told by a son of Mr. Vignes that a Mr. Fuller Maitland was also interested in the *Cambridge Confessor*. This I take to be William Fuller Maitland, Esq., of Stansted, Essex, who died in 1876, and was well known as a collector of pictures.

Perhaps these few facts relating to an enterprise which might have achieved great results may be worth recording in your pages.   R. B. P.

"WAGUES."—This word, employed as the equivalent of the stangs or single-trees used to assist in the propulsion of the rush-cart, is of great interest, if only on account of its obsolescence. It had a derivative *waguers*, meaning the men who pushed at the wagues, and it was used also in the order to the waguers before starting, "Hold up your wagues!" The custom in parts of South Lancashire and the West Riding was for thirty or forty men to help to move the rush-cart in its ceremonial progress. The assistants at the front were the waguers, and at the back were the *thrutchers*. *Thrutch*=thrust; and one is irresistibly reminded of the local description of the trombone as a *thrutch-an-poo* (thrust-and-pull); the waguers, however, were pushers, not pullers. At the order "Hold up your wagues!" the stangs were raised above the heads of the waguers, and they danced forward, covering the road from side to side by an alternate divagation in their progress. So much was this indirect method of advancing a custom that it frequently degenerated into a marlock, and resulted on one occasion in the upsetting of a temporary fair-stall by the wayside, in consequence of the ropes or traces attached to the wagues becoming entangled in the structure of the stall. At the present day one may hear such an expression as "Hold up your wagues. You're first, if you keep moving!" Sometimes the last four words are omitted. The expression has several shades of meaning. Perhaps it is most frequently employed as a non-committal remark in a friendly cross-examination that is found to be objectionable on account of its categorical character. The derivation is probably from the A.-S. *wagian*=to move. The waguers were the movers, and the wagues were the means by which the cart was moved. The only glossary in which I find *wagues* and *waguers* is Taylor's 'The Folk-Speech of South Lancashire.'

ARTHUR MAYALL.

DARLEY, A FORGOTTEN IRISH POET.—May I again, as a sort of "Old Mortality," ask the Editor of 'N. & Q.' to find a corner for a dead-and-gone "brother of Bohemia"? The following paragraph is from the *Freeman's Journal* of 26 November, 1901 :—

"George Darley, whose name was mentioned in this column on Saturday last, the fifty-fifth anniversary of his death, was considered by leading English *littérateurs* to be one of the best poets of his day, amongst the majority of whom he was a great social favourite. Yet to his own country people his name is an unknown one, nor is he remembered to any extent in England. The number of Irish poets who have made big reputations in England during their lives, to be almost completely forgotten after death, is a remarkable feature to the student of Anglo-Irish literature. Darley was the son of an Alderman Darley, of this city, and was a Trinity College man, where he graduated B.A. in 1820. He went to London early in life, and contributed to the leading magazines, a number of his poems appearing in the *Athenæum* between 1835-40

over his initials. A selection from his numerous volumes was printed for private circulation in 1890 as a memorial volume, with the title 'Poems of the late G. D.' Darley was also a very skilled mathematician and the author of some scientific works."

This may interest some of the Irish readers of 'N. & Q.' HERBERT B. CLAYTON.
39, Renfrew Road, S.E.

[We do not think Darley entirely forgotten, having read more than one of his works and possessing some of them. Darley's 'Nepenthe: a Poem in Two Cantos,' was republished by Mr. R. A. Streatfeild, and reviewed at length in the *Athenæum*, 18 Sept., 1897.]

THE SEAL OF THE GREAT STEWARD OF SCOTLAND.—The *Daily Telegraph* of the 18th of February contained the following, which is of such historical interest that it is worthy of a note in 'N. & Q.' :—

"When the Prince of Wales became Great Steward of Scotland the officials at the General Register House in Edinburgh were instructed to return the seal which the King had used as the previous occupant of that office, as it was the private property of Edward VII. It was made in London in 1863, is of silver, weighing 14 lb., and cost over 100*l*. On one side His Majesty (then Prince of Wales) is represented on horseback, dressed in Highland costume, with a peep of Holyrood and Arthur's Seat beyond. On the counter-seal the arms of Scotland and Great Britain are represented, with the Scottish lion on the right and the Prince of Wales's feathers on the left. The seal which the new Grand Steward has decided to use is the old one of George IV., showing the obsolete fleur-de-lis of France and the white horse of Hanover, both now dropped from the royal insignia."

A. N. Q.

CAMBRIDGE HEATH, SOUTH HACKNEY.— MR. GEORGE SWINTON'S interesting note on Kimmerghame (*ante*, p. 156) reminds me of an extract I once made from the Hundred Rolls regarding Cambridge Heath, a name which is difficult to account for, as the place has no connexion with the university town which is its apparent *eponymus*. The following is the finding of the commissioners :—

"Dicunt quod Egidius de Wodeham miles fecit quoddam fossatum super regalem viam que vocatur Kyngesteslane decem annis elapsis Ph's Linde manet in quadam domo que sita est super coam [communiam] pasture que vocatur Campricthesheth apud Hakeneye."—'Rot. Hund.,' i. 413, 426.

I take Campricthesheth to be the heath of Cynebeorht or Cynebriht, a well-known Saxon name, which I judge from the authorities given by MR. SWINTON to bear a closer responsibility for Kimmerghame than Cyneburh. The earliest form of Kimmerghame seems to be Cynebrihtham.

The thoroughfare called Kyngesteslane is doubtless the modern Mare Street, which, according to Robinson's 'History of Hackney,'

i. 5, is called Gaviston Street in some ancient records.   W. F. Prideaux.

The First British Subject born in New South Wales.—In the obituary notice of Charles Kent in last week's number of 'N. & Q.' mention is made of his father, William Kent, R.N., who was born at the old Government House in Sydney on December 23rd, 1799. He was the first British subject born in the colony, his great-uncle, Admiral John Hunter, being at that time the Governor of New South Wales. Charles Kent's grandfather, Capt. Kent, was the first Government Surveyor of the Australian coast, and was the discoverer of Kent Islands and the Gulf of St. Vincent. His wife is buried in St. Mary's, Paddington Green, where a mural monument commemorates her travels.   N. S. S.

Mistakes in Michelet.—I should be sorry to be considered one of those envious individuals who think to detract from the fame of a great writer by disclosing unimportant errors, yet when I find them the temptation to send them to 'N. & Q.' is not to be resisted. Here are two small ones from Michelet's 'Histoire de France':—

"La dupe universelle Henri VIII. voit qu'on l'a joué, qu'on se soucie peu de sa fille......De rage il donne sa fille à qui? au pauvre Louis XII."—Vol. ix. p. 287.

For "fille" of course sœur should be read.

"La reine Catherine d'Aragon était une sainte espagnole du XIIᵉ siècle d'une perfection désolante; son mari ne pouvait la joindre qu'à genou au prie-Dieu. Ni jeune, ni féconde, du reste: un seul enfant qui était une fille."—Vol. x. p. 130.

Catherine had several children.
    T. P. Armstrong.

Royal Adjectives.—It is strange that neither the force of character of some of our sovereigns nor the exigencies of literature should have provided us with a complete set of adjectives derived from their names, in order to describe the manners and influence of their times. Of William, Henry, Stephen, Richard, John, and Anne there are none. An adherent of William III. was called a "Williamite" in 1689; the 'N.E.D.' gives one solitary quotation for "Henrician" of 1893; "Johannine" relates to the Apostle only. "Edwardian" does not occur until 1861, but "Marian" was certainly known in the seventeenth century. "Elizabethan" is no older than 1817, and although a "Jacobite" was so called in 1689, "Jacobean" did not come in until 1844. "Caroline," however, is as old as 1652. A follower of the great Protector was termed a "Cromwellian" in 1725. "Georgian," used earlier of the star, was not applied to the period until 1855. "Victorian" is now in common use. When did it rise?
    W. C. B.

The National Anthem. — Considerable attention is being paid just now to the subject of the National Anthem and its various versions, and before long the public will be in possession of the accredited and authorized text.

There has always been much speculation as to its origin. Nothing seems positively known, except that it came into vogue during the reign of the early Georges. But expert opinion appears now to incline strongly to the theory that it sprang at the outset from a purely Jacobite source, and was subsequently adopted by the Whigs for the benefit of the Hanoverian monarchs.

This curious and remarkable conclusion is greatly strengthened by an analysis of some of the verses. For instance,

Send him victorious, happy, and glorious;
Long to reign over us,

punctuated, as is usual, like the above, is not English at all, but ungrammatical nonsense, whereas

Send him (victorious, happy and glorious)
Long to reign over us,

is intelligible and good sense.

As the Georges were already on the throne when the anthem was written, they were scarcely in need of an invocation to send them there; and if the latter punctuation is correct, the lines can only refer to some uncrowned king, like the Chevalier St. George, for whose restoration the Deity is thus entreated. The following also—

O Lord our God, arise!
Scatter his enemies—

is peculiarly applicable to the case of the unhappy fugitive Stuarts, who were, indeed, urgently in need of such an interposition of Providence on their behalf; whilst, on the other hand, the Georges succeeded to the crown in peace and quietness, had few serious enemies, and were well established in this country before the rising of the '45 took place, which happened late in the reign of the second George, and from the start had little chance of success.

Again, instead of the modern reading—

On Thee [God] our hopes are fixed,

it ran in the first known editions

On him [the king] our hopes are fixed—

implying some one about whose future there still existed much doubt and anxiety.

The point is an interesting one, although there is small likelihood now that it will ever be definitely settled ; but of one thing we are assured on the best critical authority, that it was an Englishman and not a German who composed the tune, and that the Prussians have borrowed it from us, not we from them. It seems almost a pity that the Kaiser William II., universal genius as he is, does not himself invent a national anthem for the use of his own people, so that the English and the German airs might for the future be separate and distinct.   PERCY CLARK.

['God save the King' was discussed at great length in 8th S. x., xi., xii.]

Queries.

WE must request correspondents desiring information on family matters of only private interest to affix their names and addresses to their queries, in order that the answers may be addressed to them direct.

DEFOE AT TOOTING.—An obstinate local tradition asserts that Daniel Defoe was living at Tooting-Graveney about the year 1688, and that he was active in the formation of the first Nonconformist congregation there. Mr. Thomas Wright and the other biographers of Defoe accept the story, but, apparently, on grounds of tradition alone. Morden's 'History of Tooting - Graveney' (1897) contains unqualified statements to the effect that neither in the parish records nor elsewhere is there any evidence of Defoe's residence or his association with the Nonconformist meeting, and that the house (Tooting Hall) which was thought to have been Defoe's was, in fact, built a century later, and used as the parish workhouse. Is any evidence of the tradition accessible ?   S. K. R.

PRECEPTORY OF DINMORE. — I shall be grateful for information of any history or records of this ancient religious establishment in Herefordshire, the grant for which was made to the Knights Hospitallers of St. John by Richard I. Lord Coningsby's 'Marden' and Duncumb's 'Herefordshire' give only meagre information. I cannot find any reference in Dugdale.
ARTHUR GROVES.
Alperton Park, Wembley.

HIGH STREET, OXFORD. — No. 90, High Street, adjoins the western wall of Barry's new buildings at University College on the south side of the street, and, standing upon land which belongs to Christ Church as the successor to Oseney Abbey, apparently occupies the site of Broadgates Hall in St. Mary's parish. Wood mentions this hall as a special abode of illuminators. Two large panelled rooms form the width of the second and third stories, respectively, of the present frontage, which immediately faces the gateway-tower of All Souls'. The upper room, the walls of which are entirely panelled in wood, stained white, is divided into an eastern and a western portion by folding-doors. The plaster ceiling is divided into compartments by beams, but only the plaster upon the beams is now decorated with patterns once probably coloured or gilt. The western fireplace has an elaborate carving above it of the temptation of Eve. The figures of Adam and Eve—Jacobean, I suppose, in date—almost stand out in the round from the panelling at their backs. The subject of the eastern chimney-piece is Abraham's sacrifice, and is in two compartments. The figures contained therein are quainter in design than those of Adam and Eve, but are not carved in nearly such bold relief. On the left appears the procession to the place of sacrifice : Isaac first with the laden ass ; secondly, accompanying his father. A scroll attached to Isaac's mouth asking "Where is the Lam" is answered by one issuing from Abraham's, saying "God wil provide." On the right Abraham's sword is arrested in act to strike by the angel, who cries "Abraham, Abraham" ; while the ram is shown caught in a thicket. Below the figures appear the following verses. On the left :—

Behold the father of the faithful scede.
Was heere approued : to be sound in deede.
For being warnd of God : to sacrifice.
His sonne Isaack : most pretious in his eyes.
Forthwith obedient was at his command.
And slayes his sonne had not God stayd his hand.

On the right :—

The antitipe of Christ : was he in this.
For God His only Sonn : did slay for his [?].
And if Christ crucifid : thou desirst to see.
This to a Christian : crucifix may be.
Not for to worship : as ...... intent.
But only for thy chambers ornament.

Do these lines occur elsewhere in this connexion, and what is the missing word in the penultimate line ?   A. R. BAYLEY.

CARLYLE AND SCRIPTURE.—Encouraged by the fully satisfactory reply of my friend W. S. S. to the query 'Carlyle on Symbols' (ante, p. 27), I would broach another question as to the writing of the same philosopher, even though in doing so I expose my ignorance. There are two books which in England perpetually offer themselves to proverb, illustration, and metaphor — the Bible and Shakespeare ; the adaptability of their sayings is simply wonderful. Of course, we do not like a flippant and too familiar recourse to either, and particularly are we inclined to resent the use of terms we have all our life regarded as sacred ; yet so aptly do they arise in their literary excellence that, as we cannot deny them to ourselves, we must be tolerant of their use by others, and even by the newspapers, their frequency in which (so it seems to me) has in late years augmented. Thus my excellent friend and daily visitor, the *Daily Telegraph*, on 3 February, in a very able, lucid, and accurate article on the Prime Minister, relates the chain of circumstances which tended towards the elevation of Lord Salisbury to his present position. And thus explaining, the writer—probably the same who prompted my previous question on symbols—again quotes Carlyle and his historical theory that "all things work together for good." Here the sage, like simpler folk, drops into Scripture. Let me once more exercise the learning of the student (W. S. S., if he will) to furnish this reference ; and should any similar instance of Scriptural quotation be remembered it will be welcome.

W. L. Rutton.

Bards.—It is, I think, generally taken for granted that originally the Druid was at the same time a *bard*. Is it known whether bards existed as distinct personalities from Druids *before* the introduction of Christianity into Britain? Or is the bard, as a separate person from the Druid, to be considered as the result of the destruction of Druidism by Christianity? Wülcker ('Geschichte der engl. Litteratur,' Leipzig, 1896, pp. 4 and 5) seems to be of the latter opinion.

M. Basse.

Tongeren, Belgium.

Batty, Printer, 159, Fleet Street.— From 1849 to 1863 there was a family of the name of Batty (styled successively Henry, Joseph Henry, and Batty Brothers), printers and publishers, at 159, Fleet Street. They subsequently moved—I believe about 1863-4 —to 32, Bouverie Street, E.C. I am desirous of obtaining the exact dates of publication of two editions of a pamphlet on the question of marriage with a deceased wife's sister printed by them about the years 1859-61. Can any one tell me the name and address of their successors in business, from whom, perhaps, I might obtain this information?

C. W. H.

Post-fine.—Can some reader enlighten me as to what a post-fine is? Among some MSS.

of the Rev. Joseph Greene, of Welford, of 1730 and thereabouts, I find the following receipt, endorsed "A Copy of an Acquittance for a Post-fine for Lands of ye Rev: Mr. Greene at Long-Marston & Mickleton in ye County of Glocester, signed Septr. 14, 1738." The document is within :—

Of Robert Martin to Accord with Joseph Greene Clerk and his Wife for one Messuage, one Barn, one Stable, one Garden, one Orchard, 40 Acres of Land, 10 Acres of Mead, 20 Acres of Pasture, in Long Marston otherwise Marston Sicca and Mickleton 0 15 0

The 14th of September 1738 Received the above Post-fine for the use of His Majesty and in behalf of Mr. Robins Under Sheriff of the County of Gloucester.
By Henry Green.

Received for the Receipt 0 1 0
————
0 16 0

I have no access to the 'H.E.D.' here, I am sorry to say.   W. H. Quarrell.

Ashby de la Zouch.

[Annandale's four-volume edition of Ogilvie, *s.v.* 'Post-fine,' says : "In Eng. law, a fine due to the king by prerogative : called also the *King's Silver* (which see under King)." *King's Silver* is defined as "the money which was paid to the king in the Court of Common Pleas for a license granted to a man to levy a fine of lands, tenements, or hereditaments, to another person ; and this must have been compounded according to the value of the land, in the alienation office, before the fine would pass."]

"Multiplicands."—What people were designated by this term? The word occurs in the records of a Quaker Church meeting of 1698, as follows :—

"This Meet: being informed by Danˡ Quare who hath of late had occasion upon his outward affairs to Travell into fflanders That the People were greatly Ignorant of ffrids Principles and Practice and had a Notion yᵗ ffrids were *multiplycands*," &c.

Norman Penney.

Friends' Institute, 13, Bishopsgate Without.

Montgomery MSS.—The following is taken from the Rev. George Hill's elaborate note to p. 306 of the Montgomery MSS. (1869) :—

"On the 10th December, 1610, Brian Oge McRowrie Magennis of Edenticullo, near Hillsborough, received a grant of the entire cantred, lordship, precinct, or circuit of Kilwarlin, containing 43 townlands, at the yearly rent of 20*l.*, Irish, to hold for ever in common socage. This is now the Kilwarlin estate of Lord Downshire. The late George Stephenson's mother was a Magennis lineally descended from this Brian Oge McRowrie, and *he held the original patent*, which had been handed down in the family. These lands are situated in the parishes of Hillsborough, Blaris, Dromore, Dromara, and Annahilt."

Perhaps some reader of 'N. & Q.' can give further information regarding this document.

If it has been in existence so recently it ought to be forthcoming. The patent has, of course, only an antiquarian value, as the lands were forfeited owing to the part taken by the then owner in the rebellion of 1641. In the proclamation of the Lords Justices dated 8 February, 1641 (O.S), one of the names on the long list of the proscribed is "Rory MacBrian Oge Magennis, late of Edentecullagh," and a reward of 400*l*. offered for his head, if brought in before 25 March following (300*l*. for killing and not bringing in the head). THOMAS FITZPATRICK.

KNOLLYS ROAD, STREATHAM —I should like to know the origin of the name given to this road. I have asked a member of the Knollys family, but he cannot inform me.
A. N. Q.

HODGES FAMILY.—Can any of your readers tell me the maiden name of Ann, wife of James Hodges, of Masulipatam, and mother of Lady William Murray? A monument in Bath Abbey to James Hodges gives the date of her death 11 November, 1823, and her arms Sa., a chev. engr. between three lions pass. guard. arg. To what family do these arms belong? E. H. FELLOWES.
The Cloisters, Windsor Castle.

AUTHORS WANTED.—Who are the author and the publisher of a poem commencing—

A fire-mist and a planet,
A crystal and a shell?

Also—

The bud on the bough,
The song of the bird?
J. B.

DESCENDANTS OF SIR WILLIAM DE LA POLE, DIED 1329.—This Sir William had three sons: Sir Richard (chief butler to the king, 1327-38), Sir William (father to the first Earl of Suffolk), and John. Sir Richard had two sons and three daughters: William, 1316-66 (the father of John, who married Joan Cobham), John, Joan (who married Ralph Basset, of Weldon, Northamptonshire), Elizabeth (a nun), and Margaret. Is anything known of the descendants, if any, of Sir Richard's brother John and of Sir Richard's children?
RONALD DIXON.
46, Marlborough Avenue, Hull.

PINS AND PINCUSHIONS.—Can any one give me the names of some books that would contain the history of pins and pincushions? Is there any national collection of pincushions; and, if so, where is it? I should be glad of any information on this subject.
(Miss) ELEANOR D. LONGMAN.
18, Thurloe Square, S.W.

Replies.

MICHAEL BRUCE AND BURNS.
(9th S. vii. 466; viii. 70, 148, 312, 388, 527; ix. 95.)

THE following extract from 'Literary Coincidences; and other Papers,' by W. A. Clouston, pp. 44, 45 (Glasgow, Morison Brothers, 1892), will serve to dispel the notion that Burns was indebted to Michael Bruce for the idea that

The best-laid schemes o' mice and men
Gang aft a-gley.

Mr. Clouston says :—

"Blair's 'Grave' seems to have been a great favourite with Burns, since he quotes frequently from it in his Commonplace Book, and in one instance he has imitated that author, where he says, in his 'Address to a Mouse' :—

The best-laid schemes o' mice and men
Gang aft a-gley.

Blair has :—

The best-concerted schemes men lay for fame
Die fast away.

Here Burns has improved upon Blair, for it is more correct to say that men's objects often miscarry than that they 'die fast away.'"

In December, 1901, Mr. Henry Grey Graham, author of 'The Social Life of Scotland in the Eighteenth Century,' issued his volume entitled 'Scottish Men of Letters in the Eighteenth Century' (London, A. & C. Black). This work deals, *inter alia*, with Michael Bruce and John Logan, but in some points it is not quite accurate. For instance: Bruce was born in 1746 and died in 1767, aged twenty-one years and three months. Mr. Graham says "he was but twenty years old"; and at another place, "only twenty-one years old." Logan was born in 1748 and died in London in 1788, aged forty; but Mr. Graham states that he died "at the age of fifty-one." Minor inaccuracies also occur, such as "Kinneswood" (for Kinnesswood); "Mr. Thomas Main" (for Mair); "Dr. John Brown" (this John Brown had not the degree of D.D.); "4th of July, 1767," instead of 6th, for the date of Bruce's death. He is called "a delicate, ill-fed lad," and is described as "a lad" when he "wrote his touching 'Elegy'" in the spring before he died. Logan, on the other hand, is termed "a clever, uncouth young man of nineteen" when he visited Kinnesswood. Mr. Graham repeats the usual apocryphal stories regarding "a leathern-covered quarto" and the "singed fowls," but he is mistaken in his reference to Logan's 'Poems,' issued in 1781. He avers that "in this volume eleven of the seventeen pieces in Bruce's 'Poems' (1770) were inserted as Logan's own—leaving only six to have been by his friend and the other 'different authors' spoken of in the old preface." As a matter of fact, only one piece—'The Ode to the Cuckoo'—appeared in both volumes, but several alterations were made in the later version. Both differ from that printed in Ruddiman's *Weekly Magazine* for 1774, which is believed to be in reality from one of the copies in MS. which Mrs. Hutcheson, Logan's cousin, told Dr. Anderson in 1795 she knew had been circulating in East Lothian in 1767, before Logan obtained Bruce's MSS.

The fourth verse appears as follows in the three versions already mentioned :—

1774.
The school-boy, wand'ring in the wood
  To pull the cowslip gay
Starts when thy curious voice he hears,
  And imitates thy lay.

1770.
The schoolboy, wand'ring in the wood
  To pull the flow'rs so gay
Starts, thy curious voice to hear,
  And imitates thy lay.

1781.
The school-boy, wandering thro' the wood
  To pull the primrose gay,
Starts, the new voice of Spring to hear,
  And imitates thy lay.

Mr. Graham concludes by asking, " Was it the poor schoolmaster lad of Kinross-shire or the brilliant, dissipated clerical failure who wrote 'The Ode to the Cuckoo'?" The latter, I maintain. although I do not admit that he was a " failure."

The articles in the *Scots Magazine* are as under :—

*Smeaton (James), 'A Letter on the Authorship of the " Ode to the Cuckoo,"' Jan., 1892 (published by Cowan & Co., Perth, N.B.).

Hewison (Rev. J. King, M.A.), 'John Logan, the Poet,' Nov. and Dec., 1894, and Jan., 1895.

"Inquirer" (Dr. A. M. McDonald), 'The Ode to the Cuckoo,' Nov. and Dec., 1897.

Smail (Adam), 'The Bruce-Logan Controversy—a Notice of some Recent Writings,' Dec., 1897, and Jan., 1898.

—— 'Some Early Notices of Michael Bruce and the Rev. John Logan,' Feb., 1898.

*Mearns (Rev. P.), 'The Poet of Lochleven,' Feb. and March, 1898.

Smail (Adam), 'Michael Bruce and Rev. John Logan,' March and May, 1898.

Hewison (Rev. J. King, M.A.), 'The Michael Bruce Forgeries,' May, 1898.

"Inquirer" (Dr. A. M. McDonald), 'The Bruce-Logan Controversy,' July, 1898.

—— 'Anent some of the Scottish Paraphrases,' Feb., 1900.

A careful perusal of the above - named articles will prove that recent criticism has

---

* These two writers uphold the claims of Bruce.

done something to dispel the cloud of obloquy which too long had gathered round the name and fame of Logan. It has lately been conclusively shown that the charges of plagarism against Logan with reference to Zollikofer's 'Sermons,' Rutherford's 'View of Antient History,' the 'Scottish Paraphrases,' and some of his poems are not in accordance with facts. The *United Presbyterian Magazine* from August, 1896, to January, 1900, contained some very important material on "this ancient controversial matter." MR. THOMAS BAYNE therefore scarcely does justice to his opponents when he remarks that " nothing new on the problem has come to light since Dr. Grosart advanced his damaging indictment of Logan in his edition of Michael Bruce's poems." MR. BAYNE allows that "he [Dr. Grosart] may have been wrong, but his error is still to be proved." Dr. Robertson, of Dalmeny, was by no means "a very insignificant factor in the discussion." Fortunately for the reputation of Logan he did not deal with Bruce's MSS. unaided, as the annexed letter of his friend Mr. Robertson to Dr. Baird fully proves :—

" Dalmeny, 22nd February, 1791. Bruce was my class-fellow at college, and very particular acquaintance. He shewed me all his pieces himself. After his death, Mr. Logan and I looked over all his MSS., and selected those which are published. The rest we judged not in a state to be seen by the public, and I believe they were all destroyed, among which I remember to have seen the poem on the 'Last Day,' a long work, and very unequal. I have none of his pieces in my own hands, and never had."

It will be remembered that Mr. Mackelvie on Birrell's authority says that Logan returned "a few loose papers, containing among other poems 'The Last Day.'"

Dr. Grosart evidently stands high in the good graces of MR. BAYNE, but this favourable view was not taken by Dr. David Laing, Signet Library, Edinburgh, who, in his privately printed brochure entitled 'Ode to the Cuckoo: Edinburgh, 1770, with Remarks on its Authorship, in a Letter to Principal Shairp,' Edinburgh, 1873, says : "Like the critic who reviewed Grosart's volume in the *Athenæum* for 1865, p. 48, I may apply to the 'Hymn question' what he said respecting that of the authorship of the 'Ode to the Cuckoo,' that it is one 'so unimportant that we do not care to waste time upon it.' And truly Mr. Grosart's statements and conclusions are so preposterous as not to be worthy of notice." Dr. Laing also blames Dr. Grosart for reiterating "at great length all the charges against Logan made by Mr. (afterwards Dr.) Mackelvie, and that in a most offensive style, while adducing vague tradi-

tions and allusions as 'incontrovertible facts.'"
There is much truth in this criticism.

Mr. Douglas J. Maclagan, in his painstaking and accurate work on 'The Scottish
Paraphrases' (Edinburgh, Andrew Elliot,
1889), devotes chap. v. to Logan and Michael
Bruce. The two specimens of hymns remembered by David Pearson were said to have
been considerably altered by Logan. "And
yet" these, says Mr. Maclagan, "are unaltered." What becomes of the memory
of "John Birrel, the Bickertons, Arnots,
Hendersons, and, indeed, the whole community" of Dr. Grosart? Could none of
them corroborate the statement of Pearson?
Could none of them remember the *unaltered*
Hymns which they learned in that music
class? (Buchan's, at Kinnesswood.) "Truly,
on such hearsay evidence as has been advanced, we cannot assign the Paraphrases or
yet Logan's Hymns to Michael Bruce. The
one point in Bruce's favour seems to us to
break down on examination. Logan was in
possession; he is, to our mind, in possession
still of the title to the authorship of the
Paraphrases."

In view of such arguments as have recently
been advanced by Drs. Small and Sprott,
Messrs. Hewison, McDonald, Maclagan, and
others, I am firmly of the opinion that
Logan claimed nothing more than his due in
his various publications.   ADAM SMAIL.
Edinburgh.

MR. BAYNE has certainly not been able to
acquaint himself with all that has been done
recently towards establishing the case in
favour of Logan as author of the various
compositions claimed for Bruce. Even should
the papers connected with the interdict
(1782) remain inaccessible, much has been
brought forward to show upon how unsatisfactory a foundation—one composed chiefly
of tradition intermixed with some astounding
errors — Mackelvie built a superstructure
called by Bruce's latest biographer (Stephen)
a "great work." As "qualified specialists"
Drs. Mackelvie and Grosart are unfortunate
in their treatment of the case. The attempt
to blacken Logan's character as much as
possible in one glaring instance shows the
careless manner in which Mackelvie gathered
his material. At paragraph 100 of the 'Life'
this sentence appears :—

"To these instances of his free use of other
men's works, we have to add that a great portion
of the fourth sermon in volume second is copied
verbatim from Zollikofer......slavishly transcribed
from Tooke's English translation of that author's
works."

In the *United Presbyterian Magazine*,
January, 1900, the Rev. Dr. Small, in an
interesting article detailing the steps taken
in the investigation, has at length not only
disproved this charge, but has shown that it
was Tooke who purloined from Logan in a
second edition, "corrected and improved,"
of Zollikofer's sermons, the passage being
wanting from the original. Logan was dead
before this second edition appeared. In regard
to the 'View of Antient History,' in which
is to be found incorporated almost the whole
of Logan's 'Synopsis of Lectures on the
Philosophy of History,' acknowledged in a
foot-note as Logan's, it is only necessary to
point out, in refutation of the charge that
Logan had delivered as his own lectures belonging to Dr. Wm. Rutherford, that Logan's
lectures, of which the incorporated synopsis
was an outline, were not upon ancient history,
but upon a subject with which he was well
able to deal—namely, the 'Philosophy of
Ancient History.' Two gross errors on the
part of Mackelvie are thus disposed of. His
apology to Mr. Douie, of the Glasgow Grammar School, written February, 1838, advertised in the public journals, and printed as
an addendum to, and bound up with, unsold
copies of Bruce's 'Poems,' does not increase
one's confidence in the methods pursued in
preparing his work. For Mackelvie says,
"I had no definite person whatever in view,
having of my own knowledge no acquaintance
with the statements made, which I am now
satisfied were unfounded." Bruce died in 1767;
Mackelvie published in 1837. Writing thus
after an interval of seventy years, it must
have been exceedingly difficult to verify oral
statements. One is therefore not surprised
to find that much of Mackelvie's work is
based on local tradition.

MR. BAYNE's reference to the MSS. having
been committed to Logan's care in 1767 puts
him on the horns of a dilemma. He must
either admit that Mackelvie is in error or
that Logan executed his task in a much
shorter space of time than that usually
stated. In any case, eighteen months, not
three years, is the limit. Paragraph 67
says, "Logan, then a tutor in the family of
Sir John Sinclair." "Then" is significant.
For it was not until some time in 1768, probably the summer, that Logan, on the recommendation of Dr. Blair, entered upon his
duties as tutor to the Sinclairs. Here, again,
in his foot-note to this paragraph, Mackelvie
is in error in saying that no reference to
Logan is to be found "in a recently published 'Life and Correspondence of Sir John
Sinclair, Bart.'" Pp. 15, 16, 17, refer to
Logan's introduction to this family. So

much for Mackelvie and some of his more palpable errors. Dr. Grosart follows suit ; but in addition he has attempted some literary criticism, the result of which is certainly not favourable to Bruce. In the *Scots Magazine*, December, 1897, the four known versions of the 'Ode to the Cuckoo' were published—namely, those of 1770, 1774, 1781, and 1837. That of 1837 (Mackelvie's) is singular in this respect that it professes to be Bruce's, yet contains words which Grosart maintained were Logan's—*e g*, "grove," "what time," and in the last line a most unaccountable alteration, for there we have "attendants" instead of *companions*, which appears in all the others. Dr. Grosart never attempted to account for this version. His argument on some other points shows how little *he* deserves the name "qualified specialist." I quote again from the *Scots Magazine*, November, 1897, to which interested readers are referred for Dr. Grosart's argument. The writer says :—

"What does this amount to, but that in a MS. that was never seen by Logan there occurs, according to Dr. Grosart, his [Logan's] defacement 'beauteous,' and Bruce's improvement 'cowslip'—a Logan-Bruce production in a MS., according to Dr. Grosart, 'independent of Logan.' Say 'independent of Bruce' and the difficulty vanishes."

Dr. Grosart's article upon this part of the subject will be found in the *United Presbyterian Magazine*, February, 1897. MR. BAYNE's extract from Grosart's edition of Bruce's 'Poems' merely shows that Grosart depended upon Mackelvie for information regarding Bruce's MSS. As I have already clearly shown, 1768, at the earliest, was the year in which they came into Logan's possession. It may even have been as late as 1769, when he was returning from Caithness, that he received them. Of course, when MR. BAYNE says, "This controversy......has made no progress in thirty years," he may have in view that the admirers of Bruce have been unable to advance their case by any fresh argument since Grosart published his remarkable volume. On the other hand, Logan's case grows stronger and stronger the more Mackelvie is analyzed. From a short correspondence I had upon this subject with Dr. Grosart I quite agree with MR. BAYNE that he would in any future edition of Bruce's 'Poems' have emphasized his own view of the authorship of the 'Ode to the Cuckoo,' nor should I have expected him to retract one iota of all that he had penned against Logan. Yet the expunging of these charges of plagiarism from Mackelvie removes two of the strongest buttresses by which the fabric built upon tradition was supported.

This foundation of tradition is itself also seriously undermined, and what has been reared upon it becomes untrustworthy, when the manner of transmission of the tradition is seriously investigated.

A. M. McDONALD.

"ENDORSEMENT" : "DORSO - VENTRALITY" (9ᵗʰ S. ix. 64). — Some banks require the endorsement of the payee of a cheque in addition to his discharge on the face of it, especially when the latter takes the form of a stamped receipt. The instructions on the dividend warrant referred to may therefore have been quite in order, seeing that the back demanded attention as well as the front—a clear case of "dorso-ventrality."

CHAS. GILLMAN.

Salisbury.

I do not think any banker would admit that a cheque can be endorsed by the payee signing a receipt at the foot of it. Where cheques are in the form mentioned at the above reference they must be receipted and endorsed before payment can be obtained. The words "This cheque requires endorsement" have no reference to the receipt on the front of the cheque. The same words constantly appear on cheques to which a receipt form is not attached. I remember reading an election petition case in which counsel contended that certain endorsements required by the Ballot Act ought to be made on the front of the ballot paper, but (as might be expected) he failed to carry the court with him.

F. W. READ.

UNCOVERING AT THE NATIONAL ANTHEM (9ᵗʰ S. ix. 109).—Fifty odd years ago it was rare to hear in country places 'God save the Queen' sung ; hardly ever was it called 'The National Anthem.' We were taught that it was "respectful" to stand in a room when 'God save the Queen' was sung, and for boys and men to take off their hats when the hymn was heard out of doors. The custom of uncovering was not much observed, so far as I remember, and at big gatherings out of doors never a hat was removed, except on the platform, and then all were not of one mind. There was not any intention of disrespect in keeping the hat on, so far as I remember. But 'God save the Queen' was rarely heard out of doors.

THOS. RATCLIFFE.

Worksop.

WEEKS'S MUSEUM (9ᵗʰ S. ix. 8, 97).—This museum was established as early, at least, as 1803, for in that edition of the 'Picture of

London' it is stated, although the exhibition was already open, that "when complete it will form an interesting object to the curious"; and the grand room was not 117, but 107 ft. long—at least so it appears in my own copy of that year of this most valuable compendium of the time. In another copy in my possession, dated 1818, the "show" was still prospering, and the grand room is still described as 107 ft. long. The error with regard to the date is, however, traceable, probably, to Timbs's 'Curiosities of London.'

J. HOLDEN MACMICHAEL.
Wimbledon Park Road.

BELL INSCRIPTION AT PUNCKNOWLE, DORSET (3rd S. vii. 137; 9th S. vii. 365; viii. 22, 153).—It has occurred to me that "lathers," in "must ancient lathers still maintayne," should perhaps be read "leathers," and be understood as referring to the whit-leather bawdricks by which the clappers were commonly suspended in 1629, and which required a great deal of "maintaining" in order to keep them in repair.
J. T. F.
Durham.

WINDOW GLASS (9th S. ix. 87, 150).—The unexpected always happens was the veritable dictum of one of our greatest statesmen, and it certainly has happened, so far as I am concerned, in the communications of MESSRS. ST. CLAIR BADDELEY and R. B—R in your issue of 22 February. Until I read them I had fully believed the Romans were not acquainted with window glass. I had some correspondence with my friend MR. G. C. WARDEN upon the matter, and had referred to Pliny as the earliest and best authority. That indefatigable author, in naming all kinds of glass made up to his time, omits all mention of the use of it for windows. He mentions mirrors, but says they were made of obsidian, and that imitation obsidian was made. He speaks of Scaurus, the stepson of Sylla, having built a temple, and says the first story was of marble and the second story of glass (book xxxvi. c. 24); but in c. 64 he explains this by saying "*mosaic pavements* were made in the time of Sylla, but now they have been transferred to arches and panels, as seen in the *walls of the temple of Scaurus.*" I looked at Rees's and other works of the same kind, and found only negative information; and, lastly, I cannot remember, after thirty-six years' regular study of 'N. & Q.,' to have seen anything of an affirmative character. Small pieces of glass of various colours were undoubtedly used in mosaic work, but this fact does not indicate window glass. One would like to know something more about MR. ST. CLAIR BADDELEY's find. Would it be too much to ask him if the date of the destruction of the villa at Antium is known to him? A villa might have been built many years before A.D., and if it were not destroyed for some three or four hundred years there was time for the use of glass for the windows to have been adopted. May I be permitted to ask MR. BADDELEY further if the panes of glass found at Pompeii are still in existence?
F. CLAYTON.
Morden.

SLEEPING GARMENTS (3rd S. iv. 246, 332, 439; vi. 316; xi. 51; xii. 175).—A quarto volume of Bible pictures, to which I drew attention in 8th S. x. 435, was published at Amsterdam about the year 1700. In plate 16 Jacob blesses his sons, sitting up in a canopied bed, supported by a pillow like a small cotton-bale. He is evidently nude, though the part of him from the waist down is covered up by the bedclothes. But in plate 71 Hezekiah lies in a canopied bed, clothed in an ample nightgown, and receives the prophet. His crown and sceptre are laid on an ornamental chest, and there are other signs of modern work which cannot be specified here.
RICHARD H. THORNTON.
Portland, Oregon.

LADY NOTTINGHAM (9th S. ix. 128).—This lady's thirty children do not constitute a record in maternity. I quote from the 'Dict. Nat. Biog.,' vol. xxiii. p. 80, as follows:—

"Thomas Greenhill, writer on embalming, son of William Greenhill, of Greenhill, at Harrow, Middlesex, a counsellor-at-law and secretary to General Monck, was born in 1681, after his father's death. His mother was Elizabeth, daughter of William White, of London, who had by one husband thirty-nine children, all (it is said) born alive and baptized, and all single births except one. An addition was made to the arms of the family in 1698 in commemoration of this extraordinary case of fecundity. There are portraits of Elizabeth Greenhill at Walling Wells, near Worksop, and at Lowesby Hall, Leicestershire."

One of this family, a William Greenhill, was an early Governor of Harrow School (1586-1613); and in 1621 Joseph Greenhill was the first university scholar elected from that school.
A. R. BAYLEY.
St. Margaret's, Malvern.

CHOCOLATE (9th S. viii. 160, 201, 488; ix. 53).—Evidence of a still earlier use of chocolate is intimated by the publication in 1652 of a book entitled 'Chocolate, the Nut of the Cocoa Tree, manufactured in a peculiar manner' (*vide* Robert Watt's 'Bibliotheca Britannica,' *s.v.* 'Chocolate'). This would be ten years before the issue of Dr. Stubbe's 'Indian Nectar,' 1662, and seven years before Thomas Rugge's 'Mercurius Politicus Redivivus,' quoted by W. I. R. V. Then again, in the *Public Advertiser* of 16 June, 1657, the following advertisement is said to occur :—"In Bishopsgate Street, in Queen's Head Alley, at a Frenchman's house, is an excellent West India drink, called chocolate, to be sold, where you may have it ready at any time, and also unmade at reasonable rates" ('Ency. Brit.,' ninth edition, *s.v.* 'Cocoa'). Chocolate houses began to spring up in Queen Anne's reign, sometimes assuming the sign of the "Cocoa Tree," as in the case of the now historic club of that name, transferred, before its clubhood, from Pall Mall to its present abode in St. James's Street. The chocolate-house sign of the "Cocoa Tree" survived as late as 1808, when it distinguished the shop of a tea-dealer at 302, Holborn ('Banks Coll. of Shop-bills,' 3). There was a chocolate house in St. Martin's Lane, "next to Slaughter's Coffee-house" (*Daily Adv.*, 15 Oct., 1742), and another at Blackheath ('O. and N. Lond.'), and no doubt many other such houses could be named, but the high price at which the new preparation was retailed kept it for a long time out of the reach of any but the most wealthy. A silver chocolate mill was apparently among the necessaries of a wealthy traveller's outfit, but so rare was it that the present-day dealer in antique silver does not seem to be aware of an example which has survived the melting-pot. It was, however, probably like a Queen Anne coffee-pot, and used to beat up chocolate by putting its particles in a circular motion with a stick rubbed between the hands. Such a utensil is advertised, among other articles for the recovery of which twenty - five guineas reward is offered, as having been stolen from the "One Bell" in the Strand. It was engraved with "three boars' heads on fess in a lozenge" (*Daily Adv.*, 25 March, 1742). It was after the dried kernels of the cocoa tree had been pounded in a mortar that the mill came into use. The powdered chocolate was "steeped in a little water and worked well with the little mill, whence they abstract a very large scum, which is so much the more augmented by how much the Cacao is the more old and rotten. This scum they put into a dish a part, mixing therewith a sufficient quantity of Sugar, which done, they set it up for their use, and drink it cold......not in Winter, but in the greatest heat of Summer." This was one of several ways of making chocolate described in a little book entitled 'The Manner of Making of Coffee, Tea, and Chocolate,

newly done out of French and Spanish,' 1685. There is an excellent account of 'Chocolate and Cocoa' in the *Gentleman's Magazine*, vol. xlv. (New Series).

J. Holden MacMichael.

Wimbledon Park Road.

Mr. Edward Forbes Robinson in his 'Early History of Coffee-houses in England' (London, 1893) tells us (p. 73) that "about the year 1650 coffee and chocolate began to be frequently taken" at Oxford. His authority is Anthony à Wood. In the appendix to this book Mr. Robinson reprints part of 'The Character of a Coffee-house,' first printed in 1665. It contains the following allusion to chocolate :—

> The Player calls for Chocolate.
> All which the Bumpkin, wondering at,
> Cries, ho, my Masters, what d' ye speak,
> D' ye call for drink in Heathen Greek?
> Give me good old Ale or Beer,
> Or else I will not drink, I swear.

Charles Hiatt.

Ships of War on Land (9th S. vii. 147, 235, 296, 354, 431 ; viii. 128).—When this query appeared I did not happen to see it, and the replies which have from time to time been proffered have not enlightened me as to the exact form of the original question. Being now better informed, I offer the following. An account of Emanuel Swedenborg's engineering feat at the siege of Frederickshall is to be found in the collection of documents concerning his life and character made by the late Rev. R. L. Tafel, A.M., Ph.D., and published by the Swedenborg Society in 1875–7, vol. i. pp. 554, 555. The account is translated from Fryxell's 'Berättelser ur Svenska Historien,' part xxix. pp. 128, 129, and describes the *modus operandi* thus :—

"Charles [XII.] then hit upon the same idea which Peter tried to carry out near Twerminne in 1713. Over heaps of brushwood, by means of rollers and through flowing water, he dragged and carried two galleys, several large boats, and a sloop overland from Strömstad to the Iddefjord, about two and a half Swedish miles [about seventeen English miles]. Polhem had formed the plan, and he sent Swedenborg to execute it. At first the work went on very slowly ; but soon Charles came himself, and urged on the work in person. For every yard over which any of the craft was carried he gave to each man engaged in the work a small remuneration ; and they raised a loud huzza when the first galley shot down into the waters of the Iddefjord. 'You see now,' said the king, 'that it goes ; and now the other craft must come also.' And so they did."

Charles Higham.

Chalices of Wood (9th S. ix. 89).—The eighteenth canon of the Council of Tribur, A.D. 895, in Gratian's 'Decretum,' iii. Dist. i.

c. 44, is as follows done into English. Its language may explain some of the conflicting statements of the authorities. The vessels in which the most holy mysteries are consecrated are chalices and patens, as to which Boniface, bishop (of Mainz) and martyr (A.D. 755), when asked whether it were lawful to consecrate the sacraments in wooden vessels, made answer: "Formerly golden priests used wooden chalices; now, on the contrary, wooden priests use golden chalices." Zephyrinus (A.D. 202-219), the sixteenth Roman bishop, appointed the use of glass patens in celebrating Mass. Afterwards Urban, the seventeenth Pope (A.D. 223-230), caused all the sacred vessels to be made in silver. In this, as in all other matters connected with worship, with lapse of time the magnificence of the churches has grown. Nowadays, in order that the splendour of Mother Church may not be lessened, but may be increased and multiplied, we, who are the servants of the householder, decree that henceforth no priest in any way presume to consecrate the holy mystery of the body and blood of our Lord Jesus Christ in wooden vessels, lest the service whereby God is to be appeased should stir Him to anger.

The forty-first of King Edgar's canons in 960, following the above, runs: "And that every chalice in which the Housel is hallowed be molten, and that no man hallow it in a wooden chalice." OSWALD J. REICHEL.

In the maritime museum at Madrid there is exhibited a chalice made of the wood of the tree in the shade of which was celebrated the first Mass in Havannah on 19 March, 1519. B. D. MOSELEY.

Information on the prohibition of the use of chalices of wood and references to Cardinal Bona's work and other authorities will be found in the *Transactions* of the Glasgow Archæological Society, N.S., vol. iii. p. 215, *sqq.*
DELTA.

If MR. BLACK will turn to 'N. & Q.,' 2nd S. i. 211, 340, 440; 4th S. iii. 597; iv. 46, he will find many long and interesting replies to an inquiry bearing the title 'Wooden Chalices.'
EVERARD HOME COLEMAN.
71, Brecknock Road.

ISLE OF ROSENEATH (9th S. ix. 128).—Roseneath was called an isle long before Sir Walter Scott's day. On 25 August, 1548, Mary, Queen of Scots, confirmed to Gilbert McKynne a charter, dated the 16th, of the lands of Knockdoire "in insula de Rosneith vic. Dunbertane." In a retour of the following year certain lands "jacentibus in insula

de Rosneth" are referred to. In another, dated 1663, reference is made to the "parochia et insula de Rosneth." It was not uncommon to apply the term "isle" to a wing of land, like Roseneath, stretching out into the water, though not entirely surrounded by it. In these more exact days we should call it a *pen*-insula. But our forebears split no hairs in a trifle of that kind. Then, in Scots, an aisle of a church—*ala*, a wing—is called an isle, and is latinized *insula*. The fancy is the same. J. L ANDERSON.
Edinburgh.

I would suggest that Sir Walter was right, and that Roseneath was commonly spoken of as an island because it was originally quite surrounded by water. A similar case is that of the peninsula of Pendinas, at St. Ives, Cornwall. It is, and always has been, called "The Island," though it has never been anything but a peninsula within historic times. Geology, however, shows that its designation is a memory of very ancient days.

It may be of interest to refer here to the St. Ives family of Ninnis, or Ninnes. They are so called after a male ancestor who resided on The Island—Cornish *an Enys*. The surname is, therefore, as strictly local as any could well be.
JOHN HOBSON MATTHEWS.
Town Hall, Cardiff.

"BAR SINISTER" (9th S. ix. 64, 152).—Your correspondent COL. PRIDEAUX is, I think, in error in asserting that Catherine Sedley, Countess of Dorchester, died childless. Her daughter Catherine, Duchess of Buckingham, is a well-known historical character, the "old Princess Buckingham," as Horace Walpole called her. COL. PRIDEAUX adds that no descendant of James II. sits, or has sat for 200 years, in the House of Lords. He appears to have overlooked the fact that Sir Henry Waldegrave, created Baron Waldegrave of Chewton 20 January, 1685/6, married Henrietta FitzJames, natural daughter of James by Mrs. Arabella Churchill; and the descendants of this marriage include the present Earl Waldegrave, Lord Radstock, Earl of Selborne, Earl Powis, Lord Windsor, and possibly other peers. H.

COL. PRIDEAUX refers to the term "bar sinister" at p. 21 of Lord Rosebery's 'Napoleon,' and thinks that "his lordship may have supposed that the literary poise of this passage would suffer if, with pedantic accuracy, he had used the correct term, 'bâton sinister.'" Lord Rosebery certainly errs in good company, for Walter Scott uses the same expression in the twenty-third chapter of 'Woodstock':—

"But then her father—the stout old cavalier—my father's old friend—should such a thing befall, it would break his heart. Break a pudding's end. He has more sense. If I give his grandson a title to quarter the arms of England, what matter if a bar sinister is drawn across them?"

JAMES WATSON.

The *barre* is a sign of illegitimacy in France, but whether it is actually the same bearing as the English *bar*, I am unable to say. The *Intermédiaire* for 30 January (cols. 107, 108) contains an interesting article on the signs of mourning introduced into their arms by the suffering Protestants after the revocation of the Edict of Nantes. "Finally," says the writer,

"Louis XIV. having had the registers of the Protestants' *Etat-civil* seized, they could not prove their filiation and were presumed to be bastard: the inhabitants of Bagnols protested; many took for arms the *barre*, ordinary sign of bastardy, *mais occupant le tiers de l'écu*; now in this case the *barre*, according to the laws of blazonry, is one of the most honourable bearings."

M. P.

FIREPLACES IN CATHEDRAL CHURCHES (9ᵗʰ S. ix. 88).—If your correspondent will turn to 'N. & Q.,' 2ⁿᵈ S. x. 186, 256, 393, he will find that at the under-mentioned places a fire-cradle or grate, or the remains of one, were to be seen, but generally in the church towers. Various suggestions as to their use are also given: Bradeston, Ranworth, Thorpe Abbotts, Tunsted, all in the county of Norfolk; Mettingham, Suffolk; Battlefield, Salop; and Bedlake, Yorkshire.

EVERARD HOME COLEMAN.

Exeter Cathedral contains no ancient fireplace, and only one mediæval instance exists in any church in Devon. It is at St. Andrew's, Colebrooke, and occurs in the north wall of the Copleston chantry situated to the north of the chancel. There used to be a similar one in the chantry at Luton Hoo (Beds), but that was destroyed by fire in November, 1843. Colebrooke now claims to be unique in this respect amongst all the old parish churches of England.   HARRY HEMS.

Fair Park, Exeter.

THACKERAY QUOTATION (9ᵗʰ S. ix. 107).— "The first ambassador whom the New World of Letters sent to the Old" is in 'Nil Nisi Bonum,' in the number of the *Cornhill Magazine* for February, 1860. In the twenty-four-volume edition of Thackeray, begun in 1878, it is included in the 'Roundabout Papers,' but in the *Cornhill* itself it is not included in that series.   Y. Y.

"YCLEPING" THE CHURCH (9ᵗʰ S. viii. 420, 486; ix. 55).—Unless the church tower were detached it would be difficult for people to clip or embrace it, as MR. F. T. ELWORTHY supposes that they did. It requires a very accommodating imagination to see in a tower attached to a church and set "four square" such likeness to a maypole as would qualify it to share the same symbolic honours.

ST. SWITHIN.

"LUDI MAGISTER" (9ᵗʰ S. viii. 516; ix. 86). —The head master of Winchester was thus styled upon the Long Rolls, or annual official lists of the college, 1653-89 inclusive, so far as the series is complete. Since 1690 the term "Informator," which was that used by William of Wykeham in his statutes for the college in 1409, has been used on these documents. I have been informed that the terms "Ludi magister," "Archididascalus," "Hypodidascalus," and "Pædagogus" came into fashion with the Renaissance.

C. W. H.

LORD MAYORS' "PAGEANTS" (9ᵗʰ S. ix. 68). —The pageant for 1609 was 'Camp-bell, or the Ironmongers Faire Feild,' by Anthony Munday, of which there is an imperfect copy* in the British Museum; that for 1621 was 'The Sunne in Aries,' by Thomas Middleton, reprinted in Dyce's edition of Middleton's works and in Nichols's 'Progresses of James I.'; that for 1622 was 'The Triumphs of Honor and Virtue,' by Thomas Middleton, of which the British Museum possesses an imperfect copy; and that for 1623, also by Thomas Middleton, entitled 'The Triumphs of Integrity,' which is reprinted by Dyce. Curiously enough, however, there appear to exist two pageants for the inauguration of Lord Mayor Lumley (1623), as the British Museum Catalogue gives one by Anthony Munday, entitled 'The Triumphs of the Golden Fleece.' It would be interesting to learn which of these was the official version, and why the Drapers' Company placed the commission in the hands of two City poets.

EDWARD M. BORRAJO.

The Library, Guildhall, E.C.

The printed "pageant" for the inauguration of Sir Thomas Cambell's mayoralty, 1609, was written by Anthony Munday, and is entitled 'Camp-bell, or the Ironmongers Faire Feild.' It is extremely rare, and practically unknown. I have never met with a perfect copy, nor, indeed, any but that in the National Collection, containing only sheet B (four leaves). The shows, long left

[* The only one known.]

off, were on this occasion revived by order of the king. Respecting that of Sir William Craven, 1610, I have no note, although it would appear that there was such a one. Sir Edward Barkham's, 1621, was 'The Sunne in Aries,' by Thomas Middleton (seven leaves without pagination = sig. A—B), which is very rare. That of Sir Peter Proby, 1622, also by Middleton, is entitled 'The Triumphs of Honor and Vertue,' and is of extreme rarity. Hazlitt calls it "unique." There is an imperfect copy of seven leaves (wanting the title) in the British Museum. It has been reprinted in the Shakespeare Society Papers. ii. That of Sir Martin Lumley, 1623, 'The Triumphs of the Golden Fleece' (four leaves without pagination), was by Munday, a copy of which is in the National Collection. There was also another "pageant" for the occasion, written by Middleton, entitled 'The Triumphs of Integrity' (nine leaves), and the Duke of Devonshire possesses a copy. I may add that the libraries of the British Museum and the Guildhall, London, contain the finest collections of Lord Mayors' "pageants" extant. Some of those at the Museum belonged to the well-known Humphrey Dyson. W. I. R. V.

The Lord Mayor's pageant for the year 1621 was reprinted in Nichols's 'Progresses, Processions, and Magnificent Festivities of King James I.' It is also given, together with that for the year 1623, in the 'Lord Mayors' Pageants,' by F. W. Fairholt, issued by the Percy Society in 1843. Both of the above-named volumes are in the Corporation Library, Guildhall.

Reference should be made to 7ᵗʰ S. vii. 47, 211, 294, for the titles of other works treating on this subject.

EVERARD HOME COLEMAN.
71, Brecknock Road.

STAUNTON, WORCESTERSHIRE (9ᵗʰ S. viii. 383, 510 ; ix. 11, 92, 110, 170).—I think your correspondent has proved his case.
CHARLES W. DILKE.

"BEANFEAST" (8ᵗʰ S. xii. 64, 174, 312, 371). —In 'Time's Telescope for 1820,' p. 247, I find this term applied to the celebrated Fairlop Fair. The extracts refer to Daniel Day, the founder of the fair, who died in 1767 :—

"Mr. Day was the possessor of a small estate in Essex, at no great distance from Fairlop Oak. To this venerable tree he used, on the first Friday in July, annually to repair ; thither it was his custom to invite a party of his neighbours to accompany him, and, under the shade of its branches and leaves, to dine on beans and bacon."

"Mr. Day, during his life, annually visited his favourite spot ; and, in memory of its origin, never

failed, on the day of the fair, to provide several sacks of beans, with a proportionate quantity of bacon, which he distributed, from the trunk of the tree, to the persons there assembled. For several years before the death of the benevolent, although humorous, founder of this public beanfeast, the pump and block makers of Wapping, to the number of thirty or forty, went annually to the fair in a boat made, like that of Robinson Crusoe or an Indian canoe, of one entire piece of fir. This amphibious vehicle was covered with an awning, mounted on a coach-carriage, and drawn by six post-horses, the whole adorned with ribands, flags, and streamers. It was furnished with a band of musicians, and attended, as may be supposed,

By whifflers and staffiers on foot."

If Fairlop Fair was known as a beanfeast, the transfer of the term to other annual outings appears to me natural. W. H. DAVID.

CHRISTMAS DECORATIONS AND SHROVE TUESDAY (9ᵗʰ S. ix. 86).—There is an interesting allusion to the custom at Oxford with regard to Christmas decorations in the last number of the Historical Manuscripts Commission Reports. Dr. Stratford, Canon of Christ Church, Oxford, writing to Lord Harley, afterwards second Earl of Oxford, 3 February, 1719/20, says :—

"It has been usual for our choristers to burn the day before Candlemas the greens which are put up in the hall at Christmas. They did so on Monday at noon. There was no fire in the hall at supper time, being fast night......Nothing appeared till Tuesday morning about 5 o'clock, when the lanthorn appeared all in a flame......I bless God he quenched it, but not without the loss of that part of the roof on which the lanthorn stood and of the breadth of a window on each side of the lanthorn."—Report of the MSS. of his Grace the Duke of Portland, part vii. p. 269.

G. F. R. B.

"HIGH-FALUTING" (9ᵗʰ S. viii. 505 ; ix. 176). —There is but one objection to Dr. Brewer's derivation from the "Du. *verlooten*, high-flown"; but it is sufficient. The word is a ghost-word, with a wholly imaginary meaning. To launch such words is a common device, and often succeeds with the simple.

At the same time the notion that the prefix *fa-* represents the unaccented Du. prefix *ver-* is not a bad one. And if Dr. Brewer, instead of trusting to his creative fancy, had only consulted a Dutch dictionary, he might have found something better. Thus Calisch's dictionary (1875) has Du. *verluchten*, to air ; *verluchting*, an airing. Also *luchten*, to air, ventilate ; *luchtig*, airy, thin, light, unsubstantial, careless, unsteady, flighty ; from *lucht*, air, atmosphere. Supposing that *lucht* could easily pass into *lute*, by neglect of the guttural, we may easily imagine that *high-faluting* would mean "going high in air," or "soaring" or "flighty"; and *high-faluting words* would mean "flighty talk." This is, of course, a guess; but it has the advantage of starting from a Dutch word that is perfectly real and common, and not one that was constructed for the purpose of mystifying the credulous.   CELER.

WIDOW OF PROTECTOR DUKE OF SOMERSET, HANWORTH, MIDDLESEX (9ᵗʰ S. ix. 148).— Hanworth House was built originally as a hunting-box by King Henry VIII. Towards the end of his reign it was settled in dower upon Queen Katherine Parr, who frequently resided there after the king's death with her second husband, the Lord Admiral Seymour, brother of the Protector, and the Princess Elizabeth, whose education was entrusted to her care. It was at Hanworth that the harmless familiarities took place between Elizabeth and the Lord Admiral and his wife —a molehill which was transformed into a mountain at the admiral's trial. The manor of Hanworth was granted for life to Anne, Duchess of Somerset, the widow of the Protector. In 1578 the duchess entertained Elizabeth at Hanworth, when the queen, at the request of the Countess of Hertford, the duchess's daughter-in-law, sat to Cornelius Ketel for her portrait. She again visited Hanworth in September, 1600, when William Killigrew was in possession of the manor, and hunted in the park. The Newdegates were then settled at Harefield Place, a few miles off. The old house at Hanworth was burnt down by accident on 26 March, 1797. Little of the ancient structure remained, as extensive repairs and alterations had been effected by the Killigrews and subsequent proprietors.   W. F. PRIDEAUX.

The manor of Hanworth was granted to Anne, Duchess of Somerset, for life in 1558, and in 1578 she entertained Elizabeth there. Hanworth House was destroyed by fire on 26 March, 1797, but, according to Thorne's 'Handbook to the Environs of London' (1876), part i. p. 314, "the moat and a few vestiges of the house may be seen immediately W. of Hanworth Ch."   G. F. R. B.

BÉRANGER: 'LE ROI D'YVETOT' (9ᵗʰ S. ix. 88).—MR. BOUCHIER will be amused to hear that one of our local "historians" boldly claims the hero of Béranger's poem for the Isle of Axholme. We are told in the appendix to Read's history of the isle that, according to a local tradition—which I think I may say survives only in the work named, and probably originated in the writer's own head —the real name of this potentate was Ornulff, who reigned over the isle in the time of the Heptarchy, and that it was in his honour that "the late Baron-de-Berenger" wrote the verses, of which a free rendering is there given. I quote the first stanza only :—

> 'Tis really a great while
>   Since there reigned in Axholme's Isle
> A king but little spoken of in story,
>   Who betimes he went to bed,
>   And was slow to raise his head,
> Nor lost a wink of sleep for lack of glory.
>   And a nightcap which Dame Fate
>   Made to fit upon his pate
> Was all the crown, they say, of this wondrous
>   potentate.
>   Oh la! oh la! oh dear! oh dear!
> What a funny little king in Axholme's Isle was
>   here!
>   What a funny little king was here, oh dear!
>   What a funny little king was here!

The "legend" is evidently founded upon the well-known story of Edgar and Elfrida, but many additional circumstances are added to account for Ornulff, who is the son of Elfrida and the king's emissary; and both the time and the place are changed. The whole business was probably intended for a joke; but whether the historian was himself the wag, or some foreign wit imposed upon his "islonian" simplicity, I cannot say.   C. C. B.

Lovers of Béranger will find much profitable and interesting matter in his preface to the 'Chansons Nouvelles et Dernières' (Garnier, 1876). He there discourses at some length on his political creed and his *chansons*, and pays the Frenchman's tribute to the genius of Napoleon. Chambers speaks of Béranger's devotion to the Napoleonic legend; but his *craintes*, as expressed in the 'Traité de Politique à l'Usage de Lise,' show that he was not blind to the emperor's grave errors, and did not hesitate to point them out. In 'Le Roi d'Yvetot' he likely enough portrayed the antithesis to Napoleon.   B. D. MOSELEY.
Burslem.

M. Gustave Masson, in 'La Lyre Française,' 1867, p. 407, has a note: "This masterpiece of satirical songs, composed in 1813, was evidently directed against the insatiable ambition of the Emperor Napoleon."   W. C. B.

PORTUGUESE NAVAL SUPREMACY (9ᵗʰ S. ix. 147).—The empire of the Portuguese in the East seems to have been as short-lived as their discoveries were brilliant. They had incessantly to fight with the natives, and were hard pressed later on by the Dutch and to a less extent by the English. According to one authority it was impossible that a nation so small and without liberty should long maintain her supremacy over so widespread an area. The story of the fall of their Eastern empire is related in Danvers's 'History of the Portuguese in India,' for the author does not confine himself to that country, but tells us much about Macao, the Malay Peninsula, Ternate, Amboyna, and Tidore, as well as about Africa. Brazil, of course, was lost in comparatively recent times. The 'History of Spain and Portugal,' in the "Cabinet Cyclopædia," is supposed, I believe, to be a work of considerable merit.

T. P. ARMSTRONG.

Mr. R. S. Whiteway's 'Rise of the Portuguese Power in India' (Constable, 1899) may be of use.　　　　　HIPPOCLIDES.

See upon the Portuguese military and mercantile supremacy over the world's seas the books of Hugues (professor at the University of Turin) and Ulisse Grifoni (Professor of Geography), *passim* in the *Rivista Marittima* of Rome.　　　BARON ALBERT LUMBROSO.
Frascati, Italy.

"SKIRRET" (9th S. ix. 108).—This is more usually known as a garden-reel and line. It is an instrument which acts on a centre-pin, whence a line is drawn, chalked, and struck to mark out the ground for the foundation of the intended structure. It is from this use by builders that Freemasons draw certain moral deductions from the use of this tool.　　　J. G. WALLACE-JAMES.
Haddington.

"Skirret" is the name of a plant of the parsnip character, which it resembles in flavour. It was formerly much used, but has now gone out of favour. Drayton (1563–1631) says: "The Skirret, which some say in sallads stirrs the blood."

EVERARD HOME COLEMAN.
71, Brecknock Road.

EARL OF CROMARTIE (9th S. ix. 107, 172).—Col. PRIDEAUX, in correcting Miss Bagot's error, has fallen into one himself. Anne, Duchess of Sutherland (who was paternally a Hay, and only a Mackenzie through her grandmother), was not created Countess of Cromartie in 1849, the year of her marriage to the duke, but twelve years later, in 1861. Col. PRIDEAUX speaks of the "revival" of the earldom, and says it was "necessary" (owing to the Act of Union) to make it a peerage of the United Kingdom. May I point out that it was never intended to be anything else? It was a new creation, not a revival; and the terms of the patent of 1861 specially disclaimed any intention of reviving the Scottish earldom and other honours of 1701, of which the original remainder was to heirs male general. Those honours are still dormant, and have in no sense been "revived" by the more recent creation.

OSWALD HUNTER-BLAIR, O.S.B.
Oxford.

"CE N'EST QUE LE PREMIER PAS QUI COUTE" (9th S. ix. 165).—I quoted this once to the celebrated Princesse de Sagan, and she replied: "Tu as tort, mon cher, c'est le seul qu'on nous ne paye pas!"

EDWARD HERON-ALLEN.

Miscellaneous.

NOTES ON BOOKS, &c.

Notes on Staffordshire Place-Names. By W. H. Duignan. (Frowde.)

TIME was—and that not so long ago—when we took up a new book about place-names with premonitory misgivings which were too often justified. Light-hearted guesses founded upon the modern forms of the names, and backed up by ætiological myths or stories invented to account for those forms, did duty for patient research. Even so critical a writer as the late Bishop Creighton walked unwarily into many of these pitfalls laid for him by his predecessors, as Mr. Duignan here shows (p. ix). The present writer is a representative of the new school which bases itself on philological canons and the historical method, and consequently gives us a book of value. He only makes his guess when facts fail him.

We are not always able to agree with Mr. Duignan's conclusions. Why should he throw over Freiford, the twelfth-century form, in favour of Friesforde, the sixteenth-century spelling, in order to explain Freeford? He takes Eccleshall, originally Egleshale, to mean the hall of one Æcle or Ægel. It is surely simpler to understand it as the meadow (A.-S. *healh*) of the church (*ecclesia*), that being the usual meaning of Eccles in place-names, as in Ecclesfield, Eccleshill, Eccleston. Showells, the name of a manor, may or may not be the same as *shewelles*, scarecrows to keep deer within bounds, but it is a mistake to suppose that this meant things which "show" or "exhibit" (? themselves). That word is rather akin to the old German *-sciuhen*, to scare or frighten (our rustics still "shoo" birds), and Gothic *skohsl*. The latter part of the hamlet name Small-rice is much more likely to be *ris*, underwood (A.-S. *hris*), than "rise" in the sense of elevation; and it would take a good deal to persuade us that Silkmore ever meant a moor of silken softness. Mr. Stevenson's suggestion that it may be "Seolca's moor" is much more probable. To say that "the evidence that Druids ever had any existence is very slight" (p. 53) is scepticism pushed to extremes. Among Mr. Duignan's good things is an article on Watling Street, which is a complete disquisition on the subject; but he puts the cart before the horse when he suggests that the name was applied first to the Milky Way and afterwards transferred to the great pilgrim road; it is certain that the reverse was the order of procedure.

The New Testament in Braid Scots. Rendered by Rev. William Wye Smith. (Paisley, Gardner.)

WE thought that the language of the old revisers of the Bible was familiar everywhere and considered unsurpassable. But a body of modern innovators has recently produced a 'Twentieth Century Testament,' and now we have the New Testament presented to us in broad Scotch. The translator rendered, it appears, various pieces of the Bible before, and was asked for the whole, which "the Scots blude and the Scots tongue, wi' the American edication," enabled him to supply. To those who like to return to the tongue of their early days the book may be a boon, but we do not see that the ordinary Englishman needs more "unco tenderness or wondrous pith" than James's revisers secured. If he cannot see the extraordinary force and sweetness of their rendering, he may not be much more charmed and edified by the dialect of the "kailyard," which has emptied the pockets of the Southron bookbuyer so often that he is a little tired of its appeal. Also we find ourselves somewhat irritated by the translator's commentary, which seems often otiose. He preaches in little notes, moral and controversial, which we do not want. As soon as Matthew has reached its twenty-first verse, we are told in a note that "the dourness o' the Jews......was unco strange." Notes by way of exegesis, especially in the Epistles, are tolerable, and perhaps desirable, but reflections we can make for ourselves, such as that "this Agrippa had some gude things aboot him." Is it necessary to say that the Romans were wise in their generation, or to add to Acts xxiii. 14 the comment, "What an awfu' state o' public morals! Nae wonder the wrath fell!" We are not aware, as a matter of history, that there is a record of any special judgment on the occasion. We gladly recognize that the translation approaches in several places nearer to the original meaning, as Greek scholars conceive it, than the older versions, as in Acts xxvi. 28. Here, however, an evident point is missed. Agrippa says, in this version, "Wi' a wee mair fleechin think ye to mak me a Christian?" Where is the "mair" in the original? Not in Westcott and Hort's recension, or the Vulgate, or the Revised Version, or, we think, any good MSS. At any rate, the phrase ἐν ὀλίγῳ is taken up and repeated by St. Paul in the next verse, a characteristic of his speaking which should be exhibited, and which the translation, by rendering "wi' little" in the next verse, loses altogether. There is an ample glossary of Scotch words at the end, and the volume is beautifully printed. We should add that some of the equivalents adopted for the terms of the early Church are likely to cause misconception; but this is perhaps inevitable, and the Scotch mind may enjoy the discussion of such liberties.

A History of Modern Europe. By T. H. Dyer. Revised by Arthur Hassall. Vols. III. and IV. (Bell & Sons.)

THE third and fourth volumes are now before us of the history, the earlier part of which we noticed last September (9ᵗʰ S. viii. 235). The work retains its value as the best summary known to us of a mass of detail, confusing often to the expert historian, and more often, perhaps, unknown to the general reader. The volumes together cover the period from 1576 to 1789, the later date bringing us up to more British authorities than are available for earlier periods. Dyer's style is adequate, and though not brilliant, at any rate lucid. The importance of the manner of exposition, which is denied in some quarters, we must emphasize in history, if history is to be read by the average reader. A great man gives the world the task of understanding him, it is said; but if he does, it is a defect in him, not a merit. We can read this present work with ease, and think this no small recommendation. We differ about certain details, but where we do differ we often find the competent hand of Mr. Hassall referring to later authorities or suggesting a doubt as to the validity of the evidence proffered. Generally he supplies ample means for testing conclusions in other sources open to those who can read French and German. The index, as to which we have already expressed anxiety, is still deferred, presumably for the last volume, and we expect that Mr. Hassall will make as thorough a business of it as he has of the references to the *Quellen* indispensable to a modern scholar. We are a little disappointed at the brevity of the final notices of Gustavus Adolphus and the man whose career was cut short by Ravaillac, because the characters of the great men who made history interest us more than anything else. Usually these notices are judicious, though rather too short. More might be said in defence of the foreign policy of Charles II. of England. The incompetence of Louis XVI. amounted to a crime, as did the insolence of Marie Antoinette, however atoned for afterwards.

As before, several celebrated remarks are pronounced to be inventions, but even so we are glad to have the words "Moriamur pro rege nostro Maria Theresa." There is a useful map of Europe in the eighteenth century attached to vol. iv.

Notices to Correspondents.

LONDON, SATURDAY, MARCH 22, 1902.

CONTENTS. — No. 221.

Notes.

CORONATION PEERAGES.

The precedent as to the number of peerages
created at the coronation of George IV. was
strictly followed at that of William IV., and
formed the basis of the creations made at
that of Queen Victoria, when, however, the
number was reduced by half, owing, presumably, to the quantity of peerages that would
otherwise have thus been created within the
short space of seventeen years, during which
no fewer than three coronations occurred. It
is therefore of some interest to set forth the
statistics of these creations, more especially
as, no peerages having been conferred at the
coronation of George III. or George II., these
three (being all that have taken place for
nearly two hundred years) form practically
the only precedents for the forthcoming
coronation.

At the coronation of George IV., 14 July,
1821, there were twenty-two creations, six of
which number (the Marquessate of Ailesbury
and five earldoms) were bestowed on holders
of hereditary peerages of Parliament, while
sixteen (one viscountcy and fifteen baronies)
were additions to the House of Lords ; of
this sixteen, however, one half (two for Scotland and six for Ireland) was bestowed on
Scotch or Irish peers.

At the coronation of William IV., 8 September, 1831, there were (as above) twenty-

two creations, five of which number (the
Marquessates of Ailsa, Breadalbane, and Westminster, as also two earldoms) were bestowed
on holders of hereditary peerages of Parliament (two of them being also holders of Scotch
earldoms), while seventeen (one earldom, conferred on the younger son of a duke, and sixteen baronies) were additions to the House
of Lords ; of this seventeen, however, nearly
one half (one for Scotland and six for Ireland)
was bestowed on Scotch or Irish peers. The
"promotion" (under the Act of Union) of
the *Irish* Viscountcy of Northland to the
Irish Earldom of Ranfurly should, though
not affecting the House of Lords, be reckoned
also among the peerages then conferred.

At the coronation of Queen Victoria, 28 June,
1838, the creations were exactly half the
number of those made at the two preceding
ones, amounting only to eleven, three of
which number (the Marquessate of Nor-
manby and two earldoms) were bestowed on
holders of hereditary peerages of Parliament,
while eight (all of them baronies) were additions to the House of Lords ; of this eight,
however, one half (one for Scotland and
three for Ireland) was bestowed on Scotch or
Irish peers. A full account of the peerages
conferred on these three occasions will be
found in 'The Complete Peerage,' by G. E. C.,
vol. ii. pp. 351, 312, and 145.

An able and most interesting article by
Mr. J. H. Round entitled 'Coronation Peerages,' and dealing not only with the above,
but with all previous ones, is in the *Monthly
Review* for February. From this it can be
ascertained that the number of such creations
at the earlier coronations was as under.

The number at that of George I., in 1714, was
fourteen—viz., eight (earldoms) bestowed on
holders of hereditary peerages of Parliament
and six (one viscountcy and five baronies) additions to the House of Lords ; of this six, however, no fewer than four were bestowed on
Irish peers.

At the coronation of William and Mary, in
1689 (Queen Anne as well as her father
James II. having refrained from coronation creations), the number (exclusive of
the *Irish* Viscountcy of Hewett) was ten
(two dukedoms, five earldoms, two viscount-
cies, and one barony), six of which number
were bestowed on holders of hereditary
peerages of Parliament, while four were
additions to the House of Lords, these
four being (1) the Duke of Cumberland,
brother-in-law to the Queen ; (2) the well-
beloved Earl of Portland ; (3) Viscount Sydney ;
and (4) Lord Cholmondeley, which last (as well
as Lord Lumley, one of the two English vis-

counts now made) already possessed an *Irish* viscountcy.

At the coronation of Charles II., 23 April, 1661, twelve peerages were created (six earldoms and six baronies), three of which number (earldoms) were bestowed on holders of hereditary peerages of Parliament, while the other nine (three earldoms and six baronies) were additions to the House of Lords ; one of these nine, however, the Earldom of Anglesey, was conferred on an Irish viscount. Of the two remaining earldoms, one (Bath) was given to the son and heir of the gallant Sir Bevill Granville, and the other (Carlisle) to the renegade Charles Howard, " who, even less than three years before, had stooped to accept a peerage from Cromwell himself."

At the coronation of Charles I., in 1626, eight earldoms were bestowed on holders of hereditary peerages of Parliament, but no other peerage was created, so that there was no addition to the House of Lords. At that of James I., 25 July, 1603, eleven peerages (three earldoms and eight baronies) were created, of which two (earldoms) were bestowed as above, while the other nine were additions to the House of Lords ; of this nine, however, the Earldom of Southampton was conferred (with the ancient precedence) on one who, but for his attainder in 1601, would have been such earl.

At the coronation of Queen Elizabeth, in 1559, four peerages (one earldom and three baronies) were created, all being additions to the House of Lords, though the earldom (Hertford) was granted to one who, but for his father's attainder, would have been Earl of Hertford as well as Duke of Somerset. Queen Mary, some four weeks before her coronation (30 September, 1553), conferred the (now existing) Earldom of Devon on Edward Courtenay, who but for his father's attainder would have been such earl as well as Marquess of Exeter.

At the coronation of Edward VI., in 1547, eight peerages were created—viz., the (now existing) Dukedom of Somerset, the Marquessate of Northampton, and the Earldoms of Warwick and Southampton, all four being bestowed on holders of hereditary peerages of Parliament ; as also four baronies, these last being additions to the House of Lords. As to the previous coronations, no peerages were made by Henry VIII. ; Henry VII., however, in 1485, conferred (1) the Dukedom of Bedford on his uncle, the Earl of Pembroke, and (2) the Earldom of Derby (still existing) on the Lord Stanley ; while Richard III., in 1483, conferred (1) the Dukedom of Norfolk (a

title still held by the heir male of the grantee's body) on John, Lord Howard ; (2) the Earldom of Nottingham on William, Viscount Berkeley ; and (3) the Viscountcy of L'Isle on Edward (Grey), Lord L'Isle.

" With Richard III. we begin the long series of precedents [for creation of peerages at coronations] which, however fitful at first, have now crystallized into custom." There was, however, one " anticipation " of this practice, about 100 years prior to Richard III.—viz., at the coronation of Richard II., 13 July, 1377, when four earldoms (Buckingham, Northumberland, Huntingdon, and Nottingham) were conferred respectively on the king's uncle, Thomas of Woodstock (afterwards Duke of Gloucester) ; on Henry, Lord Percy ; on Sir Guichard D'Angle ; and on John, Lord Mowbray. Nine *chevaliers* were made at the same time, while at the next ensuing coronation, that of Henry IV., 13 October, 1399, no fewer than forty-six persons were, after bathing, made Knights of the Bath, the creation of *knights* (not of peers) being, as is pointed out in the valuable article above quoted, " the essential feature " of the early coronations, and one which continued in them down to and including that of Charles II.

As to baronetcies, Mr. Round mentions that the number conferred at the 1821 coronation was twenty-four, increasing at that of 1831 to twenty-eight, and (" instead of undergoing, like the peerage honours, a sharp reduction ") at that of 1838 to thirty.   G. E. C.

SHAKESPEARIANA.

'Antony and Cleopatra,' II. ii. 211–16.—

Enobarb. Her gentlewomen, like the Nereides,
So many mermaids, tended her i' the eyes
And made their bends adornings : at the helm
A seeming mermaid steers : the silken tackle
Swell with the touches of those flower-soft hands
That yarely frame the office.

This is unquestionably the greatest crux in the play. The 'Variorum Shakespeare' devotes six pages to the conjectures of various critics. The difficulty is " tended her i' the eyes and made their bends adornings." Steevens and the majority of modern editors interpret the words thus : " The gentlewomen waited upon Cleopatra's looks, and each inclined her person so gracefully that the very act of humiliation was an improvement of her own beauty." But Shakspere is here following North's ' Plutarch ' very closely, as a reference to the corresponding passage will show, and it is expressly stated of Cleopatra's gentlewomen that there were " some steering the helm, others tending the tackle and ropes."

Steevens would leave one solitary overworked "gentlewoman" to mind the helm, pull the ropes, and lay on to the tackle with her "flower-soft hands," while her lazy companions, intent on mere eye-service, kept bowing to Cleopatra, with no other end in view, it would seem, than to make the scene more attractive to a beholder. Hardly a fair division of labour. Observe, too, that Cleopatra is already waited on by pretty dimpled boys, and yet Steevens wants to add "sweets to the sweet."

But suppose we look at the question in a more practical way. In those "spacious times" of wild sea-roving and adventure, when every morning brought home a Drake or a Raleigh with his crew of hardy mariners, and every evening closed with its sailor's yarn spun to an eager group around the inn fire, seamen's terms and seamen's language were familiar in the mouth as household words, and that Shakspere was not ignorant of them the first scene of the 'Tempest' amply shows. In the play before us he is also dealing with a ship and her crew. The ship is Cleopatra's barge, and the crew are Cleopatra's gentlewomen (*vide* North's 'Plutarch'). Let us be on the lookout for nautical terms then ; and I say that here we have them in plenty—"the eyes," "bends," "helm," "steers," "tackle"; and even "hands" seems to fit not unnaturally into the sense of the passage.

If we ask any seaman what he means by "the eyes," he will tell us that they are the "hawse holes"—*i.e.*, the holes or eyes in the bow through which the anchor cables are run. Again, any good dictionary informs us that in olden days ships were adorned with painted eyes on the bows—a supposed protection against "the evil eye." This custom is still extant in the Mediterranean, and, I believe, in Chinese waters. "The eyes," then, signify "the bow."

Now, if we ask our A.B. what "bends" are, he will tell us that a bend is a knot, that there are various kinds of bends—*e.g.*, the carrick-bend, the sheet-bend, &c. If he is of an instructive mind he will add that "bends" is a term applied also to the small ropes used to "clinch" the anchor cables. But let me give chapter and verse. In Falconer's 'Dictionary of Marine Terms' (1769) I find the following :—

"*Bend*, the knot by which one rope is fastened to another, or to the anchor.

"*To bend*, to fasten one rope to another.

"Bends are of various denominations, such as—the carrick-bend, the fisherman's bend, the sheet-bend."

I take Enobarbus's words to mean that the crew were busily engaged "i' the eyes" (*i.e.*, in the bow) attending to the various bends or the rigging (North, "ropes"); and by throwing over the whole process the indescribable charm that is all a woman's, especially when she is occupied with a work that we are accustomed to see performed by an ordinary rude ship's hand, these gentlewomen actually made the object of their work an additional ornament to the scene.

But the 'New English Dictionary' steps in to throw an obstacle in our path. That indisputable authority says that "bends" does not appear in print previous to 1769 (the date of Falconer's 'Dictionary'). But "eyes" here comes to our help. The 'New English Dictionary' says that "eyes" first appears in print, with the meaning attached to it by our intelligent A.B., in the year 1840. Now, if so well-known a term as "the eyes of a ship" does not appear till 1840, may not "bends" have been equally well known in olden times, in speech if not in print?

But I have another assistant. From the verb *to bend* (meaning to incline the body) we make the noun *bend*, and so Steevens has understood the word here. Similarly, I presume, so great a lord of language as Shakspere could make the noun *bend* from the verb *to bend* (meaning to tie ropes together), provided that such a word was at that time in the English vocabulary. To return to our dictionaries. I find in Sir Henry Manwayring's 'The Seaman's Dictionary' (published in 1644) the following remark : "To bend two Cabells or Roapes together, that is, to tye them together with a knot, and so to make their own ends fast upon themselves." Is it too much to conclude that a marine term, known to a lexicographer in the year 1644, was in common use among seamen in 1607–8?

I may add that Dr. Ingleby ('Shakespeare Hermeneutics') has already adopted the explanation of "eyes" given above, and had, indeed, come halfway to the conclusion that we have reached ; but he stopped by the wayside to pluck at the tempting fruit of textual emendation.

N. Hancock Prenter.

Trinity College, Dublin.

[This passage was discussed at much length in 7th S. x., xi., xii.]

'Cymbeline,' I. iii. 8–10 (9th S. ii. 524).— Dr. Johnson's note on this passage is as follows :—"Sir T. Hanmer alters it thus :

for so long
As he could mark me with his eye, or I
Distinguish.

The reason of Sir T. Hanmer's reading was,

that Pisanio describes no address made to the *ear.*" MR. THISELTON suggests the retention of the original "make," with practically the same meaning as "mark" proposed by Hanmer.

When Pisanio says, in the accepted reading, that Posthumus remained on deck "for so long as he could make me with this eye or ear distinguish him from others," he states something within his knowledge. As Posthumus at first, when the ship was near, made him hear his voice, and later, at a distance, caught his eye by signals. Pisanio knew that Posthumus stood on deck at least that long. If he were to say, however, that Posthumus stood there "for so long as he could make [mark] me with his eye," Pisanio would be going beyond his actual knowledge, and stating a mere conjecture, which he would hardly presume to do.

To me, "*this* eye or ear" is expressive of Pisanio's loyalty and devotion to his master.

E. MERTON DEY.

St. Louis.

THE JAPANESE REGALIA.—In the *Daily Telegraph* of the 15th inst. is an interesting account of a lecture given by Mr. Goji Ukita, Chancellor of the Japanese Legation, on the Imperial regalia of Japan. It appears that these emblems consist of the Mirror, symbolic of Knowledge; the Sword, for Courage; and the Divine Jewels, for Mercy. They are merely of copper, steel, and stone. The regalia have the highest significance, it being held that no Emperor can rule without the three virtues which they represent.

N. S. S.

"CROSSING THE BAR."—In 1680 a Scottish Presbyterian minister, the Rev. Donald Cargil, wrote to a friend who was under sentence of death :—

"Fairwell, dearest friend, never to see one another any more, till at the right hand of Christ. Fear not, and the God of mercies grant a full gale and a fair entry into his kingdom, that may carry you sweetly and swiftly over the bar, that you find not the rub of death."

The passage is to be found in the 'Cloud of Witnesses' (p. 8 in the 1836 edition).

W. S.

CONTEMPORARIES IMPERSONATED ON THE STAGE.—Has the subject of impersonating living celebrities on the stage been dealt with recently in the pages of 'N. & Q.'? In a dispatch from Amsterdam dated 24 February, and printed in the *Daily Chronicle* of the following day, we read :—

"In an operetta entitled the 'Carnival at Rome,' which is going on at one of the theatres here, one of the actors represents Mr. Chamberlain. The *Handelsblad* reprehends this proceeding, and says that whatever political differences of opinion may exist, there is always a limit to the permissible."

During, or immediately after, the Dreyfus court-martial at Rennes, a series of plays in Yiddish, dealing with the subject, were performed at the Britannia Theatre. Zola—played by a most pronounced Jew—was the hero. The representations, which formed a sort of trilogy, were followed by crowds of Jewish spectators with intense interest. The programme was printed in English and Hebrew.

CHARLES HIATT.

"GALILEE." (See 'N. & Q.' and elsewhere, *passim.*)—While we have been guessing for years and years about the origin of the term "Galilee," as applied to a part of a church, we have all the while had the true explanation ready to hand in some easily accessible books. It is simply that as Sunday is the weekly festival of the Resurrection, so the Sunday procession, in which the person of greatest dignity goes first, represents the going of our Lord before the disciples into Galilee, and hence the part of a church where the procession ended was called the "Galilee." See Rupert of Deutz, 'De Div. Off.' (Migne, 'P.L.,' vol. clxx.), lib v. cap. 8, and lib. vii. cap. 21-24 (quoted in Ducange, *s.v.*); Rud., 'Catal. of Durham MSS.,' 66; Hutchinson, 'Hist. of Durham,' 1787, ii. 71n.

J. T. F.

Durham.

MRS. SIDDONS'S HOUSE, UPPER BAKER STREET.—It is stated that when the arrangements for the electrization of the Metropolitan Inner Circle Railway are completed, one of the first houses to be demolished will be No. 27, Upper Baker Street, at the corner of Allsopp Place, which was the last residence of Mrs. Siddons, the actress, who died there 8 June, 1831.

"In 1817 Mrs. Siddons took the lease of a house, pleasantly situated, with an adjoining garden and a small green, at the top of Upper Baker Street, on the right side towards the Regent's Park. Here she built an additional room for her modelling."—Campbell's 'Life of Siddons,' p. 360.

Mrs. Siddons appears to have resided in Gower Street during the early part of her married life, and afterwards, from 1790 to 1802, at No. 49, Great Marlborough Street.

On Mrs. Siddons's death the house in Upper Baker Street was purchased by a "Mr. Gowan from India" for 2,150*l.* "It was," according to Boaden, Mrs. Siddons's biographer,

"fitted up with a plainness that has seldom attended rooms of equal grandeur—the tone of the whole house was that of wainscot, and the Muse of Tragedy, instead of 'sweeping by in her sceptred pall,' amused her retirement with the *simplex munditiis* of quaker affluence. In her drawing-room hung the portrait of her brother John [J. P. Kemble] as Hotspur, on horseback, which the late Sir Francis Bourgeois painted when M. Desenfans became possessed of the wonderful sketch by Vandyke now at Dulwich."—*Gent. Mag.*

JOHN HEBB.

"KEMP."—This word, incidentally mentioned in a contribution by MR. PLATT (*ante*, p. 74), is defined by Dr. Murray as a "coarse or stout hair occurring in wool." Our Bradford woolsorters would define it as "hair which has become detached from the skin before shearing, dead hair which will not take the dye and shows white or grey in the woven fabric." CHARLES A. FEDERER.
Bradford.

APPEASING A GHOST. — The 1231st 'Celebrity at Home' of the *World*, 15 January, was the Earl of Orford at Mannington Hall, Norfolk. With the writer of the article, I think

"it is interesting to note, in connexion with the late Earl's burial, that his coffin when brought from London, where he died, was not driven three times round the church at Wolterton, although this is the first time the formality has been omitted. The tradition held that Horatio, second Earl of Orford, destroyed the tombs of the Scalmers, former possessors of the place, and one of the unhappy ladies of this family, finding no rest, is said to still haunt the churchyard, always searching for the remains of her relations. To mollify her uneasy spirit, every Earl of Orford at his burial is driven in his hearse three times round the church before he is laid to his rest."

ST. SWITHIN.

THE O.P. RIOTS. — A graphic picture of these disturbances occurs in the second volume of (Lord) Campbell's 'Law Reports':

"Mr. Clifford, a gentleman of great eminence at the bar, on the 31st of October [1809], between nine and ten in the evening, went into the pit of Covent Garden Theatre, which had been lately rebuilt. On this, as on every night from the first opening of the house, great noise and confusion prevailed, on account of the prices of admission to the pit and boxes being raised, and the public being excluded from a number of boxes which were let to particular individuals for the season. The performance on the stage was inaudible; the spectators sometimes stood on the benches, and at other times sat down with their backs to the performers; while the play was representing, 'God save the King!' and 'Rule, Britannia!' were sung by persons in different parts of the theatre; horns were blown, bells were rung, and rattles were sprung; placards were exhibited, exhorting the audience to resist the oppression of the managers; and a number of men wore in their hats the letters O.P. and N.P.B., meaning *Old Prices* and *No Private Boxes*. But although there were some sham-fights in the pit, no violence was

offered to any person either on the stage or in any other part of the house, and no injury was done to the theatre itself, or any of its decorations. When Mr. Clifford entered, there was a cry of 'There comes the honest counsellor!' and, a passage being opened for him, he went and seated himself in the centre of the pit. Soon afterwards, a gentleman asked him if there was any harm in wearing the letters O.P. He answered 'No.' The gentleman then asked him if he had any objection to wear them himself. He said he had not. The letters O.P. were then placed in his hat, and he put it on thus ornamented. He continued, however, to sit without taking any part in the disturbance, and he persuaded a person who was near him to desist from blowing a trumpet. Having conducted himself in this quiet manner while he remained in the theatre, he was retiring from it."

Thereupon one Brandon, the box-keeper, gave Mr. Clifford in charge. He was taken to Bow Street, where the magistrate, Mr. Read, set him at liberty. Then he sued Brandon for the assault and false imprisonment.

The case was heard before Sir James Mansfield, in the Common Pleas at Westminster. Serjeant Best, being retained for Mr. Clifford, contended that, within the walls of a public theatre, the public have a right to express their approbation or disapprobation without limit or control; and that, as there had been no pulling up of benches, or breaking of chandeliers, or bloodshed, there had been no riot.

"The people were only expressing, according to ancient usage, their sense of what they disapproved. The noise was great, but not greater than is frequently heard at the condemnation of a new play. Bells and rattles may be new to the pit, but catcalls, which are equally stunning, are as old as the English drama."

Besides this, Mr. Clifford's conduct had been quiet. He had even stopped the blowing of a trumpet.

"By wearing O.P. in his hat, he simply expressed his opinion, that the old prices were sufficient, and ought to be restored. If this were illegal, it would soon be a misdemeanour to wear a blue cockade at an election, or a white favour at a wedding."

Sir James Mansfield held that there had been a riot, and said :—

"It is not easy to see that the plaintiff [Mr. Clifford] had no intention to encourage the rioters. How happened it that at his entrance he was saluted with the exclamation, 'Here comes the honest counsellor!' How had he deserved this peculiar panegyric? How came it that a word from him was sufficient to prevent a man from blowing a trumpet?"

These were awkward questions; but the jury cut the knot by giving Mr. Clifford damages in the sum of five pounds.

RICHARD H. THORNTON.
Portland, Oregon.

OLD SCHOOL RULES.—As a pendant to the rules of Heyford Free School (*ante,* p. 41), the following rules for the management of the school of Prestonkirk parish may be of interest :—

19th May, 1703.

Rules for the Management of the School.

1. The School must be convened at seven in the morning, and dismissed at five o'clock in afternoon.

2. The Master must pray with his scholars morning and evening, when he convenes the school, and dismisses.

3. He must cause his scholars get the catechism exactly and distinctly by heart, and hear them repeat the same on the Saturday forenoon.

4. He must gather his scholars on the Sabbath morning before sermon, and pray with them, and then take them to the church with him, when, after he hath sung a psalm, the catechism must be repeated by two of them—one asking and the other answering.

5. He must enjoin such as can write to write the sermon, and on Monday morning cause his scholars give an account of what they mind theirof, and subjoin some pious exhortations and advices to them.

6. He must punish severely any vice that any of them may be guilty of, such as banning, swearing, lying, fighting, and the like.

7. He must discharge them to play too near the water, or within the churchyard.

8. He must not leave the school but on a necessary occasion, and then he must acquaint the minister.

9. He must not grant the vacancie without acquainting the session, and they are to judge when and how long; and then some of the scholars are to give evidence of their proficiency in their learning.

10. Censors must be appointed for the observation of the manners of the rest, and there must be examinations once every week.

11. Those that learn Latin must be accustomed to speak it.

J. G. WALLACE-JAMES, M.B.

Haddington.

LEMAN SAND.—Dryden twice alludes to the shipwreck of James II. when, as Duke of York, he was voyaging from England to Scotland in the month of May, 1682. In part ii. of 'Absalom and Achitophel' it is mentioned in the lines—

Yet fate for ruin takes so still an hour,
And treach'rous sands the princely bark devour.

Again, in 'Britannia Rediviva,' written to celebrate the birth of the prince (called in later times the Old Pretender) on 10 June, 1688 (the longest day of the year by O.S., then observed in England), the actual place is alluded in the lines—

Methinks had we within our minds no more
Than that one shipwreck on the fatal Ore.

And a note in Scott's edition explains this to be "the Lemmon Ore, on which the vessel of King James was lost in his return from Scotland" (should be *to* Scotland, whither he was returning to bring back the duchess). The vessel was the Gloucester frigate. According to Knight's 'Pictorial History of England' she "struck upon a sand-bank called the Lemon and Ore [Lingard has Lemon - and - Ore], about twelve leagues from Yarmouth." The 'Dictionary of National Biography' (vol. xxix. p. 187) says that the place was "off the Yorkshire coast." As a matter of fact the Leman sand-bank or Ore is somewhat more than twenty miles (N.E. by E.) from Cromer, in Norfolk. "Ore" is from the A.-S. *óra,* a bank, and "leman" from the adjective *læ'men,* earthy or made of clay, whence our word "loam."

W. T. LYNN.

Blackheath.

"PULQUE."—Prescott repeatedly mentions *pulque,* or wine made from the aloe, as the national beverage of Mexico. The origin of this term is far from clear. It occurs in Spanish as early as 1535, in Oviedo ("Pulque ques su vino," edition of 1851, iii. 536). I know of three possible etymologies.

(*a*) Clavigero (English translation of 1787, i. 435) says, "*Pulque* is not a Spanish nor Mexican word, but is taken from the Araucanian language, in which *pulcu* is the generic name for the beverages these Indians use to intoxicate themselves."

(*b*) Mr. Payne ('History of the New World called America,' i. 364) objects to Clavigero's suggestion on the ground that the Araucanian word means *chicha,* which is not the same drink as *pulque.* Mr. Payne thinks *pulque* is corrupted from the Aztec word *octli.* This seems too violent a corruption to be probable.

(*c*) In the Maya language of Yucatan the word for *pulque* is *ki.* I have sometimes thought that this might account for the second syllable (-*que*) of *pulque,* but the first syllable (*pul-*) would still remain a difficulty. There is, I am told, a full list of the Spanish words derived from Maya appended to Mendoza's 'Catalogo Razonado de las Palabras Mexicanas introducidas al Castellano,' Mexico, 1872, but I cannot get to see it in London. Perhaps some reader of these lines may be in a position to say whether it includes *pulque.*

JAMES PLATT, Jun.

THE LAST OF THE PRE-VICTORIAN M.P.s.—By the death—on 20 February—of the sixth Earl Fitzwilliam, the last, or the last but one, of the pre-Victorian members of Parliament has passed away. The late earl — then Viscount Milton—was elected for Malton, in Yorkshire, in January, 1837, some six months before the dissolution of the last Parliament of William IV. Some five years ago it was pointed out (8th S. xi. 465) that nine persons were then living who had held seats in that Parliament. Unless Mr. J. T. Leader be living (of which fact there appears some doubt), the late Earl Fitzwilliam was the last of the nine there enumerated, as indeed (with the like possible exception as to Mr. Leader) he was also the last of the first Victorian House of Commons.

W. D. PINK.

INITIAL FOR FORENAME IN SERIOUS VERSE (See 9th S. iv. 184).—Is it not possible that Lydgate, in the passage given at the above reference, wrote Agellius? Cf. Teuffel's 'History of Roman Literature,' revised by Schwabe, Warr's translation, § 365. "In the MSS. and throughout the Middle Ages A. Gellius, in consequence of a jumble of his prænomen and gentile name, is frequently called Agellius." EDWARD BENSLY.
The University, Adelaide, South Australia.

Queries.

WE must request correspondents desiring information on family matters of only private interest to affix their names and addresses to their queries, in order that the answers may be addressed to them direct.

JOHN LAUGHTON, one of the most eminent of English scholars in the closing years of the seventeenth, and the opening years of the eighteenth, century, was Librarian of the University of Cambridge, 1686–1712, and Prebendary of Lichfield and of Worcester. Is any portrait known of him? R. S.

SCOTCH CHURCH IN LONDON.—Can any one tell me the name and site of a Scotch church in London, of which Dr. Rutherford was minister? He died in 1820, being at that time minister of Muirkirk parish church, Ayrshire. W. M. J.-F.

"LIMBERHAM."—This word, with allusion sometimes to Dryden's use of it as the name of the principal character of his play of 1678, and sometimes to its etymological meaning, occurs so frequently as an appellative in the literature of the eighteenth century that it seems to have a sufficient claim to a place in the English dictionary. I am surprised to find that it was not, as I had supposed, invented by Dryden. A "Master Limberham" is mentioned (though not brought on the stage) in Wycherley's 'Country Wife,' Act II. (p. 27 of the edition of 1675), three years before the performance of Dryden's comedy. If no earlier instance can be found it is possible that Wycherley invented the name,

and that Dryden took it from him. On the other hand, the word may already have been current before 1675 as a nickname for a person of the type of character depicted by Dryden. I should be glad to know whether the example in Wycherley is the earliest that is extant. HENRY BRADLEY.
Clarendon Press, Oxford.

JOHN KING, LANGUAGE MASTER, LONDON, 1722.—I had recently in my hands the MS. of "A German or High Dutch Grammar, For English Gentlemen to learn the German Language, by John King, Language Master in London, 1722." It is dedicated to "the Right Honourble John Lord Carteret, Baron of Hawnes, One of the Lords of His Majesty's most Honble Privy Council, and Principal Secretary of State." Can any one tell me anything about the author, John King, and whether this grammar ever appeared in print? It affords further corroboration of the phonetic value of the combination ea (cf. Pope's rime tea : obey), and shows that aw had not yet reached its modern pronunciation, the first letters of the German alphabet being spelt aw, bea, tsea, dea. F. J. C.
Frankfurt-a.-Main.

STAR-LORE. — Can any correspondent of 'N. & Q.' inform me in what counties of Great Britain and Ireland it is supposed to be wrong to point at the heavenly bodies, and for what reason this action is forbidden?

Miss Burne records a Shrewsbury belief that it is wicked to point at the moon ('Shropshire Folk-lore,' part ii. p. 258), and quotes Kelly's 'Indo-European Tradition,' p. 21, to show that in Germany it is held wicked to point at the stars, "because they are angels' eyes." (See also E. Gerard's 'Land beyond the Forest,' vol. i. p. 311 ; Birlinger's 'Volksthümliches aus Schwaben,' vol. i. p.190 ; and Folk-lore, vol. i. p. 151.)

In 'The Poet at the Breakfast Table,' p. 5, O. W. Holmes says :—

"I remember that when I was a child the tradition was whispered round among us little folks that if we tried to count the stars we should drop down dead. Nevertheless, the stars have been counted and the astronomer has survived."

In Melanesia the stars are called "dead men's eyes" (R. H. Codrington, 'The Melanesians,' p. 349), and in Tana, a volcanic island in the New Hebrides, Mr. Turner was told by an old man that the stars were the eyes of their forefathers looking down on the people ('Samoa,' pp. 319, 320), while in Samoa they are the spirits of the departed (ibid., 273). In South America a rather different theory seems to hold. Monsignor Lasagna says, in his account of the Coroados of Brazil, that they affirm that when a *Baire* or magician dies his soul passes into a star. Hence when a shooting-star flashes across the sky they are filled with terror and confusion, and, turning out of their huts, they weep, shriek, and gesticulate so as to exorcise the soul of the *Baire* and impede his return among them to work evil (*Salesian Bulletin*, vol. ii. p. 55).

What I want to know is whether the super-stition that it is not right to point at the stars is widely spread with us, and why it is deemed to be wrong to do so.   G. W.

G. HERBERT'S 'FLOWER.'—

> Grief melts away
> Like snow in May,
> *As if there were no such cold thing.*

Does not the last line of this read somewhat like an echo of a passage in Lord Vaux's ballad 'The Aged Lover Renounceth Love'? The third verse of that poem (altered in the gravedigger's song in 'Hamlet,' V. i.) is as follows :—

> For Age with stealing steps
> Hath clawed me with his crutch,
> And lusty Life away she leaps
> *As there had been none such.*

So in Staunton's Shakspeare. But in Percy's 'Reliques' the third line is—

> And lusty Youth away he leaps.
>   C. LAWRENCE FORD, B.A.

Bath.

SALT FOLK-LORE.—A friend of mine writes to me from Hampshire to the following effect : "Our maid tells me that a plate of salt should always be put on the floor under the coffin containing a body awaiting burial, as it prevents swelling." Is not this a variant of an old custom? The more generally known practice, I believe, is to put a plate of salt on the corpse itself.   M. P.

CELTS AND THE MASSAGETÆ.—The pressure forwards of peoples appears to have been always from East to West. The Celts had their precursors, who were driven to inhos-pitable fastnesses and to distant shores. Who were the Massagetæ; and is there any modern people representing them, as the Gaels, Kymri, Erse, Manx, Bretons, &c., are representative of the Celts? We read in Gibbon that in the reign of Justinian

"the Massagetæ (not Huns) appear in history driving the Celtic Kymri westward, many years before any Huns were heard of (see Herodotus, i. 1, c. 6, 15, 16; but these chapters must be studied carefully). They were a section of the great Gothic race."—Edition 1854, vol. iv. p. 365.

These Massagetæ were considered of the highest courage and the most formidable of warriors. At the taking of Carthage 600 of them were placed in the vanguard under John the Armenian. Belisarius employed them largely in his war against the Vandals. They were a distinguished and conspicuous people about A.D. 530. They drove the Celts further West. Is there, as I have just asked, any modern population representing these Massagetæ? Some correspondent of 'N. & Q.' might kindly enlighten me hereon.
                    R. DE PAYEN PAYNE.
12, Victoria Grove, Southsea.

ROBERT DODSLEY.—Wanted, an authorita-tive statement as to the date of Dodsley's death. 23 September, 1764, seems most likely to be correct, but many books give 25 Sep-tember. In 7ᵗʰ S. x. 406 is a copy of the entry of his burial from the Durham Cathe-dral Register : "1764, 26 Sept. Mr. Robert Doddesley, Stationer, London, bur." 'Cham-bers's Encyclopædia,' like the 'D.N.B.,' gives 25 December as the date of death.
                    JOHN T. PAGE.
West Haddon, Northamptonshire.

PICTORIAL POSTCARDS.—Can any reader of 'N. & Q.' tell me when the first pictorial post-cards came into existence? They are num-bered now by many thousands, and embrace views of almost every place of importance in the world; while the collection of them has become a recognized hobby, and has a monthly journal, the *Picture Postcard*, de-voted to its interests.
                    FREDERICK T. HIBGAME.

HUGH POULTRELL.—Can any of your readers kindly give me information as to Hugh Poultrell, who held land in Lancashire in the eleventh century, and appears to have been a baron?   K. TRICE MARTIN.

FASHION IN LANGUAGE.—May I ask if any contributor has ever made a list of pet words in literature—words which become the fashion for a time and then take rank again in obscurity? Thus in the eighteenth century we find such words as "vastly," "hugely," "the quality," "genteel," &c. "Elegant" still lingers conspicuously in America, and in England at the present time special favour seems to be shown to "con-vincing," "weird," and "strenuous." Perhaps one of your readers could supply a full list of such words, with brief notes on the rise and fall thereof.   SIGMA.

BROWN FAMILY.—I am anxious to obtain some information about people of the name of Brown. There was a Major-General Brown. A sister, I think, married a Mr. Graham

(related to the Montrose family), and another sister lived with Mrs. Graham at Barnstaple, Devonshire, for years. Papers relating to this family were unfortunately mislaid. I should also like to know particulars of the Sir Samuel Brown who built the old pier at Brighton.   E. C. WIENHOLT.
6, Girdler's Road, W.

EAST WIND IN WELSH.—A writer in a Welsh newspaper states that "in some parts," presumably of Wales, "the east wind is called *Gwynt traed y meirw*"— that is, "the wind of the feet of the dead." He suggests that the origin of this may be that as a rule the dead are buried with their feet towards the east. What is the origin of this saying, and is the suggestion probable?   JEANNIE S. POPHAM.
62, Rutland Gate, S.W.

ITALIAN QUOTATION. — Where does the following Italian quotation occur?—

L' astro che in sul mattin lieto scintilla,
Annunziator dell' alba desiata.

Is it from Metastasio? Can any of your readers kindly tell me?   S. M.

LLYN COBLYNAU: KNOCKERS' LLYN.—Can any one identify this Snowdonian lake, mentioned in 'Aylwin'? It might be Glaslyn, but I am pretty well acquainted with Snowdon after fifty ascents, and I never heard of Knockers' Llyn until I read 'Aylwin.' Mr. Watts-Dunton says it is also called "Kissing Llyn."   E. W.

"CHAMPIGNY": "BUGGY."—

"He expressed his fear that the terrific rattling of barouches......curricles, tandems, *buggies, full, half, or sweep-panelled*, and *champignys*, would unquestionably, by their irresistible concussion, destroy the ramparts of Fort William!"—Lieut.-Col. Davidson, 'Travels in Upper India,' ii. 209, published 1843.

What kind of carriage was a *champigny*? I do not find it in the 'N.E.D.' What is the distinction between the different kinds of *buggy* noted above?   W. CROOKE.
Langton House, Charlton Kings.

MATHEWS OF TRURO.—I beg to be allowed to repeat a query propounded in these columns some seventeen years ago, to which the reply is still wanting. Is anything known about Thomas Mathews, of Truro, in the county of Cornwall, yeoman, who died there in the year 1788? In 1772 he purchased the small estate of Pithenlew, on which Truro's suburb of Ferristown now stands. He was a renowned nurseryman gardener, and is said to have introduced into Cornwall the culture of turnips as a field crop. According to the family tradition he came from Norwich, but careful search there and in the county of Norfolk has failed to discover his parentage. His third son, William Mathews, was baptized at Truro in 1747; and previous to that date nothing is known of the family. Wills and parish registers in Cornwall and Norfolk have not helped. Any information will be most gratefully appreciated.
    JOHN HOBSON MATTHEWS.
Town Hall, Cardiff.

Replies.

THE AUTHOR AND AVENGER OF EVIL.
(9ᵗʰ S. ix. 22.)

SOME points in the note under this heading confessedly stand in need of further elucidation, so I will not apologize for the following remarks.

The "confused ideas with regard to the *rôle* acted by" the Evil One are due, in a great measure, to the various sources from which the popular notions of the devil are derived, being not only the Jewish and Christian Scriptures, but also ancestral tradition—not only ecclesiastical teaching, but poetry and folk-lore as well. The ordinary Englishman has formed his "confused" picture of the Prince of Darkness from Milton (generally second hand), Bunyan, and the opera of 'Faust,' rather than from a study of his Bible. In the Bible itself the evolution of Satan from an agent of disease and death, who receives a direct commission from the Almighty, into "the irreconcilable foe of God and man" is a gradual one; and the systematic divine naturally finds it difficult to harmonize the "Adversary" of the book of Job with "the Prince of this World" as presented in the fourth Gospel.

As to the personal appearance of the devil, it is probable that he owes more in popular belief to Teutonic or Keltic than to Greek or Roman elements. The cunning and malicious Loki, whose name is still a common one for Satan in Norway, is the prototype to some extent of the wily tempter of mankind. Skratt, the shaggy spirit of Scandinavian wastes and forests, has left his name, in the form of "Old Scratch," to his semi-Oriental supplanter, no less than his hairy hide; for Pan and Faunus had their representatives in Northern lands, and Dutchman and Italian can visualize the arch-fiend in much the same way. Minor differences, indeed, occur even between Germans and ourselves in diabolical insignia; the cloven hoof may become solidungulous like that of the horse, and instead of a pitchfork he may brandish a fiery sword. Not only have conquered gods and demigods contributed characteristic features to the vulgar conception of the devil, but trolls or giants have handed down to the same detested personage the stupidity and awkwardness of their kind. Hence the ludicrous stories told of Satan's discomfiture at the hands of old women and born idiots, to the scandal of many pious souls who have been taught to treat the devil with respect, like the clergyman of whom MR. MARCHANT tells us, and who cannot for the life of them see anything amusing in the author of all evil. The ease with which such a *dummer Teufel* is tricked by his intended victims contrasts indeed strangely with the character for consummate cunning attributed to the deceiver of mankind, whose very name of "the Old Serpent" is suggestive of his subtlety.*

Ancient Egypt, too, had its great serpent, Apap, the power of darkness opposed to the sun-gods, as well as Set (Typhon). So in Greek mythology Python is a mighty dragon or snake slain by the solar deity Apollo, and the Gigantes (not the Titans) are represented as monsters of Ophidian form below the waist, when attempting to storm the heavens.

"The quaint ideas of children" on the personal behaviour of the devil are generally no more than a too literal belief in what they are told. A mother warns her little boy that Satan is everywhere seeking to destroy souls, and then relates with amusement how the child asked whether he ever travelled in a railway carriage, and got under the seats. Mere infants are taught to repeat—

> And Satan trembles when he sees
> The weakest saint upon his knees.

Yet it is thought odd that a triumph over some juvenile temptation is followed by a "crow over Satan's discomfiture," which at least shows that the pupil has grasped the meaning of the couplet better than the little maid who wanted to know why Satan should tremble to take a poor saint on his lap!

The inclusive term "devil" for the infernal king, as well as for his inferior agents, is unfortunately used in our English Bibles

* The theory which was current in early patristic literature as to the method of man's redemption, by which the devil was ignominiously duped, may have had some influence in lowering the standard of infernal wisdom. See more on this subject in the *Open Court* for August, 1900 ('The Evolution of Angels and Demons in Christian Theology,' by R. Bruce Boswell).

(even in the text of the Revised Version), both for Διάβολος, never found in the plural, and δαίμων or δαιμόνιον. The Latin Vulgate with greater discrimination translates by *diabolus* and *dæmonium* respectively. There is one devil, but many demons. To the emissaries of Satan derived from foreign sources, like Beelzebub, were added, as Christianity prevailed over paganism, the fallen deities or dæmons of Greece and Rome, of Teuton and of Kelt, and even the fantastic denizens of fairyland (faërie), who, though called "the good people," perhaps to appease their malice, were nevertheless more often formidable than frolicsome in the days when they received real religious homage.

How the prince of darkness came to act "as an infernal *bourreau*" in popular imagination is no very difficult matter to understand, when the gradual descent of Satan is studied from the dignity of one who is admitted into heaven itself with the sons of God, down to the contemptible position of an inveterate trickster and buffoon, sometimes baffled and outwitted, sometimes successful, in his plots to get possession of a human soul. It is no long step from such a conception to that of the torturer gloating over his long-expected prey, with the lurid pictures of a material hell,

> Where sinners must with devils dwell
> In darkness, fire, and chains,

such as the imagination of divines and poets and painters elaborated, to scare the wicked and warn the weak. Is it surprising that the devil and his angels should share the congenial task of chastising those committed to their tender mercies by a superior power? Moreover, the earliest idea of the evil one seems to have been as an agent of Divine punishment, doing *con amore* the dirty work which no respectable angel would desire. This makes him hateful in the eyes of men, and his moral character deteriorates along with his dignity. He tempts mankind for his own ends, he thwarts instead of promoting the designs of Providence, he carries off his victims with delight, and torments them with the most savage ferocity. Though "their companion in misery," he wields the scourge with no less zest for that, any more than Sambo or Quimbo spared the back of Uncle Tom. But most probably the idea of the "infernal *bourreau*" belongs to a different pedigree from that of "the arch-rebel," and is an incongruous element in Divine justice.

In Psalm lxxviii. 49, quoted by MR. MARCHANT, "sending evil angels among them," the Revised Version renders "evil angels" as "angels of evil." Their mission was to work destruction, but they have not yet become, in the evolution of ideas, essentially evil in their own nature.

R. Bruce Boswell.

Chingford.

The subject Mr. Marchant raises is discussed in chap. xv. of Mr. Moncure D. Conway's 'Demonology and Devil-Lore.' It is, perhaps, inadvisable to reproduce Mr. Conway's argument here, but he essays to show how the Jewish Satan, originally an accusing spirit, became next an opponent, and finally an executioner. This development, or degradation (Mr. Conway uses both terms), does not appear to be peculiar to Satan, for Mr. Conway finds a parallel to it in Magian mythology (whatever that may be), and, if I understand him, in the Greek ideas of Nemesis.

C. C. B.

CHRIST'S HOSPITAL (9ᵗʰ S. viii. 283).—On Sunday last the boys of the Bluecoat School attended service at Christ Church, Newgate Street, for the last time previous to their removal to Horsham. The Lord Mayor and Sheriffs were present, and the sermon was preached by the Bishop of London, who referred to the fact that his predecessor, Bishop Ridley, in 1552 preached at the opening of the school before King Edward VI., and now in the reign of Edward VII. it fell to his lot to bid the scholars farewell. The Bishop stated that one of the old chalices which Christ's Hospital had used for 350 years would accompany the school down to their new chapel, and closed his address with the wish that "the Hospital of Christ, most beautiful of names, may continue to teach and train up many and many brave and great young Englishmen for generations yet unborn."

A. N. Q.

HARVEST BELL (9ᵗʰ S. viii. 201, 308, 427; ix. 15).—Accuracy in 'N. & Q.' is, so far as possible, essential. Neither Mr. Breslar nor Mr. Ackerley correctly gives the motto of the city of Ripon. It should be "Except ye Lord keep ye Cittie, ye Wakeman waketh in vain." I think Mr. Breslar is in error also about the hour when the Ripon horn is blown. I was at Ripon in 1897, and heard the horn blown first at the Mayor's house at 8 o'clock, and shortly after at the Obelisk in the Town Hall Square.

T. Cann Hughes, M.A., F.S.A.

Lancaster.

BIBLIOGRAPHY OF THE BICYCLE (9ᵗʰ S. viii. 304, 490, 530; ix. 36, 117, 171).—I have just spent some time carefully examining the Stoke Poges window. It is now in a modern Tudor setting, the top bits too small to make anything of; then a couple of heraldic shields surrounded by Grinling Gibbons style of ornament, and labels bearing the words "Dvcie and Pipe" and "Dvcie and Pyott." Beneath these, arranged in an oval, are larger pieces of coloured glass, as follows : (1) a duck with a green wreath (broken); (2) a bull's head with immense horns thrust through scrollwork; (3) a naked, childish figure blowing a clarion or post-horn and seated on a hobby-horse, the head of the horse like a violin's scroll, but double, the post-horn being placed between the parts of the head. A wheel with six spokes turns on an axle attached to the front of the horse, and is between the figure's feet, which reach to the ground. The back of the hobby-horse, cut off by lead round the fragment, is part of a larger back wheel, but no spokes are visible. In the left top corner of the piece is a block in yellow glass, and through a hole in this runs a string which has a small circular object on it. This arrangement does not appear to have any connexion with the rider. The figure and horse are in fawn-coloured glass with a lilac tinge, the clarion and hair are yellow. A little below on either side are pieces of scrollwork in the same colour, which, however, may have no connexion with our subject. On the left one are the letters "amm," "ann," cut short by leading; the right has "Berghen, 1642"; near this a bit with Dutchman under a tree. The centre of the present window is a circular piece with a fine yellow griffin, seated and holding the guige of a heraldic shield in his beak, while he steadies with his claw the shield itself, which bears a chevron between two flowers in chief, and in base a well (?). Other fragments are two birds' wings, yellow, architectural fragments, and at the bottom the rest of the duck's green wreath. The window faces north, is quite close to the ground, and is protected by wire outside.

Ibagué.

[We insert this as a detailed description, though we do not admit the presence of a hobby-horse in view of the communications of F. G. S. at 8ᵗʰ S. x. 318, and recently at 9ᵗʰ S. viii. 530.]

Let me refer your readers and the public generally who are interested in this subject to 'Old-Fashioned Children's Books,' p. 426, where they will find illustrations of the velocipede, which seems to have been the precursor of the bicycle. The probable date is 1819, and a gentleman is depicted as spinning along at a marvellous speed upon one amid a cloud of dust. On the other side a gentleman is represented as having come to grief, the velocipede having been upset, showing that it had its dangers like the bicycle in the present day.

Almost within the memory of man the Rev. Joseph Coltman, incumbent of Beverley Minster, who had attained an enormous bulk, used to go about the streets of the town on a velocipede. Certainly within the last twenty years a silhouette of this might have been seen in a broker's shop in Beverley. He was said to have been the biggest man in England next to Daniel Lambert.

John Pickford, M.A.
Newbourne Rectory, Woodbridge.

The inquirer on this subject should consult the sections on the literary history of the bicycle which are contained in a volume by Karl Kron, entitled '100,000 Miles on a Bicycle' (New York, 1887). They occupy pp. lxxii–lxxvi and 653–700.

W. P. Courtney.
Reform Club.

Sir William Damsell (9ᵗʰ S. ix. 169).—Richard Brandesby, writing to his friend Roger Ascham, says that he was met near Louvain by George Gilpin, "secretarius, una cum nostro Damosello." The date would be about 1553. See 'R. Aschami Epistolarum Libri Tres,' Hanov., 1602, p. 576.   W. C. B.

Portraits of Early Lord Mayors (9ᵗʰ S. viii. 485; ix. 173).—A complete list of portraits of the Lord Mayors of London, with their present owners, would be interesting and useful. I may add that I possess a fine oil portrait by Sir James Thornhill of Sir Samuel Garrard, Bart., before whom Dr. Sacheverell preached his famous sermon, for which he had to stand his trial.

Thomas Turner.
Mill Hill Road, Norwich.

Author of Books Wanted (9ᵗʰ S. ix. 188).—The author of 'Experiences of a Gaol Chaplain' is Erskine Neale (1804-83). The book was published in three volumes in 1847 and again in 1849, and, I believe, again later. It is a work of fiction. For a bibliography of this author's works see Allibone's 'Dictionary of Authors' and the 'D.N.B.,' vol. xl.

Archibald Sparke.
Bury.

The "Gaol Chaplain" and the "Coroner's Clerk" was the Rev. Erskine Neale; see 6ᵗʰ S. xii. 465; 7ᵗʰ S. i. 32.   W. C. B.

"Barracked" (9ᵗʰ S. ix. 63, 196).—It may be interesting to point out that my late friend Prof. Morris, in his 'Austral English,' states that "to barrack" is an Australian football term dating from about 1880. He derives it from a native word "borak," meaning "to banter." It certainly was not used commonly before 1883 in Victoria.

The accepted derivation of "larrikin," when I was resident in Australia, was that the word is an Irish pronunciation of *larking*. An Irish constable charged a youth with "larrakin" about the streets. The police reporter used the word and it stuck. Prof. Morris is disinclined to accept this derivation, but it is certainly believed in in Australia. It always seemed to me that the French "larron" had served at once to perpetuate the word and to affect its meaning.   H. A. Strong.
University College, Liverpool.

FitzGerald Quotation (9ᵗʰ S. ix. 189).—The passage quoted by Mr. Asquith occurs in FitzGerald's translation of 'Attār's 'Mantik-ut-Tair,' which he called 'Bird-Parliament.' It will be found on p. 457 of the second volume of the 'Letters and Literary Remains of Edward FitzGerald,' 1889.

W. F. Prideaux.

The lines quoted are to be found in 'Bird-Parliament,' p. 457, vol. ii. of 'Letters and Literary Remains of Edward FitzGerald,' edited by W. Aldis Wright, 1889.

R. A. Potts.

The Parentage of Cæsar Borgia (9ᵗʰ S. viii. 524; ix. 176).—As Baron Corvo devotes five pages of his book to arguments in support of Varillas's theory, and all the way through writes "Cardinal" or "Duke Cesare (detto Borgia)," I may perhaps be pardoned for supposing him to have been convinced by Varillas. The latter's tale was ignored as worthless by such writers as Creighton, Symonds, Villari, Gregorovius, Roscoe, &c.; it has remained for the keen eye of *Corvus* to detect that "it very likely is not fiction, historical or otherwise, but the blind and naked Truth emerging from her well unabashed." Baron Corvo's note at the last reference given above is no answer to my query; but if you allow, I will so far trespass on your space as to answer some of the statements on this point contained in his *satura*.

In the first place, nothing is proved either one way or the other by the fact that "in no official document is he [Cæsar] named as the son of" Alexander VI. On what authority does Baron Corvo state, with regard to Vanozza, "that she was the mistress first of Cardinal Giuliano della Rovere, second of Cardinal Rodrigo de Lançol y Borgia"? Even granting this, for the moment, to be true, and that the father of her first son was

Rovere, and of her second son, Borgia, all the historians mentioned above, and all others that I know of, agree that Giovanni Francisco Borgia, afterwards Duke of Gandia, was the *eldest*, and Cæsar the *second* of her sons, and Villari gives the date of the birth of the former as 1474, and that of Cæsar as 1476. If either of them was Rovere's son, it must be then the Duke of Gandia, and not Cæsar Borgia.

Moreover, contrast the treatment Cæsar received at the hands of the two Pontiffs. Alexander bestowed honours and wealth upon him, and helped him in all his schemes of aggrandizement; Julius, immediately he had the power, "demanded of Duke Cesare the renunciation of his duchy of the Romagna," "despoiled him of all fiefs and dignities held from the Holy See, and confiscated all his personal property." Cæsar escaped from Rome in disguise, but by the intrigues of Julius he was rearrested and imprisoned in Spain. In fine, the weight of all the presumptive evidence is on the side of Alexander, and Machiavelli, who had at least two personal interviews with Cæsar, and was a shrewd man, well informed of state affairs, actually refers to him in his 'Principe' as the son of Alexander VI. His testimony may safely be believed before that of the "proverbially discredited" Varillas.

It is to be noted that BARON CORVO himself calls his book a gallimaufry, which, according to Webster, is "an absurd medley." "So mote it be!" CHARLES R. DAWES.

"INTENTIONS" (9th S. v. 434; vi. 435, 504). —All the passages quoted hitherto for intentions matrimonial are of the nineteenth century. There is an earlier instance in 'Peregrine Pickle,' c. xxviii. Mr. Gauntlet, brother of Peregrine's flame, asks for satisfaction:—

"I demand it in the capacity of a brother, jealous of his own honour, as well as of his sister's reputation; and if your intentions are honourable, you will not refuse it."

HIPPOCLIDES.

GORDON RIOTS (9th S. ix. 68).—I have a small tract of 32 pp. which mentions several of the houses destroyed. It bears the following explicit title:—

"Riots. | A Genuine | Account | of the | Proceedings | of the late | Disturbances and Riots | in the | Cities of London and Westminster, | and | Borough of Southwark. | Containing | an Account of the burning of Newgate, the King's | Bench, the Fleet, and New Bridewell Prisons. Like- | wise the Houses of Lord Mansfield, Sir John Fielding, | Messrs. Langdale, Rainsforth, Cox, Hyde, &c. Romish | Chapels, Schools, &c., with an Account of the Com- | mitment of Lord George Gordon to the | Tower. |

And Anecdotes of his Life. | To which is added, | An Abstract of the Act lately passed in favour of the Ro- | man Catholicks. | London: | Printed by O. Adams & Co. 1780. | [Price Six-Pence.]"

JOHN T. PAGE.
West Haddon, Northamptonshire.

Many, if not all, of the houses destroyed by the mob, are given in Kirby's 'Wonderful and Eccentric Museum,' 1820, vol. ii.; also in Wilson's 'Wonderful Characters,' 1821, vol. i.

EVERARD HOME COLEMAN.
71, Brecknock Road.

Consult 7th S. ii. 341-3. W. C. B.

FRENCH NOVEL (9th S. ix. 148). — The title of the French novel is 'Les Inconsolables.' The author is Henry Lavedan (de l'Académie Française). The first publisher was *La Revue Illustrée*, fifteen years ago. The novel is now published in a volume in-16

BARON A. LUMBROSO.
Frascati, Italy.

UNE ANGLAISE will find 'Les Inconsolables' (comedy, not novel) in vol. ii. of Scribe's 'Collected Works,' Dentu's edition.

CHARLES A. FEDERER.
Bradford.

In answer to the query, I am glad to say that the book 'Inconsolables,' by Henri Lavedan, was published in 1886, in-16.

ABBÉ BENOIT.
Arcueil, Seine.

"FOOT-CLOTH NAG" (9th S. ix. 69). — Your correspondent should refer to Halliwell's 'Dictionary of Archaic and Provincial Words,' 1878; Archdeacon Nares's 'Glossary of the Works of English Authors'; and 3rd S. v. 461, where the following quotation is given:—

Nor shall I need to try
Whether my well-grass'd, tumbling *foot-cloth nag*
Be able to outrun a well-breath'd catchpole.
'Ram Alley,' 'Old Plays,' v. 473.

EVERARD HOME COLEMAN.

"O SAW YE MY FATHER" (9th S. ix. 147). —This song was published in Horsfield's 'Songster's Companion,' second edition, 1772, and is claimed as a lyric of English origin by Chappell in his 'Music of the Olden Time.' It was included by David Herd in his 'Ancient and Modern Scottish Songs,' 1776, and it has since appeared in all comprehensive Scottish anthologies. Allan Cunningham palmed off on Cromek a variant, probably of his own composition, for the 'Remains of Nithsdale and Galloway Song,' 1810, but he gave Herd's lyric in his own 'Songs of Scotland, Ancient and Modern,' 1825. See also Johnson's 'Musical Museum,' Chambers's

'Scottish Songs' and his 'Scottish Songs prior to Burns,' Blackie's 'Book of Scottish Song,' and so on. It is noteworthy that Ritson omits the piece from his 'Scottish Songs,' 1794, his decision probably being due to his doubts regarding its origin. Whether the English version or Herd's is the original form is a question still awaiting the decision of experts, from whom one would gladly have an authoritative deliverance on the subject. Meanwhile, as given by Herd, the song is entitled 'The Grey Cock,' and consists of seven stanzas, the first two of which (inaccurately quoted by BENEDICK) are as follows :—

O saw ye my father, or saw ye my mother,
  Or saw ye my true love John?
I saw not your father, I saw not your mother,
  But I saw your true love John.

It 's now ten at night, and the stars gie nae light,
  And the bells they ring ding, dong.
He 's met wi' some delay that causeth him to stay,
  But he will be here ere lang.

THOMAS BAYNE.

A history of the ballad from which BENEDICK gives an extract will be found in the late Prof. Child's monumental work 'The English and Scottish Popular Ballads,' iv. 389. Its usual title is 'The Grey Cock ; or, Saw you my Father?' A portion was published by Herd in 1769, and the whole, consisting of seven stanzas, by the same editor in 1776. According to Mr. Chappell ('Popular Music,' p. 731), the song was printed on broadsides, with the tune, and in 'Vocal Music ; or, the Songster's Companion,' second edition, 1772, ii. 36. Reference may also be made to 1st S. vi. 227, and to a paper of mine on 'Anglo-Irish Ballads' (which, according to Prof. Child, "brought together most of the matter pertaining to this ballad") in 6th S. xii. 223.   W. F. PRIDEAUX.

STONING THE WREN (9th S. ix. 108, 234).— Sixty years since, in the west of Ireland, it was a custom amongst boys to go on St. Stephen's Day (26 December) into the country lanes, amongst the hedgerows, to "hunt the wren." On such occasions they used to repeat a piece of doggerel commencing

    The wren, the wren, the king of all birds,
    St. Stephen's Day was caught in the lurch.

I do not know whether this amusement is still practised. It may be worth noting that the peasantry of that district pronounced "wren" so as to rime with *pan*.

                                HENRY SMYTH.
Harborne.

In the Isle of Man parties of boys, carrying a green bough, decked with coloured paper and fixed on the end of a pole, go from house to house soliciting "coppers" on St. Stephen's Day. They sing a doggerel song, the words and music of which are both in Moore's 'Manx Ballads' and Gell's 'Manx National Songs.' A wren is supposed to be hidden in the bough; but that part of the ceremony is generally left to the imagination.   F. G.

When I was a lad in Derbyshire this cruel sport was a very common amusement with big lads and young fellows, who turned out on Christmas Day and Pancake Day for that purpose. The band used to divide and hunt on both sides the hedge. Some called the sport "hunting God's little wren," and some of the hunters appeared to be imbued with a superstitious notion that bad luck to them might be the result. I have heard it called— many years ago—"devil's sport." Many parents warned their boys against the custom.

                            THOS. RATCLIFFE.
Worksop.

There is an account (perhaps the best) of this interesting superstition in 'Provincial Names and Folk-lore of British Birds,' by the Rev. Charles Swainson, 1885. The reference in the Catalogue of the British Museum Library is Ac. 99, 35/9.

                        J. HOLDEN MACMICHAEL.

GREEN AN UNLUCKY COLOUR (9th S. viii. 121, 192).—The notion, illustrated by MR. HERON-ALLEN at the last reference, that green bodes "desertion" in love, serves to explain ll. 5 and 6 of the second stanza of 'Holiday Gown,' a ballad by John Cunningham (1729–73), printed in the author's 'Poems' (Newcastle, 1771). I take the lines from the 'Goldsmith Anthology' ("British Anthologies," No. ix.), p. 201 :—

Fond SUE, I 'll assure you, laid hold on the boy
    (The vixen would fain be his Bride !) ;
Some token she claimed, either ribbon or toy,
    And swore that she 'd not be denied !
A top-knot he bought her, and garters, of *green* ;
    Pert SUSAN was cruelly stung !
I hate her so much that, to kill her with spleen,
    I 'd wed, if I were not too young !

                        THOMAS HUTCHINSON.

MINIATURE OF COL. GEO. FLEETWOOD (9th S. ix. 48, 154, 175).—In reply to MR. W. D. PINK, I based my remarks on information given in the 'Dictionary of National Biography,' where George Fleetwood, the regicide, is stated to have been "the son of Sir George Fleetwood, knt., of The Vache, near Chalfont St. Giles, Buckinghamshire, and Catherine, daughter of Henry Denny, of Waltham, Essex." His father's will describes him as his third son, but Edward and Charles, his elder brothers, appear to have died without issue. "His life was spared, but his estate of The Vache confiscated and given to the Duke of York." Lipscomb's 'History of the County of Buckingham,' vol. iii. p. 227, also says the estate was forfeited to the Crown, but gives the name of the regicide's father, according to Willis, as Charles, though the pedigree on pp. 227-28 makes him the son of Sir William Fleetwood. The pedigree also appears to be inaccurate in regard to the father of General Charles Fleetwood, Cromwell's son-in-law, and George, the Swedish general.

The 'Dictionary of National Biography' says Charles Fleetwood, Cromwell's son-in-law, was "third son of Sir Miles Fleetwood, of Aldwinkle, Northamptonshire, and of Anne, daughter of Nicholas Luke, of Woodend, Bedfordshire."

Sir Miles's eldest son, Sir William, was a Royalist, whilst George, the second son, was the Swedish general and baron. A foot-note to the biography of this George Fleetwood says, "Burke, in his 'Extinct and Dormant Baronetcies,' repeats genealogical errors of Mark Noble." I specially mention this as Mr. Pink cites Noble's 'Lives of the Regicides.' It may interest him to know that the 'Dictionary' gives biographies of eight members of the Fleetwood family.

My notes from the wills are incomplete, as I have not had time to examine all the wills and administrations. At present the results are so fragmentary that they do not appear to me to be of general interest. I hope later to make further search, but if the miniature could be traced some of the notes would probably become at once of value.

R. W. B.

The Rev. Edward Fleetwood, who was rector of Wigan from 1571 to 1604, is said to have married Christian, daughter of Paul Wentworth, of Lillingston, Bucks. Doubtless he is the "Fleetwoode of Wygan" inquired after by D. Paul was younger brother to Peter Wentworth. Both were Elizabethan M.P.s and leaders of the Puritan opposition. I have no present means at hand of testing if the wrong brother has been assigned for Mrs. Fleetwood's father. Edward Fleetwood was third son of Thomas Fleetwood, of The Vache, Bucks, and of Rossal, Lancashire (died 1 Nov., 1570), by his second wife, Bridget, daughter of Sir John Spring, of Lavenham, Suffolk. Two of his many brothers were Sir George Fleetwood, of The Vache (died 1620), and Sir William Fleetwood, of Cranford, Middlesex, Receiver of Wards, the grandfather of the celebrated Crom-

wellian officers. The Wigan parish registers give the following family to the Rev. Edward Fleetwood: Theodor (Theodora), baptized 6 Aug., 1591; Christian, baptized 29 March, 1594, buried 13 Nov., 1599; Elizabeth, baptized 13 June, 1596; Bridget, baptized 13 Nov., 1597; Dorothy, baptized 20 May, 1599; Edward, baptized 4 July, 1602. He is said, however, to have been survived only by one son and two daughters.   W. D. PINK.

"LURDEN" (9th S. ix. 185).—The silly story about *lurden* being derived from *Lord Dane* has often been quoted, but the reference to Grafton is useful. It also occurs in Fabyan's 'Chronicle,' ed. Ellis, p. 205. It is easily seen to be an invention by observing that the vowel in *lurd-* is different from that in E. *lord*, and the diphthong *ey* in the old spelling *lordeyn* is not the same thing as the *a* in *Dane*. The spelling *lordeyn* as a variant of *lurden* shows that we really have to do with the O.F. *ou*, and the spelling with *-eyn* also points to a French origin.

The word is perfectly well known. It occurs several times in 'Piers the Plowman,' spelt *lordein*, *lordeyn*, *lordeyne*, *lourdein*, *lurdeyn*, and the derivation from the O.F. *lourdein* is duly given in the glossary. The same derivation is given in Stratmann's 'Old English Dictionary,' with five references. It is given as *lourdeine* in the 'Concise Dictionary of Middle English,' by Mayhew and Skeat, with the etymology from O.F. *lourdein*. It is a mere derivative of O.F. (and mod. F.) *lourd*, explained by Cotgrave as "dull, sottish." Indeed, Cotgrave actually gives "*Lourdin*, lourdaine, blunt, somewhat blockish, a little clownish, lumpish, rude, smelling of the churl or lob-cock." It is not worth while to say more, though the number of allied words is very large. We have the variants *lourde*, *lourdart*, *lourdel*, *lourdet*, *lourdier*, *lourdin*, *lourdinot*, *lourdois*, all in Godefroy, and all with the same sense; and the modern F. *lourdaud*. Then there is the verb *lourder*, with the substantives *lourdece*, *lourderie*, *lourdeté*, *lourdie*, *lourdise*, *lourdoiement*. Altogether, the Latin *luridus* had a numerous progeny (see Diez and Godefroy). The 'English Dialect Dictionary' gives *Lurdan*, *Lurdane*, with over twenty references, refers to 'Piers the Plowman,' and quotes the O.F. form.   CELER.

SUNFLOWER ORNAMENT ON CRUCIFIX (9th S. ix. 67).—The second-hand bookseller probably mistook a radiating nimbus behind the head of a crucified Christ for a sunflower. The nimbus is, of course, one of the many Christian symbols derived from pagan

sources. In Gothic art a simple cross within
a circle almost invariably marks the nimbus
that surrounds the sacred head. Miss
Twining, in her 'Symbols and Emblems of
Early and Mediæval Christian Art' (1885),
gives an illustration of an instance of this
from a sixth-century mosaic in the church of
S. Lorenzo at Rome. Pugin, in 'Glossary of
Ecclesiastical Ornament' (1868), has beautiful
illuminated illustrations of various nimbi for
the Eternal Father, our Lord, our Lady, for
apostles, and for saints respectively. Those
for our Lord he describes as "a circular halo
......within it a cross, more or less enriched,
and sometimes extending beyond the circumference." Although neither sunflowers nor
any other flower occur behind the head of
Christ crucified, Pugin tells us the nimbi of
angels often have "an outer circle of quatrefoils, like roses, interspersed with pearls."
HARRY HEMS.

Fair Park, Exeter.

ULISSE BARBIERI (9ᵗʰ S. ix. 149).—Not only
is Edmondo di Amicis not dead, but he has
recently composed an ode on Victor Hugo.
MR. McGOVERN refers to him as a prolific
author. Certainly in a book he has written
about his impressions of the French capital
he shows himself possessed of a marvellous
capacity for producing an infinite amount
of mellifluous matter with a minimum of
meaning. Some critics think that his work
'La Vita Militare' will live as literature. It
is well worth reading, and contains two
chapters (one describing a march under a
blazing sun, and the other the attitude of an
Italian officer towards his manservant) which
are very striking and not easily forgotten.
T. P. ARMSTRONG.

South Kensington.

Ulisse Barbieri, who was living in 1878, and
of whom De Amicis speaks in his book
'Memorie,' died in the year 1900 of a cancer.
See De Gubernatis, 'Dizionario degli Italiani
Viventi.' BARON ALBERTO LUMBROSO.
Frascati, Italy.

THE OLDEST BOROUGH IN ENGLAND (9ᵗʰ S.
ix. 9, 114).—The first existing charter of
Shrewsbury is that granted by Richard I. in
the first year of his reign, 1189, 11 November,
a lithographed facsimile of which may be
seen in Owen and Blakeway's 'History of
Shrewsbury.' These authors say :—

"We are sure that a written charter of Henry II.
once existed, for it is mentioned in one by his son
John, and it protected the free customs of the burgesses of Salopesbury by a penalty of 10l. denounced
against any who should presume to violate them :
but that document has long since perished (at

least as long ago as the reign of Elizabeth, when
the charters were copied into a quarto volume),
and that of Richard I. is the earliest now preserved
in the archives of the Corporation."—Vol. i. p. 82.

There are two charters of John, both in
the first year of his reign : one, 13 April,
dated Farendon ; the other, 20 April, dated
Westminster. In the first of these is a recital
of the free customs of Henry I. and a confirmation of the charter of Henry II. The
date of Henry I.'s charter is not mentioned
in John's, but as he died in 1135, it must
have been granted before that date.
WILLIAM PHILLIPS.

Canonbury, Shrewsbury.

Lancaster may claim to be "the oldest
town in the North, and possibly in England,"
on the strength of a charter granted in 1193,
but I think Newcastle-upon-Tyne, to use a
common expression, can go one better, for
we have here a copy of a charter of King
John, dated 9 February, in the second year
of his reign, confirming a charter granted by
his father, Henry II., who died on 6 July,
1189. It is quoted by Brand ('History of
Newcastle,' vol. ii. p. 133) as follows :—

"Johannes Dei gratia, &c. Sciatis nos concessisse
et presenti carta confirmasse burgensibus nostris
de Novo Castello super Tinam et omnibus eorum
rebus quas ipsi poterint assecurare suas esse domi-
nicas, quietanciam de theolonio et passagio et pon-
tagio et de ansa et de omnibus aliis consuetudinibus
per totam terram nostram et prohibemus ne quis
eos inde vexet vel disturbet super forisfactura
nostra sicut carta Henrici Regis patris nostri
rationabiliter testatur," &c.

"From a copy remaining," adds Brand, "in
the archives of the Corporation of Newcastle,
collated with the original in the Tower of
London by N. Punshon, Esq., under-sheriff
of Newcastle." RICHARD WELFORD.
Newcastle-upon-Tyne.

The Town Clerk of Lancaster makes this
claim for his borough on the ground of a
charter dated 1193. I enclose, however,
translation of charter granted to the Borough
of Oswestry, 1190, by William Fitzalan. It is
generally called the "Charter cwtta"—i.e.,
the short charter. As will be borne in mind,
the Fitzalans are now represented by the
Duke of Norfolk, "Baron of Oswaldestre."
The other branch of the family, "Walter
Fitzalan," is the ancestor of the Stewarts,
having left Oswestry for Scotland :—

"Let these present as well as future generations
know that I William, son of William, son of Alan,
have received under my hand and protection my
burgesses of Blanc Minster by name, those who
have received messuages in my borough for the sale
of my merchandise, and I will defend them against
all [persons] as far as I lawfully shall be able.

Wherefore I myself wish and firmly give command as long as the aforesaid burgesses hold their messuages lawfully and in peace and honourably that they live freely and quietly in field, in plain, and in places elsewhere. I have also granted to the same burgesses that they hold the aforesaid messuages from me according to the laws and customs and liberties which the burgesses of Salop hold in their borough. I have expressed it as my wish that the Charter be ratified for the future. And have confirmed [it] by the placing of my seal and by the subscription of the witnesses John stranger in blood, Ham' his brother, Helie de fes, Philip son of William Reginald de he, William de Verden, Reginald......de Hesse and many others."

J. PARRY-JONES,
Mayor of Oswestry.

The precise antiquity of any given borough must surely be a most difficult point to ascertain. It is more than a mere question of the date of the earliest known charter. Cardiff had a charter from the Earl of Gloucester about the year 1145—probably a few years earlier—and its inhabitants were then styled "burgenses." It was at that date certainly a borough in the military sense, and had laid the foundations of its municipality also. (See 'Cardiff Records,' edited by the present writer, vol. i. p. 2.)

JOHN HOBSON MATTHEWS.
Town Hall, Cardiff.

Apparently the question does not apply to "municipal boroughs," strictly so called by the Act of 1835, as no precedence could exist on these terms. This distinction is, however, technical only, and, of course, communities in this country governed their local affairs hundreds of years prior to that date. One means of earning the title of borough was the right of parliamentary representation. In earlier times any walled city was a borough, but if it were under the charge of a borough reeve and owed dues to the sovereign it did not possess self-government. On the side of antiquity the question merges itself into a study of the period when the Roman colonies were formed here, and as these were at first little better than camps, and the earliest were established about the same time, it is impossible to answer the question categorically. There are many interesting side issues to the case, and for these it is worth while to consult works of reference under the words "colony," "borough," and "municipal."

ARTHUR MAYALL.

This subject has been exhaustively treated by Mr. Horace Round as a specialist, and he draws attention to the origin of the municipality of London in 1191, when Prince John, acting as viceroy for his brother, King Richard, conferred a commune on London,

founded on similar experiences in France and Flanders. This is two years earlier than Lancaster, cited as 1193; but the first charter of William the Conqueror recognizes the burgesses of London as then self-governing, and exempt from the feudal laws.

ABSENS.

PORTRAITS OF JOANNA BAILLIE (9ᵗʰ S. ix. 129).—In vol. v. of Chambers's 'Biographical Dictionary of Eminent Scotsmen' (Edinburgh, 1855) is a memoir of this lady, to which is prefixed a steel engraving representing her, and underneath is inscribed "Masquerier," "H. Robinson," the names of the painter and engraver; lower down, "Joanna Baillie, from the picture in possession of W. H. Baillie, Esq." Though this does not answer the query, yet it may prove some little guide to its locale. She died at Hampstead, in her ninetieth year, in 1851.

JOHN PICKFORD, M.A.
Newbourne Rectory, Woodbridge.

"AS MAD AS A TUP" (9ᵗʰ S. viii. 501; ix. 98).—Any one who keeps his eyes open in the country in the spring must have noticed the antics of hares at that particular season of the year, rare though these animals now are in many parts, owing to the effects of Sir William Harcourt's Act. Heywood evidently gave a correct explanation of the proverb.

H.

MUMMERS (9ᵗʰ S. ix. 87).—Besides the references given, H. W. will find accounts of mummers in the following places: 2ⁿᵈ S. x. 464; xii. 487, 493; 4ᵗʰ S. x. 487; 5ᵗʰ S. ii. 505; iv. 511; x. 484, 489; *Folk-lore Record*, 1881; *Folk-lore Journal*, 1884; 'Shropshire Folklore' (Burne and Jackson), part iii. p. 482 *sqq.* A long list of references is given in the last named to other sources, of which there are many containing isolated accounts. The Plough Monday mummeries noticed in 9ᵗʰ S. vii. 322 are essentially the same as the ordinary mummers' play. There are also a few accounts in Hone's 'Every-Day Book.'

E. H. BINNEY.

BIBLE: AUTHORIZED VERSION (9ᵗʰ S. ix. 147).—As accuracy is most desirable in dealing with so nice a subject as the history of the English Bible, I venture to recast MR. PAYNE'S second query. "Which version," then, "did the revisers of 1611 take as the basis of their work?"
The answer is found in No. 1 of the fifteen rules drawn up for their guidance, probably under the direction of Archbishop Bancroft: "The ordinary Bible read in the Church, commonly called the Bishops' Bible, to be

followed, and as little altered as the truth of
the original will permit."

"The Bishops' Bible" (popularly so called
because some eight of the revisers were
bishops) appeared, under Archbishop Parker's
supervision, in 1568. New editions, in which
the *New* Testament was carefully revised,
were published in 1572 and 1578.

Mr. Payne's first query may now be passed
by. But it is of importance to remember
the pre-eminent merit of Tyndale as the first
of this series of translators. The following
appreciation is taken, as are the previous
statements, from a volume now rare, 'A
General View of the History of the English
Bible,' by B. F. Westcott, B.D. (then a Harrow
master), first edition, 1868, p. 210 :—

"In rendering the sacred text he remained
throughout faithful to the instincts of a scholar.
From first to last his style and his interpretation
are his own, and in the originality of Tyndale is
included in a large measure the originality of our
English Version. For not only did Tyndale contribute to it directly the substantial basis of half
of the Old Testament (in all probability) and of
the whole of the New, but he established a standard
of Biblical translation which others followed. It
is even of less moment that by far the greater part
of his translation remains intact in our present
Bibles, than that his spirit animates the whole."

Coverdale was not an independent translator. His Bible was, as the title-page bears,
"faithfully translated out of Latin and
Dutch" (=German, viz., the Swiss-German
version of Zwingli and Leo Juda, and also
Luther's ; in Latin, Pagninus and the Vulgate). But "his phrasing is nearly always rich
and melodious" (Westcott, p. 217). The Prayer
Book version of the Psalms is a favourable
specimen of his style.   C. P. Phinn.
Watford.

Burial of a Suicide (9ᵗʰ S. viii. 502 ; ix.
96, 158).—In referring to the "story" mentioned by Mr. Harry Hems, Mr. F. Clayton
has, I think, confused two distinct traditions.
In Murray's 'Surrey' (fifth edition, p. 114)
it is stated that Tallis says Leith Hill is
crowned by a small structure traditionally
supposed to mark the spot where a farmer of
the neighbourhood was buried on horseback
upside down ('Topographical Dictionary of
England and Wales'). Mr. Hems referred
to Box Hill, as to which Murray says (p. 93)
that on the N.W. brow of the hill, and nearly
in a line with the stream of the Mole, was
buried, 11 June, 1800, a Major Labellière, who
had lived for some years at Dorking, and
whose mind had become unsettled in consequence of "an unrequited attachment." He
was buried here at his own request, and with
his head downwards. Like the Leith Hill

farmer he hoped that as the world was
"turned topsy-turvy" he would come up
"right at last." Mr. Clayton's details as
to the burial in Leith Hill Tower are correct,
but they do not dispose of the story mentioned by Mr. Hems.   G. T.

Tennis : Origin of the Name (9ᵗʰ S. ix.
27, 75, 153).—Your correspondent Mr. Julian
Marshall inadvertently states that *tiens* and
tenez are mere expressions of surprise. The
statement is only true of the former expression, *tiens*. As for the plural form *tenez*, it
denotes not surprise, but a desire to draw
the hearer's attention to a statement about
to be made, an appeal *ad captandum*, *e.g.*,
"Tenez, voici des preuves irrécusables" =
'Now look here, these proofs cannot be
gainsaid."   Charles A. Federer.
Bradford.

Antinomian Sect (9ᵗʰ S. ix. 108).—This
sect was so named by Luther when John
Agricola, in 1538, maintained that under the
Gospel dispensation the moral law is of no
use or obligation, as doctrines superseded the
necessity of good works and a virtuous life ;
"that it mattered not how wicked a man
was, if he had but faith." The Antinomians
were condemned by the British Parliament
in 1648.   Everard Home Coleman.
71, Brecknock Road.

Tib's Eve (9ᵗʰ S. ix. 109).—Jamieson, in his
'Dictionary of the Scottish Language,' says
that *Tibbe*, *Tibbie*, are corruptions of the
name Isabel. If this be so, the irresponsibility of one who promises to do anything on
Tib's Eve is obvious, as there is said to be no
such saint in the calendar. The phrase will
be found in the 'Antrim and Down Glossary'
(W. H. Patterson). I was at first under the
impression that "Tib" was an abbreviation
of Theobald, by way of "Tibbald," but it
appears to have been a common feminine
name. "Tib and Lal" is a jocular name
given to a man and woman in the neighbourhood of Sheffield ('Glossary,' S. O. Addy);
and in Bohn's edition of Ray's 'Proverbs'
there is a proverbial phrase, "He struck at
Tib and down fell Tom." In the game of
gleek Tib is the ace of trumps and Tom the
knave of trumps. Hence the derivation from
"Tibba," the Saxon saint, is, I think, very
improbable, and if it can be shown that Tib
was really a familiar form of Isabel, it will,
perhaps, give the advocacy of the "St. Tibba"
theory its *coup de grâce*. At previous references I do not see the equivalent phrases
"When three Thursdays meet," "In a
month of Sundays," "To-morrow come never,"

all which, of course, mean that the matter or promise "on the *tapis*" is deferred *sine die*.

A similar saying that has not been noted is "Johnny Pyot's term day"—*i.e.*, the day after the Day of Judgment—a somewhat profane form of "never" and "for ever." It is used in Banffshire (see Jamieson's 'Dictionary').

J. HOLDEN MACMICHAEL.

CROSS ON THE CARNEDDAU HILLS NEAR BUILTH (9th S. viii. 505).—The following from Camden's 'Britannia,' under 'Radnorshire,' may explain what W. O. wishes to know :—

"On the top of Gwastedin hill, near Rhaidr Gwy, are three large heaps of stones, such as are common on mountains in most if not all the counties of Wales, called in South Wales Karnen and in North Wales Karnedheu. They consist of stones from a pound to a hundredweight collected from the neighbourhood and confusedly thrown together in heaps, &c. Most if not all the Carnedhew seem intended as memorials of the dead, &c. It is still the custom to throw heaps of stones on the graves of malefactors and self-murderers."

JOHN RADCLIFFE.

"FLITTINGS" (9th S. ix. 49).—A quotation in the 'E.D.D.,' *s.v.* 'Flit,' reads (n. Lin.) : "Upo' th' eäst side o' th' Trent sarvants flits the'r plaaces at Maay-da'-time, but e' th' Isle it's at Martlemas." "Lucy's Flittin'" was, of course, a different matter. The word there meant her death. From 'The Imperial Dict.' one gathers that the "mop" was the mopping-up or second day's hiring. I see that my quotation (*ante*, p. 56) is given in the 'E.D.D.' in the forms "Better rew sit nor rew flit" and "Hit's better ta roo-sit den roo-flit."

ARTHUR MAYALL.

BISHOPS' SIGNATURES (9th S. ix. 9, 118).—Worcester will be found in King Ælfred's translation of Gregory's 'Pastoral Care' (E.E.T.S., p. 3) as Wiogora Ceastre, a corruption of Hwic-wara (Taylor's 'Words and Places').

H. P. L.

Miscellaneous.

NOTES ON BOOKS, &c.

Westminster. By Reginald Airy. (Bell & Sons.)
To the series of "Great Public Schools" 'Westminster' has now been added. The writing of the book has, we imagine, been an easier task than some others of the sort, because the literature of the subject is already large and excellent. Mr. Sargeaunt has written his admirable 'Annals,' while numerous other contributions of merit are available, as was to be expected in the case of a history so notable. Mr. Airy's account is clear and interesting, and will suffice for the average parent who has or desires to have a boy at Westminster. For ourselves we wish—and we think that old Westminster boys will be with us—that more had been made of the school traditions, glorious as they are, than the

scanty opening chapters afford. Other establishments of merit now compete with the great schools of ancient days in the training of soldiers and citizens, and the records (more admired by the every-day world) of sport and scholarship. But traditions they have not, and no historian of the older schools should fail to dwell on these as constituting a chief part of his pride and distinction. There is a good chapter on Busby, who enjoys as a type in literature a fame almost equal to that of "plagosus Orbilius." He figures, by the way, by an anachronism, for the Horatian pedant in Bailey's spirited translation of Erasmus's 'Colloquies,' where John says to Sylvius, in the dialogue 'On Scholastic Studies,' of their pedagogue: "He's a greater Whip-Master than Busby himself." Busby has his monument in the Abbey, which is reproduced here. The last time that we were there the lettering on the tomb was by no means distinct, and we hope that due care is taken, by recutting or some other method, to preserve such records, or we may be soon lamenting ἀμυδρὰ γράμματα like Thucydides. There is a just though rather too brief appreciation of the work of Dean Liddell as head master, a work all the more creditable because it was difficult and uncongenial to him; and we are rather surprised to find so little about the strong and excellent head master who has but just left Westminster to new hands. But perhaps it was felt that Dr. Rutherford's work is so much a thing of to-day as to be apparent to all, even the casual outsider.

Will Westminster ever sever herself from the shadow of the Abbey? Some have long expected it, and the writer of this volume recognizes that her growth is hampered by her position. Still, we would not do anything to encourage the loss of so fine a tradition, and though the numbers of the school have for the last fifty years sunk in comparison with earlier times, successes of all sorts can be pointed to to-day, and 1901 saw 232 boys as compared with 221 in 1883 and 67 in 1841.

Little more than a page is devoted to the school slang, a section to which we always turn with interest in these volumes, but we dare say more might be said, and there are only some 160 pages in all. Another feature which we miss here is a short list of more recent old boys who have become eminent in various ways. A few names in sport are supplied, but we expect more—*e.g.*, we should certainly mention A. H. Harrison, the best full back we ever saw in the Association game, and we have seen a good many. Here and there famous alumni are mentioned in due course, but more might be done in this way. In the notice of school papers it should be mentioned that Gilbert Abbot A'Beckett, at Westminster from 1820 to 1828, edited, with his brother William, the *Censor* and the *Literary Beacon.* Were not Cowper and Warren Hastings, an odd pair, at school here together? Prior is, of course, mentioned, but nothing is said of the unusual circumstances of his schooldays. He went to Westminster, but had only reached the middle of his third term when his father died, and his mother was unable to pay the necessary fees, so he left for the care of his uncle, the keeper of a Rhenish wine house in Westminster, and so early ripe was his graceful scholarship that his translations of Ovid and Horace became, Mr. Dobson tells us, a feature of the said tavern. Dr. Sprat and one of the Westminster masters got to hear of this, and he returned to school at Westminster under the ferule of Dr. Busby. This is interesting as showing that Prior had no objection, apparently, to the doctor's severity. A list of alumni might make another appendix with advantage. There are already sections at the end on the Latin Play, the Deans of Westminster, numbers of the school at different periods, head masters and present house masters. The illustrations give an excellent idea of the various school buildings. There are also engravings of Dr. Rutherford and the present head master, Dr. Gow, for whom we wish a repetition of the success he had at Nottingham. The volume is appropriately clad in the pink associated with Westminster sports.

The Moors. By Budgett Meakin. (Sonnenschein & Co.)

This is the concluding volume of Mr. Budgett Meakin's Moorish trilogy, the first and second volumes in which were respectively 'The Moorish Empire' and 'The Land of the Moors.' Broadly speaking, we may say that the first volume was political, the second physical, whilst the third is mainly ethnological. The three represent an important addition to the literature dealing with little-known Morocco: probably the most important addition of modern times in the English language. They represent a vast amount of painstaking labour and research, backed by a knowledge of the main highways of Morocco superior to that of most writers on the subject, and only to be obtained by prolonged residence in the country. Indeed, there are features in Mr. Meakin's work which suggest that he must be possessed of that intimacy with the Moors and with Morocco which comes only to him who is familiar with both in childhood or, at all events, in very early youth. Regarded from the purely literary standpoint, the trilogy calls for little comment. If Mr. Meakin's writing lacks distinction—and one is bound to admit that it does—it is at least free from glaring blemishes. It also lacks altogether the distinction and light which are due to imaginative force and artistic insight. It is, by the same token, devoid of the superficiality which so often mars impressionistic work; and, upon the whole, the three volumes may be said to disarm criticism to some extent by reason of the evidence they offer upon every page of perseverance, patience, and rigid fidelity to mathematical truth. These are qualities which demand and deserve cordial recognition and respect.

Considered separately, these three volumes may be said to have been presented to the public in the order of their merit, the weightiest and best coming first. The present volume is considerably less comprehensive and exhaustive than either of its predecessors, and that is probably due to the fact that the study of the human animal makes greater demands upon the imagination, and upon intuitive and sympathetic understanding, than does the study either of empires or the physical features of a country. Research, the only sound basis of exact knowledge, will not carry its most devoted disciple all the way into the soul of a people. Statistics and the study of every available authority made really exhaustive compilations of the first two volumes in this trilogy, and have given us as much as they could in this concluding volume. They have not brought us any nearer to the heart of the people of El Maghrib, however. They have not even given us those intimate glimpses which Mr. Walter B. Harris succeeded in conveying once (see

his 'Tafilet'), and which, curiously enough, another traveller, whose knowledge of the country cannot approach that of either Mr. Meakin or Mr. Harris, managed to give in his 'Mogreb-el-acksa'—Mr. R. B. Cunninghame Graham. None the less, for the reader who would learn something of the manners and customs of a people whose history is one long romance, and whose country is at once the nearest and the remotest point of the East, Mr. Meakin's works, this last volume among them, may be unreservedly commended. To the student, also, who requires exact and tabulated information conveyed as tersely and lucidly as possible, 'The Moors' and its two companion volumes should come as a real treasure. One word as to Mr. Meakin's system of transliteration, which he hopes may be accepted as a standard of spelling. The care and labour that have been expended upon it are obvious, but we venture to think it a little cumbersome, and lacking in some of the merits of the Royal Asiatic Society's system, as simplified by Hunter, and used generally in India. 'The Moors,' like the two volumes which preceded it, is handsomely printed and generously illustrated. Such types as 'Moorish Snake Charmers,' slave girls (who, "with any promise of beauty, are carefully fattened," in accordance with the Oriental love for adiposity), jugglers, water-carriers, and other conventional specimens drawn from the every-day crowd of Morocco market-places, are well exhibited; while numerous characteristic scenes are included which will surprise the ordinary reader by reminding him of the fact that within a day's journey from British Gibraltar men and women, down to the veriest details of their dress and manners, are living to-day precisely the life which is so beautifully described in the books of the Old Testament.

Notices to Correspondents.

We must call special attention to the following notices:—

On all communications must be written the name and address of the sender, not necessarily for publication, but as a guarantee of good faith.

We cannot undertake to answer queries privately.

To secure insertion of communications correspondents must observe the following rules. Let each note, query, or reply be written on a separate slip of paper, with the signature of the writer and such address as he wishes to appear. When answering queries, or making notes with regard to previous entries in the paper, contributors are requested to put in parentheses, immediately after the exact heading, the series, volume, and page or pages to which they refer. Correspondents who repeat queries are requested to head the second communication "Duplicate."

H. F. ("There goes......but for the grace of God"). — Dean Farrar attributes this to John Bradford (9ᵗʰ S. vii. 269).

NOTICE.

Editorial communications should be addressed to "The Editor of 'Notes and Queries'"—Advertisements and Business Letters to "The Publisher"—at the Office, Bream's Buildings, Chancery Lane, E.C.

We beg leave to state that we decline to return communications which, for any reason, we do not print; and to this rule we can make no exception.

LONDON, SATURDAY, MARCH 29, 1902.

Notes.

ARMS OF ETON AND WINCHESTER COLLEGES.

KING HENRY VI., in 1440, granted to the
College of St. Mary at Eton the following
coat : Sable, three garden lilies argent ; on a
chief per pale azure and gules, a fleur-de-lis
of France and a lion of England. (See
Woodward's 'Heraldry : British and Foreign,'
ed. 1896, vol. i. p. 352.) And Dr. Woodward
adds : "Sable, three lilies proper, are the
arms attributed to Winchester College." I
should like to ask what authority Dr. Woodward had for this latter statement.

One is aware of the close connexion that
has always existed between the Plantagenet
king's foundation at Eton and its elder sister,
founded by William of Wykeham in the
previous century ; but it can hardly be that
in those days, when heraldry was a much
more exact science than it is now, the royal
founder followed his model so closely that
he assigned it a portion of its armorial
insignia.

I have not Mr. Kirby's 'Annals of Winchester College' by me, or any means of
reference to the volume here. Mr. A. F.
Leach's 'History of Winchester College'
(1899) does not touch upon the arms borne

by the school of which he writes so well ; but
in Mr. R. Townsend Warner's smaller handbook in the "Great Public Schools" Series,
published by Bell & Sons (1900), the author
devotes an appendix of several pages to the
consideration of the college arms. It is so
much to the point that I could crave leave to
reproduce the greater portion of it here. He
says :—

"There is still a question with regard to the arms
of Winchester College, namely, whether Wykeham's 'episcopal' arms ought to be used, as is the
present practice, or whether Winchester (like New
College, Oxford) ought to use the Founder's
personal coat only—i.e., the roses and chevrons not
impaled by the swords [? sword] and keys of the see
of Winchester. Ancient examples of the college
arms almost all give the Founder's personal arms
only—e.g., the original Common Seal of the college,
Fromond's chantry roof (fifteenth century), a fragment of
carving (date circa 1536) now in Porter's Lodge, the
portrait of the Founder in Hall (not later than
1597), and the two old pictures in the Warden's
Gallery, college plate (1629), the arms in School,
two forms of the college bookplate (eighteenth
century), and the Trusty Servant picture. This
last was repainted in 1800 ; the old picture had no
arms on it. In fact, there is no old work or picture
about college with the Founder's episcopal arms.
The earliest example of these (date circa 1800) is in
college kitchen.

"On the other hand, the earliest evidence in
support of the present user of the 'episcopal' arms
by the school is the fact that in 1678 they appeared
as the heading of Long Roll, the official roll of the
school in its most complete form. In any case it is
quite certain that Wykeham himself never used his
so-called 'episcopal' arms ; for the arms of the see
of Winchester were not in his time in use, and the
practice of bishops impaling the arms of the see
with the personal coat was not general till at least
a century and a half after Wykeham's time.

"On the whole, it appears that there is no authority previous to 1678 for the present user of the
episcopal arms by the school. There was never any
definite grant of arms to Winchester as there was
to Eton, and therefore there is no absolute authority on the subject, but the earliest and therefore
most binding assumption of arms by the college
was clearly that of the Founder's personal arms,—
the only arms known to him, whether as bishop or
in his private capacity."

From this it will be seen that the question
discussed by Mr. Warner was whether
the college was justified in using—"as is
the present practice "—the arms of the see of
Winchester (the crossed sword and keys),
together with the founder's personal arms
(the chevrons and roses, "like New College,
Oxford "), and not whether the college was
ever entitled to, or had ever used, the arms
now attributed to it by Dr. Woodward of
Sable, three lilies proper, which coat has,
of course, a strong family likeness to that of
Eton College, and of which attribution Mr.
Warner does not seem to have been aware.

Mr. Warner states that "there was never any definite grant of arms to Winchester as there was to Eton, and therefore there is no absolute authority on the subject"; but he prefaces his remarks on the college arms (of which he gives a drawing at the head of the appendix, showing the shield encircled by the motto of the Garter, and, beneath, the college motto, "Manners makyth man") by the following quotation from Guillim's 'Display of Heraldry':—

"These arms pertain to the Colledge of *Winchester*, founded by the renowned Architect, *William Wickham*, Bishop of *Winchester*, who contrived those many and curious Castles and other Buildings of King *Edward* the Third's. And besides this goodly Colledge of *Winton*, built another magnificent Colledge (called the *New Colledge*) in the University of *Oxford*; two such absolute Foundations, as never any King of this Land did the like."

But the arms referred to by Guillim, Mr. Warner says, are not those which he depicts at the head of the appendix, which are taken from the Long Roll already mentioned.

It is a pity that Mr. Warner did not describe, heraldically, the arms which Guillim did attribute to Winchester College, and I am sorry that I have no means here of finding out what they were, as my copy of Guillim is "at home." But Mr. Warner gives some clue as to what those arms were when he states that "Guillim confused the arms with those of Magdalen College, Oxford, founded by the Wykehamical Bishop, Waynflete, and originally called Winchester College, Oxford." If I remember rightly (but here again I have no means of testing the accuracy of my memory), the arms of Magdalen College, Oxford, do contain lilies of some kind. If this be so, and these arms of lilies were given by Guillim as those of Winchester College, it may be that Dr. Woodward has relied upon Guillim for his authority for the statement which I have called in question. My question, then, involves another—Whence did Guillim obtain his authority for imputing these arms to Winchester College; or was he merely confusing them with those of Magdalen College, Oxford, as Mr. Warner believes?

J. S. UDAL, F.S.A.

Antigua, W.I.

ST. MARGARET'S CHURCH AND WESTMINSTER BENEFACTORS.
(*Continued from p. 182.*)

ON the north wall of the church, about a fourth of the length from the west end, will be seen the monument to the memory of Thomas Arneway, who, to quote again from the extremely useful and valuable vestry report of 1890,

"by his will dated 2nd Oct., 1603, after giving certain legacies, left all his goods, ready money, and chattels of what nature or kind soever, to be converted into money, as well as considerable real estate to be let for the greatest rent possible without racking the same, the proceeds to be lent to honest young men, being occupiers or traders within the City of Westminster, in sums not exceeding 50*l*., for one or two years at the most, at the rate of five pounds in the hundred."

From time to time changes were made, and in 1703 "a commission of charitable uses held an inquisition into the affairs of this bequest," and it was found that in 1676 the "stock arising from rents and interests on loans amounted to 1,347*l*."; and also, on going further into the matter, it was discovered that "from that time to the year 1700 the successive trustees received the rents of the charity houses and the interest of the charity money, and applied the said interest to their own use." This was stated to be an appalling result of the inquiry, and no wonder it has been put upon record that "on the ground of this inquisition the commission made a decree, dated 16th April, whereby...... they ordered that 3 per cent., being half the then usual rate of interest, should in future be charged." They also ordered, as was clearly within their right, that "certain sums, amounting in all to 1,490*l*. 3*s*. 6½*d*., which had been misappropriated, should be refunded," and thenceforward to 1790 the accounts were well and honestly kept; but, from a variety of causes, heavy losses were incurred, although the stock was kept up and increased by judicious investments. There was a disagreement between the treasurer and one of the trustees in 1806, and their meetings ceased, and from 1797 to 1812 no loans were granted. Suggestions were made that the "charity would be rendered more beneficial if the trustees were authorized to increase the amount of loan, and if the benefit of the charity were extended beyond the two parishes." These suggested improvements were ultimately carried out, the Court of Chancery, in 1856, ordering that the scope of the fund should be extended to the whole of the "City" of Westminster, and the amount of loan increased to 100*l*. A further enlargement of its operation was ordered in 1875, so as to include the area of the metropolis

"as defined by the Metropolis Local Management Act, 1855; but preference is given to residents within the City and Liberty, and sums of not less than 50*l*., and not more than 200*l*., are now advanced at 3 per cent. to poor occupiers and traders, repayment being secured by the bond of the borrower and two substantial householders, or by mortgage."

The endowment of 1676 was 1,347*l.* 7*s.* 3*d.* ; the capital in 1890 was over 37,000*l.*, and the annual income about 950*l.* The monument to this benevolent old worthy represents two figures in ruffles at prayer, kneeling on either side of a prie-dieu, but, strange to say, there is no regular inscription of names, dates of death, or age of either Arneway or his wife.

> Interred here in grave, doth Thomas Arnwaye lye
> Who in his lyfetyme loved the poore and in that
>   love did dye,
> For what he left, to helpe the poore ; he did devise
>   the same
> Not idell folke, bvt svch as wovlde themselfs to
>   goodness frame,
> The thriftie peopell, by his will that in this parishe
>   dwell,
> Fyvte poundes for their comfort may have if yt
>   they vse it well.
> From yeare to yeare carefvllie they looke unto their
>   charge
> Of svche men as this Arnwaye was, God make the
>   number large.

The present is the third monument, and dipping again into the notes of the late Mr. Poole, we find it stated that

"the second was dated 1703, when the first was *repaired and beautified* by scraping away the very interesting old inscription, so as to render it hardly visible, and then making a new slab of stone, giving only the names and dates of husband and wife. To protect it a screen of iron bars was placed in front of it. On removing this screen and monumental tablet, in 1878, the first one was found behind. It was so illegible that it could scarcely be deciphered, but after awhile it was accomplished. A new slab of marble-like stone was prepared of the same size, and it was engraved identically in all respects with the original one of 1603 and placed on the north wall. So interesting a relic as the original one could not but be esteemed, so it has been placed for future examination in the vault under seat No. 40. The iron grille has been—very improperly —placed in front of an ancient 'Easter Altar' near, without any affinity, and the pedestal of this altar, having been found some years before under the floor, was with reverential care placed at the east end of the south wall, after the broken pieces had been collected and joined together. With reference to the curious last line of the inscription and the prayerful ejaculation, there was such another in the Chapel of the Savoy, quoted in Seymour's 'Stowe,' vol. ii. p. 279, commemorating Humphry Gosling, of London, Vintner, servant to Lord Hunsdon, 1586. The inscription ended with this couplet :—

> So well inclined to Poore and Rich
> God send more Goslings to be sich."

The word "sich" for *such* is heard very frequently, even now, in various parts of the country, being a well-known provincialism, and also often used by the lower orders in London. The St. Margaret's burial register records that Thomas Arneway was buried on 8 December, 1603, and his wife Margaret on 19 August, 1596. W. E. Harland-Oxley.

(To be continued.)

Honorificabilitudinitas.—More than fifty years ago this leviathan of language, in its fullest inflection and with an inseparable conjunction at the end, was sounded in my ears by one from whom I could least have expected such an utterance—namely, a nonagenarian Quakeress who was equally innocent of both Latin and of Shakespeare. In conversation I had asked her about the dame-school near Boston to which she had gone in colonial days.

The last daily function, she said, was to stand up and in chorus to intone "Honorifi-cabil-itu-dini-tati-busque !" the last two syllables in this quatuorsyllabic locution being rounded up right gladsomely.

Thanks to Du Cange, 'H.E.D.' traces this longest of words to its earliest known use in Italy about A.D. 1300, but is silent as to how the vocable could have become known to an Englishman of "small Latin" nearly three centuries afterward. How did it come within the grasp of Shakespeare ?

There seems to me a guiding clue on this question in what I heard from the Quakeress.

The word may be translated "And with cordial compliments," addressed by scholars, on being let loose from school, both to each other and to their teacher.

The ponderous word may have seemed a fitting farewell-greeting onward from the first establishment of English schools, and to have held its own through English conservatism to the Stratford school refounded nine years before Shakespeare's birth. If there was this sort of apostolical succession the custom would bear transportation into the colony of Massachusetts, and would naturally have a new lease of life there.

The word in Shakespeare is addressed to a schoolmaster and regarded as one well known to him. It seems to me the terminal word of her school-sessions was said by the Quakeress to be printed in a school-book, perhaps Dillworth, and at its close.

On the whole, it may be very possible that Shakespeare was here a snapper-up of a word that was no trifle, as in many other cases, without moving foot or finger.

Some reader of 'N. & Q.' I trust will inform me when Dillworth was first published, what primary book preceded it, whether in that or any other school-book the magnitudinous vocable is discoverable, and whether any reminiscences like those of my Quakeress can be detected in England, as well as whether anything to confirm or confute my theory can be found in standard comments on 'Love's Labour's Lost.' In Wimborne Minster I note that books are still set up with their backs to the wall, and so the "honorificabilitu-dinitatibusque," which hath no fellow in our verbal firmament, may still remain in some secluded schools familiar as a household word.

Information sent to me personally will reach me months sooner than through 'N. & Q.,' but my hope is that it will be vouchsafed in both ways.

JAMES D. BUTLER.

Madison, Wisconsin, U.S.A.

"GUARDHOUND."—This word was used by Coventry Patmore in his lines from 'An Evening Scene,' running

And far, far off, to the slumbrous eve,
Bayeth an old guardhound.

The 'H.E.D.' gives "guard-dog" under the compounds of "guard," and indicates that it is obsolete. The queried meaning "a watch-dog" would seem to be confirmed as correct by the quotation here given. "Guardhound" is possibly a nonce-word only.

ARTHUR MAYALL.

A ROYAL YACHT.—King Charles II., like many of his ancestors, was devoted to the sea, and an enthusiastic yachtsman. Queen Elizabeth, we are told, had a pleasure yacht, and so we understand had James I. But Charles II. was the earliest of our sovereigns to enjoy yachting as a sport, and we read in Pepys of his racing matches on the Thames with yachts from Holland, and also of the easy victory obtained by the latter. This, however, only seems to have added to his zest, for comment is made later concerning various craft designed and built to his orders, as well as to those of the Duke of York, his brother.

He may therefore in a sense be regarded as the founder of yacht racing in this country, and, *pace* the shade of Lord Macaulay, that amongst other good qualities should certainly be placed to his credit. The first yacht club that was started in the United Kingdom was the Royal Cork in 1720, not thirty-five years after King Charles's death, and I consider that amongst the toasts which are annually given at meetings of the present-day wet-bob fraternity that of the Merry Monarch should always find an honoured place.

A paper recently read at the Society of Antiquaries by the President, Viscount Dillon, on some unpublished correspondence of Charles II. and his brother James, touched on a point of some interest in these matters. Mention was made in the royal letters of a certain yacht belonging to the king called "The Fubbs."

One of the fellows of the Society was able to throw a light on this curious word. It appears to have been the favourite nick-name bestowed by Charles on the Duchess of Portsmouth, and, without a doubt, his yacht with the same title was christened thus in her honour. At Greenwich, too, there still exists a well-known hostelry ycleped "Fubbs's Yacht," showing what a tenacious grip the nomenclature of many old inns holds upon the otherwise almost forgotten traditions of the past. PERCY CLARK.

ROYAL WALKS.—In the dim and dingy neighbourhood of Ball's Pond Road there is a winding thoroughfare called King Henry's Walk. Passing through this some little way, one is struck with another named Queen Margaret's Grove. To complete these associations with royalty in bygone days, there is Queen Elizabeth's Walk in the neighbourhood of Clissold Park. It is difficult for us moderns to conceive what charms these spots had to endear them to the royal persons whose names they now bear. If there be any authentic history, perhaps some one will favour us with the interesting particulars.

M. L. R. BRESLAR.

Percy House, South Hackney.

CLIFFORD'S INN. — This oldest Inn of Chancery (a view of which was given in 8th S. i. 267) was the subject of an action in the Court of Appeal on Wednesday, the 19th inst. Along with New Inn it is the only Inn of Chancery remaining out of ten that fulfils its original functions as a kind of preparatory school to the Inns of Court. The question before the Court was whether the Inn belongs to the individual members for their own personal benefit, or whether, as Mr. Justice Cozens-Hardy had decided, it was held subject to a trust for charitable purposes. At present there are only sixteen members, of whom four were plaintiffs in the action and the remainder defendants.

The *Daily Telegraph* of the 20th contains an interesting report of the action. Mr. Ralph Nevill, K.C., on behalf of the appellants, stated that in 1345 the property was let to members of the society, one of the Inns of Chancery, by Isabella de Clifford, at a rent of 10*l.* a year. From time immemorial the society had been governed by a principal and twelve "rules" or "antients," who formed the upper ten or "upper mess." The rest formed the "lower mess" or "Kentish mess." Originally all the members were engaged in some way in the practice of the law. The property itself upon which the Inn stood was granted by Edward II. to Robert de Clifford in

1310. In 1618 the land leased was granted by Francis, Earl of Cumberland, and Henry, Lord Clifford, to the twelve "rules." The society was not incorporated, but was a voluntary society, their powers concerning admission being delegated by the judges. Before the end of the thirteenth century these Inns of Chancery had seen their best days, and became merely meeting-places for social purposes and for the encouragement of the study of the law. In 1884 there were only nine members in the "Kentish mess" remaining. Mr. Nevill gave some curious quotations from the rules, going back to 1485. The fee for admission was forty pence; penalty for staying out after the gates were shut at nine o'clock sixpence; a member who tore or spoiled a table-cloth was fined twopence; for being late at dinner the fine was one penny. The game of "tables" might be played "in an honest manner without gambling."

The Master of the Rolls in giving judgment said that the evidence, in his opinion, that Clifford's Inn was charged to a charitable trust, was abundantly clear—so clear, indeed, as to be beyond controversy. For these reasons the decision of Lord Justice Cozens-Hardy was perfectly right, and ought to be affirmed.　　　　　N. S. S.

A GEOGRAPHICAL PUZZLE.—It occurs to me that the following cutting from the *Daily Mail* may supply an interesting note in 'N. & Q.' illustrative of the extraordinary way in which new place-names may originate at the present time:—

"For some time past puzzled geographers have wondered whence 'Cape Nome' in Alaska derived its strange appellation. An American professor, Prof. Davidson, arrived at the conclusion that the name was probably given during the voyage of the Franklin relief ships Herald and Plover in the years 1845-51, and thought it likely that it might have been given in honour of one of the officers on board one or other of these ships. He accordingly wrote to the Hydrographer of the Admiralty in London asking if any officer of that name was on the list of officers on these vessels. The professor's surmise proved incorrect, but indirectly, says the *Scotsman*, his inquiry has led to a solution of the problem. It appears that when the manuscript map of the coast was prepared from surveys made by officers of the Herald it was found that the headland had no name. The officer making the chart wrote opposite it '? name.' This was inked in by a draughtsman on the ship as 'C name,' and when the map went to the Admiralty another draughtsman there, the 'a' being indistinct, copied it on to the chart as 'C Nome,' and the name has continued in use ever since."—*Daily Mail*, 27 Dec., 1901.

　　　　　　　　LL. LLOYD.

CAXTON RECORD PRICE.—On Thursday, the 20th inst., Messrs. Sotheby, Wilkinson & Hodge sold what is probably the finest existing copy of 'The Ryal (or Royall) Book, or Book for a King,' printed by William Caxton at Westminster, 1487. Of the other recorded four perfect copies, one fetched last year 1,550*l.*; the others are in public libraries. The copy sold on the 20th was at the Caxton Exhibition in 1877. The biddings rose to 1,800 guineas, after which the fight was between Mr. Quaritch and Messrs. B. F. Stevens, when it was eventually knocked down to Mr. Quaritch for 2,225*l.*　　　　N. S. S.

SHAKESPEARE *v.* BACON.—

"When the Baconians can show that Ben Jonson was either a fool or a knave, or that the whole world of players and playwrights at that time was in a conspiracy to palm off on the ages the most astounding cheat in history, they will be worthy of serious attention."—Sir Henry Irving's Lecture at the Princeton University in New Jersey on the 19th inst., *Daily News* report.

Is it not time that what Sir Henry well calls "the grotesque gabble of the cipher" should cease?　　　　　　　　Q. A.

HOW TO DEAL WITH DIFFICULT QUESTIONS OF PEDIGREE.—There is no royal road in pedigree work. When obvious sources of information have been exhausted, the only way is to collect every scrap of detail you can gather relative to persons of the name and of the period in question.

To do this the more effectually the following suggestions are made:—

Print your crux, accompanied by a bit of tabular pedigree, and citing authorities for your statements.

Or copy it very distinctly upon a sheet of hand-made foolscap.

Send to genealogists as many copies as you can circulate, for a well-printed or clearly written authenticated scrap of pedigree is almost always sure of careful preservation.

Let professional record agents know what you seek, that they may report from time to time any "documents" relating to the family with which, in their researches amongst the records, they may meet. Order from them abstracts or copies of any likely documents which may be so reported, and thus keep the interest of the record agent alive, even if the point in question is not greatly elucidated by the information so gathered.

Be very careful as to clear copies, and a distinct, intelligible statement of your case. Careless handwriting and the use of wretched paper discount the value of much of the genealogical work done nowadays. If any progress is to be made, system and accuracy are essentials.　　GEORGE F. T. SHERWOOD.

50, Beecroft Road, Brockley, S.E.

THE KING OF TORELORE.—To modern taste
the sojourn of Aucassin and Nicolete in the
castle of Torelore is a curious and uncouth
episode in so lovely a tale. "The custom of
the couvade," says Mr. Andrew Lang in a
note to his charming translation,

"was dimly known to the poet. The feigned lying-
in of the father may have been either a recognition
of paternity (as in the sham birth whereby Hera
adopted Heracles), or may have been caused by the
belief that the health of the father at the time of
the child's birth affected that of the child."

Aucassin roughly arouses the king from his
"man-childbed," and, mounting his horse,
puts the country's enemies to flight; for,
while her lord lay at home, the queen was
fiercely engaged in fighting his foes, warring
upon them with baked apples, mushrooms,
eggs, and fresh cheeses :—

> Whoso splasheth most the ford
> He is master called and lord.

Dr. Tylor says, "The country where Marco
Polo met with the practice of the couvade
in the thirteenth century appears to be the
Chinese province of West Yunnan." Apollonius Rhodius, too, in 'The Tale of the Argo-
nauts,' sings :—

> Round the headland of Zeus the All-begetter swept
>   they then ;
> And safely they sped by the land of the Tibarenian
>   men.
> When a woman in that land beareth a child to her
>   lord, on his bed
> Doth her husband cast him adown, and he groaneth
>   with close-swathed head
> As in anguish of travail, the while the woman with
>   tender care
> Doth nurse him and feed, and for him the child-
>   birth bath doth prepare.

Mr. Arthur S. Way's translation, 1901.
A. R. BAYLEY.

THE CORN-LAW RIMER. — The enclosed
cutting from the *Irish Times* of 23 November
seems worth notice in the pages of 'N. & Q.':

"Curious reminiscences are evoked by the death,
at his residence in Hemel Hempstead, of the Rev.
Edwin Elliott, a son of the once famous Ebenezer
Elliott, the 'Corn-Law Rhymer,' whose verses even
called forth the praises of Carlyle himself. His
poems and writings are supposed by some to have
had as great an influence in promoting Free Trade
as the famine in Ireland, and seventy years ago
were sung in chapels and meetings, and quoted from
a thousand platforms. Although the 'Corn-Law
Rhymer' was himself a sturdy Nonconformist, as
his ancestors had been before him, his son, who
has now joined the majority, entered the Church of
England and laboured for a long period as the
rector of St. John's, in Antigua. He was eighty-
five years of age."

Ebenezer Elliott had a family of thirteen
children, two of whom were brought up as
clergymen of the Established Church.
HERBERT B. CLAYTON.

Queries.

WE must request correspondents desiring information on family matters of only private interest
to affix their names and addresses to their queries,
in order that the answers may be addressed to them
direct.

CELTIC.—In a notice of 'Poems,' by Mr.
W. B. Yeats, which appeared in the
Athenæum of the 8th inst., the reviewer
objects to the use of "Celtic" as a handy
definition for certain poetic qualities, and
remarks :—

"The author of ' The Epic of Hades,' for instance,
is Celtic to the marrow, and yet he is devoid of the
qualities which Arnold labelled 'Celtic,' while the
author of 'Aylwin,' a romance saturated with
'Celtic' qualities, is an unadulterated East
Anglian."

What I desire to know is, How many
pedigrees of poets, or of men less gifted, can
be safely termed "unadulterated" in such a
cross-bred nation as that which inhabits
Great Britain and Ireland?
The hymn-writing Wesleys, Tennyson, and
Miss Ingelow were all natives of Lincolnshire,
but how much of their blood was really
Mercian-Danish? Take another instance.
Mr. —— comes of a family which has been
settled in a county bordering on the German
Ocean for many centuries. His name may be
traced back in ancient documents as far as
the reign of Edward I., if not further ; yet
to superficial observation he shows no indication, either physically or mentally, of the
Teutonic stock which he represents in the
male line. His type must have been inherited
from some family to which he has kinship
through the very mixed blood of his female
ancestors. Again, his wife, who was an East
Anglian in direct male descent, came, like her
husband, of all sorts and conditions of men,
from kings and queens of foreign descent,
and Norman barons downwards, in the
female lines, and it amuses her children that
one of them has been considered like an
Egyptian in facial type, another like an
ancient Roman, a third a Frenchman, and a
fourth a Jew. Yet another instance, also
drawn from an Eastern county. Mr. —— is
tall, fair, and blue-eyed. His wife, a native
of the same shire, is small and dark, but
with aquiline features, unlike those of the
short pre-Celtic stock which she otherwise
seems to represent. Of their children three
are very fair and three dark, but it is
noticeable that two of the latter do not inherit
their mother's features. They resemble a
dark second cousin on the fair father's side
of the family. In the districts of England

considered the most purely Teutonic dark individuals, and dark families of the tall or short type, are to be found. Not infrequently these people inherit a mental quickness which differentiates them from their rather stolid neighbours; but then, again, this very quality may appear in a blue-eyed, fair-haired person showing no outward trace of non-Teutonic ancestry. Has any one ever attempted to estimate the number of strains of foreign blood which came into England at, and after, the Conquest? This blood must have considerably leavened the English, Danish, Celtic, and pre-Celtic stock. English poets have frequently sprung from families more or less affected by neurotic taint, which adds to the difficulty of deciding what manner of men they truly were; but when they were healthy themselves, and of healthy kindred, researches into their ancestry in all lines might prove of great scientific value.

EASTWARD HO!

IMAGINARY CHURCH-LORE. — Is there any foundation for this piece of church-lore from 'The Mighty Atom'?—

"'Just watch these 'ere gates as I pull 'em to and fro. Do what ye will wi' 'em, they won't shut —see!' and he proved the fact beyond dispute. 'That shows they was made 'fore the days of Cromwell. For in they times all the gates of the altars was copied arter the pattern of Scripture which sez—"An' the gates o' heaven shall never be shut either by day or by night." Then when Cromwell came an' broke up the statues an' tore down the picters or whited them wheresever they was on the walls, the altars was made different wi' gates that shut an' locked—I spose 'e was that singler afraid of idolatry that 'e thought the folks might go an' worship th' Communion cup on th' Lord's table. So now ye'll be able to tell when ye sees the inside of a church, whether the altar gates is old or new by this one thing—if they can't shut they're 'fore Cromwell's day—if they can they're wots called Jacobean gim-crackery.'"—P. 97.

Imagine any altars, "different" or otherwise, or any chancel screens, with gates that locked, or even without gates, being made in Cromwell's time, or any "Communion cups" being suffered to remain on any Lord's tables behind chancel screens during his dictatorship. For by the "altar gates" are meant the gates in the chancel screen of Combe Martin Church, which screen, of course, dates from pre-Reformation times. "Pre-Reformation" apparently means, according to Reuben Dale or the author, "'fore the days of Cromwell." It is interesting to know also of this infallible test for the date of a screen, and to learn that Jacobean woodwork is "gim-crackery," and that it dates from after the time of Cromwell. There was danger of idolatry, apparently, only from the cup, not

from the Host. This sexton was too intelligent. But has his notion that chancel gates were, as a piece of symbolism illustrating a Scripture text, purposely made not to shut properly ever been heard of before, or has it any foundation in fact? Antiquity and warping of the wood might perhaps claim to have some voice in the matter.

I must confess to being sceptical as to the genuineness of this "lore"; also as to whether Combe Martin Church really has a "weeping chancel." It is not very apparent: "The ancient roof with its crookedly planned out architecture of the very earliest English style of architecture" (p. 77). Ecclesiastical lore is hardly, I should imagine, the author's strong point or accuracy in regard to it: "Ecclesiastes the Preacher and his incessant cry of *Vanitas Vanitatem*" [sic] (p. 15). Was "the real old chest" in the vestry ever used for Peter's pence? The "few old bits of tarnished silver lying at the bottom [of this chest], the fragments of a long-disused Communion *service*," I took to be pewter, but I may have been mistaken. And why should Bishop Heber's hymn, "Holy, Holy, Holy," "allus" have been sung in the church on harvest thanksgiving, instead of on Trinity Sunday, as usual elsewhere (p. 100)?

J. P. L.

[Miss Corelli's verger and his traditions formed the subject of a query in 9th S. i. 428, and the resulting discussion ran through the next two volumes.]

LAUDERDALE FAMILY. — John Maitland, third son of John, fifth Earl of Lauderdale (died 1710), was, according to Douglas's 'Peerage of Scotland,' "a colonel in the Guards." Can any one tell me if he married, and if he had a daughter Margaret? When did Col. John die?

L. G. P.

COUNTESS OF DENBIGH.—The Countess of Denbigh died in January, 1725/6, in Cavendish Square, London. Is the house she died in still in existence; and if so, on which side of the square is it, and what number does it now bear? Will COL. PRIDEAUX, REV. WM. LOFTIE, MR. PHILIP NORMAN, MR. WHEATLEY, or any other antiquary learned in Old London kindly help me? I may mention that I applied at the Vestry Hall of St. Marylebone parish for permission to consult the rate-book in order to find the reply to this query; that I was informed in reply the fee would be one guinea; and that I would not be allowed to examine the book myself, but that a clerk would do so! A guinea is a very heavy fee for such a trifle of trouble, and in these days a prohibitive one. I may further mention that I have searched personally (as a stranger), for a week or ten days at a time, all the records of several large parishes in London and in the country without any fee whatever having been demanded of me.   C. MASON.

29, Emperor's Gate, S.W.

"THE COCK AND CRYER."—I read recently that some silver plate had been lost in February, 1718/9, from the royal household, and that it was "ordered to be cried by the Cock and Cryer" with a view to its recovery. What is the full meaning of this phrase?

C. MASON.

29, Emperor's Gate, S.W.

"MERESTEADS" OR "MESESTEADS."—In a review of Mrs. Alice Morse Earle's 'Old Time Gardens,' just published, I find that the following passage from the book is quoted :—

"The first entry in the Plymouth records is a significant one. It is the assignment of 'Meresteads and Garden Plotes,' not meresteads alone, which were farm lands, but home gardens. The outlines of these can still be seen in Plymouth town."

The word "merestead" is new to me ; but it will be seen by a reference to 9ᵗʰ S. v. 349 that "meestead" (*i.e*, *messuage*) occurs with some frequency in the Court Rolls of the manor of Dewsbury in Yorkshire in the sixteenth century. Have these New England records been correctly edited, or is "merestead" an erroneous reading of "mesestead" or "meesestead"? Perhaps Mrs. Earle or some American scholar would kindly verify the original record.   S. O. ADDY.

3, Westbourne Road, Sheffield.

DUMAS IN ENGLAND.—Dumas *père* visited England in 1833, and again in 1857 (the last few days of May and first few days of June). Can your readers refer me to any English record of either of these visits?   H. A. S.

SIR ALAN DE HEYTON.—Can any of your readers tell me the descent of Sir Alan de Heyton, of whose daughters and coheirs one married Sir John Fenwick (in the reign of Richard II.), and another married Thomas, son of John Middleton, of Belsay?

M. J. N. H.

NEWARK ABBEY, SURREY. — There is a portion of boundary wall, and a stone coffin-slab with an incised cross with fleur-de-lys hard by, near the five-barred gate opposite the abbey (on the narrow road from Pyrford to Ripley). Is it known from whose tomb the slab came, or from what part of the abbey? Are there any prints in books showing the monastic buildings or plan thereof (including

boundary wall) previous to S. and N. Buck's view? If so, please quote chapter and verse.

J. A. RANDOLPH.

128, Alexandra Road, Wimbledon, S.W.

"G.R." — In some letters written by an artillery officer serving in Flanders with the English army in 1793 the following sentences occur :—

" I lost my horse in that affair : I did not regret his loss much as he was a G.R."

"I am very tired, having been on horse-back ever since five the morning, and have got a very unruly G.R."

A note by the editor of the letters says that G.R. is "apparently the slang term for a troop horse"; but what do the letters actually stand for?   J. H. LESLIE, Major.

Hathersage, North Derbyshire.

COOPER'S 'ATHENÆ CANTABRIGIENSES.'—The second volume of this work was published in 1861. At the end of the book is printed the following note: "A third volume of 'Athenæ Cantabrigienses' is in preparation and will shortly be sent to press." This promise was never fulfilled ; but I should be glad to know if the MS. of this third volume has been preserved, and, if so, in whose custody it now is.   BERNARD P. SCATTERGOOD.

Moorside, Far Headingley, Leeds.

KENYON'S LETTERS. — Can you tell me to what the following refers : "Mr. Kenyon's Letters, Pap. Reg."? It is a reference given in 'Notitia Cestriensis' (Chetham Society Publications, vol. xix.) under "Ellenbrook Chapel."   K. TRICE MARTIN.

CHESS PLAYING : A LEGEND.—Will some one kindly refer me to the passage in Huxley's works where he speaks of Nature and man as if playing a game of chess? Where can I find the old legend of Satan playing at chess with a man for his soul?

LUCIS.

[For the devil and chess see 8ᵗʰ S. xii. 251, 354.]

BARROSA TOKEN.—A few years ago a box, of the Empire style, was given to me. It appears to have been made to hold playing cards. In it was a quantity of metal tokens to be used as card counters. They are of two kinds. On the obverse of one is a representation of the French Imperial eagle perched on a scroll bearing the name "Barrosa." It is surrounded by the words "The French Imperial Eagle." On the reverse, "Taken at Barrosa by the British troops commanded by Genˡ Grayham." The other pattern has under the scroll "March 5, 1811." I shall be glad to know if these tokens were

made for other purposes, and whether any similar ones were struck for other battles of the Peninsula. The victory of Barrosa was a great one. Lieut.-General Thomas Graham, afterwards Lord Lynedoch, deserted by the Spanish commander La Pena and his forces, in less than two hours completely defeated the French under Marshal Victor, and captured Generals Rufin and Rousseau, various officers. 420 rank and file, took six cannon, and killed about 3,000 men. The eagle of the 8th French Light Infantry Regiment was taken by Sergeant Patrick Masterson, of the 87th Regiment, and, as this was the first eagle captured in battle in the Peninsula, he was promoted to be lieutenant. A medal was struck and issued to certain officers (see Memo., dated Horse Guards, November, 1811).   HERBERT SOUTHAM.
Shrewsbury.

EARLE.—I should be glad to obtain any information relating to James William Earle and George Earle, who were respectively admitted to Westminster School in 1817 and 1819. The latter is said to have been a son of Edward Earle, of High Ongar, Essex.
G. F. R. B.

HULME FAMILY. — My father, Thomas Hulme, lived in his youth in Marchington, Staffordshire. He had two brothers, George and John. I wish to learn something of the family, and shall be grateful for information about it.   E. M. H.
Ithaca, New York.

ERSKINE.—I am desirous of ascertaining— or being placed in the way of ascertaining— some particulars as to Alexander Erskine, who in 1648 represented Sweden at the signing of the Treaty of Münster, the close of the Thirty Years' War. Some few details are given as to his history in J. Hill Burton's 'Scot Abroad' (1864) in the chapter headed 'The Statesman,' for though Erskine was primarily a soldier, his services were chiefly conspicuous as a politician. Anderson, in his 'Scottish Nation,' 1877, vol. ii. p. 145, states that he was of the family of Erskine of Kirkbuddo, cadet of the house of Dun, that he was ennobled in Sweden, and that his descendants were settled at Bonn in Germany. Burton says he died childless in 1657, but refers neither to the date nor place of his birth. There are two engravings purporting to be his likeness, of which one before me gives the idea of a fancy portrait. It was published in London, 1796, in octavo, and may be one of a series of portraits. Another of greater interest is in the Scottish

National Gallery, one of a series of all the ambassadors at the Treaty of Münster, engraved by C. Galle, jun., after Von Hulle. The bust is surmounted by a coat of arms and a coronet. The charges on the coat have no similarity to the well-known Argent, a pole sable, of Erskine, but seem to copy or follow the three crowns of Sweden and the lion rampant of Norway quarterly. They may have been specially granted to him by Gustavus Adolphus. Terburg's celebrated picture in the National Gallery of the signatories of the Treaty of Münster contains no doubt Erskine's person, but I do not know of any key to the various personages of the assembly.   W. C. J.

Replies.

CHRONOGRAMS.
(9th S. ix. 127.)

THE question as to the originator of these curious and sometimes very useful devices is, I fear, insoluble. At this distance of time we cannot fix upon any one person as the absolute inventor, or attempt to give the name of the author of the first chronogram. His contemporaries did not trouble themselves to hand down his name to us, and I fear that no trouble of our own would enable us now to discover him. However, we know when chronograms first came into fashion, and also what led up to their being used. Our good friends the literary monks deserve, I think, the credit of having prepared the way for the future chronogram. Every large monastery had a *scriptorium*, and often when a *scriptor*, who had been for many weeks or months hard at work on a precious manuscript intended for some library, at last came with joy to the end of his labour, he would proceed to crown his work by a jingling leonine distich which included in it the date of the completion.

Thus, for instance, a fine *Codex membraneus* of the Latin poet Statius in a Thuringian monastery had this distich at the end :—

Bis quingento bis trino, bis quoque bino
Nascentis Christi, Thebais, scripta fuisti,

which told the knowing ones that the MS. was written in 1010. For $(2 \times 500) + (2 \times 3) + (2 \times 2)$ amounted to that figure even in days when Cocker was unknown. There are hundreds of similar examples in mediæval times, on sepulchral monuments as well as on MSS., and while these were the fashion chronograms were non-existent. Later on the Roman numerals crept into the inscriptions, and we are thus getting nearer to the chronograms that were to come. For example, here is a date from a tomb in Gough's ' Sepulchral Monuments ':—

> M anno C quater bis XI ruit iste
> Luce bis X et 1 April,

which corresponds to 21 April, 1422.

But not till about the middle of the sixteenth century did chronograms come to the front, and succeed in ousting, most likely for ever, the rather childish jingles and doggerel of the monks from their tombs and their books. Josephus à Pinu deserves the credit of the first important work in which chronograms occur to any great extent, and all that we know about him is duly recorded by Mr. Hilton in his monumental and exhaustive book on 'Chronograms,' which is alone in the field, and not likely to be superseded for many a long day. The editorial note referred to it as one volume only, but it consists of three thick quartos, and is full of excellent illustrations and engravings.

It is surprising how many otherwise well-informed people will either stare with surprise if the subject of chronograms is casually mentioned in conversation, or else blurt out, as I have heard more than once, "Oh, yes, I know. I used once to try and guess them every week in the *World*; but they make them so awfully hard now!" The subject is really a most curious and interesting one, and covers a larger ground than one would imagine. Whole books have been written which were entirely chronogrammatic from cover to cover. Plays have been written, and acted as well, where every line in the play was a chronogram, and, to make matters more difficult, a Dutch one. Fine flowing Latin poems of many thousand lines of excellent elegiacs have been written altogether in chronograms. Biographies of saintly and courtly men and women have been given to the world (in very few copies) by ardent devotees of this literary artifice; and I know of a scholarly bibliophile who even now, in these realistic and materialistic times, will produce week by week a batch of excellent chronograms, both in Latin and English, on the current events of the day. They are to be found in many buildings, both old and new, on the Continent, and sometimes reward a searcher in some few of our own village churches. They are found on coins and rings, on keys and spades—the spade that cut the first sod for a canal was often decorated with one as a memento—on bells and foundation stones, on cups and platters and book-plates, and on the title-pages of books most of all. They abound in the records of festivities at births and marriages of the mighty in the land, and they often acted the part of the recording angel when death came to the distinguished ruler or ecclesiastic. They have preserved the date of many a tomb and many a book, and have pleasantly and harmlessly occupied the leisure hours of many a student. They have adorned numerous costly pageants, and have literally crowded the windows at many a public evening illumination abroad. They enlightened the public in a double sense then. But the English public, whether cultured or not, is here still very much in the dark.　　　　Ne Quid Nimis.

Sathalia (9ᵗʰ S. viii. 423).—This place, seen on the voyage from Rhodes to Cyprus, is apparently the ancient Attaleia in Pamphylia, identified in Pauly's 'Real-Encyclopädie der classischen Alterthumswissenschaft' (ed. Wissowa, vol. ii., 1896) with the modern Adalia. Meyer's 'Conversations-Lexicon' (Original-Ausgabe) gives Antalia, Attalia, Satalia, as different forms of the name. In the last-mentioned work of reference and in Smith's 'Dictionary of Greek and Roman Geography' (unfortunately I have no more special treatise at hand at this moment), the site of the earlier town is said not to coincide exactly with that of the modern. Could ruins of Attalus's town have given rise in mediæval times to a story to account for its destruction?　　　　Edward Bensly.

University, Adelaide, South Australia.

"Saulies" (9ᵗʰ S. ix. 108, 151).—Celer tells us that "to obtain the dissyllabic word *saulie* we must go back to a dissyllabic French form." If *saulie* has anything to do with willow, it may, of course, be the Scotch rendering of the English word *sallow* applied south of the Tweed to *Salix caprœa*.

If Celer had not decided otherwise, I would suggest that the French word *saule* may at some time have been used in Scotland alternatively with *saugh* as the word for willow. If so, *saulie* in Scotch would have been applied to a man connected with willows or carrying a willow wand, for neither before nor since the Union have we been bound by any such law as Celer enunciates.

My reason for thinking so is that the great French willow herb (*Epilobium angustifolium*) is always known with us as the "muckle saulie," and I have always supposed that we were indebted for this name to our old league with France. South of the Border you called it "great French willow herb"; here we seem to have elegantly expressed "French willow" by coining a name from a naturalized (French) form *saule*, rather than from our Scottish *saugh*, to denote the *osier Saint Antoine*. I do not think that *saulie* in this case is a local rendering of *sallow*, for, as far as I know, the name *sallow* is applied only to the broad (ob-ovate) leaved *Salix capræa*. The willow herb has linear lanceolate leaves, like *Salix viminalis*, the *osier blanc*. My theory involves a further departure from CELER's rule that we must not form dissyllables from monosyllabic French forms; but we are a law to ourselves in Scotland in the matter of adding *ie* to any word we see reason to appropriate.

J. M. T.

Colinton, N.B.

It is scarcely probable that this word is derived from the French *saule*, seeing that the native word *sauch* (=willow) is so generally in use all over Scotland. Having this word at hand, the Scotch would not be likely to adopt the French word for willow to mean a man who looks like a willow. F. J. C.

GREEK PRONUNCIATION (9th S. vii. 146, 351, 449; viii. 74, 192, 372, 513; ix. 131).—In reply to W. H. B.'s courteous rejoinder to my comments on one of his former notes, I must remark that he does not adhere to the principal point of the note in question. This clearly was that the French word *sel* would be *more* likely to be nearer in sound to the Latin original than the English *salt* (assuming, as he did, that *salt* came from *sel*). In answer to my argument that it would then follow that the Italian word *sale* was still more likely to have kept nearer to the Latin sound, W. H. B. now says that he conceives the Italian word would not be more likely than the French to have retained the old Latin sound, but *less* likely. I will, however, not insist upon what seems to me a contradiction, but endeavour to reply to what W. H. B. says about the French *sel*. To begin with, W. H. B. thinks it strange that the Latin *sal*, if pronounced with the Italian *a*, can have become *sel* in French. But *sel* is only one of a class of French words in which the Latin *a* has become *e* in French (see par. 295 of Hatzfeld and Darmesteter's 'Dictionnaire Général de la Langue Française'). As to the nature of the *a* in *sal*, we find in the same dictionary, firstly, that the French language has been formed from popular Latin; in the second place, that the five vowels of classical Latin, which, according to the authors of this excellent dictionary, were at first either long or short, but without difference of sound (*timbre*), had in the imperial

period come to be pronounced open (*ouvertes*) or shut (*fermées*), the long vowels having become "shut" and the short "open," *with the exception of ā, ă, which both appear to have merged (about) into one sound only—the open sound* (italics mine). It is further remarked in this dictionary that there was in the Latin spoken in Gaul the peculiarity that the *ū* of classical Latin, pronounced like the French *ou*, took the sound of the actual French *ü*. I note this last point because I see no more difficulty for the broad *ā* to have toned down into *e* than for the broad *ū* to have become *ü*. And, indeed, to any one acquainted with the actual pronunciation of French by Parisians, the change of *ā* into *ă* and then into *ē* can only appear most natural, as the present French *ā* is daily becoming finer and finer. Even in certain words written with *â* the *â* is no longer pronounced by Parisians so long as it used to be: witness the words *gâteau*, *château*. It is needless to add that where the *a* has no circumflex accent its thinness is *extreme*. In conclusion, I should be very glad if one of the readers of 'N. & Q.' would tell us how the Anglo-Saxon word *sealt* was pronounced. M. HAULTMONT.

CHRIST'S HOSPITAL (9th S. viii. 283; ix. 231).— The following appears in the *Daily Telegraph* of Saturday last :—

"Mr. R. L. Cassie, Churchwarden of Christ Church, Newgate Street, writes to correct the notion generally held that the farewell sermon preached before the boys of the Blue Coat School by the Bishop of London on Sunday was the last time the scholars of the famous institution would attend their parish church. Such, however, is not the case, and the boys will take part in the services as usual until Sunday, April 13. On Easter Tuesday the Lord Mayor and Sheriffs are to be present in state."

A. N. Q.

DISAPPEARING CHARTISTS (9th S. ix. 144).— Since I wrote concerning Mr. Bartlett, another real old Chartist has died—Charles Junius Haslam. George Julian Harney was always called "Julian," like some others I could mention who were known best by their second name. But Haslam was never called Junius, but always spoken of as "C. J. Haslam." As he was also known for his literary performances, he deserves the passing record of your interesting pages.

Haslam was born at Waddrington, Northumberland, in 1811, and was ninety-one years of age at his death. His father was the village schoolmaster at Waddrington, and he probably inherited a taste for letters. Few persons were able to read or write then, and the villagers used to come to his father's house to hear the newspaper read—which was *Cobbett's Register*. Its price was then 7*d.*, and afterwards 1*s.* 2*d.* His father's house was the only one where the paper was taken in. Young Haslam served a seven-year apprenticeship to a Mr. Blakey, a hatter and furrier in Morpeth, who was the first mayor of the town. He lost business through being an agitator for the Reform Bill. Being a Poor Law guardian, he was for mercy when his colleagues were cruel to the poor, which caused him to lose more trade. In 1829 young Haslam went to Manchester, where he joined the Radicals, and often heard Henry Hunt and William Cobbett speak. He never heard of the Charter until the report of the public meeting in London introducing it made it known to all. Then he said, "We all became Chartists." Afterwards he spoke at meetings of Socialists, as co-operators were then called. They were advocates of industrial cities, not exponents of what is now known as Socialism, which the State is to administer. Haslam was many times in Robert Owen's company. At that time Haslam wrote 'Letters to the Clergy of all Denominations.' There were twenty-four letters in all, setting forth that the writer did not believe in the Scripture being divinely inspired, and his dislike to persons preaching as though it was, when it was not. The Bishop of Exeter, then Dr. Phillpotts, thought it necessary to bring these letters before the House of Lords. The bishop represented that the letters would obliterate morality and religion. Their intention was the very reverse, for Haslam believed in rational religion and morality, and remained a believer in God all his life. Yet Henry Hetherington, a London bookseller, was imprisoned nine months for selling these letters. Haslam resided in Manchester from 1829 to 1860. He was afterwards in business as a chemist in Newcastle-on-Tyne. Gamage, a Newcastle Chartist, qualified himself as a physician, and probably Haslam took lessons in chemistry. In 1879 he was able to retire, and was hale and hearty until within a few years of his death. In addition to the 'Letters to the Clergy' he wrote 'The Moral Catechism,' a substitute for the Church Catechism, and the 'Light of Reason.' He died at the house of his son-in-law in Bulmer Street, Newcastle-on-Tyne, 22 Feb., 1902.

G. J. HOLYOAKE.

Eastern Lodge, Brighton.

ST. CLEMENT DANES (9ᵗʰ S. vii. 64, 173, 274, 375; viii. 17, 86, 186, 326, 465; ix. 52, 136).— A curious freak of nomenclature, like that pointed out by COL. PRIDEAUX with regard

to the absence of "castle" and "street" from that of Southern Europe, occurs in England and Germany with reference to names derived from *fons, fontana*=fountain, which in England are replaced by *spring, bourne, well*, in Germany by *Brunne, Quelle;* nor have we any names derived from *aquæ*, corresponding to the Aigue, Aigues, Aix, Dax, Ax, Acqui, Aguas, of the Continent. This is the more remarkable because Bath (Aquæ Sulis) was not taken by the Saxons until A.D. 577, and the Germans, who usually use *Baden* or *Bad*—like the Spanish and Portuguese *Caldos* and *Calida*—have kept the name Aachen for Aix-la-Chapelle (Civitas Aquensis). What is *Spa* derived from? When, moreover, the Dutch colonized South Africa, a region so like Southern Europe in its physical geography, they at once adopted the word *fontein* = "spring" in their place-names, though I do not think the word occurs as a termination in either the Netherlands or Flanders. Fontaine, of course, is often found in Walloon districts of Belgium. The fact is the more remarkable, as the termination is not common, if it occurs at all, in the well-watered districts of the Cape peninsula, which were the first colonized by the Dutch and Huguenot settlers, whilst it is universal over the Karroo, which was not reached by the Dutch, except as hunters or traders, until long after the French language had died out at the Cape. Can any reason be given why they should have adopted the word *fontaine* to designate the isolated springs in the Karroo, whilst retaining the Dutch word *pan* for waterholes? There were very few Walloons in the service of the Dutch East India Company, nor do I think *fontaine* is a commonplace termination in either Languedoc or Dauphiné, from which most of the Huguenots settled at the Cape appear to have come.

As regards *wich, wick*, I quite agree with your correspondent that there is room both for the Norse and the Latin words in England. If we omit North Northumberland, the term *wich* = vik is certainly found on our east coast within geographical limits corresponding generally with those of the "Saxon shore" of the latest Roman period, whilst the western limits of *wick*=vicus, in the south-western peninsula, at all events, viz., the Devon Axe and the Parret, agree fairly well with the limits of Roman settlement (of which comparatively few traces occur either in West Somerset, Devon, or Cornwall), corresponding with the old territories of the Damnonii and Cornubii, throughout which Cornish continued to be spoken sporadically far down into the Middle Ages, and, geologically, with those where chalks and oolites give place to older rocks. In Roman times, when wolves and bears abounded in the larger forests, open villages could hardly have existed except in treeless districts like those of the chalk downs. In France also the various "Vics," save those in Auvergne, which are upon volcanic rocks of tertiary origin, appear generally to occur in districts of secondary formation.

The quotations given as to Clapham certainly point to the persistence of the Danish settlement tradition in reference to that spot.

I note, with reference to the Gothic language spoken in the Crimea, of which Busbecq gives a vocabulary, that he himself seems to have thought it resembled his native Flemish, whilst the speakers might have been either "Flander sive Brabantirius" (Ep. iv., Elzevir, Leyden, 1633). The numerals are certainly Low German. The article was (tho the). As the difference between High and Low German was perfectly well known in the sixteenth century, and is, indeed, discussed by Busbecq himself in this very connexion, this is at least curious.

Your readers may like to know, on the authority of an ex-vice-chairman of the London County Council, that the excavations for the County Council's new street through Wych Street, Holywell Street, and the neighbourhood of St. Clement Danes have now been carried down to the sand, but not a single archæological relic of any importance has been found, although the County Council use every means to induce workmen employed by them to report such finds. The same things occurred in the excavations for the new public offices on the site of King Street, Westminster. Considering how constantly such objects are found in excavations in towns like Chester, Gloucester, and Colchester, this fact seems difficult to explain. Certainly from the plates (after contemporary paintings) of the 'Coronation Procession of Edward VI.,' now on view in the New Gallery, Regent Street, one would feel inclined to believe that much of the neighbourhood of St. Clement Danes, to the north of the Strand, was unbuilt upon in A.D. 1547; and, to judge from their representations of Cheapside as compared with the view of that street in the 'Entry of Queen Marie de Medicis' in 1638, given in Chambers's 'Book of Days' (vol. ii.), those pictures seem to be fairly faithful to nature. Is anything really known as to the date of the first buildings on the Via de Aldwych? I see *Aldwick*,

near Bognor (Sussex), was lately up for sale. Was Holywell Street built before the Reformation? Are any derivatives from *fons, fontana, aquæ*, found in Welsh or other Celtic place-names?

Other Latin words found in the place-names of Southern Europe, but not in England or Germany, include *forum* (with us Chipping), *silva, pons* (of course I know Welsh *pont*), *vadum, murus* (as in Murviedro), and *vallis*. *Mons* is only found in post-Conquest names like Montacute. There is a curious exception for *portus* in Porchester, Portsmouth. It would be interesting to know the reason for this, as derivatives from all these names are found in Normandy; some also in Belgium. Do any of them survive in our Celtic districts? H.

To make a quotation from 'Waverley,' this subject would seem to "partake of what scholars call the periphrastic and ambagitory, and the vulgar the circumbendibus." In pursuing it we have got far away from the Strand, have reached the southern suburbs of London, and are now making a compass for the mouth of the Thames and the east coast. Proceeding first to Clapham, I may point out that thirty hides at "Cloppaham" were bequeathed by Ælfred Aldorman to his wife Werburg and his daughter Alhdryth in the will which he executed some time between 871 and 889, more than a hundred and fifty years before the days of Osgod Clapa. He also stipulated that whatsoever man might enjoy the land at Clapham after his day should give two hundred pence every year to Chertsey in aid of the sustenance of the monks (Thorpe's 'Diplomatarium,' pp. 480, 481).

I quite agree with H. in the explanation given by him for the comparative absence of compounds of "street" and "castle" in the nomenclature of Southern Europe. But with regard to local names ending in -*wich*, I think the probability is that the termination is Anglo-Saxon. Ipswich was originally Gippeswīc, and is probably derived from a personal name, while Harwich (Here-wīc), Dunwich (Dūne-wīc), Greenwich (Grēne-wīc), Woolwich (Wūle-wīc), and Sandwich have Anglo-Saxon words as the first constituents of their names, and it is not unreasonable to infer that they received their appellations from Anglo-Saxons or Anglo-Jutes. Wick in Caithness stands in a different category, but Wick in Worcestershire appears as Wīc in the charters.* W. F. PRIDEAUX.

* The following quotation from Norden's 'Speculum Britanniæ,' Middlesex, ed. 1723, p. 27, is cor-

I do not know whether you may think that enough space has already been devoted to this subject, but the following extract from the 'Table Talk of S. T. Coleridge,' ed. 1852, p. 276, seems worth considering :—

"Horne Tooke was once holding forth on language, when turning to me, he asked me if I knew what the meaning of the final *ive* was in English words. I said I thought I could tell him what he, Horne Tooke, himself thought. 'Why, what?' said he. '*Vis*,' I replied, and he acknowledged I had guessed right. I told him, however, that I could not agree with him ; but believed that the final *ive* came from *ick—vicus*, οἶκος; the root denoting collectivity and community, and that it was opposed to the final *ing*, which signifies separation, particularity, and individual property, from *ingle*, a hearth, or one man's place or seat ; οἶκος, *ricus*, denoted an aggregate of *ingles*. The alteration of the *c* and *k* of the root into the *v* was evidently the work of the digammate power, and hence we find the *icus* and *irus* indifferently as finals in Latin. The precise difference of the etymologies is apparent in these phrases :—The lamb is sport*ive*; that is, has a nature or habit of sporting ; the lamb is sport*ing*, that is, the animal is now performing a sport. Horne Tooke, upon this, said nothing to my etymology ; but I believe he found he could not make a fool of me, as he did of Godwin and some other of his butts."

G. H. Thompson.

CHARLES V. ON THE DIFFERENT EUROPEAN TONGUES (9ᵗʰ S. viii. 523 ; ix. 152).—Side by side with these fine sayings of Charles V. on the characteristic merits of the various languages of Western Europe, and the desirability of learning them, it is interesting to note Michelet's opinion (exaggerated perhaps) that the emperor was no linguist, for he applies to him the words which Rabelais puts into the mouth of Picrochole :—

Tu sais toutes les langues et pas une.

According to the same author even his written French was bad, although French as it was spoken at Brussels was his native tongue.

T. P. Armstrong.

SONG WANTED (9ᵗʰ S. viii. 364, 510 ; ix. 77). —The verses sent by MR. PIERPOINT appear to contain a part only of the original. In my copy of 'Songs, Comic and Satyrical,' by

roborative of my view that *wīc* was applicable to a row of houses along a high road :—" *Kingstonwyke* is a Hamlet neere *Kingstone* vpon *Thamis*, standing in *Myddlesex*, and is so called, for that it is a rowe of houses leading into *Kingstone*, which rowe of houses in Lattine is called *Vicus*, in our toong *Vyke* or *Wyke*, of the Saxons *wyc*. *Vadianus* an excellent Geographer, saith that *Vicus in opido* [*sic*] *via est domorum seriem complexa*, *Vike* is a way or passage in a towne being orderly compact of houses, which we also cal a streete. In *Rome* are divers of these streetes, as *Vicus affricus*, *Vicus ciprius*, & *Vicus celeratus*, *Vicus sceleratus Roma*."

George Alexander Stevens, 1788, instead of the four eight-line stanzas there are sixteen verses of four lines each, and the production seems so much more complete than in its shortened form that I am tempted to send you a full copy, headed as in the book. The verses appear precisely the same in a later edition of 1807.

ORIGIN OF ENGLISH LIBERTY.

To its own Tune.

Once the gods of the Greeks, at ambrosial feast,
  Large bowls of rich nectar were quaffing,
Merry Momus among them appeared as a guest,
  Homer says the Celestials lov'd laughing.

This happened 'fore Chaos was fix'd into form,
  While nature disorderly lay :
While elements adverse engendered the storm,
  And uproar embroil'd the loud fray.

On every Olympic the Humourist droll'd,
  So none could his jokes disapprove ;
He sung, repartee'd, and some odd stories told,
  And at last thus began upon Jove ;

" Sire, mark how yon matter is heaving below,
  Were it settled 'twould please all your Court ;
'Tis not wisdom to let it lie useless you know ;
  Pray people it, just for our sport."

Jove nodded assent, all Olympus bow'd down,
  At his fiat creation took birth ;
The cloud-keeping Deity smil'd on his throne,
  Then announced the production was Earth.

To honour their Sov'reign each God gave a boon ;
  Apollo presented it light ;
The Goddess of Child-bed despatch'd us a Moon,
  To silver the shadow of Night.

The Queen of Soft-wishes, foul Vulcan's fair bride,
  Leer'd wanton on her Man of War ;
Saying, as to these Earth-folks I 'll give them a guide,
  So she sparkled the Morn and Eve Star.

From her cloud, all in spirits, the Goddess upsprung,
  In ellipsis each Planet advanc'd ;
The Tune of the Spheres the Nine Sisters sung,
  As round Terra Nova they danc'd.

E'en Jove himself could not insensible stand,
  Bid Saturn his girdle fast bind,
The Expounder of Fate grasp'd the Globe in his hand,
  And laugh'd at those Mites call'd mankind.

From the hand of great Jove into Space it was hurl'd,
  He was charm'd with the roll of the ball,
Bid his daughter Attraction take charge of the world,
  And he hung it up high in his hall.

Miss, pleas'd with the present, review'd the globe round,
  Saw with rapture, hills, vallies, and plains ;
The self-balanc'd orb in an atmosphere bound,
  Prolific by suns, dews, and rains.

With silver, gold, jewels, she India endow'd,
  France and Spain she taught vineyards to rear,
What was fit for each clime on each clime she bestow'd,
  And Freedom she found flourish'd here.

The blue-eyed celestial, Minerva the wise,
  Ineffably smil'd on the spot ;
"My dear," says plum'd Pallas, "your last gift I
      prize,
  But, excuse me, one thing is forgot.

" Licentiousness Freedom's destruction may bring,
  Unless prudence prepares its defence ;"
The Goddess of Sapience bid Iris take wing,
  And on Britons bestow'd Common-Sense.

Four Cardinal Virtues she left in this isle,
  As guardians to cherish the root ;
The blossoms of Liberty gaily 'gan smile,
  And Englishmen fed on the fruit.

Thus fed, and thus bred, by a bounty so rare,
  Oh preserve it as pure as 'twas given ;
We will while we 've breath, nay we 'll grasp it in
      death,
And return it untainted to Heaven.
                                    W. B. H.

OBELISK AT ST. PETER'S, ROME (9th S. viii.
405, 505 ; ix. 109).—The account of the inscriptions which has already been given may
be supplemented by the following extract
from Prof. Lanciani's 'The Ruins and Excavations of Ancient Rome' (Macmillan & Co.,
1897), p. 552 :—

"A whole cycle of legends was formed about the
obelisk in the early dawn of the Renaissance.
Giovanni Dondi dell' Orologio (†1389) asserts having
seen engraved in the middle of the monolith the
distich—

    ingenio, Buzeta, tuo bis quinque puellæ
    appositis manibus hanc erexere columnam.

Another even more absurd inscription is given by
Giambullari ap. Mercati—'Obelischi,' p. 139. A
third appears in the early epigraphic manuals of
Metello, Lilius the gouty, Ferrarino, &c.—

    orbe sub hoc parvo conditur orbis Herus.
    si lapis est unus, dic qua fuit arte levatus,
    et si sunt plures, dic ubi contigui."

It will be seen that these last two lines are
a different version of the couplet quoted on
p. 507 of the last volume. Prof. Lanciani and
the late Prof. J. H. Middleton ('The Remains
of Ancient Rome,' vol. ii. p. 59) draw attention
to a very interesting fact in the history of
this obelisk. Among all the obelisks in Rome
this is the only one which has never been
thrown down.   EDWARD BENSLY.
  The University, Adelaide, South Australia.

"YARD OF ALE" (9th S. ix. 84).—A yard-of-
ale glass, somewhat like a post-horn in shape,
was exhibited by Mr. Hillyar Chapman,
Kilhendre, Ellesmere, at the Loan Exhibition
of Shropshire Antiquities held at Shrewsbury, 10–21 May, 1898, and I presume it is
still in his possession. HERBERT SOUTHAM
              (Hon. Sec. to the Exhibition).
  Shrewsbury.

BULL-BAITING (9th S. ix. 188).—I am not
aware of any statute ordering bulls to be
baited as a condition precedent to their flesh

being exposed for sale ; but there were
numerous borough or town laws to that effect.
In some towns the butcher who sold the
flesh of a bull in the market without having
produced the animal on the previous market
day to be baited was liable to a penalty,
the reason being that the flesh of a baited
bull was universally considered more tender
and nutritious than that of animals slaughtered without being first submitted to the
process. The belief, while it does not excuse
the brutality of the act, was probably founded
on fact. Many still assert that the flesh of
hunted hares, deer, and rabbits is preferable
to that of tame or snared animals. In reply
to G. T.'s further inquiry, the baiting was
undoubtedly by dogs, and not by being fed
in a stall.   F. A. RUSSELL.
  49, Holbeach Road, Catford, S.E.

"WAGUES" (9th S. ix. 204).—In this highly
interesting article the proposed etymology
is, unfortunately, impossible. It is a pity
that Anglo-Saxon should be quoted without
any regard to its pronunciation. The A.-S.
ag becomes *aw*, and *wagian* is no exception,
the M.E. form being *wawien* or *wawen ;* see
wagien in Stratmann. But the spelling
wagues was presumably adopted to show that
the *g* is hard ; so the word must be Norse.
  The Icel. *vagar* (orig. *wagar*) is a fem. plural,
but it means "a kind of bier or handbarrow."
The Norw. *vaga* is a fem. sb., meaning "a
short sledge for the conveyance of timber,"
but is more common in the pl. form *vage*, in
which, as Aasen remarks, the *g* remains hard.
Consequently, *wagues* originally meant the
rush-cart itself, but the plural form was
naturally embarrassing, and a new sense had
to be found for the singular, the sense chosen
being that of one of the stangs by which
the rush-cart was propelled. At least, such
seems to be the solution which alone will
suit the facts.
  The etymology is from the Icel. *vaga*, cognate with A.-S. *wagian*, and having the same
sense. It makes all the difference to the
phonology.   CELER.

PINS IN DRINKING VESSELS (9th S. iv. 287,
358, 484 ; ix. 10, 136).—It is worthy of note
that the phrase "to put in the pin," meaning
to refrain from drinking, is evidently in
allusion to the rows of pins or pegs designed
to regulate the amount which each person
was expected to drink from the "peg tankard." The original sense apparently having
been lost sight of, it is now applied merely
to any habit or course of conduct which it is
desirable should be stopped, as "to put in
the pin at the New Year"—*i.e.*, to turn over a

new leaf. "He had two or three times resolved to......put in the pin" (Mayhew's 'London Labour and London Poor,' i. 345). "Putting in the peg" is, according to Barrère and Leland's ' Dict. of Slang,' military slang, meaning "taking a pull at one's self; being on the sober or quiet tack, voluntarily or by superior orders." Still another phrase derived from the custom of the peg tankard is apparently that of "to peg out"—he who in drinking was overcome by too many pegs, and succumbed to their influence, being said to be "pegged out." Before this stage was arrived at the convivial were said, by having another peg, "to screw themselves up a peg" in the event of feeling "a peg too low":—

Come, old fellow, drink down to your peg!
But do not drink any further, I beg.
Longfellow, 'Golden Legend,' iv.

Cf. also " to be in a merry pin ":—

"The Dutch, and English in imitation of them, were wont to drink out of a cup marked with certain pins, and he accounted the man, that could nick the pin; whereas to go above or beneath it, was a forfeiture."—Dr. Fuller's 'Eccles. Hist.,' lib. iii. p. 17.

The ornamental band round the modern tankard appears to be a survival of the hooped drinking-mug, in which the hoop served a purpose similar to that of the peg or pin. Nash, in his ' Pierce Penniless,' says, " I believe hoops in quart-pots were invented that every man should take his hoop, and no more." (See further Timbs's 'Things not Generally Known,' Second Series, 1861, p. 41.)
J. HOLDEN MACMICHAEL.

With reference to the Glastonbury cup, I shall be glad if I may be allowed to correct an error in my reply, printed at the last reference. I then represented Lord Arundell of Wardour as having spoken of the author of the 'History of Winchester' as Dr. Milman. That was incorrect, as, of course, Lord Arundell of Wardour referred to him as the Right Rev. Dr. Milner, Bishop of Winchester.
RONALD DIXON.
46, Marlborough Avenue, Hull.

"PATTLE" (9ᵗʰ S. ix. 105).—It is worthy of note that Sir Walter Scott uses both "pattle" and "pettle." He may have simply followed Burns; but as he had a direct knowledge of agriculture, his employment of the term in both spellings probably illustrates a usage in the Scottish Border counties. In 'The Monastery' (chap. xi.) he says, in his own character of narrator, that if young Halbert Glendinning "liked a book ill, he liked a plough or a pattle worse." In chap. xiii. Dame Glendinning, talking with the miller of her son Edward's future, observes, " He

will take to the pleugh-pettle, neighbour "; but why it should be the " pleugh-pettle," and not simply the " pleugh," the uninitiated reader may be at a loss to know. It may be that at one time the ploughboy learned his business by walking at the side of the man engaged in ploughing, and using the pattle or plough-spade, as occasion required, to clean the refuse from the coulter.
THOMAS BAYNE.

GORDON, A PLACE-NAME (9ᵗʰ S. ix. 29, 133). —Before sending you a reply on this query I waited until the Gordonia in Macedon, the De Gourdon in France, and the Gore-down theories should all have been advanced. But, seriously, is there any reason to suppose that Chalmers, in his 'Caledonia,' vol. ii. p. 385, was wrong when he said that Gordon in Gaelic signifies "upon the hill"; and, in vol. i. p. 544, that the renowned family, who from that small beginning have almost girdled the earth with their name, derive it from the Berwickshire village? The last seems to me capable of proof, but it depends on one thing—the date of the earliest De Gordun whose existence can be proved. For the place of Gordun we find mentioned in a charter of Cospatric the earl, who died in 1147, and apparently then owned by him (' Liber de Calchou,' ch. 288).

Can any human being named Gordon or De Gordun be dated, in Scotland, before 1200? That is the approximate date which, by comparing the witnesses with other dated charters, I give to ch. cxvii. in Raine's 'North Durham,' in which Richard de Gordun and Adam de Gordun, the traditional brothers, make what is, I believe, their first appearance. Anyway, this charter cannot be earlier than 1182, in which year its grantor, Patrick, Earl of Dunbar, greatgrandson of the above-mentioned Cospatric, succeeded.

I am aware that Douglas, in his ' Peerage,' puts down the charter in which this same Richard de Gordun appears as granting land to the church and monks of Kelso, in combination with the church of Gordun (' Liber de Calchou,' ch. 118), as between 1150 and 1160; but the charter is undated, and, as whoever transcribed it into the chartulary omitted the names of the witnesses, it is practically undatable. Moreover, the church of Gordun was under the priory of Coldingham up to 1171, in which year it was transferred to Kelso in exchange for Ercildoun (Raine, ch. dcxliii.). Richard's charter must, at any rate, be after that transfer. I am aware also that it is a tradition that De Gorduns fought under Malcolm Caenmore and at the Battle of the Standard. That ancestors of the Gordon family so fought is most probable; but is there any record or authority for the statement that they then bore the famous name? But all this should be capable of proof, and, in the interests of Scottish history and correct genealogy, should be proved.

While we are on the subject, can any one tell me what is the earliest appearance of De Gordon arms in Scotland, whether the boars' heads or anything else? I ask because I notice that Mr. Joseph Foster, in his new book on 'Feudal Coats of Arms,' puts in an Adam de Gordon, who bore, in the time of Henry III., and so presumably in England, Gules, three fleurs-de-lys argent; but it would appear as if in the actual Roll the name is spelt Gurdun, perhaps correctly.

G. S. C. S.

James B. Johnstone, in his 'Place-names of Scotland,' gives the following:—

"Gordon (Earlston). 1250, Gordin; 1280, Gordun. Welsh *gor din*, 'spacious hill,' or perhaps like Gourdon, Gaelic *gobliar* (pronounced *gore*), goat; *dun*, a hill, meaning goat hill; but Killgordon in Ireland is Irish, Coill-na-genirdin=wood of the parsnips, a word which does not seem to be in the Gaelic."

John Radcliffe.

Royal Personages (9th S. viii. 184, 252, 349; ix. 89).—A. W. B. asks, among other things, where the Duke of Cumberland, brother to George III., was married to the Hon. Anne Horton on 2 October, 1771. It was at her house in Hertford Street, Mayfair. I should much like to know what number the house at present bears.

E. F. Du Cane.

An Old Charm (9th S. ix. 49, 158).—In answer to Mr. Matthews (whom I thank heartily for his interesting reply), I think there is no doubt that my reading of the two words in question is correct, but their form may have been due to errors in copying. Their resemblance to the Welsh phrases Mr. Matthews quotes can scarcely be a mere accident.

C. C. B.

Cuckland (9th S. viii. 384, 510; ix. 155).— I agree with Mr. Harrison that we must not derive all our *cuck* names from Cwichhelm. In King Eadgar's Hampstead charter to Mangoda we find that one of the boundary limits is the "coccing pól." In the very interesting paper on this and another Hampstead charter which was contributed by Prof. J. W. Hales to the *Transactions* of the London and Middlesex Archæological Society, vi. 560,

the learned writer discusses this place-name without coming to any definite conclusion. The "cucking-stool" is brought forward, and other meanings are suggested, while the most obvious one, that derived from *cock*, is passed over. I believe that Coccing Pól has much the same meaning as the Hanewelle of Domesday, the modern Hanwell. The Domesday Haneworde (Hanworth) may in like manner be compared with the old Devonshire family name Cookworthy, which was formerly spelt Cokworthy or Cockworthy. The termination *-ing* may at first sight present a difficulty, but if we accept the dictum of Mr. W. G. Searle in his invaluable 'Onomasticon Anglo-Saxonicum,' introduction, p. xv, that it is occasionally the equivalent of a mere genitive singular in place-names, the difficulty disappears.

W. F. Prideaux.

"The moss-covered bucket" (9th S. ix. 148).—This poem is by Samuel Woodworth, of Scituate, Massachusetts, 1785–1842, and is as follows:—

How dear to this heart are the scenes of my childhood,
  When fond recollection presents them to view!
The orchard, the meadow, the deep-tangled wildwood,
  And every loved spot which my infancy knew;
The wide-spreading pond and the mill which stood by it,
  The bridge, and the rock where the cataract fell;
The cot of my father, the dairy-house nigh it,
  And e'en the rude bucket which hung in the well;
The old oaken bucket, the iron-bound bucket,
  The moss-covered bucket which hung in the well.

That moss-covered bucket I hail as a treasure;
  For often, at noon, when returned from the field,
I found it the source of an exquisite pleasure,
  The purest and sweetest that nature can yield.
How ardent I seized it, with hands that were glowing!
  And quick to the white-pebbled bottom it fell;
Then soon, with the emblem of truth overflowing,
  And dripping with coolness, it rose from the well;
The old oaken bucket, the iron-bound bucket,
  The moss-covered bucket, arose from the well.

How sweet from the green mossy brim to receive it,
  As, poised on the curb, it inclined to my lips!
Not a full blushing goblet could tempt me to leave it,
  Though filled with the nectar that Jupiter sips.
And now, far removed from the loved situation,
  The tear of regret will intrusively swell,
As fancy reverts to my father's plantation,
  And sighs for the bucket which hangs in the well;
The old oaken bucket, the iron-bound bucket,
  The moss-covered bucket which hangs in the well.

J. de Berniere Smith.

Bartlett's 'Familiar Quotations' gives two lines of these verses as the production of Samuel Woodworth, 1785–1842.

W. C. B.

THE DUCHY OF BERWICK (9th S. viii. 439, 534; ix. 130).—I think that on further inquiry H. will discover that the dukedom of Berwick has no claim to be a Spanish title. The attainder of the English Parliament in 1695 was not recognized in the French and Spanish Courts, and to create as a foreign dignity an English dukedom which, in the opinion of the Spanish king, had never been legally forfeited, would not have been regarded as a compliment by the recipient. The 'Almanach de Gotha' for 1902 says James FitzJames "fut créé Duke of Berwick (Écosse méridionale; titre angl.) 1688, Grand d'Espagne de Ire cl. au titre de Duque de Liria et de Xerica, 16 oct. 1707." The 'Almanach' makes a mistake with regard to the date of the creation, which was 1687; but it correctly expresses the fact that it was an English title, and that therefore James FitzJames was an English "duke" as well as a Spanish "duque." On 23 May, 1710, he was further created a French "duc," with the title of "Duc de FitzJames-Warty"; but the lands of Warty, which constituted the *pairie*, no longer belonging to the family, the second part of the title has been dropped, and a second *pairie* was created by Louis XVIII. on 4 June, 1814.*

I agree with H. that the prefix "Fitz" is by no means a sign of illegitimacy. In early times it was rather a proof of legitimate status; but there were, of course, exceptions. One of the illegitimate sons of Henry I. was known as Robert FitzEdith.

The information given by H. regarding the marquisate of Jamaica is exceedingly interesting, but the 'Almanach de Gotha' does not record it as one of the titles of the present Duke of Berwick.

The Order of the Garter has been very seldom conferred on any foreign subjects since the days of the Plantagenets. I can only find the following instances: Philippe de Chabot, Comte de Neublanche, 1532; Anne de Montmorency, Comte de Beaumont and Duc de Montmorency, 1532; François, Duc de Montmorency, 1572; Claude de Lorraine, Duc de Chevreuse, 1625; Bernard de Nogaret de Foix, Duc d'Épernon, 1644-5; Henri Charles de la Tremouille, Prince de Tarent, 1653; and Jean Gaspar Ferdinand de Marchin, Comte de Graville, 1657-8. The last two knights, having been created by Charles II. during his exile, were installed

* Since writing this note, I have read a couple of excellent articles in the *Royalist* on the Dukes of FitzJames. The designation of FitzJames seems to have been given to lands of Warty by the first duke.

by dispensation in 1661. The Duke of Berwick was elected a Knight of the Garter in 1688, but he was never installed, and his election was declared void in 1689-90. I presume that Louis de Duras, Marquis de Blanquefort, who was created Baron Duras by Charles II. in 1673, and succeeded his father-in-law as Earl of Feversham in 1677, was technically a British subject when he received the Garter in 1685. After his abdication, I believe, King James II. bestowed the Garter on the Duc de Lauzun and some other foreigners, but these appointments were not officially recorded. W. F. PRIDEAUX.

Though this heading may be slightly misleading, yet my remarks bear on the subject discussed, for it comes under the category of British subjects bearing titles taken from foreign places.

The late Marquess of Dufferin was also Marquess of Ava; the great naval hero was Viscount Nelson in the peerage of England, and Duke of Brontë in Sicily; the Bennets are Earls of Tankerville, a place, I believe, in Normandy. At the coronation of William IV. in 1831, Alexander Humphreys, *alias* Alexander, claimed to do homage as hereditary lieutenant of Nova Scotia. He asserted that he was lineally descended from William Alexander, created by Charles I. Earl of Stirling and Viscount Canada, and with these titles had the right of creating Nova Scotia baronets, a right which he exercised. It may be worth noting here that Nova Scotia was formerly called Acadia or Acadie.

The trial connected with this claim took place before the High Court of Justiciary in Edinburgh in 1839, and is one of the most remarkable in criminal jurisprudence. The documents put in as evidence were proved to be forgeries; but there was some doubt as to whether the panel had knowingly uttered them, and a verdict of "Not proven" was returned. There are full accounts of this important trial, which lasted for six days, given in 'Modern State Trials' (vol. ii.), by W. C. Townsend, and in 'Miscellanies' Critical, Imaginative, and Juridical' (vol. ii.) by Samuel Warren.

JOHN PICKFORD, M.A.
Newbourne Rectory, Woodbridge.

At the last reference H. asks whether there was any earlier instance of the use of Fitz in England to denote illegitimate descent from royalty than that of Henry Fitzroy, Duke of Richmond, son of Henry VIII. by Elizabeth Blount. Henry Tudor was only following the example of his ancestor, the first Henry who called his famous bastard Robert Fitzroy. Robert, who was the eldest of all Henry I.'s sons, by his marriage with Mabel, daughter and heiress of Robert FitzHamon, the builder of Tewkesbury Abbey, became the owner of vast possessions in Normandy, Wales, and England. Chief among these was the honour of Gloucester, which Henry formed into an earldom for his son. That Fitz is not always a sign of illegitimacy appears to be illustrated by the case in point: Gloucester's father-in-law was FitzHamon; while his own lawful son and heir, the second earl, was surnamed William FitzCount.

A. R. BAYLEY.

Miscellaneous.

NOTES ON BOOKS, &c.

Tribal Custom in Anglo-Saxon Law. By Frederic Seebohm, LL.D. (Longmans & Co.)

THIS scholarly and important work is modestly announced as an "essay supplemental" to 'The English Village Community' and 'The Tribal System' in Wales' of the same author. The three works are, indeed, spoken of by him as a "trilogy." In this third and presumably concluding portion the Anglo-Saxon laws are studied from the point of view of tribal custom. So established an authority upon the subjects with which he deals is Dr. Seebohm that the task of the reviewer scarcely extends beyond registering his decisions. In his opening pages he developes his previous conclusions as regards Cymric tribal custom, especially as regards the "gwely," or family unit of tribal society, and "the methods of payment of the galanas, or death-fine for homicide in lieu of the blood-feud between kindreds." In the first chapter an account is given of the wer-geld of the continental tribes and the currencies in which this death-fine was paid. The Cymric death-fines were reckoned in cows; the "eric" fine of the Breton laws was stated in *cumhals*, or female slaves, lesser payments being in cows or heifers, these being all equated with silver. Anglo-Saxon wer-gelds were generally in silver marks, ores, and orlugs, and those of continental German tribes in gold solidi. In the East a hundred head of cattle was a customary wer-geld. A hundred camels between two Meccan tribes is the price of freedom from the blood-feud; while, according to the laws of the Manu, one of the highest of the twice-born Brahman class might purge himself for the involuntary slaying of one of the warrior class by a payment to the priests of 1,000 cows and a bull. One hundred cows and a bull served for the death of one of the agricultural or trading class, and ten cows and a bull for one of the servile class. Lycaon, a son of Priam and Laothoe, taken and ultimately slain by Achilles, was redeemed by Eëtion of Imbros for a "great sum" (see 'Iliad,' xxi. 39), which great sum Lycaon declares to have been a hundred oxen (*ib.*, 71), and was ransomed as a king's son for three hundred oxen. In the Mosaic law the redemption of a man dedicated by vow to the service of the sanctuary was "fifty shekels of silver: that is the light mina of silver." It is obviously impossible to follow further these questions of monetary systems or to deal with matter which, apart from context and argument, is as devoid of intelligibility as of interest. Very clearly established by these payments are the solidarity of kindred under tribal law and the family character of the system of landholding. The constitution and working of the gwely are fully explained, and the liability in case of homicide of the wider kindred is shown. Chapter iii. is of great interest, showing the evidence of 'Beowulf' on tribal custom, regulating feuds, &c. In 'Beowulf' is shown the depth of the tribal feeling that homicide can only be expiated by revenge and feud, and that it is a hard thing for a father to abstain from revenge on his son for accidental fratricide. There is, however, no feud within kindred when one kinsman slays another, and the punishment must be left to fate or chance. Accidental homicide is not even followed by exile. Murder within the kindred "breaks the tribal tie and is followed by outlawry." The wer-gelds of the Burgundian and Wisigothic laws occupy the fifth chapter. Succeeding chapters treat of Franks, the tribes conquered by the Merovingian kings or by Charlemagne; of the oldest Scandinavian laws; of Scotland; of Anglo-Saxon custom from Norman, Danish, and Viking points of view; and the laws of the Kentish kings. The conclusion from the study of the currencies in which wer-gelds were paid is that there was a pretty general correspondence in the amount of the wer-gelds of the tribes of Western Europe, tenaciously adhered to by them, whether remaining in their old homes or settled in newly conquered countries. The amount of the fine seems not to have been a matter of race. Cymric and German customs were singularly similar. The normal wer-geld of the full freeman was 200 gold solidi, representing 100 head of cattle, an amount too large for the individual to pay, and possible only as a "payment from one group of kindred to the other. In the solidarity of kinsmen is found the strongest instinct" which everywhere moulded tribal society. We have dealt with one or two points only in a book claiming and repaying the closest study, a work of highest authority, and indispensable to the student of the origin of primitive communities.

History of the Conquest of Peru. By William H. Prescott. Edited by John Foster Kirk. 3 vols. (Bell & Sons.)

AN indispensable supplement or companion to the 'History of the Conquest of Mexico' of the same author, Prescott's 'History of the Conquest of Peru' deserves and obtains a place with that work in "Bohn's Standard Library." To the inclusion of Prescott's earlier work in that admirably selected and in its line unequalled collection we drew attention 9th S. viii. 315. What was there said concerning his 'Mexico' is also true of his 'Peru.' While equally unsatisfactory from the point of view of ethnology and kindred subjects, both are models of historical composition. They may be perused with unbroken delight, and though no longer in the full sense authoritative, and certain to be replaced by later compilations, they will long maintain their places on the shelves of the student and in the affection of the reader. The edition reprinted is that of John Foster Kirk, Prescott's secretary, whose notes do much to atone for Prescott's inevitable shortcomings. No temptation exists to deal afresh with a book that has been in the possession of readers for more than half a century. Those anxious to judge of the good faith and impartiality of the historian and of the narrative gifts of the chronicler will naturally turn to the account of the assassination of Pizarro, which will be found vol. ii. pp. 160–88. We are glad to see announced in the same "Library" the 'Ferdinand and Isabella' of Prescott, his earliest work, which first attracted to him the attention of readers. Though more *arriéré* than its author's subsequent writings, this work has not lost its attraction for students of Spanish history.

Westminster Abbey. By Charles Hiatt.—*The Cathedral Church of Chichester.* By Hubert C. Corlette, A.R.I.B.A.—*Amiens : its Cathedral and Churches.* By the Rev. Thomas Perkins. (Bell & Sons.)

These three volumes constitute the latest additions to the delightful "Cathedral Series" of Messrs. Bell and to cognate series. Mr. Hiatt's 'Westminster Abbey' may claim to be one of the best written of the series. In the matter of the illustrations, which constitute a special attraction, a uniform standard of excellence is preserved. In the case of Westminster, however, matter is superabundant, and the task of choosing from authorities early and late has offered little difficulty to a practised writer. The history of Westminster is, moreover, itself of exceptional interest, the building being, as Mr. Hiatt says, more than any other edifice "representative of the history and genius of the English race." Like many other noble fanes, and more than most, it has suffered from the restorer. The destruction of exquisite details by Wren and his successors is a matter of unending regret. The pre-eminence of Westminster as a Campo Santo has done something to lower the popular estimate of it as a cathedral church. As such, however, it is pronounced the equal of Lincoln, Ely, Salisbury, Peterborough, Durham, and Canterbury. Its situation and the vicinage of other buildings do something to prevent full recognition of its external majesty.

With its magnificent situation Chichester constitutes a lovely landmark, and its campanile and its environments generally are delightful. In spite of the ravages of fire and of storm and the consequent restoration, it remains a building of singular interest and beauty, while its proximity to Brighton renders it an object of frequent pilgrimage. The bell tower is the only one of its kind in England, and the central tower and spire, modern as they are, reproduce faithfully the features of the old.

It is astonishing to think how few of the thousands of Englishmen who hurry through to Paris remain to see the noble shrine of Amiens. The same is true of Abbeville and of many cities of interest in the Isle de France. Amiens, however, is one of the noblest religious edifices in France, and a visit to it to the lover of ecclesiastical architecture is as much a duty as an annual excursion to Chartres. We can only advise one who has not made the pilgrimage recently to slip into his pocket this useful little volume and go there this Easter. Should he take our advice, we are certain of earning his gratitude. Books on Amiens are abundant, but there is room for this of Mr. Perkins, the designs and letterpress of which are alike commendable. Our interest in these admirable works augments as the series extends.

The most important article in this month's *Antiquary* is the one in which Mr. Neilson undertakes to show that, although Huchown's 'Morte Arthure' was "centrally concerned with the King Arthur of Geoffrey of Monmouth," yet it "drew largely for its amplifications of detail......upon the circumstances of its own time"; so that the chief figure may be considered a blend of the traditionary hero of romance and Edward III.

The *Giornale di Erudizione* still gives us a very useful biographical bulletin in addition to its notes, queries, and answers. In one of the later numbers there is a question as to a passage in the 'Heptameron' in which the phrase "Car le feu auprès des estoupes n'est point seur" occurs. It would be interesting to know when the comparison of the love of man and woman to fire and tow was first made use of in literature.

The discussion of that vexed question, the *jus primæ noctis*, still continues in the *Intermédiaire*, and the evidence given suggests that certain overlords may have imagined themselves to possess the right, but this abuse of feudal power is scarcely to be regarded as a recognized institution. It is not unlikely that the payment of marriage-fees to the lord of a manor when a girl wedded outside its bounds, and thus brought about the loss of services due from her on his estate, led to the assumption that he had theoretically a more personal claim on her than ancient custom and law in reality allowed.

Notices to Correspondents.

We must call special attention to the following notices :—

On all communications must be written the name and address of the sender, not necessarily for publication, but as a guarantee of good faith.

We cannot undertake to answer queries privately.

To secure insertion of communications correspondents must observe the following rules. Let each note, query, or reply be written on a separate slip of paper, with the signature of the writer and such address as he wishes to appear. When answering queries, or making notes with regard to previous entries in the paper, contributors are requested to put in parentheses, immediately after the exact heading, the series, volume, and page or pages to which they refer. Correspondents who repeat queries are requested to head the second communication "Duplicate."

Nemo.—("Oil on Troubled Waters.")—See 6th S. x. 351, 360, 460, and innumerable other references.

Corrigenda.—P. 60, col. 1, l. 9, for "J. Rawson Lumley" read *J. Rawson Lumby ;* p. 218, col. 2, l. 11, for "Fate" read *Kate.*

NOTICE.

Editorial communications should be addressed to "The Editor of 'Notes and Queries'"—Advertisements and Business Letters to "The Publisher"—at the Office, Bream's Buildings, Chancery Lane, E.C.

We beg leave to state that we decline to return communications which, for any reason, we do not print; and to this rule we can make no exception.

LONDON, SATURDAY, APRIL 5, 1902.

CONTENTS. — No. 223.

Notes.

AN UNKNOWN FLEETWOOD PEDIGREE.

(See 'Miniature of Col. Geo. Fleetwood,' *ante*, pp. 48, 154, 175, 234.)

SINCE my last communication (p. 234), by the courtesy of Capt. Robert Harding Evans, Honorary Clerk to the Glass Sellers' Company, I have been enabled to examine the records of the company, and the following notes therefrom, combined with particulars from the wills and other sources, may, if MR. W. D. PINK's view be correct, be of some interest.

'The Book for Entry of Apprentices to Freemen of the Company of Glass Sellers, London,' contains the following entries :—

" Fleetwood, Robert, sonne of George Fleetwood, late of Chalfont in the County of Bucks, Gent., decd., putts himself apprentice to John Angevine for Eight years from the xxiii day of June last by Inde date 9th (?) November, 1674."

" To Kempster. But to serve with and be turned over to John Kempster."

" Fleetwood, Robert, the sonn of Robert Fleetwood, citizen and glass-seller of London, putts himself apprentice to his said father for seaven years from the date of his Indentures. dated the xxº March, 1700."

" Fleetwood, John, the sonn of Robert Fleetwood, Citizen and Glass Seller of London, putts himselfe Apprentice to his Father the said Robert Fleetwood for seaven yeares from the date of his Indentures. Date xviith June, 1708."

" Fleetwood, Robert, son of Robert Fleetwood, late Citizen and Glass Seller of London, deceased, putts himselfe Apprentice to Miles Halsey, Citizen and Glass Seller, of London, for seven Years from the Date of his Indentures. Dated 18th June, 1734."

" Fleetwood, John, Son of Robert Fleetwood, late a Member of this Company, deceased, putts himself Apprentice to Mr. John Fleetwood, Citizen and Glasseller [*sic*] of London, for seven years from the date of his Indentures. Dated 19th June, 1735."

The Minute Book of the Courts shows that John Fleetwood (the elder) was chosen and sworn Master 28 September, 1738, and 27 September, 1739, so that he served for two years.

In old directories between 1749 and 1760 I find " John Fleetwood Leadenhall Street," and in directories between 1763 and 1770, " John Fleetwood Ludgate Hill " (No. 12 in 1768 and 1770).

In the Poll of the Liverymen of the City of London at election of Members of Parliament, begun Tuesday, 10 April, 1722, is " Fleetwood, John, Glass Sellers " (no address given) ; and in the Poll 16-23 March, 1768 : " Fleetwood, John, Glass Sellers, Ludgate Hill ; Fleetwood, Robert, Glass Sellers, Ludgate Hill."

The following are abstracts of two wills : John Fleetwood, citizen and glass seller of London. Will dated 27 December, 1759 ; proved 17 January, 1760, by the executor. To nephew Robert Fleetwood, eldest son of late brother Robert Fleetwood, 1,000*l.* To niece Jane Fenton. widow, 50*l.*, " in case she gives my executor hereinafter named, within one month after my decease, the picture for a watch of my late grandfather, Colonel George Fleetwood, deceased, otherwise the said legacy of 50*l.*" to sink into residuary estate. To grandniece Jane Fenton, daughter of Jane Fenton, 50*l.* To Mrs. Mary Wiggan, 50*l.* Remainder of estate to John Fleetwood, youngest son of late brother Robert. Sole executor, John Fleetwood, the nephew. Witnesses : Maria Barton, Reginald Dennison.

Robert Fleetwood, of Ludgate Hill, merchant. Will dated 13 April, 1769 ; proved 15 March, 1771, by the three executors. Bequeaths all freeholds, &c., and real estate to his wife Sarah for life, with remainder to his only child Jane. To wife one-third and to daughter one-third of personal estate by custom of the City ; and as to wife, in accordance with ante-nuptial settlement of 3 October, 1757. Out of remaining third : To brother John Fleetwood, 50*l.* To sister Fleetwood (wife of John ?), 50*l.* To sister-in-law Miss Mary

Purvas, 20 guineas. To Mr. Miles Halsey, 20 guineas. To brother John Fleetwood, as executor, 20 guineas. To John Roberts, as executor, 20 guineas. After legacies, remainder invested for wife's life interest, and then to daughter Jane if married with consent of guardians (his wife and Mary Purvas); contingent remainder to children of John Fleetwood. Executors, wife, John Fleetwood, and John Roberts. Witnesses: Michael Clarke, S. Barker, Regd. Dennison.

The first Robert Fleetwood appears to have succeeded his master, as in 'Genealogical Gleanings in England,' by Henry F. Waters, in the will of John Kempster, of Plaistow, in Essex, citizen and glass seller of London, 7 March, 1686, proved 6 June, 1687, there is a bequest :—

"......To my grandson John Whiston and his heirs, &c.......and also the lease of my house in Leadenhall Street, now in possession of Robert Fleetwood, glass seller......"

The following, from the same valuable work, is interesting :—

"Will of John Oldfield of London, Esq., 30 ——, 1656, proved 3 Novr., 1657.

"......To my two grandchildren John and Ann Fleetwood, son and daughter of my daughter Katherine, wife to Col. George Fleetwood, I say to John Fleetwood 500l., to be paid to his father, now Sir George Fleetwood, upon security, &c., and to Ann Fleetwood 500l., payable (as above)."

In a foot-note Mr. Waters says :—

"Col. George Fleetwood, otherwise called Sir George Fleetwood, was, I suppose, that regicide, one of Cromwell's lords, who is said to have died in America."

From the above notes I compile the following pedigree :—

Col. George Fleetwood, of Chalfont, co. Bucks, died in or prior to 1674.

Robert Fleetwood, son of above, apprenticed 23 June, 1674 (indenture dated 9 [?] November, 1674).

Robert, son of Robert above named, apprenticed to father 20 March, 1700 ; John apprenticed 17 June, 1708.

Robert the second died in or prior to 1734, and left issue :—

1. Robert, eldest son, of Ludgate Hill, married Sarah Purvas, and had only one child Jane.

2. Jane married —— Fenton, and had issue a daughter Jane. It is not absolutely clear that she was daughter of Robert the second.

3. John, youngest son, apprenticed to uncle John Fleetwood 19 June, 1735 ; residuary legatee and executor under uncle's will.

John (the elder), son of Robert (the first) ; will proved 17 January, 1760 ; Master of the Glass Sellers' Company, 1738-9 and 1739-40.

In his will occurs the bequest subject to the return of the miniature.

I have purposely omitted the grandchildren mentioned in the Oldfield will, though the regicide had a daughter named Ann, as I have not seen the full text of the regicide's will. The only point which seems to require explanation is the description of George Fleetwood in the register of apprentices as "gentleman" simply ; but there is no real difficulty in this, as his colonelcy was in the Parliamentary army, and the knighthood was conferred by Cromwell in the autumn of 1656 ('Dictionary of National Biography').

I submit that the evidence all points to the miniature being a portrait of George, the regicide, and in all probability a replica by Cooper. Is it still in existence? If it can be found, it will be most interesting to compare it with the only other known portrait of him by Samuel Cooper.

In conclusion, I desire to express my indebtedness to Mr. Gery Milner-Gibson-Cullum, F.S.A., for information regarding his miniature, and also to Capt. Evans for permission to examine the records of the Glass Sellers' Company, without which I could not have filled in the missing links in the pedigree.   R. W. B.

ADDITIONS TO THE 'N.E.D.'

(Continued from p. 144.)

Aerograph (not in).—1898, *Brit. Journ. Photog.*, 29 April, p. 274, "Enlargements finished with the aerograph in water colours and monochrome."

Aich metal (not in).—1895, Bloxam, 'Chem.,' p. 441, "Aich metal is a kind of brass containing iron."

Air-brush (not in).—1901, *Brit. Journ. Photog.*, 1 November, p. 696, "The aerograph is probably better known to the majority of photographers as the air-brush......It may be summarized as an instrument producing a spray which issues from a minute nozzle, and which can be directed wherever desired."

Alerce (*Libocedrus tetragona*); also *Alerse.*— 1893, Spon, 'Mechanic's Own Book,' p. 127 (fourth edition).

Alerce-wood (*Callitris quadrivalvis*).—1893, Spon, *ut supra*, p. 127, "This was the celebrated citrus-wood of the ancient Romans, the timber of the gum sandarac tree."

Ambitti (not in).—1893, Spon, *ut supra*, p. 630, "Ambitti (single and double) is a sheet glass, originally of Italian manufacture, and much prized by glass-painters."

Ananas oil (not in).—1895, Bloxam, *ut supra*, p. 623, "Ethyl butyrate......is sold as ananas oil, or essence of pineapple."

Antigraph (earlier).—*C.* 1600 (title), 'The Comparison betwene the Antipus and the Antigraphe, or Answere thereunto."—Lowndes, *s.v.* 'Antipus.'

Apple.—1893, Spon, *ut supra*, p. 127, "The so-called apple-tree of Queensland (*Angophora subvelutina*) yields planks 20 to 30 in. in diameter."

Apple oil (not in).—1895, Bloxam, 'Chem.,' p. 623 (eighth edition), "Amyl valerate, or apple oil."

Aurantia (not in).—1899, 'Orthochromatic Phot.' (ed. Tennant), p. 281, "Aurantia is an orange-yellow coal-tar dye much used in dyeing leathers."

Auxochrome (not in).—Bloxam, *ut supra*, p. 662, "An acid auxochrome will yield an acid dyestuff."

Avidity (=affinity of acids for bases).—Bloxam, *ut supra*, p. 285, "If the avidity of nitric acid be taken as 1, that of sulphuric acid is 0·5."

Bacillicide (not in).—1894, *Lancet*, 3 Nov., p. 1022, "Sunshine and pure air are the best bacillicides." Also attrib., p. 1021.

Back, v. (techn. sense, not in).—1892, W. K. Burton, 'Mod. Phot.' (tenth ed.), p. 106, "In the case of an attempt being made to photograph a very trying object, such as the interior mentioned, it is well to back the plate; that is, to paint or otherwise cover it at the back with some substance that will absorb light."

Backage (not in).—1894, Du Maurier, 'Trilby,' in *Harper's Mag.*, June, p. 68.

Bacteriophobia (not in). — 1894, *Lancet*, 3 Nov., p. 1072, "Your readers will accuse me of bacteriophobia."

Baisoned (not in).—1894, S. R. Crockett, 'Raiders,' p. 270, "I ken the breed [of horses] by the bonny baisoned face o' him."

Bald-pate, the American wigeon (*Mareca americana*, Gmn.). — 1889, H. Saunders, 'Man. Brit. Birds,' p. 428.

Balliage.—See 'Bailage' in 'N.E.D.'

Barker, the avocet (*Recurvirostra avoceta*, L.).—Saunders, *ut supra*, p. 546.

Barkometer (not in).—1853, Morfit, 'Arts of Tanning,' &c., p. 318, "Burbidge regulates the strength of the extract [of oak-bark] by a hydrometer especially adapted to the purpose, which he calls a barkometer"; *ibid.*, p. 329, "That [hydrometer] referred to above has been styled by its maker [W. Pike, of New York] a barkometer, because it is specially adapted to testing the strength of bark lyes."

Basiliskishly (not in).—1844, Hewlett, 'Parsons and Widows,' xxxiii., "Jonathan, looking at me basiliskishly."

Bask (later).—1894, S. R. Crockett, 'Raiders,' p. 24, "It was a bask day in early spring."

Bathmism (not in).—1887, E. D. Cope, 'Origin of Fittest,' in Wallace, 'Darwinism,' p. 421, "A special developmental force termed 'bathmism,' or growth force."

Bawn is explained in a note to Swift's 'Grand Question Debated,' 1729 (ed. 1778, ii. 220), as a cattle-fold.

Bearding (earlier). — 1711, Sutherland, 'Shipbuilder's Assistant,' p. 53, "Placing one limb on the bearding"; *ibid.*, p. 52, "This is termed bearding the channel-wales."

Becket (earlier).—Sutherland, *ut supra*, p. 145, "Beckets upon the cap, as big as the lifts."

Beckhorn (=Bickern).—1893, Spon, 'Mechanic's Own Book,' p. 193, "Beckhorn and swivel-joint attachment."

Beddy (not in).—1829, Glover, 'Hist. Derby,' i. 88, "The freestones......often called building stone, or ashler (in distinction from beddy stone, flags or paviers, and slate or tile stones)."

Bee (earlier).—1848, G. Biddlecombe, 'Art of Rigging,' p. 81, "Fore topmast stays set up through the bees of the bowsprit, through which the stays pass."

Belland (not in, cf. Bellon). — 1829, Glover, 'Hist. Derby,' p. 68, "The fourth [kind of lead ore], which is caught by a very slow stream of water, and is as fine as flour, is termed belland; it is inferior to all the others, on account of the admixture of foreign particles."

Bellite (not in).—Bloxam, *ut supra*, p. 322, "The explosive Bellite consists of 5 parts of ammonium nitrate and 1 part of di-nitro-benzene."

Belting (not in, cf. Belt, sb. 3).—See 'Birling' below.

Bench, v.—1891, *Times*, 28 October, p. 11, col. 5, "Almost every breed of spaniel is benched."

Bend (not in, cf. Bend, 6). — 1711, Sutherland, 'Shipbuilder's Assistant,' p. 158, "Bend of Moulds, or a whole Suit; one of every sort. Bend of Riders, one of a sort of each side."

Bend (earlier).—1711, Sutherland, *ut supra*, p. 131, "Cable-bends."

Bensilling (not in, cf. Bensel).—1894, Crockett, 'Raiders,' p. 74, "The bensilling wind off the Baltic lands."

Bermy (cf. Berm).—1890, *Century Mag.*, November, p. 125, "Finally the pleasant bermy banks gave out entirely" ('In a Canyon').

Bevering Moth (not in, *Acherontia atropos?*).—1791, *Trans. Soc. Arts*, ix. 115, "To keep out the bevering moth, which you may often see, at the latter end of August......standing at the mouth of the hive, bevering their wings as if just flying in among the bees."

Bieldy (later).—1894, Crockett, 'Raiders,' p. 368, "The place was bieldy."

Bifurcature (not in).—1819, G. Samouelle, 'Entomologist's Compendium,' p. 159, "Bifurcature of the sternum lanceolate."

Bike.—Slang for bicycle.

Bindles (not in).—1890, F. Anstey Guthrie, 'The Pariah,' p. 192, "Bindles, my dear fellow!......Sheer bindles."

Biograph (not in). — 1898, *Brit. Journ. Photog. Alm.*, p. 655, "The exhibition of animated photographs on a larger scale than usual, by the biograph, the invention of an American, Mr. Casler."

Birling (not in).—1829, Glover, 'Hist. Derby,' i. 213, "The long tails of the male sheep are separately sheared; and the wool, which is called birling or belting, is sold for carpet-making."

Bisontine (not in).—1890, R. C. Auld in *American Naturalist*, September, p. 790, "Compare the animal in his natural bisontine condition with the fleshless results among the bovines under the same conditions."

Black Curlew (not in).—1889, H. Saunders, 'Man. Brit. Birds,' p. 379, "The glossy ibis (*Plegadis falcinellus*, L.)......was known to gunners and fishermen as the 'black curlew.'"

Black Fly (not in).—1892, Sutton, 'Cult. Veget. Flow.' (fifth edition), p. 380, "The Blue and the Black Fly are common plagues of the peach-house and the orchard" (Aphis).

Blaff, sb. (not in).—1894, Crockett, 'Raiders,' p. 23, "Many the time also that I have fallen with an unco blaff (serious downfall) because I have neglected to heed his warnings."

Blaff, v. (cf. Blaff, v.). — Crockett, *ut sup.*, p. 70, "They [pistols] 'll be gaun blaffin' aff when there's mair need to be as quiet as an ashleaf."

Blastie (rare).—Crockett, *ut sup.*, p. 76, "Yae word, ye crawlin' blastie, an' I'll let the life oot o' ye."

Blateroon (obs.? Survives in America). — 1890? Roland Wood (P. Cushing), 'Dr. Cæsar Crowl, Mind-Curer,' ii. 200.

Blay (not in).—1789, *Trans. Soc. Arts* (second edition), i. p. 206, "When I mention white flax, I do it in opposition to that which, being steeped in the bags, has the appellation of blay."

Blaze, a saw (not in).—Spon, *ut supra*, p. 66, "Saws are hardened in oil, or in a mixture of oil with suet, wax, &c. They are then heated over a fire till the grease inflames. This is called being blazed."

Blazer (small cooking apparatus).—1895, *Harper's Mag.*, May.

Block (earlier of sense 8).—1711, Sutherland, 'Shipbuilder's Assistant,' p. 158, "Blocks, sometimes hard knotty timber to lay under a ship."

Blond-metal (earlier).—1778, 'England's Gazetteer' (second edition), *s.v.* 'Wednesbury,' "Here is that sort of iron ore called blond-metal, used to make nails and horseshoes."

Blue.—Saunders, *ut supra*, mentions the following bird-names : p. 617, the Blue Darr, the black tern (*Hydrochelidon nigra*, L.); p. 7, the Blue Felt, the fieldfare (*Turdus pilaris*, L.); p. 655, the Blue Maa, the common gull (*Larus canis*, L.); p. 469, the Blue Rock (a misnomer), the stock-dove (*Columba œnas*, L.); p. 35, the Bluethroat (*Cyanecula suecica*, L.).

Bobble.—1836, T. Hook, 'Gilbert Gurney,' iii. 316, "The ship was comfortably bobbling herself about at Spithead."

Body (later in sense 10).—1758, Reid, trl. Macquer, 'Chym.,' i. 302, "We directed the gold to be dissolved in a tall body." 1827, J. Mitchell, 'First Lines of Science,' 231, "Cucurbits, matrasses, or bodies, which are glass, earthen-ware, or metalline vessels, usually shaped like an egg, and open at top."

Boheic (not in).—1853, Morfit, 'Arts of Tanning,' &c., p. 78, "Rochelder found boheic acid, also, in the latter [black tea]."

Bolivite (not in).—1895, Bloxam, 'Chem.' (eighth edition), p. 400, "Bolivite is an oxysulphide [of bismuth]."

Bollow (not in).—1711, Sutherland, 'Shipbuilder's Assistant,' 158, "Bollow, the opposite to hollow."

Boom (cf. Boom, vb. 2).—1831, E. J. Trelawny, 'Advent. of Younger Son,' xxx. (ed. 1890), "Four or five irregular yellow-crusted tusks boomed from his jaw, like a wild hog's."

Boracised (not in).—1901, *Daily Mail*, 27 November, p. 3, col. 3, "Boracised milk has an injurious effect upon the health of very young children."

Bore (person ; earlier).—1799, H. More, 'Female Education' (fourth edition), i. 18, "Every individual......must earn the title of pleasant, or...... must be consigned over to ridicule under the vulgar and inexpressive cant word of a bore."

Bornite (not in).—1896, *Times*, 21 August, "The wealth and working of the great bornite mine at Nelson (British Columbia)."

Bostle (not in).—1894, *Athenæum*, 19 May, p. 636, and 'Glimpses of Sussex Ancestors,' i. 97.

Boul (later).—1894, Crockett, 'Raiders,' 205, "Wi' my broth in a tin can that she was carryin' by the bool (hoop)."

Bracket (= Brachet).—1778, 'England's Gazetteer,' *s.v.* 'Grafton.'

Brandly (not in).—1645, Tullie, 'Siege of Carlisle' (1840), p. 38, "Ye enemy fired brandly upon him."

Brank (obs.).—1893, *Times*, 11 July, p. 4, col. 1, "Brank, or buckwheat, may......be grown with advantage."

Branning (no quot.).—1853, Morfit, 'Arts of Tanning,' &c., 410, "They [the skins] are now ready for the branning, and for this purpose undergo a steeping......in a 'drench' of forty pounds of bran and twenty gallons of water."

Brash (also Braish, cf. deriv.).—1793, *Trans. Soc. Arts*, iv. p. 21 (second edition), "The soil, a stone braish, inclining to sand."

Brass (sense 1e, earlier).—1829, Glover, 'Hist. Derby,' i. 234, "Many of the coal-seams......have considerable quantities of brasses or drosses in them, which are lumps of iron pyrites."

Brawl (ppl. 'Braling' in).—1645, Tullie, 'Siege of Carlisle' (1840), p. 47.

Breast (earlier).—1711, Sutherland, 'Shipbuilder's Assistant,' 158, "Breast of a Ship, see Bow. Breasthooks, large Knees fitted to the foremost Part within. Breast-backstay, that which is placed at the side of the Mast, stopping the fore Part as well as the aft."

Breech (sense 5c, no quot.). — Sutherland, *ut supra*, 158, "Breech, the outward Bending of Knee-Timber."

Bridge (not in).—1901, Prof. Hoffmann, 'Bridge Whist,' p. 4, "Bridge is a game for four players."

Brime (not in, cf. Briming).—1893, R. Kipling, 'Many Inventions,' p. 11, "Dowse could see him of a clear night, when the sea brimed, climbing about the buoys, with the sea-fire dripping off him."

Broadleaf.—Also a New Zealand tree (*Griselinia littoralis*). Spon, p. 129.

Bronzing.—1892, W. K. Burton, 'Mod. Phot.,' p. 140, "Bronzing is an appearance which is seen only in the shadows of prints got from negatives showing very bold contrasts......The appearance is that of a metallic lustre in the deepest shadows."

Brunneous (earlier).—1819, Samouelle, 'Entom. Comp.,' 234, "Body brunneous, sometimes inclined to a rust colour."

Brunolic Acid (not in).—1865, Gesner, 'Pract. Treat. Coal, Petroleum' (second edition), p. 94.

Budgerigar (not in), a parrakeet.—1891, *Bazaar, Exchange, and Mart*, 20 Feb., "Adult pair of budgerigars."

Buffle (cf. the word).—1765, 'Treat. on Domestic Pigeons,' p. 97, "The powter that buffles, which is, being stiff-winded, fills his crop so full of wind that it is thereby strained."

Bug (not in as an instrument for cheating at cards).—1894, illustrated in Maskelyne, 'Sharps and Flats,' p. 81.

Bull, v. — 1831, Trelawny, 'Advent. Younger Son' (1890), ch. lxviii. p. 286, "His messmates having bulled an empty rum cask, that is......put in a gallon of water, there to remain, with an occasional roll, for twenty-four hours, when it turns out good stiff grog."

Bullion (cf. the sense).—Spon, p. 630, "Roundels and bullions are small discs of glass, some made with a knob in the centre, and used in fretwork with cathedral glass."

Bumble-bee, v. (not in).—1844, J. T. Hewlett, 'Parsons and Widows,' ch. x., "He bumble-bee'd and tromboned through the prayers."

Bunkering (not in).—1893, *Times*, 11 July, p. 3, col. 6, "The ordinary rate of bunkering coal by manual labour."

Bunting-Lark, the corn bunting. — 1889, H. Saunders, 'Man. Brit. Birds,' p. 199.

Burl (cf. the sense).—1893, Spon, 'Mechanic's Own Book,' p. 350, "The log, or burl, being 10 ft.

long." *Ibid.*, "The ash-burls are brought in from the surrounding country."

Burlesquecal (not in).—1747, *Gent. Mag.*, 40, "A satirical, burlesquecal, ironical, dogmatical translation."

Burner (earlier).—1778, 'England's Gazetteer,' *s.v.* 'Westminster,' "32 lamps with each 3 burners."

Burr (veneer, not in).—Spon, *ut supra*, p. 357, "When French walnut burr is buckled or cockled." *Ibid.*, "Walnut burrs are best cut with scissors."

Burrel-fly (later).—1829, Glover, 'Hist. Derby,' i. 177, "*Œstrus Bovis*, Whame or Burrel Fly.—Lays eggs on horses in August."

Bushelage (no quot.).—1778, 'England's Gazetteer,' *s.v.* 'Lostwithiel,' "Its once flourishing trade is decayed, but it holds the bushelage of coals, salt, malt and corn in the town of Fowey."

Butter-ball, the buffel-headed duck (*Clangula albeola*, L.).—Saunders, *ut supra*, p. 442.

Butterick (not in, but see 'Butter-rigged' and quot.).—1901, J. L. Ford, in *Munsey's Mag.*, July, p. 534, "What is technically known as the 'butterick,' a picture of two or more persons in conversational attire [*sic*], and usually amid the most luxurious surroundings. They are supposed to be 'getting off' the humorous dialogue that accompanies it. There is no attempt at humour in the drawing of the butterick."

Butt-joint (v., not in).—Spon, *ut supra*, p. 361, "There are 3 or 4 ways of butt-jointing curls."

J. DORMER.

Redmorion, Woodside Green, S.E.

(*To be continued.*)

"ANCE" AND "ANE."—In the glossary appended to his edition of Burns's 'Poems and Songs' the late Mr. Scott Douglas says that "ance" and "ane," the Scottish spellings respectively for *once* and *one*, are usually pronounced "yince" and "yin." This is somewhat too absolute, and may mislead incautious readers. In a note the editor says that he had satisfied himself that such was the pronunciation in use among the poet's countrymen of Ayrshire and Dumfriesshire. He indicates also that this conclusion is supported by the practice of dwellers in the Lothians, but he hesitates regarding Lowlanders north of the Forth. The rimes in Burns's lyrics raise some difficulty against the establishment of Mr. Scott Douglas's theory in the poet's case. "Ance" occurs less frequently as a terminal word than "ane," and when so used it does not give definite guidance in the matter of sound. In 'Hallowe'en,' stanza iv., it rimes to "anes," from which no inference as to pronunciation is possible apart from what may be gathered otherwise with reference to "ane." Again, in 'The Kirk's Alarm,' stanza xv., "ance" responds to "sins," a fact which may or may not favour the contention of Mr. Scott Douglas. With regard to "ane" it is possible to be more decided. Mr. Douglas adduces in support of his view the penulti-

mate stanza of the song 'Philly and Willy,' in which the swain protests in these terms :—

> Let fortune's wheel at random rin,
> And fools may tyne, and knaves may win ;
> My thoughts are a' bound up in ane,
> And that's my ain dear Philly.

All that needs to be said regarding this is that, while those who use the pronunciation "yin" will find a perfect rime in the stanza, the thousands of Scotsmen who make "ane" rime to "mane" are not likely to cavil at the arrangement as it stands. Should they be critically disposed, they will regard the structure as illustrative of a legitimate assonance, and quietly pass it by. There is a similar indefiniteness in the accord of "ane" and "mine" in the second stanza of the song 'Gala Water,' of "braw ane" and "thrawing" in the twenty-third stanza of 'Hallowe'en,' and of "new ane" and "ruin" in the fourth stanza of the ode 'To a Mouse.' Similar to this last is the rime in the third stanza of the P.S. to the 'Epistle to William Simpson,' where "new ane" is made to respond to "viewin"; and towards the end of 'The Twa Herds' we find this, which may be placed with the example given by Mr. Scott Douglas from 'Philly and Willy' :—

> Forbye turncoats amang oursel',
>   There's Smith for ane,
> I doubt he's but a gray-nick quill,
>   And that ye'll fin'.

Probably the ordinary versifier would find it as difficult to discover a rime for Ecclefechan as for the proverbial "porringer," but Burns readily accomplished the feat, duly adjusting in the proper place the guttural "laigh ane," and producing this :—

> My gutcher has
> A hich house and a laigh ane,
> A' forbye my bonnie sel',
> The toss o' Ecclefechan.

There does not seem to be here the sound desiderated by Mr. Scott Douglas. On the other hand, there is no doubt whatever as to the pronunciation requisite in the second stanza of the song 'As I was a-wandering' :—

> Weel, since he has left me, my pleasure gae wi'
>   him ;
> I may be distress'd, but I winna complain ;
> I flatter my fancy I may get anither,
>   My heart it shall never be broken for ane.

The rime in stanza xvi. of 'Death and Dr Hornbook' is equally clear :—

> 'Twas but yestreen, nae farther gane,
> I threw a noble throw at ane ;
> Wi' less, I'm sure, I've hundreds slain :
>   But de'il-ma'-care,
> It just play'd dirl on the bane,
>   But did nae mair.

On the whole, if judgment is to be given

from the manifest practice of the poet, one is inclined to decide against rather than for the proposition of one of the most competent among Burns's editors. It may be well to rest our conclusion on a compromise. As Burns's father belonged to Kincardineshire he probably said "ane" and "ance," as is the custom on the east coast of Scotland, north-wards of the Forth, while his mother, an Ayrshire woman, would pronounce the words "yin" and "yince," if the editorial informa-tion regarding the practice in the south-western counties is correct. Both from his upbringing and from his experience of Scottish cities and men, the poet would be familiar with the two methods of pronuncia-tion, and, according to his wont, would treat the matter easily, leaving readers to decide for themselves. But he could hardly fail to think "yin" and "yince" erroneous.

THOMAS BAYNE.

'THE NORWICH ROAD,' BY C. G. HARPER.—In this interesting book a curious mistake occurs at p. 120. Anthony Trollope is made to kill Mrs. Proudie in 'Barchester Towers.' As a matter of fact, that well-meaning woman lived through 'Barchester Towers,' 'Dr. Thorne,' and 'Framley Parsonage,' and died in 'The Last Chronicle of Barset.'

GEORGE ANGUS.

St. Andrews, N.B.

BATTLE OF MELITENE.—In the *Philosophical Transactions* for 1853 (vol. cxliii. part i.) there is a paper by the last Astronomer Royal (afterwards Sir George Airy) on ancient eclipses. In discussing the locality of one of these he says (p. 193): "At Melitene was fought the important battle. A.D. 572, between the Emperor Tiberius and Chosroes Nushirvan." An ordinary reader would be somewhat amazed at this passage, as the name Tiberius suggests the stepson of Augustus, who ruled the Roman world when our Lord was crucified. But those familiar with the history of the later empire would perceive that the monarch in question was the one who reigned at Constantinople, and is called, for distinction's sake, Tiberius II. Airy, however, is not quite accurate in his statement. The reign of Tiberius II.—of the prudence of whose rule Mr. Bury takes a much less favourable view than did Gibbon—commenced in A.D. 578, and lasted only four years, until A.D. 582. The reign of the King of Persia, Chosroes Nushirvan, extended from A.D. 531 to 579. During his last war with the Romans, which commenced in A.D. 572, Justin II. was Emperor of Constantinople; he adopted Tiberius as Cæsar in 574; but the general who commanded in the Persian war was Justinian, the son of Germanus. Melitene, or in the Oriental form Malathiah, which was destroyed by Chosroes in his retreat, is in Lesser Armenia, near the Upper Euphrates.

W. T. LYNN.

Blackheath.

"FLAPPER," ANGLO-INDIAN SLANG.—The following seems to be an example of English slang revived in the East, shorn of the offen-sive implication which once attached to it, for which see Barrère and Leland's 'Dic-tionary of Slang,' *s.v.* 'Flippers':—

"'But you're a butterfly in Society, and this may give you something to do, when you are off duty with the flappers.' 'Flapper' is elegant Anglo-Indian for any spinster from home."—*Temple Bar*, February, 1902, p. 157.

W. CROOKE.

Langton House, Charlton Kings.

OWENS COLLEGE JUBILEE.—Full reports have appeared in the press of the jubilee of Owens College, but 'N. & Q.' should have a short note by way of reference.

A complete history of the college down to 1886 has been written by Mr. Alderman Thompson, who has been associated with it from its earliest years, and who has always been among its most ardent promoters. To him I was indebted for much information concerning the college when compiling my book on the fifty years' work of the *Athenæum*. On the 12th of March he had the satisfaction of handing the keys of the Whitworth Hall to the Prince of Wales.

The success of the college is now so com-plete that it is hard to realize the struggle it had for very life in its early years. The *Manchester Guardian* in its leading article on the 9th of July, 1858, distinctly pro-nounced the college to be a failure, and the *Manchester Examiner* on the 20th of the same month stated that "the most that can be said of the college is that it is too good for us......The crowd rolls along Deansgate heed-less of the proximity of Plato and Aristotle." Owens College, however, was not to be a failure, thanks to the undaunted zeal of the men associated with it. The *Athenæum* of the 19th of October, 1872, records that "its coming of age has been properly signalized by its change from a private to a public in-stitution by special Act of Parliament; the old trustees have abolished themselves in favour of forty-two governors......Thus has the simple scheme of the executors of Mr. Owens developed in twenty-one years into an in-stitution possessing most of the elements of a university."

The first Principal of the college, Alexander John Scott, M.A., was a man who exercised great personal influence and won much affection. Maurice dedicated to him his 'Mediæval Philosophy,' Baldwin Brown his 'Home Life in the Light of the Divine Idea,' and George Mac Donald his 'Robert Falconer.'

The first two scholarships founded were to commemorate the visit of Queen Victoria to Manchester in 1851. One, the Victoria (Classical Scholarship), was given by Samuel Fletcher, and the other, the Wellington (Greek Testament) Scholarship, in memory of the Duke of Wellington, who accompanied her Majesty. This was the gift of George Faulkner.

The recent celebration was in every way in accord with the directions left by the founder, that the college should be "free from the religious tests which limit the extension of university education." The opening service was held in the Cathedral, when the preacher was the Bishop of Manchester; the closing service, "by the request of the Court of Governors," was held in Union Chapel, Dr. Maclaren, the President of the Baptist denomination, upon whom the college has conferred the degree of Litt.D., being the preacher.

JOHN C. FRANCIS.

Queries.

WE must request correspondents desiring information on family matters of only private interest to affix their names and addresses to their queries, in order that the answers may be addressed to them direct.

HARRIETT POWELL. — Can any of your readers inform me through your columns where information can be obtained relating to Harriett Powell, afterwards Countess of Seaford, a notable actress and singer, whose portrait was painted by Sir Joshua Reynolds in 1796? I have searched all the usual sources of information, but can find no record of her or her career. I am also desirous of ascertaining the present location, if possible, of the above-mentioned portrait, or of either or both of the other two portraits of this lady, painted by C. Read and the Rev. W. Peters respectively.

W. H. W. P.

[Consult John Chaloner Smith's 'British Mezzotinto Portraits,' 1884, vol. ii. p. 682, &c.]

ST. BEES.—Who was this saint? A place named after her is in Cumberland, and is celebrated for a divinity college. Is it the same as St. Bede? G. A. BROWNE.

[Consult, under St. Bega or Bee, Baring-Gould's 'Lives of the Saints,' 6 September, vol. x. p. 92.]

RICHARD AND ED. ORIEL COWLAM. — In the 'Medical Register' of 1780 these two gentlemen appear under the heading of 'Surgeons and Apothecaries,' and as then being at "Newport. Isle of Wight." Richard Cowlam was the Mayor of Newport, but I am not sure of the years (? 1756 and 1764, and perhaps oftener). I much desire information as to their birth, baptism, parentage, marriage, death, place of burial, and any biographical particulars; also their relationship to each other. Does "Ed." stand for Edmund or Edward in this particular instance? C. MASON.

29, Emperor's Gate, S.W.

"ASTONISH THE NATIVES."—What is the origin of the proverbial use of the expression "to astonish the natives"? It occurs in inverted commas in 'The Ingoldsby Legends' ('Legend of St. Gengulphus'). I have found the expression in Gibbon's 'Decline and Fall,' chap. lii., under the sub-heading 'Magnificence of the Caliphs': "But his train of camels, laden with snow, could serve only to astonish the natives of Arabia," &c.

T. M. KOUGH.

MISPLACING OF A COMMA.—In a book by Robert Barr entitled 'The Mutable Many,' published by Methuen, on p. 109 the author commences a paragraph thus: "It is said that the misplacing of a comma in an Act of Parliament once cost the country a hundred thousand pounds." Will some courteous reader inform me what was the Act of Parliament referred to, and also the occasion of the assumed loss? F. CLAYTON.

Morden.

HEARTSEASE —Is there any legend of the heartsease or pansy in which the flower is named heartsease through having eased an aching or a wounded heart?

(Miss) L. TUCK.

New Barnes, Ely, Cambs.

AMELIA OPIE'S NOVELS.—Can any reader tell me whether any of the novels of Mrs. Opie have been reprinted? They seem to have been very largely read when first published, and it was proposed, I fancy by Routledge, to include them in the sixpenny edition of well-known novels which they brought out some twenty years since, but for some reason or other this was not done. I think that 'Temper,' which some consider her best work, has been reprinted in America, but I cannot find that either this or, indeed, any of her other works have ever been reprinted in England, though, of course, it is quite possible they may have been.   FREDERICK T. HIBGAME.

WYCH STREET.—In a report of the Building Act Committee of the London County Council, which appeared in the *Daily Telegraph* on 24 March, Wych Street, near St. Clement Danes, is mentioned as having "a characteristically Danish name." It would be interesting to know with what Danish word the name of this London street is connected. On what authority or on what evidence is this statement made?   COMESTOR OXONIENSIS.

INTRODUCTION OF TROUSERS.—Mr. Leader, in his 'Sheffield in the Eighteenth Century,' gives an amusing account of the introduction of trousers to the town. Are particulars recorded when they were first worn in other places?   WILLIAM ANDREWS.
Royal Institution, Hull.

[Trinity College, Cambridge, in October, 1812, made an order that any student appearing in hall or chapel in pantaloons or trousers should be deemed absent, from which it appears that they were beginning to oust briefer garments.]

QUOTATIONS. — Can you tell me where Ariston says?—

Θαρσί [?] βοηθεῖν πᾶσι τοῖς ἀξίοις
εἴωθεν ὁ θεός.

Also where Gregorius Nazianzenus says?—

Μήτε τὸ ἀλγεῖν ἀπαραμύθητον
μήτε τὸ εὖ πράττειν ἀπαιδαγώγητον μενέτω.
     DR. LOESCHE.
Vienna.

GIPSY VOCABULARY.—Will some kind gipsy scholar look through the list of words given in Dr. Richard Bright's 'Travels from Vienna through Lower Hungary' (Edinburgh, 1818), beginning on p. lxxx of the appendix, and inform me whether they are still in use among English gipsies? I fear that there is some confusion, but I may be wrong. Any additions to or corrections of the list will be gratefully received.   L. L. K.

ELLIOT. — Alexander Elliot and Robert Elliot were respectively admitted to Westminster School in 1769 and 1772. Can correspondents give me any information concerning them?   G. F. R. B.

DARCY OF HARVERTON.—I should be much obliged if any of your readers would inform me whether any record exists of the descent of Robert Darcy, of Harverton, co. Durham,

whose sister Katherine married John Hedworth. John Hedworth died in 1401, and it appears from Foster's Durham Visitation pedigrees that the Hedworths assumed the arms of Darcy.   G. O. B.

TOKEN FOUND IN THE STRAND.—In the rebuilding after the recent fire in New Inn, Strand, a bronze token was found imbedded in the brickwork. On one side was a representation of Norwich Castle and date 1794, and on the obverse a hanging sheep and the inscription "Good times will come." On the rim is inscribed "Richard Bacon Cockey Lane." Perhaps some of your East Anglian readers could throw some light on this. I believe the building where the fire occurred was erected over two hundred years ago.   ASHLEY H. JOHNSTON.

WINDSOR UNIFORM.—Can any reader tell me what was the "Windsor uniform," and who was entitled to wear it? An old portrait (about 1786) shows a blue coat with red collar, said to be this uniform. Any reference to books bearing on the subject would be acceptable. (Lieut.-Col.) G. S. PARRY.
18, Hyde Gardens, Eastbourne.

"LITTLE WILLIE."—Can any reader tell me where occur the words of a prayer?—

And please not to say
Little Willie almost stole an apple to-day.
     GEO. WASHINGTON MOON.
Hove, Sussex.

FIELD-NAMES, SOUTH-WEST LANCASHIRE.— Can any light be thrown on the following? Cadix Meadow; Loton (has this anything to do with an ambush?), was a wooded district in early times; Wrangling Croft; Bicol (called Bycall in 1597), anything in reference to the sea, which can be seen from the spot? Lum Hey; Long Shoot (three instances); Locker Field; Steven Stones, at base of a hill; Mars Croft; Big Sum Field; Formery; and four fields bearing the name Avorill.
     COULTHARD.

ADMIRAL FONTE'S VOYAGE.—Can any reader refer me to any works, other than the *Monthly Miscellany* (published in 1708), which treat of the voyage of Admiral Bartolomeo Fonte in the ship Holy Ghost?   C. KING.
Torquay.

GOVERNOR MICHAEL LAMBERT.—Is anything known of the parentage and of the history, public or private, of Michael Lambert, who was Lieutenant-Governor of St. Christopher's (St. Kitts) early in the eighteenth century, and died 6 March, 1723/4, in the seventieth year of his age, as recorded on his tombstone in the churchyard of the parish of St. Thomas in that island? Also, of what family was his wife Priscilla? Both are mentioned, and his monumental inscription is given, in the notes to Oliver's 'History of Antigua,' 3 vols. folio, London, 1894-9, and the names of three of their daughters, Mrs. Weatherill, Mrs. Douglas, and Mrs. Pym, appear, but without any account of the parents, who did not belong to the island of which Mr. Oliver has written the history so copiously and so well.

R. MARSHAM-TOWNSHEND.

GENESIS I. 1.—A rabbi of my acquaintance insists that the first three words mean "In the beginning He created *elohim, i.e.,* gods or powers." The word for "the heavens" is preceded by a particle, usually untranslated, which might mean "with relation to." Not being a Hebrew scholar, I ask whether the grammar of the passage, apart from theology, will bear such a rendering.

RICHARD H. THORNTON.
Portland, Oregon.

GENIUS AND INSANITY. — Seneca, quoting Aristotle, says: "Nullum magnum ingenium sine mixtura dementiæ fuit" ('Dialogues,' ix. § 17). Where is the sentence in the Stagirite from which the Roman translated this passage, which has been echoed ever since? Dryden put it :—

Great wits are sure to madness near allied,
And thin partitions do their bounds divide.

Shakespeare, who could not read either Aristotle or Seneca, after all had hit on the same idea, as he shows by classing together

The lunatic, the lover, and the poet.

JAMES D. BUTLER.
Madison, Wis.

SATIRICAL COLOURED PRINTS. — I have half a dozen old coloured prints, quarto size, each representing, in a spirit of satire, a man on horseback. Only one of them presents man and horse in a favourable light. This one shows a young buck, in a wide hat, green coat, and top boots, on the back of a sturdy brown cob, walking quietly along a country road. The title printed underneath is 'The Mistaken Notion.' What does this refer to? And from what book or collection of prints do these engravings come? They bear the inscription "H. Banbury, Esq., Delin. W. Dickinson Excudit," but no date. One of the prints is of an ugly man on an ugly horse, at cross-roads. The rider is awkwardly endeavouring to pull the horse's head in the direction of one turning, while the sorry hack is evidently determined to choose

another. In the background is an inn, the sign of which is a Golden Cross with the legend "In hoc signo vinces." The title at foot reads 'A Horse with a Nose.' From their appearance I should judge the date of these prints to be about 1780. Can any one enlighten me? JOHN HOBSON MATTHEWS.
Town Hall, Cardiff.

COURT ROLLS OF THE HONOUR OF RAYLEIGH, ESSEX.—In one of the MS. volumes of the late H. W. King, bequeathed to the Essex Archæological Society, of which he was hon. secretary for many years, are some extracts entitled 'Brief Notes taken by me 19 Aug., 1880, on a Casual Inspection of Two Large Volumes of Rolls of the Court Baron of the Honour of Raleigh.' Unfortunately, no reference is given as to the ownership or the place of custody of these rolls ; and hitherto all inquiries have been fruitless. I shall be thankful if any one can inform me of their present habitat. In his diary the last entry is dated just two months previous to the above. WALTER CROUCH.
Wanstead, Essex.

Replies.

THE WEST BOURNE.

(9ᵗʰ S. viii. 517 ; ix. 51, 92, 190.)

I THINK that COL. PRIDEAUX and readers to whom this question may be interesting (as doubtless it especially is to those who, like myself, live in the Westbourne district) must, for evidence of the original name of the stream, be content to find it in the name of the district. It is agreed, I think, that the territorial word "bourn," of French extraction, was not ingrafted on English stock until our own similar word, as an indigenous plant, had flourished for centuries. At the date of the first mention found of Westbourne—viz., 1222, it is not thought that the alien word had been imported, and for this reason, if for no other, the second syllable of the name cannot refer to land, or a land boundary, but to water—*i.e.,* a stream or bourne. Had there not been a western bourne the name Westland or Weston or Westham might have been naturally applied to the vil or manor, but not Westbourne. Thus reasoning, we may think that, while yet the virgin ground or primeval forest lay undisturbed, the London native, venturing thus far from his defended settlement, knew this stream as the western bourne ; and that in like manner it would be known to the mediæval citizen, who from his city gate went forth into the wide country a-fowling, a-maying, or perhaps attracted by the grim spectacle of the gallows.

Three streams of London vicinity would be known to the travelling citizen: (1) The River of Wells or springs, known also as the Hole-bourne, the bourne of holes or hollows, which, when it experienced the influence of the tidal Thames, became the Fleet, wherein small ships could float; (2) the bourne called, perhaps later, The Ey Bourne, or Tyburn, a name and subject highly charged with argument; and (3) the western stream or West Bourne would be reached, three and a half miles from the city walls, half a mile beyond the Ultima Thule of the condemned, and perhaps as far as the excursionist would venture. The name West Bourne was very simple, almost as primitive as that of the great river which absorbed its affluent, the Thames, the Tam-ese, the tranquil or spreading water. I learn from Isaac Taylor.

Having first mention of Westbourne as a vil belonging to the Abbot of Westminster in 1222, we continue to find record of it at later dates, and by the transmutation ably interpreted by SIR HERBERT MAXWELL at the third reference, the name, having been transferred to the vil or manor, appears to have been lost by the bourne itself. It would, then, seem to have become known simply as the bourne of the Westbourne manor. In the reign of Henry VIII., as we learn, there existed a messuage or country house called Westbourne Place, which survived, but rebuilt, until the making of the Great Western Railway. A scattered hamlet arose in the neighbourhood, the houses standing at intervals along a common of considerable length, through which wound the road to Harrow, and by one of these houses, a wayside inn, called the "Red Lion," flowed the old but, perhaps, now nameless stream. The hamlet was known as Westbourne Green.*

In the course of time, though not till after the pleasant hamlet had had many years of quiet existence, street after street was built, taking the name Westbourne with every possible change of suffix. But the old bourne, which has fitly been termed the *eponymus* of the district, the once pure stream which had flowed down from Hampstead heights, sometimes openly through meadows, sometimes occultly between elm-shaded banks, and had afforded to "Caroline the Illustrious" (George II.'s queen) a copious stream for her memorable work, the Serpentine, fared badly.

* An article on Westbourne Green, by myself, is found in the *Home Counties Magazine*, vol. ii., 1900.

In 1834, a hundred years after the making of the Serpentine, the West Bourne makes an almost unaltered and complete appearance on the map, and the elms are seen at intervals along its course, but the name written on it is "Bayswater Rivulet." The name Bayswater, derived from that of a spring and conduit on the slope of Craven Hill, and carefully preserved for human use during many centuries, had supplanted the name Westbourne in the southern part of the area. So, also, had it become the name of the old bourne; yet as "Bayswater Rivulet" it did not long visibly survive. For as London spread itself over the district the underground works of sewers and railways "tapped" the stream almost to extinction, until finally, in its impoverished and polluted condition, it was cut off from the Serpentine and committed to the flushing of the Ranelagh Sewer.

Thus was extinguished the West Bourne. Its name—which is our subject—had been lost to it. I do not think it will be found on any map, and it does not even seem to have had the recognition of the earliest topographers of the last century. Lysons, for instance, writing in 1811 the second edition of his 'Environs,' has it nameless as "a little brook which runs by Kilburn and Bayswater." Peter Cunningham is, I think, the first to give it its name, and in his 'Handbook' of 1850 has: "Westbourne......a bourne, brook, or streamlet......now the Ranelagh Sewer." Alas! In 1890 Mr. J. G. Waller did full justice to the bourne by a valuable article in vol. vi. of *Transactions* of the London and Middlesex Archæological Society.

Here I think we must rest content. And although neither in books nor maps previous to 1850 may we find the name West Bourne given to the stream, yet so surely as in the name of the district the second syllable implied water—not land—so surely we may conclude that primarily West Bourne was the name of the stream.   W. L. RUTTON.

If this is the continuation of the river that runs through Cassiobury Park and has its rise in the meadows at Great Gaddesden, it certainly is the River Gade I have before me an old map of "Hartford Shire. By Rᵗ Morden at the Atlas in Cornhill, London." attached to a description of Hertfordshire taken from some work, as it is paged 965 to 1038, the printer's marks I iiiii to s sssss, with no date to it, but separately bound. In describing Hemel Hempstead Church it states, "From this Place, which is washed by the River Gade, we pass to the Hunton, which leads to Kings Langley." But in the description of "Rickmansworth—and in old records Rickmeres-wearth or Rickmeresweard—so called from its situation in a nook of land where a little river without name falls into the Colne, and makes a rich pool of water, as the name imports."

It therefore appears to me to have a name at its source and for a long part of its course, but finally, when it joins the Colne, it has no name. I have another old book from which I give an extract : "Nordens Preparatiue To his Speculum Britanniæ. Printed in the year MDCCXXIII," apparently a reprint of an older work, dated 4 November, 1596.

Map of Hartfordshire.—The River Gade is shown, but not named, and in describing the rivers of the county Norden states that the Colne "ere it commes to Rickmansworth devoureth Caishoo river."

W. J. GADSDEN.

19, Middle Lane, Crouch End.

WINDOW GLASS (9th S. ix. 87, 150, 213).—I am pleased to reply to MR. F. CLAYTON. Pliny is a good and useful authority on a vast number of points of detail, and his omission to mention the use of glass in windows rightly gives one pause. Did he, perhaps, object to it? As long as (perhaps a little longer than) mica was cheaper than glass the former was used, and Pliny's failure to mention the use of glass for panes is a remarkable one. He only mentions that in Arabia there is "lapidem vitri mox trans-lucidum, quo utuntur pro specularibus" (lib. 36, 30). Seneca ('Q.N.,' iv. 13, 7) writes: "Quamvis cænationem velis ac specularibus muniant." Here, perhaps, we ought to understand not the use of glass panes, but only those of mica. Neverthe-less, by the dates of these two writers, glass had become very common. From before the foundation of the empire there was a street devoted to the glass trade—Vicus Vitrarius —in Rome, though, doubtless, this trade began as an industry of Southern importa-tion. Still, the all-powerful fact being proven that Pompeii and Herculaneum (cf. Winckelmann, 'Werke,' ii. 343) used glass panes when Pliny was living and familiar with their neighbourhood, while certifying us on the subject, only makes Pliny's omission the more striking. For, if a town like Pompeii used glass panes in Ves-pasian's day, Rome must in all probability have used them also, at least in her wealthy palaces. It is well-nigh impossible to think she had not. The panes found at Pompeii duly appear in the catalogue of the Museo Borbonico ; but the museum is just now undergoing rearrangement, so that the old numbering will be changed. As a matter of fact, many more of these panes have been forthcoming, and the museum of Pompeii itself contains good enough specimens. In passing, let me venture to recall the kindred application of glass mentioned by Martial ('Epig.,' 4, 21, 5)—

Condita sic puro numerantur lilia vitro
Sic prohibet tenuis gemma latere rosis—

for protecting the more delicate plants from cold, especially at night. I confess I am unable to quite follow MR. CLAYTON in his references. Pliny (lib. 36) is not speaking of the building of a temple, but of a theatre. But it is not important to our point. As to the destruction of the villa at Anzio, I am unable to assert anything, except that it is a villa of early imperial date, and that the pottery, &c., found above and below the pane of glass is of imperial days also. I therefore pass on to the more decisive refer-ence of Lactantius, a writer who, I believe, is held to have died *circa* A.D. 325. He writes ('De Op. Dei,' 8, 11), "Et manifestius est, mentem esse, quæ per oculos ea quæ sunt opposita transpiciat, quasi per fenestras perlucente vitos aut speculari lapide, ob-ductas."

This seems to me especially interesting for the double reference, to the talc windows and the glass ones. And I venture to think one may infer that both kinds subsisted, sometimes in the same dwelling. It is un-fortunate that we have no means of deter-mining the precise moment when glass panes came into competition with their predecessors made of *lapis specularis*. But, on the other hand, the discoveries above referred to prove beyond question that the desired date must be placed before A.D. 79. In a letter of the younger Pliny (lib. 2, epist. 17), descrip-tive of his Laurentine villa, he says that an excellent store chamber in it is furnished "specularibus, ac, multo magis, imminentibus tectis." It would be interesting to know if this older word became used in a wide sense to include both talc windows and glass ones. Prof. Mau, probably second to no living authority on the subject of Pompeii, writes, "Small panes of glass were found in the openings of the baths near the Forum ; had the central baths been finished, glass would undoubtedly have been used for the windows of the caldarium" ('Pompeii,' p. 273, 1899). On p. 351 the same writer states, "In the tepidarium [of the house of Diomedes] were found four panes of glass about 10½ in. square, together with the remains of the wooden frame in which they were set."

Let me trust that if other evidence be needed, and is in the possession of more learned readers of 'N. & Q.,' we may be favoured with it.   ST. CLAIR BADDELEY.
Hotel Eden, Rome.

In the seventh century Benedict Biscop brought glaziers from the Continent to contribute to the glory of his foundations at Wearmouth and Jarrow.   ST. SWITHIN.

THE FIRST BRITISH SUBJECT BORN IN NEW SOUTH WALES (9ᵗʰ S. ix. 206).—A few weeks ago, in an obituary notice in the *Manchester Guardian*, a man born in 1824 was said to have been the first British subject born in New South Wales. I let that pass; but when it is stated in 'N. & Q.' that Charles Kent, who was born in 1799, was the first British subject born in the colony, I feel bound to demur. In 1854 I knew Daniel Nowlan and his wife. The husband was a mail contractor living in Musselbrook, Hunter River, and both he and his wife were born in 1794. His father was a sergeant in the army, who went out with the first batch of convicts (800) in 1788. Doubtless many of your Australian readers could give similar instances of persons born before 1799.
ALFRED F. CURWEN.

BATTY, PRINTER, 159, FLEET STREET (9ᵗʰ S. ix. 208).—So far as my memory goes some pamphlets were published about 1859, on behalf of the High Church party, relating to the great question, then, as now, before us, of marriage with a deceased wife's sister. I cannot recall anything regarding those publications beyond the fact that there were a few printed and published for private members of the party in those days. Perhaps such firms as Masters & Co., Rivingtons, and Burns & Oates may have a knowledge of the pamphlets alluded to.
JOSEPH HENRY BATTY.

I remember in about the year 1850, when serving my apprenticeship to Joseph Masters, being frequently sent to the above-named firm of printers with advertisements for a newspaper entitled the *English Churchman*, which I see is now published at No. 74, Strand, and is called the *English Churchman and St. James's Chronicle*.
I think if your correspondent would refer to the file of that newspaper at about that date he might obtain the information he is seeking. About that period Masters published a monthly magazine called the *Ecclesiastic*, and Burns, of Portman Street, a quarterly review called the *Christian Remembrancer*, edited by Wm. Scott, of Hoxton

(Clement Scott's father), and most likely these pamphlets would be advertised and noticed in them.   ROBERT BURNINGHAM.

BISHOPS' SIGNATURES (9ᵗʰ S. ix. 9, 118, 239). —At the last reference we are told, on the authority of Taylor's 'Words and Places,' that *Wiogora-ceastre*, *i.e.*, Worcester, is a corruption of *Hwic-wara-ceastre*. Of course this is clean impossible, and Canon Taylor acknowledged that many of his early guesses were untenable. If by "corruption" is meant a total disregard of all phonetic laws, it may be doubtful if any clear case of it can be made out for Early English. As a fact, the two forms were contemporaneous : "in hwicca máegthe in......weogernacester" (Kemble, 'Codex Diplom.,' i. 114).   CELER.

ARMS OF DUTCH EAST INDIA COMPANY (9ᵗʰ S. ix. 9, 118).—I cannot say whether the company used any coat of arms as their own. Their coinage bore, besides the V. O. C. monogram described by MR. J. P. LEWIS, sundry coats of arms—perhaps those of governors.   LOBUC.

A kind friend has sent me a photograph of the device of this old company, taken from a carving, dated 1669, above the gateway of a fort in Ceylon. It consists of the letters V. O. C., interlaced in the manner described by your last correspondent, within an oval frame, on an elaborate mantling between two lions as supporters, and surmounted by a crest—a cock, I believe.   L. L. K.

TENNIS : ORIGIN OF THE NAME (9ᵗʰ S. ix. 27, 75, 153, 238).—I must admit the justice of MR. CHARLES A. FEDERER'S criticism, so courteously expressed. I find that Littré gives similar quotations, as, *e g.*, "Tenez, je vais vous dire......Tenez, tous vos discours ne me touchent point l'âme," &c. I must, however, maintain that the word has never been used in French courts in the same sense as our word "play," or at least that there is no evidence of such use, unless the word "excipe" be admitted without corroboration.
JULIAN MARSHALL.

DESCENDANTS OF SIR WILLIAM DE LA POLE, DIED 1329 (9ᵗʰ S. ix. 209).—Since this query was written I have obtained from Sheahan's 'History of Hull' (1864) the following additional information respecting the eldest son of the above Sir William and his descendants :—

"Richard de la Pole died in 1345......and his son, William de la Pole (afterwards knighted), succeeded to the possession of his wealth. The male branch of Richard's descendants soon ran out, but the female branch is represented amongst the nobility of our own times. Richard's great-granddaughter, Joan, was, by right of her mother, the Baroness Cobham. This lady had five husbands—viz., Sir Robert Hemengdale, Sir Reginald Braybrooke, Sir Nicholas Hawberke, Sir John Oldcastle (the martyr to Lollardism), and Sir John Harpden......Joan had a daughter by her second husband, who married Sir Thomas Broke, and the representative of this pair in the female line was the late extravagant Duke of Buckingham and Chandos."

RONALD DIXON.

46, Marlborough Avenue, Hull.

GREEK EPIGRAM (9th S. ix. 147).—The epigram beginning Τέσσαρες αἱ Χάριτες, Παφίαι δύο, καὶ δέκα Μοῦσαι, is No. 95 of the 'Erotica' in the 'Greek Anthology' (3 vols., Leipsic, 1829).   H. A. STRONG.

University College, Liverpool.

The following by Callimachus ('Anth. Pal.,' v. 146) is very similar to the epigram required:

Τέσσαρες αἱ Χάριτες· ποτὶ γὰρ μία ταῖς τρισὶ κείναις

ἄρτι ποτεπλάσθη κῆτι μύροισι νοτεῖ

εὐαίων ἐν πᾶσιν ἀρίζαλος Βερενίκα

ἇς ἄτερ οὐδ' αὐταὶ καὶ Χάριτες Χάριτες.

JOHN B. WAINEWRIGHT.

The description here of the Graces as *four* and of the Muses as *ten* seems to show that the poem was a humorous parody—perhaps of this by Meleager of Gadara ('Anthologia Græca,' ix. 16, ed. Tauchn., Lips., 1872, t. ii. p. 62), which may, however, possibly be itself the epigram sought for:—

Τρισσαὶ μὲν Χάριτες, τρεῖς δὲ γλυκυπάρθενοι Ὧραι·

τρεῖς δ' ἐμὲ θηλυμανεῖς οἰστροβολοῦσι Πόθοι.

ἦ γάρ τοι τρία τόξα κατείρυσεν, ὡς ἄρα μέλλων

οὐχὶ μίαν τρώσειν, τρεῖς δ' ἐν ἐμοὶ κραδίας;

JOHN MAC-CARTHY.

Sunnyfield, Clapham Park.

This anonymous epigram is in the 'Greek Anthology':—

Τέσσαρες αἱ Χάριτες, Παφίαι δύο, καὶ δέκα Μοῦσαι·

Δερκυλὶς ἐν πάσαις Μοῦσα, Χάρις, Παφίη.

There is a version by Jonathan Swift, which is probably that desired by MR. FURRAN:—

Two goddesses now must Cyprus adore;
The Muses are ten, and the Graces are four:
Stella's wit is so charming, so sweet her fair face,
She shines a new Venus, a Muse, and a Grace.

This may be compared with the epigram of Callimachus in praise of Berenice, and with that in which Plato styles Sappho the tenth Muse.   WILLIAM E. A. AXON.

[Other replies acknowledged.]

The idea implied in the epigram has been well reproduced in the following lines :—

Now the Graces are four, and the Venuses two,
  And ten is the tale of the Muses,
For a Muse, and a Grace, and a Venus are you,
  My dear little Molly Trefusis.

PATRICK MAXWELL.

Bath.

"PROSPICIMUS MODO" (9th S. viii. 445 ; ix. 34). —In the fourteenth letter of his ninth book Sidonius, who has been asked by a friend to explain with an example what are meant by "versus recurrentes," after quoting the well-known pentameter

Roma tibi subito motibus ibit amor

as a specimen of a line which can be read backwards "metro stante neque litteris loco motis," produces as an example of another class of "versus recurrentes," where the original words are retained, but their order reversed, the following distich of his own composition, with the prefatory remark "qualia reor equidem legi multa multorum":

Præcipiti modo quod decurrit tramite flumen,
  Tempore consumptum iam cito deficiet.

It will be seen that the structure of this couplet bears a close resemblance to that cited at the first reference.

For other elaborate inanities of this sort see Burman's 'Anthologia' (1759), vol. i. p. 542 ; H. Meyer's 'Anthologia Veterum Latinorum Epigrammatum et Poematum' (1835), vol. i. Nos. 236–9 ; Riese's 'Anthologia Latina,' pars i., fasciculus i. (1869), No. 81. See also Sirmond's note to Sidonius's 'Epistles,' viii. xi. ; Burman's note in his 'Anthology,' where some modern imitators of this style are mentioned ; and Lucian Müller, 'De Re Metrica,' pp. 466–70.

Those who delight in this kind of literature would probably be pleased by a highly ingenious method of making Latin verses by machinery of which an account was given at least twenty years ago in an English magazine (? *Chambers's Journal*). Perhaps some reader of 'N. & Q.' could supply the exact reference.   EDWARD BENSLY.

The University, Adelaide, South Australia.

CHILDREN'S AFFIRMATIONS (9th S. ix. 185). —No doubt a considerable number of affirmations of truth used by children past and present may be given. In Derbyshire fifty years ago the wet-finger oath was mostly used. "Is my finger wet?" "Yes."—"Is my finger dry?" "Yes."—"May I cut my throat before I'd tell a lie!" The last sentence was accompanied by the making of a cross on the throat, head tilted back. A shorter form: "Finger wet; finger dry; cut my throat if I lie." This was used when the oath-maker was in a hurry. A more elaborate form was:—

> Sure an' certain
> Bout to death;
> Eat awt worlds
> If I tell a lie.

Sometimes instead of the last two lines it was:—

> May the devil fetch me
> If I tell a lie.

There was another: "May I drop down dead if I tell a lie." These are also known in Notts, Stafford, and Yorkshire.

THOS. RATCLIFFE.

Worksop.

SIR HENRY CROMWELL (9ᵗʰ S. ix. 166).— D. J. may like to see a quotation from the Rev. W. H. Hutton's history of his college (1898), p. 87:—

"The Cromwell family had sent many members to S. John's. The daughter of Sir Thomas White's second wife, Joan Warren, married Sir Henry Cromwell, of Hinchinbroke. Her son Henry was elected a Law Fellow in 1581; his younger brother Philip became Fellow in 1594. Both were Oliver's uncles. It was from Sir Oliver, another uncle, that the living of Crick, Northamptonshire, was bought by Sir William Craven, a rich merchant, and bestowed on the college in 1613. In the last years of the sixteenth century it is clear that Buckeridge resided constantly in the college. He was very likely the tutor of the younger brother, as he was of Laud; and the family association may well have led the great Oliver to S. Giles's, Cripplegate, where, on 22 August, 1620, he married Elizabeth Bourchier."

John Buckeridge, a distinguished theologian, and also akin to the founder, was the eighth President of the college (1605-11), immediately preceding Archbishop Laud, his former pupil, in that office. Besides several country livings, he held, from 1604, that of St. Giles's, Cripplegate. He gave three MSS. to the college library, and Henry Cromwell, the fellow, gave one MS.   A. R. BAYLEY.

Joan, the daughter of Sir Ralph Warren, Lord Mayor of London in 1537 and again in 1544, by his second wife Joan, daughter and coheir of John Lake, married Sir Henry Williams, *alias* Cromwell, of Hinchingbroke, co. Hunts. Sir Ralph Warren died 11 July, 1553, and his widow remarried, 25 November, 1558, Sir Thomas White, Lord Mayor of London 1553, and founder of St. John's College, Oxford. Sir Thomas White died at Oxford, 11 February, 1566, and his widow

died at Hinchingbroke, the house of her son-in-law, on 8 October, 1572, and was buried with her first husband in the church of St. Benet Sherehog, in the City of London.

Sir Henry Cromwell, therefore, married the stepdaughter of Sir Thomas White. He had by her six sons and five daughters. Oliver the Protector was the eldest son of Sir Henry's second son Robert, and Elizabeth, Sir Henry's second daughter, was the mother of John Hampden.

W. F. PRIDEAUX.

A RIME ON EDWARD VII. (9ᵗʰ S. viii. 445, 532; ix. 52).—When I was at Oxford— now, alas! forty years ago—I remember frequently hearing the rime:—

> In Edward VII.'s reign
> Mass will be said again.

OSWALD J. REICHEL.

ARTISTS' MISTAKES (9ᵗʰ S. iv. 107, 164, 237, 293; v. 32, 317, 400; vi. 44; vii. 423, 471; viii. 171, 328).—According to the *Illustrated London News* of 14 December, the Prince of Wales, on his visit to the City on 5 December, when abreast of Christ's Hospital, wore a naval uniform with the usual cocked hat, but on his arrival at the Guildhall it was changed to a round felt one. The two illustrations being on opposite pages, the mistake is most conspicuous.   EVERARD HOME COLEMAN.

71, Brecknock Road.

NAPOLEON'S LAST YEARS (9ᵗʰ S. viii. 422, 509).—In my little library is a 'History of Napoleon,' in 2 vols. large 8vo, by George Moir Bussey, published in 1840. remarkably well written, and copiously illustrated by Horace Vernet. The illustrations are graphic, and the head and tail pieces of the chapters descriptive. The likeness of Napoleon is well preserved, though it is difficult to identify the conqueror of Marengo and Austerlitz in the plain and simple dress worn by him at St. Helena when walking about or dictating his history to Las Cases.

Antommarchi, the Italian physician, arrived there in 1819, and continued as the medical attendant of Napoleon until his death, 5 May, 1821. One vignette engraving represents the Abbé Vignali administering to the prisoner the sacrament of extreme unction, and another depicts his death surrounded by his faithful followers, Madame Bertrand amongst them. Marchand, St. Denis, and Antommarchi watched daily and constantly by the bedside of the emperor. The greatest of the lyrics of Alessandro Manzoni, 'Il Cinque Maggio,' commemorates the day, and one stanza of the noble ode may be quoted, showing that Napoleon was a believer on his deathbed :—

> Bella, immortal, benefica
> Fede ai trionfi avvezza,
> Scrivi ancor questo, allegrati,
> Chè più superba altezza
> Al disonor del Golgota
> Giammai non si chinò.

The 'History of Napoleon' alluded to concludes with the prompt and graceful answer of the Government of England in 1840 to the request made by M. Thiers, Prime Minister of France, for the removal of the remains of Napoleon.   John Pickford, M.A.
Newbourne Rectory, Woodbridge.

Of course, the great emperor's illness accounted for the unusual torpor which marked the last period of his life. Had it not been for this Waterloo, perhaps, had been a different tale. Wellington might have stood out to the last man, but Napoleon would have swept that last man from before his path. There is not a shadow of a doubt that this fatal ailment influenced the seeming sulkiness of Napoleon towards his warder Sir Hudson Lowe. Lord Rosebery's account is biassed from beginning to end. Sir Hudson did his best to ameliorate Napoleon's position at St. Helena, but his best was necessarily his worst in the eyes of his illustrious captive under these circumstances. Quite recently I called his lordship's attention to the damaging article of Mr. Reade (9th S. viii. 190), but the only reply vouchsafed to me was that he had not seen the article in question, nor had he any reason to modify his opinions. Of such stuff is history made. A peck of preconception evidently equals a bushel of truth.   J. B. McGovern.
St. Stephen's Rectory, C.-on-M., Manchester.

"Rather" (9th S. ix. 7, 137).— Mr. Elworthy, in his interesting reply, speaks of "the broad *a* in the modern *rather*," and seems to imply that the local pronunciation with long *a*, as in *pave*, is due to the conservatism of the dialect. Is this so? Dialects certainly are conservative, but they are also slovenly and incorrect. I have often thought that there is a tendency to over-estimate the value of dialects in this respect. The change of *rathe* to *rave* in Somerset should warn us not to attach too much importance to local pronunciation as a guide to the older forms of words. If *rayther* was the old pronunciation of *rather*, we might argue that *father* was originally *feyther;* but was it? How is it that *enough* is pronounced *eniff* in one county and *enew* in the next? With regard to *rather* it is worth noting that in Chamber-

layne's 'Pharonnida' (see Nares) *rath* is made to rime with *bath*.   C. C. B.

The comments of Mr. Elworthy and Lobuc are very pleasing to the writer of this item. The "dialects" of England "are the great repository of old English," says the former ; while the latter emphasizes very properly the "steadfastness with which poorer folk adhere to ancient pronunciation, while the more educated classes make changes." "Poor folk still say *rayther*." Quite so. They say "a" is *ā*, so "ra" is *rā*. Fifty years ago, in the North, "rathe" was *rāthe*, as to sound. Possibly it is "correct" to say "rắth" now. Some few years ago I heard one of our greatest actors say, "Hell itself doth *garp* contagion," &c. I prefer *gāpe*, but perhaps I am "behind the times." Even if you cannot say *rāthe, rāther, rāthest, rathe* and *rather* are closely connected, and *ready* is a near relation. Indeed, does not *rathe* mean *soon ready*, and does not "I would *rather* do so-and-so" mean "I would more *readily* do so-and-so"? Lobuc says, "The higher ranks are accustomed to pronounce *rather* as *rarther*." The fact that by sticking in the *r* there he can give the sound that the "higher ranks" want is a proof that, if we *must* have the Italian *a* sound to please the "educated classes," it can be got by the not very costly addition of an *r* in most cases. There is very little difference between *ar* and the continental *a* if the second letter in *ar* is not "rolled."

The following remarks in the *Spectator* for 15 February by H. C. Tierney may be conveniently added to those of Mr. Elworthy and Lobuc: "Many old English customs, and numbers of Anglo-Saxon words, &c., which have died out in England itself, still survive in 'Little England beyond Wales'" (*i.e.*, Pembrokeshire, &c.).   W. H. B.

Earliest Printed Instructions to Sunday-School Teachers (9th S. ix. 69, 154).—In 1880 my friend the late Mr. John Taylor, of Northampton, compiled and issued a valuable pamphlet on 'Robert Raikes and Northamptonshire Sunday Schools.' To it is added an appendix containing "A List of Publications by Northamptonshire Authors, or issued from the Press in Northamptonshire, relating to Sunday Schools ; Books printed by the Raikes Family at Northampton and Gloucester ; a Brief Account of the Originators of Sunday Schools ; Historical Notes ; &c., &c." I cannot find any notice of the "Instructions" therein ; but it seems to me that their existence may appropriately be noted under this heading.   John T. Page.

BLACK BOTTLES FOR WINE (9th S. ix. 7, 175). —Some years ago my brother, the late Mr. Clement Southam, was given a dark green squat bottle, which is now in the possession of his son. It is said to have been taken out of the lake at Ellesmere. In shape it is like some old liqueur or wine bottles that I have seen in Holland, but with a deep hollow butt, the total height being 6⅝ in., of which 2¼ in. are neck ; the circumference is about 18¼ in. On the shoulder the letters "E. A." are deeply scratched, and a little lower down, in another part, the following name and date in the characters of the period, "John Joyce 1714." My brother always thought that the bottle had contained ale, and had been dropped by some excited angler into the lake, probably by one of the family of Joyce, who have been noted clockmakers at Whitchurch (Salop) for some generations.

HERBERT SOUTHAM.

Shrewsbury.

I have a black glass bottle of a rather unusual shape. It stands 7 in. high, with a long neck, and a squat body 4 in. in diameter. It has a date impressed upon it in the shape of a seal the size of a crown piece, with "E. C. 1731" on it. It came from the village of Warkworth, Northumberland. This is no great distance from Seaton Delaval in the same county, and may probably have been manufactured there, according to the statement in the *Times* that making black glass bottles was commenced there. May not the initials refer to the Clutterbuck family, which has for a very long time been connected with Warkworth ?

G. H. THOMPSON.

A LINE OF BROWNING (9th S. ix. 47, 173).— The fact that MR. EAMES and ST. SWITHIN take diametrically opposite views about the meaning of this line is proof that Browning does not make his meaning clear to all readers. Yet I cannot think it doubtful which interpretation is correct. Browning never would set himself down as a "driveller." The words are governed by the interrogation point at the end of the line, and form a second question, succeeding that in the previous line. Browning's punctuation may not show this to a casual reader. But is MR. EAMES justified in calling it simply "bad" ? A writer in the *Edinburgh Review* lately asserted that Browning had no idea of punctuation. We know, on the contrary, that he had a very great care for punctuation, and attended to this himself in his proofs (Mrs. Orr's 'Life,' p. 381). Only, as in other matters, he had views of his own, and was a law to himself. An observant reader, I think, will find a very careful punctuation running through all Browning's poems, and it is worth trying to grasp its principle. For one thing—which bears on the line in question—he clearly used the *dash*, not disjunctively, as I have just done, but connectively. He employs it to link two ideas, not to separate them. Any one accustomed to Browning's usage would see at once that "did I drivel—Being—who ?" is meant to run together, not to be parted.

Whether any writer is justified in thus inventing a system of his own may be open to question. Yet our present system has neither age nor authority behind it, and is in many ways defective. It takes note solely of grammatical construction, and practically compels a reader to punctuate mentally for himself. Older writers were quite different. They punctuated for rhetorical pause instead of grammar. They would say, for instance, "To err, is human"—which we should now write "To err is human." Browning read deeply in old English poets, and probably drew some of his notions from their usage. At all events, his punctuation seems an attempt to supply that rhetorical arrangement of clauses which modern stopping altogether ignores. If MR. EAMES will study it in this way, he may find it a help rather than a hindrance in obscurely worded passages. That such help should be so often required is a misfortune, and I personally think MR. EAMES has rightly stated one great cause of the necessity. But at least we can use the stepping-stones which the poet himself laboured to place at our disposal.

T. S. OMOND.

TINTAGEL (8th S. i. 434 ; 9th S. ix. 194).— Borlase, 'Antiquities of Cornwall,' 1754, p. 320, spells this "Tindagel *alias* Tindogel," and adds in a foot-note "Rectius f. Tintughel, viz., the high fortify'd hill." Polwhele, 'Cornish-English Vocabulary,' 1808, p. 59, has "*Tin*, a fortified place ; Tintagel, the castle of deceit." This corresponds with the translation "castle of guile," mentioned by MR. LEWIS at the last reference, and is also confirmed by Williams, 'Lexicon Cornu-Britannicum,' 1865, where I find "*Tin*, a fortified place, a castle ; another form of *din* ; hence Tintagel in Cornwall."

JAS. PLATT, Jun.

LADY MARY TUDOR (9th S. viii. 484 ; ix. 72, 194).—In vol. ii., facing p. 256 of the 'History of English Dress,' by Georgiana Hill, is a full-length engraved portrait of this lady, representing a very beautiful woman. Underneath is inscribed "Lady Mary Tudor,

Daughter of King Charles 2nd. From the original at Slindon House, Sussex.— L. S. Costello, pinxt.—C. Cook, sculp." In the list of illustrations prefixed it is stated, "In the Court dress of the period, trimmed with ostrich feathers, the bodice embroidered with pearls, the sleeves open to the elbow, and turned back over an undersleeve of lace or embroidered muslin." Though the date of the work is said to be 1893, yet in all probability the engraving had done duty long before that date. The portrait was presumably copied by Miss Louisa Stuart Costello, once so well known a writer. Lady Mary Tudor was the mother of James Radcliffe, third Earl of Derwentwater, beheaded in 1715-16.

JOHN PICKFORD, M.A.
Newbourne Rectory, Woodbridge.

LE NEVE FAMILY (9th S. ix. 129).—The name Neve, without the prefix "Le," occurs in the parish of Sculcoates, now in the city of Kingston - upon - Hull. Parish register, burials :—

1759. Dec. 9, Winifred Neve, Gentlewoman.
1769. Oct. 12, Robert, son of Henry Neve, Mercht.

Tombstone in the churchyard of the old parish church, St. Mary's, Sculcoates :—

Winifred Neve, died 7 December, 1759, aged 67.

W. C. B.

For much information respecting this family see 1st S. i., v., x. ; 2nd S. xi., xii. ; 3rd S. v. ; 5th S. v. ; 8th S. vii.

EVERARD HOME COLEMAN.
71, Brecknock Road.

The late Mr. Francis Rye published a calendar of correspondence and documents relating to the family of Le Neve. It was published by A. H. Goose, Norwich. If not now to be procured, I shall be happy to lend it to P. L. N. F.   E. A. FRY.
172, Edmund Street, Birmingham.

WEEK (9th S. ix. 147).—Mr. A. H. Mann in the illustrated edition of Traill's 'Social England,' vol. i. (1901), says :—

"With but slight variations we find the days of the week named after the same deities in all Teutonic countries. These names must have been substituted for those of Roman gods by the German tribes on the frontier of the Empire (for this, apparently, was the immediate source of the week of seven days), and by them handed on to our own ancestors, who then dwelt along the shores of the Northern Sea."

Hence we get the days of the week named as follows : Sunday and Monday from sun and moon, viz., Balder and his wife Nanna, taking the place of Phœbus Apollo (Sol-Helios) and his twin-sister Diana (Artemis-Selene) ; Tuesday from the war-god Tiw (Norse, Tyr), or Ares (Mars) ; Wednesday from Woden (Norse, Odin), who was eventually identified by the Teutons themselves with Hermes (Mercury) ; Thursday from Thunor (thunder ; Norse, Thor), or Zeus (Jupiter) ; Friday from Fricge, the wife of Woden, or Hera (Juno) ; Saturday from Sætere, whose name also appears in Satterleigh and Satterthwaite ; but, as nothing is known concerning this god, the name may well be a corruption of the Latin "Saturn's day" (Kronos).

Our Easter is, of course, from Eostre, who was probably goddess of dawn (Aurora-Eos) and the returning year.   A. R. BAYLEY.

With regard to the names of the days of the week one might ask M., Would he have expected otherwise? Would he expect us to have Hebrew names? Or where would he expect our pagan ancestors to go for Christian names of the days?

SIMPLICISSIMUS.

PRICE OF EGGS (9th S. ix. 147). — In the 'Chronicon Preciosum' is an account of a feast which the Prior of St. Augustine's, Canterbury, made on his installation day in 1309, at which feast 9,600 eggs were used, costing 4l. 10s., or about nine for a penny. Five years later Parliament fixed the price of provisions, beginning with "a stalled or corn-fed ox, 1l. 4s. 0d.," and ending with "24 eggs (in the City but 20) for 1d." At the nearest date to that of O. O. H., namely, in 1595, the 'Chronicon,' quoting from Stow, has this entry :—

	l.	s.	d.
Wheat (by much Transportation) the Quarter, at	02	13	04
A Hen's Egg at	00	00	01
Or, at best, 3 Eggs for	00	00	02
A Pound of Sweet Butter	00	00	07

Our sins (as Mr. Stow says) deserving it.

But note the difference in the value of money in 1309 and 1314 when comparing with prices in 1595.   RICHARD WELFORD.

William Herbert in his 'History of the Twelve Livery Companies' gives a copy of "A Bill of Fare for Fifty People of the Company of Salters, A.D. 1506," in which "½ hundred eggs" are priced at "2d½." From the same work I find that on St. Dunstan's Day (19 May), A.D. 1518, at a feast given by the Goldsmiths' Company, 200 eggs cost twenty-two pence ; and at the dinner held on the same day, in 1527, 260 eggs were priced at 2s. 6d. For two similar feasts, which required 850 eggs each, 7s. 4d. and 6s. 10½d. appear in the bills of expenses.

The Morning Advertiser of 10 May, 1843,

published a copy of the bill of fare of "William Mingay, Esq., Mayor of Norwich, at which he feasted the Duke of Norfolk, the Lords, Knights, and Gentry of the County," A.D. 1561, in which 34 eggs were charged at 1s.

EVERARD HOME COLEMAN.
71, Brecknock Road.

Ray has the proverb "You come with your five eggs a penny, and four of them be rotten." According to Mr. Sidney Lee, money had in Shakespeare's time eight times its present purchasing power; but this is hardly borne out, I think, by the accounts given in Mr. Hubert Hall's 'Society in the Elizabethan Age' of Will Darrell's expenses in London in 1589. These, however, do not enable us to do more than guess roughly at the price of eggs. There are such entries as the following :—

Munday dyner Junij 9.

Egges at Brekefast	...	...	jᵈ
2 peces bief	...	...	ijˢ ijᵈ
A loyne of Veale	...	...	xxijᵈ
A Rabbett	...	...	viijᵈ
A quart of Strawberries	...	...	vjᵈ

And so on. Again :—

Supper eodem.

Egges	...	...	...	ijᵈ
A Shoulder of Mutton	...	...	xviijᵈ

And so on. We are not told how many partook of these meals; but since we find in other of Darrell's accounts "20 hens and 1 cock" valued at 5s., and "6 geese and other poultry" at 2s. 4d., we may safely conclude that one egg for a penny would be a very bad bargain. C. C. B.

At Canterbury, in 1536, the price of eggs was fixed by the Corporation : "No person allowed to buy or sell less than six eggs for a penny, on pain of 12d." (Goulden's 'Guide to Canterbury,' p. 68). KNOWLER.

Paul Delahay must not be taken too literally. "Five eggs a penny and four of them addle" is an old saying. See the 'N.E.D.,' s.v. 'Egg.' J. DORMER.

PICTURE RESTORING IN FRANCE UNDER NAPOLEON I. (9ᵗʰ S. ix. 184).—My first visit to London was made for some law matters in June, 1864. On that occasion private circumstances took me to the rooms of one who was then a well-known picture-restorer. This person succeeded his father in the business, and he worked for many distinguished owners of pictures, a vast number whereof passed under his hands. He had a very competent knowledge of schools and styles, and his judgment was often sought at sales. The minute and scrupulous care with which he restored the decayed portions of valuable

pictures was, I believe, exemplary. I noticed that the backs of the panels and canvases of most of the important specimens were either sealed with the owners' private signets or bore autograph signatures. In this way some pictures had their pedigrees traced on them. No such tricks as shaving the back or stripping the canvas could be attempted in these cases without either permission or discovery. Part of his business was to supply copies of pictures submitted to his charge. These were sometimes so well executed that on an occasion or two the copy, by mistake, found its way for a time into the gallery of the owner of the original. The man of whom I write died in 1887. W. C. B.

"OLIVER" (9ᵗʰ S. ix. 127, 194).—Probably there are not now "olivers" in the hand-nailmaking trade. The "oliver" was used in striking the heads of hob-nails. These nails, when made by hand, were the work of girls and women, and the celerity with which they turned out nails was marvellous. Hob-nails were made out of very slender iron rods, and each girl had half a dozen irons in the fire in a literal sense. The rods were whipped out of the fire to the "stiddy" (small anvil), three or four deft blows formed the "shank," then a cut-off blow, the shank placed in a small hole in the stiddy, and down came the "oliver," in which was a matrix forming the head, and a touch on a spring jerked out the finished "hob." The "oliver" was worked with the foot, and every time it came down seemed to be within an inch of smashing the worker's head.

THOS. RATCLIFFE.
Worksop.

BARON DE GRIVEGNÉE AND POWER (9ᵗʰ S. vii. 409, 476; viii. 170; ix. 91).—Can your correspondent MR. SCOTT give me any information as to the daughters of the Baron de Grivegnée other than Fanny, who married William Kirkpatrick, and as to the baron himself, with his wife's names and some dates? I possess a copy of the 'Chronicles of the Kirkpatrick Family,' by Capt. Alexander de Lapere Kirkpatrick, who in October, 1901, was at Fourteen Streams, Warrenton, South Africa.

REGINALD STEWART BODDINGTON.
15, Markham Square, Chelsea.

DALRYMPLE ON THE FUR TRADE (9ᵗʰ S. ix. 87).—'Plan for promoting the Fur Trade and securing it to this Country by uniting the Operations of the East India and Hudson's Bay Companies,' 1789, 4to.

JOHN RADCLIFFE.

Miscellaneous.

NOTES ON BOOKS, &c.

The English Dialect Dictionary. Edited by Joseph Wright, M.A., Ph.D.—Parts XI. and XII. *Ha—Jinkeling*; Parts XIII. and XIV. *Jinkes—Lyven.* (Frowde.)

SPLENDID progress is being made by 'The English Dialect Dictionary,' which has now overtaken and passed the great 'Dictionary' of Dr. J. A. H. Murray and his collaborators. The two double parts now issued comprise the letters *H, I, J, K,* and *L,* and constitute the third volume. Half the work is now in the hands of the subscribers, and the whole, consisting of 4,600 pages, may be expected before the close of 1905. Vol. IV., *M* to *Q,* is already in type, and Vol. V., *R* and *S,* is in course of being printed. The sixth and concluding volume will comprise the letters *T* to *Z,* the supplement, a bibliography of the many thousands of books specially excerpted for the 'Dictionary,' and a comprehensive comparative grammar of all the dialects treated historically. We have followed carefully the progress of the dictionary, which, since the initial stages were passed, has been creditably rapid, and have expressed frequently our sense of the thoroughness of the workmanship and the energy and enterprise of Prof. Wright, to whom the inception and the execution are due. In more than one respect the task of classifying, explaining, and illustrating a vocabulary so fluctuating is more difficult than that of supplying a complete lexicon of the written language. At any rate, Prof. Wright will soon be able to boast of having supplied his countrymen with a possession such as no other country can boast—a complete and scientific treatment of the whole of our dialects. It is needless to dwell on the labour that has been involved, first in the collection of materials, and then in classification, arrangement, and explanation. It suffices to say that to the philologist and to the student of local customs the dictionary is indispensable; and that the general student will find in the illustrative quotations matters of unending interest. It is pleasant to think that as the merits of the dictionary become more widely known the amount of support accorded it augments. Not yet is this nearly adequate to repay or to clear from heavy responsibility those who have undertaken and accomplished a task of importance truly national. A scheme is, however, advanced by which with a minimum of trouble and outlay adequate support may be accorded. In addition to a complete vocabulary of all the dialect words which are known to have been in use in England, Scotland, Ireland, and Wales during the last two hundred years, the dictionary includes American and colonial dialect words which are still in use in this country or are to be found in early printed dialect books and glossaries. Popular customs and superstitions, rural games and pastimes, and the like are all dealt with, and the work is thus commended to the ethnologist and the folklorist as well as the general reader. Before it is complete it is computed that over 100,000 words and about 500,000 quotations and references will be supplied. Dialect and folk-speech are rapidly disappearing, and had the task now in course of accomplishment been much longer delayed its execution would have been impossible. The book will, accordingly, be final, and can never grow out of date. The very extent of the information supplied prohibits us from giving an idea of the contents. We could select scores—nay, hundreds—of words of unfailing interest and importance which are rich in illustrations of country occupations and pursuits. It is natural to find that very many of the words have been the subject of discussion in our columns. See, for instance, *hodmandod,* in its first meaning of a snail with its shell, and innumerable others. To *take one's hair off*=to surprise greatly, suggests by contrast the modern slang "Keep your hair on." *Headache* as a name for the common red poppy is common (see 3rd S. viii. 274). *Letter-gae* for a precentor has been discussed in the Eighth and Ninth Series, and *level best* in the Eighth Series. Scarcely a page is there in which reference is not made to our columns, and there is none which does not supply matter curious, instructive, or edifying.

Chr. Fr. Grieb's Dictionary of the English and German Languages. By Arnold Schröer, Ph.D. 2 vols.—Vol. 1. *English and German.* (Frowde.)
FOR practical purposes the student finds the 'English and German Dictionary' of Herr Grieb the most trustworthy and generally available. Testimony to its merits is found in the fact that it has now reached a tenth edition. Under the direction of Dr. Schröer, the Professor of English Philology in the University of Freiburg, this has been rearranged, revised, and enlarged, to the great gain of the student. To judge of the full effect of the additions we must wait for the second volume, German and English, which is necessarily the more serviceable to the English scholar. With its 1350 pages, the present volume is the most comprehensive with which we are acquainted. It is also the most scientific and up to date, the 'New English Dictionary,' so far as it has progressed, having been laid constantly under contribution. Reference to any familiar word will show how full is the information imparted. For scholastic purposes and for private study it will, when completed, be the best English-German dictionary available.

The English Catalogue of Books for 1901. (Sampson Low & Co.)
THIS indispensable companion of the bookseller and the bibliophile has reached its sixty-fifth year of issue. We draw annually attention to its merits and make constant use of its pages. For our own purposes we find it the most prized and trustworthy of authorities.

MR. W. L. COURTNEY, the editor, writes in the *Fortnightly* on 'Modern Social Drama as Influenced by the Novel.' To the influence of the novel Mr. Courtney attributes the fact that the modern drama, instead of ending on a clear and unmistakable note, now more often than not finishes with a note of interrogation. It might, perhaps, be urged in answer that novel and drama both share the absence of conviction which is the difficulty of modern life. It is true, as Mr. Courtney maintains, that a dramatist must not be content to paint with servile fidelity what he sees, but must bring something out of his own genius. Another article on the condition of theatrical art is Dr. Todhunter's 'Poetic Drama and its Prospects on the Stage.' This, as will be expected by the reader, deals with the dramatic work of Mr. Stephen Phillips, the success of which is one of the signs of the time. Criticism in England — we suppose theatrical criticism is meant—is said to be in a rather chaotic condition, and Dr. Todhunter, aspiring presumably to make up for its shortcomings, passes in review the dramatic productions of Mr. Phillips, of which he forms a favourable estimate. Other theatrical experiments are the subject of comment, and the writer's mood is not wholly despondent. 'Away,' by Mr. W. B. Yeats, deals with quaint forms of pagan superstition still existing in Ireland. Mr. J. L. Bashford arrives at the rather sanguine conclusion that Anglophobia in Germany is on the decline. Dr. William Wallace notes some curious transformations in the temperament of the Scot, and holds that Scottish enthusiasm has been diverted from dogmatic religion and Radical politics and now goes out to music, to athletics, to sport. Mr. Witt's 'Concerning the Value of an Old Work of Art' is fruitful in suggestion.—The *Nineteenth Century* has also an article on the theatre. This is by Mr. Frederick Wedmore, and is entitled 'Literature and the Theatre.' Not too optimistic is Mr. Wedmore, who, though recognizing an advance in the drama, sees the necessary limitations, and is more readily disposed to seek for "Art" and discover it in story than in play. In the estimate of playwrights Mr. Grundy is credited with special gifts as an adapter. Mr. Pinero is held to be nearly always strong in stage technique and weak in psychology. Of 'The Liars' and 'The Case of Rebellious Susan' of Mr. Henry Arthur Jones it is asserted that they are "of the truest comedy," and the fact, for fact it is, that they are delightful in perusal is recognized. Some sound criticism is found in Mr. Percy F. Rowland's 'Literature of the Australian Commonwealth.' In 'Where are the Village Gentry?' Col. Pedder returns to the charge and maintains his former contention maugre the opposition of Col. Harcourt and Mr. Waters. Miss Goodrich-Freer depicts 'The Hobson-Jobson,' an Eastern holiday ceremony, in which quaint title it is not easy to recognize the names of Hassan and Hussein. Mr W. H. Mallock has a characteristic paper on 'The Latest Shipwreck of Metaphysics'; Miss M. F. Johnston voices the popular cry against hospital nurses; Mr. G. A. Raper gives some interesting statements concerning 'Freemasonry in France'; and Mrs Popham is mystical in 'Crossing the River.'—In the *Pall Mall* Mr. J. Holt Schooling reports upon Mrs. Gallup's application to certain works of Bacon's bi-literal cipher, and states that "as her mode of applying the cipher is not only lacking in any justification by fact, but is also shown to be wholly erroneous by fact, it follows that all her conclusions are proved to be without foundation, and that Mrs. Gallup's book 'Francis Bacon's Bi-literal Cypher' can be regarded only as a phantasy of her imagining, wholly unworthy of credence." Mrs. Gallup has promised further explanations. We are curious to see what she can say. 'As Others See Us' supplies an account of Lords Salisbury, Curzon, Cromer, and Lansdowne, Sir Michael Hicks-Beach, Sir William Harcourt, and Messrs. Brodrick and Wyndham as seen through American spectacles. Portraits of all are supplied. Mr. Douglas W. Freshfield gives particulars of 'A Holyday Tour in the Himalayas.' It is illustrated by photographs of stupendous peaks. A botanical article of interest is 'The Plants that Walk' of Mr. Edward Step. Mr. C. F.

Keary has an excellent contribution on 'Homer at Her Majesty's.' Another illustrated article of great interest is 'The Panama Canal,' showing the progress that is being made with the great undertaking. Mr. Archer's "real conversation" is with Mr. Heinemann. The reason why America has half a dozen first-class illustrated magazines against one in England is in this attributed to the facilities for distribution afforded by the American post office. —The *Cornhill* opens with 'At Casterbridge Fair,' a poem by Mr. Thomas Hardy. Dr. Garnett's 'Alms for Oblivion,' part ii., deals with the record by Leodius of the adventures in Spain of Frederick II., Elector Palatine, and of his brief visit to England. Many of the facts narrated are very curious. Lady Lisle, his hostess, presented him with a toothpick which she had used for seven years. 'In Praise of Birds,' by E. V. B., bewails the recognized impossibility in the matter of fashion of teaching women any lesson of humanity. The Viscount St. Cyres writes concerning 'Madame de Maintenon.' Part xv. of a 'Londoner's Log-Book' preserves a full measure of interest. Among 'A Few Conversationalists' are mentioned Browning, Leighton, Chorley, and Lord Coleridge.—Barbara Clay Finch deals in the *Gentleman's* with 'Bells' and their mottoes. Mr. S. E. Saville writes on that interesting figure Thoreau, and Mr. Attenborough on 'The Sonnet from Milton to Wordsworth.' The specimen sonnets given are not those ordinarily selected.—In *Longman's* the Rev. J. Isabell discusses 'Why are Sea Birds White,' and the Rev. J. Vaughan has an essay on 'Mary Rich, Countess of Warwick.' Mr. Lang's 'At the Sign of the Ship' is now, as always, the most interesting and readable portion of the contents.

Notices to Correspondents.

We must call special attention to the following notices:—

ON all communications must be written the name and address of the sender, not necessarily for publication, but as a guarantee of good faith.

WE cannot undertake to answer queries privately.

To secure insertion of communications correspondents must observe the following rules. Let each note, query, or reply be written on a separate slip of paper, with the signature of the writer and such address as he wishes to appear. When answering queries, or making notes with regard to previous entries in the paper, contributors are requested to put in parentheses, immediately after the exact heading, the series, volume, and page or pages to which they refer. Correspondents who repeat queries are requested to head the second communication "Duplicate."

J. W. H. ("*Sun* printed in Gold, Coronation, 1838").—We have no idea of the value.

NOTICE.

Editorial communications should be addressed to "The Editor of 'Notes and Queries'"—Advertisements and Business Letters to "The Publisher"—at the Office, Bream's Buildings, Chancery Lane, E.C.

We beg leave to state that we decline to return communications which, for any reason, we do not print; and to this rule we can make no exception.

LONDON, SATURDAY, APRIL 12, 1902.

CONTENTS. — No. 224.

Notes.

LITERARY FINDS AT MELBOURNE.

AN interesting find occurred lately in connexion with the Melbourne Public Library. A second-hand volume, which had been offered to the trustees for purchase, was referred by them to Prof. Tucker, who occupies the Chair of Classics in this University. The professor discovered on one of the fly-leaves the following Greek epigram, written with the contractions usual in the sixteenth century :—

Βάρβαροϛο ὐ πέλομαι, ἀλλ' οὐδέ τε εὔχομαι εἶναι

οὐδ' ἂν ἀμειψαίμην πρὸς Κρονίωνα πάτρην·

ἦν δὲ κλιμακοφόρων θείων γένος, ἔρνος Ἄργος,

Φοῖβον ὅλωϛ κατέχων στήθεσι, παῖγμα Τύχης.

The professor guessed that κλιμακοφόρων must be the græcized form of the name Scaliger, and was not thrown off the scent by the double error in prosody, as he was aware of the Scaligerian weakness in that respect. In another part of the book a not very happy attempt has been made by the author of the epigram to rewrite the third line, the error in which he had apparently discovered. In this later version the third line begins Ἢν γὰρ σκαληνῶν.

The book was sent to the British Museum for report, and it has lately been returned to the Melbourne Library, accompanied by a letter from Mr. F. G. Kenyon, who confirms fully Prof. Tucker's clever conjecture. Mr. Kenyon pronounces the numerous MS. notes in the volume to have been written by the hand of Julius Cæsar Scaliger, the elder of the two famous scholars. The book is a Latin translation of the ' Problemata ' of Aristotle, published at Paris in 1520. It was offered for sale by the bookseller for 2l. 12s. 6d. One would not have thought Melbourne to be a likely place for such literary treasure-trove.

ALEX. LEEPER.

Trinity College, Melbourne University.

[In a letter to the *Melbourne Argus* DR. LEEPER adds :—

" Our own University professors, curiously enough, have enjoyed a large share of the romance of literary discovery. It may be remembered by some that Prof. Jenks during his brief sojourn among us lighted upon a rare treasure in the shape of a little MS. book, containing several of Keats's poems in the poet's own handwriting. They included ' The Pot of Basil,' ' The Lines on the Mermaid Tavern,' and ' The Eve of St. Mark's.' There is the strongest reason to believe that the volume was owned by the poet's brother, George Keats, and was brought to Melbourne from America. What made it specially interesting was the fact that it contained an unpublished stanza of ' The Pot of Basil,' which would seem to have been struck out by the poet himself before printing. Prof. Jenks at the time gave good reason for his opinion that both ' The Pot of Basil' and ' The Eve of St. Mark's ' in the volume were the oldest autographs existing of those pieces.

" Another of our professors, the late Dr. Morris, whose loss the University will long mourn, had an experience of a somewhat similar kind. Some three years ago a curiosity shop in Melbourne offered him for sale the first log-book kept by Capt. Cook when he was an A.B. on board H.M.S. Eagle. The discovery was of peculiar value to Dr. Morris, as he was at that time engaged upon his biography of Capt. Cook, which is at present on the eve of publication by a London firm. The newly found log supplies details of a period in Cook's life which all his previous biographers had regarded as a blank.

" The most recent literary find in Melbourne occurred within the University precincts, though in this case the lucky digger was not a professor. Mr. Sugden, the Master of Queen's College, showed me a few days ago an interesting volume, in which he has made a discovery which does credit to his keen-sightedness, both physical and mental. The book, which is a beautiful copy of Robert Stephens's ' Editio Regia ' of the Greek Testament (Paris, 1550), was presented in 1895 to the library of Queen's College. On the title-page, beneath the date, there was a scrollwork ornamentation in vermilion paint. Looking at this closely one day, Mr. Sugden detected traces of writing underneath, and, after carefully washing off the coloured scrollwork, he brought to

light an inscription in very minute characters. The
words thus disclosed showed that the book had
once been the property of the great Isaac Casaubon,
'the most learned of all living men,' as Scaliger
styled him. Mr. Sugden gave a description of his
discovery in the *Athenæum* last year.

"Perhaps I may mention, in conclusion, a small
find of my own, of which I gave an account at the
last meeting of the Australian Library Association.
Some years ago a bundle of second-hand theological
works of little value somehow came to our college
library, I forget whether by gift or purchase. Between the pages of one of the volumes were some
loose charred sheets. On examination they turned
out to belong to the first edition of the famous
sermon preached by Dr. Sacheverell before the
Lord Mayor in St. Paul's Cathedral on 5 November,
1709, 'On the Perils of False Brethren in Church
and State.' Readers of Macaulay will remember
his summary description, 'A foolish parson preached
a foolish sermon.' Sacheverell was impeached before
the Lords, convicted, and inhibited from preaching
for three years. According to the custom of the
day, the punishment of the Court fell on not only
the preacher, but the sermon, and it was condemned to be burnt by the common hangman. The
copy which came into my hands, and is now in
Trinity College Library, had evidently been in the
fire, but had escaped destruction by being somewhere near the middle of the heap. Only the mar-
gins were burnt. The letterpress was intact. The
paper, however, was so scorched that it crumbled
in the fingers. For a time I could not think how it
could be preserved. Even handling it seemed to
threaten fatal injury. An ingenious bookbinder,
Mr. Cassidy, of Richmond, to whom I showed it,
asked to be allowed to try his skill upon it, and I
consented. He took the sheets away, soaked them,
I believe, in alum water, and gave them firmness
enough to make binding possible. The letterpress
can now be read comfortably, and the book handled
without risk. There is no reason why it should not
last as long as a work that never felt the hangman's
fire."

Mr. Sugden's letter appeared in the *Athenæum* of
28 September, 1901, p. 416.]

SHAKESPEARE AND BEN JONSON: DID THEY QUARREL?

THERE is a more or less vague tradition
that Jonson was indebted to Shakespeare
for the first opportunity to get a hearing
for his plays, and that 'Every Man in his
Humour,' with Shakespeare in the cast, is
the particular play which first drew attention
to Rare Ben's work. It is certain, however,
that Shakespeare took no part in Jonson's
next play, 'Every Man out of his Humour.'
Mr. Fleay, with probable reason, regards this
play as the cause of the so-called Elizabethan
poetomachia; and Shakespeare's participation in the quarrel has been regarded as
somewhat doubtful, despite Kemp's emphatic
declaration in the (Second) 'Return from
Parnassus.' As a contribution to the literature of the subject, the following notes are
offered for what they may be worth, the italics

in every instance being those of the present
writer. In 'As You Like It' (II. vii.) Jaques
rails partly as follows:—

A fool, a fool!—I met a fool i' the forest,
A motley fool;—a miserable world!
As I do live by food, I met a fool,
Who laid him down and bask'd him in the sun,
And rail'd on lady Fortune in good terms,
In good set terms,—and yet a motley fool.

'Every Man out of his Humour' gives us
glimpses of Jonson himself in the characters
of Asper and Macilente, and in the following
citations it is always Macilente who is
speaking, his second speech at the beginning
of Act I. being as follows:—

Soft, who be these?
I'll lay me down awhile, till they be past.
[*He lies down.*

He goes on throughout the play to rail on
Fortune in these various terms. His speech
which begins the play being over-long, the
opening Latin line only is given:—

Viri est, fortunæ cœcitatem facile ferre.

Who can endure to see *blind fortune* dote thus?
To be enamour'd on this dusty turf?—I. ii.

See how the *strumpet fortune* tickles him
And makes him swoon with laughter.—I. iii.

I see no reason why *that dog (call'd Chance)*
Should fawn upon this fellow more than me.—II. iv.

Out on thee, dotard! What star rul'd his birth?
That brought him such a star? *Blind fortune* still
Bestows her gifts on such as cannot use them.—II. iv.

O that there should be *fortune*
To clothe these men so naked in desert!—IV. vi.

These extracts do not exhaust Macilente's
allusions to fortune; but Jaques, in this same
scene of 'As You Like It,' goes on to declare
that

When I did hear
The motley fool thus *moral on the time,*
My lungs began to crow like chanticleer,
That fools should be so deep contemplative;
And I did laugh, sans intermission,
An hour by his dial.—O noble fool!
A worthy fool! Motley's the only wear.

Asper (Jonson), in the Induction, thus
morals on the time; and in view of Jaques's
words, it seems possible to determine definitely at whom Jonson was girding:—

O, how I hate the *monstrousness of time,*
Where every servile imitating spirit
(Plagu'd with an itching leprosy of wit),
In a mere halting fury, strives to fling
His ulc'rous body in the Thespian spring,
And straight leaps forth a poet! but as lame
As Vulcan, or the founder of Cripplegate.

Earlier in the Induction Asper declares
his intentions, in part as follows:—

My soul
Was never ground into such oily colours,
To flatter vice and daub iniquity:
But (with an armed and resolved hand)
I'll strip *the ragged follies of the time*

Naked as at their birth, and with a whip of steel
Print wounding lashes in their iron ribs.
I fear no mood stampt in a private brow,
When I am pleased to unmask a public vice.

Or yet again in the Induction :—

Do not I know *the time's condition?*
Yes, Mitis, and their souls ; and who they be
That either will or can except against me.
None but a sort of fools, so sick in taste
That they contemn all physick of the mind,
And, like gall'd camels, kick at every touch.

There would seem to have been another tilt between the poets in the play on the words *stature, just,* and *melancholy.* Jonson goes on in this style :—

Punt. What complexion or what *stature* bears he?
Gent. Of your *stature,* and very near your complexion.
Punt. Mine is *melancholy.*
Cor. So is the dog's, *just.*

And in 'As You Like It' there is this badinage :—

Jaques. Rosalind is your love's name?
Orl. Yes, *just.*
Jaques. I do not like her name.
Orl. There was no thought of pleasing you when she was christened.
Jaques. What *stature* is she of?
Orl. Just as high as my heart.

. . . .

Orl. I am glad of your departure ; adieu, good monsieur *melancholy.*

Carlo in Jonson's play (V. vi.) makes this reference to natural philosophy :—

"'Tis an axiom in *natural philosophy,* 'What comes nearest the nature of that it feeds, converts quicker to nourishment, and doth sooner essentiate,'"

which nonsense seems to be pointed at in Corin's speech (III. ii.) :—

That the property of rain is to wet, and fire to burn; that good pasture makes fat sheep, and that a great cause of the night is lack of the sun ; that he that hath learned no wit by nature nor art may complain of good breeding, or comes of a very dull kindred.
Touch. Such a one is a *natural philosopher.*

The exact date of 'All's Well' appears to be indeterminable ; but in the brief scene of II. ii. Shakespeare plays upon the words "O Lord, sir," in a way that may have brought out Jonson's reply in III. iv. of 'Every Man out of his Humour.' Certain is it that in this scene he is burlesquing Marston (Paunch of Esquiline, Synderisis, mincing capreal, circumference, intellectual, zodiac, ecliptic, tropic, mathematical, and demonstrate being favourite words of his). Jonson's scene is too long to bear repetition here, but the responses of Orange to Clove's fustian speeches are respectively as follows :—

O lord, sir.
It pleases you to say so, sir.

O God, sir.
O lord, sir.

Moreover, if Shakespeare's clown was highly fed and lowly taught, Clove would "sit you a whole afternoon sometimes in a bookseller's shop, reading the Greek, Italian, and Spanish, when he understands not a word of either." Jonson returns to this phrase in his "comical satire" of 'Cynthia's Revels' (I. iv.), wherein Asotus partly replies to Amorphous's various speeches in this fashion :—

O God, sir.
O lord, sir, there needs no such apology, I assure you.
O 'tis your pleasure to say so, sir.
I do purpose to travel, sir, at spring.
O God, sir, &c.

To all of which Crites (Jonson again) attaches this comment :—

O, here's rare motley, sir.

Shakespeare in 'All's Well,' anticipating somewhat Polonius's advice to his son, causes the countess to bless her son Bertram in these words :—

    Love all, trust a few,
Do wrong to none : be able for thine enemy
Rather in power than use ; and keep thy friend
Under thy own life's key : be check'd for silence,
But never taxed for speech.

And Carlo in Jonson's play, III. iv., misanthrophizes in this fashion :—

Love no man, trust no man. Speak ill of no man to his face, nor well of any man behind his back. Salute fairly on the front, and wish 'em hanged upon the turn. Spread yourself upon his bosom publicly, whose heart you would eat in private. These be principles ; think on them ; I'll come to you again presently.

In 1599 Shakespeare had finally been granted a coat of arms, and we seem to get glimpses of the incident in 'As You Like It' and 'Every Man out of his Humour.' Shakespeare's motto was "Non sans droict," and in Jonson's play, III. i., we have an intensely satirical scene which, I believe, was written to ridicule his colleague's social aspirations. After derisively discussing Sogliardo's escutcheon, there appears to be this very pointed allusion to Shakespeare's motto :—

Sog. How like you them, signor?
Punt. Let the word be *not without mustard ;* your crest is very rare, sir.
Car. A frying-pan to the crest had had no fellow.

And Shakespeare reverts to the mustard and frying-pan in 'As You Like It,' I. ii.:—

Clo. No, by mine honour, but I was bid to come for you.
Ros. Where learned you that oath, foole?
Clo. Of a certain knight, that swore by his honour they were good Pan-cakes, and swore by his honour the Mustard was naught. Now Ile stand to

it, the Pan-cakes were naught, and the Mustard was good, and yet was not the knight forsworne.

Shakespeare emphasizes the oath " by mine honour," and, to make the allusion all but certain as referring to the two playwrights, it need only be said that the knight from whom the clown learned the oath was the vainglorious Puntarvolo, who uses it in V. ii.!   Chas. A. Herpich.
18, Irving Place, New York City.

"Maceron": "Mucheron."—May I point out that Mr. Edmund Gosse, in his ' Life and Letters of John Donne' (published 1899, vol. i. p. 132); Mr. E. K. Chambers, in his edition of Donne's 'Poems' ("Muses' Library," vol. ii. pp. 240, 241); and also the late Dr. A. B. Grosart, in his edition of the 'Poems' ("The Fuller Worthies Library," vol. i. p. 69), commenting on the 'Epistle,' "Infinitati Sacrum," &c., prefixed to 'The Progress of the Soul,' all overlook the fact that the word which is spelt *maceron* in the 1635 edition is spelt *mucheron* in that of 1633, and remark that it means *fop?* *Mucheron, i.e., mushroom,* is undoubtedly the correct reading, and *maceron* only a misprint.

In support of this view I would cite Burton's 'Anatomy of Melancholy,' part i. sec. 1, mem. 2, subsec. 9, where, on the subject of metempsychosis, he writes :—

> " Lucian's cock was first Euphorbus a captain :
> Ille ego (nam memini) Trojani tempore belli
> Panthoides Euphorbus eram.
>   Ovid, 'Metam.,' xv. 161.
> A horse, a man, a *sponge*," &c.

In this passage *sponge* is used as equivalent to *fungus,* with which it is cognate (*vide* Skeat's 'Etymological Dictionary'), and therefore meaning *mucheron,* as Donne has it, or, as we should now say, *mushroom.* The whole point of the argument from a Pythagorean point of view is lost if the word is to be taken as =*fop.* In subsec. 5 of the same part of the 'Anatomy' Burton says : "The common division of the soul is into three principal faculties—vegetal, sensitive, and rational, which make three distinct kinds of living creatures — vegetal plants, sensible beasts, rational men."

In Donne's 'Epistle' the order is the same, but reversed, viz., "an Emperour, in a Post-horse, and in a Mucheron" (*i.e., mushroom*), man, beast, vegetable, and to treat the word *maceron* as, in this connexion, meaning *fop, i.e.,* as a human being, and not merely as a misprint, is a self-evident mistake, and I am somewhat surprised that it should not have been noticed before.   C. S. Harris.

"Sesame."—The ultimate origin of the name of this seed, which we have received through the Latin *sesamum,* from the Greek *sēsamon,* has not been pointed out. At least it is not in Devic's supplement to Littré of 'Words of Oriental Origin,' nor in Skeat. Mahn-Webster gives an Arabic *simsim.* I believe it is of Assyrian origin, as in the cuneiform *shamash-shammu, i.e.,* "sun-plant," is the word for sesame seed; and if the first syllable be read according to its syllabic value, which is *she* (see L. W. King, 'Assyrian Language,' p. 89), we have *she-shammu,* which is still nearer to our "sesame." The plain of Mesopotamia was renowned for its marvellous produce of all kinds of grain (see Jastrow, 'Religion of Babylonia and Assyria,' p. 30).
    A. Smythe Palmer.
S. Woodford.

'The Trial of the Spirits.'—Among the books attributed to Robert Hindmarsh in the 'D.N.B.' article *sub nomine* is one bearing the title prefixed to this paragraph and published in 1825. The real author of the book, however, was the Rev. William Ettrick, of High Barns, near Sunderland, and instead of the name of its supposed author and its title-page, casually read, would indicate — an "appreciation" of Emanuel Swedenborg, it is a bitter depreciation of that much-discussed writer. The artfully concealed secret of the authorship was promptly exposed in the *Intellectual Repository* for July, 1825, and it was briefly discussed by Robert Hindmarsh himself in his 'Rise and Progress of the New Church,' posthumously published in 1861 (pp. 430-1). The Rev. William Ettrick published 'Two Apologetical Replies' to his first Swedenborgian critic, respectively in 1825 and 1826. He was also the author of 'The Second Exodus,' 3 vols., published in 1810-14; 'The Season and Time,' in 1816; 'Scripture Proofs of the Pre-Existence and Deity of Christ,' 1819; and 'A Fragment of the History of John Bull,' in three parts, 1820-1; all of which, if contemporary gossip be trustworthy, the world of that day "willingly let die." The innocent fancy—or impudent fraud—which gives rise to the present paragraph forms also the subject of an article appearing in the *New Church Magazine* for last month, where the matter is treated at greater length than is here desirable or possible.
    Charles Higham.

Blanche Parrye. (See *ante,* p. 181.)—Mr. W. E. Harland-Oxley and others interested in the above-named lady may be pleased to know that the stained-glass window erected to her memory in Bacton Church is now in Atcham Church, near Shrewsbury, having been removed, it is stated for safety, by a former Mrs. Burton, of Atcham.

HERBERT SOUTHAM.

Shrewsbury.

"YUCCA."—In the second volume of an authoritative work, 'Central and South America,' by A. H. Keane, 1901, p. 79, it is stated that "the yucca yields......the tapioca of commerce...... Yucca is originally a Peruvian (Quichua) word now current in the Southern United States, and in Mexico." If this were true it would be of great importance, but no evidence is adduced, and all I can find is against it. A Peruvian word could not have travelled so far from its home before the arrival of the Spaniard, and although there are several terms (such as maguey and pulque) which appear to have been picked up by Europeans in one part of America and transferred to another, this can scarcely be one of them, as there are chronological difficulties. Yucca is among the very earliest native American words on record. It is quoted by Amerigo Vespucci in his famous 'First Letter,' date 1497, as heard by him in the West Indies thirty years before Pizarro set foot in Peru. This fact may be of interest to the editors of the 'N.E.D.'

JAS. PLATT, Jun.

CROMWELL FLEETWOOD. — It is a little singular that in the various attempts to enumerate the descendants of the great Protector this undoubted grandson should, so far as I am aware, have escaped notice. He is certainly not mentioned by either Noble or Waylen. Yet his identity is not obscure. He was admitted to Gray's Inn, 19 April, 1671, as "second son of Charles Fleetwood of Feltwell Norfolk esq." On 22 February, 1678/9, the licence was issued from the Vicar-General's office to marry "Cromwell Fleetwood of Stoke Newington, Midx esq. bachr about 26, and Mrs Elizabeth Nevill of Little Berkhampstead, Herts, Spr about 24, daughter of George Nevill of Staple Inn, London, gent. who consents," at All Hallows in the Wall, London, or Bayford, Herts. His age, twenty-six, fixes Cromwell Fleetwood's birth in 1653. General Fleetwood married Bridget Cromwell, it is usually thought, early in 1652, so that there can be no doubt that this son was the first child of that marriage. His description in the Gray's Inn register as "second son" of his father possibly has reference to his elder half-brother, Smith Fleetwood, the general's son by his first wife, Frances Smith.

The two elder sons of Charles Fleetwood were thus called after the maiden names of their respective mothers.

Some little further light is cast upon this branch of the Fleetwoods by a most interesting paper printed in No. 1 of the Transactions of the newly formed Congregational Historical Society. A MS. volume there quoted, called 'Dr. Watt's Church Book,' gives a list of the members of the church then in Bury Street, Duke's Place, when under the pastorate of Dr. John Owen (1673-83), together with the time of their decease. Among these are several old Cromwellians. The Fleetwoods named are: "Charles Fleetwood esq. dyed Oct. 4th 1692." "Mr. Smith Fleetwood dyed Feb. 1708/9." "Mrs Fleetwood [the general's third wife, Mary Hartopp] dyed 10 Jan. 1680." "Lady Hartopp [sister to Smith Fleetwood] dyed 9 Nov. 1711." "Mr Cromwell Fleetwood received into Church fellowship June 1673, dyed 1 June, 1688."

It would thus appear that Cromwell Fleetwood survived his marriage nearly ten years. Whether or not he left issue is an interesting query. So far as is known for certain, the descendants of Charles Fleetwood and Bridget Cromwell died out in the first generation.

W. D. PINK.

Lowton, Newton-le-Willows, Lancashire.

"COMICALLY."—This word appears to be used by T. Fuller in a peculiar sense, unknown to the dictionaries, at the beginning of his 'Second Reconciler' ('A Triple Reconciler,' London, 1654). At p. 58, describing the three "adventures" of Barnabas and Saul, he says:—

"His next voyage ends sadly, and sorrowfully with Blasphemie and Persecution from the Jews at Antioch, though it began Comically and courteously with this fair invitation in my Texte, and after the reading of the Law and the Prophets," &c.

It is possible that this word is a misprint for comitally, which would be a regularly formed adverb from comital, the adjective of comes. Comital is given in the 'N.E.D.' as the adjectival derivative from comes, with the meaning pertaining to or of the rank of a count or earl. This would be nonsense; but Fuller may have intended the meaning companionably or sociably. Comitably would be a possible form. Supposing the word derived from the adjective comis through comitas, "courteousness," "friendliness," the correct form would be comitarily, on the analogy of sanitary, hereditary, &c. The termination -ical seems to be properly derived in med. Latin only from words of Greek origin, which must needs confine comical, from κῶμος, κωμικὸς, to

its ordinary senses; cf. *heretical, physical, cynical,* and dozens of other words from Greek roots. If Fuller was coining a new sense for *comical* he was in error.   C. DEEDES.
Brighton.

"THE BISHOP OF BROOKS."—In a recent volume issued by the Historical Manuscripts Commission ('Report on the Manuscripts of Mrs. Frankland-Russell-Astley,' 1900) there is a letter, or rather a long disquisition, upon war addressed to Charles I., and attributed to Sir John Melldrum, in which occurs the following remarkable passage :—

"Such counsellors [who advised war] were the late bishop of Rosse to the late Queen of Scots, the bishop of Brooks to the Lady Jane, that miserable King of Hungaria, who were the occasion of bringing of Turks into Hungary and the French nation into Scotland, two guests that both nations may wish they never know the way thither again."

The letter is assigned by the editor or editors to the year 1639, and the following startling comment is added in a foot-note in explanation of the name of Lady Jane : "*Sic* in MS., but the proper reading no doubt is 'to King Ladislaus.'"

I have often had opportunities to point out that Hungarian history is not a strong point with the editors employed by the Historical Manuscripts Commission, and on this occasion, too, I am afraid they have gone hopelessly wrong.* There are five kings of the name of Ladislaus known in Hungarian history, four of whom reigned long before any Turk set foot in Europe. The fifth and last was Ladislaus Posthumus, who certainly did not call the Turks into his kingdom, but, on the contrary, his lieutenant, Hunyady János (*i.e.*, John of Hunyad), did his best to keep the infidels out of the country.

My humble opinion is that "Lady Jane" should read "Lord John," whose title to the crown of Hungary has not yet been recognized by all the editors in Fetter Lane, some of whom only dub him "Count of Scepuse" (*sic*) and "the Voyvode," though even his rival, Ferdinand of Austria, and his rival's brother, Charles V., had acknowledged him as king of his own part of Hungary.

"The Bishop of Brooks" is more difficult to identify because, although King John had several bishops, the diocese of "Brooks" is totally unknown in Christendom.
L. L. K.

"ST. JAMES STREET." — MR. HARLAND-OXLEY, in his interesting notes on St. Mar-

* In another part of the same volume there is a foot-note in which the capture of "Buda-Pesth" is mentioned in 1686 ! An arrant anachronism !

garet's, Westminster (*ante*, p. 182), quotes, from the 'Will Book' of that parish, an entry regarding Cornelius Vandon, who "did give eight almshouses in Pettie France, next to the end of St. James-street, for the use of eight poor women." This St. James Street is, of course, the street which was subsequently known as James Street, and which the late vestry of Westminster, with an extraordinary want of the sense of historic perception, amalgamated with Buckingham Gate. Authorities generally state that the street derived its name from its proximity to the park. Mr. Mackenzie Walcott, in his 'Memorials of Westminster,' ed. 1851, p. 292, calls the thoroughfare "St. James's Street," though in the index it figures as "James Street." The change of name probably originated after the better-known St. James's Street, connecting Pall Mall with Piccadilly, was built. In the Parish Clerks' 'New Remarks of London,' 1732, p. 277, we find the intermediate form "James's Street." It is interesting to learn from the authority quoted by MR. HARLAND-OXLEY that the street was in existence in the days of Elizabeth. In Newcourt's map, engraved by Faithorne, the western side is covered with houses, from Tothill Fields to Tart Hall, but there are no buildings on the eastern, or park, side.
W. F. PRIDEAUX.

A PARLIAMENT OF BIRDS. — Reference is made in 3ʳᵈ S. v. 409 to a tract printed in 1682 and entitled 'Concavum Cappo-cloacorum ;......being a Dialogue between Trueman and Cappo-cloak-man.' The author of it is plainly Roger L'Estrange, for his speech bewrayeth him. Here is one of his illustrations :—

"The Commonwealth of Birds, to redress some Grievances, call'd a Parliament, where, after they had taken their Places that were Representatives, and Elected *nemine contradicente* the Parrot for their Speaker, because of its excellent Qualifications of calling Names, and Collecting others Voices : All the Members were called over, and made their personal Appearance before Mr. *Speaker*. Amongst the rest appears a round fac'd Animal, that look'd as big as a Burgess, commonly call'd an Owl. All the rest of the Birds were amazed very much, as not being acquainted with any such Corporation that could be represented by it. Resolving therefore themselves into a Committee of Elections, consisting of the whole House, they began to debate the Matter before the Chair-Bird, who was a Creature of the same kind with Mr. *Speaker*. The Swallow and the Magpie chatter'd to this purpose, that they had flown far and near, but never saw any such Creature amongst the Birds. The Jay, the Goose, and the Jack-daw being also Leading Members of that Committee, concurring with the former, the pretty King in the Chair was presently for clearing the House of such an uncouth Member, and began to cry *Walk Knave Walk:* Whereupon the Owl thinking it hard Measure, before he was well seen, or at all heard, to be ejected, began to set a good Face of the Business; and raising his Ruff to shew its Feather, and stretching out its Neck, to exalt its Voice, look'd so frightfully, and made so hideous, loud, and screeching a Noise, that all the Birds were so terrified, that they presently left all their Places, and the poor *Parochete* fell out of the Chair in a Swoon, altering its Note from *Walk Knave* to *Poor Pall*, and was taken up in a very sad Condition; and so all the Debates ended, and the whole Assembly dissolved themselves."

Although *Concavum* is so printed both in the title and on the first page, I incline to think it a misprint for *Conclavum*. Allusions are made (p. 26) to *Old Nobs* and *Brisk Hall*; (p. 28) to the slapping of pew-doors during the prayers; (p. 30) to the "Churchwardens Half-pint in the Vestry"; (p. 31) to "Humming in the Church"; and (p. 55) to *Dick Medler* and *Harry Monkey-face*. There is scarcely a dull page in the tract.

RICHARD H. THORNTON.
Portland, Oregon.

"BLOCKHEAD" APPLIED TO A WOMAN.—The 'H.E.D.' gives no instance of this. See, however, Boswell's 'Life of Johnson' (Dr. G. Birkbeck Hill's edition), vol. ii. p. 456, where Boswell, after recording that Johnson addressed the very stupid maid who opened the door at Mr. Hector's as "blockhead," comments as follows:—

"I never heard the word *blockhead* applied to a woman before, though I do not see why it should not [*sic*], when there is evident occasion for it."

Compare Carlyle's 'History of Friedrich II. of Prussia,' book xx. chap. x. :—

"The reigning Czarina, old *Catin* herself, is silently the Olympian Jove to Catharine, who reveres her very much. Though articulately stupid as ever, in this Book of Catharine's, she comes out with a dumb weight, of silence, of obstinacy, of intricate abrupt rigour, which——who knows but it may savour of dumb unconscious wisdom in the fat old blockhead?"

EDWARD BENSLY.
The University, Adelaide, South Australia.

WASSAILING THE APPLE-TREE.—The following from the *Western Morning News* of January may be worth preserving in 'N. & Q.' :—

"The ancient custom, now fast dying out, of wassailing or toasting the apple-trees, is still observed in some of the outlying parishes of North Devon and Somerset, and probably nowhere with more ceremony and solemnity than at Wootton Basset, near Minehead. Old Twelfth-eve, Thursday last, twelve days after Old Christmas-eve, is the usual day, and in the evening well-nigh all the folk of the parish assemble at the farmhouse, and, after a good square meal, start in procession for the nearest orchard. A goodly supply of cider is carried by the stronger men of the party, 'the butler' brings a two-handled mug and some pieces of toast,

and the 'master' walks in front with the light, whilst a number of men with guns, old muzzle-loaders, blunderbusses, or anything that will make a noise, form the rearguard. Arrived at the orchard, the party all form in a ring, joining hands, and the master in the middle seizes a branch of the tree, and more or less out of tune sings the following words:—

O apple-tree, I wassail thee,
   In hopes that thou wilt blow,
To blow and to bear well,
   So merry let us be;
For the Lord doth know where we shall be
   To be merry another year.

Then all the folks standing round holloa, shout, or sing:—

Hatfuls, capfuls, three-bushel bagfuls,
   Barn floorfuls, tullet holefuls,
   And a little heap under the stairs.

Deafening cheers are then given, and the men who have been standing outside say, 'Now, Tom Pod, we wassail thee!' and then they let off their blunderbusses and other weapons. The health of the apple-tree having been solemnly drunk, the master blowing off the froth, and the two-handled mug having gone right round the ring, the butler takes a piece of toast, and, pouring cider over it (called 'basting'), hands it to the master, who sticks it up in the tree for the robins, in the hope that it will bring luck. The ceremony completed, the procession moves off to the next orchard, and so on until each has been visited and wassailed."

R. BARCLAY-ALLARDICE.
Lostwithiel.

[See 7th S. xi. 103, 217, 337.]

"BY ROTE."—To say or learn anything by rote means by memory, without attending to the meaning. What is the etymology of "rote"? The word is generally explained in the dictionaries as a doublet of "route," Fr. *route* (Lat. *rupta*); so Skeat, Annandale, Webster, Wedgwood, Richardson. The lexicographers say that this word "rote" is identical in form with Old French *rote* (modern *route*). But I think that when we come to look into the matter we shall find that the English word is not identical in form with the French word. The evidence goes to show that the two words differ in the quality of the root vowel, the English word having an open *o* (=Latin *ŏ*), the French word a close *o* (=Latin *u*). For evidence of the open *o* in the English "rote" I may cite Chaucer's rime *rote: cote* ('C.T.,' Prol., 327). Tyndale, Surrey, Shakespeare, Drayton, spell the word "roat" (see Nares, Richardson, and Schmidt). It is, therefore, impossible that our "rote," with an open *o*, can be a doublet of "route." "Rote" is not derived from a Latin form *rupta*, but is a learned form of Latin *rŏta*, a wheel, which in the Middle Ages was used in the sense of a regular course or order (see Ducange).

COMESTOR OXONIENSIS.

Queries.

We must request correspondents desiring information on family matters of only private interest to affix their names and addresses to their queries, in order that the answers may be addressed to them direct.

"Only too thankful."— Expressions of this type appear to be very recent; I seem to remember "only too true" in the sixties, but of such no quotations before the eighties have been sent in for the dictionary. Will readers of 'N. & Q.' try to find, or to remember, how far back the idiom goes? And we shall be glad of any light upon the sematology. What does *too* here mean? and what does *only* mean? Why *too*? and why *only* too? When a man is "only too glad" to get something to do, why is he *too* glad; and if he is "too glad" to refuse it, why is he *only* too glad? What does the "only" limit or exclude? Or is it ironical in its origin, like "Has he lost anything?" "Only his life; that's all," or "Did he speak long?" "Only till everybody was asleep." Help with this idiom will be "only too thankfully" received.
                 J. A. H. Murray.

Oxford.

Carducci's Library.—The Queen Dowager of Italy has lately bought the library of the poet Carducci and all his published and unpublished manuscripts. Her Majesty has done this so that the library may not be divided. The books are to remain in the poet's possession until his death, when they are to be transferred to the Bologna Museum. Can any reader of 'N. & Q.' give some indication as to the nature of the books and MSS.?   A. N. Q.

Tablet in West-End Square. — To the front of the house No. 35 in Bryanston Square is affixed a small framed relic, the motive for whose preservation has often puzzled me. It has the appearance of a portion of some mural adornment, and depicts sundry nude infants toying with bunches of grapes. Can any reader of 'N. & Q.' satisfy my curiosity in respect of this rather unique attraction to a private residence?   Cecil Clarke.

Junior Athenæum Club.

"Ratlings."—In this part of the country lumbermen call kindling that is tied up in bundles about four feet long "ratlings" (sometimes spelt "rattlings"). I have not been able to trace this word. Is it possibly connected with the nautical term *ratlines* and its variants *ratlins, ratlings, rattlings?* I con-

jecture, though, that it may be akin to M.E. *rattes*, rags; M.E. *ratten*, to tear; Icel. *hrat, hrati*, rubbish, trash; Norw. *rat*, rubbish (cp. *ratgods*, refuse goods); Sw., Norw., *rata*, to reject, refuse; Eng. *rate*, to refuse, to find fault with.   Charles Bundy Wilson.

State University of Iowa, Iowa City, Iowa.

Epigram on Women. — I shall be very much obliged if you can favour me with the name of the author of the following epigram upon women. It has, I fancy erroneously, been ascribed to Love Peacock :—

Oh the gladness of their gladness when they're glad,
And the sadness of their sadness when they're sad;
But the gladness of their gladness and the sadness
    of their sadness
Are as nothing to their badness when they're bad.
               Stephen Simeon.

Fleet, Hants.

'Jenny of Monteith.' — Wraxall in his 'Memoirs' speaks of the "once well-known ballad 'Jenny of Monteith.'" Where can I find a copy of it?   J. M. Bulloch.

118, Pall Mall.

Doset Hall. — In J. Rocque's map of Surrey, "compleated and engraved by J. Andrews" (date 1765?), I find, alongside Merton Abbey site, the name of Doset Hall, just on the Wimbledon side of the turnpike a little to the west of Abbey Lane. Can any reader of 'N. & Q.' supply particulars of the history of it?

I do not find Doset Hall in Norden and Spede's Surrey sheet of their 'Atlas of England' (1610?), in Schenk and Valk's 'Surria vernaculè Surrey' (1680?), nor in Kip and Norden's map of 'Surrey olim Sedes Regnorum' in Camden's 'Britannia,' sixth ed., fol. 211, date 1607. (My dates are as given in the B.M. Map Catalogue.) In these latter maps I find Merton is sometimes given as Martyn, Martin, or Martin Nevell. Can that be explained?   John A. Randolph.

Sale of Stamps forbidden by the Inland Revenue.—I find in a recent number of *Hobbies* an article on the subject of forbidden stamps. I should be glad if any reader of your paper could give the date of the order by the Inland Revenue forbidding stamps to be sold to collectors, and tell me what object is gained by it.   B. Y.

Montesquieu in England : Unprinted MSS. — If any of your readers could help me to any unprinted manuscript material throwing light on Montesquieu's residence in England between October, 1729, and 1731, I should be very grateful. It is

only unprinted manuscript material that I
require. J. C. COLLINS.
51, Norfolk Square, W.

CORONATION OF GEORGE IV.—I have a
gilt metal medallion, 2⅓ in. diameter, struck
or cast on one side only, bearing in the centre
a crown over a double line entwined and
reversed cipher G.R., under which is No. 143;
round the same in Roman capitals "Coronation of H.M. King George IV." What is the
history of it? J. ARROW.
85, Union Grove, Clapham, S.W.

MANOR COURT ROLLS OF BRADFORD AND
WILSDEN, YORKS.—I should be glad to know
of the place of deposit of above rolls, if any
such exist. These manors were sold in 1795
by John Marsden, of Hornby Castle; but the
respective rolls do not appear to have passed
with the conveyances to the present owners,
and I am unable to elicit any information
respecting them through the ordinary chan-
nels. NATHANIEL HONE.
The Limes, Ellerton Road, Surbiton.

ANDREW WILSON—I am anxious to trace
the parentage, &c., of the Rev. Andrew Wilson,
vicar of Easingwold, Yorks, 1685-1713. He
graduated at St. John's College, Cambridge,
B.A. 1680, M.A. 1684, and married at Leeds
Parish Church, 5 September, 1687, Elizabeth
Foster, of Leeds. Any further information
as to his own or his wife's family, and the
date and place of their burial, will be very
gratefully received. JOHN COMBER.
Myddleton Hall, near Warrington.

ANTWERP CATHEDRAL.—I have read somewhere that the reason why the second tower
of Antwerp Cathedral is not completed is
from the treacherous nature of the ground,
and that the one tower caused the former
tower to lean. There was, too, a rather
interesting account of the curriers supplying
thousands of hides to make the foundations
secure. Unfortunately, I did not follow Capt.
Cuttle's advice; and as I cannot put my
hand on the story—I have referred to guide-
books, Fergusson's 'Architecture,' and encyclopædias—will one of your correspondents
please say where it is, and if authentic?
LUCIS.

HARRY ST. LAWRENCE. — Could any of
your readers kindly give me information
as to parentage, &c., of Harry St. Lawrence,
who was owner of an estate in the parish
of St. Andrew's of 207 acres, and one
in St. Patrick's, 95 acres, island of St. Vincent, W.I.? He had a daughter born
there in 1765, and christened Britannia

—the first entry in the parish register of
St. Andrew's. E. METCALFE.

KIPLING'S 'CITY OF DREADFUL NIGHT.'—
Was not the Allahabad edition of this book
on sale about 1891 at one or more of Messrs.
Willing's bookstalls on the Metropolitan
Railway, or of Messrs. Smith's on the District?
I understand the book is now very rare; but I
have a recollection of buying on the Underground what was certainly an Indian edition
of something (with some mention of rupees
or the like on cover), and I seem to remember
the title in question. R. J. WALKER.

CRAPELET BIBLIOGRAPHY. — Can any one
give me a reference to a tolerably complete
list of the Old French publications of Crapelet
in the forties? R. STEELE.

DUTCH REFUGEES IN LONDON IN 1566.—
Strype's 'Life of Grindal,' 1710, Appendix,
p. 28, contains a list of 310 names of these
refugees. On p. 111 of the 'Life' the author
intimates that many of them planted themselves in Southwark, and founded families of
wealth and reputation. Some of the names
are decidedly outlandish, such as Breckpott,
Geluius, Kabeliauw, Kraanmeester, Maalsack,
Pannekoeck, Sciynwerker, Schuddemate,
Theeuwes, Van Kerssbeke, Van Verdebau,
Van Wimmepen. Either these families died
out, or the names have become metamor-
phosed in process of time. Can any contributor suggest a solution of this dilemma?
Such names as Broeck, De Vischer, Janssen,
Jacobsen, Voss, Van Kassel, &c., would be
easily anglicized. But who shall anglicize
Kabeliauw or Theeuwes?
RICHARD H. THORNTON.
Portland, Oregon.

SIBYLLINE ORACLES.—Is there a translation
into English or French later than Floyer's
1713 English version? PRESBYTER.

LATIN SENTENCE MISSPELT.—In a genealogy of a Highland family in manuscript,
after a reference to a "William Mcdhoam-
hail McFheanlay," i.e., William son of Donald,
son of Finlay, occurs a remark which appears
to be in very corrupt Latin. So far as can
be made out it is: "Pæcite varbarici vel in
nominando gentile monticcolis inevitabili."
Can any reader suggest what it should be?
J. McG.

COMBERMERE CHAIR.—"Some ladies dispense with the milliner's aid, and lounge all
day in Combermere chairs, indifferent to
their husbands' hints about dowdyism"
('Society, Manners, Tales, and Fictions of

India,' published 1844, i. 240). What was a Combermere chair? I suppose it took its name from Lord Combermere, the conqueror of Bhurtpur, Commander-in-Chief of India 1825-30.   W. CROOKE.

Langton House, Charlton Kings.

"ROMANS DES DOUZE PAIRS."—What is the name of vol. x. of this series? The 'Romancero' of Paulin Paris, sometimes given, was not originally part of the series.
   R. STEELE.

PONTIFICAL PRIVILEGES.—The *Pall Mall Gazette* of 12 February reports a determination on the part of Pope Leo XIII. to nominate his successor. Can any one give me chapter and verse for maintaining that the right of nominating a successor is included in the Pontifical prerogative?
   FREDERICK WILLIAM ROLFE.

"ENGLAND'S DARLING."—Of whom is this title properly used? Is it not a designation of Alfred the Great? Dr. Brewer in his 'Dictionary of Phrase and Fable' assigns it to Hereward the Wake. To whom does it really belong; and what is the earliest instance of its occurrence?   PERTINAX.

BROWNE FAMILY ARMS. — In Fairbairn's 'Crests' a crest of a demi-lion rampant, chained, is ascribed to a Browne family. Will any reader kindly inform me what arms are borne by the family that bears this crest?
   GENEALOGICUS.

LAURENCE FAMILY. — I should be grateful if any one would tell me the parentage of the Rev. John Laurence (or Lawrence), instituted to the living of St. Martin's, Stamford Baron, in 1666, and sometime prebendary of Lincoln. I should also be glad to know anything with regard to the family of Elizabeth his wife, or with regard to the family of Mary, the wife of his son, the Rev. John Laurence, rector of Bishop Wearmouth, the author of well-known works on gardening.
   FRANCIS P. MARCHANT.

51, Medora Road, Brixton Hill.

ST. PAUL AND SENECA.—In Henryk Sienkiewicz's romance 'Quo Vadis?' chap. xv., with reference to the desire of certain patricians at Rome to see St. Paul, we read, "So does Seneca, who heard of him from Gallo[*sic*]." Apart from the tendency of the early fathers to claim Seneca as almost their own, is there any evidence or authority for the belief that St. Paul ever held personal intercourse with Seneca?   C. H. WILLSON.

Elstow.

Replies.

HERALDRY BEFORE THE CONQUEST.
(9ᵗʰ S. ix. 124.)

I QUITE sympathize with MR. ALFRED CHAS. JONAS with regard to the "bald statement" that he complains of. It is fearful the snubbing one gets for venturing to believe that heraldry existed before 1066. No doubt all the arms he quotes of Egbert and the rest of the Saxon and Danish kings, down to Edward the Confessor in 1042, will be set down by the iron rule of heraldic authority as proleptic — that is, the writers of the centuries from 1200 to 1600 were so saturated with the heraldic ideas prevalent during those centuries that they transferred them to their ancestors as a matter of course, for they were themselves so familiar with armorial bearings as a part of a gentleman's inheritance, that they could not conceive it possible for the grandfather of a man bearing arms, say with King Richard I., to have had no armorials himself of any kind. And there is a good deal of plain common sense in their ignorant conclusion. It is certain that the bald statement that heraldry did not exist before 1066 would have been received in 1166 with derision. Nor would the monastic writers—ignorant monks of course—of the fourteenth century have given such a statement a moment's tolerance.

The bald statement will have to be qualified, and that very considerably, if it is to continue in force. In short, it will have to drop its baldness. The fact is it began as an opinion, and for want of proper treatment at first has settled down into a dogma. Of course, everybody knows that absolute and unalterable identity of form, method, and purpose from age to age is impossible. The course of nature forbids the possibility. But that every child has had a parent must be admitted, although parent and child may not be absolutely alike. Now the Planché faction of heraldists want to make us believe that, because the child in 1066 had not a father in 1030 or a grandfather in 1000 exactly like himself, therefore he had no father or grandfather at all. They talk of "regular and systematic use of arms" and "regular heraldic figures or disposition of figures," which, if they mean anything, must mean that the usage in 1066 must be precisely the same in every respect as it was in 1166, or it cannot be proper heraldry. But the great point they make is that to be proper heraldry the bearing must be heritable and transmitted from father to son. And they contend that before the time of Richard I. arms were borne anyhow—at the choice and option of the bearer—and that there was no recognized title or property in such possessions. That is the opinion in some parts of America at the present moment, so it is possible that several persons might have acted upon it in the eleventh century. But if armorials in the eleventh century were wild and disorderly, they seem to have been tolerably well regulated in the tenth, which is a little argument in favour of their existence previous to 1066. We need not worry about the true date of early armorial seals, many of which can be duly and regularly proved from pedigrees, such, for example, as that of Waleran, Earl of Mellent.

But what is the meaning of the following document of the year 938 if it does not refer to hereditary heraldic bearings in the same sense as employed in " regular heraldry "?—

"Henrici I. Aucupis Imperatoris Augusti Leges Hastiludiales sive de Torneamentis Latæ Gottingæ in Saxonia anno Domini DCCCCXXXVIII. cap. xii.

"[De hominibus novis.] Quisquis recentioris et notæ nobilis et non talis ut a stirpe nobilitatem suam et origine quatuor saltem generis auctorum proximorum gentilitibus insignibus probare possit, is quoque ludis his exesto.

"The Hastiludial Laws or Laws for the Regulation of the Tournaments held at Gottingen, in Saxony, in the year 938, under the Emperor Henry I., called the Fowler.

"Chapter xii. [concerning new men.] Whatever noble is of recent and known family, yet not such as can prove his nobility from stem and origin of at least four generations of a race of immediate ancestors with family insignia (or armorial bearings), he also must be excluded from these games."

It is only an extract, but it will serve as a sample of the whole. What can the upholders of the bald statement have to say after this dated document?

To argue on the general question of symbolism, &c., which is as old as the hills, is to miss the point. I do not intend to waste time and space by dealing with it. I want to show by dates that heraldry did exist as clearly heraldry as it is at the present moment before 1066, without reference to any prolepsis or ignorant assumption. If what I have given is not evidence I do not understand the meaning of the term. I should like the opinion of other reasonable readers of ' N. & Q.'   CHEVRON.

The fact that the nations of classic antiquity were accustomed to use pictorial symbols for denoting a family or *gens* no more proves that the Egyptians, Greeks, and Romans were familiar with heraldry than the designs painted on their shields prove that the Norman warriors of the eleventh and twelfth centuries possessed hereditary coats of arms and practised heraldry in the full sense of the word. Dr. Woodward, in his ' Heraldry, British and Foreign,' clearly shows the later rise of coat-armour as we understand it. True, the subject is complicated by the late mediæval practice of attributing to such personages as King Arthur and King Edward the Confessor arms which those monarchs never used ; but this need not confuse us when we remember that even Adam, Noah, and the Virgin Mary were similarly distinguished by the same heralds. The Welsh heralds also attributed fixed and hereditary coats to British princes who died long before heraldry was practised even in France ; and it is really wonderful with what consistency and unanimity the old Welsh genealogical MSS. assign a particular coat to each such chieftain. But this only shows the ingenuity and care of the inventors of those armorial bearings. No one really believes that Jestyn ab Gwrgan in the eleventh century went to battle with a shield bearing Argent, three chevronels gules. Yet all the heralds agree in assigning those and no other arms to the last *de facto* Prince of Glamorgan, and many native families bear the same as his actual or presumptive descendants.

For my own part I never could understand why the designation "science" should be refused to heraldry. Perhaps it is because quacks and faddists have done so much to bring it into contempt, and genuine heralds so little to advance its prestige. Until Dr. Woodward's book appeared one had to go to French works to learn much about the art, craft, or mystery of blazonry. Is it that its title to be called a science is withheld by those whose perseverance has been unequal to a mastery of its details?

JOHN HOBSON MATTHEWS.
Town Hall, Cardiff.

THE WEST BOURNE (9th S. viii. 517 ; ix. 51, 92, 190, 269).—There can be no doubt that the river was once so called right down to its mouth, where it formed, till Sir Hugh Owen's changes, the west boundary of Westminster (St. George's, Hanover Square, parish). The name was preserved by the terrace at the Chelsea boundary at Bloody Bridge. But in my childhood it was called "the Ranelagh River" from Sloane Square to its mouth.   CHARLES W. DILKE.

THE FIRST BRITISH SUBJECT BORN IN NEW SOUTH WALES (9th S. ix. 206, 272).—MR. CURWEN should read more accurately. The note stated that it was William Kent, not Charles, who was born in New South Wales. Charles Kent, the well-known author and friend of Dickens, was born, as stated in the obituary notice in 'N. & Q.,' in London on the 3rd of November, 1823. In the absence of more confirmation I am still disposed to believe that William Kent was the first British subject born in New South Wales.   N. S. S.

WINDSOR UNIFORM (9th S. ix. 268). — The Windsor uniform has for coat an old-fashioned swallowtail of dark blue with red collar and cuffs, and is often jestingly called "the two-penny postman." It is worn at Windsor by the household with pantaloons. The present King, in London, ordered for gentlemen black "frock dress," i.e., ordinary evening coat, worn with breeches and black silk stockings, or with pantaloons. This costume was worn at Windsor by guests. Mr. Gladstone always wore pantaloons at Windsor for dinner. It is probable that Windsor uniform may be superseded by the Buckingham Palace uniform, which has a velvet collar of the same blue as the coat.   D.

"OLIVER" (9th S. ix. 127, 194, 278). — The oliver is still used, and still used in England by women and girls, although in France the Factory Acts forbid this practice.   D.

SNOW-FEATHERS (9th S. viii. 403, 494; ix. 112). — Fifty years ago the rime quoted at the last reference as popular in Sheffield was common in the Midlands; but the words were :—

> Snow, snow, faster !
> Sally, Sally Blaster !
> Picking geese in [Bedford]shire,
> Send us all yer feathers here !

The "air" comprised three notes, beginning with the fifth, descending to the third, and ending on the key-note or octave, thus :—

> 5,   5,   3,   1
> 5-5, 5-5, 3,   1
> 5-5, 5-5, 3-3, 1
> 5-5, 5-5, 3-3, 1

The name of the county in the third line was changed to suit the locality of the reciter, it being usual to select one to the north or east, whence the snow appeared to come. But it must end in "shire," or you would be told that it was not "poetry."

RICHARD WELFORD.

It is quite worth while to add the following. 'Gotthold's Emblems,' by Christian Scriver, of Magdeburg, were written in 1671. No. ii. is on 'Snow,' and contains this remark: "The royal prophet says, *The Lord giveth snow like wool;* and country people predict a fruitful season when the *White Goose* hatches a numerous brood."—English trans. by Robert Menzies, Edin., 1857, p. 14.

W. C. B.

PICTORIAL GRAMMAR (9th S. ix. 49). — I have two pictorial grammars :—

1. "The Pictorial Grammar, by Alfred Crowquill. London: Harvey and Darton, Gracechurch Street." It is full of highly coloured woodcuts. Apparently Crowquill (Alfred Henry Forrester) was the author of both the letterpress and the pictures. No date. According to an extract from a book catalogue of Matthews & Brooke, of Bradford, 1891, the grammar was published in 184-.

2. 'The Illustrated English Grammar; or, Lindley Murray Simplified.' It is the first part of "The Book of Fun; or, Laugh and Learn for Boys and Girls. London: James Gilbert, 49, Paternoster Row." No date. The grammar takes up the first thirty-six pages. The rest of the book contains 'Rhetoric and Elocution for the Million; or, the New Speaker'; 'Illustrated Arithmetic; or, Cyphering made Comical'; and 'The Comic History of Rome, and the *Rumuns*.' Amongst the many woodcuts few have either initials or names. But there occur H., W. H., Hine, &c., also A. and H. each enclosed in a C or a part of a circle. The largest woodcut has G. C., also Thos. Williams. It is entitled 'Licensed to be drunk on the Premises.' It represents a crowd of drunken, fighting people with some building like St. Martin's Church in the background. I dare say that it is a well-known drawing by George Cruikshank which has been brought into this book. The woodcuts are not coloured. It would, I think, be interesting if correspondents of 'N. & Q.' would describe under separate headings the comic grammars, arithmetics, &c.   ROBERT PIERPOINT.

St. Austin's, Warrington.

THE EARL OF CROMARTIE (9th S. ix. 107, 172, 219). — I must plead guilty to a *lapsus calami* in regard to the date of the creation of the new earldom of Cromartie, but not with respect to the latter portion of SIR DAVID OSWALD HUNTER-BLAIR's indictment. Your valued correspondent, whose signature is too seldom seen nowadays in 'N. & Q.,' and whose authority on matters connected with the Cromartie peerage is necessarily second to none, says that I "speak of the 'revival' of the earldom." But if my letter on p. 172 is referred to, it will be seen that I only spoke of the revival of the title, which is quite a different thing. The present

Countess of Cromartie bears the same title as her ancestors, the Mackenzies, but she does not hold the same earldom. I think my language clearly showed that I was aware that the peerage was a new creation, and not a revival of the old Scottish dignity.

W. F. PRIDEAUX.

The following extracts from the 'Scottish Clans and their Tartans' (W. & A. K. Johnston) is interesting, and bears upon the points mentioned by COL. PRIDEAUX and SIR DAVID OSWALD HUNTER-BLAIR:—

"Anne (only child of John Hay Mackenzie, of Cromartie and Newhall), Mistress of the Robes to Her Majesty (1870-74), Duchess of Sutherland, became in her own right (1861) Countess of Cromartie, Viscountess Tarbet, Baroness MacLeod and Castlehaven."

"Anne, Countess of Cromartie, died in 1888, and was succeeded by her second son, Francis, as Earl of Cromartie, &c. He died in 1893, and his elder daughter Sibell was declared in March, 1895, to hold all her father's titles, and so is Countess of Cromartie."

RONALD DIXON.
46, Marlborough Avenue, Hull.

George Mackenzie, third Earl of Cromartie, joined the rising of 1745, and collected in support of Prince Charles Edward a considerable number of his (the Mackenzie) clan, who were with him at the battle of Falkirk, and, after their retreat to the North, he, with his eldest son, Lord Macleod, was surprised and taken prisoner by a party of Lord Sutherland's militia at Dunrobin Castle, 15 April, 1746, the day before the battle of Culloden. He was soon after brought to London, and was, 30 May, 1746, lodged in the Tower. On 28 July, 1746, in company with the Earl of Kilmarnock and Lord Balmerino, he was brought to trial in Westminster Hall before his peers, when he pleaded guilty to the indictment preferred against him of high treason, and on 1 August was sentenced to death, his estates and honours being by the ordinary sentence for high treason forfeited to the Crown; but whilst his two companions in misfortune were executed on Tower Hill, Monday, 18 August, the Earl of Cromartie was respited, and on 20 August received a conditional pardon. He was therefore not executed, and died peaceably in Poland Street twenty years after, on 28 September, 1766, "on the eve of S. Michael and All Angels," and sixteen years after his death his estates were restored to his eldest son.

In his speech before the House of Lords at his trial, when asked why sentence should not be pronounced against him, the Earl of Cromartie mentions that he had involved in his misfortunes not only his eldest son, but a much-loved wife and a child still unborn, and this child appears to have been born a month or two after the trial, and was his sixth and youngest daughter, Lady Augusta Mackenzie, who was married 6 March, 1770, to Sir William Murray, fifth baronet of Ochtertyre, co. Perth, and died 20 January, 1809.

Is it not very possible, not to say probable, that three or four old ladies, sitting round a tea-table on 4 August, 1823, and telling each other dramatic tales about birth-marks, should have assumed the execution, which never took place, of a man who was condemned to death seventy-seven years before the date of the conversation, in order to deepen the tragic character of their story? Had there been no execution, their gossip about the mark of an axe and three drops of blood would have been pointless.

F. DE H. LARPENT.

ARMS (9ᵗʰ S. ix. 147).—The coat of arms is probably that of the Beecher family, which Burke's 'General Armory,' p. 66 (edition 1878), gives as Beecher (granted 6 October, 1574): Vaire, ar. and gu., on a canton or a stag's head cabossed vert; and Beecher ('London Visitation, 1568') as above, except that stag's head is sable.

J. HAMBLEY ROWE, M.B.

Probably Beecher, impaling Brewes or Hankford. See Papworth and Morant, pp. 283, 360-1.   G. S. C.

CHESS PLAYING: A LEGEND (9ᵗʰ S. ix. 248).—The passage in which Huxley refers to Nature and man playing a game of chess is in the essay on 'A Liberal Education,' in the 'Essays on Science and Education' (the third volume of the 'Collected Essays'), and on p. 82 of Macmillan's edition of 1893.

N. R. U.

PINS IN DRINKING VESSELS (9ᵗʰ S. iv. 287, 358, 484; ix. 10, 136, 255). — In correcting one mistake about Dr. Milner (p. 256) MR. DIXON appears to have fallen into another in making him "Bishop of Winchester." In the first place, the name of Milner never once appears in the annals of this diocese as having been borne by one of its prelates; and, secondly, if it did, it could not be that of the individual in question, for the simple reason that he was *born a Roman Catholic*, and remained so to the last day of his life. He was the author of the well-known 'History of Winchester'; but beyond this, and the fact of his having resided there for some years, he never had anything to do with the place. He was an antiquary of considerable repute, and a dignitary of the Church to which he belonged, and held high office in the same, having at last been made a bishop, not, however, of the see to which Mr. Dixon has erroneously exalted him, but deriving his title (by Papal authority) from the name of some place "in partibus infidelium," which I have now forgotten. He was the author of one or two other works, dealing chiefly with the subject of ecclesiastical architecture, as well as of the article on the 'Glastonbury Cup' (*Archæologia*, vol. xi.), all of which may be seen in the London Library in St. James's Square.   Fr. N.

[Milner was consecrated at Winchester, as Bishop of Castabala, 22 May, 1803.]

Holts at Winchester (9ᵗʰ S. ix. 164).— H. C. is correct in his statement that the only "Mr. Holt," M.P., in June, 1689, was Richard Holt, M.P. for Lymington. Sir John Holt had been returned to the same Parliament, but had vacated his seat upon his appointment to the Chief Justiceship on 17 April previously. He had, moreover, received knighthood as far back as February, 1685/6, so under no circumstances could he be correctly styled "Mr." Holt in 1689. I regret that I am unable to afford much information anent this Richard Holt. He was M.P. for Lymington in 1685-7 and 1689-90, and for Petersfield in 1690-5 and 1695-8. According to Foster's 'Alumni Oxon.' he matriculated at St. John's College in 1652, B.A. 1655, and was admitted to the Middle Temple in 1656 as son and heir of John Holt, of Portsmouth. A pedigree in Chetham Coll. derives the Holts of Hampshire from Thomas, son and heir of Robert Holt, the fifth son of James Holt, of Griselhurst, Lancashire. This Thomas—who, it is said, went to Twyford, near Winchester, and was ancestor of the Holts of Portsmouth—was cousin-german to Sir Thomas Holt, of Griselhurst, who was knighted at the siege of Leith in 1544, and died in 1563.   W. D. Pink.

Richard Holt, M.P., and Lieut.-General Holt were members of a branch of the well-known Lancashire family of that name which settled at Portsmouth in the reign of James I. In 1619 Henry Holt, described as "Brewer at the Fower Houses,"* was admitted a burgess of the Portsmouth Corporation, and was mayor of the borough in 1622, 1627, and 1628. His wife was Alice, daughter of Thomas

* The "Fower Houses" were four of the seven "great brewing houses" mentioned by Leland as having been built by Henry VIII. to supply his navy.

Bonner, Mayor of Portsmouth, by whom he had five sons and five daughters. John Holt, the third son (Mayor of Portsmouth 1641 and 1651, Sheriff of Hants 1656, died January, 1669), married Catherine, daughter and sole heir of Anthony Bricket, of Salisbury, and had three sons, Anthony, Richard, and John, and three daughters, Catherine, Sarah, and Mary. Anthony and John died without issue. Richard, the second son (born 1639), resided at Nursted, between Petersfield and Buriton, co. Hants. He was M.P. for Lymington 1685-90, and for Petersfield 1690-8. He married Margaret, eighth and youngest daughter of Richard Whithed, of West Tytherley, co. Hants, and by her (who died in 1685) had two daughters only. He was buried at Buriton on 14 April, 1710.

John Holt (father of Richard), with his two younger brothers William and Francis, were during the Commonwealth victuallers of the Parliamentary fleet—William at Plymouth and John and Francis at Portsmouth. Francis Holt, who is described in 1650 as "agent to the Navy Commissioners," was Mayor of Portsmouth in 1654, and died in March, 1664. He had two wives: Margaret, who died in July, 1655, and Mary, who survived her husband, and was buried at Portsmouth in July, 1667. I am inclined to think that Henry Holt, the Winchester scholar, afterwards a lieutenant-general, was a son of this Francis Holt by his wife Margaret.

On 2 November, 1699, Henry Holt (then a colonel) married, at Buriton Church, Lucy Hare, niece of Richard Holt, of Nursted, daughter of his eldest sister Catherine, who had married in 1668 Hugh Hare, of Docking, co. Norfolk, younger son of the first Baron Coleraine. The Buriton registers record the baptism of their eldest son, Henry Holt, in November, 1700, and his burial the following month; also the baptism and burial of their daughter Catherine in October, 1701.

In the Portsmouth parish registers (which commence in 1653) the name of Francis Holt appears in various entries relating to marriages under Cromwell's Civil Marriage Act. One is perhaps worth placing on record here : "1654, Dec. 26. Married by Mr. Mayor (Mr. Francis Holt), Mr. Josiah Child and Mrs. Hannah Boate. Mr. Thomas Holt and Mrs. Rebecca Boate witnesses."

This was the first marriage of the celebrated merchant prince, afterwards Sir Josiah Child, Bart. Mrs. Rebecca Boate, one of the witnesses, was the bride's stepmother, and relict of Mr. Edward Boate, the Master Shipwright of Portsmouth. The other witness, the Rev. Thomas Holt, of Petersfield,

was a son of Rebecca Boate by her first husband, Mr. Thomas Holt, the eldest brother of the mayor.   ALFRED T. EVERITT.
High Street, Portsmouth.

LONDRES (9th S. viii. 443; ix. 35, 151).—I beg leave to thank MR. ALFRED CHAS. JONAS for his desire to set me right concerning certain points in the history of the family of De Londre and their doings; but inasmuch as his opinion appears to have been founded upon the so-called 'History of the Conquest of Glamorgan by Robert FitzHamon and his Twelve Paladins,' from which he quotes, his conclusions have not that weight and acceptance of which they might otherwise be worthy. Of this so-called "history" the late Mr. G. T. Clark, in his 'Land of Morgan,' speaks as the "traditional 'Conquest of Glamorgan,' a very neat, round, and circumstantial story, but as deficient in evidence as though from the pen of Geoffrey himself"; and discussing the matter many years ago with the late Mr. Robert Oliver Jones, of Fonmon, I came to the conclusion that it was invented by John le Stradling, younger brother, secretary, and literary hanger-on of his more fortunate elder, who desired to contract a marriage with Joanna, daughter of Henry Beaufort, subsequently cardinal. This story was invented for the greater glorification of the Stradling family and their connexions. MR. JONAS will observe that a "Sir Wm. le Esterling was one of the twelve knights, and is said to have acquired St. Donat's in consequence." There was no such person at the time in this county. The Sir Peter le Esterling then living was seated at Rogerston, in co. Monmouth, and the first incoming of the Stradlings in Glamorgan was by a fortunate marriage with Wenllian, heiress of the Bercherolles, about 1364. The family which held the manor of St. Donat's prior to the Stradlings was Bawddwyn, one of whose tombstones may still be seen amongst the nettles in the churchyard of Merthyrmawr.

The manor of Ogmore was held directly of the Crown by knight service. Of this there are many documentary evidences. The foundation charter of Ewenny is itself negative evidence, inasmuch as no "over-lord" gives consent to alienation of lands. There must have been a monastery of some kind at Ewenny prior to the foundation of William and Maurice de Londre in 1141, as in 1138 Stephen confirms to that house certain churches and tenths, and again in 1139 Robert Consul confirms to it the gift of a burgage and land in the vicinity of Kenfege.

There are extant letters from Adam, Abbot of St. Peter's at Gloucester, asking the sanction of the Lord of Ogmore to their nomination of John de Tewksbury as Prior of Ewenny in 1339. This is significant.

Ewenny was most likely a Benedictine house originally, but it is undoubtedly planned on the well-known Cistercian model, having its cloister garth on the south side of the church.

A fragment of the tombstone of William de Londre, the original founder (in intention), with deeply cut Lombardic lettering, may be seen in the church, evidently earlier than that of Maurice.   G. E. R.

THE DUCHY OF BERWICK (9th S. viii. 432, 534; ix. 130, 258).—At the last reference, in connexion with the use of the prefix "Fitz," COL. PRIDEAUX mentions that one of the illegitimate sons of Henry I. was known as Robert FitzEdith, and MR. BAYLEY refers to the case of another of Henry I.'s illegitimate sons—viz., the famous Robert le Fitz le Roy, the great Earl of Gloucester, who married Mabel, daughter of Robert FitzHamon, and had a lawful son and heir named William FitzCount, second Earl of Gloucester. MR. BAYLEY instances Robert FitzHamon and William FitzCount as cases in point that the prefix "Fitz" does not always denote illegitimacy. But do we know anything about the parentage of FitzHamon, and may not the surname FitzCount indicate illegitimacy? —an illegitimate grandson? In very many cases it is quite certain that the prefix denotes legitimacy rather than otherwise, but the two above cases quoted by MR. BAYLEY are not definite one way or the other. In fact, from other evidence it would seem that the name FitzCount indicated an illegitimate grandson of Henry I., for that name was borne in more than the one case mentioned by MR. BAYLEY by such a relation. Henry I. had by Sibyl Corbet, Reginald de Dunstanville, Earl of Cornwall; Rohesia, who married Johel Pomeray; Maud, the wife of Conan, Count of Rennes, and William de Tracy. This Reginald de Dunstanville had several daughters by Beatrix de Cardinan (? Beatrix de Valle), possibly five, amongst them Dionisia, the wife of Richard de Redvers, Earl of Devon, whose daughter Hawise married her cousin Robert, son of William FitzCount, second Earl of Gloucester (mentioned above). But Reginald de Dunstanville had also by Beatrix de Valle (who afterwards became the wife of William Brewer, the judge of Henry II. and one of the regents of Richard I.) an illegitimate son named

Henry FitzCount (sometimes FitzHenry), who became in after years also Earl of Cornwall. Thus we have at least two illegitimate grandsons of Henry I. bearing the name of FitzCount. As the two holders of this surname were not brothers, but only cousins, it would seem that the name had some reference to their relationship to the king, for why should they both have taken a name which certainly did not belong to either of their fathers? The name cannot be explained by the statement that it merely indicated they were the sons of counts or earls, for it was certainly not the general custom for the sons of earls to take the surname of FitzCount.

It is interesting to note the marriages of the children of William FitzCount, second Earl of Gloucester. His daughter Hadwisa, the great-granddaughter of Henry I. by Nest, married her second cousin, King John, who was the great-grandson of Henry I. by his wife and queen Matilda. Robert of Gloucester, son of William FitzCount, and also the great-grandson of Henry I. by Nest, married his second cousin Hadwise de Redvers, of Devon, who was the great-granddaughter of Henry I. by Sibyl Corbet.

It is worthy of note that Joan, natural daughter of King John, married in 1204 Lewellen, son of Jorworth, Prince of North Wales, by his wife, who was the daughter of Roger Corbet; also that David ap Owen, Prince of North Wales, and elder brother of this Jorworth, married Emma, the natural daughter of the Earl of Anjou, grandfather of King John.

So great was the profligacy of the period that the above Joan, natural daughter of King John and wife of Lewellen, son of Jorworth, was detected by her husband in a connexion with her and his near relation William de Braose, grandson of William Brewer and his wife Beatrix de Valle (former mistress of Reginald, son of Henry I. and Sibyl Corbet), and was put to death.

Charles II. and his Court bear a bad reputation in history, but many other of the kings of England and their Courts appear to have been, from a moral standpoint, no better.

Mr. Bayley does not mention that the mother of Robert le Fitz le Roy, Earl of Gloucester, was Nest, the tragedy of whose life was one of the greatest in those turbulent times. She was the daughter of the Welsh chief Jestyn, who in an unfortunate moment called in Robert FitzHamon to assist him in defeating and killing Rhys ap Tewdwr in 1093. She married her cousin Einion, who combined with FitzHamon in defeating her father near Cardiff and driving him to the neighbourhood of Bristol to die. She was carried off by another cousin, Owen ap Cadogan, but Gerald of Windsor, Constable of Pembroke, met the party and slew Owen and his men, and captured Nest in his turn. She attracted the attention of Henry I, and, after the birth of Robert le Fitz le Roy, Earl of Gloucester, she became the wife of Gerald of Windsor. Her brother Griffith, or Gruffydd, after having several times endeavoured to throw off the Norman yoke, was finally overcome and crushed by his own sister's husband, Gerald of Windsor. Finally, Nest's son, Robert le Fitz le Roy, married Mabel, the daughter of Robert FitzHamon, the man who had assisted to destroy her father Jestyn.

RONALD DIXON.
46, Marlborough Avenue, Hull.

Col. Prideaux may like to know that my authority for the statement that the Duchy of Berwick is a Spanish title is a late H.M. Ambassador in Spain, who is well acquainted with the family.

The Marquisate of Jamaica is given as an English titular title amongst the Jacobite creations in G. E. C.'s 'Complete Peerage.'

The Earldom of Tankerville, to which Mr. Pickford refers, was originally one of those created by Henry V. during his tenure of Normandy. Tancarville is on or near the Seine, below Rouen.

If the Marquisate of Ava is to be included amongst the titles derived from foreign places, I would include those of Lord Milner of Capetown, Lord Kitchener of Khartoum, and Lord Napier of Magdala.

It is curious that Canada was a French possession when Sir William Alexander was created Viscount Canada by Charles I. Nova Scotia certainly belonged to England when the Nova Scotia baronets were instituted in 1625, and was only handed over to France in 1629. The list of foreign knights is most valuable.

Lord Strathcona and Mount Royal, Lord Mount Stephen, and Baroness Macdonald of Earnscliffe also bear colonial titles. H.

H. is quite right at p. 130: "The prefix 'Fitz' is by no means a sign of illegitimacy." There are many instances of peerages with this prefix to be found in Burke's 'Extinct Peerage.'

At Middleham, in Wensleydale, co. York, Ralph FitzRibald had confirmation of lands there, and his son by his wife Agatha, named Robert FitzRalph, founded and built the castle there. Several of the benefactors of

Jervaulx Abbey, near Middleham, are buried there, as Henry FitzHenry, who died in 1352, and Henry, Lord FitzHugh, who fought at Agincourt and died in 1424. It is evident that the prefix merely meant originally son, as "filius naturalis" merely signified at one time a legitimate son.

JOHN PICKFORD, M.A.
Newbourne Rectory, Woodbridge.

MONTGOMERY MSS. (9th S. ix. 208).—About the year 1850 the late George Stephenson, seneschal of Hillsborough, co. Down, placed in safe keeping the Magennis patent, or, more properly speaking, the confirmatory grant to McRowrie Magennis. MR. FITZPATRICK, I think, errs in assuming that this document had only an antiquarian value, as, previous to its being deposited in new hands, eminent counsel had given a decided opinion to the contrary ; and this opinion was the chief reason which induced the late George Stephenson to hand over the deed to the predecessor of the present custodian. J. P. S.
Automobile Club, Paris.

SIBYL OR SYBIL (9th S. vii. 200, 317, 455).— I perceive that it was usual in those who must have known the right spelling to spell the word wrongly. Dr. Johnson, in the second edition of his 'Dictionary,' under the word *as*, quotes Dryden thus :—

> As many voices issue, and the sound
> Of Sybil's word as many times rebound.

Young, in his first epistle to Pope, wrote *Sybil*, if I may trust a late edition of his poetry. In an old edition of the *Spectator*, in a paper that was certainly written by Addison, I meet with *Sybil*. In a note to 'Macbeth,' in the edition of 1821, which has the notes of various commentators, Malone, after quoting the Latin, "Tres adolescentes concinno Sibyllarum habitu induti," proceeds to say in English, "three of whom personated the Sybills, or rather the Weird Sisters." In a translation of Juvenal's Satires, with notes, by Madan, 1807, the translator in a note says, "Juvenal here humorously parodies that passage in Virgil, relative to the Sybil." I ought, however, also to say that in another note he has *Sibyl*.
E. YARDLEY.

BIRTHPLACE OF LORD BEACONSFIELD (9th S. viii. 317, 426, 512 ; ix. 15, 297).—I regret to disagree with MR. THOMAS, but I contend that, though a tablet may not improve a street, putting up one serves to notify to passers-by the natal locality of great men. Had it not been for some such tablet I had not known where Scott was born—save through Lock-

hart and others. MR. THOMAS's logic is at fault when he alleges as his reason for such negligence that the place was quite different a hundred years ago. That, *inter alia*, is precisely what we want to know. The tablet to Mr. Gladstone's memory in Rodney Street, Liverpool, is no degradation to the locality now, nor will it be a century hence. Let us have more of such reminiscences of our great dead, and not fewer. J. B. McGOVERN.
St. Stephen's Rectory, C.-on-M., Manchester.

SMALLNESS OF THE INFANT JESUS (9th S. ix. 149).—There was a common belief that the Mother of our Lord was quite a girl at the time of His birth. In 1874 I saw among Dr. Routh's books, in the University Library at Durham, an old treatise which dealt with this subject, and gave on one page a woodcut showing the small size of her foot.
W. C. B.

'LES LAURIERS DE NASSAU' (9th S. viii. 464 ; ix. 157, 192).—The information sent respecting the above was copied from 'A New Method of studying History, Geography, and Chronology, with a Catalogue of the Chief Historians of all Nations, the Best Edition of their Works, and Characters of Them,' by Richard Rawlinson, LL.D. and F.R.S., Lond., 1730. It says 'Les Lauriers de Nassau,' 1615, is only a translation of the last piece from the Dutch edition 'Nassaure Laurekrans,' by Jo. Jans Orlers ende Henrich van Haustens, Leyden, fol., 1610. I am unable to give any opinion as to the work being of authority. JOHN RADCLIFFE.

WEEKS'S MUSEUM (9th S. ix. 8, 97, 212).— Richard Rush, the Minister from the United States from 1817 to 1825, in his book 'The Court of London,' records a visit to this museum on 5 March, 1819, pp. 19-22. He states that it consisted chiefly of specimens of ingenious mechanism—singing birds, "human figures of full size playing on musical instruments, in full band," mice made of pearl, &c.

"The outside of this museum looks like a common shop for umbrellas and other small wares; as in fact it is in front......It may be taken, perhaps, as one of the evidences of the immensity of London, that although I occasionally spoke of this collection in society afterwards, I hardly met with any one who had as much as heard of it......The interior mechanism of the little spider was said to be composed of more than one hundred distinct pieces."

B. W. DEXTER.
59, Princess Road, Kilburn, N.W.

ST. ANTHONY (9th S. ix. 69).—There are two popular saints of this name—St. Anthony, the third-century abbot, whose day is

27 January, and St. Anthony of Padua, a famous thirteenth-century Portuguese preacher belonging to the Franciscan Order. The latter's day is kept upon 13 June. Husenbeth, in his 'Emblems of Saints,' says the latter is illustrated in ancient ecclesiastical art under nineteen different circumstances, and records that both Callot and Salvator Rosa have pictured him preaching to fishes. Further, it seems he not only preached to them, but caught them too, for Velasquez is also quoted as representing him with a net, whilst a small boy stands handy with fish upon a plate. The earlier St. Anthony is never shown with fishes, but often in company with a favourite pig, sometimes two—one on each side of him!

HARRY HEMS.

Fair Park, Exeter.

MOLYNEUX (9ᵗʰ S. ix. 148).—The late Rev. Capel Molyneux was a very able preacher, whom I remember at Woolwich about 1836; but he established his reputation at St. Paul's, Onslow Square. He was born in 1804, a grandson of Sir Capel Molyneux, the third baronet; so a very distant relative of Lord Sefton.

ABSENS.

This is probably the Rev. Capel Molyneux, B.A., who conducted a proprietary chapel, now Holy Trinity Parish Church, in Woolwich, from 1834 to 1850, and who became afterwards distinguished as a preacher at the West-End of London (see Vincent's 'Records of Woolwich,' vol. i. p. 172).

WM. NORMAN.

"G.R." (9ᵗʰ S. ix. 248).—At the date referred to, 1793, horses in the military service of the Crown, such as troop and battery horses, were often marked with the letters "G.R." and a number, the letters being the initials of George, Rex. Officers' chargers were not marked as these Government horses were.

W. S.

COMPULSORY COSTUME FOR JEWS AND CHRISTIANS (9ᵗʰ S. viii. 521; ix. 157).—See the chapter headed 'Jewish Memorials in Rome' in Prof. Lanciani's latest work—'New Tales of Old Rome'—for some details as to the distinctive dress worn by the Jews in Rome.

VAPO.

"ALL COOPER'S DUCKS WITH ME" (9ᵗʰ S. ix. 127).—Since your correspondent W. I. R. V. describes this curious saying as having been used by a master-butcher, is it not probable that "Cooper's ducks" were those kept for his patrons by the owner of a ducking-pond, which were remorselessly hunted by the butchers' dogs, for duck-hunting was

especially a butchers' pastime? The butchers of Shepherd's Market, for instance, were notorious for their indulgence in this cruel sport, an amusement of absorbing interest to the brutal instincts of those whose pleasures were found in this and similar diversions. The proverbial ferocity of this canine breed is indicated in the saying "As surly as a butcher's dog." J. HOLDEN MACMICHAEL.

THE SOURCE OF THE SEVEN AGES (9ᵗʰ S. ix. 46, 197).—Tertullian, 'De Anima,' c. 56 ('Opera, ed. Leopold, pt. iv. p. 243), agrees with Shakspeare in some of the characteristic employments:—

"Si hic necesse erit ea tempora impleri, quæ fuerant destinata, num et ordinem vitæ, quem sortita sunt tempora pariter cum illis hic destinatum, pariter hic anima decurret, *ut et studeat ab infantia pueritiæ delegata, et militet ab adolescentia iuventa excitata, et censeat a iuventa senectæ ponderata,* et fœnus exprimat, et agrum urgeat, naviget, litiget, nubat, laboret, ægritudines obeat, et quæcunque illam cum temporibus manebant tristia ac læta?"

JOHN MACCARTHY.

It has been noticed that Shakspeare, when he wrote the lines in 'King Lear' which I quoted, seems to have had a passage from Holland's 'Pliny' in his mind. Perhaps I ought to have mentioned this.

E. YARDLEY.

PETER PETT (3ʳᵈ S. x. 127; 9ᵗʰ S. ix. 195).—The lines MR. THORNTON quotes occur in Marvell's 'Instructions to a Painter about the Dutch Wars, 1667.' The quotation breaks off in the middle of a sentence. C. C. B.

"BRISTOL LOOK" (9ᵗʰ S. ix. 148).—The above apparently refers to the well-known Bristol cardboard. Changing from object to subject, we have "stiff," or "starchy," which explains the phrase. *Un bristol* is in Parisian *argot* a gentleman's visiting card.

H. P. L.

Miscellaneous.

NOTES ON BOOKS, &c.

A New English Dictionary. Edited by Dr. James A. H. Murray.—*Leisureness—Lief.* Vol. VI. By Henry Bradley, Hon. M.A. (Oxford, Clarendon Press.)

THE third part of vol. vi. of the great 'English Dictionary' of Dr. J. A. H. Murray and his assistants and collaborators has now seen the light under Mr. Bradley's direction, and an instalment of vol. vii., dealing with the letter O, by Dr. Murray, may be before long anticipated. As a new editor has been added in the person of Mr. Craigie, who takes charge of vol. viii., and as the tenth volume will complete the work, the progress that is being made is sufficiently encouraging, and students who can no longer think themselves young may still hope to benefit by the greatest philological work ever given to the world. Considering that supplemental lists of words appear occasionally in our columns, it seems worth while to deal with what might possibly give rise to misconception. In the case of a language still in course of enlargement, if not of formation, absolute finality is not to be anticipated. A lexicon *totius anglicitatis* will never see the light. The constant developments of science and manufacture, the needs, the caprices, and even it may be the vanity of man, will lead to the regular increase of scientific terminology, and growths, hybrid and sometimes monstrous, continually enlarge or debase our language. In the inclusion of words the editors have certainly not erred on the side of illiberality and want of hospitality to strangers. If possible, they have been too generous, and admitted words which men have used for a solitary occasion, and which are not likely to be heard of again. It cannot be maintained that because a word can be found which is not in the dictionary, it ought to be there. For all purposes of scholarship the dictionary fulfils every requirement, and it is at least the richest and most exemplary of which any language can boast.

It is needless to say that in the present instalment the rate of superiority over existing dictionaries is maintained. The number of words is 1,769, as against 151 in Johnson and 935 in the 'Century,' while the illustrative quotations are 7,950 against 803 in the best equipped of competitors. But two words of Celtic origin are in the section, which is specially rich in words of Romance and Latin origin, and has a good many Greek derivatives, though few of these are of general currency. Though not large numerically, the English element comprises many words which are interesting on account of their sense-history. On the first page we find *leman*, originally *leofmon*=lief man=dear man. First used of both sexes as equivalent to sweetheart, and applied in religious or devotional language to Christ, the Virgin, &c., it came in time to be chiefly applied to the female sex, and to indicate unlawful love. The tender use of the word in a ballad, probably a corrupt form, will not be forgotten by the lovers of poetry :—

God send every gentleman
Such hawk, such hounds, and such a leman.

Under *lemur*, the spirits of the departed, we have, of course, Milton's splendidly picturesque and suggestive line—

The Lars and Lemures moan with midnight plaint.

Lend, length, and *Lent* have elaborate histories. A quotation for *lenity* from Shakespeare better than that given would be Romeo's

Away to heaven respective lenity,
And fire-eyed fury be my conduct now,

on account of the explanatory contrast supplied. The use of *lenvoy* with the preliminary *l* is curious. Nashe has "we shall lenvoy him." Leonine verses are supposed to be derived from some poet called Leo or Leonius, who made use of this form of composition. *Leopard*, forms of which are *labarde*, *libarde*, &c., has an interesting history. Not less noteworthy is that of *leprechaun*, one of the two Celtic words in the section. *Lesbian* is glided over, very little being said, but the lesbian rule and square, which have been dealt with in our columns, are fully explained. *Let* naturally occupies a large

space. Under *Levant* much curious information is given or suggested. The same may be said of *levee*, the ordinary pronunciation of which in America differs from that in England. *Level-headed* reaches us from America. A singularly interesting account is given of "that sea beast Leviathan." Space could not be spared for Milton's full description of him, "slumbering on the Norway foam." Under *levy* (sb.) we desiderate Shakespeare's "foreign levy," as opposed to "malice domestic." Among words with a history worth study is *libel*, which, of course, was originally a diminutive of *liber*. Under *liberal* (=becoming to a gentleman) we should like to see Ben Jonson's "learned and liberal soul." *Libertine* and *liberty* have much interest, and the application of the former term to Antinomian sects of the sixteenth century is clearly explained. We cannot say that Milton's "licence they mean when they cry liberty" does not appear, though we fail to trace it. The spelling *license* for the substantive is indefensible.

The Ancestor: a Quarterly Review of County and Family History, Heraldry, and Antiquities. No. 1. (Constable & Co.)

The Ancestor, the first number of which reaches us from Messrs. Constable, is a great advance upon existing works of its class. It is at once handsomer in appearance, more convenient in shape, and more authoritative in the information offered. A voucher for the character of the new work is supplied by the number of articles from the pen of Mr. J. Horace Round, the first of living English genealogists. An instance of the historical and critical spirit in which the whole is written, a spirit in which Mr. Round has had for associates the late Prof. Freeman and Mr. Walter Rye, is shown in 'An "Authoritative" Ancestor,' in which the decision of 'Burke' concerning Sir Geoffrey de Estmonte or Esmondeys is freely challenged. It is pointed out as a characteristic *chose d'Irlande* that Sir Thomas Esmonde, at the head of whose pedigree in 'Burke' stand the statements Mr. Round confutes, is endeavouring to secure from Government "promise of a special department for prosecuting research into Irish history." The assertion that Sir Geoffrey de Estmonte, Knt., of Huntington, co. Lincoln, accompanied Strongbow to the conquest of Ireland, A.D. 1172, and was one of the thirty knights who landed at Bannow, co. Wexford, is stated to be "a grotesque falsehood." No less destructive of myth is Mr. Round's account of 'The Origin of the Fitzgeralds,' of which the first portion appears. Dealing with the Gherardini ancestry, which originated in Ireland, not in Florence, Mr. Round is very humorous, speaking of "Irish earls panting for Roman ancestry." Such ambitions are surely superfluous in the case of a house which "not only traces its descent from a Domesday tenant-in-chief, but can make the probably unique boast that, from that day to this, descendants of his have been always numbered among the barons of the realm." Similar in spirit is the article of Mr. W. H. B. Bird on 'The Grosvenor Myth.' Is Mr. Bird, however, justified in saying that "the Scropes are almost forgotten"? Yorkshiremen, and especially dalesmen, will hesitate to believe this. 'Some Anecdotes of the Harris Family,' an illustrated paper of the Earl of Malmesbury, opens the volume. This interesting communication brings us on the track of Dr. Johnson and of Handel, a close friend of the

Harrises. Of the great musician a portrait is given. A picture by Romney of the first Countess of Malmesbury is among the many excellent illustrations. One by Joseph Highmore of Mrs. James Harris recalls strongly the portraits, of about the same epoch, of "Peg" Woffington. Lady Victoria Manners supplies a good account of the very interesting Belvoir miniatures, many of the most important of which are reproduced. Mr. Oswald Barron, F.S.A., the editor, is sufficiently iconoclastic in 'Heraldry Revived.' In the Patent Roll of 12 Henry VI. Sir George Sitwell has traced "the list of gentry of the land," which Fuller, in his 'Worthies of England,' tells us was "solemnly returned" in 1433 "by select commissioners into the chancery." Sir H. Maxwell-Lyte, K.C.B., describes 'Heraldic Glass from Lytes Cary.' Mr. W. H. St. John Hope, F.S.A., has a profoundly interesting paper, illustrated, on 'The King's Coronation Ornaments.' Mr. W. Paley Baildon, F.S.A., supplies a first instalment of 'Ancestors' Letters.' Reviewing Mr. Falconer Madan's 'The Gresleys of Drakelowe,' issued with so much privacy that no notice has previously appeared, Mr. J. Horace Round gives some admirable portraits of members of the family, one of whom, Sir William Gresley, third baronet, has a singularly pleasing and beautiful face, which, not only at the first look, one is disposed to assign to a woman. The contents of the volume are of highest value and are pleasantly varied, and the book is, in its way, a model. It is to be hoped that the plan of issuing in this form periodicals which the reader is likely to wish to keep will be generally adopted. These books are fit to be placed at once on the shelves. The only suggestion of improvement we can advance is the substitution for the uniform headline *The Ancestor* of one significant of the subject dealt with in each portion of the work.

Hans Holbein. By Arthur B. Chamberlain. — *Frederic, Lord Leighton.* By Geo. C. Williamson, Litt.D.—*Sir Joshua Reynolds, P.R.A.* By Rowley Cleeve. — *Watteau, Master Painter of the Fêtes Galantes.* By Edgcumbe Staley, B.A.—*Holman Hunt.* By Geo. C. Williamson, Litt.D. (Bell & Sons.)

FIVE new volumes have been added to Messrs. Bell's "Miniature Series of Painters," and are neither less interesting nor less valuable than the previous volumes. In each case a sympathetic and trustworthy biography, answering most purposes of the student, is followed by a critical estimate no less satisfactory, and by a reproduction in miniature of some of the best-known works of the master. Among the illustrations to Holbein are eight pictures from the National Gallery, Darmstadt, Berlin, The Hague, Hampton Court, and Windsor Castle. Those by Leighton, principally from private collections, include 'Dædalus and Icarus,' 'Portrait of Sir R. F. Burton,' 'The Arts of Peace,' 'Athlete and Python,' 'Fatidica,' 'Greek Girls playing at Ball,' 'Hercules wrestling with Death,' and 'Clytie.' Sir Joshua is represented by 'Mrs. Siddons as the Tragic Muse,' portraits of Dr. Johnson, the Duchess of Devonshire, Lady Cockburn, 'Robinetta,' and two gentlemen, principally from the National Gallery. With six characteristic productions of Watteau, including 'Gilles et sa Famille' from the Wallace Gallery, and the delightful 'Dénicheur de Moineaux' from Scotland, are given Lancret's 'Mademoiselle Camargo'

and Pater's 'Conversation Galante.' Eight illustrations of Holman Hunt include 'The Light of the World,' 'The Scapegoat,' 'The Finding of the Saviour,' and 'Isabella and the Pot of Basil.' The series answers admirably its purpose.

Scribner's Magazine, which reached us too late for inclusion last week with the April serials, opens with a good account of 'The Gloucester Fishermen Night-Seining and Winter Trawling.' 'A Story of Three States' has fine coloured illustrations. The most interesting portion of the contents consists of fiction.—In the case of the *Idler* the whole number is the brightest conceivable.

'NOTES AND QUERIES' FOR SALE (9ᵗʰ S. vii. 387, 520; viii. 76; ix. 60).—Messrs. Henry Sotheran & Co., 140, Strand, have a complete set from 1849 to 1900, with the eight General Indexes, newly bound in maroon calf gilt, price 37*l.* 10*s.*

           EVERARD HOME COLEMAN.

Notices to Correspondents.

We must call special attention to the following notices:—

ON all communications must be written the name and address of the sender, not necessarily for publication, but as a guarantee of good faith.

WE cannot undertake to answer queries privately.

To secure insertion of communications correspondents must observe the following rules. Let each note, query, or reply be written on a separate slip of paper, with the signature of the writer and such address as he wishes to appear. When answering queries, or making notes with regard to previous entries in the paper, contributors are requested to put in parentheses, immediately after the exact heading, the series, volume, and page or pages to which they refer. Correspondents who repeat queries are requested to head the second communication "Duplicate."

M. L. R. B. ("Call no man happy till he is dead").—The earliest and most succinct record of this γνώμη is in Æsch., 'Ag.,' 928 :—

$$\ddot{o}\lambda\beta i\sigma\alpha\iota\ \delta\grave{\epsilon}\ \chi\rho\hat{\eta}$$
$$\beta i o\nu\ \tau\epsilon\lambda\epsilon\upsilon\tau\dot{\eta}\sigma\alpha\nu\tau'\ \dot{\epsilon}\nu\ \epsilon\dot{\upsilon}\epsilon\sigma\tau o\hat{\iota}\ \phi i\lambda\eta.$$

Variants are to be found in Sophocles at the beginning of the 'Trachiniæ' and end of the 'Œdipus Tyrannus.' In Jebb's note to the last-mentioned passage you will find a discussion of the sentiment and references, Greek and Latin.

CECIL S. DAVIS ("J. K.," Wandsworth, Surrey, 2ⁿᵈ S. i. 335").—We have no means of tracing correspondents at that date.

CORRIGENDA.—P. 55, col. 1, l. 17, for κυνὴ read κυνῆ; p. 233, "Intentions" reference, read 9ᵗʰ S. v. 435, 504; vi. 252; p. 249, col. 2, l. 7, for "pole" read *pale.*

NOTICE.

Editorial communications should be addressed to "The Editor of 'Notes and Queries'"—Advertisements and Business Letters to "The Publisher"—at the Office, Bream's Buildings, Chancery Lane, E.C.

We beg leave to state that we decline to return communications which, for any reason, we do not print; and to this rule we can make no exception.

LONDON, SATURDAY, APRIL 19, 1902.

CONTENTS. — No. 225.

Notes.

THE ROUMANIAN LANGUAGE.

I HAVE often wondered why more attention is not paid in this country to Roumanian, a language as melodious as Italian, while the quaint Slavonic and Oriental elements in its vocabulary add, at least in some eyes, to its interest. There seems to be only one Roumanian grammar in English—viz., Torceanu's, in Trübner's series of simplified grammars. Even in German I know of only two of any value—namely, George Dan's (Vienna, 1897), used in Austrian schools, and Th. Wechsler's, in Hartleben's two-shilling series (Leipzig, 1890). The latter is commendable particularly for its literary extracts for reading practice. Roumanian accidence is for the most part like that of the other Romance tongues. Its chief peculiarity, the suffixed article, it has imitated from Albanian and Bulgarian. Excepting auxiliaries, it has no irregular verbs. The greater proportion of the words in common use is still Latin, yet on account of the weird foreign strain, to which I have already alluded, it is perhaps fortunate that the language is rich in etymological dictionaries. I can recommend Pontbriant (1862), Cihac (1870),

or Laurianu and Massimu (1873). A more ambitious etymological dictionary, Hasdeu's 'Etymologicum Magnum Romaniæ,' of which the first part was issued at the expense of the Bucharest Academy in 1885, is still in progress. For purely practical purposes the best dictionary is Damé's 'Dictionnaire Roumain-Français' (Bucharest, 1893). The 'Chrestomathie Roumaine,' by M. Gaster (Leipzig, 1891), contains extracts from 200 books and 100 manuscripts and documents, but is chiefly concerned with the ancient language, and is unhappily printed in a gratuitously ugly Cyrillic character, so that to read even a few lines of it makes one's eyes ache. Of course all modern books are printed in Roman letters. The orthography is by no means settled. The one provisionally adopted by the Roumanian Academy has always seemed to me pedantic, and I am glad to say it is being replaced by forms more in accordance with the genius of the language. My advice to any one desirous of entering upon a course of Roumanian reading is to patronize the "Biblioteca pentru Totī," a series now numbering some 200 volumes, published in Bucharest at the low price of threepence each. It includes not only masterpieces of native writers (such as Alexandrescu, Caragiale, Demetrescu, Ollanescu, Rossetti, Teleor, Zamfirescu), but also translations from English, French, German, &c. Among translations from English I notice works by Huxley, Lubbock, and Spencer, together with a creditable rendering into Roumanian verse of Tennyson's 'Enoch Arden' and specimen stories from Bret Harte and Mark Twain. 'The Luck of Roaring Camp' appears as 'Norocul Roaringcampului,' and its three principal characters respectively as "Kentuckianul," "Sarah din Ciroki" (*sic*), and "Broscoiul Draculuĭ" ("the d—d little cuss"). The pieces from Mark Twain are 'Aurelia's Unfortunate Young Man' ('Păsurile Sufletestĭ ale dreĭ Aurelia') and 'The Bad Boy' ('Băiat Rĕu Crescut'). The translator, Maiorescu, introduces into the latter an interesting bit of local colour by stating that in the Roumanian equivalents of our Sunday-school books bad little boys are called Ioan (John) or Radu (Rudolph), whereas this bad boy was called Gaga.   JAS. PLATT, Jun.

THE BACON—SHAKESPEARE QUESTION.
(*Continued from p. 204.*)

BACON notes a number of small turns of expression, but for what purpose is not known, unless he intended them for use in a treatise on grammar. They are expressions that are to be found scattered throughout the writings of all persons who have used the English speech since Chaucer, and even before, some few notes only excepted, and nearly all of these can be found in contemporary writers. I have found all or nearly all of them in Ben Jonson, Beaumont and Fletcher, Marlowe, and other poets and dramatists of the time; indeed, they are so commonly used that without them it is hardly possible to conceive how anybody could write or speak the English language. Here is a list of some of these expressions, and anybody who cares to take the trouble to search for them will find them in common use in Shakespeare's contemporaries: "What will you?" "For the rest." "Is it possible?" "All this while." "Of grace." "Let it not displease you." "All will not serve." "Where stay we?" "I find that strange." "Not unlike." "If that be so." "It comes to that." "Well remembered." "I arrest you there." "See then how." "I cannot tell." "O, the——." "O, my." "Believe it, believe it not." There are others of a similar character; but I pick out these because they are adduced by Mr. R. M. Bucke, who asserts that they were originated by Bacon, who uses them constantly both in his acknowledged work and in the work of Shakespeare. Mrs. Pott, whose lead Mr. Bucke seems to have followed, declares that,

"although diligent search has been made in the best works of the authors who flourished between the beginning of the sixteenth and the middle of the seventeenth century, only two or three of the turns of expression have been traced, and these expressions are used by a very limited number of authors, and rarely by them."

Baconians who indulge in such assertions as these must imagine that people have no eyes, that all men are fools, and that everybody wishes to be deceived. "Wherefore," to quote Bacon's own words against those who do not desire real knowledge so much as to hear themselves talk, "dogmas of this nature are rather to be condemned in the mass than refuted in detail." No dramatic writer of Shakespeare's time, who produced anything like the same volume of work as he did, or something approaching to it, can be examined who does not use every turn of expression noted by Bacon which is adduced from Shakespeare's work. And not only once, but many times.

But there are certain turns of speech noted by Bacon which are far from common in the literature of the time, and although these are habitually used by Bacon, they are altogether absent from Shakespeare's work.

Everbody used the turns that I have quoted, they were hoary with age; but here is one that is uncommon.

No. 1378, "The rather, bycause. (Continuing another's speech.)"

Mrs. Pott illustrates the entry thus:—

1. Well, you are come to me in a happy time,
The rather that I have some sport in hand.
'Taming of the Shrew,' Ind. i.

2.   I knew him,
The rather will I spare my praises of him.
'All's Well that Ends Well,' II. 2.

So that we may say Bacon not only intended to use his note as it is used in the plays, but that he actually invented the word "rather" as it appears in 'The Taming of the Shrew' and in 'All's Well'!

What a poverty-stricken language our ancestors must have spoken, to be sure! They could not say, Is it possible? Nor could they utter the word "well" without a prop of other words to hold it up. This word "well" forms an entry in the 'Promus,' No. 294, and Mrs. Pott, although she searched contemporary literature, as well as other literature previous to and following Shakespeare's time, and although she examined "328 known authors of the fifteenth, sixteenth, and seventeenth centuries, and upwards of 5,300 of their works,"—yet despite this almost superhuman feat, this labour that might have appalled a Hercules, she could only find one man, John Lyly, employing "well" alone, as a response.

Well, let me quote Bacon to show how he used his note "the rather, bycause," which appears so often in his works as a turn of expression, although the Baconians appear to have missed it; and let the reader say if this man, who employed it so frequently, could, if he wrote Shakespeare's plays, avoid using it at least once or twice in them, or even very many times.

1. "Fair and moderate courses are ever best in causes of estate; the rather, because I wish," &c.—'To the Duke of Buckingham,' 7 March, 1620.

2. "Yet I am unwilling to pu my sickle in another's harvest, but to leave it to the lawyers of the Scottish nation; the rather, because I imagine," &c.—'The Union of the Laws.'

3. "Which maketh me presume, with good assurance, that your lordship will accept well of these my labours, the rather, because your lordship in private hath often," &c.—'To the Lord Chancellor, on sending him his book of "The Advancement of Learning."'

4. "......which (I assure yourself) I desire the rather, because, being placed," &c.—'To the Lord Chancellor, Montague,' vol. iii. p. 35.

Very many more passages could be cited to show that the form of expression is a common one in Bacon ; nevertheless, it is not of Bacon's invention ; for it was used by others quite as early as Bacon wrote, and, like the word "real," by men who had received a university education. Ben Jonson also uses it :—

1. *Tub.* The rather may you judge it to be such Because the bridegroom was described, &c.
   'A Tale of a Tub,' III. i.

2. *Cic.* It shall be dearer rather, and because I'd make it such, hear how much, &c.
   'Cataline,' III. ii.

It occurs several times in Thomas Nashe and in Gabriel Harvey, as well as in Sir Philip Sidney and in 'The Epistle of Martin Marprelate,' 1588.

I turn now to the forms of salutation that are noted by Bacon. There are several of these, but I will notice only the following, viz., "good-morrow," "good-day," "good-night," and "good-even." The reason for this selection will appear presently. Because Bacon notes these forms of salutation the Baconians imagine that he coined them ; and Mrs. Pott draws us a harrowing picture to show how boorish our ancestors were in their manner of greeting each other. They could only exclaim, with more or less grace, "How now !" or make use of some such uncouth expression. But Bacon came into the world to put things right; he saw that everything was out of joint ; and he not only invented the better part of the English language, but, to show the love and care he had for his benighted countrymen, he taught them to say "good-day," "good-morrow." Mrs. Pott ought to know, for she has searched 328 known authors and upwards of 5,300 of their works. There cannot, therefore, be any doubt about the matter. Here are her words :—

"It is certain that the habit of using forms of morning and evening salutation was not introduced into England prior to the date of Bacon's notes, 1594."

Such being the case, it may be taken for granted that the following passage in Chaucer is a Baconian interpolation, and probably it contains embedded within itself the key to a cipher which runs throughout poor Geoffrey's work :—

Ther n'as no good day, ne no saluing,
But streit withouten wordes rehersing,
Everich of hem halpe to armen other,
As frendly, as he were his owen brother.
'The Knightes Tale.'

As regards Beaumont and Fletcher, the following are Mrs. Pott's results in searching for forms of salutation used by the joint authors :—

"Beaumont and Fletcher in upwards of forty

plays use *good-morrow* five times, *good-day* once, *good-night* four times, *good-even* once."

On the contrary, I examined only twenty plays by these authors, and my results are so very different from those of Mrs. Pott that I can only conclude I had on magnifying glasses, or that I saw things through a very hazy medium. Tears will cause that kind of double or even treble sight :—

Upon his hurt she looks so steadfastly,
That her sight dazzling makes the wound seem three ;

For oft the eye mistakes, the brain being troubled.
Baconspeare's 'Venus and Adonis,' st. 178.

I must have been weeping at the dethronement of *Shagspur.* Seeing, however, that I took some trouble about the matter, I cannot bring myself to withhold my figures from a gullible public. The people like to be deceived, and many will no doubt accept my statement in preference to that of Mrs. Pott. Nothing venture, nothing have.

In twenty plays Beaumont and Fletcher use *good-morrow* forty-seven times, *good-day* twelve times, *good-night* forty-five times, and *good-even* thirteen times. In the same plays they employ the variations *God save you and good-morrow* once, *God speed you and good-day* once, and *sweet-night* three times. The plays I examined are those contained in the first volume of "The Old Poets" edition.
C. CRAWFORD.

53, Hampden Road, Hornsey, N.
(*To be continued.*)

ST. MARGARET'S CHURCH AND WESTMINSTER BENEFACTORS.
(*Continued from p. 243.*)

THE next Westminster worthy to be alluded to as being commemorated in St. Margaret's Church is the Rev. James Palmer, whose name is perhaps oftener heard among our people than most of the others who, like him, have left charitable bequests behind, although in this respect it may be both thought and said that he is run very hard by Emery Hill. His monument is on the north wall of the church, and is of a very elaborate character ; most of the colour remains, and there are some traces of the gilding left. The inscription (which we may believe is truer than such things usually are) is as follows :—

"Hereunder is interred yᵉ body of James Palmer | batchelor in divinity borne in this parish of | St. Margᵗˢ in july 1585, a most piovs & charitable | man, exprest in severall places by many | remarkable actions & pticvlarly to this parish | in bvilding fayer Almes Hovses for 12 poore olde | people wᵗʰ

a Free School & a comodiovs habitation | for the
School mʳ & a convenient Chappell for | prayers
and preaching, where he constantly for |ᵈdivers
yeares before his death once a week gave | a com-
fortable sermon, He indowed yᵉ same with a |
competent yearly revenew of freehold estate |
comitted to yᵉ trust & care of 10 considerable |
persons of yᵉ place to be renewed as any dye, | he
cheerfully ended this life yᵉ 5 of Janʸ 1659.

Erected at yᵉ   Sʳ Wᵐ Playter
Charge of   Knᵗ & Baronet."

With the exception of the tablet upon which
the inscription appears, and the two smaller
ones containing the dedication, which are
of black marble, the whole is composed of
richly coloured alabaster, moulded and
artistically carved, and with some gilt work.
Altogether it is an admirable specimen of
the art of the time, and the effect produced
must be pronounced decidedly good. The
bust conveys the impression of being a true
likeness, and is painted in "proper" colours,
with a black gown and cap. In the days
before the erection of the south gallery in
1682 this monument was on the south
wall, but when that gallery was put up it
was placed high up over the stairs, where
it was certainly safe, and where for two
centuries it remained almost unknown,
and certainly unregarded even by those
who had the best possible reason for vene-
rating the name of the individual it commemorated. At the last restoration of the
church, in Dean Farrar's time, this and some
other monuments had better places found for
them. The blazonry of the arms—Sable, a
chevron between three crescents or—is still
fairly fresh. A few notes on our local benefactor may not be out of place. He was a
Westminster man, educated at Cambridge,
ordained by Bishop Bancroft, and presented by the Dean and Chapter of Westminster to the vicarage of St. Bride's, Fleet
Street, in 1616 ; but when the great rebellion
of 1642 broke out he was sequestered for his
loyalty. He is recorded to have been a pious
man, and Newcourt tells us that "he was a
painful preacher who (beside many and
great benefactions to ministers' widows)
hath built and endowed an alms-house in
Westminster." Hatton, in 'Hist. of London,'
1708, says that "he was a frugal person, and
being Vicar of St. Bride's he used to lye in the
steeple." There is no doubt that, if politically
disliked, he was exceedingly beloved in the
parish where he ministered. By a deed
dated 2 March, 1656 (Walcott, our often untrustworthy historian, gives the date wrongly
as 1566, although it may be a printer's error),
he conveyed to trustees an almshouse, then
recently erected in Tothill Fields,

"containing twelve rooms for six poor men and six
poor women ; and a messuage and garden containing
six acres, of which the rents were to be applied
towards the maintenance of the almspeople and for
educating twenty poor boys."

In the following year he conveyed an estate
of twenty acres in Berkshire, called Ash-
amstead Farm, for the same purposes. The
almspeople, who were required to have been
twenty years resident in the parishes, received
30s. a month, and had, once in three years,
the men a cloak and the women a black
gown apiece, with an annual allowance of
twenty chaldrons of coals divided among
them. They also received 5s. each for a
Christmas dinner, and 5s. on St. James's
Day, when the governors met. In 1816-18
the almshouses, chapel, and school were
rebuilt, the school being revived in 1817, and
twenty children, with the same number
belonging to Hill's foundation, admitted.
The children were clothed at the expense of
the foundation, the outfit consisting of a
jacket and trousers, shoes, shirt and band,
pair of stockings, cap, handkerchief, and a
pair of gloves yearly, and a gown once in
four years, to be worn on public occasions.
They were also allowed black linen to make
a round frock, the school being always
known as the "Black Coat School." In 1890
the messuage and garden in Tothill Fields,
consisting of six acres, were of the value of
47,518l., and the annual income 1,425l. The
estate in Berkshire was sold in July, 1873,
for 4,182l. The thoroughfare in which the
old almshouses stood, leading from Victoria
Street into Caxton (formerly Little Chapel)
Street, was known as Palmer's Passage,
with which Gardener's Lane (leading from
Caxton Street to York Street) has been
incorporated, the whole, now and for some
years past, being renamed Palmer Street.
Upon the site has been erected one of the
huge hotels for which London has become so
famous. It was at first opened as the Army
and Navy Hotel, and so it remained, scarcely
prosperous, for a while ; it then became the
Hotel Windsor, and as such it is at present
known. Upon another portion of the site
there has been erected a block of residential
flats called Iddesleigh Mansions, named after
the first Earl of Iddesleigh, better known to
the present generation as Sir Stafford Northcote. It is worthy of remark that a tablet,
re-erected on the flank wall of the new almshouses in Rochester Row, records the names
of the following persons as benefactors to
this charity : Sir John Crosse, Sir Thomas
Crosse, William Green, William Jelpes, Mrs.
Sarah Phillips, William Skelton, James
Stedman, and Thomas Wilson.

The next benefactor to the poor of the two parishes of St. Margaret and St. John, Westminster, who has a memorial in the church of St. Margaret is Joan Barnett, and the inscription sets forth as follows :—

"Here lyeth | the body of Mrs. Joane Barnet wid | dow borne in this Parish (| Daughter of Mr. Michael Simnel | and Joane his wife) who setled | by deed on Trustees of this Par | ish for ever : Severall Houses in | London for the uses following | vez^t | 40l: per ann' to be equally divi | ded every quart^r between twen- | ty of the Poorest ancient Widowes | of Civill life & conversation. In- ha | biteing in this Parish. and those | borne here to be first preferred : | 20s: for a yearely Sermon in this | parish on the feast of all Soules : | 20s: for a Collation for ye Trustees | 10s: for the Church officers : | she departed this life ye 6 of May | 1674, in the 82 yeare of her age."

It is set forth that in 1670 Joan Barnett, by deed under date 20 July, gave two houses in Robin Hood Court, near Bow Lane, and a messuage in Ivy Lane, St. Faith's, London, the yearly rents thereof (40l.) to be paid to

"twenty of the poorest and ancientest widows of Civil life and Conversation which shall be in- habitants of the parish of St. Margaret, 40s. to be paid to such alms-people a-piece—10s. on Lammas- day (1st August), 10s. on All Souls'-day (2nd Novem- ber), 10s. on Candlemas-day (2nd February), and 10s. on May-day (1st May); 20s. to the minister of St. Margaret's on All Souls'-day for a sermon, and 10s. to the Servants of the Church ; and 20s. to be spent at a dinner or Collation for the minister, trustees, and Churchwardens."

This dear old benefactress of the Westminster poor is said to have got her livelihood by selling oatmeal cakes hard by the church doors, and in memory of this circumstance a large oatmeal pudding used to be a standing dish at the "Feast." From the report of 1890 we find that the premises in Robin Hood Court were sold for City improvements in 1851 for 628l., and from the proceeds of the sale of the Ivy Lane premises 1,183l. 14s. 6d. Consols were purchased in 1883. In 1880 the quarterly payments were increased to 15s., the funds of the charity having considerably improved. The scheme of 1889 provided that the payments to the recipients at the time of the transference of the charity to the parochial trustees should be continued to them, but none others are to be elected to vacancies, so that the charity will eventually be merged in the consolidated account. In 1890 the sum vested in new Consols was 2,334l. 0s. 5d., and the annual income 64l. 3s. 0d.   W. E. Harland-Oxley.

71, Turner Buildings, Millbank, S.W.

(To be continued.)

Saxon Names for Meat still Current.— In the opening chapter of 'Ivanhoe' Sir Walter Scott, by means of the conversation between Wamba and Gurth, points out that the animals used for food, which while alive bear Saxon names, are called when dead by Norman names, showing that the Saxon serf herded the animals and his Norman master ate them. But Scott does not carry the argument one step further, and show that the inferior portions, which the serf was permitted to eat, still bear Saxon names, such as bullock's head, bullock's heart, ox tail, ox tongue, cow heels, &c. ; sheep's head, sheep's tongue, sheep's liver, sheep's trotters, &c. ; calf's head, calf's liver, calf's tail, calf's feet, &c. ; pig's head, pig's cheek, pig's liver, pig's fry, &c. ; deer's fry, for even the royal stag produces deer's fry, not venison fry.

As a boy I was duly taught the change of name between the live and dead animal, but I have never discovered any one who, when ordering a neck of mutton and a sheep's head, perceived that, while speaking of two adjacent portions of the same dead animal, he called it in the one case by its Norman name and in the other by its Saxon name.

    Edwin Durning Lawrence, Bt., M.P.
Athenæum Club.

George Sandys.—"A Paraphrase upon the Divine Poems, with Musical Notations by Henry Lawes. Folio. At the Bell in St. Paul's Churchyard, 1638." A large-paper copy of this book sold lately at Sotheby's for 4l. 10s. A note in the catalogue stated, "The present copy has portion of the suppressed leaf Aaa^2, which is always wanting." This is an error, as the Williamscote copy has the leaf intact. Will owners of the folio edition of this book look into their copies, and if they have the suppressed leaf state the fact in 'N. & Q.'? It is the first leaf of the text of the Lamenta- tions of Jeremiah.   John E. T. Loveday.

Sheridan and Maginn. — The financia. straits to which Sheridan was habitually driven sharpened his wits as well as his wit, and he created a reputation for smart things, many of which are apocryphal. Among them the famous dictum, "Thank Heaven that's settled!" seems open to attack. I confess I always credited Sheridan with its invention, and thousands of men have done the same. According to Charles Gibbon in 'The Casquet of Literature,' William Maginn claims "proprietary rights."
    M. L. R. Breslar.

"Hog."—I confess that I am somewhat surprised to notice that the 'New English Dictionary' marks this important substantive "origin unknown." With all deference to the learned editors of the great lexicon, I submit that the etymology of "hog" is much more transparent than that of a great many words. It is, of course, Scandinavian—from O. Nor. *högg*, a cut (*höggva*, to cut), whence Dan.-Norw. *hug*, Swed. *hugg*, a cut, and is therefore connected with Eng. *hew*=A.-Sax. *hedwan*, Ger. *hauen*, to cut=O. H. Ger. *houwan*. The compound terms hog-pig, hog-sheep, hog-mutton, hog-colt, hog-bull, the diminutives hogget, hoggrel, &c., and the Scot. hogg and hoggie, which we find in our dictionaries, denoted, at any rate originally, cut, *i.e.* emasculated, animals (in the case of sheep, also shorn); cf. Fr. *couper*, Ger. *verschneiden*, to cut, to geld. Note also the dial. verb "hog," to cut, as a horse's mane. Confusion as to the exact meaning of the noun has only arisen since the literal signification has been forgotten. "Hog" came to be specifically applied to swine merely from the great prevalence of that quadruped ; cf. the 'Catholicon Anglicum' (fifteenth century), *s.v.* 'Hogge,' "majalis, est enim porcus carens testiculis." The suggestion in the 'Concise Etymological Dictionary' (edition 1901) of Prof. Skeat, "prob. from an A.-S. **hocg*," seems scarcely feasible, for A.-S. *cg* generally yields Eng. *dg.*: A.-S. *ecg*=edge, *mycg*=midge, *wecg* = wedge, *hrycg* = ridge (the Northern "rigg" is from O. Nor. *hryggr*). There is no objection phonetically to deriving "hog" from O. Nor. *högg*, for Scandinavia itself has *fjord*, from O. Nor. *fjörðr*; *jord*, from *jörð*, "earth"; while O. Nor. *höfuð*, "head," has produced *hoved* in Norway and *hufvud* in Sweden ; and we have A.-S. *hold*, "freeholder," from O. Nor. *hölldr*.

The facts that we find the stream-name Hogg Beck (O. Nor. *bekkr*) in the north of England, and *hogge* and *hogastre* occurring in the dialect of Normandy, as shown in Moisy's Caen publications, tend to clinch the Scandinavian derivation. At all events, I have inserted this etymology against the name Hogg in my forthcoming 'Concise Etymological Dictionary of British Surnames.'

Since writing the foregoing I have remarked that the 'Century Dictionary' favours the notion of "cut"; but its editors did not detect the direct Scandinavian origin of "hog." 　　　　　Hy. Harrison.

The Young Pretender in London, September, 1761.—The old Duke of Norfolk told Prince John Sobieski Stuart that at the coronation banquet of King George III. he was seated in the gallery next to the Young Pretender, and that at the instant of the Champion throwing down his gauntlet Prince Charles Edward let fall one of his white kid gloves, as a challenge to any who would dispute his father's right to the throne. The above facts were related to me by Prince John Sobieski Stuart in the Reading Room of the British Museum.

　　　　　H. Syer Cuming.

Simon Fraser, Lord Lovat.—The following is a copy (from the original in my possession) of a letter which contains some interesting information concerning Lord Lovat :—

　　　　　London, March 14th, —47.

Sʳ—Since the writing my Letter I have got some intelligence of the yesterdays Proceeding against Lᵈ Lovat, which will not I presume be unacceptable to one of your Inquisitive Disposition, I shall therefore venture to detain you a little longer with such a relation as a multitude of Business & want of leisure will permit. The Evidence against him was very strong, his own Secretary swearing point blank to his signing a letter produc'd in Court, to the Pretender, wherein he declares he had been active enough in promoting his cause to behead an hundred Lords & hang fifty Commonors. Sʳ Edwᵈ Faulkoner, the Duke of Cumberland's Secretary, appeard against him, concerning his Behaviour since his being Prisoner, and deposed upon oath that upon being taken he declared, in his hearing, that the Discontents of the Nation were so great & the Grieveances sufferd so manifold, that if Kouli Kan had landed in Scotland he believd he should have join'd him: his Deportment in that Days tryal shewd he had little Concern or fear at heart for the eminent danger he was then in, but on the Contrary manifested rather an intrepidity of Mind arising either from the little appearance of making his escape out of the hands of avenging Justice or the Resolution of an inveterate offender : for when Sʳ Edwᵈ Faulk: had concluded his Evidence, Lᵈ Lovat turn'd about to him & with an air of Galantry, wish'd him Joy of his new wife. Further Proceeding are delay'd till Monday, which is only lengthening a few Days, a life already burdensome through natural Decay, for the witnesses are so numerous & Facts so plain, that all the cunning he is master of cannot clear him of the accusation : three or four Days is thought by some to be the longest his Tryal will now continue, as they apprehend he has not so many witness as he pretends, to appear in his Defence, the sooner it Ends the better, for it is at present the subject of every ones thoughts & the chief employmt of their time, & that I may not draw you into the number of those misspenders of their valuable moments I shall forthwith subscribe my self 　　　Yours to Command

　　　　　Wᵐ Gordon.

　　　　　Thomas Turner.

Mill Hill Road, Norwich.

"Chic."—It appears that this word is now recognized officially as good French, having been adopted by the French Academy.

　　　　　N. S. S.

Macaulay and Hannah More. — At the beginning of his essay on 'Burleigh and his

Times' (April, 1832), after expressing his astonishment at the bulk and weight of Dr. Nares's work, Macaulay writes :—

"Such a book might, before the deluge, have been considered as light reading by Hilpa and Shalum. But unhappily the life of man is now threescore years and ten; and we cannot but think it somewhat unfair in Dr. Nares to demand from us so large a portion of so short an existence."

This is curiously like a passage in a letter of Hannah More to the Rev. Daniel Wilson (1822) :—

"Had he [Walter Scott] written before the flood, when perhaps there were not, in all, so many books in the world as he alone has introduced into it, all would have been well; he would have been a benefactor to the antediluvian Hilpahs and Zilpahs. A life of 800 years might have allowed of the perusal of the whole of his volumes; a proportionate quantity in each century would have been delightful; but for our poor scanty threescore years and ten, it is too much."—'Memoirs of the Life of Mrs. Hannah More,' by William Roberts, Esq. In 2 vols. Vol. ii. p. 342 (1836).

Hannah More, it may be noted, has, if her letter is correctly printed, misspelt Hilpa (see *Spectator*, Nos. 584 and 585) on the analogy of Zilpah.   EDWARD BENSLY.
The University, Adelaide, South Australia.

Queries.

WE must request correspondents desiring information on family matters of only private interest to affix their names and addresses to their queries, in order that the answers may be addressed to them direct.

"OLIVE": "OLIVACEOUS."— These words are normally applied to a particular shade of green, defined as a dull yellowish green like that of the unripe olive. But since 1600, at least, they have also been freely applied to the complexions of Southern European peoples, and of the natives of various subtropical countries, who are certainly not green, but apparently brownish yellow or yellowish brown. A lady in the *Guardian*, No. 109 (1713), says, "You must know I am a famous olive beauty," and speaks of "olives and brunettes" as occurring among Englishwomen. Can any explanation be given of this curious application of *olive*? It occurs also in French with the adjective *olivâtre*, as defined and illustrated by the Académie and by Littré. Thus the latter explains *olivâtre* as "qui est de couleur d'olive," which is further said to be "couleur verdâtre, qui tire un peu sur le brun." But the examples given are of human complexions, said to be "les uns blancs, les autres noirs, les autres basanés, les autres olivâtres," and Buffon is cited to the effect that "les Tunquinois sont d'une couleur un peu olivâtre." But surely the Tonquinese are not green or greenish. Dr. Johnson defines *olivaster* as "darkly brown, tawny," but does not say where the *olive* comes in. Whence comes the confusion between green and brown, and how comes any shade of brown to be termed *olive*?
    J. A. H. MURRAY.

OSORIO FAMILY.—Is anything known of the Osorio family? I am led to believe that the first Osorio was a Portuguese Jew who came over to England in the suite of Catherine of Braganza as her physician. Are any records to be found to prove that such was the case? The last of the family, I believe, was Abraham, who became a Christian. He resided at Theobalds Road. He was elected a member of the Society of Arts in 1800, was one of the chairmen of accounts in 1807, and died about 1825.   P. L. N. F.

TRAVELS IN INDIA.—When Lord Auckland was Governor of India, before the Mutiny, his sister, the Hon. —— Eden, attending all his functions and travelling with him, wrote a book on her travels in India. What is the title of her book?   JOHN TUDOR.
1, Liverpool Lawn, Dover.

[The 'D.N.B.' quotes as an authority for the life of the second Earl of Auckland the 'Journal in India in 1837 and 1838' of his eldest sister, Eleanor; and in the notice of Emily Eden, a younger sister, mentions her 'Portraits of the People and Princes of India,' published in 1844, and 'Up the Country: Letters written to her Sister from the Upper Provinces of India,' but not issued till 1866.]

CASTOR SUGAR.—This is now an article of ordinary daily use. Can any of your readers give me the date when it was first brought into use and when the name is first to be found? 'H.E.D' does not help me in this matter.   D. M. R.

CABINET CARVED IN PRISON.—The *Illustrated News of the World* of 29 May, 1858, gives a picture of a cabinet dated 1614, and carved by one of the Gordons of Earlston, who was imprisoned for eighteen years in Blackness Castle. In 1858 it was in the possession of Mr. R. W. Train of Greenock, son of Scott's friend Joseph Train. What has become of it?   J. M. BULLOCH.
118, Pall Mall.

ALBINO ANIMALS.—I shall be grateful for references to the most complete accounts of the alleged worship of white or albino sacred elephants in Siam and elsewhere; also as to the worship of other white or albino animals, including the sacred white horses, ἱερῶν ἵππων τῶν λευκῶν, which accompanied the army of Cyrus to the siege of Babylon, alluded to by Herodotus. He also records that amongst the Egyptians purely white oxen were sacred to Epaphus; but one single dark hair was enough to exclude them as unclean. Do later historians corroborate the accuracy of these statements by Herodotus?

J. LAWRENCE-HAMILTON, M.R.C.S.

30, Sussex Square, Brighton.

WILBRAHAM TOLLEMACHE EDWARDS was admitted to Westminster School in 1779. I should be glad to have any particulars relating to him. G. F. R. B.

JAY, THE WOODLAND BIRD.—Is it known what are the origin and meaning of the word "jay"? B.

[The 'H.E.D.' declares it to be of uncertain origin. The French name is *geai*.]

CELLINI AND SHAKESPEARE. — In 'The Capitolo,' verses written by Benvenuto Cellini during his imprisonment in the Castle of St. Angelo, there are, according to Roscoe's rendering, lines strikingly anticipatory of the passage in 'Hamlet' (I. v.) wherein the Ghost declares that he could a tale unfold that would make each particular hair of his hearer stand on end "like quills upon the fretful porpentine":—

Staring aghast, I stalk about the room,
My hair with horror bristling on my head
Like quills upon the fretful porcupine.

Is the correspondence of expression due to the culture of the translator, or is it exactly justified by the original Italian?

ST. SWITHIN.

LANDGUARD FORT, IN SUFFOLK.—In 'The Coinage of Suffolk,' published in 1868, written by Charles Golding, the following sentence occurs on p. 55, in a paragraph describing the copper tokens of Landguard Fort : " A MS. of Garrison orders and parole words in use at the Fort, together with the state of the Garrison and Fort daily, from 1761 to 1766, is in the writer's Suffolk collections." In 1897 I tried to trace this MS., but failed. It had, so Mr. Golding told me, been sold, but he could not say to whom. Can any information be given as to its present possessor or whereabouts? J. H. LESLIE, Major.

Hathersage, North Derbyshire.

WELLINGTON PICTURE.—Can you inform me in what periodical there is a picture representing one of Wellington's Peninsular victories? It was after the battle of Salamanca, Vimiera, or Talavera. It is a picture representing Sir Arthur Wellesley riding, as was his custom after a battle, on horseback. He passes a drunken soldier who is partly reeling with a wine bottle, the neck broken, and as he passes the man says (the picture is worded), "Nosey, it is ours." I have asked *Army and Navy*. I think I was told it was not theirs. I thought it was—at any rate, it was a similar periodical. WM. TOWNSEND.

Surrey Street, Sheffield.

CHARLES II. ON WEIGHT OF FISH. — For generations Charles II. has been credited with puzzling the British Royal Society by a question. His question related to the weight of a fish, and he begged to know, since a dead fish in a pail of water increased its weight, how it came to pass that the same fish, if placed while alive in the same pail of water, added nothing to its avoirdupois. In reading Pepys, and indeed in other contemporary reading, I find no allusion to this royal and not uncharacteristic joke. How early a record of this anecdote is known to 'N. & Q.,' the readers of which, taken together, are so much more learned than any individual? JAMES D. BUTLER.

Madison, Wis., U.S.

[The late PROF. TOMLINSON stated at 8ᵗʰ S. ii. 526 that this story was not mentioned in the works of Wallis, Sprat, Birch, or Thomson. The subject was continued in 8ᵗʰ S. iii. 234, 377, 497.]

GANGANELLI'S BIBLE.—What are its attributes? How many known copies exist, and where? CRESCENT.

NAPOLEON AND THE TEMPLE AT JERUSALEM.—Is there any authority for the statement that Napoleon declared he would rebuild the Temple at Jerusalem ; also that he would rebuild Babylon? E. LOMAX.

SIR JOHN OLDCASTLE.—Is anything known of the descendants of Sir John Oldcastle and Joan, Baroness Cobham?

RONALD DIXON.

46, Marlborough Avenue, Hull.

ARMS OF CONTINENTAL CITIES.—Can any one refer me to any books showing the arms of continental cities, &c.? It is strange, especially when we remember how these are displayed in every place, that no reference is made to them in the guide-books (Murray, Hare, Baedeker), nor even in such encyclopædias as the 'Britannica' or Chambers's. It would, too, have been so easy just to give a woodcut at the head of each article or in the corner of each map. LUCIS.

CIGARETTE-SMOKING.—When and by whom was cigarette-smoking introduced into this country? At first the classes usually smoked

cigarettes, now the masses largely smoke them. The other day I was in the shop of a tobacconist in Hull, and noticed a carter from the Yorkshire Wolds purchase a pennyworth of cigarettes. After the customer had left, I expressed my surprise that a working man should not buy tobacco instead of cigarettes, and was told by the shopkeeper that working people were his chief customers for cigarettes.　　　WILLIAM ANDREWS.
Royal Institution, Hull.

[Cigarette-smoking, long familiar in Turkey and Russia, came in, we fancy, after the Crimean war, which led to its adoption by English officers, naval and military. Laurence Oliphant is said to have been the first notable person to smoke cigarettes in the streets of London.]

ST. PATRICK. — In 'St. Patrick's Hymn before Tara,' otherwise the 'Breastplate of Patrick,' one finds :—

So have I invoked all these powers
Between myself and every dangerous merciless
　power
Opposed unto my body and my soul—
Against the incantations of false prophets,
The black laws of heathendom,
The false laws of heresy, the craft of idolatry,
The spells of women, and smiths, and druids,
And all knowledge that hath defiled the soul of
　man.

I should be glad of information as to "the spells of women, and smiths, and druids."
　　　JAS. CURTIS, F.S.A.

AUTHOR OF BOOK WANTED. — "Classic Cullings and Fugitive Gatherings. By an Experienced Editor. London, M. Arnold, 1831."　　　JOHN TUDOR.
1, Liverpool Lawn, Dover.

SANTIAGO PENITENTS.—In his 'Narrative,' London, 1768, the Hon. John Byron (the admiral who was well known as "Foulweather Jack") describes the customs of the inhabitants of St. Jago de Chili as he saw them in 1743. Ladies attended the common diversion of "bull-feasts," &c., and he adds :

"Another amusement for the ladies here, are the nights of their great processions, when they go out veiled......I have seen fifty or sixty penitents following these processions ; they wear a long white garment with a long train to it, and high caps of the same, which fall down before, and cover all their faces, having only two small holes for their eyes ; so that they are never known. Their backs are bare, and they lash themselves with a cat-o'-nine-tails till the long train behind is covered all over with blood. Others follow them with great heavy crosses upon their backs ; so that they groan under the weight as they walk barefooted, and often faint away. The streets swarm with friars of all the different orders."

I have quoted from the first edition, p. 231. Of subsequent editions the best is the Edin-burgh one of 1812, where the passage is to be found at p. 174. Where can I find a full account of these self-flogging Santiago penitents ?　　　W. S.

STANDSFIELD. —John Standsfield, of The Cliffe, Lewes, married first Elinor, daughter of Thomas Comber, of Allington, Sussex (by whom he had a daughter Elinor, wife of Richard Evelyn, of Wooton) ; she was buried at All Saints', Lewes, 6 October, 1613. He married secondly Jane ——, who survived him, and subsequently married William Newton, Esq., of Southover. Can any of your readers give me the maiden name of the latter lady, and the date and place of her marriage to John Standsfield ?
　　　JOHN COMBER.
Myddleton Hall, near Warrington.

WHITE GLOVES AT ASSIZES. —Can any of your correspondents kindly inform me of the origin of the custom of presenting white gloves at assizes when there are no prisoners to be tried ?　　　CHARLES R. DAWES.
[Consult 1ˢᵗ S. i. 72 and General Indexes passim.]

OFFICIAL LEADERS OF THE OPPOSITION.— Can any of your readers inform me where I can get a list of the official leaders of the Opposition in the Houses of Lords and Commons for the last two centuries ?
　　　B. M. NOLAN.

Replies.

MICHAEL BRUCE AND BURNS.
(9ᵗʰ S. vii. 466 ; viii. 70, 148, 312, 388, 527 ; ix. 95, 209.)

So far as I am concerned, this discussion refers simply to the authorship of the 'Ode to the Cuckoo.' I must therefore decline to be drawn into the consideration of side issues, such as the historical accuracy of Mr. Grey Graham, the alleged dishonesty of Logan as a preacher and lecturer, and even the evidence for the composition of those hymns and paraphrases which Michael Bruce's father is said to have called his son's 'Gospel Sonnets.' I might—and, if necessity arose, I believe I could—defend the position I have taken up even with reference to the whole controversy over the relations of Logan to Bruce, but for the present I am concerned exclusively with the dispute regarding the 'Ode to the Cuckoo.' This was the question that was raised by an incidental remark of the late MR. A. G. REID, whose fatal illness prevented his making a defence for himself. As his unworthy substitute I have striven to uphold what he asserted, and have done all in my power to prevent the discussion from diverging into a quest after irrelevant conclusions. The authorship, then, of the 'Ode to the Cuckoo' is the theme under consideration, and of that theme alone will anything be said now.

It is sometimes averred that Michael Bruce lacked the genius for striking out a lyric of such dainty and winning simplicity as the 'Ode to the Cuckoo.' But the careful student of his unquestioned poems will have little hesitation in deciding that the achievement was not beyond his powers. The 'Elegy written in Spring' would alone suffice to prove his possession of the kind of poetic gift requisite for the purpose. This poem is more ambitious in character, and not infrequently more rhetorical in manner, than the 'Ode,' but it displays the same direct and candid love of natural beauty, a similar delight in birds and flowers, and an allied pensiveness with melancholy note deepened in accordance with the subject. The same spirit moves in the descriptive blank verse poem 'Lochleven.' In reading this remarkable, if somewhat immature study, it is impossible not to be struck with points of resemblance to passages in the 'Ode.' One may be selected for illustration. The fourth stanza of the 'Ode to the Cuckoo,' as issued in 1770, reads thus :—

> The schoolboy wand'ring in the wood
>   To pull the flow'rs so gay,
> Starts, thy curious voice to hear,
>   And imitates thy lay.

The heroine of 'Lochleven,' at an early stage in her career, is delineated in these terms :—

> Left by her school-companions at their play,
> She'd often wander in the wood, or roam
> The wilderness, in quest of curious flow'r,
> Or nest of bird unknown.

There is a striking similarity between these two extracts, not only in idea, but in rhythm, phrase, and diction. A long and exquisite passage on flowers follows immediately in 'Lochleven'; the heroine at a further stage is apostrophized as "fair wanderer of the wood"; and in another place we learn that

>   the bride and bridal-maids
> Stray'd thro' the woods, and o'er the vales, in
>   quest
> Of flow'rs, and garlands, and sweet-smelling herbs.

Little tricks of phrase and characteristic mannerisms of diction are always significant, and one cannot fail to notice in the 'Ode' and the first passage from 'Lochleven' the special use of the word "curious," while the attention is arrested by the reiterated statement as to wandering in the wood and the references to "flow'r" and "flow'rs." Again, in the memorial poem 'Daphnis,' Bruce tells of the days

> When o'er the flow'ry green we ran, we play'd
> With blooms bedropt by youthful Summer's hand.

No reader of the famous stanza of the 'Ode' which declares that the cuckoo's "bow'r is ever green" will fail to be struck with some of the expressions in Bruce's imitation of Ramsay's 'Yellow-haired Laddie.' Here we find not only "sweets of the flow'rs," but "blackbirds that warbled on blossoming bow'rs"; and we also learn that "Mary sings sweet as the bird in her bower." The stanza of the 'Ode' that should follow that on the green bower — complementary to it, and charged with suggestive and haunting pathos —was not printed by Logan, though found by his executors among his MSS. It runs thus :—

> Alas! sweet bird! not so my fate,
>   Dark scowling skies I see
> Fast gathering round, and fraught with woe
>   And wintry years to me.

It is inevitable that this should be compared with the following stanza of Bruce's 'Elegy written in Spring':—

> Now Spring returns : but not to me returns
>   The vernal joy my better years have known ;
> Dim in my breast life's dying taper burns,
>   And all the joys of life with health are flown.

Altogether, internal evidence supports the assumption that Bruce was the author of the 'Ode to the Cuckoo.' The wandering in the wood, the delight in "curious flow'r" and "curious voice" of bird upon the bower, while not germane to Logan's outlook, are specially characteristic of Bruce; and the "dark scowling skies," painfully imminent, in the sense used, in the case of Bruce, suffered editorial suppression at the hands of Logan, who did not discover them among his pressing anticipations.

The external proofs of Bruce's authorship are too numerous to be detailed here, but the conclusive evidence of one important witness must be mentioned. The primeval story of pastoral song, as set forth for all time in the account of Bion and Moschus, is recalled on the very threshold of this investigation. Bruce and his friend David Pearson are inseparably associated, just as is the case with Milton and King, Tennyson and Hallam, Arnold and Clough. In Pearson, Bruce had a comrade who was more than a brother, who climbed with him the selfsame hill, and to whom he unbosomed himself with implicit confidence. Of the few letters from the poet that were not finally disposed of by Logan, several are to David Pearson, whom the writer addresses as fully worthy of his very best correspondence. In one he communicates an account of a picturesque and impressive vision or dream, and in another he warmly describes his friend as his " rival in immortal hope." During an illness Pearson was attended by a medical specialist, to whom Bruce addressed, in his friend's stead, a poetical letter of gratitude. The original copy of this document was given to Logan, together with the other Bruce MSS., and sixteen lines of its somewhat rugged heroic couplets were afterwards recaptured from oblivion through the retentive memory of Pearson (Grosart's 'Works of Michael Bruce,' p. 235). Here, then, is no ordinary man. He is intellectually strong, he has deep and moving sympathies, and he enjoys the entire confidence of his devoted friend. Pearson, moreover, in common with the class to which he belonged, had stern religious convictions, and would have suffered much rather than perjure himself in any cause whatever. Now, he maintained throughout life that he was familiar with Bruce's 'Ode to the Cuckoo' before he ever heard of Logan. He knew it, as he knew the other work of his friend, because it had been submitted to him for approval, and he had it by heart as he had his Catechism. Writing to Anderson, of the 'British Poets,' Pearson said that a few days after the death of Michael Bruce the poet's father read to him some passages from the MS. book afterwards secured by Logan. The poems selected, he said, were the 'Ode to the Cuckoo' and the 'Musiad,' "at which," runs the narrative, "the good old man was greatly overcome." This is either the truth or a very heartless fabrication, and a just estimate of Pearson's character will readily help to fix the category in which it is to be placed. In another letter the same staunch witness writes :—

"I need not inform you concerning the bad treatment that his poems met with from the Rev. Mr. Logan, when he received from his father the whole of his manuscripts, published only his own pleasure, and kept back those poems that his friends would gladly have embraced, and since published many of them in his own name. The 'Cuckoo' and the Hymns in the end of Logan's Book are assuredly Mr. Bruce's productions."

Is Pearson's testimony to be ignored as a delusion or a deliberate tissue of misrepresentation? We have seen the relations that existed between Bruce and Pearson, and we have noted Pearson's literary appreciation and his excellent memory. The 'Ode to the Cuckoo' is a poem that was not likely to be forgotten after it was once heard or read, and Pearson could remember a succession of comparatively trivial heroics. His evidence for the authorship of the disputed poem is essential, stands at the very beginning of the question, and claims attention and consideration before dates and everything else. This was a man directly and closely familiar with what he discussed, and his acknowledged reputation rebuts the possibility of charging him with deliberate falsehood. Those who know what the men of Pearson's creed and manner were will admit that they would have been ready to perish at the stake rather than lend themselves to the propagation of an untruth. They were upright as Burns's cottar, conscientious as Scott's David Deans, and candid as the Ettrick Shepherd himself. Surely these are qualities before which it is becoming to make obeisance. The advocates of Logan's authorship of the poem must not only show that it is representative of his genius, but they must annul the testimony of David Pearson. Let them satisfactorily eliminate this witness from the number cited in Bruce's favour, and then they may advance a little. As matters stand, they seem to get forward only while trampling him ignominiously under foot. THOMAS BAYNE.

A ROYAL YACHT (9th S. ix. 244).—There is a long and interesting account of the Fubbs in the 'History of Music,' by Hawkins. The yacht was built at Greenwich in 1682 by Sir Phineas Pitt, rebuilt at Deptford in 1724, and was in the Navy list down to 1761.
W. H. CUMMINGS.

GREEK PRONUNCIATION (9th S. vii. 146, 351, 449 ; viii. 74, 192, 372, 513 ; ix. 131, 251).— When people look at anything from varying standpoints, that thing will often present different appearances ; and then it is difficult for them to come to an agreement as to what is seen. Referring to what I last wrote, I cannot say that I see any "contradiction." I did not mean to say that I "think it strange that the Latin *sal* could have become *sel*" in French. What I thought was that possibly the Latin *sal* never had so to "become," but that the sound of the Latin *sal*, originally, was probably much what the sound of the present French word *sel* yet is. If we consider that all languages may be expected to have had a drop in the vowel tones, and that yet we find the sounds *salz* and *sel*, for instance, still remaining, while *sal* and *sealt* stand out as guideposts from the past, one can only think of our own sound (*sorlt*) as a much-travelled, fashionable monstrosity. And surely it is the *sound* that is the really valuable thing to get at ; for, after all, *letters* are to language only what coin-metal is to "goods" (and the "words" are the coinage), the "medium of exchange." That coinage is very apt to get much worn, battered, and defaced in long usage, and apparently *sorlt* is a specimen. W. H. B.

"RATHER" (9ᵗʰ S. ix. 7, 137, 275).—At the last reference I find that, in discussing *rathe*, it is said that "*ready* is a near relation." This remark would never have been made if any reasonable dictionary had been consulted ; and it is hard that we should have such impossible crudities submitted to us. The A.-S. form of *rathe* begins with *hr ;* but the A.-S. form of *ready* begins with *r.* Every beginner in Anglo-Saxon knows that words commencing with *hr* are distinct from those that commence with *r.* Hence the absurdity of the remark is obvious. Q. E. D.

PARENTAGE OF CÆSAR BORGIA (9ᵗʰ S. viii. 524 ; ix. 176, 232).—I confess that I wrote the major part of 'Chronicles of the House of Borgia'; but I will not pretend to provide my readers with ability to read intelligently. I do not seek to convert any one. I merely express my proper opinion. In the present case I myself believe Varillas. Some of my grounds for believing him are stated in the book. MR. DAWES does not believe, does not want to believe him. He asserts that Creighton, Symonds, Gregorovius, Roscoe, Machiavelli, give Varillas the lie. I admit it. But does MR. DAWES dare to claim infallibility—an infallibility more ample than that of the Holiness of the Pope of Rome— for Creighton, who mistook a draught of blood for transfusion ; for Symonds, who sacrificed fact to fiction *in re* Xystus P.M. IIII. and Cardinal Sclafenati ; for Gregorovius, who squared the circle *in re* Pintorricchio's Madonna of the Borgia Tower ; for Roscoe, who is " a back number"; or for Machiavelli, who wrote two self-contradictory accounts of the *colpo di stato* of Sinigaglia ? I hardly think it.
"Ὅτι τοιαῦτα αὐτοῖς τὰ ὄντα, οἷα ἂν ὑπολάβωσι. MR. DAWES appears to be anxious to attack Varillas (or me). I, on the contrary, find Varillas very credible. An habitual liar occasionally errs into truth. I think that Varillas has so erred in the present case. It is human to err, as the copybooks say. Varillas was human. Ergo : —. And as Creighton, Symonds, Gregorovius, Roscoe, Machiavelli, also were human, MR. DAWES might as well fit his champion quincunx with a similar simple syllogism.

These remarks are intended, not as a defence of 'Chronicles of the House of Borgia,' a work which I despise, but as an intimation to MR. DAWES that, though he persist in thrumming his stringed instrument never so wisely, I decline to argue with one who cannot even cite his Webster accurately *in re* my deliberately selected word "gallimaufry." I am not a Freemason, but a Roman Catholic.
Ἄσβεστος δ᾽ ἄρ ἐνῶρτο γέλως μακάρεσσι θεοῖσιν. FREDERICK BARON CORVO.

ARMS OF DUTCH EAST INDIA COMPANY (9ᵗʰ S. ix. 9, 118, 272).—The coats of arms borne on the copper coinage of the Dutch current in Ceylon were those of Holland, Zeeland, Friesland, Guelderland, and Utrecht. On the other side is the monogram of the company.

The carving referred to by L. L. K. is over the gateway of the old fort at Galle. He is correct in supposing that it is surmounted by a cock as a crest. This device is intended to represent the town of Galle—an idea which the Dutch seem to have taken over from the Portuguese, who adopted that bird as the badge of the town, either from a notion that the name Galle had something to do with the Latin for a cock or as a punning allusion to that word. The Galle Club has recently adopted the same device for its note-paper, at the suggestion of a member with historical tastes.

I see that my account of the origin of the monogram reads as if the relative dimensions of the letters were fixed by the resolution of the company referred to therein. This I did not intend. I merely meant to describe the form of the monogram usually found. The colours, however, were prescribed.
J. P. LEWIS.

SWIFT'S VISITS TO ENGLAND: THE "FOUR CROSSES" INN (9ᵗʰ S. ix. 186).—The lines relating the story of Swift's witty couplet were sent to the *Gentleman's Magazine* by Mr. Thomas Deacon, a native of Willoughby. They appeared in the issue for November, 1819. Mr. Deacon also wrote a 'History of Willoughby,' which was published in 1828, and therein a portion of his poem was reprinted. I have seen it stated that Mr. William Cropper, father of the gentleman to whom MR. HARPER refers, was at one time landlord of the "Four Crosses" at Willoughby.
JOHN T. PAGE.
West Haddon, Northamptonshire.

EAST INDIA BADGE (9ᵗʰ S. ix. 67, 155).—This badge is the commercial or merchant's mark adopted by the United Company of Merchants trading to the East Indies up to the Act of Parliament which terminated the existence of that company in 1858-60. It also appeared upon the penknives, scissors, &c., supplied by that company to their servants in their home establishment in Leadenhall Street, but the reversed 4 stood on the centre of the superior (upper) part of a heart which was divided by two lines (one perpendicular and one horizontal) into four equal parts, the first having U in it, the second E, the third I, and the fourth C, which letters stood for United East India Company, but which were jestingly interpreted by those servants, from a very early period, as four idle, eating, cheating villains, the origin of which I know not.   C. MASON.

29, Emperor's Gate, S.W.

CHARLES WESLEY, GEORGE LILLO, AND JOHN HOME (9ᵗʰ S. viii. 402, 492 ; ix. 51).— Carlyle, in his 'French Revolution,' describing the death of Marat, says : "His life, with a groan, gushes out indignant to the shades below." The same author in the same work also transfers a phrase from Horace : "Strike the stars with sublime head," which in English seems mere nonsense.

REGINALD HAINES.
Uppingham.

"THE COCK AND CRYER" (9ᵗʰ S. ix. 248).— For an explanation of this phrase see Chambers's 'Book of Days,' i. 240, from which it appears that there was an official so named in the Lord Steward's Department of the Royal Household so lately as 1822.

H. P. L.

ITALIAN SUNDIAL INSCRIPTION (9ᵗʰ S. ix. 127).—MR. HEMS says this inscription was "half obliterated," and it is evident that many letters are missing from the end of each line. It seems to be Italian, and to run thus :—

OMBRA ONDE L............
ME FECE M............
(A shadow whence........
M............ made me.)

The last letter but two must be c, not G, and the last line must state the name of the man who made the sundial.

JOHN HOBSON MATTHEWS.
Town Hall, Cardiff.

FILBERT (9ᵗʰ S. ix. 125, 177). — MR. LYNN says that Syme's 'English Botany' gives preference to the derivation *fill beard*. As seconding that judgment may one call attention to the fact that a kindred people (the German) calls this fruit the *Bard-nusz* (or beard-nut)? An old dictionary at my side does not spell the word "filbert," but "filberd." This brings us nearer still to the *Bard* and *beard*. If we allow for the old name-sound in the *e* of *berd*, we have the *beard* (sound) of to-day pretty closely ("*beard*-nut." Compare "the *bearded* barley").   W. H. B.

WARREN AND CLEGG (9ᵗʰ S. ix. 187).—It may safely be assumed that Esther Clegg was not a descendant of Benulf de Clegg who was living in the time of Stephen, and who certainly was not the founder of Clegg Hall. The men who took their name from the hamlet of Clegg in the thirteenth century conveyed their lands there to Adam de Belfield by charters dated in 10 Edward I. and 4 Edward II., and consequently in the Subsidy Roll of 1332 not one of the family is named. The Belfield family lived in Clegg for several generations, until the estates passed by marriage to the Assheton family at the end of the sixteenth century. The house in which they lived in 1618 was described as "Clegg Hall," and probably it stood on the site of the ancestral home of the Belfields. For long after the Belfields acquired their lands in Clegg, people living there would be described as of Clegg, and consequently in the seventeenth century Clegg was one of the most common names in Rochdale, and in parish registers from 1582 to 1616 the name occurs no less than 470 times, whilst in the neighbouring parish of Bury there are only five entries of the name in the registers from 1590 to 1616.

HENRY FISHWICK.

"HIGH-FALUTING" (9ᵗʰ S. viii. 505 ; ix. 176, 217).—It is probable that Dr. Brewer adopted *verlooten* from Hotten's assertion that this "Dutch" word had produced *highfaluten* ('Slang Dictionary'). Mr. John S. Farmer, compiler of 'Americanisms,' inclines to the opinion that *highfalutin* is from high-flighting or -floating.   ST. SWITHIN.

CELER'S guess seems as good as Dr. Brewer's was bad ; but is it necessary to go so far afield as Holland for the explanation of the word ? It is, I believe, of American growth, and I do not remember meeting with it before the days of Sam Slick. My guess is that it is a pompous or intensive pronunciation of "high fluting"—*i.e.*, pitching one's pretensions, or boasting, or patriotic utterances in a high key. The transition is not difficult from the sound of the flute to the *vox humana*.   ALDENHAM.

St. Dunstan's.

[The 'H.E.D.' suggests : "Perhaps a whimsical pronunciation of *fluting*, or a grandiose equivalent of *flying* or *flown*."]

APPLE-TREE FOLK-LORE (9ᵗʰ S. ix. 169).—
The following refers to the fruit rather than
the tree. We were always told in South
Notts that we must not eat apples until they
had been christened—that is, until after
St. Swithin's Day. Sometimes, however, we
did so, with results resembling those so
graphically described by Mr. Henry S. Leigh
in his "lines after Ache-inside." C. C. B.

"Wassail, a drinking song, sung on Twelfth
Day Eve, throwing toast to the apple-tree,
in order to have a fruitful year, which seems
to be a relic of the heathen sacrifice to
Pomona" ('Gloss. of Exmoor Dialect').
　　　　　　J. HOLDEN MACMICHAEL.

This subject has been fully discussed in
'N. & Q.' on more than one occasion. See
1ˢᵗ S. iv., v., xi.; 2ⁿᵈ S. i.; 4ᵗʰ S. viii., x.;
5ᵗʰ S. xii.; 6ᵗʰ S. vii., viii., ix.
　　　　　EVERARD HOME COLEMAN.
71, Brecknock Road.

There is a note about apples at Christmas
at 6ᵗʰ S. xii. 491.　　　　　　W. C. B.

"LIMERICK" (9ᵗʰ S. ix. 188).—Is not the
reason for this name to be found in the fact
that nonsense verses of a certain form used
to be sung to an air of which the refrain
was :—

　　Won't you come up, come up,
　　Won't you come up to Limerick? (bis).

I presume the tune is that of some brisk air,
which is probably well known, but on this
point I can say nothing. The tune as applied
to "Limericks" was certainly in vogue twenty-
five years ago, and may be so at the present
time for all I know.　J. R. FITZGERALD.

SIR THOMAS MORGAN, OF ARKSTONE (9ᵗʰ S.
ix. 9, 158).—An account of this family is
given in Harl. MSS. 6596, fo. 184, and 1545,
fo. 18 and 19. They differ slightly in the
descent, but both make the wife of Sir Thos.
Morgan, father of Anne Carey, to be Elizabeth, daughter of Sir James Whitney. The
latter gives the arms of Morgan as Per pale
arg. and gu., three lions counterchanged, a
star for difference. Arkstone is an estate in
the parish of Kingston, and was afterwards
acquired by Serjeant Hoskyns, a well-known
lawyer and politician in the reign of James I.
　　　　　　J. H. PARRY.

BULL-BAITING (9ᵗʰ S. ix. 188, 255). — I am
indebted to MR. F. A. RUSSELL for his
reply. It may be that baiting by dogs
improved the quality of the bull's flesh; in
reality, I believe, the excited state of the
animal just before death would tend to

hasten putrefaction, and, as in the case of a
hunted hare, deer, or rabbit, the flesh would
have to be cooked soon or it would be unfit
to eat. But in asserting that baiting was
"undoubtedly" by dogs, MR. RUSSELL still
leaves unexplained the Cambridge ordinance
of 1376, where "baiting" is defined as being
fed with grass in a stall.　　　　G. T.

Bulls were baited by dogs to make their
flesh tender for food. That solemn and
severe old Puritan, William Perkins, who
thought that the heathen were bound to
know God, and that atheists ought to be
tortured, and that anger was only a physical
defect, and that baiting the bear was sinful,
yet allows "the bayting of the bull hath his
vse, and therefore it is commanded by ciuill
authoritie." See all this in his 'Cases of
Conscience,' 1619, p. 346, and more of the
same subject in 3ʳᵈ S. i. 346, 417.
　　　　　　W. C. B.

At a Manor Court of the Dean and Chapter
of Durham held at South Shields in a list
of "Certaine orders and penalties" the following appear :—

　"It. if any bocher doe hereafter blow any meate
they shall fyne to the Lords of the mannor vjs. viijd."
　"It. if any butcher or other doe kill any bull
vnlesse hee bee first bayted that then hee or they
soe killing the same shall fyne to the Lords xs."
　　　　　　R. B—R.

"HOP THE TWIG" (9ᵗʰ S. ix. 189).—See the
amusing anecdote related by De Quincey in
his essay on 'Coleridge and Opium-Eating'
('Collected Writings of Thomas De Quincey,'
ed. Masson, 1890, vol. v. p. 201) concerning a
wife-hunting German, whose English education had been neglected :—

　"It turned out that the Dictionary he had used
—(Arnold's, we think), a work of one hundred and
fifty years back, and, from mere German ignorance,
giving slang translations from Tom Brown, L'Estrange, and other jocular writers—had put down
the verb *sterben* (*to die*) with the following worship-
ful series of equivalents:—1. To kick the bucket;
2. To cut one's stick; 3. To go to kingdom come;
4. To hop the twig; 5. To drop off the perch into
Davy's locker."

The 'N.E.D.' quotes from Mary Robinson's
'Walsingham' (1797), vol. iv. p. 280 : "[He]
kept his bed three days, and hopped the
twig on the fourth." The 'Craven Dialect'
(1828) gives, "'Hop the twig,' to run away
in debt." The 'N.E.D.' also cites an instance
of the phrase in the sense of "to die" as
recent as 1870.　THOMAS HUTCHINSON.

If, as applied to death, it were desirable
that one phrase more than another should
be in abeyance, surely that phrase would be
"To hop the twig," although one has cer-

tainly somewhere seen the expression so used. It is, however, I think, more generally employed in the sense of departing suddenly without notice, as a bird from the twig in eluding the fowler, and is said of one who runs away from his creditors :—

"I have lost my ticker; and all my toggery has been boned, I am nearly as naked as when I was born—and the cause—the lady bird—has hopped the twig."—Pierce Egan's 'Finish to Life in London,' 1830, p. 217.

J. Holden MacMichael.

An exact equivalent for this expression occurs in Scott's 'Pirate,' chap. xl. When Fletcher unexpectedly dies in the presence of Cleveland and Jack Bunce, the effect on the latter is given thus :—

"'I always thought him a d—d fool,' said Bunce, as he wiped a tear from his eye, 'but never such a consummate idiot as to hop the perch so sillily. I have lost the best follower'—and he again wiped his eye."

The metaphor is thus used as suited to the quarter-deck of a pirate vessel.

Thomas Bayne.

May I refer to my note (9th S. v. 346, 'Hopping the Wag') for a local reference to this slang term? It is still very common, expressing unusual speed in driving, or dramming, or dying. George Marshall.
Sefton Park, Liverpool.

Bible: Authorized Version (9th S. ix. 147, 237).—The 'Encyclopædia Britannica,' under the heading of 'English Bible,' gives us the list of committees engaged in this translation, and states that they were employed four or five years, "some parts being brought back to the anvil to be hammered as much as fourteen, and some as much as seventeen times." Notwithstanding the great number of scholars who thus worked, the ordinary reader finds the result homogeneous; nor would he, I think, suspect, from the translation itself, that all had not been done by one man. I trust I shall not seem foolish if I ask whether one part of the work is at all distinguishable from another by mannerisms, archaisms, or dialectic peculiarities. If not, the amount of collaboration and of mutual correction, as between the separate committees, must have been very great.

Richard H. Thornton.
Portland, Oregon.

Sleeping Garments (3rd S. iv. 246, 332, 439; vi. 316; xi. 51; xii. 175; 9th S. ix. 213).—In one of the windows in Eton College Chapel, given by the Rev. John Wilder, one of the Fellows, some forty to fifty years ago, is a

figure lying on a bed—Isaac, if I remember rightly. This window is, I think, the second from entrance of the choir on the north side. I used to sit opposite it and to think it a strange thing that Isaac should be represented stark naked. However, having returned to Eton after an interval of holidays, I discovered that a brilliant nightgown had been substituted for the naked body. My impression is that it was of a ruby colour. This must have been in or about 1862.

Robert Pierpoint.
St. Austin's, Warrington.

In a book about Malta I find a sketch of the hospital of the Knights Hospitallers, 1676. The patients are in bed, and physicians and attendants are waiting upon them. Some are sitting up in bed, and there is no appearance of nightdresses. Men and women are naked, and covered from the waist downwards by the bedclothes. George Angus.
St. Andrews, N.B.

"Tolpatchery" (9th S. vii. 170). — This word, with its plural form "tolpatcheries," occurs frequently in Carlyle's 'History of Friedrich II. of Prussia.' See, amongst other places, book xiii. ch. xii. and xiv., book xv. ch. vii., book xviii. ch. i. In book xv. ch. ix. Uhlans are defined as "the *Saxon* species of Tolpatchery." With "Tolpatchery" may be compared "Croateries" (book xxi. ch. vi.), "Pandour doggery" (book xv. ch. ix.), "Pandour Tolpatch tagraggery" (book xiii. ch. xiv.). For "tolpatch" see Kluge, 'Etymologisches Wörterbuch der deutschen Sprache' (sixth edition, 1899), and Moritz Heyne, 'Deutsches Wörterbuch,' vol. iii. (1895). The latter connects it with the Hungarian *talpas*. In that case, if Carlyle's liberal employment of the word could be said to have endenized (or endenizened, with C. L.) "tolpatchery" in our own language, it would be one of the very few English words of Hungarian origin. Edward Bensly.
The University, Adelaide, South Australia.

"Bar sinister" (9th S. ix. 64, 152, 215). — I am much obliged to H. for conveying a warning that any looseness of expression in historical or genealogical matters will not be tolerated in the columns of 'N. & Q.' Catherine Sedley died childless only in a heraldo-legal sense, and the descendants of the first Baron Waldegrave and Henrietta FitzJames still sit in the House of Lords. I may, however, observe in defence that my statement that no descendant of James II. sits in that House was made in reference to the assertion of the *Daily Chronicle* that that monarch "contributed a good many bars sinister to the arms of the members of the House of Lords." I considered that this assertion implied that there were illegitimate male representatives of James II. in the Upper House, just as there are illegitimate male representatives of Charles II. in the persons of the Dukes of Richmond, Grafton, and St. Albans, and I used the word "descendants" in that sense. The Earl of Waldegrave does not carry any mark of illegitimacy on his escutcheon, and the "old Princess Buckingham" died childless in the usual signification of that word. But I fully admit that the language I used was open to misconception. W. F. Prideaux.

I question if you can have a bar—singular —in blazonry at all. You can have bars and barry and barwise, but the moment you use a bar by itself you change its name. Put it across the shield diagonally, and you have a bend or bend sinister. Put it perpendicular, and you find a pale. Place it at the top of the shield, and it becomes a chief ; in the centre, and you have a fesse ; at the bottom of the escutcheon, and there is a base. I write under correction, but I cannot remember any example of a bar called a bar standing alone. What is called the bar sinister is a bend or bendlet or ribbon, as a mark of illegitimacy, in modern blazons superseded by a border wavy in England and a border compony in Scotland.

George Angus.
St. Andrews, N.B.

The mural monument of Henrietta, wife of Henry Waldegrave, Baron Waldegrave of Chewton, illegitimate daughter of James II. by Arabella Churchill, and sister of James FitzJames, Duke of Berwick, may yet be seen in the chancel of the retired church of Navestock, co. Essex. Underneath the inscription are the arms of Waldegrave : Per pale, arg. and gules; impaling the royal arms of England ensigned by a baton sinister debruised. In those days, and subsequently, the brevet title of "Mrs." was often given to unmarried ladies. From her are descended the Earls Waldegrave whose remains repose in a vault adjoining the chancel of the church.

I should certainly say that "baton sinister debruised" is the more correct heraldic term, in the form in which it may be seen at this day on the arms of several dukes. Sir Walter Scott, in the 'Antiquary,' seems to use the terms "baton" and "bend" without making any difference between them (Oldbuck loquitur): "Ah, poor lad ! that was the cause, then, that he seemed so absent and

confused, while I explained to him the reason of the bend of bastardy upon the shield yonder on the corner turret" (chap. xiii.). And again in the same novel (Oldbuck loquitur) : "Very true, Sir Arthur ; and here is the baton sinister, the mark of illegitimacy, extended diagonally through both coats upon the shield. Where can our eyes have been, that they did not see this curious monument before ?" (chap. xxiv.)

John Pickford, M.A.
Newbourne Rectory, Woodbridge.

Pontefract-on-Thames (9th S. ix. 121).— It may be of service to add the following to the references given by Col. Prideaux to this place : Archæologia, xxxvi. 248 ; 'Three Fifteenth-Century Chronicles' (Camden Soc.), xvi. I have not either of the volumes at hand, so cannot tell whether they will throw light on the whereabouts of this place.

Astarte.

There is a fair account of John Abel, custos of the queen's lands, &c., 1301-2, in Foss's 'Judges.' It does not seem probable that any real "broken bridge" in Stepney Marsh could become historical ; it is rather to be supposed that the name of the manor, as Pontefreit, was imported ; there was a family named Pomfret in Essex. Absens.

Arms of Le Neve Foster (9th S. ix. 169). —Argent, on a cross sable five fleur-de-lis of the field ; a white lily, seeded gold, stalked and leaved vert, are the arms and crest of Le Neve of Ringland, co. Norfolk, and Neave of Dagnam Park, co. Essex, baronet. The motto is "Sola proba quæ honesta."

John Radcliffe.

Post-fine (9th S. ix. 208).—In the 'Law-French Dictionary,' second edition, 1718, is the following :—

" Post-fine, Is a Duty belonging to the King for a fine formerly acknowledged before him in his Court, which is paid by the Cognizee after the Fine is fully passed, and all things touching the same wholly accomplished. The Rate thereof is so much, and half so much, as was paid to the King for the Fine, and is gathered by the Sheriff of the County where the Land, &c., lyeth, whereof the Fine was Levyed to be answered by him into the Exchequer."

E. E. Street.
Chichester.

Pd the 22th of January [1628] to Mr Trapps for a post fine for the house bought of Micha : Davy ... ... 0 . xs . 0
Pd Mr Trapps for his paines ... ... 0 . js . vjd

The above entry is copied from the churchwardens' accounts of Wandsworth for 1627-8. From the time of Edward VI. quitrent had been paid to the reigning sovereign for a house belonging to the church. The quitrent was collected by Alexander Colston at this time; so that this "post fine" does not appear to have been paid to the king. The house mentioned in the above extract was bought with a bequest of 50*l.* by Mrs. Tyroe.

LIBRARIAN.

Wandsworth.

HOUR OF SUNDAY MORNING SERVICE (9ᵗʰ S. ix. 67, 155).—James Paterson's 'Pietas Londinensis,' 1714, gives the fullest information as to the practice in London at that time. For the benefit of those to whom the book may not be known I have taken about twenty churches at random, and find the greatest possible diversity as to times of services. A very large percentage had no morning prayer on Sunday; five of them held it at 11 o'clock. St. Andrew's (Holborn), St. Andrew Undershaft, St. Anne's (Soho), and St. John's (Walbrook) had those services at 6 or 7 and 11 o'clock; St. Clement Danes at 7 and 11; St. Christopher's (Threadneedle Street) at 6; whilst two others were at 10 and one at 8. I find that on weekdays eighteen held the service at 11 and two at 10 o'clock.

WM. NORMAN.

Plumstead.

THE LOCOMOTIVE AND GAS (9ᵗʰ S. vi. 227, 358; ix. 118).—Murdock's model locomotive is in the Birmingham Art Gallery, and there is an exact reproduction in the Machinery and Inventions Department of the Victoria and Albert Museum at South Kensington. My grandfather was a Soho man, and he knew Murdock well. I was acquainted with the late Mr. William Murdock, a great-grandson of the engineer, who died 31 October, 1895. I mention these facts in order to show that *prima facie* I am not likely to belittle any of Murdock's claims as an inventor. But I cannot allow it to go forth without a protest that Murdock is to be regarded as the inventor of the locomotive. This is not the place to discuss questions of priority of invention, and I refer your readers to the labours of Trevithick, as set out in his 'Life' by his son, and to the collection of old locomotives at South Kensington.

I do not remember to have seen the snuffbox alluded to by W. G. D. F. (*ante*, p. 118), though Mr. W. Murdock showed me several interesting memorials of his great-grandfather. Your correspondent asserts at the above reference, on the authority of Mr. John Murdock, that the snuffbox in question was "the only reward his father ever received for his invention of gas." It should, however, be

remembered that the Royal Society awarded the Rumford Medal to Murdock for a paper on the manufacture of gas, which will be found in the *Phil. Trans.* for 1808. The manufacture of gas-lighting plant subsequently became an important Soho industry, and Murdock, no doubt, profited directly or indirectly by it. It is quite right that a tablet should have been placed on Murdock's house at Redruth, but it must not be inferred that "the invention of gas," as it is oddly styled by some of your correspondents, was perfected there. It was, moreover, known long before that an inflammable gas was given off during the dry distillation of coal, and what Murdock did in Cornwall was to try the experiment on a large scale, thus demonstrating its practical usefulness.

I am sending you with this a copy of the reprint of a tract on gas-lighting, originally published by Murdock in 1809, which perhaps you will be good enough to transmit to your correspondent W. G. D. F. with my compliments. It will be seen that Murdock makes no reference whatever to his early experiments at Redruth.　　R. B. P.

[The pamphlet has been forwarded.]

BRISTOW FAMILY (9ᵗʰ S. viii. 404; ix. 171). MR. RADCLIFFE gives valuable information regarding the Bristow family—very complete so far as it goes. Can he tell me if any of the family are living? John Bristow had at least six grandsons. Surely there must be some descendants alive.　　OWEN ROSS.

"A MAD WORLD, MY MASTERS" (9ᵗʰ S. ix. 68).—Confirming the Editor's statement that the expression appears to have been proverbial, it may be mentioned that "'Tis a mad world, my masters," occurs as the first line of Taylor's 'Western Voyage,' written by the Water Poet (1580–1654).

ARTHUR MAYALL.

CELTIC (9ᵗʰ S. ix. 246). — The *Athenæum* reviewer says, in the passage quoted, that Sir Lewis Morris is "Celtic to the marrow." Grant Allen, however, used to contend that there is not a pure-blooded Celt in Wales, and I fancy he was right. Judging by my own experience, I should say that neither of Welsh nor English families is it safe to say that they are pure-blooded. My wife's father was proud of his "pure" Welsh descent, and each of his first two wives was as Welsh as he. He was tall and dark; they also were dark, but not so tall. The only child of the first wife was very dark, short, and stout. Most of the children of the second marriage were also dark, but inclined to be tall. Three or four of the daughters, however, were very fair, with hair varying from flaxen to a deep, ruddy golden hue. The children differed as widely in character as in appearance: some were markedly Welsh, others of them would never have been taken for Welsh if met with in England. Most of them married Welsh-men or Welshwomen, and the children of the third generation vary in a similar way. As my father-in-law was blest with twenty-one sons and daughters (sixteen of whom lived to grow up), and his two eldest daughters with twelve and ten respectively, I have had a fairly wide field of observation on them alone, and I do not suppose that this family differs in these respects from others. But if the case be so with the Welsh, what must it be with us English?   B.

AUTHORS OF QUOTATIONS WANTED (9th S. viii. 326).—The line should be :—

Each word-catcher, that lives on syllables,

and is l. 166 of Pope's 'Epistle to Dr. Arbuthnot.' Could "Now Sirius rages," the author of which is wanted by the same correspondent, be a memory-quotation of "The Dog-star rages!" in the third line of this poem?
                    EDWARD BENSLY.
The University, Adelaide, South Australia.

GEORGES I.-IV. (9th S. ix. 164).—Did not Landor write these lines? I find them attributed to him, and copied as follows in my commonplace book :—

George the First was always reckoned
Vile. But viler George the Second;
And what mortal ever heard
Any good of George the Third?
When from earth the Fourth descended,
Heaven be praised! the Georges ended.
                    JOHN T. PAGE.

DEFOE AT TOOTING (9th S. ix. 207).—There does not seem to be any known evidence to support the theory that Daniel Defoe was living at Tooting-Graveney about the year 1688. He was probably born in the parish of St. Giles, Cripplegate, in 1661, where his father (who bore the surname of Foe only) carried on the trade of a butcher, and attended the services of Dr. Annesley, the Nonconformist. From 1675 until probably the year 1680 the son was at Mr. Morton's academy at Newington Green. He tells us that he took part in the rebellion of the Duke of Monmouth in 1685. In the same year he began business as a hose-factor (not a shopkeeper, he tells us) in Freeman's Court, Cornhill, and, except for one or two visits to Spain, he seems to have remained there until he fled to Bristol from his creditors in 1692. Shortly

afterwards he started a manufactory of bricks and pantiles, "near Tilbury Fort in Essex," and carried on those works until he was imprisoned in Newgate in 1703. There he remained until August, 1704. In 1707 he was living in Edinburgh. He soon returned to London, and, though he paid other visits to Scotland, we hear, in 1712, of his being forcibly and with difficulty taken out of his fortified house at Newington by the officers of the Court of Queen's Bench. No doubt it was at Newington that he wrote 'Robinson Crusoe' (1719), 'Moll Flanders' (1721), 'Adventures of Roxana' (1724), &c. About 1724 he built himself a large house at Stoke Newington, with stables and pleasure grounds, and kept a coach. Mr. Henry Baker, the naturalist, who in that year set up a school for the deaf and dumb there, speaks of him as

"Mr. Defoe, a gentleman well known by his writings, who had newly built there a very handsome house, as a retirement from London, and amused his time either in the cultivation of a large and pleasant garden, or in the pursuit of his studies, which he found means of making very profitable."

Henry Baker there met and eventually married Sophia, one of Defoe's

"three lovely daughters, who were admired for their beauty, their education, and their prudent conduct; and if sometimes Mr. Defoe's disorders made company inconvenient, Mr. Baker was entertained by them either singly or together, and that commonly in the garden when the weather was favourable."

In September, 1729, Defoe suddenly fled from his house, and in August, 1730, he was in a hiding-place "about two miles from Greenwich." On 26 April, 1731, he died at a lodging in Ropemaker's Alley, Moorfields. So it would seem almost certain that Defoe did not live at Tooting-Graveney in 1688 or at any time in his career.   RONALD DIXON.
46, Marlborough Avenue, Hull.

"WAGUES" (9th S. ix. 204, 255).—It seems to me that CELER's proposed etymology for this word is, to say the least, no better than the one he condemns, unless he can support it by something more convincing than his mere statements. Apart from his very far-fetched explanation of the meaning, by what right does he assert that because the g in *wagues* is hard, therefore the word "must be Norse," and that "the etymology is from [sic] the Icel. *vaga*"? If this be so, then doubtless *vague*, *plague*, *league*, &c., must likewise be Norse! And what right has CELER to assume that a Norse *vaga* or *vagar* would produce a M.E. form with *ag* (instead of *aw*) any more than an O.E. *wagian*? Do not Norse *agi* and *lagu* produce Engl. *awe* and *law* respectively?

Surely Celer cannot yet afford to boast that he has found a "solution which alone will suit the facts."   F. J. C.

Gwyneth (9ᵗʰ S. ix. 109).—Genaeth is a common word used in North Wales for a girl. In Dr. Owen Pugh's great 'Dictionary' the meaning is given :—

"Geneth, plural Genethod (gân, capacity, or what hath the power to contain), a damsel, a maid, a girl, a daughter."

In this case it may signify daughter, but without the context in the inscription one cannot say whether or no it is used as a Christian name (I never heard it so used) or simply as "daughter."   William Payne.

Gwynedd, signifying blessed or happy, is the early form of the word. Gwynaeth, meaning a state of bliss—a female name still in use—is often written Gyneth. Gwynnedd or Gwent, a district in Wales (cf. Vannes in Brittany); Gwen, meaning white; and "gwenith," wheat, should not be confused with Gwynnedd, the personal name. See 'History of Christian Names,' by the late Miss Yonge.   Arthur Mayall.

In the late Miss Yonge's 'History of Christian Names' Gwynaeth and Gyneth are given as alternative forms of a Welsh female name, meaning bliss or blessed. I have never met with the name in actual use. Gwynnedd is certainly the name of one of the ancient divisions of Wales, but two of the most famous Welsh kings had it for surname—Maelgwn Gwynnedd in the sixth century, and Owain Gwynnedd in the twelfth. May not the Christian name have had the same origin ?   C. C. B.

Re-reading the copy I made of the inscription previously referred to, I find that I should have read the name "Jenett," and not "Geneth." This supposed example of the name therefore fails.   J. P. Lewis.

Miscellaneous.

NOTES ON BOOKS, &c.

The Old Royal Palace of Whitehall. By Edgar Sheppard, D.D. (Longmans & Co.)
The history of Whitehall Palace by the Sub-dean of the Chapels Royal is a companion volume to the 'Memorials of St. James's Palace' of the same author (see 8ᵗʰ S. vi. 480). Associated as it must ever be with the death of Charles I., the history of Whitehall will remain the more tragic record. The period during which it was a home of English kings was limited, the fire which in the reign of William III. destroyed all except the Banqueting House of Inigo Jones narrowing its connexion to monarchs of Tudor or Stuart strain. Small as is the surviving portion, it is rich in historical memories, which, moreover, are not necessarily confined to the Banqueting House. Apart from the earlier scenes which it witnessed when, at the height of his fortunes, Wolsey entertained that "crowned Moloch," his royal master, the scenes under Stuart monarchs may never be forgotten. First of all stands the death of Charles, which, as described in the noble and pathetic words of Andrew Marvell, seems to redeem a life of error. We then hear of Cromwell entertaining "gaudily" the Commons, and his wife, the Lady Protectress, with bourgeois thrift watching the servants through the "little labyrinths and trap stairs by which she might, at all times unseen, pass to and fro, and come always upon her servants and keep them vigilant in their places and honest in the discharge thereof." We can see again Charles II. sleeping without curtains, which had been pulled down during the progress of the Fire of London in order to facilitate removal should the flames, as was hardly probable, extend to Westminster; Monmouth, his hands tied behind him with a silk cord, brought captive into the presence of James II., in order that the caitiff king might rejoice in the humiliation of the nephew whom he had already doomed to death; and James's own "craven terrors and final flight from his crown and country." In the Banqueting House, moreover, the Lords and Commons tendered to William III. and the Princess Mary the crown. With this solemnity the historic record of Whitehall practically ceases. With regard to the execution of Charles I., naturally the matter of most importance with which the volume is concerned, the author draws largely upon 'N. & Q.,' in which the question is fully discussed as to which was the exact spot of the decollation, and which the place through which an opening was broken in order to admit of the passage of the monarch. The question who were the king's executioners is also decided in favour of — or, perhaps it should be said, against — Richard Brandon, the ordinary executioner, in spite of his reported refusal to have anything to do with the deed. From the literary standpoint the most interesting thing in connexion with Whitehall is the performance of the masques which it witnessed in the times of Elizabeth, James I., and Charles I. The scene of these was generally the Tennis Court, concerning which and the performance of Restoration comedy Pepys has many quaint entries. York House was, it is known, the original title of the palace, which only took the name of Whitehall on its transference from Cardinal Wolsey to Henry VIII. Attention is drawn by Dr. Sheppard to the fact that the present name of Charing Cross is misleading, and that the original Queen Eleanor's Cross stood where the equestrian statue of King Charles I. now stands, facing Whitehall. Had the scheme of Inigo Jones for rebuilding the whole of Whitehall, entertained by King James, been carried out, the palace would have covered near twenty-four acres, whereas Hampton Court comprises but eight to nine acres, St. James's Palace about four, and Buckingham Palace about two and a half. The account of the Cockpit is both interesting and valuable, and must be regarded as a contribution to the history of the stage. In dealing with the associations of Elizabeth with Whitehall it is said that the princess was "detained a prisoner there for the part she had taken in Sir Thomas Wyatt's conspiracy, and was

conveyed thence to the Tower on Palm Sunday, 1554." Does not this involve a begging of the question, and would it not be better to say the part she was alleged to have taken in Sir Thomas Wyatt's conspiracy? The name Whitehall is, as is pointed out in the opening chapter, in no sense individualizing, being associated with all the royal palaces in England, with the place of assembly for peers in Parliament, and with many old castles. Of the royal residents in Whitehall, and of those who have died there, a full account is supplied; a chapter is devoted to the royal Maundy, and one to the pictures and art treasures and the royal library. The celebrated houses within the precincts of Whitehall occupy two chapters. A feature of special interest consists of the illustrations. The photogravures comprise Charles I., Whitehall, Cardinal Wolsey, Princess Elizabeth (daughter of Charles I.), Oliver Cromwell, and Charles II. The other illustrations include very numerous views of the palace at different dates, with portraits of Inigo Jones, Sir John Vanbrugh, King James II., Queen Mary II., and King Henry VIII. As a record concerning a spot of undying interest and an historical monument of the highest value, and as a veracious chronicle, Dr. Sheppard's book is equally attractive and trustworthy.

History of Scotland. By P. Hume Brown, M.A., LL.D. Vol. II. (Cambridge, University Press.)
THE second volume of the 'History of Scotland' of the Fraser Professor in the University of Edinburgh completes the work which he contributes to the "Cambridge Historical Series," issued under the direction of Dr. G. W. Prothero. At 9ᵗʰ S. iii. 358 we drew attention to the merits of the new work, chief among which are the qualities (indispensable in a history that is to make general appeal) of trustworthiness and veracity. We welcome the appearance of the second volume, which in every respect save one is exactly what we want. It supplies in compendious form a chronicle such as is not elsewhere obtainable. The one defect which goes far to minimize its utility is the absence of an index. The compilation of this would, we grant, add greatly to the expense of the book. It would, however, repay the cost, whatever this might be. of the work, and we commend the undertaking to some of the zealous index-makers who occasionally consult us as to where to bestow to best advantage their energies. Beginning with the accession of Mary Stuart, and ending with the Revolution of 1689, the second volume comprises the most picturesque and romantic, as well as the most humiliating portion of Scottish annals. For the first time in history we are shown the full effects of the English raids in 1545 under the Earl of Hertford. Not, as is the accepted tradition, to the iconoclastic zeal of the followers of Knox is attributable the ruin of the abbeys of Kelso, Melrose, Dryburgh, Roxburgh, and Coldingham, but to the miscellaneous and irreverent host which, under the conduct of Hertford, crossed the border at Wark. Concerning the murder of Cardinal Beaton, Dr. Brown quotes from the 'Diurnal of Occurrents' of the Maitland Club a poem which seems to convey the general impression:—

But of a truth, tho' sooth to say,
Although the loon was well away,
The deed was foully done.

In the progress of the Reformation in Scotland

Prof. Brown is struck with the singular moderation of the representatives of the old and new religions. The same will not hold true of subsequent attempts to impose episcopacy upon Scotland. The estimate formed concerning Mary is that which all must accept. Prof. Brown attaches comparatively little importance to the famous "Casket" letters, and is reticent concerning the threat against Darnley, said to have been uttered by Mary upon the death of Rizzio, that "a fatter than he" should lie in the same place. Of the "Casket" letters he says that the course of history would not have been greatly altered had the discovery of them never been made. With Mr. Lang he holds that the mystery of these letters is practically insoluble. Of the manner in which in the matter of religion James VI. sat upon a fence, Dr. Brown has much that is worth saying to say. That the second Solomon was the most despicable of his race is apparent throughout, and there was never, probably, a moment when he would not have professed whichever religion seemed most to his advantage. James's letter to the Pope from Holyrood, dated 19 February, 1584, is properly called "an astounding document." James never was, moreover, privy to a plot in 1593 for sending over from Philip II. an army to co-operate with the Catholic earls. Much of interest is said concerning Scottish persecutions for witchcraft. Now and then, but not very often, Dr. Brown falls into the error of picturesque history. When dealing with Wishart it is said, "His fate was a foregone conclusion, and on the 1st of March he sealed his testimony in front of Beaton's own castle of St. Andrews." There are some doubtless, though perhaps not many, who, in spite of Knox and Foxe, do not know the manner of Wishart's death, and it would be better simply to say that he was burnt.

Notices to Correspondents.

We must call special attention to the following notices:—

ON all communications must be written the name and address of the sender, not necessarily for publication, but as a guarantee of good faith.

WE cannot undertake to answer queries privately.

To secure insertion of communications correspondents must observe the following rules. Let each note, query, or reply be written on a separate slip of paper, with the signature of the writer and such address as he wishes to appear. When answering queries, or making notes with regard to previous entries in the paper, contributors are requested to put in parentheses, immediately after the exact heading, the series, volume, and page or pages to which they refer. Correspondents who repeat queries are requested to head the second communication "Duplicate."

L. K. ("Droppings of warm tears," &c.).—See Mrs. Browning's 'Wine of Cyprus,' stanza 12.

ENQUIRER ("The mill cannot grind with the water that is past").—'The Lesson of the Water-Mill,' by Sarah Doudney. See 7ᵗʰ S. iii. 299.

NOTICE.

Editorial communications should be addressed to "The Editor of 'Notes and Queries'"—Advertisements and Business Letters to "The Publisher"—at the Office, Bream's Buildings, Chancery Lane, E.C.

LONDON, SATURDAY, APRIL 26, 1902.

CONTENTS.—No. 226.

Notes.

QUEEN CANDACE.

(See 2nd S. xi. 468, 515.)

THE meaning of this name should probably
be sought for in the ancient language of Nubia,
the Hent or South Land of the Egyptian
monuments, rather than in so-called Ethiopic.
Lepsius discovered in 1844 at Meroe, inscribed
in hieroglyphic letters, the name of a queen
Kenthahebi, which he thinks is intended for
Kenthaki (=Candace), the Ethiopian scribe
having mistaken one Egyptian character for
another closely resembling it (' Letters from
Egypt,' English translation, p. 196).

A strange confusion between their names
runs through the accounts of the Ethiopian
queen and the eunuch mentioned in the eighth
chapter of the Acts. Gregory of Nazianzus
(' De Sacro Baptismo,' ch. xxvi.) calls the
eunuch Candaces, Φίλιππός εἰμι· γενοῦ Καν-
δάκης—unless we assume δυνάστης to be understood or have dropped from the text, and
render, " I am Philip ; be thou (the courtier)
of Candace." So also Anastasius Sinaita
(in ' Hexam.,' vi. 882): " Eiusmodi volucris
erat Philippus, qui volans per aërem et veniens
ad Candacem Æthiopem," &c. The same
statement, probably taken from Gregory, is
also found in Euthymius (in Ps. lxvii., LXX.),
the Greek Menology, &c. The confusion
might, of course, be partly due to the ambiguity of the termination -ης, which expresses
the nom. masc. as well as the gen. fem., the
final ς being, indeed, retained in the Coptic
and Ethiopic versions. As is well known,
however, the terms Ethiopia and India are,
in the Greek geographers, often almost
synonymous, and in the Syriac version of the
Old Testament כּוּשִׁי (Ethiopian) is rendered
הנדויא, hendoyo (Hindu), as in 2 Chron. xiv. 8
and Jerem. xiii. 23. In some form of the
tradition, therefore, the name or title Ἰνδικός
may have been applied to the eunuch, and
for this some transcriber may have substituted the more familiar name of the queen.
The confusion would be very easy in an
Aramaic original.*

There seems to be some, though slight,
evidence of this. In two of Smith's invaluable
dictionaries (' Dictionary of the Bible,' second
edition, vol. i. part ii. p. 1005 ; ' Dictionary
of Christian Biography,' vol. ii. p. 234b) we
are informed that Eusebius names the eunuch
Indich. The reference is apparently to ' Hist.
Eccles ,' ii. 1 ; but neither there nor in any
other passage of Eusebius is this statement
to be found. It seems to have originated
with Damianus a Goes, a writer of the sixteenth century, whose work ' De Religione
et Moribus Æthiopum ' (included in ' Hispania
Illustrata,' Francof., 1603-6, vol. ii. part ii.
p 1306, and also in his ' Opuscula,' Coimb.,
1791, p. 251) contains an account of their
religious belief, purporting to be given by
the Ethiopians (i.e., Abyssinians) themselves,
in which they say : " Nos ferme prius cæteris
Christianis omnibus baptismum ab eunucho
Candacis Reginæ Æthiopiæ, cui nomen erat
Indich, accepimus." Now, certainly the most
natural interpretation of this is that the
eunuch was named Indich, and this is the
sense in which it is taken by the learned
contributors to Smith's dictionaries, who
evidently had this passage of Damianus in
view, though they inadvertently ascribe the
statement to Eusebius. Cornelius a Lapide,
however, who cites it in his commentary on
the Acts, understands it to mean that the
queen was named Indich, and he immediately
refers to the ' Theatrum Orbis ' of Abraham
Ortelius (Antwerp, 1603, p. 116 ; English
translation, London, 1606, p. 118) for a similar
statement, noting, however, that the Dutch
geographer calls the queen, not Indich, but

---

* Or was the queen herself Βασίλισσα Ἰνδική,
הַנְדְּקֵיה being afterwards read חַנְדְּקֵה?

Iudith ;* and in Larousse's 'Grand Diction-naire' (*s.v.* 'Candace') we are told (no authority being cited) that the eunuch was called Judas. If Indich, however, be the true reading, and is to be referred to the queen, as A Lapide supposes, it may simply represent the mode of spelling the name adopted in the Ethiopic version of the New Testament. For there, though the Greek K is regularly represented in other proper names, such as Caiaphas, Cana, Cornelius, by the letter corresponding to the Hebrew ק, in this passage of the Acts Philip's convert is described as "eunuch of Queen *H*endeke" ("·Hezewä ba 'Hendekēs negesheta-"), the initial of Κανδάκη being here represented by the rough breathing (corresponding to the Hebrew ח, Arabic *khā*), and the -ς of the genitive, as previously stated, retained, as it also is in the Coptic (Boheiric) version.

Bruce also writes ('Travels,' vol. iv. p. 529):

"There is a tradition at Chendi that a woman whose name was Hendaqui once governed all that country ; whence we might imagine that this was part of the kingdom of Candace; for if we write this name in Greek letters, it will come to no other than Hendaqui, the native or mistress of Chendi or Chandi."

Several legends connect the eunuch with India. In the 'Synopsis de Apostolis et Discipulis Domini,' ascribed to Dorotheus Tyrius, it is stated that he preached in Arabia Felix, in the island of Taprobana (Ceylon), and throughout the whole Erythræan region. His tomb in the island just mentioned became famous for miracles, and, according to the 'Historiæ Indicæ' (vol. iii.) of Petrus Massæus, cited by A Lapide, *l.c.*, the footprint on Adam's Peak, said by the natives to be the Buddha's, was claimed for him by the Christians. As this celebrated mountain was in the territory of the ancient kingdom of Kandy, the resemblance of that name to the queen's may have helped to localize the story. Names similar in sound occur also in Buddhist literature, Gautama's charioteer being called *K*andaka, his horse Ka*m*thaka, &c.; and it is a somewhat curious coincidence that, while the sixtieth chapter of the first book of the 'Mahavagga,' one of the most ancient scriptures of the southern Buddhist Church, contains a reference to the transgressions of a novice named Ka*n*daka and of a Bhikkhuni, also named Ka*n*dakâ, the very next chapter (the sixty-first) states the law regarding the exclusion of eunuchs from orders, agreeing

* So the name Judith is invariably printed in works of the sixteenth and seventeenth centuries, and it is obvious that one of these names, more probably the latter, may be the result of a typographical error.

with that in the Apostolical Canons ('Const. Apost.,' book viii.).

Candace seems to be the New Testament antitype of the Queen of Sheba. Josephus ('Antiquities,' ii. 10, 2) identifies Σαβά with Meroe, and in another place ('Ant.,' viii. 6, 5) represents the queen who visited Solomon as reigning over Egypt and Ethiopia. The Evangelists seem to have taken the same view. Whiston holds that the expressions "Queen of the south" and "Came from the uttermost parts of the earth" (Matthew xii. 42, Luke xi. 31) must refer to the Arabian Saba ; but the former would have been the Ethiopian queen's Egyptian title, and the latter reminds us of the Homeric description ('Od.,' i. 23) of her people as ἔσχατοι ἀνδρῶν. Fuerst, too, inclines to identify with Meroe the Sheba of Ezekiel xxvii. 22, whence spices, precious stones, and gold were brought to Tyre. Compare the queen's costly gifts to Solomon (1 Kings x. 2), the allusions in Psalm lxviii. (lxvii., Sept.) 29, 31, and the reference to the queen's treasures in Acts viii. 27.

Has the introduction of the name into Longfellow's poem 'Helen of Tyre' any other source than the poet's fancy? Simon Magus *loq.*, addressing his Helen:—

> Thou hast been Queen Candace,
> And Helen of Troy, and shalt be
> The Intelligence Divine!

It seems doubtful which queen of the name is here alluded to. A reference to her who was the first royal convert to Christianity (unless Abgar of Edessa is ungallant enough to claim precedence) would not very well accord with the fact that the Acts and ecclesiastical tradition represent her as a contemporary of the Father of Heresy. But we must remember Horace's dictum, 'A. P.,' 9, 10.

JOHN MAC-CARTHY.

"J. HALLS BOOKE."

SUCH is the inscription on the back of the engraved title-page in a copy of Edmund Bolton's 'Nero Cæsar,' 1627, in my hands. This inscription is repeated on the reverse side of the printed title-page, dated 1624, in the same volume. Besides, there are a number of manuscript marginal annotations scattered throughout the work, which I shall print entire in this note. If "J. Hall" was the annotator, the two autograph inscriptions are in a firm, clear, bold hand ; while the annotations themselves, as might be expected, are written in a much smaller and more contracted character. If I might venture an opinion, I should say that they both belong to the first half of the seventeenth century.

I never meet with an autograph in an old book but I try, if I can, to identify it. I have several of these about the period indicated, and this "J. Hall" is as welcome to me as the rest. But who was he? One would like to imagine that he had been some distinguished man. If the initial letter of his Christian name were to stand for "John," there was John Hall, the author of that singularly interesting and precocious little book—he was only nineteen on its publication—'Horæ Vacivæ,' 1646. Then there was John Hall, doctor of medicine, and Shakespeare's son-in-law, who died in 1635. This initial might, too, stand for "Joseph," and the famous Bishop of Norwich, who bore that Christian name, did not die until 1656. But as imagination, in the absence of fact, is apt to play us tricks more or less fantastic, I shall not pursue the speculation further. When these annotations come to be read, making every allowance for their somewhat elliptical and enigmatical construction, I think it will be admitted that the annotator, whoever he was, must have been both a thoughtful and a cultured man. I wish his annotations had been much more numerous.

Let it be understood, in what follows, that each passage of Bolton's printed text is given first, while the annotator's remarks appear immediately thereafter. I quote in every case verbatim.

P. 108. "Right historie deals in particulars, and handles limb by limb. Generalities are for summists. The odds fall out as great, as between a glimmering twilight, and a bright noon-day; or as between a bare nomination of parts, and their precise dissection."

"and this booke is rather an argument of a history, then ittself."

P. 110. The heading to chap. ix. is entitled "The Druids of Britain parties in this reuolt." In the first sentence the word "blacke" has been struck out, presumably by the annotator. It reads thus : "The head and members of this blacke agreement were fastned together in a most bloudie knot with speciall rites, and ceremonies." The marginal annotation evidently applies to the whole chapter :

"they were borne free princes and what tytle had the romane sword amongst them more then de jure gladij, and therefore nature and their more rationall lawes urge them to quitt. the eating fetters layd upon them and their posterity for eternity if possible by their tyranous foes, and therefore the expressions of ye author are not just unlesse hee will putt all tenor of life and liberty into the temper of the sword, and Guilty [?] seruice."

P. 111. "Bloud was the seale of this coniuratorie secret, and this a season of all other the most likelie for the wiues, and daughters in lawe of the wilde and ruder Britanns (of which sort Boadicia's forces did principallie consist) to celebrate those rites in which Plinie saith they were wont to goe naked, their bodies coloured ouer with oad. A grizlie ceremonie for a gastlie purpose."

The annotation is written opposite the last sentence :—

"yet thrives as well as Grose flattery yn great mens groser sins."

P. 113. "One hundred and twentie thousand men appeared now for warre at Boadicia's musters. An admirable effect of a close and sodein conspiracie."

The annotation opposite these opening sentences of chap. xi. partakes of the character of a general reflection :—

"the fullnes of the history the authour looses in ye mojety [?] of his stile : like ye spanyards pace a man must tread euery stepp after him to toe his."

P. 114. "Impossible therfore that so huge a force should rise on a sodein within so narrow a circuit, as six of our present shires ; specially, where very many thousands held loyall to the death, and where so many impediments of free assemblies interposed themselues in the Roman forts, and garrisons about."

The annotator draws an ink line under the word "loyall" in this sentence, and the marginal note is opposite the line in which it occurs :—

"loyall against their country and birthright."

P. 114. "And by that qualitie which is assigned to the materials of this militarie throne, it may be well suspected, that the place it selfe of this camp was some where in Marshland, or the ile of Elie, as a place among all other the Icenian countreyes, one of greatest safetie. For those turfes were cut vp out of plashie, or fennie grounds, and shee her selfe also assignes in her speach a refuge to bee had in the like, if the worst should happen."

"and why not ye place told as well as the strickt obseruation of her habitt, and generally in this abridgment there wants the notion of ye tymes ye best glasse of History."

P. 147. "For how doth that reason hold good which Svetonivs rendred as the finall cause of his quitting London, *By the losse of one towne to saue the whole residue, if* Vervlam was ouerwhelmed after?"

Against the words in italics the annotation reads :—

"his speech intended so much but that concludes nil, it fell out so."

P. 190. "For, vntill then, that was iust resistance, which seemed afterwards plaine rebellion."

The annotator draws an ink line under the words "plaine rebellion":—

"if ye sword or ambition bee a iust title when and where itt list."

P. 223. "Theyr ouer common pursuit is in our owne times growne the errour, and vice of wits; among whom nothing now hath taste, but (as they are called) *fine conceipts.*"

"yet whoe more affected then the authour may

seem in many expressions, nay euen poeticall almost to the taste of hyperbole."

P. 231. "Looke vpon the motiues of this knot, as Tacitvs himselfe hath assigned them, and particular aims will be found the principall ingredient, how much soeuer the publicke good was pretended : as in such cases when is it not?"

An ink line is drawn under the word "particular":—

"contradiction to his former assertion where he putts Good and all good men into the composition."

P. 233. "And although it may concerne mankinde, that the good which comes by the writings of any great author, should not be empaired by the contradiction of his deedes, yet there belongs no such priuiledge to words, that for their sakes the report of facts should be falsified, or (which amounts to a forgerie) that a part of the truth should be withdrawn, or smothered."

"the authour a great Anti-Seneca."

P. 234. "It were to be wisht that all the money of the world were at wise mens dispose."

"fooles doe but hold itt for wisemen."

P. 236. "As for Lvcan (the other of those two famous writers) whose mortall quarell to his prince was nothing else but an indignitie, forsooth, offred about verses, he stirred not so hotly among the complices for incensing hatred, as hee coldly suncke at his arrest, into ignoble feeblenesse."

"hee that can wryte good verse, questionles can dissolue them into happy prose."

A. S.

MERRY TALES.
(Continued from 9ᵗʰ S. viii. 382.)
'*Tales and Quicke Answeres.*'

XXII. 'Of the corrupte man of lawe.'—The story given by Hazlitt is hardly a parallel, but it may be worth while to remark that in Fowler's 'Reminiscences,' 1892, the same story is given as a true one of the original Arkwright. The story in the text has some resemblance to the twenty-first of the 'Pleasant Conceites of Old Hobson,' &c. Hazlitt, in his edition of that work ('Shakespeare Jest-Books'), refers to Wright's 'Latin Stories' (Percy Society), p. 73. It is also in 'Jack of Dover's Quest of Inquirie,' ed. Hazlitt ('Shakespeare Jest-Books,' Second Series, 334). It is tale 256 of Poggio, and appears in two forms in Pauli (Nos. 125 and 128). Oesterley refers under No. 125 to Vinc. Bellovac, 'Spec. Mor.,' 1138; Bromyard, A, 14, 4; Wright, 'Latin Stories,' 81; Joh. Herolt, 'Sermones Discipuli de Tempore et de Sanctis et Promtuarium Exemplorum,' Nuremb., 1486, fol., J. 42; Bernardinus de Bustis, 'Rosarium Sermonum,' i. 2, Hagen, 1503, fol., ii. 251, B.; 'Scala Celi,' 20a; Ulr. Boner, 'Der Edelstein,' hg. von Fr. Pfeiffer, Leipzig, 1844, 8vo, 95; 'Enxemplos,' 241; Seb. Brant, 'Fabulæ,' Basil., 1501, fol., A. 6;

'Scherz mit der Wahrheit,' 71b; Mart. Montanus, 'Das ander Theyl der Gartengesellschaft.,' Strasb., s. a., 8vo, ii. 65; H. W. Kirchhof, 'Wendunmuth,' i. 2, Frankf., 1573, 8vo, i. 126, fol. 136; Memel, 327, and cf. 343; 'Lyrum Larum Lyrissimum,' '550 kurtzweilige Geschichten,' s. l. et a., 8vo, 243; Eutrapel., i. 905; 'Zeitverkurzer, der ganz neu ausgeheckte, kurtzweilige, von Philander,' s. l., 1702, 8vo, 255; 'Lustigmacher, der Allzeit fertige,' s. l., 1762, 8vo, 147; Schreger, 'Lustig- und nützlicher Zeit-Vertreiber,' Stadt am Hof, 1753, 8vo, 17, 67, p. 549; 'Compl. Lond. Jester,' 1771, p. 99. The tale as from Pauli is to be found in 'Conceits, Clinches,' &c. ('Shakespeare Jest-Books,' p. 24). Pauli in his notes to No. 128 refers also to Franc. Guicciardini, 'Hore di Recreatione,' Antv., 1583, 8vo, 85b; 1588, p. 37; Franc. de Belleforest, 'Heures de Récréations et Après-dinées du Guicciardin,' Anvers, 1605, 8vo, 43; Federmann, 66; Casp. Ens, 'L' Hore di Recreatione, oder Erquickstunden desz Herrn L. Guicciardini,' Cöln, 1650, 8vo, 51; 'Scelta di Facetie,' 1579, 8vo, p. 170; Brant, A., 5b; Joh. Geiler von Keisersberg, 'Pater noster,' Strasb., 1515, fol., Alphab. i. G. sig. ciiij, Sp. 2; 'Sunden des Munds,' 41; Gv. Sp. 2; Eutrapel., ii. 8; Memel, 342, 448; Vorrath, 'Ein reicher, Artlicher Ergötzlichkeiten,' &c., s. l., 1702, 66; 'Lustigmacher,' ii. 34; Schreger, 17, 171, p. 609.

XXIII. 'Of kynge Lowes of France, and the husbandman.'—This is a literal translation from Domenichi, p. 73 verso.

XXIV. 'Of an other picke-thanke, and the same kinge.'—This also is translated from Domenichi, p. 16 verso, and is told of Old Hobson in his 'Conceites,' &c., No. 17.

XXV. 'Of Thales the astronomer that fell in a ditch.'—This is the thirty-eighth of the 'Cento Novelle Antiche.'

XXVIII. 'Of him that dreamed he fonde golde.'—This is Poggio's No. 130, but in that there is not the latter part which commences " Tibullus says," &c.

XXX. 'Of hym that fell of a tre and brake his rybbe.'—This is reproduced in 'Pasquil's Jests,' p. 42. It is taken from Poggio, No. 39.

XXXI. 'Of the frier that brayde in his sermon.'—Clouston, in his 'Flowers from a Persian Garden,' 1894, p. 71, refers to Gladwin's 'Persian Moonshee,' and also to the 'Katha Manjarí,' a Canarese collection, but without giving any more detailed reference. It is also in Poggio, No. 230, and in Pauli, No. 576. Oesterley in his notes there refers to Gabr. Bareleta, 'Sermones tam Quadragesimales quam de Sanctis,' Lugdun., 1505,

8vo, 25c; Hollen, 'Godscaldus, Preceptorium,' Colon., 1489, fol., 110a; 'Scala Celi,' Cantus vanus, l.; Fel. Hemmerlin, 'De Nobilitate et Rusticitate,' s. l. et a., fol. c. 2, fol. 8a; 'Speculum Exemplorum,' ed. Major, Duaci, 1611, 8vo, 108, ix.; 'Contes du Sieur d'Ouville,' p. 76, p. 128; 'Nouveaux Contes à rire et Aventures Plaisantes,' Cologne, 1702, p. 130; Boner, 82; Brant, E.; J. Wickram; 'Das Rollwagenbüchlein,' hg. v. Kurtz ("Deutsche Bibliothek," Bd. 7), Leipz., 1865, 8vo, 63; Memel, 164; Abraham a S. Clara, 'Judas der Ertz-Schelm,' 1-4, 1687-95, 3, 107; Eutrap., i. 552; 'Joe Miller,' 384. It is also No. 56 of Vitry, ed. by Crane, 1890.

XXXVI. 'Of the marchant that made a wager with his lord.'—This, with the exception of the moralization at the end, is translated from Poggio, No. 184.

XXXVII. 'Of the friere that gaue scrowes agaynst the pestilence.'—This is from No. 233 of Poggio. It is differently told in Pauli, No. 153. Oesterley refers to Hollen, 21d; Enr. Gran, 'Gran Specchio d' Essempi,' trad. da Astolfi, Venet., 1613, 4to, 10, 16; Brant, B. 8a; Montan., 740; Wolgemuth, '500 frische und ergötzliche Haupt-Pillen,' s. l., 1669, 5, 75; 'Lyrum Larum,' 305; 'Lustigmacher, der Allzeit fertige,' s. l., 1762, 8vo, 76.

XXXVIII. 'Of the phisitian, that vsed to write bylles ouer eue.'—This story, without the application, is No. 203 of Poggio.

XXXIX. 'Of hym that wolde confesse hym by writinge.'—This is the 299th of Pauli. Oesterley refers to Vinc. Bellovac., 'Spec. Mor.,' 3, 3, 10, 8, p. 1433; Joh. Eleemos., Norimb., 1483, fol. 77a; Brant, Gvi; Eutrap., i. 844; Poggius, 174, p. 468.

XL. 'Of the hermite of Padowe.'—This is also from the 142nd of Poggio, and is retold in the 'Apologie pour Herodote,' chap. xxi. (p. 23, vol. ii. of ed. cited). The editor refers to 'Chronique Burlesque,' Londres, P. du Noyer (Hollande), 1742, in 12, p. 293, 'La Curiosité bien Payée'; Mérard de Saint-Just, 'Espiègleries, Joyeusetés,' &c., 1764, t. i., 'La Curiosité Punie.' It is retold in 'Pasquil's Jests,' p. 63. Hazlitt in a note says it is found in the 'Heptameron.' I think this must be a mistake; I cannot find it in that work. There is also a similar tale in 'Pasquil's Jests,' p. 50, called 'A Tale of a Gentleman and his Man.' The jest also forms the latter portion of the eighth tale of 'Conde Lucanor,' by Don Juan Manuel, translated by James York, 1868, Pickering. Clouston, 'Flowers from a Persian Garden' (p. 81), gives a Persian story to the same effect, but without any references.

XLIII. 'Of the deceytfull scriuener.'—This is in Poggio, but I cannot at present find the reference.

XLIV. 'Of hym that saide he beleued his wyfe better than other, that she was chaste.' —This is the forty-first of the 'Poesies' of Marie of France, 'Dou vilain qui od sa fame vit aler son dru' (vol. ii. p. 209 of the edition by Roqueford).

XLV. 'Of hym that payde his dette with crienge bea.'—It is in 'Pasquil's Jests,' p. 45. A note in the edition by Hazlitt says it is also in the 'Family Jo Miller,' 1848, 12mo, p. 139, and that it is in the celebrated farce called 'Maître Pierre Patelin,' 1474, modernized in 1706 by Brueys under the title of 'L'Avocat Patelin,' whence was taken the farce of 'The Village Lawyer.' It will also be found in the first "Nouvelle" of 'Grand Parangon des Nouvelles Nouvelles,' and in Parabosco, Day 1, Nov. 8.

XLVII. 'Of the olde woman that prayde for the welfare of the tyrant Denise.'—This is similar to the fifty-nrst of Wright's Latin stories; No. 52 has also some resemblance. It is in 'Libro di Novelle Antiche,' &c., 1868, edited by Zambrini, Nov. 23, taken from Bosone da Gubbio, 'Fortunatus Siculus,' Firenze, 1832, and Milan, 1833.

XLIX. 'Of Socrates and his scoldinge wyfe.'—This is No. 471 of Pauli. Oesterley there quotes Seneca, 'Dialog. Creatur.,' 81; Joh. Sarisberiensis, 'Opp. Omnia,' coll. J. R. Giles, i. 2, Oxon., 1848, 8vo, 2, 8, 8, p. 268; Joh. Gallensis, 'Communiloquium siue Summa Collationum,' Argent., 1489, fol., 2, 4, 1; 'Rosarium,' 2, 205, E.; Herolt, 'Serm. de Temp.,' P. ii.; 'Conviv. Serm.,' i. 273; Guicciardini, 24b; Bellfor., 132; Federmann, 222; 'Lyrum Larum,' 221; Eutrap., i. 694; Joh. Val. Meidinger, 'Pract. französ. Grammatik,' 23 Aufl., Leipzig, 1808, 8vo, 90. It is told of a labouring man of Lincoln in 'Jack of Dover,' &c. (Hazlitt, 'Shakespeare Jest-Books,' Second Series, 327).

A. Collingwood Lee.

Waltham Abbey, Essex.

(*To be continued.*)

CECIL RHODES'S ANCESTORS.—Many of these lie buried in Old St. Pancras Churchyard, the earliest recorded member being William Rhodes, a dairy farmer residing in that parish, who died in 1769. His farm stood upon the site of the present Foundling Hospital. Samuel Rhodes, of Islington, was William's great-grandchild and Cecil Rhodes's great-great-grandfather. He died in October, 1822. He combined the avocations of brickmaking and dairy farming. Nelson, who just before his death wrote 'The History and Antiquities of the Parish of Islington,' thus refers to the farm :—

"Adjoining to Pullin's-row is an extensive dairy, or grass farm, belonging to Mr. Rhodes. This farm has been for many years, and is at this time, one of the largest establishments for supplying the London milk dealers in the vicinity of the metropolis......The stock of the present proprietor consists of from 4 to 5 or 600 cows, according to the season of the year, the greatest number being kept in the winter time ; amongst these are to be seen the finest specimens of large and handsome cattle in the environs of the metropolis, or, perhaps, in the whole kingdom. Many acres of land are rented by Mr. Rhodes in this parish, from which a great quantity of hay is procured, as the large stacks of that commodity annually deposited on his premises, near the S. end of Colebrooke-terrace, abundantly testify. On the waste ground in front of this farm is a pound for strayed cattle."

HARRY HEMS.

Fair Park, Exeter.

MIDDLE TEMPLE PRIVILEGES.—The Middle Temple Benchers have refused permission to the Post Office authorities to open the roads and lay telephone wires within the precincts over which they have control.

A. N. Q.

A SAYING ATTRIBUTED TO JESUS BY PHILOXENUS.—In the edition of the 'Discourses' of Philoxenus, Bishop of Mabbôgh (A.D. 485–519), edited and translated from the Syriac by Dr. E. A. Wallis Budge for the Royal Society of Literature (London, Asher & Co., 1894), there are two unidentified quotations of an interesting character. The 'Discourses' contain a large amount of valuable material, and Dr. Wallis Budge's translation is one of many services for which students owe him a debt of gratitude.

It is an undeniable fact that the citations of Philoxenus are often very loosely made ; but with these two exceptions Dr. Budge has been able to give precise references to them all. The index to these passages—so numerous are they—occupies nearly fifteen columns. The first of those not identified occurs in this passage: "'If ye wish to go away, depart,' He once said to them, and by reason of the hardness of His word many left Him and departed." If Philoxenus could be relied upon, this would supply a link in John vi. 65–9, R.V. Thus :—

"For this cause have I said unto you, that no man can come unto me, except it be given unto him of the Father. [If ye wish to go away, depart.] Upon this many of his disciples went back, and walked no more with him. Jesus said therefore unto the twelve, Would ye also go away? Simon Peter answered him, Lord, to whom shall we go? thou hast words of eternal life. And we have believed and know that thou art the Holy One of God."

The other quotation is a Pauline saying.

Philoxenus cites the words of Paul from 1 Thess. v. 16 and from Romans v. 3, and between them observes :—

"And in another place he has also said, 'Rejoice in your hope and endure patiently your tribulations ; for from the patient endurance of tribulations the hope concerning the things which are to come increaseth in us.'"

This has a Pauline ring about it, and recalls the account in Acts xiv. 22 of the preaching of Paul and Barnabas " that we must through much tribulation enter into the kingdom of God."

It would not be safe to be at all positive ; but the precise nature of these alleged quotations makes them noteworthy, and the first strikes one as a possible addition to the *agrapha* of Jesus. WILLIAM E. A. AXON.

BRITISH EPITAPHS IN CATALUÑA.—Having lately copied the following epitaphs of two famous Englishmen who lie buried in Cataluña (or *Catalunya*, as Catalans write it), and being unaware if their text has been published in any work in the English language, I submit them to the notice of the readers of 'N. & Q.' The first, in roman capitals, is on a stone slab in the pavement of a chapel of the great Aragonese Cistercian Abbey of Poblet, an hour's walk from the railway station of Espluga, in the province of Tarragona. Some of the letters are much worn out :—

Hic . iacet . ex'mvs .
D. Philippvs . de Whar
ton . Anglvs . Dvx
Marchio . et . comes
de Wharton . Marchio
de Malsbvrsi . et . *Cachar* (?)
loch . comes . rathas
easnvm . viceco
mes . de . Winchindon
Baro . de . Trim . eqves de
S. Georgii . (alias
de . la . Gerratera)
obiit . in fide . ec
clesiæ . Catholicæ
Romanæ . Popvleti
die . 31 . Maii . 1731.

The text of this was published, with some misprints, on p. 38 of a book entitled 'Restos Artísticos é Inscripciones Sepulcrales del Monasterio de Poblet,' by Angel del Arco y Molinero (Barcelona, 1897).

The other, also in roman capitals, is on a slab of white marble which is fixed into the front of the cavalry barracks at Vilafranca del Panadés, in the province of Barcelona, and a copy of it, with a few slight inaccuracies, may be seen on p. 158 of 'Apuntes Históricos de Vilafranca del Panadés y su Comarca' (Vilafranca, Imprenta y Librería de Pedro Alegret y Vilaró, 1887, 2ª edicion) :—

D.O.M.
Inclytvs
D. Gvlielmvs . Hanson . Anglvs
D. Ioannis . Filivs
Rei . Militaris . Peritissimvs
Centvrio . Alæ . xx. Britannorvm
in . Acri . Pugna
Adversvs . Gallos . Britanniæ . Hispaniæque
Hostes
in . Campo . Oppidi . Monachorvm
ivxta . Villafrancam . Pœnorvm
in . Catalonia
idibus . Septembris . an . MDCCCXIII
svb . dvoe . d . Friderico Bentinck
fortiter . occvbvit
ætatis . svæ . an . xxv
vt . strenvi . adolescentis
nomen . et . honos . exstent
eivsdem . pvgnæ . comilitones
mœrentes . posvervnt
annvente . illvst . episcopo . Barcinonensi.

Archæologists sometimes have to collect epitaphs, so it is best to commit copies of them to paper, which in some circumstances is more lasting than stone or metal.

E. S. Dodgson.

Ateneo Barcelonés.

Pseudo-Burnsian Songs.—Every student of Robert Burns will be familiar with that pretty little song beginning

The tither morn, when I forlorn
Aneath an aik sat moaning,

as, indeed, this song is to be found in most of the collections of Burns's poetry (cf. Robert Chambers's 'Burns,' iv. 343 ; 'The Centenary Burns,' iii. 104). Its authenticity, assumed by Stenhouse, had been questioned by Scott Douglas, whose arguments, however, do not seem to have met with general approval. I had quite forgotten this fact, so I was not a little astonished when, turning over the leaves of the 'Chearful Companion' (Perth, 1780 ; third edition, 1783), I came across three stanzas headed 'The Surprise,' which at first sight proved identical with our song, barring one or two insignificant differences only, such as "fu trig" instead of *sae trig*, or "cock'd spruce" instead of *cock'd spunk*. I have no doubt that the song occurs in other song-books of the period, although, at present, I can only refer to the 'Chearful Companion.' At all events, the question may be now looked upon as finally settled.

Another song which appears in many editions of the poet, and which probably is not Burns's own, is the one beginning

Wherefore sighing art thou, Phillis?

Its two stanzas strike one from the first as rather un-Burnsian in respect to both style and sentiment, nor have they ever been claimed by Burns. I have sought for them in vain in Scott Douglas's Library Edition and

in Chambers's 'Burns'; they are, however, included in 'The Centenary Burns' (vol. iii. p. 169). It has been assumed generally that the song was first published in the fifth volume of the 'Scots Musical Museum,' in the autumn (or winter ?) of 1796 ; but, as a matter of fact, it had made its appearance as early as 1792—viz., in vol. ii. of William Napier's 'Selection of the Most Favourite Scots Songs,' where it is stated, moreover, to be "by P. P." (qy. Peter Pindar ?).

I beg leave to add that I have succeeded in finding out the originals—hitherto unknown, so far as I can see—of some others of Burns's songs, such as "Open the door to me, O," "Charlie he's my darling," "The tailor he cam here to woo," "Jockie's taen the parting kiss," "Ay waukin, O," &c. I hope to be able before long to lay these finds before the public.
Otto Ritter.

Berlin.

'Ben-Hur.'—The *Jewish World* of 4 April states that "there was only one real Ben-Hur in Jewish history, and he lived in the time of Joshua." It continues :—

"This is the third Jewish historical play presented in London in a few years. More intense than either, but never so elegantly mounted, is a Yiddish opera-drama, 'The Fall of Jerusalem,' which in its turn is succeeded by the 'Bar Cochba' opera. Next in chronological order is Lessing's 'Nathan the Wise,' which deals with the Crusading time in Palestine. Emma Lazarus wrote a play of the same period concerning the Jews in Germany, so that if an attempt were made Jewish history could be put upon the stage in something like its sequence. Dr. Herzl's 'Modern Ghetto' and Dr. Nordau's 'Dr. Kohn' are the expression of the beginning of the twentieth century."

Are readers of 'N. & Q.' aware that there is a daily Jewish paper published in London, in Hebrew, the *Jewish Express?*
A. N. Q.

Queries.

We must request correspondents desiring information on family matters of only private interest to affix their names and addresses to their queries, in order that the answers may be addressed to them direct.

Tracing from Giotto.—In 1841, at the time of the discovery of the fresco of Dante painted by Giotto in the Bargello, Florence, Mr. Seymour Kirkup, the English artist, made a tracing of the fresco, which he sent to Gabriele Rossetti. His son had it subsequently in his possession, but at his death it was sold along with many other works of art of the painter-poet. Mr. W. M. Rossetti himself does not know for certain what has become of the original tracing. Could any one say who owns it now? A reproduction, as is known, was made by the Arundel Society. Great value is attached by Italians to the tracing, as Prof. D'Ancona, the eminent scholar, in an article in *La Lettura*, claims for Mr. Kirkup the discovery of Giotto's fresco.   ETRUSCO.

"IN AN INTERESTING CONDITION."—This happy and graceful equivalent for the older and more homely phrase "in the family way" does not appear to be registered in 'H.E.D.,' so it is difficult for those who are interested in the history of English phraseology to find out when the phrase was first introduced, and gradually took the place of its older synonyms. I notice that it is the usual way in which the situation is referred to in the public press. In the *Daily Telegraph*, 28 March, it occurs in a telegram from The Hague. The French also speak of a woman being "dans un état intéressant." See, for example, 'Le Crime de Sylvestre Bonnard,' by A. France, p. 9. The Germans, too, use "in interessanten Umständen." Was the English phrase borrowed from France, or did the French borrow from us? When did the phrase first appear in French or English literature? I was surprised to find that the phrase "to be in an interesting situation" occurs in 'The Slang Dictionary.' Well, it is no longer slang. The *Daily Telegraph* is incapable of such an indiscretion.
    COMESTOR OXONIENSIS.

NAT LEE.—What is known of Nat Lee; and in which of his tragedies do the following lines, ascribed to a man angry with a cardinal, occur?—

Stand back, and let me mow this poppy down,
This rank, red weed, that spoils the Church's corn.

The passage is quoted in Browning's 'Letters to his Wife,' and the metaphor it points must strike one for its beauty and originality.
    L. K.

[A full account of Lee is supplied in the 'Dict. Nat. Biog.' The lines you seek occur in 'Cæsar Borgia,' Act I. sc. i., and are spoken by Orsino. For "down" substitute *off*. Lee's 'Works,' vol. ii., edition 1736. They are p. 25, each play being separately paged.]

PORTRAIT OF CHARLES I.—I should be grateful for information as to the artist and the engraver to whom we are indebted for the portrait of Charles I. prefixed to his 'Large Declaration' (1639). The portrait in question is very handsome, and it brings out Charles's likeness to his father, which is not very easily traceable in the portraits by Vandyke and Vander Werff. I should also

like to know if this portrait has been reproduced in any modern book dealing with the history of Charles I.   JOHN WILLCOCK.
Lerwick.

'THE FAIRIES' FERRY.'—Some time in the year 1847 there appeared in a Dublin newspaper a translation from the German, entitled 'The Fairies' Ferry' or something to that effect. The following lines are remembered, and I should be glad if any of the readers of 'N. & Q.' could give the entire poem:—

Then a voice was heard, "Oh, ferryman dear,
Here we are waiting, all of us here,
    With our pots and pans
    And little gold cans;
    And our swift caravans
    Run swifter than man's."
    MICHAEL FERRAR.
Little Gidding.

THE MAN IN THE IRON MASK.—Will any reader give me information on the Man in the Iron Mask other than that which I find in 8ᵗʰ S. iv. and v.? There is, I believe, an article on the subject in *Temple Bar*, May, 1872.   AMY TASKER.
Colly Weston House, near Stamford.

[There is a book on the subject by Tighe Hopkins (Hurst & Blackett, 1901), reviewed in the *Athenæum* of 18 May. Later there was an article by Mr. Andrew Lang in the *Monthly Review*.]

EULOGIES OF THE BIBLE BY HUXLEY AND DARWIN.—I am looking for a eulogy on the Bible by Prof. Huxley, also one by Darwin as to its value as a guide to this life.
    G. A. M.

ARMS OF KNIGHTS.—Will any of your readers tell me the arms of the following knights, with the source from which the information has been obtained? Thomas Esturmey (Sturmy), Theodore le Tyes, 1204; Stephen de Valinis, John de Sunnevil, 1249; Matthew Hanybal, 1254; Peter le Foix, 1302; Peter Skerk, 1304; Guy de Wolston, 1487.
    JOHN RADCLIFFE.
Furlane, Greenfield, *via* Oldham.

SIR GEOFFREY POLE.—This knight married Edith St. John, half-sister of Margaret Beaufort, the mother of Henry VII. Is anything known as to his ancestry and as to whether he had any other children than Sir Richard Pole, who married Margaret, Countess of Salisbury?
    RONALD DIXON.
46, Marlborough Avenue, Hull.

'OLD FRIENDS AND NEW FRIENDS.'—Could you inform me where I might be able to obtain a copy of a short poem entitled 'Old Friends and New Friends'? I do not know who the author is, but it runs on the lines that new friends are silver, but old friends are gold.   PERCY MEREDITH.

LONDON LIBRARIES IN THE ELIZABETHAN ERA.—Commentators on Shakespeare explain many allusions and facts by references now to one and again to many recondite authors, to more, indeed, than can be now found in the British Museum. How far could such works have been within the possible reach of the dramatist? This question, I trust, will induce 'N. & Q.,' or some of its argus-eyed readers, to tell us whether any libraries existed in London three centuries ago. Were any such libraries accessible to the public or to players? How readily could they have been consulted in private or noble houses? 'H.E.D.' finds no earlier use of many words than in Shakespeare. Where did he get them? There are well-nigh forty such words compounded with the prefix *en-*, as "enwheel." These I hold to be Shakespearian creations. But there are a dozen more which 'H.E.D.' has detected in earlier writers. As those writers can hardly have been known to our dramatist, may not the making of those additional instances be also set down to his credit? If we suppose him conversant with all the writers who are set down as using his words before him, we make him one of the greatest of book-worms. A further question which I beg 'N. & Q.' to answer is, What libraries existed in Elizabethan London? and how far were such collections accessible to our dramatist? Answers will be helpful in determining his place as coiner of English words, as well as otherwise.   JAMES D. BUTLER.
Madison, Wisconsin, U.S.

BARKER CHIFNEY.—In the years 1801, 1803, and 1804 patents were granted for covering roofs with slate, and for a washing compound, to Barker Chifney, who is described as "of the city of London, gentleman." Who was he? I thought that he might be related to the celebrated jockey of the same name, but there is no mention of Barker Chifney in the notice of his distinguished namesake Samuel in the 'Dictionary of National Biography.'   R. B. P.

RENE = A SMALL WATERCOURSE.—I am told that this word (I am not sure as to the spelling) is current in Gloucestershire. Halliwell, in his dictionary, gives *rin* in the same sense, and *rindel*, a rivulet. From the *Intermédiaire*, 10 Dec., 1901, col. 874, it is clear that *ru* and *rin* also mean a watercourse in the old language of France. Whence was

the word derived? The writer in the *Intermédiaire* to whose words I am referring also speaks of the use of *rime*=hoarfrost in "notre vieille langue."   T. R. E. N. T.

"DUKE."—Can any reader give me an explanation of the meaning of the title "duc" or "duke" or "dux"? Does it mean chief or leader? Any information as to its origin and its application will oblige.
GEORGE.
[Consult 'H.E.D.,' *s.v.*]

SWAYLECLIFFE. — What is the probable origin of the name of this parish, situated to the east of Whitstable, in Kent? In a charter of King Eadred (946–55) the name is Swalewanclife (Birch's 'Anglo-Saxon Charters,' iii. 25); and at the Domesday Survey, Soanclive. The "cliff" and "clive" terminations are both used at a later time. This cannot be from a cliff, as it is situated on low ground, and at the present day there is no high cliff, neither is the place on the Swayle estuary, but on the open sea-coast. The coast-line is being washed away, so that, perhaps, a thousand years ago there may have been some high cliff. But Cliffe, near Rochester, is also in a marshy tract.   ARTHUR HUSSEY.
Tankerton-on-Sea, Kent.

INSCRIPTION ON SEAL —A friend of mine has a seal on which are engraved the words "Ofa taitoogoo." Can any one translate this inscription or tell what language it is?
E. MONTEITH MACPHAIL.
Madras.

"BUFF WEEK."—In mining districts in the north of England, where wages are paid fortnightly, the alternate weeks are called "pay week" and "buff week" respectively. I do not find this expression in the 'H.E.D.,' nor any use of the word "buff" which seems to account for it. In the South Wales coal districts the expressions "pay week" and "blank week" are used.   H. A. HARBEN.

BRISTOW FAMILY.—Could any one give me any information regarding a Henry Bristow living at Yarmouth at the latter part of the seventeenth and beginning of the eighteenth century, and tell me whether he was connected with the Bristows of Ayot St. Lawrence?   G. H. W.

"LUPO-MANNARO."—A correspondent of the *Antiquary* of February writes:—
"In Italy, however, the same expression, lupo-mannaro, is applied to unfortunate persons who are periodically afflicted with a form of madness apparently peculiar to that country......The attack of madness comes on when the moon is full.

......When the lupo-mannaro grows restless, the paroxysm seizes him, and he begins to howl like a wolf; his face becomes distorted......and he runs along on all fours."

It would be interesting to know if this form of madness exists in other lands, a fact I have been unable to discover. Is this extraordinary form of madness confined to Italy?

O. S. T.

LINES ATTRIBUTED TO DR. JOHNSON.—I find the following unpublished (?) lines of Dr. S. Johnson (in the calligraphy of a lady) in an old copy of Arthur Murphy's 'Life of David Garrick,' as a kind of note or introduction to Murphy's remarks on 'Irene':—

Dear is memory whene'er we wish to trace
Receive those lines, which time cannot erace [sic]
May that friend be happy (long absence may detain)
Is every wish, that centres yet in Jane.

The lady's remarks below the lines are: "Johnson wrote those lines for you M. W. D., with the very nice pen you made me—Adieu." Who are "Jane," "Adieu," and "M. W. D."? There being no need for a capital if At is meant, I interpret it M. W. D. The punctuation, if there was more than is here given, is now faded out.　　　JAMES HAYES.

Ennis.

[The ascription of the lines to Johnson needs corroboration. Does not "adieu" simply mean farewell?]

Replies.

ARMS OF ETON AND WINCHESTER COLLEGES.
(9ᵗʰ S. ix. 241.)

THE arms attributed to Winchester College (St. Mary of Winton, near Winton) in Guillim's 'Display of Heraldry' (edition 1724), p. 132, are thus described:—

"The Field is *Sable*, three Lilies slipped, their Stalks, Seeds, Blades and Leaves, *Argent*. These Arms pertain to the Colledge of Winchester," &c.

In Mr. C. W. Holgate's 'Winchester Long Rolls, 1653-1721,' pp. xix-xxi, there is a valuable note upon the arms used on these rolls, which have never been other than the well-known roses and chevrons, either with or without the sword and keys. In the course of this note, which is too long to reproduce here in its entirety, Mr. Holgate says:—

"Here I may mention that there seems to be little, if any, foundation for the statement originally, I believe, made by Guillim, 'that the Arms which pertain to the Colledge of Winchester' are Sable, three Lilies slipped, Argent. This question has been recently treated at some length in a paper by the Rev. E. E. Dorling, printed in the *Wykehamist* for Nov., 1898, No. 352."

It may be observed that Guillim's editor was unfortunate in his dealing with the real Wykehamical arms, the roses and chevrons; for on p. 21 of the 'Display' (1724) he gives a drawing and description of these arms, and states that they formed

"the coat of Robert Pynk, D.D., Warden of *New Colledge*, who dy'd the 3ᵈ of November 1647. S.P. and was buried in *New Colledge* Chapel, near the Pulpit."

In support of this statement he refers to a "MS. of Ant. à Wood's Remarks de Com. Oxon., p. 82," which he apparently misunderstood; for the reference is presumably to the "note in Wood, MS., F. 4, p. 82," the effect of which is thus reproduced in 'Wood's Life and Times,' Oxford Hist. Soc., i. 133, note 2:—

"Wood gives in colour the arms: 'argent two chevronells sable between 3 roses gules seeded or barbed vert [New College]: impaling, argent 9 lozenges in pale gules, on a bordure sable nine crosses patée fitchée or [Pynke].'"

See also Wood's 'Colleges and Halls' (by Gutch, 1786), p. 209, where, at the foot of a copy of the memorial inscription in New College Chapel to Warden Pynke, his arms are given thus:—

"Arms—Arg. five Lozenges in pale Gul. within a Bordure Az. charged with eight Crosses patée fitchée Or."

MR. UDAL mentions Mr. R. T. Warner's statement in his excellent handbook, p. 212, that Magdalen College, Oxford, was "originally called Winchester College, Oxford." I should be grateful for some instances of this manner of denoting Magdalen College. "Winchester College, Oxford," in passages in which I have met with this title, has meant New College (St. Mary of Winton in Oxford).

H. C.

Mr. Perceval Landon, in *Archæologia Oxoniensis*, part iv., 1894, p. 203, remarks that the arms of Magdalen College—Fusilly, ermine and sable, on a chief of the last three lilies argent—

"record the connexion [the College having been founded in 1458 by William Patten of Waynflete, sometime Provost of Eton] in a singularly graceful way, the paternal arms of the founder being charged with a chief to commemorate the College of which he had been the first head master......Guillim, quoting Buddenus, remarks, 'A parentibus accepit hujus vitæ usuram, a collegio decus et dignitatem...... Gessit idcirco in eodem clypeo utriusque insignia, Rombos cum liliis.' This is the received interpretation, but it is often forgotten that the chief corresponds more closely with the old arms of Winchester College—Sable, three lilies argent—where he had been educated. Winchester now uses the same coat with New College—Argent, two chevronels sable between three roses gules, seeded or, barbed vert."

And elsewhere he says :—

"The Wykehams, an Oxfordshire family whose remotest ancestor is supposed to have lived in the time of King John, are found bearing the present arms of New College with *red* chevronels, and the great Bishop of Winchester, whether his connexion with the family is clearly to be shown or not, adopted them, with the black ordinaries as a distinction, both for his College of St. Mary the Virgin of Winchester in Oxford, and for his College of St. Mary the Virgin in Winchester."

The great building bishop is supposed to have been the son of a carpenter, one John Longe, and some Heralds have asserted "that in these arms we have the chevronels used in their primitive form as rafters or braces to indicate a mighty builder"; but the above quotation is sufficient to rebut this pleasing fiction.

With regard to the paternal arms of Bishop Waynflete — who, like Wykeham, as was indeed usual with ecclesiastics, took his surname from the place of his birth—Mr. H. A. Wilson, in his recent (1899) 'History of Magdalen,' contends that

"the earliest representations of the coat [*e.g.*, that on Waynflete's episcopal seal, and that on the seal of his College] show the rhombi in the 'lozenge,' not in the 'fusil' form, having their horizontal diameter about equal to their sides. But this use of the arms appears to have had no sanction by way of grant or confirmation till 1574, when Richard Lee, Portcullis, describes himself as having 'ratified, confirmed, and recorded' in his 'Visitacion made of the Universitie' a coat which he declares to be 'thauncient Armes belonginge' to the College. ......Lee's drawing and attestation are preserved in the College of Arms : the field, in this drawing, is manifestly lozengy, and the lilies on the chief are argent, *stalked and seeded or.* This last feature (probably a slight variation from Waynflete's arms, intentionally made by Portcullis in 'confirming' a coat used without authority) appears in one or two representations not only of the College arms, but of the arms of the Founder (distinguished by the presence of the Garter, or of a mitre) in the glass of the Hall windows."

Mr. W. H. St. John Hope gives the first shield of King's College, Cambridge, the sister of Eton, from the seal made in 1443, and still in use, as Sable, a mitre pierced by a crozier (*sic*, pastoral staff ?), for St. Nicholas, between two lily flowers proper, for Our Lady ; a chief per pale azure, with a fleur-de-lis of France, and gules a lion of England.

The present arms, granted in 1449, are Sable, three roses argent ; the chief as before.

A. R. BAYLEY.

"ENDORSEMENT": "DORSO - VENTRALITY" (9th S. ix. 64, 212).—"It is not essential to the validity of an endorsement that it should be on the back of a bill or note ; it may equally well be on the face"—'Byles on Bills,' p. 176

(16th edition, 1899), citing R. *v.* Bigg in 1717, where the head-note (1 Str. 18) is, "The writing cross the face of a bank-note is properly called an indorsement." In old cases even signatures on the face of a negotiable instrument are (I think) sometimes so called. Another decision to the same effect as that cited is in *ex parte* Yates (2 De G. and J. at 192) in 1857. And so Judge Willis ('Negotiable Securities,' 1896, lecture v., first paragraph) :—

"I am bound to tell you that an acceptance may be as well on the back as on the face of the bill, and that which people call an endorsement may be on the face of the instrument. Still I myself have never seen a bill of exchange in which the acceptance was not on the face of it ; I have never seen an endorsement which was not on the back."

HERMAN COHEN.

GREEK EPIGRAM (9th S. ix. 147, 273).—MR. STRONG'S, MR. WAINEWRIGHT'S, and MR. AXON'S replies (not mine) are, of course, correct. Of the Ep. v. 95, imitated by Swift, the following anonymous translation, which appeared in the *London Magazine*, February, 1734, is included in Dr. Wellesley's 'Anthologia Polyglotta' :—

Cyprus must now two Venuses adore,
Ten are the Muses, and the Graces four.
So charming Flavia's wit, so sweet her face,
She's a new Muse, a Venus and a Grace.

This version, by Prof. Goldwin Smith, of the Ep. of Callimachus (v. 146) is given in the same collection :—

The Graces, three erewhile, are three no more ;
A fourth is come with perfume sprinkled o'er.
'Tis Berenice blest and fair : were she
Away the Graces would no Graces be.

Dr. Burges has another by F. H. M. :—

Four are the Graces. With the three of old
Be Berenice's heavenly form enrolled,
Breathing forth odours. They no more would be
Graces themselves without her company.

J. MAC-CARTHY.

SIR WALTER SCOTT (9th S. iii. 346, 434 ; iv. 31, 134). — The play upon the words σκότος and σκοτία in the epigram on Scott occurs also in the following elegiac distich on Buchanan by Johannes Lundorpius. I copy it from an edition of Buchanan's 'Poemata,' published at Amsterdam in 1687. It is to be found near the beginning of the book among other "virorum doctorum de Buchanano testimonia" :—

Κᾶν, Βυκανᾶνε, πατρὶς Σκοτίη σοι, κᾶν ὀνομάζῃ
Σὺ Σκότος, οὐ σκότος εἶ, ἀλλὰ φόως Σκοτίης.

Possibly Lundorp wrote εἶς.

EDWARD BENSLY.
The University, Adelaide, South Australia.

"Bristol look" (9th S. ix. 148, 298).—The ridiculous explanation that appears in your impression of the 12th inst. in regard to the above quotation makes a correction necessary. I annotated the original query a few days after it appeared, but it hardly then seemed to require further notice. It puts "Harvey" instead of Hervey. The title "Lord" is naturally omitted. Lord Hervey is the third title of the Marquess of Bristol. The person referred to in the paragraph is the present Lord Bristol, who possibly was surprised at Dicky Milnes's (not then Lord Houghton) observation. Lord Bristol was Lord Hervey till 1859, his father and grandfather being both alive. This is a singularly apposite instance of how myths originate. Cardboard and *argot* have as little to do with the expression as cabbages and cauliflower, or, for a matter of that, the town of Bristol itself. I enclose my card and beg to subscribe myself,
A. H. D.

"Say not that he did well" (9th S. ix. 87).—Mr. F. M. Camilleri Major asks for the authorship of the following quotation :—

Say not that he did well or ill,
But say he did his best.

I have looked in vain in each succeeding issue of 'N. & Q.' for a reply, being desirous to discover if my impression that the lines occur in a poem by Miss Mulock (Mrs. Craik) is correct. There is not much doubt, I think, as to this ; but I should like my verbal knowledge of the stanza in which the lines cited occur rectified. I am almost certain the following is not the exact reading :—

And when I lie in the green kirkyard
With the sod above my breast,
Say not that he did well or ill,
Only he did his best.

John Grigor.
105, Choumert Road, Peckham.

Greek Pronunciation (9th S. vii. 146, 351, 449 ; viii. 74,192, 372, 513 ; ix. 131, 251, 311).—This discussion, which has wandered rather far away from its subject, might be considerably shortened if your correspondents W. H. B. and M. Haultmont, before attempting to trace the origins of English words, would first make themselves acquainted with a few elementary things in philology, and would look at such books as Skeat's 'Etymol. Dict.' and Sweet's 'Hist. of English Sounds'; they would then not suggest such an impossible origin for *salt* as Fr. *sel*, and would see that it really comes from Anglian *salt*, not West Saxon *sealt*. Apparently there are still many who do not yet recognize that there were several dialects of O.E., and that modern standard English forms are not, as a rule, to be traced back to West Saxon forms.
F. J. C.

Sir Edmund Berry Godfrey (7th S. xii. 314 ; 9th S. ii. 367, 414 ; iii. 16, 96).—A short time ago I bought a "lot" of old deeds, and among them I found an indenture

"made the fifth day of November In the yeare of our Lord God According to the Accompt used in England one Thousand six hundred fiftie and seaven Betweene John Iles of Stanwell in the County of Middlesex Esquire of the one part and Edmund Berrey Godfrey Citizen and Woodmonger of London on the other part."

Was the latter the Sir Edmund Berrey Godfrey, or "Sir Edmondbury Godfrey," as he used to be called when the writer was at school, who has become known to history through his sensational murder on 17 October, 1678—twenty-one years later ?

He is described in the document in question, which is a conveyance by gift to him of the estate of John Iles at Stanwell in Middlesex, as "sister's sonne of him the said John Iles."

The estate consisted of :—

1. "The Farme house called Ludlowes."
2. "That Pightell or Parcell of Pasture adjoining to the Orchard [?] of the said Farme house."
3. "One Little Close of Pasture with sods [?] adjoining to the River there, called Great Besses [?] Containing by Estimation Thirteene Acres with the Coppices and springs of the wood thereunto adjoining."
4. "One other close adjoining unto Great Besses [?] aforesaid with a Sawpitt now or heretofore in the same, commonly called or known by the name of Little Besses [?]."

All the above premises were at the time or late in the occupation of Richard Finch and Thomas Russell.

5. "That water-mill......late or sometime called ......Peacockes Mill......late in the tenure of one Thomas Holland."
6. "That dwelling house adjoining to the said Mill And......all Buildings &c. thereunto belonging."
7. "Three Acres of Arable Land in Stonehillshott abutting south upon Iverhedge,"
8. "Two Acres Lieing in Dymeadshott [?] abutting south upon Dymead."
9. "One Acre of Land in Longrope Feild near Broomhedge."

These three "parcells" of land were heretofore in the occupation of John Clarke and George Clarke.

10. "One half acre of Arable Land......likewise in the Tenure or Occupation of the said John Clarke."

All these

"Messuages, &c., with all Manner of Woods, Underwoods, Timber......Hedgerows, Woods [?], Commons, Commons of Pasture......Reversions...... Fishinge, Woodes [?] Profits, Commodities, Advantages, Emoluments, Privileges and Hereditaments whatsoever," are transferred to Edmund Berrey Godfrey, his heirs and assigns, for ever,

"and to and for none other use and behoofe intent or purpose whatsoever."

It would be interesting to know whether this is the Sir Edmund Berrey Godfrey of history; whether the places named, situated in the parish of Stanwell, can be identified; and if so, in whose occupation they are and to what "use and behoofe" they are now put.

Unfortunately the signature and seal of John Iles, or of Edmund Berrey Godfrey—whichever it was who signed this particular document—have been torn out (accidentally, I think), and only those of the witnesses, "Jam: Harrison," "John Smith," and "Geo: Cooper, servᵗ to Mʳ Brome Councellʳ," remain.

J. P. Lewis.

Pins and Pincushions (9ᵗʰ S. ix. 209).— For the prehistoric pin Munro, 'Lake-Dwellings of Europe' (1890), and similar works should be consulted. Part of vol. ii. of 'British Manufacturing Industries,' edited by G. P. Bevan (1878), gives some information as to production.

J. D.

The Last of the Pre-Victorian M.P.s (9ᵗʰ S. ix. 226).—For many years there has been a great doubt as to whether Mr. John Temple Leader is alive or dead. A question was asked by a correspondent in *Westminster*, a monthly illustrated review — unhappily since dead—on 1 September, 1897, concerning this gentleman, and it was there pointed out that a correspondent in 'N. & Q.,' signing H. T., at 8ᵗʰ S. xii. 91, for 31 July, 1897, stated that "J. T. Leader is still living, and was one of the stewards at the last dinner of the Newspaper Press Fund. He is also one of the three surviving original members of the Reform Club." A reply to the query in *Westminster* was forthcoming in the following month, and in it were some very interesting notes on the various squibs and lampoons that appeared from time to time on account of the many and prolonged absences of this M.P. for Westminster—1837–47—from his Parliamentary duties. It is stated that he became a stock subject for ridicule in *Punch*, and on 8 February, 1845, there was a burlesque advertisement under the head of 'The Absent One' to this effect :—

"Mr. John Leader, you are earnestly implored, if you will not come home to your misrepresented constituents, at all events to send back the representation of the City you have taken away with you. Please address to the Steward of the Chiltern Hundreds."

Other squibs of a like character appeared at intervals, one stating "Gone to Cannes. Won't be back till next election." A London paper (I believe the *Daily News*) recorded about 1897 that he was alive and residing near Florence, but there really appeared to be no certainty as to his whereabouts, although it was "probably not in this country, as his fondness for the Continent was well known."   W. E. Harland-Oxley.

71, Turner Buildings, Millbank, S.W.

A Seventeenth - century Plagiary : 'Vindex Anglicus' (9ᵗʰ S. viii. 457; ix. 112). —The first edition of Camden's 'Remaines' was published in 1605, and the second in 1614. The writer's own words are decisive, one would think, on that point. In his dedication to Sir Robert Cotton he says :—

"Pardon me, Right Worthy Baronet, if at the Printers request, I addresse these Remaines with some supplement, to you againe in the same wordes, I did ten yeares since."

It is clear from this statement that there could have been no other edition published between the dates mentioned. Even if there had been a reprint of the first (of which there is no record) it would have been, to use the poet's phrase, "Only this and nothing more." The interesting dedication from which I have quoted is thus dated : "From my Lodging, xxx. Iunii. 1614," and has the letters "M. N." appended, which are the finals of William Camden. This curious manner of concealing the authorship from all but intimate friends is doubtless to be explained by the fact that the compiler of the volume considered it to be of little value. He calls it "this silly, pittifull, and poore Treatise,......being onely the rude rubble and out-cast rubbish (as you know) of a greater and more serious worke." From what has been said it is evident that the 'Dictionary of National Biography' must be wrong when it speaks of a second edition of the 'Remaines' in 1605, in which Carew's 'Epistle' appeared. It would have been correct in saying "the first edition," for, as the paper is not marked with an asterisk, it forms no part of the "supplement" to which the writer refers, and must therefore have been printed in 1605. It has already been noted that all fresh matter incorporated in the edition of 1614 is thus distinguished. I have seen a copy of the one edited by Philipot in 1637 : "The fift Impression with many rare Antiquities never before imprinted. By the industry and care of Iohn Philipot, Somerset Herald." He has taken considerable liberties in the way of omission and commission, but has nothing to say regarding the history of the volume or its author.

By the way, I observe that there is a sketch of the two Sir Henry Goodyers in one of the supplementary volumes of the 'Dictionary of National Biography,' in which the epitaph printed in Camden's 'Remaines,' 1614, p. 377 (and also, for the reason already given, in 1605), is once more gravely applied to the second Sir Henry, who died " March 18, 1627," according to the writer. Your esteemed correspondent MR. PERCY SIMPSON gives the following year as the date. It is a matter dealing with the " Old " and the " New Style," I take it, so the latter statement is no doubt correct. If reference had been made to this series of 'N. & Q.' the repetition of the ludicrous blunder regarding the epitaph would have been avoided, for in this one thing at least MR. SIMPSON and myself agreed, that the lines could not have been written in 1614 (not to speak of 1605) in commemoration of a man who ended his career in 1628. Apart from this mistake, one regrets that the sketch is so meagre and unsatisfactory, especially so far as the elder Sir Henry Goodyer is concerned.

JOHN T. CURRY.

THE MITRE (9ᵗʰ S. viii. 324, 493, 531; ix. 174).—John Sharp, who succeeded Thomas Lamplugh as Archbishop of York in 1691, is also represented in a mitre on his monument in the Ladye Chapel of York Minster. He died in 1713. An engraving of the tomb will be found in Drake, p. 468. The effigy, of the lively kind, has supported itself in a very uncomfortable semi-recumbent position on its elbow for well-nigh two centuries. Looking at it, one remembers a striking passage in Mr. George Gilbert Scott's 'History of English Church Architecture' touching " the resurrection of effigies." Let me have the pleasure of repeating it :—

" In the earliest monumental figures the hands are crossed upon the breast, and the attitude is that of death-like rest. Then, though this quiet slumber is still unruffled, there are signs as of a half-consciousness, and the hands are joined in prayer. The knight reposing upon his tomb becomes aware of his lady lying by his side, and, half in tenderness, half in sleep, he lays his hand in hers. But the hour of waking is at hand, the stony figures turn upon their sides, they raise themselves slowly upon an elbow, and gaze, still somewhat drowsily, about them. Ere long they rise, now fully awakened, and pose upon their knees in prayer; soon, grown weary of the pious posture, they seat themselves in curule chairs, with a cold *sic sedebat*. At the last, clad in toga, or in breeches, as the case may be, they stand erect upon their feet, and marshal armies or harangue senates, in all the affected realism of the stage."—P. 166, foot-note.

ST. SWITHIN.

STAUNTON, WORCESTERSHIRE (9ᵗʰ S. viii. 383, 510; ix. 11, 92, 110, 170, 217).—The only correspondent who has been able to locate

this parish is SIR CHARLES DILKE. It is eight miles north of Gloucester. Although once, according to Nash, it was granted a charter to hold a market every Wednesday throughout the year, and a fair during the week after St. James's Day, the authorities since have succeeded in making it lost and unknown. Roman remains have been found here, and the church is partly Saxon. The Whittingtons held the manor for some time, but the manor house would appear to have been built by a family whose arms are over the door—viz., a lion rampant between crosses fitchy. The doorway is Norman. Gazebrook attributes the arms to De Hauteville.

One Hawkinus de Hawville was King John's falconer when that monarch hunted at Gloucester, and the question arises whether this was not his residence, being in the Chase of Cors and near unto the Malvern Chase. The arms on a monument in the church are those of the Whittingtons, St. Lowes, Hortons, and Stauntons.

I believe that residents in this forgotten parish were disqualified from the office of coroner for Worcestershire because of their distance from Worcester; and this fact is recorded of Roger de Staunton, 1316. William Whittington married the heiress of John de Staunton, 1399, and held the manor under Roger Mortimer, Earl of March. Any information would be greatly valued.

J. G. HAWKINS.

QUEEN CUNEGUNDA (9ᵗʰ S. ix. 189).—Lutburg might be an abbreviation of Lutzemburgum—*i.e.*, Luxemburgum, the birthplace of Queen Cunegunda, whose burial-place was, however, Bamberg.   H. K.

PORTRAITS OF FEMALE FIGHTERS (9ᵗʰ S. ix. 68, 156).—In the list of female warriors given at the first reference I do not see the name of Mrs. Christian Davies. The second edition of the 'Life and Adventures' of this British amazon was published on 25 September, 1741 (*Daily Advertiser* of that date). This Mrs. Davies served as a foot soldier and dragoon in several campaigns under King William and the Duke of Marlborough. She was made a pensioner of Chelsea College by Queen Anne, and so continued till her death. Possibly it contained a portrait for frontispiece. There is a steel-plate portrait of the Chevalier d'Éon in the *New Wonderful Magazine* vol. ii.   J. HOLDEN MACMICHAEL.
Wimbledon Park Road.

If my memory does not play me false, there is, in one of the cases in the Castle Museum at Lewes, a painting of Phœbe Hassel on

glass. Her gravestone, it will be remembered, is still to be seen in Brighton Churchyard. Your correspondent will find numerous portraits of the Chevalier d'Éon, one from the painting by Angelica Kauffmann, in 'The True Story of the Chevalier d'Éon,' by E. A. Vizetelly, 1895.   Chas. H. Crouch.
5, Grove Villas, Wanstead.

May I direct Mrs. Emily Kerr's attention to a German "woman who fought"? She was Eleonore Prochaska, born 11 March, 1785, at Potsdam, as the daughter of a sergeant. After being brought up in the military orphanage of that town, she became a cook in some citizen's house. When the great war against Napoleon broke out in 1813 she was led away by enthusiasm to quit her town secretly; by selling her poor belongings she procured male attire and weapons, and enlisted under the name of August Renz in the Lützow Corps. On account of her tall slender figure her sex was not discovered until she was mortally wounded. This happened in the encounter in the Göhrde Forest, Regierungsbezirk Lüneburg, Kreis Dannenberg (16 Sept., 1813). The Prussians were there attempting to storm a hill occupied by the French, she acting as a drummer. In 1863 a monument in memory of her was erected in the churchyard at Dannenberg, and another in 1889 in the old churchyard of Potsdam. When a boy I often saw cheap illustrations representing her, and my mother told me about her.

Another German heroine was Johanna Staegemann, "the maiden of Lüneburg." The allies under Dörnberg's command met the French under Morand (2 April, 1813), and the engagement ended in a victory for them. When ammunition became scarce in the front, Johanna, a young peasant girl, helped her fighting countrymen by carrying cartridges in her apron from the rear. If further particulars or references are wanted I will try to provide them.   G. Krueger.
Berlin.

"Rout" (9th S. ix. 65, 198).—This word survives also in "rout-cakes," which are still sold by confectioners. They are sweet biscuits shaped somewhat like a bunch of filberts.
F. J.

"Keep your hair on" (9th S. ix. 184).—My earliest recollection of this saying traces it no further back than the fall of 1871. At the Lord Mayor's Show in 1869 it was not heard in the streets. On Thanksgiving Day, February, 1872, it became a sudden furore. During the crush at the procession, and the even worse crush at the illuminations, people were sometimes hard put to it to "keep in their rag." But then, as since, the customary reply from the good-tempered sort (of whom there are numbers in the world), when told to "keep their hair on," was "Haven't lost it yet." Some few years ago Lord Goschen said, in one of his public speeches, that many of the slang or "cant" words in popular use originated in the schools and colleges of this country. He instanced "bloke" and "mug" ("mugster"). To show that "keep your hair on" had probably a likewise collegiate (or academic) origin, I should like to quote a few lines from Barrère's 'Argot and Slang: a New French and English Dictionary of Cant Words,' 1887:—

"The English public schools, but especially the military establishments, seem to be not unimportant manufacturing centres for slang. Only a small proportion, however, of the expressions coined there appear to have been adopted by the general slang-talking public, as most are local terms, and can only be used at their own birthplace......At Harrow......a man who is vexed or angry 'loses his shirt' or his 'hair'; at Shrewsbury he is 'in a swot'; and at Winchester 'front.'"
Herbert B. Clayton.
39, Renfrew Road, Lower Kennington Lane.

More than twenty years ago I was coming down one of the poorer streets of Hull and met a boy going to school smoking. I vainly tried to snatch the pipe out of his mouth. When the lad had got a safe distance from me he lifted his right hand to his nose, extended his fingers fan-like, and called out to me, "Keep your 'air on." I am able to fix the period in my mind, as I well remember the house in which I then lived.
William Andrews.
Royal Institution, Hull.

I certainly recollect hearing this phrase used in the sense of "Don't be too excited" as far back as 1853, and have no doubt it was then well established.   E. F. D. C.

No doubt the slang sense illustrated in 'N.E.D.' is distinct from the literal meaning in Holcroft. But the underlying thought which gave rise to the expression in 1799 must surely have led directly to the slang sense long before 1883. A man is bidden to "keep his hair on"—i.e., not to allow himself to be ruffled by the storm of a sudden passion. The thought, which is exaggeration of fact in the one case, becomes metaphorical in the other, but the thought is the same.
W. C. B.

Tib's Eve (9th S. ix. 109, 238).—Jamieson is correct in saying that Tib or Tibbie is used in Scotland as a variant on Isobel or

Isabella. I know several instances of the usage at the present time. Paterson, in his 'Contemporaries of Burns,' introduces the notice of Isobel Pagan of Muirkirk with the remark, "Isobel or Tibbie Pagan is the reputed authoress of the following version of 'Ca' the Yowes to the Knowes.'" Throughout his article he uses Tibbie as often as Isobel, thus, no doubt, recording the name by which the beldam had been familiarly known in her lifetime.   Thomas Bayne.

In the spurious second part of 'Don Quixote' there is a passage, bk. vi. chap. iii. p. 348, of Capt. John Stevens's translation (1705), which may be of use in discussing this expression. Sancho Panza is made to say, "What will my poor master Don Quixote be in the hands of that confounded Goliah, who is like to sell all our guts for fiddle-strings, if good Saint Tib does not assist us?" I am unable to refer to the original or to any of the three other English translations. Perhaps some of my fellow-readers will do so and let us know the result. "Saint Tib" might be a similar translation to "By Jingo," into which the "Par Dieu" of Rabelais was turned.   E. G. B.

"Pulque" (9ᵗʰ S. ix. 226).—Though not bearing upon the point in question, the following extract from Ruxton's 'Mexico' may be found interesting :—

"From every Pulque-shop is heard the twanging of guitars, and the quivering notes of the *canta lores*, who excite the guests to renewed potations by their songs in praise of the grateful liquor."

The popular chorus of one of these is :—

     Sabe que es pulque?
     Licor divino—o !
     Lo beben los angeles
     En el sereno—o,

which is thus poetically rendered :—

     Know ye what pulque is?
     Liquor divine !
     Angels in heaven
     Prefer it to wine.

         N. Buchanan.

Comic Annual (9ᵗʰ S. ix. 188).—The work about which Pomander is seeking information, "which appeared about sixty years ago," was Hood's 'Comic Annual,' 1830–42. It was run upon very similar lines to Cruikshank's 'Comic Almanack,' but without the artistic aid of King George. The illustrations, the literary part, the jokes, and so on, were, with a few exceptions, entirely the work of Tom Hood. His drawings, though cut by the best engravers of the time—Bonner, Branston, and others—were strangely crude; yet they were full of originality, wit,

and true genius. He has had as an artist (although at the period shamefully pirated from) only one genuine imitator. As the last-named artist is still with us I refrain from mentioning names. In "Dicks's English Library" (published quite recently) will be found many of the poems and drawings of Hood which appeared in his 'Comic Annual.' To the best of my knowledge it was in Hood's 'Comic Annual' that Sir John Gilbert (frontispiece, 1839) and John Leech, who illustrated the entire volume for 1842, made their (almost) maiden attempts at woodcut illustrations. It is true that Leech had drawn for *Punch* early in 1841; but his talents were not at the time appreciated very highly by the promoters of the *London Charivari*. The publishers of Hood's 'Comic Annual' were : 1830, Hurst, Chance & Co.; 1831–4, Charles Tilt ; 1835–9, A. H. Baily & Co.; 1842, Henry Colburn. The 'Annual' did not appear in 1840, and seems to have been finally discontinued in 1842, probably owing to Hood's unfortunate illness. Original copies of the 'Comic Annual' are now very scarce ; bound volumes in "mint" condition should be of some value.
         Herbert B. Clayton.
39, Renfrew Road, Lower Kennington Lane.

Mathews of Truro (9ᵗʰ S. ix. 229).—The two following extracts from a catalogue recently received from Mr. James Coleman, of Tottenham Terrace, Tottenham, London, N., may afford some clue to Mr. Matthews, as Norfolk and Cornwall have been tried without success :—

"11. Berkshire. Deed between Anne Lane, of Banbury, and Sarah Playdell, of the city of Oxford, and Edward Bacon, of Milton, in the county of Berks, gent., relates to land, &c., there in the tenure of William Mathews, in the town of Abingdon, with signatures and seals of Sarah Playdell and Edward Bacon ; dated 1695."

"283. Mathews [*sic*] Family and their Estates, in the county of Essex, in the parishes of Kelvedon, Coggeshall, Witham, Boxted, and places adjoining, sold by the Court of Chancery in January, 1785 ; gives the names of the tenants and farms, the rentals and terms, quantities, acres, &c., &c. [of] the estates of the late Daniel Mathew, Esq. This is in [a] good state, 16 pages folio. The trial took place in 1784 and the sale in 1785."

Note. "Maybe there is a good balance waiting in the Court for some fortunate family of Mathew yet."

I understand my uncle-in-law, the Rev. Joseph Hardinge-Matthews, of Hollywood, near Birmingham, and his brother William (?) were born at Newbury, Berkshire. Their father, I believe, had grounds for thinking he was the heir of a relation who died many years ago, leaving large estates in Jamaica

or elsewhere. He is reported to have spent a fortune of several thousands of pounds in trying to prove the claim and in searching registers, but he failed, I understand, owing to the absence of the connecting link of one entry, which he knew to exist, but could not find.   RONALD DIXON.
46, Marlborough Avenue, Hull.

CHRIST'S HOSPITAL: THE LAST OF THE "BLUES" (9th S. viii. 283 ; ix. 231, 251).—The *Standard* of April 21st contains the following interesting account of the closing of the old school :—

"Only a few boys had remained within the gates during Friday night, a portion of which was spent in the observance of a custom which will, no doubt, appeal to the sympathies of 'Old Blues' all over the world. The 'Grecians' formed a long single file, each youth carrying a candle, and as they beat the boundaries of the hospital they kicked at walls of well-known spots bearing such mystic geographical expressions as 'Gymmer Door,' 'Sixes Tubby's Hole,' 'The Rid's Staircase,' 'The Z Minor,' and 'Haggery Stairs.' The perambulation having been completed to the intense satisfaction of all concerned, the boys stretched hands across the playground, and, marching up and down three times, sang 'Auld Lang Syne.' The quaint ceremony concluded with lusty cheers for the pious founder and benefactors."
A. N. Q.

PARISH REGISTERS: THEIR CARE AND PROTECTION (9th S. ix. 168).—The case cited by H. G. K. is certainly scandalous in the last degree, but it is not worse than two or three that have come to my knowledge in the course of twenty years' experience. I also could give the name of a parish whose registers were deliberately burnt by the incumbent only a few years ago — but without the somewhat palliating circumstance of a copy previously prepared. I know another instance where the parish registers are kept at a farmhouse.
Another aspect of this urgent question is the frequent practice of exacting prohibitive fees from genealogists and antiquaries whose work necessitates a general search through the registers. This is commonly supposed to be legal, but I doubt it very much. The fees fixed by statute were never intended to apply to a literary search. It is absurd to suppose it. They were meant to be charged for particular entries required for legal purposes. Yet historical investigation is often checked in mid-stream by a hopelessly conscientious insistence, on the custodian's part, that the full fees are to be paid—amounting to many pounds in an ordinary case. I admit that such custodians are a minority of the clergy. Courteous and intelligent liberality is much more common.

But cases of the other sort are numerous enough and sufficiently scandalous to call urgently for a remedy. What antiquarian workers want to know is, When are we to expect the introduction into Parliament of a Bill similar to that drawn years ago by the late Mr. William Copeland Borlase, M.P., with the object of giving us relief in this respect? It is monstrous that records of such priceless value as church registers should be left in any custody but that of the Master of the Rolls. They are perishing by the dozen every year. I could furnish abundant evidence of their rapid and irrecoverable loss. If they are to be saved, it must be done at once.
JOHN HOBSON MATTHEWS.
Town Hall, Cardiff.

Is H. G. K. aware that the existing form of entry in marriage registers does not go back further than the year 1754, having been prescribed in the Marriage Act passed in 1753? He does not mention the year to which his inquiry related, but the names of witnesses and other matter not judged material, as he supposes, are not to be found recorded before the date above mentioned. The book in use in my parish from 1754 to 1812, in pursuance of the Act of 1753, was published by Joseph Fox, "Parish Clerk to the Honourable the House of Commons" and "Bookseller in Westminster Hall," and also by Benjamin Dod, "Bookseller to the Society for Promoting Christian Knowledge." There is also a register of banns similarly published. Probably the proceeding which appears to H. G. K. to be "monstrous" is only an evidence of the care of the curate at the time, who, finding the old registers tattered and decaying, may have copied them for preservation, attesting them by his own signature and those of the churchwardens in accordance with the canon of 1603. But, nevertheless, the originals should also have been carefully kept.   W. D. MACRAY.
Ducklington Rectory, Oxon.

There can, of course, be only one answer to H. G. K. The copy to which he refers is useless alike for law and history. Why nothing is done for the protection of parish registers is a mystery, and now that the Church is every year admitting more and more uneducated men the danger is growing. I know a Cornish parish where the old registers lie about, part on the vestry floor and part in an open box, yet the vicar, instead of being suspended, has just received a good promotion. Not all the clergy are thus ignorant and selfish. In another Cornish parish where the old volumes are very worn the vicar has had a copy made, that you may search that first and only turn to the original when you know that what you seek is there. Two years' "hard" would be a mild punishment for H. G. K.'s vicar.   YGREC.

WIND FOLK-LORE (9ᵗʰ S. ix. 148). — On 25 March, 1901, a working man remarked to me, in the course of conversation about the cold wind then prevalent, "The sun crossed the line to-day, so we shall have these east winds for the next three months." So far as this district was concerned his prophecy was wonderfully correct. On two occasions the wind blew hard from the south-west for a day or two, but during the remainder of the time it came most persistently from the east or north-east.   F. R. R.
Betchworth, Surrey.

One of our local sayings is to the following effect: "Where the wind is on Martinmas Eve there it will prevail all through the winter." (See 8ᵗʰ S. xii. 88, 158, 212.)
JOHN T. PAGE.
West Haddon, Northamptonshire.

It is a common belief among Suffolk fishermen that if the wind is in the east at the vernal equinox it will remain in the east till the turn of the sun.   F. J. C.

The north-east winds that prevail in the spring about the time of the blowing of the blackthorn were known to our rural forefathers as the "blackthorn winds"; and in White's 'Selborne' (Warne's Chandos Classics, p. 429) we are told that the blackthorn usually blossoms while the cold north-east winds blow, so that the harsh, rugged weather obtaining at this season is called by the country people blackthorn winter.
J. HOLDEN MACMICHAEL.

The same superstition has been already recorded in 6ᵗʰ S. i. 254, but the query elicited no reply.
EVERARD HOME COLEMAN.
71, Brecknock Road.

HUXLEY AS REVIEWER (9ᵗʰ S. ix. 168).—In 1884 my friend Alexander Ireland published the twelfth edition of the 'Vestiges,' giving in a long introduction an account of the authorship. In an appendix to the introduction, p. xxix, he quotes from a letter, "The April number of the *Edinburgh Review* (1860) ......Prof. Huxley, of the School of Mines, has become an ardent apostle of this doctrine." This may give PROF. FRANCIS DARWIN a clue to the review inquired after.   CLIO.
Bolton.

WASSAILING THE APPLE-TREE (9ᵗʰ S. ix. 287). —It may be as well to note that "Wootton Basset, near Minehead," is evidently a mistake for Wootton Courtney, a village some four miles inland from that town. Wootton Basset is a well-known station on the Great Western Railway, six miles from Swindon.
SHERBORNE.

Miscellaneous.

NOTES ON BOOKS, &c.

Extracts from Account Rolls of the Abbey of Durham. Edited by Canon Fowler, D.C.L. 3 vols. (Durham, Andrews & Co.)

CANON FOWLER is a laborious and learned antiquary. He has already edited for the Surtees and other societies more manuscripts relating to the north of England than we have space to name. Ripon and Selby will be indebted to him for ever for the work he has accomplished in elucidating their monastic history, and his edition of the Latin life of St. Cuthbert, with the companion volume containing the Middle English life, is, as all students know, valuable for the knowledge supplied and the careful manner in which both are edited. We think we have read all that Canon Fowler has published, and must say without hesitation that the volumes before us are by far the most important contribution to history that he has yet produced. The labour expended in compiling the work would have overwhelmed most of us, however enthusiastic we may have felt ourselves to be. There were many hundreds of rolls before the editor, not a few of them in a mutilated and frail condition. Every line of all these had to be carefully pondered over before the extracts for publication could be copied for the press, for we need not say that, with such a vast mass of evidence to deal with, Canon Fowler found it impossible to give everything. We cannot but wish that the whole series could have been preserved in type, but neither the Surtees nor any other society could have ventured on the great outlay which would have been requisite. A time may, and we trust will soon, come when the minds of the rich have become sufficiently enlightened to appreciate the value of historical documents alike for ourselves and those who come after us, at home or far away. When that period arrives we shall doubtless have the Durham rolls printed in their entirety. For the present it is but a counsel of perfection to say that, whatever text is printed, every word of it should be given. The editor of these volumes has gone as near to this as was possible: he has given his readers everything that he regarded as of importance, including all the Middle English words which are blended with the text. Of these there are not a few, for when the mediæval accountants failed to remember or invent a suitable Latin term they never had any hesitation in diverging into the vernacular. This, as has been pointed out by Dr. Murray, has been "of immense value in enlarging our knowledge of the English vocabulary of the fourteenth, fifteenth, and early sixteenth centuries." The older school of antiquaries, when they printed ancient documents, rarely furnished their books with an index, and when they did so it was usually of a very imperfect character. Canon Fowler has avoided this error.

His index is copious and, so far as we have tested it, extremely accurate. But the great feature of the work is the glossary. We are constrained to say that it is at once the amplest and most scholar-like production of its kind with which we are acquainted. There does not seem to be an out-of-the-way word in the whole of the three volumes that has not been explained or, when that was found impossible, at least recorded, so that the student of the future, who may be so fortunate as to come upon it elsewhere, may have all the help which these rolls can supply. So eminently serviceable will this glossary be found, that we would suggest that it should be issued in a separate form, that students of language may have it at hand for instant reference.

Under 'Pestell' there is some curious information, as it witnesses to the survival of a word which has long dropped out of what people perversely call "good English." The monks of Durham were wont to speak of pigs' feet and shanks as pestles, though, we believe, the word does not survive in this sense in the local dialect of the bishopric. It still lives, however, in the West Riding of Yorkshire, and we are informed that in North Lincolnshire you may still hear people say to those who are over-eager in their work, and consequently always in a bustle, "Do it by degrees, as the cat ate the pestle." The intermingling of bones and flesh in the feet and legs of a pig is complex, and a cat has to spend a long time over a pestle, when one is given to her, before she has disentangled what she wants. There is an interesting note on 'Green Wax,' which was used for sealing certified extracts relating to fines. Canon Fowler finds that green wax was manufactured in the monastery. Was this wax tinted green, or was it wax in a fresh state that is meant by this name? We have read of green candles being used in the services of the Church; but there is another suggestion that ought not to be passed over in silence. It is probable that wax of a green colour may have been required for official purposes. The Bishop of Durham exercised princely authority, and it may well be that wax of this tint was used by his officials, as it was in the Exchequer of Westminster. We have somewhere seen the royal Court official who gave out these documents called "Master Green-wax" or the "Greenwax Man," but cannot remember where the entries are to be found. *Thill* or *thyll*, "the bottom of a coal-seam," is a dialect word at present in use in the north of England and in Scotland. The present form is *till*. It was used by Sir Walter Scott to indicate the hard, stony clay which in many places underlies the surface soil. Like many other words which have survived on the lips of the peasantry, it has been promoted from its low estate in recent days, and is now commonly used by geologists to indicate the glacial drift.

The introduction is very able. We wish it had been longer. It is in great part occupied by an account of the duties of the various officers of the monastery. We do not remember elsewhere anything relating to Benedictine officialdom at once so complete and so lucid. The reader must, however, bear in mind that he has not here an account of the establishment as it existed in an ordinary Benedictine monastery. Durham was one of the greatest and most wealthy houses of the order in the island, so that we must not suppose that a staff such as Canon Fowler describes was to be found in the ordinary Benedictine houses which studded the land. The Lord Prior, "besides being an eminent ecclesiastic, was a great county magnate, ranking with the Nevilles of Raby and Branspeth, the Percys of Alnwick, and the rest of the Northern nobles, while in Durham itself he kept a state only a little inferior to that of the great Prince Bishop himself."

One of the great charms of the book is that it treats of men of all ranks and conditions, from English and Scottish royalties down to Thomas Talpator, the molecatcher, who represented a state of life which we may assume, in all confidence, was a far older one than that of kings, as we know of them in times to which history reaches.

Lives and Legends of the Evangelists, Apostles, and other Early Saints. By Mrs. Arthur Bell. (Bell & Sons.)

In the great rush of new books that marked the beginning of the present season Mrs. Arthur Bell's work on the saints in Christian art was passed over, a fate it is far from deserving. It is, indeed, a valuable and an important contribution to our knowledge of the symbolism of Christian art. It also claims, with justice, to throw fresh light upon the evolution of popular belief. During years comparatively recent great additions have been made to the exact knowledge of symbolism by the publication of authoritative works such as the 'Caractéristiques des Saints' of Père Cahier, a splendid and almost exhaustive compilation which every subsequent writer on Christian imagery is bound to consult. Attention is drawn by Mrs. Bell to the manner in which legends, filched by the zeal of devotees from one saint in order to enrich the reputation of another, have been restored to their rightful owners. Another point now settled in orthodox fashion is the non-interference of Heaven to save the lives of those saints it had sustained unharmed through terrible torture. The sword as the emblem of civil power is recognized by Christ Himself, and the pagan right to inflict death is conceded, while that to inflict torture is denied. Celestial emissaries accordingly, who sustained the martyr's faith through manifold torments, were not allowed to interfere with the carrying out of a death sentence legally pronounced. If to the profane mind not quite logically conclusive, this theory is at least adequate to convince the firm believer in Christian legend. In dealing with the saints a chronological order is observed, the first chapter being assigned to St. John the Baptist and his parents, and the last five chapters to the various martyrs of the third century. The illustrations constitute naturally an eminently attractive feature. These are drawn from a great variety of sources. St. Sebastian, by Giovanni Antonio Bazzi, known as Il Sodoma, and half derisively as Il Mattaccio, from the Uffizi Gallery, constitutes an appropriate frontispiece. This is avowedly the best of the innumerable St. Sebastians in existence. Among the many masterpieces of Raphael, Pinturicchio, Lucas della Robbia, Perugino, Andrea del Sarto, Correggio, Rembrandt, Luini, and others, chiefly of the various Italian schools, appear some few works of the English Pre-Raphaelite school: the strangely treated but striking 'Nativity' of Sir E. Burne-Jones; the 'Christ in the Home of His Parents' of Sir J. E. Millais, once known, if we rightly recall, as 'The Carpenter's Shop'; Holman Hunt's 'Flight into Egypt'; and Madox Brown's

'Christ washing the Feet of Peter.' The selection of legends that is made by Mrs. Bell is the best easily conceivable, and the book is interesting as well as instructive and edifying. It is pleasant to know that a second volume from the same pen, dealing with the Fathers of the Church, the great hermits, and other early saints, is in preparation.

The History of the Parish of Hailsham, the Abbey of Otham, and the Priory of Michelham. By L. F. Salzmann. (Lewes, Farncombe & Co.)

In writing an account of the East Sussex parish of Hailsham and the two adjacent ecclesiastical edifices (now converted into farmhouses) of Otham Abbey and Michelham Priory Mr. Salzmann has been influenced by Macaulay, whose words he quotes as a motto upon his title-page, "It is unprofitable to study the history of a state in isolation; not wars and treaties only, but the internal vicissitudes of the commonwealth, form the real subject-matter of inquiry, and the smallest details, biographical, economical, or topographical, may have the greatest value." His own work illustrates forcibly the truth of his citation. Thanks to its numerous extracts from original documents, and to its ample indexes, it is of high antiquarian and the highest genealogical interest. Mr. Salzmann rightly describes as little known the part of Sussex with which he deals, and though we are familiar with places included in his survey, such as Battle and Pevensey, the spots with which he is specially concerned are unvisited by us. Of Michelham Priory, founded in 1229 by Gilbert de Aquila, the remains consist principally of the crypt, a room above with a massive stone fireplace, and a large parlour with Tudor windows. Otham, founded by Ralph de Dene in the reign of Henry II., became the nucleus of a monastery of Premonstratensian canons. From the names affixed to the foundation charter Mr. Salzmann assumes the date of foundation to have been about 1180. Fragments only of the stonework of the original building and the shrine of St. Lawrence, now or recently used as a stable, are all that are traceable. Prehistoric remains in Hailsham seem confined to a few flint implements and fragments of crockery, some of which may be Roman. The Amber Stone at Magham Down is said to have "abrogated [qy. arrogated] to itself the dignity of a Druidic monument," but its claims are unsupported by evidence. We could draw from the volume many illustrations of ancient customs, but with most of these the readers of 'N. & Q.' are familiar: such matters include the persecution of the Jews, the rebellion of Jack Cade, Puritan nomenclature, &c. It is for genealogical information that the book will be most prized, and the pedigree of the family of Medley, and the information concerning Aquila, Marmion, &c., have abiding value. In appendixes are supplied 'Marriages, 1558–1601,' and 'Consents of Marriage, 1653–1658.' The views of Hailsham and the buildings mentioned are an enhancement of the pleasure to be derived from the book.

The latest number of *Folk-Lore* affords very varied reading. 'More Folk-lore from the Hebrides' and 'Unlucky Children' are followed by Mrs. Gomme's summary of the antiquated medical beliefs of the Boers, recorded in the reports on the working of the refuge camps in South Africa; after which come an account of the rice harvest and other customs in Ceylon, and a Hindu story called 'The Tiger Prince.' At p. 94 there is also given an interesting description of the "vessel cup" custom as it still exists in East Yorkshire.

The *Antiquary* for April contains, with other papers, a brief notice, illustrated with a photogravure, of a rock-cut wine-press discovered on Mount Carmel. The Palestine mountain-sides are studded, it seems, with wine-fats as well as cisterns and rock-tombs; but wine-fats are now no longer hewn, since the owners of the existing vineyards are usually Mohammedans, who may not make wine out of their grapes.

Among the many diverse subjects discussed in recent issues of the *Intermédiaire* are fashion in the choice of baptismal names, the use of the same churches by Catholics and Protestants, and the wife of Heinrich Heine, "Mathilde," whose real name was Crescence Eugénie Mirat.

Under the title 'Rariora' Mr. John Eliot Hodgkin, F.S.A., promises a series of notes on some of the printed books (incunabula, &c.), manuscripts, broadsides, engravings, historical documents, coins, medals, &c., in his remarkable collection. The work, which is of singular interest, may be subscribed for at Messrs. Sampson Low, Marston & Co.'s It will appear next month in artistic form, with many hundreds of illustrations, coloured and other, and is a work to be prized by collectors.

Notices to Correspondents.

We must call special attention to the following notices:—

On all communications must be written the name and address of the sender, not necessarily for publication, but as a guarantee of good faith.

We cannot undertake to answer queries privately.

To secure insertion of communications correspondents must observe the following rules. Let each note, query, or reply be written on a separate slip of paper, with the signature of the writer and such address as he wishes to appear. When answering queries, or making notes with regard to previous entries in the paper, contributors are requested to put in parentheses, immediately after the exact heading, the series, volume, and page or pages to which they refer. Correspondents who repeat queries are requested to head the second communication "Duplicate."

G. A. M. ("Mostly fools").—'Latter-Day Pamphlets,' No. 5, 'Stump Orator,' about half a dozen paragraphs from the end.

Edith Mary Shaw, Jamaica ("Value of Coin"). —We cannot reproduce your design.

P.—We cannot answer such queries. Procure a book on the point.

NOTICE.

Editorial communications should be addressed to "The Editor of 'Notes and Queries'"—Advertisements and Business Letters to "The Publisher"—at the Office, Bream's Buildings, Chancery Lane, E.C.

We beg leave to state that we decline to return communications which, for any reason, we do not print; and to this rule we can make no exception.

LONDON, SATURDAY, MAY 3, 1902.

CONTENTS. — No. 227.

Notes.

RICHARD HAINES.

As the 'Dictionary of National Biography' has not found room for the above-named Sussex worthy, who does not deserve to be entirely forgotten, and as corrections and additions to that useful work are admitted into your columns, may I crave room to record in them the main facts of his life?

Richard Haines was born at Sullington, Sussex, of yeoman stock, in 1633, his father being Gregory Haine (or Heine, later Heines) and his mother Elizabeth Pollard (probably *née* Bennett). In 1656 he built a farmhouse, which is still standing, called West Wantley, near Sullington. In the same year he appears to have joined the Baptists, being a member of a congregation over which the well-known Matthew Caffyn, of Southwater, near Horsham, presided as minister or "apostle." Some time subsequently Richard Haines went on a visit to the Netherlands, where he was much impressed by the Dutch administration of their poor laws in their Spin Houses and Rasp Houses (also described by John Evelyn), in which criminals and paupers were boarded and obliged to work for the benefit of the State. Later on, as we shall see, he tried to introduce similar institutions into England.

In 1673 Richard Haines, who was a farmer by occupation, took out a patent for cleansing the seed of nonsuch, a sort of yellow clover. Matthew Caffyn, who appears to have been jealous of the influence enjoyed by his fellow Baptist among "Great Persons" (as he calls them), took occasion to quarrel with him about this patent as a worldly, self-seeking thing, and excommunicated him. Richard Haines then wrote an apologia, called 'New Lords, New Laws,' in 1674, of which only one copy exists, and that is in the Bodleian. Caffyn answered with a tract called 'Envy's Bitterness' (also a single copy in the Bodleian). Haines replied in 1675 with a pamphlet called 'A Protestation against Usurpation,' of which I have been unable to discover a single copy, and which I would give a great deal to see. To this Caffyn replied with 'A Raging Wave foaming out its own Shame' (one copy in the Bodleian). Haines appealed from one Baptist council to another, carrying his case on for eight years, till he forced Caffyn to cancel the excommunication. The line he took was that Caffyn was infringing the prerogative of the king by excommunicating a loyal subject only because he had done what any citizen had a right to do.

His other books were as follows: 'The Prevention of Poverty,' 1674 ; ' Proposals for building in every County a Working Almshouse or Hospital,' 1677 ; 'Provision for the Poor,' 1678 ; 'A Model of Government,' 1678 (a single copy in the British Museum) ; 'A Method of Government for Public Working Almshouses,' 1679 ; 'A Breviat of Proposals for restoring the Woollen Manufacture ' (one copy in the British Museum), 1679 ; 'England's Weal and Prosperity Proposed,' 1681. The first of these was apparently written before the visit to the Netherlands. Haines wished to deal with the pauper question and the question of England's trade in one scheme, especially in connexion with the linen and woollen trades.

His schemes obtained much support, and were favoured by the king, who granted him a personal audience. A Bill was brought into Parliament, and would certainly have passed but for untoward circumstances, based chiefly on the political state of the kingdom. The whole scheme was well devised and quite feasible, and, had it passed, would have had far-reaching effects.

Richard Haines then went back to his farming and wrote his last book, 'Aphorisms upon making Cyder Royal,' 1684, with supplement to same, of which there is a single copy in the Guildhall Library. In it he made an attempt to substitute a home-grown spirit for foreign spirits, and he took out a patent for making this cyder spirit.

But death cut short his schemes, and he died in London, 29 May, 1685. Among his friends or acquaintances were the Rev. John Beale, D.D , one of his Majesty's Chaplains ; the Right Hon. Viscount Brouncker, President of the Royal Society ; Thomas Firmin, a well-known philanthropist ; Henry Goreing, Esq. ; Herbert Stapley, Esq. ; Thomas Peckham, Gent. ; and Richard Dereham, Esq.

Whatever information any reader of ' N. & Q.' can give me about Richard Haines or his descendants will be most gratefully acknowledged. His grandson Gregory, my own great-great-great-grandfather, married a South Carolina lady, Alice Hooke, in 1719.

REGINALD HAINES.

Uppingham.

SHERIFFS OF STAFFORDSHIRE, 1699-1730.

The following list is written on the fly-leaves of a copy of ' Nicholas Machiavel's Prince,' translated out of Italian into English, by E(dward) D(acres), London, 1640, 12mo. It was written by Oswald Mosley, who bought the book in London, 1 June, 1715, for five shillings. The note of the assizes in 1714-15 belongs to the year in which Mr. Mosley himself was sheriff.

SHERIFFS OF STAFFORDSHIRE.

1699. Oswald Mosley, of H[all (?)] Court, Rolleston.
1700. Benjamin Jolley.
1701. Thomas Nabbs.
1702. John Babington.
1703. Thomas Okeover.
1704. Mathew Ducy Morton.
1705. Thomas Crompton.
1706. William Trafford.
1707. James Wood.
1708. John Jervis.
1709. Edmond Arblaster.
1710. Walter Mosley of Mer—— (?)
1711. Legh Broke.
1712. Sʳ Edward Litleton, Barᵗ.
1713. Henry Gray.
1714. Oswald Mosley of Rolleston.
1715. Thomas, son of George Birch of Harborne.
1716. John Turton of Alrewas.
1717. Thomas Whitby of Heywood.
1718. Charles Chadwick.
1719. Edward Browne of Caverswall, Esqʳ.
1720.   Sneyd of Keel, Esqʳ.
1721. Humphry Hodgets, Esqʳ.
The three for 1715. Geor. Burge [?], Mʳ Amphlet, Mʳ Weston Bayley.
The three for 1716. John Craddock, Es., Henry Arden, Es., Joseph Amphlet, Es.
John Craddock, of Audley, Esq., is appointed Sheriffe—Excused, and John Turton of Alrewas appointed Sheriffe.

The three for 1717. Joseph Amphlet, John Crew, Weston Bayley.
The three for 1718. Yᵉ same.
The three for 1721. Thomas Jolliffe, Es. Wᵐ Robins, Es., Hum. Hodgets, Es., both of Stafford.
1722. Henry Goreing, Esq.
1723. Zachary Babington, Esq.
1724. Richard Scot, Esq.
1725. Richard Townshend, Esq.
1726. Fowke Hussey, Esq.
1727. Edward Wilson of Cannock, Esq.
1728. Samuel Newton, Esq.
1729. Hen. Arden, Esq.
1730.   Robins.
1714/5. Yᵉ Judges yᵗ came Oxf. Circuit: Lent Assises: Blencow, Bury. Summer Assises : Blencow, Dormer.
Mʳ Browne, Mʳ Holbock, Mʳ Meers, of Lᵈ Radnor's Office [?] next door to a picture shop in Pell Mell near Charing Cross.
Mʳ Beresford, Judg Dormer's Marshall.

W. C. B.

SHAKESPEARIANA.

'Antony and Cleopatra,' II. ii. 211-16 (9ᵗʰ S. ix. 222).—Why go so far as the " hawse-holes " for " eyes "? " Eye " is the common name for a loop of cord or rope, especially " the circular loop of a shroud or stay " (Admiral Smyth), as in R. Scot, ' Discov. Witchcr.' (1584), xiii. xxix. 277, " Put the eie of the one [cord] into the eie or bowt of the other " (' N.E.D.'). It serves also for the " metal ring for holding a rod or bolt, or for a rope, &c., to pass through " (' N.E.D.'). These seem more likely uses during the navigation of a ship than hawse-holes, which are only used when she is at anchor.

JULIAN MARSHALL.

"Their bends, adornings." Here is a pun, just as in ' Hamlet,' " Take his gibes for graces," punning on " gyves." The bends are bows or curtsies, as in Chaucer's " shippes hoppesteres," they " curvetted." Shakespere contrasts " eyes " and " bends," the latter nautically from the verb " to bind." The sailor's " bends " are tied knots.

ABSENS.

' Hamlet,' I. i. 115 sq. (9ᵗʰ S. viii. 237, 480).—

The graves stood tenantless, and the sheeted dead
Did squeak and gibber in the Roman streets ;

As, stars with trains of fire and dews of blood,
Disasters in the sun, &c.

Thus the passage in question stands in most editions, the asterisks representing a line or lines assumed to be lost. I do not think, however, that there is sufficient reason for this assumption, because a highly poetical reading can be had with very little alteration of the text. Thus: Dele the asterisks. Then, instead of " As, stars " in the next line read

Asters. Dele the comma at the end of the line, and for "Disasters," beginning line 118, read *Disaster'd.* The whole passage will now appear as follows :—

> The graves stood tenantless, and the sheeted dead
> Did squeak and gibber in the Roman streets ;
> *Asters* with trains of fire and dews of blood
> *Disaster'd* in the sun ; and the moist star
> Upon whose influence Neptune's empire stands
> Was sick almost to doomsday with eclipse.

That is (lines 117–18), meteors or shooting stars (*stellæ trajectionis*), or, it may be, comets, unstarred themselves, or became absorbed in the sun, "disorbed," as Troilus has it ('Troilus and Cressida,' II. ii. 46).

I think the poet adopted the Greek ἀστὴρ to differentiate from ordinary stars the portentous appearances of which Horatio speaks, and with a view to the quaint use of the word "disaster" in its primary meaning.

Though Shakespeare does not often use Greek words, yet he does sometimes, and I can imagine him listening to a discussion at the "Mermaid," between his friends Jonson and Bacon, concerning Homer's use of the word "aster," where the flight of Here is compared to that of a meteor "with trains of fire," flung as a portent by Zeus the crafty ('Iliad,' iv. 75–7).　　J. E. Smith.

In his interesting account of the comets which appeared in the reign of Justinian, and were always thought to be the harbingers of war and calamity, Gibbon, speaking of one comet, says that after its appearance there ensued a remarkable paleness of the sun. It is also said that the sun looked pale during the year that followed the assassination of Julius Cæsar ; and at that time a comet appeared which was supposed to be the soul of the dead hero. This will explain the speech of Horatio, who, after referring to the comets, says that "disasters dimmed the sun." For I believe that Capell's alteration of *in* to *dimmed* is right. As has been noticed, Shakespeare took some of the images in the speech of Horatio from Ovid ; and the verse of Homer which I quoted may have suggested to Ovid the following :—

> Sæpe inter nimbos guttæ cecidere cruentæ.
> 'Metamorphoses,' xv. 788.

It is, however, said that there was actually a rain of blood at the time of Cæsar's death. The other passage of Homer which I could not find before, and in which it is said that Zeus rained blood in order to show that he meant mischief, is in the eleventh book of the 'Iliad,' lines 53–5. With regard to the repetition of the word *star*, I would say that it is better to repeat the right word than to change it to one that is wrong or weak.

I have observed tautology in other great writers. I find the word γέρας three times in six lines in the first book of the 'Iliad.'　　E. Yardley.

'Macbeth,' I. iv. 35 (6th S. xi. 441).—If one dwells on "sons," as one would naturally do in speaking, the line does not appear defective :—

> In dróps/ of sór/row.　Só/ns, kíns/men, thánes/.
> 　　　　　　　　E. Merton Dey.

St. Louis.

'Measure for Measure,' IV. iii. 102–3.—

> At the consecrated Fount,
> A League below the Citie.

Dr. W. Aldis Wright has, in his note on 'Coriolanus,' I. x. 31 (Clarendon Press edition), remarked that in some cases of local colouring Shakespeare had probably London in his mind. It may, therefore, be not without interest to observe that both the Theatre and the Curtain (I quote from Halliwell's 'Illustrations of the Life of Shakespeare,' part i. p. 9),

"were situate in the parish of Shoreditch, in the fields of the Liberty of Halliwell, in which locality, if the Davenant tradition is in the slightest degree to be trusted, Shakespeare must have commenced his metropolitan career. This Liberty, at a later period termed Holywell, derived its name from a sacred (A.-S. *halig*) well or fountain which took its rise in the marshy grounds situated to the west of the high street leading from Norton Folgate to Shoreditch Church—*mora in qua fons qui dicitur Halliwelle oritur*, charter of A.D. 1189, printed in Dugdale's 'Monasticon Anglicanum,' ed. 1682, p. 531."

So, too, Halliwell Priory may also have suggested the "moated-Grange" of the dejected Mariana's retirement, as well as the religious house where the duke donned the friar's habit.　　Alfred E. Thiselton.

'Macbeth,' I. ii. 21.—

> Which ne'er shook hands, nor bade farewell to him.

While something might be said for "fortune" as the antecedent of "which"—although disdained by Macbeth, who fought like valour's minion, fortune smiled on Macdonwald's quarrel, and ne'er shook hands nor bade farewell to him until his death, when his supporters fled—I believe that "which" refers to "brandish'd steel," and that we are to understand from the line in question that the blows were continuous until Macdonwald fell.　　E. Merton Dey.

St. Louis.

'Macbeth,' I. v. 23–6.—Seymour says, "The difficulty here arises from the cumulative conjunction, which leads us to expect new matter, whereas that which follows is only amplification." This is not quite true. The first " that " represents the end, and the second the means to that end. Macbeth would have a prize, and as that prize entails a certain deed, he would have the deed done without involving his own guilt — would wrongly win, and yet escape the responsibility. The meaning of lines 25 and 26 would seem to be :—

And (thou'ldst have) that (done) which rather thou dost fear to do
Than wishest should be *undone*.

E. Merton Dey.
St. Louis.

Thomas à Becket and the Cathedral Church of Sigüenza.—It is a notable fact that Spain was one of the first of the continental monarchies to venerate St. Thomas of Canterbury as a martyr of the Catholic Church. The explanation is simple. The Queen of Castille at that time was the Princess Leonora, daughter of the Norman king of England. It is probable that she took with her to Spain some Anglo-Norman chaplains, and succeeded in placing them on the episcopal thrones of the Spanish Church, and, by the irony of history, it is also to be noted that it was a Spanish princess who was the innocent occasion of the suppression, in the Anglican Church, of the tomb and the commemoration liturgical of the aforesaid Primate of All England. It can be proved that St. Thomas à Becket enjoyed his popularity in Spain within a very few years of his death—in Toledo, Salamanca, Zamora, Sigüenza, &c. Don Carlos Rodriguez Tierno—who has been a canon of the Cathedral Church of Sigüenza since 9 April, 1862, and is now, by order of Pope Leo XIII., whom all the world respects, precentor (*chantre*) of that capitular corporation—has this day placed before me some documents concerning the engrafting upon Spanish Christianity of English ecclesiasticism. Most of them he had already communicated to me in May, 1897, when I was examining the remains of Byzantine (in English Norman) architecture in this Iberian city. In the chapel of St. Catherine (Santa Catalina), formerly called "de Santo Tomás Martir," in this cathedral, there is an inscription, which is quite recent, though in mediæval letters, "Hic est inclusa Joscelini præsulis vlna"—*i e.*, "Herein is enclosed the elbow of the Prelate Joscelin." Don Carlos was present when that reliquary was opened, and believes the bone which the inscription commemorates to be there. It was left where it was found. He infers from all his studies in the antiquities of Sigüenza that the said

bishop died abroad as an ambassador, probably in Germany, and that he sent his right arm to bless *post mortem* his faithful disciples of Seguntium. Don Carlos has given, in his unpublished book entitled ' Resumen de varias Correcciones y Advertencias, que en vista de los Documentos de los Archivos de la Santa Yglesia de Sigüenza deben hacerse al Cathalato [*sic*] Seguntino,' his reasons for believing that Bishop Joscelin, who ruled the see of Sigüenza from 1168 till 1179 A.D., was a Norman or English priest. He refers me to the printed books 'Santa Librada Virgen y Mártir, Patrona de la Santa Iglesia, Ciudad y Obispado de Sigüenza, por el Doctor Don Diego Eugenio Gonzalez Chantos y Ullauri' (Madrid, 1806), and 'La Catedral de Sigüenza, erigida en el Siglo XII.......por D. Manuel Pérez-Villamil' (Madrid, 1899), in which there are some things derived from himself and some faulty copies of inscriptions, &c. (see pp. 336-7 for the subject of these notes). He has shown me in the library of his cathedral—of which he is about to publish a catalogue and which contains many precious manuscripts and incunables — four volumes in parchment which belonged to Bishop Rodrigo, who was consecrated Bishop of Sigüenza in 1182, and presented many books to the library of his church. In one of these there is a minute account of the life and last moments of St. Thomas à Becket. It occupies twenty-three leaves of parchment, of small folio size, beautifully written in very large and very black letters, with numerous abbreviations. This document, of the end of the twelfth century, begins thus : "Ad laudem beatissimi Martiris Thome : et fidelium edificationem opus impar scientie mee aggredior"; and ends as follows : "Et aperte cognoscent quod non sit Ecclesia sed scismaticorum conventicula quam Martir iste respuebat; et infidelitas [*sic*] aliud sentire de Deo quam ipse prædicabat." It fixes the date of the death of St. Thomas as "quarto Kalendas Januarii, anno ab Incarnatione Domini MᵒCᵒLXXᵒ, primo die post sollempnitatem Innocentium." St. Thomas had his altar here already in 1192. The surname of Bishop Joscelin appears to have been Adelida. Can any information about him be produced from documents written in England in the twelfth century ? St. Thomas was canonized while this prelate ruled in Sigüenza, and an altar was erected in his memory in the Cathedral of Toledo while D. Cerebruno, who preceded Joscelin as Bishop of Sigüenza, was Primate of all the Spains.

Edward Spencer Dodgson.

"RUBBER."—*Rubber*, of course, is directly derived from the verb *rub*, a Gaelic word of the same meaning as the English, but the origin of the particular application of this old term to a set of games, most generally of whist, has never been satisfactorily explained. Dictionaries appear to be silent upon this particular point. The question has been put several times in 'N. & Q.,' the conclusion arrived at being that the term reached whist through the game of bowls, one explanation being the *rubbing* or contact of the balls. I suggest a simpler and more direct source. Before counters and markers came into general use, the score or tally of games was kept by the players by chalk marks upon the table, especially in taverns, &c., where chalk was used for other scores. When the contest of games was ended and settled for, the "chalks" were *rubbed* out (like the cleaning of a slate) to make room for a fresh set of marks. Hence the term *rub* or *rubber* being applied to the final act of the contest, the obliteration of the scores; hence its application to the ending or deciding game, when the time for that action arose; hence its application to the whole contest. This, I have little doubt, is the true origin of the term, which was as likely put into practice originally for card and other games as for bowls. In Cotton's 'Compleat Gamester' (1674) there will be found several references to the scoring of card games by means of chalk marks. J. S. McTEAR.

EPITAPH ON AN ATTORNEY.—We are all familiar with the epitaph composed upon Frederick, Prince of Wales, the father of George III. I was, therefore, surprised to find that it was after all only an adaptation. Thus I have recently met with the following (I preserve the spelling):—

ON EDW. HUBLAN, A CORNISH ATTORNEY.

I Faith Ned,
I'm glad thou 'rt dead,
But had it been another,
I could a wisht had been thy Brother;
And for the good of the Nation,
Thy whole generation;
But seeing thou 'rt dead
There's no more to be said.

'Sepulchrorum Inscriptiones; or, a Curious Collection of above 900 of the most Remarkable Epitaphs,' &c., vol. i. p. 35. Westminster, 1727.
OXONIENSIS.

[The similar lines quoted by GNOMON at 9th S. viii. 307 are of earlier date.]

HOT CRESCENT BUNS.—Students of the origin of Easter customs, signs, and symbols are frequently confronted with parallel sources connected with pagan rites or the ceremonies of non-Christian religious systems. It is therefore interesting to note a contra evolution in the adaptation of the hot cross bun to suit the susceptibilities of the large Mohammedan colony located in the East-End of London, by the substitution of the crescent for the cross. *Lloyd's Weekly Newspaper*, dated 30 March, is responsible for the following:—

"An East-End baker, finding that certain of his Mahommedan customers objected to the hot cross bun by reason of religious scruples, had on Good Friday a part of his stock stamped with the Prophet's crescent. The buns were promptly bought up by Moslem patrons."
G. YARROW BALDOCK.
South Hackney.

THE ORIGIN OF SWEENY TODD. (See 9th S. vii. 508; viii. 131, 168, 273, 348, 411, 512.)—Doubts existing in the mind of some correspondents as to the origin of Sweeny Todd, I have made extensive research to discover the fundamental basis, and so far succeeded. The story of Sweeny Todd was first imported from France in 1823 and appeared in a monthly publication, the *Tell-Tale*, published by Henry Fisher, printer of T. Camden's 'Imperial History of England' (1824). It was entitled 'A Terrific Story of the Rue de la Harpe, Paris,' and described the cruel murder and mutilation of a country gentleman in the *boutique* of a fiend-like Figaro, who, after appropriating a casket of pearls he carried, disposed of the corpse to his paramour in crime, a pie-maker, whose patties were the rage of Parisian society. The subsequent discovery of the remains, as well as of the skeletons and skulls of nearly three hundred human beings who had become victims to these monsters, diffused disgust and dismay through the French metropolis. Their execution and confession, with the edict prohibiting the erection of any habitations in future upon the accursed spot, duly detailed in Fouché's 'Archives of the Police,' fix the period of the crime in 1800. When Edward Lloyd started his sensational penny library, Thomas Prest, the author of 'Tom Gallant; or, the Life of a Sailor, Ashore and Afloat,' and many other contributions to fiction of that class, embodied the Gallic details of the Rue de la Harpe, in the Faubourg St. Marcelle, in an exciting tale, changing the French characters into English, and introducing several fresh individuals. The action was transferred from the Rue de la Harpe to near St. Dunstan's Church, Fleet Street, and the pie-shop to Bell Yard, Temple Bar. It was issued by Lloyd in 1840. The first dramatic version was in two acts and eight scenes, adapted from Prest's thrilling narrative of 'Sweeny Todd, the Barber of Fleet Street, and the String of Pearls,' by George Dibdin Pitt, and produced by Samuel Lane at the Britannia Saloon, Hoxton, in 1842. Mark Howard was the fiendish Figaro ; Mrs. Atkinson (mother of the celebrated Sadler's Wells actress) the pie-maker and paramour of Todd — Maria Lovett (who is shot by Sweeny, instead of being brought to the scaffold as in the French narrative) ; Charles Pitt (afterwards manager of the Sheffield Theatre) enacted the Peckham madhouse keeper Jonas Fogg ; Joseph Reynolds (an old favourite at the Brit.) was the Indian officer Col. Jeffrey; and Sam Sawford was the victim (Mark Ingestrie). Frederick Hazleton brought out a later edition of 'Sweeny Todd' in three acts at the old Victoria Theatre, George Yates taking the part of the barber fiend, and making it very popular among the patrons of fourth-rate playhouses.

HENRY C. PORTER.
14, Livingstone Road, West Brighton.

'MRS. CARNAC,' BY SIR JOSHUA REYNOLDS. —Elizabeth Catherine, daughter of Thomas Rivett, Esq., M.P. for Derby, by Anna Maria his wife, daughter of the Rev. Peter Sibley, was baptized at All Saints' Church, Derby, 8 April, 1751. She married in London, 24 July, 1769, as his second wife, Brigadier-General John Carnac, Commander-in-Chief of the Forces in Bengal, and thereafter second in Council at Bombay, who distinguished himself by the important victory gained over Shah Alum, Emperor of Delhi (the Great Mogul), and a French contingent, commanded by M. Law, who, with fifteen officers and fifty of his men, was taken prisoner near Patna, on 15 January, 1761. General Carnac died 29 November, 1800, at Mangalore (Malabar coast), where he was buried, aged eighty-four years. Mrs. Carnac died at Broach, Bombay, on 18 January, 1780, aged twenty-eight years, and was buried in Bombay. Monumental inscription to the memory of General and Mrs. Carnac in St. Thomas's Cathedral, Bombay. Vide Burke's 'Baronetage,' s.n. 'Rivett-Carnac.'

LIONEL A. V. SCHANK.

MALLET USED BY CHRISTOPHER WREN.— The Standard of the 23rd of April states that at the laying of the foundation stone of the new mission church of the Good Shepherd, Small Heath, Birmingham, which took place on the previous day with full Masonic ritual, Lord Leigh, the Provincial Grand Master of Warwickshire, made use of the mallet known as the Wren gavel, which was employed by Sir Christopher Wren at the laying of the foundation stone of St. Paul's Cathedral in 1675.

N. S. S.

JEWISH MAY MEETINGS.—On the 11th of May the Jewish community will for the first time associate itself with the May meetings customs. The Daily News of April 21st states that "the conference will be unique in the annals of English Jews......All the synagogues in the United Kingdom have been invited to the first of these forgatherings, which will be held in London on the 11th of May next." Sir Samuel Montagu is to preside. The object of the conference is to unite London and provincial Jews in the common work of the community. One of the very first tasks to which the conference will address itself will be the dispersion (so far as practicable) of the seething Ghettoes in the East-End of London and several provincial towns. It is proposed to hold the conference every year in a different town, and it will be known as the "Jewish Congregational League."

A. N. Q.

ALLEGED ECLIPSE AT THE DEATH OF QUEEN ANNE. — In Mr. Sichel's recent work on 'Bolingbroke and his Times' (which I am glad to learn is to be supplemented by a second volume on the later part of his strange career) we read at p. 497, where the author is speaking of the death of Queen Anne, which occurred on 1 August, Old Style (= 12 by N.S.), 1714, that "it was the day, as the superstitious noted, of an eclipse of the sun."

Now the moon was new that year on 30 July, so that there could have been no eclipse on 1 August ; as a matter of fact, the single eclipse of the sun that year was in December, only a small partial one and not visible anywhere in Europe. Mr. Sichel cites as his authority a letter from Swift to Pope, which is to be found in Swift's 'Works,' second edition, vol. xvi. p. 229. The letter in question is dated 28 June, 1715, and contains the passage :—

"Upon the whole, you may truly attribute my silence to the eclipse, but it was that eclipse which happened on the 1st of August."

Probably in the second clause of this sentence the word "eclipse" is used metaphorically, and is intended to refer to the queen's death itself, which produced so great a change that "Queen Anne is dead" passed into a proverb, which is still occasionally used. There was a total eclipse of the sun, the central line of which passed over England, on 22 April, 1715, and possibly Swift refers to this in the first clause of the above letter, as, of course, it made a great sensation in this country about two months before the letter was written.

Before closing my note it occurred to me to consult Mr. Elwin's edition of Pope's works. There I find (vol. vii. p. 10) the same letter from Swift, with a foot-note by the editor taking the view which I have just expressed, that the second "eclipse" is not meant for an astronomical event, but for the queen's death.   W. T. LYNN.
Blackheath.

Queries.

WE must request correspondents desiring information on family matters of only private interest to affix their names and addresses to their queries, in order that the answers may be addressed to them direct.

STRIPES ON SAILORS' COLLARS. — Is there authority for the statement that the three stripes on the collars of sailors in the Royal Navy are so placed in honour of the three victories Nile, Copenhagen, and Trafalgar, and that the black tie is in perpetual memory of Nelson? Has the collar its origin in the idea of protection against the friction of the pigtail?   ALBERT HARTSHORNE.

NAPOLEON'S FIRST MARRIAGE. — What is the most trustworthy account of the romance of Napoleon's first marriage?   L. PAGE.
Turret House, Felpham, Sussex.

DICKENSIANA: 'DAVID COPPERFIELD.' — "Long Ned Beadwood."—In chap. xxii. Miss Mowcher says, "It won't do to be like long Ned Beadwood, when they took him to church 'to marry him to somebody,' as he says, and left the bride behind." Who was Ned Beadwood? The allusion is probably to some old ballad.
'Little Tafflin' (chap. xxviii.) —This is the title of one of Mrs. Micawber's favourite songs. I should be glad to know the name of composer, &c., and date.   F. G. KITTON.
St. Albans.

KING AND PEYTON DUEL. — Where shall I find accounts of the duel in 1698 between Thomas King, Esq., of Thurlow, co. Suffolk (who married Elizabeth Cordell, the daughter of Sir John Cordell, Bart.), and Sir Sewster Peyton. Bart., of Peyton Hall, Boxford, in which the former was killed? Where was he buried?   C. MASON.
29, Emperor's Gate, S.W.

ST. OMER CONVENT, EIGHTEENTH CENTURY.—Would it be possible to get a list of the English and Scotch girls who were in a convent at St. Omer for their education in the first years of the eighteenth century? Perhaps the *Intermédiaire* might help.
                            CONSTANCE RUSSELL.
Swallowfield, Reading.

STROHLING, A SINGER.—Can any one give me particulars of a Madame Stroehling, or Strohling, who appeared in London as a singer about 1830 or a little later? Her husband was a portrait painter, a Russian or a Pole, I think.   E. ECKERSLEY.

'THE CARRION CROW.'—Can you kindly tell me where I can find 'The Carrion Crow'? I think it is a nonsense verse, but am not sure.   DENVIL.

ROBERT DAVIS'S DIVING ENGINE.—In the fifth volume of the Report of the Historical Manuscripts Commission on the papers belonging to the Duke of Portland at Welbeck Abbey, p. 350, there is a letter from Robert Davis, dated Leith, 20 October, 1713, to the Earl of Oxford, stating that the writer had invented a diving engine. The earl was at that time the holder of a patent for recovering plate lost in ships wrecked on the coast of America, and the inventor thinks that his machine may be useful. The letter is accompanied by a certificate dated 20 September, 1704, signed by "inhabitants of the Lizzard parish," Cornwall, setting forth that they saw Davis go several times under the water in his engine. Is anything known of Robert Davis or of the construction of his engine?
                                    R. B. P.

RICHARD SMITH AND HIS LIBRARY.—Dibdin, in his 'Bibliomania,' mentions a copy of Richard Smith's catalogue, 1682, with prices and purchasers' names added He refers to it as sold in the Lort sale. I should be glad to know where this or any other copies with the purchasers' names may be found. I should also like to know the present whereabouts of Richard Smith's own manuscript catalogue, with notes and observations, which was in Thomas Thorpe's 'Catalogue of Manuscripts,' 1836, No. 104.   E. GORDON DUFF.
Prince's Park, Liverpool.

INGLIS MSS. AT OXFORD.—Will some Oxford correspondent kindly give me some notes as to Esther Inglis's MSS. in the Bodleian; and also as to her copy of the Psalms in the library of Christ Church?
                          J. G. WALLACE-JAMES.
Haddington.

CURIOUS WORD-COINAGES.—(1) *Retiral.*—Is this a word recognized by Dr. Murray and the 'N.E.D.'? I made a note of it as having been used instead of "retirement" in a number of *Black and White* for June, 1895 (the date of the particular number I have lost). The writer apparently thought that if "retire" was the equivalent of "withdraw," the proper correspondent to "withdrawal" was "retiral." But then one is of Latin-French and the other of Saxon origin.

(2) *Cavilists.*—This word is used instead of *cavillers* in a book called "Ceylon and the Cingalese, by H. C. Sirr, M.A., late Deputy Queen's Advocate of the Northern Circuit," published in 1850 The graduate and learned author says: "*Cavilists* have recently endeavoured," &c. But where did he find this word? or has Dr. Murray found it?

J. P. LEWIS

[Dr. Murray has not found *cavillist*. *Retiral* is not yet reached by the 'H.E.D.,' but is in Annandale's four-volume Ogilvie, published 1882.]

OLD SPOONS. — Can any of your readers give me information as to the mark on some old silver (?) spoons in my possession, which belonged to an ancestor living in 1770? They are stamped with "J. S.," and on the teaspoons there is a double impression of what appears to be a bell. This is rather worn, but is of a rounded triangular form. On the gravy spoon it is repeated three times.

LOUISA WALLACE-JAMES.

Haddington, N.B.

CHURCH FURNITURE. — An explanation is desired of the words indicated below, occurring in an inventory of St. Peter's Church, Barnstaple, dated 1564 (from a press cutting):—

"Itm. a chis apel [chasuble] and a *tynobd* to the same."

"Itm. iiii *prosynalles*, iii manuettes," &c.

"Itm. a *nomellet* set forthe by the bishop of London [? homily]."

"Itm. a *legen* booke, an old aulter cloth of bokram in *pains* [?]."

"Itm. a per of *postefes*, an oil vat of coppar."

H. P. L.

INDEX-MAKING.—What are the books (in English) that are most desirable to be indexed? Some years ago the Index Society put out a list which included Hacket's 'Life of Archbishop Williams' (folio, 1693). I have done that work and several others, and am now ready for another. I find index-making a very pleasant occupation for

A MAN OF LEISURE

"AWAY WITH."—Mr. George Meredith, usually so carefully observant of fine distinctions, whether in language or in thought, seems to have slipped for once in his use of the phrase "away with" in 'Diana of the Crossways,' chap. i. In recounting some of the wise and witty sayings of his heroine the author tells us, "But she would have us away with sentimentalism." The context shows plainly enough that the meaning is, she would have us put it away or have nothing to do with it. Can "away with" in this sense be properly used in any other mood than the imperative? The now nearly obsolete signification of "tolerate," "put up with," is familiar from its use in the Bible and Shakespeare. "She never could away with me," says Justice Shallow, and Falstaff rejoins, "Never, never; she would always say she could not abide Master Shallow" ('2 Henry IV.,' III. ii.).

R. BRUCE BOSWELL.

HOUNDSDITCH.—Anthony Munday, in his additions to Stow ('Survey of London'), speaks very indignantly of the usurers, "a base kind of vermin," who then inhabited Houndsditch. Again, in Lupton's 'London and the Country Carbonadoed' (1632), and in one of the satires in 'The Letting of Humour's Blood in the Head-Veine' (1611), the extortions practised by the brokers are denounced. None of these authorities gives any indication of the nationality or religion of these moneylenders, but the inference is obvious. Can any reader confirm this? It is common knowledge that the street has retained this characteristic as a mart of brokers, "sellers of olde apparell and such like," from the early sixteenth century until the present day without interruption. ALECK ABRAHAMS.

39, Hillmarton Road, N.

PETER ELLERS was admitted to Westminster School in 1771. Any information concerning him is wanted. G. F. R. B.

CORONATION ITEM: PRINTERS WANTED.—A friend has shown me a coloured print of a coronation thus headed :—

"A Perspective of Westminster Abbey from the High Altar to the West End, shewing the manner of His Majestie's Crowning. Also the manner of disposing, seating and placing several of the Persons who came in the Proceeding, &c. Exactly taken from Sandford. Printed for Bowles & Carver and R. Wilkinson." No date attached.

Can any one inform me when these printers flourished? A. M. D.

WESTERHAM QUAKERS.—In the High Street at Westerham is, I believe, a chapel of the Open Brethren, and adjoining it are some cottages reached by six steps. I should be glad to know if, as I have been informed, these cottages stand on the site of a meeting-house of the Quakers, who were once numerous in

Westerham. If so, was there a graveyard attached, as was usually the case in former times? In an antique-looking house near is said to have lived one Gibbard, a shoeing smith, the last of the Westerham Quakers. There is apparently no mention of him in the Quaker registers; but he may have died before 1785, at a period when these records were very incomplete. Information would be welcomed.   GIBSON THOMPSON.
Edenholm, Thames Ditton.

GOLF.—"Golf," in the ancient 'Icelandic Dictionary' of Runolphus Jonas, is the equivalent of the Latin *pavimentum*, which I suppose we may call "floor," if not "ground," in English. Is this word the originating cause of the name of the "ancient and royal game," or is there some other meaning to that name and origin of it?
B.

[In 'H.E.D.' identified rather doubtfully with Dutch *kolf*, a club, but the origin of the word is said to be obscure.]

SPELLING REFORM.—I have given a good deal of time to this matter, which I believe of importance in education. I ask the opinion of readers on this primary question. Should any change be international—*i.e.*, should the new method be applicable to the spelling of foreign words? Most, I think, will at first be inclined to answer, Yes. But suppose we agree to adopt the Italian values of the vowel letters, and the convention that doubling a vowel indicates its lengthening, and ç as the symbol for the unvoiced sibilant heard in *ice*, *pence*, &c. Then we should write instead of *grace*, *face*, &c., *greç*, *feç*, &c. Would not so great a change make the learning of English more difficult to a foreigner who knows any Romance language, and the reading of old books in English a little more difficult to our children?   T. WILSON.
Harpenden.

THE CROSS PROSTRATE. — Reference to paintings, engravings, and other works of art in which the cross is represented as having been laid on the ground or otherwise removed from the erect position before the body of Christ was taken from it will oblige.
W. S. WATSON.
Ellis Island, N.Y.

BRIGHTWALTON.—Can any reader afford me information as to the whereabouts of a volume, printed or MS., entitled 'Curious Particulars of Brightwalton,' by Dr. R. Eyre, of Brightwalton, Berks, 1770?
GEORGE C. PEACHEY.
Brightwalton, Wantage.

Replies.

MINAS AND EMPECINADOS.
(9ᵗʰ S. ix. 188.)

FRANCISCO was the greater of the Minas. Xaviero, his nephew, after a brief and stormy career, was shot in Mexico (1817) at the age of twenty-eight. The mere history of Francisco is a thirty years' romance. He made war much as the Boer generals do in our day. With comparatively small forces, by extreme mobility he not only evaded capture, but was able to strike many telling blows at the French. When beaten his men dispersed on all sides, a meeting-place being previously arranged by Mina. He speedily eclipsed the many guerilla leaders of his time—El Empecinado, El Medico, El Marquesito, El Frayle, El Pastor, &c.—and his success was such that he was placed in command of a larger force. In these operations, however, he failed to sustain his reputation, probably because in his first exploits he had been at great pains to exclude all regular officers of the Spanish army. He was repeatedly beaten—notably by Pannetier, and again by Reille and Caffarelli (1812); and it speaks well for his system that he was still able, in some form, to take the field. After the war Mina found that all his efforts had been in vain; and his opinions (very freely spoken) were so obnoxious to the vile gang of priests and parasites who, now that the fighting was over, formed the *entourage* of the wretched Ferdinand VII., that he had to flee for his life. A futile attempt in the north followed. In the Hundred Days Mina, then in the Côte d'Or, was offered a command by Napoleon, but declined. At the restoration he found that his old enemies were his best friends, Louis XVIII. repeatedly refusing to give him up to Ferdinand. He was back again in Spain in 1820. The constitution was once more in being, and the royal power was represented by the infamous "Army of the Faith"—a collection of bloodthirsty miscreants led by a monk, Marañon ("The Trappist"). Mina drove this rabble before him. In the subsequent defence of Catalonia against Marshal Moncey he proved a worthy antagonist. He was compelled to fly on the return of Ferdinand, whose lying "clemency" he appreciated at its true value. In 1830 he again appeared in Navarre—this time unsuccessfully. A price was on his head, and he lay hidden among the rocks, hunted, like a beast, by dogs. He managed to cross the frontier, and thence to England. The year 1834 saw him once more in Spain, fighting the Carlists. But he was worn out, and though some success attended him he was unable to effect anything decisive. He resigned in April, 1835, and died a few months later.

The contrast between Peterborough and Mina seems rather strained. The latter was a guerilla leader acting in his own country. Peterborough was compelled by circumstances to become something of a " free captain " in Spain. If it is true that he was responsible for the capture of Barcelona (of which there seems to be some little doubt), Peterborough deserves a higher place than Mina. The parallel would seem to be in the contempt of both for the red tape of their day. Peterborough had his way by land and sea as long as it was humanly possible. His methods were impossible a hundred years later, even if Mina had been capable of anything outside his own experience. Mina inveighed against the officers of the regular army. They were the slaves of an unsuccessful system, and he would have none of them. He was able to create his material, while Peterborough had to work with what was to his hand ; and Marlborough. "who thought no campaigning except his own material," took care in his wretched fashion that it should be none of the best. Both made free use of the means, good and (often) bad, that came to hand. Such disgraceful incidents as Peterborough's shameless trick on Mahoni at Murviedro and Mina's destruction of Castellfollit seem merely necessary events in such stormy careers Mina, however, was made of sterner stuff than the fiery and versatile Mordaunt. "Here was Castellfollit," he wrote on one of its ruined walls. "Cities, learn by this example not to befriend the enemies of your country ! "

It may be mentioned as a coincidence that when Peterborough arrived in Spain the Portuguese general in nominal command over tough old Galway and the allies was Las Minas.   GEORGE MARSHALL.

Sefton Park, Liverpool.

The guerilla system of warfare was of a wild and romantic character. Men totally unfitted by previous habits and education appeared upon the scene, and developed talent and determination that made them a scourge to the invaders of their country. But theirs was simply a war of extermination. Expecting no quarter (they were called bandits by the French), they did not extend any to those who became their prisoners. "War to the knife" was the motto of the guerillas, and on both sides blood flowed in torrents. Several of the followers of Juan Martin Diez, the Empecinado, having been surprised in the mountains, they were nailed to the trees and left there to die of hunger and thirst. To the same trees. before a week elapsed, a similar number of French soldiers were affixed by the guerillas. Some females had been abused most scandalously by the escort of a convoy ; in return the guerilla leader drove into an *ermida* eighty Frenchmen and their officers, set fire to the thatch, and burnt them to death. Such were the dreadful enormities a system of retaliation caused. Many of the guerilla bands were actuated in every enterprise by a love of bloodshed and spoliation. Others took the field from nobler motives : a great love of their country and religion, and for vengeance against a tyranny which had become insufferable. These desperate adventurers were commanded by men of the most dissimilar professions ; and, strange to say, the most ferocious band that invested Biscay was commanded by a woman named Martina. Of all the guerilla leaders the two Minas were the most daring and successful. The younger, Xavier, had but a short career —chivalrous and romantic. The elder, Francisco Espoz y Mina, was born in 1784, and became a guerilla chief in 1809, and after obtaining several victories over the French generals was promoted to the rank of field-marshal. Mina was the idol of the Spanish people, who styled him the "King of Navarre," and extolled his deeds beyond those of the Cid or the most famous knights of Spanish chivalry and romance. Mina resided in England for some time, but returned to Spain in 1834 to oppose Don Carlos, and died on 24 December, 1836, of wounds he received at Barcelona.

      HENRY GERALD HOPE.

119, Elms Road, Clapham, S.W.

GORDON RIOTS (9ᵗʰ S. ix. 68, 233).—In the 'Annual Register' for 1780 will be found a full account (the best I have come across) of the riots, the burning of Langdale's, &c , together with a report of the subsequent judicial proceedings, names of prisoners, verdicts, sentences (where found guilty). I would have mentioned this sooner, only I was afraid of being "one among too many." A full list (but without names) of those put on trial may also be found in Thornbury's 'Old and New London' (new edition, ed. by Edward Walford, 1893, vol. vi. p 347). Langdale's is still, I believe, in the hands of the original family ; but I doubt whether the products of the firm in 1902, however much the perfumes, vanilla, &c., might tempt the fair, but frail ones among the rioters (espe-

cially the negress), would cause the brutal rowdies of 1780 to fall down on hands and knees and "lap up" the liquor. Should your correspondent have special reasons (other than the average interest we must all feel in historical matters) for seeking information on the subject, if he cares to drop me a line I shall be pleased to forward (gratuitously) one or two short extracts from the books I have named.　HERBERT B. CLAYTON.
39, Renfrew Road, Lower Kennington Lane.

The *Universal Magazine* of 1780 contains a pretty full description of these riots and a portrait of the unfortunate originator, Lord George Gordon. W. C. B. refers to 7ᵗʰ S. ii. 341-3. This, it may be observed, contains an account of them mainly drawn from 'Barnaby Rudge,' a book which may be easier of access to most readers.　JOHN PICKFORD, M.A.
Newbourne Rectory, Woodbridge.

CRAPELET BIBLIOGRAPHY (9ᵗʰ S. ix. 289).— For a complete list of G. A. Crapelet's 'Collection des Anciens Monuments de l'Histoire et de la Langue Française' (twelve different works) see Brunet's 'Manuel' *sub* 'Crapelet.'　H. KREBS.
Oxford.

"CE N'EST QUE LE PREMIER PAS QUI COUTE" (9ᵗʰ S. ix. 165, 219).—As to the origin of this saying. Gibbon, in his note 100 to his thirty-ninth chapter, says : "A lady of my acquaintance once observed [on the miracle of St. Denis], 'La distance n'y fait rien ; il n'y a que,'" &c. Gibbon seems to imply that he either knew or regarded it as ascertained that the lady made the observation, and that he thought it an original one on her part. Guizot is quoted, on this note, in Milman and Smith's Gibbon, as stating that the lady was Madame du Deffand.
　　　　　　　　　　　　　C. O. R.

CLEBURNE : BOWES : WARD (9ᵗʰ S. ix. 189).— For pedigree of Bowes of Streatham see Foster's 'Visitations of Yorkshire,' p. 597. Hutton of Marske, Burke's 'Commoners,' vol. iii. p. 303. Cleburn, the above 'Visitations,' p. 255, and O'Hart's 'Irish Landed Gentry *temp.* Cromwell,' 1884, p. 203. Ward, Burke's 'Landed Gentry,' ninth edition, but it does not mention Bridgetta (of Kilkenny). The pedigree of Ward, of Newcastle and Stromshall, co. Stafford, and Ogborn, Great Bedwin, &c., co. Wilts, may include her name, &c.　JOHN RADCLIFFE.

A reference to J. Foster's 'Pedigrees of Yorkshire Families,' Hutchinson's 'History of Durham,' and Surtees Society's *Trans-*

actions, vol. xvii., will enable MR. WALTER J. BURKE to obtain much of the information he seeks.　MISTLETOE.

FIRST BRITISH SUBJECT BORN IN NEW SOUTH WALES (9ᵗʰ S. ix. 206, 272, 291).—N.S.S. is quite entitled to rebuke me for writing Charles instead of William Kent, though it is obvious that it was an error, not of inaccuracy of reading, but carelessness in transcribing. Governor Arthur Phillip founded Sydney on 26 January, 1788, with a mixed company of men and women, 1,030 in number. N. S. S. is unwilling to believe that any child was born before 23 December, 1799. I thought my statement would have been sufficient to have dispelled his extraordinary incredulity ; I hope in the course of the summer to have proof from Australia that will convince him.　ALFRED F. CURWEN.

WARLOW FAMILY (9ᵗʰ S. ix. 9, 155).—The little river alluded to in Mecklenburg has the name of Warnow, it is true, but there is no town so called ; the little port at the mouth of the Warnow, which belongs to Rostock, bears the name of Warnemünde, a favourite Baltic seaside resort. Warnow is not Norse, but Slav, like all the old names of the above-named country, which was in times of yore inhabited by the Slavic tribes of the Obotriten and Wilzen.
　　　　　　　　　　　　　G. KRUEGER.
Berlin.

ST. PAUL AND SENECA (9ᵗʰ S. ix. 291).— The legend of the intercourse between Paul and Seneca finds its fullest expression in the apocryphal Epistles of St. Paul to Seneca and of Seneca to St. Paul. These are printed by Fabricius, by Jeremiah Jones in his book on the New Testament Canon, and also appear elsewhere. These epistles led Jerome to include the philosopher in his catalogue of saints.　WILLIAM E. A. AXON.
Manchester.

This interesting question is fully discussed in the late Bishop Lightfoot's dissertation 'St. Paul and Seneca' in his commentary on the Epistle to the Philippians (published in 1868). His conclusion is that "no great stress can be laid on the direct historical links which might connect Seneca with the Apostle of the Gentiles." The article 'Seneca' in 'Dict. Christian Biog.,' iv. (1887), says :—

"There is, of course, no impossibility in the supposition that St. Paul and Seneca met between A.D. 61 and A.D. 65 ; but there is no evidence for it except the spurious letters ; there is nothing in the works of Seneca which requires such a supposition, though they do not absolutely forbid it."

The "spurious letters" (between St. Paul and Seneca), Lightfoot says, "betray clearly the hand of a forger." C. S. WARD.
Wootton St. Lawrence, Basingstoke.

On the fictitious letters between St. Paul and Seneca see 1ˢᵗ S. vii., viii., and Dean Farrar's 'Seekers after God,' under 'Seneca,' chap. xiv. pp. 167-73. W. C. B.

SALT FOLK-LORE (9ᵗʰ S. ix. 228).—The old Germanic races considered salt-springs holy and worshipped around them (cp. Gummere, 'Germanic Origins,' New York, 1892, p. 69). Tacitus tells a story of a desperate war waged over the ownership of a salt-spring (cp. 'Annals,' xiii. 57). Salt was made by setting fire to logs which had been saturated with salt-water from these sacred springs, and was held to be a product given to man by special favour of the gods. Homer calls salt divine. In the ceremony of baptism a small amount of salt was placed in the mouth of the one baptized (cp. Schultz, 'Das höfische Leben zur Zeit der Minnesinger,' Leipzig, 1889, vol. i. p. 148). Many other examples from Greek, Roman, and Oriental sources could be quoted to show that a peculiar religious significance has long been attached to salt. These facts may assist in explaining the custom of placing salt under a corpse.
CHARLES BUNDY WILSON.
State University of Iowa.

BROWN FAMILY (9ᵗʰ S. ix. 228).—There is a notice of Sir Samuel Brown in the 'Dictionary of National Biography,' but his merits as an inventor will only become fully apparent after the perusal of the specifications of his numerous patents. R. B. P.

"BORE" OR "BOAR," AND OTHER FASHIONABLE SLANG (9ᵗʰ S. viii. 481; ix. 152).—I am glad to be able to supply the omission of R. B. The passage occurs in 'The Life and Letters of Lady Sarah Lennox,' vol. i. pp. 179, 180, and is from a letter written by Lady Sarah to Lady Susan O'Brien, 9 January, 1766.
ST. SWITHIN.

METRICAL SERMONS (3ʳᵈ S. vii. 76, 143, 308; ix. 208).—I read in Evelyn's 'Diary,' 1665, 24 February (Friday), that "Dr. Fell, Canon of Christ Church, preach'd before the King on 15 Romans 2, a very formal discourse, and in blank verse, according to his manner." One would like to know how many of such sermons he preached, and whether any of them are extant. RICHARD H. THORNTON.
Portland, Oregon.

ANTWERP CATHEDRAL (9ᵗʰ S. ix. 289).—Antwerp Cathedral's north-west spire is reputed to be 402 feet high, and its southern neighbour, so high as it goes—i.e., some little way above the nave ridge—is of similar design, but neither is out of the perpendicular. The northern towers and spires of continental west fronts are often more ornate than are their fellows. At Rouen we find the northern tower (built 1485-1507) exceedingly rich in detail, whilst its southern companion is poor in comparison. The former is known as the "Butter Tower," much of the cost of its erection having been defrayed by market tolls put upon butter brought into the city by the country folk. At Chartres the north-western spire (375 feet) is as beautiful as is Antwerp's, whilst the southern one (350 feet), perfectly plain, is as pure in outline as is Salisbury's central spire (404 feet).

If proper precautions are taken, treacherous ground does not necessarily seriously affect foundations. Boston "Stump," the fairest and tallest of our church towers (300 feet), was built A.D. 1309 upon mud, close by the river Witham, and is still practically plumb; further, all the "sky-scrapers" in Chicago (the tallest edifices in the world), and, indeed, the entire city itself, stand upon slob-land.
HARRY HEMS.
Fair Park, Exeter.

"ROMANS DES DOUZE PAIRS" (9ᵗʰ S. ix. 290).—This series does not appear to have been distinguished throughout by the number of different volumes. One of the series, for instance, 'La Mort de Garin, le Loherain: Poème du XIIᵉ Siècle,' published by E. du Méril 1846 (which is the sequel of 'Li Romans de Garin le Loherain,' ed. P. Paris, in 2 vols., 1833-5), bears the general title "Romans des Douze Pairs de France" upon the leaf preceding its title-page, but without indicating the volume of the series. H. KREBS.
Oxford.

FASHION IN LANGUAGE (9ᵗʰ S. ix. 228).—In reply to your correspondent I may say that I have collected a list of "pet words" in German, among which are *leise, sanft, Ruhe, balde,* and *zieht.* Some of these have brought themselves into favour on account of sound, others through association. At the last meeting of the Modern Language Association of America Prof. F. N. Scott, of the University of Michigan, read an interesting paper on 'Hated Words.' His list was compiled from the testimony of about two hundred and fifty trustworthy informants. The reports showed great diversity of taste. The principal cause of dislike was unpleasantness in sound, in appearance, in association, or in early impressions. The following may serve as specimens of the "hated words" submitted : *program, victuals, beau, cuddle, swab,* and *goitre.*

Charles Bundy Wilson.
State University of Iowa.

"Buff Week" (9th S. ix. 329).—This is a mistake for "baff week." No one in Durham or Northumberland has ever been able to tell me the derivation of "Baff Saturday." May I suggest that replies should be indexed under "Baff," not "Buff," or no one will ever find them ?   Charles W. Dilke.

Satirical Coloured Prints (9th S. ix. 269).—These are excerpts from

"An Academy for Grown Horsemen, containing the Completest Instructions for Walking, Trotting, Cantering, Galloping, Stumbling, and Tumbling. Illustrated with Copper Plates and adorned with a Portrait of the Author. By Geoffrey Gambado, Esqre, Riding Master, Master of the Horse, and Grand Equerry to the Doge of Venice. London : Printed by W. Nicholson, Warner Street, for W. Baynes, 54, Paternoster Row. 1st ed. 1787."

Henry William Bunbury (1750–1811), the illustrator of this work, was a celebrated caricaturist. The engravings in the book in question are seventeen in number, and are mezzotints; those of Mr. Matthews seem to be coloured by hand.

Harold Malet, Colonel.

Llyn Coblynau : Knockers' Llyn (9th S. ix. 229).—I have ascended Snowdon thirteen times from various points, and know all its llyns well. None of them, I think, corresponds exactly to Mr. Watts-Dunton's descriptions of "Llyn Coblynau," but Glaslyn is almost certainly intended. Only from it would the description of Y Wyddfa standing out against the sky "as narrow and as steep as the sides of an acorn" be correct, but from the north and north-west sides of Glaslyn this answers with quite curious exactness to the appearance of the mountain. We must suppose the action of the story to have taken place before the revival of the copper-mining industry on Snowdon. May I be allowed to dwell for a moment upon my first ascent, some thirty-two years ago? I had walked from a point about three miles below Bettws-y-Coed, and had as companion in my climb a son of the late Henry Owen, of Pen-y-Gwryd. We went up in a dense mist, doing the whole distance from the inn in an hour and twenty minutes. The mist was thicker than ever when we reached the hut, and the cold intense. Five minutes afterwards the man in charge called us out from our cheese and beer to see "the sight of the season" (it was in July).

The mist was then clearing, and in a few moments was entirely gone. So marvellous a transformation scene, and so immense a prospect, I have never beheld since. For the first and only time in my life I saw from one spot almost the whole of North and Mid Wales, a good part of Western England, and a glimpse of Scotland and Ireland. The vision faded all too quickly, but it was worth walking thirty-three or thirty-four miles, as I did that day, for even a briefer view than that.   C. C. B.

In reply to E. W., none of us are very likely, I fear, to succeed in "placing" this llyn, because the author of 'Aylwin,' taking a privilege of romance often taken by Sir Walter Scott before him, probably changed the landmarks in idealizing the scene and adapting it to his story. It may be, indeed, that the Welsh name given to the llyn in the book is merely a rough translation of the gipsies' name for it, the Knockers being gnomes or goblins of the mine; hence "Coblynau"=goblins. If so, the name itself can give us no clue, unless we are lucky enough to secure the last of the Welsh gipsies for a guide. In any case, the only point from which to explore Snowdon for the small llyn, or perhaps llyns (of which Llyn Coblynau is a kind of composite ideal picture), is no doubt, as E. W. has suggested, Capel Curig ; and I imagine the actual scene lies about a mile south from Glaslyn, while it owes something at least of its colouring in the book to that strange lake. The "Knockers," it must be remembered, usually depend upon the existence of a mine near by, with old partly fallen mine-workings where the dropping of water or other subterranean noises produce the curious phenomenon which is turned to such imaginative account in the Snowdon chapters of 'Aylwin.'   Sion o Ddyli.

Queen Candace (9th S. ix. 321).—In addition to my note of last week I may say that the name was also borne by private persons. In the British Museum (Second Egyptian Room) may be seen the mummy and coffin of a young lady named Cleopatra, otherwise Candace, a member of the family of Soter Cornelius Pollios, archon of Thebes, dated by Dr. Wallis Budge about the year 100 A.D. She was probably the granddaughter of another Cleopatra-Candace, wife of the archon, whose mummy and coffin are at Leyden, and after whom she may have been named, in accordance with Egyptian custom. Reuvens suggested that the name Cleopatra was chosen as the Greek equivalent for Candace (originally the dynastic title of the

Ethiopian queens or queen - mothers) on account of its having been borne by so many of the wives of the Ptolemies.

JOHN MAC-CARTHY.

CHAPMAN FAMILY (9ᵗʰ S. ix. 187).—There is, or was some twenty years ago, a Checkley Hall, then used as a farmhouse, at Checkley-cum-Wrinehill, formerly known as Checkleigh, a township in the parish of Wybunbury, co. Chester. CHAS. HALL CROUCH. Wanstead.

GEORGES I.-IV. (9ᵗʰ S. ix. 100, 164, 318).—MR. PAGE is quite right. Walter Savage Landor wrote the stinging epigram on the Georges in the form quoted by him, and sent it to the *Atlas* newspaper somewhere in the later fifties of last century. I copied it at the time, but have "God be praised" in the last line instead of "Heaven." Ever since then I have been trying to hunt down a stupid version of the same epigram which is usually attributed to Thackeray, owing, no doubt, to his having lectured on the four Georges about the same time that Landor wrote. I heard those lectures, and can testify that Thackeray did not even quote the lines while on the platform, nor did he add them to his text when the lectures were published in the *Cornhill Magazine* in the summer of 1860. But in January, 1861, a reverend lecturer at Darlington, referring to the palmy days of the Georges, quoted from "Thackeray" what he called a new Georgic, as follows :—

George the First was vile—viler George the Second ;
Whoe'er heard any good of George the Third ?
And when from earth the Fourth ascended
God be praised the Georges ended.

Being at that time literary manager of the *Newcastle Daily Chronicle*, I published the correct version from the *Atlas*, made fun of the rhythm in the substitute, and sent a marked copy to the lecturer. A few years later the reverend misquoter lectured near my house, and I took the chair. To my amazement he trotted out the Thackerayan Georgic, word for word, and told me afterwards that he had given it thus many scores of times and knew he was right! Since that time his wretched version, with variations, has often appeared in the newspapers. Upon the last occasion that I saw the lines they had been much improved and were correctly attributed to Landor. Still, the first line did not rhyme with the second, and the second did not scan. That was in a paper on 'The Literature of Epigram' contributed to a magazine for Christmas, 1900, by a well-known journalist, himself the author of more

than one booklet of respectable poetry. His excuse to me was the old story. that the printers had made a hash of it. Here is the " printers' hash ":—

George the First was reckoned vile,
    Viler George the Second ;
And what mortal ever heard
Any good of George the Third ?
    When from earth the Fourth ascended,
    God be praised the Georges ended.

It is worthy of note that in every misquotation I have seen the sting of the satire in the fifth line—"When from earth the Fourth *descended* "—has been lost. Thanks to MR. PAGE we now have the correct version, and if our indexer will put a cross-reference to Landor there is some hope that the epigram may be properly quoted in future.

RICHD. WELFORD.

Newcastle-upon-Tyne.

The verses on the four Georges were certainly by Walter Savage Landor, though they are not to be found in any of his books or in Forster's edition of his collected works (1876). They were printed in the *Atlas* of 28 April, 1855, with his signature, " W. S. L.," in the form given by MR. PAGE, with the exception that the last line runs—

(God be praised) the Georges ended.

The former owner of my copy of 'Imaginary Conversations' (first edition, 1824) has written the following note on a fly-leaf :—

"Landor was with Thackeray after his lectures on the Georges were delivered, and said :—

I sing the Georges Four,
For Providence could stand no more.
Some say that far the worst
Of all the Four was George the First.
But still by some 'tis reckon'd
That worser still was George the Second.
No mortal ever said one word
Or good or bad of George the Third.
When George the Fourth from Earth descended,
Thank God the line of Georges ended.
    Extempore by Landor."

STEPHEN WHEELER.

Oriental Club, Hanover Square.

PORTRAITS OF JOANNA BAILLIE (9ᵗʰ S. ix. 129, 237).—Your correspondent would most probably get the information he desires from Miss Hunter Baillie, Duntisbourne House, Duntisbourne Abbotts, Gloucestershire.

A. A. H.

MRS. SIDDONS'S HOUSE, UPPER BAKER STREET (9ᵗʰ S. ix. 224).—What is the authority for the statement that Mrs. Siddons was living in Gower Street in 1817 ? I am aware that Campbell says she was living there at that date, but I want something more definite. Fitzgerald in his 'Lives of the Kembles,' vol. ii.

p. 292, quotes a letter from Mrs. Siddons to Lady Harcourt, dated 26 September, 1784, and written from Gower Street. This is borne out by the rate-books of the parish of St. Giles-in-the-Fields, in which parish the southern end of Gower Street is situate, William Siddons being rated in that year in respect of a house (unnumbered) on the east side of Gower Street. In 'Holden's Triennial Directory' for 1805 and 1808 I find "Siddons, W., Gower Street and Putney Heath," but this could not have been the husband of the great actress, as he died at Bath in March, 1805. In 'London Past and Present,' under 'Gower Street' it is stated that "Mrs. Siddons bought a house in Gower Street, and she wrote, 'The back of it is most effectually in the country, and delightfully pleasant,'" but my friend Mr. Wheatley is unable to say where Cunningham got his information ; but it is possible that the letter may still be in existence. Can any of your readers give the date of the letter ?

R. B. P.

A slight error occurs in Mr. John Hebb's communication anent the last residence of the famous actress. The house which, to the regret of many, is likely to be razed ere long is situate at the corner of Allsop, not "Allsopp," Place, Marylebone. From the spelling it would thus appear that the firm of brewers is not indicated.

Cecil Clarke.

"Barracked" (9ᵗʰ S. ix. 63, 196, 232).—It is at least a little astonishing that in these days, in the year of grace 1902, such very improbable explanations should be seriously offered in 'N. & Q.' as those suggested by Boscombrosa and by Mr. G. Y. Baldock, the one suggesting that *lark*=to play tricks, a word used in all, or nearly all, dialects, and *larrikin*, a specially Australian word, are to be derived from a local N.C. *lāke* (N.B., pronounced *lēk*, not *lāk !*), with a remarkable intrusion of an *r* from goodness knows where, and the other that *barrack* comes from a French law term *barreter*, with a no less remarkable change from *t* to *k !* These gentlemen should at least bring forward some support for such extraordinary assumptions as they make.

There seems to be no objection, from the phonetic point of view, to the explanations from *bark* and *lark* respectively. For such changes *analoga can* be found. But Prof. Morris's explanation seems to settle the one word satisfactorily enough (though it should be noted that the 'E.D.D.' gives *barrack* as a N. Irish dialect word=to brag), and it is

strange that, if *larrikin* is to be explained from *lark*, the 'E.D.D.' gives no instance of this word appearing in any dialect as a dissyllable. Further, is not *larrikin* in the first place the name of a person ? If so, it is not to be so easily explained from *lark*, vb. It is difficult, too, to see how Prof. Strong can imagine that a French word *larron* can have had any influence on a word so specifically Australian. After all, is it not possible that the *larrikin*, like his brother the *hooligan*, may derive his name from some former notorious chieftain of his tribe ?   F. J. C.

Prof. H. A. Strong says Prof. Morris, in 'Austral English,' derives *barrack* "from a native word *borak*, meaning 'to banter,'" "the term only dating" (which is curious) "from about 1880." Prof. Strong, however, informs us that "it certainly was not used commonly in Victoria before 1883," *i.e.*, less than twenty years ago. If the word is that said native one, why should it have been thus altered in sound ; and how is it that it has only so very recently been taken into English use ? For *borak* to have become *barrack* involves the raising of the first vowel from a lower tone to a higher one (not, as in *tobacco*, the lowering from a native higher one). As this is quite contrary to the rules of the philological game as expounded by the schoolmen, one does not feel over ready to accept Prof. Morris's theory. Even in the same number of 'N. & Q.' that Prof. Strong's letter appears in we have evidence in John King's 'Grammar' (ante, p. 227) of how higher tones in vowels tend to become lower ; but this change would be the other way about. John King's *ar* sound has become our *or*, but here, according to Prof. Morris's theory, we have *or* converted into *ar*.

Boscombrosa.

American Words (9ᵗʰ S. viii. 183, 267, 448). —I am not concerned to vindicate for America the honour of inventing the word "linkum-fiddle." Of course these notes are a bid for information, and I am glad of the light thrown on my own curios as on others'. But I am not quite convinced that my etymology is wrong. It hardly seems probable that Colman's play (which I have not seen) was the source of a term in the colonies that must have been at least as old as itself ; and the nonsense chorus of the Scotch song would hardly have been turned into a term for a fool, except by assimilation, which is probable enough. That is, "ninkum" being an old abbreviation for "nincompoop," and currently used, the names "ninkumfiddle" and "linkumfiddle" may have been suggested by the old chorus. In the absence of any evidence as to the orignal date of a term like this, proof is impossible, of course.　F. M.

"Flittings" (9ᵗʰ S. ix. 49, 239).—Concluding his account of Isobel Pagan in the 'Contemporaries of Burns,' Paterson says that an old quern at the door of her last dwelling-place "had been carefully conveyed along with her in all her 'flittings.'" This is the common use of the word *flitting* in Scotland, where it is not applied to the feeing-market or (except figuratively) to death. Thus Laidlaw, in celebrating 'Lucy's Flittin',' enlarges merely on the maid's departure from the situation which she had held throughout the summer :—

'Twas when the wan leaf frae the birk tree was
　　fa'in',
　And Martinmas dowie had wound up the year,
That Lucy row'd up her wee kist wi' her a' in,
　And left her auld maister and neebours sae dear.

The song, no doubt, concludes with the report of the heroine's death, but the Ettrick Shepherd (to whose 'Forest Minstrel' the lyric was contributed) used to say that he added the stanza containing this announcement. But whether this was the case, or whether the author himself was responsible for the whole song as it now stands, the stanza is essentially extraneous to the motive of the ballad. Lucy flits from her situation, heavy at heart because of an unfaithful Jamie whom she leaves behind her, and whose "Fare ye weel, Lucy," haunts her as she goes. The conduct of her faithless lover may have been the proximate cause of her death, but the fact of her *flittin'* is not of itself indicative of that issue. It should be added that the term *flittin'* is also applied in Scotland to the goods of the flitter, and it is so used by Laidlaw in his song, thus :—

As doun the burnside she gaed slow wi' the flittin',
　Fare ye weel, Lucy ! was ilka bird's sang,
She heard the craw sayin't, high on the tree sittin',
　And robin was chirpin't the brown leaves amang.
　　　　　　　　　　Thomas Bayne.

I used to hear in Derbyshire of "flittings and quittings"—servants leaving their old farm places for new ones. After a "long jaw" gossips said, "Ah'l flit," or "It's abart time ah flitted." There were "moonlight flitters" — householders who flitted their goods by night in order to evade the rent due to the landlord, or cheat the "bumbailiff" when his coming was expected.
　　　　　　　　　　Thos. Ratcliffe.
Worksop.

Stone Pulpit (9ᵗʰ S. viii. 325, 394, 489 ; ix. 56, 157).—John Britton in his 'Dictionary of Architecture and Archæology of the Middle Ages,' 1838 (*s.v.* 'Crosses'), says :—

"Attached to the wall of the Abbey at Shrewsbury is an octagonal stone pulpit, ascended by a flight of steps, covered with a canopy, and open at the sides, although from its situation it is not strictly a preaching cross. The preaching crosses still remaining at Hereford and at Iron Acton, Gloucestershire, may be considered the most perfect examples."

The former was attached to the monastery of Blackfriars in that city, whilst the latter is represented in plate i. fig. 6 of 'Crosses,' and was probably erected in the reign of Henry IV. There is still another at Holbeach in Lincolnshire. A fine specimen of the Shrewsbury Abbey class, says Britton, is that now placed in the grounds of Stourhead, Wiltshire, taken from the College Green, Bristol. But Britton states elsewhere, I believe, that the Hereford and Iron Acton examples were the only perfect ones that had come under his notice. The former stood in a garden belonging to Coningsby Hospital, in the northern suburbs of the city. On the dissolution of the monasteries the site and buildings were granted to John Scudamore, Esq., of Wilton, and William Wygmore, gent., of London ; but early in the reign of Elizabeth they came into the possession of the Coningsby family, from whom the estate descended to the Earl of Essex.　　　J. Holden MacMichael.

In 'Sixty Views of Endowed Schools,' by J. C. Buckler, quarto, published in 1827, are two engravings of the Grammar School at Chester, formerly the refectory of the Abbey of St. Werburgh, one of the interior and another of the exterior from the cloister court. The following description of the school seventy-five years ago, and thirty years before the description given in Parker's 'Mediæval Architecture of Chester,' may prove of interest :—

"Part of the Refectory (about two-thirds of the original room) is used as the School-room. Prior to its being reduced in size the dimensions of the apartment must have been upon a noble scale. At the east end of the south wall are the remains of a stone staircase with trefoil-headed arches open to the Hall. This might have served the purpose of the Reader's pulpit, as well as an ascent to the Dormitory over the adjoining cloister."

The book is scarce, and very useful as showing how many of the buildings of ancient schools have either been altered in modern times or improved off the face of the land.
　　　　　　　　　　John Pickford, M.A.

The Hawson Oak and its Greek Cross (9ᵗʰ S. viii. 522).—Mr. W. G. Thorpe's story relative to the interesting fragments of an old cross near Holne—the Devonshire village where Charles Kingsley was born, 12 June, 1819—is not without interest. But it requires some little correction. In the first place, this old Dartmoor grey granite cross is *not* Greek in either outline or character. The portions still existing suggest a complete cross of the usual local design and conception. Further, the anecdote relative to the iconoclastic stone-breaker and the "then" (and present) vicar of Staverton is simply a myth. The actual facts are simply as narrated below.

An old gnarled oak—maybe two or three hundred years old—stands at a point where three roads meet, a mile or thereabouts from Holne. It was possibly planted upon the site of the old cross after the latter was torn down and broken into fragments. But, speaking from some intimate local knowledge, the name "Hawson oak" is unknown to me. The tree certainly does not stand upon the Hawson estate. At the time the old cross was destroyed—at what date there is no record—the arms were broken from the parent shaft, and this with the die and base stones was scattered to the winds. The arms themselves were preserved and placed in an adjoining bank. There they remained until, perhaps, ten years ago, when one stormy day they fell out into the road. Happily my venerable friend the Rev. John Bickley Hughes, M.A.—who since 1874 has been vicar of Staverton, and who with Mrs. Hughes celebrated the fifty-fourth anniversary of their wedding-day on 12 Jan.— happened to drive by and became aware of the catastrophe. He met the late Earl (Reginald) of Devon at Ashburton the same day. Now Lord Devon all through his long life was a zealous conservator of local antiquities. Urged, therefore, by a kindred feeling, the pair sought out Mr. Tanner, the squire of Hawson, explained to him the peril the cross was in, and extracted from him a promise that it should be promptly cared for. So eventually it was built up into the wall by the side of the road to Holne.

HARRY HEMS.

Fair Park, Exeter.

"OLIVE": "OLIVACEOUS" (9ᵗʰ S. ix. 307).— Though the ordinary use of these words connotes a peculiar green tint, as a matter of fact the olive itself, as provided for consumption (on the counter of a wine-shop, for instance) in Southern European countries, has always struck me as more brown than green; in fact, as a brown with green shadows rather than as a green with brown shadows, as it is usually considered. The phrase is not used with precision, nor is the French *olivâtre*, but both fairly describe a type of complexion common in Southern Europeans, and to be met with in more northern climes. In such complexions, if carefully studied and analyzed, I think there will be found a faint tinge of green, showing, as it were, through the tawny skin.   E. E. STREET.
Chichester.

CROSSING KNIVES AND FORKS (9ᵗʰ S. viii. 325, 433; ix. 14).—I was brought up to believe that it was good manners to leave knife and fork side by side upon my plate when I had finished eating. I cannot think that either religion or superstition had anything to do with the prescription fifty years ago: it conduced merely to seemliness and order.   ST. SWITHIN.

In my young days children were told that a crossed knife and fork on the dinner plate brought bad luck to the house, and caused "rows" amongst the members of the household. If any of the table cutlery, knives and forks, were found crossed, every one made a dash to uncross them with the inquiry, made with concern, "Who's done that?" On the other hand, if spoons were found crossed that was considered to be a sign of a wedding. To drop a fork mostly drew from some one, "There's a stranger coming."
THOS. RATCLIFFE.
Worksop.

That it is unlucky to cross knives is a very widespread superstition. I have met with it, I may say, almost all over England.
C. C. B.

Here knives accidentally crossed are said to be unlucky.   R. B—R.
South Shields.

STAR-LORE (9ᵗʰ S. ix. 227).—Fifty years ago it was held to be unlucky to point at the moon and count the stars. Derbyshire girls and boys "dared" each other to do it. To point at the moon properly it was necessary to get as near it as possible, and gates, fences, and walls were mounted before the pointing was begun. They might point six times without ill effect, but at the seventh "you would be struck blind"! This pointing seemed to have some connexion with "the man in the moon," so far as talk went, who had been sufficiently punished for his sin without being pointed at. Amongst the folk to point the finger at any one was an offensive action at all times, and was always resented. The more daring children evaded the probable consequences by "hooking"

the finger at the seventh pointing—going through the motion, but not having the fore-finger extended ! It was bad luck to " count out " the stars up to one hundred, and " you might be struck down dead " for it. Gene-rally the counting stopped at ninty-nine, only a few venturing beyond " in fear and trembling." Mothers used to say, " Don't point at moon ! " " Don't count stars ! " Except that in pointing the " man in the moon " was taken into consideration, reasons why the stars should not be counted were never given. THOS. RATCLIFFE.
    Worksop.

There exists a kindred superstition among Jews to that of star - pointing. On certain days of the high festivals, such as Passover and Tabernacles, there is a survival of one, the Temple ordinances lingering in the custom of " Duchaning," or " priestly benediction." Gentlemen who claim descent from the sons of Aaron ascend the steps of the Ark and bless the congregants in a chant which is more antique than musical. On these occasions the worshippers are supposed to turn their backs towards the " Cohanim," and by no means to allow their gaze to stray in that direction, lest the result may be disastrous to those misguided persons. The tradition runs that some one was struck blind for committing this supposed offence. I am not ashamed to own that I have repeatedly looked at the Cohanim without taking hurt. M. L. R. BRESLAR.

I remember being rebuked more than once for pointing at the stars when a child. This would be in South Notts, and probably in Warwickshire too. I do not think any definite reason was given, but I was made to feel that I had been guilty of shocking irreverence. C. C. B.

" RATLINGS " (9ᵗʰ S. ix. 288).—This word from America is but another instance of the many survivals there of original importations from the old country. Of course, *ratlings* or *rattlings* is but New-World pronunciation of old West-Country *raddlings*, a term still in common use in Somerset (see ' West Somerset Word-Book,' p. 609). The lumbermen retain the name, though they no longer remember the Old-World use to which the word belongs. To *raddle* is almost identical with to *wreathe ;* at least, so it would appear to the educated observer who does not appreciate technical niceties. The latter is to interweave more or less prepared brushwood with some care as to interweaving, whereas to *raddle* is to per-form the same act with rougher material and

in a rougher manner. A *wreath-hurdle* is well known, but a hedge made with roughly interwoven untrimmed sticks is *raddled,* and the material which would otherwise go for firewood and be bound up into faggots is when so used called *raddling.* In America they only look on brushwood as kindling, having no longer any use for it as a fencing material, while they still call it by the old name when tied up in bundles.
        F. T. ELWORTHY.

" PROSPICIMUS MODO " (9ᵗʰ S. viii. 445 ; ix. 34, 273).—I cannot give the reference to *Chambers's Journal,* but the book referred to must surely be ' Artificial Versifying,' by John Peter, almanac maker, &c., three editions of which appeared in 1677, 1678, and 1679 (a copy of the last is in the British Museum). It is an extraordinary little book, professing to teach " a new way to make Latin verses " by means of certain tables, from which a patient reader can spell out, letter by letter, words which scan as Latin hexameters and pentameters. The process is purely mecha-nical, and would seem capable of giving neither pleasure nor profit. It might, however, be worth while for some student of " magic squares " and the like to solve the mystery of its mechanism. The peculiar properties of the figure 9 seem to have something to do with it. T. S. OMOND.

Miscellaneous.

NOTES ON BOOKS, &c.

English Book Collectors. By William Younger
    Fletcher, F.S.A. (Kegan Paul & Co.)
To " The English Bookman's Library " of Mr. Alfred Pollard Mr. Fletcher, well known for valuable works on bibliographical subjects and for the ser-vices he rendered to students in the Printed Book Department of the British Museum, has added a series of memoirs of English book collectors. Something of the kind had previously been done by the late Mr. Quaritch in his ' Contributions to a Dictionary of Book Collectors.' The present work seems, however, more ambitious in scheme and is up to date. It is, moreover, fully illustrated with portraits of eminent bibliophiles, devices, and book-plates and book-stamps of collectors. A portrait of Lord Spencer, the founder of the great Althorp library, serves as frontispiece, other portraits in-cluding those of Prince Henry of Wales, Archbishop Parker, Dr. Dee, Lord Lumley, Sir Robert Bruce Cotton, Archbishop Usher, Archbishop Williams, John Bagford, the Duke of Roxburghe, William Beckford, and many others, down to Frederick Locker-Lampson. In addition to these we have reproductions of the book-stamps or book-plates of Lord Burghley, the Earl of Leicester, Sir Kenelm Digby, Samuel Pepys, and various other notabilities. In the case of most of these all the particulars to be desired by the reader are supplied. Concerning men of more modern days Mr. Fletcher is more

reticent. In the case of the late Robert Samuel Turner, one of the most princely of collectors, we should like to have seen an account of those Saturday-afternoon symposia, confined to book lovers and buyers, at which one used to meet Lord Houghton, Don Pascual de Gayangos, H. S. Ashbee, and many others, and look·over the finest collection of French books in England. Ashbee himself, an indefatigable collector, deserved a few sentences. The sad death of poor Turner adds a tragic note to the record, but the mention of this may have been omitted out of regard to surviving relations. Mr. Fletcher has supplied a book of lasting interest to bibliophiles. It is well got up, moreover, and will grace the shelves of the most esoteric of collectors.

Reading Abbey. By Jamieson B. Hurry, M.A., M.D. (Stock.)

VERY quaintly Dr. Hurry dedicates to "The Memory of Reading Abbey" the handsome volume he has consecrated to its description. Few monastic piles have a record more interesting and important than this, and still fewer have undergone more complete destruction and desolation. Of its innumerable halls, cloisters, and galleries, the scenes of hospitable entertainment and historic pageantry, scarcely one is now distinguishable. The chapter-house has still some recognizable traces, and the inner gatehouse, which has been restored by Sir Gilbert Scott, stands erect and serviceable. As a result of so complete destruction the historical associations of a building which, at the period of the dissolution of the monasteries, had a revenue of close on 2,000*l.*, had fallen almost into oblivion. Most of these have now been recovered, thanks, in part, to the zeal of the latest historian. The precincts included thirty acres. The length of the abbey church was 450 feet, and the breadth, exclusive of the transepts, 95 feet, the entrance-porch being a deeply recessed semicircular Norman doorway, with abundance of ornament and moulding, and specimens of rich Norman carving being found among the debris. Ruins thickly clad with ivy are all that now survives of the noble edifice. The remains of the chapter-house constitute the most picturesque portion. Of the hospitium, at which, according to William of Malmesbury, guests arrived every hour and consumed more than the residents, of the original guest-house erected by Henry I., as of the leper-house and other portions, all that is ascertainable is told, and as to what is not known there is plausible conjecture. In the Chartulary of Reading Abbey, preserved in the Cottonian MSS. in the British Museum, is set forth the "Modus recipiendi fratres vel sorores in Hospitio Sancti Johannis," a building which was set apart for the reception of twenty-six poor brethren or sisters. Full particulars concerning them and other matters are given. A full history of Reading Abbey, founded 11 June, 1121, by Henry I, and colonized by monks of the Cluniac Order, up to the period of dissolution in 1539, follows. Refusing "for conscience' sake" to submit to the order of Henry VIII., with whom he was said to be a favourite, Hugh Faringdon, the last abbot, with two of his monks, was hanged, drawn, and quartered. Of his well-known death a good account is supplied, and is accompanied by a portrait and a plate (coloured) of his arms. A struggle which for two hundred and fifty years raged between the abbot and the guild merchant is also fully described. Other chapters are devoted to the establishment of the abbey, its

endowments, armorial bearings, relics, library, &c. Many of the valuable documents and MSS. of the library have been lost, but many are preserved in the British Museum, Bodleian, &c. Among the illustrations which constitute a striking and most acceptable feature in the volume are facsimiles of illuminated MSS. in the Bodleian, and one with the musical notation of the famous "Summer is icumen." The book, which is well executed and admirably got up, will be a treasure to the antiquary.

The Cambridge Platonists. Edited by E. T. Campagnac. (Oxford, Clarendon Press.)

MYSTICISM, as the term is generally understood, has never flourished in England. John Bull is a healthy animal, even in his melancholy fits proclaiming a constitutional indisposition to divine madness. The middle path of temperate commonsense removes him equally from the visionary raptures of Catholic Spain and the extravagant speculation of mediæval Germany, while the East, uniting these extremes, is still further out of his ken. We have individual mystics, of course, and some of these are "God-intoxicated" enough—*e.g.*, Shelley; but who will maintain that Shelley was a typical Englishman? It is hardly possible to speak of a school of English mystics, yet the word seems natural when we recall the Cambridge Platonists, who "attempted to effect a union between philosophy and religion, and formulated a kind of 'moral divinity,' which found little acceptance at the moment, but which, like a stream running underground, has, though seldom detected, given a freshness and life to the ground subsequently trodden by those who have pursued either theological or philosophical inquiries."

Of the chief members of the group—Cudworth, More, Whichcote, Smith, and Culverwell—only the last three are represented here. Mr. Campagnac has shown excellent judgment in choosing from their writings "extracts which should illustrate as fairly as possible the teaching and style of each, and the relation in which they stood to one another." These men were rational mystics. They claimed "that reason must not be fettered; that in the conscience of the individual, governed by reason, and illuminated by a revelation which could not be inconsistent with reason, itself 'a seed of Deiform nature,' lay the ultimate seat of authority in religion." Thus without any sacrifice of spiritual freedom they escaped the dangers to which uncontrolled mysticism is liable. It would be no bad thing if our clergy might be induced to return now and again to the wholesome and inspiring doctrine of these unjustly neglected writers, which is full of sap and is often embodied in passages of incomparable eloquence.

Mr. Campagnac's introduction is a scholarly piece of work, and we feel especially grateful to him for the sympathetic way in which he has brought out the character of Whichcote. It is not very honourable to Cambridge, still the home of Platonic studies, that this volume should have been edited by an Oxonian and published by the Clarendon Press.

Scottish Cathedrals and Abbeys. By M. E. Leicester Addis. (Stock.)

OVERPOWERED by the splendour of their English rivals, the Scottish cathedrals and abbeys have attracted little attention. No comprehensive account, such as has frequently been given of English ecclesiastical edifices, is accessible in the case of the Scottish buildings, many of which are no less rich in historical and romantic associations. In the case of the Border counties the buildings best known to English travellers—Melrose, Dryburgh, &c.—are in ruins, not, as is sometimes supposed, through the iconoclastic zeal of Knox and his followers, but through the destruction wrought by English invaders. Further north, however, and in the western islands buildings of great beauty and historic interest are still found. It has been reserved for an American newspaper, the *Public Ledger* of Philadelphia, to start a series of papers, which have been expanded into what claims to be the first popular work dealing on a comprehensive scale with the Scottish abbeys and cathedrals. Iona, spoken of at times as "the cradle of Western Christianity," is one of the most interesting ecclesiastical ruins of the United Kingdom, and one also of the richest in historic associations. The fine old cathedral of St. Mungo or St. Kentigern in Glasgow, an early English building of great architectural value, comes foremost in importance, and was saved from destruction by the devotion of Glasgow citizens. One of two excellent views of this constitutes the frontispiece to the volume. Of Brechin Cathedral and Round Tower; St. Machar's Cathedral, Aberdeen; Dunblane and Dunkeld; St. Giles's, Edinburgh, more interesting for its monument to Montrose, modern as this is, than its architecture; Kirkwall; Dunfermline Abbey, unique in historical associations; and Paisley Abbey—one or more designs are given. Mr. Addis shows no lack of enthusiasm, and his book, which is obviously a labour of love, will appeal to a large number of readers.

History of the Parish of Bampton. By Mary E. Noble. (Kendal, Wilson.)

A RESIDENT in the parish of Bampton, in Westmoreland, with which her family has long been connected, Mrs. (?) Mary Noble, to whom is owing the publication of the Bampton registers, has undertaken and accomplished a history of the place, the materials of which are chiefly derived from her previous work. To the traveller for pleasure the valley through which runs the Lowther, though it contains Hawes Water, the highest lake in the district, and has some lovely views, is comparatively little known. Of its close on 11,000 acres, some 8,000 are moorland and 233 are rocks. Bampton is noted for the variety and richness of its flora, which, owing to its remote position, has suffered little from the ravages of female collectors of plants and ferns. Like other places in the neighbourhood, it supplies slate of good quality, which has occasionally been worked. For a description of these and other possessions we must refer the reader to the book. Early British remains are found at Burnbanks, Whinyates, and elsewhere, the best known being what are called "The Giants' Graves." Such explorations as have been undertaken have not been very remunerative. To residents in the district the book will appeal. Its literary pretensions are not high, and its index is, according to modern views, inadequate.

Le Verbe Basque. (Oxford, Parker & Co.)

THE author of this *brochure*, whose name is not on the title-page, but who, we discover incidentally, is Mr. E. S. Dodgson, has set himself the task of making "a synopsis, analytical and quotational, of the 130 forms of the Baskish verb in the Epistle to the Philippians, as found in Leiçarraga's New Testament, A.D. 1571," and the same of the 119 forms in the Epistle to the Colossians. We infer that this is a portion of a larger work of a grammatical nature, but as the writer does not inform us here of the object he has in view we are unable to say how far he has succeeded in attaining it.

The Babylonian Conception of Heaven and Hell. By Alfred Jeremias, Ph.D. (Nutt.)

THIS, the fourth issue of Mr Nutt's popular, but thoroughly trustworthy, "Ancient East" series, has appeared with commendable promptitude, and is in no way less interesting than its predecessors. Dr. Jeremias's 'Babylonian-Assyrian Conception of Life after Death' has long been a standard book in Germany on this department of eschatology, and the present little volume, which is beautifully printed on good paper, gives us the pith of his larger work. What makes it particularly interesting is that the ideas of the Babylonians on Hades and the life to come were shared to a great extent by the Hebrews, either through borrowing or, more probably, by common inheritance from a primitive Semitic stock. Even some of our own popular customs seem to be traceable to the same remote original—*e.g.*, the refusal of the usual rites of burial to one who had committed suicide (p. 15). We can reiterate our strong recommendation of this excellent series to all Bible students, and to the many who are interested in the fascinating sciences of comparative religion and folk-lore. Miss Hutchison, the translator, has done her part well.

Notices to Correspondents.

We must call special attention to the following notices:—

ON all communications must be written the name and address of the sender, not necessarily for publication, but as a guarantee of good faith.

WE cannot undertake to answer queries privately.

To secure insertion of communications correspondents must observe the following rules. Let each note, query, or reply be written on a separate slip of paper, with the signature of the writer and such address as he wishes to appear. When answering queries, or making notes with regard to previous entries in the paper, contributors are requested to put in parentheses, immediately after the exact heading, the series, volume, and page or pages to which they refer. Correspondents who repeat queries are requested to head the second communication "Duplicate."

ALEX. PARK ("'Twixt the devil and the deep sea").—Used in 1637 and 1697. See 7ᵗʰ S. i. 453. See also 'H.E.D.' under 'Devil,' 22 b.

NOTICE.

Editorial communications should be addressed to "The Editor of 'Notes and Queries'"—Advertisements and Business Letters to "The Publisher"—at the Office, Bream's Buildings, Chancery Lane, E.C.

We beg leave to state that we decline to return communications which, for any reason, we do not print; and to this rule we can make no exception.

LONDON, SATURDAY, MAY 10, 1902.

CONTENTS. — No. 228.

Notes.

DICKENS'S OPIUM DEN.

EXCEPT a short note of my own, which appeared in the *Globe*, 25 March, 1895, there is, I think, no account in existence of the subsequent fortunes of the opium den so graphically described by Dickens in 'Edwin Drood' A few additional details may, therefore, be considered not inappropriate to these more permanent columns, especially as the den was pulled down some years ago to make room for a Board-school playground, so that no one will ever see it again. It was situated in New Court, Victoria Street. I visited it many times, and was personally well known to the old couple who kept it. It was worth going to, if only to see a Chinaman and an Englishwoman so sincerely attached to one another. They might without impropriety have been called Darby and Joan. I once took a lady artist to see this interesting pair. She was delighted with them, and they with her. The Chinaman even went the length of allowing her to sketch him in the act of smoking. Those who know the dread this people have of anything that suggests publicity will appreciate this con-cession at its full value. The lady never revisited them, but they often spoke of her, and always wished to be kindly remembered to her when they saw me. Another former visitor whom they were never tired of recalling was no less a person than our present King. Upon his departure, it appears, His Royal Highness (as he then was) gave the old man a sovereign. He had never forgotten that coin, although in the lapse of time it had acquired something of a mythological halo. Johnson (for so we always called him) was an epicure, eating very little, but requiring that little to be of the best. He was a literary man, of course from the Chinese point of view, and had quite a small library of Chinese books. One of the works on his shelves ran to as many as twenty volumes, and was an historical compilation bearing the mellifluous name 'San Kwo Che.' He had a taste for art, and displayed conspicuously upon his wall for twenty years an amateur effort (the work of a Chinese sailor), being, curiously enough, the picture of an English church. It is now in the possession of a friend of mine. It was sold, with other effects, upon his eviction from his old quarters, including his scales for weighing opium, his opium lamp, his gambling cards and dominoes, two photographs, &c. A fatality seemed to pursue him, for not long had he moved to another den in Angel Gardens before that also was condemned. In fact, he never settled down again, but wandered from lodging to lodging. I never lost sight of him till the day of his decease, which took place in Cornwall Street, in his sixty-fourth year, and after that I traced his widow from one address to another until she was taken in charge by some charitable ladies.

The poor old man's opium pipe was as admirable an example of Oriental ingenuity as I have ever seen or heard of. Unable to afford a real pipe, he manufactured a "scratch" one out of an old flageolet and a door-knob. He drilled a small hole in the top of the door-knob, and affixed it by way of bowl to the flageolet (its holes stopped up), which served for stem. The result was a most capable and workmanlike pipe. This is the veritable flageolet pipe alluded to in the 'Dictionary of London,' while the door-knob which served for its bowl is doubtless what Mr. J. T. Fields mistook for an ink-bottle. The passage is in his 'In and Out of Doors with Dickens,' p. 106. "In a miserable court, at night," Mr. Fields tells us,

"we found a haggard old woman blowing at a kind of pipe made of an old ink-bottle, and the words that Dickens put into the mouth of this wretched creature in 'Edwin Drood' we heard her croon, as we leaned over the tattered bed on which she was lying."

Jas. Platt, Jun.

THE BACON—SHAKESPEARE QUESTION.
(Continued from p. 303.)

Since I commenced this series of papers a copy of Dr. R. M. Theobald's recent book, 'Shakespeare Studies in Baconian Light,' has come into my hands, and I have been invited to notice and reply to it. I accept the invitation.

From a literary point of view Dr. Theobald's book is a piece of good work, and he has made the best of a very bad case. His parallels from Bacon and Shakespeare are at times striking and interesting—almost as striking and interesting as those which I have been able to find in several other authors whose works I have compared with Bacon. If they are not so valuable as those which can be picked out of the work of other contemporary authors, the fault is solely, or almost solely, to be attributed to the fact that Shakespeare did not trouble himself to make an acquaintance with what Bacon had written; or that he was not conversant with the Latin, Greek, and other foreign authors with whom Bacon was familiar. As Ben Jonson has said, Shakespeare's knowledge of Latin was "small," and his acquaintance with Greek "less." His learning was derived mostly from translations or was cribbed from English writers.

Dr. Theobald's work displays an intimate knowledge of the writings of Bacon and Shakespeare, as was to be expected; but the fault of his whole argument is that he ignores the writings of other authors of the period. Shakespeare and Bacon occupy the whole of his mental vision, and beyond them he can see nothing. Hence we find him adducing a long list of words, phrases, and even common English proverbs to show that the dramatist must have had an intimate acquaintance with Latin and Greek authors in the original. If Dr. Theobald had taken the trouble to compare Shakespeare as closely with other writers of his time or previously as he has done with Bacon, he would have discovered that his book is a waste of good paper. The vocabulary of Shakespeare, which has called forth such a learned treatise as that of Dr. Theobald, was the vocabulary of the time; and the learning in the plays and poems, which startles the Baconians to-day, is that of the period also. All that need excite wonder in Shakespeare is the consummate art of the craftsman; and if we find him using strange words or phrases which cannot be found in other and earlier writers, we may assume, for the want of a better explanation, that he coined them.

I will now show that Dr. Theobald's researches have not extended far enough, and that he has credited Shakespeare with an amount of erudition to which the poet could lay no claim. Shakespeare was merely a scholar well versed in the commonplaces of his time, and he could get all, or nearly all, his knowledge of Latin and Greek authors from works written by English writers.

Many times in Shakespeare we find him making use of the proverb that companionship in misery eases grief. In 'Lucrece' the sentiment is expressed thus:—

> It easeth some, though none it ever cured,
> To think their dolour others have endured.
> Stanza 226, ll. 1581-2.

These lines, according to Dr. Theobald, are evidently a translation of a Latin motto in 'Faustus,' published in 1604, ten years after the appearance of 'Lucrece.' Here it is necessary to observe that Dr. Theobald claims the whole of Marlowe's work for Bacon, in addition to that of Shakespeare, consequently he makes a point of emphasizing the assertion that the 'Lucrece' lines are merely the translation of the Latin proverb, which was *probably invented* by Bacon:—

> Solamen miseris socios habuisse doloris.

Dr. Theobald argues that as Bacon *probably invented* the 'Faustus' motto, which has not been traced to a Latin author, he translated his own saying in 'Lucrece.' The argument assumes not only that Bacon wrote 'Lucrece' and 'Faustus,' but that the proverb was new when it appeared in the poem. "How it came to appear in 'Lucrece,'" he says, "is an enigma which awaits its solution." Prodigious!

Now this proverb, in precisely the same Latin form, occurs in Greene's 'Menaphon,' 1589, and in Lodge's 'Rosalind,' 1590; and its equivalent in English is thus expressed in John Lyly's 'Euphues,' 1579: "In misery, Euphues, it is a great comfort to have a companion" (Arber, p. 96). 'Euphues' was one of Shakespeare's favourite books, and he borrows from it in several of his plays, especially in 'Love's Labour's Lost' and in 'Henry IV.' But the proverb itself was musty with age when 'Lucrece' was written, and it had become hackneyed by common usage.

"One of Bacon's frequently recurring aphorisms is that sunshine penetrates even dunghills and *cloacæ*, and yet is not thereby defiled."

So Dr. Theobald, who devotes more than four pages of his book to show that this rusty old saying is referred to by both Bacon and Shakespeare. There are at least three allusions to it in 'Euphues':—

"Cæsar never rejoyced more, then when hee heard that they talked of his valyant exploits in simple cotages, alledging this, that a bright Sunne shineth in every corner, which maketh not the beames worse, but the place better," &c.—Arber, p. 255.

"It is the disposition of the thought, that altereth the nature of the thing. The Sunne shineth upon the dounghil, and is not corrupted," &c.—P. 43.

"Bicause you are brave, disdaine not those that are base, thinke with your selves that russet coates have their Christendome, that the Sunne when he is at his hight shineth aswel upon course carsie, as cloth of tissue," &c.—P. 443.

Bacon attributes a saying to Mr. Bettenham, "that riches were like muck; when it lay upon an heap, it gave but a stench and ill odour; but when it was spread upon the ground then it was cause of much fruit."—'Apophthegms.'

Now Bacon did not mean to state that this was an original saying of Mr. Bettenham's, he merely notices it because it was so often in Mr. Bettenham's mouth. Dr. Theobald was not able to bring a strictly parallel passage from Shakespeare, but he adduces one from 'Coriolanus,' where wealth or the spoils captured in battle are contemptuously spoken of as

The common *muck* of the world.
Act II. sc. ii. l. 128.

Although Shakespeare does not make an open use of the proverb, it could hardly be unknown to him, for it occurs in the ballad of 'Gernatus, the Jew of Venice,' which furnished hints for 'The Merchant of Venice':

His life was like a barrow hogge,

Or like a filthy heap of dung,
That lyeth in a whourd;
Which never can do any good,
Till it be spread abroad.
Percy's 'Reliques of Ancient English Poetry.'

Ben Jonson, too, alludes to the proverb :—

Sord. Though hitherto amongst you I have lived,
Like an unsavoury muck-hill, to myself,
Yet now my gather'd heaps, being spread abroad,
Shall turn to better and more fruitful uses.
'Every Man out of his Humour,' Act III. sc. ii.

C. CRAWFORD.
53, Hampden Road, Hornsey, N.
(*To be continued.*)

ADDITIONS TO THE 'N.E.D.'
(*Continued from p. 265.*)

Abdomened (not in).—1805, Kirby in Kirby and Spence, 'Int. Entomol.,' ed. 1856, p. 573, "The specimen......was a black-abdomened one."

Abrin (not in).—1886, Klein, 'Micro-Organisms and Disease' (third ed.), p. 227, "The active principle [of jequirity poison] is a proteid—abrin—closely allied to native albumen."

Acariologist (not in).—1902, *Nature*, 27 March, p. 483.

Actinium (? not in). — 1902, Becquerel in *Brit. Journ. Photog.*, p. 306, "In 1900 M. Debierne announced the existence of a new element, actinium."

Aërobic (not in).—Klein, *ut supra*, p. 55, "Some bacteria require free access to oxygen, and are called aërobic (Pasteur); others grow without free oxygen, and are anaërobic (Pasteur)."

Æsthesiogenes (not in).—1896, Baldwin, trl. Binet, 'Alterations of Personality,' p. 263, "The action of æsthesiogenes on the nervous system is still doubted by very eminent men."

Alamandine (=Almandine).—1895, J. W. Anderson, 'Prospector's Handbook' (sixth ed.), p. 96.

Amœbœic (not in).—1850, Pococke, 'Greek Pastoral Poetry' in 'Ency. Metropol.,' p. 327, "These amœbœic songs."

Amphiarthrosis (earlier).—1809, Spence, *ut supra*, p. 588, "That articulation called by anatomists amphiarthrosis."

Amyloform (not in). — 1897, *English Mechanic*, p. 554, "A substitute for iodoform has recently been prepared by Prof. Classen, of Aix-la-Chapelle, which he names 'amyloform,' and which consists of a combination of formaldehyde with starch."

Amyrine (chem., not in). — 1889, 'Chambers's Ency.,' iv. 288.

Anaërobic (not in).—See 'Aërobic' above.

Anamesite (not in).—1888, 'Chambers's Ency.,' i. 768, "Fine-grained kinds [of basalt rocks] are called anamesite."

Anarthrous (earlier). — 1809, Kirby, *ut supra*, p. 591, "This anarthrous joint."

Anastigmat. — 1897, *Brit. Journ. Photog. Alm.*, p. 625, "The term 'anastigmat' was, for the first time, employed......by Dr. Miethe." [1888.]

Angeiology (=Angiology). — 1888, 'Chambers's Ency.,' i. 254, "Angeiology describes the vessels or ducts, with their complex network and ramifications."

Anidrosis (not in).—1882, R. Quain, 'Dict. Medicine,' which also mentions numerous terms (not in), such as *adenitis, adenoma, alphosis, arthralgia,* &c.

Annihilationalism (=Annihilationism). — 1890, 'Chambers's Ency.,' v. 632.

Anytin, Anytole (not in).—1898, *English Mechanic*, p. 331, "This ammonia salt......is called by Helmers 'anytin'"; *ibid.*, "Preparations thus made soluble are called anytoles."

Aplite (not in).—1890, 'Chambers's Ency.,' vol. v. p. 353, "Aplite is a fine-grained aggregate of quartz and orthoclase."

Aplome (not in). — 1890, 'Chambers's Ency.,' vol. v. p. 89, "Aplome, green, brownish, and sometimes yellow" (Garnet).

Aristo, Aristotype (not in). — 1894, 'American Ann. Photog.,' p. 98, "Some way of mounting the aristotype without paste"; *ibid.*, p. 274, "Toning and fixing aristotype prints"; *ibid.*, p. 68, "When aristo papers were first introduced."

Arrhenite (not in). — 1901, *Brit. Journ. Photog.*, September suppl., p. 65, "Xenotime, arrhenite, sipilite."

Arrow-worm (not in).—1892, 'Chambers's Ency.,' ix. 73, "Sagitta, or arrow-worm, a genus of small pelagic worms."

Automatograph (not in).—1896, Baldwin, *ut supra*, p. 231, "Prof. J. Jastrow has invented an instrument called the automatograph, by which automatic movements may be registered."

Auxanometer (not in).—1884, Henfrey, 'Element. Bot.' (fourth ed.), p. 607, "Where great accuracy and the measurement of minute spaces [in growth] are demanded, recourse must be had to special instruments called auxanometers."

Auxospore (not in).—Henfrey, *ut supra*, p. 425, "Until the original size is restored by the production of auxospores."

Azaleine (not in).—1900, G. Iles, 'Flame, Electricity, and the Camera,' p. 283, "The dyes at present used in the preparation of orthochromatic plates are chiefly eosin, cyanin, azulin, erythrosin, azaleine, and croculein."

Baisoned (*supra*, p. 263)=Bausond.

Bally-tree (not in).—1888, 'Chambers's Ency.,' vol. ii. p. 197, "Black-bully, bally-tree wood, or sapodilla plum (*Sapota Mülleri* or *Achras sapota*)."

Bannering (not in).—1888, 'Chambers's Ency.,' vol. ii. p. 363, "At Shrewsbury the bounds-beating was called bannering."

Bark-speeler (not in).—1889, 'Chambers's Ency.,' vol. iii. p. 555, "The Scotch name bark-speeler ('climber') describes its almost constant habit" (*Certhia familiaris*, the common creeper).

Barley midge (not in).—1889, 'Chambers's Ency.,' vol. ii. p. 40, "*Cecidomyia cerealis*, sometimes called the barley midge, a brownish fly with silvery wings."

Barton (=Burton).—Spon, *ut infra*, p. 470.

Bath white (not in).—1885, Kane, 'European Butterflies,' p. 9, "*Pieris daplidice*, L., the Bath white."

Bauxite=Beauxite.

Beaum (=Balm).—Kirby and Spence, p. 417, "A fragrant odour of beaum."

Bee-martin (not in).—1892, 'Chambers's Ency.,' vol. x. p. 355, "The common American shrikebilled king-bird, or bee-martin (*Tyrannus tyrannus*)."

Bee-moth (not in).—1890, 'Chambers's Ency.,' vol. v. p. 762, "Honeycomb moth, or bee-moth (*Galleria*)."

Bell, v (cf. the sense).—1902, *Munsey's Mag.*, March, p. 765, "The night-owl solemnly bells the frogs to vespers."

Bionomics (not in).—1896, 'Hazell's Annual,' p. 73, "Bionomics, which deals with the habits and variations of animals, and their modifications."

Biscuit root (not in).—1890, 'Chambers's Ency.,' vol. vi. p 631, "The quamash or biscuit root (*Camassia esculenta*) of North America."

Blind.—1895, Anderson, 'Prospector's Handbook,' p. 154, "Blind creek—a creek, dry, except during wet weather."

Blow, v. (with blowpipe) — 1893, Spon, 'Mechanic's Own Book' (fourth ed.), p. 641, "Lead the pipe away to the main supply, and 'blow' it on by means of a union suited to the case"; *ibid.*, "One end of it is 'blown on' to an 'elbow nose-piece.'"

Borzoi (not in).—1898, *Bazaar*, 1 April, "Handsome Borzoi dog."

Brachisto-chronous (not in).—1893, McCormack, trl. Mach, 'Science of Mechanics,' p. 435, "If the whole curve is brachisto-chronous, every element of it is also brachisto-chronous."

Brasqued (not in).—Spon, *ut supra*, p. 17, "Heated in a brasqued crucible."

Briquetting (not in).—1898, *English Mechanic*, p 194, "Briquetting sawdust."

Broggerite (not in).—1901, *Brit. Jour. Photog.*, September suppl., p 65, "Alvite, broggerite, monazite."

Buckstone (not in)—1895, Anderson, *ut supra*, p. 155, "Buckstone—rock not producing gold."

Bushelage.—Hist. MSS. Com. Report on Lostwithiel Muniments, &c., p. 334.

Butterick (*supra*, p. 265).—A correspondent, Mr. H. Leffmann, of Philadelphia, U.S., informs me that this word "comes from the name of a New York dealer in patterns for fashionable clothing."

J. DORMER.

Redmorion, Woodside Green, S.E.

(*To be continued.*)

"PASCHAL": "PASCUA."—The Spanish usage of the word *Pascua*, denoting the Paschal feast and other Church festivals, is worthy of note. Originally, no doubt, it is the equivalent of the French *Pâque* and the Russian *Pascha*, which, from being the Jewish *Pasch*, has become the Christian Easter, this last name recalling an old Norse festival. (Note the misplaced occurrence of *Easter* in Acts xii. 4, A.V.) The Spaniard talks of "Pascua de Navedad," "Pascua de Resurrección"—a pleonasm at first sight — and "Pascua de Pentecostés." When an eminent Spanish professor saluted me shortly after Christmas with "¿Ha pasado V. una buena Pascua?" I thought he had made a *lapsus linguæ*, and received enlightenment. (The Italian speaks of Whitsuntide as *Pasqua rosata*.) The Russian veneration for Easter is well known. Illustrated and other journals print the beautiful greeting in prominent type, "Christos voskrese! Vo istinie voskres!" ("Christ is risen! He is risen indeed!") and the glad tidings, passing from friend to friend, breathe an influence of affection and good will throughout the great Russian land.

FRANCIS P. MARCHANT.

Brixton Hill.

EASTER DAY AT BEVERLEY.—The following cutting from the *Leeds Mercury Weekly Supplement* of 5 April may interest your readers :—

"Sunday's services at St. Mary's Church, Beverley, commenced with Holy Communion at 6.30 A.M. At the Minster the choir ascended the north-west tower, and sang the Easter Hymn. The weather was cold but fine throughout the day."

St. Mary's Church at Beverley is a fine Perpendicular building in the market-place of that town, though eclipsed by the glories of Beverley Minster. Probably the idea of singing a hymn from the top of one of the towers was taken from the time-honoured custom at Magdalen College, Oxford, of

singing the 'Hymnus Eucharisticus' at 5 A.M. on May Day. JOHN PICKFORD, M.A.
Newbourne Rectory, Woodbridge.

EASTER CUSTOMS AT TAUNTON AND HASELEY.—Every series of 'N. & Q.' contains accounts of Easter customs in various parts of the world, but among them I fail to trace any report of the annual proceedings at Taunton (Somerset) or Haseley (Warwick).

Prebendary Askwith stated, at the Easter vestry for the parish of St. Mary Magdalene at Taunton, that the vestry had been regularly held at eleven o'clock on the morning of Easter Tuesday ever since the time of Queen Elizabeth. The meeting is also by ancient prescriptive right held without any notice being given. Another peculiarity is that there are three churchwardens, all of whom are elected by the parishioners, the vicar having no power of appointment. This state of things is supposed to be almost unique in England, and Prebendary Askwith said he was informed by his legal advisers that if the slightest deviation were made in the method of procedure, such as public notice of the meeting being given, the ancient prescriptive right would be lost and the proceedings would have to be conducted in accordance with modern law.

The Rev. Edward Muckleston, rector of the parish of Haseley, Warwick, stated that after the Easter vestry meeting is held the churchwardens adjourn to the parish public-house. The parish warden there reads out the list of quarterly expenses, and the rector then invites all the parishioners to eggs and ham and tea. After that is over the churchwardens treat all the parishioners to whatever they like to drink, and then the rector does the same. The evening is spent in singing songs, &c. This custom has been carried out for sixty years. EVERARD HOME COLEMAN.

"COCKERTONIZED": "GARAGE."—The Daily News of 23 April has invented a word after the fashion of "boycotted." In the issue of that day it writes the word "Cockertonized" in relation to Mr. Cockerton's crusade against the London School Board's Pupil Teachers' Centres.

The Daily Mail of the same date, referring to "new storage accommodation for city men's automobiles," writes of such storage accommodation as a "garage." Unde derivatur?
GREVILLE WALPOLE, M.A., LL.D.
Kensington.

[For "Garage," see 9th S. viii. 143, 230.]

FLINT-GLASS TRADE. — The Birmingham Daily Post of 2 April contains an interesting article on the present state of the flint-glass trade in the Midlands. From it I extract the following :—

"The men work in turns or shifts of six hours each ; in these six-hour turns the Union has fixed the quantity of work to be done. For instance, eighty is the limit number of strawstem wineglasses to be made in six hours by a 'chair,' which consists of three men and a boy. It might be presumed that a quick man might be allowed to go on making articles, and, of course, receive extra payment, but this is not so. If he gets through his number before the expiration of the six hours the business of the glass house has no further concern for him. He has done his stint......Incidentally it may be mentioned that the earnings are good, even for skilled workmen. At one establishment in Birmingham for a week of forty hours a workman—the chief of a 'chair'—would draw about 3l., the servitor 2l., and the footblower [in another part of the article called the footmaker] 30s."

The use of "chair" in this sense is not recorded in the 'H.E.D.,' and the use of "workman" in the special sense of chief of the "chair" is interesting, as are also the terms "stint," "servitor," and "footblower" or "footmaker." BENJ. WALKER.
Gravelly Hill, Erdington.

A CURIOUS WAY OF LETTING LAND.—The enclosed cutting is from the Yorkshire Post of 9 April :—

"An ancient custom in connection with the letting of a piece of land at Bourne, known as 'The White Bread Meadow,' was observed on Monday last. The land is let by auction, and at each bid a boy is started to run to a given public-house, and the land is let to the person whose bid has not been challenged when the last boy returns. The land on Monday was let for 5l. 7s. 6d. The money is partly spent in a bread and cheese and onion supper at a public-house, and the remainder is spent in loaves of bread delivered to every house within a certain district of the town."

J. A. CROSS.

COLONIAL JOURNALISM.—The following is from the Advertiser (Adelaide), 23 December, 1901 :—

"Last night Leslie Berry, a State boy, 8½ years of age, who was boarded out with Mr. John Fernace, of Lower McDonald, was bitten by a deaf adder close to the latter's residence. He was not at first aware that he had been bitten, and died in an hour and a half afterwards."

One knows what the writer meant, but why did he express himself in this way?
EDWARD BENSLY.
The University, Adelaide, South Australia.

BISHOP WHITE KENNETT'S FATHER.—The 'D.N.B.' states that the bishop was born in the parish of St. Mary, Dover, 10 August, 1660, son of Basil Kennett, M.A., rector of Dimchurch and vicar of Postling, by his wife Mary, eldest daughter of Thomas White, a wealthy magistrate and master shipwright of Dover.

In the 'Calendar of State Papers (Domestic), 1659-60,' p. 361, I notice the following:

"13 Feb. Thoˢ White to the Admʸ Comʳˢ. Being ordered by the Navy Comʳˢ to be their Agent at Dover......I took to my assistance my son-in-law Basil Kennet as storekeeper, and he had as much employment therein as he could well perform; first in taking into the storehouse such stores as were sent from Deptford, and what we bought at Dover or elsewhere for the use of the Navy, faithfully performed by Kennett, and no man in the town being able to do the service so well, he having been trained up in it these five or six years. I entreat you to confirm him in the place of storekeeper, and allow him such salary as may allow him to subsist. There has been nothing allowed him these five years but what I have given him out of my own salary."

Again, 20 February, p. 373:—

"Now my request is that you will be pleased to continue my son as storekeeper, and allow him what you think fit."

And finally, on 21 February, p. 373:—

"My son Kennett the storekeeper has gone to London, with a request for such stores as we stand in need of; his services are very necessary both for the safety and profit of the Commonwealth; if you will examine him concerning the particulars, he will give you an account."

From the above it would appear that the bishop's father was originally a storekeeper under his father-in-law Thomas White, and subsequently took holy orders and became vicar of Postling, in Kent, where the bishop's younger brother, Dr. Basil Kennett, was born in 1674.　　R. J. FYNMORE.

Sandgate, Kent.

SNODGRASS, A SURNAME.—A notice of the 'Choice Humorous Works of Theodore Hook' in the *Athenæum* of 22 March, p. 370, makes mention of the name of Mr. Pickwick's friend Mr. Snodgrass in a manner which, whether rightly or wrongly, has left on my mind the impression that the writer imagined it to be an invention of Charles Dickens. This is certainly not the case. It occurs in the late M. A. Lower's 'Dictionary of Family Names'; and in Bohn's 'Lowndes's Bibliographer's Manual' a James Snodgrass, D.D., and a Major J. J. Snodgrass appear as authors.

It is probable that if search were made nearly every name in 'Pickwick' could be proved to be that of a real family.　　ASTARTE.

MOURNING SUNDAY.—The following paragraph from the *St. James's Gazette* of 11 April refers to a custom which is perhaps worth noting, if it has not been noted before in 'N. & Q.':—

"A curious custom exists amongst the peasantry of the Isle of Man, and it is probably only of recent years that the better classes have given up its observation. The Sunday following the funeral of a relative is called 'Mourning Sunday,' and as many of the dead person's relations as are available meet together and go to church. The extraordinary part of it, however, is that throughout the entire time they remain seated, and do not enter at all into any outward participation in the service. It would be interesting to know whether any similar custom prevails in other countries of the United Kingdom, or whether it is a Scandinavian relic."

The same custom is observed in North Devonshire. There was an instance of it at Tawstock Church, near Barnstaple, in November last year. In that case a child had died of scarlet fever, yet the parents were in church the day after the funeral, which was a Sunday. They remained seated throughout the service.　　J. P. LEWIS.

GREEN CANDLES IN CHURCH. (See *ante*, p. 339.)—I do not know what is the custom now, but green tapers used to appear on the altar at All Saints', Margaret Street. In the late fifties, when Archbishop Tait (then Bishop of London) had some trouble regarding what is now called ritualism, he was represented in a cartoon in *Punch* as driving out of church sundry clergymen carrying candlesticks, &c., and then was given a rime

Yon Barney must not here be seen
With Christmas candles red and green.

The church was St. Barnabas's, Pimlico.
　　GEORGE ANGUS.

St. Andrews, N.B.

AN INDUSTRIOUS LITTÉRATEUR.—It will interest numerous readers of 'N. & Q.,' I am sure, to learn that Mr. Thomas Bayne, an exceptionally well-informed and always interesting contributor—as is shown by his latest article, in which he contends, against some formidable opponents, that the 'Ode to the Cuckoo' is the work of Michael Bruce—has completed a series of sketches of 'Literary Churchmen' in *Saint Andrew*. Beginning with Blair, Robertson, and Home, the series closes with Principal Caird and Dr. Boyd, the genial essayist known to the literary world as A. K. H. B. It is to be hoped Mr. Bayne will publish these literary portraits in volume form. Some readers of 'N. & Q.' will likewise be interested to hear that the March *Temple Bar* contained an article on 'James Macfarlan, the Pedlar Poet,' from the pen of Mr. Bayne.　　JOHN GRIGOR.

105, Choumert Road, Peckham.

DRYHURST: COLUMBELL.—In Ashover, near Chesterfield, is a farm called Dryhurst, which is bounded on the west by Columbell Lane. The soil is peaty, and beneath it fallen trees are sometimes found. The farm is about one thousand feet above the sea level, and much exposed to westerly winds. In seeking for the meaning of the word it has occurred to me that the first syllable may be the O.N. *draug-r*, a dry log, so that Dryhurst would mean "dry log (dead log) copse." A place called Deadshaw Sick, near Dronfield in the same county, lends support to the suggestion which I am making. To the south and west of Dryhurst are two other farms called Brockhurst and Peasunhurst. I may say that Peasunhurst is not at all a likely place for growing peas.

The inhabitants of the district accent the word Columbell on the penultimate, as though it were derived from the Lat. *columna*. The Lat. *columna* is found in O.E. in the forms *columne* and *columbe*, so that Columbell may be Columb-well, the *w* being thrown out by the accent on the penultimate. Accordingly the meaning seems to be " pillar field " or " post field," the termination " well " being, as is often the case, the O.N. *völl-r*. At Darley, two or three miles to the west of Dryhurst, there was an ancient family called Columbell. Their evidences go back at least to the thirteenth century.   S. O. Addy.

Queries.

We must request correspondents desiring information on family matters of only private interest to affix their names and addresses to their queries, in order that the answers may be addressed to them direct.

Downie's Slaughter.—A legend of Aberdeen University tells of a college servant, by name Downie, who, having rendered himself obnoxious to the undergraduates, was one evening forcibly conducted by a party of students into one of the college rooms, and after a mock trial sentenced to death. He was then led into another room, draped with black, and containing a block and a masked executioner with an axe. Downie was blindfolded and made to kneel at the block. After an interval, the executioner struck his neck with a wet towel. The farce was at an end, but Downie was found to be dead. The terrified students swore a solemn oath of secrecy, and the real circumstances of the death were revealed only after many years by one of the participators on his deathbed. This story, told with much circumstantial and picturesque detail, appears for the first time in print (so far as I have been able to discover) in a curious book, 'Things in General' ('N. & Q.,' 4th S. xi. 156, 510; xii.

19; 5th S. vii. 488; viii. 14), published anonymously in London in 1824, but now known to have been written by Robert Mudie (2nd S. xii. 257; 4th S. xii. 83). It is also dished up in varying forms in Colburn's *New Monthly Magazine* for June, 1830, p. 508 (? by Pryse Gordon); in *Household Words* for 24 July, 1852 (? by Andrew Halliday); and in ' Life at a Northern University,' by Neil N. Maclean, 1874. Mr. George Walker, in his entertaining volume ' Aberdeen Awa',' 1897, p. 355, suggests that the legend " owes its creation to that clever wag Sandy Bannerman [afterwards Sir Alexander Bannerman, M.P. for Aberdeen], and that if it is the poorest history, it is a bit of the richest romance." Bannerman, according to Mr. Walker, invented the story and told it to Mudie, who was not a university man. But, apart from the question whether Bannerman can be credited with originating so remarkably dramatic an incident, it is not easy to reconcile a first appearance of the story in a somewhat obscure book published anonymously in London with the fact that but a very few years later, as Mr. Walker tells me from his own recollection, the legend was such a household word in Aberdeen that students were habitually greeted by schoolchildren with the cry, "Airt an' pairt in Downie's slaughter," or the query, " Fa [Aberdonian for " who "] killed Downie ? " Further, Dr. John Cumming, in his ' Millennial Rest,' relates the story (drawing a moral therefrom) as one current when he was an undergraduate. He matriculated at King's College, Aberdeen, in 1822. Again, a correspondent assures me that his father had the story from John Bowman, schoolmaster of St. Vigean's, as a tradition of his university days (1783–7).

Not a hint of the tragic occurrence is to be found in any college record, and it is difficult to understand how there came to be localized in Aberdeen a legend the machinery of which smacks rather of German student life or the Holy Vehm. Can any reader recall, in history or in fiction, the incident of a pretended execution causing actual death?
P. J. Anderson.
Aberdeen University Library.

Black Malibran.—Can any reader give me information concerning a vocalist thus named who sang in London about 1857? I desire her true name, date of death, or any biographical data concerning her.
Edward Denham.
New Bedford, Massachusetts.

Reaches of the Thames.—Can any reader give the origin of the names of some of the reaches of the river Thames below London? Such names as Limehouse, Greenwich, or Blackwall speak for themselves; but not so with Bugsby's, Gallions, or St. Clement's, sometimes called Fiddler's Reach. Erith Rands no doubt means the shoals below the town of that name. The title of "Hope" given to the two reaches above and below that of Gravesend is sufficiently obscure.

P. L. N. F.

FRANCESCA DA RIMINI.—The Paris correspondent of the *Times*, in his letter of 22 April, speaks of having read in his youth, at Ravenna, a sixteenth-century manuscript violently attacking the tragic adventure of the beautiful daughter of Polenta, the lord of Ravenna. I should like to know where that manuscript is to be found, and whether it has been translated into English.

RICHARD EDGCUMBE.

33, Tedworth Square, Chelsea.

ENGLISH TRANSLATIONS.—I shall be glad if any one can inform me if English translations, in whole or in part, have ever been published of the following works: Grimmelshausen's 'Simplicissimus,' 'Cent Nouvelles Nouvelles,' Cabet's 'Voyage en Icarie.'

NOVEL.

AUTHORS OF BOOKS WANTED.—1. 'Two Old Men's Tales' (Bentley, 1844). 2. 'Oakfield; or, Fellowship in the East,' by Punjaubee (Longman, 1853, 2 vols.). R. S.

[1. By Mrs. Anne Marsh. 2. By W. D. Arnold.]

PORTRAITS WANTED.—Are any portraits extant of the following; if so, where?

Henry Dene, Archbishop of Canterbury, 1501-3.

John Carpenter, Bishop of Worcester, 1443-76.

John Chedworth, Bishop of Lincoln, 1452-1471.

Thomas Ruthall, Bishop of Durham, 1509-1523.

Edward Fox, Bishop of Hereford, 1535-8.

Admiral Sir William Penn, father of the founder of Pennsylvania. INQUIRER.

OMAR QUERIES.—1. In which translation of Omar is the expression "Sanctuary from self" to be found?

2. In FitzGerald's version, among the metaphors of the potter's clay (the vessels are discussing "whence" and "whither') runs a line:—

Hark to the porter's shoulder-knot a-creaking.

I should be glad to know who is meant here by the porter, and also what a shoulder-knot may be. Does the moon, which is subse-

quently mentioned, throw any light on this obscure matter? L. K.

[The porter is going to the well to water the dried-up pots after a month of abstinence (Ramazan). The new month is indicated by the new moon. The shoulder-knot, or porter's knot, is a pad worn on the shoulder to ease the carriage of the burden.]

GENERAL SIR WILLIAM FAWCETT.—I should be glad of any information about the family of General Sir William Fawcett. He came from Shipden Hall, near Halifax, Yorks, was Governor of Chelsea Hospital, and died in 1804. M. F.

ARMS WANTED.—Dexter, A lion rampant between three fleurs-de-lis. Sinister, On a field azure, a chevron or between three windmill sails (or crosses). These arms are on a piece of silver plate perhaps 150 years old.

T. WILSON.

Rivers Lodge, Harpenden.

MARRIAGE LICENCES.—The ages of the contracting parties are usually given as "about," and two or three places are mentioned, at any one of which the marriage is to take place. Why "about," and why more than one place? Were they used in compliance with any rules of the offices granting the licences, and what period of time did "about" embrace? Also, did a spinster, no matter what her age may have been, require by law the "consent" of her parent or parents, or other person, to her marriage? C. MASON.

29, Emperor's Gate, S.W.

RICHARDSON FAMILY.—Wanted the pedigree of the Richardsons of Warmington, Warwickshire, and co. Armagh, Ireland; also of the Richardsons of Toldish Hall, Coventry. Also particulars of Lady Elizabeth Percy, who married the Rev. William Nicholson about 1620.

(Mrs.) ETHEL M. RICHARDSON.

The Grove, Trefnant, N. Wales.

AUTOGRAPH COTTAGE. — William Upcott (1790-1854), sometimes styled the king of autograph collectors, spent the last years of his life in an old mansion in Upper Street, Islington, which he quaintly denominated Autograph Cottage. Can any reader identify this house or its site? ALECK ABRAHAMS.

39, Hillmarton Road, N.

FASHIONABLE SLANG OF THE PAST.—With reference to my query on 'Fashion in Language' (*ante*, p. 228), which I see quoted in the *Daily Mail* of 24 March, will not some expert contributor also tell us the life story of a selected number of fashionable slang words which from time to time have had their little day among the *jeunesse dorée* of both sexes and then died out? "Rippin'" had a great vogue. "The cheese," now obsolete, was, I suspect, of Anglo-Indian origin, as "No. 1" (*Ichiban*) is from Japan. Many of the best, I doubt not, hail, with other good things, from the United States.

C. SWYNNERTON.

"MASE."—Can any of your readers kindly give me information as to the origin of the word "mase" in the family name of Masefield? Can it have any connexion with Maserfield, near Oswestry? Any information will be gladly received by

(Rev.) F. J. WROTTESLEY.

Denstone Vicarage, Uttoxeter.

"POTION FOR THE HEALTH OF ENGLAND."— A fragment of a printed sermon, pasted upon the inside of the front and back covers, and filling two fly-leaves of John Udall's (anonymous) 'Commentarie upon the Lamentations of Jeremy' (195 pages, in small 4to, Lond., 1593), is headed by the drastic title "A Private man's potion for the health of England." Could some one kindly find out the author and date of this sermon or pamphlet? Is it perhaps another work of John Udall, author of various sermons, and a great sufferer for his Nonconformity, who was condemned, for one of his works, to die, but was respited, and died 1592 in prison? I may just add that one passage of this fragment is addressed to the "good Queene and praiseworthie princesse." Another speaks of "our gracious Queene," and expresses the belief that "Christ Jesus will suffer no violence to bee done unto his deare spowse, our Queene and governesse," by whom probably Elizabeth is meant.

H. KREBS.

Oxford.

EXHUMATION OF HENRY IV.—Is there any authentic contemporary account of the exhuming of the body of Henry IV. by the Dean of Canterbury, in Canterbury Cathedral, in 1830? Any information will much oblige. ANTIQUARY.

MADAME DE WARENS.—I find a portrait of the lady mentioned above as a frontispiece to vol. ii. of an unabridged translation of the 'Confessions' of Jean Jacques (privately printed, 1901). Could any of your readers inform me by whom the original was painted, and where the picture is now to be found?

J. R. FITZGERALD.

NEWCASTLE SILVER MARKS.—I have two or three pieces of silver plate, all bearing the Newcastle mark of the year 1788, and the maker's mark M & R in Roman capitals on an oblong punch. Can any one say to whom this mark belonged? It is not in my edition of Cripps. E. R.

"YE GODS AND LITTLE FISHES!"—What is the origin of this familiar exclamation? It is not to be found in the ordinary dictionaries of quotations. Q. R. B.

'AYLWIN.'—It is generally understood that Darcy in this novel is intended for a portrait of D. G. Rossetti. Are any of the other characters capable of being identified in the same way? FRED. G. ACKERLEY.

Seemannsheim, Libau, Russia.

LADY ELIZABETH TALBOT.—I am anxious to ascertain the maiden name of Lady Elizabeth Talbot, wife of Thomas Talbot (who died 23 July, 1487), and mother of Sir Peter Talbot, Knt., ancestor of Lord Talbot de Malahide. Can any reader of 'N. & Q.' kindly assist me? WM. JACKSON PIGOTT.

Dundrum, co. Down.

[Burke's 'Peerage,' *s.v.* Talbot de Malahide, says that the mother of Peter was Thomas Talbot's first wife, whose name was Sommerton. Thomas Talbot's second wife was Elizabeth Buckley.]

SIR ISAAC NEWTON: 'COMMERCIUM EPISTOLICUM.'—I want to know of copies of the "Commercium Epistolicum D. Johannis Collins, et aliorum de Analysi Promota...... 1712, 4to." I shall be glad if any person possessing a copy, or knowing of one, will communicate with me. G. J. GRAY.

14, Church Street, Chesterton, Cambridge.

'HISTORY OF AYDER ALI KHAN.'—Who was the author of the following book?—

"The History of Ayder Ali Khan Nabob Bahader, or New Memoirs concerning the East-Indies, with Historical Notes, by M. M. D. L. T., General of Ten Thousand Men in the Army of the Mogol Empire, and formerly Commander in Chief of the Artillery of Ayder Ali, and of a Body of European Troops in the Service of that Nabob."—2 vols. 6½ in. by 4 in., Dublin, 1774.

W. CROOKE.

Langton House, Charlton Kings.

DRAGON TREE.—I am told that the first specimen of this curious plant brought over to Europe was the one to be found to this day in the gardens of the Marquis of Sabugosa, near Lisbon, and that among other books that called 'Child's Guide to Knowledge,' published some ninety years ago, mentions the fact. Can any of your complaisant readers give me some information on the subject and tell me where this book can be found? TYRONE.

Replies.

"ONLY TOO THANKFUL."
(9ᵗʰ S. ix. 288.)

I REALLY think that DR. MURRAY is making a *nodus in scirpo* of this matter, and that, after swallowing many sematological (the word is his) camels, he is now straining at a sematological gnat.

In this elliptical colloquialism it seems to me that the word "only" is used in order to denote that the sentiment expressed is the least that the speaker can say on the subject, while the word "too" implies that the speaker is more thankful than he can express, or—in certain cases—too thankful to dream of declining any proffered boon. The phrase might be resolved as follows : "All that I can say, or the only thing I can say, is that I am too thankful for adequate expression—or too thankful to dream of declining such and such a thing."

Similarly in the phrase "only too true" the idea implied is that the least, or the only thing, that can be predicated of the subject is that it is too true to be doubted or disputed, as in the Italian phrase *troppo vero*, or *pur troppo vero*.   PATRICK MAXWELL.
Bath.

It seems to me that in this now very common expression the "only" and the "too" are to be taken separately as qualifying the "thankful." "Only" means that the feeling of thankfulness so dominates the heart of the speaker that there is no room for any other ; he or she is nothing but thankful. And the "too" means that this feeling is too strong to be expressed in words. The "only" may, however, be taken to mean that this "too" is so in a unique sense. But in "only too true" the "too true" undoubtedly means that the matter alluded to is true, but that the speaker wishes it had not been so ; it is too true to please him or her. Here again the "only" probably means that this feeling is entertained in a unique sense, intensifying (as the speaker supposes) the "too." But what it really does intensify is the feeling, or express even more strongly the wish that the matter in hand had not been true. For a thing can only be true or false ; "very true" is a redundant expression, like "infallible" as applied to "proof," which the revisers have properly removed from Acts i. 3.
    W. T. LYNN.
Blackheath.

I cannot give the exact date of the first time I heard an expression of this kind, but am certain that it was between the years 1849 and 1853. I had made a trivial present to a cousin, and she said on receiving it, "Oh, Edward, you are only too good to me." What the present consisted of I have long forgotten, but her words impressed me at the time, for I had never heard the idiom before, though of course I became very familiar with it not long after. A friend has shown me since DR. MURRAY's question appeared an instance of the kind in one of G. Lawrence's novels. I give the extract : "This fancy the other was only too ready to indulge" ('Sans Merci,' by the author of 'Guy Livingstone,' chap. xvi. Tauchnitz edit., 1866, vol. i. p. 209).
    EDWARD PEACOCK.

I have asked several people what they mean by "only too thankful," and all who have thought of the meaning at all agree in explaining the phrase in this sense: to be "too thankful" is to show or feel gratitude in excess of what the occasion demands ; "only" in this connexion means "simply." A lady who had sent a poor neighbour a dinner was asked if the man was thankful. "Only too thankful," she replied ; "he simply overwhelmed me with his gratitude." To be "too glad" may be explained similarly, or as meaning "too glad for words," though this is less likely, I think.   C. C. B.

There is an analogous idiomatic expression in German, "nur zu froh"=*sehr froh*, which is understood to be used ironically. See H. Paul's sematological 'Deutsches Wörterbuch' (Halle, 1899), *sub* 'Nur,' p. 332. H. KREBS.
Oxford.

"COMICALLY" (9ᵗʰ S. ix. 285).—There can be no doubt that Fuller wrote this word in the passage quoted, and that there is no need for change. He says that a voyage "ended sadly and sorrowfully" (in the manner of a tragedy) which had "begun comically"—*i.e.*, pleasantly and cheerfully, in manner of a comedy. This sense of the word was quite common in the late sixteenth and early seventeenth centuries, and, howsoever "unknown to the dictionaries" generally, is certainly not unknown to the 'N.E.D.,' which, amongst other examples, quotes Fuller, stating that Job's end was "comicall." To our ears the use sounds even laughable, but how strange are the whirligigs of sense which some words pass through ! Often and often have I heard a rustic say, "I felt so comical, I thought I was going to die."   C. B. MOUNT.

MR. DEEDES appears to have overlooked the fact that this word had once the sense of happily, fortunately. The 'H.E.D.' gives several instances, one of them from Fuller himself : "But Comicall was the end of Job, and all things restored double to him." This is followed by another from Hale : "The Comical part of the Lives of Men are too full of Sin and Vanity, and the Tragical part thereof too full of Sin and Misery."

C. C. B.

GORDON, A PLACE-NAME (9th S. ix. 29, 133, 256).—In the 'Scottish Clans' (W. & A. K. Johnston) is the note :—

"The first Gordon of whom there is any distinct trace is Richard of Gordon, said to be the grandson of a famous knight who slew some monstrous animal in the Merse in the time of Malcolm III. That Richard was Lord of the Barony of Gordon in the Merse is undoubted, as between 1150 and 1160 he granted from that estate a piece of land to the monks of St. Mary at Kelso, a grant confirmed by his son Thomas. Other Gordons figure in history about this time, apart from Bertram de Gordon, whose arrow in 1199 wounded Richard of England at Chalons."

'Chambers's Encyclopædia' says :—

"No proof has been found of any connection between the Gordons of France and the Gordons of Scotland. There is little or no doubt now that the Scottish Gordons took their name from the lands of Gordon in Berwickshire. Their earliest historian, writing in the sixteenth century, says that these lands, together with the arms of three boars' heads, were given by King Malcolm Ceanmohr (1057-93 A.D.) to the progenitor of the house, as a reward for slaying, in the forest of Huntley, a wild boar, the terror of all the Merse. But in the eleventh century there were neither heraldic bearings in Scotland nor Gordons in Berwickshire. The first trace of the family is about the end of the twelfth century, or the beginning of the thirteenth century, when it appears in record as witnessing charters by the great Earls of March or Dunbar, and as granting patches of land and rights of pasturage to the monks of Kelso."

The earliest historian of the Gordon family was an Italian monk of the Cistercian monastery of Kinloss in Moray, whose account, written in the middle of the sixteenth century, is still in manuscript, and is entitled 'Historiæ Compendium de Origine et Incremento Gordoniæ Familiæ, Johanne Ferrerio, Pedemontano, authore, apud Kinlos A.D. 1545, fideliter collectum.' Consequently, as he mentions that the earliest Gordon bore the three boars' heads, those arms must have been, in any case, in use in 1545 (the date of his manuscript) and before. They are still borne by the Marquis of Huntly and the Earl of Aberdeen.   RONALD DIXON.
46, Marlborough Avenue, Hull.

GORDON AS A RUSSIAN SURNAME (9th S. ix. 148).—MR. BULLOCH is right. The name Gordon is fairly prevalent among Jews. We have a young novelist of that name. I remember also reading a brilliant Hebrew novel written by a Russian writer of that name. My own impression is that the name is generically Hebraic in formation, evolving itself possibly out of "Yardine"=Jordan. Perhaps the Y and the J are difficult of pronunciation by Russians, and so became hardened into G. Jews are wont to play tricks with their names in this way for prudential reasons. The theory of transposition from "Grodno" may be dismissed for the reason that MR. BULLOCH so learnedly recognizes.

M. L. R. BRESLAR.

NAPOLEON'S FIRST MARRIAGE (9th S. ix. 347).—Probably your querist, if he wants "the romance of Napoleon's first marriage," will not be satisfied with a "trustworthy account" of the marriage, as there was, indeed, no romance about it. A sufficiently accurate account of the facts, as now known from the most recent publication of original documents, is to be found in the latest life of Napoleon—namely, 'Napoleon,' by Mr. Watson, just published by the Macmillan Company.   D.

DELAGOA AND ALGOA (9th S. v. 336, 424 ; vi. 16, 479).—There seems to be no disposition to dispute the supposed derivation of these South African place-names from Goa, the capital of the Portuguese settlements in India, so that it is perhaps worth while accentuating the supposition by quoting the following from an article in the *Empire Review* of December, 1901, by Mr. J. B. Firth, on 'The Nomenclature of South Africa' :—

"Cape Agulhas, the most northerly promontory, takes its name from the needle-shaped rocks of the headland, and the little island of St. Croix in Algoa Bay is the spot where Diaz landed and set up a huge cross to mark his zeal for the Christian religion. But the Portuguese passed on and left the great prize to others. Their goal was India, and two place-names survive to tell the story of their ambition in the most succinct form. Algoa was their port of call on the way to Goa, in India ; Delagoa was their port of call on the return voyage. These two words are an epitome of Portuguese colonial policy."

J. HOLDEN MACMICHAEL.

HONORIFICABILITUDINITAS (9th S. ix. 243).—I am inclined to think that this word was familiar in Shakespeare's time from its use in some well-known medical book. The following passage, which I quoted in the *Literary World* on 15 February, 1901, from Thomas Nash's 'Lenten Stuff,' would appear to favour that supposition. "Physicians," says that lively writer, "deafen our ears with the *honorificabilitudinitatibus* of their heavenly *panacea*, their sovereign guiacum, their treacles, their mithridates compacted of forty several poisons; their bitter rhubarb, and torturing stibium." I quote from the 'Harleian Miscellany,' ii. 305; but Nash's pamphlet was published in 1599, and Shakespeare's 'Love's Labour's Lost' in the preceding year. Still, it is impossible to think that Nash, who knew Latin well, borrowed the expression from the dramatist. His citation is so precise that it must have been taken from one of the medical books in vogue in those days, with which both writers were more or less acquainted. John T. Curry.

Arms of Le Neve Foster (9th S. ix. 168 316).—In describing the arms of the Le Neve family Mr. John Radcliffe has omitted the ducal coronet of the crest, which is Out of a ducal coronet or, a white lily, seeded or, stalked and leaved vert. P. L. N. F.

Latin Sentence Misspelt (9th S. ix. 289).—The sentence was probably "Parcite barbarismo vel in nominando gentili monticolis inevitabili" ("Be indulgent to a barbarism unavoidable by Highlanders even when naming a clansman"). H. A. Strong.
University College, Liverpool.

Erskine (9th S. ix. 249).—Your correspondent W. C. J. will find much of considerable interest anent Alexander Erskine (1648), the representative of Sweden at the Treaty of Munster, in a work lately published by Otto Schulze, of Edinburgh, entitled 'Scots in Germany,' by Fischer, on pp. 201, 318, with an account of his tomb and inscription thereon, p. 310. Herbert H. Flower.

Amelia Opie's Novels (9th S. ix. 267).—Her first novel, 'The Father and Daughter,' 1801, went through eight editions. Most probably 'The Memorials of the Life of Mrs. A. Opie,' by Miss C. L. Brightwell, Norwich, 1854, published a year after Mrs. Opie's death, would give the information desired.
R. A. Potts.

Gwyneth (9th S. ix. 109, 319).—Mr. Mayall writes as if Gwynnedd and Gwent were both names of the same division of Wales, which is, of course, not the case. Gwynnedd comprised the north-western portion of what is now known as North Wales, Gwent the south-western portion of South Wales. What is the meaning of Gwynnedd, the place-name? It is not yet clear to me that it is not the same as Gwyneth, the personal name. C. C. B.

John King, Language Master, London, 1722 (9th S. ix. 227).—The following may be the person required: John King, of Stamford,

in Lincolnshire, said to be a physician. He wrote several works, and one was an English and High German grammar, 1706, 8vo, London; 1716, 8vo. Died 1728. He was the son of John King, D.D. (a native of St. Columb, Cornwall), rector of Chelsea and prebendary of York. The MS. mentioned probably was intended for the third edition.
John Radcliffe.

The Locomotive and Gas (9th S. vi. 227, 358; ix. 118, 317).—Another claimant to the invention of "gaz" was Frederick Winsor, who was first to display practically its utility by lighting up Pall Mall in the early part of the last century. On his memorial in Kensal Green Cemetery (for he died abroad) is the text (from Zechariah xiv.), "At evening time it shall be light." R. B.
Upton.

Authors Wanted (9th S. ix. 209). — The poem beginning

　　The bud on the bough,
　　The song of the bird,

is in 'Five Minutes' Daily Readings of Poetry,' by H. L. Sidney Lear, under date 26 April, the author's name Gwen. W. M. J.-F.

"Buff Week" (9th S. ix. 329, 353).—The expression is "baff week," as is suggested at the last reference. Your correspondent will find it fully treated under 'Bauch' in the 'H.E.D.,' and under the headings 'Baff' and 'Bauch' in the 'E.D.D.'
R. Oliver Heslop.

[In the West Riding sixty years ago an imposition in a game of forfeits was to repeat with a grave face

　　Buff says Baff,
　　And gives me his staff,
　　And bids me neither smile nor laugh.

This is not advanced as contributing information as to "Buff Week." See, under 'Buff,' Gomme's 'Traditional Games,' vol. i. p. 48.]

Greek Epigram (9th S. ix. 147, 273, 331).—Neither of the translations of Callimachus's epigram given by Mr. Mac-Carthy gives any force to the ἔτι in the second line. What is its meaning? Were the makers of images accustomed to anoint their completed works? Jacobs says the meaning is that Berenice was fashioned by the gods, about whom everything is fragrant; but this seems far-fetched.
John B. Wainewright.

Artists' Mistakes (9th S. iv. 107, 164, 237, 293; v. 32, 317, 400; vi. 44; vii. 423, 471; viii. 171, 328; ix. 274).—At the last reference a correspondent describes what he considers to be an inaccuracy in the *Illustrated London News* of 14 December, a copy of which I send you. I am sure that if you refer to the two illustrations under discussion you will agree that your correspondent is under a curious misapprehension. You will understand that the very brief and transient glimpse afforded by a rapidly moving scene makes the seizing of every detail a matter of great difficulty, but it is the particular pride of the special artists of all the better-class weekly illustrated papers that very few of these details are omitted or incorrectly drawn. It is, therefore, on their behalf that I beg you to insert this refutation.

BRUCE S. INGRAM, Editor.

[The hat in the second picture is not over-clear, but we agree that it is distinctly a cocked hat, as in the picture on the opposite page, so that the inaccuracy disappears.]

JOHN KIRKBY, AUTHOR OF 'AUTOMATHES' (6th S. xii. 68, 177).—In the life of Kirkby given in the 'Dictionary of National Biography' he is stated to have been of St. John's College, Cambridge. The error seems to be of long standing; see Nichols's 'Literary Anecdotes,' ii. 56, where the translation of Barrow's lectures is ascribed to John Kirkby, of St. John's. Nichols states that this volume issued from the press of William Bowyer in 1735. On the title-page it is stated to be "Printed for Stephen Austin at the Angel and Bible in St. Paul's Church-yard MDCCXXXIV.," and the translation is stated to be by "the Rev. Mr. John Kirkby, of Egremond in Cumberland." Kirkby's name does not appear on the title-page of 'Automathes,' but the dedication, to the Right Hon. Lewis, Earl and Baron of Rockingham, &c., is signed John Kirkby. The 'Dictionary of National Biography' identifies this John Kirkby with the J. K. who was collated vicar of Waldershare 8 December, 1739, and rector of Blackmanstone 19 November, 1743, both in Kent. And this seems probable. But in the 'Act Book' of the Archbishop of Canterbury Kirkby is stated to have been ordained deacon 28 July, 1723, and priest 1 August, 1725, by Francis (Gastrell), Bishop of Chester. Now John Kirkby, of St. John's, entered the college 4 May, 1723, aged eighteen, so that it is clear he was not the vicar of Waldershare. Moreover, he was ordained deacon 28 May, 1727, by the Bishop of Lincoln, and licensed next day to the curacy of Pilham, co. Lincoln. I have not yet succeeded in tracing his further career, but suspect that he was the John Kirkby who was instituted vicar of Stoke Holy Cross and vicar of Trowse, both in Norfolk, 2 June, 1729, in both cases on the presentation of the Dean and Chapter of Norwich, so that he was probably a Minor Canon of that cathedral. Curiously enough he died in the same year as the vicar of Waldershare, for he is almost certainly the "Rev. Mr. Kirkby of Norwich, who died of grief [in 1754] from a dishonourable circumstance happening in his family" (Gent. Mag., 1755, p. 570b). Both Stoke and Trowse were filled up again in 1754. The vicar of Waldershare died 21 May, 1754 (Hasted's 'Kent,' iii. 432). A manuscript note inserted in the British Museum copy of one of Kirkby's pamphlets, 'A Demonstration from Christian Principles,' &c., states that it "was wrote by a Rev. Mr. Kirkby, father of Messrs. K. the Printers."

R. F. SCOTT.

St. John's College, Cambridge.

TOKEN FOUND IN THE STRAND (9th S. ix. 268).—The token was issued by Richard Bacon, of Cockey Lane (now called London Street), Norwich. He is described in the 'Norwich Directory' for 1802 as an auctioneer, appraiser, printer, bookseller, binder, and stationer. Wyon was the die-sinker and Kempson the manufacturer. About a ton was struck.

JOHN RADCLIFFE.

"FLAPPER," ANGLO-INDIAN SLANG (9th S. ix. 266).—MR. CROOKE has found a mare's nest. A "flapper" is only a young duck.

G. S. C. S.

SIR THOMAS SMITH, OF PARSON'S GREEN (9th S. ix. 29, 132).—This Sir Thomas Smith, who married the Hon. Frances Brydges, is not identical with his namesake who was Secretary of State to Queen Elizabeth. The lives of both are given by the 'D.N.B.' It is a remarkable fact that each was Public Orator in his university; the Sir Thomas whose name is at the head of this reply at Oxford, and the more famous Sir Thomas Smith, whose name will always be connected with the study of Greek in England, at Cambridge.

EDWARD BENSLY.

The University, Adelaide, South Australia.

NAPOLEON'S LAST YEARS (9th S. viii. 422, 509; ix. 274).—What proof is there that Napoleon's illness, from which he died six years later, affected his movements at Waterloo? It is easy to make confident assertions that Napoleon would have swept away Wellington's last soldier from the field, but mere assertion is not proof. Napoleon did not always fight successful battles. His strategy and tactics in the Moscow and Leipsic campaigns were of the most second-rate description. I doubt whether he was anything like as good a tactician as Wellington, though a far greater strategist. Why his torpor, allowing that he was torpid, should have caused him to make disjointed attacks with infantry and cavalry separately, and fight the battle generally in a blundering fashion, I cannot for my part see. Napoleon had shown no torpor in his escape from Elba and the one hundred days of preparation. It is true he did not follow up the Prussians at Ligny, and showed little of his old activity then; but it must be remembered that his troops had been severely mauled in the encounter, and, having driven off the Prussians, he hoped to crush the British.

I should much like an expert medical opinion as to how long before its fatal termination cancer in the stomach can show sensible effects upon a man's vital powers. The great Roman Emperor Marcus Aurelius, who, I believe, died of this complaint, conducted a series of severe campaigns against the fierce tribes of Central Europe with conspicuous success till he died in camp. It appears to me that Napoleon as a commander and statesman comes below, instead of above, Cæsar and Alexander, and morally he is infinitely lower. REGINALD HAINES.
Uppingham.

WINDOW GLASS (9th S. ix. 87, 150, 213, 271). — An affirmative answer to your correspondent's question as to the use of window glass by the Romans is given in the third edition of Smith's 'Dictionary of Greek and Roman Antiquities,' vol. i. p. 686, col. 2 (*s.v. domus*), and vol. ii. p. 974, col. 2 (*s.v. vitrum*), where it is stated that "a few specimens of window glass may be seen in the glass collection of the British Museum."
EDWARD BENSLY.
The University, Adelaide, South Australia.

"HAKATIST" (9th S. ix. 145).—This is not an adjective, but a substantive, denoting a member of the league called "Verein zur Förderung des Deutschtums in den Ostmarken," founded by the three gentlemen Von Hansemann (not Hannemann), Von Kennemann (not Kinnemann), Von Tiedemann (not Tidemann). The accent is on the last syllable. G. KRUEGER.
Berlin.

IN PRAISE OF BURNS (9th S. ix. 185).—There are several errors in MR. J. GRIGOR'S note on the above. First of all I may say that the author of the verses is the late John Nicholson, the "Airedale poet," whose life and full bibliography will be found in my 'Poets of Keighley, Bingley, and District.' Nicholson was born at Weardley, near Harewood, on 27 November, 1790, and lost his life by drowning in the River Aire on Good Friday, 13 April, 1843. It is quite an easy matter to confound Airdrie with Airedale. I give the whole and correct version of Nicholson's tributary lines to Burns, taken from Dearden's edition of his life and poems published in 1859 :—

LINES.
Spoken at the anniversary meeting at Leeds, to celebrate the birthday of Burns, 1826.

Learning has many a rhymer made,
    To flatter near the throne,
But Scotia's genius has display'd
    A poet of her own.

His lyre he took to vale and glen,
    To mountain and the shade ;
Ages may pass away, but when
    Will such a harp be play'd ?

His native strains each bard may try,
    But who has got his fire ?
Why, none—for Nature saw him die,
    Then took away his lyre.

And for that lyre the learned youth
    May search the world in vain :—
She vow'd she ne'er would lend it more
    To sound on earth again ;

But call'd on Fame to hang it by—
    She took it with a tear,
Broke all the strings to bind the wreath
    That Burns shall ever wear.

CHAS. F. FORSHAW, LL.D.
48, Hanover Square, Bradford.

EULOGIES OF THE BIBLE BY HUXLEY AND DARWIN (9th S. ix. 328).—A eulogy by Huxley will be found in 'Critiques and Addresses' (1873), article 'The School Boards,' first published in the *Contemporary Review*, 1870. Dr. John Murdoch's booklet, 'Testimonies of Great Men to the Bible and Christianity,' contains a number of similar eulogies by scientists and others ; but no expression of opinion by Darwin is included.
H. JOHNSON.

LECTERN IN DURHAM CATHEDRAL (9th S. viii. 483 ; ix. 135).—At the risk of being pedantic I may remark that one statement given at the last reference is not strictly correct. The coat of Bishop Fox, of Winchester, is Azure, a pelican or, vulning herself proper ; and not a pelican in her piety. The latter description implies that the bird is in her nest, surrounded by her young ; but she is represented as indicated above upon the Corpus Christi College arms at Oxford, and also at other places associated with Fox, as Taunton, Durham, Winchester, Grantham, and Netley. The Corpus coat (like those of the Lincoln foundations of Lincoln College and B.N.C.) is tierced in pale, the central division being occupied by an escutcheon of the arms of the see of Winchester, the dexter by Fox's own coat, and the sinister by the (canting) three silver owls and three red roses on a chief of Bishop Oldham, of Exeter.

Among the most interesting lecterns is that in use at Southwell Cathedral. It is not wrought, however, in the form of a pelican, but in the more common shape of a brazen eagle with expanded wings. Presented in 1805 by Sir Richard Kaye, subsequently Dean of Lincoln, it bears the inscription "Orate pro an'a Radulphi Savage, et pro an'abus 'Omn. Fidelium Defunctorum.'" It was formerly the property of the neighbouring abbey of Newstead; and at the dissolution the monks hid some documents inside and threw it into the lake. In the eighteenth century it was discovered, and passed into the hands of a Nottingham dealer.

A. R. Bayley.

There was another pelican in Durham Cathedral long before the placing there of that dreadful bird now used as a lectern. (See 'Bishop Cosin's Correspondence,' vol. i. p. 168 n., Surtees Soc , 52.) Peter Smart complains :—

"They have taken out of the cathedrall church the old holy Font which was comely, like to that at St. Paul's at London, and in other cathedralls, and instead thereof they erected a mausoleum, towring up to the roph of the church......and disfigur'd it, not only with uncomely braveries, but with abominable idols, one of a dove, which they call the Holy Ghost (set there by Mr. Cosen, to cross the Dean, whose pellican he pul'd down feeding her yong ones with her own blood)."

Ibagué.

This was designed by Sir Gilbert Scott after the pattern of the ancient lectern which is described in the 'Rites of Durham.' It is of pale brass enriched with silver and jewels. At the time when it was erected it was unique in England.   St. Swithin.

Representations of the pelican are also to be found—in stone, wood, glass, or metal—in churches at Freiburg, Strasburg, Nuremberg, Magdeburg, Basle, and Lund. They are described in Evans's 'Animal Symbolism in Ecclesiastical Architecture,' pp. 66, 83, 128.

W. S.

The Smallest Church in England (9th S. ix. 47).—Since the claim put forward by the Bishop of Carlisle that the church of Wasthead (it was given as Wasdale Head in the paper I saw) is the smallest church in England, the subject has several times been discussed in the public press. It would appear that there is at least one equally small church —that of Lullington, Sussex—but as this is only the chancel of the original edifice its claim is somewhat weakened. The churches

at the following places are, I believe, very small : Greensted, Essex ; Perivale, Middlesex ; Hulcote, Beds ; St. Lawrence, Isle of Wight ; Chilcombe, Dorset ; Hazeleigh, Essex ; Grosmont, Monmouth ; Warlingham, Surrey ; Wythburn, Cumberland ; Kilpeck, Hereford. An extension of this list, with any particulars concerning those mentioned, would be welcomed by   John T. Page.
West Haddon, Northamptonshire.

Children's Affirmations (9th S. ix. 185, 273).—This deeply interesting question will, I hope, receive the attention of many contributors. I am conversant with the wet and dry finger affirmation, but this method was far from common here in my young days. In order to prove that a boy was telling the truth we used, after a statement had been made which seemed in any way doubtful, to ejaculate, "What'll you eat?" The reply would generally be, "Fire," but in extreme cases the formula would be, "Fire and brimstone and all the very world."
John T. Page.
West Haddon, Northamptonshire.

The following scale of affirmations is not unknown among schoolboys : "Is that true?" "Yes."—"Will you take your oath on it?" "Yes."—"Will you take your Bible oath on it?" "Yes."—"Will you cut your throat if it isn't true?" "Yes."—"Will you bet a penny on it?" "No, I'll not go that length"!
J. G. Wallace-James.
Haddington.

Sir John Oldcastle (9th S. ix. 308).—Sir John Oldcastle, who was hanged as a traitor and then burnt as a heretic in December, 1417, was the fourth husband of Joan, Baroness Cobham, and left no issue. Lady Cobham, however, by her second husband, Sir Reginald Braybrooke, Knt., had a daughter and heiress, also called Joan, who married Sir Thomas Brooke, Knt., and their eldest son was summoned to Parliament 13 January, 1445, as "Edwardus Broke, de Cobham, Chivalier." His descendants are, I believe, very numerous, though the Barony of Cobham, a barony by writ, was forfeited by the attainder of Henry Brooke, sixth Lord Cobham, in 1604.   F. de H. L.

The West Bourne (9th S. viii. 517 ; ix. 51, 92, 190, 269, 291).— I have to thank Mr. Rutton for his kindly attempt to dispel the doubts which I expressed in my first paper on this subject, but I fear that the reasons which he gives for his somewhat dogmatic conclusion that "primarily West Bourne was the name of the stream" will not carry conviction to the minds of those who, like myself, require proof of a statement before accepting it. The strong searchlight which is now being thrown on the fictions which figure as historical genealogies in our popular peerages is in course of extension over the wide field of historical topography, and probabilities and assumptions no longer pass muster as "authoritative" facts.* Mr. Rutton begins by saying that the territorial word "bourn," of French extraction, was not engrafted on English stock until our own similar word, as an indigenous plant, had flourished for centuries. But is there any evidence that the word "bourn," of French extraction, was ever a constituent of English place-names? A few instances showing how and when the French "bourn" was engrafted on English stock would be welcome. The picture which my friend draws of the "London native" emerging from his shell, and in the course of an afternoon's ramble settling the local nomenclature of the district, is an attractive one; but is it history? It must be remembered that in primeval times many more streams were known to the "travelling citizen" of London than the three named by Mr. Rutton. The two great arms of marshland which, on east and west, grasped London in their clutches were a maze of tiny rivulets, some of which trickled from the northern heights into the Thames, while others were affluents of the larger streams. The eastern and western boundaries of the London district were respectively the Lea and the Brent. A walk to either was within the capacity of an ordinary ablebodied, long-legged Anglo-Saxon, and if he started, as we may suppose, from that important stream the Walbrook, which practically divided ecclesiastical London from the trading emporia on the river, he might have called all the rivulets in the Brent direction "West Bournes," while those in the opposite direction would be "East Bournes." No satisfactory reason has been given why the stream afterwards known as the Bayswater Rivulet should have been arbitrarily designated the West Bourne. Why not, for instance, the brook, afterwards canalized, which divided the parishes of Chelsea and Fulham?

There are few, if any, rivers in England whose names are identical with the names of the districts through which they flow. The Anglo-Saxon "burne" is, of course, a common

* I use the adjective in the sense employed by Mr. J. Horace Round in his instructive paper on 'An "Authoritative" Ancestor' in the *Ancestor* for April, p. 189.

factor in place-names, but in the majority of instances it occurs in the names of towns and villages, and not in the names of streams. I am abroad at present, and have not access to an English gazetteer, but, writing from memory, this is my impression. In my last note I gave the names of a group of villages in East Kent having the terminal "bourne," but at this moment I cannot recall the name of a single streamlet in the district which ends with that word, though doubtless some exist.

It is quite true, as Mr. Rutton says, that this termination implies water, but this fact is perfectly consistent with the hypothesis which, with Bosworth at my back, I provisionally put forward—namely, that the old thirteenth-century manor of Westbourne derived its name from its situation on the western bank of the rivulet. But I am open to conviction on the production of the evidence for which I asked. It would be very satisfactory if some Eastbourne correspondent of 'N. & Q.' could assist us with information on the following points: (a) was that town originally situated on a brook called the East Bourne, from which it has derived its name; or (b) was the first settlement made on the eastern bank of a brook, nameless or not?

There are one or two other points in Mr. Rutton's pleasantly written note from which I must regretfully express my dissent, such as the identity of the Holebourne with the River of Wells — another subject "highly charged with argument," on which I have already recorded my opinion in these columns —and the origin of the name "Thames," on which the latest word has perhaps been said by Mr. W. H. Duignan in his valuable little book on 'The Place-names of Staffordshire' (*sub voce* 'Tame'), which was recently reviewed in 'N. & Q.' But these points are, of course, beside the main question at issue.

W. F. Prideaux.

Villa d'Este, Cernobbio, Como.

"Bar sinister" (9ᵗʰ S. ix. 64, 152, 215, 315). —A correspondent of the *Intermédiaire* for 10 March, in treating of the "barre," wrongly considered to be a mark of "bastardy," observes that "a certain incoherence reigns in what has been said by classic and contemporary *héraldistes* regarding this charge." He then goes on to ask for an examination of the question, and commences the discussion by quoting the article 'Barre,' with the accompanying remarks, by the Count A. de Foras ('Le Blason, Dictionnaire et Remarques,' Grenoble, 1883, pp. 47 and 48), to show that the *barre* is an honourable bearing. It is the *bâton*, or *filet*, placed like a *barre*, which has been used as a token of illegitimacy. "Presque toujours les bâtards ont brisé les armes paternelles d'un bâton ou filet mis en barre ou en traverse."   M. P.

It is said to be "difficult to prove a negative," though in Aldrich's 'Artis Logicæ Compendium' the second figure is devoted to that purpose.

1. Charles Powlett, Marquess of Winchester, and the first Duke of Bolton, in Wensleydale, married as his second wife Mary, illegitimate daughter of Emanuel Scrope, Earl of Sunderland and Lord Scrope of Bolton, by whom he acquired the large estates in Wensleydale.

2. Thomas Orde, of the ancient Northumbrian family of that name, married Jean Mary, illegitimate daughter of Charles Powlett, fifth Duke of Bolton, and acquired with her extensive estates in Hampshire.

The "baton sinister debruised," or, in fact, any mark of cadency, is ignored in both these cases, the arms of Lord Bolton, the present representative, being Sable, three swords in pile, points downwards, argent, pommels and hilts or ; on a canton of the second, an escocheon of the field, charged with a salmon hauriant ppr. (for Orde). Motto, "Aymez loyaulté," with reference to the chivalrous defence of Basing House by John Powlett, Marquess of Winchester. The name is spelt both Powlett and Paulet, and, as is well known, the sword is the emblem of St. Paul, as the keys are of St. Peter.

It is more correct to write Earl Waldegrave than Earl of Waldegrave.

JOHN PICKFORD, M.A.
Newbourne Rectory, Woodbridge.

ANDREW WILSON (9th S. ix. 289).—Andrew Wilson was admitted a pensioner at St. John's College, Cambridge. 25 September, 1676, and in the Register of Admissions (printed 1882) is described as of Easingwood, presumably Easingwold, Yorkshire, as the son of George Wilson, deceased, as sixteen years of age, and as having been "bred at Pocklington." He was instituted vicar of Easingwold in 1685 (Gill's 'Vallis Ebor.,' 93).   F. DE H. L.

DARLEY, A FORGOTTEN IRISH POET (9th S. ix. 205).—An appreciative obituary notice of George Darley appeared in the *Athenæum* of 28 November, 1846. A note from his pen on 'Dante's Beatrice,' probably the last he ever wrote, was published in the previous issue of that paper. It was "written from his deathbed," being dated 18 November. Darley's reputation both as a poet and as a

critic was of a very high order, and I cannot refrain from appending the closing sentence from the notice in the *Athenæum* :—

"Intolerant of pretension, disdainful of mercenary ambition, and indignant at sluggishness or conceit —he would be often referred to by the sincere and generous spirits of literature and art, as one whose love of truth was equalled by his perfect preparation for every task that he undertook ; and whose praise was worth having—not because it was rarely given, but because it was never withheld save upon good grounds."

JOHN T. PAGE.
West Haddon, Northamptonshire.

MR. CLAYTON and others among your readers may like to read the following paragraph relating to George Darley, which I have extracted from the Rev. A. G. L'Estrange's 'Life of Mary Russell Mitford' (1870) :—

"'Sylvia, or the May Queen,' published in '27, by George Darley. Did you ever hear of it? I never did until the other day. Mrs. Cary has given it to me. It is exquisite—something between the 'Faithful Shepherdess' and 'Midsummer Night's Dream.' Would you like to see it? The author is the son of a rich alderman of Dublin, who disinherited him because he would write poetry; and now he supports himself by writing for the magazines."—Vol. iii. p. 56.

I have read 'Sylvia,' and think very highly of it. Darley's other works are unknown to me.   EDWARD PEACOCK.
Wickentree House, Kirton-in-Lindsey.

By virtue of one of his songs, at least, "It is not beautie I demande" (which deceived Palgrave), Darley lives in many of our popular anthologies, including the most recent of them, Sir Mountstuart Grant-Duff's. In Mr. Miles's 'The Poets and the Poetry of the Century' he has six pages of notice and fifteen of selections. He is remembered, too, by his introduction to Beaumont and Fletcher's 'Works,' which, if not all that an introduction should be, is yet worth having.

C. C. B.

GENESIS I. 1. (9th S. ix. 269).—Literally rendered, and in the order of the Hebrew words, the sentence is, "In-the-beginning created Elohim the-heavens and the-earth." Before "the-heavens" is the particle *ayth*, which shows it to be accusative. This particle, combined with the conjunction "and," is repeated before "the-earth," making it accusative. "Elohim" has no such prefix, and is nominative (or subject) to "created." A glance at a Hebrew accidence will suffice to satisfy MR. THORNTON about this.

C. S. WARD.

It is scarcely conceivable that any rabbi in his right senses could have proposed so maladroit a translation as your correspondent asserts that he did. It is preposterous. Are we to imagine that the masterminds originally at work in translating the Scriptures, and their successors in revising the version, were so stupid as to boggle over the very first verse of the Pentateuch? The translation as we find it is absolutely correct. The particle *eth*, twice repeated in the verse, is known to the merest tiro in Hebrew as representing the accusative case, "heaven" and "earth" being the direct objects of the verb "created."

M. D. Davis.

Epigram on Women (9ᵗʰ S. ix. 288).—I do not know the author, but pray let me cap it :—

Oh, the shrewdness of their shrewdness when they're shrewd,
And the rudeness of their rudeness when they're rude;
But the shrewdness of their shrewdness and the rudeness of their rudeness
Are as nothing to their goodness when they're good.

F. P.

Swaylecliffe (9ᵗʰ S. ix. 329).—The sense is "swallow-cliff." *Swalewan* is the gen. case of *swalewe*, usually *swealwe*, a swallow. *Cliff* does not always mean "escarpment"; it also meant, formerly, a shore, bank, strand. See 'Cliff' in 'H.E.D.'   Celer.

The Last of the Pre-Victorian M.P.s (9ᵗʰ S. ix. 226, 333).—Mr. J. Temple Leader was alive and in Florence in January, 1898. I have a letter from him addressed to my father, to whom he was sending a copy of his life of Sir John Hawkwood, of whom my father was a lineal descendant.

E. E. Street.

Chichester.

Royal Walks (9ᵗʰ S. ix. 244). — "King Henry's Walk" probably takes its name from having been a favourite spot of Henry VIII., who, tradition has it, occupied an old house at the corner of Newington Green as a rural resort for his illicit amours. This tradition, which was strongly held throughout the neighbourhood in John Nelson's time, is handed down to us in that writer's 'History of St. Mary, Islington,' 1811, pp. 187-8. Be this as it may, Henry Algernon Percy, Earl of Northumberland, gave away a great part of his lands and inheritance to the king and others when living probably at the house alluded to (Nichols's 'Hist. of Canonbury,' 'Bibliotheca Topographica Britannica,' vol. ii. p. 9). And this, says Thomas Cromwell in his 'Walks through Islington,' 1835, p. 122,

"is evident from letters in the Earl's own writing still extant; it is therefore not unlikely that in this manner these premises might have come into the possession of the Sovereign. Again, the tradition receives no little sanction from the circumstance, that a path (of late partly converted into a road) from the south-east corner of the Green to the road near Ball's Pond, has been, time out of mind, called 'King Harry's Walk.'"

Thomas Edlyne Tomlins, in his 'Perambulations through Islington,' frequently mentions this walk, but makes no attempt to assign any reason for its being so called. Queen Margaret's Grove is, no doubt, named after Margaret Tudor, Queen of Scotland and eldest daughter of Henry VII., who may, either voluntarily or compulsorily, have stayed here during her sojourn in London about the year 1515.

J. Holden MacMichael.

Miscellaneous.

NOTES ON BOOKS, &c.

In a Minster Garden: a Causerie. By the Dean of Ely. (Stock.)

In a preface with a pleasantly antiquarian flavour the Dean of Ely describes the conditions under which were written the gossiping confessions, meditations, reflections, and dreams which constitute what he calls a *causerie.* Excogitated during the enforced leisure of convalescence in the course of repeated strolls down the Cloister Walk at Ely from Prior's Door to Refectory Wall, they deal with the manuscript treasures of the cathedral library, the beauties of the garden of what is called the Liberty House (a name now all but forgotten in Ely), sunset on the river, some verses ('The Carol of King Canute') inspired in part by Milton's 'Hymn on the Nativity,' together with criticisms, narrations, correspondence, speculation, what not, the whole constituting a book agreeably varied and readable throughout. There are, under 'On the Walsingham Way,' some serious reflections on women and the stupidity of the early Churchmen, "with their unnatural and unwholesome views of ascetic discipline, and their foolish confusion of the fact of virginity with the virtue of chastity"; an insistence on the strangeness of the fact that "it was in the earlier and ruder and more barbarous, as we should say, periods of Grecian history [or, in more precise language, in the Homeric writings], not in the later and more refined, that the ideal of womanhood is to be found in its highest perfection," and other matters, including the influence of Mariolatry on the mediæval conception of women. Numerous illustrations depicting portions of the cathedral, one of the loveliest and most majestic of Eastern England, add to the attractions of a book that solicits and deserves a leisurely perusal.

Church Folk-lore. By J. E. Vaux, F.S.A. (Skeffington & Son.)

Though Mr. Vaux writes about folk-lore he is hardly a folk-lorist, nor indeed does he claim to be considered such. He has industriously collected a number of isolated facts—many from our own columns—which bear one way or another on Church matters and practices, but he makes no attempt to co-ordinate them into any connected system, or make them illuminate one another. For the most part he does not try to discover the origin or meaning of the curious customs and quaint rites which he registers, but is content to purvey the material on which others may generalize or base deductions. But it is only just to say that the author does not pretend to be more than a diligent compiler. A little research into mediæval sources would often have shown him the rise and rationale of many of the usages which, as it is, remain unexplained; but by not extending his investigations, of set purpose, beyond the Reformation period he leaves those upper reaches of the stream outside his ken. This is a pity, as wider knowledge would have cleared up some of the present anomalies and obviated not a few mistakes. It is all very well to repeat for the hundredth time the hoary guess that the proverbial "nine tailors" which make a man are only a corrupt rendering of the "nine tellers" of the passing bell; but what about the same phrase turning up in Brittany, where there is no such convenient assonance? The derivation of the North-Country word "arval" Mr. Vaux thinks "somewhat doubtful." Why not have resolved his doubts by an easy reference to Dr. Murray's or Dr. Wright's monumental dictionaries? "Derivations," as so often in these popular works, have proved a snare to the author. *Funus* and "funeral" are not so obviously related as he assumes to the Latin *funis*, a rope (p. 170). The "coom" of a bell is not "a sort of secretion of moss" (p. 398), but the black grease that accumulates round its bearings. "Greelith," meaning weepeth (p. 400), whether due to Mr. Vaux or the authority which he quotes, is a misprint for "greeteth."

Wrekin Sketches. By Emma Boore. (Stock.)

THIS work, to which on its first appearance we drew attention (see 8th S. xii. 160), has received the honours, to which it is entitled, of a cheap edition. We are sorry to find that inaccuracy and defects in the earlier edition to which we drew attention remain uncorrected in the later.

PROF. BRADLEY sends to the *Fortnightly* a paper on 'The Rejection of Falstaff,' delivered in March last in Oxford. His views concerning the fat knight and his relations to Prince Hal are original and ingenious, if not always convincing. Falstaff, he holds, is not, in the full sense, either a liar or a coward. His lies are those of a humourist, and are not intended to be believed. By solemn statements he will make truth appear absurd, and he shares the amusement which his preposterous assertions beget. As regards the charge of cowardice, it is shown that he remains a person of consideration, and that when he is in request "twelve captains hurry about London searching for him." Henry V. sinks in consideration in consequence of his treatment of Falstaff. In the Falstaff scenes Shakespeare overshot the mark. When, in order to elevate Henry, he sought to dethrone Falstaff, he failed. We cannot, even at the bidding of Shakespeare, change our attitude or our sympathies, and at the close "our hearts go with Falstaff to the Fleet, or, if necessary, to Arthur's bosom, or wheresoever he is." Mr. Charles Bastide supplies an admirable estimate of M. Waldeck-Rousseau. A comparison is suggested between the French states-

man and our own Halifax, and the former is declared to be "the ablest trimmer that France has known since Gambetta." M. Waldeck-Rousseau is also dealt with in the remarkable article of Calchas on 'The Revival of France.' Mr. W. S. Lilly has joined the ranks of those who see grave menace to the future of England. Under 'New Forms of Locomotion and their Results' the Hon. John Scott Montagu, a well-known authority, deals with the opposition experienced in England by those who drive motor-cars, and is of opinion that one hundred or one hundred and fifty miles an hour may easily in time be possible with the use of rails. His ideas take away the breath, but so doubtless did, eighty years ago, those of the advocates of railways. Two opening articles deal with the late Cecil Rhodes, and a third, on 'A Cosmopolitan Oxford,' is also concerned with him.—In the *Nineteenth Century* Mr. Havelock Ellis writes on 'The Genius of Spain.' He has much that is of extreme interest to say upon a great subject, and his observations and conclusions repay study. Due importance is naturally attached to the fact that the persecutions of the Inquisition under Ferdinand and Isabella were responsible for the shaping of subsequent Spain; but we fail to recognize the force of the assertion that the "new light" took its rise in Spain, and that to the suppression of this, thoroughly accomplished, it is due that when the trumpet-blast of Reformation sounded Spain was the only country in which it awoke no echoes. Jews were as much an object of suppression as Moors, and the extirpation of the two races was largely responsible for the decline of the country. There is originality in the plea for the cruelty of the Spaniard that the Spaniard can be as cruel to himself as he is to others, and is only indifferent to the pain of others because he is indifferent to his own. There are many conclusions of the writer on which we should like to dwell did space permit. Mr. Wilfrid Scawen Blunt analyzes the new rendering of Lady Gregory's translation of 'The Life and Death of Cuchulain' just issued by Mr. Murray. He finds the translation excellent in almost every respect, but holds that when the great Irish epic has taken its place, as it is bound to do, with the sagas and romances of Norway, France, and Germany, it may be necessary to have a hardier translation in respect of sexual matters. Lady Gregory's work will in due course come under our own observation. Writing on 'Dante and the Fine Arts,' Mr. Alfred Higgins disputes Mr. Berenson's theory that the form of Dante's imagination was largely conditioned by his knowledge of contemporary works of painting. Two writers appear to oppose the views concerning hospital nurses lately put forth in the *Nineteenth Century*. Mr. Frederic Harrison deals with Newton Hall, until recently a home of English Positivists. Sir Wemyss Reid continues his survey of 'The Month.'—The *Pall Mall* opens with a further section of 'The Rebuilding of London,' by Mr. Hugh B. Phillpott, and furnishes many views of the new Piccadilly for the Coronation, including a sketch of Hyde Park Corner, which serves as a frontispiece. One can only hope that the improvements will be adequate, but recent experiences make us hesitate to accept such a conclusion. Miss Katherine Brereton, of Guy's Hospital, gives a very pleasing and encouraging account of 'Life in the Concentration Camps' of South Africa. Great progress in soothing racial hostilities and inspiring confidence has obviously been made. Miss Brereton is able to speak with authority on the subject with which she deals. Mr. H. W. Brewer has a well-illustrated paper on 'The Tower.' 'Sarah Siddons's Tryst' is ascribed to Clara Morris. Having regard to the subject, we are disposed to question if the author is the famous American actress. If so, the fact might as well have been stated. The illustration to 'The Dead Bird' seems to be a view of Scarborough. 'Recollections of the Royal Academy,' by Mr. G. A. Storey, A.R.A., are followed by some original studies by Sir E. J. Poynter, P.R.A. Mrs. Gallup combats all comers in favour of her biliteral cipher.—In the *Cornhill* No. XVI. of 'A Londoner's Log-Book' is most amusingly continued. It will be a subject of regret when these papers are at an end. Mr. Alexander Innes Shand gives a spirited account of Field-Marshal Sir Neville Chamberlain. Writing of 'Literary Forgeries,' Mr. Charles Whibley depicts the career of George Psalmanazar, William Ireland, and Vrain Lucas. The account of the last, who is now quite forgotten, is a strange romance. Mr. Stephen Gwynn has an essay, at once thoughtful and entertaining, on 'A Century of Irish Humour.' A curious paper that may be read with much pleasure is that on 'The Language of Schoolboys,' by Mr. Nowell Smith. Mr. S. G. Tallentyre follows up other notes on French subjects by 'The English Friends of Marie Antoinette.'—The *English Illustrated* opens with an account of 'Famous Foreign Coronations,' which comprises, among others, those of Charlemagne, Frederick I. of Prussia, and the first Napoleon. An account of Victor Hugo has many portraits and other illustrations. Mrs. Steuart Erskine's account of 'Mrs. Watts's Terra-Cotta Industry' has a sketch of Mr. G. F. Watts in a garden.—To *Longman's* Mr. Fred Whishaw sends the first part of 'In a Devonshire Garden.' In this, while learning much about potato growing, we scrape acquaintance with many interesting specimens of bird and animal life. It constitutes delightful reading. 'La Grande Mademoiselle' of Miss Eveline C. Godley is very spirited. Mr. Lang in 'At the Sign of the Ship' has a harrowing paragraph to the effect that there is a possibility that the famous Casket Letters, though now destroyed, were in existence only twelve years ago. —The Rev. Dr. Smythe Palmer has in the *Gentleman's* a brilliant paper on 'The Aspen Tongue,' by which he indicates the tongue of women. Gerarde in 'The Herball' justifies the use of the phrase, and Sir Thomas More says of women that "those aspen leaves of theirs would never leave wagging." The paper is short, but has high literary flavour. Mr. W. Bradbrook has a contribution on 'Watling Street in Bucks,' and Mr. Ransom one on 'Village Chronicles.'—A large portion of the contents of *Scribner's* consists of fiction, either brief story or serial. The remainder of the number aims at being spring-like. Among the more serious portions are a conclusion of President Gilman's 'Pleasant Incidents of an Academic Life' and an essay by Senator Cabot Lodge, entitled 'Some Impressions of Russia.' Mr. Lodge finds that the territory which Russia adds to herself is an encumbrance, and will remain so until her people learn to develope personal energy and industrial force. While she remains as she is better organized nations have nothing to fear from her trade competition. The illustrations to the entire number have great interest.

'DURHAM ACCOUNT ROLLS.'—CANON FOWLER writes:—"In the very kind review of 'Durham Account Rolls,' *ante*, p. 338, the reviewer is mistaken in saying 'his edition of the Latin life of St. Cuthbert,' for there are several Latin lives of that saint, and I have not edited any of them."

LONDON, SATURDAY, MAY 17, 1902.

CONTENTS. — No. 229.

Notes.

SHELLEY'S ANCESTRY.

ALTHOUGH no respecter of pedigrees, yet Shelley was proud of his supposed relation-ship to Sir Philip Sidney ; but the connexion must have been spiritual rather than physi-cal, for he was mistaken in his pious belief that the authentic blood of Astrophel flowed in his veins. His grandfather, Sir Bysshe Shelley, had won (" eloped with," Medwin says) two heiresses in succession : the first, Mary Catherine Michell, was the poet's grand-mother ; the second, Elizabeth Jane Sidney Perry, ancestress of Lord de L'Isle and Dudley, was the descendant of Sir Philip's younger brother, Robert Sidney, Earl of Leicester.

Shelley was, however, the direct descendant of John Shellie, M.P. for Rye in the first quarter of the fifteenth century, by his wife Beatrix, the daughter of the famous Sir John Hawkwood (Acuto). Called by Hallam " the first real general of modern times," Hawk-wood was captain of the White Company, which fought for the Visconti of Milan. Although his bones lie, probably, in his ancestral church at Sible Hedingham, Essex, the counterfeit presentment of the great

captain in his armour as he lived may be seen to-day in Paolo Uccello's fresco, now at the west end of the Duomo of Florence.

Another ancestor of the poet, Edward Shelley, of Worminghurst (late the property of the convent of Sion), grandson of the above John and Beatrix, was one of the four Masters of the Household to Henry VIII., Edward VI., and Queen Mary. He was buried in the chancel of Worminghurst Church, Sussex, in 1554, with his wife Joan Iden. Her father, Paul Iden (" Pawle Yden "), in civilian costume, with Agnes his wife and one daughter, are represented on brasses in the south chancel of Penshurst Church, Kent. The date of Paul's death is given by Haines as 1514.

Readers of Shakespeare will remember the name of Iden. In ' 2 Henry VI.,' Act IV. scene x., Alexander Iden slays the notorious Jack Cade. Hasted, in his ' History of Kent,' says :—

" The Idens were a family of great antiquity and good estate about Iden, in the county of Sussex, and Rolveden in this county, and in them it con-tinued down to Alexander Iden, who resided here in the twenty-eighth year of K. Henry VI., the latter half of which year he was Sheriff of this county, being appointed to that office on the death of William Crowmer, Esq., who had been put to death by the rebel Cade and his followers."

And elsewhere he adds :—

" Jack Cade, deserted by his followers, concealed himself in the woods near this place [Hothfield], belonging to Ripley Manor, in Westwell, soon after which he was discovered by Alexander Iden...... as some say, in a field belonging to that manor in Westwell parish, but by others in a field of this parish, still named from that circumstance Jack Cade's field."

Holinshed the chronicler records this event as taking place at Hothfield (or Heathfield), Sussex. Iden married the widow of his predecessor—miscalled by Shakespeare, fol-lowing Hall, Sir James Cromer—the daughter of that Lord Treasurer Say who was also murdered by the rebels. Subsequently appointed Governor of Rochester Castle, Iden was again Sheriff of Kent in 1456-7. Barbara, the eldest daughter of a later William Crowmer (or Cromer), of Tunstall, Kent, became the second wife of Henry Shelley, of Worminghurst (who died in 1623), and thereby direct ancestress of the poet. But it is possible that Shelley's sympathies would have lain rather with the rebel Cade than with his respectable Iden and Crowmer ancestors.

An earlier poet was closely allied to characters even more warlike : Edmund Waller was not only a kinsman of the Parliamentary general Sir William Waller, but also cousin to John Hampden, and, by marriage, a connexion of Cromwell. Some have thought that Shakespeare himself was related to John Hampden ; but, in spite of heroic efforts, the Shakespearean pedigree still lies seething in the crucible. Byron, through his mother, was descended from that great poet-king, James I. of Scotland, who wrote 'The Kingis Quair,' and whose foul murder is so beautifully chronicled in Rossetti's ballad of 'The King's Tragedy.' William Cowper (also through his mother) claimed descent from an earlier poet, the great Dean of St. Paul's, John Donne ; and Donne again had an interesting pedigree, being grandson to old John Heywood, the epigrammatist, whose wife (Elizabeth Rastall) was granddaughter of Elizabeth More, sister of the martyred Sir Thomas More, Lord Chancellor.   A. R. BAYLEY.

ST. MARGARET'S CHURCH AND WEST-MINSTER BENEFACTORS.
(Continued from p. 305.)

THE last benefactor of our city's poor having a monument in our old parish church is Emery Hill, whose name is more often on the lips of our citizens than almost any other, and whose memory is generally beloved and blessed. The monument is of white marble and is attached to the last pillar westwards and northwards. It is of chaste and handsome design, with the following inscription :—

"Sacred | to ye memory of that great | Example of piety and true Christianity | Mr Emery Hill | Late Inhabitant of ye Parish & worthy benefactor of ye Same who departed ye | life upon ye 27 day of June Ao Dm. 1677, in ye 68 year of his age & lies here interred | A person accomplished wth all Chr'ian graces & vertues & most eminent for his | charity besides wt hee gave in his Life time he Left by his will at his death | 1st the Revenue of severall howses in Westminster for ever for the use of | the poor Childrenn of the Kings Hospitall in tuttle fields of wch hee | was one of ye Governrs 2ly ye Sume of 100li for ye building of three Almes | houses in Petty france. 3ly 7li p. an. in fee for ye teaching of ye poor Childrens | of ye Parish 4ly 100li for A stock of Coales for ever for ye use of ye Poor of ye | Parish. 5ly 50li to the Children of Christ church hospitall in London | 6ly A bountifull guift for ye setting upp of poor decayed Tradesmen | he Left plentifull for ye building of Twelve | Almeshouses, A Chappell & schol for six poor men & their | wifes, six poore widdowes & teaching of 20 poore | children wth Sufficient maintenance | for the same for ever | More 50li for ye use of ye poore of ye | Company of Brewers | Besides | Severall other | charitable bequests | which we have | not rowme to | mention."

This handsome tablet is adorned with his arms, Vert, three talbots passant argent, two and one. The various benefactions of this notable son of our city extend over a very wide area, many of them sounding very quaint and peculiar to our twentieth-century ears, but all of them tending to the use and comfort of our less fortunate fellow-creatures ; and, to quote again and at length from the Report of 1890 — now, I believe, out of print and not very easily procurable — we find it recorded that by his will, dated 10 April, 1677,

"he directed the Governors of the Hospital of Green Coates, in Tuttle Fields, to allow the Church-wardens for the time being from time to time 20s. a yeare forever, to be spent in a Collation with the Treasurer and ancient Vestrymen, to be spent in June, then 'before dinner' to take a view of all the gifts given to the parish by any man or woman, and see whether they be truly entered in a book kept for that purpose, and whether the gifts be applied justly and according to the donors' intention."

The benefactor goes on to state that

"I know for want of such a yearly inspection there is a great neglect of many good works, and many a pound lost to the parish for want of looking after guifts and wills."

It may be presumed he knew what he was saying ; he was an excellent parish man, and had been churchwarden of St. Margaret's in 1651-2. If the good work just referred to was neglected, the 20s. was to go to the church-wardens of St. Martin's-in-the-Fields. He also gave 100l.

"for an everlasting stock, for Sea Coales for the only use of the Poore of St. Margaret's, West-minster, that I am sure hath neither stock nor store-house. And my will and meaning is that this Hundred Pounds, noe nor any part thereof, noe nor the least proceed thereof, be ever imployed or made any other use of whatsoever so long as the world endureth......as they will answer the breach of this trust at that great and dreadful day of Judgment when and where every man must give an accompt of all his actions whether good or bad."

He was very particular and precise as to when the coals should be laid in, which was to be

"between April and August when they were cheapest, and sold in winter at the same rate they cost, provided the Charges for laying them in and delivering the same out be saved and alwaies excepted."

The vestry report tells us that the coals were deposited in a storehouse built (50l. being left by will for that purpose) on part of the ground belonging to the Red Lion Alms-houses (Van Dun's), the rule being that no individual should receive more than three bushels, and it is stated that in mild seasons the stock was not distributed at all. After the demolition of the almshouses the 100l. was invested in an Exchequer bond, and the interest applied towards the purchase of coals, which were distributed at a suitable time with other charitable gifts of a like character. The parochial trustees now get the 2*l.* 10*s.* on this bond yearly, the charity being included in what is known as their "Consolidated Account." Among his benefactions was one of 20*s.*,

"to be distributed to the prisoners in the Gatehouse, and 20*s.* to the prisoners in the Bridewell, Tothill Fields, to buy them twelve pieces of Beefe to be spent on Twelve Sundays."

In 1674, in the schedule to the deeds, under date 8 March, by which the Grammar School was established, it was provided that the Governors of the School

"should obtain a licence from the Dean and Chapter of Westminster for building six almshouses on the Common in Tothill Fields for six poor old men, or six men and their wives, and six houses for poor old widows."

No one under sixty years of age was to be admitted, nor any who had not been at least for twenty years honest housekeepers in the parish of St. Margaret. At the establishment "the six poor men and six poor women were to receive 8*s.* per month apiece, if man and wife then 12*s.*" Thirteen chaldron of coal were to be laid in; gowns were to be supplied, "not to exceed 10*s.* 6*d.* per yard"; and 10*l.* was set aside to be spent at "two collations for the governors and their wives." These almshouses were built by the trustees in the year 1708, and occupied the same site as do the present United Almshouses, on the north side of Rochester Row, opposite the well-known church of St. Stephen, the gift to Westminster of the Baroness Burdett-Coutts. The original tablet, replaced on the new almshouses, bears the inscription, still legible,

Mʳ Emery Hill
late of the Parish of
Sᵗ Margaret, Westminster,
founded these Almshouses
Anno Domini 1708
Christian Reader
In hopes of thy assistance.

By his will he not only stated his wish for "shady rows," but desired that the almshouses should have a courtyard, "and that without the courtyard may be planted with good elme, and not with lime trees, for elmes is a better greene and more lastingly."

W. E. Harland-Oxley.
71, Turner Buildings, Millbank, S.W.

(To be continued.)

"Frieze."—What is the etymology of the architectural term "frieze"? The word is generally defined as that part of the entablature of an order which comes between the architrave and cornice, and is usually enriched with figures or other ornaments. The usual etymological account given in the dictionaries is that the word is related in some way to the synonymous Italian *fregio*, which also means "border, fringe, ornament," and that *fregio* is the phonetic equivalent of the Latin *Phrygium* (sc. *opus*), "a Phrygian work" (cp. *Phrygiœ vestes*, "embroidered garments"). So 'H.E.D.,' Skeat's 'Dict.' (ed. 1901), and Hatzfeld's 'French Dict.' (*s.v.* 'Frise'). This account is not satisfactory, for it seems to involve serious phonetic difficulties. A French *frise* related to an Italian *fregio* which is identical with a Latin *phrygium*? Such an etymology would imply that a Latin -*igium* could become -*ise* in French. No doubt Latin -*si*- before a vowel becomes regularly -*gi*- in Italian—*e.g.*, Latin *Parisii, Perusia, Blasius, cerevisia*, become in Italian *Parigi, Perugia, Biagio, cervigia*. But the converse is not the case. No instance can be found of a Latin -*gia*- becoming -*se* in French. The equivalent of Italian *fregio* (from a Latin *phrygium*) in French would have been **frei*, later **froi;* the *g* would have been vocalized; cp. Fr. *essai*, the representative of Latin *exagium*, and O.Fr. *navei* (Eng. *navy*), Lat. *navigium*. There is another difficulty in admitting relationship between *fregio* and *frise*, and that is the quantity of the accented vowel: *fregio* supposes a Latin type **frĭseum*, *frise* a Latin type *frīsea*. It may be noted also that the two words differ in gender.

I would suggest that the Latin original of the Italian *fregio* may be found in the Med. Lat. *fresium*, "fimbria" (Ducange). *Frisium* (Ducange) is doubtless another spelling of the same word (with *ĭ* for *ē*). The French *frise* (Eng. *frieze*), if connected with this Med. Lat. *frisium* (*fresium*), shows an unexplained lengthening of the root vowel. I think if any one will examine the meanings of French *frise* in Hatzfeld he will come to the conclusion that the radical idea of *frise* (our *frieze*) is "a border, band," and not "something embroidered," as suggested in 'H.E.D.' In Spanish and Portuguese we find the form *friso*, agreeing with the French form in all but gender. To the Spanish word is doubtless due the Arabic *'ifrīz*, frieze, cornice, registered by Steingass, p. 62, a word without Semitic etymology.

Comestor Oxoniensis.

Sir Benjamin Rudyerd, 1572-1658.—It is said of him in his life in the 'D.N.B.,' xlix. 385, that

"on 18 April he was admitted to the Inner Temple, and on 24 October, 1600, was called to the bar (Manning, 'Memoirs of Sir Benjamin Rudyerd,' p. 5)."

This statement is probably not strictly accurate, for no entry of admission of Sir Benjamin Rudyerd to the Inner Temple is to be found in the books of that Inn. According to Foster's 'Alumni Oxon.,' he became a student of the Middle Temple in 1590, and was entered there as third son of James Rudyerd, of Winchfield, Hants.

The 'Visitation of London, 1633-4' (Harl. Soc. Publ., xvii. 215), and the 'Visitation of Berkshire, 1664-6' (by Metcalfe, 85), contain pedigrees of Rudyerd, in which Sir Benjamin, his wife Elizabeth, and his son William are mentioned. Is anything known of the wife's parentage beyond that she was a daughter of Sir Henry Harington?   H. C.

SHIELDS, DERIVATION OF THE PLACE-NAME.— In Tanner MSS. xlv. 22, as quoted in Cosin's 'Correspondence' (Surtees Soc., ii. 134, note), referring to the plague, it is said :—

"The sickness hath been a fortnight at St. Hild's (commonly called Sheelds), which is a town belonging to the Dean and Chapter betwixt Gateside and the sea month."

Now there is a church of St. Hilda at South Shields, and the above derivation seems inherently probable. But in 'Cassell's Gazetteer' (not, we may suppose, a scientific authority on the etymology of place-names) I find :—

"South S. (anciently written 'Le Sheels') originated with the fishermen of the Tyne, who built here, along the southern shore, sheds (provincially termed 'sheelds' or 'shields') to defend themselves from the weather."

I have not access just now to the late Canon Taylor's 'Words and Places'; still this note may not be altogether valueless.

JAMES HOOPER.

Norwich.

[In 'Names and their Histories' (1896) Canon Taylor said: "North Shields......probably takes its name from some fishermen's huts or 'shiellings.' South Shields......was called St. Hild's from a chapel dedicated to St. Hilda. The similar names of the two contiguous towns were inevitably assimilated, Shiels becoming North Shields, and St. Hild's becoming South Shields. Two centuries ago South Shields was officially designated as St. Hilds, commonly called Sheelds. The d in North Shields is intrusive, and is absent in Selkirk and in Galashiels, the 'huts on the River Gala.'"]

"MESS OF POTTAGE."— This phrase, frequently used, does not appear to have been noticed in 'N & Q.' It is found so far back as Coverdale's Bible (1535), at Prov. xv. 17 : "Better is a meace of potage with love, then a fat oxe wᵗ evell will." In Matthew's Bible (1537), at Gen. xxv., the title has "Esau selleth his byrthright for a messe of potage"; and Prov. xv. 17 stands as in Coverdale. The same title and rendering appear in Cranmer's Bible (1539). The Geneva Bible (1560) has at Gen. xxv. the same title, but in Prov. xv. "a dinner of greene herbes." The Bishops' Bible (1568) drops out of the title the words "for a messe of potage"; and so does the Authorized Version. It seems probable that the phrase became current chiefly from the heading to the passage in Genesis, as this is retained in the Geneva version, which for fully half a century was the Bible in popular use.   R. D. WILSON.

[The late Mr. R. Roberts, of Boston, pointed out in 9ᵗʰ S. ii. 17 that the phrase occurred in Matthew's Bible, 1537; but MR. WILSON carries the usage back two years. Coverdale rendered Gen. xxv. "a meace of meate."]

SOLDIERS' CARD-GAMES.—A soldier recently returned from Africa told me that when camping out the men occasionally played cards. I asked, "What games?" and was answered, "Pontoon and fat." "Pontoon" is simply Thomas Atkins's corruption of *vingt-et-un* — thus, "vingtoon," "vontoon," "pontoon," a word which comes easily to him. "Fat" is the game of "five or nine," but my friend could give me no reason for the name.   F. J.

[Half a century ago *vingt-et-un* was occasionally contracted into *Van-John*.]

BOOK-TITLES CHANGED.—The changing of the name of a book seems to me a most reprehensible practice. The name of a book has doubtless got something to do with its popularity, and an author is justified in asking the opinion of friends, and taking a hint from his publisher, with regard to the title. Thus Stevenson's 'Treasure Island' was intended by the author to be named 'The Sea Cook,' but Mr. Henderson, the publisher, in one of whose publications it first appeared as a serial, suggested the present felicitous title. One might even excuse such a change as the title of one of Reade's novels underwent. 'Hard Cash' first appeared as a serial with the title 'Very Hard Cash.' The dropping of the "very" was an improvement, and was justifiable enough when adopted in time— that is, before the appearance of the novel in book form.

I had heard of a romance by Oliver Madox Brown called 'The Black Swan.' I could not obtain it, but I succeeded finally in getting possession of 'Gabriel Denver' by the same author, which is 'The Black Swan' under a different name. If the title in the second instance had been 'Gabriel Denver; or, the

Black Swan,' it would not have been misleading, which a total change of name is bound (more or less) to be. 'The Collegians,' again, is sometimes published under Griffin's title, more frequently under that of the, perhaps, better-known dramatized version. Mrs. Radcliffe's novel 'The Italian' (by some considered her best work) has been published as 'The Italian Monk.' A cheap edition recently appeared under the title 'A Sicilian Romance.' I have seen a version of St. Pierre's 'Paul et Virginie' called 'The Shipwreck,' and one of Dumas's 'Count of Monte Cristo' called 'Edmond Dantès.'

In cases where the author's name is well or fairly well known, and is still appended to the work, one cannot be led far astray; but where the name is not used, or where (as in some library catalogues) it does not appear with the title, a change is apt to confuse many readers. The custom is, I assert, reprehensible, and ought not to be followed by any respectable publisher.

Doubling or reduplicating the titles of books is another fruitful cause of confusion. Thus the 'Canterbury Tales' of Chaucer and the 'Canterbury Tales' of Miss Lee are not quite the same. So, too, we have the 'Teares of the Muses' by Spenser, and 'Lachrymæ Musarum' by an old poet and also by a modern one. Even such an innocent and trifling matter as that of Stevenson borrowing the title of 'Underwoods' from Ben Jonson is not to be commended. Let every man keep his own beauties.

Another matter somewhat analogous, though not so important, which sometimes leads to confusion, and is also censurable, is the custom of referring to ancient authors by different titles. Thus we can say Tully (like Goldsmith) or Cicero and be equally correct; but surely Virgil (or Vergil) is better than Maro, and Ovid than Naso, because they are more in accordance with the prevailing practice of our best scholars. I have heard a man say that he was acquainted with Suetonius, but had never read Tranquillus, yet in a good (that is, a carefully compiled) catalogue I have seen a reference to the latter, but none to the former. In such a case (though we could not say there was any error) we might say that if we must have Tranquillus, we might be complemented with Suetonius also, as the more common and more generally used name.

A very interesting volume might be written on book-titles. Concerning misleading titles some interesting notes have appeared in 'N. & Q.' We cannot read the title of a book with the contents of which we are wholly unacquainted (especially if the title be a striking one) without forming some idea of the contents. Thus I had heard of 'The Scarlet Letter' for many years before I read Hawthorne's romance; and I had woven (I cannot tell how) around the name a romance of my own. I had come to believe that 'The Scarlet Letter' was an epistle written in his own blood by an unfortunate prisoner. The rest of the story followed as a matter of course. I only mention this as an example of what I mean. I am sure other readers of 'N. & Q.' have been thus not unpleasingly led astray by the titles of works which they have not read if they would but confess it.

THOMAS AULD.

[Most well-known classical authors have names which may be regarded as the recognized English forms, having beaten others out of the field. We should say Virgil, Cicero, and Ovid; we have never seen "Tully" or "Naso" in a modern book.]

KNURR AND SPELL.—In the course of conversation with a Yorkshire friend some time ago about this game, which is still played with keen enthusiasm in the more countrified parts of the West Riding and on the outskirts of the large manufacturing centres, my attention was caught by the use of the expresion *on avont* (pronounced by my friend *on a vont*) in the sense of the French phrase *en avant* and the golfer's *fore*. I know little of the origin of the game of knurr and spell, but think it well, invited by your motto "When found, make a note of," to communicate this in the hope that it may serve some reader. Halliwell does not afford any light on it under O, A, or E. Possibly Wright may. Skeat says *knurr* is of O.L.G. origin.

LIONEL CRESSWELL.

Wood Hall, Calverley, Yorks.

"MUNTJAC."—The origin of this well-known zoological term, since 1780 the usual European name of a small Japanese deer, has hitherto been involved in obscurity. The word is omitted from Yule's 'Hobson-Jobson,' just the work in which one would expect to find it, and it is absent even from Scott's 'Malayan Words in English' (American Oriental Society's *Journal*, 1897). The 'Imperial Dictionary' calls it a "native name." The 'Encyclopædia Britannica' says "one of the native names." The 'Century Dictionary' calls it Javanese, but I do not find it in the 'Javanese Dictionary' of Jansz, 1876; on the contrary, the Javanese equivalent is *kidang*, as explained by Dr. Murray in the latest volume of the 'N.E.D.' There are, however, two other languages spoken in Java, Madurese and Sundanese, and I have ascertained that this mysterious *muntjac* belongs to the latter. Thus Riggs, 'Sunda Dictionary,' 1862, has " *Minchek*, an animal of the deer kind, called in Malay *kidang*."

Jas. Platt, Jun.

Colne Grammar School Boys and Weddings.—Perhaps the following may be of interest, and be worth preserving now that Colne Grammar School is extinct. The buildings were sold recently. I take it from the 'Literary Corner' of the *Burnley Express* :—

"Weddings at the Parish Church seem to have been recognised as having a special claim for the boys of the Grammar School. At Burnley, in the days gone by, it was the custom of the pupils of the Grammar School to mulct the happy bridegroom in a donation, and the same custom prevailed at Colne. It was formerly the custom here, says Mr. Carr, whenever there was a fashionable wedding, for the senior scholar of the adjoining Grammar School to come into the church at a given signal, and thus address the newly married pair as they left the altar :—

> God prosper these your nuptials
> With much peace ;
> And grant that love
> Between you may increase.
> May happy minds and virtuous hearts
> Unite in virtuous love,
> And may you love your bridegroom,
> And you your lovely bride,
> And ever bless the day
> The nuptial knot was tied.
>
> May happiness on earth
> Your portion be,
> And may you always live
> In endlesse felicitie.
> We wish you health,
> Wealth, worth, and gold,
> As apples in bright
> Orchards may be told.
> We wish that you
> May never disagree
> Till lambs and wolves
> Do dwell in unitie.

At the close the bridegroom was expected to give the boy at least one of the larger silver coins. In fact, one hardly sees how he could be churlish enough to refuse, after such a poem of good wishes and flattery."

J. Langfield Ward.

Weston Lawn, Bath.

[For the Burnley custom see Mr. Langfield Ward's contribution at 9ᵗʰ S. vii. 273.]

Yarrow Unvisited.—There are evidently others besides Wordsworth who meditate on the glamour of Yarrow from afar. Speaking of conspicuous pictures now on exhibition in the Royal Academy, a writer in the *Academy* of 29 March, p. 327, overflows in this fashion :—

"One of Mr. David Murray's large canvases shows 'The Dowie Dens' of Yarrow, in whose vale the Ettrick shepherd [*sic*] was born and lies buried, a romantic district associated alike with the Border Minstrelsy, the writings of Thomas Logan, Scott, and Wordsworth. It was also the birthplace of Mungo Park, the house of whose sisters, shadowed by trees, is seen in the right of the picture."

When Yarrow is visited it is readily found that there is a considerably far cry from the birthplace of the Ettrick Shepherd to that of Mungo Park. The Ettrick Shepherd was a native of Ettrick, as his familiar designation indicates, although he farmed in Yarrow Vale, and a monument to his memory appropriately overlooks St. Mary's Loch and the historic hostelry of Tibbie Shiels. But who is "Thomas Logan"? This reference seems to call up him who left half told the story of Michael Bruce and the 'Ode to the Cuckoo,' and, if so, one trembles for what may yet befall. Logan under his own colours was serious enough, but his activities when protected by an *alias* may imply infinite complications. *Absit, procul absit.*

Thomas Bayne.

Queries.

We must request correspondents desiring information on family matters of only private interest to affix their names and addresses to their queries, in order that the answers may be addressed to them direct.

Ceiling Inscription in Shropshire. — In the old house of Wilderhope, in the parish of Rushbury, in Shropshire, which was erected by the Smalman family and finished in 1593, are some fine plaster ceilings with various devices and inscriptions. Amongst others these occur : fleur-de-lis, portcullis, roses, the three feathers, iesu on a shield, also fs in a circle, and qev . est . vem . iam . droit round. This last inscription is difficult to make out, the ceiling having been repeatedly whitewashed. What is its meaning? Another rendering of it is v . ist . vem . an . droit. The letters fs in the centre stand for Francis Smalman. There were also formerly shields of the Smalman arms, with "Deus est meus mali defensor" round the shields. The ceilings are very fine, and some have thought they were done by Italian workmen. Any suggestions as to the meaning of the inscriptions will be welcomed.

W. G. D. F.

Arms of Dutch and Flemish Towns.—I should be glad to know of any illustrated work, either English or foreign, dealing with the municipal heraldry of the Continent, and more especially of Holland and Belgium, with a view to identifying the various town marks stamped on antique Dutch and Flemish silver. Rosenberg's 'Der Goldschmiede Merkzeichen,' published at Frankfort in 1890, treats exhaustively of German assay offices and the heraldic marks used by the respective municipalities in stamping plate, but in the chapter on Holland omits all mention of the town marks formerly used at Leyden, Dordrecht, and several other places in the Low Countries where the silversmith's art long flourished. ARTHUR DASENT.

REGINALD SCOTT'S 'DISCOVERIE OF WITCHCRAFT.'— Is there an accessible edition of Reginald Scott's 'Discoverie of Witchcraft,' and, if so, who published it? C. W.

[A limited reprint of the first edition of this work was published in 1886 by Elliot Stock, of Paternoster Row, edited by our late friend Dr. Brinsley Nicholson. It is an admirably executed work, for which application may be made to the publisher, though we fear it is out of print.]

BOSWELL'S 'JOHNSON' AS A TOUCHSTONE OF TASTE.—It is told of some one that when he met a new acquaintance he would ask him his opinion of Boswell's 'Johnson,' and framed his estimate of his new friend according to the answer. Of whom is this related?
DEBONNAIRE.

JACK-IN-THE-PULPIT.—A friend is anxious to know what wild flower is called—we believe locally somewhere—" Jack-in-the-Pulpit."
(Miss) L. M. KNOCKER.

[Many different flowers bear this name, e.g., Arum maculatum in the Midlands.]

'OLIVER AND ARTHUR.' — Can any contributor oblige me with information as to an ancient romance, 'Oliver and Arthur,' originally in French, translated into German, Basel, 1521, and, again, Frankfurt. 1568? Is there any entire translation into English, or abstract of it, and, if so, where could I find it? If not separately published, there might be one in some collection of romances, or an abstract used illustratively in the introduction, or in the notes, to a work of similar character. W. T. S.

MANNERS AND CUSTOMS IN SHAKESPEARE'S TIME.—What book besides Harrison's 'Elizabethan England' gives the best account of English manners and customs in Shakespeare's time? C. W.

[Among others, see M. Jules Jusserand's 'English Novel in the Time of Shakespeare' and 'English Wayfaring Life in the Middle Ages.']

GYE FAMILY.—Who was Gye of the Cellar, who, according to Papworth, bore Az., on a chev. arg., between three leopards' heads or, as many fleurs-de-lis gu.? Papworth quotes Glover's 'Ordinary' as his source of information. LEO CULLETON.

AMERICAN EDITION OF DICKENS. — Where can I get full particulars of the 130-volume edition of Dickens on parchment now preparing in America? C. W.

BUILDING IN GOTHIC PERIOD. — Can any reader give references to books or MSS. containing the actual rules of appreticeship and guild rules of masons, carpenters, &c., during the Gothic period, or any information as to the organization of labour and purchase of materials for mediæval buildings? A. T. GRIFFITH.

"'TWAS APRIL, ON THE VERGE OF MAY."— Can any of your readers tell me where the above line appears? I remember learning it sixty or seventy years ago. I fancy it was in an 'Ode to the Cuckoo.' G. C. W.

ANNUNCIATION. — Being near a Roman Catholic church in my own neighbourhood on 11 April. I looked at the week's notices in the porch, and was surprised to see 7 April marked as "Annunciation B.V.M." It at once occurred to me that our 7 April is, in the Julian reckoning observed in the Eastern Church, 25 March, which is the feast of the Annunciation. But as the style was altered by the authority of the Pope, it is not likely that any part of the old reckoning is observed in the Western Church. Hook, in his 'Church Dictionary,' says that the Council of Toledo (A.D. 656) changed the date of the festival to 18 December, so that it might never fall during Lent (surely a less drastic change would have secured that), but that the Council in Trullo (A.D. 692) restored it to 25 March, allowing it to be the only festival, except Sunday, observed during Lent. Can one of your readers explain my difficulty?
W. T. LYNN.
Blackheath.

MIDDLETON FAMILY OF DERBYSHIRE.—Information is desired respecting the ancestry of Bishop Middleton of Calcutta, who was the son of the Rev. John Middleton, vicar of Kedleston, Derbyshire. Did he spring from a family of that name in Derbyshire who bore for arms Fretty sable, and for crest a garb or, banded vert, between two wings? One Richard Middleton, vicar of a Derbyshire parish, had three sons and a daughter— viz., (1) Samuel, who died in 1758, leaving a son Nathaniel, who held important posts in India under Warren Hastings, and became High Sheriff of Hants in 1800; (2) Richard; (3) a son, name unknown, in holy orders;

and (4) a daughter, who married a director of the H.E.I.C. Was the bishop a son or grandson of the third son of Richard Middleton? Any information will be thankfully received.   W. M. ROBERTS.
Morwylea, Aberdovey, N. Wales.

H. WHITRIDGE, PUBLISHER. — Is anything known of H. Whitridge, whose name I find in the *Gentleman's Magazine* for October, 1739, as the publisher of 'A Plain Address to the Followers and Favourites of the Methodists,' and again as selling 'Poems on Various Subjects,' by Moses Browne, of which Cave was the publisher? Mr. Whitridge was of Cornhill. So far as I know there is only one family of Whitridges in the country, and many of them belonged to Cumberland.   E. W.

ARTHUR'S CROWN.—In Mr. Owen M. Edwards's 'Wales' ("Story of the Nations" Series), p. 190, "the crown of Arthur and the precious portion of the true cross" are mentioned as the last heirlooms of the royal house of Gwynedd, which Dafydd, brother of the second Llewelyn, carried with him from fastness to fastness when hunted by Edward I.; and at p. 208 it is stated that when Edward, after the final conquest of Wales, took possession of his new land, Arthur's crown, "among other jewels," was given up to him. Does this reputed crown of Arthur still exist; and if so, where is it?
          C. C. B.

'THE PARLIAMENT OF CRITICKS.'—Is there any record of the authorship of the following work?—

"The | Parliament | of | Criticks, | The Menippæan Satyr | of | *Justus Lipsius* | in a | Dream; | Paraphras'd: | in a | Banter | Upon the | Criticks of the Age | London: Printed for J. Hartley, next Door to | the King's-Head Tavern in Holborn. 1702."

Halkett and Laing, Cushing, the B.M. Catalogue, &c., are silent.   G. G. S.

WATSON OF BARRASBRIDGE, NEWCASTLE-UPON-TYNE. — Could any of your readers possessing old army lists, magazines, &c., give me information respecting my great-uncles, as to dates of entering army, where stationed, dates of promotion, death, or any other notes they may happen to have?

1. John Blackett Watson, lieutenant Royal Marines, who was second in command of the division of Marines at the storming of the Diamond Rock by Admiral Ganteaume in 1806. The fatigue and exposure he there underwent laid the foundation for a decline, and he died at his father's house in Bishop Wear-mouth, co. Durham, in 1808, aged twenty, and was buried in the churchyard at that place.

2. Charles Mitford Watson, lieutenant 83rd Regiment, who died in the island of Ceylon, 17 June, 1824, where he was on the staff of Col. Greenwell. Could any of your Ceylon readers inform me whether there is any tombstone to his memory, or whereabouts he is buried there?

They were sons of Ralph Watson, of H.M. Customs, of Percy Street, Barrasbridge, Newcastle-upon-Tyne, and grandsons of William Watson, of Percy Street, Sheriff of the Corporation of Newcastle, 1747, who was son of Stephen Watson, of North Seaton Hall, Northumberland, by his wife Diana, daughter and at length coheir of Robert Mitford, of Seghill Towers, by his wife Christian, second daughter of Sir William Blackett, Bart., M.P., of Grey Friars, Newcastle, and of Woodcroft, co. Durham.   H. REGINALD LEIGHTON.
East Boldon, R.S.O., co. Durham.

OLD SONGS.—A song used to be sung in Lincolnshire which began:—

Come, all ye lads of high renown,
That love to drink good ale that 's brown,
And pull the lofty pheasant down
          With powder, shot, and gun.

In what collection can I find it?
I am also anxious to know the source of:—

My father kept a horse,
My mother kept a mare,
My brother kept a grew [greyhound],
My sister kept a hare,

which is still known in the same county. Whence also come two others?—

There was a miller, he had three sons,
He found his life was almost gone,

and

The doctor [?] his medical man doth tend,
The parson doth with him pray;
And the farmer doth to market ride
          Upon the market day.

This last was printed as a Lincolnshire song in 8ᵗʰ S. ii. 44, but its origin was not traced.
          M. P.

ARMORIAL.—Can any reader of 'N. & Q.' assign this armorial bearing? On a shield three arrows per bend. Seventeenth century, tinctures unknown, Sussex family.
          W. HENEAGE LEGGE.

ELIZABETH, LADY MORLEY.—The writer in the 'Dictionary of National Biography' states that William de la Pole, first Duke of Suffolk (murdered 1450), by his wife Alice Chaucer had only one child, John, who eventually became the second duke and died in 1491. But I have seen it stated elsewhere ('Early Genealogical History of the House

of Arundel,' by J. Pym Yeatman) that
William, the first duke, had also a daughter
Elizabeth, who married Henry, Lord Morley.
Is anything known of this daughter and of
her descendants? RONALD DIXON.

"AVOID EXTREMES," &c.—Can any one tell
me the author of the following lines?—

Avoid extremes; and shun the fault of such,
Who still are pleased too little or too much;
At every trifle scorn to take offence,
That always shows great pride, or little sense.
S. T. LAND.

[These lines, slightly altered by us, are in Pope's
'Essay on Criticism,' part ii.]

TEDULA, A BIRD.—In Spenser's 'Visions of
the World's Vanitie,' stanza iii., occur the
lines:—

I saw a little Bird cal'd Tedula,
The least of thousands which on earth abide, &c.

It is the common story of the crocodile's
teeth being picked by small birds. As to
the word, I can only find in my Latin
dictionary *tœdulus* = squeamish, fastidious;
but that does not appear to throw any light
on its origin. H. P. L.

[*Tedula* in Ducange is given as a diminutive of
tœda (*teda*), a torch, but this does not seem to help.]

"THE FIRST WAR."—Amongst the Royalist
Composition Papers in the Public Record
Office the expression "the first war" fre-
quently occurs. Thus it is stated of one
Shropshire Royalist in 1649: "His delin-
quency that he was in armes against the
parliament in the first warr." In his petition
he states "that your peticoner was in armes
against the Parliament in the former warr."
Which was considered to be "the First (or
Former) War," and when did it end?
W. G. D. F.

[From Edgehill, 1642, to the surrender of Charles's
army in Cornwall, March, 1646. See S. R. Gardiner's 'Student's History.']

JOHN DOVE, THE REGICIDE.—He was alderman and M.P. for Salisbury in the Long
Parliament. What was his parentage?
Robert Dove, son of Henry Dove, of Salisbury—matriculated at Magdalen Hall, Oxon,
in 1623, aged seventeen, and afterwards
rector of Elme, co. Cambridge—is stated to
have had a brother John (Foster, 'Alumni
Oxon.'). W. D. PINK.

FRANCIS SPIERA'S DESPAIR.—Sir Simonds
D'Ewes, in the 'Autobiography' printed by
Halliwell (i. 283), writes of "Francis Spiera's
despair, so much enfamoused by the pens of
many learned men." I should be glad to know
who this Francis Spiera was, and what
authors have written of him. L. B. C.

Replies.

CLIFFORD'S INN.
(9ᵗʰ S. ix. 244.)

REFERRING to N. S. S.'s note under the
above heading, may I be allowed to supplement the same with the following?

The late Alexander Pulling, serjeant-at-law
—whose acquaintance, by the way, I had the
privilege and honour to make at Swansea in
the early eighties—in his erudite and valuable
work entitled 'The Order of the Coif' (London, Wm. Clowes & Sons, 1884), in treating
of the early history of the Inns of Court,
amongst other things, states:—

"The possession of most of the smaller hostels or
Inns seems to have been originally acquired by the
apprentices of the law in somewhat the same way
as Thavies Inn, viz. by mere hiring from the actual
owners: this temporary possession being in after-
times made permanent by lease or purchase.
Thus Clifford's Inn was so acquired in the time
of Edward III., Furnival's *temp.* Henry IV.,"

and so on, naming the rest of the Inns of
Court, and in a foot-note appended:—

"Thus Clifford's Inn was in 1309 Crown Property,
and granted by Edward II., at a rent service of one
penny, to Robert de Clifford, whose widow, Isabell
Lady de Clifford, in 1345 demised it *Apprenticiis
de Banco* at a yearly rent of 10*l.*, which Lease was
from time to time renewed. It was sold to Nicholas
Sulyard for 600*l.*, and 4*l.* per annum — Dugdale,
'Orig.,' 187."

And afterwards, in treating of the law
affecting the Inns of Court, the learned
serjeant says:—

"Whilst almost every other collegiate institution
in this country is regulated by prescribed legal provisions, express statute, or governing charters, the
Inns of Court, founded on and fostered by no royal
bounty or state concession, have lived for so many
centuries, honourable and learned Societies, the
only recognised guardians of the honour and independence of the English Bar, practically exempted
from the orders, jurisdiction, or interference of the
Courts, and allowed to constitute, on all occasions
of dissension or irregularity, a sort of domestic
forum, whose conduct has in almost every known
case been fully acquiesced in as lawful and right.
The decisions of the Courts at Westminster with
reference to the Inns of Court have always been
based on the presumption that such institutions
are in a legal sense voluntary societies, over which
the ordinary tribunals have no jurisdiction, as in
the case of corporations or colleges. This remarkable feature in the constitution of the Inns of Court
is no doubt to a great extent anomalous, and if it
has rarely produced the usual evils of anomalous
institutions, it is only fair to attribute this happy
escape to the prudent conduct of these honourable
and learned societies in the management of their
affairs, and the maintenance of government and
discipline. Sir William Dugdale has carefully
compiled from various sources full information as
to orders and regulations in any way relating to

the Inns of Court, their order of government, and duties and powers, both in regard to legal education, the admission and rejection of members, and the preserving proper discipline among them; and none of such regulations dates back beyond the seventeenth century. No ordinance with reference to these institutions emanating from the Crown or the Privy Council, the Judges or the Benchers has an earlier date than the reign of Philip and Mary; and the Inns of Court are not even mentioned in any Act of Parliament before the next reign. There is no reference in any law report before that time to the Inns of Court as legally constituted institutions; and a sort of return made to the Crown in the time of Henry VIII. on this subject seems very distinctly to show that there was not any reliable previous account of the Inns of Court or their system of rule."

The talented and industrious author further appends, *inter alia*, the following foot-note :

"In the Cott. MS. Vitellius C 9, pp. 319b–321b, is the description given to Henry VIII. 'of the Inns of Court and the manner of study and preferment therein.' This MS. was much damaged in the fire that took place some years ago, but Dugdale, p. 193, gives all that relates to the Middle Temple. It is not easy to make out, from what remains of the MS., what this information was as to the other Inns."

Pulling, created a serjeant-at-law in 1864, was, if not the survivor, one of the last of the serjeants-at-law not raised to the judicial bench, and he continued from his creation to his decease one of the most zealous upholders of all the dignities, precedence, and privileges pertaining to his order. It was interesting and delightful to converse with him thereon, and to hear him refer with pride and pleasure to his call "ad statum et gradum servientis ad legem," as he termed it. and his assertion that the Order of the Coif came into being prior to the oldest title in the English peerage, and centuries before any order conferring a title of honour was instituted in England.

In Herbert's 'Antiquities of the Inns of Court and Chancery' (London. printed for Vernor & Hood, Poultry, and others, 1804), chap. iv., under headings of 'Inns of Chancery belonging to the Temple,' 'Clifford's Inn,' pp. 272-3, what Mr. Neville, K.C., mentioned in the Court of Appeal on 19 March is corroborated; also the sale to Nicholas Sulyard. Esq., the Principal of the House and a Bencher of Lincoln's Inn, Nicholas Guybon, Robert Clinche, and others, the then seniors of it. Mr. Herbert also states (p. 274) :—

"This Society was governed by a principal and twelve Rulers. The Gentlemen were to be in commons a fortnight in every term; and those that were not, paid about 4s. a week, but not always certain. They sell their chambers for one life, and formerly had *mootings*. Their armorial ensigns are Chequy or and az., a fess gules, within a border of the third."

And after speaking of the Hall of the Inn he proceeds (p. 275) :—

"In this Hall Sir Matthew Hale and the principal judges sat after the great fire of London, to settle the various differences that occurred between Landlord and Tenant, and to ascertain the several divisions of property; which difficult and important business was performed by them so much to the satisfaction of the City, that the mayor and commonalty, in gratitude for so signal a service, ordered their portraits to be painted and hung in the Guildhall. In this momentous employment it is but justice to the memory of Judge Hale to say, that he was the first that offered his service to the City: and this measure certainly obviated numerous difficulties that would otherwise have occurred concerning the rebuilding of it; insomuch, says the Author of his life, 'that the sudden and quiet building of the City, which is justly to be reckoned among the wonders of the age, is in no small measure due to the great care which he and Sir Orlando Bridgeman, then Lord Chief Justice of the Common Pleas, used, and to the judgment they shewed in that affair.'"

G. GREEN SMITH.

MOURNING SUNDAY (9ᵗʰ S. ix. 366).—I have seen this ceremony within the last ten years at St. Briavels. The male members of the family wear crape weepers on their tall hats, even longer than those of undertakers' "mutes." Mutes themselves are, however, disappearing. I am told that in Warwickshire the family still all go, sit together, and wear their funeral "trappings," but rise and kneel with others. CHARLES W. DILKE.

BLACK MALIBRAN (9ᵗʰ S. ix. 367).—Madame Malibran was, of course, not black. The lady meant by MR. DENHAM was, doubtless, a later singer of negro race, thought by admirers to be comparable with the great operatic artist of the previous generation. D.

JOHN GARRATT, LORD MAYOR OF LONDON (9ᵗʰ S. vii. 447).—This gentleman died at Cleevemont, Cheltenham, in February, 1859, aged seventy-two (*Gent. Mag.*, March, 1859, p. 334). His name is in the 'London Directory' as well as the 'Royal Kalendar' up to 1861. There is a pedigree of his family in Burke's 'Landed Gentry,' ninth edition, vol. i. p. 571 (1898). FREDERIC BOASE.

'OLD FRIENDS AND NEW FRIENDS' (9ᵗʰ S. ix. 328).—The following lines, I presume, are those which MR. MEREDITH desires to obtain. I chanced upon the "poem," if the lines may be so designated, in a provincial paper some weeks ago. Underneath it there was what I supposed to be a familiar signature, and on chaffing a lady friend on becoming a poet, I learned that the poem—which is a favourite, I believe, in young folks' autograph albums—had been enclosed in a letter sent by her to a friend in the country, and somehow got into the local paper, the editor, presumably regarding the poem as original, adhibiting the initials of the sender's name, which he knew. The lines—I do not know who is their author—as in my possession are headed 'Friendship':—

> Make new friends, but keep the old,
> Those are silver, these are gold.
> New-made friends, like new wine,
> Age will mellow and refine.
> Friendships that have stood the test,
> Time and change, are surely best.
> Brow may wrinkle, hair turn grey,
> Friendship never owns decay:
> For 'mid old friends kind and true
> We once more our youth renew.
> But, alas! old friends must die—
> New friends must their place supply;
> Then cherish friendship in your breast,
> New is good, but old is best.
> Make new friends, but keep the old,
> Those are silver, these are gold.

JOHN GRIGOR.
105, Choumert Road, Peckham.

WHITE GLOVES AT ASSIZES (9ᵗʰ S. ix. 309).—So much has appeared in 'N. & Q.' with reference to this custom it can scarcely be necessary to reopen the subject. See 1ˢᵗ S. i., ii., iii.; 2ⁿᵈ S. i.; 8ᵗʰ S. vii.; also Brand's 'Popular Antiquities'; 'Gloves,' by S. William Beck, 1883, 'Gloves on the Bench,' chap. v.; and many other publications.
EVERARD HOME COLEMAN.
71, Brecknock Road.

FIELD-NAMES, SOUTH-WEST LANCASHIRE (9ᵗʰ S. ix. 268).—Cadix Meadow, so called from the family of Cadick of Melling; Loton = Low town-field; Wrangling Croft, a disputed parcel of ground (cf. Threaplands); Bicol or Bycall = the field "by the caul" or weir (vide 'N.E.D.,' s.v. 'Cauld'); Lum Hey = the loamy enclosure or close; Long Shoot = the shot or furlong in the town-field having long ridges; Locker Field, probably "Lower" field pronounced gutturally; Steven Stones = Stephen's stones; Mars Croft = marshy croft (marys = mere-ish, being the older form of marshy); Big Sum Field, where "big" possesses the adjective termination "some," as handsome; Formery or Farmery, a corruption of "infirmary," a field lying near the infirmary of a religious house; Avorill = haver hill, a hill upon which oats (haver) were grown. Many of the above names occur in the parish of Aughton, in South-West Lancashire.
W. FARRER.
Leyburn.

LINES ATTRIBUTED TO DR. JOHNSON (9ᵗʰ S. ix. 330).—I have not made myself explicit. I have personified "Adieu," the lady who copied the lines and wrote the remarks which follow them. Her correspondent, to whom she apparently presented the 'Life of Garrick,' is M. W. D. If M. is replaced by At, which it very closely resembles, or with which it is identical, in many MSS. of the eighteenth and early part of the nineteenth century, then "At W. D." means a house visited by Dr. Johnson and the initials of which are W. D. This supposition involves the use of a capital "A" for a small "a," a venial sin in those days.
JAS. HAYES.
Ennis.

DICKENSIANA : 'DAVID COPPERFIELD' (9ᵗʰ S. ix. 347).—The song referred to is probably 'Little Taffline with a Silken Sash,' which occurs in Prince Hoare's farce 'The Three and the Deuce.' The music is by Stephen Storace.
WM. DOUGLAS.
125, Helix Road, Brixton Hill.

'Little Taffline' was composed by Stephen Storace, and sung by Mrs. Bland in the operetta called 'Three and the Deuce' at Drury Lane. It was published by Goulding & Co. No date is given.
W. T.

SIBYLLINE ORACLES (9ᵗʰ S. ix. 289).—A translation of the Sibylline oracles into English blank verse by Prof. Milton Spenser Terry was published at New York in 1890.
WILLIAM E. A. AXON.
Manchester.

DISAPPEARING CHARTISTS (9ᵗʰ S. ix. 144, 251).—One or two small mistakes in recent references to old Chartists by MR. CECIL CLARKE and MR. GEORGE JACOB HOLYOAKE (pp. 86, 251–2) should be corrected. MR. CLARKE is wrong in assuming that it was claimed for the late George Julian Harney that he was "the oldest survivor of those connected with the famous movement"—the movement for the People's Charter. What was claimed for Mr. Harney was that he was the last survivor of the members of the Chartist Convention of 1839. And this was true. There must be a good many old Chartists still living, meaning by old Chartists members of the National Chartist Association, which began in 1838 and lasted till the middle of the fifties. John Cleve, mentioned by MR. HOLYOAKE, should be John Cleave; Waddrington, the birthplace of Charles Julius Haslam, should be Widdrington; and R. G. Gammage was a Northampton, not a Newcastle Chartist. Widdrington, in Northumberland, was the home of that hero of the ballad

of 'Chevy Chase' who, in "fearful dumps," when his legs were stricken off, "fought upon his stumps." Mr. Gammage, who wrote a 'History of Chartism,' afterwards studied medicine, obtained the necessary qualification, and practised for some years as a surgeon in Sunderland. W. E. Adams.
Newcastle-on-Tyne.

"All Cooper's ducks with me" (9ᵗʰ S. ix. 127, 298).—I doubt whether the chance use of this curious expression by a master butcher who is also a native of Kent throws any real light upon its origin. I have known for many years an Essex man occasionally employ it in the sense ascribed to it by your correspondent W. I. R. V., and he tells me that, though he never hears it now, it was constantly in use among certain of his associates some thirty or forty years ago at Walthamstow, but he cannot offer any explanation of its derivation. I have sometimes wondered whether it had any connexion with the saying "chance the ducks"—that is, "chance the consequences," which the author of 'Popular Sayings Dissected' states

"is in reference to a boat's crew arrayed in clean white jumpers ready for inspection, when it is discovered that some duty involving the possible soiling of their garments has been neglected, and they accordingly say 'we must do it and chance the ducks,' that is, run the risk of our ducks being splashed."

Could it be that one of their number named Cooper in so chancing it came to grief, and thus gave its signification to the expression under notice? E. C. N.
Broxbourne.

Heartsease (9ᵗʰ S. ix. 267). — The query regarding "Heartsease" involves a rather apt and interesting example of what logicians call the "fallacy of equivocation." The beautiful and unobtrusive little pansy has always been so great a favourite with botanists and herbalists, as well as lovers, poets, and gardeners, that it has become known by an unusually large number of romantic epithets. Among these we find: Three-Faces-under-a-Hood, Flamy, Pink-of-my-John, Tittle-my-Fancy, Forget-me-not, Call-me-to-you, Cuddle-me-to-you, Love-and-Idle, Love-in-Idleness, Live-in-Idleness, Jump-up-and-kiss-me, Kiss-me-ere-I-rise, Kiss-me-at-the-Garden-Gate, Herb-Trinity, and Heart's-ease. But, although this beautiful and interesting favourite of St. Valentine, and special floral decoration of Trinity Sunday, has for so many centuries occupied a very conspicuous position in romantic literature, I have not been able to find so interest-

ing a tale connected with its past history as that which has become attached to a nominal rival. I refer to the wallflower, which, among other names supplied by the riotous imaginations of the herbalists of olden time, also received that of "Hartis Ease." The traditional origin of this appellation was that in the good old days of Border chivalry a kind of Montague-and-Capulet feud existed in the vicinity of the river Tweed. The Caledonian Juliet was kept in close imprisonment within the walls of the paternal castle. The love-lorn gallant, after many efforts, at last gained entrance, in disguise of an errant minstrel; sang before his lady-love, who made the usual arrangements for escaping—with the assistance of the faithful maid—over the wall and into the arms of her languishing Adonis. The sequel of the story has been quaintly and pathetically versified by Herrick:—

> Up she got upon a wall,
> Attempted to slide down withal,
> But the silken twist untied,
> So she fell and, bruised, she died.
> Love, in pity of the deed,
> And her loving luckless speed,
> Turn'd her to this plant we call ;
> Now the Flower of the Wall.

We are also told that minstrels and troubadours generally were in the habit of wearing the wallflower as the emblem of an affection which is proof against time and misfortune. This custom was probably due to the fact that it was usually found on the walls of old castles and abbeys.

John Parkinson, *Botanicus Regius Primarius* of Charles I., and author of the 'Theatrum Botanicum,' tells us, in the pages of that vast storehouse of herbal lore, that

"Pansyes or Hearts Ease is like unto Violets in all the parts thereof, but somewhat hotter and dryer, yet very temperate, and by the viscous or glutinous juice therein doth somewhat mollifie, yet lesse then Mallowes : it is conducing in like manner as violets to the hot diseases of the lungs and chests, for agues, for convulsions, and the falling sicknesse in children: the places also troubled with the itch or scabs being bathed with the decoction of them doth helpe much: it is said also to soder greene wounds, and to helpe old sores to use the juyce or the distilled water."

Such would appear to form the leading items in the romantic and medicinal history of "heartsease." John Knott, M.D.
34, York Street, Dublin.

Bunyan, in 'Pilgrim's Progress,' refers to the name in the sense of easing an aching heart. When Christiana in the Valley of Humiliation hears a shepherd boy singing, Greatheart says,

"Do you hear him? I will dare say this boy leads a merrier life and has more of that herb called hearts-ease in his bosom than he that is clad in silk and velvet."

Shakspere makes Oberon bid Puck fetch the pansy love-philtre, that he may drop some of it on the closed eyelids of Titania :—

> The juice of it on sleeping eyelids laid
> Will make a man or woman madly dote
> Upon the next live creature that it sees.

With the old herbalists the pansy was used to "conglutinate blood" for falling sickness and other kindred ailments. Culpepper, in speaking of it, says :—

> "This is that herb which such physicians as are licensed to blaspheme by authority, without danger of having their tongues burned through with an hot iron, called an Herb of Trinity......In Sussex we call them Pancies."

Philip Miller says of heartsease, "This plant is placed amongst the Officinal Simples in the College Dispensatory."   ANDREW HOPE.
Exeter.

I have never heard of such a legend as MISS TUCK inquires after. None is given in Phillips's 'Flora Historica,' or in any of the more recent collections of flower-lore which I possess. The nearest approach to one is in Herrick's verses 'How Pansies or Hartease came first':—

> Frolick virgins once these were,
> Overloving, living here ;
> Being here their ends deny'd
> Ran for sweet-hearts mad, and di'd.
> Love, in pitie of their teares,
> And their losse in blooming yeares,
> For their restlesse here-spent houres
> Gave them hearts-ease turn'd to flow'rs.

The real reason for this flower-name is probably more correctly shown in his verses 'To Pansies':—

> Ile......to Pansies come ;
> Comforts you'l afford me some :
> You can ease my heart, and doe
> What love co'd ne'r be brought unto.

The old name "pansy" (*pensées*) no doubt suggested the other. Thus Bernard Barton, addressing the flower :—

> Thou styled by sportive fancy's better feeling,
> A Thought, *The Heart's Ease*, or *Forget me not*.

How the flower first got the name *pensez à moi* is another question, and one I cannot answer.   C. C. B.

'THE CARRION CROW' (9ᵗʰ S. ix. 347).—It was a Winchester College song in the forties. I have never seen it in print. If DENVIL cares to send me his address, I will write out for him from memory the words and music.
W. TUCKWELL.

Waltham, Grimsby.

One version appears in 4ᵗʰ S. viii., and another from Grose's 'Olio' is given in the same volume. It will also be found in 'Ballads and Songs of the Peasantry of England.' It is explained that the "Carrion Crow" was thought to be Charles II. in his Boscobel refuge, in the guise of a voracious bird, who made the Puritan clergy disgorge their benefices ; perhaps, also, because he ordered the bodies of the regicides to be exhumed, as Ainsworth says in one of his ballads :—

> The carrion crow is a sexton bold,
> He taketh the dead from out of the mould.

EVERARD HOME COLEMAN.
71, Brecknock Road.

[Many other replies acknowledged.]

BARROSA TOKEN (9ᵗʰ S. ix. 248). — MR. SOUTHAM asks if tokens similar to his that he describes were struck for other battles of the Peninsula. I have—the gift of a "Waterloo man"—a cylindrical brass case, 1½ in. high by ¾ in., containing twenty-five commemorative tokens, all gilt, one for each of the following battles : Roliea (*sic*) and Vimiera, Corunna, Oporto, Talavera, Buzaco, Coimbra, Almeida, Albuhera, Barrosa, Fuente de Onor, Almaraz, Madrid, Salamanca, Arroyo del Molino, Ciudad Rodrigo, Orthes, Badajos, Neive, Castalla, Vittoria, St. Sebastian, Biddassoa, Pyrenees, Toulouse, Waterloo. Each token has on one side a figure of a flying Victory, with the words around it "By the mercy of God" ; on the reverse the date, place, and year ; that for Waterloo alone has laurel leaves round the word. Outside the case, on the top, is a medallion of the Duke, with the words "The Duke of Wellington" around it. At the base is "First battle, Portugal, Aug. 17, 1808. Last battle, France, April 10, 1814." All this is in relief. Around the case is "British Victories" in writing characters. MR. SOUTHAM in mentioning the capture of the French eagle by Sergeant Masterson of the 87th, at Barrosa, reminds me of the following episode. At Vittoria the baton of Marshal Jourdan was captured by a corporal of the 18th Hussars, who took off the gold ends, leaving the wooden part in its case in his tent, this latter being stolen from him by a friend in the 87th. This stick in its case was presented to Lord Wellington by the colonel of the 87th. Was Wellington ever undeceived?   HAROLD MALET, Colonel.

I have had in my possession for more than half a century some metal tokens to be used as card counters. Each of the three — I lost the fourth in 1848 — struck in commemoration of Ciudad Rodrigo, Coimbra, Roliea (*sic*) and Vimiera, respectively, is about the size of the old fourpenny piece, and bears the device of a winged figure, with a wreath, and the inscription "By the Mercy of God."

P. J. F. GANTILLON.

Hawthornden, Cheltenham.

SHERES : KNYVETT : DOWNES (7th S. iii 348). —Can the first name be identical with that of Sears or Sayers ? See Burke's 'Vicissitudes of Families,' third series, p. 288, article 'The Pilgrim Fathers,' where we are told that

"Richard Sayers's wife, Anne Bourchier, daughter of Edmund Knyvet, Esq., of the ancient family of Ashwelthorpe, co. Norfolk, incurred the lasting displeasure of the Knyvets, because she clung faithfully to her husband in his adversity......her descent in the female line was from Sir John Bourchier, Lord Berners, K.G., fourth son of William, Earl of Ewe, by Anne Plantagenet, his wife, granddaughter of King Edward III."

The story goes on to tell of Richard Sayers's flight to Amsterdam, and his grandson's ultimate voyage to America as one of the Pilgrim Fathers, where he founded a family, one of whose representatives was the Hon. David Sears, a senator for Massachusetts. Sir Bernard Burke quotes from a "little volume of singular interest and fascination by Edmund H. Sears, entitled 'Pictures of the Olden Time.'"

R. J. FYNMORE.

Sandgate, Kent.

ST. CLEMENT DANES (9th S. vii. 64, 173, 274, 375 ; viii. 17, 86, 186, 326, 465 ; ix. 52, 136, 252). —If I may sum up the discussion as to St. Clement Danes in a few words, I would say that it seems established—

1. That the church was dedicated to the saint as patron saint of the Danes and Norsemen, who derived their knowledge of him both from the Teutonic colonists, whether Goths or Saxons, as Busbecqius says, of the Crimea and from the great church of the Northern nations at Rome erected over the Oratory of St. Clement, in which the incidents of his life and martyrdom in Dacia were represented in frescoes dating from A.D. 863.

2. If a Danish or Norseman colony was established in the Vicus Dacorum, afterwards represented by Aldwych Street, near the church, it was probably founded shortly after Alfred had made peace with the Danes at Wedmore and the conversion of their leader Guthrum. This date renders a dedication to St. Clement very natural.

3. Aldwych Street, of course, bears a name connected with the termination -wich, but whether the termination is, in this instance, of Latin or Scandinavian origin it is not easy to determine. In other parts of England

the meaning of the termination may usually be gathered from the geographical position of the locality.

4. The choice of St. Clement as patron saint of the Danes opens up the much wider question why very early saints—e.g., St. Andrew in Russia and Scotland, St. Joseph of Arimathea at Glastonbury, St. James and St. John Mark in Spain and Portugal, St. Lazarus and his sisters in Provence, and the like—are so often identified with peoples and localities with which they can never have had any real connexion, and with which they are not identified even in the apocryphal Gospels and Acts. This subject would well repay detailed investigation, as, for instance, the legends connected with Glastonbury may contain a germ of truth in connexion with the early Roman lead mines in the Mendips.   H.

"YCLEPING" THE CHURCH (9th S. viii. 420, 486 ; ix. 55, 216).—Referring to the criticism of ST. SWITHIN, although I gave our local term as "clipping the tower," it must be understood that by "tower" we mean the entire fabric—we have no detached towers ; and an "accommodating imagination" is not necessary, inasmuch as the setting "four square" is so uncommon that church towers so placed can have had no part in the original practice. The fact remains that "clipping the tower"—i.e., the tower and church—was not long ago practised by joining hands and dancing round it, in the same manner as that conventionally understood as dancing round a maypole.

F. T. ELWORTHY.

This interesting ceremony was observed at St. John's Church, Buckhurst Hill, Essex, on 27 June, 1895. The children of the National schools, carrying wands bedecked with flowers and greenery, marched to the church, where a short service was conducted by the rector, the Hon. Canon Pelham.

"After the service the children, standing outside the west door, sang 'The Parish Song' and a hymn. Then, forming a ring round the church, they, at a given signal—when the bell had tolled three times—stepped forward and touched the walls of the edifice. The rector explained to the congregation in the church, before the 'clipping' took place, that they were going to resuscitate an old English church custom—the custom coming from the Midland counties of 'clipping the church,' which meant embracing the church. The reason he believed in the old custom was this : That every child in the parish should feel in his or her early days that the church which their forefathers placed for God's glory and honour was theirs ; not belonging to one particular class of people, and certainly not to the clergyman, but that it was the church of the parishioners."

The preceding extract is quoted from an account of the proceedings which appeared in the *Essex Times* of 29 June, 1895, and was copied thence into the *Essex Review* for January, 1896. I should much like to know if the statement as to the "custom coming from the Midland counties" is correct. I have never heard of it taking place in North-amptonshire. JOHN T. PAGE.
West Haddon, Northamptonshire.

May not this arise from the commemora-tion of a saint's day, the anniversary of a dedication, as we now notice a foundation? Discarding A.-S. *clyppan*, to embrace, we have *clypian*, *cleopian*, to call, so naming a church; and *clep*, *clepe*, "to name," may be found in modern dictionaries. "Ycleaped" is in Bailey. ABSENS.

ENGLISH CONTINGENT IN THE LAST CRUSADE (9th S. viii. 343; ix. 55, 177).—In "The Jerusa-lem Delivered of Torquato Tasso. Translated ......by J. H. Wiffen. Third Edition. London ......1830," vol. i. p. lxxiii, is

"A List of such of the English Nobility and Gentry as went to the Crusades. Gathered from Abbas Gemetriensis, Annales Waverleienses, Bene-dictus Abbas, Brompton, Dugdale's Baronage, Henry of Huntingdon, Matthew Paris, Ordericus Vitalis, Robert of Gloucester, Roger de Hoveden, Vinisauf, William of Tyre, Du Moulin, Weever's Funeral Monuments, MSS. in the Ashmolean Museum, &c., &c."

Following the above appears this note:—

"From Du Moulin, who gives a full list of Norman Crusaders, I have selected such only as, by the evidence of Charters, I know to have possessed English fiefs."

The list gives the names of the English Crusaders in the reigns of William Rufus, Henry I., Stephen, Henry II., Richard I., John, Henry III., followed by "Uncertain Reigns." The Henry III. list numbers fifty-eight, including Eleanor, wife of Prince Edward. Of the knights given by MR. RADCLIFFE (p. 55) from Dansey's 'English Crusaders' the following appear in the list:—

Chaworth, Pain, Hervey, and Patrick de, brothers; Gorges, Ralph de; Grandison, Otho de, Governor of Guernsey; Latimer, William, ancestor of the great Reformer; Leiburne, Roger de; Fiennes, William de.

Perhaps the others given from Dansey did not possess English fiefs, and so were excluded from the list given in Wiffen's 'Tasso.'
ROBERT PIERPOINT.
St. Austin's, Warrington.

ROYAL PERSONAGES (9th S. viii. 184, 252, 349; ix. 89, 196, 257).—At p. 196 MR. COLYER-FERGUSSON says:—

"Prince Octavius was buried 10 May, 1782."

"Prince Alfred died at Windsor, buried 27 August, 1783."

In the 1847 edition of Lodge's 'Peerage,' however, are the entries:—

"Prince Octavius, b. 23 Feb., 1779, d. 2 May, 1783."

"Prince Alfred, b. 22 Sept., 1780, died 26 August, 1782."

A. W. B. at p. 89 confirms the last date. Is the old Norroy King of Arms correct when he says Prince Octavius died in 1783? If so, this prince could not well have been buried the year before.

The following additional dates may also be useful to A. W. B.:—

Anne, Princess Royal, born 22 October, 1709; married 14 March, 1734; died 12 January, 1759.

Mary, Princess of Hesse-Cassel, born 22 Feb-ruary, 1723; married 8 May, 1740; died 14 June, 1771.

Louisa, Queen of Denmark, born 7 Decem-ber, 1724; married 30 November, 1743; died 8 December, 1751.

A. W. B. speaks of two of the children of George II. as Amelia Sophia and Caroline Elizabeth. Debrett's 'New Peerage' (1823) names them as Amelia Sophia Eleanora and Elizabeth Caroline. The same authority gives the full names of the late Duke of Cumber-land as George Frederic Alexander Charles Ernest Augustus. Debrett differs from A. W. B. very considerably with reference to the brothers and sisters of George III. For instance:—

1. A. W. B. states Louisa Anne was born 8 March, 1749. Debrett says 8 March, 1739.

2. A. W. B. states Elizabeth Caroline was born 10 January, 1740. Debrett says 30 Decem-ber, 1740.

3. A. W. B. states Frederic (? should be Frederick) William was born 24 May, 1750. Debrett says 10 May, 1750.

4. A. W. B. says Henry Frederic (Duke of Cumberland). Debrett says Henry Frederick.
RONALD DIXON.
46, Marlborough Avenue, Hull.

GEORGE SANDYS (9th S. ix. 305).—My copy has the leaf Aaa² intact.
W. H. CUMMINGS.

"PILLAGE, STALLAGE, AND TOLL" (9th S. viii. 420; ix. 35). MR. PENNY is correct in regard to the utility of Bailey's dictionary for old law terms, and he will find the term *s.v.* 'Pickage' therein, as rightly suggested by Q. V. H. P. L.

"SHIMMOZZEL" (9th S. vi. 266, 371; vii. 10; viii. 471; ix. 12).—MR. PLATT has been kind enough to refer to my Anglo-Yiddish term *noff*.

I am unaware of the nature of the explanation offered in the *Academy.* I have since thought over the matter, and come to the conclusion that it might also mean "thief"—being a clipping of *gonnof.* In other words, a *noff* would be a creature who joins thieving to vileness of living. If I am wrong, probably MR. PLATT will kindly correct me. I notice he mentions *schickster.* This is unknown to me otherwise than as *schikser* = a servant girl. No self-respecting Jew ever uses the word nowadays. It is a vile word. I may add another to the growing list of "Yiddishisms"—viz., *gyver*=pride or side, from the Hebrew *gangavah.*   M. L. R. BRESLAR.

SIR ALAN DE HEYTON (9ᵗʰ S. ix. 248).—Sir Alan de Heton was lord of Ellingham, co. Northumberland, 1 Richard II., in which year he served under Henry, Earl of Northumberland, at the siege of Berwick, and, taking a leading part in the assault, he acquired considerable notice by his courage.

In 1376, on the day of the Assumption of the Blessed Virgin Mary, Sir Alan, with thirteen other knights—viz., Henry, Lord Percy, Richard Tempest, Ingilram de Umfranville, John Conyers, John Heron, Thomas de Uderton, Walter Blount, &c.—were entertained at a banquet given by Walter de Hepscotts, Abbot of Alnwick.

He left at his death three daughters and coheirs: (1) Elizabeth, married Sir John de Fenwick, of Wallington ; (2) Margaret, married first Sir William de Swinburne, Kt., and secondly Thomas Middleton, of Silksworth, co. Durham ; (3) Joan, married Sir Robert Ogle, Kt., of Bothal Castle, who had livery of their property 12 Richard II.

A Sir Henry Heton, Kt. (query, if son of Sir Alan ?), married Isabel, daughter and eventual coheir of Bertram Montboucher, lord of Beamish, co. Durham, but died without issue, his widow remarrying Sir Robert Harbottle, Kt., of Preston, of which marriage there were at least two sons: Robert Harbottle, who continued the line, and Thomas, trustee to the entail made by his brother of the estates, 17 Henry VI. This Thomas Harbottle is presumably the mysterious —— Harbottle, whose Christian name does not appear in any of the visitations, who left three daughters and coheirs, of whom one married Thomas Riddell, ancestor of the eminent Nova-Castrian family of that name ; a second, Isabel, was the wife, first of Robert Musgrave, of Ryall (by whom she had two daughters and coheirs: Joan, wife of John Fenwick, of Wallington, and the other, wife of Robert Milford, of Seghill, which families

quartered), and secondly of Nicholas Radcliffe ; and the third, Agnes, married Sir Roger Fenwick, Kt., of Stanton.

The Heyton or Heaton arms were Vert, three lions rampant argent. It may here be remarked that in the Carr MS. Roll of the Arms of the Mayors and Sheriffs of Newcastle-upon-Tyne, printed as an appendix to Tonge's 'Visitation of the North' by the Surtees Society, the sheriff for 1508, who there occurs as Thomas Heighton, should read Thomas Leighton. Of the arms assigned to him, Argent, a chevron between three popinjays gules, beaked or, I can make nothing. The coat is evidently only a variation of that of the Northumbrian family of Wallington. The sheriff, whose name stands corrected in Mr. Richard Welford's 'History of Newcastle and Gateshead,' probably belonged to the Leightons or Lightons, of Lemmington, Rothbury Forest, &c., who traditionally derive from the same stock as the Barons of Ullyseshaven (?), in Forfar, in which case his arms would be Argent, a lion rampant gules, armed or.
     H. REGINALD LEIGHTON.
East Boldon, R.S.O., co. Durham.

ST. PATRICK (9ᵗʰ S. ix. 309).—"Women, smiths, and Druids" were the chief agents of magic in the Celtic world. The smiths held this position because they dealt with iron, which (even more than other metals) was hostile to the unseen powers of evil. For the ethnological reason of this circumstance see Rhys's 'Folk-lore, Welsh and Manx.' In the Middle Ages, and later, the village smith still kept something of his original character of a witch-doctor.   JOHN HOBSON MATTHEWS.
Town Hall, Cardiff.

PINS IN DRINKING VESSELS (9ᵗʰ S. iv. 287, 358, 484 ; ix. 10, 136, 255, 293).—I thank FR. N. for his correction (*ante*, p. 293). I was, however, quite aware that Dr. Milner was a Roman Catholic, and that he was not the Church of England Bishop of Winchester. To have been exactly correct I should have said that he was consecrated at Winchester on 22 May, 1803, as Bishop of Castabala, and that as the Catholic Vicar Apostolic of the Midland District of England he had episcopal jurisdiction including Winchester, his headquarters. Strictly speaking, therefore, your last correspondent is correct, but seemingly he overlooked the fact of Dr. Milner's appointment as Vicar Apostolic. 'The Life of the Right Rev. John Milner, D.D., Bishop of Castabala, Vicar Apostolic of the Midland District of England,' was published by James Duffy, of Dublin and of 22, Paternoster Row, in 1862, I believe. I understand from Lord

Arundell of Wardour that Dr. Milner's museum, adjoining the Catholic Church at Winchester, contains many articles of great interest. RONALD DIXON.

46, Marlborough Avenue, Hull.

THE MITRE (9th S. viii. 324, 493, 531; ix. 174, 334).—The late Bishop Forbes, of Brechin, is commemorated by a recumbent effigy in St. Paul's Episcopal Church, Dundee. He wears cope and mitre; but I do not think he ever wore these in life. Mitred abbots, certain canons in cathedral churches, and cardinals not bishops—Newman is a case in point—have the right to wear this head-dress; but I do not think it is ever worn apart from chasuble or cope.

GEORGE ANGUS.

St. Andrews, N.B.

GANGANELLI'S BIBLE (9th S. ix. 308).—Just fifty years ago this volume formed the subject of a question in 'N. & Q.,' for which refer to 1st S. v. 466 (not 463, as given in index to half-yearly volume and Index to First Series). According to the inquirer it was published in 1784, and a copy from the Duke of Sussex's library was sold to the British Museum for 30*l*. See above reference for any further information which may be required. EVERARD HOME COLEMAN.

71, Brecknock Road.

THE BIBLIOGRAPHY OF THE BICYCLE (9th S. viii. 304, 490, 530; ix. 36, 117, 171, 231).—It seems to be pretty generally agreed that for the genesis of the bicycle we have to go back to 1819. I have before me an extract from the *Literary Gazette* for the above year, headed 'The Pedestrian Carriage, or Walking Accelerator,' in which the "dandy horse" of that day is designated "a new invention." "It was originally," it says,

"the invention of an ingenious German, M. Drais, but has been introduced into this country and improved by Mr. Johnson, coach maker, in Long Acre, who has secured it by taking out letters patent. The machine is of the most simple kind, supported by two light wheels running on the same line, the front wheel turning on a pivot, which, by means of a short lever, gives the direction in turning to one side or the other, the hind wheel always running in one direction. The rider mounts it and seats himself on a saddle conveniently fixed on the back of the horse, if allowed to be called so, and placed in the middle between the wheels; the feet are placed flat on the ground, so that, in the first step to give the machine motion, the heel should be the first part of the foot to touch the ground, and so on with the other foot alternately as if walking, observing always to begin the movement very gently. In the front, before the rider, is placed a cushion to rest the arms on, while the hands hold the lever; the cushion should be properly called a balance, as it answers that purpose;

for, in giving a short turn, if the machine inclines to the left, the right arm is pressed on the balance, which brings the machine upright again, and so *vice versa*."

The paragraph goes on to state that it is easy to travel fifty or more miles a day on these "German horses," and that, as a riding-school was about to be opened for them, it was expected that they would be brought into extensive use.

ALEXANDER PATERSON.

Barnsley.

ISLE OF DOGS (9th S. ix. 165).—A spot that had for centuries been known as the richest piece of marsh land in England is hardly likely to have derived its name from a situation which formed, though this is pure conjecture, "a trap for every dead dog or cat that came down the river." Such "a fine rich level for fattening cattle," as Strype calls it, must have been regarded *en beau* rather than with the contempt that such a theory implies, and an utter disregard for the picturesque in their place-nomenclature is not a sin that can be laid at the doors of our less Thames-factory-and-other-refuse afflicted forefathers. It is in the 'Circuit Walk,' at the end of Strype's 'Stow,' p. 102, that indebtedness is expressed to Dr. Josiah Woodward, minister of Poplar, for the belief that

"the Isle of Dogs was so called, because, when our former Princes made Greenwich their Country Seat, and used it for Hunting, (they say) the Kennels for their Dogs were kept on this Marsh; which, usually making a great Noise, the Seamen and others thereupon called the Place the Isle of Dogs: Though it is not an Isle, indeed, scarce a Peninsula, the Neck being about a Mile in Length."

Why this tradition from so respectable a source should, in the absence of more trustworthy data, be contemned one cannot understand. It is apparently Lysons, in his 'Environs of London,' who first casts doubt upon it, "as it would have been," he says, "more convenient to have had their dog-kennels on the other side of the water" (p. 467, note), and Wheatley ('London Past and Present') repeats this in different words. But surely the fact of the barking of so many dogs in the vicinity of the "Manor of Pleasaunce," as the royal palace at Greenwich was called, was enough to cause their removal to a conveniently adjacent place like Poplar Marsh, which is alluded to as early as the year 1611 as if it were a matter of common knowledge that it was a home for dogs, at any rate of some, if not royal, degree : "*Moll Cutpurse.* O Sir, he hath been brought up in the Isle of Dogs, and can both fawn like a spaniel and bite like a mastiff as he finds occasion "

(Middleton and Dekker, 'The Roaring Girl,' 4to, 1611). There seems to have been some earlier authority, apparently unknown to the writers on the topography of London's environs, if one may judge from the following circumstantial description of the uses to which the marsh was put, from the *Evening Mail* of 17-19 September, 1800 :—

"The Isle of Dogs, now converting to the first commercial purposes [the first stone of the West India Docks was laid in 1800, and the West India Dock Canal, which was cut across the peninsula, converted it into an island], derived its name from being the depôt of the spaniels and greyhounds of Edward III. as lying contiguous to his sports of woodcock shooting, and coursing the red deer at Waltham, and other Royal Forests in Essex; for the more convenient enjoyment of which he generally resided in the sporting season at Greenwich."

That the river itself was, at the time the marsh received its name of the Isle of Dogs, in the putrid condition at this spot generally associated with dead dogs is improbable, from the fact that as late as the year 1736 a peter-boat fisherman caught a salmon 38 in. long and about 17 in. round off Cuckold's Point, which sold for thirty-six shillings (*St. James's Evening Post*, 30 September, 1736); and between Limehouse and Deptford another fisherman caught in a common net a large salmon 34 in. long and 15½ in. round, which sold for two guineas (*Grub Street Journal*, 2 October, 1735). In 1754, says Mr. Marston in the *Nineteenth Century*, "the take of fish was so great at London Bridge that the price of salmon fell to sixpence a pound. In one day in July, 1760, 130 salmon were sent to Billingsgate Market." J. HOLDEN MacMICHAEL.

CHESS PLAYING: A LEGEND (9ᵗʰ S. ix. 248 293).—Thank you for your reference to 8ᵗʰ S. xii. 207, 251, 354. These do not at all answer my query as to Huxley's use of the simile, which, for the benefit of future inquirers, I may say I have found in his 'Liberal Education,' the fourth chapter in the volume of his collected works—*i.e.*, the one on 'Science and Education,' p. 82. As I believe this passage of Huxley's applied to nature and man is considered the most eloquent he wrote, I make no apology for fixing the reference in 'N. & Q.'

As I do not wish to trouble you unnecessarily, I will leave for awhile the references to which you refer, till I have searched out what I can by their help. They hardly seem, though, to say where the story really comes from; and when we consider what the game of chess is, and that the stake was entirely one-sided—"heads you win, tails I lose,"

almost—the story is, to say the least, curious, and I should like to know how it originated.

I notice that Huxley refers to this "famous picture of Retsch," and his essay was written in 1868. In view of your references, is it not worth while to know where this picture really is? LUCIS.

Cannock.

[The reference to Huxley is supplied *ante*, p. 293.]

ARMS OF KNIGHTS (9ᵗʰ S. ix. 328).—I presume the Suffolk family of Esturmy, of which Sir William Esturmy was High Sheriff of Norfolk and Suffolk in 1214, is referred to. Sir Richard Gipps, in his 'Essay towards recovering some Account of the Ancient Families in the County of Suffolk' (British Museum Add. MS. 20,695), gives the arms of the family thus : "They bore quarterly gules and or, upon a Bendy az. 3 Plates." And he adds a note : "Sir Roger Sturmyne, a Suffolk knight in the time of Edw. I., he bare quarterly or and gu., a bend az. bezanted." On a pedigree prepared in the Heralds' College I have seen the arms displayed thus : Quarterly, gu. and or, upon a bend az. three bezants ; but a note made some years ago states that the arms of the family really were Quarterly, or and gu., upon a bend az. three bezants, differing, therefore, from any of the above authorities. Your correspondent will find something respecting the Esturmy family arms in *Archæologia*, vol. iii. p. 26 ; copies of charters, 1330-1334, Brit. Mus. Add. MS. 24,481 ; and seal of Henry Esturmy, 1355, Brit. Mus., xliii. 189.
W. A. COPINGER.

Kersal Cell, Manchester.

WILBRAHAM TOLLEMACHE EDWARDS (9ᵗʰ S. ix. 308).—A marriage licence was granted, in the diocese of Dublin, in the year 1797, to the above-named and Henrietta Burrowes. See the Appendix to the Twenty-sixth Report of the Deputy-Keeper of Public Records (Ireland). J. N. DOWLING.

67, Douglas Road, Handsworth, Birmingham.

Miscellaneous.

NOTES ON BOOKS, &c.

The New Volumes of the Encyclopædia Britannica. Constituting, in Continuation with the Existing Volumes of the Ninth Edition, the Tenth Edition.—Vol. XXV. of the Complete Work. (A. & C. Black and the *Times*.)

IN these days, even of elaborate literary undertakings, the bringing up to date of the 'Encyclopædia Britannica' constitutes noteworthy accomplishment. Within a space of time briefer than has ever been devoted to any similar or commensurate labour, eleven volumes will be added to the twenty-four constituting the ninth edition. The whole will, it is calculated, form the tenth edition, final so far as the present generation is concerned. The additions will consist of 10,000 articles by 1,000 contributors, 2,500 new maps, plates, portraits, and other illustrations, in all about 7,000 pages of the same size as those in the previous edition. Such a work is necessarily an inestimable boon to the student and, indeed, to all serious readers and searchers after information. Great as is the outlay incurred, it is guaranteed beforehand, the number of subscribers to what must now be considered the preliminary portion rendering it certain that the concluding portion will be in immediate demand. Not wholly satisfactory from the English standpoint are the statistics supplied concerning the subscription to the ninth edition. According to these the United Kingdom has taken 50,000 copies, against upwards of 400,000 copies dispersed through the United States. For well on to 500,000 probable subscribers the management has accordingly to cater. The editors of the new volumes represent, to a certain extent, three or more great corporations, Sir Donald Mackenzie Wallace being officially connected with the *Times*, Dr. Arthur T. Hadley being the president of Yale University, and Mr. Hugh Chisholm a former scholar of C.C.C., Oxford. In addition to these, who are principally responsible for the work, there are four associate editors, two sub-editors, and nineteen departmental editors of varying degrees of capacity or fame.

Vol. I. of the present publication extends from 'Aachen' to 'Australia,' thus all but covering the letter A. The first article of importance is 'Abyssinia,' for the history of which Count Gleichen is responsible, the geography being by Prof. A. H. Keane. This article, which is accompanied by a map, is typical of the kind of changes that have been made since the appearance of the ninth edition of the 'Encyclopædia.' Recent years have witnessed the disastrous Italian campaign and the subsequent arrival of various European missions, including that of Sir Rennell Rodd, to which the preponderating influence of England in Abyssinian councils is due. The centre of interest has shifted, as Count Gleichen says, from the northern to the southern provinces. What will be the future of the country depends on who is the successor of the "present enlightened emperor." Completely modern is Mr. Hibbert's account of 'Accumulators.' An important contribution on 'Acoustics' is by Prof. J. H. Poynting. Under 'Admiralty Administration,' 'Admiralty Jurisdiction,' &c., is much information not easily accessible elsewhere. Recent legislation upon adulteration of food is fully described under 'Adulteration,' as are the scientific attempts to combat interference. 'Aeronautics' is profusely illustrated with views of gliding and flying machines, including pictures of the flight of the balloon of M. Santos-Dumont over Nice. Sir Alfred Lyall deals with the history of Afghanistan, of which also a map is furnished. In the case of Africa, on which, naturally, much advance in knowledge is observable, Mr. Heawood deals with the geography, Dr. Scott Keltie with the history, and Prof. A. H. Keane with the ethnology. Under the last heading the professor holds, with M. A. Dumont and Sir John Evans, that the origin of man in Mauritania "must be set back to an age which deranges all chronology and confounds the very fables of the mythologies." Negroes claim

a separate heading, as do South, Central, and East Africa. 'Agnosticism,' as a term, is correctly attributed to Huxley, whose views an anonymous opponent is allowed to answer. 'Agriculture' and 'Agricultural Machinery,' two very important articles, are in the hands of Americans. The illustrations to these are the best executed, the most striking, and the most serviceable in the volume. 'Algebraic Forms' are treated by Major MacMahon, F.R.S. 'America,' an enormous subject, is dealt with by American writers, the anthropological section being allotted to Prof. O. T. Mason. 'Anthropology' itself is in the admirably competent hands of Prof. Tylor. It is chiefly supplementary to what appeared in the previous volumes. 'Classical Archæology' gives the results of recent discoveries. Under articles such as 'Athens,' 'Eleusis,' &c., information must be sought as to the conclusions of modern research, which, under this heading, are treated principally in regard to sculpture and art generally. This portion of the volume is profusely illustrated, though the designs are in some cases less clear than might have been desired. 'Architecture' is also profusely illustrated, the designs being principally of modern edifices. Under 'Armour' much novel and important information is furnished, especially as to the results of the trial of armour plates. 'Astronomy' is also a contribution of highest importance. No task of greater difficulty than that of giving an insight into or estimate of the claims of an encyclopædia can well be devised. To deal with almost every question demands a separate expert. We may not, accordingly, go further into the merits of the work. As regards the new features, the most important consist of the illustrations and maps, which add greatly to the utility of the work. Some of the illustrations, like those supplied in a selection of specimen pages which accompanies the first volume, give a good idea of the wealth which will be found in the entire work. The account of 'Colour Printing' is deeply interesting; the picture of the *Okapia johnstoni*, discovered by Sir H. H. Johnston in the Semliki Forest, is beautiful; and the reproductions of designs by Sir E. Burne-Jones in the Kelmscott Chaucer, of book-plates, &c., are of special value and interest. Not a few of the portraits are excellent. The editors pride themselves on the addition of biographies of men still living or recently dead. These as a rule are hardly up to the level of the other contributions. They scarcely seem to form an indispensable portion of an encyclopædia, and would not be necessary if we had anything approaching to an adequate biography of contemporaries. There is some justice in the view that before dealing with the characters of yesterday and to-day it is expedient to get an historical perspective in which your poet, novelist, or so-called statesman is sure of his immortality, or likely to present himself to our successors in the same light in which he is seen by us. It is, however, well for the encyclopædia, as for other things, to give us too much rather than too little. A hedge is more easily pruned than fostered. A worthy, important, and necessary undertaking is spiritedly and admirably begun, and will doubtless be brought to a satisfactory termination.

The *Quarterly Review* for April is a strong number. It contains eleven articles of real merit. We regard "The Sacred Books of the East" as one of the most important contributions to the explanation of Oriental thought to the Western mind with which we have become acquainted. The writer evidently knows thoroughly the whole series of translations edited by the late Prof. Max Müller, and has turned his knowledge to good account. We have but one depreciatory remark to make. The Koran has received scant measure, and has been dealt with in a way far less enlightening than the more mystical literature of the Further East. This is to be regretted, as, in the words of the reviewer, "the late Prof. Palmer's translation is one which more than any other reveals to us the spirit and power of the original." We may add, too, that Mohammed's utterances, though deeply impregnated with the higher mysticism, are far more in line with Western thought than the older imaginings of the great prophets of the Further East. In treating of this vast mass of Oriental teaching the writer points out that to those who can enter into its spirit it disposes—as we may hope, for ever—of the dream-and-ghost theories of the origin of religion. As to what we must provisionally accept as its true source, so very much depends on what is meant by the word "religion" and on the point of view of those who endeavour to form a coherent picture, that we can give no answer except by saying that whatever awakened the latent faculty in man, it was mainly, though perhaps not entirely, reduced into form by the contemplation of "the great objects of nature, especially the sun; that its root is in the feeling after, and of, the Infinite." 'The Gaelic Revival in Literature' has interested us very much, because it establishes incidentally the fact, so often denied by incompetent folk, that Celtic literature contains a great mass of poetry, legend, and history which we can on no account consent to lose. The influence of Celtic ideals on those who have written in French and English has frequently been exaggerated by those who have been not unnaturally revolted by people who have advocated for social and political objects the stamping out of a group of noble languages, but we believe that modern discoveries—or theories only, if you will—have all but demonstrated that the Celt has impressed his dream-world on many of us who have, so far as we know, no strain of Celtic blood, who do not know a word of any one of his languages, and have read little or nothing of his literature, even in a translated form. 'The Oxford Historians' deals justly, and therefore appreciatively, with John Richard Green and Samuel Rawson Gardiner. Green was the more brilliant personality, and for those who read mainly for the purpose of storing their minds with historic pictures was no doubt the more serviceable writer. His books have had an immense influence for good, as he was almost always accurate as well as highly picturesque; but we are compelled to say—if a comparison must be made which we regard as useless, if not positively harmful—that Gardiner ranks the higher of the two, for though not so impressive, he brings before the reader the times to which he gave his special attention in a manner no other historian has done hitherto, and he has the great advantage of being almost entirely free from the baneful tendency to speculate as to motives. This is a gain which we may hope future ages will appreciate more highly than many do at present. To tell how people acted and what they did is a comparatively easy task if we have the raw material before us, but to fathom the motives of their actions is in most cases impossible. Even personal friendship is a very slight help. We all of us make childish blunders when we comment on the conduct of our most intimate friends. 'Mediæval Libraries' is the work of one who has evidently a true appreciation of the learning of the Middle Ages. Books were far more common before the art of printing was discovered than people formerly thought. Some of the monasteries had considerable collections of volumes. The books which remain now are but a very small portion of those which have perished. One of the evils of the Renaissance was that it caused almost everything written in mediæval Latin or the vernacular to be treated with contempt; then followed the religious turmoils of the sixteenth century, when many of those who were in opposition to the old order of things thought it an act of virtue to destroy the literature of the past. When these things are remembered, coupled with the carelessness of custodians in more recent days, it is not wonderful that so little remains; the surprising thing is that time has spared so much. The papers on 'Zionism and Anti-Semitism' and on 'Turkey and Armenia' contain valuable information, but make too near an approach to modern political life for us to do more than mention them.

THE King has graciously accepted the dedication of the Coronation Prayer Book which is now being prepared at the Oxford University Press.

Notices to Correspondents.

We must call special attention to the following notices:—

ON all communications must be written the name and address of the sender, not necessarily for publication, but as a guarantee of good faith.

WE cannot undertake to answer queries privately.

To secure insertion of communications correspondents must observe the following rules. Let each note, query, or reply be written on a separate slip of paper, with the signature of the writer and such address as he wishes to appear. When answering queries, or making notes with regard to previous entries in the paper, contributors are requested to put in parentheses, immediately after the exact heading, the series, volume, and page or pages to which they refer. Correspondents who repeat queries are requested to head the second communication "Duplicate."

H. HARE ("Award of Nobel Prizes").—Apply to the Secretary of the Society of Authors, 39, Old Queen Street, S.W.

GEORGE PRICE ("Welshing": "Welsher").—See 3ʳᵈ S. ix. 433; 6ᵗʰ S. vii. 189; viii. 116; 9ᵗʰ S. iv. 208.

A. BYGATE.—Apply to one of the numerous translation bureaus which advertise.

A. G. ("William Bent").—This query appeared *ante*, p. 188.

NOTICE.

Editorial communications should be addressed to "The Editor of 'Notes and Queries'"—Advertisements and Business Letters to "The Publisher"—at the Office, Bream's Buildings, Chancery Lane, E.C.

We beg leave to state that we decline to return communications which, for any reason, we do not print; and to this rule we can make no exception.

LONDON, SATURDAY, MAY 24, 1902.

CONTENTS. — No. 230.

Notes.

LADY NAIRNE'S JACOBITE SONGS.

In the *Athenæum* of 22 February, p. 233, a reviewer of Mr. Graham's 'Scottish Men of Letters in the Eighteenth Century' shows a strange lack of familiarity with the writings of Lady Nairne. "That Lady Nairne," he says, "wrote 'Will ye no come back again?' is news to us; and if she wrote 'Charlie is my Darling,' which form of the words is hers?" To say of any statement that it "is news to us" is indicative of one of two things: it means either that the critic considers the information offered erroneous or that he has at length gained knowledge of which he was not formerly in possession. It is to be feared that readers of the *Athenæum*, otherwise unacquainted with the subject, will infer that the critic convicts Mr. Graham of error, and it would have been well if the implied objection had been more explicitly stated. If the reviewer considers that Lady Nairne did not write 'Will ye no come back again?' it would have been easy for him to say so, and to state his reason for his belief. On the other hand, if he now learns for the first time that the authorship of the song is believed to be

settled as Mr. Graham states, then he admits a curiously limited knowledge of the subject he undertakes to discuss. It is also singular that a critic in a leading literary journal should have to ask which particular version of 'Charlie is my Darling' was the work of Lady Nairne. This is a point that has been perfectly clear to readers of Scottish song during something like half a century.

Hogg included in his 'Jacobite Relics,' vol. ii. p. 195, a song entitled 'Will he no come back again?' In a note he says: "This old song was never published till of late years. I had it in manuscript; but a copy, scarcely so perfect, is to be found in a late Paisley publication." With the exception of the chorus appended to the first stanza, which reads "Will you no," &c., this lyric is narrative throughout, "Will he" and not "Will you" being used in the refrain. This is the opening quatrain with chorus :—

Royal Charlie 's now awa,
  Safely owre the friendly main;
Mony a heart will break in twa,
  Should he ne'er come back again.
Will you no come back again?
Will you no come back again?
Better lo'ed you 'll never be,
And will you no come back again?

The second stanza suggests disloyalty on the part of the islesmen, many of whom, it is asserted, "sought to wear his life awa"; the third tells of the hills, the birken tree, and the sheltering bush, which "none on earth can claim but he"; and the sixth and concluding quatrain rings with genuine pathos:

Sweet the lav'rock's note and lang,
  Lilting wildly up the glen;
And aye the o'erword o' the sang
  Is, "Will he no come back again?'

The song thus given by Hogg is sometimes entitled in reprints 'Will you no come back again?' but its strictly narrative character cannot be altered. 'Will ye no come back again?' is another and different lyric, and will be found in Charles Rogers's 'Life and Songs of the Baroness Nairne,' 1869-86. Lady Nairne's reticence about her work and her persistent anonymity made it somewhat difficult for her editor to complete his task of collecting her lyrics. With the expert help, however, of her relatives—including the distinguished scholar Mr. T. L. Kington Oliphant, of Gask—he at length achieved a satisfactory result. In the preface to the revised edition of the 'Life and Songs' he unhesitatingly says that "the public may confidently accept all the songs contained in the present volume as being certainly composed by the gifted Baroness." As this has not been refuted, the student of Scottish song has come to regard it as definite and final, and he accepts as Lady Nairne's not only 'The Hundred Pipers,' 'He's owre the Hills,' and 'The Women are a' gane wud,' but 'Charlie is my Darling' and 'Will ye no come back again?' It is characteristic of the last-named lyric that it is throughout composed in the form of an appeal. The writer utilizes Hogg's opening, but changes "Royal" to "Bonnie," and gives "Will ye," not "Will you," in her chorus, the third line of which gets its classic form "Better lo'ed ye canna be." There is no hint of traitorous associates, and the unswerving loyalty of adherents is thus proclaimed :—

> We watched thee in the gloamin' hour,
>   We watched thee in the mornin' grey ;
> Tho' thirty thousand pounds they'd gi'e,
>   Oh there was nane that wad betray.

The last stanza of Hogg's version is used, with some slight variations.

With regard to 'Charlie is my Darling' little needs to be said. Burns supplied Johnson's 'Musical Museum' with a song under this title, and this has therefore historic if but small poetical value. Hogg gives it as "original" in the 'Relics,' furnishing a "modern" reading of his own which is not very successful. Lady Nairne's lyric, with its bright movement and its steadily recurring "young Chevalier," appeared anonymously in R. A. Smith's 'Scotish Minstrel,' 1821–4, and it straightway took its place as the outstanding song on the theme. It is this "form of the words" that everybody learns and that singers deliver on the concert platform. A fourth version by Capt. Charles Gray, given in G. Farquhar Graham's 'Songs of Scotland,' 1849, has been forgotten. Thomas Bayne.

ADDITIONS TO THE 'N.E.D.'
(*Continued from p. 364.*)

Cabriolean (not in).—1786, *Times*, in Larwood, 'London Parks' (188–), p. 180, "One female cabriolean gave a very pretty lecture on the art of driving."

Cacker (not in).—1894, Crockett, 'Raiders,' p. 132, "I hear the horses' cackers [shoes] ringing on the granite."

Calcimine (no quot.).—1893, Spon, 'Mechanic's Own Book' (fourth ed.), p. 612, "The wash or calcimine can be used for ordinary purposes"; *ibid.*, p. 610, "Calcimining or distemper painting."

Calcitratorily (not in).—1844, J. T. Hewlett, 'Parsons and Widows,' chap. xxxiii., "I felt calcitratorily inclined."

Calico-bush (not in).—1890, 'Chambers's Ency.,' vol. vi. p. 389, "*Kalmia latifolia*, the mountain laurel, or calico-bush, occupies large tracts in the Alleghany Mountains."

Callevine (not in).—Crockett, *ut supra*, p. 46, "He made marks on it [paper] with a callevine [pencil] as if he were drawing a map."

Calm, sb. 2 (obs.).—Spon, *ut supra*, p. 630, "The use of lead calmes for fixing window-panes is of venerable antiquity"; *ibid.*, "Glaziers differ as to the best tool for soldering the calmes."

Calorifer (not in).—1826, in Lady Granville, 'Letters' (1894), vol. i. p. 383.

Calyptrate (earlier).—1806, J. Galpine, 'Brit. Bot.,' p. 106, "Seed calyptrate."

Camel (nowhere found wild).—Found wild in Central Asia by Przhevalsky. 1898, Sven Hedin, 'Through Asia,' vol. ii. p. 833, "A herd of wild camels two hundred paces away"; *ibid.*, p. 837, "We surprised a second herd of five wild camels."

Cameloid (not in).—1885, O. Schmidt, 'Mammalia,' p. 156, "The cameloid type of ruminants."

Camptonite (not in).—1901, *Nature*, p. 513, col. 1, "The sills of camptonite and felsite intrusive in the Cambrian rocks."

Cantaloon (later).—1778, 'England's Gazetteer' (second ed.), ii. *s.v.* 'Somersetshire,' "The manufactures are chiefly fine cloths......serges, cantaloons, knit stockings," &c.

Capitalize (nonce-use). — 1890, Baring - Gould, 'Pennycomequicks,' p. 238, "Capitalize a Q."

Carbolite (not in). — 1898, *English Mechanic*, p. 490, "Carbolite is a combination of carbon, calcium, aluminium, and silicon, and from it is produced ethylene gas"; *ibid.*, "A 150-ton-a-day carbolite plant will cost 150,000 dollars."

Carbonado (not in). — 1895, J. W. Anderson, 'Prospector's Handbook' (sixth ed.), p. 95, "Carbonado is a black diamond." Also 1895, Bloxam, 'Chem.,' p. 71, "A dark amorphous diamond (carbonado) found at Bahia in the Brazils."

Carborundum (not in).—Bloxam, *ut supra*, p. 127, "Silicon carbide (carborundum), SiC, is prepared by heating silicon or silica with carbon in the electric furnace."

Cardiologist (not in).—1885, *Lancet*, 26 September, p. 576, "The great cardiologist."

Carmagnole.—1895, Baedeker, 'Northern Italy' (tenth ed.), p. 55, "Carmagnola...... The 'Carmagnole,' the celebrated republican dance and song of the French Revolution, was named after this town, the home of most of the street-musicians of Paris."

Carriage, v.—1902, *Daily Mail*, 13 March, "Many continental monarchs......have been 'horsed' and 'carriaged' by East's."

Carton pierre (not in).—Spon, *ut supra*, p. 608, "Carton pierre is a species of papier-mâché made with paper pulp, whiting, and size, pressed into plaster moulds."

Cat, v. (earlier). — 1711, Sutherland, 'Shipbuilder's Assistant,' p. 159, "Catting the Anchor, is haling the Stock up to the Cathead."

Catabolism=Katabolism.

Catalogist (earlier).—1804, *Trans. Lin. Soc.*, vol. vii. p. 120, "We have omitted, however, mere catalogists."

Catalyst (not in).—1902, *Nature*, 3 April, p. 523, col. 1.

Cataractal (not in).—1888, W. C. Russell, 'Death Ship,' vol. iii. p. 46, "Cataractal roaring of water."

Catechin.—Also "catechuine" in 1853, Morfit, 'Arts of Tanning,' &c., p. 69.

Catenulated (not in).—1819, G. Samouelle, 'Entom. Compend.,' p. 145.

Cats (=Cat-salt).—1894, Baring-Gould, 'Queen of Love,' vol. ii. p. 14, "The salt that forms round the side of the pans is termed 'cats.'"

Cauling (not in).—Spon, *ut supra*, p. 361, "Before cauling, raise the veneer and glue the ground well."

Celloidin (not in).—1898, *English Mechanic*, p. 64, "Celloidin is practically collodion, being prepared from pure pyroxylin."

Chalazogam, Chalazogamic, Chalazogamy (not in). —1894, *Times*, 11 August, p. 11, col. 3, "Treub's division into chalazogams and porogams"; *ibid.*, "the chalazogamic Amentiferæ"; *ibid.*, "inclined to regard chalazogamy as an adaptation."

Chalk.—Also 1895, Anderson, *ut supra*, p. 154, "Black chalk—a variety of clay containing carbon."

Chatsome (not in).—1810, in Lady Granville, 'Letters' (1894), vol. i. p. 2.

Check, v. (cf. the sense).—Spon, *ut supra*, p. 678, "The covers to be droved, and in 3 pieces, one of which to cover the building on one side and half of the well, and to be half-checked where the other 2 stones meet it in the middle, and they are to be half-checked into it, also half-checked into each other where they meet in the middle, and to cover the other side of the building."

Chestnut-oak (no quot.).—1853, Morfit, 'Arts of Tanning,' &c, p. 99, "*Quercus Prinus Monticola*...... In Pennsylvania, Virginia, and Maryland it is called chestnut-oak, on account of the resemblance of the bark to that of the chestnut."

Cheval (not in).—1747, *Gent. Mag.*, p. 437, "A cheval fill'd with powder, and furnish'd with bombs, grenades, and other fire-works, to be roll'd in upon a breach, where it kills or wounds all about it."

Chine (earlier).—1711, Sutherland, 'Shipbuilder's Assistant,' p. 159, "Chine; that part of the waterway, or any thing that is channel'd, which is thicker than the other part."

Chirt.—1894, Crockett, 'Raiders,' p. 78, "He's gotten an unco chirt [sudden squeeze], puir laddie"

Chlamydospore (not in).—1884, Henfrey, 'Element. Bot.' (fourth ed.), p. 160, "Chlamydospores, when fully formed, are still enclosed within their parent cells."

J. DORMER.

Redmorion, Woodside Green, S.E.

(To be continued.)

HOLLICKE OR HOLLECK, TOTTENHAM.

THREE centuries ago the manor and parish of Tottenham in Middlesex (then vested in William, Lord Compton, as lord of the manor) contained within itself the remains of a miniature "town," named Hollicke. Adjoining it, moreover, was a wood—long since disappeared — perfectly distinct from the historic Hornsey and Tottenham woods, known as Hollicke or Holleck Wood. Ample evidence is extant showing that this town (not mentioned in any published local history) was situate at the western boundary of the "ancient parish of Tottenham," which included a portion of Harringay, the whole of Wood Green. and an important part of Muswell Hill. This extensive area is to this day comprised in the "Tottenham Parliamentary Division," although recently Tottenham and Wood Green have, by 51 & 52 Vict., c. clxxxvii., been separated for parochial administrative purposes. Hollicke was, in fact, situate at or near Wood Green, this latter district originally having been simply one of the four wards of Tottenham parish. In Norden's 'Speculum Britanniæ (A.D. 1593) a reference is made to it as follows :—

"Hollicke D. 18. there is noted the foundations of ancient buildings affirmed by some aged men that it hath been a Towne, but oftentimes *Immensa cani spirans mendacia.*"

The above initial and figures—D and 18— have reference to the divisions of a map of Middlesex comprised in Norden's treatise, and indicate that portion thereof where Hollicke is delineated. The name is also marked with an asterisk, a sign adopted by the topographer and draughtsman to denote that Hollicke was one of several "decayed places" then much in evidence in this county. This circumstance partially corroborates the affirmations of the "aged men," and reduces the force of implied doubt suggested by the old Latin quotation. Hollicke likewise appears in another map of Norden's "augmeted" by Speed ; also in an old (undated) map by Ric. Bloome. In each instance it is placed between a sub-manor of Duccatts—modernized Ducketts—and Muswell Hill, this sub-manor, like Muswell Hill, being partly in Tottenham and partly in Hornsey. The name of such sub-manor is perpetuated by a newly formed road (Ducketts Road) in the Green Lanes, Harringay ; but Hollicke having been forgotten, the "powers that be" may well be pardoned for not adopting it in our local street nomenclature. Up to within a hundred years ago there was also a "Holleck" Wood, skirting the southern extremity of the town bearing the same name, though variously spelt. It was not far removed from Hornsey Wood, now the site of Finsbury Park, a small portion of the latter, as testified by the existing boundary stones, being in Tottenham parish. Reference is incidentally made to Holleck Wood in a quaint old document under date 22 May, 1802, entitled 'Remarks on the Perambulation of the Parish of Tottenham made by the Parishioners' (see Dr. Robinson's 'History of Tottenham,' edition 1840). This valuable literary relic has reference to the custom of "beating the bounds," which our forefathers considered an excellent method of keeping in remembrance ancient landmarks, maintaining local rights, and preserving public privileges. It is to be regretted that this time-honoured and estimable custom, with all its interesting associations, has in some urban districts died out, though it lingers still in certain rural and more conservative parishes. After minutely describing the Tottenham boundaries the 'Remarks' wind up with the following interesting disclosure, "After which we dined at the 'White Hart,' and the Churchwardens paid all the expenses." This inn was situate on the east side of the high road, within a short distance of All Hallows (the old parish church), and has only recently been demolished. A modern structure, retaining the original name, so reminiscent of the sporting and rustic character of the ancient manor in bygone days, now occupies the identical site. The "White Hart" was also very near to Tottenham Wood, the latter having been a favourite hunting-ground of King James. No longer, however, can it be said,

The morning wakes, the huntsman sounds,
At once rush forth the joyful hounds ;
They seek the wood with eager pace,
Through bush, through briar, explore the chase,

for Tottenham Wood has long since ceased to exist. Unhappily this is not, however, the only cause for regret, so far as the antiquary is concerned. Alas ! like Goldsmith's "deserted village," the ancient town Hollicke, with its sylvan wood, has undergone such a marvellous transformation that it reminds one of the prophecy of Lucan respecting certain towns connected with ancient Rome :—

Nor after length of years a stone betray
The place where once the very ruins lay.

As regards the derivation and signification of Hollicke (which is also a surname), *holl* is probably another form of *hill*, and *icke*, or *eck*, a variation of *ock*. This would, of course, signify a little hill. Assuming, however, the first syllable to be a corruption of the Anglo-Saxon *holt*, it might be rendered a small woody hill. It is important to bear in mind that Hollicke, or Holleck, was not only built on a slight elevation, but was also located in the vicinity of a wood.   J. Basil Birch.

56, Vale Road, Finsbury Park, N.

Proverbs XXVI. 4–5.—One of the least appreciated of a clever band of magazine writers in the latter part of the Victorian era, William Kirkus, starts a bright essay on 'Satire' (Longmans) by seeking to reconcile the seeming hostility of these two passages in the Book of Proverbs. Let me say broadly that in respect of all word-problems in the Hebrew Scriptures one must never forget that the real difficulty confronting the investigator is to discover the precise sense in which any given author applied a given word on a given occasion. The Hebrew vocabulary is limited, yet it is notorious for possessing a disproportionate number of words representing sometimes a distressingly large variety of senses. Fortunately, the words "kesil," "evayless," and "angnah," which form the objects and predicates of these sentences, do not offer a very large field of selection. Likewise it is not proved that the Proverbs of Solomon have come down to us unmutilated and line for line as they were penned by their royal author. For aught we know to the contrary certain passages have been excised between verses 4 and 5: so much so that the precise objects the moralist had in mind to castigate were at that time heterogeneous, albeit they seem to-day to be homogeneous as to mode and composition by reason of accidental juxtaposition. Warranty for this hypothesis may be drawn from the Talmudic dictum, "The Rabbins were for excluding Ecclesiastes from the Canon on account of inherent inconsistencies." In all likelihood the larger work found a more experienced editor, so that the framers of our Canon were in no such quandary.

At the period under review (*circa* 800 B.C.) the intellectual condition of the Hebrews may be summarized within three separate categories. There were (1) the "Nebeehim" or prophetical school—a distinct class ; (2) the "Chachameem" and "Nevouneem" —under this heading the literati, the statesmen, and men of professional rank were currently known ; (3) the masses, comprising among others the "Kesilleem" ("upstarts") and the "Bangareem" (peasantry). These *novi homines* or "Kesilleem" were men aping the manners, ideas, and virtues of the "Nevouneem"; overweening idlers, ambitious nobodies, seeking by their impertinent vulgarities to be somebodies, a despicable class whom moralists from Solomon to Aristophanes, from Juvenal to Pope, have lashed furiously with their wit. Moving serenely along the uneven tenor of their devious ways, they resist reformation, and survive the fusillade of ridicule. A *Kesil*, derived from *kaysel*, may have meant to the Hebrew satirist (who saw enough of him dangling about the royal courts) a parasitic person or pompous upstart, half-educated, full of conceit and bland self-assurance, quick enough in the art of fence, skilled in the lower forms of casuistry, obstinate in his prejudices, a dissolute scoffer, and a dangerous libertine. Hanging on the skirts of the cultured classes (the Chachameem), these parasitic units were just smart enough to lord it over the "Bangareem," or herdsmen, to whom they were wont to discourse portentously of the marvels of the Court or to retail the tittle-tattle of the upper circles. The self-sufficiency and pomposity of these ignoramuses made Solomon often wince for want of power to cope successfully with so undesirable a class, against whom repressive measures were discounted by the etiquette of the unwritten law.

I have already explained what was meant by *kesil* = fool, A.V. *Évayless*, rendered "folly" in A.V., calls for a note. It may mean two distinct things, (1) vicious living, (2) ritual errors or ignorance. The verb *angnah* likewise comes out in dual lights, (1) of encouraging, (2) of reasoning. Finally, if we suppose a probable error in transcription in verse 4, whereby " b'ēvoltou " got rounded into "k'ē-voltou" in the text, the way is clear for summarizing all the points. Wherefore, in all humility, we may translate verse 4 thus : "Don't encourage the upstart in his vices lest you be accounted like unto him." Any other method of managing him might result in your friends failing to understand your motives. Verse 5, however, would then read thus : " Confute the scoffer by his own error lest he think himself a 'Chacham.'" You are to persevere with him until you convince him of his error, in a calm, resolute, and philosophic spirit, which is in contradistinction to the summaries drawn up by Mr. Kirkus, who says, "There are times when flippancy must be rebuked by solemn gravity ; and there are times when the lightest jest would be sufficient for its discomfiture." I prefer Solomon's method to that of Mr. Kirkus, and most of my readers will be of the same opinion, I believe.   M. L. R. Breslar.
Percy House, South Hackney.

" Babies in the eyes." — I was permitted in 8th S. iii. 181 to attempt at some length an explanation of that cryptic and puzzling expression of several of the seventeenth-century poets, "the babies in the eyes." I there came to the conclusion that "to look babies in the eyes" probably meant to kindle desire by amorous and enticing glances. I have recently come across a very strong confirmation of this view in some verses in the *Gentleman's Journal* for April, 1693, in imitation of the twentieth ode of Anacreon :—

> How blest were I, could but my Face
> Be chang'd into your Looking-Glass,
> That there you might reflected view
> Those Beauties I admire in you,
> And I each Morn in this Disguise,
> Might thus look Babies in your Eyes.

The writer's fancy obviousl is that amorous inclinations would be excited in the lady by the contemplation in her lover's face of those beauties which had excited them in himself.
W. C. Bolland.
Lincoln's Inn.

A " Wild-Cat " Company.—During a recent trial the question arose : "What is a wild-cat company ?" Although both sides agreed that the term was not complimentary, the designation was not precisely definable. Some said one thing, some said another. The origin and meaning of the term were never explained. Under these circumstances perhaps the following, for which I am indebted to the *Financial News*, may be found worthy of a corner in ' N. & Q.' :—

" Mr. Justice Lawrance and others may be interested to know that in the early fifties a large bank in Michigan had a vignette on its notes representing a panther, which is, or was then, known in the Western States as a wild cat. The bank failed, having a large number of its notes in circulation, and these were afterwards known as 'wild-cat' money, and the bank that had issued them was called a 'wild-cat' bank. Other banks were compelled to stop payment soon after in consequence of the want of confidence in them, and the term 'wild-cat' became general in Michigan to denote banking institutions of an unsound character. In time the term came to be applied throughout the United States to all bogus and swindling concerns, and was, I believe, first employed in England in the columns of the *Financial News* in connection with the Harney Peak and other mining bubbles."
Richard Edgcumbe.
33, Tedworth Square, Chelsea.

Coincidences. — I happen to be able to vouch for the truth of the following strange series of coincidences. Some years since a number of business friends who habitually lunched together in one of our large provincial cities, upon the casual proposition of one of their number, adjourned to a photographer's and were taken in a group, their individual positions being determined by no design, but standing or sitting as it chanced. Not long afterwards one who had occupied an extreme end of the group died ; and within a comparatively short time the whole of the persons who had been photographed died, without a single exception, in the exact order they had there occupied. The last survivor died in 1900, and then from relatives of his I learnt the foregoing. To avoid possible pain to persons living I abstain from specifying more than the general facts, but for saying that these happened as I have stated there is indisputable authority.   W. B. H.

Macaulay in German.—In Moellenhoff's German translation of Macaulay's essay on Frederick the Great (Leipzig, Philipp, Reclam, jun., no date) there are one or two curious slips. Saxe (the victor of Fontenoy, the son of Aurora von Königsmark and the "Saxon man of sin") is transformed into "der sächsische Hof." When the English writer, with an obvious allusion to Horace, 'A. P.,' 372–3, describes the king's verses as "hateful to gods and men," this by a strange mistake appears as "voller Erbitterung gegen Gott und Menschen."

In quoting these errors no disparagement is intended to Reclam's "Universal-Bibliothek," that wonderful series of cheap literature to which we have at present no parallel in England. EDWARD BENSLY.

The University, Adelaide, South Australia.

BOON FOR BOOKWORMS. — I have just come across what will doubtless be hailed as a welcome innovation in the reading world. This is a marker of narrow ribbon which a thoughtful firm of publishers has attached to the covers of a couple of volumes recently issued. When the unsatisfactory nature of various expedients employed for keeping one's place, such as the elusive paper-knife, clips, turned-down edges, and the like, is considered, the appearance of so neat and simple an indicator should certainly be welcomed with gratitude. May the entire book-trade adopt the plan ! say I. CECIL CLARKE.

Junior Athenæum Club.

ITALIAN BELL. — I do not know whether the foreign bells in English churches have ever been catalogued, but it may not seem unworthy of record in 'N. & Q.' that one brought by me from Rome two years ago has been hung recently at Hendon. It is a Sanctus bell, measuring in height 1 ft. 4½ in., and in rim circumference 4 ft. 2½ in. It belonged to the church of S. Giovanni Calabita on the Tiber Island. It bears the following encircling inscription in three lines :—

1. DEO + MENTEM . SANCTAM . SPONTANEAM . HONOREM.
2. ET . PATRIE . LIBERATIONEM . A.D . MDLXXVII.
3. JOANNES . MELO . VERVLANVS.*

Below this occurs a shield bearing in chief two stars above a melon. Above is a half-figure, in relief, of Christ, with hands bound in front. The bell was in danger of being sold for "breaking up" when rescued.
ST. CLAIR BADDELEY.

BREAKING BREAD AT TABLE. — The practice of breaking one's bread at table may be commended on the score of elegance, but few people would suppose that there may some-

* Of Veroli, near Frosinone.

times be a deeper reason for doing so. Once, however, I heard a Russian girl say to her little brother at dinner, "Jesus Christ broke His bread, He did not cut it, and you should do the same." T. P. ARMSTRONG.

SHORTHAND IN THE FOURTH CENTURY. — That shorthand was used in the ancient world is well known, but our information is still scanty and any addition is welcome. It may, therefore, be worth noting that there is in the Armenian 'Acts of St. Callistratus' a reference to the employment of stenography. A translation of this is included in Mr. F. C. Conybeare's 'Armenian Apology and Acts of Apollonius and other Monuments of Early Christianity' (second edit., London, 1896, p. 331), a book for which all students of the early ages of the Christian Church must be grateful. The account of Callistratus was probably written in the first half of the fourth century. It includes several long addresses of Callistratus to his fellow-soldiers, in explanation of the mysteries of the new faith for which he and forty-nine of his comrades became martyrs. Perhaps with a view to giving them authority as verbatim reports the compiler says :—

"But there was a certain scribe of the law court, who was near to the prison, and he listened to the discourse of Callistratus, and wrote it down in shorthand on paper, and gave it to us; and we set in order, with all accuracy, the record and outline of his thought."

My good friend the late Sir Isaac Pitman, the inventor of phonography, would, I think, have been delighted with this reference to the art which he so greatly improved and so widely popularized. WILLIAM E. A. AXON.

Manchester.

"METROPOLI."—The following extract is taken from the *Advertiser* (Adelaide, South Australia) of 14 March :—

"A Melbourne paper writes: — 'The mutual jealousy of Melbourne and Sydney prevents either of these fine cities becoming the capital. Why not then select one of the smaller metropoli of the States?'"

I do not know whether this curious plural is confined to the Southern hemisphere or has appeared elsewhere. Certainly the daily newspapers of Australia are at least as fallible as their contemporaries in other lands, especially when they leave the safe ground of the King's colonial English. Volksraad has been known to disguise itself as Yolksroad ; Appendicitis has masqueraded as a South African place - name ; a democratic statesman out of office has been happily compared to Coriolanus(!) returning to the plough;

while various specimens of popular etymology which have been effectually slain in your columns by Prof. Skeat receive here a new lease of life, and, introduced by the ominous words "It is not generally known that," are presented to the philological curiosity of the ingenuous Australian.   Edward Bensly.
The University, Adelaide, South Australia.

Queries.

We must request correspondents desiring information on family matters of only private interest to affix their names and addresses to their queries, in order that the answers may be addressed to them direct.

English Gladiators. — In the just published letters of César de Saussure, issued in a translation by Mr. John Murray as 'A Foreign View of England in the Reigns of George I. and George II.,' the writer speaks of gladiators, both male and female, exhibiting on a stage (see pp. 276 et seq.). They fought with

"a sort of two-handed sword, three or three and a half feet in length; the guard was covered, and the blade was about three inches wide and not too sharp—only about half a foot of it was, but then that part cut like a razor."

The whole description is animated, and it "seemed really surprising that neither man should be killed." Grave wounds were naturally inflicted. Where can I obtain further particulars of a class of entertainment of which I have not previously heard?
H. T.

England with Many Religions and One Sauce. — Who described England as "a country of —— religions and only one sauce —melted butter"?   Debonnaire.

[James Payn says it was a distinguished Frenchman. Qy. Voltaire?]

"Grey city by the Northern Sea."— Where do the lines occur (as applied to St. Andrews) beginning "Grey city by the Northern Sea"?   Debonnaire.

Archery.—
And when he fand the bridges broke,
  He bent his bow and swam;
But when he fand the grass growing,
  He slacked it and ran.

And when he came to that lord's gate,
  Stopt not to knock nor call,
But set his bent bow to his breast,
  And lightly lap the wall.

In these verses, taken, I believe, from the 'Ballad of Lady Maisey,' and in others of the same period, the condition of the bow is often mentioned, and evident importance is attached to it. What is the exact reason that the bow is bent for swimming and leaping, and slacked for running?
D. G. Lange.
11, St. Julian's Road, Willesden Lane, N.W.
[Surely the tension of the bow for immediate action varies according to the tension of the mind, as impressed by various circumstances.]

Royal Colour.—Will you kindly tell me what is the true royal colour? Is it the same as the old imperial purple, which is (is it not?) crimson? The newspapers speak of the coronation robes of the peeresses as crimson, and of those to be worn by their Majesties as somehow differing from these, calling them sometimes purple, sometimes crimson.
R. C.

"Moniales de Clinton."—In 'Testa de Nevill,' p. 323, referring to Welleby, now Welby, in Lincolnshire, is the following entry: "Ite' moniales de Clinton tene't ibide' totu' residuu' de soka de Grah'm in pur' elem' de vel'i feoff'." Can any one say what this monastic house was, and whether there is any other record of this gift to it? Was it Kenilworth?   A. E. Welby, Lieut.-Col.
26, Sloane Court, S.W.

Martigny Priory.—This Cluniac house was granted the manor of Welby by King Stephen, because his mother Adela there laid aside "worldly desire and the purple of secular glory," though only for a brief time. The prioress transferred the manor in exchange for a pension to the Priory of Farley, Wilts, before 1291. The house is variously called Marcigny, Monteganiacum, Martiginacum, Mortignatum, Mortigamatum, Martney, &c. It was situated on the Loire in the diocese of Autun. I shall be much obliged for references to any history of this priory or to documents connected with it.
A. E. Welby, Lieut.-Col.
26, Sloane Court, S.W.

Bilingual Wills, Latin and English.— John Cosin, Prince Bishop of Durham, wrote his will, dated 11 December, 1671, partly in Latin and partly in English; this he thus explains in the final paragraph of the Latin section :—

"Hæc præfatus, quæ ad Religionem et animæ meæ statum ac salutem spectant, quæque Latino sermona à me dictata atque exarata sunt: reliqua, quæ ad sepulturam corporis, et bonorum meorum temporalium dispositionem, attinent, sermone patrio perscribi faciam, ac perorabo." — Cosin's 'Correspondence, &c., part ii., 1872, p. 293, Surtees Society.

Was it a custom, or at all usual, for testators

to make their spiritual dispositions in Latin and their temporal in their mother tongue? Cosin was a past master in all that pertained to exact ecclesiastical usage, and for that reason was chosen as Magister Ceremoniarum at the coronation of Charles I.

JAMES HOOPER.

Norwich.

KNIFE UNDER BOULDER. — Can any one inform me where I may obtain an authentic account of the finding of a flint knife under a boulder stone? It is fairly common knowledge, and a geological friend told me lately he thought it was found so in France. Any information (and the more full the better) will oblige.   B. WELLS.

Crawley.

"PUBLISH" IN RIME.—Is there a legitimate rime for "publish," or is it to be added to the two or three English words, including *window* and *orange*, which are legitimately unrimeable?   A. F. R.

NAPOLEONIC QUOTATION.— Wanted the exact words and authorship of the quotation about Napoleon I. which is parallel to Cicero's eulogy on Pompeius, "Qui non modo eorum hominum qui nunc sunt, gloriam, sed etiam antiquitatis memoriam virtute superavit."

C. H. WILLSON.

Elstow.

LETHBRIDGE.—Can any of your readers say who was the Lethbridge to whom W. M. Praed refers in his 'Song of Impossibilities'? The lines are :—

When Huskisson is heard to say
That Lethbridge understands.

Wherein lay the peculiar obtuseness of this Lethbridge?   W. L.

"COTEMPORARIES."—When I was a lad I frequently heard my father use the words "cotemporary" and "cotemporaries," which seem to have been their current forms in the sixties and seventies. Was this form still in use during the eighties? If my memory is worth trusting, I should say that no leading writer of that time would be found guilty of such an anachronism. For my own part, I must avow that even when a mere boy I had a great aversion for the word.

M. L. R. BRESLAR.

[See the full note under 'Contemporary' in the 'H.E.D.']

CANTERBURY RECORDS. — Are there any known printed or MS. records of family or domestic life in the city or neighbourhood of Canterbury about the latter half of the six-

teenth century? Historical or biographical records, and not works of fiction.   I.

['The Canterbury Marriage Licences,' 1568-1700, are compiled and issued by Mr. Joseph Meadows Cowper, of Canterbury, to whom apply.]

WHITSUNDAY, 1593.—Can any one tell me on what month and on what day of it Whitsunday fell in 1593?   I.

INQUESTS. — Where were the reports of coroners' inquests preserved in olden times? Are any dating back to the sixteenth century known to be in existence anywhere?   I.

[Inquests in the thirteenth and fourteenth centuries occur in the City Letter-Books, Calendars of which are being edited by Dr. R. R. Sharpe.]

'HOSANNAS TO THE KING.'—I am compiling an anthology of coronation odes with the above title. I shall be glad if any reader will draw my attention to applicable poems which meet his eyes. Answers direct to

CHAS. F. FORSHAW, LL.D.

48, Hanover Square, Bradford.

PRESENTATION AT COURT. — It has been thought desirable to ascertain, for family reasons, if a certain person was presented at Court during the latter half of the eighteenth century. What steps should be taken to ascertain this? Are there any periodicals of the date likely to contain entries of presentations?   X. Y. Z.

ANDREW FITZHERBERT EVANS was admitted to Westminster School on 7 June, 1779. I should be glad to obtain particulars of his parentage and career.   G. F. R. B.

SWORN CLERKS IN CHANCERY BEFORE 1765. —The names of the sworn clerks are given in the 'Court and City Kalendar' for 1765, but I have not been able to meet with an earlier list of them. Can any reader tell me where I can find one? I wish to ascertain when the John Wainwright who died 8 October, 1760 (*London Mag.*, vol. xxix. p. 556), entered the office—I think it was in 1745 or 1746—and whether he succeeded any one of the same name.   J. B. W.

HERRICK'S 'HESPERIDES': "LUTES OF AMBER."—In the "Canterbury" edition of Herrick's 'Hesperides' the editor, Mr. H. P. Horne, gives the following note on the poem 'Upon Julia's Voice,' which ends with the lines :—

But listen to thee, walking in thy chamber,
Melting melodious words to lutes of amber.

"The word 'amber' must have been used here merely from stress of rhyme. Mr. A. J. Hipkins, a first authority on these matters, tells me that though a lute was commonly inlaid with ivory, tortoiseshell, and mother-o'-pearl, yet he does not remember a single example in which amber was used, not only in that, but in any other musical instrument. It had been ingeniously suggested to him that the amber varnish used in the making of the lute might here be meant, but I am afraid this would be taking Herrick too literally."

It certainly does not seem likely that Herrick would use an inappropriate word simply for the sake of a rime. Is it not possible that he may have come across an instance of ἤλεκτρον in some Greek poet as the material, wholly or in part, of a harp? Liddell and Scott distinguish two meanings of the word, (1) amber, (2) "a metallic substance compounded of four parts gold and one silver," referring for their authority to Pliny, 'N.H.,' xxxiii. 23, xxxvii. 2, 11. It seems highly probable that the ἤλεκτρον of Homer, which along with gold, silver, copper, and ivory we find adorning the walls of Menelaus's palace, was the second kind. Herrick may, perhaps, have met with some such use of the word, and, taking it in the old sense of "amber," have thus arrived at his phrase "lutes of amber." Is there any instance of ἤλεκτρον as part of the material of a lute or harp?   H. I. B.

AINSWORTH THE NOVELIST. — I should be glad of any information respecting William Harrison Ainsworth. He wrote. I believe, forty-one novels (together with other works), commencing with 'Sir John Chiverton,' 1826, and 'Rookwood,' 1834, and finishing with 'Stanley Brereton,' 1881. Has there been any complete collective edition of his novels, and by whom published? After the period of Cruikshank, Franklin, Johannot, Phiz, and Sir John Gilbert, were his works illustrated, and by what artists? Was his life ever published?   R. D.

[A new edition of Ainsworth's novels, the "Windsor," is being published by Messrs. Gibbins & Co., and will be finished by next September. In the 'D.N.B.' you will find details of him and of the scanty biographical memoirs available. He figures in many contemporary records, e.g., Maclise's 'Portrait Gallery,' Friswell's 'Modern Men of Letters,' and Horne's 'New Spirit of the Age.']

ARMORIAL BEARINGS OF RAILWAY COMPANIES.—Those of the Great Northern of Ireland being Quarterly: 1, Dublin; 2, Londonderry; 4, Belfast, what town is 3 (a castle bearing a banner)? Those of the Great Southern and Western being Quarterly: 1 and 4, Dublin, what town is 2 and 3 (again a castle with banner)? Those of the Midland Great Western being Quarterly: 1 and 4, Dublin; 3, Longford, what town is 2 (Az., three horses' heads couped or, 2 and 1)?

Those of the Donegal Railway being the shield of arms of Londonderry, beside a shield Ar., a pall between three mullets sa. (?), whose is the latter? In the armorial bearings of the Midland, what is the origin of the wyvern as crest and of the fish and salamander in flames of fire, displayed as it were as supporters on either side the shield? Those of the London and South-Western, not as at present, but up to perhaps fifteen years ago, being Quarterly: 1, London; 2, Winchester; 3, Portsmouth, what town is 4 (apparently identical with Hastings)? Those of the North London being quarterly, 3 is London; but what are 1, an anchor charged with an escutcheon bearing a lion rampant; 2, extremely like Birmingham; 4, an archway, thereon a three-masted ship? Are they arms of London boroughs?

H. H. BRINDLEY.

Replies.

PARISH REGISTERS: THEIR CARE AND PROTECTION.
(9ᵗʰ S. ix. 168, 337.)

THE older portions of these "priceless" records are due entirely to the voluntary care of the clergy. A few cases of gross neglect do not prove general carelessness. They are rendered comparatively insignificant by the vast number of unnoticed cases of extreme care. Moreover, central authorities have been quite as guilty as individual clergy. The bishops' transcripts are in far worse condition than the original registers, and the early reports of the Deputy-Keeper of the Public Records tell a pitiful tale.

The agitators for the removal of parish registers to London forget that they are not national records; they are the Church's own records of her own children and her own sacraments, and are strictly parochial. We may as well be asked to deposit our ancient chalices, and the like, in the British Museum. Such a removal would be a great hardship to the poor, who very often need certificates for which the clergy seldom make any charge, whereas the public registrar demands 3s. 7d. The interests of mere genealogists, amateur and professional, which are almost wholly private, ought not to weigh against these things.   W. C. B.

The whole question of the care and protection of our priceless parish registers demands immediate and energetic action. Without doubt the great majority of the registers are most carefully kept and preserved, and our thanks are due to their custodians. But unfortunately in some cases, equally without doubt, these records are, and have been, treated as if they had little or no value. One aspect of the question has not as yet been mentioned by your correspondents. It is instanced in the case of the registers of a Perthshire parish. In those books not a single entry of baptism was made for thirty-five years (1720-55), nor a single marriage entry for thirteen years (1744-57). The times were turbulent, but the omission is grave. It has much affected certain investigations of mine, and has also had some serious consequences to me personally.

I agree entirely with Mr. Matthews in his protest against the prohibitive fees demanded — "legal fees" they are always named — from genealogists and others whose work, often undertaken solely for the benefit of — shall I say? — the world at large, necessitates a general search. Recently I had occasion to think that the registers of two parish churches in the north of England probably contained certain entries I was anxious to discover. The first vicar asked for "the legal fee," and said the charge would "mount up considerably." The second vicar referred me to the parish clerk, who demanded for "opening books" a fee of 21s.. in addition to 1s. for every hour, and 2s. 6d. for the certificate, should the necessary entry be found. It should be noted also that this parish church had for generations been liberally supported by the people at large, without any distinction of creed, just because it had been so connected with their past history and traditions.

I very much doubt whether any vicar or any parish clerk has any legal right — certainly he has no moral right — to impose such excessive charges on historical investigations, and so further hamper searches which are often difficult and expensive enough without such hindrances. A small fee is reasonable enough in these seemingly general commercial days, but to attempt to exact "corner" fees is quite another matter.

Vigorous action both to preserve the priceless registers still existing and to investigate the legality of "legal charges" in the case of general searches for literary purposes is most desirable. Ronald Dixon.

46, Marlborough Avenue, Hull.

This question might be solved if indexes of their contents were made and deposited in some central place. Then the registers might remain in their own parishes, and on payment of 2s. 6d. postal order the complete entry could be obtained. I made indexes of a number of Berkshire parishes with the approval of the late Bishop Stubbs, but it is too expensive to print them.

(Mrs.) J. H. Cope.

13c, Hyde Park Mansions, W.

Samuel Taylor, Shorthand Writer (7ᵗʰ S. ii. 308, 377, 457).—I send details concerning Samuel Taylor. Can any one tell me where he was buried?

"Died lately, in Palace Street, Pimlico, aged sixty-two, Mr. Samuel Taylor, professor and author of several treatises on shorthand writing."—*Sun*, Saturday, 24 August, 1811, p. 4, col. 4.

"Taylor, the shorthand teacher, whose death we recently announced, was a very eccentric character. He never would tell whence he originally came, or whether he had any relations. He was constantly employed as a shorthand writer, and must have received a good deal of money, but nobody could tell how he disposed of it, and he was always in debt. It would be impossible to count the number of houses in which he had lodged, even if he had been less mysterious in his operations. His reputation was high as a teacher of shorthand, but he never would take a pupil who came to him in consequence of that reputation. He seemed to have an odd pleasure in hunting out scholars for himself, and was always offended with those who recommended him. His manners were so strange and rough to those whom he permitted to employ him, that if it had not been for his skill in teaching, he must have been discarded by everybody. He had two children, whom he left to the care of chance, for he always went out very early in the morning, and returned late at night. He was supposed to have been seventy years of age, and upwards of fifty of them must have passed in this manner."—*Sun*, Monday, 2 September, 1811, p. 2, col. 4.

"Taylor, le fameux tachygrafe, vient de mourir aussi pauvre qu'il avoit toujours été pendant sa vie. Il n'a pas été possible de savoir de lui ni le lieu de sa naissance, ni le véritable nom de sa famille. Cet homme mystérieux changeait secrètement de logis plusieurs fois dans l'espace d'un mois. On ne le voyait faire aucune dépense, et on ignore ce qu'il a pu faire des sommes considérables qu'il gagnait." —*Journal de Paris*, Jeudi, 12 Septembre, 1811, p. 1825.

Matthias Levy.

English Translations (9ᵗʰ S. ix. 368).— A magnificent edition of 'Cent Nouvelles Nouvelles' exists in English. It is in two octavo volumes, with fifty coloured illustrations by Léon Lébègue, and was published by C. Carrington, in Paris, last year. The literary part of the work has been very well done by Robert B. Douglas.

J. de Villiot.

1, Rue Montaigne, Paris.

There is a complete translation into English of 'Les Cent Nouvelles Nouvelles,' by Robert B. Douglas, which claims to be the first. It was published in Paris by Charles Carrington in 1899, and called 'One Hundred Merrie and Delightsome Stories.'

CHARLES R. DAWES.

DRAGON TREE (9th S. ix. 369).—TYRONE may still obtain the 'Child's Guide to Knowledge' from Simpkin & Marshall. It will tell him very little about the dragon tree. There are five plants bearing that name. The best known are *Calamus draco* and *Calamus rotang*, palms with reed-like stems, and *Dracœna draco*, a liliaceous tree, which attains extraordinary size. To this last belonged the famous dragon tree of Teneriffe, seventy-eight [*sic*] feet in circumference, in whose hollow stem an ascending staircase was constructed. It was believed to be the oldest tree in the world, but was destroyed by a storm in 1867.

W. T.

The following interesting account of this tree, accompanied by an illustration, appears in Dr. Annandale's 'Imperial Dictionary':—

"A genus of endogenous, evergreen trees, nat. order Liliaceæ, remarkable for their elegant palm-like appearance. As formerly constituted the genus contained thirty-six species, but, as remodelled by Dr. Planchon, it includes only the dragon tree of Teneriffe (*D. draco*), celebrated for producing the resin called dragon's blood, and for the age and immense proportions of an individual at Orotava in Teneriffe, totally destroyed by a hurricane in 1867, which was forty-eight [*sic*] feet in circumference and seventy feet high. It was hollow inside, and ascended by a staircase. It was of the same circumference in 1402."

EVERARD HOME COLEMAN.
71, Brecknock Road.

"HOG" (9th S. ix. 305). — MR. HARRISON expresses his surprise "that the 'New English Dictionary' marks this important substantive 'origin unknown,'" and kindly tells us of his discovery that "it is, of course, Scandinavian—from O.Nor. *högg*, a cut," &c. He omits to say that the 'N.E.D.' has dealt with that suggestion in the words :—

"Some have thought *hog* possibly related to *Hag, v.*[1],* with the notion of castration. But the notion of 'yearling' seems to run through most of the uses. Cf. 2b, 4, 4b, 5, 13b."

MR. HARRISON does not say why this evidence should be set aside. Nor does he attempt to solve the difficulty of a word implying castration being applied on the one hand to a *chilver-hog*, a *ewe hog*, and a *gimmer-hog*, and, on the other hand, to a *tup-hog*. He seems to run counter to the ordinary phenomena of language in his theory that one and the same word may be treated as meaning *castrate* when you want it for the

* "*Hag, v.*[1], north. dial. [a. O.N. *hoggva* (:—*hagg-wan* :—O. Teut. *hauwan*)......] To cut, hew, chop."

etymon of the name of a gelded animal, and *shear* when a shorn animal is in question.

Perhaps he will give us details and quotations from "Moisy's Caen publications." Few of us have access to them. I have not time just now to find out whether or not they are accessible to me, but I shrewdly suspect that the words occur only in an inventory compiled in England, and entered in the cartulary of the Abbey of the Holy Trinity of Caen for Benedictine nuns, in the diocese of Bayeux (Bibliothèque Nationale, MS. Lat. 5650), from fo. 45vo of which Du Cange gives a quotation, which is transferred in part to the 'N.E.D.,' *s.v.* hoggaster.

Round's 'Calendar of Documents preserved in France,' &c., 1899, describes the document from which the quotation is taken (which covers folios 41 to 87 of the cartulary) as a

"detailed inquest on the manors of the abbey in England, evidently made under Henry II......This inquest is followed by one precisely similar for the Norman manors" (*op. cit.*, p. 144, No. 430).

Q. V.

The derivation from O.Nor. *höggva* (base *hagg-*) is not satisfactory, as the vowel does not correspond. A better solution is to derive it from the Norwegian *hogga*, to cut; for which see Ross and Aasen. Rietz, *s.v. hagga*, to cut (whence E. *hag*, to cut), notes that some Swedish dialects likewise employ the form *hogga*. The *o* appears as *u* in Dan. *hugge*. An A.-S. *cg* appears as E. *g* in a few cases, as in *docga*, a dog; *frocga*, a frog; but both these nouns are weak.

CELER.

To the list of surnames beginning Hog may be added "Hogg-gogin," which appears among the list of deaths in a recent number of the *Church Times*. The Rev. J. F. Hogg-Goggin, J.P., is rector of Rufford.

J. A.

BLACK BOTTLES FOR WINE (9th S. ix. 7, 175, 276).—In January, 1901, some workmen, while demolishing some old buildings in Gallowgate, Newcastle, broke into a cellar in which were many of these squat early eighteenth-century black bottles, filled with some kind of liquor, said to have been ale. Some of the workmen imbibed rather too freely. Three of these bottles—two empty and one full—were presented to the Museum of the Newcastle Society of Antiquaries. An illustration of the bottles is given in the *Proceedings* of the society, vol. x., facing p. 2.

R. B—R.

ARMS OF DUTCH EAST INDIA COMPANY (9th S. ix. 9, 118, 272, 312).—It appears doubtful if this Company ever had a regular coat of arms. The regiment "de Meuron" was raised by the Company for duty in its Eastern territories, and was taken into the English service about 1795, when quartered in Ceylon. Its principal colour, or standard, was plain white, bearing in the centre the capital letters V. O. C. interlaced. A correspondent at The Hague, well qualified to know, tells me that this particular cipher was the well-known badge, or insignia, of the old Dutch East India Company, its full title being "Vereenigde Oest Indisches Compagnie." The three capital letters, interlaced, formed its device.　　　　　S. M. MILNE.

"ENGLAND'S DARLING" (9ᵗʰ S. ix. 290).— I have always understood that Edgar Atheling, son of Edward the Outlaw, was "England's darling.' He was the true heir and actually elected king, but not crowned; nor could he have held it against William the Conqueror; but, as the last known survivor of the royal house of Egbert (A.D. 836) and Alfred (A.D. 901), he would naturally be looked up to by the people, and, so to speak, live in memory for generations. What is known of him after Tenchebrai in 1106?　ABSENS.

PRICE OF EGGS (9ᵗʰ S. ix. 147, 277).—The following quotation from an old ballad in the 'Reliques of Ancient English Poetry' may prove illustrative, though scarcely trustworthy. It is there said to be taken from the 'Garland of Goodwill.' The dialect is broad Somersetshire, and the scene the ruins of Glastonbury Abbey :—

IGNORANCE.
Ch' ill tell thee vhat, good vellowe,
　Before the vriers went hence,
A bushell of the best vheate
　Was sold vor vourteen pence
And vorrty egges a penny,
　That were both good and newe;
And this che zay my zelf have zeene
　And yet ich am no Jewe.

Glastonbury Abbey was dissolved in 1539, and seems to have been one of the richest monastic establishments in England. The conversation recorded may be supposed to have taken place some forty years later.
　　　　　JOHN PICKFORD, M.A.
Newbourne Rectory, Woodbridge.

COUNTESS OF DENBIGH (9ᵗʰ S. ix. 247).— The Countess of Denbigh of the period did not die in January, 1725/6, in Cavendish Square, London. The countess of that time was Isabella, daughter of Peter de Jonge (or Young), of Utrecht, in Holland; her husband was William, the fifth Earl of Denbigh, who succeeded to his titles 18 March, 1716. She did not die until 16 May, 1769. Possibly the lady who died in Cavendish Square in 1725/6

was the Countess Dowager of Denbigh—*i.e.*, Hester, daughter of Sir Basil Firebrass, Bart., and widow of Basil, fourth Earl of Denbigh and third Earl of Desmond.
　　　　　RONALD DIXON.
46, Marlborough Avenue, Hull.

PORTRAITS OF EARLY LORD MAYORS (9ᵗʰ S. viii. 485; ix. 173, 232).—I doubt if it would be possible to compile "a complete list of portraits of the Lord Mayors of London." I trust, however, that a list of those in existence may be gradually built up under this heading in the pages of 'N. & Q.' Doubtless there are many such portraits in the custody of the numerous City companies, and it is to be hoped that a record of their existence may be forthcoming I append a few rough notes which may be of service.

The Mercers' Company possesses a copy of the ordinances of the almshouses founded by Sir Richard Whittington, "thrice Lord Mayor of London," who died in 1423. On these ordinances is depicted, by a contemporary artist, a representation of Whittington's deathbed,

"surrounded by his executors, his chaplain, his doctor, the master of his almshouses, and his twelve bedesmen. The picture is interesting for the portraits it contains. The fine, but wasted face and frame of Whittington himself; the small figure, instinct with energy and capacity, of John Carpenter, the Town Clerk, to whom we owe the 'Liber Albus,' and who was himself a member of the Mercers' Company; the characteristic expressions and attitudes of John Coventry and William Grove, the other executors, are well worthy of notice."*

The portrait of Sir Lionel Duckett, Lord Mayor in 1572,

"in his robes as Lord Mayor, said to have been painted by Holbein, was for many years in the possession of his descendants, and was recently sold by Sir George F. Duckett, Bart., F.S.A., to the Mercers' Company."†

"The ceremony of administering the oath to Alderman Newnham (Lord Mayor in 1782) is commemorated in a curious picture in the City Art Gallery, presented to the Corporation by Alderman Boydell, painted by William Miller, and containing upwards of 120 portraits."‡

A portrait of Sir John Guyer, Lord Mayor in 1646, is in possession of his descendant —— Biggs, Esq., of Stockton, Wilts.

At the Bethlem Hospital may be seen a portrait of Sir William Withers, Lord Mayor in 1707.

The Skinners' Company possesses a full-length portrait of Sir Thomas Pilkington,

* 'The Mercers' Company and some of its Eminent Members,' by E. W. Brabrook, F.S.A., F.R.S.L. Privately printed, 1889.
† *Ibid.*　　　　　‡ *Ibid.*

Lord Mayor in the years 1689, 1690, and 1691. A copy of this picture is given in Wadmore's 'Account of the Skinners' Company.'

In the Guildhall hangs a fine portrait of Sir Robert Clayton, Lord Mayor in 1679. It was painted by order of the Governors of the London Workhouse, and removed to its present quarters on the breaking up of that establishment. The frame was carved by Grinling Gibbons. In the British Museum collection is a mezzotint portrait of Sir Robert, drawn by Riley, and engraved by Smith. A process picture of this appeared in the *Pall Mall Magazine* for November, 1894 (p. 358). There is a life-size statue of Sir Robert Clayton in the central court of St. Thomas's Hospital. It is of white marble, and was erected by the governors during his lifetime. Sir Robert Clayton is buried at Bletchington [?], Surrey. In the south chancel of the church is a large monument to his memory, on which appears his figure in white marble, clad in the insignia of office as Lord Mayor of London.

In 'Memorials of Stepney Parish' (Hill & Frere, 1890-1) is an engraving of Sir William Ryder, Lord Mayor in 1600. It is taken from a portrait published by G. Richardson in 1797.   JOHN T. PAGE.

West Haddon, Northamptonshire.

PRONUNCIATION OF "SEA" (8th S. viii. 4, 109, 151, 209).—At the third of these references PROF. SKEAT asked,

"for the sake of the information of us all, what quotations, later than 1780, can be found in which some standard author, using a pronunciation that is neither provincial, nor Irish, nor intentionally comic, clearly shows that he meant the word *sea* to be pronounced as *say*."

One quotation was furnished (8th S. viii. 210) in reply from a poem published in 1825; and I would add another from 'The Rover; or, a Pirate's Faith,' by Thomas Ansell, issued two years later by William Sams, "Bookseller to the Royal Family, St. James's Street, London." In this it was written :—

> Thus many a boisterous hour was spent
> In strife upon the weltering sea:
> For storm was the Pirates' element;
> And war to them but casual play.

But elsewhere in the poem Ansell gave the usual pronunciation by riming *sea* with *lee*; while, as if in anticipation to justify PROF. SKEAT's declaration (8th S. viii. 152) that "the rhyme of *seas* with *ease* proves nothing at all," he spoke of

> Revelling in the spicy breeze,
> In wanton luxury of ease,
> Sweetly breath'd o'er Levant seas.
>   ALFRED F. ROBBINS.

CAMBRIDGE HEATH, SOUTH HACKNEY (9th S. ix. 205).—COL. PRIDEAUX quotes from certain Hundred Rolls—*re* Hackney—showing that Egidius de Wodeham made a foss, ditch, or moat at Kyngesteslane (Hackney), which, we are told, is doubtless the modern Mare Street. This brings forward a question I have often wished to ask, What is the origin of this name, Mare Street, and the meaning? Probably I may be told that the question has been raised and answered in 'N. & Q.' before. If so, I beg pardon. If not, I would, while raising the question, suggest the answer that Conjecture (precocious hussy!) has supplied me with. Mare Street she takes to be Mær Street. And if so it is noticeable that just as Hake(neye) has become lowered in the vowel-tone to Hack, so Mær has become lowered in tone to Mare. The ditch, or moat, or foss of Egidius de Wodeham would presumably be or form a landmark, instituting a boundary (mere) of some nature and purport.   B.

"MACHINE" = PUBLIC COACH (9th S. viii. 462; ix. 37, 116).—Tramping from Strome Ferry to Balmacarra, co. Ross, in September, 1899, approaching the latter village, I asked a boy belonging to the place whether I could there obtain a *vehicle* to convey my party back to Strome. The boy looked puzzled, evidently not at all comprehending at first what I meant by a "vehicle." At length he replied, "Do you mean a machine, sir? Oh, you can get a machine at the hotel."
                    W. W.

Lewisham.

"Machine" is still in use nearly, if not quite, all over Scotland, in the sense of "carriage," particularly of a four-wheeled carriage. I have heard it all over the west, and also in the east and centre. "To hire a machine" is the regular phrase for hiring a carriage.   F. J. C.

The name "machine," given to public coaches, appears to have been much earlier than stated by any correspondent, so far, and really to have been contemporary with their introduction. The word "machine" really expresses the astonishment of the time at what was thought an extraordinary invention. Swift, writing about the year 1700, uses the word, applying it to the Chester stage coach, in a satirical description of a journey to Chester :—

> By steps and lanthorn enter the machine,
> And take my place—how cordially!—between
> Two aged matrons of excessive bulk.
>   CHARLES G. HARPER.

Petersham, Surrey.

THE KING OF TORELORE (9ᵗʰ S. ix. 246).—This curious circumstance seems to be alluded to in 'Hudibras,' part iii. canto i. 705-10 :—

> But all the mischief is the doubt
> On whose account they first broke out.
> For tho' Chineses go to bed,
> And lie-in in their ladies' stead,
> And, for the pains they took before,
> Are nurs'd and pamper'd to do more, &c.

JOHN PICKFORD, M.A.
Newbourne Rectory, Woodbridge.

JAY, THE WOODLAND BIRD (9ᵗʰ S. ix. 308).—For the origin of Jay as an English surname and for the name of the bird, see 5ᵗʰ S. i. 128, 195, 336, 437.
EVERARD HOME COLEMAN.
71, Brecknock Road.

DUTCH REFUGEES IN LONDON IN 1566 (9ᵗʰ S. ix. 289).—Try the 'Registers of the Dutch Church in Austin Friars,' by Mr. Moens ; also the Southwark Cathedral Registers.
C. MASON.
29, Emperor's Gate, S.W.

MICHAEL BRUCE AND BURNS (9ᵗʰ S. vii. 466 ; viii. 70, 148, 312, 388 527 ; ix. 95, 209, 309).—With reference to the Bruce-Logan 'Ode to the Cuckoo,' I may mention that some years ago, when at Blair Adam with the late William Adam, M.P., we had some conversation on this subject, when he told me that Michael Bruce had been born close there, and that he had gone very carefully into the subject, and was perfectly satisfied that Michael Bruce was the author and not Logan.
G. C. W.

OSORIO FAMILY (9ᵗʰ S. ix. 307).—*Vide* Dr. Moses Gaster's 'History of the Synagogue,' lately reviewed in 'N. & Q.,' pp. 146-8 in the volume noticed.
M. D. DAVIS.

STANDSFIELD (9ᵗʰ S. ix. 309).—A licence was issued at Lewes, 20 March, 1597/8, for the marriage of John Stanfelde, of Clive, merchant, to Ellinor Comber, of St. John sub Castro, Lewes, virgin. The sureties to the bond were the said John Stanfelde and Thomas Comber, father of the maiden. This information appears in a volume of marriage licences I am now editing for the Sussex Record Society. Though not a reply to MR. COMBER's query, a note of this licence will probably be of interest to him.
E. H. W. DUNKIN.
The Heath, Fairlight, Hastings.

William Newton, of Gray's Inn and Southover, who died 24 May, 1648, aged eighty-four, married Jane, daughter of William Apsley, of Thackham, but Horsley does not speak of her as a widow. She is the only Jane mentioned by him as marrying a Newton. From them descended the Newtons of Lindfield. John Stansfield died 23 Feb., 1626, and was buried at All Saints', Lewes, as was his first wife.
CAROLINE STEGGALL.

ARMS OF CONTINENTAL CITIES (9ᵗʰ S. ix. 308).—' Il Dizionario Corografico dell' Italia,' by Prof. Amato Amati, which is to be found on the bookshelves of the Reading-room of the British Museum, contains the arms of the principal cities and towns of Italy with their proper tinctures.
JOHN HEBB.

The armorial bearings of many German cities figure in the various editions of the artistic 'Münchener Calendar,' published annually for the last ten years or so. The arms of some French cities appear in ' Les Français peints par Eux-mêmes,' in the ' Noblesse et Chevalerie de Cambrai,' and in most of the admirable French heraldry books produced in the seventeenth century.
JOHN HOBSON MATTHEWS.
Town Hall, Cardiff.

SHAKESPEARE v. BACON (9ᵗʰ S. ix. 245).—Following up Q. A., may I mention that Wordsworth in referring to Bacon says, "The most singular thing is that in all the writings of Bacon there is not one allusion to Shakespeare." Now as Bacon survived Shakespeare ten years, and never even mentioned his name, it is surely a proof that Bacon had nothing to do with Shakespeare's plays, notwithstanding the "grotesque gabble of the cipher," as Q. A. aptly quotes from Sir Henry Irving's lecture.
GEORGE WATSON.
Penrith.

LONDON LIBRARIES IN THE ELIZABETHAN ERA (9ᵗʰ S. ix. 329).—The query propounded by PROF. JAMES D. BUTLER is one of those which, for lack of any satisfactory solution hitherto (*pace* the theorizings of oversure Shakespearians), have led many to doubt as to the traditional authorship of the Shakespearian plays, and largely contributed to the rise of the troublesome and pestilent sect of literary heretics known as " Baconians "—a sect which, though, like the Nazarenes of old, "everywhere spoken against," seems largely on the increase. Assuredly there were no libraries in the London of Elizabeth, such as the British Museum and the like, open to the public, to which a player in the interval of learning his part, or of other stage business, could resort for study or literary reference, or, if there were, there is no record of them. The man of mystery, therefore, from Stratford, if he were the

author of the plays he took part in or placed upon the stage, must either have had other sources of information peculiar to himself or must have acquired his all-pervading knowledge, philological and otherwise, by pure inspiration, or, on the Dogberrian theory, from the light of nature—alternatives which a plain man may surely have some hesitation in accepting without being writ down an "ass," or pronounced a "candidate for Bedlam." JOHN HUTCHINSON.
Middle Temple Library.

In chap. iii. of vol. i. of Macaulay's 'History of England' one of the complex queries under the above heading will find solution if the paragraph 'Scarcity of Books in Country Places' be read. STAPLETON MARTIN.
The Firs, Norton, Worcester.

'MRS. CARNAC,' BY SIR JOSHUA REYNOLDS (9ᵗʰ S. ix. 346).—If interest attaches to the subject of Sir Joshua's well-known portrait, the following details may be added to the note of MR. L. SCHANK in a recent issue. General Carnac was the descendant of an *émigré* belonging to a noble Huguenot family in Brittany, who settled in Ireland after the revocation of the Edict of Nantes. Having served, as stated, with distinction in the army in India, and as Clive's lieutenant at Plassey, General Carnac returned to England, and sat as member of Parliament for Tewkesbury. He married Elizabeth (the subject of the picture), daughter of Thomas Revett, M.P. and High Sheriff of Derbyshire, whose election in opposition to the Devonshire and Chesterfield interest caused some stir at the time, as noticed by Horace Walpole in one of his letters, and as described in Mr. Rathbone's 'Correspondence of Lady Jane Coke.' Mr. Revett married, according to the *Gentleman's Magazine*, "the celebrated Miss Sibley," but inquiry in your columns has not elicited any information as to her claim to celebrity. Mr. Revett was of the branch of the ancient Suffolk family of Stowmarket and Branderton which settled in Derbyshire. On the death of General Carnac without issue, his property passed to his brother-in-law, Mr. J. Rivett, my grandfather, on the condition of his assuming the name of Carnac in addition to his patronymic; so that the Rivett family, although in no way connected with the Carnacs in blood, bear that additional surname. According to Collins the picture was sold by Sir Joshua for 73*l.* 10*s.* It was, unfortunately, resold by the late Sir J. Rivett-Carnac, Bart., M.P., to Lord Hertford for 1,795*l.* 10*s.*, and is now the property of

the nation as a part of the Wallace bequest. Last year, at Christie's, a mezzotint by Smith of the picture realized the record price of 1,160 guineas, or some sixteen times as much as was originally paid for the portrait itself.
J. H. RIVETT-CARNAC,
Col. (Vols.), Aide-de-Camp to the King.

SHERIFFS OF STAFFORDSHIRE (9ᵗʰ S. ix. 342).—A complete list of the sheriffs of Staffordshire, from the accession of Henry I. to the year 1798, is given in Stebbing Shaw's 'History of Staffordshire.'
B. D. MOSELEY.
Burslem.

AN HEUSKARIAN RARITY IN THE BODLEIAN LIBRARY (9ᵗʰ S. viii. 378; ix. 111).—In reply to MR. R. L. POOLE, I have only to say that I asked Mr. E. W. B. Nicholson whether he did not think the marginal notes, to which I referred, to be written in Mr. Thomas's hand (with which I was well acquainted during the period when he worked at Bask in the Bodleian), and found him inclined to attribute them to him. If MR. POOLE is sure that they were written by a member of the librarian's staff, had that person any right to do so? Was it not "an 'illegal' act," to use MR. POOLE's words? I did not charge Mr. Thomas with it *before* his much-lamented death, because I never saw the notes in question until last autumn. Having occasion to mention them for their critical value, I thought it right also to point out that they were a breach of the rules of the library.
E. S. DODGSON.
Hotel Peninsular, Madrid.

"ENDORSEMENT": "DORSO-VENTRALITY" (9ᵗʰ S. ix. 64, 212, 331).—The warrants issued to incumbents by the Ecclesiastical Commissioners require the signature of the payee upon the face, and no indorsement is demanded by the bankers. The same is true of railway companies' dividend warrants.
W. C. B.

INTRODUCTION OF TROUSERS (9ᵗʰ S. ix. 268).—If the following extract from the article entitled 'Clothing—Costume,' by William and Robert Chambers, in their 'Information for the People,' vol. i. (1857), is correct, the authorities of Trinity College, Cambridge, were somewhat behind the times when in October, 1812, they objected to the wearing of "pantaloons or trousers":—

"The comparatively simple form of dress of the Sans Culottes found many admirers in England, and soon became common among young men; the change from antique fashions was also greatly helped by the imposition of a tax on the use of hair-powder, which was henceforth generally abandoned. Pantaloons, which fitted closely to the leg, remained in very common use by those persons who had adopted them till about the year 1814, when the wearing of trousers, already introduced into the army, became fashionable. It is proper, however, to mention that trousers had for the previous 15 or 20 years been used by boys, and were perhaps from them adopted by the army. Previous to the French Revolution, the dress of boys was almost the same as that of men."

RONALD DIXON.
46, Marlborough Avenue, Hull.

If MR. ANDREWS will take the trouble to turn to 3rd S. v.; 5th S. xii.; 6th S. x.; 7th S. vii.; 8th S. ii., he will find all particulars respecting this comparatively modern article of men's attire.

EVERARD HOME COLEMAN.
71, Brecknock Road.

OLD SPOONS (9th S. ix. 348). — The marks are probably foreign. Each silver piece marked at Goldsmiths' Hall has five marks: (1) the sovereign's head (after 1784); (2) the lion passant (the standard mark), probably introduced between 1538 and 1558; (3) the standard mark, fixed 8 & 9 William III., 1696–7; (4) leopard's head, the hall-mark; (5) the maker's mark (an old custom).

The London district mark is a leopard's head; for York, three lions and a cross; for Exeter, a castle with three wings; for Chester, three wheatsheaves; for Newcastle, three castles; for Birmingham, an anchor; for Sheffield, a crown; for Edinburgh, a castle and lion; for Glasgow, a tree, salmon, and ring; and for Dublin, the figure of Hibernia. (See Cripps's 'Old English Plate.')

EVERARD HOME COLEMAN.
71, Brecknock Road.

BENJAMIN HEATH, OF EXETER (9th S. iv. 379, 485). — Reference having already been made to the brothers Benjamin and John Heath— successively Town Clerks of Exeter during the latter half of the eighteenth century—the following (cut from the *Western Times* for 5 April) appears to have some interest :—

"The portrait of ' Thomas Heath, Esq.,' who was Mayor of Exeter in 1738, and again in 1747, is to be presented to the City, on behalf of subscribers, by Mr. John Gidley. The portrait of the Mayor is three-quarter length, and his Worship is represented sitting in his robes in the pose customary with artists of the period. The picture is chiefly valuable for its local association, and for the fact that it was painted by Hudson, under whom the great Sir Joshua Reynolds commenced his studies in London in 1741. Of Hudson, Allan Cunningham, in his ' Lives of British Painters,' says, ' He was the most distinguished portrait painter of that time; was, nevertheless, a man of little skill and less talent, who could paint a head, but without other aid was unable to place it upon the shoulders. He

was, in truth, a mere manufacturer of portraits...... Reynolds proceeded with his studies under Hudson; but it seldom happens that a man of no genius and moderate skill can give counsel to one who longs for distinction and has the talent to obtain it.' Whatever may be thought of Hudson's paintings as works of art, it is well that the City should have in its keeping all portraits of its past Mayors, even if the heads only are worthy of admiration from the art critic's point of view."

HARRY HEMS.
Fair Park, Exeter.

" GENTLE SHEPHERD, TELL ME WHERE " (9th S. viii. 423, 530; ix. 113). —The last words of ch. xi., bk. ii., ' Past and Present,' are " Gentle shepherd, tell me what!" Is it too much to presume that Carlyle had the words of ' The Wreath' running through his mind at the time he was writing?

JOHN T. PAGE.
West Haddon, Northamptonshire.

CELLINI AND SHAKESPEARE (9th S. ix. 308). —Roscoe's translation of the ' Capitolo,' addressed to Luca Martini, is in no sense a literal one. The line

Vo per la stanza, e cigli e capo arriccio

is well rendered by John Addington Symonds as follows :—

My cell I search, prick brows and hair upright.

Symonds has been, as he points out, at pains to preserve the roughness of the original, whereas Roscoe rewrites it. " Capo arriccio" simply means the hair standing on end with horror, and the comparison to the quills on a porcupine did not occur to Cellini. We may safely acquit Shakespeare, therefore, of any suspicion of plagiarism, nor need we ascribe to Bacon the authorship of the ' Vita di Benvenuto Cellini,' and thus add to the burden which Mrs. Gallup has already placed upon his broad shoulders.

EDWARD M. BORRAJO.
The Library, Guildhall, E.C.

In the edition of ' La Vita scritta da lui Medesimo' published by Suc. Le Monnier (Firenze, 1891) there is nothing resembling the lines quoted by ST. SWITHIN in the ' Capitolo' of Cellini in praise of prison life, for a short term at least as a salutary lesson. Can it be a ludicrous blunder in the translation of the first line of the eighteenth triplet?

Vo per la stanza, e' cigli e 'l capo arriccio,

which expresses no horror, but elation or alertness in hitting on the means of providing writing appliances such as prisoners in romance resort to. It is not credible that Cellini wrote so long a poem on the fly-leaves of a Bible with a splinter torn from the door

with his teeth and a mixture of triturated paving-stone and urine.   B. D. MOSELEY.
Burslem.

The resemblance to Shakespeare which ST. SWITHIN notes in Cellini's verses must, I think, be due to the translator. The late Mr. J. A. Symonds's version gives no hint of it :—

> My cell I search, prick brows and hair upright,
> Then turn me toward a cranny in the door,
> And with my teeth a splinter disunite.

One would, in fact, scarcely recognize this as the same passage, but Mr. Symonds usually stuck close to his original, I understand, and there can hardly be a doubt that he is here translating almost literally.   C. C. B.

Symonds's translation of the 'Capitolo' of Cellini has one line,

> My cell I search, prick brows and hair upright,

in place of the three in the version by Roscoe. I have not the original Italian here, but am sure the fretful porcupine is Roscoe, and not Cellini.   S. C. H.
Burlington, Vermont.

THE MAN IN THE IRON MASK (9th S. ix. 328).—Your correspondent may find additional particulars in *Chambers's Journal*, First Series, iv. ; 'Chambers's Book of Days'; Kirby's 'Wonderful Museum,' ii. ; *Cornhill*, vol. xxi. ; *Temple Bar*, May, 1872 ; *All the Year Round*, Second Series, xvii. ; Granger's 'Wonderful Museum,' v. i. ; and 'N. & Q.,' 1st S. v., vii., viii., xi., xii. ; 4th S. iv., v., xii.   EVERARD HOME COLEMAN.
71, Brecknock Road.

Any one seeking information on this subject should not overlook Gibbon's dissertation thereon, entitled 'A Dissertation on the Subject of L'Homme au Masque de Fer.' This is in vol. v. of the 1814 edition of the 'Miscellaneous Works,' p. 41, and at p. 693 of the 1837 edition (where the title is given differently).   A. N. O.

There is an account of the "Iron Mask" in the 'Book of Curiosities,' by the Rev. I Platts.
J. HOLDEN MACMICHAEL.

SEASALTER (9th S. ix. 189).—I take the following from Virtue's 'National Gazetteer' for 1868 :—

"Seasalter Liberty, a par. in the hund. of Whitstable, lathe of St. Augustine, co. Kent, 5 miles N.W. of Canterbury, its post town. It is a coastguard station and considerable fishing village. The land is chiefly in meadow, with a small proportion of arable and garden. It is mentioned in Domesday Book, and comprises the hmts. of Harwick and Seasalter. On the shore is an extensive Oyster bed, called the Pollard, belonging to the Dean and Chapter of Canterbury, who let it to the Whitstable company of free dredgers. The appropriate tithes belonging to the Dean and Chapter of Canterbury have been commuted for a rent charge of 225*l.*, and the vicarial one for 160*l.*, besides an impropriate glebe of 39 acres. The living is a vic. in the dioc. of Canterbury, val. 130*l.*, in the patron. of the dean and chapter. The church is dedicated to St. Alphage. The Independents have a place of worship. There is a school endowed by Mrs. F. Fagg in 1794. The fairs formerly held here have been discontinued."
ARTHUR FORSHAW.
48, Hanover Square, Bradford.

MINIATURE OF COL. GEO. FLEETWOOD (9th S. ix. 48, 154, 175, 234, 261).—It seems evident that a son of the above settled to trade in London, and it is of interest to note that a great-uncle of the father had preceded this line of glass-sellers therein. I refer to Robert Fleetwood, citizen and merchant tailor of London, who was a brother to Thomas of the Vache, reputed parent of thirty-two children by two wives. Such fecundity is a terror to genealogists. Now the above Robert was father to Sir William of Missenden, born 1535, died 1593, Recorder of London, and also a merchant tailor. It is alleged that of this couple father or son was illegitimate. What is known thereon? For myself, I have not traced the name of any alleged wife of Robert who thus settled in London.
ABSENS.

CASTOR SUGAR (9th S. ix. 307).—A diligent reader of, and occasional writer in, 'N. & Q.,' I have heard of ghost-words. I think this *castor* may be one. We all know the pepper caster, but we do not all know the sugar caster, an old-fashioned ornament of the dessert table, out of fashion in the forties, but brought back in the seventies of last century. In the sixties cook pounded the sugar, and the sugar spoon with its pierced bowl scattered it, the grocer knowing nothing of this. The demand at last came to the grocer. He had heard of castor oil, and perhaps of castor, the beaver, and he labelled his sugar dust "castor sugar." The people swallow and pay for it as labelled.
JOHN P. STILWELL.
Hilfield, Yateley, Hants.

This name must be of recent date, having not yet found its way into any modern English dictionary. The usual spelling *castor* is evidently misleading with regard to its origin, since it derives its name from the "caster," or strainer, through which it is strewn. The corresponding German name, *Streu-Zucker*, is properly rendered by "powdered sugar, or caster sugar," in Muret-Sanders's new encyclopædic German - English dictionary, which was completed last year.

H. Krebs.

Harvest Bell (9th S. viii. 201, 308, 427; ix. 15, 231).—Long ago in Swiss pedestrianism, in addition to the noonday village bell, I heard one rang one hour earlier. To my question as to the ground of this custom, it was answered that many women worked in the fields side by side with their husbands, and that it was necessary for them to go home an hour before noon for preparing the midday meal as well as to care for the children.   James D. Butler.

"Giglet" (8th S. viii. 271; ix. 114).—The following extract from the criticism furnished in the *Era* of 12 April, by its Paris correspondent, of 'Gigolette,' an Ambigu drama, by MM. Pierre Decourcelle and Edmond Tarbé, is a striking addition to what has already been written as to the meaning of the word *giglet* :—

"An interesting melodrama, one of the best M. Decourcelle ever wrote, which obtained great popular favour when originally produced at the Ambigu nine or ten years ago, has been revived there with equal promise of success. Its title needs explanation, I should think, for English readers, and the task is both risky and unpalatable. Some dozen years ago the word was added to Parisian slang by a song that obtained popularity in the music-halls. It signifies a woman of the lowest class, one of those wretched beings who ply their miserable trade on our outer boulevards, under the ægis of a protector or 'bully,' who lives on the unfortunate creature's earnings, and wallops her into the bargain. He is a gigolo, she a gigolette. When the piece first appeared a discussion was opened in one of the Paris papers regarding the etymology of the word, and its origin seems to date back much further than the song which brought it into common use. The reader has only to take up his English dictionary, however, and he will discover it there as 'giglot,' derived from 'giggle,' while Shakespearian scholars may remember that the immortal bard used it occasionally. In 'Cymbeline' (Act III. scene i.) we find the Queen exclaiming: 'The famed Cassibelan, who was once at point—O giglot fortune!—to master Cæsar's sword'; in '1 King Henry IV.' (Act IV. scene vii.) John Talbot tells Joan of Arc that he 'was not born to be the pillage of a giglot wench'; and in 'Measure for Measure' (Act V. scene i.) Escalus says, 'Away with those giglots,' alluding to Mariana and Isabella, who, by-the-by, were nothing of the sort. Everything is to be found in Shakespeare, as we know, but who could have dreamt of his supplying titles for café-concert ditties and Ambigu melodramas, as seems to have been really the case in the present instance?"

The word, of course, is still used in some parts of this country as signifying young people in general and female farm-servants in particular; and its employment by the town clerk of a municipal body is to be found in the following official advertisement, issued in December, 1896 :—

"Launceston Christmas Market.—In consequence of Christmas Day next falling on a Saturday, notice is hereby given that the Launceston Christmas Market, which would otherwise be held on that day, will be held on Thursday, the 23rd day of December next. No alteration will be made in the date of the Launceston Giglet's market, which will be held on Saturday, the 1st day of January, 1897. By order of the Town Council.—C. H. Peter, Town Clerk."

Alfred F. Robbins.

Tennis : Origin of the Name (9th S. ix. 27, 75, 153, 238, 272). — If the O.H.G. *tenni*, modern German *die Tenne*, threshing-floor, had been taken over by Old French, it would have been organically changed; besides, there is no indication of its existence there. And if it had been adopted from German at a much later period by the French without organic alteration, it ought to be shown, first, when and why this took place, that in Germany the word *Tenne* was ever connected with the game of tennis, and that the French made the acquaintance of the latter through their eastern neighbours.

Mr. Julian Marshall is not right in his statement that the word *tenez* never meant and never means "take it." He need only take up Littré's great dictionary; this is what he will find under *tenir*, 1, p. 2181, second column :—

"Absolument. Tiens, tenez, *prend, prenez.* 'Tiens, voilà de quoi vaincre et taureaux et gens d'armes.'—Corneille, 'Toison d'Or,' iv. 4. 'Tenez, lui dit-il, votre anneau.'—Fénelon, t. xix. p. 29, 'Rosimond et Braminte.' Il s'emploie aussi à une personne que l'on frappe, qui subit quelque mauvais traitement. 'Tiens, tiens, voilà le coup que je t'ai réservé.' —Racine, 'Andromaque,' v. 5."

And this meaning *tiens, tenez,* have kept; you may hear it used every day for *voilà, prends, prenez.* With this I do not intend to say, of course, that modern French tennis-players employ it when serving a ball.

G. Krueger.

Miscellaneous.

NOTES ON BOOKS, &c.

The Mystery of William Shakespeare. By his Honour Judge Webb. (Longmans & Co.)

It is narrated concerning some humourist that, weary of the discussion concerning the authorship of the plays attributed to Shakespeare, he declared that he had come to the conclusion that they were not written by William Shakespeare, but by another man of the same name living in the same epoch. So strangely does "the whirligig of time" bring "in his revenges" that the *jeu d'esprit* of yesterday is the sober argument of to-day. In a book which he qualifies as "a summary of evidence," and in which he treats with respect his immediate predecessors in the study of Shakespeare, Judge Webb presents as two separate men the Stratford player and the author of 'Venus and Adonis,' 'The Rape of Lucrece,' and the plays contained in the first folio. In order to avoid the possibility of mistake the player is always spoken of as Shakspere, the name into which that of the Stratford family ultimately crystallized. The author meanwhile is as invariably called William Shakespeare. Starting from this point, Judge Webb has produced an ingenious, erudite, and closely reasoned book, the aim of which is to establish that William Shakespeare is, in fact, Francis Bacon. Of the numerous volumes *pro* and *con.* on the question which crowd our table soliciting our attention this is the most considerable. Its arguments are not to be answered off-hand, and a complete refutation of what is advanced would involve a labour from which all but intentional participators in what after all is a silly discussion will be disposed to shrink. We find the writer, however, an advocate rather than a judge, and hold much that he says to be prejudiced and unfair. As regards the difference in name on which Judge Webb elects to dwell, he will scarcely deny that in Elizabethan names spelling is a matter of no consequence. Dekker's name was spelt a dozen different ways, and a century later a name so plain as Cibber could be converted into Keyber. We do not assert that Judge Webb founds what can exactly be called an argument upon the spelling of the names, but he obviously regards it as of importance. Like a skilled counsel, moreover, he unduly depreciates and disparages the position of the defendant, as we must hold Shakespeare to be if we assume this to be an action. To speak of Shakespeare—we beg pardon, we mean "Shakspere"—as "the uneducated or half-educated young countryman from Stratford" involves what our author must see is a *petitio principii.* Again, we are told that "all the traditions about the young man are of a degrading character," a view which we immediately reject. The fact that when a youth Shakespeare with other lads chased the king's deer, probably in sport, no more stamps him as a poacher than the fact that some of us in boyhood robbed an apple orchard stamps us as thieves. If there is one thing which mislikes us in the treatment of Shakespeare by his biographers in general, it is the effort to free him from every customary infirmity of adolescence in early manhood and show him as a "faultless monster which the world ne'er saw." Whatever else Shakespeare was he was not a Puritan. So strong is Judge Webb's animus against "Shakspere" that he seems to regard it as telling against him that Stratford in the time of "Shakspere," according to the showing of Mr. [Halliwell-] Phillipps, was a town of "fetid watercourses, piggeries, and middens." Far too much is made of Greene's petulant utterances, probably due to misconception, while everything that tells in favour of "Shakspere" is deprived of significance, and those who express a favourable opinion concerning him are the subjects of depreciation or attack. Davies of Hereford identifies the player with the poet, and is therefore dubbed "the Hereford Poetaster." William Camden even incurs a sneer, perhaps merited, in consequence of praising the Stratford writer's "genius and great abilities." Fuller's utterances concerning the wit combats between Shakespeare and Jonson are characterized as "apocalyptic," and the attitude of the Drydens,

Tates, and others who arranged Shakespeare's plays is, unintentionally no doubt, misrepresented. Scarcely one of these men is there who in modernizing Shakespeare, or "tagging" his lines with rimes, does not express his admiration for his original and assume it to be shared by the public. It was while perverting 'The Tempest' that Dryden wrote:—

> But Shakespeare's magic could not copied be;
> Within that circle none durst walk but he.

We acquit Judge Webb of anything more than an over-anxious desire to establish his case, which renders him something less than fair. His book is fruitful in suggestion, and may be studied with pleasure and in some respects with profit. If we have not dealt with its main theme it is because we do not wish to embark upon what we seriously regard as a futile controversy, and because we feel that in getting rid of one set of difficulties we encounter another set not less formidable. In his endeavour to prove "Shakspere" little more than a clown Judge Webb falls into that common error of making inadequate allowance for exceptional natures. It is only in degree that Shakespeare is more of a miracle than Burns or than James Ferguson.

The Prose Works of Jonathan Swift. Edited by Temple Scott. Vol. IX. (Bell & Sons.)
The ninth volume of the convenient and attractive edition of Swift's 'Prose Works' added to "Bohn's Standard Library" consists of Swift's contributions to the *Tatler,* the *Examiner,* the *Spectator,* and the *Intelligencer.* These constitute some of the most characteristic, most brilliant, and most readable of Swift's writings. To judge how true this is the reader has only to turn to the account of 'La Platonne' (*Tatler,* No. 32), with which the volume opens. Mr. Temple Scott rightly disputes the appropriateness of the term "Prince of Journalists" applied to Swift, declaring it both misleading and inaccurate. His introduction is indeed excellent in all respects. For ourselves, after skimming afresh a portion of the contents, we sigh for an opportunity of rereading them through. The style is admirably pellucid and furnishes a lesson how to write. It is simply the best.

Butterflies and Moths of Europe. By W. F. Kirby, F.L.S. (Cassell & Co.)
In a brilliant cover appears the first instalment of a valuable and attractive work. Three plates, two of them superbly coloured, are given, and with them the introduction. If the work is continued as it begins it will be a delight to the naturalist.

We are most of us very ignorant of all things which relate to Abyssinia. The fact that the people profess a form of Christianity believed to be of a Monophysite type, and that the nobles regard themselves as descended from Solomon and the Queen of Sheba, about exhausts our knowledge; even the war which we carried on there some years ago excited little permanent interest regarding either the country or a people which, whatever their faults may have been, have worked out for themselves a civilization of a highly interesting character. The writer of 'The Recent History of Abyssinia,' in the *Edinburgh Review* for April, is one of the few who have studied not only the race, but the land itself. As to whether he has travelled therein we are of course ignorant, but at any rate he has acquired a surprising amount of knowledge on a very difficult and confusing subject. 'The Rabbit' is a sporting article of a kind which even non-sporting men will enjoy. The writer naturally speculates as to the native home of the rabbit, but wisely hesitates to express a confident opinion. That it is not a native of the North is certain. So far as is known at present it seems probable that it arrived in Europe, by way of Spain, from Northern Africa. Before the great enclosures of the eighteenth century rabbit-warrens were very common, from the East Riding of Yorkshire to the Thames, but new processes of agriculture have in most districts supplanted the warren by crops of barley and turnips. A few still remain, and their denizens are an interesting study for those who care to observe animals in a wild state. The hearing of the rabbit is as acute as that of the cat, but we do not think its eyesight reaches far. On a summer's evening we have watched them from very near at hand without their being in the least degree alarmed, but when the very slightest noise was made they at once fled to their holes. We have an excellent piece of work in 'The Death Legend in Folk-lore.' It seems but a short time ago when the very few people who cared at all about the belief of those who continued to accept the misconceptions of nature which they had derived from a remote ancestry thought either that each separate story represented an isolated superstition, or that the whole of them were derived from what were called classic sources. We are in a far different position now. Many highly competent persons are doing their best to elucidate the folk-lore of all countries by scientific methods, and as a consequence, though there is, as was to be expected, much difference of opinion on many points, these crude theories have fallen into the background and the books containing them have been discarded, and are now of no value whatever except for the records of fact which they preserve. The folk-lore which has gathered around death, the grave, and the disembodied spirit is vast beyond comprehension: some little of it is touchingly beautiful, but the greater part inspires in the believer abject terror. The writer of the present article has gleaned in many far-separated fields samples which give his readers a by no means exaggerated picture of the kind of dream-world in which our forefathers lived, and by which many in lands called Christian are still haunted. The labour has been well bestowed, for what he has garnered will form a centre around which new facts, as they come in, will arrange themselves almost automatically. The paper on 'Forests and Forestal Laws' will well repay study, although it is by no means easy reading. The forest laws, tyrannous as they were in some of their provisions, might not have been unbearable had they been honestly and reasonably administered, but in the Middle Ages even wise and strong kings had little control over their subordinates, except when they were close at hand; thus an amount of wrong was inflicted for which the laws themselves were only in an indirect way responsible. This forestal tyranny had a long life, and even when decrepit was very hard to kill. We owe to it the harsh game-laws, which remained practically unaltered until our grandfathers' time. There have been frequent mistakes as to the right of free-warren, which certain lords of manors have claimed, even in recent days. It is far too thorny a subject for us to discuss, but readers interested in this curious survival

will find here incidental information of no small value. The paper on 'Assyrian Politics' shows how far deeper as well as wider was the civilization of ancient Assyria than we had any idea of but a few years ago. When we compare the state of that interesting land as it was in the seventh century before our era with what it has now become, painful thoughts arise, and we feel at times inclined to question whether what is called progress is in every case a march upwards. The documents here made use of have been translated into French by the Rev. A. J. Delattre, S.J. Their general sense is beyond dispute, but such translations are extraordinarily difficult, and as further texts come to light some slight corrections may be called for.

The *Playgoer* for May reproduces some of the more striking scenes in 'Ben-Hur,' and has much theatrical information.

By the death of Sir George Floyd Duckett, Bart., in his ninety-first year, England loses a distinguished archæologist and 'N. & Q.' an old friend. Sir George, who was the third baronet, was educated at Harrow and Christ Church, was a knight of various orders, was appointed by the French Government an officer of Public Instruction, and a major in the German Legion. His books included a 'Technological Military Dictionary' and contributions to many literary and antiquarian societies. He was specially interested in the Cluniac foundations in England, on which he wrote much. Owing to his advanced age he wrote of late but seldom in our columns, though a communication from him appeared in the last volume, 9th S. viii. 141. A few years ago his name—or more often his initials G. D.—frequently occurred.

Notices to Correspondents.

We must call special attention to the following notices:—

On all communications must be written the name and address of the sender, not necessarily for publication, but as a guarantee of good faith.

We cannot undertake to answer queries privately.

To secure insertion of communications correspondents must observe the following rules. Let each note, query, or reply be written on a separate slip of paper, with the signature of the writer and such address as he wishes to appear. When answering queries, or making notes with regard to previous entries in the paper, contributors are requested to put in parentheses, immediately after the exact heading, the series, volume, and page or pages to which they refer. Correspondents who repeat queries are requested to head the second communication "Duplicate."

C. L. F. ("Gilbertian").—After the fashion of Mr. W. S. Gilbert, topsy-turvyish.

NOTICE.

Editorial communications should be addressed to "The Editor of 'Notes and Queries'"—Advertisements and Business Letters to "The Publisher"—at the Office, Bream's Buildings, Chancery Lane, E.C.

We beg leave to state that we decline to return communications which, for any reason, we do not print; and to this rule we can make no exception.

LONDON, SATURDAY, MAY 31, 1902.

CONTENTS. — No. 231.

Notes.

A BIBLIOGRAPHICAL ACCOUNT OF THE WORKS OF CHARLES DIBDIN.

(*Continued from* 9ᵗʰ S. viii. 281.)

A SUCCESSION of untoward events, coinciding with my arrival at a very rough place on my bibliographical road, brought me to a dead halt; and the many occupations of a busy autumn and winter have deterred me an unduly long time from making a fresh start. To those who have taken interest in my task I owe an apology for this, and also for the fact that the section of the bibliography now to be presented is very imperfect. The period of experiment between Dibdin's final break with Covent Garden Theatre in 1781 and his success with 'The Oddities' in 1789 was one of great effort and little success. The first part of it was devoted to the Royal Circus Playhouse. He produced an opera, 'Liberty Hall,' at Drury Lane Theatre in 1785; composed six pieces for the Dublin Theatre Royal in 1786; attempted a satirical and critical journal the *Devil*, produced 'Harvest Home' at the Haymarket, and commenced a musical tour, all in 1787; set out for India in 1788; and in January, 1789, commenced his first table entertainment in London, 'The Whim of the Moment.' I do not pretend to have entirely disentangled Dibdin's own confused account of this period of about seven years, or to have traced all his publications (many of an ephemeral character) during it. As regards the Royal Circus productions I am not even certain in some cases as to the dates or order of production, or if they were printed. It may be well to repeat that, as hitherto, all entries which I have not been able to authenticate by personal scrutiny will be marked with an asterisk. I take this opportunity of acknowledging that I have already received from readers of 'N. & Q.' since I commenced the publication of this bibliography very valuable help, in materials for it and for my forthcoming Life of Charles Dibdin.

1782. (British Museum date.) *The Graces, an Intermezzo, by C. Dibdin. 8vo.

— The Progress of Love, containing Love's Approach, Anxiety, Rapture, and the Wedding Day; composed by Mr. Dibdin. Price 1*s*. 6*d*. London. Printed & Sold by J. Preston at his warehouses 97 Strand & Exeter Change. Where may be had all this Author's works. Oblong folio, n.d., 12 pp.; pp. 2, 3, and 12 blank.

I include this here, because one song is from 'The Graces.'

1783. The Cestus: a Serenata, performed at the Royal Circus, in St. George's Fields. MDCCLXXXIII. 8vo, paged 13 to 36.

Author's name not stated. This seems to have been part of a collection of Circus pieces.

— The Cestus A Serenata as performed at the Royal Circus composed by C. Dibdin. Price 5*s*. London: Printed for S. A. & P. Thompson No. 75, St Pauls Church Yard. Oblong folio, n.d., engraved title in an upright oval, pp. ii and 26; pp. ii, 1, and 26 blank.

1783. *Harlequin the Phantom of a Day. 8vo. ('Biog. Dr.')

1783. *Lancashire Witches. Pantomime. 8vo.

1783. *The Long Odds. Serenata by C. Dibdin. 8vo. ('Biog. Dr.')

1784. *Tom Thumb.

— The favorite songs sung at the Royal Circus, in Tom Thumb; Composed by Mr. Dibdin. Price 1*s*. London: Printed & sold by J. Preston, at his Music Warehouse, No. 97 Strand. Folio, n.d., 12 pp.; pp. 8 and 9 blank.

Separate sheet song :—

— The Tinker......London. Printed & sold by Preston, at his warehouses, 97 Strand & Exeter Change. Folio, n.d., 4 pp.; front blank. Price erased and 1*s*. substituted in ink. Watermark date 1799.

This song has recently had a fresh lease of popularity in a clever arrangement by Mr. H. Lane Wilson, published by Boosey & Co. The above was from plates not engraved before 1788.

1784. Royal Circus Epitomized. London: Printed for the Author; and sold by all Booksellers in Lond [torn] Westminster. 1784. Price Two shillings and six pence. 8vo, pp. xx, 79.

1784. (?) 13 Favorite Songs for the Voice and Harpsichord composed by, [sic] C. Dibdin. Price 4 Shillgs N.B. All the Above Songs may be had separate as also those of the Padlock, by the above composer Price 6d. each. And every new work as soon as Published. London Printed & Sold by J. Bland, at his Music Warehouse 45 Holborn. Where may be had Bland's Melodious Entertainᵗ for the Flute or Violin No 1 & 2 by Dibdin Carter &c. each 2⁄6 Do. do—for the guitar No 1. 2 6. Folio, n.d. Watermark date 1794. 28 pp.

The contents chiefly from Royal Circus pieces.

1785. *The Two Houses. Name afterwards changed to A Game at Commerce; or, the Rooks Pigeoned. Comedy. "Not printed" ('Biog. Dr.').

1785. *The Talisman, and *The Honest Imposter. Both in G. Hogarth's list under date 1782. Possibly the former may be identical with 'The Talisman,' farce, produced at the Haymarket 1784 ('Biog. Dr.'), or more probably

1785. *The Talisman of Orosmanes; or, Harlequin Slave & Sultan, grand grotesque pantomime performed at the Royal Circus 28th March, 1785.

1785. *The Olive Branch. An Occasional Allegory, performed at the Royal Circus 28 March 1785.

1785. *The Statue; or, The Bower of Confidence. Mus. Ent. performed at the Royal Circus 15 Apl. 1785. "Not printed" ('Biog. Dr.').

1785. *The Land of Sorcery; or, Harlequin Will o' the Wisp. Pantomime, produced at R. Circus 16th April 1785.

1785. *The Maid of the Skylight; or, The Devil among the Lawyers, performed at R. Circus, 1785.

It is possible that this was 'The Land of Sorcery' under another title.

1785. Clump and Cudden; or, The Review: a Comic Musical piece, in one act. As it is performed at the Royal Circus. Written and composed by Mr. Dibdin. Printed in the year MDCCLXXXV. 8vo, 30 pp.

1785. The favorite songs sung at the Royal Circus, in Clump & Cudden. Pr. 1s. 6d. [altered with a pen to 2s. 6d.]. Composed by Mr. Dibdin. London: Printed & Sold by J. Preston, at his Music Warehouse, No. 97 Strand. N.d. Folio, ii, 10 pp.; pp. ii, 1, and 10 blank.

1785 *The Benevolent Tar; or, The Miller's Daughter, performed at R. Circus 8 June, 1785.

1785. *The Metamorphoses of Harlequin. Pantomime. Written & Composed by C. Dibdin. Performed at Royal Circus 12 Sep. 1785.

The dates of the seven following pieces cannot be stated more exactly than as having been produced between 1782 and 1785 at the Royal Circus:—

— *Pandora. Musical Entertainment by C. Dibdin. "Not printed" ('Biog. Dr.').

— *The Regions of Accomplishment. Musical Entertainment by C. Dibdin. "Not printed" ('Biog. Dr.').

— *The Refusal of Harlequin. Pantomime by C. Dibdin. "Not printed" ('Biog. Dr.').

— *The Land of Simplicity.

— *The Milkmaid. A Serenata by C. Dibdin. "Not printed" ('Biog. Dr.').

— *The Barrier of Parnassus.

— *The Saloon. Musical Entertainment by C. Dibdin. "Not printed ʔ ('Biog. Dr.').

Separate songs from 'The Saloon':—

Robin-Hood. A Favorite Song Sung by Miss Romanzini, Written & Composed by Mr. Dibdin. Price 6d. (Preston) folio, n.d., 4 pp.; front blank.

A favourite Song sung by Miss Wilkinson in The Saloon an Entertainment Performed at the Royal Circus Composed by C. Dibdin. Price 6d. Printed by John Welcker, Music seller to their Majesties; and sold by Bland, No. 45 Holborn; Birchall No. 129 New Bond Street; S. Vache, St Albans Street Pall Mall; Smart, the Corner of Argyl Street, Oxford Street; and Fentum, the Corner of Salisbury Street, Strand. Folio, n d., 2 pp.; outside blank.

The first line of the song is "Kind melancholy soothing sigh."

— *The Passions. A Musical Entertainment, by C. Dibdin. "Not printed" ('Biog. Dr.').

This may have reference to the following publication :—

— Hope Revenge & Chearfulness from Collins's Ode on the Passions the Music with Serenity an additional Character written by Mr Dibdin. Price 3s. London Printed & Sold by Preston & Son, at their Wholesale Warehouses, 97 Strand. Folio, n.d., pp. ii, 16; pp. ii, 1, 15, and 16 blank.

1785. A Novel & Interesting Musical Work. To be published in six numbers, intituled The Pupil's Compendium, or The Bee of Apollo. to consist of Italian, French and English Music, such as have been The most reigning & popular favorites at the Theatres of Rome Florence, Naples, Paris, and London adapted to the Harpsichord with occasionally an accompanyment for the Violin, Flute or Guitar. Half of the music will be composed The remainder selected, and the whole published under the conduct & Inspection of Mr Dibdin. No — Pr 2 6. London Printed & Sold by Jno Preston at his Music & Musical Instrument Warehouse No. 97, Strand, and sold by all Music-Sellers, Booksellers, Stationers & News Carriers in the Kingdom. Initialled (with a pen) "C. D." Part 1 is folio, n.d., 16 pp., dedicated to Mrs. Sheridan, and has a long preface.

I have not seen any other parts. My date is conjectural, but probably correct.

1785. *Liberty Hall; or, The Test of Good Fellowship. Comic opera in two acts, written and composed by C. Dibdin. 8vo.

1785. Liberty Hall, or the Test of Good-Fellowship; a Comic Opera as performed with Universal Applause, at the Theatre-Royal, Drury-Lane; being entirely an Original Composition by Mr. Dibdin. Price 8s. London: Printed & Sold by J. Preston, No 97 Strand. Oblong folio, n.d., pp. ii, 42; pp. ii and 42 blank, p. iii occupied by publisher's advertisement, which mentions 'The Pupil's Compendium.' Some copies have on the title "Entered at Stationers' Hall."

This opera contained the very popular song 'The High-Mettled Racer,' long a stock piece in song collections. It has been illustrated and separately published, e.g., as follows :—

1831. By Robert Cruikshank. Ten designs engraved on wood by G. W. Bonner. London: William Kidd, 6, Old Bond Street. 12mo, 36 pp.

N.d. By J. B published by Richard Griffin & Co. London & Glasgow. Oblong 4to, yellow paper cover.

Separate sheet songs :—

N.d. Jack Ratlin a favorite Song sung by Mr Bannister in Liberty Hall, Composed by C. Dibdin. Pr. 6d. London Printed & Sold by Preston at his Music Warehouse, No. 97 Strand. Where may be had just publish'd by the above author *The Race Horse. Price 1s. *The Bells of Aberdovy. Price 6d.

— Jack Ratlin, A favorite song. Sung by Mr Bannister in Liberty Hall, composed by C. Dibdin. Price 1s London Printed & Sold by W. Boag at his Music Shop No 11 Great Turnstile Lincoln's Inn Fields.

— Jack Ratlin......London Printed and Sold by Preston. Pr. 1s.

All three versions of ' Jack Ratlin' folio, 4 pp., front blank. On fourth page are versions for " Guittar " and Flute.

1785. (Museum date, doubtful.) *The Fisherman, Song, words beginning " I am, d'ye see," by Mr. Lonsdale, music by C. Dibdin. Folio.

1786. A Match for a Widow: or, the Frolics of Fancy. a a [sic] Comic Opera, in three acts. As performed at the Theatre-Royal, Dublin London: printed for C. Dilly, in the Poultry. MDCCLXXXVIII. [Price one shilling and six-pence.] 8vo, viii and 64 pp. Three acts and an epilogue.

Dedicated to Richard Daly, Esq., Patentee and manager of the Theatre Royal, Dublin. Here the author says of the piece : " It was then transmitted to Mr. Dibdin in London, who embellished it with his harmony...... you in the spring of 1786 gave it a fair trial before an Irish audience." This is the only trace I have been able to find of a great deal of work done by Dibdin for Daly (most of it not paid for) under an agreement entered into on 1 October, 1785. Can Irish antiquaries help me to further particulars ?

1786. *The Fortune Hunters ; or, You may say That. musical piece written and composed by C. Dibdin. performed at Sadlers Wells.

1786. The Devil: containing a Review and Investigation of all Public Subjects whatever calculated to Furnish the World with every material intelligence and Remark, relative to Literature, Arts, Arms, Commerce, Men, Measures, the Court, the Cabinet, the Senate, the Bar, the Pulpit & the Stage : which together with all other of the various Topics that excite universal Curiosity will be treated with no less firmness and freedom than fairness and candour.—The whole self-evidently intended as a disinterested & handsome Tribute to the Liberty of The English Press By a Society of Literary Gentlemen. Printed by Denew & Grant No 91 Wardour Street & sold by W. S. Fores No. 3 Piccadilly C Couch Stationer Curzon St Mayfair & by all the Booksellers in Town & Country.

The first number, 12mo, 16 pp., price twopence-halfpenny, was published 2 October, 1786, " to be continued weekly." No. 1 seems to have reached a third and Nos. 2 and 3 a second edition. The first volume was completed by the thirteenth number. The whole seems to have been reprinted. No. 14 had 24 pages. No. 16 was priced threepence and published for the proprietors by J. Stevenson, Martlet Court, Bow Street, and sold at their office, the Pandemonium, the corner of New Round Court in the Strand. The last number I have seen is No. 9 of vol. ii., dated 18 February, 1787. The Devil was chiefly, if not entirely, written by Dibdin.

1787. Harvest - Home. A Comic opera, in Two Acts. As performed, with universal applause, at the Theatre-Royal, in the Hay-market. By Mr Dibdin. London: Printed for Harrison and Co. No. 18 Paternoster-Row. MDCCLXXXVII. 8vo, 27 pp. First performed 21 May, 1787.

This brings the record of Dibdin's activities up to the commencement of his musical tour.

E. RIMBAULT DIBDIN.

Morningside, Sudworth Road, New Brighton.

(To be continued.)

THE BACON—SHAKESPEARE QUESTION.

(Continued from p. 363.)

MRS. POTT would not allow that Bacon used many of his ' Promus ' notes in his acknowledged work, but Dr. Theobald admits that at least 500 of them can be traced. In his book Dr. Theobald has made out a list of such notes as have been traced by Baconians ; but it is quite clear from this list that the followers have been too busy groping blindly into other men's works to be able to find time to devote to the master himself. Hundreds of notes, some of which Bacon uses many times over, are not mentioned in Dr. Theobald's list. It is very strange that so many willing workers, in all parts of the world, who profess to know Bacon's work so well, should be ignorant of matters which so vitally concern Bacon's own work ; for I need hardly observe that a thorough knowledge of the manner in which a man uses his notes is absolutely necessary in cases where it is desired to reclaim other work, supposed to be his. The omission to work the ' Promus ' properly with Bacon is so strange to me that I often ask myself whether the Baconians have essayed the task and stopped short because they perceived that such conscientious work would be fatal to their theories.

One note very frequently used by Bacon, and which Baconians could not help recording, although they fail to remark on the marvellous number of times it figures in the master's work, is the following : 375. " Declinat cursus aurumque volubile tollit." Bacon's note, of course, has reference to the fable of Atalanta and Hippomenes, which he details and explains in 'The Wisdom of the Ancients.' He uses this note in the 'Advancement of Learning,' in the 'De Augmentis,' in 'Filum Labyrinthi,' twice in the 'Interpretation of Nature,' and twice in the 'Novum Organum,' besides elsewhere; and each time that he uses it he does so in a fixed manner. In the 'Novum Organum' he, in a manner, excuses his fondness for the illustration, for he brings it in with the remark "to use a common allusion of ours." The following quotation shows how Bacon uses his 'Promus' jottings:—

"But here by use and action, we do not mean the applying of knowledge to lucre, for that diverts the advancement of knowledge, as the golden ball thrown before Atalanta, which, while she stoops to take up, the race is hindered.
Declinat cursus, aurumque volubile tollit."
'Advancement of Learning,' book i.

Surely, if Bacon wrote Shakespeare, we should be able to find something better to fit the 'Promus' entry than the following, which Mrs. Pott, who forgot, or did not know, that Bacon used his note and used it often, adduces from the plays: "You have a nimble wit: I think 'twas made of Atalanta's heels" ('As You Like It,' Act III. sc. ii.).

Besides, among Shakespeare's contemporaries the allusion to the fable is very common, Lyly referring to it many times. Here is one case:—

"Let Atalanta runne never so swiftelye, shee will looke back upon Hyppomanes."—'Euphues and his England,' 1580.

If the following occurred in Shakespeare it would be fatal to his claims, and a large library would be speedily stocked with the books that would dethrone him:—

"The onely enemie to sloth is contention and emulation; as to propose one man to my selfe, that s the onely myrrour of our age, and strive to out goe him in vertue. But this strife must be so tempred, that we fal not from the eagernes of praise, to the envying of their persons; for, then, we leave running to the goale of glorie, to spurne at a stone that lyeth in our way; and so bid Atlante, in the midst of her course, *stoup to take up* the golden apple her enemie scattered in her way, and was out-runne by Hippomenes." — Thomas Nashe, 'Pierce Penilesse,' 1592.

Dr. Theobald deals with the following 'Promus' notes:—403, 1,168, "Art of forgetting"; 114, 1,232, "Well to forget"; and remarks:—

"Artificial forgetfulness is not, I believe, referred to in the prose works: nor is it likely to appear except in 'Works of Invention,' but it is frequent in Shakespeare."

Now "artificial forgetfulness" *is* referred to in the prose works; it does *not* occur in 'Works of Invention,' and Bacon's manner of using his note is not only characteristic of himself, but it is altogether different from the manner of Shakespeare. The note is used in a letter from Essex to the Queen, written by Bacon:—

"And, indeed, madam, I had never thought it possible that your majesty could have so disinterested yourself of me; nor that you had been so perfect in *the art of forgetting*," &c.—Montague, vol. iii. p. 55, col. 1.

Passages illustrative of the art of forgetting are to be found not only in Shakespeare, but in almost every writer of the time. In Sidney's 'Arcadia,' book ii., Pyrocles, after making a hasty rejoinder to Philoclea, regrets his speech, and Sidney writes, "And then he fain would have *remembered to have forgot* himself." The saying was a proverbial one, and it occurs in Young's 'Night Thoughts,' iv. l. 57:—

I've been so long remembered I'm forgot;

and, more closely, Dr. Wolcot's 'George III.':

"Remember to forget to ask Mr. Whitbread to dinner."

Frequently we come across notes in the 'Promus' which, at first sight, seem to be original or Bacon's own; but further research proves them to be merely common sayings. The following is a good case:—

No. 152. "All is not in years to me; somewhat is in houres well spent."

Bacon uses the note several times, and in a variety of ways; nevertheless the Baconians, who have the sight of eagles for coincidences, or what they believe to be coincidences, in Shakespeare and Marlowe, have been as blind as moles once more. They do not seem to think that Bacon was wise when he wrote that it is better to milk the standing cow than to make a blind rush after the cows that are running away. For the sake of comparison I will quote one passage from Bacon and one that Mrs. Pott adduced from Shakespeare:—

"I make not love to the continuance of days, but to the goodness of them."—Essay of 'Death.'
"I am only old in judgment and understanding."
—'2 Henry IV.,' Act I. sc. ii.

The Shakespeare quotation is a threadbare saying, and it has no relation to the 'Promus' entry. The saying in the 'Promus' is from Seneca, and it is alluded to twice in 'Euphues.' Ben Jonson, too, makes use of it in 'Catiline':—

"The chiefe beauty of life consisteth not in the numbring of dayes, but in the using of vertuous dooings."—'Euphues,' p. 183.
"*Cicero.* The vicious count their years, virtuous their acts."—'Catiline,' Act III. sc. i.

C. Crawford.

(*To be continued.*)

IN PRAISE OF 'N. & Q.'—There are more than a few readers of 'N. & Q.,' I am sure, who can recall the pleasurable anticipations with which, away back in the early nineties, they were wont to open each Thursday's *Star* and discover the column 'Books and Bookmen,' contributed, over the pseudonym "Tatler," by Mr. Clement Shorter to that lively evening paper. To some readers, too, and certainly to the writer of this note, the most attractive feature of the *Illustrated London News* for a number of years was the 'Literary Letter,' which Mr. Shorter wrote during a portion of the time he was editor of that journal. It is not too much to assert that the *Sphere* — conducted by Mr. Shorter — the youngest, but, alike on account of its excellence as a pictorial record of current events and the literary character of its letterpress, the foremost of English, if not, indeed, of all illustrated weeklies, would to many of us lack its chief interest did it not contain C. K. S.'s 'Literary Letter.' On somewhat similar lines is his column 'Jottings of a Journalist' in the *Tatler*, which he also edits. With this long preamble I introduce Mr. Shorter's "praise." In the issue of the latter journal of 14 May, under 'Jottings,' he writes:—

"In that interesting little paper *Notes and Queries*, a paper that is a perpetual joy to me, I find some discussion as to the famous epigram on the four Georges, which has often been incorrectly attributed to Thackeray, doubtless from the rough and ready recollection that he lectured about those monarchs. The epigram, of course, was by Walter Savage Landor......Mr. Stephen Wheeler, who is the best living authority on Landor, or, at least, shares that distinction with Prof. Colvin, sends to *Notes and Queries*,"

C. K. S. informs readers of the *Tatler*, "an interesting verse written on the fly-leaf of the first edition of Landor's 'Imaginary Conversations.'" 　　JOHN GRIGOR.
105, Choumert Road, Peckham.

ROSSETTI'S 'RUGGIERO AND ANGELICA.'—
　One rock-point standing buffeted alone,
　Vexed at its base with a foul beast unknown,
　Hell-birth of geomaunt and teraphim.

These lines occur in Rossetti's well-known sonnet entitled 'For Ruggiero and Angelica, by Ingres,' one of his 'Sonnets on Pictures.' The sonnet gives us in words what the picture gives us in form and colour—the delivery of Angelica from the foul sea-beast the Ork by the knight Ruggiero on his griffin-horse. As everybody knows, the story may be found in Ariosto's 'Orlando Furioso,' x. 92–113. It had been told before by Greek and Latin poet of a knightly hero Perseus and a king's daughter Andromeda. I write now to draw attention to Rossetti's mysterious description of the foul sea-monster, Ariosto's "Orca":—

Hell-birth of *geomaunt* and *teraphim*.

The "Ork" was sent to devastate Ebuda (the Hebrides) by Proteus :—

　Proteo marin, che pasce il fiero armento
　Di Nettuno che l' onda tutta regge.

What in the world has Proteus to do with "geomancy" and the Jewish cult of "teraphim"?

Where did Rossetti find the word "geomaunt"? The word occurs nowhere else in any English author. It looks like the Italian word "geomante," a word occurring in Dante's 'Purgatorio,' xix. 4. This "geomante" means a geomancer, one who practises geomancy. Geomancy was a kind of divination by means of certain arbitrary arrangements of dots on the ground, one of which was known as "the Greater Fortune" ("la Maggior Fortuna"). The word "teraphim," with which "geomaunt" (a geomancer) is strangely coupled, denotes properly images representing the household gods of the ancient Hebrews. I suppose that Rossetti may have vaguely connected both the words "geomaunt" and "teraphim" with the idea of magic. But it may be that what Rossetti really wrote was "*geomaunce* and teraphim." Compare Gower's 'Confessio Amantis,' vi. 1295 :—

　The craft which that Saturnus fond,
　To make prickes in the Sond,
　That *Geomance* cleped is.

Readers of Rabelais will remember the use made of this mode of divination in bk. iii. ch. xxv. 　　COMESTOR OXONIENSIS.

ROBERT BUCKENHAM. — In the 'D.N.B.,' vol. vii. p. 199, there is an account of Robert Buckenham, D.D. (Cambr., 1531), who in March, 1535, "crossed the seas to Louvain to assist in the prosecution of William Tyndale." In a letter dated 31 July, 1535, he is described as "Dr. Bockenham, late prior of the Black Friars at Cambridge" ('Cal. of Letters and Papers, Henry VIII.,' vol. viii. No. 1151 ; see also vol. ix. No. 1097). Was this Buckenham identical with the Robert Buckenham whose name appears in the lists of archdeacons of Lewes in Hardy's 'Le Neve,' i. 263, and in Dallaway and Cartwright's 'City of Chichester,' 109 ?

These lists assign different dates to Archdeacon Buckenham. Hardy's list runs thus : Edward More, 1528 ; Robert Buckenham, S.T.P., 1531 ; John Shirry, 1547. In Dallaway and Cartwright's list the dates are : 1531, Edward More ; 1547, Robert Buckenham, D.D. ; 1551, John Sherrey. Perhaps neither list is free from error; for Edward More (as to whom see 'D.N.B.,' xxxviii. 413) appears as Archdeacon of Lewes in 'Valor Ecclesiasticus' (1535); and the 'Composition Books' at the Record Office show that John Shereye, clerk, compounded for the first-fruits of the archdeaconry on 17 January, 33 Hen. VIII. (1541/2), about the date of More's death. Shereye's successor, Richard Brisley, compounded on 10 September, 5 Edw. VI. (1551).   H. C.

TOAD FOLK-LORE.—The following occurs in the *Lindsey and Lincolnshire Star* of 29 March, p. 6 :—

"The Leytonstone guardians have discovered a primitive cure for smallpox in one of their registers for the year 1700. The recipe was evidently placed on the minutes as being a standard remedy. 'Take thirty to forty live toads and burn them to cinders in a new pot ; then crush into a fine black powder. Dose for smallpox, 3 oz.'"
      N. M. & A.

"UNEDA" AND OTHER OLD CONTRIBUTORS TO 'N. & Q.'—Some of your most valued correspondents have chosen to use initials or fictitious names as a signature. A writer may have good reason for concealing his identity while living; but such reason will usually lose its force after his decease. I therefore suggest that an effort be made to preserve the memory of HERMENTRUDE, JUXTA TURRIM, MELETES, and a score of others who in their day did good service to the literary world. A very learned contributor was F. C. H, who, as I gather, was Dr. Husenbeth. "In memoriâ æternâ erit justus." Will not some one write a memoir of him? My excellent friend Dr. Horace Howard Furness informs me that UNEDA, a Philadelphia correspondent, was Mr. William Duane, son of William J. Duane. The latter was a lawyer, the draughtsman of the famous will of Stephen Girard. He married a granddaughter of Benjamin Franklin. UNEDA was married, but left no children. He was a strange, solitary, unsociable man, but a man who read with a pen in his hand. Another Philadelphia correspondent of the last generation was BAR-POINT, who perhaps was Mr. Ashworth.
      RICHARD H. THORNTON.
Portland, Oregon.

[Appreciative notices of Dr. Husenbeth appeared in 4ᵗʰ S. x. 365, 388, 441, at the time of his death in 1872. Biographies of him are supplied in the first volume of Boase's 'Modern English Biography' and in the 'D.N.B.' HERMENTRUDE was Miss Emily S. Holt. A short obituary notice was given 8ᵗʰ S. v. 20.]

HOYLE ON BACKGAMMON.—I have had occasion to refer to the notice of Edmond Hoyle in the 'Dictionary of National Biography, and I find it there stated that the first edition of his treatise on backgammon appeared without a title-page. The writer has evidently followed the erroneous statement in 'N. & Q.,' 7ᵗʰ S. viii. 201, which, so far as I know, has not been contradicted. My copy of the treatise has the title-page as follows :—

"A Short | Treatise | on the Game of | Back-Gammon. | Containing | a Table of the thirty six chances, ... | By Edmond Hoyle, Gent | London : | Printed for F. Cogan, between the two | Temple-Gates in Fleet-Street, 1743. | [Price 2*s*. 6*d*.]"

I have also a copy of the sheet of the 'Laws of Whist,' designed for framing (7ᵗʰ S. viii. 144), dated 1746. The price has been reduced to a shilling. I know of the existence of a similar copy.   F. J.

YTTINGAFORDA.—This place, mentioned in the 'Saxon Chronicle' under anno 906, has not hitherto been identified, so far as I can discover. Thorpe gives it Hitchin, which is miles away from any "ford." Dr. Giles has Hitchingford, without suggesting the locality. T. Miller thinks it is Ulting or Maldon, places far removed from the probable scene of the treaty between King Edward and the Northumbrians and East Anglians.

I would suggest Wittingford or Wittenford, at the northern extremity of Minstead parish, as the probable site. It is close to Cadnam, where several important roads meet, and should form a suitable gathering-place. The circumstance that Ytene was an early name for the New Forest has given rise to a notion in my mind that Yttingaforda is in this district, and a careful examination of the Ordnance map has revealed the existence of Wittingford. (The old one-inch map is the one consulted.) It is an obscure little corner of England now, but it is worth while putting on record that the place may be of great historic interest.   EDWARD SMITH.
Walthamstow.

"WISDOM" IN ECCLESIASTICUS.—A verse in the apocryphal Book of Ecclesiasticus, vi. 22, has hitherto proved a puzzle to the commentators. In the Authorized Version it runs, "For wisdom is according to her name, and she is not manifest unto many." The Greek is : Σοφία γὰρ κατὰ τὸ ὄνομα αὐτῆς ἐστί, καὶ οὐ πολλοῖς ἐστι φανερά. Dr. Edersheim, commenting on this in the 'Speaker's Commentary' edition, edited by Dr. Wace, says :—

"It seems impossible by any critical ingenuity to explain the first clause of this verse, since there is not any Hebrew or Greek word which would admit of a play upon the word 'wisdom.'"

He refers to some unsuccessful attempts at explanation by Hitzig and Horowitz. The case is, I think, not so hopeless if we remember what philologists tell us, that σοφία, wisdom, is akin to σαφής, clear, manifest, originally full of flavour, tasty, and both from a base *sap*, to taste (see Curtius, 'Greek Etymology,' ii. 64). If σαφής was in the original text, or in the mind of the writer, instead of the synonymous word φανερά, the play upon words would be natural, and better grounded than paronomasias generally are : "Wisdom is according to her name [viz., tasteful, to the wise or men of taste], and (yet) to many she is not tasty." Or, to use a Latinized version, " *Sapientia* secundum nomen est ejus, et non est multis *sapida*"; *sapience* (*sapidness*) to many is *insipid* ; σοφία οὐ σαφής.   A. Smythe Palmer, D.D.
S. Woodford.

Queries.

We must request correspondents desiring information on family matters of only private interest to affix their names and addresses to their queries, in order that the answers may be addressed to them direct.

Dawbarn's 'Builder's Price List.'—Can any one say when a series of nine letters on 'Public Health from a Builder's Point of View' were published in the 'Builder's Price List' by Messrs. W. Dawbarn & Co.? I have reason to believe they were written by Dr. Metcalfe Johnson, long a very respected medical practitioner in this town, and at the time of his death on 18 January last almost the senior member of our borough bench. I am desirous of annotating as fully as possible the copy of the reprint of these letters which it is proposed to place in our local free library with a portrait of the old doctor.   T. Cann Hughes, M.A., F.S.A.
Lancaster.

"Sixes and sevens."— Has the saying "Things were at sixes and sevens" ever been satisfactorily explained ?   G. Krueger.
Berlin.
[See 1ˢᵗ S. iii. 118, 425; 5ᵗʰ S. ii. 20. Suggestions are supplied at the second reference, but the question remains unsolved. Consult Brewer's 'Dictionary of Phrase and Fable.']

Cartwright John William Ellis was admitted to Westminster School on 27 January, 1813. Any information concerning his parentage and career is desired.   G. F. R. B.

Euston Road.—What is the history of the New Road, between the Angel, Islington, and Portland Road (now Euston Road)? Who is responsible for allowing this once fine boulevard to become one of the ugliest roads in London ? Who is the ground landlord, and what were the terms in the original leases respecting building on forecourts ?
                              A. Masson.
[The Duke of Grafton and the Earl of Euston have, we believe, no property in the district.]

Talboys Pedigree.—Information required as to the relationship between Thomas Talboys, of Doughton (sometimes spelt Dufton) Manor, Tetbury, Gloucestershire, who died in 1765, and his kinsman Thomas, son of Charles, to whom he left his property.
                    C. T. Getting & Sons.
4, Corbet Court, Gracechurch Street, E.C.

Sir Archibald Alison's Rectorial Address at Aberdeen.—Sir (then Mr.) Archibald Alison was elected Rector of Marischal College and University, Aberdeen, on 1 March, 1845 (his opponent being the Right Hon. T. B. Macaulay) ; and his inaugural address was delivered on 17 March. In his 'Some Account of my Life and Writings : an Autobiography' (Edinb., 1883), vol. i. p. 530, is the statement :—
"The speech which I made on my installation, *which was afterwards printed in my Collected Essays*, bore internal evidence, &c.......The speech, *which will be found in my Collected Essays*, was listened to," &c.
In spite of the reiterated assertion which I have italicized, the address is not to be discovered either in Alison's 'Essays, Political, Historical, and Miscellaneous' (3 vols. Edinb., 1853), or in 'Modern British Essayists,' vol. ii. (Philadelphia, 1850). Where was it printed ?
                              P. J. Anderson.
University Library, Aberdeen.

"Cradel grass."—In Du Bartas's 'Divine Weekes,' ed. 1641, p. 130, col. 2, l. 54 ('The Colonies,' day 2, week 2), "cradel grass" is mentioned. What is it ?—some particular sort of grass formerly used for lining a cradle ?
                              S. L. Petty.
Ulverston.
[Cradle-dock is the common ragwort. See 'E.D.D.']

Marks on Table Linen. — I have some table linen with the motto "Nemo me impune lacesset," the border composed of thistles and leaves. In the centre is a large thistle, surmounted with a crown ; on each side of the crown is a circle, in the border of which there are small squares and crosses. In the centre of this circle is a cross, on which there is the figure of a man. In the lower corners there

are suns, in the centre of each a thistle.
They belonged to a great-great-grandmother
of mine, but I do not remember whether a
Robertson of Struan, or a Hutton of that
ilk, or my ancestors the Lidderdales of St.
Mary's Isle. Some of your readers may be
kind enough to explain the meaning of this.
                           E. C. WIENHOLT.

OVERLAND JOURNEY TO INDIA : FIRST LADY
WHO PERFORMED IT.—Mrs. Col. Elwood, in
her 'Narrative of a Journey Overland from
England, by the Continent of Europe, Egypt,
and the Red Sea, to India' (2 vols., London, 1830), vol. i. p. 1, writes:—

"I believe I may safely say, that I am the only
lady who ever travelled thither overland, by this,
or perhaps by any other route: and probably mine
was the first journal ever kept by an Englishwoman
in the Desert of the Thebais, and on the shores of
the Red Sea."

Are these statements correct? She left England on her travels in 1825.   W. CROOKE.
    Langton House, Charlton Kings.

CURIOUS BEQUEST. — In his will dated
2 January, 1644, Martin Whiteway, yeoman,
of the parish of Milford, near Southampton,
bequeaths to his son William

"the tablebord in the hall, with all seelings, benches,
formes, doores, windowes, glasse, and all other implements that are fastened to the house, and not
fitting to be removed; together with the cupbord
in the hall, the greatest brasse pott, and the furnace.
All to remayne and contynue in the house as belonging thereunto.'—P.C.C., 112 Rivers.

Is not this an unusual bequest, as the premises were apparently held on lease and were
not freehold?   R. H. E. HILL

CASTLE CAREWE, PEMBROKE. — Was the
name of this castle originally Castle Huel or
Hoel? The first known holders of it were the
Hoels, princes of South Wales, descendants of
the ancient line of the princes of Brittany.
The Anglo-Norman Fitz-Geralds obtained
Carewe Castle by marriage with the Hoels.
Carhuel is another form of Carel.
                              T. W. C.

AQUARIUM CARTOONS.—I am informed that
within a year or so a London periodical published a clever cartoon anent the Westminster
Aquarium. I am told it represented various
kinds of "fish" dressed up as men and
women, walking "arm in arm," coupled
together by their fins and flappers, endeavouring to get into the Aquarium. These personages, being regarded as "fishy" characters,
were, however, prevented from entering by
policemen in uniform stationed at the doors
of the building. One of these guardians of
public purity pointed to a notice-board

stating that "certain classes of 'fish' were
desired to keep outside the Aquarium," or
something to that effect. I shall be grateful
to learn where and when this alleged cartoon
was published, and if there are any similar
satirical cartoons upon this topic.
       J. LAWRENCE-HAMILTON, M.R.C.S.
    30, Sussex Square, Brighton.

JAMES ECCLESTON. — Will any reader of
'N. & Q.' tell me where I may learn something about James Eccleston, B.A., at one
time head master of Sutton Coldfield Grammar School, and the author of 'An Introduction to English Antiquities,' published in
1847? I wish specially to know the dates
and places of his birth and death, and
whether he was the author of any other
published works.   S. W. R.

[A James Eccleston, apparently the same, published through Simpkin, Marshall & Co. before 1851
'Questions on Mosheim and Burnet,' 12mo, 2s.]

'THE DIRTY OLD MAN.'—Can any of
your readers inform me as to the title and
author of a small 8vo book, issued in or after
1854, containing thirty-two poems, the first
of which is 'The Valley Stream' and the last
'Autumnal Sonnet'? That, however, by
which it will be more readily identified is
No. 'XVIII. The Dirty Old Man. A lay of
Leadenhall,' which, alluding to Nathaniel
Bentley ("Dirty Dick"), and commencing

In a dirty old house lived a Dirty Old Man,

is well known, and first appeared in
Household Words My copy of this apparently very scarce and probably privately
printed book is imperfect, but should contain, I believe, thirty-two leaves (unpaged).
It is dedicated "To my friends, known and
unknown"; and at the end of the "Contents"
we are informed that

"some of these poems appeared in a volume
published in 1850, which has since been withdrawn;
others in *Household Words, Fraser's Magazine*, &c.
All these are now revised, and some new compositions are added."

I should also be glad to know further about
the "volume published in 1850" referred to
above.   W. I. R. V.

"THE" AS PART OF TITLE.—In the title of
newspapers, companies, &c., as, for instance,
The Times, "The Union Bank," does the
word "The" correctly form part of the
quotation, or should the title be written
the *Times*, the "Union Bank"? What are
the authorities on the question?   S. W.

COCKADE OF GEORGE I.—Can you inform
me if the cockade introduced into this
country by George I. was given by him as a

special mark of distinction to his officers of the naval and military services, and fashioned differently for each? If so, his orders on the subject, or references to them, will be information which will greatly oblige.

C. Sharp.

Dr. Morse, of Barnet. — During some recent research in the records of the Foundling Hospital I discovered that the organ presented to the chapel of that institution in the year 1750 by Handel was built by a Dr. Morse, of Barnet. The committee's minutes of 2 May, 1750, record that Handel, who was present at the meeting, acquainted the committee that "Dr. Morse had not finished the organ......pursuant to the contract he made with him [Handel] in July last for that purpose." On 30 May Dr. Morse himself attended the committee and promised to proceed with the work ; and on the following 6 February it was reported that Morse had delivered all the pipes, and that he was paid 20l. "for the diapason stop." The name of Dr. Morse, of Barnet, is quite new as an organ builder, and all biographical dictionaries appear to be silent about him. Was he an amateur organ builder? And is there anything known in regard to him or his achievements in any other occupation?

F. G. Edwards.

3, Canfield Gardens, Hampstead.

Proscenium Doors at Drury Lane.—The apparently insoluble mystery attached to Cruikshank's plate of 'The Last Song' in 'The Memoirs of Joseph Grimaldi'—that is, relative to the plate in some copies of the first edition bearing the grotesque border, and not in others—has already been alluded to in 'N. & Q.' But another curious matter in connexion with the plate has never yet been referred to. The illustration deals with Grimaldi's farewell benefit at Drury Lane on Friday, 27 June, 1828, and is seemingly inaccurate in its details. Cruikshank shows the presence of the old proscenium doors, while as a matter of fact they were banished from old Drury in October, 1822. The occasional address, written by George Colman, and spoken by Terry on the opening of the season, referred at length to this vital change. Am I correct in assuming that Cruikshank erred in showing these doors in 1828 ; or is there any evidence to prove that they were replaced in their old position? W. J. L.

Anchoress in the Land of Leodium.—In Bale's 'Select Works' (1849, p. 168) is a reference to the doctrine of the Real Presence, and the statement that no great honour was given to it of the common people "till a sorry solitary sister, or anchoress, in the land of Leodium, or Luke, called Eva, after certain visions," procured of Urban IV., in 1273, the feast of Corpus Christi to be holden solemn all Christendom over. Bale quotes for this Arnoldus Bostius, Epist. vi., 'Ad Johannem Paleanydorum.' Who was this anchoress Eva? James Hooper.

Norwich.

Replies.

AN UNKNOWN FLEETWOOD PEDIGREE.
(9ᵗʰ S. ix. 261.)

R. W. B.'s interesting note is an important and valuable contribution towards an obscure section of the pedigree of this historical family. It is now no longer doubtful that Col. George Fleetwood, the Regicide, was of Chalfont, co. Bucks, and therefore the third (or possibly the fourth) son of Sir George Fleetwood of the Vache, who died 21 December, 1620. This I find—but had somewhat foolishly omitted to note—is the parentage correctly assigned to him by the able writer of his biographical sketch in 'D.N.B.' I am now inclined to the opinion that the Col. George Fleetwood, the alleged brother of "Lord" Charles Fleetwood, is altogether a creation of Noble, and had no existence in fact. The two Parliamentary officers were thus cousins-german. The regicide George must, however, still be distinguished from the Swedish baron of that name, who was another cousin, admitted to Gray's Inn 2 February, 1619/20, knighted 27 May, 1632, and died in Sweden in 1667. The regicide was admitted to Gray's Inn 22 November, 1613, and received knighthood from Cromwell 15 September, 1656, a title, of course, not allowed after the Restoration. If, after his liberation from prison, he retired to America and there died—as not unlikely—it is now clear that he left behind him a family whose descendants continued in London until at least the close of the eighteenth century.

There is, however, still a point in connexion with the regicide's history that requires a little elucidation. It is stated, both in the 'D.N.B.' and in Lipscomb's 'Bucks,' that he held the Vache estate, which upon his attainder was forfeited to the Crown. It is quite certain that this estate did fall into the hands of the Crown at about this period, and was bestowed upon James, Duke of York. But when and how did the regicide become possessed of it? His father, Sir George, had a family apparently of fourteen children, of whom eight were sons. Three of these were older than the regicide—viz., 1. Arthur, who matriculated at Oxford 24 May, 1605, aged seventeen, entered Gray's Inn in 1607 as "son and heir of Sir George Fleetwood of the Vache," and was dead before 1620 ; 2. Edward, of whom I know nothing, and who perhaps died young ; 3. Charles, who succeeded his father at the Vache and died 28 May, 1628. Will dated the day of his death. Inq. p.m. taken 26 July, 1628 (see *Genealogist*, vol. xviii. 129), mentions George, his son and heir, "aged 5 years and 26 months" (*sic*), a second son, David, and a daughter, Catherine. This daughter afterwards married (see *Miscell. Genealogica*, second series, iv. 73) George Clerk, a merchant of London, and died in 1678, leaving issue. Did the sons George and David die in youth, and their uncle inherit ?

The Vache Fleetwoods must at one time have been very numerous Several of the eight sons of Sir George Fleetwood are known to have left issue. In addition, Sir George had apparently no fewer than seven or eight brothers, one of whom, Sir William of Cranford, Middlesex, had also a family of five or six sons, whose descendants in the next generation became very widespread in the counties of Middlesex, Northampton, Bedford, Bucks, and Oxford. It is hardly likely that these lines have all failed. Noble's account of these—upon which most modern pedigrees are based—is, as we have seen, both meagre and incorrect. That given in Lipscomb's 'Bucks,' though somewhat fuller, contains so many incongruities and contradictions that it cannot be relied upon. Evidently it is largely a guesswork compilation, George the regicide being identified in the same pedigree in three different places, while George the Swedish baron and general is placed a generation too early. The late Mr. J. P. Earwaker commenced the compilation of a pedigraic account which, if completed, would doubtless have removed most of the difficulties in the somewhat involved and complicated descent of this historical family. His untimely death, however, occurred before the work had proceeded much beyond the initial stages. In the meantime contributions like that of R. W. B. are of great value towards the ultimate compilation of a complete pedigree.

W. D. PINK.

Lowton, Newton-le-Willows.

In the middle of the seventeenth century a Robert and a Charles Fleetwood were in the service of the East India Company. Robert was Chief at Masulipatam, and Charles was a Senior Merchant at Fort St.

George. Robert left sons and daughters, whose names figure in the St. Mary's register books until the middle of the eighteenth century. See 'History of Fort St. George,' by Mrs. Frank Penny.   F. P.

INGLIS MSS. AT OXFORD (9ᵗʰ S. ix. 347).—Mr. WALLACE-JAMES will find these MSS. fully described by my old friend the late Dr. David Laing in the sixth volume of the *Proceedings* of the Society of Antiquaries of Scotland, pp. 284-309, where he gives an account of all the existing specimens of the lady's writing that he knew of. Of the volume preserved in the library at Christ Church he supplies a description with which I furnished him, having examined it at his request for the purpose. I have notes of two other MSS. not found in his list : 'Argumenta Capitum Geneseos,' in Bishop van Mildert's sale in 1838, and 'Argumenta Psalmorum,' sold at Mr. Edw. Quaile's sale, 11 May, 1901, for 93*l.*   W. D. MACRAY.

GENIUS AND INSANITY (9ᵗʰ S. ix. 269).—The passage quoted from Seneca is, I think, easier to find if the reference, 'De Tranquillitate Animi,' cap. 15, sect. 16, is given. The following is the note in Ruhkopf's 'Seneca':—

"*Aristoteli.* Lipsius laudat Stagiritæ hunc locum 'Cur homines, qui ingenio claruerunt, vel in studiis philosophiæ, vel in republica administranda, vel in carmine pangendo, vel in artibus exercendis, melancholicos omnes fuisse videmus.' (Aristot. Problem. sect. 30, Quæst. i., pag. 815, B, tom. 2, edit. Paris, 1629.) Quo respexit Cic Tusc. Dispp. lib. i. cap. 33, ubi confer. Intpp."

Compare Aulus Gellius, xviii. 7, where is told an anecdote concerning "Domitius, a learned and renowned grammarian, to whom was given the name of Insanus, because he was by nature somewhat rough and testy." Compare also Cicero, 'De Divinatione,' i. 37.

ROBERT PIERPOINT.

St. Austin's, Warrington.

THE SMALLEST CHURCH IN ENGLAND (9ᵗʰ S. ix. 47, 375).—Until actual measurements are forthcoming this question will remain one for discussion and rivalry. Some, but not all, of those MR. PAGE enumerates are quite familiar to me, and, judging from the known to the unknown, the bulk of them seem to come nowhere near the place claimed for them. St. Lawrence, Isle of Wight, is the one best known, and has the commonly accepted reputation of being the smallest parish church in England ; but those who know both are well aware that St. Lawrence is a large and commodious edifice in comparison with Culbone, or, as it is called in

Ecton's 'Thesaurus' and other eighteenth-century documents, Kitnor, on the north coast of Somerset between Porlock and Lynton. This latter is out of the way of the tourist, and, though often seen by stag-hunters, has been quite overlooked by archæologists. It is locally said that the parson of Culbone can stand in his pulpit and shake hands with all his congregation. For a complete parish church, steeple and all, it is much the smallest I have ever seen, and one feature in it has, so far as I am aware, never been made public: it has on the south-east side, low down, a window, now walled up, which can have had no other purpose than that of the well-known leper window of the Middle Ages.

The seating accommodation in Culbone Church, to the best of my recollection, is limited to six oak benches, of probably fourteenth-century date, on each of which no more than two persons can find room.

Much of the quaintness of this very curious little church has, within the writer's recollection, been destroyed by a new road and sundry new adjoining buildings, but those who have seen it, even as it is, will have no doubt as to which is the smallest parish church in England. Still it is to be desired that exact plans and measurements should be taken of any church for which supremacy in minuteness is claimed.

F. T. Elworthy.

To the list furnished by Mr. Page I would add Mappleton Church, Derbyshire, a tiny place of worship served from Ashbourne and situate about a couple of miles from the entrance to lovely Dovedale; also the small church which stands within the grounds of Okeover Hall—almost on the lawn, indeed—in the same village. Close to the picturesque old house lie buried many ancestors of the honoured family of Okeover. I think the rector of Blore, not far distant, holds the services in this little edifice.

Cecil Clarke.

Junior Athenæum Club.

The churches of Mardale, at the head of Haweswater, and of Swindale in the next valley are both as small as, or smaller than, that at Wastdale Head. Mardale is a chapelry in the parishes of Bampton and Shap, and the church is said to have been built by Holm to serve as an oratory; the old oak beams of the roof have obviously been trimmed with the axe, not cut with the saw. Swindale, also in Shap parish, is of much more recent date, and adjoining it at one end is the building where is still carried on

the old grammar school, founded by Richard Baxter in 1703.

M. E. Noble.

The same claim is, or used to be, made for the church at Wythburn. When I told this to the Rev. Mr. Pigott, the "eccentric" vicar of Burnthwaite, some thirty years ago, his reply was that of the Sacristan in the 'Ingoldsby Legends.'

C. C. B.

Mr. J. T. Page, I am afraid, can never have seen Grosmont Church. Instead of it being a very small church, it is a church "of unusual size, consisting of nave, aisles, transept, and chancel" (Murray's 'South Wales,' 1890, p. 75). If I remember rightly, the nave is not used, and when I was there it was screened off from the rest of the church by means of a wood and glass partition.

G. F. R. B

"In an interesting condition" (9th S. ix. 328).—As applied to a woman *enceinte* this expression occurs at the end of the last chapter of 'Roderick Random': "My dear angel has been qualmish of late, and begins to grow remarkably round in the waist, so that I cannot leave her in such an interesting condition [?]" But "happy and graceful," and all that is requisite, as the phrase may be, one of a still more reserved nature has to some extent apparently superseded it. A woman is now often said to be "in a delicate state of health," with sometimes the addition of "owing to an interesting event being expected." The young Queen Wilhelmina of Holland was, I think, thus, before her illness, alluded to in the newspapers. Older far, however, even than being "in the family way," is to be "in the straw," from the days when straw was almost the only material used for beds—an expression equivalent to the more general one of being "brought to bed"—*i.e.*, "of a child." "Brought to bed" occurs as early as the fourteenth century. See the 'H.E.D.,' *s.v.* 'Bed.'

J. Holden MacMichael.

The last words of Smollett's 'Roderick Random' (1748), referring to the condition of health of the hero's wife, are, "I cannot leave her in such an interesting situation [?], which, I hope, will produce something to crown my felicity."

George Price.

31, Paignton Road, Birmingham.

Golf (9th S. ix. 349).—The question as to the derivation of "golf" from the Icelandic equivalent for *pavimentum* was raised by Pinkerton in a note in his edition of the 'Maitland Poems.' "Is it not," he said, "from *Golf*, Isl. *pavimentum*, because it is played in the *level* fields? Perhaps the game was originally played in paved areas." Jamieson, in the 'Scottish Dictionary,' deprecates this explanation, and thus discusses the probable origin of the word :—

"It is more natural to derive it from Germ. *Kolbe*, a club ; Belg. *kolf*, a club for striking bowls or balls, a small stick ; Sw. *kolf*, properly a hooked club, which is the form of that used in this game. Isl. *kylba, kylfa, kylva*, clava. Germ. Su.-*G. klubba* is certainly radically the same. Wachter derives it from *klopp-en*, to strike."

The root idea of striking, as Jamieson mentions, is supported by the pronunciation of the word as *gouf*, which is in common use in Scotland to-day, both for the game and for a contemptuous box on the ear. "A gouf i' the lug" may still be heard in the provinces, the word thus surviving exactly in the sense in which it was used by Nicol's henpecked husband in 1739 :—

She lends me a gouf, and tells me I 'm douf,
I 'll never be like her last Goodman.

THOMAS BAYNE.

PORTRAITS OF JOANNA BAILLIE (9ᵗʰ S. ix. 129, 237, 354).—A fine engraving of Joanna Baillie is prefixed to Longman's edition of 'The Dramatic and Poetical Works of Joanna Baillie,' 1851. The engraving is quite in accord with Samuel Carter Hall's description of Joanna Baillie in his 'Book of Memories,' 1871 :—

"I remember her as singularly impressive in look and manner, with the 'queenly' air we associate with ideas of high birth and lofty rank. Her face was long, narrow, dark, and solemn, and her speech deliberate and considerate, the very antipodes of 'chatter.' Tall in person, and habited according to the mode of an olden time, her picture, as it is now present to me, is that of a very venerable dame, dressed in coif and kirtle, stepping out, as it were, from a frame in which she had been placed by the painter Vandyke."

F. E. MANLEY.

Stoke Newington.

THE SOURCE OF THE SEVEN AGES (9ᵗʰ S. ix. 46, 197, 298).—In the south transept of Siena Cathedral there was, until some forty years ago, an incised pavement of great beauty, representing the seven ages of man—infancy, childhood, adolescence, youth, manhood, old age, and decrepitude—designed and executed by the sculptor Antonio di Federigo or Federighi in 1475. This pavement was removed from the cathedral between 1869 and 1878, and was replaced by what is called a copy of the original work, executed by two native artists, at a cost, according to the guide-books, of about 900*l.* Federighi's pavement may be seen nearly complete in the cathedral museum to which it has been relegated, together with part of the frieze of

stags in front of the Porta del Perdono, which is of the same period. Fragments of the other friezes and borders are also to be found, laid down outside the north aisle of the cathedral, in the little courtyard between it and the present palace of the archbishop. There are a description and photograph of this pavement in the 'Pavement Masters of Siena (1369-1562),' by R. H. Hobart Cust, M.A., pp. 84-6 (Bell & Sons, 1901).

It is evident from the archives of the cathedral that the seven ages of man was a familiar subject at the time that the commission was given for the execution of this pavement. Under the date of 24 April, 1475, there is an entry of a disbursement of "libre diciotto di pecie si diè a maestro Antonio [Federighi] capomaestro di buttiga nostra per impeciare la storia dell' ettade."

JOHN HEBB.

"FIVE O'CLOCK TEA": WHEN INTRODUCED (9ᵗʰ S. vi. 446; vii. 13, 96, 176, 332). — Dr. Somerville, minister of Jedburgh, was born in 1741, and, writing of social habits in Scotland in his "early life," he says :—

"Most families, both in the higher and in the middle ranks, used tea at breakfast ; but among the latter it was only recently introduced, or beginning to be introduced, in the afternoon, and then exclusively on the occasion of receiving company."—'Life and Times,' p. 329.

More explicit is his mention of the custom of afternoon tea at Buxton in 1793 :—

"While at Buxton, I had great pleasure in the society of Sir John and Lady Clerk. At their lodgings I was introduced to the company of Miss Seward, a lady of literary celebrity, Mr. Seward, author of the 'Anecdotes,' Sir Adam Ferguson, Sir Archibald Grant, and Baron Gordon. Miss Seward spoke a good deal to the persons near her, but no literary subject was introduced, nor had I any opportunity of taking part in the conversation, or breaking that silence which she imputes to me, in a letter in which she characterizes all the individuals who met at a tea-drinking party one afternoon."—P. 280.

Carlyle of Inveresk mentions the custom as existing at Harrogate thirty years earlier. Writing of society there in 1763, he says : "The ladies gave afternoon's tea and coffee in their turns" ('Autobiography,' p. 434).

W. S.

EULOGIES OF THE BIBLE BY HUXLEY AND DARWIN (9ᵗʰ S. ix. 328, 374). — Will MR. JOHNSON kindly inform me where to procure the article named and the booklet, as I have tried in vain ?   L. A. M.

BOOK-TITLES CHANGED (9ᵗʰ S. ix. 384).— MR. AULD will find 'The Black Swan,' by Oliver Madox Brown, in the second volume of the posthumous collection of the young author's writings issued in 1876 as 'The Dwale Bluth, &c.' Why it was first published as 'Gabriel Denver' is fully explained in my 'Biographical Sketch' of its author, published by Elliot Stock in 1883.

J. H. Ingram.

Mr. Auld says he has seen a version of St. Pierre's 'Paul and Virginia' entitled 'The Shipwreck.' I have such a copy, published in Edinburgh in 1808; but the first edition of this story in English was entitled 'Paul and Mary,' and was "printed for J. Dodsley, London, 1789," in 2 vols. fcap. 8vo.

John Gilpin.

"Brod" (9th S. ix. 162).—Two distinct words are alluded to under the above reference :—

(1) *Brod*=spike or goad, from Icel. *broddr*, appearing in our *brad*.

(2) *Brod*, or *braid*=*per metathesin*, board. See Jamieson, *s.v.* 'Braid,' sb. The last four instances given show plainly *board*. With *dambrod* cf. Ger. *Dambrett, Damenspiel* (Fr. *jeu de dames*). *Alm'd leither*=alumed—*i.e.*, white (Jamieson). H. P. L.

Exhumation of Henry IV. (9th S. ix. 369). —A complete account of this matter will be found in Felix Summerly's 'Handbook for Canterbury,' a new edition revised by John Brent, jun., F.S.A., pp. 102-5, 1860. A more marvellous exposition of the occasional unfaithfulness of contemporary evidence than the record adduced by Felix Summerly it would be difficult to find. J. H. I.

See 'Links with the Past,' by Mrs. Charles Bagot, p. 301. Her husband was present at the opening of the coffin in 1832, not 1830, as Antiquary states. Vapo.

The 'D.N.B.' mentions the fact of the king's tomb being opened in 1832, and refers the reader to *Archæologia*, xxvi. 440-5.

A. R. Bayley.

Annunciation (9th S. ix. 387).—In reply to Mr. Lynn, I beg to inform him that not only in the Roman, but also in the English Church Holy Week is too solemn a fast in which to keep a feast. The festival of the Annunciation falling this year during that week, it was therefore transferred to the first vacant day after Low Sunday, and was kept on either 6 April or 7 April. At the parish church which I attend (St. Michael, in Lewes) it was held on 6 April. Caroline Steggall.

Lady Day fell this year in Holy Week. Its observances—mass and office—were transferred to the Monday following Low Sunday, the usual "Alleluias" of Eastertide being added. In the Roman Calendar 18 December is marked as "The Expectation of B.V.M."— *i.e.*, about to be delivered of her Son.

George Angus.

St. Andrews, N.B.

Tedula, a Bird (9th S. ix. 389).—Beyond all doubt the right name of the bird is *trochilus* (Pliny, book viii c. 25). It would seem that it was wrongly made feminine, and so took the form *trochila*. Any one who will write down the word may see that this form (entirely strange, because wrong) might be misread as *taedula*. The change of *o* to *e* is common; the *c* and down-stroke of the *h* make a *d*, and the rest of *h* and the *i* make a *u*. This gives *tredula*, which is not far off. Celer.

Richard Smith and his Library (9th S. ix. 347).—In an early number of 'N. & Q.' it is stated that Richard Smith or Smyth died on 26 March, 1675, aged eighty-five years, and was buried on the north side of the chancel of St. Giles's, Cripplegate. His library was sold by auction at the "Swan" in Bartholomew Close by Richard Cheswelly, bookseller, of St. Paul's Churchyard, in May and June, 1682. The sale catalogue, with prices in manuscript, is now in the British Museum. Richard Smyth's 'Obituary' was edited by Sir Henry Ellis for the Camden Society. See also Wood's 'Athenæ Oxonienses,' iii. 1031, and 1st S. ii.; 2nd S. iii., viii, xi. Everard Home Coleman.

71, Brecknock Road.

Antwerp Cathedral (9th S. ix. 289, 352).— Mr. Hems's theory about the northern towers and spires of continental west fronts being often more ornate than their fellows does not find support, as he believes, in the case of Rouen Cathedral. Le Tour de Beurre is to the south-west, and it is generally asserted that it was due to fines paid for permission to eat butter in Lent, and not to market tolls. It is not often that self-indulgence provides so fair a monument. St. Swithin.

Doset Hall, Surrey (9th S. ix. 288).—The above appears, at the position indicated, in Cary's 'Actual Survey of the Country Fifteen Miles round London,' published by J. Cary, 181, Strand, 20 June, 1800. W. B. H.

The Duchy of Berwick (9th S. viii. 439, 534; ix. 130, 258, 295).—With reference to my previous reply it is interesting to note that Debrett, in his 'New Peerage,' 1823 ('Duke of Leinster,' 'Viscount Mountmorres'), and in his 'Baronetage,' 1824 ('Gerard of Bryn'), gives further particulars of Nest, or Nesta, the mother of Robert le Fitz le Roy, Earl of Gloucester. He variously calls her father by the names of Rees ap Gryffyths and Reese ap Theodore. He says that, besides the Earl of Gloucester and other children, she had by Henry I. a daughter Aline, "whom the Montmorencys of England procured in marriage for the chief of their house in France, Matthew, sire de Montmorency." Debrett further states that by her only husband, "Gerald, sometimes surnamed Fitz-Walter" (in another place "Gerard Fitzwalter"), Seneschal of Pembrokeshire, Nesta had three sons :—

1. "William, ancestor of the Carews, formerly earls of Totness, &c.; of the Graces, formerly barons of Courtstown; of the Fitzmaurices, earls of Kerry and marquesses of Lansdown; and of the Gerards, earls of Macclesfield, &c."

2. "Maurice, ancestor to the noble families of Fitzgerald, Fitzgibbon, and Mackenzie."

3. "David, Bishop of St. David's."

Debrett also tells us that, after the death of her husband Gerald in 1118, Nesta fell into the hands of Stephen de Marisco or Montmorency, Constable of Cardigan and Earl of Pembroke ("slain by the Welsh 1136"), and had issue by him,

"besides several daughters married to the lords de Barry, de Carew, de Cogan, and others, one son, Robert Fitz-Stephen, the renowned colleague and precursor, in the conquest of Ireland, 1169, of Earl Strongbow, which Robert was created Duke of Cork by King Henry II., and is the first Montmorency in France or England who, by creation, ever bore the ducal title; he left no surviving issue."

We are finally told that Nesta, the ancestress of all these great men, died in 1136.

It would be interesting to know how far the 'Debrett' of 1823-4 will withstand the criticism of the present day in the matter of these other descendants of the mother of Robert le Fitz le Roy, Earl of Gloucester.

RONALD DIXON.
46, Marlborough Avenue, Hull.

My instances in support of the proposition that the prefix "Fitz" is not always a sign of illegitimacy were doubtless unconvincing, and FitzHamon's parentage is a matter of controversy. But I did not mention Nest as mother of Robert, Earl of Gloucester, because modern historians have generally denied that she stood in any such relationship to him. The late Prof. Freeman, in his 'Norman Conquest,' set aside this tradition for the very good reason that Nest's own grandson, Giraldus Cambrensis, in his minute account of her family, makes no mention of the great earl. Robert, probably born at Caen before his father's accession, was most likely the son of a French mother.

Nest, too, was daughter of Rhys ap Tewdwr, King of Deheubarth, and not of Jestyn. She had, apparently, been married for some ten years to Gerald of Windsor before she was abducted by her cousin Owen, son of Cadwgan. Gerald died before 1136, and thereafter Nest was wife—or, more probably, mistress—of Stephen, Constable of Cardigan, and was a mistress of Henry I. By the king she was mother of Henry (*filius regis*), who was slain in Anglesey in 1157.

A. R. BAYLEY.

In addition to the titles mentioned by H. at p. 296 is one from two widely remote places—Earl Roberts of Kandahar and Pretoria. Until the present campaign that British combination of Nestor and Agamemnon was Lord Roberts of Kandahar.

FRANCIS P. MARCHANT.
Brixton Hill.

"OLIVE": "OLIVACEOUS" (9ᵗʰ S. ix. 307, 357). — I have just come on a passage in Alphonse Daudet's 'Numa Roumestan,' 1881, p. 78, which may be of use :—

"Sa figure fine, régulière, allongée et verte comme une olive à l'arbre, ne marqua ni joie ni surprise, garda l'expression concentrée qui rapprochait ses épais sourcils noirs, les nouait tout droit, au-dessous du front entêté, comme d'un lien très dur."

The woman spoken of is a peasant of Provence.

M. P.

KENYON'S LETTERS (9ᵗʰ S. ix. 248).—There appear to be several references to Ellenbrook Chapel (see index) in Mr. Hardy's 'Report on the Manuscripts of Lord Kenyon' (Hist. MSS. Comm., Fourteenth Report, App. IV., 1894). Probably these will give a clue to the information required.

O. O. H.

RENE=A SMALL WATERCOURSE (9ᵗʰ S. ix. 329).—Spelt *rean* in Halliwell, who quotes the M.E. dat. *rene* from a copy of 'Floris and Blancheflur.' Probably a variant of E. *run*, a small stream, better known in the dimin. form *runnel*, which answers to *rindel*. The A.-S. form is *ryne*; M.E. *rune*. The A.-S. diminutive is *rynel*. The word *rime*, hoarfrost, bears no relation to it; neither does the O.F. *ru* or *riu*, and the alleged O.F. *rin* is probably a misprint for the latter. CELER.

This term is of every-day occurrence in the flat portion of Somerset; also, I believe, in Gloucestershire. It is, however, spelt *rhine* or *rhyne*, pronounced *rheen*. The Ord. Survey adopts *rhyne*.

The Somersetshire levels (extensive flat districts between the hills and the sea) are under the control of commissioners acting under early Acts of Parliament and having extensive powers. The main water-channels are known as "rivers" or "yeos" (Kenn River, Little River, Great Yeo, Middle Yeo, &c.). These are more or less artificial. Then there are smaller, but frequently important, rhynes receiving the water from ditches and gripes (small surface drains), and forming secondary mains to the yeos and rivers. The yeos and rhynes are kept in order by the owners of property within the district liable to be affected by flooding, being known as "river-work" or "rheen-work." The banks have to be made up, weeds cut, &c , under the supervision of parochial juries, presided over by an experienced foreman. These report to the commissioners, who fine where they see cause, without appeal. The liability for "commission work" is frequently very heavy, as the whole work of a farm is often (by contract) charged on a small part, to the exclusion of the remainder.

In sheet x. N.E. 6-inch Ord. Survey, now before me, I observe "Binhay Rhyne," "Biddlestreet Rhyne," "Wemberham Rhyne," with many others. The name appears to have nothing in common with *rime*=hoarfrost, but to be one of the many signifying a watercourse or stream.

Mr. Ayshford Sanford, the well-known geologist, in his paper 'On the Course of the Rivers in Western Europe during the Pleistocene Period,' abstracted in the *Proceedings* of the Som. Arch. and N. Hist. Soc., xiii. 9, states that he "had come to the conclusion that......the main river of this part of the world was then the Rhine," the river *par excellence*. JAMES R. BRAMBLE, F.S.A.

Hon. Sec. Som. A. and N. H. Soc.
Weston-super-Mare.

This word is familiar to all country people in Herefordshire as well as Gloucestershire. Sir G. C. Lewis, who spells it *reen*, defines it as the "interval between ridges of ploughed land," from which it serves to carry off the water. With the spelling *rean*, Halliwell gives it in his dictionary, citing an example of its use from the 'Chester Plays' (i. 36). JOHN HUTCHINSON.
Middle Temple Library.

FASHION IN LANGUAGE (9th S. ix. 228, 352). —Under this head it may be well to draw attention to the fact that there were and still are persons who, for some reason which I cannot fathom, persist of set purpose in using words which they are well aware have come into the language as it were by stealth, and, if not in themselves objects of reprobation, are useless and accompanied by associations which render them when heard painful

to those who regard our tongue as a possession to be kept, so far as may be, incorrupt. "Reliable" and "dependable" are of this class. They are possibly capable of defence, as are most evil things, but if used at all, for which there seems no occasion, should be confined to the hurried writing of those who make copy for the daily press and the advertisements which disfigure the walls of our streets.

Another set of people will argue with you that it is not only permissible but elegant to use phrases such as "If I was" and the like, and will quote examples from writers whom we all respect, thinking thereby they prove their case. Such persons do not bear in mind that there is hardly any writer of English who has not made mistakes, and that expressions of this sort may often be charitably accounted for by negligent proofreading.

Another set of people constantly err regarding titles. Commonly this is mere innocent blundering, but sometimes it has its origin in deliberate purpose. I have myself known persons who have persisted in calling the author of the ' Novum Organum ' "Lord Bacon," although they were careful to point out that they knew his proper title was Viscount St. Albans. The defence they vouchsafed was that " Lord Bacon" was the name by which the philosopher was popularly known. Mr. Gladstone fell into this error, but whether by mistake or with deliberation it perhaps does not become me to speculate. Another instance of this may be given. Many of those who have written concerning the history of the seventeenth century speak of General Monck when referring to times succeeding the Restoration. In most cases this cannot be accounted for by ignorance. Whatever the truth may be, it is but kindly to assume they were aware that when the Stuart monarchy was restored Monck was created Duke of Albemarle. To be consistent such people should tell us that Sir Arthur Wellesley defeated the Emperor Napoleon I. at Waterloo. ASTARTE.

'HISTORY OF AYDER ALI KHAN' (9th S. ix. 369).—With reference to my query as above, I have since found that the authorship of this book was settled by MR. ALLNUTT (5th S. ii. 396). The author is M. Maître de la Tour. If we had a complete General Index, say to the end of last century, much waste of space would be saved. W. CROOKE.
Langton House, Charlton Kings.

I find in my notes that M. M. D. L. T. stands for Monsieur le Maître de la Tour,

This work was also published by J. Johnson, No. 72, St. Paul's Churchyard, 1784, and reprinted by Sanders & Co., No. 7, Mission Row, Calcutta, 1848. W. C. L. Floyd.

Cecil Rhodes's Ancestors (9th S. ix. 325).— Some discussion has lately been going on in the *Times* as to the locality of the dairy-farm carried on by Mr. Rhodes, ancestor of Mr. Cecil Rhodes. The following extract from 'The Book of Table Talk,' p. 281, published by Charles Knight in 1836, would seem to prove that originally it was at Islington. Later the progress of building may well have compelled him to seek pastures new. The writer, speaking of the Arab notion that anything perfect in quantity is particularly affected by the evil eye, continues :—

"It is curious to recognize this superstition of the desert in the neighbourhood of London. We remember when we were children there was a great cowkeeper at Islington of the name of Rhodes, who had no difficulty in keeping nine hundred and ninety-nine cows all safe and sound; but, do what he would, he could never keep a thousand. If he bought one to make up the number, two or three others were sure to die; nay, if he purchased ten or twenty at a time, before he could get them home a sudden mortality would dispose of other ten or twenty; thus always keeping the number down to the charmed nine hundred and ninety-nine. At least so went the story, which no cook-maid, house-maid, or old maid in the neighbourhood seemed to doubt."

J. H. Parry.

A picture of the altar-tomb erected by the late Mr. Cecil Rhodes in St. Pancras Church-yard to the memory of his ancestors appeared in *Black and White* of 5 April. At the south end of the tomb are the words "Erected to replace two decayed family tombs by C. J. R., 1890." Almost all the available space is occupied by the names of those buried beneath and of some interred at other places. Three valuable articles on the Rhodes family appeared in the *St. Pancras Guardian* of 5 Feb., 5 March, and 2 April, 1897. I believe these have since been reprinted in a local magazine.

John T. Page.
West Haddon, Northamptonshire.

The following anecdote relating to Samuel Rhodes, of Islington, great-great-grand-father of the "Colossus," may be of interest. It was popularly said that he could never successfully keep a thousand cows, a belief, in accordance with the superstition as to un-lucky numbers, which was held by Samuel Rhodes himself, who said that he was tired of trying to increase his stock to 1,000 or up-wards. So surely as he did some misfortune would happen; his cows would sicken, or meet with a series of accidents, until the number had sunk below the fatal standard, when all would go well again. His answer to the jests which such an assertion produced was that he was the best judge, as the loss was his, and that for several years he had uninterrupted good fortune even when his stock stood at 999, and misfortune as in-variably when he reached 1,000.

J. Holden MacMichael.
Wimbledon Park Road.

Greek Pronunciation (9th S. vii. 146, 351, 449; viii. 74, 192, 372, 513; ix. 131, 251, 311, 332).—F. J. C. should "verify his references." If he had read my letter appearing at 9th S. viii. 513 he would have seen that I am in no way responsible for the derivation of *salt* from the Latin *sal*. I then said, and I maintain that, according to Prof. Skeat, *salt* is derived from A.-S. *sealt*. Since reading F. J. C.'s reply I have again consulted Skeat's 'Etymol. Dict.,' second edition (1884); also his 'Principles of English Etymology' (1887). *Salt* is given as a Modern English word, the Middle English form of which was also *salt* (the Middle English period being considered by Prof. Skeat as extending roughly from 1200 to 1460). *Salt* is then put as derived from A.-S. *sealt*, and absolutely no mention is made of any Anglian word *salt*. I have not been able to consult Sweet's 'History of English Sounds.' M. Haultmont.

An old dictionary was responsible for the derivation of English *salt* from Latin *sal*, and not the present writer; and another con-tributor to 'N. & Q.' was responsible for its derivation from *sealt*. Whether those deri-vations are correct or incorrect does not, I think, much affect the arguments submitted by me, which were concerned with changes in vowel sound, not with letters or deriva-tions. W. H. B.

St. Bees (9th S. ix. 267).—Authorities agree that St. Bees was Bega or Begga, but differ as to her day and generation. Dr. Owen, in his 'Sanctorale Catholicum,' quotes her death as occurring upon 6 September, 560, and remarks :—

"In Cumberland, S. Bega, a virgin, was patroness of the goodly church and monastery of S. Bees, which was a famous place of pilgrimage for the people of the north of England."

Dr. Husenbeth, in his 'Emblems of Saints,' describes her as a widow who passed away 17 December, 689, and quotes 'Chorographia Sacra Bradantiæ,' in which she is repre-sented as a crowned abbess, holding a model of a monastery in her hands. Lewis, in 'A Topographical Dictionary of England,' under 'St. Bees,' says :—

"The church was formerly the conventual one of a monastery, founded about 650 by Bega, or Begogh, an Irish female, who subsequently received the honour of canonization. This monastery was destroyed by the Danes, but restored, in the reign of Henry I., by William de Meschines, Lord of Copeland, as a cell to the abbey of St. Mary at York : and in 1219 it was pillaged by the Scots."

HARRY HEMS.

Fair Park, Exeter.

See Sandford's MS. in the library of the Dean and Chapter, Carlisle. Also refer to an old copy of a St. Bees 'Calendar,' obtainable from Mr. R. W. Broomfield, St. Bees ; also my 'St. Bees, and other Poems,' 1891, a copy of which I shall be glad to lend MR. G. A. BROWNE if he will communicate with me. The college is now defunct.

CHAS. F. FORSHAW, LL.D., F.R.Hist.S.

48, Hanover Square, Bradford.

In the 'Dictionary of Christian Biography' the late Bishop Stubbs, s.v. 'Bega,' said :—

"A Cumbrian saint of whom nothing is clearly known, and whom the endeavours of the hagiographers have only succeeded in investing with a history which belongs to several other saints."

The article in Baring-Gould is from Montalembert.

C. S. WARD.

Wootton St. Lawrence, Basingstoke.

"MERESTEADS" OR "MESESTEADS" (9th S. ix. 248).—MR. ADDY will find merestead defined in the 'Standard Dictionary' as "a farm," and in the 'Century Dictionary' as "the land within a particular mere or boundary ; a farm"; and in the latter dictionary is given an extract from Longfellow's 'Miles Standish.' In the 'E.D.D.,' however, under mear, the combination mear-stead is not recorded ; but the word mear-stone there given was not uncommon in the American colonies in the seventeenth century. MR. ADDY asks whether the word merestead, which Mrs. Earle says ('Old Time Gardens,' p. 3) occurs in the 'Plymouth Colony Records,' is correctly given. The passage referred to by Mrs. Earle is as follows : "The meersteads & garden plotes of [those] which came first layd out 1620" (' Plymouth Colony Records,' xii. 3). This entry, in the handwriting of Governor W. Bradford, was presumably made in or about 1620, and shows that Mrs. Earle has altered the original spelling. That the form meerstead is not an error of the copyist is proved by the facsimile given on p. 2.

What, so far as I am aware, has never before been pointed out is the fact that the words meadstead and misted occur in the same 'Records.'

Whether misted is a corruption of meerstead or of meadstead is a point I will not venture to determine, and whether meadstead occurs in the original, or is a copyist's error for mearstead, is a question I cannot answer, because the original records, being at Plymouth, Mass., cannot be consulted by me. The following extracts are of interest :—

"Richard Higgens hath bought of Thomas Little his now dwelling howse & misted, for & in considerac'on of twenty-one bushels of merchantable corne." 1633, Oct. 7 (i. 16).

"At the same Court, a misted that was granted formerly to Richard Warren, deceased, & forfeited by a late order, for want of building, the said misted was granted to Mr Raph Fog & his heires forever, provided the said Raph wthin twelue monethes build a dwelling howse upon the same." 1633, Oct. 28 (i. 18).

"Whereas Kanelm Wynslow & Josias Wynslow, by a joynt purchase, bought of Francs Eaton his then dwelling,......the said Josias hath sold vnto the said Kanelm his p't of the said purchase, as also of all & singular the moveables in & about the said dwelling howse & misted in joynt p'tnershipbetween them......In consid' whereof the said Kenelm & his heires to haue, hold. occupie, enjoy, the said dwelling howse & misted, &c., to him & them forever." 1633/4, Jan. 22 (i. 24, 25).

"At the same time Rich. Beare allowed to erect a dwelling howse, & to haue a misted appointed in place convenient." 1636, Oct. 6 (i. 45).

"A midstead is graunted to George Russell in the towne of Plymouth, and to haue land assigned vnto yt in a convenient place." 1637, April 3 (i. 57).

"Thomas Starr......Hath......sould vnto Andrew Hellot One frame of a house wth a chymney to be set vp and thacked in Yarmouth in the place appoynted and seaventeene acrees of vpland in two divisions and twelue acrees of Marsh & meaddow vnto the said house and......meadstead belonging in Yarmouth aforesaid......To haue & to hold the said house & meadstead seaventeene acrees of vpland and twelue acres of Marsh & meaddow." 1639, Nov. 25 (xii. 50).

"Will'm Sherman is graunted a meadstead about the Stony Boooke, in Duxborrow." 1640, April 6 (i. 145).

"Will'm Hiller & Georg' Pollerd are graunted a p'cell of vpland......The said lands lye betwixt John Irish & John Caruers meadsteads." 1640, July 6 (i. 158).

"John Irish doth acknowledg that for and in considerac'on of the dwelling house wherein Will'm Hiller now dwelleth in Duxborrow and the meadstead or garden adjoyneing wth the fruits thereon groweing hath......sold vnto the said Will'm Hiller & George Pollerd......tenn acrees of vpland." 1641, June 11 (xii. 74).

"Peter Brown, whose first house and 'meerstead' was on the south side of Leyden Street, near the water-side in Plymouth, afterwards moved to Duxbury." 1883, 'New Eng. Hist. and Gen. Register,' xxxvii. 277.

The above are the only examples of the words meadstead, meerstead, and misted known to me, and the extracts show that the words were used for about twenty years

near Plymouth, Mass., after which time they disappeared.　　　ALBERT MATTHEWS.
Boston, U.S.

HOUNDSDITCH (9ᵗʰ S. ix. 348). — Thomas Lodge, in his 'Alarum against Usurers' (first published in 1584), does not expressly state to what nationality they belong, but one gathers that they were Englishmen. He begins by describing the "state within this our common wealth" (I quote from the "Defence of Poetry, Music, and Stage-Plays, &c. London: Printed for the Shakespeare Society," 1853, p. 43):—

"I meane the state of Merchants, who though to publyke commoditie they bring in store of wealth from forrein nations, yet such are their domesticall practises, that not onely they inrich themselves mightelye by others misfortunes, but also eate our English gentrie out of house and home."

Their method was (p 44) to

"finde out......some olde soaking undermining solicitour:......this good fellowe must haunt Ordinaryes, canvasse up and downe Powles, and as the catte watcheth the praye of the mouse, so dilygentlye intendes hee to the compassing of some young novice."

The result was as to be expected (p. 48):—

"Purchased arms now possess the place of ancient progenitors, and men made rich by young youth's misspendings doe feast in the halls of our riotous young spend thrifts."

Again on p. 68:—

"If it be true that the nobilitie of the father worketh in the childe, I cannot see howe these upstartes maye anie waies employe themselves in honourable actions, when as neither their aunces-tours ever knewe more then their beads, or their fathers other then unlawfull gaines."

The above extracts seem to show that the usurers were English. I will now give one quotation on their religion (p. 70):—

"Yet some will here adde and inferre (though unnecessarily) that those whom I heere so asperlye reprehend are as religious as the best, haunt the church with the most, at their buriall be as bountifull as the goodliest; and therefore it may not be thought, that seeing so many goods, they should follow the bad. To whom I aunswere— If they beare correction of sin by often haunting of sermons, yet continue their wickednesse when they know what it worketh, their actions are wicked, their lives dissolute, their endes desperate."

W. R. B. PRIDEAUX.

PARENTAGE OF CÆSAR BORGIA (9ᵗʰ S. viii. 524; ix. 176, 232, 312).—For amazing epithets and equally astounding logic commend me to BARON CORVO's reply at the last reference given above. He confesses to the deliberate selection of "gallimaufry," a pedantic expression beyond the ken of most readers. I wonder whether he has "deliberately selected" "quincunx," which in its position here conveys to my mind no meaning whatever. I

should suggest that he meant "quintette," which, at any rate, would convey the five names which he has just mentioned, and not five-twelfths ("quincunx"). He finds Varillas "very credible," yet in the very next sentence he infers that he is an habitual liar, and then gives us the first and second premisses of a syllogism built thereon, which is almost as logical as that he should write 'Chronicles of the House of Borgia,' and then himself describe it in the reply about which I write as "a work which I despise." Truly, here is a reductio ad absurdum.

I am not at all anxious to assail either Varillas or BARON CORVO, but I certainly cannot congratulate the latter upon keeping to the point, and I seem to read between the lines of his latest lucubration a soreness at my own presumption in even venturing to question a conclusion arrived at in a work which he "despises," and concerning an historian whom he practically dubs "an habitual liar."

In conclusion, I beg to state that my quotation from Webster was perfectly accurate, even if restricted; "gallimaufry = any absurd medley" is one of the meanings given therein.

CHARLES R. DAWES.

STAMP COLLECTING (8ᵗʰ S. xii. 469; 9ᵗʰ S. i. 115; v. 404, 501).—To the references already given of the earliest mentions in 'N. & Q.' of stamp collecting, an interesting one is to be added in 3ʳᵈ S. v. 418.

ALFRED F. ROBBINS.

Miscellaneous.

NOTES ON BOOKS, &c.

Bluebeard; an Account of Comorre the Cursed and Gilles de Rais. By Ernest Alfred Vizetelly. (Chatto & Windus.)

MR. VIZETELLY's book on Bluebeard is a quaint and deeply interesting mixture of folk-lore and history. The Breton peasant has insisted on finding in Gilles de Montmorency de Laval de Rais, Marshal of France, the prototype of Bluebeard in Perrault's immortal tale. In point of fact, the resemblance between the pair is so slight as to be non-existent, since Gilles de Rais, as he is generally known, was the husband of but one wife, who survived him and married a second husband. Our own Henry VIII. might with much more cause have been accepted as the prototype of this wife-slaying tyrant. So bloodthirsty, ferocious, and infamous was, however, this distinguished warrior, a sharer in the triumphs of Joan of Arc, that no conceivable injury can be done to his memory by the association. In very fact, the atrocities of Gilles de Rais belong to the mysteries of devil-worship, which seems at one time to have been prevalent in France, and to have extended its ramifications into high quarters. His victims, almost exclusively children, were all slaughtered in the cult of the devil, and in the hope of inducing him to appear and supply his worshipper with money for his extravagances and debaucheries. Whether these victims were, as Mr. Vizetelly supposes, two or three hundred, or, according to what is said to be the criminal's own estimate, six times that number, there is no doubt that he spread consternation over Western France, from Brittany to Poitou, and made a profound impression upon the popular mind. Each of his castles was a shrine of Moloch. It is probable enough that he grew in time accustomed to murder, and that, instead of performing a mere perfunctory ritual in honour of Satan, he took pleasure in the blood of his victims. At any rate, his name of "the exterminating beast" is appropriate, and his death by hanging and burning, though chiefly attributable to his ecclesiastical offences, was richly merited. So emphatically is he a real character that he figures largely in historical compilations. In this country a full record of his misdeeds is not easily obtained, and Mr. Vizetelly's book will be eagerly consulted by the students of human perversity. In opposition to Mr. Vizetelly, we are disposed to regard him as mad, though his madness furnishes no excuse for his iniquities, and fortunately did not procure him any immunity from punishment. He stands in this respect near the Marquis de Sade, the Chemos to this Moloch, the mere mention of whose name almost constitutes an offence. Mr. Vizetelly himself has hesitated to describe all the actions of "the exterminating beast," a full record of whose crimes is, so far as we understand, only to be found in the Latin of the proceedings on his trial.

To the life of Gilles de Rais Mr. Vizetelly has prefixed that of Comorre the Cursed, another Breton, who lived between 515 and 535, or nine hundred years earlier than Gilles de Rais. Concerning this scarcely less execrable being, who also is supposed to have furnished a possible prototype of Bluebeard, ordinary books of reference are silent, and it is in 'The Life, Deeds, Death, and Miracles of the Saints of Armorican Brittany' that we find the best account. Not that Comorre was a saint—far from it. St. Gildas was, however, so far concerned with his crimes as to restore to life Tryphine, the last of the wives whom he beheaded. On Comorre, according to pious legends, the saints of Brittany called down judgment, debarring him from access either to heaven or purgatory, with the result that the Breton peasants saw him, in the guise of a wolf, prowling in search of human prey.

In his opening chapter Mr. Vizetelly treats the histories he narrates and the story of Bluebeard from the point of view of folk-lore. In the later and more interesting portion of his work he gives a full account of the crimes of Gilles de Rais. His book will appeal strongly to a wide public. We are not quite sure as to some of his references. Is Ducange responsible for a 'Glossaire Français'? The volume is enriched with an alleged portrait of Gilles de Rais from Montfaucon and eight illustrations by the author of spots in Brittany connected with the deeds he describes.

How to Make an Index. By Henry B. Wheatley, F.S.A. (Stock.)

Of the three works which Mr. Wheatley has contributed to his own "Book-Lover's Library" the third is in almost all respects the best. 'How to Form a Library' (to some extent a matter of will or taste) and 'How to Catalogue a Library' were the previous volumes, the second having naturally much in common with the present. Good indexes are, however, less common than good catalogues, and the information Mr. Wheatley supplies should lead to a notable improvement of the art. With most of the indexes to which he refers with praise we are familiar, from that to the translation of Pliny's 'History of the World' (which is called a "table") to the really magnificent index to Boswell's 'Johnson' of Dr. Birkbeck Hill, the utility of which extends far beyond either Johnson or his biographer. The earlier and more amusing portion of Mr. Wheatley's work deals with the history of index-making, and constitutes delightful reading; the later and more useful section consists of information how an index should be made. The whole, it is to be trusted, will be widely studied and effect great improvement in a neglected or misunderstood art. Among things Mr. Wheatley might have mentioned are the eminently useful indexes *verborum* which accompany some classics—*e.g.*, the Horace of Doering of 1838. Materials for this, which serves most purposes of a concordance, are furnished in the 'Horace of the Forty Commentators,' once famous, but now, it is to be feared, forgotten. Mr. Wheatley draws attention to the difficulties to readers resulting from the incapacity of index-makers, and mentions, among others, that resulting from using the Christian name instead of the surname of a writer. A curious instance of this is supplied in the 'Bibliotheca Scriptorum Societatis Jesu' (Antwerp, 1643), which is, in a sense, one prolonged index. In this the Christian name has always to be sought, so that in looking for, say, the famous Father Gerard (1564-1637), unless one knows that his name is John, in Latin Joannes, research is practically futile. Mistakes in indexing such as Mr. Wheatley points out are not confined to indexes. Not at all uncommon is it in dictionaries to find opposite a word, say, in French, the same word in English. On turning to the English section, however, the word does not appear. In Eadie's 'Dictionary of the Bible' (1850), Mr. Wheatley points out, under 'Dorcas' you are referred to 'Tabitha'; but under 'Tabitha' there is no entry at all. So common and aggravating is this form of error that some of our own books of reference are scored with comment that we fear might incur the charge of ribaldry. There is but one adjective to be applied to Mr. Wheatley's volume, and that adjective is "excellent."

The Owens College Jubilee. Being a Special Issue of the *Owens College Union Magazine* to commemorate the recently accomplished Jubilee of the College. (Manchester, Sherratt & Hughes.)

The Owens College, Report of the Council. (Manchester, Gill.)

On the 12th of March, 1851, when London was full of excitement and anticipation as to the result of the forthcoming Great Exhibition, a good work in Manchester was commenced. On that day the doors of Owens College were for the first time opened in the old building in Quay Street, a house that had been Richard Cobden's. Of the founder, John Owens, very little is known, except that he lived in Nelson Street, was a merchant apparently, and had a warehouse near Shudehill. The first article in this Jubilee number of the College magazine is by the Principal of the College, Dr. Hopkinson, entitled 'The University and the City.'

In it he states that "after a quarter of a century, first of struggle, and then of growth—during which the ideals of the founder and first directors of the College were never forgotten—the time arrived for making the claim for recognition as a University. A clear account of the movement is given by Mr. Alderman Thompson in his history of the College—a record inspired by his affection for it and devotion to its interests."

Other articles are 'The Case for a Federal University,' by Dr. Wilkins; 'The Work of the Manchester School of Chemists,' by Sir Henry Roscoe; 'The Medical School and the Jubilee,' by the Professor of Anatomy, A. H. Young; 'The Manchester Royal School of Medicine,' by Dr. Dreschfeld; and 'Recollections of the Old College,' by Mr. Alderman Thompson. Prof. Dawkins relates 'The Story of the Boulder-Stone,' which stands on end by itself in the quadrangle: "It was found in 1888, in making a sewer in Oxford Road, opposite No. 226. It was met with in tunnelling through the sand, gravel, and clay, at a depth of twelve feet from the surface, and was presented by the Manchester Corporation to the College. It consists of a block of hard crystalline volcanic rock, called andesite, and weighs about 25 tons......The groovings are the unmistakable marks of ice, and were formed while it was at the bottom of a glacier, while the iron-stained crust is the equally unmistakable result of the decomposition of the surface before it was embedded in the ice, and before it formed a portion of the glacial drift of the Lancashire and Cheshire plains." Contributions signed by Edith Lang and Catherine Chisholm show the progress in the "Women's Department." The early reminiscences are somewhat amusing: "We never thought of entering Owens by the principal door, but always that to the right of the quad., and we were always ushered out of the History Theatre by the professor." A book could not be demanded from the library "in the hardened manner now usual." A voucher had to be filled up, and "a dear little maid-of-all-work, aged about 13, went to the library with it......it was never suggested that she should be chaperoned." "The first two women had not even an umbrella stand to call their own, and had to go to lectures with dripping macintoshes, making little pools around them." Now in the Jubilee year a woman may enter practically every department of the College, and the "ancients" remind their younger sisters that the battle has been fought, and the science door has been opened by them: "We petitioned for the associateship with all its privileges, we who dreamt of a 'settlement of Owens women,' and made tentative efforts in that direction at a Working Girls' Club, and, though you have gone far ahead of us in old paths and new, despise not your elder sisters." The number contains many portraits and views of the College buildings.

The Report of the Council shows how splendidly the financial portion of the work of the College has been conducted. The treasurer, Mr. Alderman Thompson, may well be congratulated on the result. Under the Report of Public Health we find much to interest us. During the last official year four thousand six hundred and fifty-two official reports have been issued. Out of these typhoid and diphtheria exceeded three thousand.

Scottish Art and Letters has issued an interesting Coronation number. In order to make room for the historical matter the serial fiction and other familiar features are for once postponed. Among the contents are 'The Last Four Scottish Coronations,' by Prof. Cooper; 'The Crowning of the King'; 'In Praise of Follies,' by Sir George Douglas, &c. A great feature in the number is the portraits, which are numerous and excellent, some of them being in colours. The number itself contains portraits of James VI., Charles I., Charles II., Anne of Denmark, Regent Mar, Archbishop Spottiswood, and Drummond of Hawthornden. In a portfolio are further likenesses of Charles I., Lord Chancellor Thirlestane, Marquis of Argyle, Regent Mar, Earl of Eglinton, Dr. John Craig, and the Marquis of Montrose, a curious combination, which tempts an irreverent joke concerning the Evil One's opinion of the Commandments. The book and portfolio should, however, be got and preserved. The cover has a bright-coloured picture of Anne of Denmark, after Van Somer. She can scarcely be regarded as Scotch. We should have expected to find Mary Stuart.

To their "Life and Light" books Messrs. Bell & Sons have added a pocket edition of Mrs Browning's *Aurora Leigh*, with an introduction by Misses Charlotte Porter and Helen A. Clarke.

Lady Renouf (46, Roland Gardens, S.W.) writes: "You would confer a great favour on me if you would kindly make it known in 'N. & Q.' that we should be glad to obtain on loan all letters received from my late husband, Sir Peter le Page Renouf, the first volume of whose collected works is about to appear under the editorship of Messrs. Naville, Maspero, and Rylands. The letters might be sent to me at the above address, or to the Secretary of the Society for Biblical Archæology, 37, Great Russell Street. They will, of course, conscientiously be returned."

Notices to Correspondents.

We must call special attention to the following notices:—

On all communications must be written the name and address of the sender, not necessarily for publication, but as a guarantee of good faith.

We cannot undertake to answer queries privately.

To secure insertion of communications correspondents must observe the following rules. Let each note, query, or reply be written on a separate slip of paper, with the signature of the writer and such address as he wishes to appear. When answering queries, or making notes with regard to previous entries in the paper, contributors are requested to put in parentheses, immediately after the exact heading, the series, volume, and page or pages to which they refer. Correspondents who repeat queries are requested to head the second communication "Duplicate."

Alfred B. ("Conjugis haud immemor desideratissimi").—Not unmindful of a most lamented husband.

NOTICE.

Editorial communications should be addressed to "The Editor of 'Notes and Queries'"—Advertisements and Business Letters to "The Publisher"—at the Office, Bream's Buildings, Chancery Lane, E.C.

LONDON, SATURDAY, JUNE 7, 1902.

CONTENTS. — No. 232.

Notes.

ARCHBISHOPS OF CYPRUS.

"The ancient and autocephalous Orthodox Church of Cyprus sustained the loss of its Archbishop Sophronios. His Beatitude had been elected in 1865, when he was appointed under an Imperial Berat which conferred various privileges, and he had, therefore, served in his high office for more than thirty-five years. On the occasion of his funeral obsequies the ancient character of the Church was notably marked. According to ancient custom, the Archbishops are buried sitting in a chair and clasping a copy of the Gospels. The corpse is brought into the church clothed in full pontifical robes, and before the corpse is borne the sceptre surmounted by an Imperial orb, as used by the Eastern Emperors, in right of the decree of the Emperor Zeno, who, about the year A.D. 480, conferred this privilege as well as that of signing all Ecclesiastical orders or communications in the Imperial purple. These and other marks of special distinction which are still continued, were conferred by the Emperor Zeno for the discovery of a copy of Saint Matthew's Gospel upon the breast of Saint Barnabas, the first Archbishop of Cyprus, in his own handwriting, tradition stating that the manuscript was placed there by Saint Mark himself. However these things may be, these ancient distinctions were conferred by the Imperial authority for the reasons so stated, and have continued for more than fifteen centuries in the unchanging Orthodox Church of Cyprus."— 'Cyprus, Report for 1900-1901,' presented to Parliament April, 1902, p. 59.

The writer of the preceding extract is Sir William Frederick Haynes Smith, K.C.M.G., LL.D., High Commissioner of Cyprus.

As to the special privileges of the Archbishops of Cyprus I give the following extracts :—

" Anciently a very great contest happened in this island about jurisdiction : the Archbishop pretended to be independent of any patriarch, whereas the Patriarchs of Antioch and Alexandria no less violently insisted that this church was subordinate to them. The pretentions of the three contending parties were laid before the Grecian Emperor at Constantinople for his decision. In the meantime an affair happened which occasioned a great deal of talk. The monks of a certain convent, whether in building or repairing it, by accident found a coffin, and in it a body with a leaden plate on it, signifying that in this coffin was deposited the body of the apostle St. Barnabas. About the neck of the Saint was also a chain fastened to a leaden box, which was found to contain an Arabic copy of St. Matthew's Gospel, written by St. Barnabas himself on parchment. The clergy of Cyprus very dexterously availed themselves of this discovery, sending to the Emperor Zeno both the sacred relicks and the manuscript ; with which present that devout prince was so pleased that he gave a charter to the Church of Cyprus, declaring it independent of any patriarch." —' Travels through Part of Europe, Asia Minor, the Islands of the Archipelago, Syria, Palestine, Egypt, Mount Sinai, &c.,' by the Honourable J. Ægidius van Egmont (Van der Nijenberg) and John Heyman, translated from the Low Dutch, and printed at London, 1759, vol. ii. chap. xviii.

It is probable that the authors' visit to Cyprus was within the first quarter of the eighteenth century.

" In the time of the latter Byzantine Emperors of Constantinople the church there having no authentic copy of the Gospel of S. Matthew issued orders for the seeking of one throughout the Empire. The priest of a convent near Famagosto dreamed that if he dug under his church in a spot pointed out, he should find it. Next day he obeyed the injunctions of the Angel who had appeared to him a vision [*sic*], and found the tomb of S. Barnabas, with the Gospel of S. Matthew laid on the bosom of the dead saint. The Archbishop wrote this to Constantinople, whence the royal galleys were immediately sent, on board of which he carried the treasure to the capital, and in return for his present, he was made independent, and presented with a red vest, which he still has the prerogative of wearing, and allowed the privilege of writing with red ink, which he has ever since continued. He has a third privilege, that of bearing the arms of the Greek Church (very like the Russian Eagle) on his chair, like a Patriarch."— 'Journal of a Tour in the Levant,' by William Turner, Esquire, pub. by John Murray, London, 1820, vol. ii., under date 16 and 17 Oct., 1815.

William Turner was attached in 1812 to the staff of Sir Robert Liston, H.M.'s Ambassador to the Porte. He obtained permission "to change his official labours for the pleasures of travelling." His two visits to Cyprus took place in 1815.

"A proof of some such intention on the part of the Porte is that it receives very graciously their *arz* or petition about taxes, and all complaints they may make, if so be they be sent to it direct under ther [*sic*] seals, the Archbishop's name being written in Turkish with red ink (his seal alone is found imprinted in the Imperial *qayul* or register in red ink, while all the seals which accompany it, including those of the Patriarchs, are impressed in black ink) and those of his three suffragans in black. So that we may conclude that the Ottoman Porte was certainly assured after the conquest, the fact being of course confirmed by the Patriarch, that the Archbishop of Cyprus enjoyed *ab antiquo* the privilege, given him by the sovereigns on account of the loyalty and devotion of himself and his flock, and which he has preserved without a break up to the present day, to sign and seal with red ink : and this same vermilion seal is recognized by the Porte and by all its subjects. And I do not believe that any other red seal will be found in the registers."—Translated from a 'History of Cyprus,' by Cyprianos, an Archimandrite of the Church of Cyprus, printed at Venice in 1788.

The extract is from that part of the history which is "A Narrative of an Old Rebellion in Cyprus, which Monsieur Astier, Consul of France, set down on December 20, 1764."

I take the above extracts, the first, of course, excepted, from 'Excerpta Cypria,' translated and transcribed by Claude Delaval Cobham (Nicosia, Herbert E. Clarke, 1895), pp. 117, 315, 257.

On p. 76 is given a letter, dated 13 May, 1806, written in Greek by Chrysanthos, Archbishop of Cyprus. The signature is printed in Greek capitals in red ink.

Mr. Cobham is, and has been for many years, Commissioner of Larnaca. He has recently issued some additional 'Excerpta Cypria' in loose sheets, one of which (No. 2) gives the following :—

"The Island of Cyprus was in its ecclesiastical government subjected once to the Patriarch of Antioch, but afterwards by the Council of Ephesus as canon the eighth, and the same again confirmed by the grace and favour of Justinian the Emperour (whose mother was a Cypriot by birth) this church was made absolute and independent of any other, and a privilege given to Anthemius, the Archbishop in that age, to subscribe his name to all publick acts in red letters, which was an honour above that of any Patriarch, who writes his name or firm in black characters, the which was afterwards confirmed by the authority of Zeno the Emperour : this favour and indulgence was granted in honour to the Apostle Barnaby, who primarily governed this diocess, where now his sepulcher remains."— "The Present State of the Greek and Armenian Churches, Anno Christi 1678, p. 89 or 90. This book was written, at the command of his Majesty Charles II., by Paul Ricaut, Esquire, late Consul at Smyrna, and Fellow of the Royal Society...... London, 1679."

Mr. (now Sir) Robert Hamilton Lang, K.C.M.G., formerly English Consul in Cyprus, in his 'Cyprus: its History, its Present Resources, and Future Prospects' (London, 1878, p. 166), chap. viii., says :—

"It was in A.D. 477, when the Bishops of Cyprus were struggling to prevent their subjection to the Patriarch of Antioch, that a shepherd at Salamis discovered the body of St. Barnabas, and with it a copy of the Gospel of St. Matthew, written by the hand of the Cyprian Saints. In gratitude for this precious relic the Emperor Leno* confirmed the Church of Cyprus in its absolute independence, and conferred upon its head peculiar honours which he still enjoys. Amongst these were the assumption by the Archbishop of Cyprus of purple silk robes, a gold-headed sceptre, the title of Beatitude, and the privilege, only customary with the Emperors, of signing in red ink."

In "Cyprus, Historical and Descriptive. Adapted from the German of Franz von Löher. With much Additional Matter by Mrs. A. Batson Joyner. London : 1878," p. 27 (chap. iii.), is the following :—

"I afterwards found that the head of the Cyprian Church is a worthy and distinguished man, who well deserves his title of μαχαριωτατος ...... The Archbishop of Cyprus......signs his name with red ink, seals with the imperial double-headed eagle, carries a shepherd's crook, surmounted by a golden orb, and bears a title enumerating his saintly and lordly attributes."

The writer of the above meant, no doubt, μακαριώτατος, *i.e.*, "most beatified." Μακαριότης is the word for "beatitude."

The Archbishop is a Μακαριότης, a "Beatitude," in common with the other Patriarchs, except the Patriarch of Constantinople, who is a Παναγιότης, a "Holiness."

In addressing the Archbishop you would say, Μακαριώτατε ; in speaking to him of himself you would say, ʽΗ ʽΥμῶν Μακαριότης ; in speaking of him to others you would say, ʽΗ Αὐτοῦ Μακαριότης. It would appear that the difference between Μακαριώτατε and ʽΗ ʽΥμῶν Μακαριότης is somewhat analogous to that between "My Lord Archbishop" and "Your Grace."

I had occasion some five years ago to send a telegram from Larnaca to the Archbishop at Nicosia. I well remember using (under advice) the expression "your Beatitude"; my telegram was in English.

I had the pleasure of calling on Archbishop Sophronios. As I remember him he was a courteous, pleasant old man, living without any appearance of grandeur, such as his privileges might suggest. He also called on me. Unfortunately our conversation had to be carried on through an interpreter. I find in my diary of February, 1896, a reference to an old Greek church in Nicosia, in which were

---

* "Leno" should no doubt be *Zeno*.

"many coarsely painted frescos, one or two representing the Archbishop of Cyprus receiving his special privileges from the Emperor, *e.g.*, wearing the purple, carrying the sceptre, signing with red ink."

I have not got the name of the church.

In 'Excerpta Cypria,' pp. 339–42, is a translation of the "Imperial Berat issued to His Beatitude Sophronios, the present Archbishop of Cyprus, after his proclamation in 1865." This *berat* concerning the Archbishopric of Cyprus, "the last, we may believe, which will ever be issued, is a document of some historical interest." It begins as follows :—

"Seeing that, in consequence of the news of the death of the monk Macarios, Archbishop of the island of Cyprus, &c., which was recently announced, it was necessary that another should be chosen in his room, and as, by the common voice and assent, there has been elected the bearer of this our Imperial *Berat* (may the strength of this Christian Primate be stablished !) the monk Sophronios (may his dignity be prolonged !) WE, having received news of this by a memorial (*Mazhar*) signed by all the deputies appointed to this end by the rayahs of Cyprus, who have humbly tendered their report, as well as by notice received in a resolution (*Mazbata*) of the common council of the said island, after the archives had been searched, and it was found that there really stood recorded a grant of the Archbishopric of the island to the aforenamed monk deceased, and having obtained the necessary assurance and report that the customary douceur of one hundred thousand aspers has been paid in cash to the proper office, as it was agreed, and was laid down in the original *firman*, WE give this our Imperial *berat*, and WE command......"

Then follow forty-five clauses. The first is :—

"That the said monk Sophronios do take up the said Archbishopric of Cyprus, &c., according to the custom existing *ab antiquo*."

This clause presumably includes the ancient privileges of the purple robes, the red ink, &c.

The end of the berat is as follows :—

"So let them know.
Let them respect our holy sign.
Written at the beginning of the month Shawwal, in the year 1282."

The beginning of the month Shawwal (or Chawal), Anno Hegiræ 1282, would fall between 17 and 26 February, Anno Domini 1866, the fifth year of the reign of Sultan Abdul Aziz.

I do not know what is the value of an "asper" or "aspre." In 'Les Voyages du Seigneur de Villamont,' Arras, 1598, about p. 300 (?) (see 'Excerpta Cypria,' p. 23), is the following :—

"The gold *sultan* is worth about as much as the Venetian *sequin*......It passes for 120 *aspres*, the *aspre* being a little coin of pure silver less in size than half a *denier*. Eight *aspres* make a *seya*, and

fifteen *seyas* are worth a *sequin*......The *aspre* is worth about six French *deniers obole*."

Mr. Cobham, in his introduction to the extract from the 'History of Cyprus' by Cyprianos quoted above, says that three aspers or aqches made a para or medin, forty paras a piastre, that the piastre of 1788 was worth about 1*s.* 10½*d.*, and that five piastres made a Venetian gold sequin of 9*s.* 5½*d.* Perhaps De Villamont unintentionally omitted the piastre item.

Mr. H. A. Grueber, Assistant-Keeper of Coins and Medals at the British Museum, has been good enough to send me the following information :—

"In the fourteenth century this name ["aspre" or "asper"] was given to a silver coin current at Rhodes and in the East of about the value of the groat of Edward III.; but of late years, *circa* 1865, it was used to denote a small copper piece, which like the Portuguese reis was only a money of account. Its value appears to have been :— 3¼ aspre=1 kharoobeh; 16 kharoobeh (or 52 aspre) =1 piastre; and 100 piastre=18*s.* English. This was the reckoning at Tunis in 1859; and I should say it was the same at Cyprus; but it would make the sum paid by the Archbishop rather small."

It would be about 17*l.* 6*s.*

In Murray's 'Handbook for Travellers in the Ionian Islands, Greece, Turkey,' &c. (1845), p. 156, 120 aspers are said to make a piastre. With the exchange at 110 piastres to 1*l.* sterling, 100,000 aspers would equal about 7*l.* 10*s.*

I should think that the word as used in the berat has a meaning *ab antiquo*, and has no reference to any modern value. Perhaps 100,000 aspers in the berat equal some 78*l.* according to the value of the asper in 1788, given by Mr. Cobham. But even that sum would appear to be small if Mrs. Scott-Stevenson, in 'Our Home in Cyprus,' London, 1880, p. 307, note, is correct when she says :—

"The Bishop of Larnaca caused one thousand pounds to be distributed through a friend among the electors, and the Bishop of Baffo's election cost him one thousand five hundred pounds."

It would be more correct to call these two Bishops of Kition and Papho. I should think that the election expenses of the two are fabulous.   ROBERT PIERPOINT.

"BUCKS" AND "GOOD FELLOWS" IN 1778.
(*Continued from* 9th S. viii. 480.)

Gregorians.—

"The Brethren of the Pope's Head Chapter of the Antient and Honourable Order of Gregorians are desir'd to meet at the Fountain Tavern on Ludgate Hill, this Evening at Six o'Clock, to proceed from thence to visit the Globe Chapter in Fleet Street."—*Daily Advert.*, 18 Feb., 1742.

Griggs and Gregorians here their meetings hold,
Convivial Sects, and Bucks alert and bold ;
A kind of Masons, but without their sign ;
The bonds of union—pleasure, song, and wine.
Crabbe, 'The Borough,' Letter X.

The Historical Society.—See the Mathematical Society.

Hook and Eye Club.—Douglas Jerrold's club held its weekly meetings at the "Albion Tavern and Hotel," No. 26, Russell Street.

Horseshoe.—"The Knights Companion of the Most Honourable Order of the Horseshoe" met at the "White Horse," King Street, Golden Square, in 1782 (Banks Coll. Admission Tickets, portfolio 2).

The House of Lords Club held their meetings at the "Fleece" or "Golden Fleece" in Cornhill. It appears to have been known as the "Fleece Tavern" Club in 1736, the membership being composed, in its earlier times, of influential citizens, for in the *St. James's Evening Post* of 6 May in that year we are told that

"the Gentlemen of the Common Council, belonging to the 'Fleece Tavern Club'—waited upon the Lord Mayor to desire his Lordship would call a Common Council to congratulate his Majesty upon the happy Nuptials of his Royal Highness the Prince of Wales with her Royal Highness the Princess of Saxe Gotha [mother of George III.], and......his Lordship was pleased to receive them in a very handsome Manner and to promise to speedily call a Common Council for that purpose."

Ned Ward, however, says it was composed of tippling citizens and jocular Change brokers, who met every night

"to wash away their consciences with salubrious claret ; that the mental reservations and fallacious assurances the one had used in their shops, and the deceitful wheedles and stock-jobbing honesty by which the others had outwitted their merchants, might be no impediment to their night's rest ; but that they might sleep without repentance, and rise next day with a strong propensity to the same practice."

One of the last houses where the House of Lords Club met was the "Yorkshire Grey" (Daniel's Livery Stables) in Fetter Lane. But they had previously removed from the "Fleece" to the "Three Tuns" in Southwark to escape the sarcastic attentions of the London apprentices. But as late as 1825 there was a tavern with the sign of the "Abercrombie" in Lombard Street where a House of Lords Club appears to have survived, or had, perhaps, only been revived ('Tav. Anecd.'). Its heyday was evidently at the "Fleece" in Cornhill before its down-grade period set in, when it was broken up for a time through the leading members having committed suicide ! See 'Compleat and Humorous Acc. of Club Societies,' by Ed. Ward, 'Knights of the Golden Fleece.' There is a

card in the Banks Collection of Admission Tickets, showing that the House of Lords Club held their anniversary dinner as late as 1786.

The Royal Humane Society.—The "Chapter Tavern and Coffee-House" is further remarkable (see Conger Club) for having seen the formation of the Royal Humane Society. It was in 1773 that the benevolent Dr. Hawes, whose father was the landlord of the "Old Thatched House Tavern" in Cross Street, Islington, began to call attention to the means of resuscitating persons apparently drowned, encountering, of course, much ridicule and opposition. In 1774 Dr. Hawes and his friend Dr. Cogan, who subsequently became registrar of the society, each brought fifteen friends to a meeting at the "Chapter Coffee-House," when the society was at once formed. Dr. Hawes's zeal and benevolence in advertising rewards to persons who, between London and Westminster Bridges, should, within a certain time after the accident, rescue drowned persons from the water and bring them to places appointed for their reception, irresistibly remind one of a story told by Sir Wemyss Reid concerning a shrewd Novocastrian known as "Cuckoo Jack." Jack lived upon the Tyne in a well-patched boat, picking up any trifle that came in his way from a derelict log to a corpse. One day an elderly and most estimable Quaker of Newcastle, in stepping from a river steamboat to the quay, slipped and fell into the stream. "Cuckoo Jack" was at hand with his boat and quickly rescued the luckless "Friend," landing him dripping on the quay. The good man drew half-a-crown from his pocket, and solemnly handed it to his preserver. Jack eyed the coin for a moment with lack-lustre gaze, spat upon it for good luck, and, having placed it safely in his pocket, said in a matter-of-fact tone to the soaking Quaker, "Man, ah 'd hev gotten five shillin' for takin' ye to the dead-house."

The Humdrum Club of the *Spectator* held its silent meetings in Ivy Lane.

The "Je ne sais quoi" Club (1797) met at the "Star and Garter" in Pall Mall.

The Judge and Jury trials.—For full accounts of these disreputable proceedings see *Sporting Life*, 7 October. 1848, 'A Night at Baron Nicholson's' ; *Daily Telegraph*, 28 August, 1894, G. A. Sala, 'Things I have Known,' and 20 November, 1896, Clement Scott, who gives a graphic description of Baron Nicholson and his infamous judge and jury trials. Baron Nicholson was at one time landlord of the "Wrekin" (*q.v.*). There is still a Judge and Jury Club which holds its meetings at a little public-house near Victoria Park, an account of which will be found in the *Evening News* of 26 February, 1901.

The Keep - the - Line Club in the early part of the nineteenth century consisted of wits, artists, actors, authors, gentlemen, and peers. Its object was

"enjoyment and preservation of temper, by putting it to the severest trials. One of the rules was that, whenever a member was insulted by another, however grossly, the insulted person should rise and offer his best thanks to the offender. Another rule imposed a fine of a dozen of claret to the club on the member who published any literary composition of his own. Samuel Rogers, Topham, Miles Peter Andrews, Merry, Morton, Reynolds, Fitzgerald, Horace Smith, Boaden, Kenney, and others, paid the fine willingly whenever it was fairly due. The penalty was once demanded of Wilson (the surgeon) and of John Tufton. The first had issued an advertisement announcing a course of lectures; Tufton had addressed an electioneering handbill to his constituents. Both publications were pronounced to be literary. The authors had not only to pay the penalty in claret, but to profess their unfeigned delight at its being imposed on them."— Dr. Doran, 'In and About Drury Lane.'

Kentish Club.—In 1756

"the Gentlemen of the Kentish Club dine together at the 'St. Alban's Tavern,' according to agreement last year, on 20th January, the 3rd of February, the 2nd of March, and the 6th of April."— *Whitehall Evening Post*, 13 January, 1756.

It was a general custom for county folk to hold their convivial meetings and public feasts—the latter once a year—at the better-class taverns, and the "St. Alban's" was a famous home of the tavern sodality, and one of those which gave its immediate origin to the modern club. It was situated, not in the thoroughfare now known as Pall Mall, but in St. Alban's Street. This street was wiped out of the map of London to make way for Waterloo Place and Regent Street. The sign of the tavern was doubtless suggested by the name of the street in which it was situated, which in its turn was thus named, not after the proto-martyr, but after Henry Jermyn, Earl of St. Albans, who, however, took his title from the town so named in honour of the saint.

The King of Clubs. — "Bobus" Smith's King of Clubs, of which Samuel Rogers the banker-poet was a member, met at the "Crown and Anchor Tavern" at the corner of Arundel Street in the Strand. Bobus Smith was the brother of Sydney Smith. See further Timbs's 'Clubs and Club Life.'

The King's Club. — 'Tav. Anec.,' 1825, p. 130.   J. HOLDEN MACMICHAEL.
Wimbledon Park Road.

(To be continued.)

STEPMOTHER = MOTHER-IN-LAW.—The use of *mother-in-law* for *stepmother* has been more than once referred to in 'N. & Q.' A flagrant instance of the less usual substitution of *stepmother* for *mother-in-law* occurs in Smollett's translation of 'Gil Blas,' book x. ch. ii. Asked the hero of his mother :—

"'Will you not on all occasions be absolute mistress in my household?' 'May be so, and may be not,' rejoined she; 'you have only to fall in love with some flirt of a girl, and then you will marry: then she will be my daughter-in-law, and I shall be her stepmother; and then we shall live together as stepmothers and daughters-in-law usually do.'"

Smollett's mind, on the evidence of his rendering of 'Gil Blas,' appears to have been thoroughly imbued with Shakespeare phraseology.   ST. SWITHIN.

GENDER OF NOUNS IN GERMAN AND RUSSIAN.—It may perhaps be worth while pointing out briefly that the different methods of expressing the grammatical gender of nouns in German and in Russian find their respective antecedent and model in Greek and in Latin. For just as the Germans use their threefold definite article to denote the gender of every noun—not an easy, but an indispensable task to the foreign student who has to learn it by heart—so did and still do the Greeks, whilst, on the other hand, the Russians—in strange accordance, not with Greek, but with Latin—lack the definite article, but express the different gender of nouns by means of their different terminations. In this respect, we may assert, the acquisition of Russian presents a minor obstacle to the classical scholar than does that of German.   H. KREBS.
Oxford.

EVOLUTION OF A NOSE. — Lord Ronald Leveson-Gower, in his gossipy volume of 'Old Diaries,' recently published, speaking of a visit he paid on one occasion to Mr. Finch, of Barley-on-the-Hill (a grandson of the sixth Duchess of Beaufort), remarks of his host, "He has the Somerset nose," in allusion, of course, to what has been in modern times a very prominent distinguishing feature of the ducal house in question.

But it is curious that Lord Ronald should be apparently in ignorance that the well-known Beaufort nose is in reality a Leveson-Gower nose, having been brought into the Somerset family by the very Duchess of Beaufort above referred to, who was a daughter of the first Marquis of Stafford (Lord Ronald's great-grandfather). The Sutherlands, oddly enough, have lost the famous nose, at least in the present generation; but it survives conspicuously not only in the Beauforts, but in other branches of the family, notably the Galloways ; for it is as unmistakable a feature in Lord Galloway's brothers and sisters as it was in his mother (born a Somerset), and in his brother, the late earl.

Apropos of Lord Ronald's book, I cannot refrain from adding that I have never in my experience seen in a single volume such a collection of misspelt proper names, English, French, German, and Italian. In German the noble author's rule seems to be, "When in doubt put a double dot"; hence such weird forms as Nassau Höf, Bayerischer Höf, Scöttischer, and Schlöss Eltz, to say nothing of Karlsbruke and Dusseldorff. "Lettres Atheniens" is a typical bit of French ; while in Italian we have a "terra motta," Borghesi for Borghese, Peatti (the violoncellist) for Piatti, "feminili" for *feminile*, del Angeli for degl' Angeli, Olivetto for Oliveto, Catterina for Caterina, and (indifferently) Ponti Konisi and Pontoi Konosi (this perhaps is meant for Greek). But English names fare little better, even those of the "high nobility" with whom Lord Ronald is presumably conversant. The Marchioness Conyngham twice figures as Cunningham, Mr. Philip Stanhope as Phillip, Lord Erroll as Errol, Lord Plunket as Plunkett, Lord Saye and Sele as Say and Sele, Lord Revelstoke as Revelstroke, and so well-known a lady as Madame de Navarro (Mary Anderson) as Navarino ! The Empress Frederick is Frederic as often as not, and Magdalen College, Oxford, is Magdalene.

These instances, noted and quoted almost at random, will show what a curiosity of inaccurate spelling the book is. The grammar, too, is often "sadly to seek"; but, *en revanche,* the 'Old Diaries' are often interesting, even amusing, and they are not at all ill-natured.

D. Oswald Hunter-Blair, O.S.B.
Oxford.

Gavarni and Ballooning. — In view of the recent artistic ball in Paris, taking place as it did at a time when flying machines are (both metaphorically and literally) "in the air," it may not be uninteresting to the readers of 'N. & Q.' if I venture to quote two or three lines from the 'Imp. Dict. Univ. Biog.' concerning the "sunset" of the great caricaturist's life : "Of late Gavarni is said to have returned to his mechanical pursuits, being deeply occupied in solving the problem of rendering balloons navigable."

Herbert B. Clayton.

"Hateful." — The 'H.E.D.' gives no example of "hateful" used in the sense of full of hate, cherishing hatred, malignant, from any nineteenth-century prose writer (the passage quoted from the *Universal Review,* 15 June, 1890, is apparently in verse). There is a good instance in R. L. Stevenson's 'Strange Case of Dr. Jekyll and Mr. Hyde,' paragraph 8 of the first chapter ('Story of the Door'): "I never saw a circle of such hateful faces." The context makes it clear that the adjective here bears the meaning "full of hate."

A German writer has said, "Ein untrügliches Kennzeichen eines allgemein gewordenen Citats ist die Veränderung seiner ursprünglichen Form." If the same holds good of characters in fiction, one need not be surprised at the appearance of "Jekyl-Hyde [*sic*] dogs" in a recent American book ('Wild Animals I have Known,' by E. S. Thompson, Nutt, 1901). Edward Bensly.
The University, Adelaide.

William IV. — Anent the numerical objection that has been raised to the title of Edward VII. in Scotland, it is interesting to note that when Queen Victoria's predecessor came to the throne it was pointed out that he was at the same time William I., II., III., and IV. : I., as King of Hanover, which was not added till the first George ; II., as King of Ireland, which was not conquered till Henry II. ; III., as King of Scotland ; and IV., as King of England. I take this note from p. 9 of Sir John Mowbray's 'Seventy Years at Westminster.' St. Swithin.

"Upwards of." — A correspondence that has recently been carried on in the *Yorkshire Post* reveals the curious fact that in that county and the neighbouring parts of Lincolnshire (and possibly over an even wider area) this phrase is commonly used in the sense of less than, or rising towards. As one correspondent puts it, "'Upwards of' means (to a thorough country-bred Yorkshireman) 'almost,' or 'approaching to,' or, as we say in some parts of Yorkshire, 'close on.'" It is still more curious to hear it asserted that this use of the phrase is "good colloquial" English, and quite as defensible as the established use. C. C. B.

Shorthand in the Third Century.—To the interesting note (*ante*, p. 406) of Mr. Axon on the Armenian 'Acts of St. Callistratus' I have an analogue out of Eusebius, who writes in his 'Historia Ecclesiastica,' vi. cap. xxiii., 'De Originis Studio':—

"Ex eo tempore etiam Origenes in divinas scripturas commentarios cœpit conscribere, Ambrosio innumeris stimulis eum incitante, nec solum verbis atque hortationibus, sed etiam largissimis rerum necessariarum præbitionibus. Quippe septem et amplius notarii dictanti illi præsto aderant, qui præstituto tempore sibi per vices succedebant: nec pauciores antiquarii simul cum puellis elegantius scribere assuetis," &c.

Here we have in the beginning of the third century (Origen was born 185/6 A.D.) not only stenographers (*notarii*) succeeding one another, in the manner of modern Parliamentary stenographers, in predetermined sections and times (*præstituto tempore*), but we can also find an anticipation of one of our most modern institutions, since the "puellæ elegantius scribere assuetæ" can be described as a sort of "typewriting girls," who give in an easily legible text what the *antiquarii* have translated from shorthand in ordinary handwriting. "Puellas notarias" (stenograph girls) I cannot find in ancient times. An excellent note 'On Old Greek Tachygraphy,' by F. W. G. Foat, and the whole literature (mostly German) of Greek and Latin tachygraphy, are to be found in the English *Journal of Hellenic Studies*, 1901, p. 238.　　　　　Dr. MAX MAAS.
Munich, Bavaria.

SIR GEORGE FLOYD DUCKETT, BART. (See *ante*, p. 420.)—Sir George Duckett was born on 27 March, 1811, and died on 13 May, 1902, in his ninety-second year. 'N. & Q.' being a work of reference, I venture to send these dates.　　　　　W. C. L. FLOYD.

"ARTLANDISH," A LOW GERMAN DIALECT.— It may be worth noting that H. Middendorff, in his work on Anglo-Saxon place-names ('Altenglisches Flurnamenbuch,' Halle, 1902), makes frequent reference to "artländisch," which he explains as "niederdeutscher Dialekt des Artlandes, Provinz Hannover, Regierungsbezirk Osnabrück."
　　　　　HY. HARRISON.

LADY-DAY DAY.—In a reply on ' "Ycleping" the Church' (*ante*, p. 55) the above phrase was used intentionally, with "(as we say)" after it. This was carefully edited to "Lady Day (as we say)." It may be worth while to record a peculiarity of our West-Country dialect which was omitted (*inter alia multa*) in my 'West Somerset Word-Book,' and has escaped the notice of Prof. Wright in the 'E.D.D.' When it is desired to emphasize the day of any event, if it should happen upon one of the periods when "day" is conventionally used, it is usual here to consider the ordinary expressions May Day, Christmas Day, &c., merely to apply to the season, and consequently, if the reference is made to the actual day, that word is duplicated. Thus an old soldier of my acquaintance used always to lament his ill luck by saying, " I

was born 'pon the very worst day in all the year—Lady-day Day, 'cause the rent wadn' never ready." So it would be said of any event so happening, " 'Twas 'pon Michaelmas-day Day, beyun' all the days in the wordle," or, " The last time I zeed 'n was last Christmas 'pon Old Christmas-day Day," *i.e.*, 6 January. So we say Midsummer-day Day, and I have heard Whitsun-Monday Day.
　　　　　F. T. ELWORTHY.
Foxdown, Wellington, Somerset.

Queries.

BAPTISMAL FONTS.—I should be glad to know if there is any full list of ancient baptismal fonts in any good work later than Simpson or Paley; if not, on what lines one should be made. Kindly answer direct.　　　(Miss) B. C. WROUGHTON.
Woolley Park, Wantage.

ANN KINDON.—I wish to find the parentage of Ann Kindon, of Bromsgrove, county Worcester, widow of Joseph Kindon. She died about 1790, and was buried in the chancel of Chaddesley-Corbett Church. Her maiden name was Fox. Her descendants believe her to have been the granddaughter of Sir Stephen Fox. Can any of your readers give me information about her?
　　　　　A. L. KNIGHT.

LATIN VERSES.—Can any one help me to find these verses?—

Quid faculam præfers, Phileros, qua nil opus nobis?
　Ibimus, hoc lucet pectore flamma satis.
Illam non potis est vis sæva extinguere venti,
　Aut imber cælo candidus præcipitans.
　　　　　S. D.

COAT OF ARMS.—L. B. D. in the *Standard* last week "thinks there can be but little doubt that the term 'coat of arms' is a corruption of *côte d'armée*. The cognizances or devices of soldiers commanding forces even before the Crusades were painted on their shields on the sides towards the army." Has 'N. & Q.' had any reference to this?
　　　　　Q. N.

[The 'H.E.D.' states that "coat of arms" is a translation of the French *cotte d'armes*.]

CAPT. ARNOLD.—The Rev. W. H. Fitchett, in his 'Tale of the Indian Mutiny,' speaks of a Capt. Arnold, of the 2nd (Madras) Fusiliers, who was killed before Lucknow.

Can you tell me whether this officer was a descendant—probably a grandson—of Benedict Arnold? As three of Benedict's sons—Edward, James, and William—did serve in India, it is not impossible that he was a son of one of these. I am particularly interested in this matter, and shall be glad of any information.   W. ABBATT.

281, Fourth Avenue, New York.

SAN SEBASTIAN, SPAIN.—Can any of your readers furnish me with the titles and dates of authoritative or trustworthy works by English authors (not reckoning Napier's 'Peninsular War') giving particulars of the siege and capture of this town in 1813?   W. SANDFORD.

Clapham.

SIR FRANCIS WRONGHEAD.—Macaulay says at the close of his essay on the 'War of the Spanish Succession':—

"Parson Barnabas, Parson Trulliber, Sir Wilful Witwould, Sir Francis Wronghead, Squire Western, Squire Sullen, such were the people who composed the main strength of the Tory party."

Can any one tell me in what work of imagination Sir Francis Wronghead occurs?   F. C. M.

[Sir Francis Wronghead is a character in 'The Provoked Husband,' begun by Vanbrugh and finished by Colley Cibber. On its production at Drury Lane 10 January, 1728, Cibber played the part.]

VERSES BY ARTHUR O'SHAUGHNESSY. — I should be very grateful to any of your readers who could give me information as to the holder of the copyright of a lyric by Arthur O'Shaughnessy, entitled 'If She but Knew.' These verses appear in the second volume of Macmillan's 'Golden Treasury,' but Messrs. Macmillan inform me they do not know the owner of the copyright.   EDWIN GREENE.

[Arthur O'Shaughnessy died *sine prole*, and without, we believe, any surviving relative. We doubt whether any claimant for the copyright will be found.]

BISHOP SANDERSON'S DESCENDANTS. — I have been much puzzled by the following note from the *Gentleman's Magazine* for 1815, and shall be extremely grateful to any reader who can prove or disprove the descent contained therein :—

"At Bourne, aged 84, Mrs. Pare. This pious and benevolent woman was the last surviving daughter of the Rev. J. Sanderson, rector of Addington, co. Northampton, and fifth in descent from the learned Bp. Sanderson."—Vol. lxxxv. pt. ii. p. 88.

Any information regarding male or female descendants of the good bishop and great Lincolnshire collector Dr. Sanderson would be most welcome. I may add I have seen the previous references to this family in 'N. & Q.'   CHAS. H. CROUCH.

5, Grove Villas, Wanstead.

WALDBY ARMS.—Can any reader explain the reason for the difference in the arms of Waldbye of Waldbye, given in Stowe and Lansdowne MSS. as Argent, on a chevron sable three crosses pattée or, and another coat for Waldbye in the same MSS., viz , Argent, a chevron sable? On the seal of Archbishop Robert Waldby in the British Museum the arms of Waldby are a lion rampant gutte, crowned, within a bordure compony. Were these different families?   YORK.

'HISTORY OF MANSELL.'—Was the second part of the 'History of Mansell, Maunsell, or Mansel,' by W. W. Mansell, ever published? The first part was issued in 1840 or 1850. It is reported that the author died before he had completed the second part. It is a book of interest to genealogists.   WELSHMAN.

MAJOR MACDONALD, of Terndreich, who was taken prisoner after the battle of Falkirk and executed at Carlisle in 1746, had married secondly a cousin, Miss Macdonald, of Killichonat. Could any of your readers state how the relationship existed?

(Major) R. S. CLARKE.

Bishops Hull, Taunton.

CERNEY MANOR, CIRENCESTER. — Can any of your readers supply me with information relating to South Cerney Manor, Cirencester, until lately in the possession of the Sutton family? The house itself dates back to the time of Elizabeth, and is constructed with gable ends and mullion windows. I shall also be glad to learn if it is mentioned in any county or antiquarian history, and if any print of it exists.

REG. C. C. HOCKLEY.

CRESHELD DRAPER, M.P. WINCHELSEA, 1678 TO 1687.—He married Sarah, daughter of Sir Dennis Gauden, of Clapham, Surrey, who was Sheriff of London in 1667-8. Licence (Vicar-General) 24 March, 1665/6, he about twenty, she sixteen. Any further information about this M.P. will be esteemed.

W. D. PINK.

TERIN.—Mirth's garden in the 'Romaunt of the Rose' is brightened with the songs of various birds :—

For there was many a bridde syngyng,
Thorough-oute the yerde al thringyng.

Nightingales, finches, turtledoves, larks, and others are enumerated as choristers. One line groups "thrustles, terins, and mavys."

The terin is by some authorities said to be the siskin; but would the siskin be singing along with nightingales and the others mentioned? The poet gives his assurance on the point, for he says:—

> And, trusteth wel, that I hem herd
> Ful lustily, and wel I ferde.

Is, then, the terin the siskin; and, if so, does it mingle its voice with those of the spring songsters in the English woodlands?

THOMAS BAYNE.

SPIDER POISON.—The poison of the spider is said by Alexander Rosse to crack glass. Is this a piece of British folk-lore, or did Rosse gather it, like so much else, from some classic source? 'Mel Heliconium,' 1643, p. 34.

N. M. & A.

DIXON OF NEWCASTLE AND ATKIN OF NORTHUMBERLAND.—Capt. James Dixon, of Newcastle, is supposed to have gone down with his vessel in Boston Deeps some time between 1823 and 1845. His mother's maiden name was Atkin, and his son James was born in 1823. Is anything known of Capt. James Dixon, his parentage, his wife's name, and anything about his mother's family?

RONALD DIXON.

46, Marlborough Avenue, Hull.

'STRAY LEAVES.'—Who was the author of 'Stray Leaves from a Freemason's Note-book,' by a Suffolk Rector, published by Spencer, London, 1846? The work is mentioned by Lowndes, but no author given. W. B. H.

JACOBITE LINES.—Will some correspondent give the exact date and authorship of the Jacobite effusion 'As the D—l was marching o'er Britain's Fair Isle'? The line

> Look down on my offspring, there's F—y my son,

must have been written before 20 March, 1751, and subsequent to Culloden, as G—'s laudatory mention of "B—y my darling" shows. W. G. BOSWELL-STONE.

Oxford.

SHROPSHIRE PLACE-NAMES. — I should be glad of a reference to any recent book on this subject. More especially I desire an explanation of Ruyton-of-the-XI.-Towns and of Eaton Constantine. Has either of these curious names been discussed in 'N. & Q.'? CHARLES HIATT.

[At 5th S. i. 275 H. W. A. gave the following quotation from Gough's manuscript 'History of Myddle, co. Salop' (1701): "I shall sometimes mention the Eleven Towns. I will here give an Account of what they are, and first their names are Old Ruyton, Cotton, Shelvocke, Shottatton, Wykey, Eardeston, Tedsmeare, Rednall, Haughton, Sutton, Felton. These Eleven Towns make up the Manor or Lordship of Ruyton, and they are an allotment in the Hundred of Oswestry." A. R. added: "All the names given by Gough remain, but some of them do not represent even villages in the present day."]

'GULLIVER': EARLY EDITIONS.—Can any reader supply me with the dates of publication of the early editions of 'Gulliver's Travels'? E. B.

[The first edition appeared London, B. Motte, 2 vols., 1726-7, with plates by Sturt: the second in 1727. Other editions followed in 1731, 1747, 1751, 1766, &c. Consult 'Book-Prices Current.']

DESERTER AND SPY.—Of whom, by whom, and upon what occasion was it said of an English public man that he had left his party as a deserter, and that they would take care he did not return to them as a spy? I find that "He came into the Camp like a Spy, and went out of it like a Deserter," is quoted as from *Town-Talk*, No. IX., on the title-page of 'The Pretender's Flight......or, a Mock Coronation,' a tragi-comical farce by John Phillips, published by Curll in 1716. POLITICIAN.

SEA BEGGARS.—In his 'Progress of South Africa' Dr. Theal, speaking of President Boshof, says, "He was wanting in that perseverance under difficulties which has always been a characteristic of the majority of the sons of the sea beggars in South Africa." Who were the sea beggars, and why were they so called? C. S. WARD.

Wootton St. Lawrence, Basingstoke.

[Sea beggars (Gueux de la Mer) were the seamen of the small fleet organized by William of Orange in 1572 in order to combat the Spaniards under Alva. See Ruth Putnam's 'William the Silent,' ii. 2, *et seq.*, or Motley, *passim*.]

CATHERINE BABINGTON.—It is stated in the Supplement to the fourth edition of Burke's 'Landed Gentry' for 1863, and no other, that

"William Babington, of Greenfort and Urney, co. Donegal, who died in 1710, had an eldest son Thomas Babington, born *circa* 1701, who died childless, leaving Urney to his widow, who married a Mr. Pigott, and sold the estate, which thus passed from the Babingtons."

In the Dublin Diocesan Marriage Licence Bonds appears the marriage in 1740 of Catherine Babington and John Pigott, evidently the same persons. Can any correspondent of 'N. & Q.' kindly give me the maiden name of this Catherine, or say if she was a widow when married to Thomas Babington?

WM. JACKSON PIGOTT.

Dundrum, co. Down.

BOX HARRY.—The other day I was talking to an old woman on the subject of planting potatoes. She was telling me that she had only by her a very poor supply of seed, and

finished up by ejaculating, "Never mind, I must box Harry." When questioned as to the meaning of the last two words, she said their equivalent was that she must needs do without. As this was the first time I had heard the expression, I turned, on arriving home, to Miss Baker's 'Glossary of Northamptonshire Words and Phrases.' "The origin of this phrase," says she, "I know not, but it means to go without dinner." I have since discovered another person who was conversant with the phrase, and who said that it meant to go without food. The old woman whom I first heard employ it evidently used it in a much wider sense. Can 'N. & Q.' throw any light on its origin?   John T. Page.
West Haddon, Northamptonshire.

Replies.

'AYLWIN.'
(9ᵗʰ S. ix. 369.)

Ever since the publication of 'Aylwin' I have, at various times, seen in 'N. & Q.,' the *Daily Chronicle*, the *Contemporary Review*, and other organs, inquiries as to the identification of the characters that appear in that story. And now that an inquiry comes from so remote a place as Libau in Russia, I think I may come forward and say what I know on the subject. For I enjoyed the intimate friendship of D. G. Rossetti and knew a great deal of some of the other characters in 'Aylwin.' But, of course, within the limited space that could possibly be allotted to me in 'N. & Q.,' I can only say a few words on a subject that would require many pages to treat adequately. Until 'Aylwin' appeared Mr. Joseph Knight's monograph on Rossetti in the "Great Writers" series was, with the sole exception of what has been written about him by his own family and by my late father, Dr. Gordon Hake, in his 'Memoirs of Eighty Years,' the only account that gave the reader the least idea of the man—his fascination, his brilliance, his generosity, and his whimsical qualities. But in 'Aylwin' Rossetti lives as I knew him; it is impossible to imagine a more living picture of a man. I have stayed with Rossetti at 16, Cheyne Walk for weeks at a time, and at Bognor also, and at Kelmscott—the "Hurstcote" of 'Aylwin.' With regard to "Hurstcote," I well knew "the large bedroom with low-panelled walls and the vast antique bedstead made of black carved oak" upon which Winifred Wynne slept. In fact, the only thing in the description of this room that I do not remember is the beautiful 'Madonna and Child' upon the frame of which was written "Chiaro dell' Erma" (readers of 'Hand and Soul' will remember that name). I wonder whether it is a Madonna by Parmigiano, belonging to Mr. Watts - Dunton, which was much admired by Leighton and others, and has been exhibited. This quaint and picturesque bedroom leads by two or three steps to the tapestried room "covered with old faded tapestry—so faded, indeed, that its general effect was that of a dull grey texture"—depicting the story of Samson. Rossetti used the tapestry room as a studio, and I have seen in it the very same pictures that so attracted the attention of Winifred Wynne: the "grand brunette" (painted from Mrs. Morris) "holding a pomegranate in her hand"; the "other brunette, whose beautiful eyes are glistening and laughing over the fruit she is holding up" (painted from the same famous Irish beauty named Smith who appears in 'The Beloved'), and the blonde "under the apple blossoms" (painted from a still more beautiful woman—Mrs. Stillman). These pictures were not permanently placed there, but, as it chanced, they were there (for retouching) on a certain occasion when I was visiting at Kelmscott. With regard to the green room in which Winifred took her first breakfast at "Hurstcote," I am a little in confusion. It seems to me more like the green dining-room in Cheyne Walk, decorated with antique mirrors, which was painted by Dunn, showing Rossetti reading his poems aloud. This is the only portrait of Rossetti that really calls up the man before me. As Mr. Watts-Dunton is the owner of Dunn's drawing, and as so many people want to see what Rossetti's famous Chelsea house was like inside, it is a pity he does not give it as a frontispiece to some future edition of 'Aylwin.' Unfortunately, Mr. G. F. Watts's picture, now in the National Portrait Gallery, was never finished, and I never saw upon Rossetti's face the dull, heavy expression which that portrait wears. I think the poet told me that he had given the painter only one or two sittings. As to the photographs, none of them is really satisfactory.

I have often seen on the whatnot in the breakfast-room at "Hurstcote" the "French novels in green and yellow covers," and they were always, I believe, the novels of Dumas. I have spent delightful evenings at "Hurstcote" listening to Rossetti's talk about Dumas, his favourite novelist. The "young gentleman from Oxford who has been acting as my secretary," as mentioned in 'Aylwin,' was my brother. With regard to the two circular mirrors surrounded by painted designs telling the story of the Holy Grail, "in old black oak frames carved with knights at tilt." I do not remember seeing these there. But they are evidently the mirrors decorated with copies of the lost Holy Grail frescoes once existing on the walls of the Union Reading - Room at Oxford. One of these mirrors has been photographed, and is given in Mr. Marillier's charming book on Rossetti. These beautiful decorations I have seen at "The Pines," but not elsewhere. I have often seen "D'Arcy" in the company of several of the other characters introduced into 'Aylwin'; for instance, "De Castro" and "Symonds" (the late F. R. Leyland, at that time the owner of the Leyland line of steamers, living at Prince's Gate, where was the famous Peacock Room painted by Mr. Whistler). I did not myself know that quaint character Mrs. Titwing, but I have been told by people who knew her well that she is true to the life. With regard to "De Castro," it is a matter of regret to those who knew him that, after giving us that most vivid scene between "D'Arcy" and "De Castro" at Scott's oyster - rooms (a place which Rossetti was very fond of frequenting in those nocturnal rambles that caused "De Castro" to give him the name of Haroun al Raschid), the author did not go on and paint to the full the most extraordinary man of the very extraordinary group, the centre of which was Rossetti's Chelsea house. Rossetti was a well-known figure at Scott's and at Rule's oyster-rooms at the time he encountered "Aylwin." That scene at Scott's is, in my opinion, the most living thing in the book—a picture that whenever I turn to it makes me feel that everything said and done must have occurred. "De Castro" seemed to belong not merely to the Rossetti group, but to all groups, for he was brought into touch with almost every remarkable man of his time, and fascinated every one of them. Literary and artistic London was once full of stories of him, and no one that knew him doubted he was what must be called a man of genius—although a barren genius. Among others, he was brought into close relations with Ruskin, Burne-Jones, and, I think, Smetham ("Wilderspin"), and others. Rossetti used to say that since Blake there has been no more visionary painter in the art world than Smetham.

Rossetti had a quite affectionate feeling towards Smetham, and several of his pictures (small ones) were on Rossetti's studio walls.

I remember one or two extraordinary pictures of his—especially one depicting a dragon in a fen, of which Rossetti had a great opinion; and I believe this, with other pictures of Smetham's, is in the hands of Mr. Watts-Dunton. The author of 'Aylwin' would have been much amused had he seen, as I did, in an American magazine the statement that "Wilderspin" was identified with William Morris—a man who was as much the opposite of the visionary painter as a man can be. Morris, whom I had the privilege of knowing very well, and with whom I have stayed at Kelmscott during the Rossetti period, is alluded to in 'Aylwin' (chap. ix. book xv.) as the "enthusiastic angler" who used to go down to "Hurstcote" to fish. At that time this fine old seventeenth - century manor house was in the joint occupancy of Rossetti and Morris. Afterwards it was in the joint occupancy of Morris and (a beloved friend of the two) the late F. S. Ellis, who, with Mr. Cockerell, was executor under Morris's will. But "Wilderspin" was Smetham with a variation : certain characteristics of another painter of genius were introduced, I believe, into the portrait of him in 'Aylwin'; and the story of "Wilderspin's" early life was not that of Smetham. The series of "large attics in which was a number of enormous oak beams" supporting the antique roof was a favourite resort of my own; but all the ghostly noise that I there heard was the snoring of young owls—a peculiar sound that had a special fascination for Rossetti; and after dinner Rossetti, my brother, and I would go to the attics to listen to them.

But a more singular mistake with regard to the 'Aylwin' characters than that of Morris being confounded with "Wilderspin" was that of confounding, as certain newspaper paragraphs at the time did, "Cyril Aylwin" with Mr. Whistler. I am especially able to speak of this character, who has been inquired about more than any other in the book. I knew him, I think, even before I knew Rossetti and Morris, or any of that group. He was a brother of Mr. Watts-Dunton's—Mr. Alfred Eugene Watts. He lived at Park House, Sydenham, and died suddenly either in 1870 or 1871, very shortly after I had met him at a wedding party. Among the set in which I moved at that time he had a great reputation as a wit and humourist. His style of humour always struck me as being more American than English. While bringing out humorous things that would set a dinner table in a roar, he would himself maintain a perfectly unmoved countenance. And it was said of him, as "Wilderspin" says of

"Cyril Aylwin," that he was never known to laugh. The pen-picture of him in 'Aylwin' is so vivid that I am tempted to reproduce it here :—

"Juvenile curls clustered thick and short beneath his wideawake. He had at first struck me as being not much more than a lad, till, as he gave me that rapid, searching glance in passing, I perceived the little crow's feet round his eyes, and he then struck me immediately as being probably on the verge of thirty-five. His figure was slim and thin, his waist almost girlish in its fall. I should have considered him small, had not the unusually deep, loud, manly and sonorous voice with which he had accosted Sinfi conveyed an impression of size and weight such as even big men do not often produce. This deep voice, coupled with that gaunt kind of cheek which we associate with the most demure people, produced an effect of sedateness......but in the one glance I had got from those watchful, sagacious, twinkling eyes there was an expression quite peculiar to them, quite inscrutable, quite indescribable."

With regard to the most original character in the story, those who knew Clement's Inn, where I myself once resided, and Lincoln's Inn Fields, will be able at once to identify Mrs. Gudgeon, who lived in one of the streets running into Clare Market. Her business was that of night coffee-stall keeper. At one time, I believe—but I am not certain about this—she kept a stall on the Surrey side of Waterloo Bridge, and it might have been there that, as I have been told, her portrait was drawn for a specified number of early breakfasts by an unfortunate artist who sank very low, but had real ability. Her constant phrase was "I shall die o' laughin'—I know I shall!" On account of her extraordinary gift of repartee, and her inexhaustible fund of wit and humour, she was generally supposed to be an Irishwoman. But she was not: she was cockney to the marrow. Recluse as Rossetti was in his later years, he had at one time been very different, and could bring himself in touch with the lower orders of London in a way such as was only known to his most intimate friends. With all her impudence, and I may say insolence, Mrs. Gudgeon was a great favourite with the police, who were the constant butts of her chaff.

With regard to the gipsies, although I knew George Borrow intimately, and saw a great deal of Mr. Watts-Dunton's other Romany Rye friend, the late Frank Groome, I did not know Sinfi Lovell or Rhona Boswell. But I may say that those who have said that Sinfi Lovell was painted from the same model as Mr. Meredith's Kiomi are mistaken. Sinfi Lovell was extremely beautiful, whereas Kiomi, I believe, was never very beautiful. But that they are represented as being contemporaries and friends is shown by D'Arcy's mention of Kiomi in Scott's oyster-rooms. The characters who figure in the early Raxton scenes I cannot speak of for reason which may be pretty obvious; nor can I speak of the Welsh chapters in 'Aylwin,' which have been a good deal discussed in recent numbers of 'N. & Q.' (ante, pp. 229, 353). But being myself an East Anglian by birth—one of my Christian names is St. Edmund, because I was born at Bury St. Edmunds—I can say something about what the East Anglian papers call "Aylwinland," and of the truth of the pictures of the east coast to be found in the story. Since 'Aylwin' was published an interesting attempt has been made by a correspondent in the *Lowestoft Standard* (25 August, 1900) to identify Pakefield Church as the "Raxton" Church of the story, and the writer of the letter mentions the most remarkable, and to me quite new fact, that although the guide-books of Lowestoft and the district are quite silent as to a curious crypt at the east end of Pakefield Church there is exactly such a crypt as that described in 'Aylwin,' and that in the early days of the correspondent in question it was used as a storehouse for bones. The readers of 'Aylwin' will remember the author's words : "The crypt is much older than the church, and of an entirely different architecture. It was once the depository of the bones of Danish warriors killed before the Norman conquest."

With regard to the heroine, Winifred Wynne, I could not say anything without the author's permission. But it is well known that the description in the story of the unequalled beauty and charm of this Snowdonian maiden is not in the least exaggerated. But here I must stop for want of space. Should any correspondent of 'N. & Q.' want enlightening upon any matters within my knowledge in connexion with 'Aylwin,' I shall be pleased to come to his assistance. THOMAS ST. E. HAKE.
Craigmore, Bulstrode Road, Hounslow, W.

KNURR AND SPELL (9ᵗʰ S. ix. 385).—Fifty years ago this game was played by hundreds, often before thousands of spectators, in the outskirts of Leeds, Bradford, Halifax, Huddersfield, and other towns and villages in that part of the "clothing district." There were crack players, just as at cricket and football now, and often there was playing for considerable stakes, and much betting as to results. I remember some thirty years ago a remark in the *Globe* newspaper

showed that the writer of the passage had no idea of what the game was, and I in a short letter enlightened him. A hard wood ball, rather less than a full-sized billiard ball, is sprung, by a touch from the player, from a holder suitably contrived, and then struck by him when it is about two to three feet from the ground as far as possible. The striking implement used to be a long tapering stick, not much unlike a billiard cue, with a short little bat, not unlike the half of a small beer-bottle in shape, the neck part being that by which the whole is bound on to the stick at the smallest end of it, the round side of the half bottle being the back of the bat in striking. The ball was usually made of hard heart of holly tree, and was often brought into shape by repeated and innumerable cuts of the knife, presenting thus to the eye hundreds of tiny facets. Mr. Lionel Cresswell mentions a modern dictionary that does not give the meaning of the name of this game, and does not show the origin of the name. Can he tell one who has not leisure to hunt them up of one that does? I remember I looked in vain, but that was many years ago, and every one is much more cocksure now. The *Standard* of 2 April last made the remark that "people who are always 'cocksure' are somehow less convincing than those who affect or feel a certain intellectual diffidence." I endorse the sentiment. I do not know the origin of the name knurr and spell, but I told the *Globe* (I remember) that I surmised that the name was nothing but an English rendering of *Knorren Spiel*, meaning the game with the wooden knots, and I expressed a wish that it might be ascertained if in old time in Germany or in Holland such a game so named had been played. I suppose it is extremely unwise in the columns of 'N. & Q.' to hazard such a speculative inquiry; but, in the light of Mr. Cresswell's remarks, I will venture it. I might say that in Yorkshire the words *knurr and* are pronounced by the people as *knurren—i.e.*, much as *Knorren* is pronounced by Germans — and any man knowing Low German can or could understand a good deal of the Yorkshire "lingo."
B.

[The 'H.E.D.' says M.E. *knorre, knurre ;* ulterior etymology uncertain.]

WHITSUNDAY, 1593 (9ᵗʰ S. ix. 408).—Between 1582 and 1752 Easter (and therefore Whitsuntide) was not kept at the same time in England and in Western and Southern Europe, all Roman Catholic countries having adopted, at the former date, the new or Gregorian style of the calendar, whilst we in England adhered to the old or Julian style, which even now continues to be observed in Russia.

In 1593 Whitsunday fell by new style on 6 June, but in England it was kept according to old style on 3 June, which by the new style corresponded to 13 June, the reckoning of days differing at that time by ten, whilst it now differs by thirteen, so that 18 May (our Whitsunday this year) was called 5 May in Russia, and their Whitsunday is 2 June in their reckoning, but 15 June in ours.

Let me call your correspondent's attention to a most handy book in such inquiries, the Rev. W. A. Whitworth's 'Churchman's Almanac for Eight Centuries (1201 to 2000),' in which are given the dates of all the Church festivals by both styles of the calendar between the above dates. It was published by Wells Gardner & Co. in 1882, and should be more extensively known.   W. T. Lynn.
Blackheath.

According to Sir H. Nicolas's 'Chronology of History,' p. 65, Easter Day in 1593 was 15 April. This being so, Whitsunday was 3 June.   Celer.

BOON FOR BOOKWORMS (9ᵗʰ S. ix. 406).—Where has Mr. Cecil Clarke been biding all these years that he should hail the ribbon markers attached by "a thoughtful firm of publishers" to their books as being an innovation? Messrs. J. M. Dent & Co. must have used up thousands of yards of Chinese ribbon on the *agrément* of their reprints, on their "Temple" Shakespeare, Dramatists, and Classics, &c. Not seldom the date is omitted from their title-pages, but I have an edition of Miss Ferrier's novels which is markered, and which owns to 1894. I had imagined the Junior Athenæum Club to be in London.
St. Swithin.

OSORIO FAMILY (9ᵗʰ S. ix. 307, 414).—It may interest P. L. N. F. to know that there was an Abraham Osorio living in Nottingham in 1780. There are several baptisms of his children in the registers; *vide* 'Notes on Registers of St. Mary's, Nottingham,' by J. T. Godfrey, p. 65, published 1901.
T. Colyer-Fergusson.
Ightham Mote.

ENGLISH GLADIATORS (9ᵗʰ S. ix. 407).—These bloodthirsty contests, which even foreign observers like Misson allow were to a certain extent serious, appear to have been a survival of the sword-and-buckler days, when serving-men carried a sword with a buckler slung at their back, a custom again which was itself a survival from feudal days and the joust and tournament of the gentry. The champions mounted a raised platform which served as a stage. The bear-garden at Hockley-in-the-Hole, the "Great Booth" at Tottenham Court, Figg's "Boarded House" in Marylebone Fields, &c., were the favourite resorts of the "back-sword" fancy. The following advertisement is from the *St. James's Evening Post* of 9 February, 1738 :—

"At the Great Booth in Tottenham Court Road near S. Giles's Pound at 3 o'clock......Will be performed a Trial of Skill between the two following Masters of Sword and Gafflet, at an inch Lance clear from the Button, for the sum of Forty Guineas, viz. (Some Time after Mr. Sullivan and Mr. Vantrogan fought the Small-Sword and Gafflet at Tottenham Court, there happened a Dispute between two of their Scholars which Dispute occasioned a Wager of Forty Guineas to be laid between these two Gentlemen which of these two Masters should get the better at that Exercise; this is to certify the Publick that they will meet at the aforesaid Time and Place, then and there will decide that Wager, with an Inch of a Lance clear from the Button, the most Thrusts in Nine Assaults).
"Mr. SULLIVAN and Mr. VANTROGAN.
"Attendance at One, and the Masters to mount precisely at Three."

See further Harl. MSS., 5931, 50; Palmer's 'Hist. of St. Pancras'; Capt. Godfrey's 'Science of Defence'; *Spectator*, No. 449; John Ashton's 'Social Life in the Reign of Queen Anne' and his 'History of the Fleet River'; also numerous announcements of the challengers in the *Daily Advertiser* of 25 Sept., 1741; 30 March, 5 April, 12, 13, and 17 July, 1742. In Hone's 'Every-Day Book,' vol. ii., 9 June, there is an advertisement conveying a challenge to a sword combat in the usual bombastic style. In this case it was the notable Figg himself who was challenged. J. HOLDEN MACMICHAEL.

"ENGLAND'S DARLING" (9th S. ix. 290, 412). —No reason or quotation has been adduced in favour of the guess that Edgar Atheling was called "England's darling." That King Alfred was so called is a solid fact. In the poem entitled 'The Proverbs of Alfred,' printed at p. 103 of 'An Old English Miscellany,' edited by Dr. Morris in 1872, we find in ll. 9–11 "Alfred......Englene derling" —*i.e.*, Alfred, darling of the Angles or English. See the whole passage. CELER.

TENNIS: ORIGIN OF THE NAME (9th S. ix. 27, 75, 153, 238, 272, 418).—I should like to make clear my views concerning the etymology of this word. There is not an atom of evidence (so far as I know) to show that the word is of Old Central French origin. The word is rather of Anglo-French origin, and

therefore confined to England. Even if *tenez* was never used in France when serving a ball, that is no reason at all why it may not have been so used in England in Plantagenet times. Any one who wishes to understand that Anglo-French was a living language, with ideas and forms of its own, may study the history of the word *duty*.

Now the point is exactly this, that in the best and earliest MS. of the line in which the game is mentioned for the first time, the spelling used is precisely *tenetz*. I will not refer to my own edition, but rather to Macaulay's edition of Gower's poem in 'Praise of Peace,' vol. iii. p. 490, l. 295 :—"Of the *tenetz* to winne or lese a chace Mai no lif [person] wite er that the bal be ronne." The spelling *tenetz* represents the Anglo-French *tenez*, just as *fitz* is now usual in place of A.-F. *fiz*; and the A.-F. *z* was pronounced as *ts*, as it still is in German. If the A.-F. *tenez* is not the imperative plural of the A.-F. *tenir* (L. *tenēre*), perhaps MR. JULIAN MARSHALL, who alone is competent to decide, will kindly tell us what it is, and how the spelling is to be explained. WALTER W. SKEAT.

AUTOGRAPH COTTAGE (9th S. ix. 368).— William Upcott lived at Autograph Cottage, No. 102, Upper Street, Islington, and there died 23 September, 1845. He was buried at Kensal Green Cemetery on Wednesday, 1 October, 1845. I can with pleasure show his portrait and catalogues, formerly belonging to Abraham Lincoln, to MR. A. ABRAHAMS, if he wishes to see them.
JULIAN MARSHALL.

GREEK EPIGRAM (9th S. ix. 147, 273, 331, 372).—The looseness of the poetical versions of the second line may be due to the writers having followed Liddell and Scott in taking ἄρτι ποτεπλάσθη to mean "has just been added." For we should, perhaps, adhere, as MR. WAINEWRIGHT suggests, to the fuller sense of the verb, and render the clause "one has lately been formed (or moulded) in addition to the well-known Three"; and we might then, with him, suppose the epigram to relate to the inauguration of a statue of the queen. Madame Dacier, however, in a note given in Ernesti's edition of Callimachus, takes the second member of the pentameter, "and still drips (or is moist) with myrrh (or unguents)," as an amplification of the first (which she evidently understands to mean "one has lately been formed, or created "), and refers it to the custom of anointing new-born infants. Μύρον appears to have been profusely used by the luxurious Egyptian Court, and Athenæus (xv. 38) ascribes the excellence of the brand for which Alexandria was once famous to the care and encouragement given to the manufacture by Arsinoe, one of the wives, and Berenice, probably the mother of Ptolemy Philadelphus. If, as some think, Psalm xlv. was composed in honour of this prince, there would be a special appropriateness in the reference it makes to "robes (scented with) myrrh and aloes and cassia."

It seems, however, to be undecided whether the Berenice of the epigram was Soter's wife, whose character is eulogized by Plutarch ('Pyrrh.,' 4), and who appears, indeed, not to have been unworthy even of the courtly praise of Theocritus, or her granddaughter, the wife of Euergetes.   J. M. C.

GORDON RIOTS (9ᵗʰ S. ix. 68, 233, 350).— Barnaby Rudge,' referred to in one of the replies, is hardly to be depended upon for historic information. Dickens threw a glamour over the somewhat sordid story of the riots, allowing himself a novelist's licence in dealing with facts. Whence came his ever-memorable record of the rioters' visit to Chigwell? Certain strong negative evidence tends to prove that no such visit was paid.
    I. C. GOULD.

LADY NOTTINGHAM (9ᵗʰ S. ix. 128, 213).— This lady's thirty children, and Mrs. Green-hill's thirty-nine children, do not appear to state the limit of maternity :—

"In Aberconway Churchyard, Carnarvonshire, a stone records
Here lyeth the body of
Nicholas Hooks of Conway, gent.,
who was
the one-and-fortieth child of his Father
William Hooks, Esq. by Alice his Wife
and the father of seven-and-twenty children
he died the 20ᵗʰ day of March, 1637."

From "Here lies: being a Collection of Ancient and Modern Humorous and Queer Inscriptions on Tombstones. Compiled and edited by W. H. Howe. New York, A.D. 1901."
    JOHN TOWNSHEND.

"DUKE" (9ᵗʰ S. ix. 329).—This word, as also French *duc*, Italian *duca*, and Latin *dux*, are from Latin *duco*, "I lead." Welsh, with its natural tendency to assimilate Latin nouns, has its equivalent *duc*. There is a Welsh root *dyg-*, formerly *dyc-*, with the idea of "leading," the third pers. sing. perf. ind. whereof is *dwg*; but this is an indigenous root, cognate with, but not derived from, the Latin *ducere*.   JOHN HOBSON MATTHEWS.
    Town Hall, Cardiff.

"FLAPPER," ANGLO-INDIAN SLANG (9ᵗʰ S. ix. 266, 373).—In my day in India, at Benares and elsewhere, 1860-63, we used a "fly-flapper" with which to kill the common house fly—swarms of them infesting bunga-lows in the hot weather. The fly-flapper was a short cane wand, having a stiff piece of leather attached to the top, wherewith a fly, when settling anywhere (and they settled everywhere), was promptly smashed.
    GEORGE ANGUS.
    St. Andrews, N.B.

BISHOP WHITE KENNETT'S FATHER (9ᵗʰ S. ix. 365).—In stating that the bishop was born in August, 1660, at Dover, and was son of Basil Kennett, vicar of Postling, the 'D.N.B.' followed Wood, 'Ath. Oxon.,' iv. 792 (Bliss). The statement that the bishop's mother was Mary White apparently comes from another source. According to Hasted's 'Kent,' iii. 404, 429, Basil Kennett, M.A., became vicar of Postling in 1668, and rector of Dimchurch in 1676, and died, while in-cumbent of both livings, in 1686. He is not in 'Graduati Cantab., 1660–1823,' nor in Foster's 'Alumni Oxon.,' except as father of White Kennett, the bishop, and of Basil Kennett, who became president of Corpus Christi College, Oxford. In 5ᵗʰ S. viii. 117 it is said that his will was proved at Canterbury 3 December, 1686, and some particulars of its contents are given : "He left his son White Kennett lands and tenements at Folkestone and elsewhere." It is further said that "his wife's will is also at Canterbury (viz., Eliza-beth), proved Aug. 23, 1694-5." Did the bishop's father try two wives as well as two walks in life ?   H. C.

"COMICALLY" (9ᵗʰ S. ix. 285, 370).—Miss Baker gives the local meaning of "comical" as "odd, singular, ill-tempered." It is still used in this sense here, and also, probably more frequently, as indicating a slight illness or sudden qualm.   JOHN T. PAGE.
    West Haddon, Northamptonshire.

PINS AND PINCUSHIONS (9ᵗʰ S. ix. 209, 333). —Pins of bone and bronze have been fre-quently encountered in British sepulchral mounds, but far more frequently in circum-stances making it evident that they were in general use for the hair (*acus crinalis*)—as well as for those purposes of dress to which the pin is put to-day—by the Romans during their occupation of this country. Seven hair-pins in blue and green glass were found near Dorchester in 1835 (Roach-Smith's 'Collec-tanea Antiqua' and 'Illust. of Roman Lon-don'). The pin was passed through the back of the hair after it had been plaited or turned up, in order to keep it neatly arranged, as appears from the fragment of a statue in the Ducal Gallery at Florence. A great variety are engraved in the ' Museo Borbonico' (ix. 15) and in Guasco ('Delle Ornatrici,' p. 46). As to the pin for ordinary fastening purposes, I often encountered, during a constant attendance on excavations in the City some years ago, a type of pin from about two or three to six inches in length, which, with the exception that it is made of bronze and has a larger head, bears a remarkable resemblance to the modern draper's pin, perhaps a trifle finer and very flexible. It was, no doubt, used to fasten parts of the female dress, and appears to be the prototype of the modern pin, such pins as were used prior to this, at all events in Britain, having been evidently and invariably for the toilet. In Rich's 'Dictionary of Greek and Roman Antiquities,' s.v. 'Acus,' there is an illustration representing a vessel containing pins found at Pompeii, which apparently exactly resemble those in my possession. Miss Longman will find a good deal of information on the subject in Fosbroke's 'Encyclopædia of Antiquities' and Planché's 'Cyclopædia of Costume'; something, I think, likewise in Meyrick's 'Costume of the Britons.' See also J. Y. Akerman's 'Archæological Index,' 1847; Abraham Hume's 'Antiquities found at Hoylake in Cheshire,' 1847; and similar works concerned with the minor antiquities of Britain.

J. Holden MacMichael.

Sir Benjamin Rudyerd, 1572-1658 (9th S. ix. 383).—There is no doubt that Mr. Foster is right, and the 'D.N.B.' wrong, as regards the Inn to which this celebrity belonged. His name appears on the Admission Book of the Middle Temple, 18 April, 1590, as "Benjamin Rudierde, late of New Inn, the third son of James R. of Winchfield, co. Hants"; and he was called to the bar there 24 October, 1600. John Hutchinson.
Middle Temple Library.

The West Bourne (9th S. viii. 517; ix. 51, 92, 190, 269, 291, 375).—I am sorry that my concluding sentence (ante, p. 270) should have appeared "somewhat dogmatic" to Col. Prideaux, and, reading it again, I think that perhaps it errs a little in excess of emphasis. My wish was to express agreement with him as to the absence of any early written evidence that the stream was called West Bourne, but to add that of its having been so called there seemed to me sufficient proof in the name given to the adjacent land, which would not have had that name if there had been no stream known as the western bourne. I over-

looked his conjecture that the stream never had a name, and that the land was designated Westbourne simply because it lay west of a bourne; or as if the term "west of the bourne," originally used to define the land, had by contraction lapsed into the name "Westbourne."

Well, there are the two views, and choice may be made between them. That which I have supported appears to me the more reasonable, that which would be naturally held, which therefore has been generally held, and which a fresh conjecture is not sufficient to supplant. In the names of places having bourne as termination is not the prefix a qualification or definition of the bourne which has been the feature of the locality and origin of its name? As many think that the bourne we discuss was defined as the western bourne, so we find others defined as the little bourne (Littlebourn), the black bourne (Blackburn), and the red (?) bourne (Radbourn). The Bishop's bourne was probably the feature of ecclesiastical property, and, not to risk definitions in the absence of a sufficient glossary, there may be mentioned Patrixbourn, Beakesbourn, Winterborne, Swanbourne, Sherborne, &c. Are we not to think that all these were first the definition of streams, and afterwards the names of the localities they watered? Bosworth ('A.-S. Dict.') is not to the contrary. He states that "bourne, as a prefix or termination to the names of places, denotes that they were situate near a stream," and I think it would do no violence to his meaning to add, "the distinctive names of which they took."

That names are lost, especially of small streams, we know, and Sir Herbert Maxwell's experience in Cassiobury Park (third reference) is typical. The "Dang me if I remember!" would be the answer in most cases of inquiry, and only by diligent search in the village the stream's old name, far on its way to oblivion, might be evoked from the oldest inhabitant. But it is probable that to Peter Cunningham the name of the forgotten stream (it was extinct or out of sight when he wrote) appeared sufficiently obvious in Westbourne, the surviving name of the district, so that no inquiry was suggested.

I am quite of accord with my kind correspondent in hoping that we have arrived at a time when no statement can be allowed currency without the credentials of sound evidence, and by "evidence" is generally meant that of document. Yet I think there may be evidence that is not written, and that although West Bourne is not on any map or, in reference to the stream, in any early book or manuscript, yet that in the surviving name there is evidence which weighs more than conjecture. Not that conjecture is to be contemned when thus earmarked; it is at least interesting, and may be useful as tending towards the ultimate discovery of fact.

My correspondent does not seem to think much of the "long-legged Anglo-Saxon" who would get no further from primitive London than the stream which we (at any rate) know as the West Bourne. It was not far enough west to be known to A.-S. as *the* western bourne, and he could easily have stridden on to the Brent. Of course; but in many cases might not the distance have been found sufficient? The ground was rough in those days, and A.-S., with the lowering sun before him, may have considered that the return to his home required daylight and circumspection. Besides, if he did call it the Western Bourne, he need not be thought to have been ignorant of other streams more westerly; even as, doubtless, the "Man of Kent" knew of bournes more northerly than his North Bourne.

I was rash to name the other streams on this west side of London. One and all are, to repeat my borrowed phrase, highly charged with argument, and so, like dangerous sleeping dogs, it is best to leave them undisturbed. Perhaps West Bourne may be now allowed to sleep with them. But I feel sorry that dear old "Tamese" should have been assailed. It is well that Canon Taylor (whose loss we regret) should have passed to his rest. The meaning was so intelligible, and, moreover, poetical. We questioned, perhaps, whether it was the character of our river to be tranquil and spreading in its normal condition; but we know that much of it is subject to flood, and that the region now South-West London was seen by A.-S. in a chronic state of overflow. Thus we were satisfied. The sturdy Saxon, however, did not give the name, and we are now told that its barbarian root and meaning is lost and "irrecoverable."

I may just add that the late Canon, in his 'Names and their Histories,' says: "Eastbourne, in Sussex, is called *Burne*, the 'brook,' in the Chronicle. The prefix is a later addition which may have served to distinguish the stream from another burn further west, now called the Cuckmere River."

W. L. RUTTON.

GENERAL SIR WILLIAM FAWCETT (9th S. ix. 368).—General Sir William Fawcett was the son of William Fawcett, of Halifax, and Martha, daughter of James Lister, apothecary in the same town, afterwards of Shibden Hall, his wife. Born at Shibden Hall 30 April,

1727, at the age of sixteen he entered the army as an ensign in General Oglethorpe's Regiment of Foot. Served in Flanders, then resigned his commission, but, being dissatisfied with a civilian's life, joined the 3rd Regiment of Guards as ensign. He was aide-de-camp to General Eliott and the Marquis of Granby, and was appointed to bear the news to England of the battle of Warburgh, fought 31 July, 1760. He gave King George II. a graphic account of the battle in the German language. Created K.B. 20 December, 1786, general 3 May, 1796, and 12 July following was made a Governor of Chelsea Hospital; sworn a Privy Councillor 23 January, 1799. He married Susanna, daughter of William Brooke, of Hampstead, in 1749. Died 22 March, 1804, and was buried at Chelsea Hospital.

JOHN RADCLIFFE.

"PASCHAL": "PASCUA" (9th S. ix. 364).—In the 'Metrical Life of St. Cuthbert,' edited by me for the Surtees Society, and issued in 1891 (vol. lxxxvii.), we find *Pace, Pase, Pasche*, and *Pasce* used for Easter (glossary, p. 267). But *Pace* is once used for Christmas, as I then thought "in error," thus: "Done solempnite of pace, To farne agayne he takes his trace" ("peracta die solemni nativitatis Dominicæ," Bæda, 'Vit. S. Cuthb.,' cap. xxxvii.). But it was the editor who was "in error"; "adsum qui feci." Ducange says that *Pascha* may mean "quodlibet magnum festum." Hence *Pascha floridum, P. rosarum*, Fr. Pasque de Noël, Sp. Pascua de Natividad. See also Sir H. Nicolas, 'Chron. Hist.,' 128, for some more valuable information on this point.

J. T. F.

Durham.

"ONLY TOO THANKFUL" (9th S. ix. 288, 370).—I think that we must decompose this remarkable phrase into its two distinct elements. The desire to express themselves very forcibly drives men to choose words which in themselves would be too strong for the occasion. Wishing to say "You are very kind," they say "You are too kind." In many cases this "too" may make sense still. But owing to exaggeration, which is such a favourite in conversational speech, *too* has come to mean often not an excessive, but a high degree of some quality. Women especially indulge in that sort of overdoing statement. Instead of simply asserting that they are happy, they are "too happy." This would account for the *too*. Now for the *only*. When asked, "Was it not hot?" we Germans often answer by way of irony, "No, it was not hot, it was only *very* hot." This produces, of course, a comical effect, as we pretend to regard that which is the highest degree of some quality as its lowest, and therefore substitute *only* for *even*. Irony is everywhere the same, and for this reason the development may have been identical in English, German, and French, for "es ist nur zu wahr" and "il n'est que trop vrai" are quite as common idioms as "it is only too true." With this I do not intend to imply that all the three invented this turn of speech independently; I am convinced, on the contrary, that one of them has the priority— but which? Continual borrowings have been going on between the different nations of culture. Whether the solution offered holds good I am uncertain, but my sincere thanks are due to DR. MURRAY for having set me thinking.   G. KRUEGER.

Berlin.

PORTRAITS OF EARLY LORD MAYORS (9ᵗʰ S. viii. 485 ; xi. 173, 232, 412).—I should have written Bletchingley, not Bletchington.
J. T. PAGE.

West Haddon, Northamptonshire.

BRIGHTWALTON (9ᵗʰ S. ix. 349).—Possibly the information required might be obtained from Mr. T. Wareing, who published a paper on the brasses in Brightwalton Church in the Monumental Brass Society's *Transactions*, vol. ii., 1899.   EVERARD HOME COLEMAN.

Miscellaneous.

NOTES ON BOOKS, &c.

Cuchulain of Muirthemne: the Story of the Men of the Red Branch of Ulster. Arranged and put into English by Lady Gregory. (Murray.)

THIS rendering by Lady Gregory of the Cuchullin saga is likely to do more to popularize these impressive legends among English readers than any treatment previously accorded them. The best-known translation is that executed by various scholars, edited by Miss Eleanor Hull, and issued by Mr. Nutt in 1898 as the eighth volume of the "Grimm Library" (see 9ᵗʰ S. iv. 138). To this scholars will still turn. For the general reader, however, Lady Gregory's work, which is converted into what may be called colloquial Irish—that is, English as familiarly spoken by Irish lips—offers singular attractions. We are almost disposed to echo Mr. W. B. Yeats, who thus opens his eulogistic, but critical and discriminating preface: "I think this book is the best that has come out of Ireland in my time. Perhaps I should say that it is the best book that has ever come out of Ireland, for the stories which it tells are a chief part of Ireland's gift to the imagination of the world—and it tells them perfectly for the first time." There is about these narratives in their present form a great, if not easily definable charm. No attempt is made now, as in previous renderings, to depict things such as the means by which Cuchullin at the outset of his career finds his modesty subject to so severe a strain by the unpardonable proceedings of the women of Emain. For a full account of such things one must turn to a scholarly rather than a popular work. None the less, the description generally of the women, and their influence in stirring up strife, is admirable. No chapter is more interesting or better in any respect than that of the 'War of Words of the Women of Ulster,' brought about by the malicious representations of Bricriu. We are reminded of the vauntings of Tamburlaine when we read the boasting of these ladies. Emer, the wife of Cuchullin, "spoke, and it is what she said: 'There is no woman comes up to me in appearance, in shape, in wisdom; there is no one comes up to me for goodness of form, or brightness of eye, or good sense, or kindness, or good behaviour. No one has the joy of loving or the strength of loving that I have ; all Ulster desires me ; surely I am a nut of the heart. If I were a light woman, there would not be a husband left to any of you to-morrow.'" The sad fate of Deirdre, the Irish Juliet, and her lover Naoise is delightfully narrated. Here is the picture of Deirdre when she is fourteen, the age of Juliet: "And Deirdre grew straight and clean like a rush on the bog, and she was comely beyond comparison of all the women of the world, and her movements were like the swan on the wave, or the deer on the hill. She was the young girl of the greatest beauty and of the gentlest nature of all the women of Ireland." Her wail over Alban, when "she cried pitifully, wearily, and tore her fair hair," is one of the most touching things in fiction, and her suicide after the slaughter of the sons of Usnach is harrowing. It is interesting to folklorists to hear how Fingan, the Druid physician of Conchubar, could tell what a person's sickness was by looking at the smoke of the house he was in, and knew also by looking at a wound what sort of person gave it. Very spirited is the description of the great combat for the bull of Cuailgne. For days Cuchullin, single-handed, except for his charioteer, defends Ulster against the men of Connaught, executing deeds unparalleled except among the feats of the Paladins of Charlemagne, as told in 'La Légende des Siècles.' Knowledge of the great Irish saga is confined in England to comparatively few. It should now be widely extended. The description of feastings and slaughter is apt to become monotonous. This is as true of Homer as it is of Irish or Scandinavian bards. The fights in Cuchullin are, however, varied as well as spirited, and the atmosphere of the work in its latest form is enchanting.

Huchown of the Awle Ryale, the Alliterative Poet. By George Neilson. (Glasgow, MacLehose & Sons.)

ONE of the keenest, most assiduous, and most erudite of Scottish antiquaries, Mr. Neilson has undertaken, and in part accomplished, the solution of many problems of national importance. His latest endeavour has been to prove the identity of Huchown of the "Awle Ryale" with Sir Hew of Eglinton, a Justiciar of Scotland, the holder of many important offices, and the husband of the half-sister of Robert the Steward, afterwards King Robert II. In addition he has sought to settle what are the works of Huchown which establish him as one of the foremost of alliterative poets. On both points great diversity of opinion exists, and very varying conclusions have been put forward by men of acknowledged position and reputation,

The points raised are mainly technical, and to pronounce upon them requires a kind of erudition rarely to be found outside a very limited circle. The critic called upon to deal with Mr. Neilson's argument may say of Mr. Neilson as Wyntoun says of Huchown, that he

> Has tretyd this mar cwnnandly
> Than suffycyand to pronowns am I.

Alliterative pieces previously claimed, directly and indirectly, for Huchown, include the following, printed by the Early English Text Society and, in some cases, elsewhere also: 'Morte Arthure,' 'Destruction of Troy,' 'Cleanness' and 'Patience' (the last two in 'Early English Alliterative Poems'), 'Gawayne and the Green Knight,' and 'The Pearl,' together with 'Golagros and Gawayne,' 'Awntyrs of Arthure,' and 'Pistill of Susan,' edited for the Scottish Text Society. To these Mr. Neilson adds 'The Wars of Alexander' (E.E.T.S.); 'Titus and Vespasian; or, the Sege of Jerusalem,' edited by Gustav Steffler (Marburg, 1891); 'The Parlement of the Three Ages' and 'Wynnere and Wastoure' (Roxburghe Club, 1897); 'Erkenwald,' included in Prof. Carl Horstman's 'Altenglische Legenden' (Neue Folge, Heilbronn, 1881); and three or four short pieces, with which, however, Mr. Neilson does not specially concern himself. Sufficiently startling are the conclusions at which Mr. Neilson arrives—so startling that we must perforce leave experts to pronounce upon them. One, perhaps the most important, is that there is being gradually revealed to us "the countenance of an immortal who ranks among the great formative forces in the literature of the English tongue, who, while Chaucer was still (to public intents) silent, had ransacked the storehouses of Latin, French, and English in the quest of material for romantic narrative, and who, no less than Chaucer, set his seal for ever on the literary art of his own generation and of the generations to follow......in romance ......a unique and lofty spirit, comparable, in respect of his greatness, only with Walter Scott." Not less remarkable are the interpretations put upon some of the Arthurian legends, recalling those which a couple of centuries earlier were forced upon 'Pantagruel' and 'Gargantua.' In the 'Golagros' poem, as we are told, the fact in substance is that "Golagros represents John of France, Arthur is Edward III., Gawayne is the Black Prince, and the duel is the battle of Poitiers, while the white horse is that ridden by the French king on that ill-fortuned day." Ill-fortuned for France, we presume is meant. In another poem, 'The Erlis Sone of Kent,' Arthur is Edward III. and Gawayne is the Black Prince, while Galleroun "is a historical and allegorical representative of Scotland." That these and other views herein put forward will meet with opposition may safely be assumed. We are in no position to challenge them. All we can do is to commend them to the consideration of the students of alliterative verse. The rich stores of Glasgow University, already laid under contribution by the Hunterian Club, have been used by Mr. Neilson, whose volume includes the substance of two lectures delivered before the Glasgow Archæological Society, in whose *Proceedings* they were first printed. Some additions have been made, an index has been supplied, and the work thus constituted has been issued in an edition practically limited to 250 copies. Facsimiles from Hunterian MSS. of Geoffrey of Monmouth, diagrams, crests,

and other illustrations add to the interest and value of the volume.

Sir Edmund T. Bewley, LL.D., has reprinted from the Cumberland and Westmorland Archæological Society's *Transactions*, vol. ii., New Series (Kendal, Wilson), *Some Notes on the Lowthers who held Judicial Office in Ireland in the Seventeenth Century*. These are of historical as well as genealogical interest, and are accompanied by a design of the Lowther monument in Lowther Church, Westmorland.

Mr. Percy Lindley's *Holidays in Eastern Counties* has been greatly enlarged, and is very likely to set one dreaming of a visit to places so pleasantly described by pen and pencil.

Honour to the season is furnished in the *Fortnightly* by a 'Coronation Ode,' the author of which is Mr. James Rhoades. Like many similar compositions it is creditable as rhetoric, if not specially noteworthy as poetry. Mr. G. Marconi writes on 'The Possibilities of Wireless Telegraphy.' He is, of course, bound to make out a case for his own invention, but some of the instances he advances of wireless communication are sufficiently remarkable. Mr. Arthur Symons contributes an article on 'Rodin,' of whom he speaks as "a visionary, to whom art has no meaning apart from truth." He is a little startling in his paradox, as when he says in reference to rhythm, the importance of which it is difficult to exaggerate, "The same swing and balance of forces make the hump on a dwarf's back and the mountain in the lap of a plain. One is not more beautiful than the other, if you will take each thing simply, in its own place." This we cannot but regard as a hard saying. An animated account is given of various works of Rodin. With Mr. Symons's conclusions we cannot deal. He quotes, however, a message from the civic authorities in Paris which is a surprising "document in the relations of art and the State." Without the absolute assurance of the writer we should hesitate to believe such a communication possible. They do not do everything better in France. Mr. Joseph Morris has an able article on 'John Webster,' in which he holds the scales successfully between the measureless enthusiasm of Mr. Swinburne and the carping discontent of Mr. William Watson. Concerning Webster Mr. Morris has no doubt. He is "infinitely the greatest of that fascinating brotherhood of playwrights who cluster, like clever and emulative children, round the gigantic manhood of Shakespeare." Mr. Courtney's treatment of the legend of 'Undine' is, too, a delightful blend of poetry and fantasy.—'George Eliot' is the subject in the *Nineteenth Century* of an essay by Mr. Herbert Paul. George Eliot's letters are pronounced "ponderous, conventional, and dull." Her style has not the magic of Rousseau and George Sand. It has, even at its best, "a hard metallic tone," and the metal is not silver. What seems to Mr. Paul most remarkable in her is that her powers of expression seldom find "a simple and natural outlet," except in the mouths of her characters. She is credited with a true and sincere sympathy with goodness of all kinds, with sorrow, with suffering, and with childhood. 'Middlemarch' is regarded as the culminating effort of George Eliot's genius. She is said to have been "always didactic," preaching "to the conventional masses of her fellow-countrymen the gospel of self-sacrifice, self-surrender, and self-restraint." She wrote, it is owned, good English, but was "apt to write it as a good classical scholar writes Latin prose." We quote these opinions as Mr. Paul's, and reserve our judgment as to their truth and justice. No one else having undertaken the defence of Thackeray against the attack of Mr. Frewen Lord, Mrs. Leche enters the field and vindicates the novelist from the charge that he loves to portray only the ludicrous and the discreditable, instancing, as any defender was bound to do, Henry Esmond, Col. Newcome, J. J., and the Warrington brothers. Thackeray is credited with "a lofty ideal of public duty," a "chivalrous enthusiasm for patriotism and self-devotion," and "an almost passionate appreciation of heroism, fortitude, and tenacity of purpose." Capt. L. Oppenheim gives a terribly realistic and striking picture of 'The Fight at Roival' and the recapture of lost guns and pompoms. Mr. E. S. Hope describes 'Some Bygone Coronation Progresses.' Mr. Laird Clowes deals with the tempestuous career of Admiral Edward Vernon, generally known as "Old Grog." Mr. Archibald Little praises the Chinese drama.—Under the title 'The New Agriculture' Mr. W. S. Harwood gives in *Scribner's* a highly interesting account of the work carried on at the fifty-six stations attached to or connected with the agricultural colleges of the United States. To the support of these the Government appropriates 15,000 dollars annually, an example we might do well to follow. Thanks to the work of these colleges, millions of acres supposed to be desert will be compelled to yield food for human or other consumption. One result of their labour appears to be that the spectre of the desolation which has hitherto followed the failure of the wheat crop seems to be laid for ever. Problems of irrigation, a subject in which India and Australia are deeply concerned, are among the subjects studied. 'The Camera in a Country Lane' gives pleasant pictures of wild flowers and other natural objects. In 'The Gulf Stream Myth and the Anticyclone' Mr. Watts says that "the Gulf Stream as an ocean current has no more influence on the climate of Western Europe than the weather-vane has on the winds that turn it." The establishment of the myth was greatly due to the 'Physical Geography of the Sea' of Lieut. Maury. At present the anticyclone is the benefactor. How long it will remain so some may see.—The *Pall Mall Magazine* is largely occupied with matter relevant to the approaching Coronation. Among articles dealing with this are one on 'The Crown as a Symbol,' by the Duke of Argyll; a second on 'The Coronation,' by Lord Esher; a third on 'India and the Coronation,' &c. Sir H. Maxwell Lyte has an interesting and well-illustrated account of Domesday Book. A notable paper is that of Mr. Ian Malcolm, M.P., on 'The Maharajah of Jaipur,' one of the most illustrious of our guests, and his vast dominions. Mr. William Archer interviews Mr. George Alexander on the conditions of theatrical art and management and on the need for a subventioned theatre. On the latter point the two dialogists are not wholly in accord. 'Domestic Service in the Middle Ages' has some excellent illustrations from the Bayeux tapestry and other sources. 'The Hidden Secrets of Creation,' by Mr. Marcus Reed, fosters the idea that flowers feel.—Mr. Sidney Low writes in the *Cornhill* on 'The Plethora of Poets.' His purpose is largely satirical, and he holds up to ridicule very much of what by the writers themselves is qualified as poetry. In vain has the lesson been preached that mediocrity in poetry is not to be tolerated. Miss Elizabeth Lee deals with the German drama of to-day, and makes the statement that "not the hardest and most prosaic facts of every-day life, not all the misery of all the world, can crush the romance that lurks in every German heart." 'A Londoner's Log-Book' is concluded, and we are sorry for it. Prof. H. C. Beeching in 'Alaric Watts and Wordsworth' gives some marvellous instances of inane criticism by the former upon the latter. 'In the Editorial Chair' describes some aspects of the life of the editor of a daily paper. The fiction generally is excellent.—A notice in the *Gentleman's* of the recent life of Napoleon by Mr. Rose, reviewed in our columns, is eulogistic, but bears a title which may be regarded as presumptuous. The title is 'Napoleon: The Last Word.' Most surely the last word concerning Napoleon has not been spoken, and will not soon be given to the world. 'The Romance of Genealogy,' by Mr. Dominick Browne, shows the pleasure of pedigree tracing. In his paper 'On the Education of the Upper Classes in France and England' Mr. Yorke holds that neither country has any manifest superiority over the other. 'A Forgotten Art Critic' describes the infamous John Williams, or Anthony Pasquin.—Mr. Lang in 'At the Sign of the Ship' in *Longman's* returns to the charge as to the Bacon-Shakespeare controversy, and is, after his wont, sufficiently outspoken. Among those whom he encounters in his career is Judge Webb, whose work on the subject we reviewed a week or two ago. He is always readable and delightful. Of a Swinburne myth he makes short work. Mrs. Lecky has an excellent article on 'Sports and Games of Ancient France,' founded upon a recent work of M. Jules Jusserand.—The contents of an amusing number of the *Idler* are principally fiction.

Notices to Correspondents.

We must call special attention to the following notices :—

On all communications must be written the name and address of the sender, not necessarily for publication, but as a guarantee of good faith.

We cannot undertake to answer queries privately.

To secure insertion of communications correspondents must observe the following rules. Let each note, query, or reply be written on a separate slip of paper, with the signature of the writer and such address as he wishes to appear. When answering queries, or making notes with regard to previous entries in the paper, contributors are requested to put in parentheses, immediately after the exact heading, the series, volume, and page or pages to which they refer. Correspondents who repeat queries are requested to head the second communication "Duplicate."

Scrutator.—We cannot enter on these highly abstruse questions.

NOTICE.

Editorial communications should be addressed to "The Editor of 'Notes and Queries'"—Advertisements and Business Letters to "The Publisher"—at the Office, Bream's Buildings, Chancery Lane, E.C.

We beg leave to state that we decline to return communications which, for any reason, we do not print; and to this rule we can make no exception.

LONDON, SATURDAY, JUNE 14, 1902.

CONTENTS. — No. 233.

Notes.

DEFOE AND THE ST. VINCENT ERUPTION OF 1718.

THE appalling consequences of the volcanic eruptions in the island of St. Vincent during the greater portion of May in this present year have served to call public attention, in a very marked degree, to one of the many literary problems associated with the name and career of Daniel Defoe. One of these I may claim to have already solved in these pages (see 8th S. viii. 221, 349), and with the other I hope not less satisfactorily to deal.

In the issue for 5 July, 1718, of the *Weekly Post, with Fresh Advices Foreign and Domestick* —commonly known, from the name of its publisher, as *Mist's Journal*—there appeared in the most prominent position a long, detailed, and (if I may use the word) moralized description of " the entire desolation of the island of St. Vincent in the West Indies, by the immediate hand of Nature, directed by Providence." This was asserted to be gathered from many letters received in London descriptive of a most destructive eruption at St. Vincent on the previous 26 March ; and as

" it would be impossible to bring the letters all separately into this journal......we have thought it better to give the substance of this amazing accident in one collection, making together as full and as distinct account of the whole as we believe is possible to come at by any intelligence whatsoever."

It has never been doubted that the writer of that account was Defoe ; but what is astonishing is that his biographers have followed one another in expressing the belief that he not merely wrote, but invented it. Mr. William Lee was not emphatic in that belief as he started, but it appeared to grow upon him as he proceeded with his monumental work. In the first volume (p. 280) he merely remarked that

" in June, 1718, an exaggerated account reached England that the Island of St. Vincent had been destroyed by an earthquake, upon which Defoe wrote a long and wonderfully circumstantial narrative of the catastrophe."

But in the preface to the second volume (p. viii) he considered that " lovers of the marvellous " would be " amused by [Defoe's] refusal afterward to admit that the story was not true "; while on p. 48, without a word of caution as to there being a doubt on the subject, he bluntly headed the narrative ' Imaginary Destruction of the Isle of St. Vincent.'

This very brusque fashion of dealing with the matter appears to have misled subsequent biographers. Prof. Minto (in the " English Men of Letters " series) wrote (p. 125) :—

" It is a notable circumstance that one of the marks by which contemporaries traced his hand was ' the little art he is truly master of, of forging a story and imposing it on the world for truth.' Of this he gave a conspicuous instance in *Mist's Journal* in an account of the marvellous blowing up of the island of St. Vincent, which in circumstantial invention and force of description must be ranked among his masterpieces."

And Mr. George A. Aitken, in his introduction to the collected edition of Defoe's works, which contains this narrative (vol. xv.), is even more precise :—

" Defoe's ' make-believe ' cannot be denied in the account of the ' Destruction of St. Vincent.' The article appeared in *Mist's Journal*, and seems to have been entirely of Defoe's invention, for no mention of any rumours about the island is to be found in the other newspapers of the day."

In face of so positive a statement, it will come upon your readers with some surprise to learn that, on the very date of the publication of Defoe's narrative in *Mist's*, there appeared in the rival *Applebee's*—the *Original Weekly Journal, with Fresh Advices, Foreign and Domestick*, for 28 June–5 July —an account of the same eruption, giving some details not possessed by the other ; and this is now of sufficient interest to be republished in full. It was as follows :—

London, July 5.

Letters from Passengers on board a Sloop, which sailed the 21st of March for Barbadoes, give us an Account, that on the 26 of the same Month, being about 5 Leagues to the Leeward of that Island, they met with a Calm, the Weather being very black till about Twelve a Clock at Night, when it looked very dismally all round the Horizon, as if it were on Fire, with a sulphurous Smell, and they heard prodigious Reports like Cannon, which were follow'd by continuous Showers of dry Dust or Ashes. About Six the next Morning, there was such a Darkness for three Quarters of an Hour, that they could not see one another without Candle Light. The Dust continued to fall upon them till seven at Night, when it lay 7 or 8 Inches thick upon the Deck. There being at that Time a little Wind, they bore up the Helm for Martinico, with a Design to get Bread and other Necessities they wanted. An Hour after, there fell Dust again, but not so violent. The Night look'd still terrible, but the Weather pretty moderate, and on the 30th they arrived at Guardaloupa, where they heard the surprizing News, that the Island of St. Vincent was blown up, and that they had an Account from Martinico, that from the Wednesday Night, being the 26 of March, to the Thursday Morning, they had heard above 1200 Reports like Cannon, and that St. Vincent was sunk. We hear since by other Advices, that the Governor of the Leeward Islands having received the like Information, sent a Sloop to see if they could discover that Island, but they could not see any Land, but where they expected to have seen the same, they saw the Sea in a Breach, so that it seems nothing remain'd of that Island but a Rock. One of our Sloops coming from Barbadoes, met with the same Showers of Dust or Ashes, and brought some of it, which is like Sand in Hour-Glasses but the Colour is like that of Ink-Powder. The Island of St. Vincent was about 8 Leagues long and 6 broad, and inhabited by Indians.

The Island of St. Vincent is blown up, which occasion'd that Shower of Ashes so much spoken of by our Sailors, who were so terrify'd thereat, and at the prodigious Reports they heard at the same time, as if a thousand or twelve hundred great Guns had been discharged, that the Accounts we have received from them, are very imperfect. We hear that nothing of that Island is to be seen but only two small Rocks.

But it happened that there was a third weekly newspaper in London in that day, generally referred to as *Read's*, and that one missed this startling piece of news altogether. That in itself would have sufficed to arouse its anger; but there was the greater reason in that the detailed Defoe narrative obviously caused a great sensation, and that this was particularly galling to the "Whigg-Writers" who had been attacked in the same number of *Mist's* in which that narrative appeared. Accordingly, the *Weekly Journal, or British Gazetteer, being the Freshest Advices Foreign and Domestick*, of the following Saturday, contained a letter addressed to "Mr. Jour-

nalist," and signed "Truth and Daylight," bitterly attacking *Mist's*, on the ground that it had become "dull, dull, very dull."

"Two Pages which us'd to contain many bright Things in Scandal ; two precious Pages, nay, two of the most celebrated Pages in his Paper, for those Occasions, are thrown away, for want of other Matter, in pitiful, stupid, and nonsensical Remarks, on the blowing up of an Island, I thank God, a good way off if true, and well worthy the grave, learned, and reputable Authors employ'd by *Mist*. In the next Line but one (that follows this News, and at this time a Day when Europe is big with many great Events, insignificant Harangue, which 20 Lines would have told as well as 2 Pages) is the lucky Appellation of Whig-Writers again; if one could but strip him of that Ornament of Speech, the Fellow would be left naked, and not have wherewithal to furnish out his weekly Scandal, without being oblig'd to take up with such bombast Stuff as the two first Pages in his last are."

No reply was made to this invective; but in *Mist's* of 19 July appeared among the ordinary news this paragraph :—

"Our Merchants have an Account, that there hath been a great Irruption at Porto Pikoe near Fial, belonging to the Portuguese, like that which lately happen'd at the Island of St. Vincent, which has made Chasmes in the Island 100 Yards every way, destroy'd and damaged several Houses, spoil'd above 1000 Pipes of Wine, and other Goods, so that the Loss is extream great."

Thus the pith of the general statement was repeated, and further independent corroboration came from *Applebee's*, which published on 26 July the following :—

"By our Letters this Week from New-England, we have the following News, viz.,......Boston, May 16. We have received here a Confirmation of the Destruction of the Island of St. Vincent, by the mighty Hand of Providence."

A week afterwards, however, it added :—

"Letters from Barbadoes mention the Eruption of a Volcano, or Burning Mountain, lately in the Island of St. Vincent; which generally happens once in Fifty or Sixty Years. And this is the only Ground of the Story of that whole Island's being blown up, which was dress'd in such Formidable Figures, in some of our News-Papers, a while ago; the said Island standing still where it ever did."

And it was to the latter paragraph that *Mist's* at once chaffingly replied :—

"They pretend to tell us a strange Story, viz., that the island of St. Vincent is found again, and is turn'd into a Volcano or burning Mountain; but we must acknowledge we do not believe one Word of it."

In face of all these facts, it should be impossible henceforward to deny the authenticity of the main narrative given by Defoe; even less should it be possible for any future biographer to follow the example of Mr. Thomas Wright, of Olney, and dismiss so brilliantly written an article merely as a "tomfoolery." ALFRED F. ROBBINS.

ST. MARGARET'S CHURCH AND WEST-MINSTER BENEFACTORS.

(Concluded from p. 383.)

UNDER date 10 April, 1677, 100*l.* was given to the churchwardens and vestrymen of St. Margaret's for the purpose of building three other almshouses, "all upon a ground floor," in Petty France, "to make the court or walks before the said houses quite through, and to plant elms before them." This legacy was received in due course, and the vestry ordered, on 21 January, 1677, the erection of the three almshouses at the west end of Cornelius van Dun's Almshouses (the Red Lion). They were pulled down in 1848, and the multi-angular building of the Petty France Workhouse erected on the site. This building is now known as Wellington House, and utilized as the Guards' married quarters. To the King's Hospital (Green Coat School) or St. Margaret's Hospital, the site of which is now occupied by the Stores of the Army and Navy Auxiliary Supply, Emery Hill proved a good friend, and, among other things, provided that

"the said Governors doe allow Ten shillings ayeare for ever to some able minister of the parish to examine the poore Hospitall Boys on that Day the Treasurer delivers up his accompts how the poore children growes and thrives in their duties to God and Man and in theire Learnings, and also keepe a checke on their Scholemaster."

So far for the mental, now for a glance at the bodily aspect of the case. He also provided for five chaldron of sea coals to be laid in "for the King's Hospital" every year,

"and that the poore children there have Rostmeate and Plumporridge every Christmas-day for ever to put the poore Creatures in mind of that extraordinary Good provided for their Soules on that Day, and that they may have green Mittens every time they have new Cloths, and that the Schoolmaster may have a new Gowne every Two years, And that care be taken to supply the poore Boys with Bookes fitt for their learning, especially with Catechisms and Bibles, And that every Boy that is putt forth may carry his Bible with him as his own proper goods."

I always feel a keen regard for this old school, for within its walls my own father received his early education, and many were the quaint stories he used to tell of his schooldays and the life that was lived there. Emery Hill left by deed dated 8 March, 1674, certain premises in Villiers Street, Duke Street, Office Alley, Buckingham Street, and the Strand, to establish—in addition to the almshouses—a

"free School to teach 20 poor town-born children born in Westminster, and a Chapel over the said School and a territt at one end of the chapel to hang a bell in, to ring the poor people to prayers, with a house for the school master to dwell in."

The children were to be taught free, both in English and Latin, to write and keep accounts, but further were to be catechized and grounded in all that appertained to religious knowledge. The school and master's house were built in 1708, and thirty years later, 1738, the Rev. Wiseman Holt was appointed schoolmaster, and for twenty-nine years had the destinies of this school in his hands, with the strange result that during those years until his death in 1767 he never educated a single boy. As a matter of fact,

"no boys appear to have been educated upon this foundation until 1817, when, the funds having got into a better state, a school was really established, and 20 boys taught in the School house of Palmer's Charity (The Black Coat School) by the same schoolmaster. For fifty-six years this arrangement worked harmoniously, but after 1873 the foundation had, for a short time, a separate existence."

Among the other benefactions of this large-hearted man was one under a deed dated 1 January, 1668, by which he transferred to the vestrymen the college lease of a tenement in the Almery of the value of 7*l.* a year, so that a school begun in 1666 for the poor parish children put out to nurse by the overseers might be continued and kept up. A penny a week was allowed the nurses for every child able to attend, which, with 5*s.* a month from the overseers,

"did well satisfie the Schoolemistress for teaching the poore Children, what nomber soever they caused to be sent. By which meanes the Seeds and Nursery of Idleness, Vice and Beggary was destroyed.'

Later on the same deed states that the school was neglected, and goes on :—

"By which meanes the sayd children were not only deprived of the meanes of their welfare for Bodies and Soules, but are exposed as heretofore to lye in the streets and at men's dores without any government or controll."

Under his will he devised a further tenement in the Great Almery, of like value, to aid in this good work, in which it is found that Dr. Busby, the eminent head master of Westminster School, was a coadjutor. Hatton, under date 1708, mentions this school, where a schoolmistress had "6*l.* per annum, a house, and a Chalder of Coal." A very exhaustive search and inquiry have been made, but no light can be thrown upon the causes which led to the extinction of this old charity school. Some of Emery Hill's benefactions have to our ears a very quaint and peculiar sound, of which some must be chronicled as lost. First may be noted his gift of 50*l.*, in trust, to be given to "some poore tradesmen and women that would faine live by their Trade if they had some small stock to help them therein, as some poore Shoo-maker or Cobler to have a good piece of Leather, or some poore Waterman to help him to a Boate, or some Herbwoman, or some that makes Buttons, or some that would Cry Things. If these and the like had some small stock to sett them at worke, it would much help them."

He appears to be rather hard upon beggars, who were to receive no benefit "unless it bee to take them quite off from theire Begging, and then it were well given." Another lost benefit to the parish is one whereby he gave to the churchwardens and vestrymen

"ffifty pounds of good and lawfull money of England to make a faire and a large Causeway, to make it at least thirty or forty feet wide, and to plant it with good Elmes, not with lime trees for they hold not green soe long, and to secure them from Cattell."

Again, he left a further 10l. for

"poor Bedridden People that have the most need of it, and none to have lesse than Two shillings six pence apiece, and that the Overseers of the Poore doe not Stop any part of such poore Allowance because of this guift not by any meanes, so that they [who] shall receive may supply with some refreshing that otherwise they never would have had."

Alas! how many poor there are now who would be glad of such monetary help! One is afraid to compute the number in the old city of Westminster, for there is a vast quantity of decent honest poverty within its area. Further, he also devised

"ten pounds to the charge in keeping upp the worke house as a worke house, it being of very good and great use if well managed to keepe the poore employed and also to keepe them from being Insolvent."

A very real and lasting memorial of this generous-handed worthy is in the new street from Rochester Row to Coburg Row and Ashley Gardens, opened in 1895, which was named after him, and so "points a moral and adorns a tale" for future generations. The value in 1890 of the funded property and Consols, and freeholds and leaseholds in the Strand district already mentioned was 79,880l., of which seven-twelfths are for the United Westminster Almshouse Endowment, and five-twelfths for that of the United Westminster Schools, and the annual income in the same year was 3,128l., while in 1824 it was only 310l., being rents 171l. and dividends 139l. As a large number of people knew the old almshouses they were neat brick cottages, a very quaint and pleasing feature of Rochester Row; but they vanished under an improvement scheme and were rebuilt in 1881, in a very picturesque style, Mr. R. R. Arntz, F.S.A., being the architect. He was a well-known figure in the parish, having been parish surveyor for some years. Not a pleasant person to deal with at times; but as the designer of these buildings he showed a good appreciation of his art and much ability in arranging the ground plan. He died before they were completed, the latter part of the work being done under the superintendence of Mr. Cole A. Adams, F.R.I.B.A., who carried out excellently the suggestions left unfinished. There is a very good picture of the old buildings in Mr. J. E. Smith's 'History of St. John's Parish'; and the new ones were figured in the *Builder* of 2 September, 1882.* For many years the superintendent of the Emery Hill Almshouses was Mr. S. Elliott, B.A.; but upon his resignation a successor was found in Mr. E. H. Fedarb, who from 1861 to 1898, a period of thirty-seven years, was the able master of St. Margaret's Church Schools, and who is admirably adapted for his present position.

So much for some of our generous benefactors who have monuments in St. Margaret's Church. There are others who have done many kindly actions; their monuments are to be found in the hearts of those who have been benefited by their wise and Christian forethought, and whose memories have been kept fresh through many generations and yet flourish as a green bay tree. Long may Westminster men, women, and children honour them, for they took thought for those who came after them, to smooth the rugged and often very rough way of the aged, and to render it possible for the children to make a fair start in the battle of life with what is the greatest blessing they can possess, a sound education founded upon a religious basis, as here provided. Our benefactors have been mindful of the poor and unfortunate, who are with us in every age, and may it be granted for some of our wealthy citizens to do for those who come after them as these worthies did centuries ago, whose benefactions are still fruitful for good!

W. E. Harland-Oxley.
C 2, The Almshouses, Rochester Row, S.W.

* At the time of the rebuilding the trustees of the almshouses were Mr. (afterwards Sir) Frederick Seager Hunt (chairman), the Venerable Archdeacon Jennings, Sir Henry Hunt, C.B., Mr. John Lettsom Elliot, Mr. James Alfred Hallett, Mr. George Taverner Miller, Mr. Herbert Thomas Steward, Mr. George Andrew Spottiswoode, Mr. Joseph Carter Wood, Mr. Edgar Horne, Mr. William Goldsmith, Mr. George Burt, Mr. George Francis Trollope, Mr. Thomas John White, Mr. R. Selby Freeman, and Mr. William Mann Trollope (clerk and solicitor), of whom a very large number are dead.

THE SONGSTRESSES OF SCOTLAND. — A writer in a London literary journal, referring to a new book entitled 'The Spindle Side of Scottish Song,' expresses the belief that Scottish poetesses have not hitherto received special and separate treatment. The subject, he says, "has not yet, I believe, had a volume all to itself." For the information of those interested in the subject, it may here be said that a work of two volumes bound in one, entitled 'The Songstresses of Scotland,' and written conjointly by Miss Sarah Tytler and Miss Jane L. Watson, was published by Messrs. Strahan & Co. in 1871. It is not satisfactory in all respects, needing revision in various *minutiæ*, as is customary with works on a large and comprehensive scale; but it displays biographical skill, taste in the art of selection, and a measure of critical accomplishment. It comprises an account of the life and writings of ten ladies, viz., Lady Grisell Baillie, Jean Adams, Mrs. Cockburn, Jean Elliot, Susanna Blamire, Jean Glover, Elizabeth Hamilton, Lady Anne Barnard, Lady Nairne, and Joanna Baillie. Had the writers included Lady Wardlaw, Isobel Pagan, Mrs. Grant of Carron, and Mrs. Grant of Laggan, their record would have been fairly complete. All are adequately represented in Mr. Grant Wilson's 'Poets and Poetry of Scotland,' 1877, and Mr. J. Ross's 'Book of Scottish Poems,' 1878. Prof. Veitch includes those that suit his purpose in his admirable 'Feeling for Nature in Scottish Poetry,' 1887.

THOMAS BAYNE.

DEATH OF THE TRUMPET-MAJOR AT BALACLAVA.—The death of Trumpet-Major Thomas Monks, of the Inniskilling Dragoons, who sounded the "charge" for the Heavy Brigade at Balaclava, may be worth recording in 'N. & Q.' For twenty years he had been trumpet-major of the Shropshire Yeomanry, his total military service amounting to half a century. His death took place at Shrewsbury on 25 May.

FREDERICK T. HIBGAME.
1, Rodney Place, Clifton, Bristol.

"CARIBOU."—This is the Canadian word for the reindeer. The 'N.E.D.' gives, as its earliest occurrence in English, a quotation dated 1774, but I find the term in use more than a century earlier, in Josselyn's 'New England's Rarities,' 1672, p. 20, as "the Macarib or Caribo, a kind of Deer, as big as a Stag." Popular etymology derives it, I need hardly say incorrectly, from "carré bœuf." The 'N.E D.' describes it vaguely as "probably of native American origin." I have traced it to the Micmac, an aboriginal

tongue of the group known as Eastern Algonquin. Elizabeth Frame, in her interesting booklet 'Micmac Names of Nova Scotia,' 1892, p. 8, gives the Micmac spelling as *kaleboo*, and states that it means "the shoveller, because they shovel up the snow with their broad feet in digging down for the moss on which they feed." These references should be of value if a supplement is projected of Dr. Murray's great work.

JAS. PLATT, Jun.

THE NEW HOURS OF BUSINESS IN THE HOUSE OF COMMONS.—There was noted in 'N. & Q.,' 7th S. v. 205, the fact that the House of Commons entered on 27 February, 1888, upon a new phase of its career, the Speaker taking the chair at 3 P.M. and public business beginning at 3.30. This may now fairly be supplemented by the fact that on 5 May last, according to the *Times* of the following day,

"in the House of Commons the sitting was the first held under the new rule, which fixes 2 o'clock as the hour for meeting. The questions on the notice paper were all disposed of at 10 minutes to 3, and the debate on the Education Bill was begun before the hour struck."

ALFRED F. ROBBINS.

"TIDAL WAVE." — The accounts of the terrible disasters in the West Indies have brought this expression again to the front. There is a very wide and almost universal misuse of the term. A wave in the sea created by an earthquake or volcanic action is an "ocean wave," a "sea wave," or a "volcanic wave," but is *not* a tidal wave. A tidal wave is the wave, and its complementary at the Antipodes, that daily travels round the earth from east to west, caused by the attraction of the moon. To call anything else a tidal wave exhibits a want of scientific information in the user. If I dump a boulder from the top of a cliff into the sea, I should be as much justified in calling the commotion thereby created a tidal wave as that made by the shock of an earthquake, &c. The difference is only one of degree, whereas the true tidal wave comes from a cause that is radically and totally distinct. The reason of the misapplication seems to arise from the confusion of the terms *sea* and *tide*. In conversation one often hears *tide* being used where *sea* is meant.

J. S. McTEAR.

"GIRAFFINE."—In the number of the *Harmsworth London Magazine* for December, 1901, Sir H. H. Johnston, K.C.B., discoverer of the much-discussed okapi, writing upon his discovery, used the expression "the giraffine family." *Giraffid* might have been more correct, as the animal is one of the Giraffidæ ; but *giraffine*, having been used under unique circumstances may be said to have obtained a footing, and being associated with the okapi—or *o'api*, as we are informed the dwarfs pronounce it—may rise to the dignity of an established unit in our language. It may be noted further that Prof. Ray Lankester has given the name *Ocapia* to the genus of which the Special Commissioner's discovery is a specimen.   ARTHUR MAYALL.

"CIRCULAR JOYS."—Crashaw has this phrase in his poem 'On the Death of Mr. Herrys' for everlasting, or, it may be, for eternal joys. I confess I have never been able to see the beauty of the simile of the circle as an emblem of eternity. It may be quite true that to the ring (or to the circumference of a circle) there is not any end ; but it always occurs to me that we are in any circle traversing the same ground again and again. I think of eternity as a perfectly straight line without termini. I know that it may be said such a thought is unthinkable ; but we can think of the station where we began our part of the journey, and of that other station where we shall end. In this idea at least we have no treadmill work—no person ever travels the same part of the journey a second time. History never repeats itself. The world since its creation has never been in the same spot two mornings in succession.
    THOMAS AULD.

" COPTIC" USED AS A TYPE OF AN OUT-OF-THE-WAY LANGUAGE OR LITTLE-KNOWN SUBJECT. — The 'H.E.D.' assigns separate sections to somewhat similar uses of the words "Greek" and "Hebrew." For "Coptic" in this typical sense see Macaulay's essay on Croker's edition of Boswell's 'Life of Johnson ' (p. 165 in the one-volume edition of the 'Essays,' 1870): "The composition of this eminent Latinist, short as it is, contains several words that are just as much Coptic as Latin."
    With this compare the following passage : "the constitution of this country (in which and the Coptick Mr. Steele is equally skilled)" (Swift, 'Public Spirit of the Whigs,' vol. viii. of 'Miscellanies,' 1751, p. 14).
    The 'Public Spirit of the Whigs' appeared in March, 1714, and Swift may have had in his mind No. 69 of the *Spectator* (a number written by Addison), where the Spectator himself in describing his visits to the Royal Exchange says, "There is indeed a Merchant of Egypt, who just knows me by sight...... but as I am not versed in the modern Coptick, our Conferences go no further than a Bow

and a Grimace." Even if there is a special reference in Swift's sarcasm to the words just quoted, it seems possible that the word " Coptick " may at the same time have been intended to bear a typical meaning.
    Perhaps, before concluding that " Coptic " is found in this proverbial sense, it would be well to ask for more examples of such a use.
    EDWARD BENSLY.
    The University, Adelaide, South Australia.

"GOD HAS THREE CHANCELLORS." — In a letter of 2 July, 1614, written from Leeds, Alexander Cook thus addresses James Usher:
    " Good sir, I read in the *Mariale*, that Deus in curià suà cœlesti habet tres Cancellarios : primus est, ad quem spectat dare literas simplicis Justitiæ, et iste est Michael Arch-angelus, &c. Secundus Cancellarius, ad quem spectat dare literas mixtas, scilicet Justitiæ & Misericordiæ, est B. Petrus apostolus......Tertius Cancellarius est ille, ad quem spectat dare literas puræ gratiæ & misericordiæ, & hoc officinm habet B. Virgo," &c.
    RICHARD H. THORNTON.
    Portland, Oregon.

THE IRON DUKE AND THE DUKE OF WELLINGTON.—I venture to think that exception should be taken in 'N. & Q.' to the bestowal of the old appellation of " the Iron Duke " (p. 473) upon the illustrious Duke of Wellington in such an important historical work (perhaps the standard life) as 'The Life of Napoleon I.' by J. H. Rose, for the simple reason that the name of " Iron Duke " was selected for a large ship launched at Liverpool, and not as a title of regard for the conqueror of such " a wonder-worker " as Napoleon the Great (the greatest name in modern history) and nearly all his marshals and generals.   HENRY GERALD HOPE.
    119, Elms Road, Clapham, S.W.

[Surely Wellington has fairly secured the title for himself, and now it would be futile to attempt to deprive him of it. Other men were just besides Aristides, but he has secured the adjective in history as his own.]

Queries.

WE must request correspondents desiring information on family matters of only private interest to affix their names and addresses to their queries, in order that the answers may be addressed to them direct.

OPTIC OR OPTICAL GLASS.—In Hermann Kirchener's 'Oration in Praise of Travell,' prefixed to 'Coryat's Crudities,' 1611, we read, " For this Counsellor is like that opticke-glasse wherein not onely the space of three or tenne miles, but also of a whole prouince, yea, and of the whole world it selfe, may be represented." Lady Luxborough, writing to Shenstone, 17 April, 1748, says : "I feel that it would give me pain to see St. James's, Vauxhall, Ranelagh, &c , &c., represented in so lively a manner as I see them through an optical glass which I have lately purchased, now that I am absent from them." That this was, or contained, a lense of some kind, appears from a later letter of 11 September, in which she says :—

"Mr. Sanders, speaking of the dimension of his Optic Glasses yesterday, put me in mind of measuring mine It is near three inches and a half diameter, convex on one side, and flat on the other."

The usual sense of "optic" or "optical glass" was, indeed, a lense, hence any instrument consisting of or containing a lense, as a microscope or telescope. As Milton has it,

the moon, whose orb
Through Optic Glass the Tuscan Artist views
At Ev'ning from the top of Fesole.

Sometimes it seems to mean a convex mirror, or any glass used for refraction or reflexion of light. But what kind of "optical glass" could that be in which a whole province or the whole world could be represented, or through which Lady Luxborough could see the fashionable resorts of London "represented in so lively a manner," now that she was absent from them ?

J. A. H. Murray.

[Is Dee's magic crystal referred to ?]

Dr. Johnson.—It would be interesting to learn who was the last survivor of persons known to have seen Dr. Samuel Johnson in the flesh. Dr. Martin Routh, President of Magdalen College, Oxford, who died in 1854 in his hundredth year, had seen the doctor, "in his brown wig, scrambling up the steps of University College." In the 'Journals of Walter White' (assistant secretary of the Royal Society, 1861–85) is the following :—

"1864, Sept. 24. To Earl's Colne......Mr. Carwardine told me he remembered having seen Dr. Johnson. He was walking, at four years of age, through St. Paul's Churchyard, holding by his father's finger, when his father, pointing to an old man dressed in a snuff-coloured suit and worsted stockings, who stood as if resting by a post, said, 'That is the great Dr. Johnson.' Mr. Carwardine also remembers Cowper."

Dr. Johnson died in 1784, and had thus been seen by one who was living eighty years later. W. B. H.

"Hopeful": "Sanguine."—I had thought that to be hopeful and to be sanguine were one and the same thing ; but in his speech at Birmingham on 16 May, Mr. Chamberlain plainly used the words to indicate two distinct attitudes of mind : "I am hopeful," he said. "but I am not sanguine. Does this strike your correspondents as it does me, as being an attempt to mark a difference where none, in reality, exists ; or do they, too, attach some signification to *sanguine* which would prevent them from employing it as an exact synonym for *hopeful?* In like manner, I confess that I always distinguish between *like* and *similar.* To my thinking, if things resemble each other precisely, they are alike ; if they differ at all they are only similar. Can nothing save us from a "combine"? St. Swithin.

Aix-la-Chapelle. — What is the correct pronunciation of this name ? English authorities (such as Chisholm, Lippincott, Smith, Webster) give *Aiks,* yet I frequently hear *Ai* from educated Londoners, while I always heard *Aiss* from speakers of French during my stay in the town in 1889, and *Aiss* is given by such French authorities as Delille, Landais, Levizac, &c. Some French orthoepists (*e.g.,* Malvin-Cazal) discriminate between the various places named Aix ; according to them Aix in Provence should be called *Aiks,* and the Isle of Aix should be called *Ai,* but Aix-les-Bains and Aix-la-Chapelle should be *Aiss.* Are these distinctions still observed by good French speakers or are they obsolete ?
Jas. Platt, Jun.

Quotation attributed to Coventry Patmore.—R. L. Stevenson, at the end of 'The Dynamiters,' makes Prince Florizel say :—

"Is it not one of your English poets, that looked abroad upon the earth and saw vast circumvallations......troops manœuvring, war-ships at sea and a great dust of battles on shore ; and casting anxiously about for......the cause of so many and painful preparations, spied at last, in the centre of all, a mother and her babe ?"

Where in Coventry Patmore's works does this occur ? C. Hudson.

Thomas Phaer, of Cilgerran. — In the list of members of Parliament ordered to be printed 1 March, 1878, appear the following entries for Cardigan : "Thomas Phayr, armiger, 2 & 3 Philip & Mary, summoned to meet 21 Oct., 1555." "Thomas Phayer, generosus, Cardigan Borough, 20 Jan., 1557/8." "Thomas Phaer, Esq., Cardigan, 1558." These three entries, in which the name has three different spellings, presumably all refer to the same person. I assume, though with some diffidence, that the M.P. referred to is identical with the famous Welsh writer who lived at Cilgerran or Kilgerran Forest, in Pembrokeshire, and died in 1560. I do not find in 'Dict. Nat. Biog.' any notice of Thomas Phaer's service in Parliament, and I have never seen any account of his armorial. Can any of your readers inform me whether more than one Thomas Phaer is known as connected with Cardigan and Pembrokeshire at this period; and, secondly, whether any account of Thomas Phaer's arms has ever been published? If these arms could be ascertained they might help to throw light on the family history of a distinguished man.

A. W. C. B.

ROMAN CATHOLIC CHAPEL, MOORFIELDS.—In what magazine, published within the last two or three years, shall I find an illustrated description of this building (now pulled down)?   EVERARD HOME COLEMAN.
71, Brecknock Road.

SECOND EARL OF ALBEMARLE. — Does any portrait exist of William Anne Keppel, second Earl of Albemarle (1702–54), who succeeded the Duke of Cumberland as Commander-in-Chief in Scotland after the battle of Culloden?   Q. K. B.

[A portrait of him as Lord Bury is described in Chaloner Smith's 'British Mezzotint Portraits,' vol. iii. p. 1146. Other portraits are mentioned in the same work, which consult.]

SIR GEOFFREY POLE, DIED 1558. — This knight was the youngest son of Sir Richard Pole and Margaret, Countess of Salisbury. He married Constance Pakenham, of Lordington, and had eleven children: Arthur (died in the Tower about 1570), Thomas, Edmund (died in the Tower about 1570), Jeffrey, and another son; Margaret (who married Walter, son of the second Lord Windsor), Katherine (who married Anthony Fortescue), and four other daughters (one a nun of Sion). Is anything known of the descendants (if any) of these children of Sir Geoffrey Pole and his wife Constance?   RONALD DIXON.
46, Marlborough Avenue, Hull.

LODGE'S 'EARLS OF KILDARE.'—Lodge, in the preface to the first edition of his 'Peerage,' published in 1754, speaks of a history of the family of the Earl of Kildare, which he had published in 1745 as a specimen of the 'Peerage of Ireland.' Can you tell me if copies of this work are rare? I do not find it in the Catalogue of Printed Books in the British Museum Library.   F. G.

TRANSLATOR'S NAME REQUIRED.—"Virgil's Husbandry, or an Essay on the Georgics: being the First Book. Translated into English Verse. To which are added the Latin Text and Mr. Dryden's Version. With Notes Critical and Rustick." Would some of your readers kindly say who is responsible for the translation? My copy contains translations of the first and second books (the former dated 1725, the latter 1724).

T. SAVAGE.
Armagh.

[The translator appears to have been William Benson, 1682–1754, for whom consult the 'Dict. Nat. Biog.']

WILLUGHBY'S 'ORNITHOLOGY.'—With reference to the missel thrush Willughby's 'Ornithology' (1678), p. 187, says: "A late English writer saith, that this bird......feeds all her young ones with misselto berries and nothing else," and adds:—

"For convulsions or the Falling sickness kill this bird, dry him to a powder, and take the quantity of a penny weight every morning in six spoonfuls of black Cherry water, or distilled water of Misseltoberries. The reason of this conceit is because this bird feeds upon Misselto, which is an approved remidy for the Epilepsie."

This is probably from a medical work. I shall be greatly obliged if any of your readers will supply me with the "late English writer's" name and a reference to the passage.   THOMAS SOUTHWELL.
Norwich.

ANALOGOUS TITLES OF BOOKS. — Does the English law of copyright include titles of books? There seems to be no such restriction over the Channel—or, at least, in France. In L'Intermédiaire of 10 March, 1897, a long list appears of analogous titles of works. Are our French neighbours less exacting and more courteous than ourselves in this matter?

J. B. McGOVERN.
St. Stephen's Rectory, C.-on-M., Manchester.

"KNIFE."—We often hear such expressions as "he always has his knife in me." Are they originally English? We are not a knife-using people. I do not find anything directly bearing on this in the 'H.E.D.'   C. C. B.

GREEN=CARY: SMYTHIES=CARY. — William Cary, of Whitechapel Common, died in 1711, leaving, amongst other relatives, two married sisters, Margaret Green and Sarah Smythies. When and where were these sisters married? Any information concerning them will greatly oblige.

GEO. S. CARY.
Laurel Lodge, Terenure, co. Dublin.

'SWEEPINGS FROM MY STUDY.'—Who is the author of this work?   JOHN TUDOR.
1, Liverpool Lawn, Dover.

'STEMMATA CHICHELIANA,' NOS. 256 AND 258.—I should be glad of any further information respecting the families of Henden, Winder, Stone, Sibley, Houghton, and Spencer (all of Kent), not easily accessible in print. I have ascertained that the copy of this book at All Souls' College affords nothing additional as regards these pedigrees.

G. W. WRIGLEY.

68, Southborough Road, South Hackney.

ALPHABET-KEEPER.—This is used as a compound word in the *Gentleman's Magazine* for January, 1731, p. 33, where the death is recorded on 11 January of William Whorwood, Alphabet-keeper to the Foreign Post Office, and again on p. 35, where the appointment of his successor, I presume, is recorded as follows : "Mr. Allan Lavalade, appointed Alphabet-keeper at the Foreign Post Office." The word *alphabet* in the sense of an index is given in the 'H.E.D.,' but not the compound word *alphabet-keeper*. Can your readers give me the exact duties of this functionary ?

D. M. R.

[See under 'Alphabet-man,' 8th S. xi. 207, 271, 318, 451; xii. 492.]

EASTGATE FAMILY. — In Gillow's 'Biographical Dictionary of English Catholics' it is said that "John Eastgate, monk of the Cistercian Abbey of Whalley, co. Lancaster, belonged to a local family now extinct, and was probably brother to Richard Eastgate, a monk of the neighbouring Abbey of Salley" —Sawley, Yorkshire. Can any one tell me what was Gillow's authority for the statements that the family was a Lancashire one, and that it has since become extinct? A number of men bearing the name were at that time settled in Norfolk. The name was then spelt Estgate.

G. E.

ERVIN.—John Ervin was admitted to Westminster School on 13 January, 1766; another Ervin, whose Christian name is omitted from the school register, was admitted on 12 January, 1767. Can any correspondent of 'N. & Q.' help me to identify these two admissions?

G. F. R. B.

DERVISH SECTS.—A correspondent writing in 1877 (5th S. vii. 473) alludes to a then recently published Blue-book on the subject of Dervish sects. Will any one kindly give a reference to it?

W. CROOKE.

Langton House, Charlton Kings.

SIR E. COKE IN THE TOWER.—I find a note dated in January, 1621/2, relating to Coke's detention in the Tower at this time. He was not released till August, 1622, but this contemporary writer, quoting the gossip of the day, speaks of him as having "the liberty of the Tower," and "excused giving his gown because it was borrowed." What does this mean?

LOBUC.

Replies.

MICHAEL BRUCE AND BURNS.

(9th S. vii. 466; viii. 70, 148, 312, 388, 527; ix. 95, 209, 309.)

THE Bruce-Logan controversy has certainly not in 'N. & Q.' been "diverging into a quest after irrelevant conclusions," but it may be well at present to confine attention to the authorship of the 'Ode to the Cuckoo.' It must be evident to the candid and unbiassed student that the adverse findings of Drs. Mackelvie and Grosart cannot longer be maintained in view of recent researches, as indicated in the various publications to which attention has lately been directed. MR. BAYNE obviously lays much stress on internal evidence, and quotes from 'Lochleven,' 'Daphnis,' and the imitation of Ramsay's 'Yellow-haired Laddie,' in support of his contention that Michael Bruce wrote the 'Ode to the Cuckoo.' In 1810 Alexander Chalmers, in his revised edition of Dr. Johnson's 'Poets' (21 vols., royal 8vo), prints the following as 'Poems attributed to Logan' (vol. xviii. pp. 67-72): 'Damon, Menelaus, and Meliboeus'; 'Pastoral Song' (the imitation of Ramsay); 'Ode to a Fountain'; 'Danish Ode'; 'Anacreontic to a Wasp'; 'The Episode of Lerina' (from 'Lochleven'); and 'Ode to Paoli.' He also admits the 'Ode to the Cuckoo' among the works of Logan, and remarks :—

"In the whole of Logan's poems are passages of true poetic spirit and sensibility. With a fancy so various and regulated it is to be regretted he did not more frequently cultivate his talents. The episode of 'Lerina,' among the pieces attributed to him, indicates powers that might have appeared to advantage in a regular poem of narration and description."

Chalmers credits Logan with that portion of 'Lochleven' commencing on p. 186 of Mackelvie's 'Bruce,'

Low by the lake, as yet without a name,

and extending to p. 196,

Of Lomond and Lerina he would talk,

which forms lines 102 to 387 of this poem. But in a foot-note (pp. 184-5) Dr. Mackelvie remarks :—

"The next twenty lines [this should be 21]—or lines 81 to 101, pp. 185-6—in the printed text are not in the original draught, and ought to have been claimed for Logan, since his friends have been disposed to claim all the alterations and improvements in the poem for him."

These twenty-one lines I now hold to be Logan's, on the ground of descriptive similarity with other portions of his writings. In them we find "the tenants of the wood" and "He roam'd the dusky wood." Further on in this poem are : " fenc'd by a wood," "made the woods enamour'd," "She'd often wander in the wood," " warbler in the verdant wood," "fair wanderer of the wood !" "wildings of the wood," " while the wood suffers," " lose me in the wood," " the monarch of the wood," "The woods among they wandered," and "Strayed thro' the woods." Parallel passages containing "wood" or "woods" may be found in " Poems by the Rev. Mr. Logan, one of the ministers of Leith " (Lond., 1781), on pp. 18, 24, 25, 26, 48, 50, 57, 61, 71, 72, 86, 88, 90 (*bis*), and 97. His lines on p. 24 are noteworthy : "The cuckoo in the wood unseen"; line 61, "A stranger, wandering thro' the wood"; and line 71, "One day, a wanderer in the wood."

The peculiar word "beauteous," applied to the cuckoo in the first line of the 'Ode,' occurs in 'Lochleven': line 127, "all beauteous with the robes of heaven"; line 157, "She'd bring the beauteous spoils"; line 171, " In beauteous clusters flourished "; line 274, "Cease, beauteous stranger !" and line 317, "Her beauteous robes of light." On p. 36 of Logan's 'Poems' is, "that beauteous bosom ever wound." Other words in the 'Ode to the Cuckoo,' such as "spring," "bowers," "vale," "grove," and "wandering," are also frequently met with in Logan's volume.

Turning now to the 'Ode to the Cuckoo,' round which so much controversy has long raged, I observe it appears in Bruce's 'Poems,' 1770, 1782 (a reprint of the preceding edition), 1796 (Baird's edition), 1807, 1837 (Mackelvie), 1865 (Grosart), and 1895 (Stephen). On the other hand, it was given in Logan's 'Poems,' 1781, 1782 (8vo and 12mo), 1789, 1795 (Anderson's collection), 1805, 1810 (Chalmers's collection), 1812, 1813, and 1823. The 'Ode' is attributed to Logan in Southey's 'Specimens of the Later English Poets,' 1807 ; 'The Cabinet of Poetry' (6 vols., Lond., 1808) ; D'Israeli's 'Calamities of Authors,' 1812-13 ; Campbell's 'Specimens of British Poetry,' 1819 ; 'The Scottish Biographical Dictionary' (12mo, Lond., 1822) ; Cunningham's 'Songs of Scotland,' 1825 ; the Rev. W. Lee, Roxburgh, editor of " My Own Life and Times : 1741-1814, by Thomas Somerville, D.D." (Edin., 1861), and by more recent writers. The 'Book of the Poets : Chaucer to Beattie' (Lond., Chidley, 1844), gives four pieces as examples of Logan's works, one of which is the 'Ode,' with a brief prefatory notice. Two specimens are given in 'The Book of Gems : Swift to Burns,' edited by S. C. Hall, F.S.A. (Lond., 1866) : 'The Braes of Yarrow'

and the 'Ode.' In the biographical sketch it is stated :—

"His 'Ode to the Cuckoo' is one of the sweetest poems in the language. Logan has been charged with having stolen this composition from the posthumous manuscripts of Bruce, the collecting and editing of which were committed to his care. His claim to it, however, is not only supported by internal evidence, but the charge was never advanced against him while he was alive to repel it."

Mr. Hall has indicated very clearly the weak part of David Pearson's claim on behalf of the Bruce authorship of the 'Ode.' He did not challenge the right of Logan to insert it in his volume of 1781, and it was not till seven years after Logan's death that he put forward his version of the events of nearly thirty years before. Dr. Mackelvie says that "he had almost no education, understanding by that term training at school." James Bruce, the poet's brother, who died in 1814, said, according to Dr. Mackelvie, that

"he, with David Pearson and others, had strung together some uncouth rhymes which have ever since [from the time his brother's devotional sentiments had been withdrawn] continued to be sung by the youths in the village [of Kinnesswood] when practising church music."

This statement, however, is contradicted by his previous assertion, wherein he declared, in the most solemn manner, that all the paraphrases published in Logan's name were written by his brother Michael, that he had often read them, heard them often repeated, and frequently sung portions of them in Buchan's class long before the addition to the Assembly's collection was heard of. Pearson testified to the Bruce authorship of the paraphrases, and says that " these hymns as they stand in Logan's works are considerably altered." The first of the two passages quoted has not been changed, and it appears in Logan's volume and in the paraphrases now in use :—

> Who from the cearments of the tomb
> Can raise the human mold ?

The other verse runs thus :—

> Logan (1781).
> The beam that shines on Zion hill
>   Shall lighten every land ;
> The King who reigns in Zion towers
>   Shall all the world command.

> Mackelvie (1837).
> The beam that shines from Zion's hill
>   Shall lighten every land,
> The King that reigns in Salem's tow'rs
>   Shall all the world command.

The current paraphrase (xviii. 3) differs in line 1 from Mackelvie, "Sion hill"; "ev'ry," line 2 ; and "who" for "that" in line 3. But no MS. evidence was ever supplied by

Bruce or Pearson in support of their confident asseverations, so far as I am aware.

The Rev. George Gilfillan, in his 'Specimens, with Memoirs, of the Less-Known British Poets' (3 vols., 8vo, Edin., 1860), supplies some information regarding the Bruce-Logan controversy, but is not quite accurate on several points. He confuses Dr. William Robertson, the historian, with Dr. Thomas Robertson of Dalmeny; gives 1782 for 1781 as the date of the first issue of Logan's 'Poems'; 1807 instead of 1796 for the publication of Baird's edition of Bruce; and says that in the former year it was published "for the behoof of Bruce's mother, then an aged widow." She had died, however, at the age of eighty-eight, in 1798. Mr. Gilfillan was of the opinion that the 'Ode'

"was originally written by Bruce, but probably polished to its present perfection by Logan, whose other writings give us rather the impression of a man of varied accomplishments than of deep feeling or original genius. If Logan were not the author of 'The Cuckoo,' there was a special baseness connected with the fact, that when Burke sought him out in Edinburgh solely from his admiration of that poem, he owned the soft and false impeachment, and rolled as a sweet morsel praise from the greatest man of the age, which he knew was the rightful due of another."

But we prefer the dictum of Thomas Campbell, who says :—

"But as the charge of stealing the 'Cuckoo' from Bruce was not brought against Logan in his lifetime, it cannot, in charity, stand against his memory on the bare assertion of his accusers."

As a foot-note he quotes Southey's observation from the *Quarterly Review*, vol. xi. p. 501:

"Because some pieces which are printed among the remains of poor Michael Bruce have been ascribed to Logan, Mr. Chalmers has not thought it proper to admit Bruce's poems into his collection."

Logan's cousin, Mrs. Hutchison, wife of Mr. John Hutchison, merchant in Edinburgh,

"informs the present writer [this was penned in 1795 by Mr. Anderson, and is printed in his 'Poets,' vol. xi. p. 1030] that she saw the 'Ode' in Logan's handwriting before it was printed......In this edition the present writer has not ventured, upon the authority of Dr. Robertson, to give him the pieces ascribed to him in Bruce's 'Poems,' which he did not think proper to claim himself; neither has he presumed, upon the authority of Mr. Pearson, to deprive him of the 'Ode to the Cuckoo,' to which he has put his name. In justice to both poets he has followed the collection of their poems, printed under their respective names, in the present edition, distinguishing the pieces which have been claimed for the one or the other by their respective friends......The 'Ode to the Cuckoo,' which he is supposed to have written, and certainly improved, is distinguished by the delicate graces of simplicity and tenderness in the highest degree."

It would have been the height of folly and the depth of meanness on Logan's part if he, who had been one of the ministers of Leith for several years from 1773, had claimed as his own the composition of another. Until contrary documentary evidence is forthcoming, I maintain that the authorship of the 'Ode' must justly be ascribed to the Rev. John Logan.   ADAM SMAIL.

Two of the lines quoted by MR. BAYNE from Bruce's 'Elegy written in Spring' are borrowed obviously from Milton :—

> Now Spring returns: but not to me returns
> The vernal joy my better years have known.
> Bruce.

> Seasons return : but not to me returns
> Day, or the sweet approach of even or morn,
> Or sight of vernal bloom.—Milton.
> E. YARDLEY.

HERRICK'S 'HESPERIDES': "LUTES OF AMBER" (9th S. ix. 408). — The passage to which H. I. B. refers is an instance of the confusion between the fossil gum "amber" and the metallic alloy "electrum," which begins in Homer and continues to the seventeenth century, causing a considerable amount of controversy amongst scholars. In this case Herrick clearly uses "amber" in the same sense as the English translators of Ezekiel, *i.e.*, that of a "shining" metal. (Luther, by the way, avoids the term in the German version.) In a rather large collection of notes on the subject made some years ago, I find this ambiguity a frequent source of misapprehension. A "chair of amber," for example, is understood to be of the fossil, though the context, "with a mirror of the same material," displays the error. An instance of the converse use of "electrum" for "amber" occurs in Greene :—

> It was her master's death
> That drew electrum from her weeping eyes.
> J. DORMER.

SAMUEL TAYLOR, SHORTHAND WRITER (7th S. ii. 308, 377, 457 ; 9th S. ix. 410).—Further search has enabled me to discover, from the burial register of St. Margaret's, Westminster, that Samuel Taylor was buried on 10 August, 1811.   MATTHIAS LEVY.

SHIPS OF WAR ON LAND (9th S. vii. 147, 235, 296, 354, 431 ; viii. 128 ; ix. 214).—W. L. Hertslet in his 'Der Treppenwitz der Weltgeschichte,' Berlin, 1886, p. 228, gives the following :—

"In the 'Muster-Roll of all the Regiments and Corps of the Royal Prussian Army,' Berlin, 1806, Himburg, p. 255, one finds among extracts from the history of the hussar regiment No. 2, formerly 'Zieten's Hussars,' the statement, taken from a

Berlin almanac for the year 1789, that the first 'battalion,' meaning one-half of that regiment or five squadrons, was lucky enough to capture a frigate during the campaign of 1787 in Holland. The said almanac, after giving a short account of the taking of the fortress of Gorkum, 17 Sept., 1787, adds this short remark: 'At the same time—as who should believe it?—a Dutch frigate on the water was taken by Prussian Hussars on the land. This was done by the Eben Hussars, who took an armed frigate in the middle of the Leck.' A poem by Koeppen celebrates this feat. In reality the affair happened thus: Major-General Freiherr von Eben, commander of the regiment in question from 1786 to 1795, happened to witness with some officers and five orderlies of his regiment the capitulation of a ship which, having struck in the Leck on a sandbank, was attacked by Prussian fusiliers and threatened by two Prussian heavy guns. This was all."

G. KRUEGER.

Berlin.

CHURCH FURNITURE (9ᵗʰ S. ix. 348).—For "tynobel" read *tynokel* (tunicle).

For "prosynalles" read *prossessyonalles* (processionals).

For "manuettes" read *manuelles* (manuals).

For "a nomellet" read *an omellet*, which must mean a homily.

For "a legen" read *a legend* (the collection of saints' lives).

For "pains" read *panes* (broad stripes of alternate colours).

"A per of postefes" is probably a pair of organs called "a positive"—*i.e.*, a fixed organ, as distinct from a "portative," or movable one.

J. T. F.

Durham.

For "chis apel" read *chisapel*. H. P. L.

[Other replies or conjectures are acknowledged.]

ENGLAND WITH MANY RELIGIONS AND ONE SAUCE (9ᵗʰ S. ix. 407).—I have it in my mind that it was the Prince de Soubise who said that England had twenty religions and only one sauce. Doubtless he little thought when he said it that his only claim to immortality would rest on his *one* sauce.

SHERBORNE.

In an old commonplace book of mine I find the following entry :—

"'England is the land where every man has the right to beg, and the liberty to starve—the land which has eighty-seven religions, and only one sauce—melted butter.'—Voltaire."

I am unable to say at the moment in which of Voltaire's seventy volumes the witticism may be found. H. JOHNSON.

"GREY CITY BY THE NORTHERN SEA" (9ᵗʰ S. ix. 407).—The poem that begins thus, and has St. Andrews for its subject, was written, so far as my memory serves me, by a distinguished alumnus of the "College of the scarlet gown," who died, regretted by all his friends, a good many years ago. Mr. Andrew Lang, in his poem 'Almæ Matres, St. Andrews, 1862; Oxford, 1865,' alludes, I think, to his dead friend. It begins

St. Andrews by the northern sea,

and is, it may be, the actual poem wanted by DEBONNAIRE. The following are two of its stanzas :—

Oh broken Minster looking forth
    Beyond the Bay, above the town.
Oh winter of the kindly North,
    Oh College of the scarlet gown !
And shining sands beside the sea,
    And stretch of links beside the sand,
Once more I watch you, and to me
    It is as if I touched his hand.

And therefore art thou yet more dear,
    Oh little city grey and sere,
Though shrunken from thine ancient pride,
    And lonely by the lonely sea,
Than these fair Halls on Isis' side,
    Where youth an hour came back to me.

JOHN GRIGOR.

ARMS OF CONTINENTAL CITIES (9ᵗʰ S. ix. 308, 414).—The arms of most continental cities can be found under their names in the latest edition of 'Meyers Konversations-Lexikon,' the volumes of which are in the reference library of the British Museum.

L. L. K.

That excellent book of reference the 'Konversations-Lexikon' of Brockhaus gives the municipal arms of many cities. I have just tested it for places in Germany, France, Italy, and England, and in each case have found that the coat of arms is given.

WILLIAM E. A. AXON.

SIR EDMUND BERRY GODFREY (7ᵗʰ S. xii. 314; 9ᵗʰ S. ii. 367, 414; iii. 16, 96; ix. 332). —There can be no doubt that the "Edmund Berrey Godfrey, Citizen and Woodmonger of London," referred to in the deed in MR. J. P. LEWIS's possession, is the man chiefly remembered for his brutal murder, which, by the way, did not happen on 17 October (the day his body was discovered), but on the night of Saturday, 12 October, 1678. In a curious little volume called 'Memoirs of the Life and Death of Sir Edmondbury Godfrey, late Justice of the Peace for Middlesex, who was Barbarously Murthered,' &c., London, 1682 (which I shall be pleased to lend MR. LEWIS if he would care to see it), the unfortunate knight is described as

"being a younger brother, and what estate he had, consisting in Moneys to the value of 1,000l. or thereabouts, was advised (as a fair way of improvement) to join Stocks with the aforesaid Gentleman [Mr. Harrison, probably the James Harrison of the deed] and to come in a partner with him, in managing the Trade of a Wood-wharf, which he accordingly did; setling themselves first at Dowgate, within the City of London."

The book is dedicated to Charles II. by its author, the curious writer Richard Tuke. As to the spelling of Godfrey's Christian name or names the book is strangely uncertain. From pp. 1 to 31 and 65 to the end at the head of the page it appears as "Edmondbury Godfrey," but on pp. 33, 37, 41, 45, 49, 53, 57, and 61 it is "Edmund-Bury-Godfrey," whilst the remaining pages give it as "Edmond-Bury Godfrey"! The frontispiece is a bust of the knight by "F. H. van Houe, Sculp."   WM. NORMAN.
6, St. James's Place, Plumstead.

The citizen and woodmonger of London mentioned in the indenture quoted at the last reference is the well-known Justice of the Peace for Westminster, who was mysteriously murdered in 1678. He was christened 13 January, 1621/2; "his godfathers," writes his father in his diary, "were my cousin, John Berrie, esq., captain of the foot company of......Lidd......his other godfather was...... Edmund Harrison, the King's embroiderer. ......They named my son Edmund Berrie, the one's name and the other's Christian names." Macaulay, J. R. Green, and others have committed the error of running the two Christian names into one as Edmundbury or Edmundsbury; but it is noticeable that, in the trial of the unhappy Robert Green and others for the murder, the notorious Lord Chief Justice Scroggs himself several times speaks of "Sir Edmundbury Godfrey." His mother was Thomas Godfrey's second wife Sarah, daughter of Thomas Isles, Esq., of Hammersmith, who may possibly have been akin to the other party of the indenture —John Iles of Stanwell to wit.
                            A. R. BAYLEY.

I fancy the Edmund Berry Godfrey mentioned was a native of Thatcham, Berks—at least one of the name was.   E. E. COPE.
13c, Hyde Park Mansions, W.

CORONATION ITEM: PRINTERS WANTED (9th S. ix. 348).—Bowles & Carver and R. Wilkinson were among the best-known printsellers in London towards the end of the eighteenth and beginning of the nineteenth centuries. Bowles & Carver carried on their business at 69, St. Paul's Churchyard, and their names are to be found in the London directories from 1796 to 1832. The business was an old-established one, being conducted so far back

as 1723 by Thomas Bowles, and subsequently, as shown by the directories of 1780 to 1793, by Carington Bowles, who himself compiled and published a 'New London Guide' of streets, public buildings, &c. I do not find the names of Bowles & Carver in the London directories after 1832; and Tallis, in his 'London Street Views,' published circa 1839, shows that No. 69, St. Paul's Churchyard was at that time occupied by Hall & Allen, silk mercers and drapers.

R. Wilkinson's name appears in the London directory of 1789, but not in that of 1787, and from 1789 until 1815 he seems to have occupied the premises No. 58, Cornhill. From Cornhill he moved in 1815 to 125, Fenchurch Street, and continued there until the year 1825, when he presumably retired from business or died, as his name is not given in the London directories after that date. A reference to his well-known work 'Londina Illustrata,' published 1819-25, will show that the earlier plates were issued from 58, Cornhill, while the later ones, from 1816 and onwards, were dated from 125, Fenchurch Street. It is probable, therefore, that the print referred to represents the coronation of George IV., which took place in Westminster Abbey in July, 1821.
                            H. A. HARBEN.

"BUFF WEEK" (9th S. ix. 329, 353, 372).—I have pleasure in sending you the following extract from Mr. R. O. Heslop's excellent compilation 'Northumberland Words,' which originally appeared in the Newcastle Weekly Chronicle, commencing in 1887. The subjoined definition of baff was published in the early part of 1888:—

"Baff, blank. A pitman, if paid fortnightly, speaks of the alternate weeks as 'the baff week' and 'the pay week.'

The baff week is o'er—no repining—
Pay Saturday's swift on the wing.
    Henry Robson, 'The Collier's Pay Week,'
        Allan's Collection, p. 237.

"'A card not a trump is a baff one. The partly decayed, split, or root end of a log or tree of timber is also called the baff end, and from the baff ends, or otherwise useless pieces or ends of timber, are cut baffs, which are used to keep the wooden cribs in position when sinking pits in our North Country.' —W., Durham, correspondent, in Newcastle Weekly Chronicle, May 15, 1886."
                        ERNEST W. ADAMS.
Newcastle-on-Tyne.

FLINT-GLASS TRADE (9th S. ix. 365).—"The limit number—to be made in six hours by a 'chair,' which consists of three men and a boy." It seems to me that there is little difficulty in this word, which, however, is not quite correctly explained. I take it to mean "a turn or stroke or 'stint' of work to be done in a given time by three men and a boy." If so, it is the same as *char* or *chare*, an example of which in spelling "chair" is given in the 'H.E.D.' Many are the cases in which words said to be "not recorded" by this thesaurus are found there on more careful search. C. B. MOUNT.

GEE FAMILY (9ᵗʰ S. ix. 10, 131).—William Gee I. was Sheriff of Hull in 1537, which is an earlier date than any yet mentioned. William Gee II. was Sheriff of Hull in 1560, and Mayor of Hull in 1562, 1573, and 1582. William Gee III. (son of William Gee II.) was M.P. for Hull in the 1588 Parliament. William Gee IV. (? really V. or VI.) was M.P. for Hull in the Parliament of 1689. Joseph Gee was Sheriff of Hull in 1854.
RONALD DIXON.
46, Marlborough Avenue, Hull.

SURNAMES FROM SINGLE LETTERS (9ᵗʰ S. vi. 264, 398; viii 232). — Amongst the names referred to by MR. HARRISON is Ell, my surname—of which I have been trying to trace the origin (strange to say, my wife's maiden name was Gee). Ferguson, in his 'Teutonic Name System,' says of the name, on p. 299: "Simple forms: — Old German, Alj, Ello, Ella, 7th century. Ang.-Saxon, Ella, Al, El= Foreigner. Eng., Ell, Elley, Ella" In Taylor's 'Words and Places' I find on p. 85: "The Edings, the Ellings, the Hardings, and the Sings in eight places"; and I gathered the following from the 'Register of Malmesbury Abbey' (a copy of which is in the General Assembly Library here), edited by J. S. Brewer, M.A. In vol. ii. p. 294, I came across the name of Aella, being the sixteenth signature to grant of tithes by Ethelwulf. And in 'Catalogue of Ancient Deeds,' Herts:—

"Grant by Ralph Cressy and Helenysa his wife, William Eyle and Helenysa his wife, and ot[her]s of a tenement with a void plot of land in Haliwellestret (St. Albans), which they inherited after the death of Robert Albyn of Hemelhamstede."—Date, Saturday after St. Vincent, 34 Edward III.

In Gough's and Camden's work the name of "Ell Lade" appears in a list of small areas of water in the Fen country of Cambridgeshire or Lincolnshire.

I came across the mention of a man bearing the name Robert Eyll; he held some office in the fourteenth century, but I have mislaid the note I took. The following note is from the 'History of Hampton Court Palace in Tudor Times,' p. 350, Appendix C:—

"Great Bay Window.—Pd to John Ells of Westmyster, fremason, for making and intayling of two bullyns in freston standing in the vowght of the Great Bay Window in the Kynges New Hall at 10s. the pece—20s."

A Mary Ell was buried in Henlow (Beds) Churchyard, and, according to the tombstone, died 7 May, 1807, aged eighty-one.

From the above I am inclined to think that MR. HARRISON is mistaken, but I should feel grateful for assistance from any of your contributors. H. G. ELL.
Christchurch, N.Z.

"SAY NOT THAT HE DID WELL" (9ᵗʰ S. ix. 87, 332).—The verse in question was written by Mrs. Craik, and was quoted in the sermon preached at Shortlands, Kent, on the Sunday after her death. It is also given in an obituary notice of Mrs. Craik in the *Athenæum* for 22 October, 1887, in what, I presume, is its correct form :—

And when I lie in the green kirkyard,
With the mould upon my breast,
Say not that she did well—or ill,
Only, "She did her best."

But it is not stated from which of her poems it is taken. ALEYN LYELL READE.
Park Corner, Blundellsands.

DARLEY, A FORGOTTEN IRISH POET (9ᵗʰ S. ix. 205, 377).—In the 'Biographical Sketch' prefixed to my edition of 'Sylvia; or, the May Queen,' are included all the known facts of Darley's life and career. Canon Livingstone and other relatives of the deceased poet kindly assisted me in furnishing this, the first faithful account of George Darley. It will be seen that I have been obliged to refute Miss Mitford's very imaginative account of the "Unrecognized Poet," as she termed Darley in her 'Recollections of a Literary Life,' vol. ii. pp. 283-91. My reprint of 'Sylvia' appeared in 1892.

Canon Livingstone, the poet's cousin, had a volume of 'Poems' by Darley printed privately. My copy is undated. A charming reprint of Darley's marvellous phantasy, 'Nepenthe,' was edited by R. A. Streatfeild in 1897. The article on Darley referred to by C. C. B. as issued in Mr. Miles's 'Poets and Poetry of the Century' was written by me. It will be seen that George Darley is not forgotten. J. H. INGRAM.

DOWNIE'S SLAUGHTER (9ᵗʰ S. ix. 367).—The idea of death being caused through the imaginary suffering of the victim is well brought out in the gruesome story of a condemned convict who was handed over to the surgeons. They pretended they were going to bleed him to death, blindfolded him, and pricked his arm slightly with a needle. The unfortunate man's illusion was maintained by the surgeons causing a constant trickle of lukewarm water to drip from his arm into a vessel. The story goes that, when a quantity of water equal to the amount of blood in the man's body had thus dripped into the vessel, the victim (who all the while had been slowly collapsing) at length expired.

JOHN HOBSON MATTHEWS.
Town Hall, Cardiff.

INQUESTS (9th S. ix. 408).—The Hull Corporation possesses a very large book, the contents of which date from the reign of Henry VI. to that of Philip and Mary, and consist mainly of minutes of the proceedings of Quarter Sessions and Sheriff Turns. But the book contains a large number of miscellaneous entries, and amongst these are many records of coroners' inquests held in the county of Kingston-upon-Hull in the fifteenth and sixteenth centuries.	J. R. BOYLE.

The records of the coroners' courts should be found among the Calendar Rolls for the county, or with the clerk of the peace for the borough, as the case may be. No great care seems to have been taken to preserve these records, and difficulty may be found in ascertaining their whereabouts. I know of the wholesale destruction of the coroners' records in one borough, where they had got into private hands. Comparatively recent records are probably in the custody of the coroners.

JOHN HOBSON MATTHEWS.
Town Hall, Cardiff.

PORTRAITS WANTED (9th S. ix. 368).—Bromley, who might be consulted in this kind of case before 'N. & Q.,' notes portraits of none of the personages mentioned at the above reference except one of "William Pen, Admiral, knighted by Charles II.?—oval, in Brachelius's 'History.'"

JULIAN MARSHALL.

There is a small mezzotint portrait of Admiral Sir William Penn, published 1811, in the portrait gallery of the Friends' Institute, 12, Bishopsgate Street Without.

P. D. LUCAS.
Claygate.

There is a portrait of Admiral Sir William Penn, father of the founder of Pennsylvania, by Sir Peter Lely, at Greenwich Hospital. A good reproduction of this may be seen in vol. v. of Mr. Wheatley's edition of Pepys's 'Diary' (1895).	CHARLES R. DAWES.

Two miniatures of the celebrated naval commander Admiral Sir William Penn (1621–70) were exhibited at the special loan collection of works of art at the South Ken-

sington Museum in June, 1862. One, by S. Cooper, was lent by the Duke of Buccleuch, and the other by the Rev. J. Beck. Both are recorded in the Catalogue, edited by J. C. Robinson, F.S.A., on pp. 191 and 198. My copy of the Catalogue is the revised edition, January, 1863.

CHAS. H. CROUCH.
5, Grove Villas, Wanstead.

BUILDING IN GOTHIC PERIOD (9th S. ix. 387). —If MR. GRIFFITH refers to Canon Jessopp's 'Trials of a Country Parson,' p. 166 (second edition, 1891), he will find some notes extracted from the muniments of the diocese of Ely of a very interesting character. I should think that the examination of the muniments in question would afford him some of the material which he requires.

CHARLES HIATT.

GREEK PRONUNCIATION (9th S. vii. 146, 351, 449; viii. 74, 192, 372, 513; ix. 131, 251, 311, 332, 436).—I deeply regret that it is possible for any one to be able to say that, "according to Prof. Skeat, *salt* is derived from A.-S. *sealt.*" For, of course, this is not *strictly* the case, though the assertion would not for a moment mislead any one who had the most elementary notions about English phonetics. I have tried to guard against such a blunder by careful explanation, which, however, has been wholly ignored. Thus, in my 'Principles of English Etymology,' series i. p. 43, I say: "It ought to be carefully borne in mind that, when we say a word is 'derived' from Anglo-Saxon, we commonly mean that it is derived from an Old Mercian form, which in some cases probably coincided with the recorded A.-S. form, but in other cases certainly *did not.*" The italics are in the original; and the caution has particular regard to the fact that the A.-S. often has *ea* where the Mercian has *a*. See the whole context.

All experience shows that such warnings are of no use, and that my countrymen deeply resent learning the most elementary facts about their own language. One result has been that I have had to rewrite my 'Concise Etymological Dictionary,' and I have endeavoured thereby to help the uninitiated by using plainer language than would otherwise have been necessary. This is why, in the new edition of that work, ed. 1901, p. 461, my article on *salt* now takes the following form: "*Salt*, M.E. *salt*, O. Merc. *salt*, A.-S. *sealt*, both adj. and sb. So also O. Fries. *salt*, Icel. *saltr*, Dan. Swed. *salt*, Du. *zout*, all adjectives, from a Teutonic type **saltoz;* cf. W. *hallt*, adj. salt, and L. *salsus*,"

&c. It will thus be seen that "A.-S." differs from all the other dialects; and I have tried to explain, over and over again, that modern English is not derived from the A.-S. or Wessex dialect, but from Mercian or Anglian. The reason why the A.-S. form is given is because it is so easily accessible, and every one ought to know at least the alphabet of it. Why pronunciation should be discussed without reference to any of the established facts about it, I do not understand.

WALTER W. SKEAT.

EULOGIES OF THE BIBLE BY HUXLEY AND DARWIN (9ᵗʰ S. ix. 328, 374, 432).—Dr. John Murdoch's booklet, 'Testimonies of Great Men to the Bible and Christianity,' is published by the Religious Tract Society.

H. JOHNSON.

"LUPO-MANNARO" (9ᵗʰ S. ix. 329).—I am interested in learning that "lupo-mannaro" is still prevalent in Italy. It is a form of werewolfism (a subject to which I have devoted much study), and, indeed, it is identical with it, for a few centuries ago a madman with such tendencies would have been accredited with a magic wolf-skin, and the devil's ointment by means of which he could drop his human form. Lycanthropy has been at one time or another prevalent in every country of Europe, England and Ireland not excepted. But the most terrible outbreak of that disease occurred in France about three or four hundred years ago, when such maniacs were treated as emissaries of Satan and enemies of God, and as loupsgarous were tortured and burnt by the hundreds. This epidemic was caused by want and the incredible hardships of peasant life. It took its imaginative form from Germany, though there can be little doubt that the dull greyness of the people's lives tempted many who were sane to mimic the doings of those who were mad, purely for the sake of the horrible excitement and notoriety which such a course brought upon them. In 1521 two men afflicted with this disease, then called zooanthropy, were burnt at Poligny in the Jura; and sixty years later the malady was spreading all over France, increased by the barbarous methods taken to stamp it out.

CLARE JERROLD.

Hampton-on-Thames.

Although Borrow in his account of the Zincali of Spain does not allude to this curious folk-name, yet wolf-madness is probably traceable to other hot countries, for, as he says, the belief in the evil eye (to which it cannot be doubted a "lupo-mannaro"

was believed to be indirectly a victim) "is all-prevalent in countries where the sun and moon are particularly dazzling." Perhaps a were-wolf was originally a man who had become mad at the glance of the moon, and had escaped to "dree his weird" of solitary madness in the depths of the forest—*i.e.*, if the etymology of "were" be accepted, that it is equivalent to the Gothic *vair* and the Latin *vir*. The operations of the "werewolf" were always at night. In the Perigord the were-wolf is called *louléerou*, certain men, especially bastards, being obliged at each full moon to transform themselves into these diabolic beasts, who will provide a supful of horrors to any one who cares to read about them in Mr. Baring-Gould's 'Book of Were-Wolves,' 1865. So let no one who wishes to avoid becoming a lupo-mannaro, and a victim to the evil eye, "sleep uncovered beneath the smile of the moon, for her glance is poisonous, and produces insupportable itching in the eye, and not unfrequently blindness"; and, in the words of Psalm cxxi. 6, "the moon shall not smite thee by night."

J. HOLDEN MACMICHAEL.

On lycanthropy, or were-wolves, the following may be consulted: Baring-Gould, 'Book of Were-Wolves,' 1865; Mayo, 'Popular Superstitions'; Pusey, 'Commentary on Daniel'; Camerarius, 'Living Librarie,' 1621; Malebranch, 'Search after Truth,' 1694, i. 267; C. Prieur, 'Lycanthropie,' 1596; Dendy, 'Philosophy of Mystery,' 1847; Begbie, 'Supernatural Illustrations,' 1851; Walton, 'Complete Angler,' 1823, pp. 124-5; Montaigne, 'Essays,' Florio, 1897, iii. 344; Gairdner, 'Early Chroniclers, England,' 1883, p. 170; J. Edwards, 'Authority of Scriptures,' 1693, i.; Willet, 'Daniel,' 1610, pp. 136-7; and the indexes of 'N. & Q.' W. C. B.

"WEEK-END" (9ᵗʰ S. viii. 162, 292, 414, 511). —I first heard this phrase at Ripley, Derbyshire, in 1884; but I now constantly hear it employed in South Wales and in London. It is evidently a case of the spread of a word owing to its usefulness.

JOHN HOBSON MATTHEWS.

Town Hall, Cardiff.

ROSSETTI'S 'RUGGIERO AND ANGELICA' (9ᵗʰ S. ix. 425).—Geomancy is a kind of divination, but I am not sure that all writers who mention it know exactly what it is. In the story of 'Aladdin and the Wonderful Lamp' the brother of the African magician discovers the death of his brother through geomancy. Greene in his 'Friar Bacon and Friar Bungay' speaks of pyromancy as the means of controlling the spirits of fire, and geomancy of controlling the spirits of earth. These, with hydromancy and aëromancy, were classical modes of divination, effected through the dæmons, who generally may be thought to be elementary beings. Burton, in his 'Anatomy of Melancholy,' says that the devils were worshipped through pyromancy and hydromancy. The note to the line in 'Hudibras,'

> But those that trade in geomancy,

tells us that geomancy is sorcery by pricks and circles in the earth; and a reference is made to a tract of Cornelius Agrippa concerning geomancy, and to other works.

E. YARDLEY.

THE ORIGIN OF SWEENY TODD (9th S. ix. 345).—A serious error occurs in this communication anent the "fiend-like Figaro" and his pie-making "paramour." It concerns two ladies with whom I was well acquainted, Mrs. Atkinson of the "Brit." and Miss Emma Atkinson of Sadler's Wells, between whom there was not the slightest relationship. I began to know Emma (then a slip of a girl), her sister Alice, and their mother as far back as 1844-5 in Newcastle. I also knew Mrs. Atkinson at the Britannia while I was under a two years' engagement to Mr. S. Lane, commencing in 1853. In my early days at the Adelphi I often visited Emma and her mother at their home near Islington Green, to chat over old days in the North. Emma was a kindly woman and a loving, dutiful daughter. Whether she is yet in the land of the living is unknown to   FATHER TOM.

PASSAGE IN THACKERAY (9th S. iv. 207).—The reference for the passage in Thackeray asked for by J. C. does not appear to have been given in 'N. & Q.' See 'Barry Lyndon,' chap. i., paragraph 46. The words, when correctly quoted, are as follows :—

"Love! sure the word is formed on purpose out of the prettiest soft vowels and consonants in the language, and he or she who does not care to read about it is not worth a fig, to my thinking."

Probably J. C. has already ascertained the source of his quotation, but, as the query has appeared, it may seem fitting that an answer should be recorded.

EDWARD BENSLY.
The University, Adelaide, S.A.

YARROW UNVISITED (9th S. ix. 386).—The *Academy* writer quoted by MR. THOMAS BAYNE at the above reference has evidently made a *lapsus*, and written "Thomas" for John. There is only one Logan associated with the minstrelsy of Yarrow—John Logan, the erstwhile minister of South Leith, whose immortal ballad 'The Braes of Yarrow' is,

perhaps, the most widely-known poem connected with the celebrated stream and valley. D'Israeli, in his 'Calamities of Authors,' includes the name of this unfortunate genius, who was driven from his ministry by the publication, and subsequent performance at the Edinburgh Theatre, of his tragedy of 'Runnimede,' while the Michael Bruce story was long since cleared up by Mr. Laing, who established John Logan's claim to the authorship of 'The Ode to the Cuckoo,' as Dr. Carruthers says in 'Chambers's Cyclopædia,' "beyond all dispute."

To those who would learn more of the peculiar power exercised by Yarrow on her votaries I would recommend a capital little anthology by the Rev. R. Borland, minister of Yarrow, entitled 'Yarrow: its Poets and Poetry,' published by Mr. Thomas Fraser, Dalbeattie, in 1890. G. YARROW BALDOCK.
South Hackney.

"AWAY WITH" (9th S. ix. 348).—Apparently Babington uses this phrase similarly in a passage quoted in the 'H.E.D.' under "away": "Yea, we would bid......away with it, and not abide the sight of it." This dated 1590. C. C. B.

MONOSYLLABLES IN LITERARY COMPOSITION (9th S. viii. 521).—To Newman's lyric "Lead, kindly light," may be added Bonar's well-known hymn "Thy way, not mine, O Lord." Comparing the two, we find that Newman's, out of 131 words, has only 10 that are not monosyllabic, while Bonar's, out of 135, has only 8 that are not monosyllables. The former, as correctly stated by MR. TAYLOR, has 30 consecutive monosyllables; the latter, in the third verse, has 32. In Coleridge's little poem 'Something Childish, but Very Natural,' out of 96 words only 7 are of more than one syllable. So far as I can tell without actually counting, monosyllables seem largely to preponderate in 'In Memoriam.'

In all such cases the Anglo-Saxon element will probably prevail, and be more simple and forcible than the ponderous Latin derivatives of the Johnsonian style. There seems, therefore, hardly room for Pope's imitative satire in his 'Essay on Criticism,'

> And ten low words oft creep in one dull line,

which, in fact, we may suppose to have mainly applied to poems written in the same decasyllabic metre which he was then using, and which was the fashionable one of the day.

However, if this be a fault, Pope himself lies open to the same censure. For in this very essay, without reckoning the imitative line, there are no fewer than two dozen exactly similar lines; and one of these is in the very same paragraph as the satire. But then Pope would perhaps have said that *his* lines were *not* "dull." Still, he might have looked to his own windows before throwing this stone. Churchill, in the 'Rosciad' (1761), seems to have copied Pope in a yet more forcible denunciation and in rougher numbers :—

In monosyllables his thunders roll,
He, she, it, and, we, you, they, fright the soul,

where we have the same illustrative imitation.

In the introduction to Sharp's 'Sonnets of this Century' may be found a "clever piece of trifling......a sonnet of single-syllable lines," *i.e.*, each line consists of *one* word only, and that a monosyllable, at least in the English sense of "syllable"—the sonnet is in French. But I have dwelt quite long enough on this trivial matter, in which we may say *chacun à son goût*. C. LAWRENCE FORD, B.A.
Bath.

"CONSERVATIVE" AS A POLITICAL TERM (8ᵗʰ S. vi. 61, 181; vii. 356; xi. 494; 9ᵗʰ S. iv. 333; viii. 489).—In MR. OWEN's communication at the first of these references an extract was given from M. Louis Simond's 'Journal of a Tour and Residence in Great Britain during the Years 1810 and 1811,' published at Edinburgh in 1815, in which a French *Sénat Conservatif* is mentioned. But as Littré described this body as *Sénat conservateur*, MR. OWEN wrote :—

"It would be interesting to get dated references, if such are known, to contemporary writings, where the 'Sénat conservateur' is loosely described as *conservatif*."

Such a reference can now be given, and it disposes of the suspicion entertained by MR. OWEN that the word was a mistake on the part of M. Simond, for the *Times* employed the term on 17 May, 1802, as if it were one in ordinary use at that period, in the following paragraph :—

"We again received Paris Journals last night to the 13th instant inclusive. No doubt can be entertained but that Bonaparte will be elected Consul for life, when we consider the means that will be used, and the power which (if necessary) is ready to be employed to carry this question in his favor. What then remains for him but to flatter, or command, for it is one and the same thing, the Conservative Senate, into another question for the popular decision, whether the Consulate should not become an hereditary settlement in his own family? That arrangement would be concluded with the same facility as the former, and the most powerful Military Government that Europe has ever known will then be established, and most probably with all the titular honours and characteristic insignia of it."

ALFRED F. ROBBINS.

WILLIAM TOLLEMACHE EDWARDS (9ᵗʰ S. ix. 308, 398).—In the 'English Registry' for the year 1810, bound with John Watson Stewart's 'Almanac' (Dublin), appears a 'List of the Army'; and on p. 176, under majors gazetted 1807, is the name "W. Tol. Edwards of the 86th regiment of Foot," which regiment is stated on p. 190 to be then (1810) serving abroad. J. N. DOWLING.
67, Douglas Road, Handsworth, Birmingham.

BRITISH EPITAPHS IN CATALUÑA (9ᵗʰ S. ix. 326).—MR. DODGSON may like to know that "Cacharloch" in the epitaph of the Duke of Wharton is really Catherlough, the old name for county Carlow. The duke was Marquis of Catherlough, Earl of Rathfarnham ("Rathaseasnum" in copy of epitaph), and Baron of Trim in Ireland. He had been created Duke of Northumberland by King James III. in 1726, and signs his request to the Inquisition at Madrid for admission into the Catholic Church, now amongst the Egerton MSS. in the British Museum, as Wharton of Northumberland, so that I am rather astonished that the latter title does not figure on his tombstone at Poblet. It is curious that the duke, who at one time had been amongst the greatest politicians of his day, had become so completely forgotten before his death that no notice of it occurs in the dispatches of Sir Benjamin Keene, then British envoy in Spain, part of whose duties consisted in keeping a very close watch upon all the Jacobite exiles in the Peninsula, whilst only the briefest mention of it occurs in the English newspapers of the day. It is a curious instance of the uncertainty of historic fame that even so able a writer as Mr. Wilkins, in his 'Love of an Uncrowned Queen,' does not mention the fact that it was chiefly owing to Thomas, Marquis of Wharton, the father of the duke, that the name of the Electress Sophia was originally inserted in the Act of Settlement. The Wharton family had become closely connected with Northern Germany during the reign of James II. I find I should have added that the Duke of Wharton was K.G only by the creation of King James III.
H.

HERRICK: SILVER-PENCE (9ᵗʰ S. ix. 49, 178).—MR. MATTHEWS's reference to the survival among the Jews of the use of a sharp flint for performing circumcision is so obscure that it may be read in two senses—one of which requires correction. Jews do not nowadays use such rude methods for so delicate an operation. The "mohel," or practitioner, is a skilled surgical operator, employing whatever is most efficient among surgical appliances. Any "mohel" who should revert to the Mosaical mode would be sent to Coventry or Jericho.

M. L. R. BRESLAR.

GWYNETH (9th S. ix. 109, 319, 372).—Gwynnedd is equated by the Breton Guened, whence Vannes, if I am not mistaken. If this is so, it may be a question whether Gwynnedd and Gwent are not, after all, related to each other, and perhaps also whether Venetia is not a distant kinswoman. A clerical error crept into the reply of C. C. B. He meant to say that Gwent is the southeastern portion of South Wales.

JOHN HOBSON MATTHEWS.
Town Hall, Cardiff.

OLD SPOONS (9th S. ix. 348, 416).— MR. COLEMAN does not appear to have stated correctly the hall-marks of the York and Chester Assay Offices. The modern York mark was, until the closing of the office, about 1856, the city arms—viz., Five lions passant on a cross. The Chester mark is a sword erect between three garbs or wheatsheaves. T. SEYMOUR.
9, Newton Road, Oxford.

Miscellaneous.

NOTES ON BOOKS, &c.

A Foreign View of England in the Reigns of George I. and George II. Translated and edited by Madame van Muyden. (Murray.)

CÉSAR DE SAUSSURE, whose view of English life, as contained in a series of letters written from this country to some friend—presumably a relative—in Switzerland, where his family had taken refuge during the persecutions of the Protestants under Louis XIV., Madame van Muyden, a descendant by marriage, has translated, belonged, apparently, to a family many of whose members were authors. He appears himself to have been a tolerably voluminous writer; but whether any of his works attained to the dignity of print we know not. His name appears in no biographical dictionary across which we have come, and no work of his is mentioned in the authoritative compilations of Quérard and Brunet. Whether the letters now published are translated from the original MSS. or a printed volume we are not informed. When first written they circulated largely in Switzerland in MS. They were then sorted by the author and bound into two volumes, and were read, at his own request, by Voltaire, who pronounced them amusing and useful. Such, indeed, they are, and their present publication is a boon, since we know no work from a foreign source which throws so strong and, in the main, trustworthy a light upon the time of the first Georges. Totally ignorant of our language when, after a dangerous sea voyage, he landed in England—so ignorant, indeed, that when he lost his way in London he could acquaint no one with his wants —M. de Saussure, at the close of a long residence, became familiar with our speech and our institutions. He was admitted to the intimacy of men of position, was fairly versed in Court secrets, supplies an animated sketch of the relations between George I. and his son, describes the coronation of the latter monarch, makes eminently intelligent observations upon matters with which foreign visitors are little apt to trouble themselves, and gives a highly edifying picture of social life and popular practices in the first half of the eighteenth century. He accompanied Lord Kinnoull when that nobleman went as ambassador to Constantinople, was first secretary to the British Embassy in that city, and was for a time secretary to Lord Cathcart, commanding a portion of the British fleet sent against the Spanish Settlements in America. Ample as were his sources of information, he is betrayed into some mistakes, and there are points at which his letters are misleading. This is inevitable in a work written under similar conditions; but the whole carries with it, as is said, "a conviction of veracity," and is eminently agreeable, readable, and instructive.

We look back with a sigh to the London described. M. de Saussure reached us by way of the Rhine and Holland, speaks of the Hague as a "village," and rhapsodizes over the Thames below London Bridge: "You can imagine nothing more beautiful than the banks of the Thames; on either side are charming country houses and many pretty towns and villages, the principal being Sheerness, Gravesend, and Greenwich; in the latter [sic] place is a magnificent hospital for seamen." Here is a description of a presentation to George I.: "Three ladies were then presented to His Majesty; he kissed them all affectionately on the lips, and I remarked that he seemed to take the most pleasure in kissing the prettiest of the three." His correspondent is not to be scandalized. "This form of salutation is common in England, and though some who have travelled much offer the cheek instead of the lips, many ladies would be displeased should you fail to salute them after the custom of the country." He says that the suburbs of Southwark are "habitually known as Sodrick," a name which conveys nothing to us; states that Queen Anne was often called "Boutique d'Eau-de-vie," because of her well-known liking for the bottle and spirituous liquors, a piece of scandal with which we were not familiar; and dwells upon the general use, even at that time, by the bargemen of "quite extraordinary terms, and generally very coarse and dirty ones," which he is unable to explain to his correspondent. A characteristic sight which he witnessed was the hanging of thirteen criminals at the same time, one of them being Jonathan Wild. With some astonishment he comments on the inconceivable amount of water used by the English for external purposes, though he states that "absolutely [sic] none is drunk." Of our proneness to fight, of our appearance, character, and amusements, he has much to say. He praises the beauty of complexion of our women, dwells upon the drunkenness generally prevalent, and says that maidservants go out on Sunday almost as well dressed as their mistresses. Of theatrical entertainments, and especially of the pantomimic performances of Rich, he has much to say; and he describes gladiatorial combats given in public, in which sharp swords were used by men and sometimes by women. Of these sanguinary entertainments he disapproves, determining never to witness any of them again; but he regards cockfights as much more diverting. The book, which is handsomely got up, and has many interesting designs of London in the period of the first Georges, is a mine of delight to the antiquary.

Biographical History of Gonville and Caius College, Cambridge. By John Venn, Sc.D., F.R.S., F.S.A., Senior Fellow of the College. 3 vols. (Cambridge, University Press.)

Our warmest congratulations are due to Dr. Venn on his successful achievement of the unique task of compiling a biographical history of the third largest college in Cambridge. In the first two volumes (it will be remembered) he gave a wonderfully ample account of all the members of the college from its foundation in 1349 to 1897. In the third and final volume he gives a biographical account of the successive masters of the college, with illustrative extracts from the annals, gesta, bursars' books, &c., which forms practically a very interesting social and architectural history of the college from the earliest times to the present day. It is followed by a full description and history of the college buildings, the endowments, offices, schools, and almshouses, the college records, the commemoration of benefactors, a list of the antiquities still remaining in the college and of the portraits it possesses, a description of the chief pieces of plate, a history of the boat club (by Mr. Roberts, senior tutor), and the livings in the gift of the college, with lists of incumbents, not to mention an appendix of transcripts of charters and other deeds.

Gonville and Caius College, founded by Edmund Gonville in 1347-8 as the Hall of the Annunciation of the Blessed Virgin, was originally located in Lurteburgh Lane (afterwards known as Free School Lane); but on the death of the founder in 1351 his executor, William Bateman, Bishop of Norwich (who was the founder of Trinity Hall), removed the Hall to its present position. The existing Gonville Court represents its condition at the beginning of the fifteenth century, the chapel walls being mainly original work of 1393 on the south side, the old hall of 1441 still existing on the west side, though cut up into chambers when the new hall was built in 1853 by Salvin. Probably the more reverent care of these later years would have kept the old hall in its original state to serve as a library, as has been wisely done at Balliol College, Oxford. The north wall of the court is also original, but the chambers were rebuilt in 1753. The second foundation by John Caius, who was President of the College of Physicians (at a festival dinner a few years ago, to commemorate the tercentenary of the admission of William Harvey to the college, the writer well remembers the then President, Sir Andrew Clarke, exhibiting the silver mace given by Caius to the College of Physicians side by side with the one which he had presented to his new foundation), and physician to Edward VI. and Queen Mary, took place in 1557, and the buildings of Caius Court are the actual ones erected by Caius after that date. The court is open to the south, a special and wise proviso of the founder, so as to admit sunlight and air. With the somewhat elaborate allegorical taste of the age, his entrance gateway in Trumpington Street was called the Gate of Humility (it now adorns the Master's garden—is this a latter-day allegory?); thence the student would proceed to the Gate of Virtue, and, turning to the left, through Caius Court, would leave the college by the Gate of Honour, leading to the Schools, and now to the Senate House—thus typify-

ing the seemly and well-ordered progress of the undergraduate in his time of residence in the university. In the third, or Tree Court, several groups of buildings known as the Perse and Legge Buildings were pulled down when the present front of the college, in the French Renaissance style, was built in 1870 from the designs of Mr. Waterhouse. This new building—admirably designed, and a splendid piece of architecture—seems singularly out of place in the main street of a mediæval English university. Caius himself, William Harvey, Jeremy Taylor, John Hookham Frere, the late Lord Esher, Lord Thurlow, and the late Sir George Paget are only a few out of many distinguished names of former members of the college.

Many interesting matters are dealt with in this volume. The first mention of bedmakers, for instance, occurs in the college chronicle of 14 April, 1702; that of "finding," the term applied to the waiters in hall, dates from 1724; while the rather handsome gown of blue faced with velvet was introduced in 1837. The history of the boat club brings out the fact that the light blue and white straw hat had been adopted by the college before the university; when the latter did so the college changed the hat for a black straw one, as at present. The old notion was that the light blue was given to the college as a distinction for its having been chosen to represent the university, as the head boat of the river, in 1844 against a Cambridge town boat club crew, which it beat.

It need hardly be added that the three volumes are produced in excellent style, with good and satisfactory illustrations, by the Cambridge University Press. An improvement would be possible in the shape of top edges gilt.

Notices to Correspondents.

We must call special attention to the following notices:—

On all communications must be written the name and address of the sender, not necessarily for publication, but as a guarantee of good faith.

We cannot undertake to answer queries privately.

To secure insertion of communications correspondents must observe the following rules. Let each note, query, or reply be written on a separate slip of paper, with the signature of the writer and such address as he wishes to appear. When answering queries, or making notes with regard to previous entries in the paper, contributors are requested to put in parentheses, immediately after the exact heading, the series, volume, and page or pages to which they refer. Correspondents who repeat queries are requested to head the second communication "Duplicate."

L. S. R.—Should we print your suggestion, you will be certain to get your knuckles rapped by philologists.

NOTICE.

Editorial communications should be addressed to "The Editor of 'Notes and Queries'"—Advertisements and Business Letters to "The Publisher"—at the Office, Bream's Buildings, Chancery Lane, E.C.

We beg leave to state that we decline to return communications which, for any reason, we do not print; and to this rule we can make no exception.

LONDON, SATURDAY, JUNE 21, 1902.

CONTENTS. — No. 234.

Notes.

MIRACULOUS LIKENESSES OF JESUS AT TIBERIAS AND AT BERITHUS.

AMONGST the mass of apocryphal literature circulating in the early ages of Christianity was a Syriac document respecting the history of a painting of Christ at Tiberias, and of the miraculous events connected therewith. The text of this curious specimen of early Christian literature has been edited and translated by Dr. E. A. Wallis Budge, and published in Luzac's "Semitic Series."* 'The History of the Likeness of Christ' professes to be written by Philotheus, the Deacon of the Country of the East, and to embody information given to him by a "messenger of God." According to this angelic communication, the document refers to the Jews of Tiberias in the reign of "the God-loving emperor Zeno." The events recorded are thus said to have happened in the last quarter of

the fifth century. The Jews of Tiberias, we are told, hired an artist to paint a likeness of Christ on a panel of wood, and set it up in the Temple and mocked at it. One of them pierced it with a spear, and straightway blood and water flowed from the wood. This, whilst convincing them that Christ was the Son of God, only excited in them a desire to conceal the miracle. Whilst they were whispering a blind man came, and, having obtained admission, smeared his eyes with some of the blood and water, and so regained his sight. The priests tried to bribe him to conceal the truth, but he gave information to a paralytic, who was also cured by the application of the blood and water applied to him by the erewhile blind man. At his prayer the door of the room in which the likeness was placed, and which had been sealed by the priests, opened spontaneously. The door-keeper was now also converted. They prayed to God to "let the likeness be taken away from here and given to a holy nation, and let these doors be shut fast again, and let the seals be found sealed in their proper places." Then the angel of the Lord came down and removed the likeness, "and no man hath ever seen it since." The doorkeeper and the ex-paralytic had a horn full of the blood and water, and with this they worked many miracles, and, persecuted by the Jews, finally went to Cilicia, where they built a monastery, dwelling there all the days of their life. Such, in brief outline, is the story of the miraculous Christ of Tiberias.

There is another story of a miraculous likeness of Christ, which is referred to by Durant in the following passage :—

"Erat et altera Christi imago, quam Nicodemus Gamalieli dono dederat, quæ cum Berithi, post multa secula pervenisset ad Iudæos, eam Iudæi in eorum Synagoga sputis fœdarunt, arundine percusserunt, crucifixerunt, lanceâ latus perforaverunt. Vnde sanguis et aqua cœpit decurrere. Quod pluribus persequitur Athanas. in libello de passione imaginis Domini, qui tum cœpisse Ecclesias extrui et consecrari in honorem Saluatoris affirmat. Tolosæ exstat et Basilica suburbana abhinc multis annis sancti Saluatoris nomine edificata. Festum verò feria 5. post festum Paschæ annis singulis celebramus. Porro eadem historia in Synodo 7. iisdem ferè verbis Act. 4. exaratur."—Joannis Stephani Duranti 'De Ritibus Ecclesiæ Catholicæ,' libri tres (Paris, 1631), lib. i. cap. v. p. 33.

This apocryphal tract, attributed to Athanasius, is included in the edition of the works of that saint printed at Cologne in 1686. Whilst the underlying idea is the same, its development is quite different. Nicodemus made an image of Christ, which he gave to Gamaliel, and it passed through a succession of inheritors. At the fall of Jerusalem it was

---

* 'The History of the Blessed Virgin Mary,' and 'The History of the Likeness of Christ which the Jews of Tiberias made to mock at.' The Syriac texts, edited, with English translations, by E. A. Wallis Budge, M.A., Litt.D., D.Lit., Keeper of the Egyptian and Assyrian Antiquities in the British Museum. London, Luzac & Co., 1899.

taken to Berithus in Syria, and the house in which it was became the habitation of a Jew. The image was subjected by the Jews to all the indignities of the Crucifixion, but when the lance pierced its side blood and water gushed forth, and by the agency of this miraculous fluid (taken to the synagogue) the blind recovered sight and the lame were healed. These miracles had the effect of converting the Jews of Berithus. Glasses filled with the blood and water of the image of Christ were sent into all parts of the world.

There is a similar story of an incident said to have occurred at Paris in 1290. A Jewish money-lender induced a woman to conceal the Host when communicating and to bring it to him. He proceeded to stab the sacred wafer and to inflict upon it the tortures recorded of the Crucifixion. Blood gushed from it, and when finally it was thrown into a cauldron of boiling water there was the appearance of a cross with the dying Christ upon it. A neighbour came in, and, after beholding the vision, received the Host again in its original form and took it to the Bishop of Paris. The Jew was burnt alive, his wife and children turned Christians, and his house was converted into the "Church of the Miracles," where the penknife and the cauldron were long preserved as evidences. One of Hone's tracts is devoted to this "miraculous Host."

Underneath what may be called the Christian mythology of these stories is the Old World idea that identified the person and his picture. Some savage races object to portraiture from a feeling that a portion at least of the individuality is abstracted from the sitter and conveyed into his counterfeit presentment.   WILLIAM E. A. AXON.
Manchester.

ADDITIONS TO THE 'N.E.D.'
(*Continued from p. 403.*)

Chock (earlier).—1711, Sutherland, 'Shipbuilder's Assistant,' p. 159, "Chok; a small piece of timber fitted to a larger to make out the substance required."

Chokiness (not in).—1844, Hewlett, 'Parsons and Widows,' ch. vi., "I felt a short, unpleasant kind of chokiness."

Chop (=dent, not in).—1893, Spon, 'Mechanic's Own Book,' p. 84, "If the hammer leaves indentations, or what are technically called 'chops'"; *ibid.*, p. 85, "distinct indentations, or chops." (In metal plate working.)

Choppiness (not in).—18—, Pinto, 'Africa,' vol. i. p. 142, "choppiness of the surface of water."

Chromo-collotypy (not in).—1896, *Brit. Journ. Photog. Alm.*, p. 572, "Chromo-collotypy and allied processes are receiving marked attention."

Chromogram (not in).—1894, *Amer. Ann. Photog.*, p. 208, "The word chromogram designates the combination or the ensemble of three diapositives made from negatives representing the action of the blues, yellows, and greens respectively of the original."

Chromograph (not in).—1899, 'Orthochromatic Photography' (ed. Tennant), p. 281, "those [screens] made of coloured glass, such as the chromograph."

Chromometer (earlier).—1797, *Month. Mag.*, iii. p. 205, "He [Lamarck] has invented a graduated scale, which he calls a chromometer, on which may be ascertained by methodical tables 2,700 shades."

Chromosome (not in).—1894, *Times*, 11 August, p. 11, col. 2, "In the case of dividing cells, achromatic filaments are seen connecting different parts of the chromosomes."

Chrysocale (not in).—Spon, *ut supra*, p 16, "Other alloys are also known in commerce, by the names of tombac, similor or Mannheim gold, pinchbeck or prince's metal (chrysocale), &c." (=Chrysocoll?)

Chunk, v. (not in).—1892, R. Kipling, 'Barrack-Room Ballads,' p. 50, "Can't you 'ear their paddles chunkin' from Rangoon to Mandalay?"

Cicatriculose (not in).—1819, G. Samouelle, 'Entomol. Compendium,' p. 190.

Cigarettiferous (not in).—1890, C. Doyle, 'Captain of Polestar,' p. 172, "He strutted, cigarettiferous, beneath the grateful shadow of his limes."

Cinematograph, cinematographer, cinematographic (not in).—1898, *Brit. Journ. Photog. Alm.*, p. 647, "A brief description of Messrs. Lumière's cinematograph." 1901, *Brit. Journ. Photog.*, p. 738, "No great event takes place nowadays without the presence of a small army of cinematographers"; *ibid.*, p. 746, "The successful cinematographic entertainment."

Cissing (not in).—Spon, *ut supra*, p. 432, "To prevent a graining coat from 'cissing' at a watercolour overgraining coat, that is, repelling the water by antagonism of the oil."

Clearcole, v. (no quot.).—Spon, *ut supra*, p. 612, "When dry, claircole with size, and a little of the whitewash."

Cleistogenous (no quot.).—1873, Asa Gray, in *Amer. Natur.*, vol. vii. p. 692, "Cleistogenous flowers."

Clerkling (earlier).—1747, *Gent. Mag.*, p. 234, "Augmenting salaries,......so as our clerklings may be the better enabled to set up their equipages."

Clinker (not in).—1889, H. Saunders, 'Brit. Birds,' p. 546, "From its cry the Avocet was formerly known as the 'yelper,' 'barker,' and 'clinker.'"

Clover, v. (later).—1793, *Trans. Soc. Arts*, vol. iv. p. 14, "It seldom being required to clover down a corn crop."

Clutch.—See 'Crutch' below.

Cobaldish (not in).—1757, trl. J. F. Henckel, 'Pyritologia,' pp. 123, 190.

Cobbly (not in).—1891, *Bicycling News*, 4 April, p. 197, "Our rough cobbly roads."

Coccineous (obs.).—1819, G. Samouelle, 'Entomol. Compendium,' p. 133.

Cochleate (earlier).—1806, J. Galpine, 'Brit. Bot.,' p. 116, "Seed cochleate."

Cock-a-hoopedness.—1890, Baring-Gould, 'Pennycomequicks,' p. 216, "Would manifest self-assertion and cock-a-hoopedness when lifted into a sphere of authority."

Coherer (not in).—1902, *Windsor Mag.*, May, p. 718, "Marconi adopted a device invented by an Italian, Calzecchi,......called the coherer."

Coke (not in; cf. *Cawk*).—1797, *Month. Mag.*, p. 432, "Soil......partly a mixture of sand, flint, and chalk, or coke, as it is commonly called here" (*i.e.*, Lincolnshire); *ibid.*, p. 431, "The roads made with coke or chalk."

Cold, v. (obs.).—1900, Huxley, 'Life,' vol. ii. p. 101, "It blew and rained and colded for eight and forty hours consecutively."

Collotypy.—See 'Chromo-collotypy' above.

Colorification (not in).—1799 [Jordan ?], 'New Observations concerning the Inflections of Light,' p. 128.

Combinability (not in).—1900, G. Iles, 'Flame, Electricity, and the Camera,' p. 255, "All the properties of matter, transparency, chemical combinability, and the rest."

Come, v. (earlier of sense 15)—1605 [S. Harsnet], 'Declar. of Egreg. Popish Impostures,' p. 135, "The butter would not come."

Commonplacely (not in).—1893, G. Travers, 'Mona Maclean,' vol. i. p. 57, "Uniformly, hideously, commonplacely yellow."

Compromisee (not in).—1893, J. K. Bangs, 'Toppleton's Client,' p. 168, "To distinguish my clients...... by calling them respectively the compromisee and the compromisor."

Comptometer (not in).—1894, *Times*, 19 March, p. 13, col. 5, "The comptometer, which is a machine specially adapted for subtraction, multiplication, and division."

Cope bead.—Spon, *ut supra*, p. 374, "The other drawers......receive a ⅛ in. mahogany beading all round. This is called a 'cope bead.'"

Corking (not in).—1902, *Munsey's Mag.*, March, p. 810, "A good show......and a corking good show at that."

Corklit (not in; cf. *Cork*, sb. 2).—1894, Crockett, 'Raiders,' p. 132, "They slide and scrape the corklit from the stones."

Corkscrew-grass (not in).—1898, *Nature*, p. 311, "Spear or corkscrew-grass (*Stipa setacea*)."

Corrosivity (earlier). — 1689, Glauber's 'Works,' part i. pp. 314, 334.

Corymbous (no quot.).—1806, J. Galpine, 'Brit. Bot.,' p. 173, "F[lowers] corymbous."

Cotton-bales (not in).—1894, *Amer. Ann. Photog.*, p. 24, "The cloud well known as 'cotton-bales,' or 'thunder-heads,' we term cumulus."

Cottonous (obs.).—1797, *Month. Mag.*, iii. p. 303, "Two indigenous and common cottonous plants."

Cotton-rose (no quot.). — 1853, Morfit, 'Arts of Tanning,' p. 79, "*Filago Germanica* (common cotton-rose)."

Coxcombishness (not in). — 1890, D. C. Murray, 'John Vale's Guardian,' vol. ii. p. 143.

Crake, v.—1892, H. Hutchinson, 'Fairway Island,' p. 2, "The landrail craked unceasing, in a field...... upon his left."

Cresylite (not in). — 1892, 'Chambers's Ency.,' vol. ix. p. 386, "The French use cresylite, a compound of cresol, as melinite is of phenol." (Explosive for shells.)

Crevicing (not in; cf. *Crevice*, 1 b).—1895, Anderson, 'Prospector's Handbook' (sixth ed.), p. 157, "Crevicing—collecting gold in the crevices of rock."

Crisp, sb.—1847, Halvorson in Morfit, *ut supra*, p. 459, "Keep it [the skin] therein (while the oil is boiling), until a white or yellowish scale or crisp begins to form on its surface."

Crocodile (sense 4, no quot.).—1902, *Windsor Mag.*, June, p. 43, "She was the left-hand girl in the third joint of the crocodile."

Crookeding (not in).—1711, Sutherland, *ut supra*, p. 50, "The Variety in the Crookeding of Ships"; *ibid.*, "Their Curving, or Crookeding the Sheer."

Crooningly (not in).—1902, *Munsey's Mag.*, April,

p. 42, "'Ah, no, ah, no,' she said crooningly, as if she comforted the child."

Cross-bar (sense 3).—For "bar sinister" read *baton sinister*.

Crotching (not in).—Spon, *ut supra*, p. 431, "The style of grain varies. Generally in panels 'crotching' is resorted to." (In graining.)

Crotch punch (not in ; for saws).—Spon, *ut supra*, p. 218, "Spread setting is generally performed by crotch punches."

Crow-fig (not in).—1895, Bloxam, 'Chem.' (eighth ed.), p. 760, "Nux-vomica, or crow-fig, contains about 1 per cent. of strychnine."

Crumpet (not in). — 1902, *Strand Mag.*, March, p. 298, "He placed his hand against his forehead. 'Barmy on the crumpet,' he observed."

Crutch (earlier).—1711, Sutherland, 'Shipbuilder's Assistant,' p. 159, "Crutches, or Clutches ; large Knees fitted in the aft part of the Ship in Hold, to bind the parts together."

Cuckle (not in).—1889, Saunders, 'Brit. Birds,' p. 719, "On Lundy, where it [the Manx shearwater, *Puffinus anglorum*] is well known as the 'Cuckle.'"

Cucumber-beetle (not in).—1852, Harris, 'Insects of New England' (second ed.), p. 110, "These striped cucumber-beetles......notorious......for their attacks upon the leaves of the cucumber and squash" (*Galeruca vittata*).

Cur (=bird).—Used by Col. P. Hawker, 'Diary,' 1893, to denote the scaup-duck.

Curdy. — 1892, Hutchinson, 'Fairway Island,' p. 17, "He'll be fine and curdy." (Of a salmon.)

Cushion (electr.; earlier).—1745, *Gent. Mag.*, p. 295, "To imitate Mr. Winkler in his precaution, which is to fasten a cushion, powder'd with chalk, against the electric globe."

Cyclostat (not in) —1899, *English Mechanic*, p. 482, "The neat and ingenious instrument......devised by Dr. Charles A. Perkins of the University of Tennessee and called by him the Cyclostat......is for continuously viewing a rotary object."

Cymbal (earlier of sense).—1690, Harris, 'Specif. Magdalen Coll. Organ,' in Grove, 'Dict. Mus.,' *s.v.* 'Organ,' "Cymbal of 2 ranks, 100 pipes." (Named by Harris.)

Cymous (no quot.).—1806, J. Galpine, 'Brit. Bot.,' p. 114, "Racemes cymous."

Cypress pine.—Spon, *ut supra*, p. 131, "Cypress pine (*Callitris columellaris*) is a plentiful tree in Queensland."

J. DORMER.

Redmorion, Woodside Green, S.E.

(To be continued.)

"FROM THE LONE SHIELING."—It has long been widely accepted that the exile poem, the best-known stanza of which begins :—

From the lone shieling of the misty island
    Mountains divide us, and the waste of seas,

was written by the Earl of Eglinton. The lines were first published in *Blackwood's Magazine* for September, 1829 ; in an altered form they appeared in *Tait's Magazine* for June, 1849, with an accompanying note : "As from the papers of the late Earl of Eglinton." Mr. Neil Munro, the author of 'John Splendid,' in one of his weekly contributions to a Glasgow journal relates that

Messrs. Blackwood recently caused a search to be made, and have discovered that the manuscript of the poem, which appeared in a 'Noctes Ambrosianæ' by Lockhart, is in the handwriting of Lockhart, who gives no hint as to its authorship further than stating that it had been sent to him "by a friend now in Upper Canada." In this statement Mr. Munro thinks there is a clue to the author's identity, "and it is significant," he adds, "that in the same number of *Maga* in which the poem first appeared, there is an article on Upper Canada from the pen of John Galt, who was certainly in that country in 1829......It is now considered by the Blackwoods certain," he concludes, "that Galt was the author of 'From the lone shieling.'" The author of 'The Annals of the Parish,' as Mr. Munro points out, wrote a good deal of verse ; and while, as he asserts, the poem "impresses a very poignant Celtic note, it does so in a fashion purely Saxon," implying that the lines came from the pen of a Lowlander. It may not be inappropriate to mention here that Neil Munro, as one of the "Blackwood group," was honoured by inclusion in the 'Noctes Ambrosianæ' which formed a feature of the thousandth number of *Blackwood* three years ago. Here is the first verse of his interlude—'To Exiles'—which shows the author of 'The Lost Pibroch' as a genuine poet :—

Are you not weary in your distant places,
  Far far from Scotland of the mist and storm,
In stagnant airs, the sun-smite on your faces,
  The days so long and warm ?
When all around you lie the strange fields sleeping,
  The ghastly woods where no dear memories roam,
Do not your sad hearts over seas come leaping,
  To the highlands and the lowlands of your Home ?

"There's an eerie sough aboot thae lines," as the Ettrick Shepherd would say.

                           JOHN GRIGOR.
[See also 6ᵗʰ S. xii. 310, 378 ; 9ᵗʰ S. vii. 368, 512.]

SIR RICHARD REDE.—In the brief account given in the 'D.N.B.,' vol. xlvii. p. 374, of Sir Richard Rede (or Reade), Lord Chancellor of Ireland, 1546-8, and afterwards a Master of the Court of Requests in England, it is stated that he died in 1579. His will, however, was proved in 1576, P.C.C. 20 Carew ; and according to the finding of the jury upon the inquisition post mortem taken at Hatfield, Herts, 13 Dec., 19 Eliz. (1576), he died on 11 July, 1576. See the 'Chancery Inquisitions,' series ii. vol. clxxvii. No. 102.
The dictionary does not refer to Rede's connexion with Sherburn Hospital, Durham. While the see of Durham was vacant by

reason of Bishop Tunstall's deprivation, Rede, who was one of the commissioners upon Tunstall's trial, obtained a grant, dated 4 Feb., 1552/3, of the mastership of this hospital for his life, without prejudice to an earlier grant he had from the king of a life annuity of 100*l.* ; Patent Roll, 7 Edward VI., part vi. ; cf. Strype, 'Eccl. Mem.,' II. ii. 276. edition 1822, where Rede is miscalled "Sir Robert." His tenure of the hospital was cut short through Tunstall's restoration to the see shortly after Queen Mary's accession. Anthony Salvayn thereupon obtained possession of the hospital, and the grant of the mastership to Rede was afterwards cancelled on the ground of a voluntary surrender, 14 Nov., 2 & 3 Ph. & M. (1555). Apparently, however, the surrender did not wholly determine Rede's connexion with the hospital ; for in 1568 he was suing Thomas Lever, who was then the master, for a pension of 40*l.* a year and fourteen years' arrears ; see 'Cal. State Papers, Dom.,' Addenda, 1566-79, p. 51. In the index to the calendar Thomas Lever, who died in July, 1577, is confused with Ralph Lever, his successor in the mastership ; see Hutchinson's 'History of Durham,' ii. 593-4.   H. C.

CROMWELLIANA.—On one of the fly-leaves of my copy of 'A Short Critical Review of the Political Life of Oliver Cromwell,' by John Banks (M.DCC.LXIX.), is written as follows : "Lord Hailes, in his 'Annals of Scotland,' says that at Halidon two Stuarts fought under the banners of their chiefs ; the one Allan of Dughom, the paternal ancestor of Charles I., and the other James of Rosythe, the maternal ancestor of Oliver Cromwell."   JOHN T. PAGE.

"BREECHIN."—Dr. John Brown's 'Rab and his Friends' has reached the classic dignity that is gained by the appreciation of the school-book compiler. The fight with the "thoroughbred white bull-terrier" is given in 'Passages from Modern Authors,' an attractive little book published by Messrs. Blackie & Son. The following passage prompts an editorial note :—

"He is muzzled ! The bailies had proclaimed a general muzzling, and his master, studying strength and economy mainly, had encompassed his huge jaws in a home-made apparatus, constructed out of the leather of some ancient *breechin.*"

The note given is, "Breechin, or brechame, the collar of a working horse." But the "breechin," of course, is the breeching, or that in which the horse sits when resisting the pressure of his load in a downhill movement. This part of the harness would suit the purpose of Rab's master much better than any portion of an old "brechame" or collar of a carthorse.   THOMAS BAYNE.

"PLOUGHING HIS LONELY FURROW."—Many guesses have been made as to the origin of Lord Rosebery's now familiar phrase of "ploughing his lonely furrow." The following lines from 'A Letter to the Right Hon. B. Disraeli, M.P.,' now known to have been written by the late Mortimer Collins, though published anonymously in 1869, may be of interest in this connexion :—

O to bring back the great Homeric time,
The simple manners and the deeds sublime :
When the wise Wanderer, often foiled by Fate,
Through the long furrow drave the ploughshare
    straight,
When Nausicaa, lovely as a dream,
Washed royal raiment in the shining stream !
Such men, such maidens, are the sort we seek :
Can English blood produce them like the Greek ?
W. B. H.

"RAMPANT."—The *Guardian* of 23 April, in a criticism of Scott's 'Waverley,' as introduced and edited by Miss E. E. Smith, calls attention to a gloss "*Rampant*, crouching ready to spring," which it says "is obviously wrong." This reminds me that in Clifton's 'Nouveau Dictionnaire' French *rampant* is defined as "creeping, crawling, cringing, mean, sloping, raking." In the English-French division of the work we have "Rampant, exubérant, effréné, rampant."
ST. SWITHIN.

'HOW TO MAKE AN INDEX.' (See *ante*, p. 439.) —In 1872 Mr. Geo. J. Armytage printed an 'Index' to Dugdale's 'Visitation of Yorkshire,' vol. xxxvi. of the Surtees Society's Publications, 1859. The index-maker mistook Thomas Lord, of Brampton, for Thomas, lord of Brampton, so that his dwelling-place is turned into his surname, and he appears under "Brampton" and not at all under "Lord," his surname.   W. C. B.

WESTMINSTER CITY MOTTO. — On Thursday afternoon, 15 May, at the usual fortnightly meeting of the Westminster City Council, the Mayor, Lieut.-Col. Clifford Probyn, J.P., presiding, the General Purposes Committee recommended that the Council adopt the motto "Regni Jurisque Sedes," which, being englished, means "The Seat of Government (or Law) and Justice," as being "both terse and apposite to the position and status of the city." This was objected to in a letter received from Councillor Lord Doneraile, it being condemned by him as bad Latin. Councillor Dean Vere, rector of St. Patrick's (R.C.) Church, Soho, proposed as an amendment "Custodi Civi-

tatem, Domine," which may be interpreted as "Lord, keep (or guard) the City." This was supported by Councillors Hayter, Spencer Smith, and Col. Hill James, and carried unanimously. I sent in a suggestion, "The Past an Earnest of the Future," but it does not appear to have been brought forward. The selection of the city motto seems to be a matter of sufficient interest to be noted in the columns of 'N. & Q.' for the benefit of our successors.
W. E. HARLAND-OXLEY.

THE NATIONAL FLAG.—In the *Standard* for June 7th it is stated that the congregation of St. Michael's, Folkestone, had purchased a royal standard to fly from the church tower, and that the Rev. E. Husband, the vicar, had written to Sir Francis Knollys, asking that permission might be granted in the case of churches to fly the flag on the occasion of royal anniversaries. To this the reverend gentleman received the following reply :—

"Buckingham Palace, June 4, 1902.—Dear Sir,— In reply to your letter, I am afraid that the Royal Standard, which is the King's personal flag, can only be hoisted at the Coronation. If permission were given in one case, it would be impossible to refuse it in many others. I must remind you that you can always fly the Union Jack.—Yours faithfully, F. KNOLLYS."

'N. & Q.' has always contended that the proper flag for British subjects to fly is the Union Jack, otherwise the Union Flag. Now that the King has declared this to be the national flag, one would hope that the long controversy is finally settled. How is it that at St. Dunstan's, in Fleet Street, and at some other churches the white ensign is displayed ? This flag belongs exclusively to the Royal Navy and the Royal Yacht Squadron.
A. Q.

[See 9th S. v. 414, 440, 457, 478, and Supplement, 30 June, 1900.]

Queries.

WE must request correspondents desiring information on family matters of only private interest to affix their names and addresses to their queries, in order that the answers may be addressed to them direct.

EDWARDIAN CHARTER. — An Edwardian charter six centuries old, exhibited recently to the Society of Antiquaries by Mr. Thorpe, F.S A., has points of human as well as historical interest, apart from its age and peerless condition, which last shows to its best in the framing and mounting by a British Museum expert.
Granted by Edward of Carnarvon, in whose name Welsh independence was strangled,

and dated four months before Bannockburn, which established that of Scotland, it runs from start to finish with the great struggle between king and Parliament for the control of taxation, which deposed four English monarchs and consigned three to violent deaths, coming in at its close as a living factor in the fight. For it was aliened for value with its other charters by the borough of Portsmouth in 1683, to avoid the surrender of them to the Crown by the hands of the infamous Jeffreys, sent round to " bring them in " by fine and imprisonment, actually enforced in some places.

The "governing" charter of Charles I., 1627, was sold to Louise de Querouaille, Duchess of Portsmouth (whose drafts on the English Exchequer were 150,000*l.* in one year only), for two massive loving cups, 175 oz., and as this controlled Parliamentary elections, it was repurchased after the Revolution. But the corporation cared not for the others, and refused to purchase this when offered to them in 1864, through Sir Frederick Madden, and they refused again in 1891 and 1898. One more point : the proclamation of 20 July, 1683, called in also the charter of Massachusetts Bay, and the king's messenger, Randolph, carried 200 copies for dispersal in New England. Do any of these exist ?

A. E. C.

St. Edward's Shrine : 'Textus Sancti Edwardi.'—By writ of *liberate* of 28 October, 1241, Henry III. ordered to be paid,

" Ricardo Abel aurifabro 30*s.* pro quodam *saphiro citrino* empto per preceptum nostrum et liberato eidem E[dwardo filio Odonis, clerico nostro], ad feretrum sancti Edwardi" ('Liberate Roll,' Exch. of Receipt, No. 5,* m. 1).

What sort of stone was this ?

In MS. Tanner, 197, ff. 61b-62, is a list of " the jewels remaining in the Wardrobe on the retirement of Robert de Wodehouse, late cofferer......at the end of the month of January [1331]," including "liber rubeus qui vocatur textus sancti Edwardi." Is it known when this MS. of the Gospels disappeared ? It seems not to have been the 'Royal MS.' (Bibl. Reg. I. A, xiv.), as the latter dates from about the time of Stephen and belonged at

* This was the reference a few weeks ago. I saw a brand-new list inserted in the P.R.O. catalogue of the Exchequer of Receipt the other day, which had not even a note of the old references appended to the entries, so I am not able to give the present one. If it is necessary to recast such lists in order to provide occupation for junior assistants, they could fill up their time still further, and avoid causing needless irritation and waste of the time of the studious, if their instructions included the addition of the old press-mark in every case.

one time to the abbey of St. Augustine, Canterbury, and afterwards to Archbishop Cranmer, whose name, "Thomas Cantuarien.," is on the first page.

One could wish it were in existence, and could be used for the Coronation oath on 26 June, instead of the "Great Bible," hot from the presses of Oxford and Cambridge.

Robert J. Whitwell.

Oxford.

Lord Frederick Markham.—Can any of your readers throw light upon the following passage from Mr. Montgomery Carmichael's ' Life of John William Walshe, F.S.A.' (Murray, 1902) ?—" My name is Markham, and I am called Lord Frederick Markham because my father was Marquis of Clitheroe " (p. 70). The book professes to be the life of a real person, and deals with a period within the recollection of persons still living, although no dates are given with reference to the subject of the biography or mentioned in it. Who was Lord Frederick Markham, whose death is described with great detail ?

L. C. R.

J. H. Eyre left Westminster School in 1809. I should be glad to obtain any information about him. G. F. R. B.

Gillespie Gruamach.—Can any of your readers give me proof that this *sobriquet* was applied to the Covenanting Marquess of Argyll ? I have proof that it was applied to his father, the seventh Earl of Argyll, whose portraits represent him as somewhat stern and "grim." The marquess, in spite of the cast in his eye, is by no means forbidding in expression, in some, at any rate, of his portraits. J. Willcock.

Lerwick.

William Baxter, of Australia.—Is anything known of the descendants of this William Baxter ? He was one of the three sons of John Baxter (b. 1768, m. 1797, d. 1855), of Findo-Gash (co. Perth), and Janet Din, his wife, and after he emigrated to Australia nothing seems to have been heard of him.

Ronald Dixon.

46, Marlborough Avenue, Hull.

J. Quant, 23 May, 1791.—This name is stamped on the cover of an old Prayer Book, dated at Oxford, 1787. Any clue to his family will oblige. A. C. H.

"Mallet" or "Mullet."—In '2 Henry IV.,' Act II. sc. iv. line 263, Falstaff says of Poins, "There's no more conceit in him than is in a mallet." Schmidt in his 'Shakespeare-Lexicon' defines conceit here as " mental faculty, comprising the understanding as well as the imagination." *Mallet* in this passage certainly does not furnish a very striking comparison. Is it not probable that *mallet* is here a typographical error for *mullet*? If Shakespeare had wished to name some inanimate thing as a simile, I think he would not have chosen a mallet. A clod, a stone, a block, would have furnished a more striking illustration. But the mullet is notably a dull, mud-loving fish, and a very fit simile for a man without "conceit."   John Phin.

Paterson, N.J., U.S.

Queen's or King's Bounty.—In Oulton's 'Memoirs of Her late Majesty Charlotte, Queen,' &c., London, 1819, p. 68, we read :—

"In this year [1762] her Majesty sent a present to the wife of the Duke of Richmond's porter, who was delivered of three daughters; and to a carpenter's wife, who had three boys: ever after applications were generally made on those occasions with success."

Are these the first known instances, and the origin, of the royal custom of giving three pounds on the birth of triplets?

H. Dalton.

Mont Pelée. — Was the name of Mont Pelée (or Peleus Mount), of the Martinique island, whose awful volcanic eruption, together with that of the Soufrière (or Brimstone Mount) in St. Vincent island, the world witnessed during the month of May, not really meant for Mount Pelion? Every one has heard of the classical myth according to which the Titans had endeavoured, in their struggle with Zeus, to heap up the neighbouring Mount Ossa upon Mount Pelion, for the purpose of reaching the higher abode of the Olympic deities. Truly, those Titanic efforts, or personified physical forces, of an ancient myth may be regarded as an allegory and simile comparable to the present volcanic phenomena and sulphuric ejections of the two mountains of Martinique and St. Vincent.

H. Krebs.

Oxford.

Royal Household.—What book will give me information as to the engaging or dismissing of a lady-in-waiting, maid of honour, or bedchamber woman? Is there a special uniform worn by females? Was there ever a custom of wearing one that has now fallen into disuse?   George Gilbert.

"Arrived."—We find it sometimes said of a successful author, artist, &c., that he has "arrived." Is this merely one more instance of that latest deposit of speech which we call slang, or is there any historic reference?

After the *coup d'état* of 18 Brumaire, Joubert said of Bonaparte, "Il n'est point parvenu, il est *arrivé.*" See 'Talleyrand,' by Lady Blennerhassett, Clarke's translation, vol. i. p. 314 (Murray, 1894).

C. Lawrence Ford, B.A.

Bath.

Milbournes of Somerset, Surrey, and Wilts.—I shall be greatly obliged for any information respecting the parentage of the following ladies, viz. :—

Isabella, the wife of John de Milbourne, of Somerset and Surrey, 1360-83. She married secondly Richard Ardern.

...... the wife of Richard Milbourne, of Laverstock, co. Wilts. He died 1451.

Elizabeth, the wife of Simon Milbourne, of Laverstock. He died 1464.

Margaret, wife of Henry Milbourne, of Laverstock. He died 1519. She married secondly Roger Yorke, serjeant-at-law.

Edithe, wife of Richard Milbourne, of Laverstock. He died without issue male 1532. She married secondly Edward Twynyho.

Also as to what became of Isabella, Joane, and Elizabeth, the three daughters of the before-mentioned Henry and Margaret Milbourne.   Thomas Milbourn.

12, Beaulieu Villas, Finsbury Park.

Heraldic.—I shall be very much obliged if any one can tell me the exact origin of the arms, Arg., a chevron sa. between three Cornish choughs proper, each holding in bill an ermine spot, and the corresponding crest, a Cornish chough proper, holding in its dexter claw a fleur-de-lys arg., borne by several Welsh families—especially how the fleur-de-lys has got into the crest. The arms are often slightly differentiated, but are all evidently originally from the same. The accompanying motto is "Duw a ddarpar i'r Brain," and sometimes "Deus pascit corvos." Has this any enigmatical or historical meaning? I shall also be glad to know why the Cornish chough appears in so many Welsh coats of arms, also the fleur-de-lys. The above arms were borne by the second Noble Tribe of North Wales, but the present families bearing them do not seem to be descended from the founder, Llowarch ap Bran.   Chough.

Trentham and Gower Families.—Wanted a pedigree of Lord Trentham of Trentham, co. Staffs; also of the Gower family.

E. E. Cope.

13c, Hyde Park Mansions, W.

"Le Fizgert."—Cresse, a London Jew, *circa* 1240, is thus described. What does the word signify?   M. D. Davis.

RIMES IN MOORE AND CAMPBELL.—In the
'Ingoldsby Legends' ('The Cynotaph') the
author says :—

Moore and Tom Campbell themselves admit
  "spinach"
Is perfectly antiphonetic to "Greenwich."

Can any one give me the exact references
to Moore and Campbell?   AYEAHR.

AUTHORS OF BOOKS WANTED —"Adrift; or,
the Rock in the South Atlantic. A Faithful
Narrative written from the Diary of Harper
Atherton, Surgeon. London, 1861." The
British Museum Catalogue enters this under
"Atherton, Harper, *pseud.*" The book is not
noted by Halkett and Laing. It is remark-
able that this striking story has never been
reprinted.
"Charles Lysaght, a Novel devoid of
Novelty. By P. M. Berton. London, 1873."
The British Museum Catalogue enters this
under "Berton, P. M."; but I have reason to
believe that the author's name was Pember-
ton. The book is not noted by Halkett and
Laing.   Q. K. B.

DEAD SEA LEVEL.—Sir David Wilkie, when
travelling in Palestine in 1841, made an
experiment with a barometer in which he
believed that he had proved the Dead Sea
"greatly below all other seas." Is there any
scientific value in this observation by Wilkie?
        W. B.

ROBERT FOOTE, son of John Foote, of Canterbury, was at Westminster School in 1798.
I should be glad to obtain further information concerning him.   G. F. R. B.

Replies.

CHOCOLATE.
(9ᵗʰ S. viii. 160, 201, 488 ; ix. 53, 213.)

IN Manget's 'Bibliotheca Scriptorum Medi-
corum' (folio, Geneva, 1731), tom. i. p. 35,
I have found a still earlier work on this subject. It is by Johannes de Cardenas, with the
title 'Del Chocolate, que provechos haga, y si
es bebida salutable, o no,' and was printed at
Mexico in 1609. It is not in the British Museum.
A book called 'Tratado de la naturaleça y
calidad del Chocolate,' by Antonius Colme-
nerus, was published at Madrid in 1631. A
French version by Réné Moreau appeared
at Paris in 1643, and it was translated into
Latin by Marcus Aurelius Severinus, Professor
of Anatomy and Surgery in the University of
Naples, and published by his friend J. G.
Volcamerus at Nuremberg in 1644. The
British Museum Catalogue in error attributes

the translation to Volcamerus. The book,
translated into English by Don Diego de
Vadesforte (*i.e.*, James Wadsworth), was published in London in 1640 (4to) and again in
1652 (8vo). The latter is probably the book
mentioned by MR. HOLDEN MACMICHAEL at
the last reference, though the title as given
in the 'D.N.B.' (under 'Wadsworth') seems
somewhat different. In the preface (I have
used the Latin edition) the author states that
the drinking of chocolate had become quite
common not only in the Indies, from which
it came, but among the Italians, Belgians,
and Spaniards, especially at Court, and that
he had seen nothing written about it before,
except by a certain doctor of Marchena. He
explains that chocolate was a sweetmeat or
a drink made from the crushed cocoa-bean,
flavoured with various substances, such as
pepper, vanilla, aniseed, and sugar, of which
last he liked a little, but not too much (p. 11).
It was made up into little balls by the Mexican
women and exposed for sale in the taverns.
        W. R. B. PRIDEAUX.

Present or future readers of 'N. & Q.' who
may be interested in the history of this
popular article of diet may find the following not unworthy of consideration, as contributing to a knowledge of its earlier manufacture :—

"His Majesty having been pleased to grant to
Walter Churchman Letters Patent for his new
Invention of making Chocolate without Fire, to
greater Perfection in all Respects than by the common Method, as will appear by its immediate
Dissolving and Smoothness on the Palate, its full
Flavour, and the Fineness of the Sediment; being
by this Method made more free from the usual
Grit and Roughness so much disliked; which he
refers to the fair and impartial Experiment. This
Chocolate he proposes for his common Standard,
which is now sold at 5s. per lb. with Vanelloes at
6s. per lb.

"N.B. The Curious may be supplied with his
Chocolate as many Degrees finer than the above
Standard, as that exceeds the finest that is sold by
the best other Makers, at 6s. and the Vanelloes
at 7s.

"To be sold (only for ready Money) at his Choco-
late Warehouse; at Mr John Young's in S: Paul's
Churchyard; and by L. Brouse, Haberdasher of
Hats in Great Turnstile, Holbourn."—*Lond. Eve.
Post,* 25 April, 1732.

This invention must have marked a decided
improvement on the crudeness of its earlier
manipulation, for ten years later the death
of the inventor is recorded, and the process
is still advertised as if it had superseded all
others :—

"His Majesty having granted to Mr Walter
Churchman, of Bristol, lately deceas'd intestate,
Letters Patent for the sole Use of his new Invention
for the expeditious, fine, and clean making of

Chocolate by an Engine to greater Perfection than any other Method hitherto in use," &c.—*Daily Advert.*, 15 October, 1742.

On 22 June, 1742, E. Bence, widow of Peter Bence, chocolate maker in Broad Street, Soho, advertises that she "continues to make and sell all sorts of Chocolate, after the Manner of Mr Alphonce, Confectioner to the late Countess Dowager of Albemarle" (*Daily Advert.*, 1742).   J. Holden MacMichael.

I have before me as I write the chocolate mill used by my great-grandmother, who died some seventy years ago. It is not silver, alas! but iron. Probably if it had been of the former metal it would not have come down to me. It is very well made. It has a flat head, and six perforated blades about two and a half inches long. Each blade is pierced with three five-pointed stars about a quarter of an inch from point to point, and with seven small holes near to the curved outer edge. The head is fitted on to a nicely turned oak handle about eleven inches long. It is in a good state of preservation.

E. E. Street.

Chichester.

There was, perhaps, no boy in London in the forties who did not know the mill that worked, to the delight and wonder of passers-by, in the front window of a celebrated chocolate house situated just at the top of Holborn Hill. I believe that chocolate and other delectable hot drinks are still disbursed from the same spot. The compound used to be stirred around by revolving mechanism that scooped up and turned over the toothsome-looking mass at every revolution. Just below, upon the same (the north) side of Holborn Hill, there existed a popular eating-house, in whose window the following tempting notice was displayed : "A la Mode Soup, and no flies, 3 pence a basin." This particular place of entertainment stood a bit higher up than Field Lane. In the midst of the latter was a gutter, said to divide the City from the county. On one side were shoemakers (mostly second-hand), on the other Jews kept slop-shops, and dealt largely in second-hand silk pocket-handkerchiefs.

Harry Hems.

Fair Park, Exeter.

Introduction of Trousers (9th S. ix. 268, 415).—The following, from the *Daily News* of 31 May, is to the point :—

"Mr. J. Scruton, of Doncaster, referring to the recent correspondence in this column on the subject of 'trousers,' states that in the original trust deed of Bethel Chapel, Cambridge Street, Sheffield, 1820, there is a clause providing that 'under no circum-stances whatever shall any preacher be allowed to occupy the pulpit who wears trousers.' The custom and propriety of that time required the ordinary breeches and gaiters. 'I remember, too,' the same correspondent adds, 'when in Hull in 1863, the late Rev. W. Garner (one of three very remarkable ministerial brothers) told me he had a letter in his possession in which the late Rev. Hugh Bourne, one of the founders of the Primitive Methodist Connexion, said of the late Rev. W. Clowes, the other founder thereof, "That trousers - wearing, beer-drinking Clowes will never get to heaven." Hugh Bourne was a rigid teetotaler (even before the Seven Men of Preston), and a rigid wearer of breeches and gaiters, whereas Clowes drank an occasional glass of ale and wore trousers.'"

C. C. B.

In view of the quotations given at 7th S. vii. 25, 75 ; 8th S. ii. 488 ; 9th S. iii. 126, 274, and earlier ones mentioned at the last of these references, the following extract from a journal called *Fashion*, of 15 May, reads somewhat singularly :—

"Quietly and without any pomp or ceremony we —that is, the masculine portion of the human race —are celebrating the centenary of the trouser. Trousers 'came in' a hundred years ago as the result of drink, and may be said to owe their origin to old-world royalty, which in those days ate, and especially drank, heavily, and was consequently afflicted with gout and other maladies of a character to swell the leg. George IV., as Prince Regent, his brothers, the Dukes of York, Clarence, Cumberland, and Sussex, the French Princes who afterwards reigned as Louis XVIII., Charles X., and Louis Philippe, King Frederick William III. of Prussia, and many other equally illustrious personages, adopted the modern form of pantaloon, which was at the time a source of no end of ridicule and entertainment to Gillray and to the other caricaturists of the age."

A. F. R.

The dress of the ancient Irish consisted of the *truis* or strait *bracca*, the long *cota*, the *cochal*, the *canabhas*, the *barrad*, and the *brôg*. The *truis* (*i.e.*, the "trowses") was made of weft, with various colours running on it in stripes or divisions. It covered the ankles, legs, and thighs, rising as high as the loins, and fitted so close to the limbs as to discover every muscle and motion of the parts which it covered. "The Celtic *braccæ*," says Whitaker, in his 'Hist. of Manchester,' vol. i. p. 267, "were so denominated from the colours running on them in stripes or divisions." In vulgar Irish we have *bhreacàn*, a plaid (see 'Historical Essay on the Dress of the Ancient and Modern Irish,' by Joseph Walker, in the Grenville Library, British Museum). Trousers were worn by the northern nations of antiquity generally, especially by the Germans and Gauls. Striped, checked, and embroidered trousers were much worn by the inhabitants of Asia. Bracata Gallia, a department of

Gaul, was so called from the long breeches or trousers worn by its inhabitants (Rich's 'Dict. of Roman and Greek Antiquities,' 1873, *s.v.* 'Bracæ or Braccæ'). "Coverings for the legs and thighs, *feminalia*, *tibiala*, were worn by the Romans only on occasion of sickness. However, under the Cæsars, *braccæ*, breeches, were introduced, being borrowed from foreign nations; but I suppose they were not very prevalent, and used at a late period" (Fuss's 'Roman Antiquities,' 1840).
J. Holden MacMichael.

"Mase" (9ᵗʰ S. ix. 369).—Masefield is certainly a place-name. It is probable that we have here one of the numerous redundancies met with in place-names. In the west of England these redundancies often consist of the conjunction of Welsh and English particles, and this seems to be a case in point. The first half of the name is pretty certainly the Welsh *maes*, a field.
John Hobson Matthews.
Town Hall, Cardiff.

Masefield or Maserfield was probably a field where the maser or field maple grew. The mediæval alms-dish, known to the virtuoso as the "mazer-bowl," was made from maser-wood roots. J. Holden MacMichael.

"Cadaver" (9ᵗʰ S. ix. 188).—The ridiculous derivation of *cadaver* from the union of the first syllable in each of the words "caro data vermibus" belongs, of course, to the prescientific days of etymology. That the word is connected with *cado* (like πτῶμα with πίπτειν) seems to be pretty certain, though the theory that it preserves traces of a perfect active participle is highly questionable.

It is interesting, by the way, to note that St. Jerome, in his commentary on St. Matthew, anticipated the philologers in assigning the origin of *cadaver* to *cado*, though he lived in an age that could derive *aurora* from "aurea hora" and *virgo* from "vir egeo."
Alex. Leeper.
Trinity College, Melbourne University.

Marriage Licences (9ᵗʰ S. ix. 368).—The phrase "about" in the recorded age of a party to a formal document of this kind was used merely to save possible error, like the words "be the same more or less" in a conveyance of land. One may safely assume that the age was accurately stated by the number of years given—in the case of a man, at all events. "Circa ætatem viginti quinque annorum vel infra" was the phrase always used in referring to the next of kin in an Inquisitio post mortem.

The same (minus the last two words) was applied to deponents in Exchequer suits. The words were purely formal.
John Hobson Matthews.
Town Hall, Cardiff.

Castle Carewe, Pembroke (9ᵗʰ S. ix. 428).—I have been unable to discover T. W. C.'s authority for his statement that "the first known holders of it were the Hoels." Carew (the usual spelling) is locally pronounced Carey—which is also the pronunciation still in use by some representatives of the ancient Carew family—and this has been held to preserve the derivation of the place-name, *caerau* ="forts." The oldest part of the existing ruins may belong to the castle of Gerald de Windsor, *temp.* Henry I. C. S. Ward.

Is your correspondent acquainted with the description of this castle from the time of its building in the reign of Henry I. (1100–35), given in *Archæologia*, iii.; also with some instructive articles in 'N. & Q.,' 6ᵗʰ S. ii.; 7ᵗʰ S. iii.? Everard Home Coleman.

Bibliography of the Bicycle (9ᵗʰ S. viii. 304, 490, 530; ix. 36, 117, 171, 231, 397).—It may interest those who are collecting facts for an early history of the bicycle to know that two specimens of the velocipede, or "walking accelerator," used to be preserved in one of the gateways at Alnwick Castle. I saw and tried them there many years ago, and I doubt not that there they still remain.
Herbert Maxwell.

Green an Unlucky Colour (9ᵗʰ S. viii. 121, 192; ix. 234).—The following couplets, indicative of what combination of colours country children in Dorset consider should be adopted or avoided, together with the belief obtaining amongst the country folk there that it is unlucky to wear a wedding dress of the last combination of colours mentioned in the rime, would seem to bear out what some of your correspondents have stated as to green being generally considered to be an unlucky colour:—

Pink and blue
Will never do.

Pink and green
Fit for a queen.

Green and white
Forsaken quite.
J. S. Udal, F.S.A.
Antigua, W.I.

"Chic" (9ᵗʰ S. ix. 306).—The attitude of the Académie Française regarding this word recalls to mind the sarcasm of Saint-Evremond: "Passer huit ou dix ans à réformer six mots." More than twenty years ago a French journalist expressed a hope that the Academy would sanction the use of "ce mot vif, spirituel, dont s'occupent les plus jolies femmes et les plus nobles gentilshommes." An erroneous notion prevailed that it was a word *sorti des ateliers.* It is given in the 'Vocabulaire Français,' seventh edition (1818), "ouvrage adopté par l'Université de France pour les Colléges et Écoles publiques," wherein it is defined as a "nom provençal de plusieurs petits oiseaux—ou chique, sub-tilité, finesse : populairement."

B. D. Moseley.

Death of the Trumpet-Major at Bala-clava (9th S. ix. 465).—Through sheer care-lessness and irresponsibility the "trumpet myth" has gained currency. It will be seen upon investigation that no "sounding" occurred on 25 October, 1854. Troop-Ser-geant-Major Keyte, of the 1st or Royal Dragoons, writes: "No trumpet or bugle sounding took place in either brigade." The Russian cavalry were making for Balaclava, but were dissuaded from their intention by a well-directed volley from the Highlanders. The Russians changed direction, and thus confronted the Heavy Brigade, who found themselves unable to put any considerable amount of speed into their impact with the enemy. With the Light Brigade I heard no trumpet sound that day ; but I heard the order of Lord Cardigan, "The Light Brigade will advance ! Walk ! March ! Trot !" of course taken up by regimental commanders. No word was ever given to increase the pace after the word "Trot !" The merit of the Light Brigade advance was its steadiness under strong incentives to confusion and dis-order. I suppose we must take it that these unworthy misstatements have been repeated so often that those giving them publicity have, as Shakespeare has it, become "such sinners unto memory" as really to regard them as true. Mr. T. H. Roberts, the pub-lisher, of Fleet Street, whose noble work in rescuing many of the Light Brigade from the ignominy of the poor-house deserves high honour, writes to me, *à propos* of the "trumpet fable," "I have done my best to refute the fallacy of 'sounding the charge'; but these old lies are like old soldiers—they die hard !" W. H. Pennington.

84, Princess May Road, N.

Francis Spiera's Despair (9th S. ix. 389). —I transcribe the following brief notice from Rose's 'Biog. Dict.' (1850) :—

"Spira (Francesco), a lawyer of Cittadella, in the Venetian state, who, being accused of heresy to the Papal nuncio, made his submission, and afterwards a public recantation. Shortly after this he fell into a deep melancholy, and died, full of horror and remorse for his apostasy, in 1548."

From the Schaff-Herzog 'Religious Ency-clopædia ' (1884) we learn that the "apostasy" for which he felt "remorse" was not his defection from Popery, but his insincere re-cantation of Protestantism, which he made "for worldly considerations." His despair is thus described :—

"Spiera believed he had committed the sin against the Holy Ghost......He held he belonged to the number of those who were lost, and lost eternally. In his assurance that God had forsaken him, he had the most painful visions. Devils surrounded him ......and in his terrible consciousness of sin he often roared like a lion."

It is added that Calvin and the other Re-formers took a deep interest in the case. The same article mentions the following writers as having given accounts of him: Vergerius, Gribaldi, Henricus Scotus, Ge-lous, all of whose accounts are contained in one work ; Roth, 1829 ; Bacon, 1665, 1710 ; and Schaff, 1841. C. Lawrence Ford, B.A.
Bath.

Francis Spiera the atheist, advocate of Cittadella in the Venetine, embraced Lutheran opinions, recanted his heresy before Giovanni Casa, Pope's legate in Venice, repented of his recantation, and died in despair soon after in Padua, c. 1548. His story, as an awful warn-ing, appeared in English as 'A Relation of the Fearful Estate of Francis Spiera,' compiled (preface) from the accounts of "Vergerius and Gribaldus, Professors of Law at Padua, Henry Scrimger a Scotchman, Sigism. Gelous a Transilvanian, and Mart. Bocha a Divine of Basil." In my copy, which lacks title-page, is bound up with it 'The Second Spiera, being a fearful example of an Atheist, who had apostatized from the Christian Religion and died in Despair at Westminster, Decemb. 8, 1692.' Printed for John Dunton at the "Raven," in the Poultry, 1693. I should imagine that the 'Relation,' &c., came out the same year. Francis King.

"Cradel grass" (9th S. ix. 427).—Mr. Petty appears to have misread his author. In my copy of Sylvester's ' Du Bartas' (1633) the couplet in which the line referred to occurs reads :—

They saw the light of *Phœbus* live-ning face ;
Having, for milk, moyst deaws ; for Cradle, grass ?
C. C. B.

Arthur's Crown (9th S. ix. 388).—As the author of this popular and interesting book on Wales, Mr. Owen M. Edwards, kindly tells me, Arthur's crown and the heirlooms of the ancient royal house of Gwynedd were probably given by Edward I., after the conquest of Wales, for his little son Edward (born at Caernarvon in 1284, the first Prince of Wales), to Westminster Abbey, whence they must have disappeared, with other relics, at the time of the dissolution of monasteries.

H. Krebs.

Oxford.

Sir Isaac Newton: 'Commercium Epistolicum' (9th S. ix. 369).—Three editions of this work, 1722, 1725, and 1787, are in the library of the Royal Astronomical Society, Burlington House, Piccadilly.

Everard Home Coleman.

71, Brecknock Road.

Old Songs (9th S. ix. 388).—My friend Mr. Bartholomew Howlett, of this town, has asked me to forward you the enclosed, which he remembers hearing sung many years ago:

THE LINCOLNSHIRE POACHER.

Come, all ye lads of high renown
That love to drink good ale that's brown,
And pull the lofty pheasant down
  With powder, shot, and gun.

Me and five more a-poaching went,
To kill some game was our intent;
Our money all being gone and spent,
  We had nothing else to try.

The moon shone bright,
Not a cloud in sight;
The keeper heard us fire a gun
And to the spot did quickly run,
And swore before the rising sun
  That one of us lads should die.

The bravest youth amongst the lot
'Twas his misfortune to be shot,
His feelings never shall be forgot
  By all his friends below.

For help he cried, which was denied;
He rose again to stem the best,
And fight again with all the rest,
While down upon his gallant breast
  The crimson blood did flow.

Edward Peacock.

Wickentree House, Kirton-in-Lindsey.

Browne Family Arms (9th S. ix. 290).—Burke's 'General Armory' gives the following families with a demi-lion ramp. for crest:
Jas. Brown, of Harehills Grove, co. York, and Wm. Williams Brown, of Chapel Allerton, near Leeds, sons of the late James Brown, of Leeds, by Anne his wife, daughter and heir of Samuel Williams: Arg., on a bend sa., cottized az., between two six-pointed mullets pierced sa., three lions ramp. of the field, quartering Williams. Crest, a demi-lion ramp. erased or, between two elephants' trunks ppr.
Browne (bart., Westminster, created 11 March, 1732): Gu., a chev. between three fleurs-de-lis or. Crest, a demi-lion ramp. gu., holding in the dexter paw a fleur-de-lis or.

J. R. Nuttall.

Though in Debrett (1824) the name under the coat of arms is spelt Browne, in the index and in the body of that work it is given as simply Brown. The following extract from Debrett's 'Baronetage' (1824), vol. i. pp. 434 and 435, answers the query of Genealogicus:

"Brown of Westminster, 11 March, 1731/2.—Sir William-Augustus Brown, bart., succeeded his father Sir James, 20 April, 1784, and has been many years insane.

"I. Sir Robert, a merchant of Venice, having been his Majesty's resident abroad, was advanced to the dignity of a bart., with a remainder in his patent, in case of failure of his own issue male, to his brothers, Colonel James Brown, and Edward. Sir Robert m. Margaret, sister of Dr. Cecil, bishop, 1st of Bristol, and afterwards of Bangor, by whom he had 2 das., who d. unm. Lady Brown d. 13 Feb., 1782. Sir Robert d. 5 Oct., 1760, and was succeeded by his nephew,

"II. Sir James, m. ——, by whom (who d. 21 Sept., 1822) he had 1 son, William-Augustus. Sir James d. 20 April, 1784, and was succeeded by his only son,

"III. Sir William-Augustus, the present bart.

"Arms—(see plate 17) Gules, a chevron, erminois, between three fleurs-de-lys, or. Crest—A demi-lion, rampant, gules, holding in its paws a fleur-de-lys, as in the arms. Motto—Gaudeo."

As no mention is made of a baronet of the name of Brown or Browne in Lodge's 'Peerage and Baronetage' of 1847, it is to be presumed that this baronetage had become extinct by then.

The peers bearing the surname of Browne in the above edition of Lodge—i.e., the Marquis of Sligo, the Earl of Kenmare, the Lord Kilmaine, and the Lord Oranmore and Browne—bear quite different arms and crests from the baronet of Westminster. A Sir Richard Broun, of Colstoun, Haddingtonshire (S. cr. 1686), is mentioned, but his arms and crest are not given.

Ronald Dixon.

46, Marlborough Avenue, Hull.

Dutton Family (9th S. vi. 409, 415; vii. 54, 117, 174, 293, 301, 433).—The author of the 'Memorials of the Duttons of Dutton' says:—

"The earliest progenitor of the Dutton family in this country was Odard, the eldest or first named of five brothers, who came over together, one of them as a priest, from Avranches in Normandy, at the time of the Conquest. They then accompanied a Norman noble named Nigel, who became Baron of Halton, and who is said to have been a kind of cousin of the Conqueror's. It has for long been doubtful whether the five brothers were related to Nigel, or whether they were his friends or vassals. ......Nigel himself appears to have been in the retinue of Hugh Lupus, afterwards Earl of Chester, and the five brothers mentioned, or at least four of them, as one was a priest, were most probably esquires to Nigel."

Sir Peter Leycester, who compiled the Dutton pedigree up to the year 1666, traces the family (through the Earls of Eu) back to Rollo, the first Duke of Normandy. He says that William, fourth Earl of Eu, married a sister of Hugh Lupus, named Jeanne, who was a niece of the Conqueror, and that there was issue of this marriage (besides William's successor in the Earldom of Eu and another child) six sons — namely, Nigel, Geoffrey, Odard (or Huddard), Edward, Horswin, and Wolfaith. These six brothers, Sir Peter says, accompanied their uncle Hugh Lupus into England in the train of William the Conqueror, their great-uncle, and on the establishment of the Norman power had various estates and honours conferred upon them, Odard being created Lord of Dutton.

I shall be glad if any of your readers can throw any further light upon the point in question—namely, whether Odard was really a brother of Nigel, or only a brother in arms. The title of Earl of Eu (Comte d'Eu) still exists in France, and I presume the bearer thereof is heir male to Nigel's brother William, fifth Earl of Eu.

CHARLES STEWART.
22, Gloucester Road, Stoke Newington, N.

MALLET USED BY CHRISTOPHER WREN (9th S. ix. 346).—This is evidently an heirloom of the Freemasons of high historic interest, for when Sir Christopher Wren was building the great cathedral he was a zealous Master of the St. Paul's Lodge, one of the most ancient in England, at which he presided for upwards of eighteen years, the meetings being held at the "Goose and Gridiron" in St. Paul's Churchyard, only lately pulled down. Besides presenting the "Goose and Gridiron" with three carved mahogany candlesticks, the great architect handed over to its custody the trowel and mallet which he used in laying the foundation stone of the cathedral in 1675 ('O. and N. Lond.') On 2 October, 1895, was begun the demolition of this old tavern, where, as we are told in the 'Vade Mecum for Maltworms,'

Dutch carvers from St. Paul's adjacent Dome
Hither to wet their Whistles, daily come.

But what has become of the three carved mahogany candlesticks? The landlord of the "Mitre," a former sign of the "Goose and Gridiron," derived from its proximity to the inn or town house of the bishops of London, issued a

"Catalogue of many natural rarities, with great industrie, cost, and thirty years travel into foreign countries collected by Robert Herbert, alias Forges, Gent., and sworn servant to his Majesty, to be seen at the place called the Musick House at the Mitre, near the west end of St. Paul's Churchyard, 1664."

This collection, or a great part of it, was bought by Sir Hans Sloane (see 'O. and N. London'). J. HOLDEN MACMICHAEL.

HEARTSEASE (9th S. ix. 267, 392).—To attribute the origin of this name to the story DR KNOTT tells of the wallflower is, I venture to say, a very apt example of what logicians call "the fallacy of equivocation." Folkard tells the same tale as DR. KNOTT, and, curiously enough, misquotes Herrick in the same way, but he does not give the story as an explanation of the name "heartsease," nor does Herrick. Herrick's verses, indeed, are headed 'How the Wall-flower came first, and why so called,' and begin :—

Why this flower is now call'd so,
List, sweet maids, and you shal know.

So far as I know, Turner (referred to by Folkard) is the first authority for the statement that heartsease is a name for the wallflower ; and, though Lyte repeats it, I do not remember having seen the name so applied by any other writer of "olden time" besides these. The earliest name for the wallflower that I have met with in English is "walfair," which occurs in the 'Alphita' glossary under 'Violaria.' C. C. B.

DARCY OF HARVERTON (9th S. ix. 268).—The manor of Harraton, or Harverton, co. Durham, at an early period belonged to the Herrington family, from whom it passed—either by marriage or grant, most probably the former, though how it works in does not at present appear—to the Darcys. Sir John Darcy, Knt., of Harraton, married and left issue :—

1. Robert Darcy, of Harraton, who died s.p. in 1414 ; his widow Margaret died 1433.

2. Isabel Darcy, daughter and coheir, married Thomas Darcy, of Park, co. Lincoln, and had issue : Rowland Darcy, of Henton, co. Lincoln, who was found coheir of his uncle Robert in 1414. Rowland left an only child Margaret, married to Robert Conyers, of Hutton-Wiske, co. York.

3. Elizabeth Darcy, daughter and coheir (so found 1414), married Robert Percy, of Rydale, co. York, and had a son John Percy, of Rydale, 1414, who as coheir of Robert Darcy, 16 Henry VI., released all his right to Harraton.

4. Katherine Darcy, daughter and coheir, married John Hedworth, of Southwick, co. Durham, and had a son John Hedworth, of Harraton, coheir of Robert Darcy, 1414.

5. Mary Darcy, daughter and coheir, married —— Semer, and had a daughter Alice, *æt.* sixteen in 1414, who married Thomas de la More, and had a daughter Margaret, wife of Richard Hansard, of Walworth Castle, co. Durham.

The ancient arms of the Hedworth family were On a bend three quatrefoils.

H. R. Leighton.
East Boldon, R.S.O., co. Durham.

'Oliver and Arthur' (9th S. ix. 387).— For a summary of the chief editions and versions of this old romance (the earliest in French, translated from Latin by Ph. Camus, is an incunabulum of 1482, and bears the title 'Le livre de Olivier de Castille et de Artus Dalgarbe, son tresroyal Compaignon'; the first translation of it into English, printed in London by W. de Worde, 1518. appeared under the title 'Yᵉ Historye of Olyver of Castylle and the fayre Helayne') see Brunet's 'Manuel,' *sub* 'Olivier,' vol. iv. col. 183–5.

H. Krebs.
Oxford.

There is a note on the literary history of this romance in Dunlop's 'History of Prose Fiction,' edited by H. Wilson (London, 1888), vol. i. p. 318.   William E. A. Axon.
Manchester.

Black Malibran (9th S. ix. 367, 390).—If I may trust a very distant remembrance. there was a portrait of this black vocalist of negro race in the *Illustrated London News* nearly fifty years ago ; but what her real name was I cannot say. She was depicted as a very ugly woman, wearing a low dress, and accompanying herself on the guitar.

Madame Malibran de Beriot was born in Paris in 1808, died at Manchester in 1836, and was buried in the south aisle of the choir of the collegiate church, now the cathedral. The stone under which she had been laid was pointed out to me when a boy, some ten years afterwards. The body only rested there for a few months, when it was exhumed and taken to Brussels.

John Pickford, M.A.
Newbourne Rectory, Woodbridge.

Curious Word-Coinages (9th S. ix. 347).— " Retiral " has long been a recognized technical term with reference to bank bills, receiving in this connexion the attention of the lexicographer. Lately it has come to be commonly used in allusion to retirement from office. Two examples occurred in the Scottish newspapers, almost simultaneously, about the end of April and the beginning of May. The Chief Constable of Glasgow and the Sheriff-Substitute of Dumbartonshire both retired, the former on the plea of failing health and the latter on account of advancing years. The newspapers of Glasgow and the county of Dumbarton appropriately referred to the " retiral " in each case.

Thomas Bayne.

Manners and Customs in Shakespeare's Time (9th S. ix. 387).—Rolfe's 'Shakspere the Boy' (Chatto & Windus) and Goadby's 'England of Shakspere' (Cassell) are both interesting books, and may be found useful.

W. E. Wilson.
Hawick.

'Society in the Elizabethan Age,' by Hubert Hall, F.S.A., with eight coloured and other plates (Swan Sonnenschein & Co., 1901).

Henry Gerald Hope.
119, Elms Road, Clapham, S.W.

Honorificabilitudinitas (9th S. ix. 243, 371). — It may interest Prof. Butler and Mr. J. T. Curry to learn that the first known appearance of the dative and ablative plural of this word in an English work—as it appears in 'Love's Labour's Lost' (1589-92, published 1598), Nash's 'Lenten Stuffe' (1599), and Marston's 'Dutch Courtezan' (1605)—is in a volume entitled 'The Complaynt of Scotland,' published at St. Andrews in 1548 or 1549, and attributed to Sir John Inglis by some and to Robert Wedderburn by others. This volume, which is of extreme rarity, and was dedicated to Queen Mary, was reprinted in Edinburgh in 1801. In the " Prolog " to the reader, the author, in railing at the use of long and out-of-the-way words by " diverse translatours and cōpilaris in ald tymys," gives as examples

" Hermes, quilk pat in his verkis thir lang tailit vordis, conturbabātur, constantinopolitani, innumerabilibus, solicitudinibus. There vas ane uthir that writ in his verkis, gaudet honorificabilitudinitatibus," &c.

It would be interesting to discover who was this " uthir." This, however, was not the earliest use of the dative and ablative plural of the word, as it appeared in the 'Magnæ Derivationes' of Uguccione da Pisa, the standard Latin dictionary in Dante's time, and also in the 'Catholicon' of Giovanni da Genova, one of the earliest of printed books.

George Stronach.
Edinburgh.

Your correspondents may be referred for information to the 'New English Dictionary' (*s.v.* 'Honorificabilitudinity'); and, for amusement, to *Pearson's Magazine*, December, 1897, pp. 653-4, and to a note by Mr. Paget Toynbee in *Literature* for 9 April, 1898, at p. 424, in which that learned Dantophilist shows that Dante makes an indirect reference to this word, actually citing the ablative singular, and that Costard's ablative plural, being anagrammatized, reads : "Ubi Italicus ibi Danti honor fit," *i.e.*, "Wherever an Italian is to be found, there honour is done to Dante."

Mr. Toynbee's 'Dante Studies and Researches' (1902, p. 113) show that Dante derived this word from Uguccione Pisano (*ob.* 1210), who says :—

"Ab *honorifico, hic* et *hec honorificabilis, -le,* et *hec honorificabilitas, -tis,* et *hec honorificabilitudinitas,* et est longissima dictio, que illo versu continetur : *Fulget honorificabilitudinitatibus iste.*"

For a pleasing illustration of the fatuity of the "universal negative" (that fallacy so dear to a certain school of Old Testament critics as well as to *Shaconians**) he may further see Mr. Edwin Reed's 'Bacon *versus* Shakspere' (1899). On p. 60 Costard's word is cited, along with an oddly truncated *honorificabilitudino* (which is said to occur on the "manuscript title-page of one of Bacon's works"), and the two are stated to be the only instances "in all the world's literature."

Q. V.

GORDON AS A RUSSIAN SURNAME (9th S. ix. 148, 371).—May I ask if it is impossible that any Russian Gordons of to-day who are Jews can owe their surname to being descended from any of the Scottish Gordons, mostly from Aberdeen, who settled in Russia and the Polish provinces in the seventeenth century ?

Military archives at St. Petersburg show that there was a Capt. William Gordon in the Russian army in 1631, and a Col. Alexander Gordon in it in 1634. The celebrated General Patrick Gordon, who became Peter the Great's commander-in-chief and intimate friend, spent the best part of his life in Russia, and died at Moscow in 1699, leaving three sons and two daughters. Both daughters married. The eldest son was for a short time in the Russian army when a youth. He left a numerous family. The second son became a colonel in the Russian army in 1690, and the third son a colonel in it a few

---

* This "portmanteau word" seems a necessary, if unfortunate addition to our vocabulary, in order to distinguish the holders of a particular view of the authorship of certain plays from the real followers and students of the great master of inductive philosophy, who have for many years been correctly known as Baconians, just as the followers of Thomas Hobbes are called Hobbesians. See, for an example of the true use of the former word, Sir Humphry Davy's 'Chemical Philosophy' (1812), p. 32: "In the spirit of the Baconian school, multiplying instances, and cautiously making inductions."

years later. A nephew became an admiral in the Russian navy. W. S.

FASHIONABLE SLANG OF THE PAST (9th S. ix. 368).— Although not specially pertinent to the subject immediately to hand, the enclosed cutting from the *Family Herald* of 17 November, 1900, may prove a slight help towards a really good slang, cant, or dialect dictionary :—

"'It's fierce' is New York's latest slang phrase. If one wears a shirt that has plenty of colour, one's friends say 'It's fierce'; if a young lady comes out with snowy shoulders and a diamond tiara, her admirers whisper, one to another,' Isn't she fierce?' If a horse shows up well on the track, the word passes along that 'Whirlwind is fierce to-day.' The golfer who succeeds in winning five out of six holes is 'fierce'; and when the baby is brought out all dressed in its downiest coat and softest laces, its beautiful auntie holds up her hands and exclaims, 'Oh, isn't the darling fierce!'"

HERBERT B. CLAYTON.
39, Renfrew Road, Lower Kennington Lane.

It is in my experience, dating back thirty-six years, that "No. 1" was common in "Pidgin English" in China for "tip-top," "very superior," long before *Ichiban* had any other but its plain, matter-of-fact meaning in Japan—viz., first of a row. "B'long number one" has been a Chinaman's highest eulogism on anything since the inception of "Pidgin English" probably. H. P. L.

ROYAL PERSONAGES (9th S. viii. 184, 252, 349 ; ix. 89, 196, 257, 395).—Lodge (Clarenceux King of Arms) is quite right as to the year of Prince Octavius's death, but wrong as to day. He died 3 May, 1783, and was buried at Westminster 10th of the same month, so that MR. COLYER-FERGUSSON is right as to day, but wrong as to year.

Prince Alfred died at Windsor 20 August, 1782, and was buried at Westminster 27th of the same month. In this case MR. COLYER-FERGUSSON is again wrong as to year and Lodge as to day of death. A. W. B. is also wrong in this respect. Lodge is correct as to dates of birth of both princes. The remains of both the royal brothers were removed to St. George's Chapel, Windsor, 20 February, 1820.

MR. DIXON is probably quite correct as to date of birth of Anne, Princess Royal. Anderson and Clay Finch both give 22 October, whilst Voigtel, Hiort-Lorenzen, Oettinger, and Chiusole give 2 November, which is the same day, New Style. Hall and Toone say 9 October, and 'L'Art de Vérifier les Dates' 13 November. All agree as to year. He is absolutely right as to the date of Anne's marriage according to Old Style. Modern writers make it 25 March; Mrs. Matthew Hall gives 24 March. All agree as to year. The date of her death is given by Mrs. Hall as 2 January. Others agree with Mr. Dixon as to 12 January. Voigtel and 'L'Art de Vérifier les Dates' say 13 January. All again agree as to year.

The Princess Mary, Landgravine of Hesse Cassel, was born, according to all authorities (excepting Toone, who says 24 February), 22 February, Old Style, or 5 March, New Style, 1723. She was married by proxy in the Chapel Royal, St. James's (her brother, the Duke of Cumberland, acting for the absent bridegroom), on 8 May, 1740, and again at Cassel on 28 June following. She died 14 January, 1772. Mrs. Hall says ('Royal Princesses of England from Reign of George I.') that she died 14 June, 1772, at the age of sixty-nine, whereas she was only forty-nine, and died in January.

Princess Louisa, Queen of Denmark, was born, as Mr. Dixon says, 7 December, 1724, Old Style, although six different days are given by historians as that on which she first saw light. She was married at Hanover by proxy 30 October, 1743 (the Duke of Cumberland again acting as bridegroom), and afterwards at Altona 11 December following. She died 8 December, Old Style, 19 December, New Style, 1751.

George II.'s second and third daughters were Amelia Sophia Eleanora and Caroline Elizabeth.

Princess Elizabeth Caroline (daughter of Frederick, Prince of Wales) was born 30 December, 1740, Old Style—so far Debrett is right—or 10 January, 1741, New Style. A. W. B. is wrong as to year.

Princess Louisa Anne (her sister) was born 8 March, 1748/9. A. W. B. is right, and Debrett wrong, as to year.

Prince Frederick William (youngest son of Frederick, Prince of Wales) was born 13 May, 1750, Old Style, 24 May, New Style, so again A. W. B. is right and Debrett is wrong.

Debrett is right as to the spelling of his elder brother's name, Henry Frederick.

H. Murray Lane, Chester Herald.

"Paschal": "Pascua" (9ᵗʰ S. ix. 364, 457). —I directed attention to this subject, with special reference to the 'Metrical Life of St. Cuthbert,' in 'N. & Q.,' 8ᵗʰ S. i. 244. I think Mr. Marchant would find my article interesting.   F. Adams.

The Mitre (9ᵗʰ S. viii. 324, 493, 531; ix. 174, 334, 397).—Mr. Angus's doubt whether a mitre is ever worn apart from chasuble or cope must relate to the present day. I have a fifteenth-century MS. Pontifical in which a bishop is depicted as consecrating paten and chalice habited in alb and girdle, and wearing a mitre.

It would be interesting to know on what F. de H. L. bases the "certainty" that mitres were not worn in the Apostolic age. This may be so, but no proof is attempted. As to the eight following centuries, learned authorities are divided, some saying that they were worn in the earliest ages of the Church, some not till the tenth century.

Aldenham.

St. Dunstan's.

Disappearing Chartists (9ᵗʰ S. ix. 144, 251, 391).—Mr. W. E. Adams, who writes concerning the note on 'Disappearing Chartists,' has spent his life in reading for "literals," and is a most useful correspondent of 'N. & Q.,' among whose merits is its love of literality. I dictated my notes, and did not conceive there was a human being who did not know John Cleave had an *a* in his name. Great was my surprise to find the *a* taken out of the name and put into Widdrington, making it into Waddrington, unknown to all good Northumbrians. The correction of errors is the establishment of truth. If truth be one, she is a lady of infinite parts.

G. J. Holyoake.

Brighton.

[The words mentioned were clearly so miswritten by the amanuensis. To employ another hand without inspecting the written result before sending it to the printer is unwise.]

San Sebastian, Spain (9ᵗʰ S. ix. 448).— Alison's 'History of Europe,' vol. xi. chap. lxxvii. ('Campaign of the Pyrenees'), 1813.   F. E. R. Pollard-Urquhart.

Castle Pollard, Westmeath.

"Pack" (9ᵗʰ S. viii. 144, 273, 433).—At the first reference is a quotation, from the presentments made at the visitations of the Archdeacon of Canterbury, of the use of this word in 1572 at Preston next Faversham, in Kent.

The word also is used at Ulcombe in 1569:

"We present that one Richard Noxe is suspected to have used and frequented the company of a light woman, who is at one Richard Walters, whom we present also for a receiver of such naughty packes into his house."

Arthur Hussey.

Tankerton-on-Sea, Kent.

Snodgrass, a Surname (9ᵗʰ S. ix. 366).—It is doubtful whether any one of the surnames he used was an invention of Dickens. A great many of them—some the most singular —have been seen by myself over shops or elsewhere. I have had a Stallabrass in my own house.

Even Bunyan may have taken many of his expressive surnames from real life. Smallpeace, Faithful, Christian, and many of the others are quite common. Some, such as Handsombody, Lightbody, Slowbilly, Hogbin, are known to myself; but the most unfortunate one of my acquaintance is perhaps the most expressive, and the family is a very large one. I can point to a shop whose owner has painted his name, Windebag, in large letters over his door.

Here in Somerset the names Halfyard and Fouracre are quite common; indeed, novelists in search of quaint surnames might glean almost a harvest in our country towns and villages.   F. T. ELWORTHY.
Foxdown, Wellington, Somerset.

According to Bowditch ('Suffolk Surnames') there were eleven families of the name of Snodgrass living in Philadelphia in 1861. The name was borne, too, by a medical attendant of Edgar Allan Poe. Several instances of its occurrence in England have recently been noted in the *Athenæum*.
    C. C. B.

Jenny Snodgrass is mentioned in a letter from Scotland in Miss Ferrier's 'Inheritance,' published in 1824.   HERMAN COHEN.

I agree with ASTARTE that many of Dickens's fantastic names were those of real persons. I remember being surprised to find several in such an unlikely place as the Glasgow 'Post Office Directory.' Quite recently I saw Chadband on a shop sign—in Lichfield, I think.   W. E. WILSON.
Hawick.

ST. PAUL AND SENECA (9ᵗʰ S. ix. 290, 351).— The following is from chap. x. of the 'Life of Lucius Annæus Seneca,' by Justus Lipsius, translated by Lodge :—

"But hearke you Sir, make you no reckoning of his Epistles to Saint Paul? Those that are now extant are not so much worth; nay, it is most certaine, that they have all of them the same Authour, and that they were written, but by some scarce learned Clerke in our disgrace. He travaileth and attempteth to speake Latine, whosoever it was, that was the Authour. Did they not therefore write one unto another? Saint Jerome, Saint Augustine, and Pope Linus (more ancient then them both) averre it, and it is a passive opinion. And John of Salisburie likewise confidently confirmeth it. 'They seeme to bee foolish, who reverence not him, who, as it appeareth, deserved the familiaritie of the Apostle.' I therefore dare not wholly reject and contemne this; it may be there were some, but others then these; if these, I required the judgement of the best Fathers."

The following are the references given in the margin, but corrected, after comparison with the 'Life' contained in Seneca, edited by Lipsius, 1615, and in that edited by Ruhkopf, 1828: to St. Jerome, "De scriptorib. Ecclesiasticis"; to St. Augustine, "Epist. 53, ad Maced. et vi De Civit., cap. 10"; to Pope Linus, "De Passione divi Pauli"; to John of Salisburie, "Lib. viii Polycrat., cap. 13." Lodge gives Polycarp for *Polycrat.* His translation as to the letters being by one author ought, according to the Latin text, to run : "Nay, it is most certaine, that they, both those of Paul and those of Seneca, have all of them the same Authour." Further, "It is a passive opinion" should be "It was formerly a passive opinion." Also, "I required the judgement of the best Fathers" should be "I require," &c. "Passive" (*passiva*) means "common" or "general."

Jeremy Collier, in his 'Great Historical ......Dictionary,' second edition, 1701, *s.v.* 'Seneca,' says :—

"There are some that take Seneca to have been a Christian, and that he had converse with St. Paul by Letters; it seems not altogether improbable, but that he might have had the Curiosity to inform himself about the Christian Doctrine, which appeared so strange and extraordinary; but as for the Letters publish'd under their names, they are unworthy of either of them. To know whether Seneca was a Christian or no, we need only observe what Tacitus relates speaking of his Death : 'As he entred the Bath,' saith he, 'he took of the Water and sprinkled his Friends that stood about him with it, saying, That he offered these Libations to Jupiter his Redeemer.'—Tacit., Lib. 12, 14 and 15, in 'Annal.' Sueton. in 'Neron.' Aul. Gellius. Just. Lipsius in 'Vita Senec.' Delrio in Comment."

The reference for the Jupiter Liberator incident in Tacitus is in the edition of Gronovius (1721), 'Annal.,' xv. 65.

Cates, in his 'Dictionary of General Biography,' fourth edition, 1885, *s.v.* 'Seneca,' says :—

"It was for centuries believed in the Christian Church that Seneca was personally acquainted with St. Paul. (See, on this interesting point, Cruttwell's 'History of Roman Literature,' second edition, 1878, p. 385.)"
    ROBERT PIERPOINT.
St. Austin's, Warrington.

MOURNING SUNDAY (9ᵗʰ S. ix. 366, 390).— This custom is still occasionally observed at All Saints' Church, Colchester. The family occupy the front seat in the nave, remain seated during the service, but take no part in it. Some thirty years ago in Wootton Bassett, Wiltshire, it was of frequent occurrence. At that time the band round the hat, with long ends hanging behind, was worn at funerals; on returning from the funeral the ends were fastened round the hat, and so worn till after the following Sunday. The family mostly occupied their own seats, and took part in the service; sometimes, however, the front seat of the nave was used — here they remained seated, and did not take any part in the service. It was the custom to toll the bell (for church people) at intervals during the day of burial, often starting as early as eight o'clock in the morning.   T. FORSTER.

Kennington.

In the parish from which I write it is the rule that the friends of the deceased who follow the body appear in church on the next Sunday after the funeral. They rise or kneel as the rest of the congregation, and wear only their mourning garments. So persistent is this custom that I frequently see persons who do not conform to the Christian Sunday in any respect come to church on these occasions.   F. CLAYTON.

Morden, Surrey.

In connexion with this subject it may be pertinent to recall a passage in Canon Atkinson's 'Forty Years in a Moorland Parish' (p. 225), in which he tells us that, when he first came to Danby, all the male relatives present at the funeral of a deceased person would sit round the coffin with their hats on during the reading of the Psalm and lesson in church. Shortly before that the vicar of Scarborough had put down the same custom in his parish.   ST. SWITHIN.

This custom has been general in Devonshire for a very long time, probably for more than a century. It seems to be gradually falling into disuse—in the towns, at least—although I have seen one instance of it in Torquay this year. As in the Isle of Man, the mourners here (and this term includes friends, sometimes to the number of twenty or more) remain seated throughout the service. The custom implies as much respect for the dead as following them to the grave, and, indeed, seems to be the proper complement of it.   A. J. DAVY.

Torquay.

In Jersey it is quite the ordinary custom in the country parishes for families, on the death of a relative, to sit together in church the Sunday following the funeral, and not to rise during any part of the service.
   C. P. LE CORNU, Colonel.

FOUNTAIN FAMILY (9ᵗʰ S. ix. 149).—In the possibility of its being of some interest to M. HUBERT DE FONTAINES, it may be mentioned that there was an old family of the name of Fountain (otherwise Fountains) two centuries ago in the district known as Craven, in Yorkshire. They then held property in the vicinity of Linton (Wharfedale).   B.

RICHARD HAINES (9ᵗʰ S. ix. 341).—There are six tracts by this author in the rich pamphlet collection of the Manchester Free Library, including some of those noted by MR. REGINALD HAINES as unique. Richard Haines is an interesting writer, and may be compared with John Bellers.
   WILLIAM E. A. AXON.

Manchester.

SHORTHAND IN THE FOURTH CENTURY (9ᵗʰ S. ix. 406).—MR. AXON will, I am sure, pardon me if I am citing a reference already known to him in drawing his attention to the *notarii* mentioned more than once by Martial, who died about 104 A.D. That these were true shorthand writers is manifest from book xiv. ep. 208, where one is mentioned as competent to report verbatim the most rapid speaker.
   A. GORHAM.

CANTERBURY RECORDS (9ᵗʰ S. ix. 408).—In the Cathedral library at Canterbury are the MS. records of the city, and also some MS. volumes of presentments made at the visitations of the Archdeacon of Canterbury, the latter covering the years 1560-1735, but not continuously. These volumes I am going through, and have copies of the East Kent parishes, but as yet not those of Canterbury. Life in rural parishes does not seem to have been very different from what it is in the present day, and complaints made "as the common fame is in our parish" seem in many cases on examination to have originated from what we should call the village gossip, unless the accused perjured himself in the Archdeacon's Court.

If your correspondent will write to me, perhaps some of my notes may be of use to him.   ARTHUR HUSSEY.

Tankerton-on-Sea, Kent.

Miscellaneous.

NOTES ON BOOKS, &c.

The New Volumes of the Encyclopædia Britannica. Vol. II. (A. & C. Black and the *Times*.)

EXTENDING from Austria-Hungary to Chicacole, a town in British India, the second volume of the complement of the 'Encyclopædia Britannica,' the twenty-sixth of the entire work, makes considerable progress in the alphabet. It opens with 'A General Survey of Recent Political Progress,' from the pen of Edward Dicey, C.B. Among the points on which, in his deeply interesting paper, Mr. Dicey longest dwells is the manner in which a policy of annexation on the part of all the powerful nations in the world has connected itself with or followed the possession of increased armaments. England and Germany, the two countries with the densest and most rapidly increasing population, take, necessarily, the lead in obeying an instinct due to what is called the contraction of the earth and the dread of being crowded out. The dislike to England felt by foreign countries is shown to be connected with English expansion, and the growth of Imperialism is stated to be due in part to the feeling that the nations of the world are, as a rule, against us, and that there is the more need we should to ourselves be true. Not only England and her colonies, but the nations generally of the world, are dealt with in an essay equally wide in observation and moderate in statement. One of the subjects in the knowledge of which conspicuous advance has recently been made is Babylonia and Assyria, which are dealt with by Prof. Sayce. Recent explorations have greatly extended the range of our knowledge. In this extension the most important and systematic work that has been done in Babylonia is that of the expedition of the University of Pennsylvania, which has been scientifically investigating the temple of El-lil, otherwise Bel, at Niffer, the ancient Nippur, one of the centres from which radiated early Babylonian culture, the other centre being Eridu, now represented by Abu-Shahrein. Ea of Eridu was a god of light, while El-lil of Nippur was that of the ghostland. Progress has been made of late in Babylonian chronology, a subject in regard to which we were until recently in almost total darkness. A list of Babylonian dynasties and kings, so far as they are at present known, is given at pp. 45, 46. A high degree of civilization appears to have been attained. There was little polygamy; torture as a means of extorting confession was unknown; education was widespread, women as well as men being able to read and write, and extinct as well as living languages were studied. Bacchylides, the Greek lyric poet, is the subject of an admirable essay by Sir Richard Jebb. Very great progress has been made during the last few years in our knowledge of bacteria, and the illustrated contributions of Profs. Marshall Ward and Robert Muir are of extreme importance. One of the points of most interest is the effect of rays of light upon these organisms. Spores of *B. anthracis* which withstand high temperatures can be killed by exposure to rays of reflected light at temperatures far below anything injurious to growth. 'Balloons, Military,' by Major Baden-Powell, late President of the Aëronautical Society, is disappointingly short. An account of Baluchistan, by Sir T. H. Holdich, is accompanied by a map. The whole of Baluchistan has now been surveyed. Passing over 'Banking' and 'Bankruptcy,' we come to 'Bantu Languages,' a term used to designate the most remarkable group of African languages. This is by Sir Harry Johnston, and is accompanied by a map of South Africa from Senegal and Abyssinia to the Cape, showing the countries in which the tongue is spoken. Accompanying the life of Antoine Louis Barye is a reproduction of his 'Lion and Snake,' and with that of Marie Bashkirtseff—to use the name by which she is generally known—is given one of her 'The Meeting.' Bayreuth is principally noticeable for the Wagner Theatre, fully described by Mr. J. A. Fuller Maitland. A portrait accompanies the life of Lord Beaconsfield by Mr. Frederick Greenwood. In this contribution an account of the Beaconsfield family and its separation from Judaism is included. The view concerning Lord Beaconsfield is sympathetic. He is, however, declared to have been thoroughly and unchangeably a Jew, and an Englishman in nothing but his devotion to England and his solicitude for her honour and prosperity. 'Bechuanaland' is another of those South African articles which occupy a considerable space in the volume. The modern literature of Belgium is discussed by Mr. Arthur Symons. Among the writers treated is naturally M. Maeterlinck, who is said to have invented a whole theatre of marionettes, "more mysteriously simple than human beings." 'Belgrade' is by the late Servian Minister at the Court of St. James's; 'Bengal' by Mr. J. S. Cotton; and 'Benin' by Col. Gallwey and Sir George S. Clarke, Governor of Victoria. The information supplied in the last article is naturally new, comprising as it does the British punitive expedition of 1897. Berlin and its environs are the subjects of plans which would be more useful if clearer in design, at any rate, so far as old eyes are concerned. Mr. Alfred Watson writes on 'Betting' and the anomalies in the law thereon. Major Broadfoot writes on 'Billiards,' and Dr. Hans Gadow on 'Birds.' Mr. J. W. Headlam contributes lives of Beust and Bismarck, the latter biography being enriched with an admirable portrait. With Marie Rosalie Bonheur are given reproductions of two famous pictures. 'Bookbinding,' by Mr. Davenport, 'Book-plates,' by Mr. Egerton Castle, and 'Book Printing,' by Mr. Charles Ricketts, are all freely illustrated. A reduced facsimile of a page of the Kelmscott 'Chaucer' accompanies the last. Much new information is furnished concerning Borneo, which also is supplied with a map. A portrait of George Borrow is furnished with Mr. Watts-Dunton's biography of that writer. A good reproduction of the 'Return of the Gleaners' appears with the life of Jules le Breton. Long articles on 'Brazil,' 'Brewing,' &c, are of little literary interest. 'Bridge,' the game, is treated, presumably for the first time in an encyclopædia. With Prof. Unwin's 'Bridges' are given designs of the Tower Bridge, the Washington and New East River Bridges, New York, and a bridge over the North Sea and Baltic Canal. Achievements more remarkable than some of these are to be found. 'The British Empire' is by Miss Flora Shaw. Madox Brown's famous 'Work,' which we were once in the habit of seeing daily, illustrates Mr. W. M. Rossetti's account of the painter. A not very striking portrait is given with Mr. Leslie Stephen's 'Browning.' 'Buddhism' is by Prof. Rhys Davids. 'Bulgaria' is treated at some length by Mr. Bourchier. 'Bull-fighting' is in the hands of Mr. Alfred Watson. 'Burma,' by Sir J. G. Scott, has two maps. The life of Burne-Jones is illustrated by a portrait and two designs. Mr. Stanley Lane-Poole, in what is, perhaps, the most judicious biography in the volume, gives a capital account of Sir Richard Francis Burton. 'Canada,' which is dealt with by three different authorities, is the most important article encountered during the short incursion into the letter C. 'Canals,' 'Caricature,' 'Ceylon,' 'Chemistry,' and 'Chess' are all of interest, as is a biography of Carlyle by Mr. Leslie Stephen, who is not quite accurately described as editor of the 'Dictionary of National Biography,' a post from which he has long retired. In interest and importance the volume claims high rank.

The Coming Unity: the Problem of the Churches.
By the Rev. Alfred J. Harvey. (Stock.)

We have read this little book with much interest. The tone of it will commend itself to Churchmen and Dissenters alike. The author seeks to draw the various churches together by love and mutual help in a union not founded by Acts of Parliament, but, as urged by the late Dr. Stoughton, "a real and visible union between Churchmen and Dissenters, distinct from comprehension — not involving the destruction or injury, and not at all threatening the independence, of any free ecclesiastical organization whatever." Mr. Harvey refers to two important changes made of late years by the Free Churches in their services and in the architecture of their buildings. In their services "not only are the Te Deum, the canticles, and Psalms rendered as in our churches, but oftentimes large portions of the Prayer Book prayers are incorporated into their supplications and giving of thanks," while "many of the noblest hymns found in Church of England hymn-books are the work of members of these Evangelical Free Churches." As regards architecture "many a Nonconformist 'chapel' of recent years is architecturally indistinguishable from an English parish church." This change was commenced as far back as 1848, when, through the liberality of Mr., afterwards Sir, Morton Peto, Bloomsbury Chapel was built. The origin of its two handsome towers is rather curious. Peto had great difficulty in obtaining a site for a Dissenting place of worship in such a prominent position. The ground was the property of the Commissioners of Woods and Forests. Lord Morpeth, who was the Chief Commissioner, had suggested that in order to protect the adjoining property the building should be veiled by a row of houses. When Peto asked Lord Morpeth for a lease, McCree, in his life of Brock, relates that "he gave a dubious look, and said, 'If it had been a building with a spire,' whereupon Peto exclaimed, 'My lord, we shall have two spires.'" Peto had like trouble when he purchased the site of the Diorama in 1852 for the present Regent's Park Chapel. The representatives of the Crown insisted that the front should be maintained as part of the terrace, and that there should be no outward appearance of its being a chapel. As showing the interest Baptists are taking in their new buildings, we have noticed that a correspondence on the architecture of chapels is now appearing in the *Baptist Times and Freeman*, and a recent number contains illustrations of the homely old chapel in which Robert Hall preached at Cambridge for fifteen years, and the very handsome new building shortly to be erected. Mr. Harvey closes his book with the wish that "both ministers and people will avail themselves of every opportunity of brotherly intercourse and co-operation."

We have received the first number of *Cambrian Notes and Queries* (Cardiff, *Western Mail* Office). The contents are of very varied character. Some of the questions might have been answered by the writers for themselves had they paid a visit to any good free library. Others are of real importance, and we trust will in due time receive satisfactory replies. Several contributors send jingles, half Welsh, half English, made for the purpose of impressing on children the English equivalents of the words they use. All these should be carefully preserved. Some of our own contributors who have discussed the subject of the ill luck which is supposed to attend those who walk under a ladder may like to know that in Carmarthen the evil influence is supposed to be averted by crossing the thumbs.

The *moulins à hosties* sometimes figured in ecclesiastical glass receive attention in the later numbers of the *Intermédiaire*. These strange symbolical representations, which seem to have no English name, show the Saviour fixed in a mill, from which Eucharistic wafers are escaping—"transformation du corps divin." Winepresses out of which the sacred blood flows in like manner are also to be met with, and a fine example of one of these Eucharistic presses is to be seen in a window of the church at Conches (Eure). The *Intermédiaire* also continues to discuss the question of the proper signification of the *barre* in heraldry, and to furnish a list of the real names of many religious communities and orders, since their popular names are often incorrect. One correspondent desires to receive information regarding women who have disguised themselves as men to serve as sailors, and quotes an instance recorded in Jurien de la Gravière's 'Souvenirs d'un Amiral,' 1872.

At an early date lists of the chief *errata* in the 'Dictionary of National Biography' will be issued. Such *errata* will deal exclusively with matters of fact and date, and will not supply new information. The publishers would be obliged if those who have not already forwarded particulars of mistakes would send them now to the Editor of the 'Dictionary,' 15, Waterloo Place, S.W.

Notices to Correspondents.

We must call special attention to the following notices :—

On all communications must be written the name and address of the sender, not necessarily for publication, but as a guarantee of good faith.

We cannot undertake to answer queries privately.

To secure insertion of communications correspondents must observe the following rules. Let each note, query, or reply be written on a separate slip of paper, with the signature of the writer and such address as he wishes to appear. When answering queries, or making notes with regard to previous entries in the paper, contributors are requested to put in parentheses, immediately after the exact heading, the series, volume, and page or pages to which they refer. Correspondents who repeat queries are requested to head the second communication "Duplicate."

H. ("For the love of God is broader").—'Hymns Ancient and Modern,' No. 634, by Faber.

W. Abbatt ("Capt. Arnold").—This query appeared on 7 June, p. 447.

NOTICE.

Editorial communications should be addressed to "The Editor of 'Notes and Queries'"—Advertisements and Business Letters to "The Publisher"—at the Office, Bream's Buildings, Chancery Lane, E.C.

We beg leave to state that we decline to return communications which, for any reason, we do not print; and to this rule we can make no exception.

LONDON, SATURDAY, JUNE 28, 1902.

CONTENTS.—No. 235.

Notes.

THE CORONATION, 26 JUNE, 1902.

We have this week to record the first coronation of an English monarch that has taken place since 'N. & Q.' came into existence. From 1838 to 1902 is a long period in a nation's history, and the world over which the British flag now waves extends beyond any limits of which those participating in the coronation of Queen Victoria could have dreamed. Some loss of romance may be felt when, for a fair queen whose youth, beauty, and inexperience touched most hearts, is substituted a monarch mature in years and wise in council. Those, however, who participated in the ceremony of Thursday can indulge in the reflection that they have seen a spectacle beside which all recorded triumphs sink into insignificance. Rome in her palmiest days can show nothing that approaches it as regards the Imperial sway which is represented. There is, moreover, this difference between a Roman triumph and the great pageant just witnessed, that those taking part in the latter are no unwilling captives dragged in the train of a conqueror. Britain herself and her stalwart sons constituted the main figures in the immense cortège. Descendants of subjugated kings were there as those who shared the benefits of British rule, and regarded themselves as bulwarks of British empire. But one feeling of regret was there that the latest recruits to the ranks of Britain's sons could not be present to stand shoulder to shoulder with those between whom and themselves joint prowess had begot mutual respect. Had they been there it would have been as freemen among freemen, inheritors of dearly won privileges and sharers in world-wide renown. It is a commonplace to say that the greeting awarded them would have been the most cordial that can be conceived. It is but natural that Imperial sentiment should prevail on an occasion such as the present. These pages will be in the hands of our readers before the rejoicings are over, and the aspects of the Coronation, archæological, historical, and ceremonial, are outside our immediate ken. The share of literature in the event is not yet evident, though it will be so hereafter, and nowhere, in all probability, more visibly than in our columns. In common with all true Englishmen, we participate in a triumph of loyal union such as a few years ago the wisest could not foresee. We share in the hope, even if it be delusive, that the Coronation may bring with it a reign of peace; and we pray for a blessing on the august heads which are lighted by the crown, and for strength for them to maintain the noblest and worthiest traditions and the greatest personal attachment that have ever descended upon a monarch.

CORONATION SERMONS.

While we are all thinking about the Coronation of King Edward VII., it may be well to place on record in 'N. & Q.' some account of the sermons preached at the coronations of former English sovereigns. Much has been written elsewhere about other details of the coronation services, but, so far as I know, little or nothing about the sermons, which have been an important and sometimes a tedious part of the service.

There was no sermon at the coronation of Edward VI., but Archbishop Cranmer, who was the king's godfather, exhorted his sovereign and godson to follow the example of King Josiah, of whom it was written in the book of Kings, "Like unto him was there no king before him, that turned to the Lord with all his heart, and with all his soul, and with all his might"(2 Kings xxiii. 25). Between two and three centuries were to elapse before another young English monarch was crowned, and at the coronation of Queen Victoria the story of Josiah furnished the text of Bishop Blomfield's sermon.

At the coronation of Queen Mary I., Day, who had recently been restored to the bishopric of Chichester, was the preacher, but I have not been able to find his text. Perhaps some other contributor can supply it. I have also failed to discover if sermons were preached at the coronations of Elizabeth and James I. At Elizabeth's coronation the see of Canterbury was vacant; Heath, Archbishop of York, refused to crown a Protestant queen, and the bishops generally followed his example. Oglethorpe of Carlisle officiated, and if there was a sermon he probably preached.

Charles I. was crowned on the Feast of the Purification. The preacher was Senhouse of Carlisle, whose text, "And I will give thee a crown of life" (Rev. ii. 10), seems, in the light of subsequent events, to have been almost a prophecy. The sermon was full of quotations from various sources — Homer, Livy, Dionysius the Areopagite, Philo, Lactantius, Jerome, Bernard, Luther, and others — as well as from the Bible. Each quotation was assigned to its author, and in many cases translated. There was one touch of humour in what was in other respects a sober, not to say a tedious discourse. The gift of life, said the preacher, was a free gift, unlike the gifts of physicians which they call "doses," though the patients have to pay for them. The bishop concluded with a solemn apostrophe to the king, "For man hast thou loss here? Thou shalt have a gift there. Hast thou contempt here? Thou shalt have a crown there. Hast thou death here? Thou shalt have life there." When, twenty-three years afterwards, on another wintry morning, the king stood beside Bishop Juxon on the scaffold at Whitehall, his last words, "I go to exchange a corruptible crown for an incorruptible one," must have seemed like an echo of the conclusion of Senhouse's sermon.

Charles II. was crowned twice—in 1651, at Scone, as King of Scotland, and on St. George's Day, 1661, at Westminster, as King of England. At the Scotch coronation the Moderator of the General Assembly preached from two texts: "And he brought forth the king's son, and put the crown upon him, and gave him the testimony; and they made him king, and anointed him; and they clapped their hands, and said, God save the king......And Jehoiada made a covenant between the Lord and the king and the people, that they should be the Lord's people; between the

king also and the people" (2 Kings xi. 12, 17). At Westminster the preacher was Morley, Bishop of Worcester, and afterwards of Winchester. His text was, "For the transgression of a land many are the princes thereof: but by a man of understanding and knowledge the state thereof shall be prolonged" (Prov. xxviii. 2). The sermon was very long, and was intended to show the evils of a multitude of rulers, and especially of "an unnatural, unreasonable, insolent, and tyrannical democracy." Examples were cited from sacred and secular history. Korah, Dathan, and Abiram, Sheba the son of Bichri, Cleon the Athenian tanner, and the Gracchi were all denounced. Charles was, of course, the man of understanding, and his comeliness, courtesy, and affability were expatiated upon. The joy of the coronation was not confined to earth. "I do verily believe," said the bishop, in concluding his sermon, "the angels in heaven have their share of it. For if there is great joy in heaven at the conversion of any one sinner, how much greater joy is there at the conversion of three so great and so sinful nations?"

The morning of the coronation had been fine, but after the king had left Westminster there was a terrible storm of thunder and lightning, which recalled to many minds— Richard Baxter's among others—the earthquake and the storm at the coronation of Charles I.

Francis Turner of Ely preached at the coronation of James II. and Mary of Modena from the words, "Then Solomon sat on the throne of the Lord as king instead of David his father, and prospered; and all Israel obeyed him" (1 Chronicles xxix. 23). Macaulay, in his account of the coronation, has devoted a paragraph to the sermon, of which he has nothing good to say. It is, I think, worthy of record that Turner denounced King John, "who meanly surrendered his imperial crown to the Pope"; and perhaps it was by way of palliation of this reference to the head of the king's Church that the preacher alluded in flattering terms to his Majesty's person, in which "we see every line of his blessed father's visage."

William III. and Mary were crowned by Henry Compton, Bishop of London, whose collateral descendant, the present Bishop of Ely, had the privilege of assisting at the present coronation. Burnet, who had recently been appointed Bishop of Salisbury, preached from the words: "The God of Israel said, the Rock of Israel spake to me, He that ruleth over men must be just, ruling in the fear of God. And he shall be as the light of the morning, when the sun riseth, even a morning without clouds; as the tender grass springing out of the earth by clear shining after rain" (2 Samuel xxiii. 3, 4). Macaulay has also referred to this sermon, and has described it as a grave and eloquent discourse, polluted neither by flattery nor by malignity. Whether the sermon was wholly free from flattery is perhaps open to question.

The Archbishop of York, John Sharp, preached at the coronation of Queen Anne from the words: "And kings shall be thy nursing fathers, and their queens thy nursing mothers: they shall bow down to thee with their face toward the earth, and lick up the dust of thy feet; and thou shalt know that I am the Lord: for they shall not be ashamed that wait for me" (Isaiah xlix. 23). Sharp's Whig principles leavened his sermon, and he insisted quite as fully upon the duties of kings to their subjects as upon the duties of subjects to their king. Some of his historical references are a little amusing. He told the congregation that the first Christian king (Lucius) was a Briton, and England had also produced the first Christian emperor, Constantine; and that the first king to throw off the yoke of Rome was also an English king. In one respect the archbishop's sermon forms a precedent. He promised to be brief, and was as good as his word; subsequent Coronation preachers have copied his example.

William Talbot, Bishop of Oxford, and afterwards of Durham, preached the Coronation sermon for George I. His text was: "This is the Lord's doing; it is marvellous in our eyes. This is the day which the Lord hath made; we will rejoice and be glad in it" (Psalm cxviii. 23, 24). Talbot's was also a Whig sermon, and the preacher had no greater difficulty in deducing Whig principles from Scriptural precepts and examples than Morley and Turner in obtaining support for their political views from the same source.

John Potter, also Bishop of Oxford, and afterwards Archbishop of Canterbury, was the preacher when George II. and Queen Caroline were crowned. His text was: "Blessed be the Lord thy God, which delighted in thee to set thee on his throne, to be king for the Lord thy God: because thy God loved Israel, to establish them for ever, therefore made he thee king over them, to do judgment and justice" (2 Chronicles ix. 8). Potter's text had been used by Burnet for his sermon preached before William III. at Whitehall on the thanksgiving day for the peace of Ryswick. Burnet had made the text the starting-point of what John Evelyn called a florid panegyric, and Potter profited by the censure Burnet had provoked, for the Coronation sermon is free from personal references to the king, and may be fairly described as a plain exposition of the text.

Robert Drummond, who preached at the coronation of George III. and Queen Charlotte, had been Bishop of St. Asaph, held the see of Salisbury at the time of the coronation, and was afterwards translated to York. His text was almost identical with Potter's text at the previous coronation, both preachers having chosen a part of the Queen of Sheba's address to King Solomon. But Potter used the version given in the book of Chronicles and Drummond's text was: "Blessed be the Lord thy God, which delighted in thee, to set thee on the throne of Israel: because the Lord loved Israel for ever, therefore made he thee king, to do judgment and justice" (1 Kings x. 9). The sermon was free from panegyric, and was described by Horace Walpole as a sensible and spirited discourse.

At the coronation of George IV., Archbishop Vernon Harcourt of York selected the same text that Burnet had chosen when William and Mary were crowned. There were in the sermon some personal references to the king, and a pathetic mention of the long affliction of his father the late monarch.

The sermons at the coronations of William IV. and Queen Adelaide, and of Queen Victoria, were preached by Bishop Blomfield of London. The first sermon was from the words: "Submit yourselves to every ordinance of man for the Lord's sake: whether it be to the king, as supreme" (1 Peter ii. 13), which form part of the epistle for the Coronation service. The sermon contained a long quotation from Cranmer's address at the coronation of Edward VI., and was criticized by Macaulay as "well enough, but not so effective as the occasion required." The sermon at the coronation of the late Queen was from the words: "And the king stood in his place, and made a covenant before the Lord, to walk after the Lord, and to keep his commandments, and his testimonies, and his statutes, with all his heart, and with all his soul, to perform the words of the covenant which are written in this book" (2 Chronicles xxxiv. 31). This was the shortest of all the Coronation sermons.

J. A. J. Housden.

THE OFFICE OF CHAMPION.

Though this office has not been exercised since the coronation of George IV. in 1821, yet much interest is attached to its possessors, who discharged the office at the coronation of most of the English sovereigns. Even prior to the Conquest it is said that the Marmions were hereditary champions to the Dukes of Normandy as Lords of Fontenaye, and the Dymokes claimed descent from them. Sir Baldwin Freville claimed the office as "Lord of Tamworth Tower and Town"; but his claim was disallowed in favour of John Dymmok—as the name was then spelt—lord of the manor of Scrivelsby.

Sir Walter Scott, in 'Redgauntlet,' has given a graphic description of the banquet in Westminster Hall after the coronation of George III., and of Lilias Redgauntlet taking up the Champion's gage of battle. He mentions Lord Erroll "rearing his gigantic form in the presence of the grandson of his father's murderer," of course, referring to Lord Kilmarnock, beheaded on Tower Hill for his share in the rebellion of 1745. The earl was six feet four inches in height, and towered over all the rest. Horace Walpole notices this circumstance also; but whether the gage of battle was taken up and another gauntlet deposited in its place is very doubtful. Another legend runs that Prince Charles Edward was himself present in London at the time of the coronation.

There is a very interesting account of the coronation of King George III. and Queen Charlotte, on 22 September, 1761, in the appendix to 'Tenures of Land and Customs of Manors,' by W. C. Hazlitt, published in 1874, a book of which only 325 copies were printed, and the names of the distinguished lords who were present are appended in the notes, and add much to the interest. The banquet took place in Westminster Hall rather late in the day, and three thousand wax lights were all kindled in less than five minutes. After the second course the Champion was brought up between the High Constable and the Earl Marshal. In the *Universal Magazine* of that date are two large folding plates representing the coronation in the Abbey, and the subsequent banquet in the Hall, with the Champion riding up the middle of the Hall, armed *cap-à-pie*.

For a good account of the family of Dymoke of Scrivelsby let me refer to Burke's 'History of the Commoners,' vol. i. pp. 32–37, published in 1836, in which there are inserted many interesting anecdotes of the ancient house. This work, though abounding with errors, yet contains much curious information and antiquarian knowledge not to be found elsewhere. In many points it much surpasses the 'History of the Landed Gentry.'

A list is appended to the pedigree of fourteen quarterings of the Dymoke family. Their coat is engraved, Sable, two lions passant arg., crowned or. Crests: first, a sword erect arg., hilt and pommel or; second, a lion passant arg., crowned or; third, the scalp of a hare, ears erect, ppr. Motto, "Pro rege dimico."

This interests me in many ways by reminding me of the past, for I can remember in 1866, when on a visit to a friend in Lincolnshire, meeting and being introduced to the Rev. John Dymoke, who in former years was rector of Scrivelsby, and at that time, owing to the death of his elder brother, Sir Henry Dymoke, was styled the Champion, and resided at Scrivelsby Court, near Horncastle. He and his only son, Henry Lionel Dymoke, have long since passed away. He did not remind me of, or look much like, the stately Lord Marmion of whom Sir Walter Scott says:—

> His square-turned joints and strength of limb
> Showed him no carpet-knight so trim,
> But in close fight a champion grim,
>   In camps a leader sage.

My late friend Thomas Adolphus Trollope, whose loss, with that of many other old and valued correspondents, 'N. & Q.' has to deplore, tells the following anecdote of meeting the Champion at Florence in his 'What I Remember':—

"I dare say that there be many now who do not know without being told that Dymock [*sic*], the last Champion—as I am almost afraid I must call him, though doubtless Scrivelsby must still be held by the ancient tenure—was a very small old man, a clergyman, and not at all the sort of individual to answer to the popular idea of a champion. He was sitting in a nook all alone by himself and not looking very heroic or very happy as we passed, and, nudging my companion's arm, I whispered, 'That is the Champion.' The interest excited was greater than I had calculated on, for the lady made a dead stop, and, facing round to gaze at the old gentleman, said, 'Why, you don't tell me so! I should never have thought that that could be the fellow who licked Heenan! *But he looks a plucky little chap!*'"—Vol. ii. p. 103.

Perhaps this occurred in 1860. But I can give an almost similar instance from my own experience in this neighbourhood. Once, when I mentioned to a friend having met Champion Dymoke in Lincolnshire, he asked whether his office was to fight with his fists *à la* Sayers and Heenan. But, as a rule, we are not literary characters in East Anglia— "The wisdom of a learned man cometh by opportunity of leisure, and he that hath little business will become wise" (Ecclus. xxxviii. 24).   JOHN PICKFORD, M.A.
Newbourne Rectory, Woodbridge.

NEWSPAPERS AT THE TIME OF THE CORONATION OF QUEEN VICTORIA.

On the 6th of December, 1837, Dr. Arnold wrote to his friend Mr. Platt, "A newspaper requires a more condensed and practical style than I am equal to." This was written in the days of small papers and small sales, and the present penny daily of from twelve to sixteen large pages would have been regarded as little short of a miracle. The *Sun* gave a full account of the coronation of the Queen, printed in letters of gold. This was limited to four pages; and the *Weekly Chronicle* of July 1st, 1838, an excellent facsimile of which was issued by the proprietors of the *Evening News* on Monday, the 16th, had a like limit. Its leader, written the day before the ceremony, states that London is teeming with life. The mass of human beings congregated within the limits of the metropolis defies calculation. The writer was evidently a veteran on the press, for he remembered the celebration of peace in 1814 and the last two coronations; "but we can recall nothing in the least comparable to the present display." "We only pray that our fickle climate may not mar the effect of these vast preparations." In the same paper it is announced "that the hour is now at hand when the last remnant of slavery will expire throughout the dominions of Great Britain." "By the last packet the gratifying intelligence has been received that in Barbadoes, as well as most of the smaller islands, the colonial legislatures have resolved to meet the wishes of the people of England by the general emancipation on the first of August of the apprentices."

A very interesting account of the Press and the last Coronation, by Henry Charles Moore, is given in the 'Newspaper Press Directory,' edited by my old friend Mr. Walter Wellsman. Mr. Moore has been at much pains in collecting extracts from the reports which appeared in the various papers. At the time the daily papers in the whole of the United Kingdom did not number twenty, the price being, for the most part, fivepence. There were no illustrated papers.

The *Globe* was the first of the important papers to publish an account of the Coronation, and, in mentioning the presence of the poet Campbell, stated that in his written application to the Earl Marshal he had remarked that there was a place in the Abbey called Poets' Corner, and suggested that room could, perhaps, be found there for a poor living poet. The *Globe* mentions that one noble lord had been detected in selling by public advertisement the order for admission which had been presented to him. The ticket was stopped, and the twenty-five guineas obtained for it had to be refunded. The *Times* devoted thirty-three columns to the Coronation. Referring to the conduct of the Westminster boys, who hailed the Queen with noisy shouts of "Regina Victoria!" it said, "It might have been as well had they been banished entirely from the Abbey, for a more murderous scream of recognition than that which they gave Her Majesty Queen Victoria was never before heard by civilized ears."

The *Morning Post* described the scene in the Abbey as being quite theatrical, asserting "that it would be difficult to arrange, with the greatest resources of the finest theatre in the world, anything capable of the same result."

The Coronation was the first public ceremony at which Press passes were issued by the police. Henry Vizetelly was provided with one in order that he might make sketches for the double number of the *Observer*. Mr. Vizetelly, in his 'Glances Back through Seventy Years,' mentions that special sketches had to be made of the State coach and the various uniforms of the Beefeaters, Gentlemen-at-arms, &c. Near the Abbey he

"encountered many ladies and gentlemen in Court and full dress—the ladies with nodding plumes on their heads and dainty white satin shoes on their feet, and with their embarrassing long trains gathered up in their arms—who, foreseeing a possible difficulty of reaching the Abbey in their carriages, were calmly proceeding there on foot, laughing among themselves at the curiosity they excited in the crowd."

Mr. Vincent Dowling, the editor of the *Observer*, wished to include a view of the procession from the roof of Apsley House, and wrote to the Duke of Wellington to grant his permission. The Duke replied :—

"F.M. the Duke of Wellington has received a letter signed Vincent Dowling. The Duke has no knowledge of the writer of the letter, neither is he interested in any way in the *Observer* newspaper. Apsley House is not a public building, but the Duke's private residence, and he declines to allow any stranger to go upon the roof.
"Apsley House, June 21, 1838."

Mr. Vizetelly had to throw many sketches aside, as they could not be used for the *Observer*. These he "utilized for a panoramic drawing in columns, a dozen or more feet in length, which was published by Tyas, who paid me for it, I remember, at the rate of so much per foot!"

Before the starting of the *Illustrated London News* on the 14th of May, 1842, occasional illustrations would appear in some of the weekly papers. Among the first and best of these was the *Athenæum*, and Mr. Clement Shorter, in 'A Literary Letter' in the *Sphere* of June 14th, gives a beautiful reproduction of two illustrations which appeared on the 12th of March, 1831, of the Lowther Arcade and the improvements at Charing Cross. Other illustrations included a general plan and a perspective view engraved on steel of the new Houses of Parliament. These engravings attracted great attention, as they were supplied exclusively to the *Athenæum.* They were given with the number for the 21st of May, 1836.

Among incidents which occurred at the coronation of Victoria is one given in the diary of Sir John Bickerton Williams, who was the first knight made by Her Majesty. He occupied a seat in the part of the Abbey allotted to the Royal family. He noticed that "when Her Majesty had to take off her crown to receive the Sacrament, she was obliged to apply both her thumbs to pinch it up ; it appeared rather too tight." Another incident will be remembered, as mentioned in 'The Greville Memoirs,' that the ruby ring was made for the Queen's little finger instead of the fourth, on which the rubric prescribes that it should be put. The Archbishop insisted upon its being placed on the fourth finger, and it was forced on and hurt her very much, and "she was obliged to bathe her finger in iced water in order to get it off."   John C. Francis.

The 'Coronation Order.'—It might be interesting to know whether any effort was made to normalize the third person singular inflexions of the verbs. The variety in, *e.g.*, the Oblation of the Sword (§ ix.), where "the King......ungirds his Sword, and *offers* it," while "the Peer, who first received the Sword, *offereth* the price of it," is singularly inelegant. And in 'The Queen's Coronation, by the Archbishop of York' (§ xvii.), that prelate, according to the first rubric, *saith* a prayer, and, according to the last rubric but one, *sayeth* another prayer.

I am copying from an edition in forty-eight pages, 7¾ by 5⅛ in., published at the Oxford University Press, which I understand to be authorized and authentic.   O. O. H.

Coronation Dress of the Bishops.—An article entitled 'The Coming Coronation,' in the *Pall Mall Gazette* of 10 June, concludes thus :—

"The bishops who are actually officiating are, as has already been announced, to wear splendid copes. The remainder of their brethren, who will be seated upon the north side of the Sacrarium of the Abbey, will be vested in their usual garb in its rather more elaborate form—that is to say, they will appear not in the black-and-white 'magpie' habiliment, but in their rochets with their scarlet chimeres, such as they wear at Convocation, placed over them. We fear that the unhappy precedent of the last three or four coronations respecting the headdress of the Episcopal bench will be followed. We can hardly imagine anything more utterly absurd than for a bishop to place a square cap upon his head at the very moment when all the temporal peers adorn themselves with their coronets. The mitre is the corresponding headgear for the spiritual peerage, and it is much to be wished that it should figure at the approaching Coronation. It is quite a mistake to suppose that this could be in any sense an innovation, for in the interesting volume recently published by Messrs. John Murray, entitled 'A Foreign View of England in the Reigns of George I. and George II.,' the writer, M. César de Saussure, who happened to be present at the coronation of the last-named sovereign, distinctly states that the bishops carried in their hands, during the procession to the Abbey, mitres composed of cloth of silver, those of the two primates being made of cloth of gold. The combination of cap and cope which it appears the bishops are going to affect on June 26 will hardly, we fear, be conducive to greater dignity."

In the official programme of George IV.'s coronation the archbishops and bishops are described as being "in their rochets with their caps in their hands." As the rochet, a surplice open at the sides, is in the case of the officiating bishops to give way to splendid copes, it seems a great pity that the caps should be worn instead of the far more interesting and appropriate mitres. There seems to be no historical reason for the use of the caps, and they are infinitely less dignified.   Charles Hiatt.

An Ode of Welcome to the Princess Alexandra. — There are some readers of 'N. & Q.' who may like to be reminded, or who may be interested to learn if they are not aware, that in the opinion of one of the ablest literary critics of the day, the best verses written on the occasion of the betrothal and wedding of King Edward VII. and his consort were not those of Tennyson or of the Honourable Mrs. Norton, but the 'Welcome' which came from the pen of the late William Forsyth, editor of the *Aberdeen Journal.* Forsyth, it may be stated, assisted Dr. Robert Carruthers in the preparation of the first edition of 'Chambers's Cyclopædia of Literature,' issued in 1842. Thackeray was one of the earliest to discern the genius of the North-Country journalist, who contributed to the *Cornhill* while conducted by the great novelist, and whose volume, 'Idylls and Lyrics,' is worthy of wider acquaintance than it has had. The 'Welcome' consists of six stanzas ; and the following is not only typical, but will, I think, be considered as appropriate in view of the Coronation rejoicings :—

> She comes in the light of her loveliness—
>   In the joy of her golden days ;
> And the hands of the people are raised to bless,
>   And their voice in songs of praise :
> And the thunder-peals of welcome swell
>   Through the cities' crimson air ;
> And the joy of the hamlets is heard as well,
>   Though 'tis simple as their prayer ;
> And the mighty voice of Welcome,
>   Of true heart and trusty hand—
> The Realm's rejoicing Welcome—
> Fills the heaven's blue vault with Welcome,
>   Like an anthem of the land :
> For who but the Sea-King's child should be
>   The Bride of the Sea-King's land ?

JOHN GRIGOR.

'THE ONLY SON.'—There was considerable questioning as to the authorship of the beautiful and apposite lines quoted by the Bishop of London in his sermon at St. Paul's Cathedral on Peace Sunday, 8 June. The poem, entitled 'The Only Son,' was published in the *Spectator* of 20 January, 1900, over the name of Mr. Henry Newbolt. As the poem, which will appear in Mr. Newbolt's forthcoming volume, has been marred by frequent transcription, it may be well to give it textually correct in 'N. & Q.' :—

> O bitter wind toward the sunset blowing,
>   What of the dales to-night ?
> In yonder gray old hall what fires are glowing,
>   What ring of festal light ?
>
> " In the great window as the day was dwindling
>   I saw an old man stand ;
> His head was proudly held and his eyes kindling,
>   But the list shook in his hand."
>
> O wind of twilight, was there no word uttered,
>   No sound of joy or wail ?
> " ' A great fight and a good death,' he muttered ;
>   ' Trust him, he would not fail.' "
>
> What of the chamber dark where she was lying
>   For whom all life is done ?
> " Within her heart she rocks a dead child, crying
>   ' My son, my little son.' "

JOHN GRIGOR.

Queries.

WE must request correspondents desiring information on family matters of only private interest to affix their names and addresses to their queries, in order that the answers may be addressed to them direct.

KING'S CHAMPION. — Was the ceremony of King's Champion instituted merely as pageantry, or was defiance in the Middle Ages really meant ? If it was, what would have been the result if the Champion had been defeated ? Would it not always have been necessary that he should be a man of great prowess and skill in arms, so as to be able to overcome any opponent who might dare to take up the gauntlet ? Supposing the first Champion to have been such a man, his descendant (the office being an hereditary one) might have been the very opposite. Does this not prove that it was always pageantry and nothing more ?

G. H. C. CRISP.

7A, St. Botolph's Lane, Cambridge.

CORONATION SONG.—Fifty years ago I used to hear sung in Yorkshire an amusing song called ' The Coronation.' It began with :—

> At home and in our village, when
>   We 'd done our daily labour,
> The barber every night would read
>   The news to each good neighbour.
> I heered it all, but wouldn't stay
>   For feyther's approbation,
> But started off to London town
>   For t' see t' Coronation.
>   Ri tol de rol de rido.
>
> But when I got there just at fust
>   I felt mysen quite flustered, &c.

I shall be much obliged if any one of your contributors will kindly send me all the verses, as I have forgotten several of them. It was an old song when I heard it, and had evidently been written at the time of the coronation of one of our kings, as in one of the verses it says :—

> I simply axed which wor the king ;
>   A man wi' irritation
> Said, " Aren't thou a pretty fool
>   To come to a coronation ? "

(Mrs.) E. JACOB.

Brooklands, Tavistock.

"DAGGERING."—This word appears in connexion with shipping or marine insurance. A correspondent, in looking over the minutes of the Merchant Venturers of Bristol, has found various entries condemning something called "daggering." For example :—

"1746, Feb. 6. The Master having acquainted the Hall that the pernicious practice of Daggering had increased greatly since the War, to the prejudice of shipowners and freighters, the standing Committee is empowered to petition Parliament, and to send up persons to prove its allegations."

Other items show that the obnoxious custom was in some way connected with the insurance of vessels, though in what way is not explained. If any of your correspondents can throw any light upon the meaning of " daggering " I shall be grateful.

H. HOZIER, Secretary.

Lloyd's, London, E.C.

GAUTIER'S 'VOYAGE EN ITALIE.'—I should be much obliged for any light on the following : " C'est un voyage dans le noir aussi étrange, aussi mystérieux que ceux qu'on fait pendant les nuits de cauchemar sur les ailes de chauvesouris de Smarra." What is Smarra?

Gautier names a novel the scene of which is laid in Venice, 'Le Confessionnal des Pénitents Noirs.' Who was the author of this?

A journey through Venice at night recalls "la tirade de Malipiero à la Tisbé." What is this?   De V. Payen-Payne.

SERJEANT EDWARD DENDY.—Is anything known of the parentage and ultimate fate of this worthy? He was serjeant-at-arms to the Commonwealth, and as such proclaimed the High Court of Justice for the king's trial. He was excepted from the benefit of the Indemnity Act, but escaped to Lausanne, where Ludlow in his 'Memoirs' tells us he met with him in 1666.   W. D. Pink.

JEWS' WAY: JEWS' GATE: JEWS' LANE, &c. —I shall feel obliged to any correspondents favouring me with references to these in the ante-expulsion period, 1290.
        M. D. Davis.

GERALD GRIFFIN. — I should be glad to know where I can find the poem by Gerald Griffin which contains the following lines :—
Wordsworth and Coleridge, and Landor and
    Southey,
Are stupid and prosy and frothy and mouthy ;
Like A and H they sit side by side,
True brotherly emblems of dulness and pride.

What is the meaning of the third line? After roundly abusing the four poets named, Griffin continues :—
Compared with such garbage, the trash of a Tenny-
    son
To me is a haunch of poetical venison ;
Or Bulwer as deep as the sky in a lake,
Till the mud at six inches reveals your mistake.
        Charles Hiatt.

"FLOWERING SUNDAY."—It is reported in the journals that on Palm Sunday it is customary in South Wales and Monmouthshire to strew flowers on the graves of deceased relatives. Did this observance originate from caprice, or has it any special significance?   B. D. Moseley.

GUEST FAMILY.—What is the origin of the surname Guest, which, though belonging to families settled in Wales, seems to be analogous to the Anglo-Saxon gest (stranger) rather than to any Welsh word?   Alpha.

MERRY ENGLAND AND THE MASS. — There is a sixteenth-century saying, though where to be found I know not, to the effect that "'twas never merry in England since the Mass was done away." Selden, I think,

repeats the mot in the form "since the priest ceased to conjure," perhaps in his 'Table Talk.' What is the particular connexion qua cause and effect? I have my own idea, which is probably wrong, and should be obliged if any one could account for the meaning of the dictum.   Philip North.

BYRON. — In the 'Bibliographie de la France,' 1824, there is a reference to 'Ode sur la Mort de Byron,' by Thomas Moore. The ode begins as follows :—

Il est mort, et la Grèce est en deuil.
Les guerriers pleurent sur leurs armes.

Is it not an error to ascribe this to Moore? Can some one tell me anything about this ode?   Leo C.

MILITARY COSTUME. — I shall be greatly obliged to any of your readers who will help me to find copies of the under - mentioned works on military costume. In several cases only the publisher's name and approximate date are known; but as they all contain plates it may be possible to trace them. Any information about them may be sent to the address below.

'Costume of the British Army,' Engelmann & Co.,
1828-9, folio.
Fores, 1844.
S. & J. Fuller, 1823.
'Costumes of the British Army and Navy,' Gam-
bart & Co., 1854-5, 8vo.
'Costumes of the British Army and Militia,' Gam-
bart & Co., 1855-6, 8vo.
Graves & Co.
Heath, 1830.
Jones, 1864.
Murray, 1813.
'Military Incidents,' Newhouse, 1845.
Robinson, of Leeds, 1814.
Ridley, 1829.
'Sketches of British Soldiers,' Stanford, 1869.
'The British Army,' Spooner, 1835.
        H. R. Plomer.
23, Fortune Gate Road, Willesden, N.W.

THACKERAY'S RESIDENCES IN LONDON.—On the front of a house now numbered 28, Clerkenwell Road (but which was formerly in Wilderness Row) is a stone tablet with the inscription :—

William Makepeace
Thackeray
lived here
1822-1824.

I cannot find any reference to this house as having been Thackeray's residence, and shall be glad to know what authority there is for the inscription placed upon it. Thackeray, who was born in Calcutta 18 July, 1811, was sent to England by his parents in 1817, and was first put to school in Hampshire, and afterwards to a school at Chiswick kept by

Dr. Turner, which is supposed by some to be the original of Miss Pinkerton's ladies' school. His mother, having married again, returned to England in 1821, and settled at Addiscombe. Thackeray was at Charterhouse School from 1822 to 1828, first as a boarder and afterwards as a day boy. During the latter part of his schooldays he lived at a boarding-house in Charterhouse Square, but there is no record of his having lived in Wilderness Row.   JOHN HEBB.

BYRON'S GRANDFATHER.—Byron's maternal grandfather, George Gordon, thirteenth Laird of Gight, Aberdeenshire, died at Bath 9 Jan., 1779. He is sometimes said to have committed suicide in the canal. What is the authority for this statement?—a very important one, as it bears on Byron's heredity. I have searched contemporary newspapers in vain.

J. M. BULLOCH.

118, Pall Mall.

THE METRICAL PSALTER.—Can any reader of 'N. & Q.' say whether the Metrical Psalter —either Sternhold and Hopkins or Tate and Brady—is still used by any congregation? Or, if not, when and where was it last in use? The substitution of hymnody for psalmody is one of the most remarkable among the changes in English religious life which the last fifty years have seen.   H. DAVEY.

MRS. THRALE'S HOUSE, STREATHAM PARK. — Where can I find the history of the above house and the land adjacent subsequent to the death of Mrs. Piozzi? When was the famous villa pulled down, and who became the owners of the property? I shall feel greatly obliged if any reader of 'N. & Q.' can afford me full details.   B. R. J.

"STEER" OF WOOD OR BARK.—Can any of your readers inform me of the meaning of the word as used in this conjunction? It appears in sec. 17 of 24 & 25 Vic., cap. 97, the Malicious Injuries to Property Act. I should be much obliged if any one would refer me to his authority.   H. E. G.

"LANGUAGE ADHERES TO THE SOIL."—In a book I have been reading there is a quotation from Sir Francis Palgrave: "Language adheres to the soil when lips which spake are resolved in dust." Can any one give me the exact reference?   AYEAHR.

CIPHER-STORY BIBLIOGRAPHY.—Would some literary expert think it worth while to compile a bibliography of all the essays, articles in periodicals and daily papers, treating the cipher questions put forward by Mrs. Gallup?

We must look to England for a thorough refutation of the latest humbug, as only Englishmen can master the details of their own history to an extent necessary for that purpose, and as only in England the documents and books relative to the question are accessible.   G. KRUEGER.

Berlin.

"POETRY NEEDS NO PREFACE."—Is "Poetry needs no preface" a "winged word"; and, if so, can any reader oblige me by naming its author and giving me a reference?

DR. C. STOFFEL.

Nijmegen, Holland.

GERMAN LETTERS.—Will some reader of 'N. & Q.' enlighten my ignorance on the following subject? I wish to learn the names of those Germans of note whose published correspondence has real literary value. Heine's letters are admirable. What other Germans have attempted to rival the French in epistolary dexterity?   G. W.

"THE BEATIFIC VISION."—According to the 'N.E.D.' the earliest occurrence of this phrase in English literature is in the seventeenth century. What is the earliest known use of the Latin or Greek expression, which is, presumably, the original of it?   PERTINAX.

"HEROINA."—I find in some seventeenth-century Latin correspondence this term applied to the wives of gentlemen and noblemen, e.g., So-and-so and "heroina sua." Was this a term in common use?   LOBUC.

Replies.

SHELLEY'S ANCESTRY.
(9th S. ix. 381.)

IN tracing Shelley's ancestry MR. BAYLEY might have gone back one step further, namely, to Bernabo Visconti, Lord of Milan. "This unscrupulous and dissolute tyrant"— to quote the chroniclers—in order to attach the redoubtable Sir John Hawkwood to the league which he had formed against Pope Urban V., gave Donnina, one of his natural daughters, in marriage to Hawkwood. This marriage, which took place at Milan, is thus described by the Mantuan ambassador in that city. The date is May, 1377 :—

"Last Sunday, Sir John Hawkwood conducted a bride with all honours to the house where he was living, that is to say, to the house once belonging to Gasparo del Conte, in which the late Bishop of Parma lived, and the wedding was honoured by the presence of the lady duchess, and all the daughters of Signor Bernabo. After the dinner the said lord Signor Bernabo, with the mother of the bride, went to the house of Sir John, where there was jousting going on all day. They tell me that after dinner the lady Regina made a present to the bride of a thousand gold ducats in a vase. The Signor Marco gave her a *zardino* of pearls, worth three hundred ducats, and the Signor Luigi* a gift of pearls of the same value, and in like manner did many of the nobles. So much silver was offered in *largesse* to the Englishmen, that it is estimated at the value of a thousand ducats. I have heard that Sir John Hawkwood was near Parma on Thursday, and according to what Signor Bernabo Visconti told me, amongst other things, he will soon be starting towards Modena with his English soldiers."

The honeymoon seems to have been passed at Cremona, where Hawkwood was making preparations for war.

Three daughters, Janet, Catherine, and Anna, were born of this marriage; also a son, John Hawkwood, who succeeded his father in 1394. He came to England, and was knighted by Henry IV. in 1407. This worthy gentleman seems to have led an uneventful life. It is recorded that in 1409 he had property at Padbury in Buckinghamshire, and that he married a certain Margaret, with whom he lived to extreme old age. In 1464 they were living at Sible Hedingham, where they enjoyed the lifehold possession of eighty acres of land. Their daughter Beatrix Hawkwood married John Shelley, Esq., M.P. for Rye, in Sussex, in the reign of Henry VI. From them are descended both branches of the Shelley family. It will be seen that Mr. BAYLEY has made a slight error in stating that Beatrix was the daughter of the famous Sir John Hawkwood (Giovanni Acuto). She was his granddaughter.

I am indebted for whatever information I may possess on this subject to that great scholar and distinguished Englishman John Temple Leader, who has written a copious and trustworthy life of my maternal ancestor Hawkwood, the most famous *condottiere* of the fourteenth century.

            RICHARD EDGCUMBE.
Edgbarrow, Crowthorne, Berks.

Supplementary to MR. A. R. BAYLEY'S very interesting note, it may be well to observe that Shelley could well afford to be no respecter of pedigrees without shocking the believer in the value of a noble descent. For besides his Sidney ancestry he was looked upon—and rightly—as a descendant of the same stock that produced the Lords Buckhurst, Cranfield, Bolebroke, and Sackville, the Viscounts Cantelupe and Bolebroke, the

* Marco and Luigi were two of the legitimate sons of Bernabo Visconti, Lord of Milan. At that epoch they held Parma as an appanage, in common with their brothers Rodolfo and Carlo ('Life of Sir John Hawkwood,' by John Temple Leader).

Earls of Dorset, Middlesex, Plymouth, and De la Warr, and the Dukes of Dorset. For Henry Shelley, son of Edward Shelley and his second wife, Joan Iden, of Penshurst, married Anne, daughter and heiress of Richard Sackville, great-uncle of Thomas, first Earl of Dorset, from whom, in the male or female line, all the above-mentioned peers descended. From Henry Shelley and his wife Anne Sackville descended John Shelley, of Fenn Place (died 1739), father of Timothy (died 1770), father of Sir Bysshe (died 1815), father of Sir Timothy, father of the poet.

            RONALD DIXON.

MR. BAYLEY remarks that "Hawkwood was captain of the White Company, which fought for the Visconti of Milan"; and "his bones lie, probably, in his ancestral church of Sible Hedingham, Essex." This information anent the burial-place of Sir John Hawkwood is not supported by Susan and Joanna Horner's charming 'Walks in Florence' (Strahan & Co., 1873), from which I quote the following (vol. i. pp. 69, 70):—

"Uccelli's most celebrated work in the Cathedral represents Sir John Hawkwood, or, as he was better known in Italy, Giovanni Aguto, *who was a tailor* from Essex in England. He served as an archer in the English wars against France. He wandered into Italy at the head of a lawless band of English lancers and adventurers. Hawkwood received the sobriquet of *Falcone del Bosco* (Hawk of the Wood) from the rapidity of his movements. After ravishing Tuscany, when commander of the Papal troops, he served the Florentines with equal fidelity, and when in 1394 he died in a villa outside the city, the grateful citizens spared no expense in his obsequies, causing his body to be wrapped in a cloth of gold, and to be laid in state in the Piazza della Signora, whence it was conveyed to the Cathedral *and buried beneath the choir.* The Signory decreed that a splendid monument of marble should be erected to his memory, and assigned dowries to his daughters. The monument, however, was never executed, but his portrait, painted by Paolo Uccelli, in terra-verde, was placed on the façade of the Cathedral. This portrait was originally in fresco, but has since been transferred to canvas, in which operation it sustained much damage."

            HENRY GERALD HOPE.

[Hawkwood died at his house called Polverosa, in the suburb of Florence known as San Donato di Torre. His monument in the Duomo was on the north side of the choir.]

"FRIEZE" (9ᵗʰ S. ix. 383). — Kluge (*s.v.* 'Fries') assumes that the German word *Fries* ("grobe Art Wollenzeug") was borrowed from the French word *frise*, which comes from the Germanic: cf. A.-S. *frise*, "gelockt"; Eng., to friz, frizzle. I know that some etymologists connect with this word "to freeze," *i.e.*, to crinkle up, and the Frisians have been held to=Cincinnati. See also Ducange, under

'Pallia fresonica.'   I find that a similar account is given in Zambaldi, ' Vocabolario Etimologico Italiano,' *s.v.* ' Fregio.'
                                        HERBERT A. STRONG.
University College, Liverpool.

Apart from "cloth of frieze," what is the origin of Friso, a personal name in the royal family of Holland, and the eponymous ancestor of Friesland? We have various mythical persons, as Frey, Freyja, and a Frisco ; but Friso seems to stand apart.
                                                    ABSENS.

GYE FAMILY (9ᵗʰ S. ix. 387).—I cannot say who Gye of the Cellar was, but I would point out—what may be helpful—that the arms stated to have been borne by him are identical with those at present used by Guy's Hospital.
   I perhaps ought to add that the leopards' heads wear antique crowns, and the motto is " Dare quam accipere."   MISTLETOE.

BISHOP SANDERSON'S DESCENDANTS (9ᵗʰ S. ix. 448).—Mrs. Pare's father was a member of a family of Sanderson which was settled at Little Addington, Northants—at any rate, in the seventeenth century and later. See the memorial inscriptions in the parish church, as given in Bridges and Whalley's ' Northamptonshire,' ii. 208. The earliest of these inscriptions relates to " Clariss. Dom. Johan. Sanderson, Armig. & Juriscons.," who died 14 January, 1672. The advowson of Little Addington vicarage belonged to this family. Anthony Sanderson (sometime fellow of Emmanuel College, Cambridge, S.T.P. 1700) became vicar in 1720. His successors include John Sanderson (1737/8), William Sanderson (1770), Thomas Sanderson (1813). The above information may possibly help MR. CROUCH to ascertain whether Mrs. Pare was really a descendant of the bishop.   H. C.

There is some account of the family of Saunderson of Addington in *Northamptonshire Notes and Queries*, i. 113-6. It is there stated that the Addington branch was connected with the Blyth branch, to which the bishop belonged, but was not descended from him, at least in the male line. Numerous references are given to printed pedigrees. There does not appear, according to the account I refer to, to have been any Rev. J. Saunderson at Addington who can have been father to Mrs. Pare, who must have been born about 1731 or 1732.   W. D. SWEETING.
Holy Trinity Vicarage, Rotherhithe.

KNURR AND SPELL (9ᵗʰ S. ix. 385, 452) —Knurr and spell may have escaped the dictionaries, but it has been caught in the net

of ' N. & Q.' ; see 3ʳᵈ S. vi. 168, 235 (' Nurr') ; 4ᵗʰ S. i. 294, 325, 468 ; 5ᵗʰ S. i. 348 ; ii. 133. It is entered in Halliwell, and in Addy's ' Sheffield Glossary.' In East Yorkshire it was known as "dab and trigger," and the implements were articles of trade, and could be bought at all toy-shops. I have played at it many times about 1855-60. Tip-cat is a humbler and more economical form of the same game.   W. C. B.

Surely " knurr " comes from the old English word *knar*, a knot in wood, and "spell," a turn of occupation, A.-S. *spëljan* (*vide* Kluge, *s.v.*). In Australia a "spell" always means a turn of rest as contrasted with a term of work.   H. A. STRONG.
University College, Liverpool.

LADY NAIRNE'S JACOBITE SONGS (9ᵗʰ S. ix. 401). — For certain family reasons among others, the note of MR. BAYNE is of considerable interest to me, and so, perhaps, you will allow me to place on record the following use of the lyric ' Will ye no come back again ?'—

"Prolonged cheering greeted General Sir Ian Hamilton (presiding at the annual general meeting of the Scottish Clans' Association of London, in the Crown Room, Holborn Restaurant, 24 July, 1901) when he rose to respond. He said that Lady Hamilton and he had enjoyed one of the happiest evenings of their lives among their fellow-Highlanders, and were now thanked for it. This, he said, was just like the Highlanders. He himself was proud of being a Highlander. He had been born in the cradle of a Highland regiment, and was always glad to come and feel at home with Highlanders. Voice from the centre of the hall : ' Will ye no come back again ?' The General : ' With the greatest of pleasure' (hearty applause)," &c.

With reference to what MR. BAYNE says about the version of ' Charlie is my Darling,' by Capt. Charles Gray, which appeared in G. F. Graham's ' Songs of Scotland ' (vol. i. p. 91) in 1849, it may be that it "has been forgotten" generally ; but it seems well to note that it was also previously published in 1841 at Edinburgh in ' Lays and Lyrics.' This, I believe, was also pointed out by Dr. Charles Rogers in his ' Life and Songs of the Baroness Nairne.'
   It may be of some interest to the few who are not aware of it that, in addition to the portrait of Lady Nairne which forms the frontispiece of Dr. Rogers's book, four portraits—entitled respectively ' Lady Nairne and her Son,' ' Lord Nairne before his Restoration,' ' Caroline, Baroness Nairne, *née* Oliphant of Gask,' and ' William Murray, last Lord Nairne '—appear in the very brief volume entitled " The Scottish Songstress Caroline, Baroness Nairne, by her Great-grand-niece " (Margaret Stewart Simpson),

published in 1894 by Oliphant, Anderson & Ferrier.   RONALD DIXON.
46, Marlborough Avenue, Hull.

WIND FOLK-LORE (9th S. ix. 148, 338).—A farmer in the Fylde district of Lancashire assured me that you could depend upon the prevalence of the wind from the quarter it was blowing from "when the equinoxes were on."   RICHD. LAWSON.
Urmston.

HARRIETT POWELL (9th S. ix. 267).—The fourth volume of 'Selections from the *Gentleman's Magazine*,' by John Walker (London, 1814), contains a list of the prints after Sir Joshua Reynolds, among which the following are named: "Powell, Miss Harriet, in the character of Leonora in the 'Padlock,' nine lines—'Say, little, foolish, flutt'ring thing,' &c. R. Houston, engraver. Ditto, 8vo. Eliz. Judkins, engraver." This may be of interest to your correspondent.
EVERARD HOME COLEMAN.
[See also Smith's 'Catalogue Raisonné.']

THE SMALLEST CHURCH IN ENGLAND (9th S. ix. 47, 375).—In answer to MR. PAGE's suggestion, I can add one particularly small church to his list—namely, that of Little Gidding, in Huntingdonshire, once so well known through Nicholas Ferrar and his family in the days of Charles I., in more modern times brought to notice through 'John Inglesant,' Miss Carter's (of Clewer) 'Life of Nicholas Ferrar,' Mrs. Marshall's 'A Haunt of Antient Peace,' and Miss Cruwys-Sharland's remarkable 'Story Books of Little Gidding, 1631–32.' The church has sittings for twenty-six persons, but could hold more. It is a parish church, and not a chapel of ease or other adjunct to a parish church.
MICHAEL FERRAR.
Little Gidding, Ealing.

A little-known instance of an exceptionally small church occurs at Snibston, Leicestershire, where the dimensions are: exterior, 32 feet by 18 feet 3 inches; interior, 26 feet by 13 feet 7 inches.   W. B. H.

CHESS PLAYING: A LEGEND (9th S. ix. 248, 293, 398).—The outline plate 'Satan playing at Chess with Man for his Soul,' by Retzsch, appeared in the *Saturday Magazine*, vol. x. p. 169, published 6 May, 1837.   W. B. H.

'THE DIRTY OLD MAN' (9th S. ix. 428).—The volume referred to by your correspondent was a series of poems written, I believe, by William Allingham. I have possessed for many years a small pamphlet issued by a publican in Bishopsgate Street, entitled

"'Ye Dirty Old Man' (Dirty Dick), a legend of Bishopsgate, from *Household Words*, conducted by Charles Dickens." It contains a poem of fifteen verses, commencing with

In a dirty old house lived a Dirty Old Man.

Could Charles Dickens have made a mistake in describing Bentley as of Bishopsgate, in lieu of Leadenhall Street; or may the pamphlet be regarded as an advertisement only?   EVERARD HOME COLEMAN.

SWORN CLERKS IN CHANCERY BEFORE 1765 (9th S. ix. 408).—The information could, perhaps, be obtained from the manuscript catalogues of Chancery Proceedings at the Record Office, where the clerks' names date back to *circa* 1650.
JOHN HOBSON MATTHEWS.
Town Hall, Cardiff.

Lists may be found in the annual volumes of Chamberlayne's 'Present State of Great Britain.'   W. D. MACRAY.

MICHAEL BRUCE AND BURNS (9th S. vii. 466; viii. 70, 148, 312, 388, 527; ix. 95, 209, 309, 414, 469).—The following misprints in my article at the last reference require correction: P. 469, for "Lerina" read *Levina*; for "Menelaus" (l. 21) read *Menalcas*; p. 470, col. 1, ll. 16 and 17, for "line" read *page*.

The fair fame and literary integrity of the Rev. John Logan have long been subjected to "the slings and arrows of outrageous fortune." The first serious assault was made by the Rev. Dr. Mackelvie in 1837. His information was largely derived from floating tradition and the verbal evidence of Mr. John Birrel (1752–1837), who, at his first meeting with Dr. Mackelvie, was about seventy-eight years of age. The other chief witness for the prosecution of Logan was Mr. David Pearson (born in 1744). The declarations of these individuals therefore require to be carefully examined. Dr. Mackelvie says (p. 20):—

"No person had better opportunities than Pearson to know what our poet [Michael Bruce] wrote, and, consequently, no one could be better able to give evidence on the subject, when evidence was wanted."

Dr. Anderson's opinion runs thus in a letter to Mr. John Birrel (Mackelvie, p. 20):—

"The friends of Logan think I have paid too much attention to Mr. Pearson's testimony; but I think he is not disqualified from giving his testimony on this point by his want of learning. His integrity is admitted on all hands."

Pearson wrote to Dr. Anderson that Logan having received from Bruce's father

"the whole of his manuscripts, published only his own pleasure, and kept back those poems that his friends would gladly have embraced ; and since published many of them in his own name."

Mr. John Birrel, also writing to Dr. Anderson on this subject (pp. 1029–30), remarked :

"Some time before the poet's father died, he delivered the book containing the first draught of some of Michael's poems, his sermons, and other papers, into my hand, desiring I would keep them. ......Some years after I entered upon terms with Mr. Morison, of Perth, to sell the MSS. for the benefit of auld Annie [the poet's mother], who was in very destitute circumstances. But in the meantime Dr. Baird wrote for them, with a view to republish Michael's poems, with any others that could be procured of his. I sent them to him gladly, hoping soon to see the whole in print, and the old woman decently provided for in consequence. The finished book of Michael's poems was given to Mr. Logan, who never returned them [sic]. Many a time, with tears trickling down his cheeks, has old Alexander told me how much he was disappointed in Logan, who came unexpectedly and got all the papers, letters, and the books away, without giving him time to take a note of the titles, or getting a receipt for the papers, &c. After the publication he went over to Edinburgh to recover them. Mr. Logan desired him to call again, and they would be ready. He did so ; but he was gone out, and no message left. He saw Mr. Logan on the street, who told him that he had left the poems with the servants, but that, as he did not get them, he was afraid the servants had taken them, and singed fowls with them."

"David Pearson," he adds, in another place, "does not remember of seeing the 'Ode to the Fountain,' 'The Vernal Ode,' 'Ode to Paoli,' 'Chorus of Elysian Bards,' or the 'Danish Odes,' until he saw them in print. But the rest of the publication he decidedly ascribes to Michael, and in a most particular manner the 'Cuckoo,' 'Salgar and Morna,' and the other 'Eclogue.'"

It will be seen that Logan is declared by Pearson to have received from Bruce's father "the whole of his manuscripts," and by Birrel to have "got all the papers, letters, and books away," and that "the finished book" was never returned ; further, that Alexander Bruce "did not get them" (the MSS., &c.) back from Logan. But Mr. Birrel received from the poet's father some time before he died "the book containing the first draught of some of Michael's poems, his sermons, and other papers." Were these returned by Logan, or had they not been seen by him ? The mention of "sermons" among the youthful poet's productions lays the testimony of Birrel open to grave suspicion. What time or opportunity or reason could Bruce have had for the writing of sermons in the course of his brief life of twenty-one years and three months ?

The foregoing narrative of Birrel is amplified in an astonishing fashion by Dr. Mackelvie in paragraphs 77, 78 (pp. 108–10). Some of the details flatly contradict Birrel, e.g. :—

"Logan took him [Alexander Bruce] to his lodgings, where he delivered to him a few loose papers containing the first draught of 'Lochleven,' 'The Last Day,' and 'Lochleven no More,' expecting he would be content with these."

Then follows the apocryphal story of the "singed fowls." It is on such conflicting testimony that the Rev. John Logan, F.R.S.E., has been charged with treachery and utter heartlessness towards his college friend Michael Bruce. A careful perusal of Dr. Mackelvie's volume does not give one a favourable impression of his qualifications as a biographer. The same remark may with even more justice be applied to Dr. Grosart.

ADAM SMAIL.

Edinburgh.

AN UNKNOWN FLEETWOOD PEDIGREE (9th S. ix. 261, 429).—Sir Robert Smyth, of Upton, Essex, first baronet, died 12 June, 1669, æt. seventy-five, having married Judith, daughter of Nicholas Walmesley. She died 1653, æt. forty-eight. They had, according to Wotton and Betham's 'Baronetages,' three sons and four daughters. One of the daughters, Hester, was married to Robert Fleetwood, of The Vache, in Buckinghamshire, Esq. Was this Robert the son of George Fleetwood the regicide ?   R. C. BOSTOCK.

ANALOGOUS TITLES OF BOOKS (9th S. ix. 468).—There is no copyright in a title per se, but the protection of the law can be claimed when it can be proved that a title is used fraudulently, i.e., "where the result is to induce the public to buy one work under the impression that they are buying another ; and this appears to be the only true ground on which titles of books can claim protection" (Scrutton, 'Laws of Copyright,' p. 30, 1883).

The following extract from the Times report of a case now before the court will serve as an example :—

"Cox v. Sports Publishing Co. (Limited).—In this action Mr. Horace Cox, the registered proprietor of the well-known weekly paper called the Field, the Farm, the Garden, the Country Gentleman's Newspaper, and generally known as the Field, moved to restrain the defendant until the trial of the action or further order from printing, producing, publishing, advertising, or selling or disposing of a monthly magazine called Field and Kennel, or any publication representing or being a colourable imitation of the Field. Mr. Justice Buckley, without calling on the defendants' counsel, on their undertaking to keep an account of profits until the trial, refused to make any order on the motion except that the costs should be costs in the action. His Lordship said that the plaintiff's well-known publication had been in existence for forty-nine years, and was published weekly. The defendants' publication had only been recently started, and was published monthly. The two publications were of different sizes and 'get-up.' No one going to a bookstall could possibly mistake one for the other. The plaintiff said his publication was always called the *Field*, and that the defendants' publication would also be called the *Field*, and, of course, the shorter title of a paper was commonly used. But the jurisdiction to interfere rested on property, and it was not shown that a person going to buy the plaintiff's paper would buy the defendants' magazine and so injure the plaintiff's property. After disposing of other points raised by the plaintiff, his Lordship said these questions might require further consideration at the trial, but on the materials before him he could not grant an interlocutory injunction."

WM. H. PEET.

ARMORIAL BEARINGS OF RAILWAY COMPANIES (9ᵗʰ S. ix. 409).—In reply to one of the points raised, I quote the following from 'The History of the Midland Railway,' by C. E. Stretton, p. 351 :—

"The dolphin is on the left, the salamander on the right, and the wyvern on the top of the shield. At the time of the Saxon Heptarchy Leicester was the capital of Mercia, and the wyvern was the crest of the Mercian kings. The wyvern is a quartering of the town arms of Leicester, and was adopted as the crest of the Leicester and Swannington line, out of which sprang the present Midland Railway. Hence its forming an important part and parcel of the Midland Company's coat of arms."

Being interested in railway history, this is a branch that I should like to know more about, and I should be very glad to hear from MR. BRINDLEY direct if he cares to write me as below. G. W. J. POTTER.

Bedford Road, South Woodford.

BREAKING BREAD AT TABLE (9ᵗʰ S. ix. 406). —When quite a child, I was told that the reason why it was more proper to break bread rather than cut or bite it was because bread was broken by Christ on the occasion of the Last Supper. At some of the "love feasts," as held in Mid-Derbyshire fifty years ago, the bread which was handed round was first broken into small portions; in some other parts of the county it was cut in small cubes. THOMAS RATCLIFFE.

Worksop.

CASTOR SUGAR (9ᵗʰ S. ix. 307, 417).—Sugar casters are now re-introduced, and very general at eating-houses kept by Swiss, French, and German proprietors; they are much larger than pepper casters, indeed somewhat bulky. ABSENS.

"BARRACKED" (9ᵗʰ S. ix. 63, 196, 232, 355). —How F. J. C. knows that the N.C. word *lake*, to play (or be "off work"), "should be pronounced *lēk*, not *lāk*," I do not gather. I am a West Riding man, and can "talk Yorkshire," and have lived half my life in York-

shire, and I never once heard it pronounced *lēk*. It was always *lā'ăke;* and a mill hand off work was *a-lā'ăkin.* I fancy thousands of North-Countrymen could tell F. J. C. that this is so, if they would take the trouble. My conjecture was that an Irishman, talking of a man "larking," would talk of him as *a-lar'r'kin;* and that, with an Australian-Irish origin, the word—spelt *larrakin*—came to represent a rough of Australian cities. Against this conjecture F. J. C., with crisp criticisms of MR. BALDOCK's items and my own, sets what, so far as I see, is only another conjecture, viz., Is not *larrakin* in the first place the name of a person? (I suppose he means a surname.) If he knows that this is so, surely he had better say so plainly. I do not know it. I have only found people asking what the origin of the word is. To the best of my knowledge the word is comparatively of recent origin. If F. J. C. ridicules the idea that *larking* comes from *lāke (lā'ăke)*, can he tell us what to *lark* (and *larking*) does come from? Webster does not tell us. F. J. C. is concerned about the intrusion of an *r*. The Irishman intrudes two *r*'s in *larking*, but then he does not bother about letters so much as F. J. C. does. The cockney intrudes one (possibly so does F. J. C.) in "Charncery Lane" and "barsket," &c. An actor of note, we saw (in these columns under the head of 'Rather,' *ante*, p. 275), intruded an *r* into *gape (garp)*; so I do not see that the matter of the *r* intruded into *lā'ăke* (whence *larking*, as I conjectured, and thence *larrakin*) is worth contesting. BOSCOMBROSA.

SHERIFFS OF STAFFORDSHIRE (9ᵗʰ S. ix. 342, 415).—See list from 31 Hen. 1. to 4 Edw. III. in 'Thirty-first Report of the Deputy-Keeper of Public Records,' published in 1870, pp. 340–343. W. D. MACRAY.

GENESIS I. 1 (9ᵗʰ S. ix. 269, 377).—There are certain grammatical nonentities which, if not explained away, serve as old bogies to dismay the neophyte; one such is the German prefix *ge, ga* in Gothic, and we are told to take no notice, it means nothing; but its origin has not been traced.

Similarly *eth* in Hebrew, a mere redundancy, is called a sign of the accusative in grammar, but we have no grammar old enough to serve as valid authority; so I take it we should resort to earlier stages of language, in which it may have represented a "determinative," in pictorial language, to point out the object indicated. In plain English, the particle "it" stands as representative, and to illustrate the usage I venture to transliterate the opening verse, in

Hebrew, as "Bereshith bara Elohim *eth* ha shammaim, waw *eth* ha erets"; and it may be surprising to find how readily it becomes anglicized. Thus B=F, read "fore-st" or "first," Scandinavian *förste*. *Bara*=bore, Gothic *bairan;* we speak of the "*birth* of creation." Elohim, *it*, the Latin *summum*, English *summit*. With Scandinavian *vid* for *vaw*, it, the earth, *erets*=*era* in Greek. Grammar is a mere clothing to the living speech.   Absens.

[We insert these speculations without endorsing them.]

Quotation attributed to Coventry Patmore (9th S. ix. 467).—It is somewhat curious that on the very day on which your correspondent's query appears the poem for which he inquires is printed in our local paper here. It is not given quite as Patmore wrote it, but I correct the few errors in the copy I enclose for Mr. Hudson. The poem is one of Patmore's miscellaneous pieces.   C. C. B.
Epworth.

Dickensiana : Phrase of Mrs. Gamp (9th S. viii. 324, 426 ; ix. 12, 172).—As a boy, I used frequently to see the "spinner" mentioned by C. C. B. There was a well-known stall at our annual "Stattis" (=Statute) Fair which always carried one of these popular attractions, and many times have I tried my luck threat. "Haddon Stattis," which bears date the last Friday in September, has, with all its accompaniment of revelry and gaiety, long ago vanished into limbo.
                                       John T. Page.
West Haddon, Northamptonshire.

Source of Quotation Sought (6th S. vi. 106).—The words for which a reference was desired were "Furem pretiosa signata sollicitant." Seneca ('Epistles,' 68, § 4) has "Furem signata sollicitant." Lodge's rendering ('The Works of Lucius Annæus Seneca, Both Morrall and Naturall,' first edition, 1614, p. 283) is worth quoting : "The coffer that is closed whetteth on the theefe to breake it open."   Edward Bensly.
The University, Adelaide, South Australia.

"Machine"=Public Coach (9th S. viii. 462 ; ix. 37, 116, 413).—In 'N. & Q.,' 1st S. vi. 99, under the heading 'Coaches,' are some interesting advertisements of a Hereford "machine," which was announced to "begin flying" to London "in a day and a half."
                                       Alfred F. Robbins.

Whilst "machine" is used in Scotland to express "coach," what in England are called "bathing machines" are north of Tweed termed "bathing coaches."   Ibagué.

Londres (9th S. viii. 443 ; ix. 35, 151, 295). —G. E. R. is satisfied that my previous note is founded on what he is pleased to designate "the so-called 'History of the Conquest of Glamorgan by Robert Fitz-Hamon and his Twelve Paladins.'" Possibly he is wrong in his judgment of appearances. However, he apparently denies that the subjugation ever took place by Fitz-Hamon, on his own authority or that of the king. Under any circumstances, I prefer to accept special and general history which has unmistakable and collateral proof to back it to any gentleman's opinion.

If G. E. R. wishes us to understand that Caradoc's history and circumstantial account is a farce; that Giraldus Cambrensis is a myth; that the 'Annales Cambriæ' are fables; that 'Brut-y-Tywysogwn' and the Iolo MSS. are spurious; that Leland is no good; that William of Malmesbury's references to Fitz-Hamon and his intimacy with the king all tend to support the invention of one man, John le Stradling, by which he, according to G. E. R., desired to raise his (Stradling's) predecessors in the estimation of his successors; that the 'Anglo-Saxon Chronicle' played a certain part in this imposition—then G. E. R. has a work of some magnitude before him.

When he has done this he will have to turn his attention to more recent writers—Camden ; Speed's 'Chronicle'; Thomas Tanner ; Sir John Doddridge ; James Moore, F.A.S. ; Dugdale ; Rev. William Warrington ; Wynne's 'Hist. of Wales'; Thomas Nicholas ; Dr. Heylyn ; Humfrey Lhuyd's 'Brev.'; last, but not least, John Rhys and David Brynmor Jones ; the 'Dictionary of National Biography' (vol. xix.), and others. After these few writers are disposed of G. E. R. may rewrite or correct the lineage of a few Welsh families, as well as several in different counties of England.

It is not new to me that the names of the twelve knights who came with FitzHamon are said to have been derived from a history attributed to Esterling, but I can add that this is also attributed to one Edward Mansell, and we do know that one Philip Mansell came with William, and we also know whom he married. G. E. R. informs us that there was not a Stradling in the county of Glamorgan at the period of which we are speaking (1090). It is unnecessary to inquire how he proves this. He admits there was a family of the name in Monmouth, a bordering county. It is a pity that G. E. R. did not tell us where *this* family came from.

It may here be stated that St. Donats was

not known by that name previous to the time in question. It certainly seems very wide of the mark to refer to the manor of Ogmore (more correctly Ogor) having been held directly "of the Crown by knight service" in the face of the then condition of the country, when FitzHamon overran and took possession of it, with no doubt the cognizance—if not the actual assistance—of Rufus.

I have already stated that, from reliable records, William de Londres founded a priory at Ewenny soon after the Conquest, and between this period and 1141 there was ample time for Stephen to "confirm to that house" certain churches, &c., to which G. E. R. makes reference.

It would be useless to add more than the fact that if FitzHamon is done away with a few years of Welsh history will require to be recast or wiped out of existence ; and the views on the question of FitzHamon and the conquest by him of Glamorgan, as expressed by G. E. R., preclude the necessity of my venturing to trespass further, now or in the future, on the pages of 'N. & Q.'

ALFRED CHAS. JONAS.

"UPWARDS OF" (9th S. ix. 446).—Very many people indeed use the words "upwards of" in the sense of nearly—a hundred, or any other quantity ; and to get exactly at their meaning it is necessary to ask questions to ascertain it. Many contend here and in the neighbouring counties that "upwards of" does not mean the "top side" of any given number, but below, or not quite up to it. "I've upwards of fifty" is often heard ; and if you query "How many?" the reply is "Not quite fifty." THOS. RATCLIFFE.
Worksop.

ANCHORESS IN THE LAND OF LEODIUM (9th S. ix. 429).—In Baring-Gould's 'Saints' (7 March) we read :—

"Eve was a recluse built up in a niche of a wall near the church of S. Martin, at Liege, and through the hole by which she received light, air, and alms besought the canons as they passed to seek out the bishop and entreat him to write to the Pope on the subject of the proposed festival. The bishop did not disdain this humble prayer, but transmitted her message to the Pope, who received at the same time the petition of the first doctor in the Church to the same effect. He wrote a letter to the poor recluse of S. Martin, in 1264, telling her of the issuing of a bull in answer to her prayer, and transmitting a copy of the office which the Angelical doctor had drawn up."

With this compare the article on St. Juliana (5 April). C. S. WARD.

The allusion is to the famous nun of Liège, whose writings led indirectly to the establish-

ment of the festival of Corpus Christi. MR. HOOPER will have no difficulty in getting information about her. See, for instance, the late Father Bridgett's 'History of the Holy Eucharist in Great Britain,' vol. ii. p. 265.
JOHN HOBSON MATTHEWS.
Town Hall, Cardiff.

"BABIES IN THE EYES" (9th S. ix. 405).—MR. W. C. BOLLAND has, I think, somewhat imperfectly apprehended the meaning of this ancient phrase in supposing it to be an allusion to the children that are the fruit of consummated love. The allusion is obviously to the cause rather than to the effect, that cause being the baby boy Cupid, whose reflection is, according to the conceit, seen in the pupil of a lover's eye—a fond fancy which originated in the minute reflection which it is said one sees of oneself in gazing into another's eyes :—

While in their crystal eyes he doth for Cupids look.
Drayton's 'Polyolbion,' song xi.

J. HOLDEN MACMICHAEL.
Wimbledon Park Road.

Burton, as "the last and best cure of love-melancholy," says :—

"What remains then but to joyn them in marriage? They may then kiss and coll, lye and look babies in one anothers eyes as their syres before them did."—'The Anatomy of Melancholy,' reprint of 1651, ed. London, 1838, p. 609.

IBAGUÉ.

Does this expression not refer to the reflection of one's own figure in miniature sometimes seen in both the eyes of another person?
J. S. McTEAR.

TEDULA, A BIRD (9th S. ix. 389, 433).—The interesting question asked by H. P. L. reminds me of the similar bird-words acredula (thrush?), ficedula (becafico), monedula (daw), querquedula (teal?), and of nitedula (dormouse?). May I enlarge his question by asking for an interpretation of the common element -edula ? C. S. WARD.

Should not the word have been written titula=a little tit? In Scotland the little bird which accompanies the cuckoo is called the tit. Cf. Norse tita, a small bird, originally "a tender thing." H. A. STRONG.
University College, Liverpool.

That CELER is correct in his interpretation is shown by reference to Herodotus, ii. 68, where the story of the τροχίλος in the crocodile's mouth is told. The bird, as shown by its derivation from τρέχω, was probably a sandpiper or wagtail, and not the wren, as the dictionaries translate Pliny's reference, and as referred to by Spenser, "the least of thousands," &c. A tame wagtail will be found on the floor of most large kitchens in Malta, &c., to keep down the bluebottle flies, which are doubtless the βδέλλαι of Herodotus.

H. P. L.

Spenser may have called the crocodile's bird-friend a torch as a poetical conceit that it was always near to light him from danger, which it is supposed to do by its cry ; or can the word be a corrupt diminutive of *tædium*, which in the plural is rendered by Littleton "vermine that breed about us and trouble us"? Ainsworth admits this meaning, but doubtfully, being careful to add, "Litt. unde non dicit." The connexion, I allow, is somewhat nebulous, as the leeches of Herodotus or the gnats of modern naturalists would be the *tædia* of the crocodile rather than the little plovers which come to his relief.

CHAS. GILLMAN.

Church Fields, Salisbury.

STEPMOTHER = MOTHER-IN-LAW (9th S. ix. 445). — Has St. SWITHIN not given poor Smollett undeserved blame? There are translations by other men (*e.g.*, Malkin) masquerading as Smollett's. The first edition (1749, anonymous) gives the passage as follows :—

"'Will you not always (said I) be mistress in my house?' 'I don't know that (she resumed), you may fall in love with some young girl, and marry her ; and then I shall be her mother-in-law ; consequently, we cannot live together.'"—Vol. iv. p. 18

Q. V.

CERNEY MANOR, CIRENCESTER (9th S. ix. 448).—On referring to my Gloucestershire note-book I find that the lands of Francis Wye, a Popish recusant, in the parish of South Cerney, in the county of Gloucester, were forfeited to the Parliament and granted to Richard Mathews in 1643. This estate remained in the Mathews family until about the middle of the eighteenth century. Other members of the family held the manor of Winstone. JOHN HOBSON MATTHEWS.

Town Hall, Cardiff.

See Samuel Rudder's 'New History of Gloucestershire,' 1779, p. 327.

J. HOLDEN MACMICHAEL.

OLD WOODEN CHEST (9th S. v. 88, 196, 275, 465 ; vi. 392).—Ancient oak chests, cut out of the solid balk, are quoted by Col. Hart, of Birmingham, in a paper entitled 'Oak Chests,' as existing in churches at Bickenhill, Curdworth, Lapworth, Maxstoke, Studley, and Offchurch, in Warwickshire, as well as at Bradford Abbas, Churchill, and Ensham Gar-

way, in Leicestershire, and at St. Martin's and at St. Margaret's in Leicester. Col. Hart also mentions the churches at Long Sutton, Corleton, Tettenhall, and Whitwell as possessing ancient chests cut out of the solid oak, as well as a very curious one of the same kind now to be seen in the kitchen of Aston Hall, near Birmingham. This latter is believed to have originally come from Baginton Church, in Warwick. Yet another of these "dug-outs" is at Spetchley Church, near Worcester. The gallant colonel mentions two French examples—neither of them probably of later date than A.D. 800—found, respectively, in the crypt of St. Etienne at Bordeaux and in a barrow at Châlons.

HARRY HEMS.

Fair Park, Exeter.

LADY-DAY DAY (9th S. ix. 447).—This duplication of the word "day" I used to hear regularly in Derbyshire when a lad, and I hear it here sometimes. It was "next Michaelmas-day Day," "It will be Christmas-day Day soon," "It wor on a Sat'dy-dey-dey," and so on with every "day-day." feast-days, and ordinary days. THOS. RATCLIFFE.

Worksop.

CECIL RHODES'S ANCESTORS (9th S. ix. 325, 436).—Many inscriptions in memory of the Rhodes family are printed by Mr. F. T. Cansick in his 'Epitaphs of Saint Pancras,' 1869, pp. 49-51. W. C. B.

LAURENCE FAMILY (9th S. ix. 290).—A John Laurence, clerk, compounded for first-fruits of rectory of Gretham, co. Lincoln, 8 Feb., 1656/7, and had for his bondsmen Andrew Arnold, of Marorre in the Fen, and Robert Burrough, of Moreby, co. Lincoln, clerk ('First-Fruits Composition Books,' xxii.).

A John Laurence compounded for prebend or rectory of Sutton, in Lincoln, and had as bondsmen Cromwell Death, of Furnival's Inn, London, gent., and Robert Stubbs, of Barnard's Inn, 1 Dec., 1668 ('First-Fruits Composition Books,' vol. xxiv. folio 271). The above may help MR. MARCHANT to identify the family of his John Laurence.

GERALD MARSHALL.

23, Trefoil Road, S.W.

MONT PELÉE (9th S. ix. 487).—Surely "La Montagne Pelée," the usual local name, explains itself. D.

MACAULAY IN GERMAN (9th S. ix. 405).—I feel ashamed to be forced to warn every English student against the German translations of English authors contained in Reclam's collection, Leipzig. All that I have tested are full of the grossest mistakes. One of the most ludicrous specimens is that perpetrated by Dr. Karl Theodor Gaedertz of Washington Irving's 'Sketch-Book.' In the 'Beiblatt zur Anglia' (Jahrgang 1900) I. Ellinger has shown up several hundreds of glaring blunders. This *traduttore* is a real *traditore*.

G. KRUEGER.

Berlin.

EUSTON ROAD (9th S. ix. 427).—Euston Road forms a portion of the New Road from Paddington to Islington, which was formed by Act of Parliament 29 George II., c. lxiii. The Act of Parliament authorizing the construction of the road prohibited the erection of buildings at a less distance than fifty feet from the roadway, and empowered the authorities of the parishes through which the road passes to pull down any such erection and to levy the expense of so doing on the offenders' goods and chattels. The restriction with regard to the erection of buildings appears to have been tolerably well maintained until some fifty years ago, when the control of lines of frontage in the metropolis was vested in the Metropolitan Board of Works, since which time some encroachments have occurred. Some of the buildings erected in advance of the fifty-feet line have been sanctioned, as in the case of the Hospital for Women and the block of shops opposite the Great Northern terminus; but in the majority of instances the buildings are unauthorized, and have in many cases been erected piecemeal, after the manner adopted by squatters in building on common land, which has rendered the task of repression difficult. An example of these tactics may be seen in the case of a fruitstall recently erected on a portion of the forecourt of one of the houses on the north side of Euston Road, between George Street and Euston Square. The London County Council took proceedings to obtain the removal of this fruitstall, but without success, and it is probable that in the process of time this stall will develope into a permanent building. It is to be borne in mind that although the New Road from Paddington to Islington was for the most part carried across open land, there were some scattered buildings abutting upon it at the time it was laid out, as may be seen in the map in the supplement to the *Gent. Mag.* for 1755, notably at the Edgware Road and Islington ends, and at the intersection with Hampstead Road, and advantage has been taken by the owners of these buildings to rebuild and extend them from time to time.

It is difficult to say at the present time to whom the unsatisfactory condition of Euston Road is to be attributed; but the London County Council must be exonerated from any blame with regard to it, that body having from its first institution shown the utmost anxiety to preserve it from further encroachment.

JOHN HEBB.

It might be supposed that the City Road, of which the Euston Road is a continuation, is older than the latter; but this is not the case, except in name only, while Pentonville Road, connecting the two, could not have been so named until after 1773, when Pentonville itself arose out of the formation of the New Road, which passed through certain fields belonging to Henry Penton, Esq. The Euston Road, now that portion of the New Road extending from King's Cross to Osnaburgh Street, was not so named until 1857, the New Road itself having been formed in 1757, whereas the City Road was not opened for passengers and carriages until 29 June, 1761. This "New Road," from Paddington to Islington, was formed under the provisions of a local Act (29 Geo. II., c. lxxxviii.), entitled

"An Act to enable the respective Trustees of the turnpike-roads leading to Highgate Gate House and Hampstead, and from St. Giles's Pound to Kilbourne Bridge, in the county of Middlesex, to make a new road from the Great Northern Road at Islington to the Edgeware Road near Paddington, and also from the north end of Portland Street, across the Farthing Pye House fields, into the said new road; and for enlarging the terms and powers granted by two several Acts for repairing the said road from St. Giles's Pound to Kilbourne Bridge."—Tomlins's 'Perambulation of Islington,' 1858, p. 43.

The site of the New Road, says Cunningham in his 'London,' is distinctly marked in the map before the 1754 edition of Stow; and in the *Public Advertiser* of 20 February, 1756, is a long account of the intended road, and the important advantages which would result from its formation. Fitzroy Square, Grafton Street, Euston Square, Euston Road, &c., were all named after the Fitzroys, Dukes of Grafton and Earls of Euston, the then ground landlords. I think this property, in all about a hundred acres in the immediate neighbourhood of Euston and St. Pancras railway stations, is now owned by the Duke of Bedford. One of Horace Walpole's letters alludes to the "new road," and to a former Duke of Bedford's connexion with it, as follows:—

"A new road through Paddington has been proposed to avoid the stones. The Duke of Bedford, who is never in town in summer, objects to the dust it will make behind Bedford House, and to some buildings proposed, though, if he was in town, he is too short-sighted to see the prospect."—25 March, 1756.

Bedford House occupied the whole north side of Bloomsbury Square.

JOHN HOLDEN MACMICHAEL.

INQUESTS (9th S. ix. 408, 475).—Coroners' Rolls exist in the Record Office, arranged by counties. Those of Lincolnshire go back to early in Edward III.'s reign, and record inquests, and often the names of the jurors.

A. E. WELBY.

Miscellaneous.

NOTES ON BOOKS, &c.

The Form and Order of the Coronation Service of their Majesties King Edward VII. and Queen Alexandra. (Frowde.)

OF the souvenirs of the Coronation which the public will keep and cherish this 'Form and Order of the Coronation Service' will make to many the most direct appeal. It is issued in a sumptuous form, on Whatman paper, rubricated throughout, and in a pure white binding. The title-page has an appropriate symbolical border. It should be in the hands of all privileged to be present in the Abbey, and should be retained almost as an heirloom. Bibliophiles will soon look on it as a treasure, seeing that it is confined to five hundred copies, all of them already absorbed by the trade, and will not be reprinted.

The Benedictine Abbey of SS. Mary, Peter, and Paul at Pershore, Worcestershire. By Francis B. Andrews. (Birmingham, Midland Educational Company; Pershore, Fearnside & Martin.)

THE useful and well-illustrated volume before us is not called a history—it has, indeed, no claim to that title—but will be of great service to any future historian. Had we been called upon to give it a name we should have called it an architectural description of the buildings now existing, accompanied by chronological notes. We say this in no spirit of depreciation, for we regard the literary portions, though mostly compiled from printed works, as useful, and the architectural illustrations as of high value.

There was a religious house at Pershore in pre-Norman times, but the name of its founder and the date of its origin are alike involved in mystery. Its earliest occupants were probably secular canons, who were displaced at the time of the great Benedictine revival in the days of St. Dunstan. These seculars, however, had sufficient influence to secure their return when political circumstances changed, but this can have been only for a few years, for we find a Benedictine abbot ruling A.D. 984. From him to the abbot who signed the deed of surrender to Henry VIII. the list is nearly, though we think not quite, complete.

The monastery and its surroundings, judging from what remains, must have been a magnificent structure. So far as our memory serves us, Mr. Andrews's descriptions are very accurate. We cannot, however, lend ourselves to giving praise to the manner in which what is called the restoration has been carried out. A Norman font of most interesting character existed here till recent days, but is now, we gather, an ornament in somebody's garden. It was taken out of the church shortly after the last restoration. The author gives an engraving of one side of it; but this is necessarily imperfect, as it is much worn and encrusted with lichen. The design seems to consist of an arcade of segmental arches canopying human figures. It is much to be desired that it should be examined and described by some competent antiquary. The names of all those who were responsible for its removal from the church should likewise be handed down to posterity. A mutilated effigy of a man clad in chain mail has had a somewhat better fate. The legs are crossed, which may be the reason of its being spoken of as a Knight Templar. An account written when the figure was entire informs us that the feet rested on a hare. If this were so, it is very curious. Some probability is, however, lent to the statement, as the right hand of the figure grasps a horn. It has, however, been suggested that during life the person represented held lands by cornage tenure. The arms of the abbey, of which an engraving is given, are highly curious. They are blazoned, "Sable, on a chevron or, between three anthills of the same, three holly leaves proper, slipped (sometimes given as vert, and at others as azure), on each hill four ants proper." We are not among those who on all occasions look for symbolism in heraldry, but in this case something more must have been intended than meets the eye.

The Berks, Bucks, and Oxon Archæological Journal for 1901. (Reading, Slaughter.)

PROF. WINDLE contributes a tentative list of early objects of interest in the above-named shires. Such a catalogue, in the present imperfect state of knowledge, cannot be exhaustive, but the attempt is praiseworthy. The list will be found very useful by the tourist, and it will direct the attention of those who dwell near them to precious relics of the past which, being familiar, they may have overlooked. The Rev. A. J. Foster continues his 'Tour through Buckinghamshire,' and, as on former occasions, records interesting facts. John Schorne was, he tells us, at one time rector of North Marston. He is, however, mistaken in regarding him as a canonized saint, unless he is using the word in that loose sense which includes such noteworthy persons as Thomas of Lancaster and Simon de Montfort. It seems certain that no official canonization was ever conferred upon this worthy, though he was an object of popular devotion in widely separated places. A well near the church at North Marston, which bears his name, was celebrated in former days for healing those sick of the ague. In the time of Browne Willis many ceremonies were connected with this well, but Mr. Foster gives no account of them. If they could be recovered they would be interesting to students of folk-lore. Several references to Schorne occur in former volumes of 'N. & Q.'

Practical Spanish. — Part I. *Nouns, Adjectives, Pronouns, Exercises.*—Part II. *Verbs, &c.* With Copious Vocabularies. By Fernando de Arteaga y Pereira. (Murray.)

OF no European language—except, possibly, Italian—is a decent smattering more easily acquired than of Spanish, and of none is a complete conquest more difficult. By the aid of this new grammar of the Taylorian teacher of Spanish in Oxford a man with a knowledge of Latin should be able in three months to read easily a newspaper and to make himself understood when he has passed from St. Jean de Luz to Fontarabia. In how short time he can obtain a mastery of the language we may not say, never having made such progress. It will depend greatly upon his aptitude for the acquisition of languages. Señor Arteaga's method is, however, admirable, and the student, the traveller, and the business man, for all of whom the work is intended, will receive from him intelligent and practical help and guidance. A more serviceable and practical work, and a better guide to the treasures of Spanish literature and the idioms of Spanish speech, is not to be hoped.

Intermediate French Grammar. By G. H. Clarke, M.A., and L. R. Tanqueray, B.-ès-L. (Murray.)

WHILE not claiming completeness so far as regards the scientific study of the language, this latest French grammar is likely to be of highest utility to the advancing student. It has one distinct advantage over previous works of its class : that it renders a full account of the decree of 26 February, 1901, by which liberties were permitted with certain rules of syntax now judged out of date. As is pointed out, the decree in question prescribes nothing—it simply tolerates. These liberties are given in an appendix which repays close study. The apostrophe need not be used in compound verbs such as *entrouvrir* ; the hyphen may be omitted in [qy. from] compound nouns, adjectives, verbs, &c., as *chef d'œuvre, ci joint,* &c. ; we may now say *le Dante, le Gnide,* as well as *le Tasse* and *le Corrège.* When we come to nouns, verbs, &c., the changes permitted are more important, and the advanced student will do well to master this part of the volume, even though permission, and not obligation, is involved. Suggestions for desirable changes in English practice may be drawn from the appendix. For general purposes the 'Grammar' is greatly to be commended.

William Hogarth. By G. Elliot Anstruther. (Bell & Sons.)
Thomas Gainsborough. By Mrs. Arthur Bell. (Same publishers.)

HOGARTH and Gainsborough are the latest additions to Bell's "Miniature Series of Painters." Both volumes are worthy of the companionship into which they are admitted. The former contains a biography derived in part from Mr. Austin Dobson's studies of Hogarth as artist, chronicler, and moralist, the location of his principal pictures, and their chronology, together with a selected bibliography. Eight designs, including the picture of the artist by himself, Garrick as Richard III., and 'A March to Finchley,' are given.

Mrs. Bell's 'Life of Gainsborough' is divided into four sections, dealing with boyhood, youth, and marriage ; at Bath ; return to London ; and last years and death. The judgments passed upon his work repay study. Among the pictures reproduced are 'The Blue Boy,' which serves as frontispiece, 'The Market Cart,' 'Mrs. Siddons,' and 'Lady Mulgrave.'

Barnaby Rudge ; Little Dorrit ; Our Mutual Friend. By Charles Dickens. (Chapman & Hall and Frowde.)

AT 9th S. viii. 416 we noticed the appearance of an Oxford-paper edition of the 'Pickwick Papers,' with reduced illustrations, published jointly by Messrs. Chapman & Hall and Mr. Henry Frowde, and commented on its convenient size and legible type. This was the second volume of the series. We

have now to acknowledge the three concluding volumes (xv.-xvii.), got up in similar style, and provided also with illustrations—in the case of 'Little Dorrit' by Phiz, in that of 'Barnaby Rudge' by Phiz and Cattermole, and in that of 'Our Mutual Friend' by Mr. Marcus Stone. The work last named also supplies a portrait of Dickens taken in 1870.

THE Coronation number of the *Lady's Pictorial* is superbly illustrated, and has remarkable interest. With it is supplied a reproduction of the design of E. T. Parris, showing the coronation of Queen Victoria. It occupies a prominent place among serial publications dealing with the Coronation.

MESSRS. T. & R. ANNAN & SONS are responsible for a photographic reproduction of William Barr's portrait of Thomas Carlyle, which is admirably executed, and presents the old Chelsea sage and cynic in his most characteristic aspect.

MR. MAX BELLOWS, of Locarno, Stroud Road, Gloucester, writes: " May I, through the medium of 'N. & Q.,' ask those who possess letters written by the late John Bellows, of Gloucester, to be kind enough to lend them for possible publication ? They may be addressed to Mrs. Bellows, Upton Knoll, Gloucester, who will return them within reasonable time."

Notices to Correspondents.

We must call special attention to the following notices :—

ON all communications must be written the name and address of the sender, not necessarily for publication, but as a guarantee of good faith.

WE cannot undertake to answer queries privately.

To secure insertion of communications correspondents must observe the following rules. Let each note, query, or reply be written on a separate slip of paper, with the signature of the writer and such address as he wishes to appear. When answering queries, or making notes with regard to previous entries in the paper, contributors are requested to put in parentheses, immediately after the exact heading, the series, volume, and page or pages to which they refer. Correspondents who repeat queries are requested to head the second communication "Duplicate."

T. W. PRESCOTT ("Heath's 'Brief Chronicle,' 1663").—This work in good condition is worth a few pounds ; but everything depends on condition. Send it, if you choose, for inspection, and we will tell you what a bookseller will give. It has sold recently from 30s. to 6l.

E. O.—Hobson Newcome, in 'The Newcomes,' lived in Bryanston Square.

CORRIGENDUM.—P. 300, col. 2, l. 42, for $\chi\rho\bar{\eta}$ read $\chi\rho\eta$.

NOTICE.

Editorial communications should be addressed to " The Editor of 'Notes and Queries'"—Advertisements and Business Letters to " The Publisher"—at the Office, Bream's Buildings, Chancery Lane, E.C.

We beg leave to state that we decline to return communications which, for any reason, we do not print ; and to this rule we can make no exception.

INDEX.

NINTH SERIES.—VOL. IX.

[For classified articles, see ANONYMOUS WORKS, BIBLIOGRAPHY, BOOKS RECENTLY PUBLISHED, EDITORIAL, EPIGRAMS, EPITAPHS, FOLK-LORE, HERALDRY, OBITUARIES, PROVERBS AND PHRASES, QUOTATIONS, SHAKESPEARIANA, and SONGS AND BALLADS.]

INDEX.

INDEX.

INDEX.

Notes and Queries, July 26, 1902.

INDEX.

INDEX.

LONDON : PRINTED BY JOHN EDWARD FRANCIS, BREAM'S BUILDINGS, CHANCERY LANE.